Online tools to help you excel!

At this book's new Web site, you participate! http://www.cj.wadsworth.com/colesmith10e

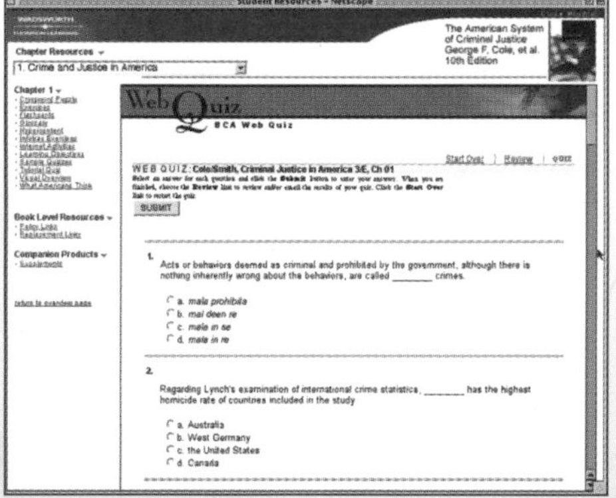

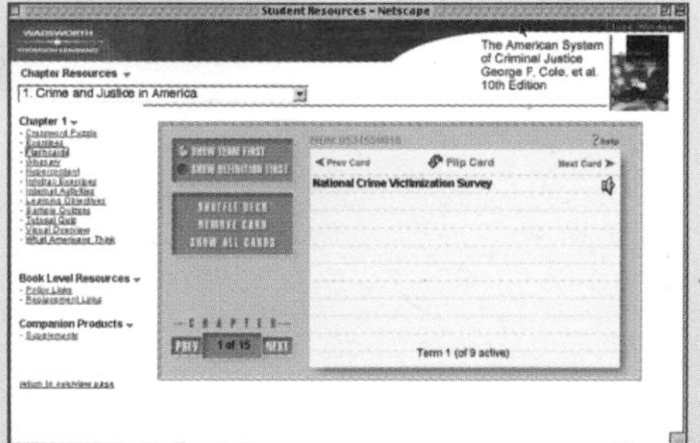

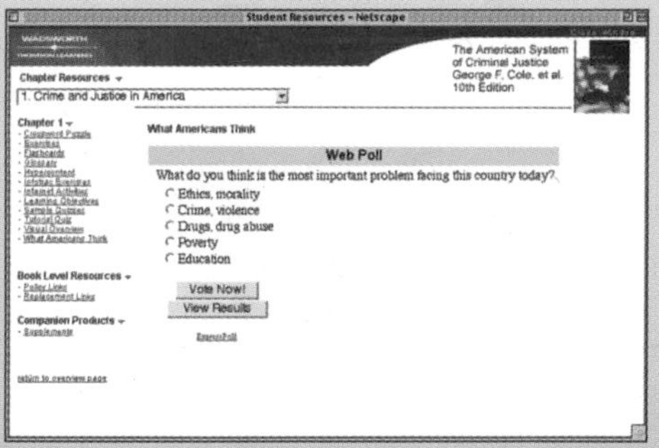

- **Tutorial Quizzes** for every chapter offer many opportunities for self-testing, even giving you feedback for each answer choice. (Self-Assessments on the enclosed CD-ROM offer additional quizzing.)
- **Chapter Outlines and Chapter Review/Summaries**—Use these as you read each chapter to reinforce your understanding of key concepts!
- **Flashcards** test your knowledge of key terms.
- **Final Exam** questions for each chapter help you better prepare for "the real thing."
- **Multi-Step Learning Modules** guide you in applying the theories and research you'll learn in this book to simulated situations you may encounter in your professional life.
- **What Americans Think** exercises allow you to participate in online polls and view tallied results to discover how your views on crime and justice compare with those of other students around the country (correlated with the "What Americans Think" poll results featured throughout the text).
- **Former inmate Chuck Terry** (now a Ph.D. and assistant professor) tells his story in "Inside the Criminal Justice System and Beyond: One Man's Journey."
- **Links to current Web sites** for every section heading within each chapter enrich your understanding of every important topic!
- **Internet and InfoTrac College Edition Exercises** sharpen your online research skills.

For information about police agencies, see the International Association of Chiefs of Police at http://www.theiacp.org.

Watch for this icon in margins of the text. Color coded (yellow for topic-related addresses and green for references to this book's Web site), they link you to interesting, pertinent information that gives you greater insight into the topics being discussed on that page of the text.

Quick access to Wadsworth's Criminal Justice Resource Center— Go directly from the book site to the Resource Center, where you'll find a newsletter that highlights current issues in criminal justice, Supreme Court updates, the Criminal Justice Library (featuring online journals, news sources, graphs, and statistics), links to exciting careers (in policing, the federal arena, academia, and protective services), a Student Lounge (offering study and career tips), and links to fun sites, such as *Disorder in the Courts* and *Help Locate a Fugitive.*

A direct link to InfoTrac® College Edition—A FREE four-month subscription to InfoTrac College Edition is included with every new copy of this book! Opening the door to complete articles (not just abstracts) from thousand of publications, this online library is expertly indexed and ready to use. You can also link to InfoTrac College Edition from this book's CD-ROM, where you'll find keyword search tips by chapter topic.

"Going Online" sections guide you to additional Web sites. Found at the end of every chapter, these sections provide you with Web addresses and quick summaries of sites that add important information about key topics in the chapter, as well as keyword search tips for accessing relevant InfoTrac College Edition articles.

Going Online

1. Write a short paper describing the organization, staffing, and facilities of the department of corrections in your state. Vivamus lobortis odio ut nisl. Nullam sit amet wisi. Cras ut diam. Praesent arcu wisi?
2. Go to the web site of the Bureau of Justice Statistics describing the organization, staffing, and facilities of the department of corrections in your state. What was the incarceration rate? Compare the numbers and rates of two adjacent states. Can you explain the differences among the three states?
3. Go to InfoTrac and log on. Search for the subject "prison reformers."

About the Authors

George F. Cole (right) is Professor Emeritus of Political Science at the University of Connecticut. A specialist in the administration of criminal justice, he has published extensively on such topics as prosecution, courts, and corrections. George Cole is also co-author with Christopher Smith of *Criminal Justice in America,* co-author with Todd Clear of *American Corrections,* and co-author with Marc Gertz and Amy Bunger of *The Criminal Justice System: Politics and Policies.* He developed and directed the graduate corrections program at the University of Connecticut and was a Fellow at the National Institute of Justice (1988). Among his other accomplishments, he has been granted two awards under the Fulbright-Hays Program to conduct criminal justice research in England and the former Yugoslavia. In 1995 he was named a Fellow of the Academy of Criminal Justice Sciences for distinguished teaching and research.

Trained as a lawyer and social scientist, Christopher E. Smith, J.D., Ph.D., is Professor of Criminal Justice at Michigan State University, where he teaches courses on criminal justice policy, courts, corrections, and law. In addition to writing more than 80 scholarly articles, he is the author of 20 books, including several other titles with Wadsworth: *Criminal Procedure; Law and Contemporary Corrections; Courts, Politics, and the Judicial Process; The Changing Supreme Court: Constitutional Rights and Liberties* with Thomas R. Hensley and Joyce A. Baugh; *Courts and Public Policy; Politics in Constitutional Law;* and *Courts and the Poor.*

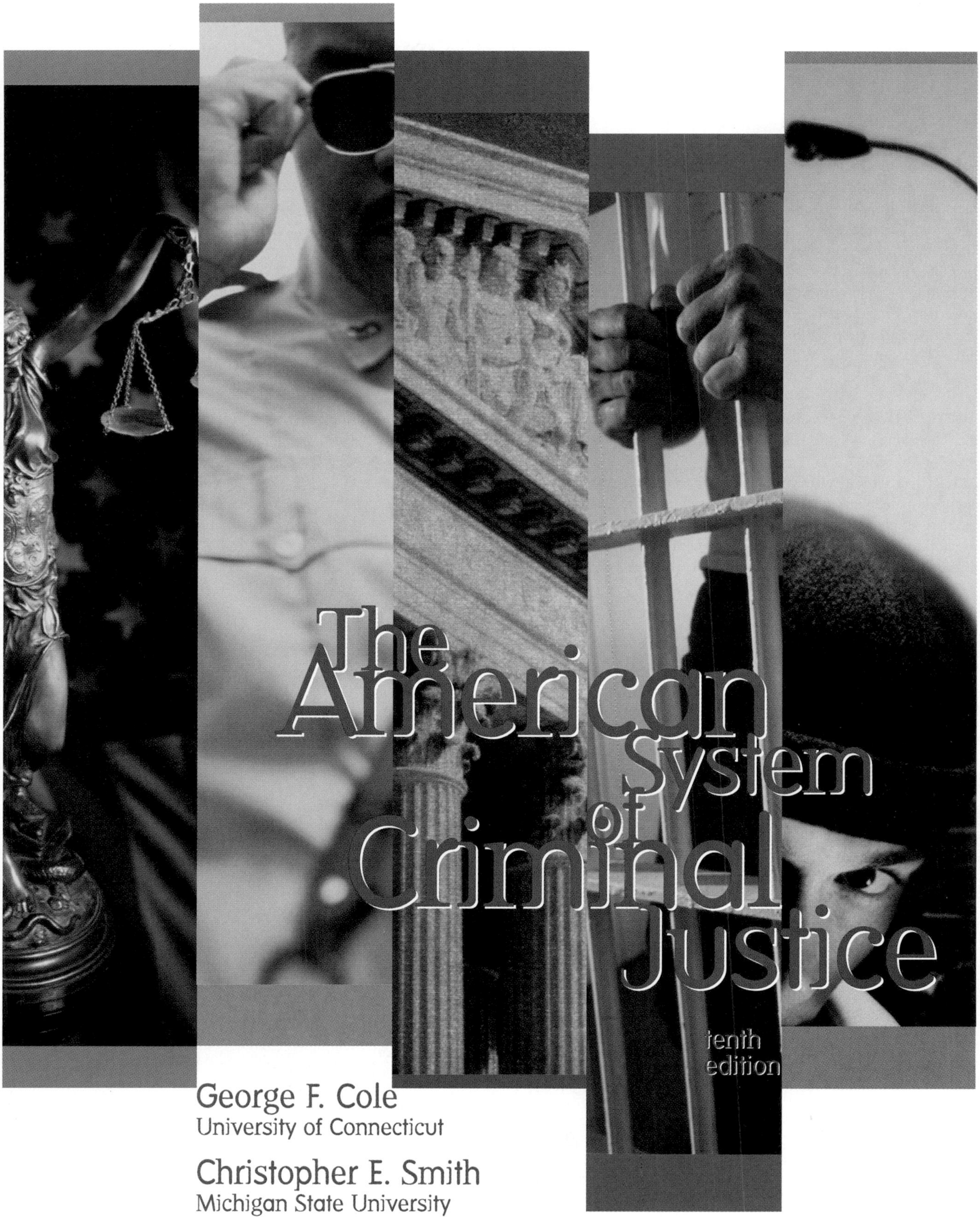

The American System of Criminal Justice

tenth edition

George F. Cole
University of Connecticut

Christopher E. Smith
Michigan State University

Australia • Canada • Mexico • Singapore • Spain
United Kingdom • United States

Senior Acquisitions Editor, Criminal Justice: Jay Whitney
Senior Executive Editor, Criminal Justice: Sabra Horne
Development Editor: Shelley Murphy
Assistant Editor: Dawn Mesa
Editorial Assistant: Paul Massicotte
Technology Project Manager: Susan DeVanna
Marketing Manager: Dory Schaeffer
Marketing Assistant: Neena Chandra
Advertising Project Manager: Stacey Purviance
Project Manager, Editorial Production: Jennie Redwitz
Print/Media Buyer: Kris Waller
Permissions Editor: Joohee Lee
Production Service: Greg Hubit Bookworks
Text Designer: Patrick Devine Design
Photo Researcher: Roberta Spieckerman
Copy Editor: Molly Roth
Illustrator: Lotus Art
Cover Designer: Yvo Riezebos
Cover Image: Cameron Heryet/Getty Images
Compositor: R&S Book Composition
Text and Cover Printer: Transcontinental Printing/Interglobe

Printed in Canada
1 2 3 4 5 6 7 07 06 05 04 03

For more information about our products, contact us at:
Thomson Learning Academic Resource Center
1-800-423-0563
For permission to use material from this text, contact us by:
Phone: 1-800-730-2214
Fax: 1-800-730-2215
Web: http://www.thomsonrights.com

Library of Congress Control Number: 2002114548

Student Edition with InfoTrac College Edition: ISBN 0-534-61533-3
Student Edition without InfoTrac College Edition:
ISBN 0-534-61540-6

Instructor's Edition: ISBN 0-534-61541-4

Wadsworth/Thomson Learning
10 Davis Drive
Belmont, CA 94002-3098
USA

Asia
Thomson Learning
5 Shenton Way #01-01
UIC Building
Singapore 068808

Australia/New Zealand
Thomson Learning
102 Dodds Street
Southbank, Victoria 3006
Australia

Canada
Nelson
1120 Birchmount Road
Toronto, Ontario M1K 5G4
Canada

Europe/Middle East/Africa
Thomson Learning
High Holborn House
50/51 Bedford Row
London WC1R 4LR
United Kingdom

Latin America
Thomson Learning
Seneca, 53
Colonia Polanco
11560 Mexico D.F.
Mexico

Spain/Portugal
Paraninfo
Calle/Magallanes, 25
28015 Madrid, Spain

brief contents

contents

Most students come to the introductory course in criminal justice intrigued by the prospect of learning about crime and the operation of the criminal justice system. Many of them look forward to the roles they may one day fill in allocating justice, either as citizens or in careers with the police, courts, or corrections. All have been exposed to a great deal of information—and misinformation—about criminal justice through the news and entertainment media. Whatever their views, few are indifferent to the subject they are about to explore.

Like all newcomers to a field, however, introductory students in criminal justice need, first, **content mastery**—a solid foundation of valid information about the subject—and second, **critical understanding**—a way to think about this information. They need conceptual tools that enable them not only to absorb a large body of factual content but also to process that information critically, reflect on it, and extend their learning beyond the classroom. This text aims at providing both the essential content and the critical tools involved in understanding criminal justice.

This new version of *The American System of Criminal Justice* has been labeled the "media edition" because it is designed so that students can take advantage of the vast resources now available on CD-ROM and the Internet. The technological changes of the last five years have revolutionized learning. Faculty can now bring to the classroom visual and print presentations that replace the lecture podium and blackboard as teaching tools. Students can be directed to original sources and databases that augment the content of textbooks and lectures, as well as to numerous interactive research tools, including a new text-specific CD-ROM and text companion Web site.

The Approach of This Text: Four Key Themes

When the first edition of *The American System of Criminal Justice* was published in 1975, it embodied three assumptions about the future direction of criminal justice as a discipline and the way the introductory course should be taught:

1. *The field of criminal justice is interdisciplinary,* with research contributions from criminology, sociology, law, history, psychology, and political science.
2. *Criminal justice involves public policies* that are developed within the political framework of the democratic process.
3. *The concept of social system is an essential tool* for explaining and analyzing the way criminal justice is administered and practiced.

In this tenth edition, greater emphasis has been placed on a fourth theme—American values, which people have always assumed to be the foundation on which criminal justice in a democracy is based. At this time, with citizens' concerns about terrorism and civil liberties at the forefront of the national agenda, we decided that making this theme explicit was important. Basic American values include individual liberty, equality, fairness, and the rule of law. These values guide the development of criminal justice policies and procedures. The application of American values creates special tensions between the civil liberties of the individual and the crime control needs of society.

Over the years the approach of *The American System of Criminal Justice* has found a degree of acceptance both gratifying and challenging. Instructors at hundreds of colleges and universities throughout the nation have chosen this book, and during its 30 years of use in their classrooms more than a half million of their students have used it. Yet textbook authors cannot afford to rest on their laurels, particularly in a field as dynamic as criminal justice. The social scene changes, research multiplies, theories are modified, and new policies are proposed and implemented while old ones become unpopular and fade away. Students and their needs change as well. Accordingly, we have made this tenth edition of the "Eagle" even more current, vital, cohesive, and appealing to students and instructors alike.

Highlights of the Tenth Edition

This new media edition encompasses major revisions in organization, content, and presentation. Users of the ninth edition will find significant changes in the reordering of chapters to equalize each part of the book, the combining of several chapters, and the addition of a new chapter on police actions and constitutional law. As just discussed, we give a more explicit focus to the role of American values in the application of criminal justice goals and to the conflicts that often ensue. We have enhanced our coverage of public policies dealing with crime and justice, as well as the role public opinion plays in the development of those policies.

As mentioned, this media edition has been designed to help students take advantage of advancements in information technology. We hope it will enhance students' learning and critical analysis by providing opportunities for interactions between the text and original data and literature sources found on the Internet.

In addition to these structural changes, the content, research sources, examples, and emphasis have been updated in every chapter. We have rewritten the text line by line to make descriptions succinct and clear and chapters and sections cohesive. The text's special features help the student see the significance of important issues and the context in which they occur. The text is also now more accessible to students at all levels. The use of full color clarifies and enhances the many graphs, photographs, and illustrations, bringing to life the text discussion of the rapidly changing aspects of criminal justice today. We hope that these changes make this tenth edition even more usable and "teachable" than its predecessors. Let's look more closely at the book's principal features and the ways they address the two main goals introduced earlier—to promote content mastery and critical understanding.

Content Mastery: Organization, Coverage, and Study Aids New to This Edition

Although current users will find the basic plan of the text familiar, this edition embodies several important changes. Study and review aids have been revised and enhanced in accordance with these changes.

Expanded Coverage of Policing

Major changes are occurring in American policing as the law enforcement and crime-fighter emphasis is supplemented by a focus on community policing and problem solving. Part 2 (Chapters 5, 6, 7, 8) has been reoriented to illustrate this shift in police operations, and the most up-to-date research has been incorporated into the text. We have strengthened the content of these chapters to give students a better understanding of the day-to-day operations of the police. Because law enforcement functions within the context of law, we have provided a new Chapter 7: "Police and Constitutional Law." Coverage of the new, enhanced role of private security as a guard against terrorism has been expanded. Police tactics—aggressive public order enforcement, high-speed chase policies, profiling—are explored more deeply than they were in previous editions.

Crime and Justice in a Multicultural Society

Disparities in the treatment of African Americans, Hispanics, and other minorities are pervasive in the criminal justice system. This issue is addressed in Chapter 3 and reexamined in succeeding chapters in discussions of what minority group members experience when they come in contact with the police, the courts, and corrections. We carefully examine the complex issue of attributing criminality to race and give special attention to the controversy over racial profiling, especially as it affects immigrants from the Middle East.

Criminal Justice and the War on Terrorism

The war on terrorism has brought about changes in the American criminal justice system. The creation of the Department of Homeland Security is reorganizing many law enforcement agencies of the federal government. Private security is playing a much greater role than in the past in protecting people and property. The courts are wrestling over issues of civil liberties and national security. Corrections, especially the Federal Bureau of Prisons, may have to deal with convicted terrorists. Public policies dealing with terrorists are changing rapidly. Throughout this new edition, we have tried to alert students to this new dimension of criminal justice.

Crime Control Policy

Recent years have seen a major shift to a greater emphasis on crime control. In response to public opinion, legislators have toughened sentences, increased the number of police officers, and reduced funding for rehabilitative programs. We examine this shift in light of the decrease in crime rates and the increase in prison populations.

This edition includes five policy issues for student discussion and debate in boxes called "The Policy Debate." In each, we describe an issue such as aggressive policing or the death penalty, outline its pros and cons, and then ask students to decide which policy they think the United States should adopt.

Study and Review Aids

To help students identify and master core concepts, the text provides several study and review aids.

- *Chapter outlines* preview the structure of each chapter.
- *Opening vignettes* introduce the chapter topic with a high-interest real-life episode.
- *Questions for Inquiry* highlight the chapter's key topics and themes.
- *Checkpoints* throughout each chapter allow students to test themselves on content.
- *Going Online* provides students with a set of exercises using the World Wide Web and InfoTrac College Edition.
- *Chapter Summaries* and *Questions for Review* reinforce key concepts and provide further checks on learning.
- *Key Terms* are defined throughout the text in the margins of each chapter and can also be located in the Glossary. *Key Cases* explain major issues decided by the courts.
- *An appendix on understanding statistical figures and tables* helps readers interpret the data presented in this text and research in other fields as well.

Enhanced Graphics

Today's students have been influenced by television all their lives. They are attuned to colorful images that convey values and emotions as well as information. For this edition, outstanding graphic artists and photo researchers have helped to develop an impressive array of full-color illustrations. Quantitative data are illuminated by conversion into bar and line graphs, pie charts, and other graphics; written summaries guide comprehension of the graphic presentations. We have taken special care to place photographs and their captions so that the images are linked to the message of the text.

Promoting Critical Understanding

Aided by the features just described, a diligent student can learn the essential content of the introductory course. While such mastery is no small achievement, most teachers aim higher: They want their students, whether future criminal justice professionals or simply citizens, to complete this course able to take a more thoughtful and critical approach to issues of crime and justice than they did at the start of the course. The tenth edition provides several features that help students learn *how to think* about the field.

Thematic Emphases

A gratifying number of instructors have welcomed the key assumptions that have guided the writing of this book. These assumptions—that criminal justice is an interdisciplinary field, that crime and justice are public policy issues, and that criminal justice can best be seen as a social system—are introduced in Chapter 1 and reiterated in the chapters that follow. The new emphasis on the role of American values in criminal justice policies and procedures provides a basis for the presentation and discussion of contemporary issues.

The text is truly *interdisciplinary* in that it draws on the research and writings of scholars from a range of academic and applied disciplines. In each chapter students can see the contributions of historians, criminologists, legal scholars, psychologists, political scientists, and others. They will recognize, for example, that the penitentiary is an American invention and that its development in the 1830s was greatly influenced by the social and political ideas of that era. They will also see how the administrative sciences have contributed to the organization and tactics of the police.

Through examples and explicit discussions throughout the text, we also explore the *role of public policy* in criminal justice. For example, we examine policies such as "three strikes and you're out," assistance to crime victims, community policing, and the death penalty for both their content and their potential impact on the system. Throughout the book, students are reminded that the definition of behaviors as criminal, the funding of criminal justice operations, and the election of judges and prosecutors all result from decisions that are politically influenced.

The *system perspective,* developed in Chapter 3, is carried throughout the book as a useful tool for analyzing criminal justice operations. The idea of the system is reinforced graphically with illustrations that remind students of exchange relationships, the flow of decision making, and the way the criminal justice system is itself embedded in a larger social context.

Close Ups and Other Real-Life Examples

Understanding criminal justice in a purely theoretical way does not give students a balanced understanding of the field. The wealth of examples in this book shows how theory plays out in practice and what the human implications of policies and procedures are. In addition to the many illustrations in the text, the "Close Up" features in each chapter draw on newspapers, court decisions, first-person accounts, and other current sources. In this edition, the Close Up boxes are smoothly integrated into the context so that students readily see their relevance.

New Directions in Criminal Justice Policy

To illustrate criminal justice policies that have been proposed or are being tested, we include a box called "New Directions in Criminal Justice Policy" in many of our chapters. Policies such as restorative justice, wrongful convictions, and the changing role of federal law enforcement are discussed so that students will be prepared to face the new realities of criminal justice.

Doing Your Part

Many Americans have contributed to criminal justice through voluntary activities or by promoting reforms. In selected chapters the roles played by individuals who are doing their part to assist the police, crime victims, courts, and prisoners are described in "Doing Your Part." We hope that these illustrations will encourage students to contribute to a just society.

A Question of Ethics

Criminal justice requires that decisions be made within the framework of law but also be consistent with the ethical norms of American society. In most chapters, boxes entitled "A Question of Ethics" place students in the context of decision makers faced with a problem involving ethics. Students become aware of the many ethical dilemmas that criminal justice personnel must deal with and the types of questions they may have to answer if they assume a role in the system.

What Americans Think

Public opinion plays an important role in the policy-making process in a democracy. As such, we present the opinions of Americans, as collected through surveys, alongside controversial criminal justice issues. Students are encouraged to compare their own opinion with the national perspective. This feature is linked to the text-specific Web site as well.

Comparative Perspective

With the move toward more global thinking in academia and society at large, students are showing new interest in learning more about criminal justice in other parts of the world. Most chapters of this edition include a "Comparative Perspective" section that describes a component of the criminal justice system in another country. In addition to broadening students' conceptual horizons, these sections encourage a more critical appreciation of the system many Americans take for granted. By learning about others, we learn more about ourselves.

Supplements

The most extensive package of supplemental aids available for a criminal justice text accompanies this edition. Many separate items have been developed to enhance the course and to assist instructors and students.

Available to qualified adopters. Please consult your local sales representative for details.

For the Instructor

Instructor's Edition

The *Instructor's Edition* includes a complete Resource Integration Guide for the text. This valuable tool will assist instructors in organizing their classroom presentations and reinforcing the themes of the course. Each chapter contains topically relevant references to all of the supplements and where they fit best in the lectures.

Instructor's Manual

A full-fledged, completely updated *Instructor's Manual* has been developed by Scott Johnson of Frostburg State University. The manual includes learning objectives, a detailed chapter outline, key terms and figures, class discussion exercises, worksheets, lecture suggestions, and a test bank. Each chapter's test bank has multiple choice, true/false, fill-in-the-blank, and essay questions. The *Instructor's Manual* is backed up by ExamView, a computerized test bank available for IBM-PC compatibles and Macintosh computers.

ExamView® Computerized Testing

Create, deliver, and customize tests and study guides (both print and online) in minutes with this easy-to-use assessment and tutorial system. ExamView offers both a Quick Test Wizard and an Online Test Wizard that guide you step-by-step through the process of creating tests, while its WYSIWYG capability allows you to see the test you are creating on the screen exactly as it will print or display online. You can build tests of up to 250 questions using up to 12 question types. Using ExamView's complete word processing capabilities, you can enter an unlimited number of new questions or edit existing questions.

Classroom Presentation Tools for the Instructor

Multimedia Manager for Criminal Justice 2004: A Microsoft® PowerPoint® Link Tool This valuable resource is a one-stop shop containing all of the art from the book as well as interactive learning tools that will enhance your classroom lectures. In addition, you can choose from the ready-made dynamic slides offered or customize your own with the art files provided from the text.

Transparency Acetates Taken directly from the text, these 50 full-color figures and tables will help bring your lectures to life.

CNN® Today: Introduction to Criminal Justice, Volume VI Now you can integrate the up-to-the-minute programming power of CNN and its affiliate networks right into your course. This video features short, high-interest clips perfect for launching your lectures. A current new volume is available to adopters each year. Ask your Thomson/Wadsworth representative about our video policy by adoption size. Also available: Volumes I–V.

America's New War: CNN Looks at Terrorism This great discussion starter includes 16 two- to five-minute segments featuring CNN news footage, commentator remarks, and speeches dealing with terrorist attacks on U.S. targets throughout the world. Topics include: anthrax and biological warfare, new security measures, Osama bin Laden, Al Qaeda, asset freezing, homeland defense, renewed patriotism, new weapons of terrorism, the bombing of U.S. embassies in Kenya and Tanzania, the American psyche, and the Arab-American response to recent events. Ask your Thomson/Wadsworth representative about our video policy by adoption size.

The Wadsworth Custom Video for Criminal Justice, Volume II Produced by Wadsworth and Films for the Humanities, this video includes short five- to ten-minute segments that encourage classroom discussion. Topics include: white collar crime, domestic violence, forensics, suicide and the police officer, the court process, the history of corrections, prison society, and juvenile justice. Also available: Volume I.

The Wadsworth Criminal Justice Video Library So many exciting, new videos... so many great ways to enrich your lectures and spark discussion of the material in this text! Your Thomson/Wadsworth representative will be happy to provide details on our video policy by adoption size. The library includes these selections and many others:

- Court TV videos: One-hour videos presenting seminal and high-profile court cases.
- Videos from the A&E American Justice series, Films for the Humanities, and the National Institute of Justice Crime File videos.

For the Student

Companion CD-ROM

Each copy of the text is packaged with a free CD-ROM. The CD-ROM provides students with Chapter Topics, Assessment Quizzing, an interactive Public Policy feature, InfoTrac College Edition research, Critical Thinking exercises, Work Perspectives, and Review Discussion Questions.

InfoTrac College Edition

Every new copy of this text includes four months of real-time access to InfoTrac College Edition's online database of continuously updated, full-length articles from hundreds of journals and periodicals. By doing a simple keyword search, users can quickly generate a list of related articles, then select relevant articles to explore and print out for reference or further study.

Study Guide

An extensive student guide has been developed and updated for this edition by Scott Johnson. Because students learn in different ways, the guide includes a variety of pedagogical aids to help them. Each chapter is outlined and summarized, major terms and figures are defined, and worksheets and self-tests are provided.

Terrorism: An Interdisciplinary Perspective, Second Edition

Available for bundling with each copy of *The American System of Criminal Justice,* Tenth Edition, this 80-page booklet (with companion Web site) discusses terrorism in general and the issues surrounding the events of September 11, 2001. This information-packed booklet examines the origins of terrorism in the Middle East, focusing on Osama bin Laden in particular, as well as issues involving bioterrorism, the specific role played by religion in Middle Eastern terrorism, globalization as it relates to terrorism, and the reactions and repercussions of terrorist attacks.

Careers in Criminal Justice Release 2.0 Interactive CD-ROM

The *Careers in Criminal Justice 2.0 Interactive CD-ROM* is filled with self-assessment and profiling activities. It is designed to help students investigate and focus on the criminal justice career choices right for them. This CD-ROM includes many outstanding features:

- The Career Rolodex features video testimonials from a variety of practicing professionals in the field and information on hundreds of specific jobs including descriptions, employment requirements, and more
- Interest Assessment gives students a direct link and free online access to the Holland Personalized Self-Assessment Test, designed to help them decide which careers suit their personalities and interests

- The Career Planner features helpful tips and worksheets on resume writing, interviewing techniques, and successful job search strategies
- Links for Reference offer direct links to federal, state, and local agencies where students can get contact information and learn more about current job opportunities.

Crime Scenes: An Interactive Criminal Justice CD-ROM

Recipient of several *New Media Magazine Invision Awards,* this interactive CD-ROM allows your students to take on the roles of investigating officer, lawyer, parole officer, and judge in excitingly realistic scenarios! Available for FREE when bundled with every copy of *The American System of Criminal Justice,* Tenth Edition! An *Instructor's Manual* is also available for the CD-ROM.

Mind of a Killer CD-ROM (bundle version)

Voted one of the top 100 CD-ROMs by an annual *PC Magazine* survey, *Mind of a Killer* gives students a chilling glimpse into the realm of serial killers with over 80 minutes of video, 3-D simulations, and extensive mapping system, a library, and much more.

Internet Guide for Criminal Justice, Second Edition

Internet beginners will appreciate this helpful booklet! With explanations and the vocabulary necessary for navigating the Web, it features customized information on criminal justice Web sites and presents Internet project ideas.

Internet Activities for Criminal Justice, Second Edition

This completely revised 96-page booklet shows how to best utilize the Internet for research through searches and activities.

Criminal Justice Internet Explorer, Third Edition

This colorful, trifold brochure lists the most popular Internet addresses for criminal justice Web sites. It includes URLs for corrections, victimization, crime prevention, high-tech crime, policing, courts, investigations, juvenile justice, research, and fun sites.

Internet-Based Supplements

WebTutor™ Advantage on Blackboard and WebCT http://webtutor.thomsonlearning.com

WebTutor Advantage takes your course beyond the classroom to an anywhere, anytime environment. You can use WebTutor Advantage to provide virtual office hours, post your syllabi, set up threaded discussions, and track student progress with the quizzing material. WebTutor's rich communication tools include a course calendar, asynchronous discussion, real-time chat, a whiteboard, and an integrated e-mail system. WebTutor Advantage offers access to a full array of study tools organized by text chapter, including glossary flashcards, practice quizzes, online tutorials, and Web links. "Out of the box" or customizable, this versatile online tool is filled with preloaded, text-specific content, including diagrams and illustrations, Microsoft® PowerPoint® files organized by text chapter, and more. Customize the content in any way you choose, from uploading images and other resources to adding Web links, to creating your own practice materials. WebTutor Advantage is flexibly designed for use in a variety of ways, from an electronic study guide for your students all the way to a tool for teaching your course online.

The Wadsworth Criminal Justice Resource Center http://www.cj.wadsworth.com

Now includes a direct link to "Terrorism: An Interdisciplinary Perspective," an intriguing new site that provides thorough coverage of terrorism in general and the issues surrounding the events of September 11. This Web site also provides a variety of tools and resources such as critical thinking exercises from Jonathan White's *Terrorism: An Introduction,* InfoTrac College Edition Exercises, and links to on-line journals for updated information.

Companion Web Site http://www.cj.wadsworth.com/colesmith10e

The book-specific Web site provides many chapter-specific resources. These include Chapter Outlines, Chapter Summary and Review, Glossary, Flashcards, Tutorial Quizzing, Final Exam, Internet Exercises, InfoTrac College Edition Exercises, Web References, and a Discussion Forum. The text Web site also offers a Multi-Step Learning Module, presenting key concepts with case examples followed by essay questions for students to apply their knowledge and critical thinking skills.

In addition to these chapter-specific resources, the site contains information on conventions and grants, as well as interactive features such as the criminal justice timeline; the Crime and Technology module, packed with resources and activities; and the CJ in the News site. It also includes the "What Americans Think" poll, where students can cast their votes on key issues. An extensive criminal justice glossary, general discussion forums, and activities specifically addressing policing, the courts, and corrections, are also provided, as well as hundreds of links to popular criminal justice sites.

A Group Effort

No one can be an expert on every aspect of the criminal justice system. Authors need help in covering new developments and ensuring that research findings are correctly interpreted. This revision has greatly benefited from the advice of two groups of criminal justice scholars. The first group were those we asked to comment on the entire manuscript, especially its organization and pedagogical usefulness. We chose these reviewers from the wide range of colleges and universities throughout the country that have used previous editions, so their comments concerning presentation, levels of student abilities, and the requirements of introductory courses at their institutions were especially useful. Reviewers in the second group we consulted are nationally recognized experts in the field; they focused their attention on the areas in which they specialize. Their many comments helped us avoid errors and drew our attention to points in the literature that had been neglected.

The many criminal justice students and instructors who used the ninth edition also contributed abundantly to this edition. Several hundred readers returned the questionnaire included in that edition. Their comments provided crucial practical feedback. Others gave us their comments personally when we lectured in criminal justice classes around the country.

Others have helped us as well. Chief among them was Senior Executive Editor Sabra Horne, who has always supported our efforts. Editor Jay Whitney helped us strengthen the focus of the book. Our Developmental Editor, Shelley Murphy, provided invaluable comments as we revised the book. The project has benefited much from the attention of Production Editor Jennie Redwitz, and Dawn Mesa was invaluable in helping us develop the supplements. Molly Roth prevented us from committing egregious errors in the use of English. As always, Greg Hubit used his managerial skills to oversee the project from manuscript submission to bound books. Patrick Devine designed the interior of the book. Finally, the following reviewers contributed valuable comments:

Jerry Armor, Calhoun Community College

Ronald Burns, Texas Christian University

William Head, Indiana University, Bloomington

Harold Nees, Metropolitan State College of Denver

Patrick O'Guinn, Sr., Howard Community College

Ultimately, however, the full responsibility for the book is ours alone. We hope you will benefit from it, and we welcome your comments.

George F. Cole
gcole281@earthlink.net

Christopher E. Smith
smithc28@msu.edu

What is the sequence of events in the criminal justice system?

This flowchart provides an overview of the criminal justice system as it will be described in this book. It is important to recognize that the system portrayed here is a social system. Each event depicted represents a complex interaction of people, politics, and procedures.

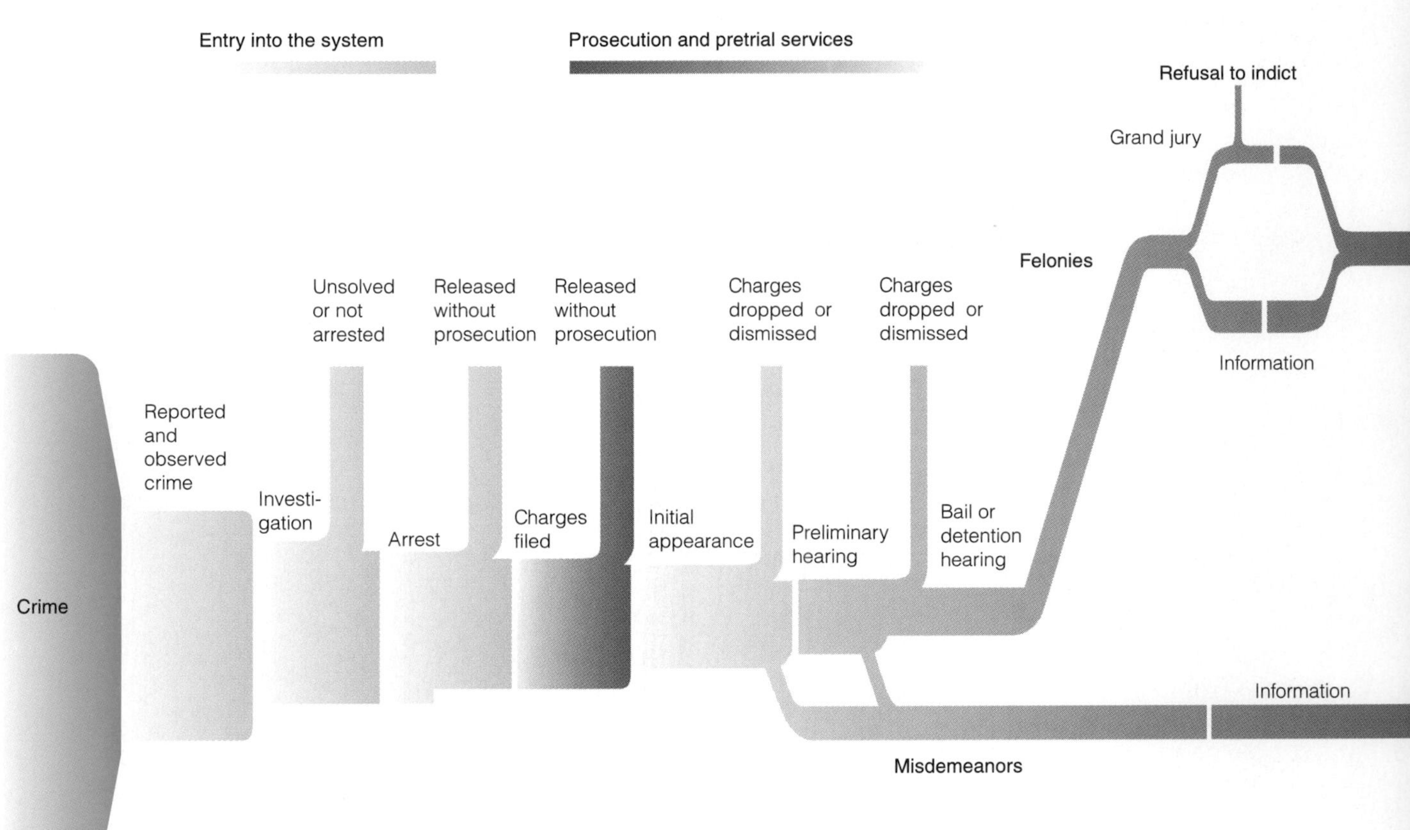

Originally published by the President's Commission on Law Enforcement and Administration of Justice in 1967, the flowchart was revised in 1997 by the Bureau of Justice Statistics.

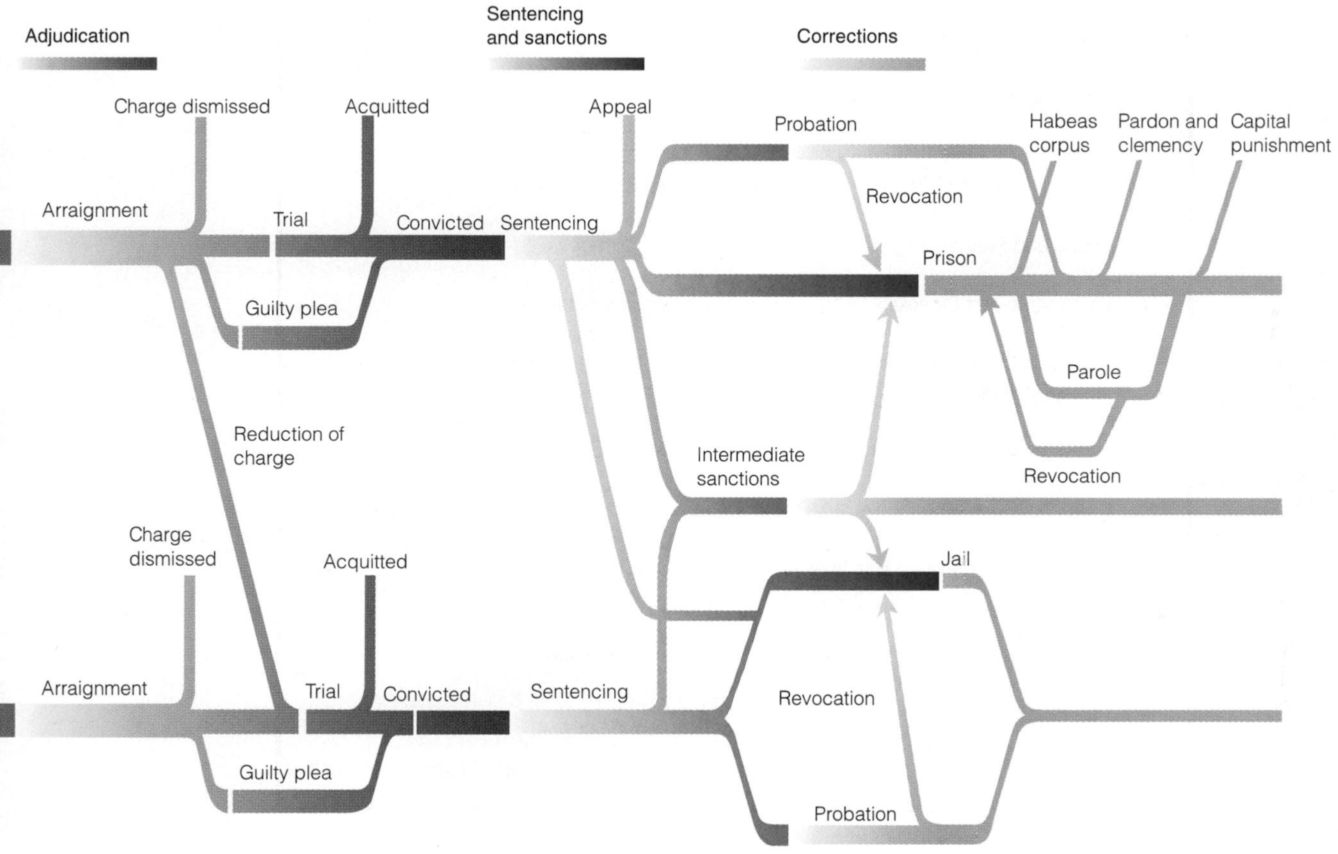

Adjudication
Sentencing and sanctions
Corrections
Charge dismissed
Acquitted
Appeal
Probation
Habeas corpus
Pardon and clemency
Capital punishment
Arraignment
Trial
Convicted
Sentencing
Revocation
Prison
Guilty plea
Parole
Reduction of charge
Intermediate sanctions
Revocation
Charge dismissed
Acquitted
Jail
Arraignment
Trial
Convicted
Sentencing
Revocation
Guilty plea
Probation

CD-ROM Cross-Reference Guide to *The American System of Criminal Justice*, Tenth Edition

PART ONE

Crime and the Criminal Justice System

The American system of criminal justice is a response to a problem that has required the attention of all societies from the beginning of time: crime. To understand how the system works and why crime persists in spite of our efforts to control it, we need to examine both the nature of criminal behavior and the functioning of the justice system itself. As we shall see, the reality of crime and justice involves much more than "cops and robbers," the details of legal codes, and the penalties for breaking laws. From defining what behavior counts as criminal to deciding the fate of offenders who are caught, the process of criminal justice is a *social* process that is subject to many influences other than written law.

Part 1, in introducing the study of this process, provides a broad framework for analyzing how our society—through its police, courts, and corrections—tries to deal with the age-old problem of crime.

CHAPTER 1

Crime and Justice in America

The Main Themes of This Book

Crime and Justice as Public Policy Issues
- The Role of Public Opinion
- Contemporary Policies
- Crime and Justice in a Democracy
- Crime Control versus Due Process
- The Politics of Crime and Justice

Defining Crime

Types of Crime
- Occupational Crime
- Organized Crime
- Visible Crime
- Crimes without Victims
- Political Crime
- Cybercrime

The Crime Problem Today
- The Worst of Times?
- The Most Crime-Ridden Nation?
- Keeping Track of Crime
- Trends in Crime

AFP Photo/Seth McAllister/CORBIS

The tragic events of September 11, 2001, changed the focus of many Americans' concerns about the world in which they live. In the aftermath of the hundreds of death caused by airline hijackers' suicidal attacks on the World Trade Center and the Pentagon, nearly half of the respondents to a June 2002 Gallup poll listed terrorism, national security, and fear as the "most important" problem facing the country (Gallup Poll, June 6, 2002). Although fear of terrorism increased after the events of 2001, these issues did not eliminate Americans' continuing preoccupation with crime.

There are two primary reasons for concluding that crime remains a paramount issue of concern for Americans. First, acts labeled as "terrorism" are themselves crimes. Hijackings, bombings, and murders violate criminal laws. Investigations and prosecutions resulting from such acts involve the Federal Bureau of Investigation (FBI), local police, prosecutors, and judges. Thus,

What Americans Think

Question: "What do you think is the most important problem facing this country today?"

Problem	Percent
Terrorism/national security/fear	46%
Economy	24%
Education	8%
Ethics/morality	7%
Poverty	4%
Drugs	3%
Crime/violence	2%
Judicial system	2%

Source: Gallup Poll, "Mood of America Becoming More Somber," *Gallup News Service,* June 14, 2002 (http://www.gallup.com).

crime in a particular form, one that involves political motivations and international organizations, has become Americans' foremost public policy concern. As indicated by "What Americans Think," if we recognize terrorism as embodying forms of crime that draw on the resources of the criminal justice system, issues of crime and public safety far exceed other major policy issues, such as the economy and education, as the foremost American concerns.

Second, Americans remain focused on other forms of homegrown crime as a major social problem. Newspaper headlines across the country continue to emphasize shootings, robberies, rapes, and drug busts. For example, on July 4, 2002, as newspapers across the country universally featured stories about Americans' renewed sense of patriotism, crime remained prominently portrayed in the day's news coverage. The *Boston Globe*'s headline, "Pair Allegedly Tried to Shoot at Rival Gang," highlighted coverage of the shotgun killing of a ten-year-old bystander. The headline in the *San Francisco Chronicle,* "Murder Suspect Called San Francisco Victim 'Mama'," concerned a man's brutal bludgeoning of his 85-year-old godmother. Across the country in Pittsburgh, the *Post-Gazette*'s headline, "Rape Suspect's Violent Trail Puzzles His Neighbors," introduced a story about a friendly ex-con who allegedly committed a series of armed robberies, home invasions, and sexual assaults before killing himself.

Americans are accustomed to reading such stories every day and seeing these themes featured in news programs, television dramas, and movies. Televised news programs depict urban neighborhoods ravaged by drugs and crime, small towns anxious about local shootouts, and citizens expressing fears about leaving their homes at night. Crime reporting has become such a staple of local television news coverage that it has acquired its own cliché: "If it bleeds, it leads" (*New York Times,* July 6, 1997:E4). Whatever else has happened, if someone is murdered, raped, or assaulted, that story will lead the newscast. These news programs do not merely demonstrate the news media's focus on crime. They also reflect the public's preoccupation with criminals, police, and courts. NBC has expanded the number of *Law and Order* programs because of the public's interest in crime, and CBS has done the same with its growing list of *CSI: Crime Scene Investigation* shows.

Parker Hank/CORBIS Sygma

Highly publicized crimes such as the murder of congressional intern Chandra Levy, killed while jogging through Rockcreek Park in Washington, D.C., are particularly frightening. How might such crimes affect public behavior?

Highly publicized crimes can readily frighten the public. As Americans read about the sniper killings in the District of Columbia, Maryland, and Virginia and the disappearance and murder of college student Chandra Levy while jogging in Washington, D.C., it is difficult to avoid wondering whether such things could happen to anyone's family. No wonder Americans go to bed fearful.

Responding to these concerns, politicians have tried to outdo one another in being "tough on crime." This toughness has led to shifts in public policies: adding 100,000 police officers nationwide, building more prisons, extending the death penalty to cover sixty federal offenses, mandating longer sentences, and requiring parolees to register with the police.

But is the concern about crime justified? Public opinion polls indicate that people remain quite fearful of crime and that they do not realize that serious crime declined steadily from the record-setting years of the early 1980s through 2000. The nation's view of crime continues to validate one reporter's observation in the early 1990s: "It is as though the country were confronting a devastating new wave of theft and violence" (*San Jose Mercury News,* October 23, 1993). In fact, however, there *is* no national crime wave. The news that crime is not rampant may surprise most Americans, but FBI data support this view. For example, property crime increased a modest 2.2 percent. Serious crime fell every year from 1993 through 2000, and violent crime increased only slightly (0.3 percent) in 2001 (FBI, 2002). By 2000, homicide rates reached their lowest point since 1969, and murders rose only 3.1 percent in 2001. The modest increase in crime rates in 2001 did not undo the large drops that had occurred in prior years. For example, in 1998 the number of violent crimes and property crimes each fell 7 percent and the number of murders went down 8 percent (Butterfield, 1999a). Further declines occurred immediately afterward in 1999 and 2000. Yet despite the generally good news about lower levels of crime than in the past, Americans "are afraid of and obsessed with crime" (Donziger, 1996:1).

To see the most recent government statistics on crime rates, see the U.S. Bureau of Justice Statistics homepage, http://www.ojp.usdoj.gov/bjs/.

The Main Themes of This Book

The study of criminal justice offers a fascinating view of a crucial social problem. Drawing from the perspectives of such academic disciplines as economics, history, law, political science, psychology, and sociology, the field of criminal justice aims to supply knowledge and develop policies to deal with criminality. But it is a challenge to a democracy to develop policies that deal with **crime** while still preserving individual rights, the rule of law, and justice. Democracy in the United States is defined and guided by historic American values, including individual liberty, the preservation of constitutional rights, an expectation of personal privacy, and the protection of private property and free enterprise. These American values guide the development of public policy in all areas of government, including criminal justice. The application of American values creates special tensions and problems in criminal justice. For example, people's sense of liberty may depend on how freely they can walk the streets without being fearful of crime; therefore, they want tough crime-control policies. On the other hand, other aspects of American values emphasize the protection of criminal defendant's rights in order to ensure that no one is improperly denied his or her liberty. Our democracy's challenge in finding the proper balance between conflicting values may become even greater in an era in which fears about terrorism have enhanced citizens' concerns about crime and public safety. Because 78 percent of Americans would be willing to give up some freedom in order to gain greater security (Gallup Poll, June 11, 2002), the nation may be experiencing an era in which a new balance will be developed between individual rights and protection of the public from crime.

crime
A specific act of commission or omission in violation of the law, for which a punishment is prescribed.

This book presents three major themes: (1) crime and justice are public policy issues; (2) criminal justice can best be seen as a social system; (3) The criminal justice system embodies society's effort to fulfill American values, such as liberty, privacy, and individuals' rights. As we shall see, these values can come into conflict as choices are made about how to operate the system and define public policies. This chapter focuses on the first theme; the third theme, American values, will be highlighted throughout each chapter. In addition, Chapter 1 examines the nature and definition of crime.

As you learn about crime and the criminal justice system, take note of the many different academic disciplines that contribute to our knowledge in these areas. For example, the study of criminal justice requires psychologists' contributions about the thinking and behavior of individuals. Criminologists develop and test theories about the causes of criminal behavior. Sociologists and economists examine the impact of society on crime as well as crime's impact on society. Political scientists explore the development of public policy and the operations of criminal justice agencies. Increasingly, chemists, biologists, and engineers play important roles in criminal justice because of the development of new scientific methods for investigating crimes and new technologies for weapons, surveillance, databases, and other essential aspects of law enforcement administration. Criminal justice is a multidisciplinary area of study that is of interest and importance to people with varied interests and expertise.

To learn about the primary organizations for criminal justice researchers, see the American Society of Criminology at http://www.asc41.com and the Academy of Criminal Justice Sciences at http://www.acjs.org.

By gaining an understanding of the crime problem and U.S. society's definition of this problem as a public policy issue, you will have the groundwork for later discussions about criminal justice as a social system in which actors and agencies interact and make decisions. To guide your study, we address the following Questions for Inquiry:

QUESTIONS for INQUIRY

- How are public policies on crime formed?
- How do the crime control and due process models of criminal justice help us understand the system?
- What is a crime?
- What are the major types of crime in the United States?
- How much crime is there, and how is it measured?

Crime and Justice as Public Policy Issues

Who bears responsibility for addressing issues of crime and justice? The answer to this question depends on the organization of a society and the nature of its governing system. Looking back at human history, one can see many approaches to crime and punishment. In a sparsely populated rural society that lacks effective control by government, crime and justice could be viewed as a private matter. When one individual harms another through violence or theft, a measure of justice might be obtained through vengeful acts by the victim's family or through the payment of compensation by the perpetrator. Such approaches were common in the centuries before central governments became dominating forces in modern nations. Alternatively, local leaders could rely on religious values or cultural traditions to impose punishments upon wrongdoers. Such approaches still exist in some communities that are isolated or otherwise guided by nongovernment leaders and organizations. For example, in 2002 news stories emerged about a young woman in Pakistan who was sexually assaulted by tribal leaders as punishment for her brother's association with a woman from a higher-status tribe, a violation of local customs (Tanveer, 2002). In doing this the leaders violated Pakistani law, but they asserted significant control over the community in a region where Pakistani officials did not have enough authority to enforce the rules of the criminal justice system. In the United States, by contrast, crime and justice are **public policy** issues because they are addressed by government. Institutions and processes of government produce laws to define crimes; create and operate agencies to investigate, prosecute, and punish criminals; and allocate resources to address the problems of crime and justice.

public policy
Policies developed by government as to the ways public resources will be used to deal with issues affecting society.

Crime and justice are important and difficult public policy issues in the United States. In a democracy, we struggle to strike a balance between maintaining public order and protecting individual freedom. Both sides of this equation represent American values. To enjoy the liberty that we value so highly, we want to feel safe to move freely in society. On the other hand, if we push too strongly to ensure safety, we could limit individual rights and liberty by unnecessarily restricting, detaining, or punishing too many individuals. For example, we could impose policies that make us feel safe from crime, such as placing a police officer on every street corner and executing suspected criminals. Such severe practices have been used elsewhere in the world. While they may reduce crime, they also fly in the face of democratic values. If we gave law enforcement officers a free hand to work their will on the public, we would be giving up individual freedom, due process, and our conception of justice. Liberty and legal rights are of such importance that they are enshrined in the nation's founding document, the U.S. Constitution. However, the protection of these democratic values can impede the ability of criminal justice officials to catch and punish offenders. Thus we continually struggle to find the proper balance between stopping crime and preventing government officials from violating individuals' rights.

Many organizations seek to influence the development of criminal justice policy. To see one example, read about the Criminal Justice Policy Foundation at http://www.cjpf.org.

Some critics of criminal justice, such as Jeffrey Reiman, argue that our system is designed "not to reduce crime or to achieve justice but to project to the American people a visible image of the threat of crime" (Reiman, 1996:1). This is done by maintaining a sizable population of criminals while at the same time failing to reduce crime. Reiman argues that we need to move away from a system of *criminal* justice to one of criminal *justice.* He urges policies that

- End crime-producing poverty
- Criminalize the dangerous acts of the affluent and white collar offenders
- Create a correctional system that promotes human dignity
- Make the exercise of police, prosecution, and judicial power more just
- Establish economic and social justice

If adopted, Reiman's thought-provoking critical perspective would revolutionize not only the criminal justice system but also many of the attitudes and customs of American society.

Dealing with the crime problem concerns not only the arrest, conviction, and punishment of offenders; it also requires the development of policies to deal with a host of issues such as gun control, stalking, hate crimes, cybertheft, drugs, child abuse, and global criminal organizations. Many of these issues are controversial; policies must be hammered out in the political arenas of state legislatures and Congress. The Policy Debate examines the pros and cons of one of these issues: "Have Tough Crime-Control Policies Caused a Decline in Crime?"

The Role of Public Opinion

In a democracy, political leaders are greatly influenced by public opinion. They know that if they develop policies not in accord with what the public thinks, elections may be lost and the legitimacy of those policies may be diminished. But legislators also know that they can cater to the American public's anxiety about crime and community safety. As a result, policies are often enacted that are popular with the general public but that are thought by researchers to have little potential impact on crime.

Throughout this book, you will find marginal notations labeled "What Americans Think." These present the results of public opinion surveys on issues concerning crime and the administration of justice. As you read each chapter, consider these expressions of public opinion. Do you agree with the majority of Americans on each issue? Or does your understanding of criminal justice give you a different perspective on the policies that might better address these problems? Do your opinions differ from those of other criminal justice students?

To find out the opinions of other criminal justice students, please go to http://www.cj.wadsworth.com/colesmith10e. Click on "Survey" and answer the questionnaire. Your responses will be collated with those of other students so that you can review the results by clicking on the Web site again. You may want to download and print out your responses as well as those of students throughout the country. Compare your opinion, student opinion, and the general public's opinion.

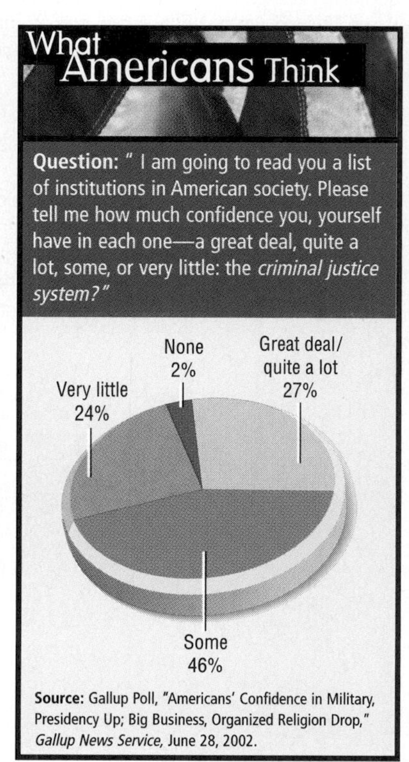

Source: Gallup Poll, "Americans' Confidence in Military, Presidency Up; Big Business, Organized Religion Drop," *Gallup News Service,* June 28, 2002.

Contemporary Policies

Over the past several decades, both conservatives and liberals have promoted policies for dealing with crime. Each group has its own perspective on what works best to advance justice.

Have Tough Crime-Control Policies Caused a Decline in Crime?

Regarding crime, there's good news and there's bad news. The good news is that there have been significant decreases in every type of violent and property crime in recent years. And virtually every demographic group has experienced drops in violent victimization. The bad news is that experts do not fully understand the causes for the decline in crime. Have the tough crime-control policies of the past 20 years been successful? Or have crime rates declined because of factors unrelated to anything criminal justice agencies have done?

Some experts point to the increasing number of police on the streets, longer sentences, and the greater probability upon conviction of going to prison. They say the police have been more aggressive in dealing with public order offenses, the waiting period for handgun purchases has been effective, and more than a million Americans are already in prison and off the streets. In other words, the police and other agencies of criminal justice *do* make a difference.

Other experts question the impact of tough policies. They point out that unemployment is low, the economy is good, and most important, the number of men in the "crime-prone" age group is low. Many also say that the tough crime policies, instead of reducing crime, have devastated minority communities and diverted resources from dealing with the poverty that underlies crime. They urge policies that "put justice back in criminal justice."

For Tough Crime Control

Supporters of tough crime control say that even though crime rates have declined, violence is still many times higher than in other developed democracies. They advocate continuing to pursue criminals through strict law enforcement, aggressive prosecutions, and the sentencing of career criminals to long prison terms.

The arguments for tough crime-control policies are as follows:

- The United States must ensure that offenders receive strict and certain penalties.
- Crime is not caused by poverty, unemployment, and other socioeconomic factors. Instead, crime causes poverty.
- The expansion of the prison population has taken hardened criminals out of the community, thus contributing to the drop in crime.
- The police must have the resources and legal backing to pursue criminals.

Against Tough Crime Control

Opponents of the "get-tough" approach believe there are better ways to deal with crime. They argue that crime is no more effectively controlled today than it was in the early 1970s and that in many respects the problem has worsened, especially in the poorest neighborhoods. Another price of the tough crime-control policies has been an erosion of civil rights and liberties—especially for racial and ethnic minorities. What is needed is an infusion of *justice* into the system.

The arguments against tough crime-control policies are as follows:

- The get-tough policies have not significantly reduced crime.
- Resources should be diverted from the criminal justice system to get to the underlying causes of criminal behavior—poor housing, unemployment, and racial injustice.
- Tough incarceration policies have devastated poor communities. When large numbers of young men are in prison, families live in poverty, and children grow up without guidance from their fathers and older brothers.
- Crime policies emphasizing community policing, alternatives to incarceration, and community assistance programs will do more to promote justice than the failed get-tough policies of the past.

What Should U.S. Policy Be?

Advocates of tough crime-control policies say the $100 billion cost of the criminal justice system is worth the price—cutting back would cost much more to crime victims and society as a whole. The crime rate is lower because of the more aggressive and punitive policies of the past two decades.

Opponents of these policies respond that the police, courts, and corrections have had little impact on crime. Other factors have been responsible for the reduction. The diversion of resources—in both money and people—to fighting crime has limited government programs that could improve conditions in poor neighborhoods where crime flourishes.

Even though they are told that crime has gone down, Americans remain fearful and have supported politicians who advocate the tough approach. No candidate wants to be labeled "soft on crime." What would be the costs—economic and human—of continuing the get-tough policies? Would that same fearful public be affected?

Go to the *American System of Criminal Justice* Web site at http://www.cj.wadsworth.com/colesmith10e to explore this question in further detail: Have tough crime control policies caused a decline in crime?

Conservatives believe that solutions will come from stricter enforcement of the law through the expansion of police forces and the enactment of laws that require swift and certain punishment of criminals (Logan and DiIulio, 1993:486). Advocates of such policies have dominated since the early 1980s. They argue that we must strengthen crime control, which they claim has been hindered by certain decisions of the United States Supreme Court and by programs that substitute government assistance for individual responsibility.

In contrast, liberals argue that stronger crime-control measures endanger the values of due process and justice (S. Walker, 1993:504). They claim that strict measures are ineffective because progress will come from reshaping the lives of offenders and changing the social and economic conditions from which criminal behavior springs.

As you consider these arguments, think about how they relate to crime trends. Crime increased in the 1960s when we were trying the liberal approach of rehabilitating offenders. Does this mean that the approach does not work? Perhaps it was merely overwhelmed by the sheer number of people who were in their crime-prone years (between the ages of 16 and 24). Perhaps there would have been even more crime if not for the efforts to rehabilitate people. On the other hand, crime rates decreased when tough policies were implemented in the 1980s. But was that because of the conservative policies in effect, or because there were fewer people in the crime-prone age group? If conservative policies are effective, then why did violent crime rates rise in the early 1990s, when tough policies were still in force? Clearly, there are no easy answers, yet we cannot avoid making choices about how to use the police, courts, and corrections system most effectively.

Crime and Justice in a Democracy

Americans agree that criminal justice policies should control crime by enforcing the law *and* should protect the rights of individuals. But these goals taken together are difficult to achieve. They involve questions such as the amount of power police should have to search persons without a warrant, the rules judges must follow in deciding if certain types of evidence may be used, and the power of prison wardens to punish inmates. These questions are answered differently in a democracy than they would be in an authoritarian state.

The administration of justice in a democracy also differs from that in an authoritarian state in the nature and extent of the protections provided for an accused person as guilt is determined and punishment imposed. The police, prosecutors, judges, and correctional officials are expected to act according to democratic values—especially respect for the rule of law and the maintenance of civil rights and liberties. But citizens must also view the criminal justice system as legitimate and have confidence in its actions.

Laws in the United States begin with the premise that all people—the guilty as well as the innocent—have rights. Moreover, unlike laws in some other countries, U.S. laws reflect the desire to avoid unnecessarily depriving people of liberty, either by permitting the police to arrest people at will or by punishing a person for a crime that he or she did not commit.

Joseph Sohm, ChromoSohm Inc./CORBIS

In a democracy, citizens should take an interest in the criminal justice system, as they are doing here in this demonstration against drug use and killings in East Los Angeles.

Although all Americans prize freedom and individual rights, they often disagree about policies to deal with crime. Our greatest challenge as we move through the twenty-first century may be to find ways to remain true to the principles of fairness and justice while operating a system that can effectively protect, investigate, and punish.

check point

1. What criminal justice policies are advocated by conservatives?
2. What criminal justice policies cause concerns for liberals?
3. What are the two criminal justice goals that Americans agree on?

(Answers are at the end of the chapter.)

Crime Control versus Due Process

In one of the most important contributions to systematic thought about criminal justice, Herbert Packer (1968) described two competing models of criminal justice

crime control model
A model of the criminal justice system that assumes freedom is so important that every effort must be made to repress crime; it emphasizes efficiency, speed, finality, and the capacity to apprehend, try, convict, and dispose of a high proportion of offenders.

due process model
A model of the criminal justice system that assumes freedom is so important that every effort must be made to ensure that criminal justice decisions are based on reliable information; it emphasizes the adversarial process, the rights of defendants, and formal decision-making procedures.

administration: the **crime control model** and the **due process model.** These are contrasting ways of looking at the goals and procedures of the criminal justice system. The crime control model is much like an assembly line, while the due process model is like an obstacle course.

In reality, of course, no criminal justice official or agency functions according to one model or the other. Elements of both models are actually found throughout the system. However, the two models reveal key tensions within the criminal justice process, as well as the gap between how we describe the system and the way most cases are actually processed. Table 1.1 presents the main elements of each model.

Crime Control: Order as a Value

The crime control model assumes that every effort must be made to repress crime. It emphasizes efficiency and the capacity to catch, try, convict, and punish a high proportion of offenders; it also stresses speed and finality. This model places the goal of controlling crime uppermost, putting less emphasis on protecting individuals' rights. As Packer points out, in order to achieve liberty for all citizens, the crime control model calls for efficiency in screening suspects, determining guilt, and applying sanctions to the convicted. Because of high rates of crime and the limited resources of law enforcement, speed and finality are necessary. All of these elements depend on informality, uniformity, and few challenges by defense attorneys or defendants.

In this model, police and prosecutors decide early on how likely the suspect is to be found guilty. If a case is unlikely to end in conviction, the prosecutor may drop the charges. At each stage—from arrest to preliminary hearing, arraignment, and trial—established procedures are used to determine whether the accused should be passed on to the next stage. Rather than stressing the combative aspects of the courtroom, this model promotes bargaining between the state and the accused. Nearly all cases are processed through such bargaining, and they typically end with the defendant pleading guilty. Packer's description of this model as an assembly-line process conveys the idea of quick, efficient decisions by actors at fixed stations that turn out the intended product—guilty pleas and closed cases.

Due Process: Law as a Value

If the crime control model looks like an assembly line, the due process model looks more like an obstacle course. This model assumes that freedom is so important that every effort must be made to ensure that criminal justice decisions are based on reliable information. It stresses the adversarial process, the rights of defendants, and formal decision-making procedures. For example, because people are poor observers of disturbing events, there is a good chance that police and prosecutors may be wrong in presuming a defendant to be guilty. Thus, people should be labeled as criminals only on the basis of conclusive evidence. To reduce error, the government must be forced to prove beyond a reasonable doubt that the defendant is guilty of the crime. Therefore, the process must give the defense every opportunity to show that the evidence is not conclusive, and an im-

Table 1.1 **Due process model and crime control model compared**

What other comparisons can be made between the two models?

	Goal	Value	Process	Major Decision Point	Basis of Decision Making
Due process model	Preserve individual liberties	Reliability	Adversarial	Courtroom	Law
Crime control model	Repress crime	Efficiency	Administrative	Police, pretrial processes	Discretion

partial judge and jury must decide the outcome. According to Packer, the assumption that the defendant is innocent until proved guilty has a far-reaching impact on the criminal justice system.

In the due process model, the state must prove that the person is guilty of the crime as charged. Prosecutors must prove their cases while obeying rules dealing with such matters as the admissibility of evidence and respect for defendants' constitutional rights. Forcing the state to prove its case in a trial protects citizens from wrongful convictions. Thus, the due process model emphasizes justice as protecting the rights of individuals and reserving punishment for those who unquestionably deserve it. These values are stressed even though some guilty defendants may go free because the evidence against them is not conclusive enough. By contrast, the crime control model values efficient case processing and punishment over the possibility that innocent people might be swept up in the process.

check point

4. What are the main features of the crime control model?
5. What are the main features of the due process model?

The Politics of Crime and Justice

Criminal justice policies are developed in national, state, and local political arenas. There is always a risk that politicians will simply do what they believe voters want to hear rather than think seriously about whether those policies will achieve their goals. For example, the crime bill passed by Congress in 1994 expanded the death penalty to cover sixty additional offenses, including the murder of members of Congress, the Supreme Court, and the president's staff. These are tough provisions, but will they actually accomplish anything? Many criminologists doubt it.

Frequently there is a "knee-jerk" quality to the political process. A problem occurs and captures significant public attention. There are calls to "do something."

J. Scott Applewhite/AP/Wide World Photos

Attorney General John Ashcroft (right) and FBI Director Robert Mueller at a news conference in which they support the new antiterrorism legislation, which will have a major impact on the criminal justice system.

For an example of a state's sex offender registry, see Iowa's registry at http://www.iowasexoffenders.com/.

Politicians respond with (1) outrage, (2) a study of the problem, and (3) a law—often poorly thought out and with little regard for unintended consequences. Politicians often propose laws without carefully studying the nature and extent of the problem that they claim to address (Gest, 2001).

Megan's Law is an example of good intentions gone awry. Though it varies from state to state, the legislation was passed in reaction to the rape and murder of a New Jersey child, Megan Kanka, by a convicted sex offender. This well-meaning attempt to deal with dangerous sexual predators has been difficult to implement fairly. For example, under Connecticut's version of the law, sex offenders who have served their sentences must report their addresses for display on a Web site for the public to peruse. The law was so poorly written that hundreds are labeled dangerous sex offenders when only a small percentage on the list might fit that category (*Hartford Courant,* September 10, 1999:A22).

The clearest link between politics and criminal justice can be seen in the statements of Republicans and Democrats who try to outdo each other in showing how tough they can be on crime (Estrich, 1998). Just as important are the more "routine" links between politics and the justice system. Penal code provisions and the budgets of criminal justice agencies are decided by legislators who are responding to the demands of voters. Congress appropriates millions of dollars to help states and cities wage the "war on drugs" but limits spending for legal counsel for poor defendants. At the state and local levels, many criminal justice authorities—including sheriffs, prosecutors, and judges—are also elected officials. Their decisions will be influenced by the concerns and values of their communities.

As you learn about each part of the criminal justice system, keep in mind the ways decision makers and institutions are connected to politics and government. Criminal justice is closely linked to society and its institutions, and to understand it fully we must be aware of those links.

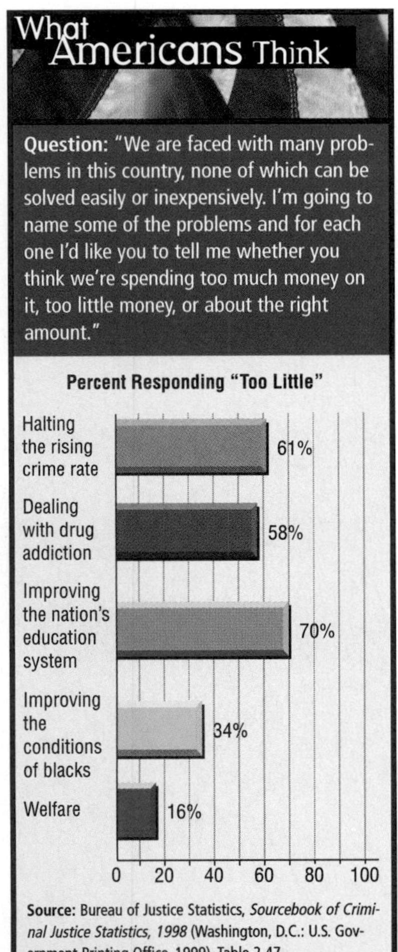

Source: Bureau of Justice Statistics, *Sourcebook of Criminal Justice Statistics, 1998* (Washington, D.C.: U.S. Government Printing Office, 1999), Table 2.47.

check point

6. At what level of government are many justice officials elected to office?
7. How do politics influence criminal justice policies?

Defining Crime

Why does the law label some types of behavior but not others as criminal? For example, many young people ask, "Why is it illegal to smoke marijuana but legal to consume alcohol?" If the answer is that marijuana might be addictive, could lead to the use of more potent drugs, and may have negative effects on health, then the questioner might point out that alcoholism is a major social problem, drinking beer can create a thirst for hard liquor, and overuse of alcohol leads to heart and liver disorders as well as many auto accidents. A parent facing such arguments from a teenager may find it difficult to explain why the parent drinks alcohol but forbids the teenager from smoking marijuana. Frequently, the parent may cut the argument short by simply declaring, "You cannot use marijuana because pot smoking is against the law, and that's that!" Criminal laws are not necessarily developed through consistent logical reasoning. Instead, they reflect societal values, some of which may be inconsistent, as well as the preferences of politicians.

To find your state's criminal laws, go to http://www.findlaw.com/11stategov/. Then click the name of your state and find the link for the state's codes or statutes.

Criminal law is defined by elected representatives in state legislatures and Congress who make choices about the behaviors that government will punish. Some of those choices reflect a broad consensus in society that certain actions, such as rape, assault, and murder, are so harmful that they must be punished. Such crimes have traditionally been called ***mala in se***—wrong in themselves.

mala in se
Offenses that are wrong by their very nature.

However, legislatures also create criminal laws concerning certain acts, the harmfulness of which the public is still debating. These crimes are referred to as ***mala prohibita***—they are crimes because they are prohibited by the government and not because they are wrong in themselves. Everyone does not agree, for example, that gambling, prostitution, and drug use should be punished. Today, some people view these behaviors as free choices that adults should be able to make themselves (see "What Americans Think"). Indeed, these behaviors have not been illegal at all times and in all places. Gambling, for example, is illegal in many states, but it represents an important legitimate business in Nevada, New Jersey, Michigan, Native American reservations, and other locations in the United States. Regulated prostitution is legal in Nevada and in many countries of the world, but not in most of U.S. states. Although the federal government has blocked the implementation of state laws that relax drug regulations, voters in several U.S. states have expressed their views on the subject by voting to permit people to smoke marijuana for medicinal purposes. Thus the designation of such activities as crimes does not reflect values that are universally shared throughout the United States.

mala prohibita
Offenses prohibited by law but not wrong in themselves.

Source: Bureau of Justice Statistics, *Sourcebook of Criminal Justice Statistics, 1998* (Washington, D.C.: U.S. Government Printing Office, 1999), Tables 2.72, 2.99, 2.100.

Evidence from a national survey helps show the extent to which Americans agree about the behaviors that should be defined as crimes. (BJS, 1988:16). In this study, respondents were asked to rank the seriousness of 204 illegal events. The results (see Table 1.2) showed wide agreement on the severity of certain crimes. However, crime victims scored those acts higher than did nonvictims. The ratings assigned by minority group members tended to be lower than those assigned by whites. Thus there is disagreement about which behaviors to punish as crimes.

American laws are often in conflict with the religious and cultural practices of recent non-Western immigrants. In Maine, a refugee from Afghanistan was seen kissing the penis of his baby boy, a traditional expression of love by his father. To his neighbors this was child abuse and the boy was taken away (*New York Times,* March 6, 1999:A15). A court in Lincoln, Nebraska, gave 4–6 year prison terms to two 28- and 34-year-old Iraqi men for sexual assault on a child. They had married the daughters, aged 13 and 14, of a fellow Iraqi immigrant in a Muslim ceremony. Their attorney argued that they were following Iraqi custom and did not know that the minimum age for marriage in Nebraska is 17 (*Kansas*

Table 1.2 How do people rank the severity of a crime?

Respondents to a survey were asked to rank 204 illegal events ranging from school truancy to planting a deadly bomb. A severity score of 40 indicates that people believe the crime is twice as bad as does a severity score of 20.

Severity Score	Ten Most Serious Offenses	Severity Score	Ten Least Serious Offenses
72.1	Planting a bomb in a public building. The bomb explodes and twenty people are killed.	1.3	Two persons willingly engage in a homosexual act.
52.8	A man forcibly rapes a woman. As a result of physical injuries, she dies.	1.1	Disturbing the neighborhood with loud, noisy behavior.
43.2	Robbing a victim at gunpoint. The victim struggles and is shot to death.	1.1	Taking bets on the numbers.
39.2	A man stabs his wife. As a result, she dies.	1.1	A group continues to hang around a corner after being told by a police officer to break up.
35.7	Stabbing a victim to death.	.9	A youngster under 16 runs away from home.
35.6	Intentionally injuring a victim. As a result, the victim dies.	.8	Being drunk in public.
33.8	Running a narcotics ring.	.7	A youngster under 16 breaks a curfew law by being on the street after the hour permitted by law.
27.9	A woman stabs her husband. As a result, he dies.	.6	Trespassing in the backyard of a private home.
26.3	An armed person skyjacks an airplane and demands to be flown to another country.	.3	A person is vagrant. That is, he has no home and no visible means of support.
25.8	A man forcibly rapes a woman. No other physical injury occurs.	.2	A youngster under 16 is truant from school.

Source: Bureau of Justice Statistics, *Report to the Nation on Crime and Justice,* 2nd ed. (Washington, D.C.: U.S. Government Printing Office, 1988), 16.

City Star, September 24, 1997:A2). Sexual practices, puberty rites, animal sacrifices, and the use of narcotics have been portrayed as traditional rituals of particular cultures. But can ethnic groups justifiably claim that their practices need not conform to the law?

check point

8. Who defines certain behaviors as criminal?
9. What is meant by *mala in se* and by *mala prohibita?*

Types of Crime

Crimes can be classified in various ways. As we have seen, scholars often use the distinction between *mala in se* and *mala prohibita.* Crimes can also be classified as either felonies or misdemeanors. A third scheme classifies crimes by the nature of the act. This approach produces five types of crime: occupational crime, organized crime, visible crime, victimless crime, and political crime. Each type has its own level of risk and reward, each arouses varying degrees of public disapproval, and each is committed by a certain kind of offender. New types of crime emerge as society changes. Cybercrimes committed through the use of computers over the Internet are becoming a major global problem.

Occupational Crime

occupational crime
Criminal offenses committed through opportunities created in a legal business or occupation.

Occupational crimes are committed in the context of a legal business or profession. Often viewed as shrewd business practices rather than as illegal acts, they are crimes that, if "done right," are never discovered. An important American value is economic liberty. Each person is presumed to have the opportunity to make his or her own fortune through hard work and innovative ideas. The success of the American economic system is built, in part, on the creativity of people who invented new products, developed new technologies, or discovered new ways to market goods. Although we admire entrepreneurial activities, some individuals go too far in using their creativity within our free enterprise system. The freedom to make financial transactions and other decisions in fast-moving private businesses also creates opportunities to steal from employers or defraud customers and investors. The U.S. Department of Commerce estimates that occupational crimes cost businesses $40 billion annually (Dumaine, 1998:193).

Crimes committed in the course of business were first described by criminologist Edwin Sutherland in 1939, when he developed the concept of "white-collar crime." He noted that such crimes are committed by respectable offenders taking advantage of opportunities arising from their business dealings. He forced criminologists to recognize that criminal behavior was not confined to lower-class people (so-called blue-collar crime) but reached into the upper levels of society (Shover, 1998:133; Sutherland, 1949).

The white-collar/blue-collar distinction has lost much of its meaning in modern society. Since the 1970s, research on white-collar crime has shifted from the individual to the organization (Friedrichs, 1996:38). Gary Green has described four types of occupational crimes (Green, 1997: 17–19):

1. *Occupational crimes for the benefit of the employing organizations.* Employers rather than offenders benefit directly from these crimes. They include price fixing, theft of trade secrets, and falsification of product tests. In these cases an employee may commit the offense but will not benefit personally, except perhaps through a bonus or promotion. It is the company that benefits. These crimes are "committed in the suites rather than in the streets."

AP Photo/Louis Lanzano

David F. Myers, former comptroller for WorldCom, is led from federal court in New York City after surrendering to face federal charges for accounting fraud.

In 2002 many Americans became more keenly aware of the impact of occupational crimes, when news reports focused on corporate misconduct that produced significant detrimental consequences for investors and pension funds. Arthur Andersen, the international accounting firm, was convicted of obstruction of justice for interfering with the federal investigation of Enron, the energy company whose collapse cost investors and employees millions of dollars (Torriero and Manor, 2002). The company faced a potential fine of $500,000 for the crime. As in the case of communications giant WorldCom, Xerox, Tyco, and other companies, Enron and its accountants relied on deceptive practices to inflate earnings reports and the value of its stock (Kadlec, 2002). These actions, some of which may have violated criminal laws, advanced the interests of the company as well as the bank accounts of many high-level corporate officials.

Some organizations attempt to monitor socially harmful activities by corporations and their executives. For one example, see http://www.corpwatch.org/.

2. *Occupational crimes through the exercise of government authority.* In these crimes the offender has the legal power to enforce laws or command others to do so. Examples include removal of drugs from the evidence room by a police officer, acceptance of a bribe by a public official, and falsification of a document by a notary public. For example, in July 2002 a U.S. Army colonel stationed in South Korea was charged with accepting bribes from Korean construction businesses that sought contracts to build military barracks at American bases. The colonel was responsible for approving more than $300 million annually in government contracts. Investigators found more than $700,000 in cash hidden in the colonel's home (Carter, 2002).
3. *Occupational crimes committed by professionals in their capacity as professionals.* Doctors, lawyers, and stockbrokers may take advantage of clients by, for instance, illegally dispensing drugs, using funds placed in escrow, or using "insider" stock-trading information for personal profit or, if their offices are not prospering, to keep their businesses going (Willott, Griffin, and Torrance, 2001). From the late 1990s onward, fraud crimes increased as financial services professionals and corporate executives took advantage of Americans' interest in investments and used that interest as a means to obtain money illegally (Labaton, 2002). For example, during 2002, federal authorities investigated Sam Waksal, former Chief Executive Officer of a company called ImClone. Authorities suspected he used "insider information" to help

family members and friends, including Martha Stewart, profit from selling company stock just before its value crashed. Stewart and her stockbroker were also targeted by investigators for both insider trading and obstruction of justice related to the criminal investigation (Naughton, 2002). The financial scandals led to calls in Congress for stronger criminal punishments for corporate executives, stockbrokers, and investors who violate the law.

Many commentators believe that the American value of economic liberty led the government to reduce the regulation of business. As a result, some individuals exploited the lack of government control to manipulate corporate stock values in ways that gave them great profits but ultimately harmed millions of investors. As a result of the scandals involving Enron and other corporations, Congress is moving toward new public policy choices that will reduce corporate executives' freedom to make decisions without supervision and accountability.

4. *Occupational crimes committed by individuals as individuals, where opportunities are not based on government power or professional position.* Examples of this type of crime include thefts by employees from employers, filing of false expense claims, and embezzlement (Wright and Cullen, 2000). Employee crime is believed to account for about 1 percent of the gross national product and causes consumer prices to be 10 to 15 percent higher than they would be otherwise. Employee theft is involved in about a third of business failures. The total loss due to employee theft therefore is greater than all business losses from shoplifting, burglary, or robbery (Friedrichs, 1996:115).

Although they are highly profitable, most types of occupational crime do not come to public attention. Regulatory agencies, such as the Federal Trade Commission and the Securities and Exchange Commission, often do not enforce the law effectively. Many business and professional organizations "police" themselves, dropping employees or members who commit offenses.

The low level of criminal enforcement of occupational crimes may result from the fact that the general public does not view them as serious. Such crimes usually do not involve violence or threats to public safety, although some may involve selling unsafe food or defective products. Many people may not realize, however, the huge costs of such crimes to society. In addition, the complex nature of financial transactions and executive decisions may make these cases difficult to investigate and prosecute. In the words of one criminologist, "Many of these cases lack jury appeal: that is the 'sexiness' of other cases, in which it is easier to identify the harm that was caused and how it was caused" (Eitle, 2000:830).

Organized Crime

organized crime
A framework for the perpetration of criminal acts—usually in fields such as gambling, drugs, and prostitution—providing illegal services that are in great demand.

money laundering
Moving the proceeds of criminal activities through a maze of businesses, banks, and brokerage accounts so as to disguise their origin.

The term **organized crime** refers to a *framework* within which criminal acts are committed, rather than referring to the acts themselves. A crime syndicate has an organizational structure, rules, a division of labor, and the capacity for ruthless violence and to corrupt law enforcement, labor and business leaders, and politicians (Jacobs and Panarella, 1998:160). Organized criminals provide goods and services to millions of people. They will engage in any activity that provides a minimum of risk and a maximum of profit. Thus organized crime involves a network of activities, usually cutting across state and national borders, that range from legitimate businesses to shady deals with labor unions to providing "goods"—such as drugs, sex, and pornography—that cannot be obtained legally. In recent years organized crime has been involved in new services such as commercial arson, illegal disposal of toxic wastes, and **money laundering.** Few organized criminals are arrested and prosecuted.

Investigations of the crime "families," which are known as the Mafia and Cosa Nostra, have yielded detailed accounts of their structure, membership, and activities. The FBI and the media give the impression that the Mafia is a unified syndicate, but scholars tend to believe that the "families" are fairly autonomous local groups (Abadinsky, 2003; Albanese, 1991). The June 2002 death of John Gotti, the imprisoned boss of New York's Gambino crime "family," led to numerous news stories reviewing the activities of "the most important gangster since Al Capone" (Pyle, 2002). Gotti's death was also treated as the end of an era, because criminal organizations no longer neatly fit the image of falling under exclusive control by the families of European immigrants.

Although the public often associates organized crime with Italian Americans—indeed, the federal government indicted 73 members of the Genovese New York crime "family" in 2001 (Worth, 2001)—other ethnic groups have dominated at various times. Thirty-five years ago, one scholar noted the strangeness of America's "ladder of social mobility," in which each new immigrant group uses organized crime as one of the first rungs of the climb (Bell, 1967:150). However, debate about this notion continues, because not all immigrant groups have engaged in organized crime (Kenney and Finckenauer, 1995:38).

Some believe that the pirates of the seventeenth century were an early form of organized crime in America. But in the 1820s the "Forty Thieves," an Irish gang in New York City, were the first to organize on a large scale. They were followed by Jews who dominated gambling and labor rackets at the turn of the century. The Italians came next, but they did not climb very far up the ladder until the late 1930s (Ianni, 1973:1–2).

Over the last few decades, the Mafia has been greatly weakened by law enforcement efforts. Beginning in 1978 the federal government mounted extraordinary efforts to eradicate the group. Using electronic surveillance, undercover agents, and mob turncoats, the FBI, the federal Organized Crime Task Forces, and the U.S. attorneys' offices, law enforcement launched investigations and prosecutions. As Jacobs notes, "The magnitude of the government's attack on Cosa Nostra is nothing short of incredible." By 1992, 23 bosses were convicted, and the leadership and soldiers of five New York City families (Bonanno, Colombo, Gambino, Genovese, Lucchese) were decimated (Jacobs, Panarella, and Worthington, 1994:4). In addition, an aging leadership, lack of interest by younger family members, and pressures from new immigrant groups have contributed to the fall of the Mafia.

Today African Americans, Hispanics, Russians, and Asians have formed organized crime groups in some cities. (See the Close Up box, "The Russian Mafiya of Brighton Beach" on page 18.) Drug dealing has brought Colombian and Mexican crime groups to U.S. shores, and Vietnamese-, Chinese-, and Japanese-led groups have been formed in California. Because these new groups do not fit the Mafia pattern, law enforcement agencies have had to find new ways to deal with them (Kleinknecht, 1996).

Just as multinational corporations have emerged during the past 20 years, organized crime has also developed global networks. Increasingly transnational criminal groups "live and operate in a borderless world" (Zagaris, 1998:1402). Senator John Kerry describes a "global criminal axis" involving the drug trade, money laundering, and terrorism (Kerry, 1997). In 1999 a federal grand jury indicted three Russian immigrants and three of their companies on money laundering charges. The indictment said that those charged had moved $7 billion through the Bank of New York over three and a half years. Investigators say the Russian funds may have involved corporate embezzlement, political graft, and organized crime. The FBI and their Russian counterparts have been investigating the source of the funds and the conduits through which they were moved (*New York Times,* October 6, 1999:A1).

In the aftermath of the events of September 11 American law enforcement and intelligence officials increased their efforts to monitor and thwart international organizations that seek to attack the United States and its citizens. Many of these organizations use criminal activities, such as drug smuggling and stolen credit card numbers, to fund their efforts. For example, in 2002 eight men in North

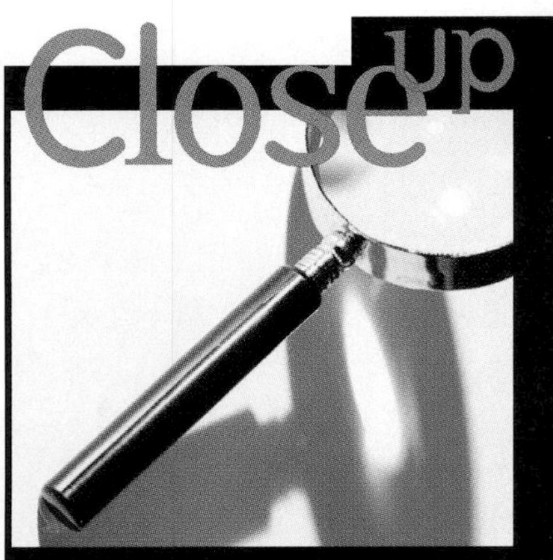

The Russian Mafiya of Brighton Beach

Brighton Beach, an immigrant neighborhood in New York City, is famous in Russia and Eastern Europe as the hub of the Russian *mafiya.* Like other Russian crime organizations in Denver, Los Angeles, and Toronto, the mafiya is involved in heroin dealing, prostitution, money laundering, and toxic waste disposal.

The 1995 indictment of 25 Russian immigrants on tax fraud charges is evidence of the growing power of these groups in the New York metropolitan area. The charges described a scheme to cheat the government out of more than $140 million in taxes on more than $500 million in fuel sales. By 2002, however, authorities had learned from informants that these groups tended to rise and fall as they competed with each other and as "turncoat" members helped American police convict their colleagues. Thus no single powerful crime organization developed in the manner that authorities had feared.

The Russians involved in these crimes are often highly educated and more sophisticated than members of some other ethnic-based crime organizations. As a result, they have emphasized insurance scams, credit card fraud, counterfeiting, and other business-related crimes. One such group had developed a clever scheme based on the fact that diesel fuel and one type of home heating oil are almost the same, but there are no taxes on home heating oil. Posing as a legitimate company, the group created Kings Motor Oils, which bought home heating oil. Through a series of dummy companies, this oil was transferred to Petro Plus as diesel fuel at the wholesale price plus 36 cents a gallon in taxes. When the Internal Revenue Service tried to collect the taxes, the dummy company disappeared.

By 2002 many law enforcement officials believed that they had increased their capacity to combat the Russian crime organizations in the United States. Because they discovered a culture of distrust and betrayal among members of these organizations, they could gain incriminating evidence from informants who struck deals in order to avoid long prison sentences. Some observers, however, still fear that these organizations can grow stronger through greater coordination with each other or through tighter connections with crime organizations in Eastern Europe and Asia.

More information on Russian criminal organizations is available from the Center for Strategic and International Studies at http://www.csis.org/tnt.

Sources: Drawn from Bill Berkeley, "Code of Betrayal, Not Silence, Shines Light on Russian Mob," *New York Times,* August 19, 2002 (http://www.nytimes.com); *New York Times,* August 8, 1995, p. A1; *USA Today,* September 14, 1995, p. A1; Julienne Salzano, "The Sludge Runners," *Heavy Duty Trucking,* August 1993, pp. 106–108.

Carolina were convicted of running a cigarette-smuggling operation that allegedly raised money for Hezbollah, a Lebanon-based organization responsible for attacks against Americans abroad and an organization that reportedly works closely with the Al-Qaida network in training people for attacks against the United States and its allies (Priest and Farah, 2002).

The attacks on the World Trade Center and the Pentagon also increased awareness of the need to address the activities of international criminal organizations. Because the flow of money and weapons to organizations that employ terrorist tactics for political purposes is so closely connected to international crime networks, the United States will undoubtedly devote additional personnel and resources to this issue. The American government seeks to cut off the supply of money and weapons to these organizations as well as avoid the worst-case scenario of a transfer of nuclear material or weapons from a Russian crime organization to Al-Qaida or other groups intent on using such materials to attack the United States.

Visible Crime

visible crime
An offense against persons or property committed primarily by members of the lower class. Often referred to as "street crime" or "ordinary crime," this type of offense is the one most upsetting to the public.

Visible crime, often called "street crime" or "ordinary crime," ranges from shoplifting to homicide. For offenders, such crimes are the least profitable and, because they are visible, the least protected. These are the acts that the public regards as "criminal." The majority of law enforcement resources are used to deal with them. We can divide visible crimes into three categories: violent crimes, property crimes, and public order crimes.

Violent Crimes

Acts against people in which death or physical injury results are violent crimes. These include criminal homicide, assault, rape, and robbery. The criminal justice system treats them as the most serious offenses and punishes them accordingly. Although the public is most fearful of violence by strangers, most of these offenses are committed by people who know their victim.

Property Crimes

Property crimes are acts that threaten property held by individuals or by the state. Many types of crimes fall under this category, including theft, larceny, shoplifting, embezzlement, and burglary. Some property offenders are amateurs who occasionally commit these crimes because of situational factors such as financial need or peer pressure. In contrast, professional criminals make a significant portion of their livelihood from committing property offenses.

Public Order Crimes

Acts that threaten the general well-being of society and challenge accepted moral principles are defined as public order crimes. They include public drunkenness, aggressive panhandling, vandalism, and disorderly conduct. Although the police tend to treat these behaviors as minor offenses, there is evidence that this type of disorderly behavior instills fear in citizens, leads to more-serious crimes, and hastens urban decay (Kelling and Coles, 1996). The definition and enforcement of such behaviors as crimes highlights the tensions between different interpretations of American values. Many people see such behavior as simply representing the liberty that adults enjoy in a free society to engage in offensive and self-destructive behavior that causes no concrete harm to other people. By contrast, other people see their own liberty limited by need to be wary and fearful of actions by people who are drunk or out of control.

Those charged with visible crimes tend to be young, low-income minority group men. Some argue that this is due to the class bias of a society that has singled out visible crimes for priority enforcement. They note that we do not focus as much on occupational crimes as on street crimes.

Crimes without Victims

Crimes without victims involve a willing and private exchange of goods or services that are in strong demand but illegal—in other words, offenses against morality. Examples include prostitution, gambling, and drug sales and use. These are called "victimless" crimes because those involved do not feel that they are being harmed. Prosecution for these offenses is justified on the grounds that society as a whole is harmed because the moral fabric of the community is threatened. However, using the law to enforce moral standards is costly. The system is swamped by these cases, which often require the use of police informers and thus open the door for payoffs and other kinds of corruption.

crimes without victims
Offenses involving a willing and private exchange of illegal goods or services that are in strong demand. Participants do not feel they are being harmed, but these crimes are prosecuted on the ground that society as a whole is being injured.

The "war on drugs" is the most obvious example of policies against one type of victimless crime. Possession and sale of drugs—marijuana, heroin, cocaine, opium, amphetamines—have been illegal in the United States for over a hundred years. Especially during the past 40 years, extensive government resources have been used to enforce these laws and punish offenders.

In "One Man's Journey Inside the Criminal Justice System" (see http://www.cj.wadsworth.com/colesmith10e), Chuck Terry describes his love of heroin and the consequences as he traveled inside the criminal justice system.

Political Crime

Political crime refers to criminal acts either by the government or against the government that are carried out for ideological purposes (F. E. Hagan, 1997:2). Political criminals believe they are following a morality that is above the law.

political crime
An act, usually done for ideological purposes, that constitutes a threat against the state (such as treason, sedition, or espionage) or a criminal act by the state.

Getty Images

Abdullah al Muhajir (aka Jose Padilla) was arrested when he returned to the United States from a trip to Pakistan. The government has labeled him an "enemy combatant" and placed him in indefinite confinement in a military jail. No formal criminal charges have been filed against him. What constitutional issues are raised by this case?

Examples include James Kopp—arrested for the murder of Dr. Barnett Slepian near Buffalo, New York, and other doctors who performed abortions—and Eric Rudolph, wanted for the bombing of abortion clinics in Atlanta and Birmingham and the pipe bomb explosion at the Atlanta Olympics. Similarly, shocking acts of violence that are labeled as terrorism, including the 1994 bombing of the federal building in Oklahoma City by Timothy McVeigh and the 2001 attacks on the World Trade Center and Pentagon, spring from political motivations.

In some authoritarian states, merely making statements that are critical of the government is a crime that can lead to prosecution and imprisonment. In Western democracies today, there are few political crimes other than treason, which is rare. Many illegal acts, such as the World Trade Center and Oklahoma City bombings, can be traced to political motives. But they are prosecuted as visible crimes under laws against bombing, arson, and murder rather than as political crimes per se.

Political crimes against government include activities such as treason, sedition (rebellion), and espionage. Since the nation's founding, many laws have been passed in response to perceived threats to the established order. The Sedition Act of 1789 made it a crime to utter or publish statements against the government. The Smith Act of 1940 made it a crime to call for the overthrow of the government by force or violence. During the Vietnam War, the federal government used charges of criminal conspiracy to deter those who opposed its military policies. The foregoing examples became obsolete as federal judges' interpretations of the Constitution expanded the definition of free speech and thereby limited the government's authority to pursue prosecutions based on an individual's expression of political beliefs and policy preferences. However, in the aftermath of September 11, the U.S. government entered a new era in which people were detained or prosecuted based on their alleged connections to organizations employing terror tactics.

In 2002 Abdullah al Muhajir, an ex-convict from Chicago who was formerly known as Jose Padilla, was arrested after arriving in the United States from a visit to Pakistan. The government alleged that he was part of a plot to build and detonate a nuclear "dirty" bomb in the United States. The U.S. government labeled him an "enemy combatant" and placed him in indefinite confinement in a military jail without any plan for formally prosecuting him on criminal charges or for providing him with any of the constitutional rights that would be available to a defendant in a civilian criminal court (Benson and Wood, 2002). Is he being detained because of his political beliefs and associations? Because the government does not intend to prove his guilt by presenting evidence to any court—civilian or military—it is obvious that the "war on terrorism" is forcing the country to reevaluate its definitions of constitutional rights, government authority, and political crimes.

Cybercrime

Go to the Public Policy feature on the American System of Criminal Justice CD to learn more about the issues surrounding cybercrime.

As new technologies emerge, so do people who take advantage of them for their own gain. One has only to think of the impact of the invention of the automobile to realize the extent to which the computer age will lead to new kinds of criminality. Today, the justice system is beginning to deal with the ramifications of cybercrimes on criminal law. To illustrate the problems that may arise, FBI Special Agent Richard Bernes of San Jose points out that "everything you touch sets a new precedent. Suppose someone accesses your computer and downloads files. What should she be charged with? Burglary or trespassing? Wire fraud or copyright violation?" (Gill, 1997:116).

cybercrimes
Offenses that involve the use of one or more computers.

Cybercrimes involve the use of computers and the Internet to commit acts against people, property, public order, or morality. Thus, cybercriminals have learned "new ways to do old tricks." Some use computers to steal information, resources, or funds. Others use the Internet to disseminate child pornography, to advertise sexual services, or to stalk the unsuspecting. (See the Close Up box

You Could Get Raped

Randi Barber, a 28-year-old woman from North Hollywood, California, started getting dirty solicitations on her answering machine. When a stranger knocked on her apartment door, she hid. When he later telephoned, she learned that he was responding to her sexy ad on the Internet.

"What ad? What did it say?" Barber asked.

"Let me put it to you this way," the caller said, "you could get raped."

Barber, who doesn't own a computer, later discovered that a stalker had assumed her identity in cyberspace and had posted ads on the Internet seeking men to fulfill her kinky sexual desires. Under such log-ons as "playfulkitty4U," sadomasochistic messages were posted. The stalker included directions to Randi's home, details of her social plans, and advice on how to short-circuit her alarm system.

Months later, the Los Angeles County Sheriff's Department arrested an acquaintance of Barber's, Gary Dellapenta, a 50-year-old security guard. He was charged under a California law that criminalizes stalking and harassment on the Internet.

Researching the Internet

The National Center for Victims of Crime provides information about stalking; see http://www.ncvc.org/special/stalking.htm.

"You Could Get Raped.") The more sophisticated "hackers" create and distribute viruses designed to destroy computer programs. In April 1999 the country was confronted by the Melissa virus created by a New Jersey hacker. People would receive an innocent-looking email message labeled "Important," but when they opened it viewers found a list of pornographic Web sites. If that was opened, Melissa sent the email virus to the first 50 names in the user's address book.

The global nature of the Internet presents new challenges to the criminal justice system. For example, through electronic financial networks that link much of the world, money launderers in Moscow can simply tap on their computer keyboard and send their money digitally to New York. A few more keystrokes and the money can be sent to an private account in Antigua where it will be shielded from the prying eyes of government agencies. In another example, stolen credit card numbers are sold on the Internet, primarily by dealers based in states that were formerly part of the Soviet Union. Computer hackers steal large numbers of credit card numbers from the computer systems of legitimate businesses and sell the numbers in "bulk" quantities to dealers who sell them throughout the world via "members-only" Web sites. Credit card fraud costs online merchants more than $1 billion each year (Richtel, 2002).

Efforts to create and enforce effective laws that will cover such activities have been hampered by the international nature of cybercrime. Agencies in various countries are seeking to improve their ability to cooperate and share information. However, law enforcement officials throughout the world are not equally committed to and capable of catching cyberthieves and hackers. Criminals in some countries may have better computer equipment and expertise than do the officials trying to catch them. In the United States, some laws intended to punish people involved in online pornography have been struck down for violating First Amendment rights to free expression.

Since the events of September 11, many countries' law enforcement agencies have increased their communication and cooperation in order to thwart terrorist activities. As these countries cooperate in investigating and monitoring the financial transactions of groups that employ terror tactics, it seems likely that they will also improve their capacity to discover and pursue cybercriminals.

Officers Tom Harrington and Don Conden patrol cyberspace, looking for child predators. Florida's Computer Child Exploration statute makes it a crime to download child pornography or solicit sex with minors online. When arresting offenders, these officers also seize the computer, using the hard drive as evidence.

Hollyman/The Gamma Liaison Network

Close up

Hate Crimes: A New Category of Personal Violence

Black churches are set afire in the Southeast; the home of the mayor of West Hartford, Connecticut, is defaced by swastikas and anti-Semitic graffiti; gay Wyoming student Matthew Shepard is murdered; a black woman in Maryland is beaten and doused with lighter fluid in a race-based attack. These are just a few of the more than 7,500 hate crimes reported to the police each year. The U.S. Department of Justice said that threats, assaults, and acts of vandalism against Arab Americans and people of South Asian ancestry increased in the months following the events of September 11. Crimes based on the victims' ethnicity may become more diversified as Americans react to their anger and fear about the threat of terrorism from foreign organizations.

Hate crimes have been added to the penal codes of 46 states and the District of Columbia. These are violent acts aimed at individuals or groups of a particular race, ethnicity, religion, sexual orientation, or gender. The laws also make it a crime to vandalize religious buildings and cemeteries or to intimidate another person out of bias. Although the Ku Klux Klan, the World Church of the Creator, and Nazi-style "skinhead" groups represent the most visible perpetrators, most hate crimes are committed by individuals acting alone.

Hate crime laws have been challenged on the ground that they violate the right of free speech. Some argue that racial and religious slurs must be allowed on this basis. In response, supporters of hate crime laws say that limits must be placed on freedom of speech and that some words are so hateful that they fall outside the free speech protection of the First Amendment.

The U.S. Supreme Court has considered the constitutionality of such laws in two cases. In *R.A.V. v. City of St. Paul* (1992), the Court ruled unconstitutional a law that singled out only certain "race baiting" words. However, in *Wisconsin v. Mitchell* (1993), it upheld a law providing for a more severe sentence in cases in which the offender "intentionally selects the person against whom the crime [is committed] because of the race, religion, color, disability, sexual orientation, national origin or ancestry of that person." By asking, "Do you all feel hyped up to move on some white people?" and by calling out, "There goes a white boy; go get him," the defendant had incited a group of young black men, who had just seen the film *Mississippi Burning,* to assault a young white man. The Court said that the penalty was appropriate because the conduct was "thought to inflict greater individual and societal harm." It rejected the argument that the law would have a "chilling effect" on free speech.

In a society that is becoming more diverse, hate crimes hurt not only their victims but the social fabric itself. Democracy depends on people sharing common ideals and working together. When groups are pitted against one another, the entire community suffers. But is criminal law the way to attack this problem?

Members of the white supremacist Aryan Nation and the Ku Klux Klan march in Cour D'Alene, Idaho. What challenges do such groups pose to American values and the ideals of democracy?

David Butow/SABA Press

Researching the Internet

The American Psychological Association provides information about hate crimes; see http://www.apa.org/pubinfo/hate.

Sources: Drawn from J. Jacobs, "Should Hate Be a Crime?" *The Public Interest,* Fall 1993, pp. 1–14; C. Newton, "Crimes against Arabs, South Asians Up," *Washington Post,* June 26, 2002 (http://www.washingtonpost.com).

Which of these main types of crime is of greatest concern to you? If you are like most people, it is visible crime. Thus, as a nation, we devote most of our criminal justice resources to dealing with such crimes. To develop policies to address these crimes, however, we need to know more about the amount of crime and all the types of crimes that occur in the United States. One of the most disturbing crimes, which has gained much attention lately, is hate crime; see the Close Up box for more.

10. What are the six main types of crime?
11. Why is the term *occupational crime* more useful today than the term *white-collar crime*?
12. What is the function of organized crime?
13. Who commits "visible" or "street" crimes?
14. What is meant by the term *crimes without victims*?
15. What are political crimes?

The Crime Problem Today

Public opinion polls show that Americans rank crime among the nation's greatest problems. Many people believe that the crime rate is rising, even though it has generally declined from the 1990s through 2000. At the dawn of the twenty-first century, however, an increasing number of Americans were recognizing that the crime rate was not rising as it had done in prior decades (see "What Americans Think"). Is crime still at record levels? Is the United States the most crime-ridden nation of the world's industrial democracies? How do we measure the amount of crime? What are the current and future trends? By trying to answer these questions, we can gain a better understanding of the crime problem itself and the public's beliefs about it.

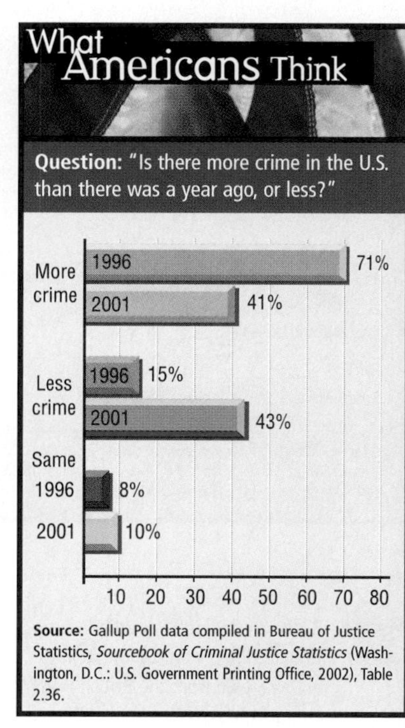

Source: Gallup Poll data compiled in Bureau of Justice Statistics, *Sourcebook of Criminal Justice Statistics* (Washington, D.C.: U.S. Government Printing Office, 2002), Table 2.36.

The Worst of Times?

There has always been too much crime, and ever since the nation's founding people have felt threatened by it. There were outbreaks of violence after the Civil War, after World War I, during Prohibition, and during the Great Depression (Friedman, 1993). But there have also been extended periods, such as the 1950s, when there was comparatively little crime. Thus, ours is neither the best nor the worst of times.

Although crime is an old problem, the amount and types of crime have not always been the same. During both the 1880s and the 1930s, pitched battles took place between strikers and company police. Race riots occurred in Atlanta in 1907 and in Chicago, Washington, D.C., and East St. Louis, Illinois, in 1919. Organized crime was rampant during the 1930s. The murder rate, which reached a high in 1933 and a low during the 1950s, rose to a new high in 1980 and has been falling since 1993 except for a modest 3.1 percent increase in murders during 2001 (see Figure 1.1).

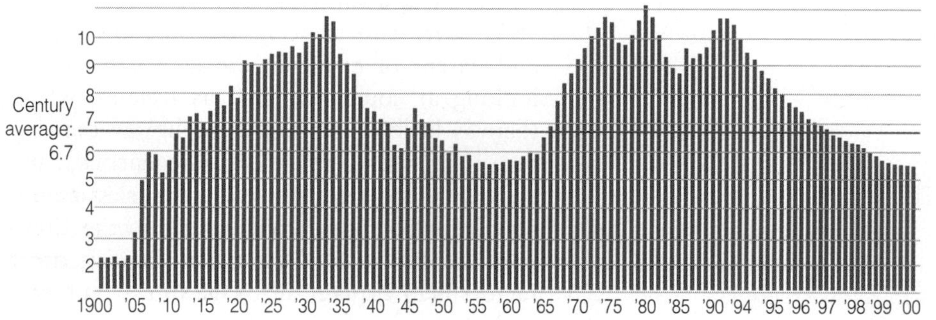

Sources: Bureau of Justice Statistics, *Sourcebook of Criminal Justice Statistics, 1999* (Washington, D.C.: U.S. Government Printing Office, 2000), Table 3.146; Federal Bureau of Investigation, *Crime in the United States, 2000* (Washington, D.C.: U.S. Government Printing Office, 2001), 15.

Figure 1.1
A century of murder
The murder rate per 100,000 people in the United States has risen, fallen, and since 1960 risen again. Data from the last several years show a decline from the peak in 1980. What causes these trends?

The Most Crime-Ridden Nation?

How does the amount of crime in the United States compare with the amount in other countries? It is often said the United States has more crime than do other modern industrial nations. But as James Lynch argues, this belief is too simple to be useful (1995:11). He points out that it is hard to compare crime rates in different nations. First one must choose nations that are similar to the United States—nations with democratic governments, similar levels of economic development, and the same kinds of legal systems (MacCoun et al., 1993). Second, one must get data from reliable sources. The two main sources of cross-national crime data are Interpol and the International Crime Survey.

Lynch compared crime rates in the United States and in Australia, Canada, England and Wales, West Germany, France, the Netherlands, Sweden, and Switzerland. Both police and victim data showed that the homicide rate in the United States was more than twice that in Canada, the next highest country, and many times that in the other countries. The same was generally true at that time for robbery, but American robbery rates subsequently declined in the 1990s to levels below that of several other countries (see Table 1.3).

When it comes to property crimes, the data are surprising. The victim surveys show that rates of property crime are lower in the United States than in several other industrialized countries. A study of crime in England found that rates for serious crimes were higher than in the United States. After dropping for six years, crime rates rose 6 percent nationally and as much as 20 percent in specific counties in Britain during 2002 ("Crime Rate Rising Again," 2002). The main difference between the countries lay in homicide rates, which were six times higher in the United States than in England. It was also found that firearms play a much greater role in violent crimes in the United States, where they were used in 68 percent of murders and 41 percent of robberies, compared with 7 and 5 percent respectively in England (BJS, 1998d). See Table 1.4 for more on non-homicide offenses.

Table 1.3 Comparative homicide rates, average rates, 1997–1999

Homicide rates in the United States exceed those of industrialized democracies, but some developing countries have higher rates.

Nation	Homicide
United States	6.3
Northern Ireland	3.1
Finland	2.6
Spain	2.6
Scotland	2.1
England and Wales	1.5
Estonia	12.2
South Africa	56.5

Source: G. Barclay, C. Tavares, and A. Siddique, *International Comparisons of Criminal Justice Statistics 1999,* May 2001, British Home Office Report, Table A (http://www.homeoffice.gov.uk/rds/pdfs/hosb601.pdf).

In sum, the risk of lethal violence is much higher in the United States than in other industrial democracies. But the risk of minor violence is not greater than in several other countries. In contrast, the United States has lower rates of serious property crime, even than in many countries that are thought to be safer (J. Lynch, 1995:17).

Research findings from the International Crime Victimization Surveys are available from the British Home Office at http://www.homeoffice.gov.uk.

Interestingly, crime rates in Western countries besides the United States may have begun to decline (Tonry, 1998b:22–23). Crime in Canada fell 4.1 percent in 1998; as in the United States, it was the seventh consecutive drop in as many years (*Halifax Chronicle Herald,* July 22, 1999:1). English and Dutch victimization data likewise show significant declines, as do data from many of the 11 industrial countries in the International Crime Victimization Surveys (Mayhew and van Dijk, 1997).

We can gain more insight into the nature and extent of crime in the United States by looking at countries, such as Iceland, where there is little crime. Some might say that because Iceland is small, homogeneous, and somewhat isolated, the two countries cannot be compared. But as we can see in the Comparative Perspective on pages 26–27, other factors help explain differences in the amount and types of crime in different countries.

Table 1.4 Percent of respondents victimized by specific crimes during 2000

These data from the International Crime Victimization Surveys indicate that the United States does not lead the world in rates of non-homicide offenses.

Nation	Auto Theft	Burglary	Robbery
United States	0.5	1.8	0.6
Australia	1.9	3.9	1.2
Canada	1.4	2.3	0.9
Denmark	1.1	3.1	0.7
England and Wales	2.1	2.8	1.2
France	1.7	1.0	1.1
Japan	0.1	1.1	0.1
Sweden	1.3	1.7	0.9
Switzerland	0.3	1.1	0.7

Source: United Nations Interregional Crime and Justice Research Institute (UNICRI), *The International Crime Victimization Surveys,* 2001, Appendix 4, pp. 178–79 (http://www.unicri.it/icvs/index.htm).

Finding the amount of crime is not as easy as it may seem. Let's look more closely at the sources of crime data and ask what they tell us about crime trends.

Keeping Track of Crime

One of the frustrations in studying criminal justice is the lack of accurate means of knowing the amount of crime. Surveys reveal that much more crime occurs than is reported to the police. This is referred to as the **dark figure of crime.**

dark figure of crime
A metaphor that emphasizes the dangerous dimension of crime that is never reported to the police.

Most homicides and auto thefts are reported to the police. In the case of a homicide, a body must be accounted for, and insurance companies require a police report before they will pay for a stolen car. But about 71 percent of rape or sexual assault victims do not report the attack; almost half of robbery victims and 60 percent of victims of simple assault do not do so. Figure 1.2 shows the percentage of victimizations not reported to the police.

There are many reasons crimes go unreported. Some victims of rape and assault do not wish to be embarrassed by public disclosure and police questioning, but the most common reason for not reporting a violent crime is that it was a personal, private matter. In the case of larceny, robbery, or burglary, the value of the property lost may not be worth the effort of calling the police. Many people refrain from reporting crimes because they do not want to become involved, fill out papers at the station house, perhaps go to court, or appear at a police lineup. As these examples suggest, many people feel the costs of reporting crimes outweigh the gains.

Until 1972, the only crimes counted by government were those that were known to the police and that made their way into the Federal Bureau of Investigation's Uniform Crime Reports (UCR). Since then the Department of Justice has sponsored the National Crime Victimization Surveys (NCVS), which survey the public to find out how much victimization has occurred. One might hope that the data from these two sources would give us a clear picture of the amount of crime, crime trends, and the characteristics of offenders. However, the picture is blurred, perhaps even distorted, because of differences in the way crime is measured by the UCR and the NCVS.

The Uniform Crime Reports

Issued each year by the FBI, the **Uniform Crime Reports (UCR)** are a statistical summary of crimes reported to the police. At the urging of the International

Uniform Crime Reports (UCR)
An annually published statistical summary of crimes reported to the police, based on voluntary reports to the FBI by local, state, and federal law enforcement agencies.

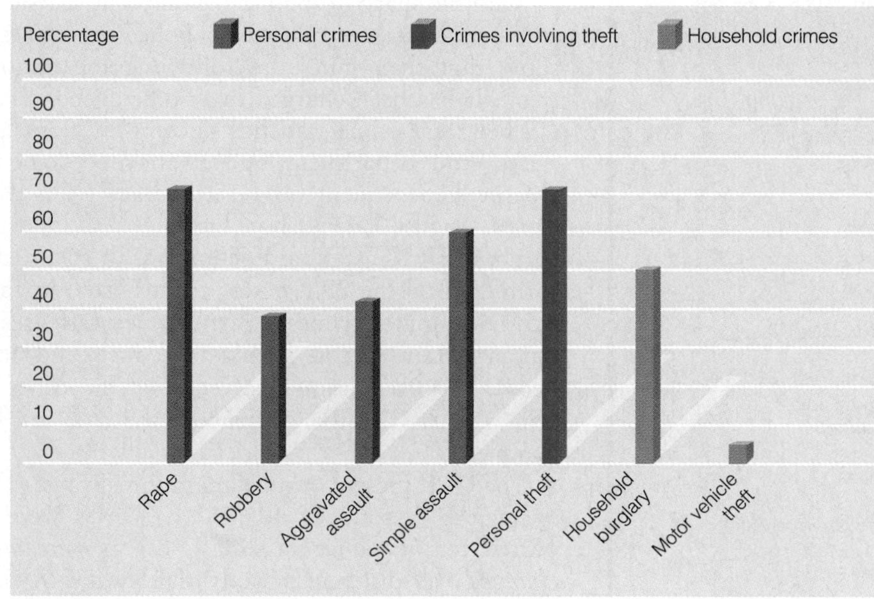

Source: Bureau of Justice Statistics, *Sourcebook of Criminal Justice Statistics, 2000* (Washington, D.C.: U.S. Government Printing Office, 2001), Table 3.38.

Figure 1.2
Percentage of victimizations *not* reported to the police
Why do some people not report crimes to the police? What can be done to encourage reporting?

Iceland: A Country with Little Crime

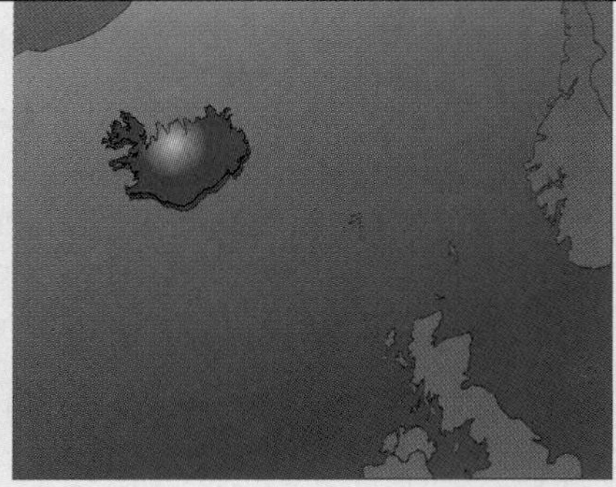

Why does Iceland have so little crime, compared with its neighbors and other developed countries? Is it the size of the population? The homogeneity of the people? The physical isolation from the major centers of Europe? What is it like to live in a country where there are only two homicides per year, and where the first bank robbery with a firearm occurred in 1984?

Iceland is an island republic the size of Virginia. It has a population of 270,000. The country retains strong cultural ties to Denmark, which ruled it from 1380 until 1944, and to the rest of Scandinavia. The Icelandic population is ethnically homogeneous, and policies have been instituted to restrict immigration. There are relatively small differences along class lines, literacy is very high, and about 95 percent of the people there belong to the Evangelical Lutheran Church. The people enjoy a high standard of living, an extensive health and welfare system, and a low unemployment rate.

Even though 90 percent of the Icelandic people live in urban areas, the society is one where extended families, strong community ties, and a homogeneous culture seem to act as effective agents of social control. Iceland is also relatively equalitarian: there are no slums, and education and health care are provided to all, thus further reducing social disparities.

After centuries of isolation, Iceland first came into extensive contact with European and North American countries at the end of World War II. The result has been a cultural lag in the shift to industrialization and urbanization. Iceland has retained many aspects of an agrarian society.

When compared with those of the United States, Icelandic crime rates are extremely low. For example, the assault rate per 100,000 people is 14, while in the United States it is 388; the rate for homicide is .73 in Iceland, and 7 in the United States; the rate for rape is 16.35 in Iceland and 36 in the United States. The country's homogeneous population, geographic isola-

Association of Chiefs of Police, Congress in 1930 authorized this system for compiling crime data (Rosen, 1995). The UCR come from a voluntary national network of some 16,000 local, state, and federal law enforcement agencies, policing 98 percent of the U.S. population. The main publication of the UCR is an annual volume, *Crime in the United States.*

Table 1.5 Uniform Crime Reports offenses

The UCR present data on 8 index offenses and 21 other crimes for which there is less information. A limitation of the UCR is that they tabulate only crimes that are reported to the police.

Part I (Index Offenses)	Part II (Other Offenses)
1. Criminal homicide	9. Simple assaults
2. Forcible rape	10. Forgery and counterfeiting
3. Robbery	11. Fraud
4. Aggravated assault	12. Embezzlement
5. Burglary	13. Buying, receiving, or possessing stolen property
6. Larceny/theft	14. Vandalism
7. Auto theft	15. Weapons (carrying, possession, etc.)
8. Arson	16. Prostitution and commercialized vice
	17. Sex offenses
	18. Violation of narcotic drug laws
	19. Gambling
	20. Offenses against the family and children
	21. Driving under the influence
	22. Violation of liquor laws
	23. Drunkenness
	24. Disorderly conduct
	25. Vagrancy
	26. All other offenses (excluding traffic)
	27. Suspicion
	28. Curfew and loitering (juvenile)

Source: Federal Bureau of Investigation, *Crime in the United States, 2000* (Washington, D.C.: U.S. Government Printing Office, 2001)

With the sharp drop in crime in recent years, new pressures have been placed on police executives to show that their cities are following the national trend. It has been charged that some agencies have falsified their crime statistics since promotions, pay raises, and department budgets have become increasingly dependent on positive data (*New York Times,* August 3, 1998:1).

The UCR use standard definitions to ensure uniform data on the 29 types of crimes listed in Table 1.5. For 8 major crimes—Part I (Index Offenses)—the data show factors such as age, race, and number of reported crimes solved. For the other 21 crimes, Part II (Other Offenses), the data are less complete.

The UCR present crime data in three ways: (1) as *aggregates* (a total of 407,842 robberies were reported to the police in 2000), (2) as *percentage changes* over different periods (there was a 0.4 percent decrease in robberies from 1999 to 2000), and (3) as a *rate per 100,000 people* (the robbery rate in 2000 was 144.9) (FBI, 2001:4).

tion, and prohibition of handgun ownership all may contribute to its low level of violence.

The Icelandic public has become most concerned by the increase in drug use during the past two decades, but such use is still minuscule compared with that of other Western countries. Marijuana use increased during the 1970s but has declined since then. Still, a study conducted in 1997 found a greater percentage of Icelanders had used marijuana at least once than citizens of the other Nordic nations had, with the exception of Denmark. However, only 1.6 percent admitted using marijuana during the last six months. This is similar to the other Nordic countries.

Although there is much concern about the use of "hard" drugs, the problem seems minor when compared with drug use in the United States. In 1984 about 4 percent of Icelanders aged 16–36 said they had consumed amphetamines. Not until 1983 did police find cocaine; the first seizure of a significant amount (one kilo) took place in 1987. Yet scholars believe that drug use has increased considerably during the past five years.

Undoubtedly the size of Iceland's population and its isolation from the major drug supply routes account for the low level of drug abuse. However, special "drug police" were established in the 1970s. Today, the Reykjavík police allocate a greater portion of their budget to drug control than do the police in Copenhagen and Oslo. But containing the "drug problem" is enhanced by the ease with which the country may be "sealed" because import routes are few, and it is difficult for drug users to hide their habit in such a tightly knit community. There seem to be no organized drug rings in Iceland.

Whereas most Western countries are preoccupied with the war on drugs, this social problem is overshadowed in Iceland by concern over the abuse of alcohol. Alcohol abuse has a high correlation with the crime rate, particularly in the form of drunken driving. Total consumption of alcohol has increased during recent decades, and public drunkenness is the most common violation of the criminal law.

With the the highest number of automobiles per capita in the world, Iceland strictly enforces its drunken-driving rules, resulting in a high arrest rate (1,400 per 100,000 people versus 386 per 100,000 in the United States). Most arrests occur as a result of intensive routine highway checks. When blood tests reveal a level of .5 to 1.2 per milliliter alcohol, drivers lose their licenses for one month. When tests show a level of more than 1.2 per milliliter, drivers lose their licenses for a year. A third offense means a prison sentence. Low levels of serious crime and a policy of treating alcohol offenses severely have resulted in the fact that 20 percent of prisoners in Iceland have been committed for drunken driving.

The number of crimes reported to the Icelandic police has reflected the rapid transformation of the society during the past 30 years. As in other countries, the crime rate increased after World War II but has leveled off during the past decade. Several factors can account for the increases in crime compared with that of a generation ago. For example, the growth in economic crime seems to be a consequence of more-complex business activities. Concern over the abuse of alcohol has resulted in proactive law enforcement policies that have contributed to the amount of crime as measured by arrests. But these "increases" must be viewed in the context of the very low levels of criminality in Iceland as compared with other developed countries. As in other Scandinavian countries, as well as such low-crime countries as Switzerland, cultural, geographic, economic, and public policy factors appear to explain the relative absence of crime in Iceland.

Sources: Drawn from Helgi Gunnlaugsson, "Icelandic Sociology and the Social Production of Criminological Knowledge," in *From a Doll's House to the Welfare State: Refllections on Nordic Sociology,* ed. Margareta Bertilsson and Goran Therborn (Montreal: International Sociological Association, 1998), 83–88; Omar H. Kristmundsson, "Crime and the Crime Control System of Iceland," unpublished paper, University of Connecticut, 1999.

The UCR provide a useful but incomplete picture of crime levels. Because they cover only reported crimes, these reports do not include data on crimes for which people failed to call the police. Also, the UCR do not measure occupational crimes and other offenses that are not included in the 29 types covered. And because reporting is voluntary, police departments may not take the time to make complete and careful reports.

In response to criticisms of the UCR, the FBI has made some changes in the program that are now being implemented nationwide. Some offenses have been redefined, and police agencies are being asked to report more details about crime events. Using the **National Incident-Based Reporting System (NIBRS)**, police agencies are to report all crimes committed during an incident, not just the most serious one, as well as data on offenders, victims, and the places where they interact. While the UCR now count incidents and arrests for the 8 index offenses and count arrests for other crimes, the NIBRS provides detailed incident data on 46 offenses in 22 crime categories. The NIBRS distinguishes between attempted and completed crimes as well.

National Incident-Based Reporting System (NIBRS)
A reporting system in which the police describe each offense in a crime incident, together with data describing the offender, victim, and property.

The National Crime Victimization Surveys

A second source of crime data is the **National Crime Victimization Surveys (NCVS)**. Since 1972, the Census Bureau has done surveys to find out the extent and nature of crime victimization. Thus data have been gathered on unreported as well as reported crimes. Interviews are conducted with a national probability sample of about 100,000 people in 50,000 households. The same people are interviewed twice a year for three years and asked if they have been victimized in the last six months.

National Crime Victimization Surveys (NCVS)
Interviews of samples of the U.S. population conducted by the Bureau of Justice Statistics to determine the number and types of criminal victimizations and thus the extent of unreported as well as reported crime.

Each person is asked a set of "screening" questions (for example, did anyone beat you up, attack you, or hit you with something such as a rock or a bottle?) to determine whether he or she has been victimized. The person is then asked questions designed to elicit specific facts about the event, the offender, and any financial losses or physical disabilities caused by the crime.

Besides the household interviews, surveys are carried out in the nation's 26 largest cities; separate studies are done to find out about the victimization of businesses. These data allow us to estimate how many crimes have occurred, learn more about the offenders, and note demographic patterns. The results show that for the crimes measured (rape, robbery, assault, burglary, theft) there were 26 million victimizations in 2000 (down from 43 million in 1973) (BJS, 2001d). This level is much higher than the number of crimes actually reported to the police suggests.

Although the NCVS provide a more complete picture of the nature and extent of crime than do the UCR, they too have flaws. Because the surveys are done by government employees, the people interviewed are unlikely to report crimes in which they or members of their family took part. They also may not want to admit that a family member engages in crime, or they may be too embarrassed to admit that they have allowed themselves to be victimized more than once.

The NCVS are also imperfect because they depend on the victim's *perception* of an event. The theft of a child's lunch money by a bully may be reported as a crime by one person but not mentioned by another. People may say that their property was stolen when in fact they lost it. Moreover, people's memories of dates may fade, and they may misreport the year in which a crime occurred even though they remember the event itself clearly. In 1993 the Bureau of Justice Statistics made some changes in the NCVS to improve their accuracy and detail.

The next time you hear or read about crime rates, take into account the source of the data and its possible limitations. Table 1.6 compares the Uniform Crime Reports and the National Crime Victimization Surveys.

Table 1.6 The UCR and the NCVS

Compare the data sources. Remember that the UCR tabulate only crimes reported to the police, while the NCVS are based on interviews with victims.

	Uniform Crime Reports	**National Crime Victimization Survey**
Offenses measured	Homicide	
	Rape	Rape
	Robbery (personal and commercial)	Robbery (personal)
	Assault (aggravated)	Assault (aggravated and simple)
	Burglary (commercial and household)	Household burglary
	Larceny (commercial and household)	Larceny (personal and household)
	Motor vehicle theft	Motor vehicle theft
	Arson	
Scope	Crimes reported to the police in most jurisdictions; considerable flexibility in developing small-area data	Crimes both reported and not reported to police; all data are for the nation as a whole; some data are available for a few large geographic areas
Collection method	Police department reports to Federal Bureau of Investigation	Survey interviews: periodically measures the total number of crimes committed by asking a national sample of 49,000 households representing 101,000 people over the age of 12 about their experiences as victims of crime during a specific period
Kinds of information	In addition to offense counts, provides information on crime clearances, persons arrested, persons charged, law enforcement officers killed and assaulted, and characteristics of homicide victims	Provides details about victims (such as age, race, sex, education, income, and whether the victim and offender were related) and about crimes (such as time and place of occurrence, whether or not reported to police, use of weapons, occurrence of injury, and economic consequences)
Sponsor	Department of Justice's Federal Bureau of Investigation	Department of Justice's Bureau of Justice Statistics

Trends in Crime

Experts agree that, contrary to public opinion and the claims of politicians, crime rates have not been steadily rising. In fact, the rates for many crimes have dropped since the early 1980s.

The National Crime Victimization Surveys show that the victimization rate peaked in 1981 and has declined since then. The greatest declines are in property crimes, but crimes of violence have also dropped, especially since 1993. The Uniform Crime Reports show similar results, revealing a rapid rise in crime rates beginning in 1964 and continuing until 1980, when the rates began to level off or decline. The overall crime rate has declined each year from 1991 through 2000, with only a 2 percent increase in 2001.

Statistics and trends in the United States from the National Crime Victimization Surveys are presented at http://www.ojp.usdoj.gov/bjs/cvict.htm.

The most surprising trend has been the 25 percent decline in violent index crimes (murder, nonnegligent manslaughter, forcible rape, robbery, aggravated assault) from 1993 through 2000. In 1993, 4.2 million of such serious violent crimes occurred. By 2000, the figure had dropped to 2.2 million. Between 1993 and 2000, every major type of violent and property crime significantly decreased, and every demographic group experienced substantial drops in violent victimization. In 2001, there was a 0.3 percent increase in violent crime and a 2.2 percent increase in property crime, but these modest increases did not return crime rates to their levels of the past.

Figure 1.3 displays four measures of violent crime, adjusted for changes made in the NCVS in 1992. The top two measures are based on the victimization survey, while crimes recorded by the police and arrests are from the UCR are presented below these. Remember that the differences in the trends indicated by the NCVS and the UCR are explained in part by the different data sources and different populations on which their tabulations are based. The UCR are based on crimes reported to the police, while the NCVS record crimes experienced by victims.

What explains the drop in both violent and property crime well below the 1973 levels? Among the reasons given by analysts are the aging of the baby boom population, the increased use of security systems, the aggressive police efforts to keep handguns off the streets, and the dramatic decline in the use of crack cocaine. Other factors may include the booming economy of the 1990s and the quadrupling of the number of people incarcerated since 1970. These final factors may also account for the slight increase in crime during 2001 because of the economic downturn in that year as well as release from prison of hundreds of thousands of parolees and offenders who had completed their sentences. Let's look more closely at two factors—age and crack cocaine—as a means of assessing future crime levels.

Age

Changes in the age makeup of the population are a key factor in the analysis of crime trends. It has long been known that men aged 16 to 24 are the most

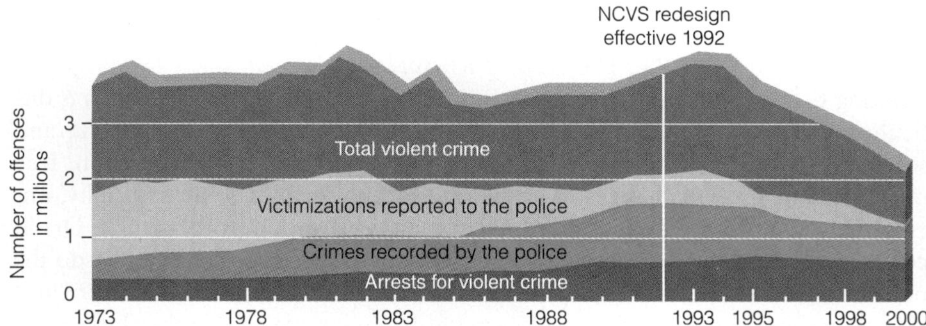

Note: The violent crimes included are rape, robbery, aggravated assault, and homicide. The shaded area at 1992 indicates that because of changes made to the victimization survey, data prior to 1992 are adjusted to make them comparable to data collected under the redesigned methodology.

Source: Bureau of Justice Statistics, October 2001 (http://www.ojp.usdoj.gov/bjs/).

Figure 1.3

Four measures of serious violent crimes

Data from both the UCR and the NCVS show that violent crime has declined in recent years. What might account for the decline?

crime-prone group. The rise in crime in the 1970s has been blamed on the post–World War II baby boom. By the 1970s the "boomers" had entered the high-risk crime group of 16–24-year-olds. They made up a much larger portion of the U.S. population than ever before. Between 40 and 50 percent of the total arrests during that decade could have been expected as a result of the growth in the total population and in the size of the crime-prone age group. Likewise, the decline in most crime rates that began during the 1980s has been attributed to the maturing of the post–World War II generation.

During the 1990s the 16- to 24-year age cohort was smaller than it had been at any time since the early 1960s, and many people believe that this contributed to the decline in crime. One controversial study argues that contributing to the small age cohort and the decline in crime in the 1990s was the Supreme Court's 1973 decision legalizing abortions (Samuelson, 1999:76). The study, by Steven Levitt and John Donahue, suggests that those who would have been at greatest risk for criminal activity during their crime-prone years—"the unwanted offspring of teenage, poor and minority women—were aborted at disproportionately high rates" (Brandon, 1999:A5). Abortions reduced the size of the 1973–1989 age cohort by about 40 percent.

In 1994 a small but influential group of criminologists predicted that by year 2000 there would be a great increase in the number of young men in the 14- to 24-year-old cohort. It was argued that the decline in crime experienced in the 1990s was merely the "lull before the storm " (Steinberg, 1999:4WK). In the words of James Fox, " To prevent a blood bath in 2005, when we will have a flood of 15-year olds, we have to do something today with the 5-year olds"(Krauss, 1994:4). However, this link between increases in the juvenile population and a rise in violent crime has not occurred. In the years since the prognostication was made, the homicide rate among teenaged offenders has been falling.

Crack Cocaine

The huge increase in violent crime, especially homicide, in the late 1980s and early 1990s is now generally attributed to killings by young people aged 24 and under. These killings were driven by the spread of crack cocaine and the greater use of high-powered semiautomatic handguns by young people in that market (Blumstein, 1996; Butterfield, 1998a). During this period hundreds of thousands of unskilled, unemployed, young men from poor urban neighborhoods became street vendors of crack. To protect themselves, because they were carrying valuable merchandise—drugs and money—they were armed. They felt they needed this protection, because drug dealers cannot call for police assistance if threatened. As shootings increased among sellers engaged in turf battles over drug sales, others began to arm themselves, and the resulting violence continued to skyrocket (Blumstein, 1996). The sharp drop in violent crime in the 1990s followed the sudden decline in the use of crack as more and more people saw the devastation that the drug brought (Egan, 1999:A1).

Crime Trends: What Do We Really Know?

Pointing to specific factors that cause an increase or decrease in crime rates is difficult. Once people thought that, with the proper tools, they could analyze and solve the crime problem. However, crime is a very complex phenomenon. Key questions remain: Do changes in crime rates occur because of demography, unemployment rates, housing conditions, and changes in family structure? Or do crime rates result from interactions among these and other factors? How do the policies of law enforcement, sentencing, and corrections affect criminality? Until we know more about the causes of criminal behavior, we can neither blame nor praise government policies for shifts in crime rates.

Go to the *American System of Criminal Justice* Web site at http://www.cj.wadsworth.com/colesmith10e to explore the topic of crime trends and policies in further detail.

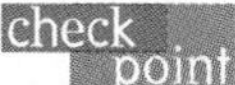

16. Has crime in the United States reached record levels?
17. For which crimes does the United States have the highest rates among industrial nations?
18. What are the two main sources of crime data?
19. What are key factors in crime trends?

Summary

- Crime and justice are high on the agenda of national priorities.
- Crime and justice are public policy issues.
- Criminal justice can best be seen as a social system.
- In a democracy there is a struggle to strike a balance between maintaining public order and protecting individual freedom, especially because of the tensions between conflicting American values.
- The crime control model and the due process model are two ways of looking at the goals and procedures of the criminal justice system.
- Criminal justice policies are developed in national, state, and local political arenas.
- Behavior that is defined as criminal varies from society to society and from one era to the next.
- There are six broad categories of crime: occupational crime, organized crime, visible crime, crimes without victims, political crime, and cybercrime.
- Each type of crime has its own level of risk and profitability, each arouses varying degrees of public disapproval, and each has its own group of offenders with their own characteristics.
- Today's crime problem is not unique. Throughout the history of the United States, crime has reached high levels at various times.
- Homicide is the primary type of crime that occurs at higher rates in the United States than in other industrialized democracies.
- The amount of crime is difficult to measure. The Uniform Crime Reports and the National Crime Victimization Surveys are the best sources of crime data.
- The complexity of crime statistics makes monitoring trends in crime a challenge.
- Crime rates are affected by changes in demography, unemployment rates, housing conditions, and changes in family structure.

Questions for Review

1. What are the goals of criminal justice in a democracy?
2. What are the major elements of Packer's due process model and crime control model?
3. What are the six types of crimes?
4. What are the positive and negative attributes of the two major sources of crime data?

Key Terms

crime (p. 5)
crime control model (p. 10)
crimes without victims (p. 19)
cybercrimes (p. 20)
dark figure of crime (p. 25)
due process model (p. 10)
mala in se (p. 12)
mala prohibita (p. 13)
money laundering (p. 16)
National Crime Victimization Surveys (NCVS) (p. 27)

National Incident-Based Reporting System (NIBRS) (p. 27)
occupational crime (p. 14)
organized crime (p. 16)
political crime (p. 19)
public policy (p. 6)
Uniform Crime Reports (UCR) (p. 25)
visible crime (p. 18)

For Further Reading

Gest, Ted. 2001. *Crime and Politics: Big Government's Erratic Campaign for Law and Order.* New York: Oxford University Press. An experienced journalist provides analytical descriptions of the political interests and events that shaped federal crime policy on such issues as gun control and narcotics laws.

Reiman, Jeffrey. 2000. *The Rich Get Richer and the Poor Get Prison: Ideology, Crime, and Criminal Justice.* 6th edition. Boston: Allyn and Bacon. A stinging critique of the system. Argues that the system serves the powerful by its failure to reduce crime.

Walker, Samuel. 2001. *Sense and Nonsense about Crime and Drug Policy.* 5th ed. Belmont, Calif.: Wadsworth. A provocative look at crime policies.

Wilson, James Q., and Joan Petersilia, eds. 2002. *Crime.* Rev. ed. San Francisco: Institute for Contemporary Studies Press. Essays by 28 leading experts on crime and justice.

Windlesham, David. 1998. *Politics, Punishment, and Populism.* New York: Oxford University Press. A distinguished British scholar who served as a visiting researcher in the United States provides a detailed analysis of the political interactions that produced the Violent Crime Control and Law Enforcement Act of 1994 during President Clinton's first term in office.

Going Online

For an up-to-date list of Web links, go to http://www.cj.wadsworth.com/colesmith10e

1. Using the Internet, access a leading national or state newspaper. Count the number of crime and noncrime stories appearing on the front page for a typical week. What percentage of crime stories do you find? What types of crimes are described? Should readers be concerned about crime in their community?
2. Enter "National Criminal Justice Commission" in any search engine to access the site. Look at the Commission's recommendations. Would you categorize the Commission's recommendations as liberal or conservative?
3. Access the United States Code at http://www.law.cornell.edu. Look at Title 18, section 1961. Examine the federal statutory definition of "racketeering activity." What activities are listed?
4. Access the Uniform Crime Reports at http://www.fbi.gov/ucr/ucr.htm. What is the crime rate for the eight index offenses?
5. Go to the Web site of the University of Dayton School of Law at http://www.cybercrimes.net. List the types of cybercrimes described there.
6. Access InfoTrac College Edition and type in the keyword *crime rate.* Then read an article from 2002 entitled "Florida's Crime Rate Plunges." What are the possible reasons for the crime statistics discussed in the article?

Checkpoint Answers

1. Stricter enforcement of the law through the expansion of police forces and the enactment of laws that require swift and certain punishment of offenders.
2. Stronger crime measures endanger the values of due process and justice.
3. That criminal justice policies should both control crime by enforcing the law and protect the rights of individuals.
4. Every effort must be made to repress crime through efficiency, speed, and finality.
5. Every effort must be made to ensure that criminal justice decisions are based on reliable information. It stresses the adversarial process, the rights of defendants, and formal decision-making procedures.
6. State and local levels of government.
7. Penal codes and budgets are passed by legislatures, many criminal justice officials are elected, and criminal justice policies are developed in political arenas.
8. Elected representatives in state legislatures and Congress.
9. *Mala in se*—offenses that are wrong in themselves (murder, rape, assault). *Mala prohibita*—acts that are crimes because they are prohibited (vagrancy, gambling, drug use).
10. Occupational crime, organized crime, visible crime, crimes without victims, political crime, cybercrime.
11. The distinction between blue-collar and white-

collar crime is no longer useful.

12 To provide goods and services that are in high demand but are illegal.

13 Usually poor people.

14 These are crimes against morality in which the people involved do not believe they have been victimized.

15 Crimes such as treason committed for a political purpose.

16 No, there have been other eras when crime was high.

17 Only violent crimes.

18 Uniform Crime Reports, National Crime Victimization Surveys.

19 Demography, unemployment, housing conditions, family structure.

CHAPTER 2

Victimization and Criminal Behavior

Casey Christie/Bakersfield Californian/Corbis Sygma

During the summer of 2002, the media gave almost constant coverage to a series of child abduction and murder cases. Although fear of child abduction seems to be growing, FBI statistics show that the number of such cases remains steady at about 115 or so each year. Of the 2002 abductions, one that occurred the night of August 1 near Lancaster, California, resulted in the kidnapper dead and the young women alive.

At approximately 1 A.M., an armed man surprised two women, aged 16 and 17, and their dates as they parked on a country road. After tying their dates to a fence post, the kidnapper bound the women with duct tape and drove them away in a Ford Bronco owned by one of their dates.

Within a few hours, television and radio warnings went out throughout the West Coast asking law enforcement officers to look for the Bronco and providing the vehicle's license number. Information was also made public about the identities and descriptions of the missing victims. The quick, widespread warning is called an "Amber Alert," because it was developed after the 1996 abduction and killing of a nine-year-old Texas girl named Amber. Several states are developing "Amber Alert" systems. California's had begun shortly before the kidnapping occurred. The alert included the activation of highway emergency signs that flash a description of the car and ask drivers to be on the lookout (Almeida, 2002).

After several reports from people who saw the vehicle, a police helicopter located the Bronco at 1 P.M. the next afternoon. Police closed in on the kidnapper near an isolated desert road. When police reached the vehicle, the kidnapper pointed a gun, so the officers fired several shots and killed him. The victims were found alive on the floor of the vehicle. Law enforcement officers told news reporters that the assailant apparently intended to kill the women and bury them in the desert. The officers believed that the women were rescued only a few minutes before they were to be killed. In addition, one county sheriff told news reporters that the women had been sexually assaulted soon after the abduction (NBC News, 2002).

The kidnapper turned out to be a man named Roy Ratliff who had spent most of the previous 13 years in prison for various burglary and drug charges. Three months after he was paroled from prison, he was charged with sexually assaulting a teenage relative, but police had not yet apprehended him at the time that he undertook the fatal kidnapping (Almeida, 2002).

This California kidnapping had a happier ending than did other kidnappings in the news during 2002. For example, later that same month, police in Oregon found the bodies of two missing 12-year-old girls buried on an ex-convict neighbor's property (D. Murphy, 2002). The California case did not represent a "typical crime." Indeed, the highly publicized incident that attracted significant mobilization of law enforcement resources and national news media attention differs greatly from most crimes, which involve the loss of property or some other less dramatic event. However, the California case provides an excellent illustration of the factors that shape the subject of crime victimization and the questions about victimization that are raised as a result.

For example, when we examine the California kidnapping, who are the crime victims? Obviously, the young women, who were terrorized and apparently brutalized by a wanted man, fit the classification of crime victims. So, too, do the young men who were with the women on the fateful night and found themselves tied to fence posts at gunpoint. What about the families of these young people? Aren't they also victims of this crime, because of the psychological stress and worry produced by the kidnapping? Would it be proper to say that all people in society are also victims of the crime? The kidnapper's actions cost the public tens of thousands of dollars to pay for law enforcement officers and helicopters to search for the women. Moreover, members of the public may feel less safe as a result of hearing about this shocking crime, which could have happened to anyone. The nationally publicized event may have led to a general loss of liberty for everyone in society. Although difficult to measure, this loss is significant because personal liberty—a highly prized American value—is diminished when people feel more afraid to leave their homes or do the things that they would normally do.

These are important questions to consider, because how we answer them will define the scope of the subject of criminal victimization. In other words, when we talk about the victimizing consequences of crime, should we only talk about the individuals most directly harmed by a crime or should we also consider people who suffer less direct, but equally real, consequences? These questions actually have practical consequences under circumstances in which we speak of crime victims as being entitled to compensation or other "victims' rights." We need to define what we mean by a "victim" before we can implement any such policy.

Another issue raised by the California case is the nature of crime victimization. Were the young women harmed only by the kidnapper or were they also victimized by the ways in which society responds to crime? For example, the young women's names were broadcast on the news when the search effort was underway. After their rescue, in violation of the rules and ethical standards for many news outlets and law enforcement agencies, a law enforcement officer told news reporters that the women had been sexually assaulted. Does the publicizing of such personal information intensify the women's pain and humiliation? Does it violate their entitlement to privacy? As you can see, the issue of crime victimization can also be affected by the responses of the news media and officials in the criminal justice system.

A further question might be whether these women bear any responsibility for their own victimization. If young women sit in parked cars in dark, out-of-the-way places, are they placing themselves at risk of victimization? Even if no kidnapper had appeared, does such a context raise the risk of date rape or some other crime? Before answering that question, we might also take one step back and ask whether it is ethically proper even to raise issues about victims' potential responsibility for the harms that they have suffered. Is such a line of inquiry unfair and inhumane?

An additional important question looms in this and every other criminal case: Why did the perpetrator do what he did? Criminal behavior is the key factor that initiates criminal victimization. Scholars, policy makers, and the public have long pondered questions such as What causes crime? and Why do criminal offenders cause harm to other human beings? These questions have significant implications for the subject of criminal victimization. Theories about crime causation often influence government policies for controlling and punishing violations of criminal laws.

In this chapter, we examine the many facets of crime victimization, including aspects that are not well recognized by the general public. In addition, we discuss the causes of crime. There are many complex and controversial theories about why people commit crimes. In considering this subject, we need to bear in mind that no single theory can be expected to explain all crimes. Remember that "crimes" are whatever actions a legislature defines as deserving punishment at a particular moment in history. Thus we should not assume that a corporate official who employs deceptive accounting practices in order to skim off millions of dollars in business profits has the same motives as the man who kidnapped the girls in California. That crime has many causes, however, does not mean that all proposed theories about crime causation are equally useful or valid. We should look closely at theories about crime and evaluate what evidence supports them.

QUESTIONS for INQUIRY

- Who are the victims of crime?
- What is the impact of crime on society?
- How has the criminal justice system responded to increasing recognition of the needs and experiences of crime victims?
- What theories have been proposed to explain criminal behavior?
- Which theories seem most applicable to specific kinds of crimes or categories of offenders?

Go to the *American System of Criminal Justice* Web site at http://www.cj.wadsworth.com/colesmith10e to explore the topic of crime victimization in further detail.

The National Center for Victims of Crime provides information about services for crime victims: http://www.ncvc.org.

Crime Victimization

Until the past few decades, researchers paid little attention to crime victims. The field of **victimology,** which emerged in the 1950s, focused attention on four questions: (1) Who is victimized? (2) What is the impact of crime? (3) What happens to victims in the criminal justice system? (4) What role do victims play in causing the crimes they suffer? We discuss research on these questions in the next section.

victimology
A field of criminology that examines the role the victim plays in precipitating a criminal incident.

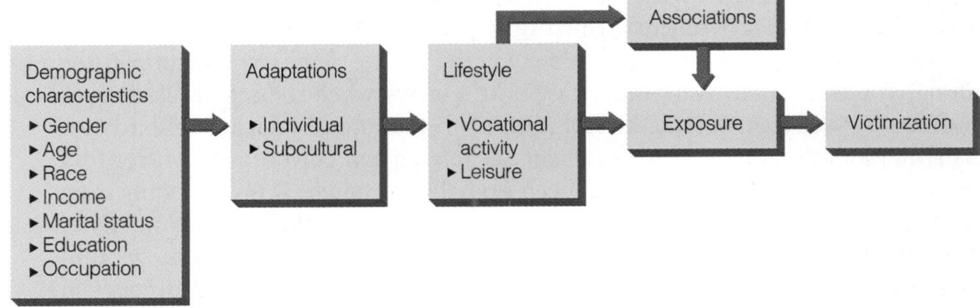

Figure 2.1
Lifestyle-exposure model of victimization
Demographic and subcultural factors determine personal lifestyles, which in turn influence exposure to victimization.

Source: Adapted with permission from Robert F. Meier and Terance D. Miethe, "Understanding Theories of Criminal Victimization," *Crime and Justice: A Review of Research,* ed. Michael Tonry (Chicago: University of Chicago Press, 1993), 467.

Who Is Victimized?

Not everyone has an equal chance of being a crime victim. Moreover, recent research shows that people who are victimized by crime in one year are also more likely to be victimized by crime in a subsequent year (Menard, 2000). Research shows that members of certain demographic groups are more likely to be victimized than others. As Andrew Karmen notes, "Victimization definitely does not appear to be a random process, striking people just by chance" (Karmen, 2001:87). Victimologists have puzzled over this fact and come up with several answers. One explanation is that demographic factors (age, gender, income) affect lifestyle—people's routine activities, such as work, home life, and recreation. Lifestyles, in turn, affect people's exposure to dangerous places, times, and people. Thus, differences in lifestyles lead to varying degrees of exposure to risks (Meier and Miethe, 1993:466). Figure 2.1 shows the links among the factors used in the lifestyle-exposure model of personal victimization. Using this model, think of a person whose lifestyle includes going to nightclubs in a "shady" part of town. Such a person runs the risk of being robbed if she walks alone through a dark high-crime area at two in the morning to her luxury car. By contrast, an older person who watches television at night in her small-town home has a very low chance of being robbed. But these cases do not tell the entire story. What other factors make victims more vulnerable than nonvictims?

Figure 2.2 **Victimization rates for violent crimes**
Black male teenagers have the highest victimization rate for violent crimes. Why are they more likely than other age, gender, and racial groups to be robbed or assaulted?

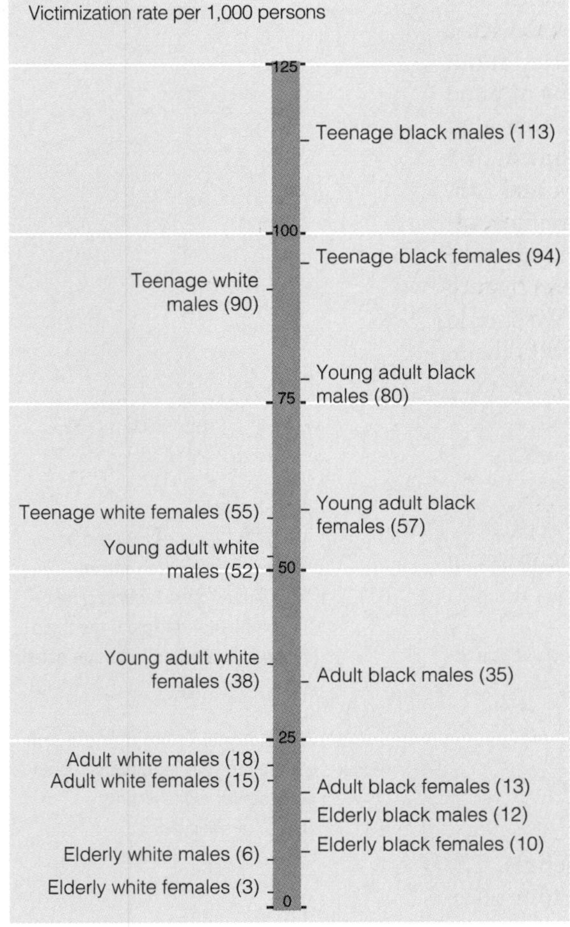

Source: Bureau of Justice Statistics, *Highlights from 20 Years of Surveying Crime Victims* (Washington, D.C.: U.S. Government Printing Office, 1993), 20.

Men, Youths, Nonwhites

The lifestyle-exposure model and survey data shed light on the links between personal characteristics and the chance that one will become a victim. Figure 2.2 shows the influence of gender, age, and race on the risk of being victimized by a violent crime, such as rape, robbery, or assault.

If we apply these findings to the lifestyle-exposure model, we might suggest that teenage black males are most likely to be victimized because of where they live (urban, high-crime areas), how they spend their leisure time (on the streets late at night), and the people with whom they associate (other violence-prone youths). Lifestyle factors may also explain why elderly white females are least likely to be victimized by a violent crime. Perhaps it is because they don't go out at night, don't associate with people who are prone to crime, carry few valuables, and take precautions such as locking their doors. Thus, lifestyle choices directly affect the chances of victimization.

Race is a key factor in exposure to crime. African Americans and other minorities are more likely than whites to be raped,

Alon Reininger/Woodfin Camp & Associates

Nonwhite men, aged 14–24 are the most criminally victimized group. What factors might account for this?

robbed, and assaulted. The rate of violent crime victimization for whites is 27 per 1,000 people, compared with 35 per 1,000 for African Americans. For Hispanics, the rate is over 28 per 1,000 (BJS, 2001d). White Americans are fearful of being victimized by African American strangers (Skogan, 1995:59). However, most violent crime is intraracial: Three of every four victims are of the same race as the attacker (see Figure 2.3). These figures do not reveal that there is a direct connection between race and crime. To the contrary, these numbers simply reflect that there is significant residential segregation in the United States, meaning that African Americans and whites often live in separate neighborhoods. And, most importantly, African American neighborhoods are much more likely to be those experiencing what scholars call "high levels of socioeconomic disadvantage" with respect to unemployment, quality of schools, quality of housing, and other factors associated with income and wealth (Lauritsen and White, 2001:53). These factors are often associated with higher levels of street crime, although obviously other kinds of crime, such as occupational crime and computer crime, appear mostly in other kinds of settings. These same factors of race

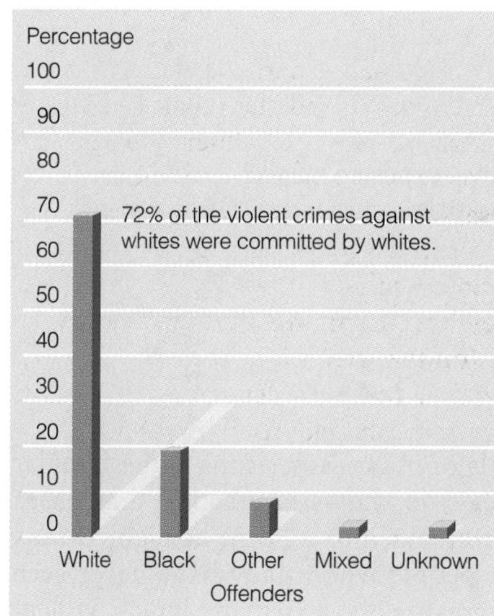

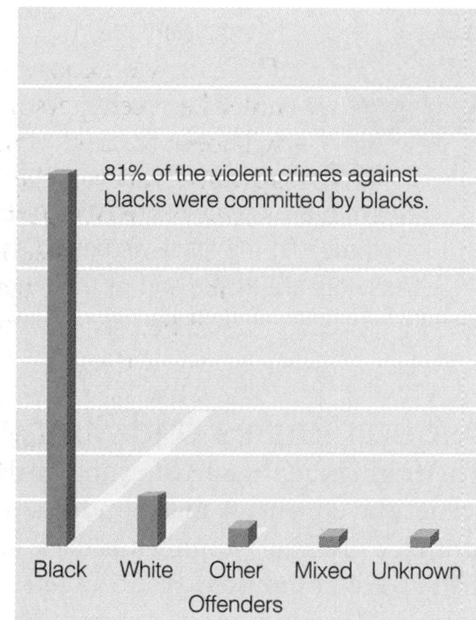

a White victims

b Black victims

Source: Bureau of Justice Statistics, *Report to the Nation on Crime and Justice,* 2nd ed. (Washington, D.C.: U.S. Government Printing Office, 1988), 21.

Figure 2.3
Victims and offenders are of the same race in three out of four violent crimes
Although whites seem most fearful of being victimized by blacks, most violent crime is intraracial. Why do people have such misperceptions?

are also associated with property crimes: Most victims and offenders are of the same race and social class. Street crimes that people fear most occur among people who are in close proximity to each other. Again, in modern America, many people come into contact mainly with others of the same race, especially in the neighborhoods in which they live.

Low-Income City Dwellers

Income is also closely linked to exposure to crime. Americans with incomes below $7,500 annually experienced a victimization rate of 60 violent crimes per 1,000 people. By contrast, those with incomes in excess of $75,000 experienced only 22 violent crimes per 1,000 people (BJS, 2001d). Economic factors largely determine where people live, work, and seek recreation. For low-income people, these choices are limited. Some have to live in crime-prone areas, lack security devices to protect their homes, cannot avoid contact with people who are prone to crime, or cannot spend their leisure time in safe areas. Poor people and minorities have a greater risk of being victimized, because they are likely to live in inner-city zones with high rates of street crime. People with higher incomes have more lifestyle-exposure choices open to them and can avoid risky situations (Meier and Miethe, 1993:468).

Living in a city is, in fact, a key factor in victimization. Violent crime occurs mainly in large cities, where the violent crime victimization rate is 35 per 1,000 people, compared with 26 per 1,000 in suburbs and 24 per 1,000 in rural areas. Urban households are also more prone to property victimization, with victimization rates more than double those in suburbs and nearly six times higher than those in rural areas (BJS, 2001d).

In the inner cities, where drug dealing and drug use have been significant, visible problems, murder rates have risen the most. Like their killers, most of the victims tend to be young African Americans. The national homicide rate among African American men aged 18 to 24 is 103 for every 100,000 of the same group, about eight times that for white men in the same age bracket (BJS, 2001e: Table 3.147). But this does not tell the whole story, because homicide rates differ by city and state. In some cities and states, the gaps between rates for African Americans and whites are even greater.

Further, we cannot conclude that crime rates will be high in all poor urban areas. There is more crime in some poor areas than in others. Many factors besides poverty—such as the physical condition of the neighborhood, the residents' attitudes toward society and the law, the extent of opportunities for crime, and social control by families and government—can affect the crime rate of a given area.

check point

1. What are the main elements of the lifestyle-exposure model?
2. What are the characteristics of the group that is most victimized by violent crime? Of the least-victimized group?

(Answers are at the end of the chapter.)

Acquaintances and Strangers

The frightening image of crime in the minds of many Americans is the familiar scene played out in many movies and television shows in which a dangerous stranger grabs a victim on a dark street or breaks into a home at night. Many crimes are committed by strangers against people whom they have never seen before. However, most Americans do not realize the extent to which violent crimes occur among acquaintances, friends, and even relatives. In 2000, for example, female victims of violent crimes were victimized by strangers in only 33

Table 2.1 Victim and offender relationship, 2000

Look at the differences in crimes by strangers and nonstrangers for various kinds of offenses. Are you surprised by the frequency with which crime victims experience harm at the hands of people whom they know?

	Percentage of Perpetrators			
Relationship to Victim	**Violent Crime**	**Rape/Sexual Assault**	**Robbery**	**Simple Assault**
All Victims				
Intimate	10%	17%	5%	13%
Other Relative	5%	2%	3%	6%
Friend/Acquaintance	38%	43%	20%	42%
Stranger	45%	34%	69%	38%
Female Victim				
Intimate	21%	18%	16%	23%
Other Relative	9%	2%	8%	3%
Friend/Acquaintance	37%	42%	14%	39%
Stranger	33%	34%	60%	27%
Male Victim				
Intimate	3%	0%	0%	4%
Other Relative	3%	0%	1%	3%
Friend/Acquaintance	38%	63%	23%	45%
Stranger	54%	37%	74%	46%

Note: Percentages do not total 100%, because the table omits offenses committed by offenders whose relationship with the victim is unknown.

Source: Bureau of Justice Statistics, *Criminal Victimization 2000* (Washington, D.C.: U.S. Government Printing Office, 2001), 8.

percent of those crimes. Acquaintances or relatives committed two-thirds of the violent crimes against female victims. Although only 44 percent of male victims suffered violent crimes at the hands of acquaintances and relatives, that figure still constitutes a significant percentage of violent crimes (BJS, 2001d). Table 2.1 shows the number and percentages of crimes committed by strangers, intimates (i.e., spouses, boyfriends, and girlfriends), other relatives, and friends and acquaintances.

As indicated by Table 2.1, victims tend to suffer different kinds of crimes, depending on whether strangers or nonstrangers are the perpetrators. Robbery victims tend to be victimized by strangers, but sexual assault victims are more likely to be victimized by someone they know. These differences reflect, in part, the contexts in which these crimes occur. In robberies, valuables are taken from an individual by force and then the robber typically runs away. Thus the scenario fits situations in which the robber hopes to escape without being caught or identified. This result is much more difficult for a robber who is known to the victim. By contrast, sexual assaults often take place in isolated or private locations. People are most likely to place themselves in isolated or private locations, such as inside a house or apartment, with someone whom they know.

As we have seen, people's odds of being victimized depend in part on the people with whom they associate. An element of the lifestyle-exposure model includes consideration of the places that people frequent and the people with whom they interact. Some people increase their vulnerability to victimization by spending time with people who steal property and commit acts of violence. In the case of female victims, who suffer more than 20 percent of their violent victimizations from husbands and boyfriends, this may mean that they misjudged their partners or that they could not anticipate how marital conflicts and other interpersonal stress would affect interactions and behavior. This does not mean,

Close Up: Victimization in the Family?

As a busy college student working two part-time jobs and living with your parents, you spend very little time at home. Your younger brother, who decided to work full-time rather than enroll in college after high school, is hanging around with people who supposedly use and sell drugs. Whenever you try to talk to your brother about his friends' reputations, he gets angry and leaves the room. You notice that household items regularly disappear and your parents immediately buy new ones. The vacuum cleaner, the lawn mower, the snow-blower, a gas grill, and the stereo have all been replaced. You can't help noticing your brother's increasingly suspicious behavior, so you lock your bedroom door whenever you leave the house. When you overhear your parents discussing missing jewelry, you ask whether your parents recognize that your brother is apparently stealing items in order to support a drug habit. You then ask, "What are you going to do about it?"

"Your brother has some problems right now. But he'll only be hurt worse if we call the police or do anything like that. We just need to give him some time to get himself together."

You shake your head and think to yourself, "I wouldn't put up with this stuff in my own house."

Shortly thereafter, you return home one evening to find your bedroom door open and several expensive items missing, including your personal CD player, laptop computer, and cell phone. Naturally, you're furious at your brother, especially because you know that you can't afford to replace these items.

If this happened to you, what would you do? Would you call the police? Would you think that your brother should be sent into the criminal justice system? Could you stand the thought that your brother is likely to steal even more items from you and your parents? Are there alternative courses of action that you could take?

Researching the Internet

Go to the Web site of the Partnership for a Drug-Free America at http://www.drugfreeamerica.org. Read the materials that advise parents about how to teach their children about drugs and determine whether their children are using drugs. Does this information help you to decide how you would handle the foregoing situation?

however, that these victims have necessarily chosen to place themselves at risk. Our legal system, at least theoretically, does not blame victims for the harms that they suffer. The individuals who commit crimes, including domestic violence, are responsible for their own behavior.

There are other contexts in which people's risk of victimization is high because of the people with whom they associate, yet they cannot readily prevent such situations from arising. For example, people who live in neighborhoods with active drug trafficking may be acquainted with neighbors, former schoolmates, and even relatives who rob and steal because they have become dependent on illegal drugs and they need money to support their drug habits. When these acquaintances commit crimes, people who live nearby may find avoiding victimization difficult. They cannot stop walking down the streets or leaving their homes empty and vulnerable to burglary when they go to work or school. Moreover, they may be reluctant to report some crimes because they fear that the offenders will take revenge. People may also be reluctant to report theft committed by a relative with a drug habit. They may be upset about losing their valuables, but they do not want to see their son, daughter, or cousin arrested and sent to prison. If the perpetrators of such crimes know that their relatives will not report them, they may feel encouraged to victimize these people further in order to support a drug habit. Thus the prior relationships among people may facilitate some crimes and keep victims from seeking police assistance. As you read the accompanying Close Up box, think about what you would do if you had a relative involved in criminal activities.

The lifestyle-exposure model helps us understand some of the factors that increase or decrease the risk of being victimized, but what is the impact of crime on the nation and on individuals? We turn to this question in the next section.

3. Which crime and category of victim is among the most likely to be committed by nonstrangers?
4. Which type of crime is among the most likely to be committed by strangers?

The Impact of Crime

Crime affects not only the victim but all members of society. We all pay for crime through higher taxes, higher prices, and fear. These factors impinge on key American values such as individual liberty and protection of private property and personal wealth. As such, many people advocate crime control policies as a means to restore American values.

As we have seen, crime can diminish our sense of liberty by making us fearful about going certain places, being out after dark, and trusting strangers. In addition, the money that we work so hard to earn is reduced by the costs of increased insurance premiums to cover thefts throughout society and increased taxes to pay for police and other governmental services. There may be other costs, too. For example, research shows an increased probability of people deciding to move to a new home after being victimized by a crime in their neighborhood (Dugan, 1999). Moving produces financial costs, personal costs in the loss of friendships and the social isolation of arriving in a new location, and the hassles of becoming settled in a new neighborhood, especially if there are children in a family. It is hard to estimate the precise impact of crime, but it is clear that we all share the burdens of crime and that these burdens clash with our ideas about the American values that we should expect to enjoy.

Costs of Crime

Crime has many kinds of costs. First, there are the economic costs—lost property, lower productivity, and the cost of medical care. Second, there are psychological and emotional costs—pain, trauma, and lost quality of life. Third, there are the costs of operating the criminal justice system.

A Justice Department study from the mid-1990s estimated the total annual cost of tangible losses from crime (medical expenses, damaged or lost property, work time) at $105 billion. The intangible costs (pain, trauma, lost quality of life) to victims were estimated at $450 billion (NIJ, 1996). Operating the criminal justice system costs taxpayers more than $146 billion a year to pay for police, courts, and corrections (BJS, 2002d). Government costs also increased in the aftermath of the September 11 tragedy as more money was spent on airport security, border patrols, and counterterrorism activities. These figures do not include the costs of occupational and organized crime to consumers. However, losses from economic crimes alone were estimated to be $200 billion in 2000, and private businesses spent more than $103 billion on consultants, services, and products to combat these economic crimes (Security Industry Association, 2000). In addition, individual citizens who install locks and alarms or employ guards and security patrols incur crime-related costs.

Fear of Crime

One impact of crime is fear. Fear limits freedom. Because they are fearful, many people limit their activities to "safe" areas at "safe" times. Fear also creates anxieties that affect physiological and psychological well-being. What are the costs to the quality of people's lives if they spend time worrying about victimization every day? What is the cost of human suffering if people cannot get a good night's sleep because they awaken at every sound, fearing that an intruder is breaking in? The very people who have the least chance of being victimized, such as women and the elderly, are often the most fearful (Miethe, 1995:14). All Americans do not

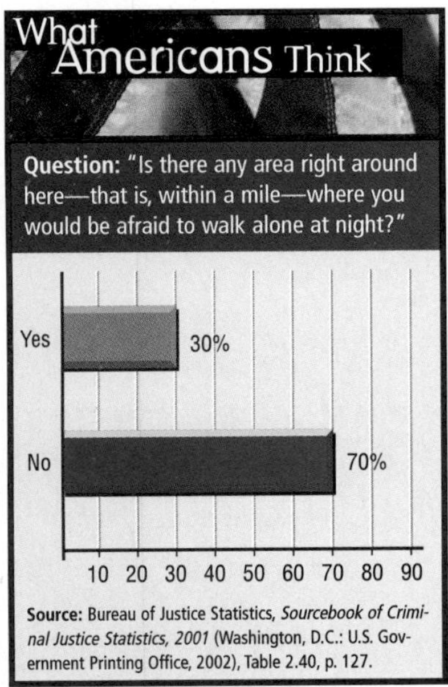

Source: Bureau of Justice Statistics, *Sourcebook of Criminal Justice Statistics, 2001* (Washington, D.C.: U.S. Government Printing Office, 2002), Table 2.40, p. 127.

experience the same fears (Lee and Ulmer, 2000), but some portion of the population adjust their daily activities to prevent being victimized.

Since 1965, public opinion polls have asked Americans whether they "feel more uneasy" or "fear to walk the streets at night" (see "What Americans Think"). From 1972 to 1993, more than 40 percent of respondents indicated that fear of crime limited their freedom. Coinciding with the declining crimes rates during the 1990s, the percentage of respondents who were fearful of walking near their homes dropped to 30 percent in 2001. Despite the improvement in quality of life indicated by the lower figure, this number still represents a significant segment of the American public. Figure 2.4 shows the results of a 12-city study of perceptions of community safety. The percentage of fearful residents differs not only by city but also by the extent to which they fear crime in their city, in their neighborhood, or on the street. In some large cities, more than 60 percent of residents say they are afraid to walk through their neighborhoods at night, while in small towns and rural areas fewer than 30 percent express this concern.

High levels of fear are found among nonwhites and people with low incomes, the groups that are most likely to be victimized. For example, in 2000, 45 percent of African Americans but only 38 percent of whites expressed fears about walking at night in their own neighborhoods. Similarly, 50 percent of those with incomes below $20,000 expressed these fears, while only 28 percent of those with incomes over $50,000 made such statements. These differences may reflect the reality of what people observe in their own neighborhoods. However, not all fears are based on realistic assessments of risk. For example, women and the elderly are more fearful than the average citizen, despite lower-than-average rates of victimization (BJS, 2001e: Table 2.41; Warr, 1993:25).

A Seattle study found that the most-feared crime was residential burglary, a crime that holds little risk of personal injury. Murder, the most serious offense, was ranked tenth. In explaining these findings, researchers suggest that the degree to which certain crimes are feared depends on two factors: the seriousness of the offense and the chances that it will occur. A Gallup poll supports this view. Thirty-five percent of those interviewed said they worried very frequently about being burglarized when they weren't home, whereas 19 percent worried about being murdered (Warr, 1993:27).

Figure 2.4 **Fear of crime in 12 cities**
Percentage of residents who said they were fearful of crime in their city or neighborhood, or of being a victim of street crime.

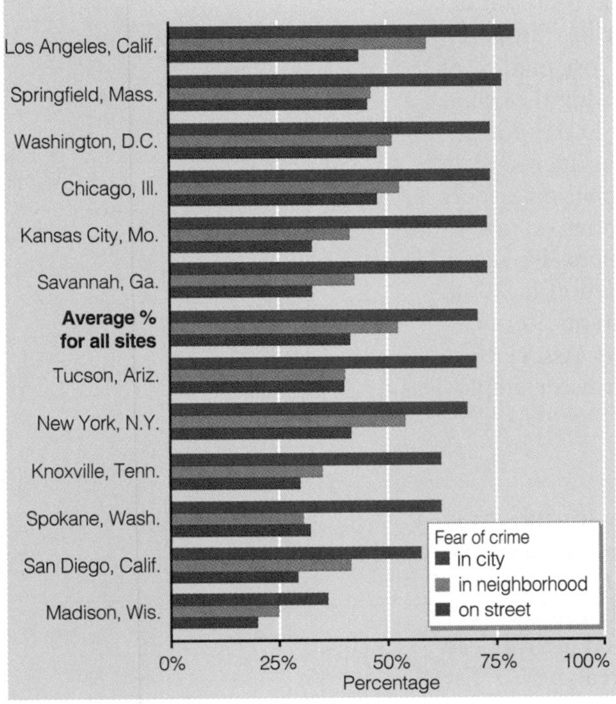

Source: Bureau of Justice Statistics, *Criminal Victimization and Perceptions of Community Safety in 12 Cities, 1998* (Washington, D.C.: U.S. Government Printing Office, 1999), 10.

Although crime rates are down, Americans' fears seem to exceed the actual victimization risks. People do not have a clear picture of the true risk of crime in their lives. They gain perceptions about crime from talk at their workplace and from politicians' statements and campaign promises. Their views about crime also seem to be shaped more by what they see on television than by reality (Chiricos, Padgett, and Gertz, 2000). Although fewer than 8 percent of victimizations are due to violent crime, such crimes are the ones most frequently reported by the media. In the mid-1990s, with violent crime in decline, television and newspaper coverage of violent crime increased more than 400 percent. One result was a jump in the percentage of Americans ranking crime as the nation's foremost problem—from 9 percent to 49 percent (Chiricos, Escholz, and Gertz, 1997:342).

The amount of news coverage of crime, compared with coverage of the economy or government, can be startling (Chermak, 1995:48). Crime stories sell newspapers, build viewership, and appeal to certain types of audiences. Data from the National Opinion Survey on Crime and Justice revealed the regular viewers of television crime programs such as *Cops* and *America's Most Wanted* showed a higher degree of fear "about the probability of being sexually assaulted, beaten, knifed, and getting killed" than did other viewers (Haghighi and Sorensen, 1996:29).

Most people do not experience crime directly but instead learn about it indirectly (Skogan and Maxfield, 1981:157). Local television news has a major impact on attitudes about crime (Kurtz, 1997). In addition, tabloid shows such as *Hard Copy* and *A Current Affair* present reports of heinous crimes almost daily (Kappeler, Blumberg, and Potter, 1996:47). Researchers believe that conversations with friends also tend to magnify the amount of local violence. Such conversations often focus on crimes against women, the elderly, and children. Stories about defenseless victims create a feeling that violent crime lurks everywhere.

The Police Foundation disseminates information about how law enforcement officials can reduce the public's fear of crime: http://www.policefoundation.org/docs/citizenfear.html.

Fear of crime may be linked to disorderly conditions in neighborhoods and communities (Skogan, 1990; Wilson and Kelling, 1982). As discussed by George Kelling and Catherine Coles, in urban areas, disorderly behavior—public drunkenness, urination, aggressive panhandling, and menacing behavior—offends citizens and instills fear. Unregulated disorderly behavior signals to citizens that an area is unsafe. Because of this fear, they "will stay off the streets, avoid certain areas, and curtail their normal activities and associations" (Kelling and Coles, 1996:20). Avoidance of "unsafe" business areas may lead to store closings, declines in real estate values, and flight to more orderly neighborhoods.

In any case, among all groups, the fear of crime outstrips the real risk of it. People do not assess the risk of crime as they do other risks, such as those caused by nature or by accident (see Table 2.2).

Actions that might reduce the fear of crime are costly, and those who can best afford to protect themselves are those who are least threatened by crime. Some responses to the perceived risk of crime may not seem costly, such as staying at home after dark. Yet even such a simple measure is often far easier for the rich than for the poor. The rich tend to work during the day, with some control over their hours of work. Poorer people are more likely to work evenings and nights as waiters, security guards, or convenience store clerks. Other measures, such as moving to the suburbs, installing home security systems, and hiring private security companies, are also most available to the rich.

Table 2.2 Rates of crime compared with rates of other events

Crime is a major concern to many Americans, but what are the risks of victimization compared with other kinds of risks?

Events	Rate per 1,000 Adults per Year
Accidental injury, all circumstances	220
Accidental injury at home	66
Personal theft	61
Accidental injury at work	47
Violent victimization	31
Assault (aggravated and simple)	25
Injury in motor vehicle accident	22
Death, all causes	11
Victimization with injury	11
Serious (aggravated) assault	8
Robbery	6
Heart disease death	5
Cancer death	3
Rape (women only)	1
Accidental death, all circumstances	0.4
Pneumonia/influenza death	0.4
Motor vehicle accident death	0.2
Suicide	0.2
HIV infection death	0.1
Homicide	0.1

Source: Bureau of Justice Statistics, *Highlights from 20 Years of Surveying Crime Victims* (Washington, D.C.: U.S. Government Printing Office, 1993), 4.

check point

5. What are some of the impacts of crime?
6. How is fear of crime shaped, and how does it relate to actual crime rates?

The Experience of Victims within the Criminal Justice System

After a crime has occurred, the victim is often forgotten. Victims may have suffered physical, psychological, and economic losses, yet the criminal justice system focuses on finding and prosecuting the offender.

Too often the system is not sensitive to the needs of victims. For example, defense attorneys may ask them hostile questions and attempt to paint them, rather than the defendant, as causing the crime to occur. Likewise, while victims are a key source of evidence, the police may question them closely—and in a hostile

Ted Soqui/Sygma

Violence against women is perpetrated mainly by those with whom they are intimate—husbands, boyfriends, lovers. Only during the past two decades have justice agencies become sensitive to the interests of female crime victims.

fashion—to find out if they are telling the truth. Often the victim never hears the outcome of a case. Sometimes a victim comes face-to-face with the assailant, who is out on bail or on probation. This can be quite a shock, especially if the victim assumed that the offender was in prison.

For an example of state services provided to crime victims, see the Web site of the New York State Crime Victims Board: http://www.cvb.state.ny.us.

Victims may be forced to miss work and lose pay in order to appear at judicial proceedings. They may be summoned to court again and again, only to learn that the arraignment or trial has been postponed. Any recovered property may be held by the court for months as the case winds its way through the system. In short, after cases have been completed, victims may feel that they have been victimized twice, once by the offender and once by the criminal justice system.

During the past two decades, justice agencies have become more sensitive to the interests of crime victims. This has happened partly because victims often are the only witnesses to the crime and their help is needed. Many victims are not willing to provide such help if it involves economic and emotional costs. Some research indicates that victims are more likely to cooperate with the prosecutor if victims assistance workers meet with them to provide comfort as well as information about how the court system operates (Dawson and Dinovitzer, 2001).

A proposed federal "Crime Victims' Bill of Rights" would grant victims the right to be informed about plea bargains, to obtain restitution for losses, and to bar offenders from earning income from books and films about their crimes. At least 20 states have amended their constitutions to achieve these objectives. As you read the Close Up box, consider how a federal constitutional amendment concerning victims' rights might affect the criminal justice system.

Programs that give information, support, and compensation to victims have been started in many states. Information programs are designed (1) to sensitize justice officials to the need to treat crime victims courteously and (2) to let victims know what is happening at each stage of a case. In some states the investigating officer gives the victim a booklet listing the steps that will be taken and telephone numbers that can be called should questions arise.

Support is most important when the victim faces medical, emotional, or financial problems as a result of a crime. Such support is offered by rape crisis centers, victim assistance programs, and family shelters. These programs may be administered by courts, prosecutors' offices, or private agencies. Often these programs rely heavily on volunteers, who may not know enough to recognize the full range of victims' needs, especially the need for psychological assistance to deal with lingering emotional harms. In most states, compensation programs help victims of vio-

Victims' Rights

In 1996 a proposed constitutional amendment was introduced in Congress. This proposed amendment sought to create constitutional rights for crime victims. President Clinton endorsed the idea when it was first proposed, and President Bush also endorsed it after he moved into the White House. To become part of the Constitution, the proposed amendment would need to be approved by two-thirds of both chambers of Congress and then ratified by three-fourths of the states through action by their state legislatures or state constitutional conventions. One version of the proposed amendment says, in part:

To ensure that the victim is treated with fairness, dignity, and respect, from the occurrence of a crime of violence and other crimes as may be defined by law pursuant to section 2 of this article, and throughout the criminal, military, and juvenile justice processes, as a matter of fundamental rights to liberty, justice, and due process, the victim shall have the following rights: to be informed of and given the opportunity to be present at every proceeding in which those rights are extended to the accused or convicted offender; to be heard at any proceeding involving sentencing, including the right to object to a previously negotiated plea, or a release from custody; to be informed of any release or escape; and to a speedy trial, a final conclusion free from unreasonable delay, full restitution from the convicted offender, reasonable measures to protect the victim from violence or intimidation by the accused or convicted offender, and notice of the victim's rights.

The proposed amendment raises many questions. Would police officers and prosecutors be subject to civil rights lawsuits if they failed to notify victims about their rights and fulfill other affirmative obligations in the amendment? Many Americans are accustomed to filing lawsuits against government officials who violate their rights. If police officers can be sued for such omissions, this may impose significant financial costs on states, counties, and municipalities. In addition, police officers may have less time to combat crime if they must spend time notifying victims and serving as witnesses in legal processes that accuse them of violating victims' rights.

Who would be defined as a "victim" entitled to the rights? This is an important issue for determining who must be notified and who might be able to file a lawsuit for a rights violation. For example, are family members or friends of a murder victims considered "victims" under the proposal?

Does the right to be present and object to pleas and sentences really constitute a significant entitlement? The proposed amendment does not guarantee that prosecutors and judges will follow the wishes of crime victims. Indeed, criminal justice officials retain the discretionary authority to ignore crime victims and do what they would have done anyway. They merely have to make sure that victims are notified and permitted to speak.

Should the criminal justice system really accommodate the wishes of victims with respect to sentencing? Would this create increased risks of unequal treatment for convicted offenders? For example, a purse-snatching victim who lost treasured family photographs may be so upset and angry that she demands a maximum sentence of incarceration for the offender. By contrast, another person who is seriously injured in a violent assault may have religious beliefs that emphasize forgiveness and therefore ask the court to send the offender to a counseling program rather than to prison. In theory, criminal punishment reflects *society's* sense of the appropriate punishment rather than that of an individual victim. In a victim-centered system that caters to the desires of individuals, "justice" may be defined in ways that treat offenders in an unequal manner.

In addition, do any of the proposed rights of victims conflict with existing rights for defendants? With respect to this final question, the victim's right to a speedy trial stands out as a possible source of problems. Could a victim force a defendant to go to trial before the defendant's attorney is completely prepared? Alternatively, would judges merely define the victim's right to a speedy trial in such a vague manner that the right would be more symbolic than substantive?

The idea of constitutional rights for victims is appealing to politicians and the public. However, the design and implementation of those rights may cause unanticipated negative consequences. As indicated by the foregoing examples, policy makers can attempt to anticipate the potential consequences of a new amendment only if they are keenly aware of the role of discretion and other characteristics of the criminal justice system. Past experience indicates that future consequences are not always adequately considered when new policies and laws are developed.

WWW Researching the Internet

For information about President Bush's endorsement of the amendment, see http://www.whitehouse.gov/infocus/victimsrights/. An opposing viewpoint is presented by scholars at the Cato Institute: http://www.cato.org/dailys/9-20-96.html.

Go to the Public Policy feature on the American System of Criminal Justice CD to learn more about the issues surrounding victims' rights.

Imagine the following scenarios: Two women, who live in different cities, arise early one morning to prepare to leave for their jobs at different insurance companies. As single parents, they both bear the responsibility of providing financial support as well as parental guidance to their children. After one woman parks in the underground garage next to her office building, an unfamiliar man sneaks up behind her, places a handgun against her face, and demands her purse and the keys to her car. Because she is startled and frightened, she drops her keys and reflexively bends to retrieve them. When she moves, the gun goes off and she is killed. In the other city, the woman is sitting at her desk in her office tower when suddenly her entire office suite bursts into flames in an explosion. She is killed instantly. The date is September 11, 2001. One woman has been killed in a parking garage in the Midwest and the other has died in the hijackers' attack on the World Trade Center in New York City.

In the aftermath of the September 11 tragedy, Congress enacted legislation to compensate victims with financial awards that exceed those of victim compensation programs and instead match the kinds of significant awards that someone might win in a wrongful lawsuit. Thus the family of the woman killed at the World Trade Center would be eligible for significant financial support from the federal government to replace the income that she would have provided for her family. By contrast, the family of the woman killed in the parking garage would receive very little. If the state's law provided for compensation, it would probably be a modest amount that might not even cover the cost of the funeral. Both women were killed in sudden attacks by strangers. Both women left behind children who had relied on them for financial support as well as emotional support and parental guidance.

→ Is it ethical for the federal government to provide financial support for one victim's family but not for the other? Are there any persuasive reasons to treat the two families differently?

WWW Researching the Internet
For information on the compensation program for September 11 victims, see http://www.ncvc.org/9-11/fed_compensation.htm.

lent crime by paying the medical expenses of those who cannot afford them. When property has been stolen or destroyed, compensation programs encourage judges to order restitution by the offender as part of the sentencing. Crime victims can also file civil lawsuits against the offenders who injured them. Such lawsuits are not difficult to win, especially after an offender's guilt has been proven in a criminal case. However, most offenders cannot afford to pay restitution, especially if they are sitting in prison. Thus victims typically do not receive full compensation for their losses and the continuing emotional harms that they suffer. See "A Question of Ethics" and "Doing Your Part" for more on victims' rights.

check point

7. Who is most fearful about crime?
8. Why do some crime victims feel mistreated by the justice system?
9. What are the main criticisms of the proposed federal Crime Victims' Bill of Rights?

The Role of Victims in Crime

Victimologists study the role victims play in some crimes. Researchers have found that many victims behave in ways that invite the acts committed against them. This does not mean that it is the victim's fault that the crime occurred. It means instead that the victim's behavior may have led to the crime through consent, provocation, enticement, risk taking, or carelessness with property.

What do studies tell us about these situations? First, some people do not take proper precautions to protect themselves. For example, they leave keys in their cars or enter unsafe areas. Using common sense may be part of the price of living in modern society. Second, some victims provoke or entice another person to commit a crime. Third, some victims of nonstrangers are not willing to help with the investigation and prosecution. These behaviors do not excuse criminal acts, but they do force us to think about other aspects of the crime situation.

Karmen points out that some victims are partly to blame for motor vehicle theft (Karmen, 2001:118). In some cases the victims are legally blameless, while in others they have posed as victims to commit insurance fraud. Victim contributions to motor vehicle theft can include *negligence* (leaving the keys in the vehicle), *precipitation* (leaving the car in a vulnerable location so it may be stolen), and *provocation* (arranging to have a vehicle damaged or destroyed). According to Karmen, survey research indicates that 75 percent of vehicle owners have not installed alarms, 30 percent do not always lock their car doors, and 10 percent admit that they sometimes leave their keys in parked cars (Karmen, 2001:119).

Victimologists now recognize that victims play a key role in many crimes. Criminologists consider this among the many other factors that contribute to crime. We now turn to the major theories of the causes of crime.

check point

10. What behaviors of victims can invite crime?

Causes of Crime

Whenever news of a crime hits the headlines, whether the crime is a grisly murder or a complex bank fraud, the first question is "Why did he (or she) do it?" Do people commit crimes because they are poor, greedy, mentally ill, or just plain stupid?

Criminology is concerned mainly with learning about criminal behavior, the nature of offenders, and how crime can be prevented. Research focuses mainly on the offender. Fewer questions are asked about how factors like the economy, government policy, family, and education affect crime (Messner and Rosenfeld, 1994:45–47). In this section we look at the two major schools of criminological thought—classical and positivist. We then examine biological, psychological, and sociological theories of the causes of criminal behavior.

When the prosecutor's office in Washington County, Oregon, sought to initiate a crime victims' assistance program in 2002, Rita and Vern Strobel became the first volunteers. The Strobels assist victims by accompanying them to court hearings, keeping them informed of the schedule for hearings and trials, explaining how the court system operates, and assisting with the paperwork necessary to get victims' compensation and other benefits. In Lafayette, Georgia, a court-established program assists both victims and witnesses. Volunteers help to fulfill the provisions of Georgia's Victims' Bill of Rights by informing victims of their rights and educating them about how the court system works. Local victims' assistance programs throughout the country rely on volunteers to provide comfort, support, and help to victims of crime. These programs are often administered by local prosecutors' offices. Other programs develop in neighborhood centers. In Buffalo, New York, Linda Kowalewski helped to found the East Side's Neighborhood Information Center in order to assist crime victims. Eventually, the center's activities expanded to include a food pantry and home energy assistance program. Agencies that administer victims' assistance program are constantly searching for dedicated volunteers interested in serving their communities by helping their fellow citizens who are experiencing the trauma and crisis that accompanies crime victimization.

Sources: D. Bonilla, "At East Side Neighborhood Center, Assistance Comes in Many Forms," *Buffalo News,* August 25, 2002, p. C4; S. Martin, "Victim Witness Assistance Program a Big Help to Those Affected by Crime in Georgia," *Chattanooga Times,* April 29, 2002, p. B3; "Meet Your Neighbor: Shepherding Crime Victims," *Portland Oregonian,* April 4, 2002, p. 12.

Classical and Positivist Theories

Two major schools of criminological thought are the classical and positivist schools. Each was pioneered by scholars who were influenced by the dominant intellectual ideas of their times.

The Classical School

Until the eighteenth century, most Europeans explained criminal behavior in supernatural terms: They saw it as the work of the devil. Those who did wrong were "possessed" by the devil. Some Christians believed that all humanity had fallen with Adam and had remained in a state of total depravity ever since. Indictments often began, "[John Doe], not having the fear of God before his eyes but being moved and seduced by the instigation of the devil, did commit [a certain crime]." Even today the media report some crimes as having been committed by members of "satanic cults." Alleged child-abuse victims have told gripping stories of ceremonies involving sex, blood, and animal sacrifice carried out in the name of the devil.

Researching the Internet

The Web site for the federal government's Office for Victims of Crime provides information about and links to victims' assistance programs: http://www.ojp.usdoj.gov/ovc/.

Before the eighteenth century, defendants had few rights. The accused had little chance to put forth a defense, confessions were obtained through torture, and the penalty for most offenses was physical punishment or death.

In 1764 Cesare Beccaria published his *Essays on Crime and Punishments.* This was the first attempt to explain crime in secular, or worldly, terms, as opposed to religious terms. The book also pointed to injustices in the administration of criminal laws. Beccaria's ideas prompted reformers to try to make criminal law and procedures more rational and consistent. From this movement came **classical criminology,** whose main principles are as follows:

classical criminology
A school of criminology that views behavior as stemming from free will, demands responsibility and accountability of all perpetrators, and stresses the need for punishments severe enough to deter others.

1. Criminal behavior is rational, and most people have the potential to engage in such behavior.
2. People may choose to commit a crime after weighing the costs and benefits of their actions.
3. Fear of punishment is what keeps most people in check. Therefore, the severity, certainty, and speed of punishment affects of the level of crime.
4. The punishment should fit the crime, not the person who committed it.
5. The criminal justice system must be predictable, with laws and punishments known to the public.

Classical ideas declined in the nineteenth century, partly because of the rise of science and partly because its principles did not take into account differences between individuals or the way the crime was committed.

Neoclassical Criminology After remaining dormant for almost a hundred years, classical ideas took on new life in the 1980s, when America became more conservative. Some scholars argue that crimes may result from the *rational choice* of people who have weighed the benefits to be gained from the crime against the costs of being caught and punished. But they also recognize that the criminal law must take account of differences among individuals. To a large extent, sentencing reform, criticisms of rehabilitation, and greater use of incarceration stem from a renewed interest in classical ideas. However, it is the positivist school of thought that has dominated American criminology since the start of the twentieth century.

Positivist Criminology

positivist criminology
A school of criminology that views behavior as stemming from social, biological, and psychological factors. It argues that punishment should be tailored to the individual needs of the offender.

By the middle of the nineteenth century, as the scientific method began to take hold, the ideas of the classical school seemed old-fashioned. Instead, **positivist criminology** used science to study the body, mind, and environment of the offender. Science could help to reveal why offenders committed crimes and how they could be rehabilitated. Here are the key features of this approach:

1. Human behavior is controlled by physical, mental, and social factors, not by free will.
2. Criminals are different from noncriminals.
3. Science can be used to discover the causes of crime and to treat deviants.

Understanding the main theories of crime causation is important because they affect how laws are enforced, guilt is determined, and crimes are punished. As we describe each of the theories, consider its implications for crime policies. For example, if biological theories are viewed as sound, then the authorities might try to identify potential offenders through genetic analysis and then segregate or supervise them. On the other hand, the acceptance of sociological theories might lead to efforts to end poverty, improve education, and provide job training.

check point

11. What were the main assumptions of the classical school?
12. What are the main assumptions of the positivist school?

Biological Explanations

The medical training of Cesare Lombroso (1836–1909) led him to suppose that physical traits distinguish criminals from law-abiding citizens. He believed that some people are at a more primitive state of evolution and hence are *born* criminal. These "throwbacks" have trouble adjusting to modern society. Lombroso's ideas can be summarized as follows (Lombroso, 1968 [1912]):

criminogenic
Factors thought to bring about criminal behavior in an individual.

1. Certain people are **criminogenic,** that is, they are born criminals.
2. They have primitive physical traits such as strong canine teeth, huge jaws, and high cheekbones.
3. These traits are acquired through heredity or through alcoholism, epilepsy, or syphilis.

Around the turn of the century, interest shifted from physical traits to inherited traits that affect intelligence. Some scholars believed that criminals commit crimes to alleviate pathological urges inherited from mentally defective ancestors. They studied genealogies to find the links between these traits and the criminal records of family members.

Two studies, first published in 1875 and 1902, of families with the fictitious names of Jukes and Kallikak, presented evidence that genetic defects passed on to offspring could condemn them to lives of crime. Richard Dugdale studied more than 1,000 descendants of the woman he called Ada Jukes, whom he dubbed the "mother of criminals." Among them were 280 paupers, 60 thieves, 7 murderers, 140 criminals, 40 persons with venereal diseases, and 50 prostitutes (Dugdale, 1910).

Similar data collected by Henry H. Goddard supported the belief that the Kallikak family, whose members were all related to the illegitimate son of Martin Kallikak, contained more criminals than did the descendants of Martin's later marriage into a "good" family (Goddard, 1902).

These early studies may no longer seem credible to us, but they were taken seriously in their time and affected criminal justice for decades. For example, many states passed laws that required repeat offenders to be sterilized. It was assumed that crime could be controlled if criminal traits were not passed from parents to children. Not until 1942 did the U.S. Supreme Court declare required sterilization unconstitutional (*Skinner v. Oklahoma*).

Renewed Interest in Biological Explanations

Although **biological explanations** of crime were ignored or condemned as racist after World War II, they have attracted renewed interest. *Crime and Human Nature,* by James Wilson and Richard Herrnstein, reviews the research on this subject (Wilson and Herrnstein, 1985). Unlike the early positivists, the authors do not claim that any one factor explains criminality. Instead, they argue that biological factors *predispose* some people to a crime. Genetic makeup, body type, and IQ may outweigh social factors as predictors of criminality. The findings of research on nutrition, neurology, genetics, and endocrinology give some support to the view that these factors may contribute to violent behavior in some people (Brennan, Mednick, and Volavka, 1995:65).

biological explanations
Explanations of crime that emphasize physiological and neurological factors that may predispose a person to commit crimes.

These new findings have given biological explanations a renewed influence and reduced the dominance of sociological and psychological explanations. Scientists are doing further research to see if they can find biological factors that make some people prone to violence and criminality (Fishbein, 1990:27). For example, a study published in 2002 found that a single gene can help to predict which abused children will become violent or antisocial adults. Although most abused children do not commit crimes, studies indicate that abused children are twice as likely as other children to commit crimes later in life. Abused children with a specific gene identified in the study were twice as likely as other abused children to commit acts of violence (Hathaway, 2002). The study does not prove that possession of the gene causes a person to commit crimes, because 15 percent of the abused children with the gene did not do so. However, it provides an interesting indication of how genetic factors (i.e., the specific gene) may interact with life experiences (i.e., victimization by child abuse) to trigger or facilitate later criminal behavior.

Policy Implications of Biological Explanations

A policy based on biological theories of crime would attempt to identify people who have traits that make them prone to crime and then to treat or control those people. This might lead to selective incarceration, intensive supervision, or drug therapies. Special education might be required for those with learning disabilities. Because modern research has never established a simple connection between biology and criminality, however, these policy approaches are highly problematic. As indicated by the recent study connecting a genetic marker in some abused children with higher rates of subsequent violent behavior, not all of the child-abuse victims with the gene committed crimes. Moreover, there appears to be an interaction between life experiences and the gene. Thus basing policies merely on the gene or some other biological connection would lead to the treatment or punishment of too many people.

13. What were the main elements of Lombroso's theory?

Psychological Explanations

psychological explanations Explanations of crime that emphasize mental processes and behavior.

People have often viewed criminal behavior as being caused by a mental condition, a personality disturbance, or limited intellect. **Psychological explanations** of crime center on these ideas.

Before the eighteenth century, as we have seen, those who engaged in such behavior were thought to be possessed by demons. However, some scholars suggested that defects in the body and mind caused people to act "abnormally." One early advocate of this idea was Henry Maudsley (1835–1918), an English psychologist who believed that criminals were "morally insane." Moral insanity, he argued, is an innate characteristic, and crime is a way of expressing it. Without crime as an outlet, criminals would become insane (Maudsley, 1974).

Sigmund Freud (1856–1939), now seen as one of the foremost thinkers of the twentieth century, proposed a *psychoanalytic theory* that crime is caused by unconscious forces and drives. Freud also claimed that early childhood experiences had major effects on personality development. Freud's followers expanded his theory, saying that the personality is made up of three parts: the id, ego, and superego. The id controls drives that are primarily sexual, the ego relates desires to behavior, and the superego (often referred to as the conscience) judges actions as either right or wrong. Psychoanalytic theory explains criminal behavior as resulting from either an undeveloped or an overdeveloped superego. For example, a person who commits a violent sex crime is thought to have an undeveloped superego, because the urges cannot be controlled. Alternatively, a person with an overdeveloped superego may suffer from guilt and anxiety. To reduce the guilt, the person may commit a crime, knowing that punishment will follow. To ensure punishment, the offender will unconsciously leave clues at the crime scene. Psychoanalysts say this occurred in the famous Loeb-Leopold murder of Bobby Franks in 1924 (Regoli and Hewitt, 1994).

Psychiatrists have linked criminal behavior to such concepts as innate impulses, psychic conflict, and the repression of personality. Such explanations propose that crime is a behavior that takes the place of abnormal urges and desires. Although the psychological approach takes many different forms, all are based on the idea that early personality development is a key factor in later behavior.

A. Fredrickson/Sipa Press

Does criminological theory help us understand what compelled Jeffrey Dahmer to drug and kill young men and boys, have sex with their corpses, then dissect and cannibalize the bodies?

Psychopathology

The terms *psychopath, sociopath,* and *antisocial personality* refer to a person who is unable to control impulses, cannot learn from experience, and does not feel emotions, such as love. This kind of person is viewed as psychologically abnormal, as a crazed killer or sex fiend.

During the 1940s, after several widely publicized sex crimes, many state legislatures passed "sexual psychopath laws" designed to place "homicidal sex fiends" in treatment institutions. Such laws were later shown to be based on false assumptions. They reveal the political context within which the criminal law is fashioned (Sutherland, 1950).

new directions in criminal justice policy

Dealing with Sex Offenders

Sex offenses are among the most shocking of crimes, especially when children are victimized by repeat offenders. Yet some sex offenders repeatedly gained opportunities to commit crimes because, after being convicted for a crime, they served their complete prison sentences and then gained release from custody. Because many criminal justice officials have concluded that repeat sex offenders are motivated by deep-seated psychological problems that are difficult, if not impossible, to cure, efforts emerged to find ways to keep repeat sex offenders confined in secure treatment centers. Many state legislatures enacted laws to provide for such custody and treatment, even for offenders who had already served their prison sentences.

People who were confined to such facilities filed legal actions claiming that, by punishing them twice for their offenses, these laws violated their constitutional right against double jeopardy. The first punishment was the prison term and the second punishment was the civil commitment and mandatory residential treatment of indefinite duration. The U.S. Supreme Court, however, has rejected those claims and approved state laws that provide for the potentially indefinite confinement in secure treatment facilities of repeat sex offenders (*Kansas v. Hendricks,* 1997). This policy is based on the presumption that repeat sex offenders suffer from severe psychological problems that require continuing confinement and treatment.

Such policies have a selective incapacitation effect by choosing specific individuals for confinement, presumably for long periods and perhaps even for life. Selective incapacitation always creates risks that someone will be confined who really would not have committed another crime. It is extremely difficult, and probably impossible, to make perfectly accurate predictions about people's future behavior. Thus the Supreme Court has warned states to be careful in defining which people are eligible for civil confinement and treatment as well as the nature of proof required before a person can be placed in custody.

Researching the Internet

To investigate the laws in your state and other states concerning sex offenders, find the links to various states' statutes at http://www.findlaw.com.

For an example of policies based on psychological theories of crime causation, see the Web site of the Texas Council on Sex Offender Treatment: http://www.tdh.state.tx.us/hcqs/plc/csot.htm.

Psychological theories have been widely criticized. Some critics point to the fact that it is hard to measure emotional factors and to separate out people thought to be prone to crime. Others note the wide range of theories—some contradicting one another—that take a psychological approach to crime.

Policy Implications of Psychological Explanations

Despite the criticisms, psychological explanations have played a major role in criminal justice policy during the twentieth century and beyond. The major implication of these theories is that people with personality disorders should receive treatment, while those whose illegal behaviors stem from learning should be punished so that they will learn that crime is not rewarded.

Policies that stress rehabilitation attempt to change the offender's personality and hence, behavior. From the 1940s to the mid-1970s, psychotherapy, counseling, group therapy, behavioral modification, and moral development programs were used in efforts to rehabilitate criminals. However, in the past two decades there has been less reliance on these policies, except as a justification to confine repeat sex offenders even after they have served their full criminal sentences. As you read about these programs in the accompanying "New Directions in Criminal Justice Policy," consider whether you think this is an appropriate application of psychological theory.

14. What is a psychopath?

Sociological Explanations

sociological explanations
Explanations of crime that emphasize the social conditions that bear on the individual as causes of criminal behavior.

In contrast to psychological approaches, **sociological explanations** focus on the way that belonging to social groups shapes people's behavior. Sociologists do not believe that criminality is inborn but instead caused by external factors. Thus, sociological theories of crime assume that contact with the social world, as well as such factors as race, age, gender, and income, mold the offender's personality and actions.

Social theorist Emile Durkheim (1858–1917) argued that when a simple rural society develops into a complex urbanized one, traditional standards decline. Some people cannot adjust to the new rules and will engage in criminal acts.

In the 1920s a group of researchers at the University of Chicago looked closely at aspects of urban life that seemed to be linked to crime: poverty, bad housing, broken families, and the problems faced by new immigrants. They found high levels of crime in those neighborhoods that had many opportunities for delinquent behavior and few legitimate means of earning a living.

From a sociological perspective, criminals are made, not born. Among the many theories stressing the influence of societal forces on criminal behavior, three types deserve special mention: social structure theories, social process theories, and social conflict theories.

Social Structure Theories

social structure theories
Theories that blame crime on the existence of a powerless lower class that lives with poverty and deprivation and often turns to crime in response.

Social structure theories suggest that criminal behavior is related to social class. People in various social classes have quite different amounts of wealth, status, and power. Those in the lower class suffer from poverty, poor education, bad housing, and lack of political power. Therefore, members of the lower class, especially the younger members, are the most likely to engage in crime. Crime thus is created by the structure of society.

What criminological theories might help explain this scene?

Larry Downing/Woodfin Camp & Associates

Sociologist Robert Merton extended Durkheim's ideas about the role of social change and urbanization on crime. He stressed that social change often leads to a state of **anomie,** in which the rules or norms that guide behavior have weakened or disappeared. People may become anomic when the rules are unclear or they are unable to achieve their goals. Under such conditions, antisocial or deviant behavior may result.

anomie
A breakdown in and disappearance of the rules of social behavior.

It is said, for example, that American society puts a high value on success but makes it impossible for some of its members to succeed. It follows that those who are caught in this trap may use crime as a way out. Theorists believe that this type of situation has led some ethnic groups into organized crime. Others argue that social disorganization brings about conditions in which, among other things, family structure breaks down, alcohol or drug abuse becomes more common, and criminal behavior increases. They assert that poverty must be ended and the social structure reformed if crime is to be reduced.

Contemporary Theories Contemporary theorists have drawn from social structure concepts and Merton's anomie theory to develop certain theories of crime causation. Prominent among modern approaches is the general theory of strain. Under this approach, negative relationships can lead to negative emotions. These emotions, particularly anger, are expressed through crime and delinquency. Strain is produced by the failure to achieve valued goals, which may particularly affect poor people in a society that values financial success. Strain is also produced by negative experiences, including unemployment, child abuse, criminal victimization, and family problems, which also may prevail in poor communities. Under the theory, those who cannot cope with negative experiences may be predisposed to criminal behavior (Liska and Messner, 1999: 36–37).

As these ideas have become more refined, they have also been applied to explain white-collar crime. Although one may assume that the affluent would be the beneficiaries of American social structure, theorists have raised the question about whether business people measure their success against the wealth and power of those that they see above them in their corporate settings and affluent communities. To achieve even higher levels of success in a structure that values ever-increasing wealth, individuals may break rules and violate laws in order to enhance their personal success. Thus structure theories have been used to explain the behavior of corporate leaders who manipulate stock prices and take other actions to add to their wealth despite already being millionaires (Liska and Messner, 1999:37).

Policy Implications of Social Structure Theories If crime is caused by social conditions, then actions should be taken to reform the conditions that breed crime. Such actions include policies to combat the effects of poverty, including education and job training, urban redevelopment, better health care, and economic development. Theorists who apply structural theories to white-collar crime are likely to see such criminality as an inevitable component of a society with a free-market economy that equates wealth with success.

Social Process Theories

Many criminologists find the social structure approach is inadequate because they believe that it does not adequately explain criminality by middle-class and affluent people. They fear that a focus on social structure erroneously emphasizes crime as primarily a problem of the poor. **Social process theories,** which date from the 1930s but did not gain recognition until the 1960s and 1970s, assume that any person, regardless of education, class, or upbringing, has the potential to become a criminal. However, some people are likely to commit criminal acts because of the circumstances of their lives. Thus, these theories try to explain the processes by which certain people become criminals.

social process theories
Theories that see criminality as normal behavior. Everyone has the potential to become a criminal, depending on (1) the influences that impel one toward or away from crime and (2) how one is regarded by others.

learning theories
Theories that see criminal behavior as learned, just as legal behavior is learned.

theory of differential association
The theory that people become criminals because they encounter more influences that view criminal behavior as normal and acceptable than influences that are hostile to criminal behavior.

control theories
Theories holding that criminal behavior occurs when the bonds that tie an individual to society are broken or weakened.

labeling theories
Theories emphasizing that the causes of criminal behavior are not found in the individual but in the social process that labels certain acts as deviant or criminal.

Go to the Web site of the National Check Fraud Center and read about different kinds of white collar crime: http://www.ckfraud.org/whitecollar.html. Which theories of crime provide the most plausible explanations for the various kinds of offenses?

social conflict theories
Theories that assume criminal law and the criminal justice system are primarily a means of controlling the poor and the have-nots.

Three Social Process Theories There are three main types of social process theories: learning theories, control theories, and labeling theories.

Learning theories hold that criminal activity is learned behavior. Through social relations, some people learn how to be a criminal and acquire the values associated with that way of life. This view assumes that people imitate and learn from one another. Thus family members and peers are viewed as major influences on a person's development.

In 1939 Edwin Sutherland proposed a type of learning theory called the **theory of differential association,** which states that behavior is learned through interactions with others, especially family members (Sutherland, 1947). Criminal behavior occurs when a person encounters others who are more favorable to crime than opposed to it. If a boy grows up in a family in which, say, an older brother is involved in crime, he is likely to learn criminal behavior. If people in the family, neighborhood, and gang believe that illegal activity is nothing to be ashamed of, this belief increases the chance that the young person will engage in crime.

Control theories hold that social links keep people in line with accepted norms (Gottfredson and Hirschi, 1990; Hirschi, 1969). In other words, all members of society have the potential to commit crime, but most are restrained by their ties to family, church, school, and peer groups. Thus, sensitivity to the opinion of others, commitment to a conventional lifestyle, and belief in the standards or values shared by friends all influence a person to abide by the law. A person who lacks one or more of these influences may engage in crime.

Finally, **labeling theories** stress the social process through which certain acts and people are labeled as deviant. As Howard Becker notes, society creates deviance—and, hence, criminality—"by making the rules whose infraction constitutes deviance, and by applying those rules to particular people and labeling them outsiders" (Becker, 1963).

Becker studied the process through which people become deviant. Social control agencies, such as the police, courts, and corrections, are created to label certain people as outside the normal, law-abiding community. When they have been labeled, those people come to believe that the label is true. They take on a deviant identity and start acting in deviant ways. Once labeled, the person is presumed by others to be deviant, and they react accordingly. This reinforces the deviant identity.

Labeling theory suggests that criminals are not very different from other people. It is only that the police or courts have labeled them as deviant. In this view, the justice system creates criminals by labeling people in order to serve its own bureaucratic and political ends. Those who support this view call for decriminalization of drug use, gambling, and prostitution.

Policy Implications of Social Process Theories If crime is a learned behavior, it follows that people need to be treated in ways that build conventional bonds, develop positive role models, and avoid labeling. Policies to promote stable families and develop community agencies to help those in need are based on this view.

Social Conflict Theories

In the mid-1960s, the biological, psychological, and sociological explanations of criminal behavior were challenged by **social conflict theories.** These theories assume that criminal law and the justice system are designed mainly to control the poor. The rich commit as many crimes as do the poor, it is argued, but the poor are more likely to be caught and punished.

Those in power use the law to impose their version of morality on society in order to protect their property and safety. They use their power to change the definitions of crime to cover acts they view as threatening.

Types of Social Conflict Theories There are different types of social conflict theories. One type, proposed by critical, radical, or Marxist criminologists, holds that the class structure causes certain groups to be labeled as deviant. In this view, "deviance is a status imputed to groups who share certain structural characteristics (e.g., powerlessness)" (Spitzer, 1975:639). Thus, the criminal law is aimed at the behavior of specific groups or classes. One result is that the poor are deeply hostile toward the social order, and this hostility is one factor in criminal behavior. Moreover, when the status quo is threatened, legal definitions of crime are changed in order to trap those who challenge the system. For example, vagrancy laws have been used to arrest labor union organizers, civil rights workers, and peace activists when those in power believed that their interests were threatened by these groups.

Policy Implications of Social Conflict Theories Conflict theories require policies that would reduce class-based conflict and injustice. Policies to help women, the poor, and minorities deal with government agencies would follow. Criminal justice resources would need to focus on crimes committed by upper-class offenders, not just on those committed by lower-class offenders.

Like other theories about the causes of criminal behavior, sociological theories have been criticized. Their critics argue that these theories are imprecise, not supported by evidence, and based on ideology. Even so, sociological theories have served as the basis for many attempts to prevent crime and rehabilitate offenders.

check point

15. What is the main assumption of social structure theories?
16. What is the main assumption of social process theories?
17. What is the main assumption of social conflict theories?

Women and Crime

Theories about causes of crime are almost all based on observations of men. This is understandable, because men commit far more crimes than do women. It also reflects the fact that until recently most criminologists were men. Only in the past few decades has research focused on women and crime. Although they have raised new questions, scholars in this field base their research on the theories just described (Daly, 1998).

Except in the case of so-called female crimes such as prostitution and shoplifting, before the 1970s little research was done on the female offenders, who account for fewer than 10 percent of arrests. It was assumed that most women, because of their nurturing and dependent nature, could not commit serious crimes. Those who did commit crimes were labeled as "bad" or "fallen" women. Unlike male criminals, then, female criminals were viewed as moral offenders. Today criminologists are looking more closely at female offenders (Daly and Chesney-Lind, 1988:497).

Two books published in 1975, Freda Adler's *Sisters in Crime: The Rise of the New Female Criminal* and Rita Simon's *Women and Crime,* led to a new view of gender and crime (F. Adler, 1975; R. Simon, 1975). Both books looked at increases in female crimes, but they reached different conclusions.

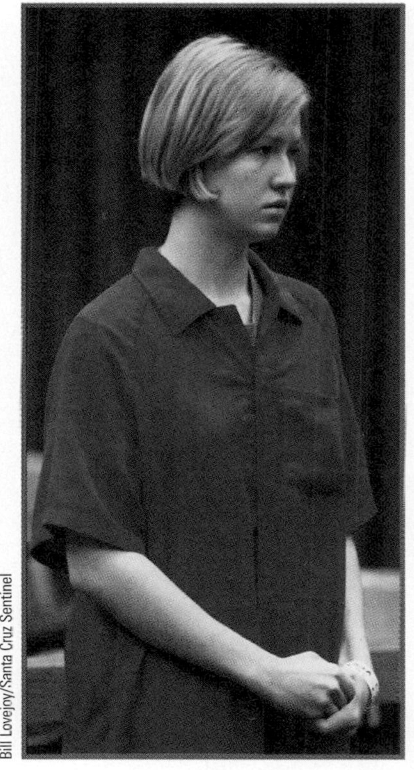

Bill Lovejoy/Santa Cruz Sentinel

University of California, Santa Cruz, student Emma Rose Freeman, 18, accused of pointing a .380-caliber Berretta semiautomatic handgun while robbing a hair salon and a Costco warehouse store with another student.

Adler stressed the impact of the women's movement. She believed that as the roles of women changed, their criminality would be more like that of men. As she noted, "When we did not permit women to swim at the beaches, the female drowning rate was quite low. When women were not permitted to work as bank tellers or presidents, the female embezzlement rate was low" (F. Adler, 1975:31). In other words, as women and men become more equal, gender differences will decrease.

According to Simon, because of recent changes, women now have greater freedom, are less likely to be victimized and oppressed by men, and are less likely to be dependent on them. Simon placed less emphasis than Adler did on the women's movement and more on changes in the job market. She argued that with new opportunities for women, the number of business-related and property crimes committed by women is likely to rise (R. Simon, 1975:19).

But has female criminality really changed? Some scholars believe that arrest data do not suggest major shifts in the types of crimes committed by women. However, from 1960 to 1990 the female share of all arrests rose from 10 percent to 20 percent. This shift was most evident among women under 18 and older women. For both age groups the greatest increase was for larceny/theft—for older women, this mainly took the form of fraud and forgery (Daly, 1998:88). From 1991 through 2000, the total number of arrests rose by 0.2 percent, arrests of men declined 3.8 percent, but arrests of women increased 17.6 percent. Even more striking, over the same period arrests of men for violent crimes declined by 17.1 percent but arrests of women for violent crimes jumped 32.7 percent (FBI, 2001). Even with these increases, however, women are still most frequently arrested for larceny/theft, and women account for only 22 percent of the total arrests. As shown in Figure 2.5, women make up a relatively small percentage of arrestees for all types of crime except larceny/theft. As Herrnstein notes, "As a rule, the more heinous the crime or more chronic the criminal, the greater the disproportion between males and females" (Herrnstein, 1995:57).

For most crimes, women remain minor players. Yet one study found that many women play a leadership role when committing crimes with male partners. Many of the women "initiated criminal behavior, led others into crime, and took primary roles in committing numerous criminal offenses" (Alarid et al., 1996:451).

As the status of women changes and as more women pursue careers in business and industry, some scholars believe that women will commit more economic and occupational crimes, such as embezzlement and fraud. However, research continues to show that arrested women, like male offenders, tend to come from poor families in which physical and substance abuse are present (J. L. Rosenbaum, 1989:31). Other researchers believe that the higher crime rates among women are due in part to a greater willingness of police and prosecutors to treat them like men. Thus far, the findings of research on gender differences in crime are not conclusive (Decker et al., 1993:142).

For information on women and crime, see the FBI's annual reports on crime in the United States at http://www.fbi.gov/ucr/ucr.htm.

Figure 2.5
How do the types of crimes committed by men and women differ?
While most arrests are of men, women make up a relatively high percentage for larceny/theft.

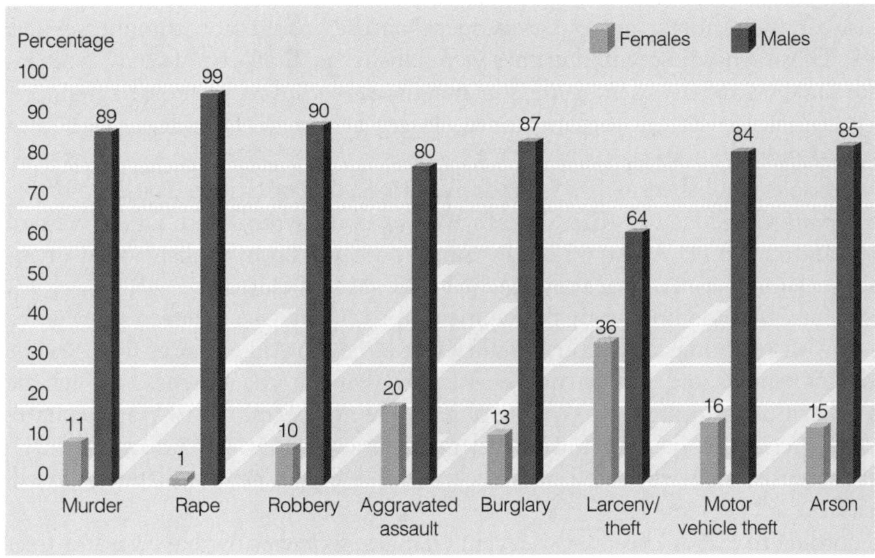

Source: Federal Bureau of Investigation, *Crime in the United States, 2000* (Washington, D.C.: U.S. Government Printing Office, 2001).

Table 2.3 Major theories of criminality and their policy implications

Scholars and the public support various types of policies. We know little about the real causes of crime, but note how many people think they have the answers!

Theory	Major Premise	Policy Implications	Policy Implementation
Biological	Genetic, biochemical, or neurological defects cause some people to commit crime.	Identification and treatment or control of persons with crime-producing biological factors. Selective incapacitation, intensive supervision.	1 Use of drugs to inhibit biological urges of sex offenders. 2 Use of controlled diet to reduce levels of antisocial behavior caused by biochemical imbalances. 3 Identification of neurological defects through CAT scans. Use of drugs to suppress violent implulses. 4 Special education for those with learning disabilities.
Psychological	Personality and learning factors cause some people to commit crime.	Treatment of those with personality disorders to achieve mental health. Those whose illegal behavior stems from learning should have their behavior punished so they will realize that crime is not rewarded.	1 Psychotherapy and counseling to treat personality disorders. 2 Behavior modification strategies, such as electric shock and other negative impulses, to change learned behavior. 3 Counseling to enhance moral development. 4 Intensive individual and group therapies.
Social structure	Crime is the result of underlying social conditions such as poverty, inequality, and unemployment.	Actions taken to reform social conditions that breed crime.	1 Education and job-training programs. 2 Urban redevelopment to improve housing, education, and health care. 3 Community development to provide economic opportunities.
Social process	Crime is normal learned behavior and is subject to either social control or labeling effects.	Individuals to be treated in groups, with emphasis on building conventional bonds and avoiding stigmatization.	1 Youth programs that emphasize positive role models. 2 Community organizing to establish neighborhood institutions and bonds that emphasize following society's norms. 3 Programs designed to promote family stability.
Social conflict	Criminal definitions and punishments are used by some groups to control other groups.	Fundamental changes in the political and social systems to reduce class conflict.	1 Development of programs to remove injustice in society. 2 Provision of resources to assist women, minorities, and the poor in dealing with the criminal justice system and other government agencies. 3 Modification of criminal justice to deal similarly with crimes committed by upper-class members and crimes committed by lower-class members.

check point

18. What have Freda Adler and Rita Simon contributed to theories of female criminality?
19. How do the number and trends in arrests compare for male and female arrestees?

Assessing Theories of Criminality

Undoubtedly all of the theories of crime described here contain at least an element of truth (see Table 2.3). However, none is powerful enough to predict criminality or establish a specific cause for an offender's behavior. The theories are limited in other ways as well. They tend to focus on visible crimes and the poor. They have less to say about upper-class or organized crime. Most of the theories also focus on male behavior. What is missing, and truly needed, is a theory that merges these disparate ideas about the causes of crime. Once we have a complete and testable account of what causes crime, we can develop better policies to deal with it.

Summary

- Young male residents of lower-income communities are among those most likely to be victimized by crime.
- Because of the connection between race and social status in the United States, African Americans are more frequently victimized by crime than are whites.

- A significant percentage of crimes are committed by acquaintances and relatives of victims, especially crimes committed against women.
- Because of the financial and other costs it produces, crime significantly affects all of society.
- Government agencies have begun to be more sensitive to the needs of crime victims. Thus there are now programs in many places to provide services and compensation.
- Scholars have begun to study the role that victims may play in facilitating crimes.
- The classical school of criminology emphasized reform of criminal law, procedures, and punishments.
- The rise of science led to the positivist school, which viewed behavior as stemming from social, biological, and psychological factors.
- Positivist criminology has dominated the study of criminal behavior in the twentieth century.
- Biological theories of crime claim that physiological and neurological factors may predispose a person to commit crimes.
- Psychological theories of crime propose that mental processes and behavior hold the key to understanding the causes of crime.
- Sociological theories of crime emphasize the social conditions that bear on the individual as causes of criminal behavior. Three types of sociological theory are social structure theories, social process theories, and social conflict theories.
- All criminal theories have implications for policy decisions.
- The criminality of women has only recently been studied. Some argue that, as women become more equal with men in society, the number of crimes committed by women will increase.
- Theories of criminality are criticized for focusing too exclusively on lower-class and male perpetrators.

Questions for Review

1. Who is most likely to be victimized by crime?
2. What are the costs of crime?
3. How does the criminal justice system treat victims?
4. What are the major theories of criminality?
5. What have scholars learned about criminal behavior by women?

Key Terms

anomie (p. 55)
biological explanations (p. 51)
classical criminology (p. 49)
control theories (p. 56)
criminogenic (p. 50)
labeling theories (p. 56)
learning theories (p. 56)
positivist criminology (p. 50)
psychological explanations (p. 52)
social conflict theories (p. 56)
social process theories (p. 55)
social structure theories (p. 54)
sociological explanations (p. 54)
theory of differential association (p. 56)
victimology (p. 37)

For Further Reading

Butterfield, Fox. 1996. *All God's Children: The Bosket Family and the American Tradition of Violence*. New York: Avon. A detailed account of the transmission of a culture of violence through multiple generations of one family.

Erikson, Kai T. 1966. *Wayward Puritans*. New York: Wiley. A classic analysis of three "crime waves" in Puritan New England.

Heidensohn, Frances M. 1985. *Women and Crime*. New York: New York University Press. An account and critique of criminological and sociological writings on women and criminality.

Katz, Jack. 1988. *Seductions of Crime: Moral and Sensual Attractions of Doing Evil.* New York: Basic Books. A challenge to positivist criminology that argues there is an emotional appeal to "being bad" and "being hard."

Messner, Steven F., and Richard Rosenfeld. 2001. *Crime and the American Dream.* 3rd ed. Belmont, Calif.: Wadsworth. Argues that high levels of serious crime result from the normal functioning of the American social system.

Rhodes, Richard. 1999. *Why They Kill: The Discoveries of a Maverick Criminologist.* New York: Knopf. Exploration of the ideas of criminologist Lonnie Athens, who challenges the theory that violent behavior is impulsive, unconsciously motivated, and predetermined.

Going Online

For an up-to-date list of Web links, go to http://www.cj.wadsworth.com/colesmith10e

1. Access Victims Assistance Online at http://www.vaonline.org and examine the kinds of victims' assistance programs that are provided in countries outside of the United States. Do you think any of the services provided elsewhere but not here should also be supplied to American crime victims?
2. Access the Crime Victims Assistance Web site for the State of Oregon at http://www.doj.state.or.us/CrimeV/welcome1.htm and read the Crime Victims Rights that are provided under Oregon law. Do you see any potential problems in implementing these rights effectively?
3. Access Crimetheory.com at http://www.crimetheory.com. Read about two theories of crime causation. Which theory do you believe helps to explain a larger number of crimes or the behavior of a larger number of offenders?
4. Using InfoTrac College Edition, enter the keywords *aged crime victims.* Read the article, "Police Practice: Assisting Senior Victims," *FBI Law Enforcement Bulletin,* February–March, 1996. How does the Senior Victims Assistance Team of the Colorado Springs police department work? What assistance to elderly crime victims does it provide?

Checkpoint Answers

1. Demographic characteristics, adaptations, lifestyle, associations, exposure.
2. Most victimized: young black men. Least victimized: elderly white women.
3. Rape and sexual assault against female victims.
4. Robbery.
5. Fear, financial costs, emotional costs, lifestyle restrictions.
6. People gain perceptions about crime through the news media, movies, and television shows; thus perceptions and fears about crime often exceed the actual risks of victimization.
7. Although residents of higher-crime areas are fearful of crime, women and the elderly also have above-average levels of fear that seem disconnected from their actual rates of victimization.
8. The system focuses on finding and punishing the offender; police and lawyers often question victims closely, in an unsympathetic manner; victims do not always receive assistance that covers their medical expenses and other losses.
9. The proposal does not guarantee how rights will be provided to victims, what the remedies will be if the rights are violated, and what will happen if the victim's rights clash with the defendant's rights.
10. Failing to take precautions; taking actions that may provoke or entice; refusing to assist police with investigations.
11. Criminal behavior is rational, and the fear of punishment keeps people from committing crimes.
12. Criminal behavior is the product of social, biological, and psychological factors.
13. Offenders are born criminals and have traits that mark them.
14. A person who is unable to control impulses, cannot learn from experience, and does not have normal human emotions.
15. Crime is caused by people's negative reactions to social inequality, lack of opportunity, and the success of others that does not seem to be attainable in a society that values wealth and status.
16. Everyone has the potential of becoming a criminal, depending on the influences, such as learning or labeling, that move one toward or away from crime, and on how one is regarded by others.
17. Criminal law and the criminal justice system are primarily a means of controlling the poor and the have-nots.
18. The idea that women would commit more crimes as they became liberated and achieved greater equality in the workplace and elsewhere in society.
19. Women constitute a small percentage of arrestees for all crimes except larceny/theft, although there have been increases in women arrested for violent crimes even as arrests of men declined.

CHAPTER 3

The Criminal Justice System

Bill Graham Photography/Athens, Ohio

Columbus Dispatch

On November 3, 2000, Gregory McKnight, the kitchen manager at a pizza restaurant in Gambier, Ohio, kidnapped Emily Murray, a Kenyon College student working part-time at the same restaurant. After McKnight took Murray's car and drove her 90 miles away to a rural trailer that he owned, he shot her to death. Her body was found in the trailer six weeks later after police discovered her car there as they looked for McKnight concerning an unrelated burglary (Dreitzler and Lafferty, 2001). Later, police discovered the remains of Gregory Julious at the trailer, and McKnight was charged with two murders.

As McKnight's case moved through the various stages of the criminal justice system toward an eventual trial, the trial judge, Vinton County Common Pleas Judge Jeffrey Simmons, ruled that the county prosecutor could not seek the death penalty against McKnight, because a capital punishment trial would be too expensive. Although the State of Ohio would pay half of the costs for McKnight's defense, the judge concluded that the cash-strapped, rural county with a total annual budget of $2.7 million would have difficulty paying its half of defense expenses, which could reach as high as $350,000 (Liptak, 2002). Capital punishment cases are often much more expensive than regular murder cases because of lengthy processes for jury selection and appeals, payments to expert witnesses, and an extra trial proceeding for the determination of final punishment.

Meanwhile, in neighboring Meigs County, a jurisdiction in such financial difficulty that 15 of the county's 20 judicial employees had to be laid off temporarily. Common Pleas Judge Fred W. Crow ruled that financial hardships would not prevent prosecutors from seeking the death penalty in murder cases within his county. The judge declared that he would make sure that the defense attorneys appointed to represent an indigent murder defendant had sufficient funds to prepare an adequate defense (T. Sheehan, 2002).

When a crime is committed, the American public expects that the person responsible for the crime will be apprehended, prosecuted, convicted, and punished. If the crime is especially horrible and was committed by an adult, the public frequently expects that the punishment will be as severe as the law allows. In fact, however, the processes used by the American system of criminal justice cannot guarantee that the proper person will be apprehended or that a convicted person will receive the maximum possible punishment. As indicated by the neighboring counties in Ohio, similarly situated defendants may receive different treatment for various reasons, including the availability of resources for specific agencies and processes in the criminal justice system. Moreover, individual decision makers can have significant influence over the fates of specific defendants as well as over the work of other officials in the system. For example, police, prosecutors, and judges make individual decisions about whom to invesigate, what charges to file, and in the case of poor defendants, which attorney will represent the defense. Each of these decisions can lead a defendant to be treated differently from a similarly situated individual being prosecuted in another state or county.

In McKnight's case, the judge's initial decision made national headlines. Two weeks later, Judge Simmons changed his mind. Despite defense attorneys' complaints that the judge lacked the authority to reinstate death penalty charges that had been dropped, McKnight was tried on October 25, 2002, and sentenced to death for killing Murray and Julious. Would other judges have held firm to their original decision in this case? We cannot easily answer this question, but such a question helps to remind us that the fates of criminal defendants are determined by human decision-makers who may be influenced by differing beliefs, sources of information, and societal pressures.

In this chapter, we examine the goals of criminal justice and how American criminal justice operates as a system. Moreover, we shall see how that system's processes are shaped by scarce resources, individual decision makers, and other factors that can lead to divergent treatment for similar criminal cases. In the United States, our history has taught us that we must be aware that differences in the treatment of suspects, defendants, and offenders may be related to issues of race, ethnicity, and social class and the interaction of these demographic factors with the criminal justice system's processes. Thus this chapter will also examine controversies about the existence of discrimination in criminal justice processes.

QUESTIONS for INQUIRY

- What are the goals of the criminal justice system?
- How is criminal justice pursued in a federal system of government?
- What are the major features of criminal justice as a social system?
- What are the main agencies of criminal justice, and how do they interrelate?
- What are possible causes of racial disparities in the criminal justice system?

The Goals of Criminal Justice

To begin our study of the criminal justice system, we must ask, What goals does the system serve? Although these goals may seem straightforward as ideas, saying exactly what they mean in practice can be difficult.

In 1967 the President's Commission on Law Enforcement and Administration of Justice described the criminal justice system as an apparatus that society uses to "enforce the standards of conduct necessary to protect individuals and the community" (President's Commission, 1967:7). This statement will form the basis for our discussion of the goals of the system. Although there is much debate about the purposes of criminal justice, most people agree that the system has three goals: (1) doing justice, (2) controlling crime, and (3) preventing crime.

Yong Kim/Philadelphia Daily News/The Image Works

The goals of criminal justice cannot be accomplished solely by the police, courts, and corrections. Here, community groups, led by C. B. Kimmons (center), march through Philadelphia's Kensington neighborhoods fighting against drug dealers who threaten residents with violence if they call the police.

Doing Justice

"Doing justice" is the foundation of the rules, procedures, and institutions that make up the American criminal justice system. Without the principle of justice, there would be little difference between criminal justice in the United States and in authoritarian countries. Fairness is essential: We want to have fair laws. We want to investigate, judge, and punish fairly. Doing justice also requires upholding the rights of individuals and punishing those who violate the law. All of these elements reflect American values and are presented in the U.S. Constitution. Thus, the goal of doing justice embodies three principles: (1) offenders will be held fully accountable for their actions, (2) the rights of persons who have contact with the system will be protected, and (3) like offenses will be treated alike and officials will take into account relevant differences among offenders and offenses (DiIulio, 1993:10).

Doing justice successfully is a tall order, and it is easy to identify situations in which criminal justice agencies and processes fall short of this ideal. In authoritarian political systems, criminal justice clearly serves the interests of those in power, but in a democracy people can try to improve the capacity of their institutions to do justice. Thus, however imperfect they may be, criminal justice institutions and processes can enjoy public support. In a democracy, a system that makes doing justice a key goal is viewed as legitimate and can therefore pursue the secondary goals of controlling and preventing crime.

Controlling Crime

The criminal justice system is designed to control crime by arresting, prosecuting, convicting, and punishing those who disobey the law. A major constraint on the system, however, is that efforts to control crime must be carried out within the framework of law. This reflects a central tension within American values, in that we do not fully enjoy our liberty if we live in fear of crime, yet the value that we place on rights may inhibit our effectiveness in controlling crime. The criminal law not only defines what is illegal but also outlines the rights of citizens and the procedures officials must use to achieve the system's goals.

In any city or town, we can see the goal of crime control being actively pursued: police officers walking a beat, patrol cars racing down dark streets, lawyers speaking before a judge, probation officers visiting clients, or the wire fences of a prison stretching along a highway. Taking action against wrongdoers helps to control crime, but the system must also attempt to keep crimes from happening.

After his jewelry store had been burglarized for the third time in less than six months, Tom Henderson was frustrated. The police were of little help, merely telling him that they would have a patrol officer keep watch during nightly rounds. Tom had added new locks and an electronic security system. After unlocking his shop one morning, he saw that he had been cleaned out again. He looked around the store to see how the thief had entered, as the door was locked and evidently the security alarm had not sounded. Suddenly he noticed that the glass in a skylight was broken.

"Damn, I'll fix him this time," he swore.

That evening, after replacing the glass, he stripped the insulation from an electric cord and strung it around and across the frame of the skylight. He plugged the cord into a socket, locked the store, and went home.

Two weeks later, when he entered the store and flipped the light switch, nothing happened. He walked toward the fuse box. It was then that he noticed the burned body lying on the floor below the skylight.

→ What are the limits to which one can go to "protect one's castle"? If the police are unable to solve a crime problem, is it ethical for individuals to take matters into their own hands?

Preventing Crime

Crime can be prevented in various ways. Perhaps most important is the deterrent effect of the actions of police, courts, and corrections. These entities not only punish those who violate the law but also provide examples that will likely keep others from committing wrongful acts. For example, a racing patrol car responding to a crime also serves as a warning that law enforcement is at hand.

Crime prevention depends on the actions of criminal justice officials and citizens. Unfortunately, many people do not take even basic steps necessary to protect themselves and their property. For example, they leave their homes and cars unlocked, do not use alarm systems, and walk in dangerous areas.

Citizens do not have the authority to enforce the law. Society has assigned that responsibility to the criminal justice system. Thus, citizens must rely on the police to stop criminals; they cannot take the law into their own hands. Still, they can and must be actively engaged in preventing crime (see "A Question of Ethics").

Any decision made in the justice system—whether in doing justice, controlling crime, or preventing crime—will reflect particular legal, political, social, and moral values. As we study the system, we must be aware of the possible conflicts among these values and the implications of choosing one value over another.

The tasks assigned to the criminal justice system are most easily performed when they are clearly defined so that citizens and officials can act with precise knowledge of their duties.

Canada's National Crime Prevention Centre uses the slogan "Safer Communities . . . Everybody's Responsibility." Its Web site is at http://www.crime-prevention.org/index_ncpc.html.

check point

1. What are the three goals of the criminal justice system?
2. What is meant by "doing justice"?

(Answers are at the end of the chapter.)

Criminal Justice in a Federal System

federalism
A system of government in which power is divided between a central (national) government and regional (state) governments.

Like other aspects of American government, criminal justice is based on the concept of **federalism,** in which power is divided between a central (national) government and regional (state) governments. States have a great deal of authority over their own affairs, but the federal government handles matters of national concern. Because of federalism, no single level of government is solely responsible for the administration of criminal justice.

The structure of the U.S. government was created in 1789 with the ratification of the U.S. Constitution. The Constitution gives the national government certain powers—to raise an army, to coin money, to make treaties with foreign countries—but all other powers, including police power, were retained by the states. No national police force with broad powers may be established in the United States.

The Constitution does not include criminal justice among the federal government's powers. However, the government is involved in criminal justice in many ways. For example, the Federal Bureau of Investigation (FBI) is a national law enforcement agency. In addition, criminal cases are often tried in U.S. district courts, which are federal courts, and there are federal prisons throughout the nation. Most criminal justice activity, however, occurs at the state rather than the national level.

Two Justice Systems

Both the national and state systems of criminal justice enforce laws, try criminal cases, and punish offenders, but their activities differ in scope and purpose. The vast majority of criminal laws are written by state legislatures and enforced by state agencies. However, a variety of national criminal laws have been enacted by Congress and are enforced by the FBI, the Drug Enforcement Administration, the Secret Service, and other federal agencies.

Except in the case of federal drug offenses, relatively few offenders break federal criminal laws, compared with the large numbers who break state criminal laws. For example, only small numbers of people violate the federal law against counterfeiting and espionage, while large numbers violate state laws against assault, larceny, and drunken driving. Even in the case of drug offenses, which during the 1980s and 1990s swept large numbers of offenders into federal prisons, many violators end up in state correctional systems because such crimes violate both state and federal laws.

The role of criminal justice agencies after the assassination of President John F. Kennedy in November 1963 illustrates the division of jurisdiction between federal and state agencies. Because Congress had not made killing the president a federal offense, the suspect, Lee Harvey Oswald, would have been charged under Texas laws had he lived (Oswald was shot to death by Jack Ruby shortly after his arrest). The U.S. Secret Service had the job of protecting the president, but apprehending the killer was the formal responsibility of the Dallas police and other Texas law enforcement agencies.

Expansion of Federal Involvement

Go to the Public Policy feature on the American System of Criminal Justice CD to learn more about the issues surrounding the federalization of criminal justice.

Since the 1960s the federal government has expanded its role in dealing with crime, a policy area that has traditionally been the responsibility of state and local governments. As Willard Oliver notes, the federal role has become much more active in "legislating criminal activity, expanding [the] federal law enforcement bureaucracy, widening the reach and scope of the federal courts, and building more federal prisons" (Oliver, 2002:1).

The report of the U.S. President's Commission on Law Enforcement and Administration of Justice (1967:613) emphasized the need for greater federal involvement in local crime control and urged that federal grants be directed to the states to support criminal justice initiatives. Since then, Congress has allocated billions of dollars for crime control efforts and passed legislation, national in scope, to deal with street crime, the "war on drugs," violent crime, terrorism, and juvenile delinquency. Although most criminal justice expenditures and personnel are found at the local level, over the past 40 years the federal government has increased its role in fighting street crime (Oliver, 2002; Scheingold, 1995).

Because many crimes span state borders, we no longer think of some crimes as being committed at a single location within a single state. For example, crime syndicates and gangs deal with drugs, pornography, and gambling on a national level. Thus, Congress has expanded the powers of the FBI and other federal agencies to pursue criminal activities that were formerly the responsibility of the states.

Congress has also passed laws designed to allow the FBI to investigate situations in which local police forces are likely to be less effective. Under the National Stolen Property Act, for example, the FBI may investigate thefts of more than $5,000 in value when the stolen property is likely to have been transported across state lines. As a national agency, the FBI is better able than any state agency to pursue criminal investigations across state borders.

Disputes over jurisdiction may occur when an offense violates both state and federal laws. If the FBI and local agencies do not cooperate, they may each seek to catch the same criminals. This can have major implications if the court to which the case is brought is determined by the agency that makes the arrest. Usually, however, law enforcement officials at all levels of government seek to cooperate and to coordinate their efforts.

Sheron Norman holds a photo of her former brother-in-law John Allen Muhammad (right) and John Lee Malvo. On the possibility that the killer was a terrorist, the hunt for the D.C. Sniper involved not only the state and local police of the District of Columbia, Maryland, and Virginia, but also more than 1,500 people working for federal agencies including the FBI, ATF, DEA, Marshal's Service, and Secret Service.

After the September 11 attacks on the World Trade Center and the Pentagon, the FBI and other federal law enforcement agencies focused their resources and efforts on investigating and preventing terrorist threats against the United States, including tightening security at airports and national borders. As a result, the role of the FBI as a law enforcement agency may be changing. One month after the attacks, 4,000 of the agency's 11,500 agents were dedicating their efforts to the aftermath of September 11. So many FBI agents were switched from their traditional law enforcement activities to antiterror initiatives that some observers claimed that other federal crimes were no longer being vigorously investigated (Kampeas, 2001). The federal government's response to potential threats to national security may ultimately diminish the federal role in traditional law enforcement and thereby effectively transfer responsibility for many criminal investigations to state and local officials.

The reorientation of the FBI's priorities is just one aspect of changes in federal criminal justice agencies to address the threat of terrorism. Congress and President Bush sought to increase the government's effectiveness by creating new federal agencies. The Transportation Security Administration (TSA), a new agency within the Department of Transportation, assumed responsibility for protecting travelers and interstate commerce. Most importantly, federal employees of the TSA assumed responsibility for screening passengers and their luggage at airports throughout the country. In light of the ease with which the September 11 hijackers brought "box cutters" onboard commercial airliners, there were grave concerns that employees of private security agencies were not adequately trained or sufficiently vigilant to protect the traveling public.

The biggest change in federal criminal justice occurred in November 2002, when Congress enacted legislation to create a new Department of Homeland Security. This department was created in order to centralize the administration and coordination of many existing agencies that were previously scattered throughout various departments. The Secretary of Homeland Security is responsible for overseeing the Coast Guard, Immigration and Naturalization Service, Border Patrol, Secret Service, Federal Emergency Management Agency, and other agencies (including the new TSA) concerned with protecting the food supply, nuclear power facilities, and other potential terrorism targets. The Department of Homeland Security will take charge of training emergency first responders, coordinating federal agencies' actions with those of state and local agencies, and analyzing domestic intelligence information obtained by the CIA, FBI, and other sources. (See Table 3.1)

The Secretary of Homeland Security faces an enormous challenge in seeking to integrate departments that previously operated separately. It remains to be seen how long it will take for the new department to handle its duties efficiently. There will undoubtedly be unanticipated problems as the combined federal agencies, as well as state and local agencies, begin to develop new working relationships.

Because both state and federal systems operate in the United States, criminal justice here is highly decentralized. As Figure 3.1 shows, two-thirds of all criminal justice employees work for local governments. The majority of workers in all of the subunits of the system—except corrections—are tied to local government. Likewise, the costs of criminal justice are distributed among the federal, state, and local governments.

For information about the responsibilities and activities of the FBI, visit the agency's Web site: http://www.fbi.gov/homepage.htm.

Table 3.1 Department of Homeland Security

Congress approved legislation to create a new federal agency dedicated to protecting the United States from terrorism. The legislation merges 22 agencies and nearly 170,000 government workers.

	Agencies to Be Moved to the Department of Homeland Security	Department or Agency They Are Now
Border and Transportation Security	Immigration and Naturalization Service enforcement functions	Justice Department
	Transportation Security Administration	Transportation Department
	Customs Service	Treasury Department
	Federal Protective Services	General Services Administration
	Animal and Plant Health Inspection Service (parts)	Agriculture Department
Emergency Preparedness and Response	Federal Emergency Management Agency	(*Independent agency*)
	Chemical, biological, radiological, and nuclear response units	Health and Human Services Department
	Nuclear Incident response teams	Energy Department
	National Domestic Preparedness Office	F.B.I.
	Office of Domestic Preparedness	Justice Department
	Domestic Emergency Support Teams	(*From various departments and agencies*)
Science and Technology	Civilian biodefense research program	Health and Human Services Department
	National Biological Warfare Defense Analysis Center	(*Proposed in fiscal 2003 budget*)
	Plum Island Animal Disease Center	Agriculture Department
	Lawrence Livermore National Laboratory (parts)	Energy Department
Information Analysis and Infrastructure Protection	National Communications System	Defense Department
	National Infrastructure Protection Center	F.B.I.
	Critical Infrastructure Assurance Office	Commerce Department
	National Infrastructure Simulation and Analysis Center	Energy Department
	Federal Computer Incident Response Center	General Services Administration
Secret Service	Secret Service including presidential protection units	Treasury Department
Coast Guard	Coast Guard	Transportation Department

Source: *New York Times*, November 20, 2002, p. A12.

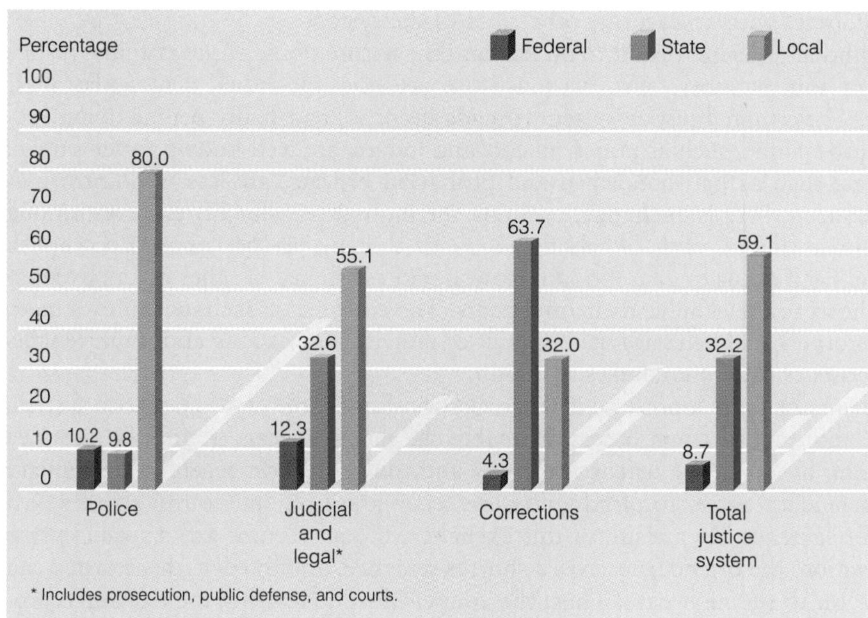

Source: Bureau of Justice Statistics, *Sourcebook of Criminal Justice Statistics, 2000* (Washington, D.C.: U.S. Government Printing Office, 2001), Table 1.19.

Figure 3.1
Percentage (rounded) of criminal justice employees at each level of government, 1999
The administration of criminal justice in the United States is very much a local affair, as these employment figures show. Only in corrections do states employ a greater percentage of workers than do municipalities.

Laws are enforced and offenders are brought to justice mainly in the states, counties, and cities. As a result, local traditions, values, and practices shape the way criminal justice agencies operate. Local leaders, whether members of the city council or influential citizens, can help set law enforcement priorities by putting pressure on the police. Will the city's police officers crack down on illegal gambling? Will juvenile offenders be turned over to their parents with stern warnings, or will they be sent to state institutions? The answers to these and other important questions vary from city to city.

check point

3. What are the key features of federalism?
4. What powers does the national government have in the area of crime and justice?
5. What factors have caused federal involvement in criminal justice to expand?

Criminal Justice as a System

To achieve the goals of criminal justice, many kinds of organizations—police, prosecution, courts, corrections—have been formed. Each has its own functions and personnel. We might assume that criminal justice is an orderly process in which a variety of professionals act on each case on behalf of society. To know how the system really works, however, we must look beyond its formal organizational chart. In doing so, we can use the concept of a **system:** a complex whole made up of interdependent parts whose actions are directed toward goals and influenced by the environment in which they function.

system
A complex whole consisting of interdependent parts whose operations are directed toward goals and are influenced by the environment within which they function.

The System Perspective

Criminal justice is a system made up of parts or subsystems. The subsystems—police, courts, corrections—have their own goals and needs but are also interdependent. When one unit changes its policies, practices, or resources, this change will affect other units as well. An increase in the number of people arrested by the police, for example, will affect not only the judicial subsystem but also the probation and correctional subsystems. For criminal justice to achieve its goals, each part must make a unique contribution; each must also have at least minimal contact with at least one other part of the system.

Although it is important to understand the nature of the entire criminal justice system and its subsystems, we must also see how individual actors play their roles. The criminal justice system is made up of a great many people doing specific jobs. Some, such as police officers and judges, are well-known to the public. Others, such as bail bondsmen and probation officers, are less well-known. A key concept here is **exchange,** meaning the mutual transfer of resources among individual actors, each of whom has goals that he or she cannot accomplish alone. Each needs to gain the cooperation and assistance of other actors by helping those actors achieve their own goals. The concept of exchange allows us to see interpersonal behavior as the result of individual decisions about the benefits and costs of different courses of action.

exchange
A mutual transfer of resources; a balance of benefits and deficits that flow from behavior based on decisions about the values and costs of alternatives.

There are many kinds of exchange relationships in the criminal justice system, some more visible than others. Probably the most obvious example is the **plea bargain,** in which the defense attorney and the prosecutor reach an agreement: the defendant agrees to plead guilty in exchange for a reduction of charges or a lighter sentence. As a result of this exchange, the prosecutor gains a quick, sure conviction, the offender receives a shorter sentence, and the defense attorney can move on to the next case. Thus, the cooperation underlying the exchange promotes the goals of each participant.

plea bargain
A defendant's plea of guilty to a criminal charge with the reasonable expectation of receiving some consideration from the state for doing so, usually a reduction of the charge. The defendant's ultimate goal is a penalty lighter than the one formally warranted by the charged offense.

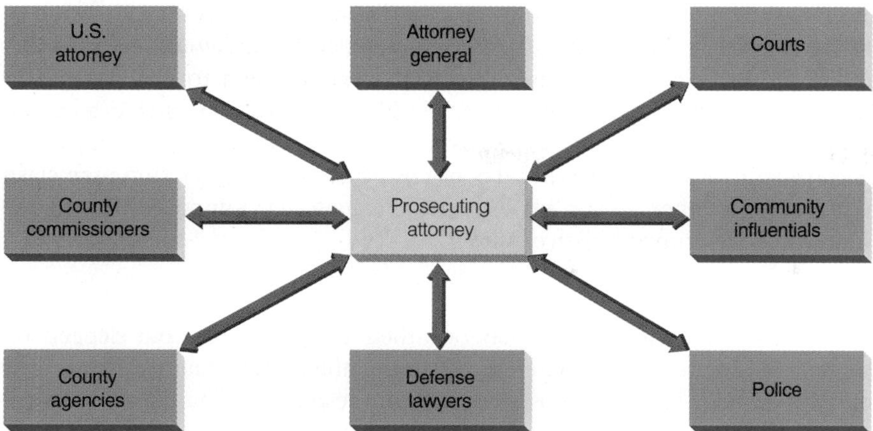

Figure 3.2
Exchange relationships between prosecutors and others
The prosecutor's decisions are influenced by relationships with other agencies and members of the community.

The concept of exchange reminds us that decisions are the products of interactions among individuals and that the subsystems of the criminal justice system are tied together by the actions of individual decision makers. Figure 3.2 presents selected exchange relationships between a prosecutor and other individuals and agencies involved in the criminal justice process.

The concepts of system and exchange are closely linked. In this book, these concepts serve as an organizing framework to describe individual subsystems and actors and help us see how the justice process really works. Let's turn now to the main characteristics of the system, all of which shape the decisions that determine the fates of defendants.

To read descriptions of the incentives that induce each participant in plea bargaining to engage in exchanges, see the description of plea bargaining under Criminal Law in the Plain-English Law Center link at http://www.nolo.com/index.cfm.

Characteristics of the Criminal Justice System

The workings of the criminal justice system have four major characteristics: (1) discretion, (2) resource dependence, (3) sequential tasks, and (4) filtering.

discretion
The authority to make decisions without reference to specific rules or facts, using instead one's own judgment; allows for individualization and informality in the administration of justice.

Discretion

All levels of the justice process reveal a high degree of **discretion.** This term refers to officials' freedom to act according to their own judgment and conscience (see Table 3.1). For example, police officers decide how to handle a crime situation, prosecutors decide which charges to file, judges decide how long a sentence will be, and parole boards decide when an offender will be released from prison.

The extent of such discretion may seem odd, given that the United States is ruled by law and has created procedures to ensure that decisions are made in accordance with law. However, instead of being a mechanical system in which the law dominates decisions, criminal justice is a system in which actors may take many factors into account and exercise many options as they dispose of a case. The role of discretion opens the door for individual police officers, prosecutors, defense attorneys, and judges to make decisions based, at least in part, on their own self-interest. They may want to save time, save resources, or hurry a case along to completion. Whenever people base criminal justice decisions on self-interest, however, they run the risk that American values, such as individual liberty and constitutional rights, will receive inadequate consideration and protection.

Two arguments are often used to justify discretion in the criminal justice system. First, discretion is needed because the

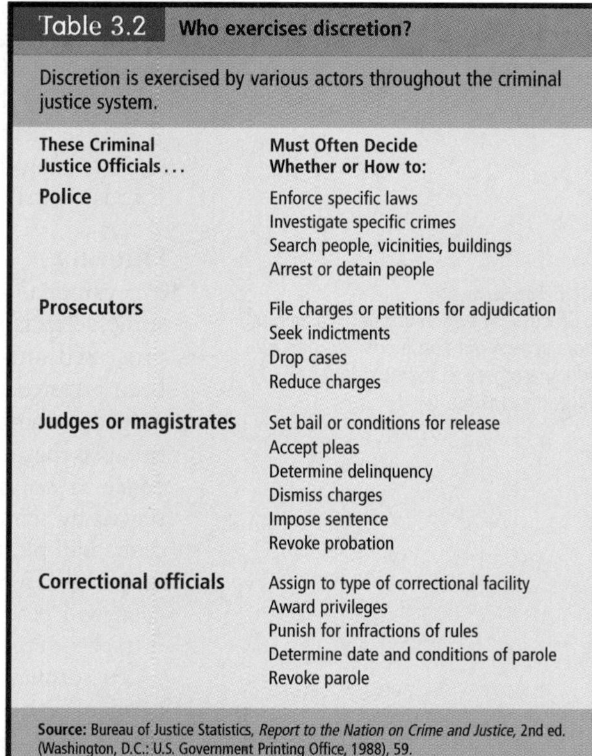

Table 3.2 **Who exercises discretion?**

Discretion is exercised by various actors throughout the criminal justice system.

These Criminal Justice Officials . . .	Must Often Decide Whether or How to:
Police	Enforce specific laws Investigate specific crimes Search people, vicinities, buildings Arrest or detain people
Prosecutors	File charges or petitions for adjudication Seek indictments Drop cases Reduce charges
Judges or magistrates	Set bail or conditions for release Accept pleas Determine delinquency Dismiss charges Impose sentence Revoke probation
Correctional officials	Assign to type of correctional facility Award privileges Punish for infractions of rules Determine date and conditions of parole Revoke parole

Source: Bureau of Justice Statistics, *Report to the Nation on Crime and Justice,* 2nd ed. (Washington, D.C.: U.S. Government Printing Office, 1988), 59.

system lacks the resources to treat every case the same way. If every violation of the law were pursued through trial, for example, the costs would be immense. Second, many officials believe that discretion permits them to achieve greater justice than rigid rules would produce. However, the second justification can only be true when officials emphasize justice in their decisions. If they emphasize other considerations, such as efficiency or cost, their use of discretion may clash with justice and other important American values that supposedly form the foundation of the criminal justice system.

Resource Dependence

Criminal justice agencies do not generate their own resources but depend on other agencies for funding. Therefore, actors in the system must cultivate and maintain good relations with those who allocate resources—that is, political decision makers, such as legislators, mayors, and city council members. Some police departments gain revenue through traffic fines and property forfeitures, but these sources are not enough to sustain their budgets.

Because budget decision are made by elected officials who seek to please the public, criminal justice officials must also maintain a positive image and good relations with voters. If the police have strong public support, for example, the mayor will be reluctant to reduce the law enforcement budget. Criminal justice officials also seek positive coverage from the news media. Since the media often provide a crucial link between government agencies and the public, criminal justice officials may announce notable achievements while trying to limit publicity about controversial cases and decisions.

As illustrated by the death penalty example at the beginning of this chapter, a lack of resources can influence decisions about how defendants are processed through the system.

Sequential Tasks

Decisions in the criminal justice system follow a specific sequence. The police must make an arrest before a defendant is passed along to the prosecutor; the prosecutor's decisions determine the nature of the court's workload; and so forth. If officials act out of sequence, they cannot achieve their goals. For example, prosecutors and judges cannot bypass the police by making arrests, and correctional officials cannot punish anyone who has not passed through the earlier stages of the process.

The sequential nature of the system is a key element in the exchange relationships among decision makers who depend on each other to achieve their goals. It thus contributes to the strong interdependence within the system.

Filtering

filtering process
A process by which criminal justice officials screen out some cases while advancing others to the next level of decision making.

The criminal justice system may be viewed as a **filtering process.** At each stage, some defendants are sent on to the next stage, while others are either released or processed under changed conditions. As shown in Figure 3.3, people who have been arrested may be filtered out of the system at various points. Note that few suspects who are arrested are then prosecuted, tried, and convicted. Some go free because the police decide that a crime has not been committed or that the evidence is not sound. The prosecutor may decide that justice would be better served by sending the suspect to a substance abuse clinic. Although many defendants will plead guilty, the judge may dismiss charges against others, and the jury may acquit a few defendants. Most of the offenders who are actually tried, however, will be convicted. Thus, the criminal justice system is often described as a funnel—many cases enter it, but only a few result in conviction and punishment.

To summarize, the criminal justice system is composed of a set of interdependent parts (subsystems). This system has four key attributes: (1) discretion, (2) resource dependence, (3) sequential tasks, and (4) filtering. Within this framework, we look next at the operations of criminal justice agencies and then examine the flow of cases through the system.

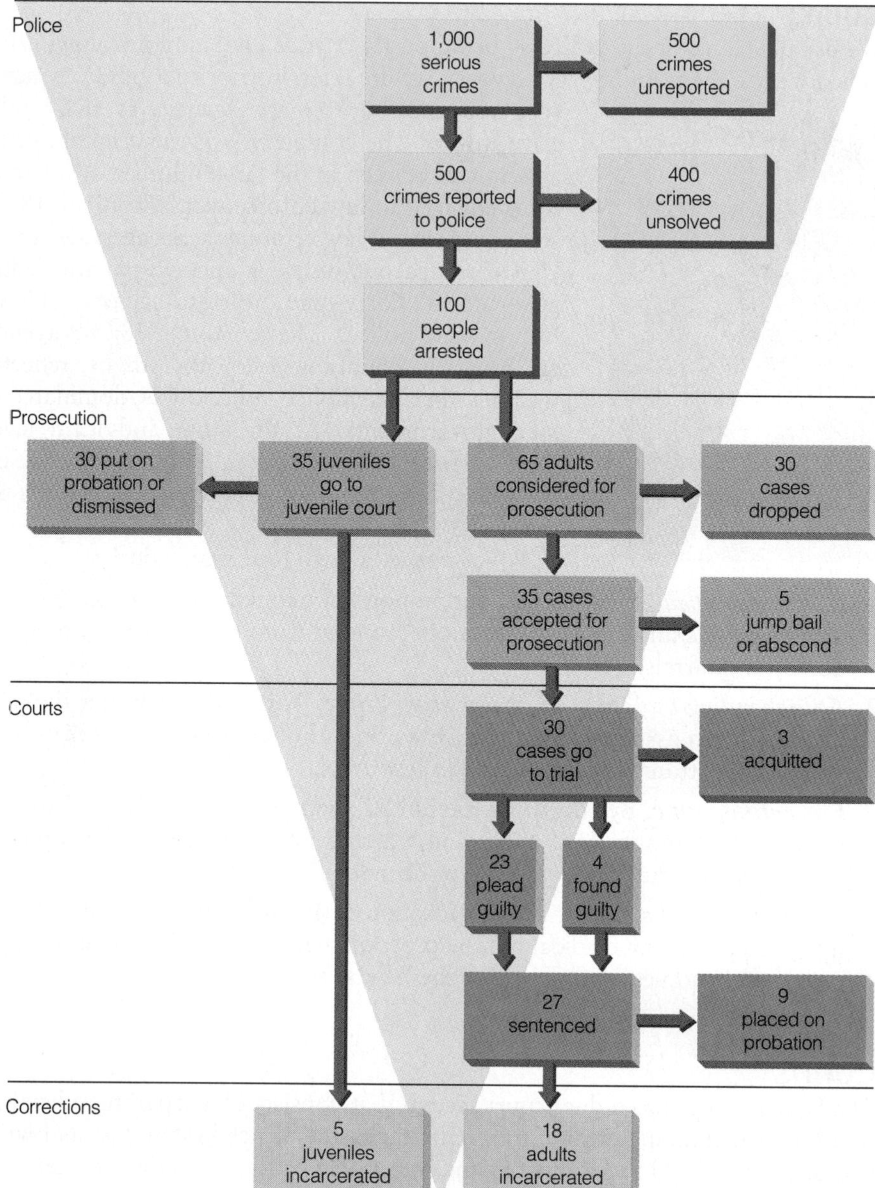

Sources: Data from this figure have been drawn from many sources including Bureau of Justice Statistics, *Sourcebook of Criminal Justice Statistics, 1998* (Washington, D.C.: U.S. Government Printing Office, 1999) and Bureau of Justice Statistics, *Bulletin*, February 1988.

Figure 3.3
Criminal justice as a filtering process
Decisions at each point in the system result in some cases being dropped while others are passed to the next point. Are you surprised by the small portion of cases that remain?

check point

6. What is a system?
7. What is one example of an exchange relationship?
8. What are the major characteristics of the criminal justice system?

Operations of Criminal Justice Agencies

The criminal justice system has been formed to deal with people accused of violating the criminal law. Its subsystems consist of more than 60,000 public and private agencies with an annual budget of more than $146 billion and more than 2 million employees. Here we review the main parts of the criminal justice system and their functions.

Police

We usually think of the police as being on the "front line" in controlling crime. When we use the term *police,* however, we are referring not to a single agency or type of agency but to many agencies at each level of government. The complexity of the criminal justice system can be seen in the large number of organizations engaged in law enforcement. There are 18,769 state and local law enforcement agencies in the United States but only 50 agencies of the federal government. Forty-nine are state agencies (Hawaii has no state police). The remaining 18,769 agencies are found in counties, cities, and towns, reflecting the fact that the police function is dominated by local governments. At the state and local levels, these agencies have more than 900,000 full-time employees and a total annual budget that exceeds $50 billion (BJS, 2001e).

Steven Rubin/The Image Works

Maintaining their peace-keeping function isn't always easy for law enforcement officers in emotionally charged situations, such as this protest sparked by an accident in which a Hasidic motorist struck and killed a black child in the Crown Heights section of New York City.

Police agencies have four major duties:

1. *Keeping the peace.* This broad and important mandate involves the protection of people and rights in situations ranging from street-corner brawls to domestic quarrels.
2. *Apprehending violators and combating crime.* This is the task that the public most often associates with police work, although it accounts for only a small proportion of police time and resources.
3. *Preventing crime.* By educating the public about the threat of crime and by reducing the number of situations in which crimes are likely to be committed, the police can lower the rate of crime.
4. *Providing social services.* Police officers recover stolen property, direct traffic, give emergency medical aid, help people who have locked themselves out of their homes, and provide other social services.

For information about police agencies, see the International Association of Chiefs of Police at http://www.theiacp.org.

Courts

dual court system
A system consisting of a separate judicial structure for each state in addition to a national structure. Each case is tried in a court of the same jurisdiction as that of the law or laws broken.

The United States has a **dual court system** that consists of a separate judicial system for each state in addition to a national system. Each system has its own series of courts; the U.S. Supreme Court is responsible for correcting certain errors made in all other court systems. Although the Supreme Court can review cases from both the state and federal courts, it will hear only cases involving federal law or constitutional rights.

With a dual court system, the law may be interpreted differently in different states. Although the wording of laws may be similar, none of the state courts interprets the law in the same way. To some extent, these variations reflect regional differences in social and political conditions; that is, although a common set of American values concerning liberty and rights exists throughout the country, the interpretation and weight of those values may vary in the minds of citizens and judges in various regions. For example, the nature of expectations about personal privacy and the role of private gun ownership as elements of liberty are viewed differently in the Northeast than in the South and West. Differences in interpretation may also be due to attempts by state courts to solve similar problems by different means. For example, before the U.S. Supreme Court ruled that evidence the police obtained in illegal ways should be excluded from use at trials, some states had already enacted rules barring the use of such evidence.

adjudication
The process of determining whether the defendant is guilty or not guilty.

Courts are responsible for **adjudication**—determining whether the defendant is guilty or not guilty. In so doing, they must use fair procedures that will produce just, reliable decisions. Courts must also impose sentences that are appropriate to the behavior being punished.

Corrections

On any given day, about 6 million (one of every 34) American adults are under the supervision of state and federal corrections systems. There is no "typical" correctional agency or official. Instead, a variety of agencies and programs are provided by private and public organizations—including federal, state, and local governments—and carried out in many different community and closed settings.

While the average citizen may equate corrections with prisons, less than 30 percent of convicted offenders are in prisons and jails; the rest are being supervised in the community. Probation and parole have long been important aspects of corrections, as have community-based halfway houses, work release programs, and supervised activities.

The federal government, all the states, most counties, and all but the smallest cities engage in corrections. Nonprofit private organizations such as the YMCA have also contracted with governments to perform correctional services. In recent years, for-profit businesses have also entered into contracts with governments to build and operate correctional institutions.

For information about corrections and links to Web sites about various aspects of corrections, go to http://www.corrections.com.

The police, courts, and corrections are the main agencies of criminal justice. Each is a part, or subsystem, of the criminal justice system. Each is linked to the other two subsystems, and the actions of each affect the others. These effects can be seen as we examine the flow of decision making within the criminal justice system.

9. What are the four main duties of police?
10. What is a dual court system?
11. What are the major types of state and local correctional agencies?

The Flow of Decision Making in the Criminal Justice System

The processing of cases in the criminal justice system involves a series of decisions by police officers, prosecutors, judges, probation officers, wardens, and parole board members. At each stage in the process, they decide whether a case will move on to the next stage or be dropped from the system. Although the flowchart shown in Figure 3.4 appears streamlined, with cases entering at the top and moving swiftly toward the bottom, the actual route may be quite long, with many detours. At each step, officials have the discretion to decide what happens next. Many cases are filtered out of the system, others are sent to the next decision maker, and still others are dealt with by informal means.

Moreover, the flowchart does not show the influences of social relations or the political environment. For example, in 1997 reports surfaced indicating that the late Michael Kennedy, then a 39-year-old lawyer and nephew of the late President John F. Kennedy, had carried on an affair with his children's 14-year-old baby-sitter. If true, Kennedy would have been guilty of statutory rape, since it is a serious felony to have sexual relations with an underage girl, even if she willingly participates. Amid reports that Kennedy's lawyers were negotiating a quiet financial settlement with the girl and her family, the local prosecutor announced that no criminal charges would be filed because the girl—now a college student—refused to provide any evidence against Kennedy.

In other cases, prosecutors and judges may pressure witnesses to testify, sometimes even jailing reluctant witnesses for contempt of court. Did the prosecutor decline to press charges because Kennedy was a member of a politically powerful family? We cannot know for sure; it is possible that political factors or behind-the-scenes negotiations influenced the prosecutor. Such factors may affect decisions in ways that a simple description of decision-making steps does not reflect. As we follow the 13 steps of the criminal justice process, bear in mind that

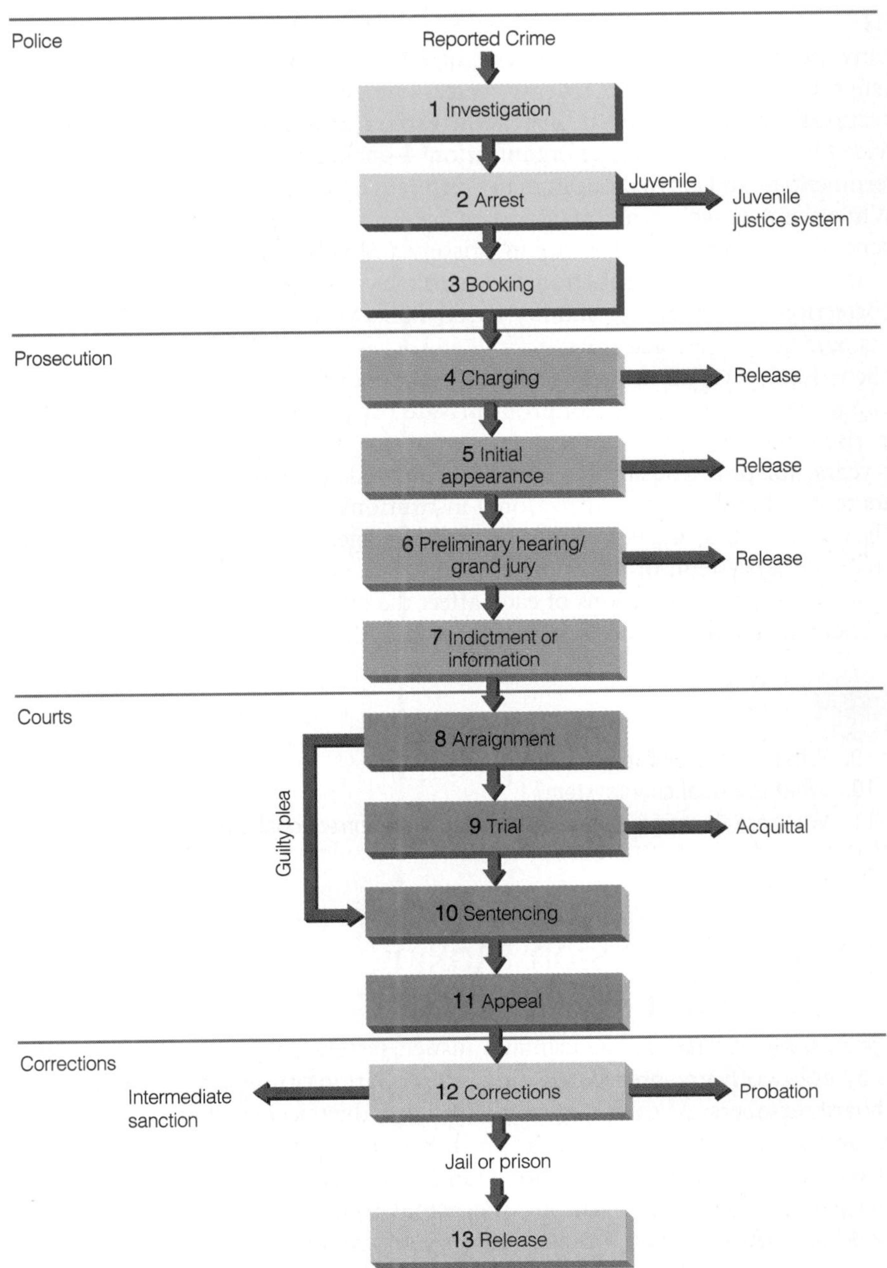

Figure 3.4
The flow of decision making in the criminal justice system
Each agency is responsible for a part of the decision-making process. Thus the police, prosecution, courts, and corrections are bound together through a series of exchange relationships.

the formal procedures do not hold in every case. Discretion, political pressure, and other factors may alter the outcome for different defendants.

Steps in the Decision-Making Process

The criminal justice system consists of 13 steps that cover the stages of law enforcement, adjudication, and corrections. The system looks like an assembly line where decisions are made about defendants—the raw material of the process. As these steps are described, recall the concepts discussed earlier: system, discretion, sequential tasks, filtering, and exchange. Be aware that the terms used for different stages in the process may differ from state to state, and the sequence of the steps differs in some parts of the country, but the flow of decision making generally follows this pattern.

1. *Investigation.* The process begins when the police believe that a crime has been committed. At this point, an investigation is begun. The police normally depend on a member of the community to report the offense. Ex-

cept for traffic and public order offenses, the police rarely observe illegal behavior themselves. Because most crimes have already been committed and offenders have left the scene before the police arrive, the police are at a disadvantage in quickly finding and arresting the offenders.

2. *Arrest.* If the police find enough evidence showing that a particular person has committed a crime, an arrest may be made. An **arrest** involves physically taking a person into custody pending a court proceeding. This action not only restricts the suspect's freedom, but it is also the first step toward prosecution.

   Under some conditions, arrests may be made on the basis of a **warrant**—a court order issued by a judge authorizing police officers to take certain actions, such as arresting suspects or searching premises. In practice, most arrests are made without warrants. In some states, police officers may issue a *summons* or *citation* that orders a person to appear in court on a certain date. This avoids the need to hold the suspect physically until decisions are made about the case.

arrest
The physical taking of a person into custody on the grounds that probable cause exists to believe that he or she has committed a criminal offense. Police may use only reasonable physical force in making an arrest. The purpose of the arrest is to hold the accused for a court proceeding.

warrant
A court order authorizing police officials to take certain actions: for example, to arrest suspects or to search premises.

3. *Booking.* After an arrest, the suspect is usually transported to a police station for booking, in which a record is made of the arrest. When booked, the suspect may be fingerprinted, photographed, interrogated, and placed in a lineup to be identified by the victim or witnesses. All suspects must also be warned that they have the right to counsel, that they may remain silent, and that any statement they make may be used against them later. Bail may be set so that the suspect learns what amount of money must be paid or what other conditions must be met to gain release from custody until the case is processed.

4. *Charging.* Prosecuting attorneys are the key link between the police and the courts. They must consider the facts of the case and decide whether there is reasonable cause to believe that an offense was committed and that the suspect committed the offense. The decision to charge is crucial because it sets in motion the adjudication of the case.

5. *Initial appearance.* Within a reasonable time after arrest, the suspect must be brought before a judge. At this point, suspects are given formal notice of the charge(s) for which they are being held, advised of their rights, and, if approved by the judge, given a chance to post bail. At this stage, the judge decides whether there is enough evidence to hold the suspect for further criminal processing. If enough evidence has not been produced, the judge will dismiss the case.

   The purpose of bail is to permit the accused to be released while awaiting trial and to ensure that he or she will show up in court at the appointed time. The concept of bail is connected to the important American value of liberty. Bail represents an effort to avoid depriving presumptively innocent people of liberty before their guilt has been proven in court. Bail requires the accused to provide or arrange a surety (or pledge), usually in the form of money or a bond. The amount of bail is based mainly on the judge's view of the seriousness of the crime and the defendant's prior criminal record. Suspects may also be released *on their own recognizance*—a promise to appear in court at a later date. In a few cases bail may be denied and the accused held because he or she is viewed as a threat to the community.

6. *Preliminary hearing/grand jury.* After suspects have been arrested, booked, and brought to court to be informed of the charge and advised of their rights, a decision must be made as to whether there is enough evidence to proceed. The preliminary hearing, used in about half the states, allows a judge to decide whether there is probable cause to believe that a crime has been committed and that the accused person committed it. If the judge does not find probable cause, the case is dismissed. If there is enough evidence, the accused is bound over for arraignment on an **information**—a document charging a person with a specific crime.

information
A document charging an individual with a specific crime. It is prepared by a prosecuting attorney and presented to a court at a preliminary hearing.

indictment
A document returned by a grand jury as a "true bill" charging an individual with a specific crime on the basis of a determination of probable cause as presented by a prosecuting attorney.

In the federal system and in some states, the prosecutor appears before a grand jury, which decides whether there is enough evidence to file an **indictment** or "true bill" charging the suspect with a specific crime. The preliminary hearing and grand jury are designed to prevent hasty and malicious prosecutions, to protect people from mistakenly being humiliated in public, and to decide whether there are grounds for prosecution. The use of the grand jury reinforces the American value of limited government. By giving citizens the authority to overrule the police and prosecutor in determining whether criminal charges should be pursued, the grand jury represents an effort to reduce the risk that government officials will use their power to deprive people of liberty in unjustified circumstances.

7. *Indictment/information.* If the preliminary hearing leads to an information or the grand jury vote leads to an indictment, the prosecutor prepares the formal charging document and presents it to the court.
8. *Arraignment.* The accused person appears in court to hear the indictment or information read by a judge and to enter a plea. Accused persons may plead guilty or not guilty, or in some states, stand mute. If the accused pleads guilty, the judge must decide whether the plea is made voluntarily and whether the person has full knowledge of the consequences. When a guilty plea is accepted as knowing and voluntary, there is no need for a trial and the judge imposes a sentence. Plea bargaining can take place at any time in the criminal justice process, but it is likely to be completed before or after arraignment. Very few criminal cases proceed to trial. Most move from the entry of the guilty plea to the sentencing phase.
9. *Trial.* For the small percentage of defendants who plead not guilty, the right to a trial by an impartial jury is guaranteed by the Sixth Amendment if the charges are serious enough to warrant a prison sentence of more than six months. In many jurisdictions, lesser charges do not entail a right to a jury trial. Most trials are *summary* or *bench trials*—that is, they are conducted without a jury. Because the defendant pleads guilty in most criminal cases, only about 10 to 15 percent of cases go to trial and only about 5 percent are heard by juries. Whether a criminal trial is held before a judge alone or before a judge and jury, the procedures are similar and are set out by state law and Supreme Court rulings. A defendant may be found guilty only if the evidence proves beyond a reasonable doubt that he or she committed the offense.

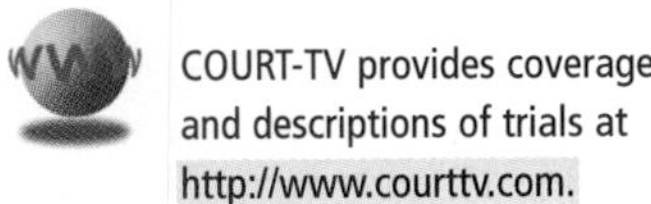

COURT-TV provides coverage and descriptions of trials at http://www.courttv.com.

10. *Sentencing.* Judges are responsible for imposing sentences. The intent is to make the sentence suitable to the offender and the offense within the limits set by the law. Although criminal codes place limits on sentences, the judge still has leeway. Among the judge's options are a suspended sentence, probation, imprisonment, or other sanctions such as fines and community service.
11. *Appeal.* Defendants who are found guilty may appeal convictions to a higher court. An appeal can be based on the claim that the trial court failed to follow the proper procedures or that the defendant's constitutional rights were violated by the actions of police, prosecutors, defense attorneys, or judges. The number of appeals is small compared with the total number of convictions, and in about 80 percent of appeals, trial judges and other officials are ruled to have acted properly. Even defendants who win appeals do not necessarily go free. Normally the defendant is given a second trial, which may result in an acquittal, a second conviction, or a plea bargain to lesser charges.
12. *Corrections.* The court's sentence is carried out by the correctional subsystem. Probation, intermediate sanctions such as fines and community service, and incarceration are the sanctions most often imposed. Probation allows offenders to serve their sentences in the community under supervision. Youthful offenders, first offenders, and those convicted of minor violations are most likely to be sentenced to probation rather than incar-

ceration. The conditions of probation may require offenders to observe certain rules—to be employed, maintain an orderly life, or attend school—and to report to their supervising officer from time to time. If these requirements are not met, the judge may revoke the probation and impose a prison sentence.

Many new types of sanctions have been used in recent years. These intermediate sanctions are more restrictive than probation but less restrictive than incarceration. They include fines, intensive supervision probation, boot camp, home confinement, and community service.

Whatever the reasons used to justify them, prisons exist mainly to separate criminals from the rest of society. Those convicted of misdemeanors usually serve their time in city or county jails, while felons serve time in state prisons. Isolation from the community is one of the most painful aspects of incarceration. Not only are letters and visits restricted, but supervision and censorship are ever present. To maintain security, prison officials make unannounced searches of inmates and subject them to strict discipline.

13. *Release.* Release may occur when the offender has served the full sentence imposed by the court, but most offenders are returned to the community under the supervision of a parole officer. Parole continues for the duration of the sentence or for a period specified by law. Parole may be revoked and the offender returned to prison if the conditions of parole are not met or if the parolee commits another crime.

Go to the *American System of Criminal Justice* Web site at http://www.cj.wadsworth.com/colesmith10e to explore the topic of decision making in the criminal justice system in further detail.

The case of Christopher Jones is described on page 80. Jones, a 31-year-old man from Battle Creek, Michigan, was arrested, charged, and convicted of serious crimes arising from the police investigation of a series of robberies. His case illustrates how the steps just discussed can play out in the "real world."

check point

12. What are the steps of the criminal justice process?

The Criminal Justice Wedding Cake

Although the flowchart shown in Figure 3.4 is helpful, we must note that not all cases are treated equally. The process applied to a given case, as well as its outcome, is shaped by the importance of the case to decision makers, the seriousness of the charge, and the defendant's resources.

Some cases are highly visible either because of the notoriety of the defendant or victim or because of the shocking nature of the crime. At the other extreme are "run-of-the-mill cases" involving unknowns charged with minor crimes.

As shown in Figure 3.5, the criminal justice process can be compared to a wedding cake. This model shows clearly how different cases receive different kinds of treatment in the justice process.

Layer 1 of the "cake" consists of celebrated cases that are highly unusual, receive much public attention, result in a jury trial, and often drag on through many appeals. These cases embody the ideal of an adversary system of justice in which each side actively fights against the other, either because the defendant faces a stiff sentence or because the defendant has the wealth to pay for a strong defense. Further, Layer 1 cases are like morality plays. People see the carefully crafted arguments of the prosecution and defense as expressing key issues in society or tragic flaws in individuals. The case of Oklahoma City bomber Timothy McVeigh and the celebrated trial of football legend O. J.

Figure 3.5 The criminal justice wedding cake
This figure shows that different cases are treated in different ways. Only a very few cases are played out as "high drama"; most are handled through plea bargaining and dismissals.

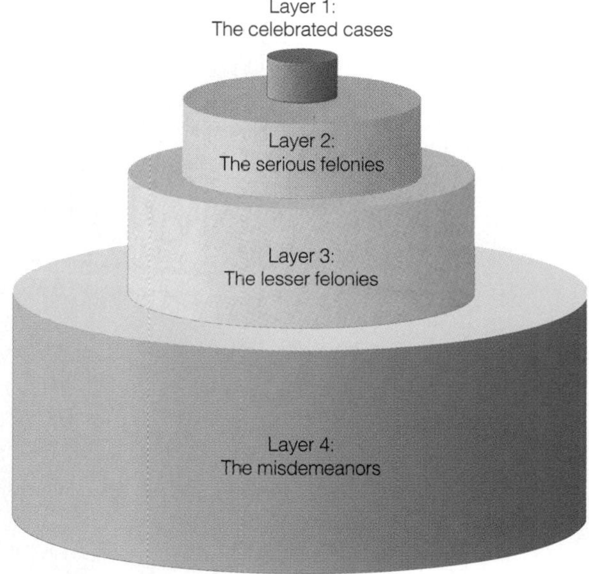

Source: Drawn from Samuel Walker, *Sense and Nonsense about Crime and Drugs,* 4th ed. (Belmont, Calif.: Wadsworth, 1998), 30–37.

Robberies Solved?

Jones Accepts Plea Agre

No Contest Plea Now Entered

the Criminal Justice Process

The State of Michigan versus Christopher Jones

Investigation

In October 1998, police in Battle Creek, Michigan, investigated a string of six robberies that occurred in a ten-day period. Assaults occurred during some of the robberies. One victim was beaten so badly with a power tool that he required extensive reconstructive surgery for his face and skull. The police received an anonymous tip on their Silent Observer hotline, which led them to put together a *photo lineup*—an array of photographs of local men who had criminal records. Based on the anonymous tip and photographs identified by the victims, the police began to search for two men who were well-known to them, Christopher Jones and his cousin Fred Brown.

Arrest

Christopher Jones had shut himself into a bedroom at his parents' house. He was a 31-year-old African American man whose life was in shambles. A dozen years of struggles with cocaine addiction had cost him his marriage and several jobs in local factories. In addition, he had a criminal record, stretching back several years, from pleading guilty to charges of attempted larceny and attempted breaking and entering in separate incidents. Thus he had a record of stealing to support his drug habit and he had previously spent time on probation and done a short stretch in a minimum-security prison and a boot camp. But he had never been caught with drugs and he had never been accused of committing an act of violence.

LOCAL Juvenile worker has charge dropped/3A

SPORTS Local football teams eye playoffs/1B

LIFESTYLE Program instills good values/1C

Battle Creek ENQUIRER

CITY EDITION

FRIDAY Oct. 30, 1998

Kellogg Co. earnings per share

Glenn relives space history

Hero is 'enjoying the show'

Kellogg's earnings expected to be low

2 charged in violent robberies

Fred Brown

Christopher R. Jones

Because his family feared that he would be injured or killed by the police if he tried to run or resist arrest, his parents called the police and told them where he was. At approximately 10 P.M. on October 28, as officers surrounded the house, the family opened the door and showed the officers the way to the bedroom. When Jones heard the knock on the door, he knew he had to face the inevitable. He surrendered peacefully and was led to the waiting police car in handcuffs.

The officers took him to the police station. A detective with whom Jones was acquainted offered him a cup of coffee and then read him his *Miranda* rights, including his right to remain silent and his right to an attorney. The detective then informed Jones that he was looking at the possibility of a life sentence in prison unless he helped the police by providing information about Fred Brown. Jones said that he did not want to talk to the police yet, and he asked to be given an attorney. Because arrested suspects are entitled to have an attorney present during questioning if they ask for one, the police ceased questioning Jones. He was taken next door to the jail.

Booking

At the jail, Jones was strip-searched. After removing all of his clothes so that officers could make sure he had not hidden weapons or drugs in his clothing or on his body, he was given a bright-orange jumpsuit to wear. He was photographed and fingerprinted. He was told that he would be arraigned the next morning. He was handed a blanket and locked in the *holding cell*—a large cell where people are placed immediately upon arrest. The holding cell was big enough to hold approximately ten people and it had four cement benches to serve as beds. As Jones looked for a space to lie down on the floor with his blanket, he estimated that there were 16 men sleeping in the crowded cell that night.

Arraignment

The next morning, the men in the holding cell were taken to a neighboring room for video arraignment. A two-way camera system permitted Jones to see the district courtroom in the neighboring courthouse at the same time that the judge and others in the courtroom could view him on a television screen. Jones was informed by the judge that he was being charged with breaking and entering, armed robbery, and assault with intent to commit murder. The final charge alone could draw a life sentence. Under Michigan law, these charges can be filed directly by the prosecutor without being presented to a grand jury for indictment as in federal courts and some other states. The judge set bond [bail] at $200,000, an amount that an unemployed, penniless person like Jones would have no hope of obtaining.

nes Arraigned by Video Connectic Judge: No Withdrawal Jones Faces Seven Count

At a second video arraignment several days later, Jones was informed that he faced seven additional counts of assault with intent to commit murder, armed robbery, unarmed robbery, and home invasion for four additional robberies. Bond was set at $200,000 for each alleged robbery. Thus he faced ten felony charges for the five robberies, and his total bail was $1 million.

Jail

After arraignment, jail officers examined Jones's current charges and past record in order to determine the level of security and supervision he would need in the jail. Prisoners charged with violent offenses or who have substantial criminal records are kept in areas separate from people charged with property crimes. Jones was placed in a medium-security area with 55 others who were charged with serious felonies. Jones would eventually spend nine months at the jail before his case was processed.

Defense Attorney

Under state court procedures, Jones was supposed to have a preliminary hearing within two weeks after his arraignment. At the preliminary hearing, the prosecution would be required to present enough evidence to justify the charges. If the evidence was inadequate, the district judge could dismiss the charges. If there was enough evidence to raise the possibility of guilt, the district judge would send the case up to the Calhoun County Circuit Court, the court that handled felony trials.

Jones received a letter informing him of the name of the private attorney appointed by the court to represent him, but he did not meet the attorney until he was taken to court for his preliminary hearing. Minutes before the hearing, the attorney, David Gilbert, introduced himself to Jones. Jones wanted to delay any preliminary hearing until a lineup could be held to test the victims' identification of him as a robber. According to Jones, Gilbert said they must proceed with the preliminary hearing in one case because the victim had traveled from another state in order to testify. The other preliminary hearings were postponed, but the out-of-town witness's testimony led the district judge to conclude that sufficient evidence existed to move one of Jones's cases to the circuit court on an armed robbery charge.

Lineup

Jones waited for weeks for the lineup to be scheduled. When he was taken to his rescheduled preliminary hearing, his attorney complained to the judge that the lineup had never been conducted. The judge ordered that the lineup be held as soon as possible.

Jones and the other men were told to stand and turn around in front of a one-way mirror. One by one, the victims of each robbery looked at the men in the room and attempted to determine if any of them were the robbers. At the end of each identification, one of the men in the lineup was asked to step forward, and Jones presumed this meant that the victim had identified that man as one of the robbers. Jones was only asked to step forward twice, and other men were asked to step forward at other times. Jones guessed that he was picked out by two of the victims, but that the other three victims either picked other men or were unable to identify anyone.

Jones's defense attorney was unable to attend the lineup. Another attorney arrived and informed Jones that he would take Mr. Gilbert's place. Although Jones protested that the other men in the lineup were much shorter and older, he was disappointed that the substitute attorney was not more active in objecting that the men looked too different from Jones to adequately test the victims' ability to make an identification. He later discovered that his substitute attorney had just entered private practice after serving as an assistant prosecutor at Jones's first preliminary hearing.

Preliminary Hearing

At the next preliminary hearing, the victims in each case provided testimony about what happened. Because the testimony generally focused on Brown as the perpetrator of the assaults and robberies, the defense attorney argued that many of the charges against Jones should be dropped. The judge determined that the victims' testimony provided enough evidence to send most of the charges against Jones to the circuit court.

Plea Bargaining

Jones waited for weeks in jail without hearing much from his attorney. Although he didn't know it, the prosecutor was formulating a plea agreement and communicating to the defense attorney the terms under which charges would be dropped in exchange for a guilty plea from Jones. Outside the courtroom a few minutes before a hearing on the proposed plea agreement, Gilbert told Jones that the prosecutor had offered to drop all of the other charges if Jones would plead guilty to one count of unarmed robbery for the incident in which the victim was seriously injured by Brown and one count of home invasion for another robbery. Jones did not want to accept the deal, because he claimed that he was not even present at the robbery for which he was being asked to plead guilty for home invasion. According to Jones, the attorney insisted that this was an excellent deal compared with all of the other charges that the prosecutor could pursue. Jones still resisted.

In the courtroom, Judge James Kingsley read the offer to Jones, but Jones refused to enter a guilty plea. Like the defense attorney, the judge told Jones that this was a favorable offer compared with the other serious charges that the prosecutor could still pursue against Jones. Jones again declined.

Jones was worried that he was making a mistake by turning down the plea offer. He wondered if he could end up with a life sentence, even for a crime he did not commit, if one of the victims identified him by mistake as having done a crime that was actually committed by Brown. Outside the courtroom, he told his attorney that he had changed his mind. They went right back into the courtroom and told the judge that he was ready to enter a guilty plea. As they prepared to enter the plea, the prosecutor said that they also expected Jones to provide information about the five robberies and testify against Brown as part of the plea agreement. The defense attorney protested that this condition had not been part of the plea agreement offered by prosecution. Jones told the judge that he could not provide any information about the home invasion to which he was about to plead guilty because he was not present at that robbery and had no knowledge of what occurred. Judge Kingsley declared that he would not accept a guilty plea when the defendant claimed to have no knowledge of the crime.

After the hearing, the prosecutor and defense attorney renewed their discussions about a plea agreement. Jones agreed to take a polygraph (lie detector) test so that the prosecutor could find out which robberies he actually knew about. Although Jones waited for weeks for the polygraph test in hopes that it would show prosecutors that his criminal involvement with Brown was limited, no test was ever administered.

Scheduled Trial and Plea Agreement

Jones waited for several more weeks in jail. When Gilbert finally came to visit, he informed Jones that the armed robbery trial was scheduled for the following day. In addition, the prosecutor's plea offer had changed. Fred Brown pleaded guilty to armed robbery and assault with intent less than murder and he was facing a sentence of 25 to 50 years in prison. Because Brown pleaded guilty, the prosecutor no longer needed Jones as a potential witness in any trial against Brown. Thus the prosecutor no longer offered the unarmed robbery and home invasion pleas. He now wanted Jones to plead to the same charges as Brown in exchange for dropping the other pending charges. According to Jones, Gilbert claimed the prosecutor would be very angry if he did not take the plea, and the attorney encouraged Jones to accept the plea by arguing that the prosecutor would otherwise pursue all of the other charges, which could bring a life sentence. Jones refused to plead guilty.

The next day, Jones was given his personal clothes to wear instead of the orange jail jumpsuit, because he was going to court for trial instead of for a hearing. Prior to entering the court, Gilbert again encouraged Jones to accept the plea agreement. He raised the possibility of a life sentence if the prosecutor pursued all of the pending charges and, according to Jones, he said that the guilty plea could be withdrawn if the sentencing recommendation made by the probation office was too high. Because he did not want to risk getting a life sentence and he believed he could later withdraw the plea if he wanted, Jones decided to accept the offer.

With his attorney's advice, he entered a plea of "no contest" to the two charges. A no contest plea is treated the same as a guilty plea for punishment purposes. However, the plea means that crime victims must prove their case in any subsequent civil lawsuit against the defendant for injuries suffered in the alleged crime rather than automatically winning the lawsuit because the offender admitted guilt.

Before taking the plea, Judge Kingsley informed Jones that by entering the plea he would be waiving his right to a trial, including his right to question witnesses and to have the prosecutor prove his guilt beyond a reasonable doubt. After Judge Kingsley read the charges of armed robbery and assault with intent to do great bodily harm and asked, "What do you plead?" Jones replied, "No contest." Then the judge asked Jones a series of questions.

Judge Kingsley: Mr. Jones, has anyone promised you anything other than the plea bargain to get you to enter this plea?
Jones: No.
Judge Kingsley: Has anyone threatened you or forced you or compelled you to enter the plea?
Jones: No.
Judge Kingsley: . . . Are you [entering this plea] of your own free will?
Jones: Yes.

The judge reminded Jones that there has been no final agreement on what the ultimate sentence would be and gave Jones one last opportunity to change his mind about pleading no contest. Jones repeated his desire to enter the plea, so the plea was accepted.

Immediately after the hearing, Jones had second thoughts about pleading "no contest." According to Jones, "I was feeling uneasy about being pressured [by my attorney] to take the plea offer. . . . [so I decided] to write to the Judge and tell him about the pressures my attorney put upon me as well as [the attorney] telling me I had a right to withdraw my plea. So I wrote the Judge that night." Jones knew he was guilty of stealing things at one robbery, but he had been unarmed. He felt as if he had been pressured into pleading guilty to an armed robbery and assault that he did not commit because the prosecutor threatened him with so many other charges and his own attorney seemed so eager for him to accept the plea agreement.

Presentence Investigation

Probation officers are responsible for conducting presentence investigations in which they review offenders' records and interview the offenders about their education, work history, drug use, and family background before making recommendations to the judge about an appropriate punishment. Jones felt that his interview with the probation officer went well, but he was dismayed to discover that his file erroneously stated that he had three prior criminal convictions instead of two. The extra conviction would mean additional years tacked on to his sentence unless he could get his file corrected. When the errors were eventually corrected, the presentence report prepared by the probation office ultimately recommended 5 to 25 years for armed robbery and 4 to 7 years for assault.

When Gilbert learned that Jones had written the letter to Judge Kingsley that was critical of Gilbert's performance in the case, he asked the judge to permit him to withdraw as Jones's attorney. Judge Kingsley initially refused to permit him to withdraw. However, when Jones spoke in open court at the first scheduled sentencing hearing about his criticisms of Gilbert as well as his complaints about the prosecution's handling of the lineup and the failure to administer the polygraph test, the judge decided to appoint a new defense attorney to handle sentencing at a rescheduled hearing. It was clear that the relationship between Gilbert and Jones had deteriorated to the point that it would be difficult for them to cooperate in preparing for the sentencing hearing.

Sentencing Preparation

The new defense attorney, Virginia Cairns, encouraged Jones's parents, siblings, ex-wife, and minister to write letters to the judge describing Jones's positive qualities and his prospects for

nes Arraigned by Video Connectic Judge: No Withdrawal Jones Faces Seven Count

successful rehabilitation after prison. Jones was pleased with his attorney. According to Jones, "She came to visit me within a week or so.... She said she would fight for me to get a lesser sentence than what was recommended."

Sentencing

Although he was arrested in October 1998, Jones's case did not complete its processing until the sentencing hearing in July 1999. When his case was called, Jones was led into the courtroom wearing an orange jail jumpsuit and escorted by a deputy sheriff. Judge Kingsley called on Jones to make his statement first. Jones faced the judge as he spoke, glancing occasionally at his family and at the victim when he referred to them in his remarks.

First and foremost, I would like to say what happened to the victim was a tragedy. I showed great remorse for that. He is in my prayers along with his family. Even though, your Honor, I'm not making any excuses for what I'm saying here today, the injuries the victim sustained were not at the hands of myself and nor did I actually rob this victim. I was present, your Honor, as I told you once before, yes, I was. And it's a wrong. Again I'm not making any kind of excuse whatsoever....

Your Honor, I would just like to say that drugs has clouded my memory, and my choices in the past. I really made some wrong decisions. Only times I've gotten into trouble were because of my drug use.... One of the worst decisions I really made was my involvement of being around the co-defendant Fred Brown. That bothers me to this day because actually we didn't even get along. Because of my drug use again I chose to be around him.

Jones also used his statement to talk about his positive record as a high school student and athlete, his work with the jail minister, and his desire to talk to young people about his experiences in order to steer them away from drugs.

Cairns spoke next. She called the court's attention to several errors in the presentence report, such as the fact that Jones had only two prior convictions rather than three. She emphasized the letters of support from Jones's family and argued that this support system would help him to become rehabilitated after serving his prison term. She argued that Jones should receive a less severe sentence than the long prison term imposed on the co-defendant Brown.

The courtroom was completely silent as the victim spoke about his severe injuries and how his $40,000 worth of medical bills had driven him to bankruptcy.

I went from having perfect vision to not being able to read out of my left eye any more. I got steel plates in my head....

They left me to die that morning. He took the keys to my car.... So today it's true, I don't think Mr. Jones should be sentenced same as Brown. That's who I want—I want to see him sentenced to the maximum. He's the one that crushed my skull with a drill. But Jones did hit me several times while Mr. Brown held me there to begin with. It's true that I did hit him with a hammer to get them off me. But he still was there. He still had the chance of not leaving me without keys to my car so I could get to a hospital. He still had the choice to stop at least and phone on the way and say there's someone that could possibly be dead, but he didn't.... You don't treat a human being like that. And if you do you serve time and pretty much to the maximum. I don't ask the Court for 25 years. That's a pretty long time to serve. And I do ask the Court to look at 15 to 20. I'd be happy. Thank you.

Gary Brand, the assistant prosecutor recommended a 20-year sentence and noted that Jones should be responsible for $35,000 in restitution to the victim and to the state for medical expenses and lost income.

After listening to the presentations, Judge Kingsley spoke sternly to Jones. He agreed that Jones's drug problem had led to his involvement in this crime and the crimes that led to Jones's prior convictions. He also noted that Jones's family support was much stronger than that of most defendants appearing in circuit court. He chastised Jones for falling into drugs when life got tougher after enjoying a successful career in high school. Judge Kingsley then proceeded to announce his sentencing decision.

You are not in my view as culpable as Mr. Brown. I agree with [the victim] that you were there. When I read your handwritten letter, Mr. Jones, I was a bit disturbed by your unwillingness to confront the reality of where you found yourself with Mr. Brown. You were not a passive observer to everything that went on in my view. You were not as active a participant as Mr. Brown, but you were not an innocent victim in the sense that "I simply walked into the store. I had no idea what was going on. I just stood there in amazement as my acquaintance brutalized this man." I don't think that's the case. But what I'm going to do, Mr. Jones, is as follows: Taking everything into consideration as it relates to the armed robbery count, it is the sentence of the Court that you spend a term of not less than 12 years nor more than 25 years with the Michigan Department of Corrections. I will give you credit for the [261 days] that you have already served.

The judge also ordered the payment of $35,000 in restitution as a condition of parole. He also noted that the sentence was within the state's new sentencing guidelines and remarked that the cost to the taxpayers would be approximately $500,000 to hold Jones in prison during the sentence. He concluded the hearing by informing Jones of his right to file an application for a leave to appeal.

Prison

After spending a few more weeks in jail awaiting transfer to the state prison system, Jones was sent to the state correctional department's classification center at a state prison in Jackson. At the center, newly incarcerated prisoners are evaluated. Based on their criminal history, presentence report, psychological and medical problems, and age, they are assigned to one of 40 correctional facilities in the state. Jones spent one month in center in which he was confined to a small cell with one other prisoner. Because there was no mirror in the cell, he shaved by looking at his reflection in the pipes on back of the toilet. Each day the prisoners were released from their cells for ten minutes at each meal and one hour in the recreation yard.

He was eventually assigned to a Level IV prison, where he lived with a cellmate in a space designed to house one prisoner. Prisons' security classifications range from Level I for minimum security to Level VI for "super maximum," high security. At prison, conditions are better than at the classification center. They are given more time at each meal and more choices of foods. There are longer periods in the mornings and the afternoon for recreation, prison jobs, and school. Because Jones is a high school graduate who had previously attended a community college—and therefore was one of the most highly educated prisoners in his institution—he became head clerk in the prison library. After serving his initial years without receiving any citations for violating prison rules, he was transferred to a Level II prison, where he seeks to take all of the vocational and psychological self-improvement courses that the institution offers.

Sources: T. Christenson, "2 Charged in Violent Robberies," *Battle Creek Inquirer*, October 30, 1998, p. 1A; Interview with Christopher Jones, St. Louis Correctional Facility, St. Louis, Michigan, October 19, 1999; Letters to author from Christopher Jones, October and November 1999; Calhoun County Circuit Court transcripts for plea hearing, May 20, 1999, and sentencing hearing, July 16, 1999.

Corbis

Michael Skakel enters court in 2002. This cousin of the famous Kennedy family was charged for the 1975 murder of his childhood playmate and neighbor, 15-year-old Martha Moxley, in affluent Greenwich, Connecticut. The tragedy of the crime, the 27-year time lapse, and the defendant's connection to a prominent family provided the elements for a celebrated case. He was found guilty and in August 2002 given 20 years to life.

Simpson on double murder charges fall into this category. Not all cases in Layer 1 receive national attention, however. From time to time, local crimes, especially cases of murder and rape, are treated in this way.

The Layer 1 cases fit the ideals of American values concerning liberty, due process, and constitutional rights. In such cases, attorneys work vigorously to make sure that the defendant's rights are protected and that the trial process produces a careful, fair decision about the defendant's guilt and punishment. The drawn out, dramatic procedures of such trials fulfill the picture of the American justice process that is taught to schoolchildren and reinforced in movies and television shows. When people in other countries ask Americans to describe the U.S. legal system, they are most likely to draw from their idealized image of American values and describe the Layer 1 process. Too often, however, the public's belief in the prevalence of idealistic American values leads to the erroneous conclusion that most criminal cases follow this model.

felonies
Serious crimes usually carrying a penalty of death or incarceration for more than one year.

Layer 2 consists of serious **felonies:** violent crimes committed by people with long criminal records, against victims unknown to them. Police and the prosecutors speak of these as "heavy" cases that should result in "tough" sentences. In such cases the defendant has little reason to plead guilty and the defense attorney must prepare for trial.

Layer 3 also consists of felonies, but the crimes and the offenders are seen as less important than those in Layer 2. The offenses may be the same as in Layer 2, but the offender may have no record, and the victim may have had a prior relationship with the accused. The main goal of criminal justice officials is to dispose of such cases quickly. For this reason, many are filtered out of the system, often through plea bargaining.

misdemeanors
Offenses less serious than felonies and usually punishable by incarceration of no more than a year, probation, or intermediate sanction.

Layer 4 is made up of **misdemeanors.** About 90 percent of all cases fall into this category. They concern such offenses as public drunkenness, shoplifting, prostitution, disturbing the peace, and traffic violations. Looked on as the "garbage" of the system, these cases are handled by the lower courts, where speed is essential. Prosecutors use their discretion to reduce charges or recommend probation as a way to encourage defendants to plead guilty quickly. Trials are rare, processes are informal, and fines, probation, or short jail sentences result.

The wedding cake model is a useful way of viewing the criminal justice system. Cases are not treated equally: Some are seen as quite important, others as merely part of a large number that must be processed. When one knows the nature of a case, one can predict fairly well how it will be handled and what its outcome will be.

13. What is the purpose of the wedding cake model?
14. What types of cases are found on each layer?

Crime and Justice in a Multicultural Society

One important aspect of American values is the principle of equal treatment. At the time of the Revolution, Americans rejected the notion of having a king, a royal family, or people with royal titles, as part of their separation from Great Britain and their establishment of their own democratic identity. The American value of equality is prominently announced and displayed in important national documents. The Declaration of Independence speaks of every American being "created equal" and the Fourteenth Amendment to the Constitution guarantees the right to "equal protection." Despite the lofty expressions of our important values, we saw in our previous discussion that defendants are not treated alike, for several reasons. The widespread application of discretion gives individual police officers, prosecutors, defense attorneys, judges, and other officials opportunities to make their own judgments about what will happen to individuals who are drawn into contact with the system.

Disparity and Discrimination

One of the most significant concerns expressed by critics of the criminal justice system is that discretionary decisions and other factors produce racial discrimination. The existence of racial discrimination in any aspect of government policies and programs is an especially troubling violation of American values. It took many years for the United States to address slavery and the widespread discrimination that existed in the decades after slavery was abolished. The Fourteenth Amendment's Equal Protection Clause was written with African Americans specifically in mind, because of fears that southern states would mistreat former slaves. When the Supreme Court finally declared that racial segregation was unconstitutional in 1954, its decision in *Brown v. Board of Education* became one of the most proudly important moments in U.S. legal history. Thus the existence of racial discrimination in the criminal justice system would dramatically call into question the country's success in fulfilling the values that it claims to regard as supremely important. As we will see, there is good reason to look closely at the possible existence of discrimination and its clash with American values.

African Americans, Hispanics, and other minorities are subjected to the criminal justice system at much higher rates than are the white majority (Cole, 1999:4–5; J. Hagan and Peterson, 1995:14). For example:

- African Americans account for one-third of all arrests and one-half of all incarcerations in the United States, although 12 percent of the people in the United States are African American.
- The per capita incarceration rate for African Americans is seven times greater than that for whites.
- Since 1980 the proportion of Hispanics among all inmates in U.S. prisons has risen from 7.7 percent to 16.0 percent.
- About one-third of all African American men in their twenties are under criminal justice supervision.

- The rate of unfounded arrests of Hispanics in California is double that of whites.
- Among 100,000 African American men aged 15–19, 68 will die as the result of a homicide involving a gun, compared with about 6 among 100,000 white men in the same age group.
- The robbery victimization rate for African Americans is 150 percent of that for whites, and they are victimized by rapes and aggravated assaults at similar rates that exceed those for whites.
- The crime victimization rate is 260 per 1,000 Hispanic households versus 144 per 1,000 non-Hispanic households.
- The violent crime victimization rate for Native Americans is more than twice the rate for the nation.

disparity
The unequal treatment of one group by the criminal justice system, compared with the treatment accorded other groups.

discrimination
Differential treatment of individuals or groups based on race, ethnicity, gender, sexual orientation, or economic status, instead of on their behavior or qualifications.

A central question is whether racial and ethnic disparities like those just listed are the result of discrimination (Mann, 1993:vii–xiv; Wilbanks, 1987). A **disparity** is a difference between groups that can be explained by legitimate factors. For example, the fact that 18- to 24-year-old men are arrested out of proportion to their numbers in the general population is a disparity explained by the fact that they commit more crime. It is not thought to be the result of a public policy that singles out young men for arrest. **Discrimination** occurs when groups are differentially treated without regard to their behavior or qualifications: for example, if people of color are routinely sentenced to prison regardless of their criminal history.

Explanations for Disparities

Racial disparities in criminal justice are often explained in one of three ways: (1) people of color commit more crimes, (2) the criminal justice system is racist, with the result that people of color are treated more harshly, or (3) the criminal justice system expresses the racism found in society as a whole. We consider each of these views in turn.

Explanation 1: People of Color Commit More Crimes

Nobody denies that the proportion of minorities arrested and placed under correctional supervision (probation, jail, prison, parole) is greater than their proportion of the general population. However, people disagree over whether bias is responsible for the disparity.

Disparities in arrests and sentences may be due to legitimate factors. For example, prosecutors and judges are supposed to take into account differences between serious and petty offenses, and between repeat and first-time offenders. It follows that more people of color will end up in the courts and prisons if they are more likely to commit more serious crimes and have more serious prior records than are whites (S. Walker, Spohn, and DeLone, 2000:15–18).

But why would minorities commit more crimes? The most extreme answer is that they are more predisposed to criminality. This assumes that people of color are a "criminal class." The available evidence does not support this view. Behavior that violates criminal laws is prevalent throughout all segments of society. Indeed, nearly every adult American has committed an act for which he or she could be jailed. For example, studies of illicit drug use find that young adults, men, whites, and those with less than a high school education are more likely to use drugs than are others. As the Clinton Administration's "Drug Czar" General Barry McCaffrey, the former director of the U.S. Office of National Drug Control Policy, has said, "The typical drug user is not poor and unemployed" (*New York Times,* September 9, 1999, A14). Furthermore, self-report studies, in which people are asked to report on their own criminal behavior, have shown that nearly everyone has committed a crime, although most are never caught. Other offenses committed by large segments of affluent people, whites, and other population groups include drunken driving, misreporting income for taxation purposes, and falsifying reimbursement forms for business expenses. Indeed, even George W. Bush, prior to becoming Governor of Texas and President of the United States, violated federal law by failing to properly report the sale of stock from a company on whose board of directors he served (*New York Times,* July 4, 2002). Some observers fear that Bush avoided prosecution because the offense occurred while his father was President of the United States and the government officials running the Security and Exchange Commission did not want to clash with or embarrass the President.

AP/Wide World Photos, Inc.

Four African Americans and their attorneys announce the filing of a civil suit against two New Jersey state troopers. The men were driving in a rented van along the New Jersey Turnpike when Troopers John Hogan and James Kenna pulled them over and then opened fire on the van, shooting three and critically injuring two. The plaintiffs charge that they were stopped because of their race. The incident brought to national attention the issue of racial profiling.

Many of these kinds of crimes are difficult to detect or are low priorities for law enforcement agencies. In other instances, affluent perpetrators are better positioned to gain dismissals because of their status within the community, social networks, or access to high-quality legal representation. When the federal government began to push for criminal investigations of executives from Enron and other companies in 2002, this action was widely regarded as based on concerns that the voters were suddenly interested in such crimes and might punish elected officials for failing to take action. Thus there were hopes that if a few key executives were sent to prison for corporate misdeeds, the public would feel satisfied by this symbolic action and the government could again regard such offenses as a low priority.

In evaluating theories about possible links between race and crime, we must be aware that many commentators may be focusing on only specific kinds of crimes, such as burglaries, robberies, and murders. In addition, analysts may focus only on crimes that resulted in prosecutions. Such limitations may distort an accurate understanding of this important issue. Race itself is not causally linked to crime. Instead, any apparent associations between crime and race relate to subcategories of people within racial and ethnic groups, such as poor, young men, as well as certain categories of crimes that are commonly investigated and prosecuted.

The link between crime and economic disadvantage is significant. Minority groups suffer greatly from poverty. Nearly half (46 percent) of African American children and 39 percent of Hispanic children are poor, compared with only 16 percent of white children (A. Sherman, 1994). Unemployment rates are highest among people of color, and family income is lowest. People in this segment of society do not have the same opportunities as affluent Americans to acquire money unlawfully through tax cheating, employee theft, and illegal stock transactions. If poor people seek to steal, it is likely to be through means available to them, such as shoplifting, street-corner drug sales, robbery, and burglary, which are more easily detected and emphasized as enforcement priorities by police and prosecutors. It was only during the booming job market of the 1990s that young African American men with little education were gainfully employed in greater numbers and committing fewer crimes (*New York Times,* May 23, 1999:A1). In light of the association between race and poverty as well as the criminal opportunities associated with economic status, it would not be surprising to find Native Americans, Hispanics, and African Americans to be overrepresented among perpetrators of certain categories of crimes.

Related to the link between crime and disadvantage is the fact that most crime in America is *intra*racial, not *inter*racial. Victimization rates, especially homicide and robbery, are higher for minorities than for whites. The lifetime risk for black men is 4.16 per 100, followed by Native American men (1.75), black women (1.02), white men (.64), Native American women (.46) and white women (.26) (Sampson and Lauritsen, 1997:319).

As John DiIulio points out, "No group of Americans suffers more when violent and repeat criminals are permitted to prey upon decent, struggling, law-abiding inner city citizens and their children than . . . 'black America's silent majority'" (DiIulio, 1994:3). The poor cannot move away from the social problems of the inner cities. As a result, victimization by one's neighbors is a tragedy faced by many African Americans.

One way to explain racial disparities in the criminal justice system, then, is to point out that African Americans and Hispanics, who are overrepresented among the poor, are arrested more often and for more serious offenses than are whites. These factors are tied to the types of crimes investigated and enforced by criminal justice officials rather than to behavioral patterns linked to race. Some analysts argue that the most effective crime control policies would be those that reduce the social problems, such as poverty and unequal educational opportunities, that appear to contribute to higher crime rates among the poor (Tonry, 1995).

For information on poverty in the United States and the people affected by it, see the Web site of the Institute for Research on Poverty at http://www.ssc.wisc.edu/irp/.

Explanation 2: The Criminal Justice System Is Racist

Other explanations focus on the possible existence of racism in the criminal justice system. Many writers have discussed and analyzed evidence concerning the existence of biased attitudes among criminal justice officials, the system's perpetuation of inequalities created by discrimination throughout American history, and other facets of racism. These explanations are particularly disturbing because they violate important American values concerning equality and fairness. These values are embodied in the Fourteenth Amendment, which purports to guarantee "equal protection" for people of different races when they are subjected to government laws, policies, and procedures. The contemporary Supreme Court has not been active in evaluating and supporting claims concerning alleged violations of equal protection in the criminal justice system. Its inaction has left open more opportunities for discrimination to be a source of racial disparities (C. E. Smith, DeJong, and Burrow, 2002).

Racial disparities may result if people who commit similar offenses are treated differently by the criminal justice system because of their race or ethnicity. In this view, the fact that people of color are arrested more often than whites does not mean that they are more crime prone. For example, although African Americans are 13 percent of monthly drug users, they represent 35 percent of those arrested for drug possession, 55 percent of convictions, and 74 percent of prison sentences (Butterfield, 1995b). One study found that the police make *unfounded* arrests of African Americans four times as often as of whites (Donziger, 1996:109). Racial profiling, as described in the Close Up box, is an example of what many people believe is a racist activity by police, and evidence of its existence has led to new laws and policies that require police to keep records about their traffic law enforcement patterns (Engel, Calnon, and Bernard, 2002).

The disparity between crime rates, arrest rates, and rates of incarceration is key to the claim by some that the criminal justice system is biased against minority groups. The arrest rate of minority citizens is indeed greater than even their higher offense rates would justify. For example, 29 percent of rape victims report that their assailant was African American, but 43 percent of people arrested for rape are African American. Similarly, 22.6 percent of assault victims say the offender was African American, but 34 percent of those arrested for assault are African Americans. In sum, the odds of arrest are higher for African American offenders than for white offenders.

Racial Stereotyping

Most people of all races and ethnic groups are never convicted of a crime, but stereotypes can brand all members of some groups with suspicion. These stereotypes are bad enough in the culture at large, but they also work their way into law enforcement through the use of criminal profiles, putting an undue burden on innocent members of these groups. Moreover, such actions produce stark collisions with important American values, especially equal treatment and fairness.

A particularly clear example of racial profiling comes from 1990s studies of the searches that Maryland State Troopers made of motorists on Interstate 95. On this particular stretch of highway, motorists were found to be speeding equally across races.

African American motorists, for example, constituted 17 percent of the motorists and 17.5 percent of the speeders. But African American motorists were the subject of 77 percent of the automobile searches made by the police looking for contraband.

Why were these motorists searched so often? The police might justify such practices on the ground that African Americans are more likely to carry contraband. And the statistics show this to be true: The police found contraband in 33 percent of the searches of African American motorists and in 22 percent of the searches of white motorists. But the mischief in this practice is quickly exposed. African Americans had a 50 percent higher chance of being found with contraband but were searched 400 percent more often. The result is that 274 innocent black motorists were searched, while only 76 white motorists were searched. The profiles apparently used by the Maryland State troopers make 17 percent of the motorists pay 76 percent of the price of law enforcement strategy, solely because of their race.

The evidence of racial profiling in the criminal justice system is not limited to traffic enforcement. A study by the U.S. General Accounting Office, the research agency that provides reports to Congress, revealed that African American women returning from abroad were nine times as likely as white women to be subjected to X-ray searches at airports, even though white women were found to be carrying illegal contraband twice as often as were African American women.

Sources: Drawn from: Christopher Stone, "Race, Crime, and the Administration of Justice," *National Institute of Justice Journal,* April 1999, pp. 24–32; Jennifer Loven, "Black Women Searched More Often," *Associated Press Wire Service,* April 10, 2000; U.S. General Accounting Office, *U.S. Customs Service: Better Targeting of Airline Passengers for Personal Searches Could Produce Better Results,* Washington, D.C.: U.S. Government Printing Office, March 2000.

Researching the Internet

One public interest legal group's reports on racial profiling throughout the United States are available at http://www.aclu.org/profiling/.

Higher arrest rates may also lead to higher incarceration rates. Some point to the fact that 50 percent of the prison population is African American as further evidence of a racist system. One study found that differences in incarceration rates of African Americans and whites reflected "significant disparities that could not be attributed to arrest charges [or] prior criminal charges" (New York Office of Justice Systems Analysis, 1991:1). Recent research has found that judges' discretionary decisions in sentencing produce longer sentences for African Americans in some jurisdictions, even when studies control for other factors (Bushway and Piehl, 2001).

Criminal justice officials need not act in racist ways to cause disparities in arrest and incarceration rates. At each stage of the process, the system itself operates in ways that may put minority group members at a disadvantage. The number of minority arrests may be greater because police patrols are more heavily concentrated in areas where nonwhites live, where drug use is more open, and where users are more likely to be observed by police. Further, a study of 150,000 cases in Connecticut found that on average an African American or Hispanic man must pay *double* the bail that would be paid by a white man for the same offense (Donziger, 1996:111). Most pretrial release practices take into account factors such as employment status, living arrangements, and prior criminal record. Poor offenders are less likely than richer ones to be able to make bail and hire their own lawyer. Prosecutors may be less likely to dismiss charges against a poor, unemployed African American or Hispanic offender than against a white or prosperous offender. Offender characteristics may further skew sentencing as well.

Is the criminal justice system racist? The result of the system's decisions cannot be disputed—African American and Hispanic men end up in prison and jails in higher proportions than can be explained by their crime and arrest rates. Recent research finds that Hispanic defendants are at greater risk of receiving severe sentences than are other offenders (Steffensmeier and Demuth, 2001). A review of 38 studies found more than two-thirds of them had uncovered biases in the system that were disadvantageous to African Americans. The authors concluded that "race is a consistent and frequently significant disadvantage when [imprisonment] decisions are considered... [but] race is much less of a disadvantage when it comes to sentence length" (Chiricos and Crawford, 1995). These conclusions do not mean that every minority defendant is treated disadvantageously compared with whites. Instead, the existence, nature, and extent of discrimination can vary by community (Britt, 2000). Thus racial discrimination may be "confined to certain types of cases, settings, and defendants" (S. Walker et al., 2000:218).

Explanation 3: America Is a Racist Society

Some people claim that the criminal justice system is racist because it is embedded in a racist society. In fact, some accuse the system of being a tool of a racist society.

Evidence of racism shows in the way society asks the criminal justice system to operate. For example, federal sentencing guidelines punish users of crack cocaine about one hundred times more harshly than users of powder cocaine, even though the drugs are virtually identical in their chemical composition and effect on users. A primary difference is that whites tend to use cocaine in its powder form, while people of color in the inner cities tend to use crack cocaine. Thus the imposition of significantly harsher punishments for one form of the drug produces racial disparities in imprisonment rates (Tonry, 1995).

In addition, sentencing studies find a stronger link between unemployment rates and rates of imprisonment than between crime rates and rates of imprisonment. This suggests that prisons are used to confine people who cannot find jobs—and many of the unemployed are African American men (Chiricos and Bales, 1991).

Finally, according to law professor Michael Tonry, the war on drugs was "foreordained to affect disadvantaged black youths disproportionately [and was based on] the willingness of the drug war's planners to sacrifice young black Americans" (Tonry, 1995:123). Others point out that enforcement of drug laws focuses "almost exclusively on low-level dealers in minority neighborhoods" (Donziger, 1996:115). Yet federal health statistics define the typical drug addict as a white male in his twenties who lives in a suburb where drug busts rarely happen (*New York Times,* May 10, 1999:A26).

One can see other evidence of racism in American society in the stereotyping of offenders. As Coramae Richey Mann points out, such stereotyping varies among racial and ethnic groups, depending on the crime and the section of the country. Americans, including police officers and other criminal justice officials, may make assumptions about the criminal tendencies of African Americans, Native Americans, and members of other minority groups (Mann, 1993:vii). Conditioned to think of social ills as minority problems, readers of a *Hartford Courant* series on drug-addicted prostitutes were stunned to learn that 70 percent were white (*New York Times,* May 10, 1999:A26).

That racist stereotyping affects police actions can be seen in cases of African American and Hispanic professionals who have been falsely arrested when the police were looking for a person of color and these individuals happened to be "out of place." Judge Claude Coleman was handcuffed and dragged through crowds of shoppers in Short Hills, New Jersey, while protesting his innocence, Harvard philosopher Cornel West was stopped on false cocaine charges while traveling to Williams College, and law student Brian Roberts was pulled over by the police as he drove in an affluent St. Louis neighborhood on his way to interview a judge for a class project (Tonry, 1995:51).

If people of color are overrepresented in the justice system because the larger society is racist, the solution may seem daunting. Nobody knows how to quickly rid a society of racist policies, practices, and attitudes.

check point

15. What is meant by racial or ethnic disparities in criminal justice?
16. What three explanations may account for such disparities?

Summary

- The three goals of criminal justice are doing justice, controlling crime, and preventing crime.
- Both the national and state systems of criminal justice enforce laws, try cases, and punish offenders.
- Criminal justice is a system made up of many parts or subsystems—police, courts, corrections.
- Exchange is a key concept for the analysis of criminal justice processes.
- Four major characteristics of the criminal justice system are discretion, resource dependence, sequential tasks, and filtering.
- The processing of cases in the criminal justice system involves a series of decisions by police officers, prosecutors, judges, probation officers, wardens, and parole board members.
- The criminal justice system consists of 13 steps that cover the stages of law enforcement, adjudication, and corrections.
- With its four layers, the criminal justice wedding cake model indicates that not all cases are treated equally.
- The existence of unequal treatment of people within the criminal justice system would clash with the American values of equality, fairness, and due process.
- Racial disparities in criminal justice are explained in one of three ways: minorities commit more crimes; the criminal justice system is racist; the criminal justice system expresses the racism of society.

Questions for Review

1. What are the goals of the criminal justice system?
2. What is a system? How is the administration of criminal justice a system?
3. What are the 13 steps in the criminal justice decision-making process?
4. Why is the criminal justice wedding cake a better depiction of reality than is a linear model of the system?
5. What is the challenge of criminal justice in a multicultural society?

Key Terms

adjudication (p. 74)
arrest (p. 77)
discretion (p. 71)
discrimination (p. 86)
disparity (p. 86)
dual court system (p. 74)
exchange (p. 70)
federalism (p. 66)
felonies (p. 84)

filtering process (p. 72)
indictment (p. 78)
information (p. 77)
misdemeanors (p. 84)
plea bargain (p. 70)
system (p. 70)
warrant (p. 77)

For Further Reading

Cole, David. 1999. *No Equal Justice: Race and Class in the American Criminal Justice System*. New York: New Press. Argues that a double standard compromises the legitimacy of criminal justice and exacerbates racial divisions.

Friedman, Lawrence M. 1993. *Crime and Punishment in American History*. New York: Basic Books. A historical overview of criminal justice from colonial times. Argues that the evolution of criminal justice reflects transformations in America's character.

Parenti, Christian. 1999. *Lockdown America: Police and Prisons in the Age of Crisis*. New York: Verso. Argues that beginning in the late 1960s American capitalism hit a dual social and economic crisis. In response was a buildup of the criminal justice system, which has led to state repression and surveillance.

Smith, Christopher E., Christina DeJong, and John D. Burrow. 2002. *The Supreme Court, Crime, and the Ideal of Equal Justice*. New York: Peter Lange. An examination of how U.S. Supreme Court decisions have alleviated, facilitated, or tolerated discrimination by race, gender, social class, and offender status in the American criminal justice system.

Walker, Samuel, Cassia Spohn, and Miriam DeLeone. 2003. *The Color of Justice: Race, Ethnicity and Crime in America*. 3rd ed. Belmont, Calif. An excellent overview of the links between crime, race, and ethnicity.

Going Online

For an up-to-date list of Web links, go to http://www.cj.wadsworth.com/colesmith10e

1. Using the Internet, access leading state or national newspapers and look for articles about criminal cases. How many articles are about trials and how many are about plea bargains? For the cases that went to trial, what kinds of charges were pressed and who were the defendants?
2. Type the phrase *police discretion* into any search engine. In the articles that you find, what kinds of concerns are raised about the nature and consequences of police discretion? What suggested remedies are provided?
3. Using InfoTrac College Edition, enter the phrase *racial profiling*. Find articles that discuss remedies for racial profiling, such as lawsuits against officers or mandatory record-keeping of the race of the persons whom they stop. Based on these articles, do you believe that racial profiling can be eliminated?

Checkpoint Answers

1. Doing justice, controlling crime, preventing crime.
2. Offenders are held fully accountable for their actions, the rights of people who have contact with the system will be protected, and like offenses will be treated alike and officials will take into account relevant differences among offenders and offenses.
3. A division of power between a central (national) government and regional (state) governments.
4. Enforcement of federal criminal laws.
5. The expansion of criminal activities across state borders.
6. A complex whole made up of interdependent parts whose actions are directed toward goals and influenced by the environment within which it functions.
7. Plea bargaining.
8. Discretion, resource dependence, sequential tasks, filtering.
9. Keeping the peace, apprehending violators and combating crime, preventing crime, providing social services.
10. A separate judicial system for each state in addition to a national system.
11. Prisons, jails, probation, parole, intermediate sanctions. Public, nonprofit, and for-profit agencies carry out these programs.
12. (1) Investigations, (2) arrest, (3) booking, (4) charging, (5) initial appearance, (6) preliminary hearing/grand jury, (7) indictment/information, (8) arraignment, (9) trial, (10) sentencing, (11) appeal, (12) corrections, (13) release.

13 To show that all cases are not treated alike.

14 Layer 1: celebrated cases in which the adversarial system is played out in full; Layer 2: serious felonies committed by people with long criminal records against victims unknown to them; Layer 3: felonies in which the crimes and the offenders are viewed as less serious than in Layer 2; Layer 4: misdemeanors.

15 That racial and ethnic minorities are subjected to the criminal justice system at much higher rates than are the white majority.

16 Minorities commit more crime; the criminal justice system is racist; American society is racist.

CHAPTER 4

Criminal Justice and the Rule of Law

Foundations of Criminal Law	Substantive Law and Procedural Law Sources of Criminal Law Felony and Misdemeanor Criminal versus Civil Law
Substantive Criminal Law	Seven Principles of Criminal Law Elements of a Crime Statutory Definitions of Crimes Responsibility for Criminal Acts
Procedural Criminal Law	The Bill of Rights The Fourteenth Amendment and Due Process The Due Process Revolution The Fourth Amendment: Protection against Unreasonable Searches and Seizures The Fifth Amendment: Protection against Self-Incrimination and Double Jeopardy The Sixth Amendment: The Right to Counsel and a Fair Trial The Eighth Amendment: Protection against Excessive Bail, Excessive Fines, and Cruel and Unusual Punishments
The Supreme Court Today	

Mark E. Gibson/CORBIS

On July 22, 2000, 40-year-old Michael Pangle spent an evening drinking heavily in New Jersey strip clubs. When he was pulled over by the police, his system contained more than double the blood-alcohol level permitted for people operating motor vehicles. Instead of placing the drunken man in jail, officers permitted Pangle's friend, Kenneth Powell, to pick up Pangle at the state police barracks. Unfortunately, Powell did not drive Pangle home as the police expected him to do. Powell drove back to his friend's car. Pangle got behind the wheel and went down the road again. Tragically, Pangle crossed the center line on a highway. His car collided head-on with a vehicle driven by 22-year-old Navy ensign John Elliott. Pangle and Elliott both died in the collision, and Elliott's girlfriend was seriously injured.

Aside from drunken driving, did any crime occur in the foregoing events? Who was responsible for the collision and Elliott's

legal responsibility
The accountability of an individual for a crime because of the perpetrator's characteristics and the circumstances of the illegal act.

death? Was it Pangle alone, the man who drank too much and got behind the wheel of the car? Was it the bartenders who served him too many drinks? Was it the state troopers who let him go when they knew he was drunk? Was it Kenneth Powell, who took his drunken friend back to the vehicle? Does anyone have **legal responsibility** for these deaths? If you were a prosecutor, would you seek to punish anyone for the death of Ensign Elliott?

The answer to the question of whether a crime occurred depends on several factors. Most importantly, the answer depends on whether the laws of New Jersey define any of the participants' actions as murder or manslaughter. The answer also depends on local prosecutors' interpretations of state criminal laws, because prosecutors must decide whether individuals will be processed through the system's steps to determine the existence of criminal guilt. Ultimately, the answer depends on the decision of a jury or judge, who must determine whether an individual's actions fit within the coverage of laws concerning crime, guilt, and punishment. Further, various laws require that an accused person must have an attorney to present arguments and that the prosecutor must present evidence that is acceptable under court rules.

In the actual case, the prosecutor charged Kenneth Powell with manslaughter, vehicular homicide, and aggravated assault, even though Powell never drove the car in question and was not present at the fatal crash. The prosecutor argued that the laws defining these crimes permitted people to be sent to prison for failing to stop drunken friends from driving vehicles and causing accidents. Do you agree with the prosecutor that criminal laws should be interpreted to punish people who fail to stop others from committing crimes?

As it turned out, the prosecutor did not persuade a jury that this interpretation advanced the interests of justice. The prosecutor argued that Powell made a series of decisions and actions that led to the deaths of innocent motorists. The defense argued that the state was desperately seeking to find someone to punish since the actual perpetrator was dead and the prosecutor did not want to focus on the state troopers' failure to prevent the drunk driver from returning to the road. Ultimately, the judge declared a mistrial because the jury was not able to reach a verdict ("Mistrial in Landmark DUI Case," 2002).

Do you think that you should be held criminally responsible for your friends' actions? Should your friends be responsible for what you do? If so, under what circumstances? Many commentators found it difficult to believe that Powell's actions, despite being irresponsible, should be considered as a serious crime. How can it be a crime for someone to fail to stop someone else from acting? Like other actions subject to punishment, it could be a crime for the same reason that any other human action becomes a crime: A legislature enacts a law declaring a particular behavior to be deserving of criminal punishment. In this case, New Jersey's laws did not clearly define Powell's actions as criminal. But such a law could be enacted. One of the primary functions of criminal law is to define those behaviors that are labeled criminal and therefore worthy of punishment. Legislatures bear primary responsibility for defining crimes, but judges frequently interpret what legislators meant in establishing criminal offenses.

In defining crimes, we often consider a person's mental status and intentions. Thus, for example, we permit the use of the insanity defense. We also punish intentional acts more harshly than inadvertent actions. Intentional crimes, such as premeditated murder, are more serious than negligent harmful acts, such as involuntary manslaughter. The definitions of crimes and people eligible for punishment are spelled out in substantive criminal law, to be discussed shortly.

A second primary function of criminal law is to describe the procedures to be followed under our adversarial system by those responsible for law enforcement, adjudication, and corrections. This type of law, called procedural criminal law, specifies the rights possessed by people drawn into the criminal justice system. Powell gained benefits from this aspect of criminal law because he was entitled to an attorney and a trial before a final judgment was made about his possible guilt. Legislatures enact statutes to establish procedures, but these procedures are frequently modified as judges determine if any processes violate the rights of criminal defendants. Procedural criminal law is also established by provisions of federal and state constitutions. One such provision, from the Sixth Amendment of the Constitution, is the right to counsel. The precise nature of individuals' rights under procedural criminal law is determined by judges' interpretations of the U.S. Constitution, state constitutions, and relevant statutes enacted by Congress and state legislatures.

In previous chapters, we saw how criminal justice operates as a system influenced by political and social forces; now we turn to a fourth ingredient of our analysis—law. This chapter explores the two main aspects of criminal law: substantive criminal law and the law of criminal procedure.

QUESTIONS for INQUIRY

- What are the bases and sources of American criminal law?
- How does substantive criminal law define a crime and the legal responsibility of the accused?
- How does procedural criminal law define the rights of the accused and the processes for dealing with a case?
- How has the United States Supreme Court interpreted the criminal justice amendments to the Constitution?

(Answers are at the end of the chapter.)

Foundations of Criminal Law

Like most Americans, you are probably aware that law and legal procedures are key elements of the criminal justice system. Americans are fond of saying that "we have a government of laws, not of men (and women)." According to our American values, we do not have a system based on the decisions of a king or dictator. Historically, presidents, governors, and mayors could not legally choose to punish people they disliked. Instead, even our most powerful leaders had to make decisions within limits imposed by law. The government could only seek to punish people who violated defined laws, and their guilt had to be determined through procedures established by law. Since the tragic events of September 11, however, some commentators have expressed fears that the federal government had moved away from traditional constitutional values by jailing people suspected of involvement in terrorism without charging them with any crimes or presenting any evidence in court to prove their involvement in wrongdoing (Turley, 2002). Thus we find ourselves entering a new era in which the government's actions against terrorism clash with traditional American values and functions of law.

Laws tell citizens what they can and cannot do. Laws also tell government officials when they can seek to punish citizens for violations and how they must go about it. Government officials, including the President of the United States, who take actions according to their own preferences run the risk that judges will order them to take different actions that comply with the law. Government officials are expected to follow and enforce the law. Thus, in a democracy, laws are a major tool to prevent government officials from seizing too much power or using power improperly.

Substantive Law and Procedural Law

Criminal law is only one category of law. Peoples' lives and actions are also affected by **civil law**, which governs business deals, contracts, real estate, and the like. For example, if you harm other people in an accident or damage their property, they may sue you to pay for the harm or damage. By contrast, the key

civil law
Law regulating the relationships between or among individuals, usually involving property, contract, or business disputes.

feature of criminal law is the government's power to punish people for damage they have done to society.

substantive criminal law
Law that defines the acts that are subject to punishment and specifies the punishments for such offenses.

Among the two categories of criminal law, **substantive criminal law** defines actions that may be punished by the government. It also defines the punishments for such offenses. Often called the *penal code,* substantive law answers the question "*What* is illegal?" Elected officials in Congress, state legislatures, and city councils write the substantive criminal laws. These legislators decide which kinds of behaviors are so harmful that they deserve to be punished. They also decide whether each violation should be punished by imprisonment, a fine, probation, or another kind of punishment. When questions about the meaning of substantive criminal laws arise, judges interpret the laws by seeking to fulfill the legislators' intentions.

procedural criminal law
Law defining the procedures that criminal justice officials must follow in enforcement, adjudication, and correction.

By contrast, **procedural criminal law** defines the rules that answer the question "*How* shall the law be enforced?" It protects the constitutional rights of defendants and provides the rules that officials must follow in all areas of the criminal justice system. It embodies the American values of liberty and individual rights by seeking to ensure that no one will be incarcerated or otherwise punished unless the government proves criminal guilt through proper procedures that respect constitutional rights. Many aspects of procedural criminal law are defined by legislatures, such as how bail will be set and which kind of preliminary hearing will take place before a trial. However, the U.S. Supreme Court and state supreme courts also play a key role in defining procedural criminal law. These courts define the meaning of constitutional rights in the U.S. Constitution and in state constitutions. Their interpretations of constitutional provisions create rules on such issues as when and how police officers can question suspects and when defendants can receive advice from their attorneys.

To read the U.S. Supreme Court's most recent decisions defining criminal procedure and individuals' constitutional rights, see http://www.law.cornell.edu.

check point

1. What is contained in a state's penal code?
2. What is the purpose of procedural criminal law?

Sources of Criminal Law

The earliest known codes of law appeared in the Sumerian law of Mesopotamia (3100 B.C.) and the Code of Hammurabi (1750 B.C.). These written codes were divided into sections to cover different types of offenses. Other important ancestors of Western law are the Draconian Code, produced in the seventh century B.C. in Greece, and the Law of the Twelve Tables created by the Romans (450 B.C.) However, the main source of American law is the common law of England.

Common Law

common law
The Anglo-American system of uncodified law, in which judges follow precedents set by earlier decisions when they decide new but similar cases. The substantive and procedural criminal law was originally developed in this manner but was later codified—set down in codes—by state legislatures.

Common law was based on custom and tradition as interpreted by judges. In continental Europe, a system of civil law developed in which the rules were set down in detailed codes produced by legislatures or other governing authorities. By contrast, the common law of England was not written down as a list of rules. Rather, it took its form from the collected opinions of the judges, who looked to custom in making their decisions. The judges created law when they ruled on specific cases. These rulings, also known as *precedents,* established legal principles to be used in making decisions on similar cases. When such cases arose, judges looked to earlier rulings to find principles that applied to the type of case they were deciding. Over time, as new kinds of situations emerged, judges had to create new legal principles to address them. As more rulings on various kinds of legal issues were written down, they grew into a body of law—composed of principles and reasoning—that other judges could use in deciding their own cases. The use of a common set of precedents made the application of law more stable and consistent. Moreover, the judges' ability to adjust legal principles when new kinds of situations arose made the common law flexible enough to respond to changes in society.

The English precedents and procedures were maintained in the American colonies, but after independence the states began to make some changes in the law. For example, the definitions of crimes and punishments in the English common law were often enacted into penal codes by state legislatures. Although these legislative actions altered the nature and force of common law, they did not eliminate the common law process. American courts still create precedents when they interpret laws and constitutional provisions. These judicial rulings guide the decisions of American courts on issues concerning both substantive and procedural criminal law.

Archive Photos

The Draconian Code, promulgated in classical Greece in the seventh century B.C., is one of the earliest foundations of Western law.

Written Law

Most people agree that having a document that clearly stated the criminal law, both substantive and procedural, would be helpful. It would allow citizens to know definitively when they might be in danger of committing an illegal act and to be aware of their rights if official action is taken against them. If such a document could be written in simple language, society would probably need fewer lawyers. However, it is not possible to write such a document. Our criminal laws and procedures are too complex to be reduced to simple terms. Further, we are constantly expanding the scope and complexity of criminal law. When we try to define new illegal acts—like pirating of videotaped films or fraud in electronic filing of tax returns—we see how the law must be able to respond to new, complex problems. Moreover, any effort to reduce rules to words on a page creates opportunities for those words to be interpreted in different ways. If we have a crime called "negligent homicide," for example, how will we define *negligence?* The need for interpretation means that lawyers and judges will always have a role in shaping—and changing—the meaning of both substantive and procedural law.

Because we cannot compile a single, complete document that provides all the details of criminal law, we continue to rely on four sources of law: constitutions, statutes, court decisions (also known as case law), and administrative regulations.

Constitutions contain basic principles and procedural safeguards. The Constitution of the United States was written in Philadelphia in 1787 and went into effect in 1789 after it had been ratified by the required number of states. It sets forth the country's governing system and describes the institutions (legislature, courts, and president) that will make its laws. The first ten amendments to the Constitution, together known as the Bill of Rights, were added in 1791. Most of these amendments provide protections against government actions that would violate basic rights and liberties. Several have a direct bearing on criminal law, because they guarantee the rights of due process, jury trial, and representation by counsel, as well as protection against unreasonable searches and cruel and unusual punishments. Most state constitutions also contain protections against actions by state and local governments. During the early 1960s the U.S. Supreme Court decided to require state and local governments to respect most of the rights listed in the Bill of Rights. (Before that time the Bill of Rights protected citizens only against actions by the federal government.) As a result of Supreme Court decisions, the power of police officers, prosecutors, and judges is limited by the U.S. Constitution and their own state constitution.

constitutions
The basic laws of a country defining the structure of government and the relationship of citizens to that government.

To read an example of a state constitution, see Vermont's constitution at http://www.leg.state.vt.us/statutes/const2.htm.

Statutes are laws passed by legislative bodies; the substantive and procedural rules of most states are found in their statutes. Although criminal law is written

statutes
Laws passed by legislatures. Statutory definitions of criminal offenses are found in penal codes.

For an example of the nature and range of criminal statutes enacted by a state legislature, see the Texas penal code at http://www.capitol.state.tx.us/statutes/petoc.html.

mainly by state legislatures, Congress and local governments also play a role in shaping the law. Federal criminal laws passed by Congress deal mainly with violations that occur on property of the U.S. government or with acts that involve the national interest (counterfeiting money) or more than one state (taking a kidnap victim across state lines). The states give cities and towns some authority to pass laws dealing with local problems. There is overlap among national, state, and local rules governing certain kinds of criminal conduct. Possession or sale of drugs, for example, may violate criminal laws at all three levels of government. In such situations, law enforcement agencies must to decide which one will prosecute the offender.

If we want to know the definition of a crime covered by a statute, we consult a state's penal code. The acts that constitute a crime and the penalty to be imposed are clearly specified. Although the laws of most states are similar, there are some differences. To make state laws more uniform, the American Law Institute has developed the *Model Penal Code,* which it urges legislatures to adopt.

case law
Court decisions that have the status of law and serve as precedents for later decisions.

Court decisions, often called **case law,** are a third source of criminal law. As noted earlier, the main characteristic of the common law system is that judges look to earlier decisions to guide their rulings. Although much of the common law of crime has been replaced by statutes, precedent is still an important aid to lawyers and judges in interpreting penal codes.

administrative regulations
Rules made by government agencies to implement specific public policies in areas such as public health, environmental protection, and workplace safety.

Administrative regulations are laws and rules made by federal, state, and local agencies. The legislature, president, or governor has given those agencies the power to make rules governing specific policy areas such as health, safety, and the environment. Most such rules have been produced in this century to deal with modern concerns, such as wages and work hours, pollution, traffic, workplace safety, and pure food and drugs. Many of the rules are part of the criminal law, and violations are processed through the criminal justice system.

As you can see, the criminal law is more than just a penal code written by a state legislature or Congress. The sources of criminal law are summarized in Figure 4.1.

check point

3. How does the common law shape criminal law?
4. What are the forms of written law?

Felony and Misdemeanor

Crimes are classified by how serious they are. The distinction between a felony and a misdemeanor is one of the oldest in the criminal law. Most laws define felonies and misdemeanors in light of the punishment that may be imposed. Conviction on a felony charge usually means that the offender may be given a prison sentence of more than a year. The severest felonies may draw the death penalty. Those who commit misdemeanors are dealt with more leniently; the sentence might be a fine, probation, or a jail sentence of less than a year. Some states define the seriousness of the offense according to the place of punishment: prison for felonies, jail for misdemeanors.

Whether a defendant is charged with a felony or a misdemeanor determines not only how the person is punished, but also how the criminal justice system will process the defendant. Certain rights and penalties follow from this distinction. For example, the conditions under which the police may make an arrest and the trial level where the charges will be heard are based on the seriousness of the charge. In 1996 the U.S. Supreme Court declared that people who face less than six months in jail for a charge are not entitled to a jury trial. The Constitution requires only that they be tried in front of a judge (*Lewis v. United States*).

CONSTITUTIONAL LAW

The Constitution of the United States and the state constitutions define the structure of government and the rights of citizens.

STATUTORY LAW

The substantive and procedural criminal laws are found in laws passed by legislative bodies such as the U.S. Congress and state legislatures.

CASE LAW

Consistent with the common-law heritage, legal opinions by judges in individual cases have the status of law.

ADMINISTRATIVE LAW

Also having the status of law are some decisions of federal and state government agencies that have been given the power to regulate such areas as health, safety, and the environment in the public interest.

Figure 4.1
Sources of criminal law
Although codes of law existed in ancient times, American criminal law is derived mainly from the common law of England. The common law distinguishes English-speaking systems from the civil law systems of the rest of the world.

The distinction between types of crimes also can affect a person's future. People with felony convictions may be barred from certain professions, such as law and medicine, and in many states they are also barred from certain other occupations (bartender, police officer, barber). Felony convictions may also keep people from ever voting, serving on juries, or running for election to public office (Olivares, Burton, and Cullen, 1996).

Criminal versus Civil Law

As mentioned earlier, the legal system makes basic distinctions between criminal and civil law. A violation of criminal law is an offense against society as a whole, while civil law regulates relations between individuals. The focus of the criminal law is on the intent of the wrongdoer. We view intentional acts as most deserving of punishment, but we may decide to press criminal charges even when a harmful event was "an accident." By contrast, in civil law the focus is on fixing the blame for the damage or harm.

In some cases, both criminal and civil proceedings may arise from the same event. When hunting, if you carelessly fire a shot that crashes through the window of a home and wounds the homeowner, the homeowner may bring a civil suit against you to recover the cost of the damage you caused. The damage could include medical bills and the cost of fixing the window. This legal action falls within the area of civil law known as *torts*, which deals with compensation for

Fred Goldman is hugged by his daughter while he pats his wife's cheek after O. J. Simpson was found liable on all counts in a wrongful death civil trial for the murders of Ronald Goldman and Nicole Brown Simpson.

injured individuals. In a separate action, the state may charge you with a violation of the criminal law because your actions violated society's rules for the lawful use of firearms.

Although criminal and civil law are distinct, both attempt to control human behavior by steering people to act in a desired manner and by imposing costs on those who violate social rules. Increasingly, civil suits are being brought against offenders who previously were subject only to criminal charges. For example, some rape victims have brought civil suits against their attackers, and some department stores are suing shoplifters for large amounts. Other rape victims successfully sue apartment complexes for failing to maintain secure conditions that would prevent criminal attacks. It is even possible for victims to win civil lawsuits against defendants who have been acquitted of criminal charges. Such was the case when the families of murder victims Nicole Brown Simpson and Ronald Goldman won a lawsuit worth millions of dollars against O. J. Simpson, despite the retired football star's acquittal after a highly publicized murder trial. To gain a criminal conviction, prosecutors must persuade the jury or judge of the existence of proof showing the defendant's guilt "beyond a reasonable doubt." The Simpson jury in the criminal case did not believe that the evidence met this high standard of proof. In the later civil trial, however, a jury believed that the evidence satisfied the lower civil law standard of showing by a "preponderance of evidence" that Simpson was most likely responsible for the two deaths.

Civil law is also important for the criminal justice system because citizens can file lawsuits against police officers, correctional officers, and other government actors if they believe those actors have violated their constitutional rights. Such lawsuits can result in multimillion dollar verdicts, especially when innocent citizens are seriously injured or killed through improper high-speed driving or the use of weapons by the police. These civil lawsuits help to shape police training and departmental policies, because government agencies want to avoid the high costs of defending and losing civil rights litigation (C. E. Smith and Hurst, 1997).

civil forfeiture
The confiscation of property by the state as punishment for a crime. In recent years the police have used civil forfeiture to seize property that they believe was purchased with drug profits.

Another example of a link between criminal and civil law is **civil forfeiture.** This concept, derived from English common law, allows for government to take privately owned property and has frequently been applied in drug law enforcement (Stahl, 1992). Forfeiture can even affect property owners who are not guilty of any crime. In 1996 the U.S. Supreme Court decided that, despite her innocence, a wife lost her ownership rights in a car when her husband used the vehicle to pick up a prostitute (*Bennis v. Michigan*). Forfeiture laws frequently permit law enforcement agencies to sell seized property and use the money for themselves. The use of forfeiture by law enforcement agencies has generated controversy, especially when applied against people who have never been convicted of any crime. In 2000 an unusual coalition of conservatives and liberals persuaded Congress to enact legislation limiting the federal government's authority to seize property. Under the law, the federal government must show by a preponderance of evidence that property it seeks to seize is linked to crimes. Previously, owners of seized property bore the difficult burden of proving that their property was not linked to criminal conduct (Abrams, 2000). The passage of the law reflected the fact that Americans across the political spectrum had come to believe that government forfeiture practices violated American values about the protection of private property and individuals' entitlement to due process of law before losing property or receiving punishment.

WWW Information about the use of forfeiture in criminal justice can be found at the Web site of the U.S. Department of Treasury's Executive Office for Asset Forfeiture (EOAF): http://www.eoaf.treas.gov.

In summary, the bases of American criminal law are complex. English common law and the laws found in such written sources as constitutions, statutes, case law, and administrative regulations all contribute to what most people call "criminal law." Within this body of law, there is a major division between substantive criminal law and procedural criminal law.

check point

5. What is the difference between a felony and a misdemeanor?
6. What types of legal issues arise in civil law cases?

Substantive Criminal Law

As we have seen, substantive criminal law defines acts that are subject to punishment and specifies the punishments. It is based on the doctrine that no one may be convicted of or punished for an offense unless the offense has been defined by the law. In short, people must know in advance what is required of them. Thus, no act can be regarded as illegal until it has been defined as punishable under the criminal law. While this sounds like a simple notion, the language of law is often confusing and ambiguous. As a result, judges must become involved in interpreting the law so that the meaning intended by the legislature can be understood.

Seven Principles of Criminal Law

The major principles of Western criminal law were summarized in a single statement by legal scholar Jerome Hall (1947). To convict a defendant of a crime, prosecutors must prove that all seven principles have been fulfilled (see Figure 4.2).

1. *Legality.* There must be a law that defines the specific action as a crime. Offensive and harmful behavior is not illegal unless it has been prohibited by law before it was committed. The U.S. Constitution forbids *ex post facto* laws, or laws written and applied after the fact. Thus, when the legislature defines a new crime, people can be prosecuted only for violations that occur after the new law has been passed.
2. *Actus reus.* Criminal laws are aimed at human acts, including acts that a person failed to undertake. The U.S. Supreme Court has ruled that people may not be convicted of a crime simply because of their status. Under this *actus reus* requirement, for a crime to occur a person must perform an act of either commission or omission. In *Robinson v. California* (1962), for example, the Supreme Court struck down a California law that made it a crime to be addicted to drugs. States can prosecute people for using, possessing, selling, or transporting drugs when they catch them performing these *acts,* but states cannot prosecute them for the mere *status* of being addicted to drugs.
3. *Causation.* For a crime to have been committed, there must be a causal relationship between an act and the harm suffered. In Ohio, for example, a prosecutor tried to convict a burglary suspect on a manslaughter charge when a victim, asleep in his house, was killed by a stray bullet as officers fired at the unarmed, fleeing suspect. The burglar was acquitted on the homicide charge because his actions in committing the burglary and running away from the police were not the direct cause of the victim's death (Bandy, 1991).
4. *Harm.* To be a crime, an act must cause harm to some legally protected value. The harm can be to a person, property, or some other object that a

Figure 4.2 **The seven principles of criminal law**
These principles of Western law are the basis for defining acts as criminal and defining the conditions required for successful prosecution.

A crime is	
1 legally proscribed	(legality)
2 human conduct	(*actus reus*)
3 causative	(causation)
4 of a given harm	(harm)
5 which conduct coincides	(concurrence)
6 with a blameworthy frame of mind	(*mens rea*)
7 and is subject to punishment	(punishment)

legislature deems valuable enough to deserve protection through the government's power to punish. This principle is often questioned by those who feel that in causing harm only to themselves they are not committing a crime. Laws that require motorcyclists to wear helmets have been challenged on this ground. Such laws, however, have been written because legislatures see enough forms of harm to require protective laws. These forms of harm include injuries to helmetless riders, tragedy and loss for families of injured cyclists, and the medical costs imposed on society for head injuries that could have been prevented.

inchoate offense
Conduct that is criminal even though the harm that the law seeks to prevent has been merely planned or attempted but not done.

An act can be deemed criminal if it could do harm that the law seeks to prevent; this is called an **inchoate offense.** Thus, criminal law includes conspiracies and attempts, even when the lawbreaker does not complete the intended crime. For example, people can be prosecuted for planning to murder someone or hiring a "hit man" to kill someone. The potential for grave harm from such acts justifies the application of the government's power to punish.

5. *Concurrence.* For an act to be considered a crime, the intent and the act must be present at the same time (J. Hall, 1947:85). Let's imagine that Joe is planning to murder his archenemy, Bill. He spends days planning how he will abduct Bill and carry out the murder. While driving home from work one day, Joe accidentally hits and kills a jogger who suddenly—and foolishly—has run across the busy street without looking. The jogger turns out to be Bill. Although Joe had planned to kill Bill, he is not guilty of murder, because the accidental killing was not connected to Joe's intent to carry out a killing.
6. *Mens rea.* The commission of an act is not a crime unless it is accompanied by a guilty state of mind. This concept is related to intent. It seeks to distinguish between harm-causing *accidents,* which generally are not subject to criminal punishment, and harm-causing *crimes,* in which some level of intent is present. Certain crimes require a specific level of intent; examples include first-degree murder, which is normally a planned, intentional killing, and larceny, which involves the intent to permanently and unlawfully deprive an owner of his or her property. Later in this chapter we examine several defenses, such as necessity and insanity, that can be used to assert that a person did not have a ***mens rea***—"guilty mind" or blameworthy state of mind—and hence should not be held responsible for a criminal offense. The element of *mens rea* becomes problematic when there are questions about an offender's capability of understanding or planning harmful activities, as when the perpetrator is mentally ill or is a child.

mens rea
"Guilty mind" or blameworthy state of mind, necessary for legal responsibility for a criminal offense; criminal intent, as distinguished from innocent intent.

Exceptions to the concept of *mens rea* are strict liability offenses involving health and safety, in which it is not necessary to show intent. Legislatures have criminalized certain kinds of offenses in order to protect the public. For example, a business owner may be held responsible for violations of a toxic waste law whether or not the owner actually knew that his employees were dumping polluting substances into a river. Other laws may apply strict liability to the sale of alcoholic beverages to minors. The purpose of such laws is to put pressure on business owners to make sure that their employees obey regulations designed to protect the health and safety of the public. Courts often limit the application of such laws to cases that involve recklessness or indifference.

7. *Punishment.* There must be a provision in the law calling for punishment of those found guilty of violating the law. The punishment is enforced by the government and may carry with it loss of freedom, social stigma, a criminal record, and loss of rights.

The seven principles of substantive criminal law allow authorities to define certain acts as being against the law and provide the accused with a basis for mounting a defense against the charges. During a criminal trial, defense attorneys often try to show that one of the seven elements either is unproven or can be explained in a way that is acceptable under the law.

These seven principles are by no means adopted throughout the world; other countries base their laws on different principles (Souryal, Potts, and Alobied, 1994). Laws typically reflect the values and traditions of a society. Criminal law may be based on religious tenets, for example, rather than on laws enacted by legislatures. The values protected by the law may also differ. In the United States, *defamation*—slander or libel by making false statements that harm someone else's reputation—is addressed by civil tort law. A person can sue to gain compensation from someone who harms his or her reputation. By contrast, under Islamic law certain kinds of defamation may be punished by society as criminal offenses.

As they do between countries, differences in traditions, values, and social structures also create variations among the state laws within the United States. While we generally think of American law as permitting drinking, for example, differences among states' laws may be influenced by religious values. Most notably, Utah significantly restricts the availability of alcoholic beverages. Liquor is served only at clubs with dues-paying members and at a limited number of restaurants that are not allowed to advertise the fact that they have a liquor license. Grocery stores can sell only low-alcohol beer. Moreover, it is a crime for anyone other than a licensed dealer to bring alcoholic beverages into the state. The restrictions on drinking in Utah are usually attributed to the political dominance of Mormons, members of a religion that forbids drinking (Foy, 1999). As you read the Comparative Perspective about Islamic law and its differences from criminal law in the United States, think about differences in the definitions of crimes and punishments in the United States that also reflect the way in which law is shaped by values and traditions.

check point

7. What are the seven principles of criminal law?

Elements of a Crime

Legislatures define certain acts as crimes when they fulfill the seven principles under certain "attendant circumstances" while the offender is in a certain state of mind. These three factors—the act (*actus reus*), the attendant circumstances, and the state of mind (*mens rea*)—are together called the *elements* of a crime. They can be seen in the following section from a state penal code:

> Section 3502. Burglary
>
> 1 ***Offense defined:*** A person is guilty of burglary if he enters a building or occupied structure, or separately secured or occupied portion thereof, with intent to commit a crime therein, unless the premises are at the time open to the public or the actor is licensed or privileged to enter.

The elements of burglary are, therefore, entering a building or occupied structure (*actus reus*) with the intent to commit a crime therein (*mens rea*) at a time when the premises are not open to the public and the actor is not invited or otherwise entitled to enter (attendant circumstances). For an act to be a burglary, all three elements must be present.

Even if it appears that the accused has committed a crime, prosecution will be successful only if the elements match the court's interpretations of the law. For example, Pennsylvania judges have interpreted the *actus reus* of burglary to include entering a building that is open to the public, such as a store or tavern, so

Islamic Criminal Law

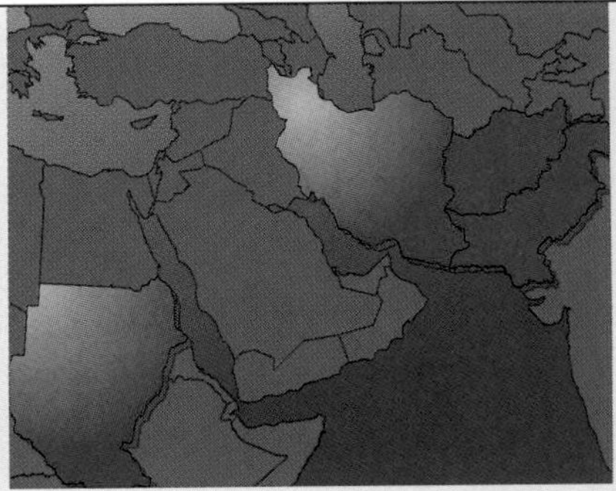

The rise of fundamentalist Islamic thought throughout the world has made Americans aware of great cultural differences between Westerners and Middle Easterners. Islamic criminal law, in particular, appears to be at odds with justice as it is administered in the West. What are some of the major differences that exist between the two systems of law? How is Islamic criminal law a reflection of Middle Eastern culture?

In November 1996, Americans were shocked to read the graphic description of the stoning of two adulterers in Afghanistan before thousands of witnesses. The condemned woman was lowered into a pit dug into the earth so that only her chest and head were above ground. Her lover was blindfolded and taken to a spot about 20 paces away and stood before the Muslim cleric who was the judge. Between the condemned were two piles of stones. The judge threw the first stone at the woman. Quickly, stones thrown by military men hailed down on the condemned. Death came after ten minutes to the man, but longer to the woman. Her son stepped forward and told the judge she was still alive. At this point one of the men picked up a large rock and dropped it on her head, killing her.

To the West, justice in Islamic states, such as Iran, Afghanistan, Saudi Arabia, and Sudan, seems harsh and unforgiving. The practices of stoning for adultery and amputation for theft often serve as examples of the ferocity of Islamic law. What most Americans do not realize is that there are judicial and evidentiary safeguards within the *Shari'a,* the law of Islam. Islamic criminal law is concerned with (1) the safety of the public from physical attack, insult, and humiliation; (2) the stability of the family; (3) the protection of property against theft, destruction, or unauthorized interference; and (4) the protection of the government and the Islamic faith against subversion.

Criminal acts are divided into three categories. *Hudud* offenses are crimes against God, and punishment is specified in the Koran and the Sunna, a compilation of Muhammad's statements. *Quesas* and *Tesars* are crimes against others such as those that threaten a family's livelihood, including physical assault and murder, which are punishable by retaliation—"the return of life for a life in case of murder." As shown below for the seven *Hudud* offenses, the Koran defines the crime, specifies the elements of proof required, and sets the punishment.

Theft

Theft is the taking of property belonging to another, the value of which is equal to or exceeds a prescribed amount, usually set at ten dirhams or about 75 cents. The property must be taken from the custody of another person in a secret manner, and the thief must obtain full possession of the property. "Custody" requires that the property should have been under guard or in a place of safekeeping.

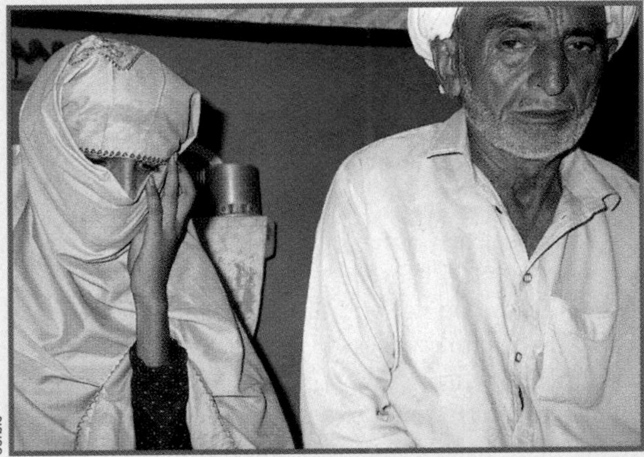
Corbis

Pakistani gang-rape victim Mukhtaran Bibi sits with her father. Tribal elders ordered the gang rape because her 11-year-old brother was seen with a woman not related to him. The incident caused a worldwide outrage and charges were filed against the four rapists and ten council members who ordered the rape.

Islamic *Hudud* offenses, required proofs, and punishments

Crime	Proof	Punishment
Adultery	Four witnesses or confessions	Married person: stoning to death. Convict is taken to a barren site. Stones are thrown first by witnesses, then by the *qadi* (judge), and finally by the rest of the community.
		For a woman, a grave is dug to receive the body.
		Unmarried person: 100 lashes. *Maliki* school also punishes unmarried men with one year in prison or exile.
Defamation	Unsupported accusation of adultery	Free person: 80 lashes.
		Slave: 40 lashes.
		Convict is lightly attired when whipped.
Apostasy	Two witnesses or confessions	Man: death by beheading.
		Woman: imprisonment until repentance.
Highway robbery	Two witnesses or confessions	With homicide: death by beheading. The body is then displayed in a crucifixion-like form.
		Without homicide: amputation of right hand and left foot.
		If arrested before commission: imprisonment until repentance.
Use of alcohol	Two witnesses or confessions	Free person: 80 lashes (*Shafi'i,* 40).
		Slave: 40 lashes.
		Public whipping is applied with a stick, using moderate force without raising the hand above the head so as not to lacerate the skin. Blows are spread over the body and are not to be applied to the face and head. A man stands, and a woman is seated. A doctor is present. Flogging is inflicted by scholars well versed in Islamic law, so that it is justly meted out.
Theft	Two witnesses or confessions	First offense: amputation of hand at wrist, by an authorized doctor.
		Second offense: amputation of second hand at wrist, by an authorized doctor.
		Third offense: amputation of foot at ankle, by an authorized doctor, or imprisonment until repentance.
Rebellion	Two witnesses or confessions	If captured: death. If surrendered or arrested: *Ta'azir* punishment.

Sources: From A. A. Mansour, "Hudud Crimes," in *The Islamic Criminal Justice System,* ed. M. C. Bassiouni (Dobbs Ferry, N.Y.: Oceana, 1982), 195.

By contrast, American criminal law focuses on ownership rather than custody, so that stealing something left in the open, including items sitting unattended in public places, clearly fall under laws against theft if the offender intends to take items known to be owned by others.

Extramarital Sexual Activity

Sexual relations outside marriage are believed to undermine marriage and lead to family conflict, jealousy, divorce, litigation, and the spread of disease.

Some American states continue to criminalize adultery and premarital cohabitation through old laws that remain on the books. However, these laws are rarely enforced, and many prosecutors doubt whether juries will convict people of such offenses because society has become more tolerant of such commonplace behavior.

Defamation

In addition to false accusations of fornication, this offense includes impugning the legitimacy of a woman's child. Defamation by a husband of his wife leads to divorce and is not subject to punishment.

Defamation under American law can lead to civil lawsuits concerning harmful falsehoods spoken or written about a person that significantly harm that person's reputation.

Highway Robbery

This crime interferes with commerce and creates fear among travelers and is therefore subject to punishment.

American robbery statutes typically apply in all contexts and are not focused on travelers. The primary exception is "carjacking" statutes that were enacted by Congress and state legislatures in response to highly publicized incidents of drivers being killed and injured by robbers who forcibly stole their vehicles as they sat at traffic lights or stop signs.

Use of Alcohol

Drinking wine and other intoxicating beverages is prohibited because it brings about indolence and inattention to religious duties.

By contrast, alcoholic beverages are legal in the United States, subject to regulations concerning the legal drinking age and criminal statutes concerning the operation of vehicles while a person is under the influence of alcohol.

Apostasy

This is the voluntary renunciation of Islam. The offense is committed by any Muslim who converts to another faith, worships idols, or rejects any of the tenets of Islam.

In the United States, the First Amendment protections for freedom of religion and freedom of speech permit people to change religions and to criticize the religions of others without fear of criminal prosecution.

Rebellion

Rebellion is the intentional, forceful overthrow or attempted overthrow of the legitimate leader of the Islamic state.

In the United States, the government can change only through the process of democratic elections. Any effort to use force as the means to overthrow the government will result in criminal prosecutions.

Sources: From *Islamic Criminal Law and Procedure: An Introduction,* by M. Lippman, S. McConville, and M. Yerushalmi, 42–43. From "Hudud Crimes," by A. A. Mansour, in M. C. Bassiouni (ed.), *The Islamic Criminal Justice System,* 195.

long as the entry was "willful and malicious—that is, made with the intent to commit a felony therein." Thus, in Pennsylvania one can be convicted of burglary for entering a store with the intent to steal even though the entry was made during business hours and without force.

Statutory Definitions of Crimes

Federal and state penal codes often define criminal acts somewhat differently. To find out how a state defines an offense, one must read its penal code; this will give a general idea of which acts are illegal. To understand the court's interpretations of the code, one must analyze the judicial opinions that have sought to clarify the law.

In the following discussion we focus on two of the eight index crimes of the Uniform Crime Reports (UCR), homicide and rape. The elements of these crimes are interpreted differently in different states.

Murder and Nonnegligent Manslaughter

The common-law definition of criminal homicide has been subdivided into degrees of murder and voluntary and involuntary manslaughter. In addition, some states have created new categories, such as reckless homicide, negligent homicide, and vehicular homicide. Each of these definitions involves slight variations in the *actus reus* and the *mens rea*. Table 4.1 defines these offenses according to the Uniform Crime Reports, which count murder and nonnegligent manslaughter as index offenses.

In legal language, the phrase *malice aforethought* is used to distinguish murder from manslaughter. This phrase indicates that the crime of murder is a deliberate, premeditated, and willful killing of another human being. Most states extend the definition of murder to these two circumstances: (1) defendants knew their behavior had a strong chance of causing death, showed indifference to life, and thus

Table 4.1 Definitions of offenses in the Uniform Crime Reports (Part I)

The exact descriptions of offenses differ from one state to another, but these UCR definitions provide a national standard that helps us distinguish among criminal acts.

1 **Criminal homicide:**

a. Murder and nonnegligent manslaughter: the willful (nonnegligent) killing of one human being by another. Deaths caused by negligence, attempts to kill, assaults to kill, suicides, accidental deaths and justifiable homicides are excluded. Justifiable homicides are limited to (1) the killing of a felon by a law enforcement officer in the line of duty and (2) the killing of a felon by a private citizen.

b. Manslaughter by negligence: the killing of another person through gross negligence. Excludes traffic fatalities. While manslaughter by negligence is a Part I crime, it is not included in the Crime Index.

2 **Forcible rape:**

The carnal knowledge of a female forcibly and against her will. Included are rapes by force and attempts or assaults to rape. Statutory offenses (no force used—victim under age of consent) are excluded.

3 **Robbery:**

The taking or attempting to take anything of value from the care, custody, or control of a person or persons by force or threat of force of violence and/or by putting the victim in fear.

4 **Aggravated assault:**

An unlawful attack by one person upon another for the purpose of inflicting severe or aggravated bodily injury. This type of assault usually is accompanied by the use of a weapon or by means likely to produce death or great bodily harm. Simple assaults are excluded.

5 **Burglary—breaking or entering:**

The unlawful entry of a structure to commit a felony or a theft. Attempted forcible entry is included.

6 **Larceny/theft (except motor vehicle theft):**

The unlawful taking, carrying, leading, or riding away of property from the possession or constructive possession of another. Examples are thefts of bicycles or automobile accessories, shoplifting, pocket picking, or the stealing of any property or article that is not taken by force and violence or by fraud. Attempted larcenies are included. Embezzlement, "con" games, forgery, worthless checks, and so on, are excluded.

7 **Motor vehicle theft:**

The theft or attempted theft of a motor vehicle. A motor vehicle is self-propelled and runs on the surface and not on rails. Specifically excluded from this category are motorboats, construction equipment, airplanes, and farming equipment.

8 **Arson:**

Any willful or malicious burning or attempt to burn, with or without intent to defraud, a dwelling house, a public building, a motor vehicle or an aircraft, the personal property of another, and so on.

Source: Federal Bureau of Investigation, *Crime in the United States, 2001* (Washington, D.C.: U.S. Government Printing Offiice, 2002)

recklessly engaged in conduct that caused death, or (2) defendants' behavior caused death while they were committing a felony. Mitigating circumstances, such as "the heat of passion" or extreme provocation, would reduce the offense to manslaughter because the requirement of malice aforethought would be absent or reduced. Likewise, manslaughter would include a death resulting from an attempt to defend oneself that was not fully excused as self-defense. It might also include a death resulting from recklessness or negligence.

PhotoEdit

L.A.P.D. officers examine the body of a man killed in a drive-by shooting. Police must find the perpetrator and prosecutors must convince a jury that the crime fits the definition of criminal homicide as outlined in the penal code.

Rape

In recent years pressure has mounted, especially from women's groups, for stricter enforcement of laws against rape and for greater sensitivity toward victims. Successful prosecution of suspected rapists is difficult because it may not be possible to prove *actus reus* and *mens rea* (Hickey, 1993). Because the act usually takes place in private, prosecutors may have difficulty showing that sexual intercourse took place without consent. Some states have required evidence from someone other than the victim. Force is a necessary element in the definition of rape. In some courts, the absence of injury to the victim's body has been taken to show that there was no resistance, which may imply that consent was given. Since the 1970s, many jurisdictions have either eliminated the traditional requirements of corroborating evidence and resistance by the victim or interpreted those requirements as demanding only minimal substantiation (Horney and Spohn, 1991).

For information about the prosecution of rape cases, see the Web page for the Rhode Island Attorney General's Domestic Violence and Sexual Assault Unit at http://www.riag.state.ri.us/criminal/domestic.html.

Another problem in prosecuting rape is that rape victims often feel humiliated when their identities are revealed and they are questioned in court about actions that could indicate consent to engage in sex. Many victims therefore are reluctant to press charges (Bast, 1995). Some victims are unwilling even to report rape because of the insensitive way victims have been treated. In recent decades many states have enacted laws that limit the kinds of questions that can be asked of rape victims in courts, especially questions concerning the victim's reputation or past sexual history.

Unlike murder, rape is not usually divided into degrees, but under some circumstances offenders are charged with other offenses, such as "deviate sexual intercourse," "sexual assault," "statutory rape," or "aggravated assault." These charges can be used to designate sexual offenses that do not contain all the elements necessary to prove rape.

From this review of the crimes of murder and rape, we can see that substantive criminal law defines the conditions that must be met before a person can be convicted of an offense. The seven principles of Western law categorize these doctrines, and the penal code of each of the states and the laws of the United States define offenses in precise terms. But as the following Close Up box shows, individual perceptions of what constitutes a crime also come into play. How can the court system determine if rape occurred when the defendant claims that the victim consented to have sex? Does the task of reaching judgment become even more difficult when the victim and alleged assailant are dating and have previously engaged in consensual sex? What if the defendant did not actually engage in any sex acts but merely videotaped others having sex with the victim? Should the defendant still be held criminally accountable?

8. What kinds of reforms have been made in criminal law concerning rape?

Acquaintance Rape

On January 31, 2002, a woman and several of her friends met Oakland Raiders professional football player Darrell Russell at a bar in San Francisco. She went with Russell and his friends to another player's house where two men had sex with her while Russell allegedly videotaped the encounter. She had been dating Russell for several months and testified in court that she had previously had consensual sex with him on three occasions. She later claimed that she could remember little about the January evening except for faint recollections of being attacked and seeing someone holding a video camera. She believed that Russell, the person who handed her a drink at the club, had drugged her with a "date rape" drug that caused her to lose consciousness and suppressed her memories. By contrast, Russell told police that the woman consented to the sexual encounter. Russell's attorneys claimed that the woman consented to sex, dressed provocatively, and bragged about posing for *Playboy* magazine. Moreover, during a tough cross-examination of the woman at a preliminary hearing, the woman admitted that she had previously had sex with Russell and another player during one 30-minute period. One defense attorney also implied that the alleged victim was just a football groupie who hoped to sue Russell for millions of dollars as a result of her allegations. Russell was arrested and initially charged with 25 felonies as an accomplice to sex crimes. His bail was set at $1.2 million.

Does the prosecutor appear to have a strong case against Russell? If the victim really only has vague memories, how can prosecutors know, let alone prove, that a rape occurred? In determining whether to proceed with charges, how should the judge and prosecutor evaluate the evidence about the woman's sexual history that was revealed during the cross-examination at the preliminary hearing? Is such information relevant to the issue of whether a rape occurred?

Sources: "Darrell Russell Told Police that Alleged Rape Victim Gave Consent," *San Jose Mercury News,* June 13, 2002 (http://www.bayarea.com); "Defense Lawyer Calls Victim 'A Willing Participant,'" February 8, 2002 (http://www.msn.espn.go.com/nfl/news); "Russell's Accuser Recalls Little of Incident," *Santa Rosa Press Democrat,* June 11, 2002 (http://www.pressdemocrat.com/raiders/stories).

Researching the Internet

To read about research on acquaintance rape, see http://www.aaets.org/arts/art13.htm.

Responsibility for Criminal Acts

Thus far we have described the elements of crime and the legal definition of offenses; we now need to look at the question of responsibility. Of the seven principles of criminal law, *mens rea* is crucial in establishing responsibility for the act. To obtain a conviction, the prosecution must show that the offender not only committed the illegal act but also did so in a state of mind that makes it appropriate to hold him or her responsible for the act. In April 1999, 11-year-old twin boys in rural Vance County, North Carolina, killed their father and shot their mother and sister in a spontaneous shooting rampage that left authorities perplexed (Griffin and Rhee, 1999). Were these young boys old enough to plan their crime and understand the consequences of their actions? Is a child capable of forming the same intent to commit a crime that an adult forms? The analysis of *mens rea* is difficult because the court must inquire into the defendant's mental state at the time the offense was committed. In other words, it must determine what someone was thinking when he or she performed an act.

Many defendants admit that they committed the harmful act but they still plead not guilty. They do so not only because they know that the state must prove them guilty but also because they—or their attorneys—may believe that *mens rea* was not present. Accidents are the clearest examples of such situations: The defendant argues that it was an accident that the gun went off and the neighbor was killed, or that the pedestrian suddenly crossed into the path of the car. As Justice Oliver Wendell Holmes once said, "Even a dog distinguishes between being stumbled over and being kicked" (O. W. Holmes, 1881:3).

The courts label events *accidents* when responsibility is not fixed; *mens rea* is not present, because the event was not intentional. But a court may not accept the claim that an event was an accident. In some cases the offender is so negligent or reckless that the court may hold him or her responsible for some degree of the resulting harm. If a passing pedestrian was killed as the result of a game of throwing a loaded gun into the air and watching it fire when it hit the ground, the reckless gun-tossers could be held responsible. If a pedestrian was killed by a car in which the driver was preoccupied with speaking on a cellular phone, the reckless driver could be charged with a crime. The court holds people accountable for irresponsible actions that cause serious harms; such actions are not easily justified as being mere "accidents" for which no one should be punished. How would you apply this concept to the actions of Kenneth Powell, the man presented at the beginning of the chapter, who facilitated the actions of a drunk driver that resulted in a fatal collision?

Note that *mens rea,* or criminal responsibility, may occur even when the defendant had no motive or specific intention to cause harm. In other words, motives do not establish *mens rea;* rather, the nature and level of one's intent do. The *Model Penal Code* lists four mental states that can be used to meet the requirement of *mens rea:* the act must have been performed intentionally, knowingly, recklessly, or negligently. Some offenses require a high degree of intent. For example, larceny requires a finding that the defendant intentionally took property to which she knew she was not entitled, intending to deprive the rightful owner of it permanently.

A major exception to the *mens rea* principle has to do with public welfare offenses or **strict liability** offenses—criminal acts that require no showing of intent. Most of these offenses are defined in a type of laws first enacted in England and the United States in the late 1800s. They dealt with issues arising from urban industrialization, such as sanitation, pure food, decent housing, and public safety. Often the language of the law did not refer to *mens rea.* Some courts ruled that employers were not responsible for the carelessness of their workers because they had no knowledge of the criminal offenses being committed by them. An employer who did not know that the food being canned by his employees was contaminated, for example, was not held responsible for a violation of pure food laws, even if people who ate the food died. Other courts, however, ruled that such owners were responsible to the public to ensure the quality of their products, and therefore they could be found criminally liable if they failed to meet the standards set forth in the law. Some experts believe that the principle should be applied only to violations of health and safety regulations that carry no prison sentence or stigma. In practice, the penalty in such cases is usually imposed on business owners only after many failed attempts to persuade them to obey the law.

strict liability
An obligation or duty that when broken is an offense that can be judged criminal without a showing of *mens rea,* or criminal intent; usually applied to regulatory offenses involving health and safety.

For an example of a court's decision upholding a conviction for strict liability offenses, see http://courtlink.utcourts.gov/opinions/mds/jeppson.htm. The offenses in question are municipal ordinances barring "animals running at large" and "dogs attacking persons and animals."

The absence of *mens rea,* then, does not guarantee a verdict of not guilty in every case. In most cases, however, it relieves defendants of responsibility for acts that would be labeled criminal if they had been intentional. Besides the defense of accidents, there are eight defenses based on lack of criminal intent: entrapment, self-defense, necessity, duress (coercion), immaturity, mistake of fact, intoxication, and insanity.

Entrapment

Entrapment is a defense that can be used to show lack of intent. The law excuses a defendant when it is shown that government agents have induced the person to commit the offense. That does not mean the police may not use undercover agents to set a trap for criminals, nor does it mean the police may not provide ordinary opportunities for the commission of a crime. But the entrapment defense may be used when the police have actually *encouraged* the criminal act.

entrapment
The defense that the individual was induced by the police to commit the criminal act.

The defense of entrapment evolved through a series of court decisions in the twentieth century. In earlier times, judges were less concerned with whether the police had baited a citizen into committing an illegal act and were more concerned with whether or not the citizen had taken the bait. Now when the police investigate a crime or implant the idea for a crime in the mind of a person who then commits the offense, entrapment may have occurred. Entrapment raises tough questions for judges, who must decide whether the police went too far toward making a crime occur that otherwise would not have happened (D. D. Camp, 1993).

The key question is the predisposition of the defendant. In 1992 the Supreme Court stressed that the prosecutor must show beyond a reasonable doubt that a defendant was predisposed to break the law before he or she was approached by government agents. The case involved Keith Jacobson, a Nebraska farmer who had ordered, from a California bookstore, magazines containing photographs of nude boys. The material did not violate the law at that time, but a few months later Congress passed the Child Protection Act, and the U.S. Postal Service and the Customs Service began enforcing it. These agencies set up five fictional organizations with names such as the American Hedonist Society and sent letters to Jacobson and others whose names were on the California bookstore's mailing list. The letters urged Jacobson to fight the new law by ordering items that "we believe you will find to be both interesting and stimulating." One postal inspector, using a pseudonym, even became Jacobson's "pen pal." Jacobson ordered the material and was arrested by federal agents. No other pornographic material was found in his home.

In the majority opinion, Justice Byron White wrote that government officials may not "originate a criminal design, implant in an innocent person's mind the disposition to commit a criminal act, and then induce commission of the crime so that the government may prosecute."

Self-Defense

A person who feels that he or she is in immediate danger of being harmed by another person may ward off the attack in *self-defense*. The laws of most states also recognize the right to defend others from attack, to protect property, and to prevent a crime. For example, in August 2002, T. J. Duckett, an African American football player for the Atlanta Falcons, was attacked by three white men who yelled racial slurs at him as he walked toward his car after a concert. Duckett lost a tooth and suffered a cut that required four stitches when he was struck with a bottle in the surprise attack. The 250-pound running back then defended himself, knocking one attacker unconscious and causing a second attacker to be hospitalized with injuries. The third attacker ran away. Although the attackers received the most serious injuries, they faced criminal charges because Duckett was entitled to defend himself with reasonable force against an unprovoked criminal assault (Winkeljohn, 2002).

The level of force used in self-defense cannot exceed the person's reasonable perception of the threat. Thus, a person may be justified in shooting a robber who is holding a gun to her head and threatening to kill her, but homeowners generally are not justified in shooting an unarmed burglar who has left the house and is running across the lawn.

Necessity

Unlike self-defense, in which a defendant feels that he or she must harm an aggressor to ward off an attack, the *necessity* defense is used when people break the law in order to save themselves or prevent some greater harm. A person who speeds through a red light to get an injured child to the hospital or breaks into a building to seek refuge from a hurricane could claim to be violating the law out of necessity.

The English case *The Queen v. Dudley and Stephens* (1884) offers a famous example of necessity. After their ship sank, four sailors were adrift in the ocean without food or water. Twenty days later, two of the sailors, Thomas Dudley and Edwin Stephens, killed the youngest sailor, the cabin boy, and ate his flesh. Four days later they were rescued by a passing ship. When they returned to England, they were tried for murder. The court found that

> if the men had not fed upon the body of the boy they would . . . within the four days have died of famine. That the boy, being in a much weaker condition, was likely to have died before them. That at the time of the act there was no sail in sight, nor any reasonable prospect of relief. That under these circumstances there appeared to the prisoners that unless they then fed or very soon fed upon the boy or one of themselves they would die of starvation. That there was no appreciable chance of saving life except by killing some one for the others to eat.

Despite these findings, the court did not accept their defense of necessity. Lord Coleridge, the chief justice, argued that regardless of the degree of need, standards had to be maintained and the law not weakened. Dudley and Stephens were convicted and sentenced to death, but the Crown later reduced the sentence to 6 months' imprisonment.

Duress (Coercion)

The defense of *duress* arises when someone commits a crime because he or she is coerced by another person. During a bank robbery, for instance, if an armed robber forces one of the bank's customers at gunpoint to drive the getaway car, the customer would be able to claim duress. However, courts generally are not willing to accept this defense if people do not try to escape from the situation. After heiress Patty Hearst was kidnapped by a radical political group and held for many months, she took part in some of the group's armed robberies. She could not use the defense of duress because, in the court's view, she took part in the crimes without being directly coerced by her captors.

Immaturity

Anglo-American law excuses criminal acts by children under age seven on the grounds of their *immaturity* and lack of responsibility for their actions—*mens rea* is not present. Common law has presumed that children aged seven to fourteen are not liable for their criminal acts; however, prosecutors have been able to present evidence of a child's mental capacity to form *mens rea*. Juries can assume the presence of a guilty mind if it can be shown, for example, that the child hid evidence or tried to bribe a witness. As a child grows older, the assumption of immaturity weakens. Since the development of juvenile courts in the 1890s, children above age seven generally have not been tried by the same rules as adults. In some situations, however, children can be tried as adults—if, for example, they are repeat offenders or are charged with a particularly heinous crime. Because of the public's concerns about violent crimes by young people, in the 1990s it became increasingly common to see prosecutors seek to hold children responsible for serious crimes in the same manner that adults are held responsible. For example, prosecutors in Pontiac, Michigan, charged an 11-year-old boy with first-degree murder and succeeded in having a court permit them to try the boy as adult, despite the fact that experts concluded the defendant had the abstract reasoning abilities of a six-year-old (Loof, 1999).

Mistake of Fact

The courts have generally upheld the view that ignorance of the law is no excuse for committing an illegal act. But if an accused person has made a *mistake of fact* in some crucial way, that may serve as a defense (Christopher, 1994). For example, suppose some teenagers ask your permission to grow sunflowers in a vacant lot behind your home. You help them weed the garden and water the plants. Then it turns out that they are growing marijuana. You were not aware of this because you have no idea what a marijuana plant looks like. Should you be convicted for growing an illegal drug on your property? The answer depends on the specific degree of knowledge and intent that the prosecution must prove for that offense. The success of such a defense may also depend on the extent to which jurors understand and sympathize with your mistake.

Intoxication

The law does not relieve an individual of responsibility for acts performed while voluntarily intoxicated. There are, however, cases in which *intoxication* can be used as a defense, as when a person has been tricked into consuming a substance without knowing that it may cause intoxication. More complex are cases in which the defendant must be shown to have had a specific, rather than a general, intent to commit a crime. For example, someone may claim that they were too drunk to realize that they had left a restaurant without paying the bill. Drunkenness can also be used as a mitigating factor to reduce the seriousness of a charge. In 1996 the U.S. Supreme Court narrowly approved a Montana law that barred defendants from using evidence of voluntary intoxication to attempt to show that they lacked the *mens rea* element of criminal offenses (*Montana v. Egelhoff*). Thus states can enact laws that prevent the use of the intoxication defense.

Insanity

The defense of *insanity* has engendered a heated debate. The public believes that many criminals "escape" punishment through the skillful use of psychiatric testimony. Yet only about 1 percent of incarcerated offenders are held in mental hospitals because they were found "not guilty by reason of insanity." The insanity defense is rare and is generally used only in serious cases or where there is no other valid defense.

Over time American courts have used five tests of criminal responsibility involving insanity: the M'Naghten Rule, the Irresistible Impulse Test, the Durham Rule, the *Model Penal Code*'s Substantial Capacity Test, and the test defined in the federal Comprehensive Crime Control Act of 1984. These tests are summarized in Table 4.2, and the tests used in the various states are shown in Figure 4.3.

Before 1843 the insanity defense could be used only by those who were so lacking in understanding that they could not know what they were doing. In that year Daniel M'Naghten was acquitted of killing Edward Drummond, a man he had thought was Sir Robert Peel, the prime minister of Great Britain. M'Naghten claimed that he had been delusional at the time of the killing, but the public outcry against his acquittal caused the House of Lords to ask the court to define the law with regard to delusional persons. The judges of the Queen's Bench answered

Table 4.2 Insanity defense standards

The standards for the insanity defense have evolved over time.

Test	Legal Standard Because of Mental Illness	Final Burden of Proof	Who Bears Burden of Proof
M'Naghten (1843)	"Didn't know what he was doing or didn't know it was wrong"	Varies from proof by a balance of probabilities on the defense to proof beyond a reasonable doubt on the prosecutor	
Irresistible Impulse (1897)	"Could not control his conduct"		
Durham (1954)	"The criminal act was caused by his mental illness"	Beyond a reasonable doubt	Prosecutor
Model Penal Code (1972)	"Lacks substantial capacity to appreciate the wrongfulness of his conduct or to control it"	Beyond a reasonable doubt	Prosecutor
Present federal law	"Lacks capacity to appreciate the wrongfulness of his conduct"	Clear and convincing evidence	Defense

Source: National Institute of Justice, *Crime File*, "Insanity Defense," a film prepared by Norval Morris (Washington, D.C.: Government Printing Office, n.d.).

Figure 4.3 **Standards for insanity used by the states**
State laws differ in the standards used to determine insanity.

Sources: Adapted from Bureau of Justice Statistics, *Report to the Nation on Crime and Justice,* 2nd ed. (Washington, D.C.: U.S. Government Printing Office, 1988), 87; Ingo Keilitz and Junikus Fulton, *The Insanity Defense and Its Alternatives: A Guide for Policy Makers* (Williamsburg, Va.: National Center for State Courts, 1984), 15, 88–89.

by saying that a finding of guilt cannot be made if, "at the time of the committing of the act, the party accused was laboring under such a defect of reason, from disease of the mind, as not to know the nature and quality of the act he was doing, or if he did know it that he did not know he was doing what was wrong." This test, often referred to as the "right-from-wrong test," is accepted by many states today.

Over the years many have criticized the M'Naghten Rule as not in keeping with modern concepts of mental disorder. Some have argued that people may be able to distinguish right from wrong and still be insane in the psychiatric sense, and that terms such as *disease of the mind, know,* and *nature and quality of the act* have not been defined adequately. Some states allow defendants to plead that, while they knew what they were doing was wrong, they could not control an urge to commit the crime. The Irresistible Impulse Test excuses defendants when a mental disease was controlling their behavior even though they knew that what they were doing was wrong. Five states use this test along with the M'Naghten Rule.

The Durham Rule, originally developed in New Hampshire in 1871, was adopted by the Circuit Court of Appeals for the District of Columbia in 1954 in the case of *Durham v. United States.* Monte Durham had a long history of criminal activity and mental illness. When he was 26, he and two companions broke into a house. He was found guilty, and the appeal judge, David Bazelon, rejected the M'Naghten Rule, stating that an accused person is not criminally responsible "if an unlawful act is the product of mental disease or mental defect." The Durham Rule defined insanity more broadly than did the M'Naghten Rule by assuming that insanity is caused by many factors, not all of which may be present in every case.

The Durham Rule aroused controversy. It was argued that the rule offered no useful definition of "mental disease or defect." By 1972 (*United States v.*

Close up: The Insanity Defense and Its Aftermath

Defendants who are judged not guilty by reason of insanity are typically committed to mental hospitals. If medical experts subsequently determine that they are not a danger to themselves or the community, they may be released. New York law provides the opportunity for a jury trial if a person acquitted through the insanity defense wants to challenge a judge's decision to extend the length of confinement in a mental hospital. In April 1999 Albert Fentress, a former schoolteacher, sought such a jury trial. Twenty years earlier, he had tortured, killed, and cannibalized a teenager, but he had been found not guilty by reason of insanity. The jury listened to four expert witnesses presented by the prosecution who asserted that Mr. Fentress had not changed during two decades in the hospital. They also listened to four expert witnesses, including doctors from the state's psychiatric facility, who said that Mr. Fentress no longer posed a danger to society. How can the average juror know which set of experts presented the most accurate diagnosis? In the end, the jury voted 5 to 1 that although Fentress was still mentally ill, he no longer needed to be confined to the hospital.

Undoubtedly, many members of the public would be shocked to think that someone who has committed an outrageous, gruesome murder could be released to walk freely in society. Many members of the public were probably equally shocked in 1999 when John Hinckley, Jr., the man who shot President Ronald Reagan in 1981, was granted permission to take supervised outings away from the mental hospital where he had been confined after successfully presenting an insanity defense. Some states have sought to prevent the release of mentally ill, violent offenders by enacting statutes that permit the state to hold such people in mental hospitals after they have finished serving prison sentences. In 1997 the U.S. Supreme Court approved the use of such laws for people diagnosed as "sexually violent predators" (*Kansas v. Hendricks*). However, such laws apply only to people who are convicted of crimes, not to those found not guilty by reason of insanity.

Brawner) the federal courts had overturned the Durham Rule in favor of a modified version of a test proposed in the *Model Penal Code*. By 1982 all federal courts and about half of the state courts had adopted the *Model Penal Code*'s Substantial Capacity Test, which states that a person is not responsible for criminal conduct "if at the time of such conduct as a result of mental disease or defect he lacks substantial capacity either to appreciate the criminality [wrongfulness] of his conduct or to conform his conduct to the requirements of law." The Substantial Capacity Test broadens and modifies the M'Naghten and Irresistible Impulse rules. Key terms have been changed to conform better with modern psychological concepts, and the standards lacking in *Durham* have been supplied. By stressing "substantial capacity," the test does not require that a defendant be unable to distinguish right from wrong.

AP Photo/Image from video pool

Andrea Yates pleaded not guilty by reason of insanity for the drowning of her five children. The prosecutor argued that Yates knew that what she was doing was wrong. The jury found her guilty but spared her the death penalty, giving her life in prison.

All of the insanity tests are difficult to apply. Moreover, as the Close Up box shows, there are significant difficulties in deciding what to do with someone who has been found not guilty by reason of insanity. It is even possible that jurors' fears about seeing the offender turned loose might affect their decisions about whether the person was legally insane at the time of the crime.

John Hinckley's attempt to assassinate President Ronald Reagan in 1981 reopened the debate on the insanity defense. Television news footage showed that Hinckley had shot the president. Yet, with the help of psychiatrists, Hinckley's lawyers counteracted the prosecution's efforts to persuade the jury that Hinckley was sane. When Hinckley was acquitted, the public was outraged, and several states acted to limit or abolish the insanity defense. Twelve states introduced the

The jury's decision in the Fentress case led the Governor of New York to complain that "individuals like Albert Fentress can hide behind an insanity plea to avoid the prison time they deserve." However, an insanity acquittal does not always lead to more-lenient treatment for people committed to mental hospitals. In Virginia, for example, one-quarter of the 239 people confined to mental hospitals after asserting the insanity defense were only accused of misdemeanors. Thus, if they had been convicted, they would have served a jail sentence of one year or less. Instead, some of them may serve much longer commitments in the hospital. A man named Leroy Turner has spent more than 13 years in Virginia's Central State Hospital after having been found not guilty by reason of insanity for breaking a window. His doctors say that his substance abuse problems are in remission and he is not psychotic. Despite the fact that some mental health experts estimate that as many as 40 percent of Virginia's sanity acquittees no longer need to be hospitalized, the state's Forensic Review Panel approves relatively few petitions for release. Is it fair for people to lose their liberty for long periods when they have been acquitted of minor crimes?

As the foregoing examples show, the insanity defense presents significant problems. How can we follow our tradition of reserving criminal convictions for those people with sufficient mental capacity yet also protect society from dangerous people and avoid unduly long hospital commitments for insanity acquittees charged with minor offenses?

These problems may be especially difficult when decision-making responsibilities are placed in the hands of jurors who lack knowledge about psychiatry and mental illness. In 1999 a jury in Sault Sainte Marie, Michigan, convicted Nathan Hanna of murdering a friend at work and sentenced him to life in prison, despite the fact that one of the state's own psychiatrists, who usually testifies for the prosecution in insanity defense cases, concluded that mental illness led Hanna to believe that the victim was "the Antichrist" whom God ordered him to kill. Did the jurors follow the proper test for the insanity defense, or were they worried that Hanna might someday be released if they found him not guilty by reason of insanity? It is impossible to know. Clearly, judges, politicians, and the public periodically show great concern about how the insanity defense works in practice. In the aftermath of public outcry about the impending release of Albert Fentress in New York, a state judge overturned the jury's release decision and kept Fentress in the mental hospital. Do these examples raise questions about society's commitment to the insanity defense? If there are so many problems, then why do we keep the insanity defense? What would you do about this issue?

Sources: Drawn from Charlie LeDuff, "Jury Decides Hospitalized Killer in Cannibalism Case Can Go Free," *New York Times*, April 22, 1999; John Flesher, "Testimony: Defendant Thought Victim Was Antichrist," *Lansing State Journal*, June 25, 1999, p. 3D; David M. Halbfiinger, "Verdict in Cannibalism Case Is Set Aside," *New York Times*, June 11, 1999; "In Virginia, Insanity Plea Can Bring Long Incarceration," *Washington Post*, June 21, 1999, p. B3; "Man Gets Life Sentence in Killing," *Lansing State Journal*, August 4, 1999, p. 3B; Bill Miller, "Judges Let Stand Hinckley Ruling; St. Elizabeths Officials Have Right to Decide on Day Trips," *Washington Post*, April 28, 1999, p.

To see how the American Psychiatric Association explains the insanity defense to the American public, see http://www.psych.org/public_info/insanity.cfm.

defense of "guilty but mentally ill" (Klofas and Yandrasits, 1989). This defense allows a jury to find the accused guilty but requires that he or she be given psychiatric treatment while in prison (L. A. Callahan et al., 1992). As indicated in the Close Up box, Hinckley gained permission to take supervised day trips away from the hospital in 1999. The fact that the man who shot the president of the United States could walk among other members of the public aroused new debates about the insanity defense.

In 1997 a Pennsylvania jury found multimillionaire John du Pont guilty of third-degree murder but mentally ill in the shooting of Olympic wrestler David Schultz. Under Pennsylvania law, a verdict of guilty but mentally ill means the defendant was sane enough to understand right from wrong. Third-degree murder is defined as killing without premeditation. Psychiatrists had testified that du Pont was a paranoid schizophrenic and that this mental illness contributed to the murder. The verdict means that du Pont will first go to a mental institution and then, if medical authorities say he is well enough, to prison to serve his sentence.

Norval Morris suggests that the defendant's condition after the crime should be taken into account in deciding whether he or she should be confined in a hospital or a prison (Morris, 1982). Illness at the time of the crime should be considered also in deciding the charge on which the defendant may be convicted. For example, a defendant found to have diminished mental capacity would be convicted of manslaughter rather than murder.

The Comprehensive Crime Control Act of 1984 changed the federal rules on the insanity defense by limiting it to those who cannot, because of severe mental disease or defect, understand the nature or the wrongfulness of their acts. This change means that the Irresistible Impulse Test cannot be used in the federal courts. It also shifts the burden of proof from the prosecutor, who in some federal courts had to prove beyond a reasonable doubt that the defendant was not insane, to the defendant, who has to prove his or her insanity. The act also creates a new procedure whereby a person who is found not guilty only by reason of insanity must be committed to a mental hospital until he or she no longer poses a danger to society. These rules apply only to federal courts, but they are spreading to several states.

The movement away from the insanity defense reduces the importance of *mens rea*. Many reform efforts have aimed at punishing crimes without regard for the knowledge and intentions of the offender.

The U.S. Supreme Court has reminded states that they cannot do away with considerations of mental competence in all cases. In the past, people who lacked the mental competence to understand the charges against them and to assist in their own defense were committed to mental hospitals until they were able to stand trial (T. Ho, 1998; Winick, 1995). In 1996 the justices unanimously declared that states cannot require defendants to meet an excessively high standard in proving incompetence to stand trial. Such standards would result in too many trials of people who lack the necessary mental competence to face charges (*Cooper v. Oklahoma*).

In practice, the outcomes of the various insanity tests frequently depend on jurors' reactions to the opinions of psychiatrists presented as expert witnesses by the prosecution and defense. For example, the prosecution's psychiatrist will testify that the defendant does not meet the standard for insanity, while the defendant's psychiatrist will testify that the defendant does meet that standard. The psychiatrists themselves do not decide whether the defendant is responsible for the crime. Instead, the jurors decide, based on the psychiatrists' testimony and other factors. They may take into account the seriousness of the crime and their own beliefs about the insanity defense. The rules for proving insanity thus clearly favor wealthy defendants who can afford to hire psychiatrists as expert witnesses.

There is nothing automatic about the insanity defense, even for defendants who engage in highly abnormal behavior (Steury, 1993). In fact, it is rare for anyone to successfully present an insanity defense. In 1991, for example, Jeffrey Dahmer was arrested for drugging and killing more than a dozen men and boys whom he had lured to his Milwaukee apartment. He had had sex with the corpses, cut up and eaten the bodies, and saved body parts in his refrigerator. Despite his shocking behavior, a Wisconsin jury rejected his insanity defense, perhaps because they feared that he might be released someday if he were not held fully responsible for the crimes.

Even when defendants are acquitted by reason of insanity, they are nearly always committed to a mental hospital (P. H. Robinson, 1993). Although the criminal justice system does not consider hospitalization to be "punishment," commitment to a psychiatric ward results in loss of liberty and often a longer period of confinement than if the person had been sentenced to prison. A robber may have faced only ten years in prison, yet an acquittal by reason of insanity may lead to a lifetime of hospital confinement if the psychiatrists never find that he has recovered enough to be released. Thus the notion that those acquitted by reason of insanity have somehow "beaten the rap" may not reflect reality.

check point

9. What kind of offense has no *mens rea* requirement?
10. What are the defenses in substantive criminal law?
11. What are the tests of criminal responsibility used for the insanity defense?

procedural due process
The constitutional requirement that all people be treated fairly and justly by government officials. An accused person can be arrested, prosecuted, tried, and punished only in accordance with procedures prescribed by law.

Procedural Criminal Law

Procedural law defines how the state must process cases. According to **procedural due process,** accused people must be tried in accordance with legal procedures. The procedures include providing the rights granted by the Constitution to criminal defendants. As we saw in Chapter 1, the due process model is based on the premise that freedom is so valuable that efforts must be made to prevent erroneous decisions that would deprive an innocent person of his or her freedom. Rights are not only intended to prevent the innocent from being wrongly convicted; they also seek to prevent unfair police and prosecution practices aimed at guilty people, such as conducting improper searches, using violence to pressure people to confess, and denying defendants a fair trial.

The concept of due process dates from the thirteenth century, when King John of England issued the Magna Carta, promising that "no free man shall be arrested, or imprisoned, or disseized, or outlawed, or exiled, or in any way molested; nor will we proceed against him unless by the lawful judgment of his peers or by the law of the land." This rule, that people must be tried not by arbitrary procedures but according to the process outlined in the law, became a basic principle of procedural law.

The importance of procedural law has been evident throughout history. American history contains many examples of police officers and prosecutors harassing and victimizing those who lack political power, including poor people, racial and ethnic minorities, and unpopular religious groups. The development of procedural safeguards through the decisions of the U.S. Supreme Court has helped protect citizens from such actions. Because of the weight it places on protecting procedural rights and preventing police misconduct, the Supreme Court may favor guilty people by ordering new trials or may even release them from custody.

Corbis/Bettmann

The Magna Carta, signed by England's King John in 1215, is the first written guarantee of due process. It established the principle that people must be arrested and tried according to the processes outlined in the law.

Individual rights and the protection against improper deprivations of liberty represent central American values. However, the protection of rights for the criminally accused can clash with competing American values that emphasize the control of crime as an important component of protecting all citizens' freedom of movement and sense of security. Because the rules of procedural criminal law can sometimes lead to the release of guilty people, some observers believe that it is weighted too heavily in favor of American values emphasizing individuals' rights rather than equally valid American values that emphasize the protection of the community.

Public opinion does not always support the decisions by the Supreme Court and other courts that uphold the rights of criminal defendants and convicted offenders. Many Americans would prefer that other goals for society, such as stopping drugs and ensuring that guilty people are punished, would take a higher priority over the protection of rights. Such opinions raise questions about Americans' commitment to the Bill of Rights. Public opinion data indicate that most first-year college students believe that courts have placed too much emphasis on the rights of criminal defendants. Moreover, this sentiment has grown over the past 30 years. In addition, although male and female students' support for rights differed in 1971, there is little difference between the two groups today. Do you agree that there are too many rights? Can you identify specific rights that give too much protection to criminal defendants? Would reducing the rights available in the criminal justice process create any risks? See "What Americans Think."

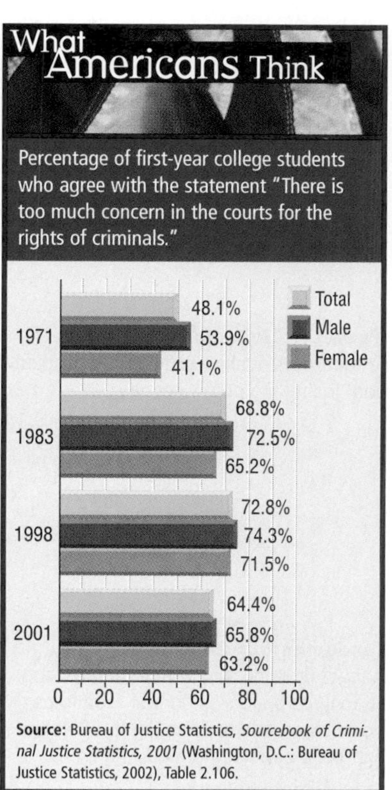

Source: Bureau of Justice Statistics, *Sourcebook of Criminal Justice Statistics, 2001* (Washington, D.C.: Bureau of Justice Statistics, 2002), Table 2.106.

Unlike substantive criminal law, which is defined by legislatures through statutes, procedural criminal law is defined by courts through judicial rulings. Judges interpret the provisions of the U.S. Constitution and state constitutions, and those interpretations establish the procedures that government officials must follow. Because it has the authority to review cases from state supreme courts as well as from federal courts, the U.S. Supreme Court has played a major role in defining procedural criminal law. The Supreme Court's influence stems from its power to define the meaning of the U.S. Constitution, especially the Bill of Rights. Although public opinion may clash with Supreme Court rulings, the

Supreme Court can make independent decisions because its members cannot be removed from office by the voters.

The Bill of Rights

The U.S. Constitution contained few references to criminal justice when it was ratified in 1788 and 1789. Because many people were concerned that the document did not set forth the rights of individuals in enough detail, in 1791 ten amendments were added that list legal protections against actions of the government. These are the Bill of Rights. Four of these amendments concern criminal justice issues. The Fourth Amendment bars unreasonable searches and seizures. The Fifth Amendment outlines basic due process rights in criminal cases. For example, consistent with the assumption that the state must prove the defendant's guilt, protection against **self-incrimination** means that people cannot be forced to respond to questions whose answers may reveal that they have committed a crime. The protection against **double jeopardy** means that a person may be subjected to only one prosecution or punishment for a single offense within the same jurisdiction. The Sixth Amendment provides for the right to a speedy, fair, and public trial by an impartial jury, as well as the right to counsel. The Eighth Amendment bars excessive bail, excessive fines, and cruel and unusual punishment.

self-incrimination
The act of exposing oneself to prosecution by being forced to respond to questions whose answers may reveal that one has committed a crime. The Fifth Amendment protects defendants against self-incrimination. In any criminal proceeding, the prosecution must prove the charges by means of evidence other than the testimony of the accused.

double jeopardy
The subjecting of a person to prosecution more than once in the same jurisdiction for the same offense; prohibited by the Fifth Amendment.

For most of American history, the Bill of Rights did not apply to most criminal cases, because it was designed to protect people from abusive actions by the *federal* government. It did not seek to protect people from state and local officials, who handled nearly all criminal cases. This view was upheld by the U.S. Supreme Court in the 1833 case of ***Barron v. Baltimore.*** However, as we shall see shortly, this view gradually changed in the middle of the twentieth century.

***Barron v. Baltimore* (1833)**
The protections of the Bill of Rights apply only to actions of the federal government.

The Bill of Rights is in the National Archives and is described on its Web site: http://www.nara.gov.

The Fourteenth Amendment and Due Process

After the Civil War, three amendments were added to the Constitution. These amendments were designed to protect individuals' rights against infringement by state and local government officials. Two of the amendments had little impact on criminal justice: The Thirteenth Amendment abolished slavery and the Fifteenth Amendment attempted to prohibit racial discrimination in voting. The other amendment, however, profoundly affected criminal justice.

The Fourteenth Amendment, ratified in 1868, barred states from violating people's right to due process of law. It states that "no State shall . . . deprive any person of life, liberty, or property without due process of law; nor deny to any person within its jurisdiction the equal protection of the laws." These rights to due process and equal protection served as a basis for protecting individuals from abusive actions by local criminal justice officials. However, the terms *due process* and *equal protection* are so vague that it was left to the U.S. Supreme Court to decide if and how these new rights applied to the criminal justice process.

For example, in ***Powell v. Alabama* (1932)**, the Supreme Court ruled that the due process clause required courts to provide attorneys for poor defendants facing the death penalty. This decision stemmed from a notorious case in Alabama in which nine African American men, known as the "Scottsboro boys," were quickly convicted and condemned to death for allegedly raping two white women, even though one of the alleged victims later admitted that she had lied about the rape (Goodman, 1994).

***Powell v. Alabama* (1932)**
An attorney must be provided to a defendant facing the death penalty.

In these early cases, the justices had not developed clear rules for deciding which specific rights applied against state and local officials as components of the due process clause of the Fourteenth Amendment. They implied that procedures must meet a basic standard of **fundamental fairness.** In essence, the justices simply reacted against brutal situations that shocked their consciences. In doing so, they showed the importance of procedural criminal law in protecting individuals from abusive and unjust actions by government officials.

fundamental fairness
A legal doctrine supporting the idea that so long as a state's conduct maintains basic standards of fairness, the Constitution has not been violated.

The Due Process Revolution

From the 1930s to the 1960s, the fundamental fairness doctrine was supported by a majority of the Supreme Court justices. It was applied on a case-by-case basis, not always in a consistent way. After Earl Warren became chief justice in 1953, he led the Supreme Court in a revolution that changed the meaning and scope of constitutional rights. Instead of requiring state and local officials merely to uphold fundamental fairness, the Court began to require them to abide by the specific provisions of the Bill of Rights. Through the process of **incorporation,** the Supreme Court during the Warren Court era declared that elements of the Fourth, Fifth, Sixth, Eighth, and other amendments were part of the due process clause of the Fourteenth Amendment. Up to this point, states could design their own procedures so long as those procedures passed the fairness test. Under Warren's leadership, however, the Supreme Court's new approach imposed detailed procedural standards on the police and courts. As it applied more and more constitutional rights against the states, the Court made decisions that favored the interests of many criminal defendants. These defendants had their convictions overturned and received new trials because the Court believed that it was more important to protect the values underlying criminal procedure than to single-mindedly seek convictions of criminal offenders. In the eyes of many legal scholars, the Warren Court's decisions made criminal justice processes consistent with the American values of liberty, rights, and limited government authority.

incorporation
The extension of the due process clause of the Fourteenth Amendment to make binding on state governments the rights guaranteed in the first ten amendments to the U.S. Constitution (the Bill of Rights).

To critics, however, these decisions made the community more vulnerable to crime and thereby harmed American values by diminishing the overall sense of liberty and security in society. Warren and the other justices were strongly criticized by politicians, police chiefs, and members of the public. These critics believed that the Warren Court was rewriting constitutional law in a manner that gave too many legal protections to criminals who harm society. In addition, Warren and his colleagues were criticized for ignoring established precedents that defined rights in a limited fashion. Some people alleged that the justices were advancing their own political views rather than following the true meaning of the Constitution.

From 1962 to 1972 the Supreme Court, led by Chief Justices Earl Warren (1953–1969) and Warren Burger (1969–1986), applied most criminal justice rights in the U.S. Constitution against the states. By the end of this period, the process of incorporation was nearly complete. Criminal justice officials at all levels—federal, state, and local—were obligated to respect the constitutional rights of suspects and defendants. Today most Americans believe that these rights are essential (see "What Americans Think").

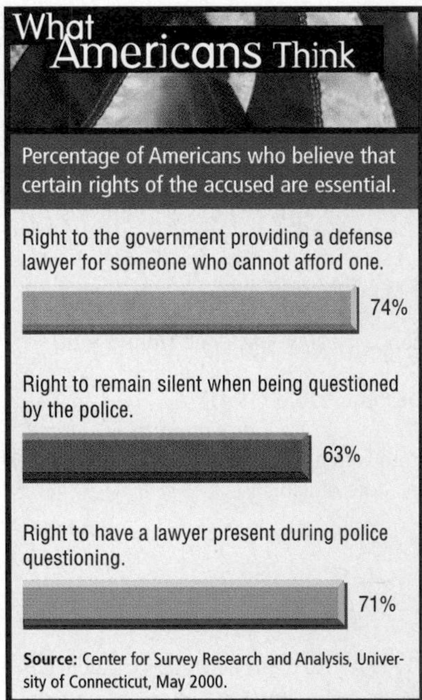

Source: Center for Survey Research and Analysis, University of Connecticut, May 2000.

check point

12. What is "incorporation"?
13. Prior to incorporation, what test was used by the Supreme Court to decide which rights applied to the states?
14. Which Supreme Court era (named for the chief justice) most significantly expanded the definitions of constitutional rights for criminal defendants?

The Fourth Amendment: Protection against Unreasonable Searches and Seizures

> The right of the people to be secure in their persons, houses, papers, and effects, against unreasonable searches and seizures, shall not be violated, and no Warrants shall issue, but upon probable cause, supported by Oath or affirmation, and particularly describing the place to be searched, and the persons or things to be seized.

Heightened airport security is an inconvenience to many but a necessary precaution for most Americans. Is there a Fourth Amendment right to resist these procedures?

The Fourth Amendment limits the ability of law enforcement officers to search a person or property in order to obtain evidence of criminal activity. It also limits the ability of the police to detain a person without justification (Perkins and Jamieson, 1995). The Fourth Amendment does not prevent the police from conducting searches; it merely protects people's privacy by barring "unreasonable" searches. It is up to the Supreme Court to define the situations in which a search is "reasonable" or "unreasonable." Because different Supreme Court justices do not always agree on the Constitution's meaning, the definitions of these words and the rules for police searches can change as the makeup of the Court changes.

The wording of the Fourth Amendment makes clear that the authors of the Bill of Rights did not believe that law enforcement officials should have the power to pursue criminals at all costs. The Fourth Amendment's protections apply to suspects as well as law-abiding citizens. Police officers are supposed to follow the rules for obtaining search warrants, and they may not conduct unreasonable searches even when trying to catch dangerous criminals.

exclusionary rule
The principle that illegally obtained evidence must be excluded from a trial.

***Mapp v. Ohio* (1961)**
The Fourth Amendment protects citizens from unreasonable searches and seizures by state officials.

In 1914 the Supreme Court declared, in *Weeks v. United States,* that federal courts must exclude any evidence that was obtained through an improper search by federal law enforcement agents. With this **exclusionary rule,** the Court created the principle that such evidence must be excluded from a trial; it was assumed that this would cause law enforcement officers to follow the dictates of the Fourth Amendment. The Supreme Court expanded this rule to include searches by state and local law enforcement officers in ***Mapp v. Ohio* (1961)** by incorporating the Fourth Amendment exclusionary rule into the Due Process Clause of the Fourteenth Amendment.

Go to the Public Policy feature on the American System of Criminal Justice CD to learn more about the issues surrounding the exclusionary rule.

To read one scholar's report arguing that the exclusionary rule is necessary and valuable, see http://www.cato.org/pubs/pas/pa-319es.html.

After being broadened during the Warren Court era (1953–1969), Fourth Amendment rights were narrowed during the chief justiceships of Warren Burger (1969–1986) and William Rehnquist (1986–present). New justices appointed to the Court during these eras defined rights less broadly. For example, in *United States v. Leon* (1984), the Court created a "good-faith" exception to the exclusionary rule. In this case police officers had used outdated information from an informant of unproven reliability to obtain a search warrant. Using that warrant, the police found illegal drugs in the course of their search. Under the rule established in *Mapp v. Ohio,* the drugs should have been excluded because the search warrant was defective. However, the justices created an exception to the exclusionary rule. Because the police had tried to follow proper procedures, and a judge, not the police, had made the error in issuing the improper warrant, the Supreme Court ruled that the evidence could be used against the defendant. Justice Byron White explained the ruling, writing that the social costs of excluding evidence outweighed the social benefits of deterring improper searches. White's claim is subject to debate because evidence is excluded in very few cases, and the police often have other evidence to support a conviction even when some evidence is barred (Nardulli, 1983; Uchida and Bynum, 1991).

This decision and others have made it easier for law enforcement officials to use evidence obtained through improper searches, but they have also made the exclusionary rule less clear (Crocker, 1993). The creation of exceptions makes it harder for police to know beforehand whether evidence obtained from an improper search can be used in a trial.

The Burger and Rehnquist Courts did not abolish the exclusionary rule, but they limited its applicability and gave police greater flexibility to conduct searches without obtaining a search warrant (Vaughn and del Carmen, 1997). For example, the Rehnquist Court made it much easier for police to conduct warrantless searches of cars and closed containers found inside cars. Such searches are often used in efforts to combat drug trafficking. In 1999, for example, the Supreme Court decided that when a police officer saw a syringe sticking out of the pocket of a car's driver, the police could search the purse of a car passenger, even though the officer had no specific reason to suspect that the passenger had any drugs (*Wyoming v. Houghton*). Officers have also used other approaches, such as stopping people who fit the profiles of suspected drug couriers. When the courts give police more flexibility in search and seizure actions, there are risks that innocent citizens will feel that their rights have been infringed (C. E. Smith, 2003).

check point

15. What controversial principle was applied against the states in *Mapp v. Ohio?*

The Supreme Court will undoubtedly continue to face new cases that force it to interpret the "reasonableness" of searches and the Fourth Amendment's warrant requirements. In recent years technological advances and new situations have led the Court to consider whether helicopter surveillance of property constitutes a search that requires a warrant (the justices said no) and whether the Fourth Amendment applies to the search and seizure of a noncitizen outside the United States by government agents (again, the justices said no). Other new issues will likely include electronic surveillance and prosecutors' efforts to gain access to computer files. Because of its composition, the Court probably will continue to tilt in favor of law enforcement officials and will not establish broader Fourth Amendment rights for criminal defendants. Despite its conservative orientation, however, the Court regularly demonstrates that it will not let police officers conduct any kind of search that they may wish to make (C. E. Smith and Dow, 2002). For example, in 2001, the Supreme Court found a constitutional violation when police officers, acting without a warrant, pointed a thermal imaging device at a house to detect the presence of heat-generating grow lights used to cultivate marijuana indoors (*Kyllo v. United States*).

The Fifth Amendment: Protection against Self-Incrimination and Double Jeopardy

> No person shall be held to answer for a capital, or otherwise infamous crime, unless on a presentment or indictment of a Grand Jury, except in cases arising in the land or naval forces, or in the Militia, when in actual service in time of war or public danger; nor shall any person be subject for the same offense to be twice put in jeopardy of life or limb; nor shall be compelled in any criminal case to be a witness against himself, nor be deprived of life, liberty, or property, without due process of law; nor shall private property be taken for public use, without just compensation.

The Fifth Amendment clearly states some key rights related to the investigation and prosecution of criminal suspects. Here we explore two of them: the protections against compelled self-incrimination and double jeopardy.

Self-Incrimination

One of the most important due process rights is the protection against compelled self-incrimination—that is, people cannot be pressured to act as witnesses against themselves (Gardner, 1993). This right is consistent with the assumption that the state must prove the defendant's guilt. It is connected to other protections, especially the Sixth Amendment right to counsel, because representation by a defense attorney is seen as a means of preventing self-incrimination during questioning by police or prosecutors (Richardson, 1993).

In the past, the validity of confessions hinged on their being voluntary, because a confession involves self-incrimination. Under the doctrine of fundamental fairness, which was applied before the 1960s, the Supreme Court was unwilling to allow confessions that were beaten out of suspects, that emerged after extended questioning, or that resulted from the use of other physical tactics. Such tactics can impose inhumane treatment on suspects and create risks that innocent people will be wrongly convicted. In the cases of ***Escobedo v. Illinois*** **(1964)** and ***Miranda v. Arizona*** **(1966)**, the Warren Court outraged politicians, law enforcement officials, and members of the public by placing limits on the ability of police to question suspects without an attorney present. The justices ruled that, prior to questioning, the police must inform detained suspects of their right to remain silent and their right to have an attorney present. In response, many police officers argued that they depended on interrogations and confessions as a major means of solving crimes (Cassell and Fowles, 1998). However, nearly four decades later, many suspects continue to confess for various reasons, such as feelings of guilt, inability to understand their rights, and the desire to gain a favorable plea bargain (Leo, 1996a; 1996b).

***Escobedo v. Illinois* (1964)**
An attorney must be provided to suspects when they are taken into police custody.

***Miranda v. Arizona* (1966)**
Confessions made by suspects in custody who were not notified of their due process rights cannot be admitted as evidence.

When they required them to read the "*Miranda* warnings" to suspects, the justices were not seeking to limit police officers' ability to investigate crimes. They were trying to satisfy the Fifth Amendment prohibition of compelled self-incrimination. They also knew that confessions can be unreliable, especially if no limits are set on questioning by the police. The justices knew that law enforcement officials often "solve" crimes when they are allowed to badger, intimidate, or coerce suspects into confessing. This may "solve" the crime, but whether the person who confessed is the one who committed the crime remains uncertain.

The Warren Court made the exclusionary rule applicable to violations of Fifth Amendment as well as Fourth Amendment rights. If police questioned suspects without giving them proper warnings and access to an attorney, incriminating statements and confessions by those suspects could not be used against them. However, just as the Burger Court created the "good-faith" exception in a Fourth Amendment case, other exceptions to the exclusionary rule were created in the Fifth Amendment context. For example, the Court created an "inevitable discovery rule" that allows police to use evidence that they would have discovered even without improper questioning of the suspect (*Nix v. Williams,* 1984). In the case in question, police learned the location of a murder victim's body by improperly questioning the suspect without his attorney present. The body was later admitted into evidence because the police convinced the Court that search parties would have inevitably found the body even without the suspect's confession. In another example, the Court ruled that evidence obtained from improper questioning could be used if the situation posed an immediate threat to public safety, such as seeking information about a gun that they knew to be hidden somewhere nearby (*New York v. Quarles,* 1984).

Although some observers expected the creation of exceptions to lead the Court eventually to eliminate *Miranda* warnings, the Court has strongly endorsed the continuation of the rule. In 2000 the Court issued a 7-to-2 decision that explicitly confirmed that *Miranda* warnings are required by the U.S. Constitution (*Dickerson v. United States*).

Double Jeopardy

Because of the limit imposed by the Fifth Amendment, a person charged with a criminal act may be subjected to only one prosecution or punishment for that offense in the same jurisdiction. As interpreted by the Supreme Court, however, the right against double jeopardy does not prevent a person from facing two trials or receiving two sanctions from the government for the same crime (Henning, 1993; Hickey, 1995; Lear, 1995). Because a single criminal act may violate both state and federal laws, for example, a person may be tried in both courts. Thus, when Los Angeles police officers were acquitted of assault charges in a state court after they had been videotaped beating motorist Rodney King, they were convicted in a federal court for violating King's civil rights. The Supreme Court further refined the meaning of double jeopardy in 1996 by ruling that prosecutors could employ both property forfeiture *and* criminal charges against someone who grew marijuana at his home. The Court did not apply the double jeopardy right in the case, because the property forfeiture was not a "punishment" (*United States v. Ursery*).

The Sixth Amendment: The Right to Counsel and a Fair Trial

> In all criminal prosecutions, the accused shall enjoy the right to a speedy and public trial, by an impartial jury of the State and district wherein the crime shall have been committed, which district shall have been previously ascertained by law, and to be informed of the nature and cause of the accusation; to be confronted with the witnesses against him; to have compulsory process for obtaining witnesses in his favor, and to have the assistance of counsel for his defense.

The Sixth Amendment includes several provisions dealing with fairness in a criminal prosecution. These include the right to counsel, to a speedy and public trial, and to an impartial jury.

The Right to Counsel

Although the right to counsel in a criminal case had prevailed in federal courts since 1938, not until the Supreme Court's landmark decision in ***Gideon v. Wainwright*** **(1963)** was this requirement made binding on the states. Many states already provided attorneys, but the Court forced all of the states to meet Sixth Amendment standards. In previous cases the Court, applying the doctrine of fundamental fairness, had ruled that states must provide poor people with counsel only when this was required by the special circumstances of the case. A defense attorney had to be provided when conviction could lead to the death penalty, when the issues were complex, or when a poor defendant was either very young or mentally handicapped.

Gideon v. Wainwright **(1963)**
Defendants have a right to counsel in felony cases. States must provide defense counsel in felony cases for those who cannot pay for it themselves.

Although the *Gideon* ruling directly affected only states that did not provide poor defendants with attorneys, it set in motion a series of cases that affected all the states by deciding how the right to counsel would be applied in various situations. Beginning in 1963, the Court extended the right to counsel to preliminary hearings, initial appeals, postindictment identification lineups, and children in juvenile court proceedings. Later, however, the Burger Court declared that attorneys need not be provided for discretionary appeals or for trials in which the only punishment is a fine (*Ross v. Moffitt,* 1974; *Scott v. Illinois,* 1979).

The Right to a Speedy and Public Trial

The nation's founders were aware that in other countries accused people might often languish in jail awaiting trial and often were convicted in secret proceedings. At the time of the American Revolution, the right to a speedy and public trial was recognized in the common law and included in the constitutions of six of the original states. But the word *speedy* is vague, and the Supreme Court has recognized that the desire for quick processes may conflict with other interests of society (such as the need to collect evidence) as well as with interests of the defendant (such as the need for time to prepare a defense).

The right to a public trial is intended to protect the accused against arbitrary conviction. The Constitution assumes that judges and juries will act in accordance with the law if they must listen to evidence and announce their decisions in public. Again, the Supreme Court has recognized that there may be cases in which the need for a public trial must be balanced against other interests. For example, the right to a public trial does not mean that all members of the public have the right to attend the trial. The courtroom's seating capacity and the interests of a fair trial, free of outbursts from the audience, may be considered. In hearings on sex crimes when the victim or witness is a minor, courts have barred the public in order to spare the child embarrassment. In some states, trials have become even more public than the authors of the Sixth Amendment ever imagined, because court proceedings are televised, and some are even carried on national cable systems through COURT-TV.

These Sixth Amendment rights obviously represent important American values related to liberty and fair judicial proceedings. In the aftermath of the September 11 tragedy, however, these values have been challenged by the federal government's antiterrorism efforts. Individuals regarded as "enemy combatants," including some American citizens, are being jailed without any prospect for a speedy trial or any public presentation of evidence against them (Liptak, Lewis, and Weiser, 2002). It remains to be seen whether judges will take action to force the government to respect the values embodied in the Sixth Amendment or whether competing concerns about national security will receive a higher priority.

The Right to an Impartial Jury

The right to a jury trial was well established in the American colonies at the time of the Revolution. In their charters, most of the colonies guaranteed trial by jury, and it was referred to in the First Continental Congress's debates in 1774, the Declaration of Independence, the constitutions of the 13 original states, and the Sixth Amendment to the U.S. Constitution. Juries allow citizens to play a role in courts' decision making and to prevent prosecutions in cases that do not have enough evidence for a proper conviction.

Several Supreme Court decisions have dealt with the composition of juries. The Magna Carta required that juries be drawn from "peers" of the accused person who live in the area where the crime was committed. However, the Sixth Amendment does not refer to a jury of one's peers. Instead, the Supreme Court has held that the amendment requires selection procedures that create a jury pool made up of a cross section of the community. Most scholars believe that an impartial jury can best be achieved by drawing jurors at random from the broadest possible base (Hans and Vidmar, 1986; Levine, 1992). The jury is expected to represent the community, and the extent to which it does so is a central concern of jury administration (C. E. Smith, 1994). Prospective jurors are usually summoned randomly from voter registration lists or drivers' license records. After the jury pool has been formed, attorneys for each side may ask potential jurors questions and seek to exclude specific jurors (C. E. Smith and Ochoa, 1996). Thus the final group of jurors may not, in fact, reflect the diversity of a particular city or county's residents (King, 1994).

The Eighth Amendment: Protection against Excessive Bail, Excessive Fines, and Cruel and Unusual Punishments

> Excessive bail shall not be required, nor excessive fines imposed, nor cruel and unusual punishments inflicted.

The briefest of the amendments, the Eighth Amendment deals with the rights of defendants during the pretrial (bail) and correctional (fines, punishment) phases of the criminal justice system.

Release on Bail

The purpose of bail is to allow for the release of the accused while he or she is awaiting trial. The Eighth Amendment does not require that all defendants be released on bail, only that the amount of bail not be excessive. Despite these provisions, many states do not allow bail for those charged with some offenses, such as murder, and there seem to be few limits on the amounts that can be required. In 1987 the Supreme Court, in *United States v. Salerno and Cafero,* upheld provisions of the Bail Reform Act of 1984 that allow federal judges to detain without bail suspects who are considered dangerous to the public.

Excessive Fines

The Supreme Court ruled in 1993 that the forfeiture of property related to a criminal case can be analyzed for possible violation of the Excessive Fines Clause (*Austin v. United States*). In 1998, the Court declared for the first time that a forfeiture constituted an impermissible excessive fine. In that case, a man failed to comply with the federal law requiring that travelers report if they are taking $10,000 or more in cash outside the country (C. E. Smith, 1999a). There is no law against transporting any amount of cash. The law only concerns filing a report to the government concerning the transport of money. When one traveler at the Los Angeles failed to report the money, which was detected in his suitcase by a cash-sniffing dog trained to identify people who might be transporting money for drug dealers, he was forced to forfeit all of the $357,000 that he carried in his luggage. Because there was no evidence that the money was obtained illegally and because the usual punishment for the offense would only be a fine of $5,000, a slim, five-member majority on the Supreme Court ruled that the forfeiture of all the traveler's money constituted an excessive fine (*United States v. Bajakajian*). It remains to be seen whether the Court's recent interest in violations of the Excessive Fines Clause will limit law enforcement agencies' practices in forcing criminal defendants to forfeit cash and property.

Cruel and Unusual Punishments

Because the nation's founders were concerned about the barbaric punishments that had been inflicted in seventeenth- and eighteenth-century Europe, where offenders were sometimes burned alive or stoned to death, they banned "cruel and unusual punishments." The Warren Court set the standard for judging issues of cruel and unusual punishment, in a case dealing with a former soldier who was deprived of U.S. citizenship for deserting his post during World War II (*Trop v. Dulles,* 1958). Chief Justice Earl Warren declared that judges must use the values of contemporary society to determine whether a specific punishment is cruel and unusual. This test has been used in death penalty cases, but the justices have strongly disagreed over the values of American society on this issue. For example, only Justices William Brennan, Thurgood Marshall, and later, Harry Blackmun felt that the death penalty violates the Eighth Amendment's ban on cruel and unusual punishments. Examine "A Question of Ethics" and consider whether the use of new technologies may raise issues concerning cruel and unusual punishment.

In 1972 a majority of justices decided that the death penalty was being used in an arbitrary and discriminatory way (*Furman v. Georgia,* 1972). After many state legislatures passed new laws that required more careful

At a June 1998 sentencing hearing in Long Beach, California, Ronnie Hawkins, a petty thief, served as his own attorney as he faced a possible sentence of 25 years to life under the state's three-strikes law. In the courtroom he had to wear chains and shackles to prevent him from escaping. He also wore a stun belt designed to deliver a high-voltage electric shock if he disobeyed law enforcement officers. When Hawkins interrupted Judge Joan Comparet-Cassani, she warned him not to interrupt again or he would receive an electric shock. When he repeatedly interrupted the judge, she ordered the bailiff to activate the belt. Hawkins was zapped with a painful 8-second jolt of 50,000 volts of electricity.

→ Is the use of electric shock devices proper under the Supreme Court's test that applies contemporary community standards to define cruel and unusual punishment? Do electric shocks constitute the sort of torture that the framers of the Eighth Amendment intended to ban? Technically, the Supreme Court applies the Eighth Amendment only to punishments inflicted on convicted offenders. Defendants who have not yet been convicted of a crime are protected against abuses by the Due Process Clause, but the courts apply the Eighth Amendment test to determine if pretrial detainees' due process rights have been violated. Stun belts are placed on both pretrial detainees and convicted offenders, especially when they are being transported and there are fears that they might try to escape. As such, they might be regarded as violating both the Eighth Amendment and the Due Process Clause. The mere threat of painful electric shocks are likely quite frightening for prisoners, because the belt's manufacturer claims that fewer than three dozen people have been subjected to the shock in the 50,000 times that the belt has been used. The human rights group Amnesty International argues that electroshock stun belts are inhumane. Should such devices be used on offenders like Hawkins who, chained and shackled in a courtroom chair, were not attempting to escape or threatening public safety? Even if it does not violate the Eighth Amendment to use such stun belts (the courts have not yet decided the issue), is it ethical to use such painful techniques in order to force defendants and offenders to cooperate?

Sources: Drawn from "Commission Investigating Judge Who Shocked Inmate," *Lansing State Journal,* August 27, 1998, p. 4A; Minerva Canto, "Federal Government Investigates Use of Stun Belt," *Lansing State Journal,* August 7, 1998, p. 4A; "Noisy Defendant Shocks Judge With Security Belt," *National Law Journal,* July 27, 1998.

decision-making procedures in death penalty cases, a majority of justices in *Gregg v. Georgia* (1976) allowed the states to reactivate the death penalty. The new procedures require a trial to determine the defendant's guilt and a separate hearing to consider whether he or she deserves the death penalty. In the sentencing hearing, the jury or judge must examine any factors that make the offender especially deserving of the most severe punishment—for example, "aggravating factors" such as an especially gruesome killing. They must also examine any "mitigating factors" that make the offender less deserving of the death penalty, such as youth or mental retardation (Acker and Lanier, 1994, 1995; Blankenship et al., 1997).

***Gregg v. Georgia* (1976)**
Capital punishment statutes are permissible if they provide careful procedures to guide decision making by judges and juries.

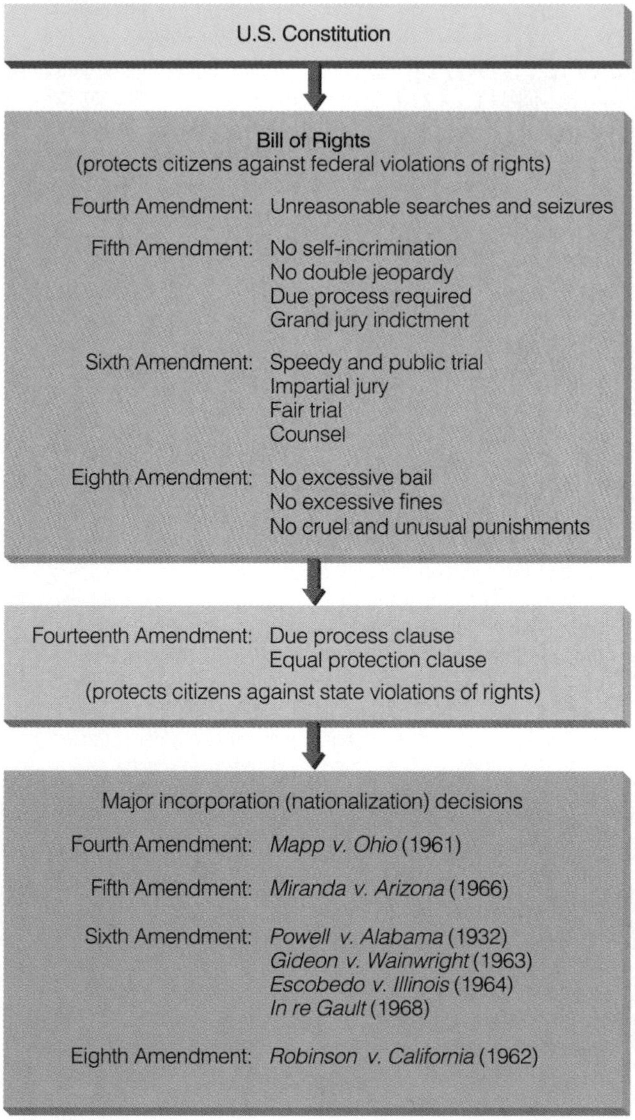

Since the Gregg decision, lawyers have brought many cases to the Supreme Court trying to persuade the justices to declare the death penalty to be cruel and unusual punishment. Throughout the 1980s and 1990s, these efforts were generally unsuccessful. Only since 2002 have there been indications that support for the death penalty, among the justices as well as in public opinion, has weakened. Most notably, in two cases the Supreme Court decided that sentencing mentally retarded people to death violated the Eighth Amendment (*Atkins v. Virginia*), and it limited the ability of states to permit judges rather than juries to make final determinations about which defendants would receive a death sentence (*Ring v. Arizona*). The death penalty controversy is fully discussed in Chapter 12.

Since the 1950s the rights of defendants in state criminal trials have greatly expanded. The Supreme Court has incorporated most of the Fourth, Fifth, Sixth, and Eighth Amendments, as shown in Figure 4.4. Figure 4.5 shows the amendments that protect defendants at various stages of the criminal justice process.

Figure 4.4
Relationship of the Bill of Rights and the Fourteenth Amendment to the rights of the accused
For most of U.S. history, the Bill of Rights protected citizens only against violations by officials of the federal government. The Warren Court began the process of incorporation, in which portions of the Fourteenth Amendment were interpreted as protecting citizens from unlawful actions by state officials.

U.S. Constitution

↓

Bill of Rights
(protects citizens against federal violations of rights)

Fourth Amendment: Unreasonable searches and seizures

Fifth Amendment: No self-incrimination
No double jeopardy
Due process required
Grand jury indictment

Sixth Amendment: Speedy and public trial
Impartial jury
Fair trial
Counsel

Eighth Amendment: No excessive bail
No excessive fines
No cruel and unusual punishments

↓

Fourteenth Amendment: Due process clause
Equal protection clause
(protects citizens against state violations of rights)

↓

Major incorporation (nationalization) decisions

Fourth Amendment: *Mapp v. Ohio* (1961)

Fifth Amendment: *Miranda v. Arizona* (1966)

Sixth Amendment: *Powell v. Alabama* (1932)
Gideon v. Wainwright (1963)
Escobedo v. Illinois (1964)
In re Gault (1968)

Eighth Amendment: *Robinson v. California* (1962)

check point

16. What are the main criminal justice rights set forth in the Fifth Amendment?
17. What are the main criminal justice rights set forth in the Sixth Amendment?
18. What are the main criminal justice rights set forth in the Eighth Amendment?

The Supreme Court Today

When William Rehnquist became chief justice in 1986, a new conservative majority on the Supreme Court began to consider issues such as preventive detention, unreasonable searches and seizures, and the death penalty. The appointments of Anthony Kennedy in 1988, David Souter in 1989, and Clarence Thomas in 1991 added more conservative justices to the Court. Even with the replacement of Byron White by Ruth Bader Ginsburg in 1993 and of Harry Blackmun by Stephen Breyer in 1994—two appointees placed on the high court by President Bill Clinton—the Court continues to lean in a conservative direction on criminal justice issues.

Despite its reputation, the Rehnquist Court has not been as conservative as many of its critics believe (Hensley and Smith, 1995). It has maintained the land-

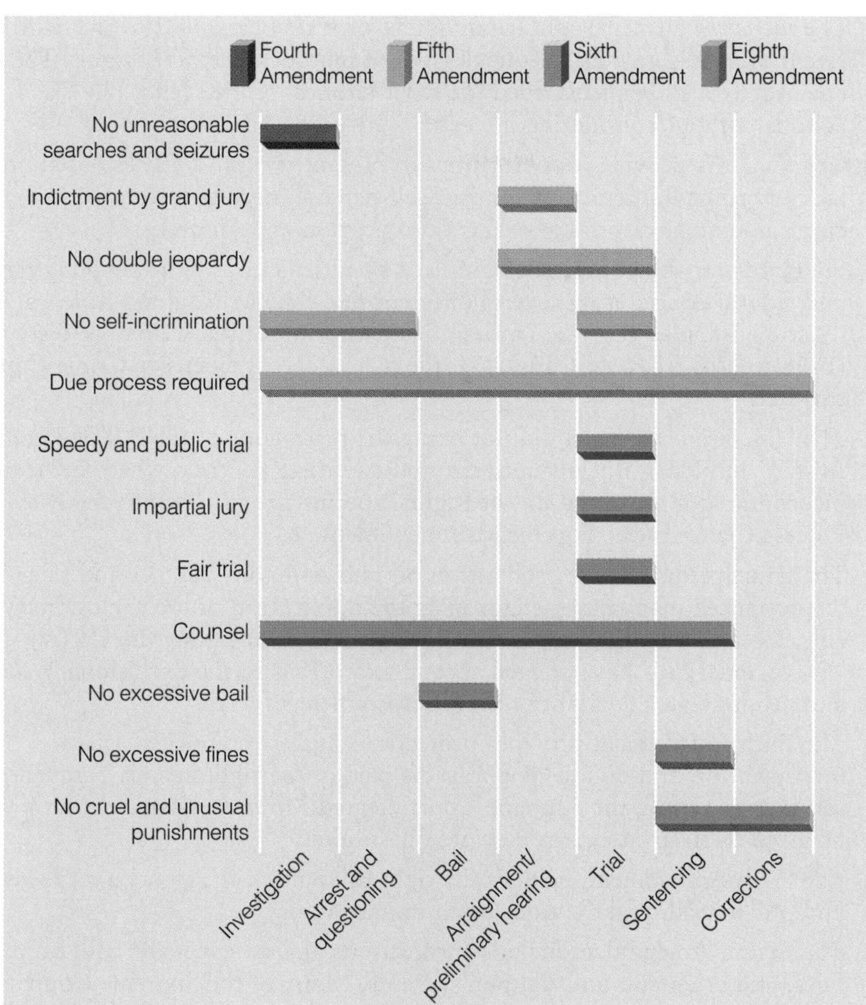

Figure 4.5
Protections of the Bill of Rights
The Bill of Rights protects defendants during various phases of the criminal justice process.

mark precedents dealing with the right to counsel (*Gideon v. Wainwright*), the exclusionary rule (*Mapp v. Ohio*), warnings to suspects (*Miranda v. Arizona*), and other rights. Although the Court has reduced the rights of defendants and given more flexibility to criminal justice officials, it still requires the authorities to be aware of the Bill of Rights in carrying out their responsibilities.

Summary

- Criminal law focuses on state prosecution and punishment of people who violate specific laws enacted by legislatures, while civil law concerns disputes between private citizens or businesses.
- Criminal law is divided into two parts: substantive law, which defines offenses and penalties, and procedural law, which defines individuals' rights and the processes that criminal justice officials must follow in handling cases.
- The common-law tradition, which was inherited from England, involves judges shaping law through their decisions.
- Criminal law is found in written constitutions, statutes, judicial decisions, and administrative regulations.
- Substantive criminal law involves seven important elements that must exist and be demonstrated by the prosecution in order to obtain a conviction: legality, *actus reus,* causation, harm, concurrence, *mens rea,* and punishment.

- The *mens rea* element, concerning intent or state of mind, can vary with different offenses, such as various degrees of murder or sexual assault. The element may also be disregarded for strict liability offenses that punish actions without considering intent.
- Criminal law provides opportunities to present several defenses based on lack of criminal intent: entrapment, self-defense, necessity, duress (coercion), immaturity, mistake of fact, intoxication, and insanity.
- Standards for the insanity defense vary by jurisdiction, with various state and federal courts using several different tests: the M'Naghten Rule, the Irresistible Impulse Test, the Durham Rule, the Substantial Capacity Test (from the *Model Penal Code*), and the federal Comprehensive Crime Control Act.
- The U.S. Supreme Court did not apply the provisions of the Bill of Rights to state and local officials until the mid-twentieth century, when the Court incorporated most of the Bill of Rights' specific provisions into the Due Process Clause of the Fourteenth Amendment.
- The Fourth Amendment prohibition on unreasonable searches and seizures has produced many cases questioning the application of the exclusionary rule. Decisions by the Burger and Rehnquist Courts during the 1970s, 1980s, and 1990s have created several exceptions to the exclusionary rule and given greater flexibility to law enforcement officials.
- The Fifth Amendment provides protections against compelled self-incrimination and double jeopardy. As part of the right against compelled self-incrimination, the Supreme Court created *Miranda* warnings that must be given to suspects before they are questioned.
- The Sixth Amendment includes the right to counsel, the right to a speedy and public trial, and the right to an impartial jury.
- The Eighth Amendment includes protections against excessive bail, excessive fines, and cruel and unusual punishments. Many of the Supreme Court's most well-known Eighth Amendment cases concern the death penalty, which the Court has endorsed, provided that states employ careful decision-making procedures that consider aggravating and mitigating factors.

Questions for Review

1. What two functions does law perform? What are the two major divisions of the law?
2. What are the sources of criminal law? Where would you find it?
3. List the seven principles of criminal law theory.
4. What is meant by *mens rea?* Give examples of defenses that defendants can use to deny that *mens rea* existed when the crime was committed.
5. What is meant by the "incorporation" of the Fourteenth Amendment to the U.S. Constitution?

Key Terms and Cases

administrative regulations (p. 100)
case law (p. 100)
civil forfeiture (p. 102)
civil law (p. 97)
common law (p. 98)
constitutions (p. 99)
double jeopardy (p. 120)
entrapment (p. 111)
exclusionary rule (p. 122)
fundamental fairness (p. 120)
inchoate offense (p. 104)
incorporation (p. 121)
legal responsibility (p. 96)
mens rea (p. 104)
procedural criminal law (p. 98)
procedural due process (p. 118)
self-incrimination (p. 120)
statutes (p. 99)
strict liability (p. 111)
substantive criminal law (p. 98)
Barron v. Baltimore (p. 120)
Escobedo v. Illinois (p. 124)
Gideon v. Wainwright (p. 125)
Gregg v. Georgia (p. 128)
Mapp v. Ohio (p. 122)
Miranda v. Arizona (p. 124)
Powell v. Alabama (p. 120)

For Further Reading

Fletcher, George P. 1988. *A Crime of Self-Defense: Bernhard Goetz and the Law on Trial.* New York: Free Press. An insightful examination of the legal issues involved in the Goetz case.

Katz, Leo. 1987. *Bad Acts and Guilty Minds.* Chicago: University of Chicago Press. Exploration of questions raised by the insanity defense.

Lewis, Anthony. 1964. *Gideon's Trumpet.* New York: Vintage Books. A classic examination of the case of *Gideon v. Wainwright* showing the process by which the issues came to the U.S. Supreme Court.

Morris, Norval. 1982. *Madness and the Criminal Law.* Chicago: University of Chicago Press. A stimulating and controversial examination of the insanity defense by a leading criminal justice scholar.

Simpson, A. W. Brian. 1984. *Cannibalism and the Common Law.* Chicago: University of Chicago Press. Exciting study of the case of *The Queen v. Dudley and Stephens* showing that there were many such incidents during the age of sailing in which punishment did not follow.

Going Online

For an up-to-date list of Web links, go to http://www.cj.wadsworth.com/colesmith10e

1. Look at the criminal laws of your state (or another state) by visiting http://www.findlaw.com. Are there any laws that some people might claim are out of step with current society?
2. At http://www.law.cornell.edu, find a U.S. Supreme Court decision from the past several years that has clarified or changed the rights possessed by suspects and defendants. How will this decision affect the behavior of police officers, prosecutors, and other officials in the criminal justice system?
3. On InfoTrac College Edition, find and read an article on the use of the insanity defense in criminal cases. Did the information or perspective provided by the article's author change your views about how the insanity defense ought to be defined and applied?

Checkpoint Answers

1. Penal codes contain substantive criminal law that defines crimes and also punishments for those crimes.
2. Procedural criminal law specifies the defendants' rights and tells justice system officials how they can investigate and process cases.
3. Based on English tradition, judges make decisions relying on the precedents of earlier cases.
4. Constitutions, statutes, judicial decisions, and administrative regulations.
5. A felony usually involves a potential punishment of one year or more in prison; a misdemeanor carries a shorter term of incarceration, probation, fines, or community service.
6. Civil law includes tort lawsuits (for example, personal injury cases), property law, contracts, and other disputes between two private parties.
7. Legality, *actus reus,* causation, harm, concurrence, *mens rea,* punishment.
8. New definitions of graded sex offenses that do not contain all the elements necessary to prove rape; new protections for victims with respect to questions asked in court.
9. Strict liability offense.
10. Entrapment, self-defense, necessity, duress (coercion), immaturity, mistake of fact, intoxication, insanity.
11. M'Naghten Rule (right-from-wrong test), Irresistible Impulse Test, Durham Rule, *Model Penal Code,* federal (Crime Control Act).
12. Taking a right from the Bill of Rights and applying it against state and local officials by making it a component of the due process clause of the Fourteenth Amendment.
13. Fundamental fairness.
14. Warren Court.
15. Exclusionary rule.
16. The right against compelled self-incrimination and against double jeopardy; the right to due process.
17. The right to counsel, to a speedy and fair trial, to a jury trial, plus confrontation and compulsory process.
18. The right to protection against excessive bail, excessive fines, and cruel and unusual punishments.

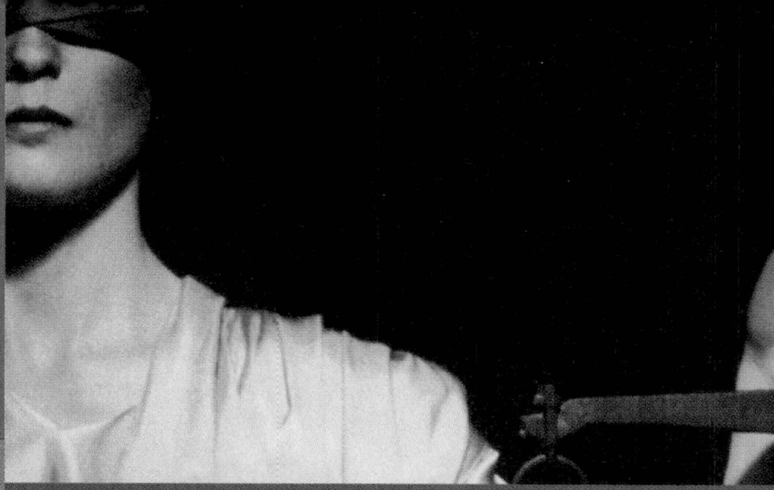

PART TWO

Police

Although the police are the most visible agents of the criminal justice system, our images of them come mainly from fiction, especially movies and television. The reality of police experiences, however, differs greatly from the dramatic exploits of the cops in *Law and Order* or *NYPD Blue*.

In Part 2 we examine the police as the key unit of the criminal justice system: the one that confronts crime in the community. Chapter 5 traces the history of policing and looks at its function and organization. Chapter 6 explores the recruitment of officers and the daily operations of the police. Chapter 7 examines the relationship between the police and constitutional law. Chapter 8 analyzes current issues and trends in policing. As we shall see, police work is often done in a hostile environment in which life and death, honor and dishonor are at stake. Police officers are given discretion to deal with many situations; how they use it has an important effect on the way society views policing.

CHAPTER 5

Police

René Clement/AURORA

At 8:45 A.M. on September 11, 2001, a hijacked commercial airliner crashed into the North Tower of the World Trade Center, a 110-story office complex in New York City. A second hijacked airliner slammed into the South Tower at 9:03 A.M. One hour later, the entire South Tower collapsed. Less than 30 minutes later, the North Tower also collapsed. Tons of debris fell to the street, destroying nearby buildings and killing nearly 3,000 people who were inside the falling structures or standing below as part of police and fire crews that had responded to the emergency. This was the deadliest act of terrorism in the history of the United States, and it revealed that Americans are at greater risk of attack on their own shores than anyone had previously imagined.

When emergencies occur, police officers are "first responders." Along with firefighters and emergency medical technicians, law enforcement officers are expected to rush to the scene, restore order, and assist in rescue operations. Hundreds of New York City law enforcement officers fulfilled their duties on the morning of September 11, many of them sacrificing their lives in the process. The tragedy of that day demonstrated that police officers throughout the United States must be prepared to face emergency situations that had been unimaginable prior to that fateful day. The aftermath of the World Trade Center attack also demonstrated the size, complexity, and specialization of the various agencies that fulfill law enforcement and emergency response responsibilities in the United States.

Within hours of the blast, units from multiple federal, state, and local agencies were on the scene to rescue survivors, remove the dead, and begin the process of tracking down the people responsible for the death and destruction. The federal agencies involved included the Federal Bureau of Investigation; Drug Enforcement Administration; Bureau of Alcohol, Tobacco, and Firearms; and Department of Defense. In addition, the New York National Guard and the New York City Police Department bore primary responsibility for order maintenance and assisting firefighters and others with the rescue operation. There were also police on the scene from the Port Authority of New York and the New York city transit system.

Before the destruction of the World Trade Center, most Americans had little reason to recognize the number of agencies with law enforcement responsibilities and their particular areas of emphasis. How many Americans previously knew about the Bureau of Alcohol, Tobacco, and Firearms of the U.S. Treasury Department and recognized that it might act in such circumstances? The swift actions of so many different law enforcement agencies demonstrated the importance of the network of relationships among national, state, and local police forces.

Many Americans think immediately of their local police department when they picture law enforcement operations. If pressed to name other agencies, many people could undoubtedly cite the state police officers who patrol interstate highways, and the FBI, whose agents have been made famous in books, television, and movies. Few people, however, have any inkling about the large number of separate law enforcement agencies, in various levels of government, that have specific responsibilities for criminal investigations.

The uniformed men and women who patrol American streets are the most visible presence of government in the United States. They are joined by thousands of plainclothes officers who share various law enforcement responsibilities. Whether they are members of the local or state police, sheriff's departments, or federal agencies, the more than 700,000 sworn officers in the country play key roles in U.S. society. Citizens look to them to perform a wide range of functions: crime prevention, law enforcement, order maintenance, and community services. However, the public's expectations of the police are not always clear. Citizens also form judgments about the police, and those judgments have a strong impact on the way the police function.

In a free society the police are required to maintain order. In performing this task, police officers are given a great deal of authority. Using their powers to arrest, search, detain, and use force, they can interfere with the freedom of any citizen. If they abuse such powers, they can threaten the basic values of a stable, democratic society.

In this chapter we examine several aspects of policing. A brief history of the police precedes discussions of the organization, policies, and functions of law enforcement.

QUESTIONS for INQUIRY

- How has policing evolved in the United States?
- What are the main types of police agencies, and how are they organized?
- What are the functions of the police?

- What influences police policy and styles of policing?
- How do police officers balance actions, decision making, and discretion?
- What role does the link between the police and the community play in preventing crime?

The Development of Police in the United States

Law and order is not a new concept; it has been a subject of debate since the first police force was formed in London in 1829. Looking back even further, to the Magna Carta of 1215, limits were placed on constables and bailiffs. Reading between the lines of that historic document reveals that the modern problems of police abuse, maintenance of order, and the rule of law also existed in thirteenth-century England. Further, current remedies—recruiting better-qualified people to serve as police, stiffening the penalties for official misconduct, creating a civilian board of control—were suggested even then to ensure that order was kept in accordance with the rule of law.

The English Roots of the American Police

The roots of American policing lie in the English legal tradition. Three major aspects of American policing evolved from that tradition: (1) limited authority, (2) local control, and (3) fragmented organization. Like the British police, but unlike police in continental Europe, the police in the United States have limited authority; their powers and duties are specifically defined by law. England, like the United States, has no national police force; instead, 43 regional authorities are headed by elected commissioners who appoint the chief constable. Above these local authorities is the home secretary of the national government, which provides funding and can intervene in cases of police corruption, mismanagement, and discipline. In the United States, policing is fragmented: There are many types of agencies—constable, county sheriff, city police, FBI—each with its own special jurisdiction and responsibilities.

Systems for protecting citizens and property existed before the thirteenth century. The **frankpledge** system required that groups of ten families, called tithings, agree to uphold the law, keep order, and bring violators to a court. By custom, every male person above the age of 12 was part of the system. When a man became aware that a crime had occurred, he was obliged to raise a "hue and cry" and to join others in his tithing to track down the offender. The tithing was fined if members did not perform their duties.

frankpledge
A system in old English law in which members of a *tithing,* a group of ten families, pledged to be responsible for keeping order and bringing violators of the law to court.

Over time England developed a system in which individuals were chosen within each community to take charge of catching criminals. The Statute of Winchester, enacted in 1285, set up a parish constable-watch system. Members of the community were still required to pursue criminals, just as they had been under the frankpledge system, but now a constable supervised those efforts. The constable was a man chosen from the parish to serve without pay as its law enforcement officer for one year. The constable had the power to call the entire community into action if a serious disturbance arose. Watchmen, who were appointed to help the constable, spent most of their time patrolling the town at night to ensure that "all's well" and to enforce the criminal law. They were also responsible for lighting street lamps and putting out fires.

Not until the eighteenth century did an organized police force evolve in England. With the growth of commerce and industry, cities expanded while farming declined as the main source of employment and the focus of community life. In the larger cities these changes produced social disorder.

In the mid-eighteenth century, the novelist Henry Fielding and his brother, Sir John Fielding, led efforts to improve law enforcement in London. They wrote newspaper articles to inform the public about crime, and they published flyers describing known offenders. After Henry Fielding became a magistrate in 1748, he organized a small group of "thief-takers" to pursue and arrest lawbreakers. The government was so impressed with Fielding's Bow Street Amateur Volunteer Force (known as the Bow Street Runners) that it paid the participants and attempted to form similar groups in other parts of London.

After Henry Fielding's death in 1754, these efforts declined. As time went by, however, many saw that the government needed to assert itself in enforcing laws and maintaining order. London, with its unruly mobs, had become an especially dangerous place.

In the early 1800s several attempts were made to create a centralized police force for London. While people saw the need for social order, some feared that a police force would threaten the freedom of citizens and lead to tyranny. Finally, in 1829 Sir Robert Peel, home secretary in the British Cabinet, pushed Parliament to pass the Metropolitan Police Act, which created the London police force.

This agency was organized like a military unit, with a 1,000-man force commanded by two magistrates, later called "commissioners." The officers were called "bobbies" after Sir Robert Peel. In the British system, cabinet members who oversee government departments are chosen from the elected members of Parliament. Thus, because it was supervised by Peel, the first police force was under the control of democratically elected officials.

Under Peel's direction the police had a four-part mandate:

1. To prevent crime without using repressive force and to avoid having to call on the military to control riots and other disturbances
2. To maintain public order by nonviolent means, using force to obtain compliance only as a last resort
3. To reduce conflict between the police and the public
4. To show efficiency through the absence of crime and disorder rather than through visible police actions (Manning, 1977:82)

In effect, this meant keeping a low profile while maintaining order. Because of fears that a national force would threaten civil liberties, political leaders made every effort to focus police activities at the local level. These concerns were transported to the United States.

check point

1. What three main features of American policing were inherited from England?
2. What was the frankpledge and how did it work?
3. What did the Statute of Winchester (1285) establish?
4. What did the Metropolitan Police Act (1829) establish?
5. What were the four mandates of the English police in the nineteenth century?

(Answers are at the end of the chapter.)

Policing in the United States

Before the Revolution, Americans shared the English belief that members of a community had a duty to help maintain order; therefore, they adopted the English offices of constable, sheriff, and night watchman. The watch system was the main means of keeping order and catching criminals. Each citizen was required to be a member of the watch, but paid watchmen could be hired as replacements. Over time, cities began to hire paid, uniformed watchmen to deal with crime.

After the formation of the federal government in 1789, police power remained with the states, in response to fear of centralized law enforcement. However, the American police developed under conditions that were different from those in England. Unlike the British, police in the United States had to deal with ethnic diversity, local political control, regional differences, the exploration and settling of the West, and a generally more violent society.

American policing is often described in terms of three historical periods: the political era (1840–1920), the professional model era (1920–1970), and the community model era (1970–present) (Kelling and Moore, 1988). This description has been criticized because it applies only to the urban areas of the Northeast and does not take into account the very different development of the police in rural areas of the South and West. Still, it remains a useful framework for exploring the organization of the police, the focus of police work, and the strategies employed by police (H. Williams and Murphy, 1990).

The Political Era: 1840–1920

The period from 1840 to 1920 is called the political era because of the close ties that were formed between the police and local political leaders at that time. In many cities the police seemed to work for the mayor's political party rather than for the citizens. This relationship served both groups in that the political "machines" recruited and maintained the police while the police helped the machine leaders get out the vote for favored candidates. Ranks in the police force were often for sale to the highest bidder, and many officers took payoffs for not enforcing laws on drinking, gambling, and prostitution (S. Walker, 1999:26).

In the United States as in England, the growth of cities led to pressures to modernize law enforcement. Social relations in cities differed from those in towns and the countryside. From 1830 to 1870 the large cities experienced much civil disorder. Ethnic conflict, hostility toward nonslave blacks and abolitionists, mob actions against banks during economic declines, and violence in settling questions of morality, such as the use of alcohol—all these factors contributed to fears that a stable democracy would not survive.

Around 1840 the large cities began to create police forces. In 1845 New York City established the first full-time, paid police force. Boston and Philadelphia were the first to add a daytime police force to supplement the night watchmen; other cities—Chicago, Cincinnati, New Orleans—quickly followed.

Culver Pictures

During the political era, the officer on a neighborhood beat dealt with crime and disorder as it arose. Police also performed various social services, such as providing beds and food for the homeless.

By 1850 most major cities had created police departments organized on the English model. A chief, appointed by the mayor and city council, headed each department. The city was divided into precincts, with full-time, paid patrolmen assigned to each. Early police forces sought to prevent crimes and keep order through the use of foot patrols. The officer on the beat dealt with crime, disorder, and other problems as they arose.

In addition to foot patrols, the police performed service functions, such as caring for derelicts, operating soup kitchens, regulating public health, and handling medical and social emergencies. In cities across the country, the police provided beds and food for homeless people. In station houses, overnight "lodgers" might sleep on the floor or sometimes in clean bunkrooms (Monkkonen, 1981:127). Because they were the only government agency that had close contact with life on the streets of the city, the police became general public servants as well as crime control officers. Because of these close links with the community and service to it, they had the citizens' support (Monkkonen, 1992:554).

Police developed differently in the South because of the existence of slavery and the agrarian nature of that region. Historians note that the first organized police agencies with full-time officers developed in cities with large numbers of slaves (Charleston, New Orleans, Richmond, and Savannah), where white owners feared slave uprisings (Rousey, 1984:41). The owners created "slave patrols" to deal with runaways. These patrols had full power to break into the homes of slaves who were suspected of keeping arms, to physically punish those who did not obey their orders, and to arrest runaways and return them to their masters.

Westward expansion in the United States produced conditions quite different from those in either the urban East or the agricultural South. The frontier was settled before order could be established. Thus, those who wanted to maintain law and order often had to take matters into their own hands by forming vigilante groups.

One of the first official positions created in rural areas was that of sheriff. Although the sheriff had duties similar to those of the "shire reeves" of seventeenth-century England, the American sheriff was elected and had broad powers to enforce the law. As elected officers, sheriffs had close ties to local politics. They also depended on the men of the community for assistance. This is how the *posse comitatus* (Latin for "power of the county"), borrowed from fifteenth-century Europe, came into being. Local men above the age of 15 were required to respond to the sheriff's call for assistance, forming a body known as a *posse.*

After the Civil War, the federal government appointed U.S. marshals to help enforce the law in the western territories. Some of the best-known folk heroes of American policing were U.S. Marshals Wyatt Earp, Bat Masterson, and Wild Bill Hickok, who tried to bring law and order to the "Wild West" (Calhoun, 1990). While some marshals did extensive law enforcement work, most had mainly judicial duties, such as keeping order in the courtroom and holding prisoners for trial.

During the twentieth century, all parts of the country became increasingly urban. This change blurred some of the regional differences that had helped define policing in the past. In addition, growing criticism of the influence of politics on the police led to efforts to reform the nature and organization of the police. Specifically, reformers sought to make police more professional and to reduce their ties to local politics.

The Professional Model Era: 1920–1970

American policing was greatly influenced by the Progressive movement. The Progressives were mainly upper-middle-class, educated Americans with two goals: more efficient government and more government services to assist the less fortunate. A related goal was to reduce the influence of party politics and *patronage* (favoritism in handing out jobs) on government. The Progressives saw a need for professional law enforcement officials who would use modern technology to benefit society as a whole, not just local politicians.

The key to the Progressives' concept of professional law enforcement is found in their slogan, "The police have to get out of politics, and politics has to get out of the police." August Vollmer, chief of police of Berkeley, California, from 1909 to 1932, was one of the leading advocates of professional policing. He initiated the use of motorcycle units, handwriting analysis, and fingerprinting. With other police reformers, such as Leonhard Fuld, Raymond Fosdick, Bruce Smith, and O. W. Wilson, he urged that the police be made into a professional force, a nonpartisan agency of government committed to public service. This model of professional policing has six elements:

1. The force should stay out of politics.
2. Members should be well trained, well disciplined, and tightly organized.
3. Laws should be enforced equally.
4. The force should use new technology.

Jeff Shere/Black Star

During the professional era, the police saw themselves as crime fighters. Yet many inner-city residents saw them as a well-armed, occupying force rather than as public servants who might be looked to for help.

5. Personnel procedures should be based on merit.
6. The main task of the police should be fighting crime.

Refocusing attention on crime control and away from maintaining order probably did more than anything else to change the nature of American policing. The narrow focus on crime fighting broke many of the ties that the police had formed with the communities they served. By the end of World War I, police departments had greatly reduced their involvement in social services. Instead, for the most part, cops became crime fighters.

O. W. Wilson, a student of Vollmer, was a leading advocate of professionalism. He earned a degree in criminology at the University of California in 1924 and became chief of police in Wichita, Kansas, in 1928. He came to national attention by reorganizing the department and fighting police corruption. He promoted the use of motorized patrols, efficient radio communication, and rapid response. He believed that one-officer patrols were the best way to use personnel and that the two-way radio, which allowed for supervision by commanders, made officers more efficient (Reiss, 1992:51). He rotated assignments so that officers on patrol would not become too familiar with people in the community (and thus prone to corruption). In 1960 Wilson became superintendent of the Chicago Police Department with a mandate to end corruption there.

The new emphasis on professionalism spurred the formation of the International Association of Chiefs of Police (IACP) in 1902 and the Fraternal Order of Police (FOP) in 1915. Both organizations promoted the use of new technologies, training standards, and a code of ethics.

Advocates of professionalism urged that the police be made aware of the need to act lawfully and to protect the rights of all citizens, including those suspected of crimes. They sought to instill a strong—some would even say rigid ("Just the facts, ma'am")—commitment to the law and to equal treatment (Goldstein, 1990:7).

By the 1930s the police were using new technologies and methods to combat serious crimes. They became more effective against crimes such as murder, rape, and robbery—an important factor in gaining citizen support. By contrast, efforts to control victimless offenses and to maintain order often aroused citizen opposition. As Mark Moore and George Kelling have noted, "The clean, bureaucratic model of policing put forth by the reformers could be sustained only if the scope of police responsibility was narrowed to 'crime fighting'" (Moore and Kelling, 1983:55).

In the 1960s the civil rights and antiwar movements, urban riots, and rising crime rates challenged many of the assumptions of the professional model. In their attempts to maintain order during public demonstrations, the police in many cities seemed to be concerned mainly with maintaining the status quo. Thus, police officers found themselves enforcing laws that tended to discriminate against African Americans and the poor. The number of low-income racial minorities living in the inner cities was growing, and the professional style kept the police isolated from the communities they served. In the eyes of many inner-city residents, the police were an occupying army keeping them at the bottom of society, not public servants helping all citizens.

Although the police continued to portray themselves as crime fighters, citizens became aware that the police often were not effective in this role. Crime rates rose for many offenses, and the police could not change the perception that the quality of urban life was declining.

The Community Policing Era: 1970–Present

Beginning in the 1970s, calls were heard for a move away from the crime-fighting focus and toward greater emphasis on keeping order and providing services to the community. Research studies revealed the complex nature of police work and the extent to which day-to-day practices deviated from the professional ideal. The research also questioned the effectiveness of the police in catching and deterring criminals.

Three findings of this research are especially noteworthy:

1. Increasing the number of patrol officers in a neighborhood had little effect on the crime rate.
2. Rapid response to calls for service did not greatly increase the arrest rate.
3. Improving the percentage of crimes solved is difficult.

Such findings undermined acceptance of the professional crime-fighter model (Moore, 1992:99). Critics argued that the professional style isolated the police from the community and reduced their knowledge about the neighborhoods they served, especially when police patrolled in cars. Use of the patrol car prevented personal contacts with citizens. Instead, it was argued, police should get out of their cars and spend more time meeting and helping residents. This would permit the police to help people with a range of problems and in some cases to prevent problems from arising or growing worse. For example, if the police know about conflicts between people in a neighborhood, they can try to mediate and perhaps prevent the conflict from growing into a criminal assault or other serious problem. Reformers hoped that closer contact with citizens would not only permit the police to help them in new ways but would also make them feel safer, knowing that the police were available and interested in their problems.

In a provocative article titled "Broken Windows: The Police and Neighborhood Safety," James Q. Wilson and George L. Kelling argued that policing should work more on "little problems" such as maintaining order, providing services to those in need, and adopting strategies to reduce the fear of crime (1982:29). They based their approach on three assumptions:

1. Neighborhood disorder creates fear. Areas with street people, youth gangs, prostitution, and drunks are high-crime areas.
2. Just as broken windows are a signal that nobody cares and can lead to worse vandalism, untended disorderly behavior is a signal that the community does not care. This also leads to worse disorder and crime.
3. If the police are to deal with disorder and thus reduce fear and crime, they must rely on citizens for assistance.

Advocates of the community policing approach urge greater use of foot patrols so that officers will become known to citizens, who in turn will cooperate with the police. They believe that through attention to little problems, the police may not only reduce disorder and fear but also improve public attitudes toward policing. When citizens respond positively to police efforts, the police will have "improved bases of community and political support, which in turn can be exploited to gain further cooperation from citizens in a wide variety of activities" (Kelling, 1985:299).

Closely related to the community policing concept is problem-oriented policing (see Chapter 8). Herman Goldstein, the originator of this approach, argued that instead of focusing on crime and disorder the police should identify the underlying causes of such problems as noisy teenagers, battered spouses, and abandoned buildings used as drug houses. In doing so they could reduce disorder and fear of crime (Goldstein, 1979:236). Closer contacts between the police and the community might then reduce the hostility that has developed between officers and residents in many urban neighborhoods (Sparrow, Moore, and Kennedy, 1990).

Cynthia Johnson/The Gamma Liaison Network

Community policing encourages personal contact between officers and citizens. How do such contacts affect citizens' expectations about relationships with police?

In *Fixing Broken Windows,* a book written in response to the Wilson and Kelling article, George L. Kelling and Catherine Coles (1996) call for strategies to restore order and reduce crime in public spaces in U.S. communities. In Baltimore, New York, San Francisco, and Seattle, police are paying greater attention to "quality-of-life crimes"—by arresting subway fare-beaters, rousting loiterers and panhandlers from parks, and aggressively dealing with those who are obstructing sidewalks, harassing others, and soliciting. By handling these "little crimes," the police not only help restore order but also often prevent worse crimes. In New York, for example, searching fare-beaters often yielded weapons, questioning a street vendor selling hot merchandise led to a fence specializing in stolen weapons, and arresting a person for urinating in a park resulted in discovery of a cache of weapons.

Although reformers argue for a greater focus on order maintenance and service, they do not call for an end to the crime-fighting role. Instead, they want a shift of emphasis. The police should pay more attention to community needs and seek to understand the problems underlying crime, disorder, and incivility. These proposals have been adopted by police executives in many cities and by influential organizations such as the Police Foundation and the Police Executive Research Forum.

Can—and should—community policing be implemented throughout the nation? The populations of some cities, especially in the West, are too dispersed to permit a switch to foot patrols. In many cities, foot patrols and community police stations have been set up in public housing projects. Time will tell if this new approach will become as widespread as the focus on professionalism was in the first half of the last century.

The call for a new focus for the police has not gone unchallenged (Reichers and Roberg, 1990:105). Critics question whether the professional model really isolated police from community residents (S. Walker, 1984:88). Taking another view, Carl Klockars doubts that the police will give higher priority to maintaining order and wonders whether Americans want their police to be something other than crime fighters (1985:300).

Whichever approach the police take—professional, crime fighting, or community policing—it must be carried out through a bureaucratic structure. We therefore turn to a discussion of police organization in the United States.

check point

6. What are the three historical periods of American policing?
7. What was the main feature of the political era?
8. What were the major recommendations of the Progressive reformers?
9. What are the main criticisms of the professional era?
10. What is community policing?

Law Enforcement Agencies

As discussed in Chapter 3, the United States has a federal system of government with separate national and state structures, each with authority over certain functions. Most of the 19,000 police agencies at the national, state, county, and municipal levels are responsible for carrying out four functions: (1) enforcing the law, (2) maintaining order, (3) preventing crime, and (4) providing services to the community. They employ a total of more than one million people, sworn and unsworn. The agencies include the following (BJS, 1998b):

- 13,578 municipal police departments
- 3,088 sheriff's departments
- 1,316 special police agencies (jurisdictions limited to transit systems, parks, schools, and so on)
- 49 state police departments (all states except Hawaii)
- 135 Native American tribal police agencies
- 50 federal law enforcement agencies

This list shows both the fragmentation and the local orientation of American police. That only 17 percent of funds for police work are spent by the national government, and only 11 percent by state governments, further reveals the local nature of law enforcement. Each level of the system has different responsibilities, either for different kinds of crimes, such as the federal authority over counterfeiting, or for different geographic areas, such as state police authority over major highways. The broadest authority tends to lie with local units. Table 5.1 shows the number of full-time sworn officers in federal, state, county, and local law enforcement agencies.

As we examine the differing law enforcement agencies, we should recognize that in the aftermath of 9-11 there has been an expansion and reorganization, especially among federal law enforcement agencies. The creation of the Department of Homeland Security, the reordering of crime control policies away from

Table 5.1 Personnel in federal, state, county, and local law enforcement agencies

The decentralized nature of U.S. law enforcement is shown by the fact that 56 percent of all full-time sworn officers are in local departments.

Type of Agency	Number of Full-Time Sworn Officers	Percentage of Total
Local Police	410,535	56%
County Police	152,922	21
State Police	54,587	7
Special Police*	43,082	6
Federal	74,493	10

*Officers in state and local parks, transportation, animal control, housing, etc.
Source: Bureau of Justice Statistics, *Law Enforcement Management and Administrative Statistics, 1999* (Washington, D.C.: U.S. Government Printing Office, 2000), 1.

Federal Law Enforcement and the War on Terrorism

In the wake of the events of 9-11, a dramatic reordering of priorities and responsibilities has taken place among federal law enforcement agencies. As a result of this shift, many federal agencies have had to reorient their focus toward addressing the issues of terrorism and away from the street crime and drug cases they had been handling prior to 9-11.

One key sign of this change is the creation of the Office [now Department] of Homeland Security and the President's budget request to allocate $37.7 billion to this new office to "develop and coordinate the implementation of a comprehensive national strategy to secure the United States from terrorist threats or attacks." In addition, dramatic budget increases have been proposed for several federal law enforcement agencies including $6.3 billion to the Immigration and Naturalization Service (INS) for 2,200 new positions, "primarily targeted at building greater homeland security and combating terrorism"; an additional $711.1 million for 1,790 new agents for the Border Patrol; and a 6 percent increase—up to $1.7 billion—for the Drug Enforcement Agency to support the war on terrorism.

Another important example is found in the Federal Bureau of Investigation. Besides a greatly increased budget, the FBI has a restructuring plan in place to "increase the emphasis in counter terrorism, counterintelligence, cyber crimes, and relations with state and local law enforcement." This new policy thrust shifts the focus of the FBI from the investigation of local street crimes to cases of international and domestic terrorism. FBI Director Robert Mueller has acknowledge that, following 9-11, many cases had to be set aside as over 4,000 of the FBI's 11,000 agents directed their attention toward Al-Qaida and anthrax cases. Further, the Bureau has come to rely on state and local law enforcement to fill the gaps where the FBI could not respond. Director Mueller and Attorney General John Ashcroft have stated that the FBI needs to retool by shedding its role in areas where the FBI jurisdiction overlaps with another agency, such as carjacking cases, auto thefts, bank robberies, weapons violations, child support matters, and drug investigations.

Although crime has historically been a state and local issue in this country, "federalization" of crime has been a mainstay of American criminal justice policy since the 1960s. With the events of 9-11 it would appear that the role of federal law enforcement agencies is being reoriented to focus more on international and domestic terrorism and less on local street crimes. This may mean that state and local police will pursue their crime control policies without conflict with federal agencies.

Source: Drawn from Willard M. Oliver, "9-11, Federal Crime Control Policy, and Unintended Consequences," *ACJS Today* 22 (September–October 2002): 1–3.

Researching the Internet

You can read about the Department of Homeland Security at http://www.whitehouse.gov/deptofhomeland.

street crime and drugs to international and domestic terrorism, and the great increase in federal money to pursue the war against terrorism are greatly affecting law enforcement at all levels of government. (See "New Directions in Criminal Justice Policy" for more on the war on terrorism.)

Federal Agencies

Federal law enforcement agencies are part of the executive branch of the national government. They investigate a specific set of crimes defined by Congress. Recent federal efforts against drug trafficking, organized crime, insider stock trading, and terrorism have attracted attention to these agencies, even though they handle relatively few crimes and employ only 74,493 full-time officers authorized to make arrests.

The FBI

The Federal Bureau of Investigation (FBI) is an investigative agency within the U.S. Justice Department with the power to investigate all federal crimes not placed under the jurisdiction of other agencies. Established as the Bureau of

The war on terrorism has greatly expanded the work of federal law enforcement agencies. Here an FBI agent talks on a cell phone as evidence gathering takes place inside a suspected Al-Qaida terrorist cell safehouse in Lackawanna, New York. Six Yemeni American men were indicted on charges of providing "material support" to a foreign terrorist organization.

AP Photo/Don Heupel

Investigation in 1908, it came to national prominence under J. Edgar Hoover, its director from 1924 until his death in 1972. Hoover made major changes in the bureau (renamed the Federal Bureau of Investigation in 1935) to increase its professionalism. He sought to remove political factors from the selection of agents, established the national fingerprint filing system, and oversaw the development of the Uniform Crime Reporting System. Although Hoover has been criticized for many things, such as FBI spying on civil rights and antiwar activists during the 1960s, his role in improving police work and the FBI's effectiveness is widely recognized.

With more than 11,000 agents and an annual budget of $3.3 billion, the FBI now places greater emphasis on five areas: white-collar crime, organized crime, terrorism, foreign intelligence operations in the United States, and political corruption (BJS, 2001b). The bureau provides valuable assistance to state and local law enforcement through its crime laboratory, training programs, and databases of fingerprints, stolen vehicles, and missing persons.

Since Hoover's death, the FBI has a been more responsive to the law enforcement policies of the presidential administration (S. Walker, 1999:57). An indication that the bureau is no longer above criticism, as it was during Hoover's reign, is the congressional investigation of the FBI's 1993 attack on the Branch Davidian compound in Waco, Texas.

To read about the FBI, see http://www.fbi.gov.

Specialization in Federal Law Enforcement

Other federal agencies are concerned with specific kinds of crimes. Within the FBI is the semiautonomous Drug Enforcement Administration (DEA), which assists state and local authorities in investigating the illegal use and importation of controlled drugs. As part of the Treasury Department, the Internal Revenue Service (IRS) pursues violations of tax laws; the Bureau of Alcohol, Tobacco, and Firearms deals with alcohol, tobacco, and gun control; and the Customs Service enforces customs regulations. Other federal law enforcement agencies include the Secret Service Division of the Treasury Department (covering counterfeiting, forgery, and protection of the president), the Bureau of Postal Inspection of the Postal Service (mail offenses), and the Department of Justice's Immigration and Naturalization Service (INS). Many of these agencies are slated to become part of the Department of Homeland Security.

Some other departments of the executive branch, such as the U.S. Coast Guard and the National Parks Service, have police powers related to their specific duties. The park officers need to enforce law and maintain order to protect people and property at national parks. In addition, few people realize that some law enforcement officers in federal agencies focus on noncriminal justice policies. For example, special agents in the U.S. Department of Education investigate student loan fraud, and similar officers in the U.S. Department of Health and Human Services investigate fraud in Medicare and Medicaid programs.

Internationalization of U.S. Law Enforcement

Law enforcement agencies of the U.S. government have increasingly stationed officers overseas, a fact little known by the general public (Nadelmann, 1993). Agents of the Customs Service, the Immigration and Naturalization Service, and the Postal Inspection Service have worked with foreign governments since the nation's founding. In recent years, however, the FBI, IRS, and DEA have also established offices overseas. In a shrinking world with a global economy, the threat of terrorism, electronic communications, and jet aircraft, much crime is transnational, giving rise to a host of international criminal law enforcement tasks. American law enforcement is being "exported" in response to increased international terrorism, drug trafficking, smuggling of illegal immigrants, violations of U.S. securities laws, and money laundering, as well as the potential theft of nuclear materials. Although global crime is not new, more and more people are seeing it as a national security issue (*New York Times,* April 17, 1995:1).

To meet these challenges, U.S. agencies have dramatically increased the number of officers stationed in foreign countries. For example, with a growing concern about Russian organized crime, the FBI has opened a full-fledged office in Budapest. The Hungarian capital is home to many of Russia's mob leaders, who use the city as a portal to Western Europe and the United States. The Hungarian government requested help from the United States and have given FBI agents the right to carry weapons and, in conjunction with their Hungarian counterparts, make arrests (*New York Times,* February 21, 2000:3).

Agencies operating overseas seek to enforce U.S. laws and protect the American people; however, they are often limited by the sovereignty of host countries. Although U.S. law may permit U.S. police to investigate, seize evidence, and make arrests abroad, foreign laws may forbid law enforcement activities by foreign agents on their territory. To deal with these issues, government officials attempt to work jointly with foreign governments on common problems.

The complexities—and risks—of working with the law enforcement agencies of several countries are seen in the DEA's efforts to gain the cooperation of Mexico to stop the flow of Colombian cocaine shipped to the United States through Mexico. In February 1997 those efforts were compromised when the head of Mexico's national drug agency, General Gutierrez Rebollo, was dismissed and detained following charges that he had protected and accepted huge payments from one of Mexico's most notorious drug barons (*New York Times,* February 20, 1997:1).

Interpol, the International Criminal Police Organization, was created in 1946 to foster cooperation among the world's police forces (L. Anderson, 1989). Based today in Lyon, France, Interpol maintains an intelligence databank and serves as a clearinghouse for information gathered by agencies of its 177 member nations. Long criticized by law enforcement experts for its outdated technology, complex bureaucracy, and unreliable protection of sensitive intelligence information, Interpol has undergone major reforms to become a "formidable instrument for combating global crime" (*Los Angeles Times,* January 4, 1998:1).

The U.S. Interpol unit, the U.S. National Central Bureau based in Washington, D.C., facilitates communication with foreign police agencies. It has a permanent staff of 85, plus officers assigned by 13 federal agencies including the FBI, the Secret Service, and the DEA. In recent years Interpol has formed links with state and local police forces in the United States (Geller and Morris, 1992:297). With criminals increasingly viewing their activities on a global scale and taking advantage of technological advances, cooperation among law enforcement agencies around the world is essential.

Since the end of the cold war, American police organizations have assisted United Nations peacekeeping operations in Bosnia, Cyprus, Haiti, Kosovo, Panama, and Somalia. In these countries more than 3,000 police officers from around the world "have engaged in monitoring, mentoring, training, and generally assisting their local counterparts" (Perito, 1999:9). American involvement has emphasized the need for policing to be conducted by civilian police forces whose officers are trained in basic law enforcement skills and who display respect for the law and for human rights.

State Agencies

Every state except Hawaii has its own law enforcement agency with statewide jurisdiction. In about half of the states, state police agencies carry out a wide range of law enforcement tasks. The others have state highway patrols with limited authority, primarily the task of enforcing traffic laws. The American reluctance to centralize police power has generally kept state police forces from replacing local ones.

Before 1900 only Texas had a state police force. The Texas Rangers, a quasimilitary force, protected white settlers from bandits and Native American raids. It had already been established by 1836, when Texas declared its independence from Mexico. Modern state police forces were organized after the turn of the century, mainly as a wing of the executive branch that would enforce the law when local officials did not. The Pennsylvania State Constabulary, formed in 1905, was the first such force. By 1925 almost all of the states had police forces.

The California Highway Patrol provides an example of a state agency: http://www.chp.ca.gov.

All state forces regulate traffic on main highways, and two-thirds of the states have also given them general police powers. In only about a dozen populous states—such as Massachusetts, Michigan, New Jersey, New York, and Pennsylvania—can these forces perform law enforcement tasks across the state. For the most part, they operate only in areas where no other form of police protection exists or where local officers ask for their help. In many states, for example, the crime lab is run by the state police as a means of assisting local law enforcement agencies.

County Agencies

Sheriffs are found in almost every one of the 3,100 counties in the United States (except those in Alaska), employing 152,933 full-time sworn officers. Sheriffs' departments are responsible for policing rural areas, but over time, especially in the Northeast, many of their criminal justice functions have been assumed by the state or local police. In parts of the South and West, however, the sheriff's department is a well-organized force. In 33 states, sheriffs are elected and hold the position of chief law enforcement officer in the county. Even when the sheriff's office is well organized, however, it may lack jurisdiction over cities and towns. In these situations, the sheriff and his or her deputies patrol unincorporated parts of the county or small towns that do not have police forces of their own.

To learn about a county sheriff's department, see the Broward County, Florida sheriff's Web page at http://www.sheriff.org.

In addition to performing law enforcement tasks, the sheriff often serves as an officer of the court; sheriffs may operate jails, serve court orders, and provide the bailiffs who maintain order in courtrooms. In many counties, politics mix with law enforcement: sheriffs may be able to appoint their political supporters as deputies and bailiffs. In other places, such as Los Angeles County and Oregon's Multnomah County, the sheriff's department is staffed by professionals who are hired through competitive civil service processes.

Native American Tribal Police

Through treaties with the United States, Native American tribes are separate, sovereign nations and have a significant degree of legal autonomy. They have the power to enforce tribal criminal laws against everyone on their lands, including non–Native Americans (Mentzer, 1996). The last national census found 1.9 million Native Americans belonging to approximately five hundred tribes. However, many tribes are not recognized by the federal government, and many Native Americans do not live on reservations. Traditionally Native American reservations have been policed either by federal officers of the Bureau of Indian Affairs (BIA) or by their own tribal police. The Bureau of Justice Statistics identified 135 tribal law enforcement agencies with a total of 1,731 full-time sworn officers. An additional 339 full-time sworn officers of the BIA provide law enforcement services on other reservations (BJS, 1999a:32). As the number of non–Native Americans entering reservations for recreational purposes (such as gambling) increases, criminal jurisdiction disputes have risen.

Municipal Agencies

The police departments of cities and towns have general law enforcement authority. City police forces range in size from more than 40,000 full-time sworn officers in the New York City Police Department to only one sworn officer in 1,657 small towns. Slightly more than half of municipal police departments employ fewer than ten sworn officers. There are 410,956 full-time sworn municipal police officers. Sworn personnel are officers with the power to make arrests (BJS, 2000e:1).

Nearly 90 percent of local police agencies serve populations of 25,000 or less, but half of all sworn officers are employed in cities of at least 100,000 (BJS, 1998b:5). The six largest departments—New York City, Chicago, Los Angeles, Houston, Philadelphia, and Detroit—provide law enforcement services to less than 8 percent of the U.S. population, yet they face 23 percent of all violent crime. These big-city departments hire 19 percent of all police employees (BJS, 2002f:10).

In a metropolitan area composed of a central city and many suburbs, policing is usually divided among agencies at all levels of government, giving rise to conflicts between jurisdictions that may interfere with efficient use of police resources. The city and each suburb buys its own equipment and deploys its officers without coordinating with those of nearby jurisdictions. In some areas with large populations, agreements have been made to enhance cooperation between jurisdictions.

In essence, the United States is a nation of small police forces, each of which is authorized, funded, and operated within the limits of its own jurisdiction. This is in direct contrast to the centralized police forces found in many other countries. For example, in France the police are a national force divided between the Ministry of Interior and the Ministry of Defense. All police officers report to these national departments, as can be seen in the Comparative Perspective.

Because of the fragmentation of police agencies in the United States, each jurisdiction develops its own enforcement goals and policies. Each agency must make choices about how to organize itself and use its resources to achieve its goals.

check point

11. What is the jurisdiction of federal law enforcement agencies?
12. Why are some law enforcement agencies of the U.S. government located overseas?
13. What are the functions of most state police agencies?
14. Besides law enforcement, what functions do sheriffs perform?
15. What are the main characteristics of the organization of the police in the United States?

Organization of the Police in France

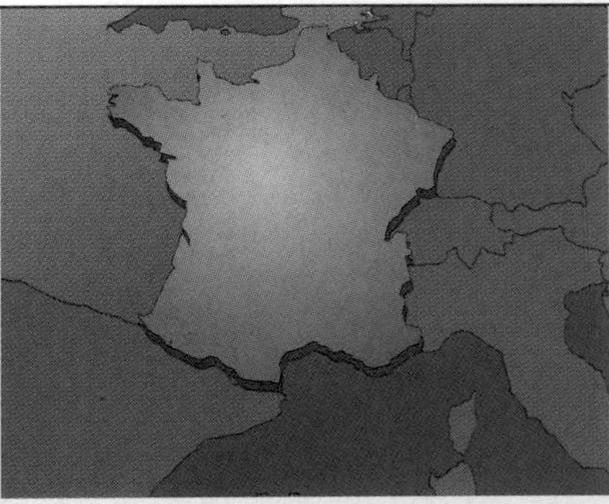

France has a population of about 52 million and a unitary form of government. Political power and decision making are highly centralized in bureaucracies located in Paris. The entire country has a single criminal code and standardized criminal justice procedures. The country is divided into 96 territories known as departments and further divided into districts and municipalities. In each district, a commissaire of the republic represents the central government and exercises supervision over the local mayors.

Police functions are divided between two separate forces under the direction of two ministries of the central government. With more than 200,000 personnel employed in police duties, France has a ratio of law enforcement officers to the general population that is greater than that of the United States or England.

The older police force, the Gendarmerie Nationale, with more than 80,000 officers, is under the military and is responsible for policing about 95 percent of the country's territory. The gendarmerie patrols the highways, rural areas, and those communities with populations of less than ten thousand. Members are organized into brigades or squads collectively known as the Departmental Gendarmerie. They operate from fixed points, reside in their duty area, and constitute the largest component of the force. A second agency, the Mobile Gendarmerie, may be deployed anywhere in the country. These are essentially riot police; their forces are motorized, have tanks, and even have light aircraft. The Republican Guard, the third component of the Gendarmerie, is stationed in Paris, protects the president, and performs ceremonial functions.

The Police Nationale is under the Ministry of the Interior and operates mainly in urban centers with populations greater than ten thousand. The Police Nationale is divided into the Directorate of Urban Police, which is responsible for policing the cities with patrol and investigative functions, and the Directorate of Criminal Investigation, which provides regional detective services and pursues cases beyond the scope of the city police or the gendarmerie. Another division, the Air and Frontier Police, is responsible for border protection. The Republican Security Companies are the urban version of the Mobile Gendarmerie but without the heavy armament.

In addition to traditional patrol and investigative functions, the Police Nationale also contains units responsible for the collection of intelligence information and for the countering of foreign subversion. The Directorate of General Intelligence and Gambling has 2,500 officers and has as its purpose the gathering of "intelligence of a political, social, and economic nature necessary for the information of government." This includes data from public opinion surveys, mass media, periodicals, and information gathered through the infiltration of various political, labor, and social groups. The Directorate of Counterespionage has the mission of countering the efforts of foreign agents on French soil intent on impairing the security of the country.

The police system of the central government of France is powerful; the number, armament, legal powers, and links to the military are most impressive. The turbulent history of France before and after the revolution of 1789 gave rise to the need for the government to be able to assert authority. Since the 1930s France has had to deal not only with crime but also with political instability—the Nazi invasion of 1940, weak governments following World War II, the Algerian crisis in 1958, and student rioting in 1968 all brought conditions that nearly toppled the existing regime. The need to maintain order in the streets would seem to be a major concern of the government.

Source: Adapted from Philip John Stead, *The Police of France* (New York: Macmillan, 1983), 1–12. Copyright © 1983 by Macmillan Publishing Company, a division of Macmillan, Inc. Reprinted by permission of The Gale Group.

Police Functions

The police are expected to maintain order, enforce the law, and prevent crime. However, they perform other tasks as well, many of them having little to do with crime and justice and more to do with community service. They direct traffic, handle accidents and illnesses, stop noisy parties, find missing persons, enforce licensing regulations, provide ambulance services, take disturbed people into protective custody, and so on. The list is long and varies from place to place. Some researchers have suggested that the police have more in common with social service agencies than with the criminal justice system.

The American Bar Association has published a list of police goals and functions that includes the following (Goldstein, 1977:5):

1. Prevent and control conduct considered threatening to life and property (serious crime).
2. Aid people who are in danger of harm, such as the victim of a criminal attack.
3. Protect constitutional rights, such as the right of free speech and assembly.
4. Facilitate the movement of people and vehicles.
5. Aid those who cannot care for themselves: the drunk or the addicted, the mentally ill, the disabled, the old, and the young.
6. Resolve conflict, whether between individuals, groups of individuals, or individuals and government.
7. Identify problems that could become more serious for the citizen, for the police, or for government.
8. Create a feeling of security in the community.

How did the police gain such broad responsibilities? In many places the police are the only public agency that is available 7 days a week and 24 hours a day to respond to calls for help. They are also best able to investigate many kinds of problems. Moreover, the power to use force when necessary allows them to intervene in problem situations.

The functions of the police can be classified into three groups: (1) order maintenance, (2) law enforcement, and (3) service. Police agencies divide their resources among these functions on the basis of community need, citizen requests, and departmental policy.

Order Maintenance

The **order maintenance** function is a broad mandate to prevent behavior that either disturbs or threatens to disturb the peace or involves face-to-face conflict among two or more people. A domestic quarrel, a noisy drunk, loud music in the night, a beggar on the street, a tavern brawl—all are forms of disorder that may require action by the police.

order maintenance
The police function of preventing behavior that disturbs or threatens to disturb the public peace or that involves face-to-face conflict among two or more people. In such situations the police exercise discretion in deciding whether a law has been broken.

Unlike most laws that define specific acts as illegal, laws regulating disorderly conduct deal with ambiguous situations that different police officers could view in different ways. For many crimes, determining when the law has been broken is easy. Order maintenance requires officers to decide not only whether a law has been broken but also whether any action should be taken and, if so, who should be blamed. In a bar fight, for example, the officer must decide who started the fight, whether an arrest should be made for assault, and whether to arrest other people besides those who started the conflict.

Patrol officers deal mainly with behavior that either disturbs or threatens to disturb the peace. They confront the public in ambiguous situations and have wide discretion in matters that affect people's lives. If an officer decides to arrest someone for disorderly conduct, that person could spend time in jail and lose his or her job even without being convicted of the crime.

Officers often must make judgments in order maintenance situations. They may be required to help people in trouble, manage crowds, supervise various kinds of services, and help people who are not fully accountable for what they do. The officers have a high degree of discretion and control over how such situations will develop. Patrol officers are not subject to direct control. They have the power to arrest, but they may also decide not to make an arrest. The order maintenance function is made more complex by the fact that the patrol officer is normally expected to "handle" a situation rather than to enforce the law, usually in an emotionally charged atmosphere. In controlling a crowd outside a rock concert, for example, the arrest of an unruly person may restore order by removing a troublemaker and also serving as a warning to others that they could be arrested if they do not cooperate. However, an arrest may cause the crowd to become hostile toward the officers, making things worse. Officers cannot always predict precisely how their discretionary decisions will promote or hinder order maintenance.

To uphold important American values of equal treatment and respect for constitutional rights, police officers must make decisions fairly and within the boundaries of their authority. Officers may be faced with a difficult, immediate situation that leads them to use force or target specific individuals for restraint. The volatile context of order maintenance situations, where emotions are running high and some people may be out of control, can produce anger and hostility toward officers. If officers must stop a disturbance in a bar, for example, they will inevitably seek to restrain individuals who are contributing to the disturbance. However, if they cannot restrain everyone, they may choose specific individuals or focus their attention on the people standing close at hand. As a result, some citizens may believe that officers are applying unequal treatment or targeting individuals because of their race or ethnicity. Thus the immediacy of order maintenance problems and the need to make quick decisions can create risks that officers will be viewed as acting in manner that is contrary to American values.

Law Enforcement

law enforcement
The police function of controlling crime by intervening in situations in which the law has clearly been violated and the police need to identify and apprehend the guilty person.

The **law enforcement** function applies to situations in which the law has been violated and the offender needs to be identified or located and then apprehended. Police officers who focus on law enforcement serve in specialized branches such as the vice squad and the burglary detail. Although the patrol officer may be the first officer at the scene of a crime, in serious cases a detective usually prepares the case for prosecution by bringing together all the evidence for the prosecuting attorney. When the offender is identified but not located, the detective conducts the search. If the offender is not identified, the detective must analyze clues to find out who committed the crime.

The police often portray themselves as enforcers of the law, but many factors interfere with how effectively they can do so. For example, when a property crime is committed, the perpetrator usually has some time to get away. This limits the ability of the police to identify, locate, and arrest the suspect. Burglaries, for instance, usually occur when people are away from home. The crime may not be discovered until hours or days have passed. The effectiveness of the police is also reduced when assault or robbery victims cannot identify the offender. Victims often delay in calling the police, reducing the chances that a suspect will be apprehended.

As in the case of order maintenance, The important American values of equal treatment and respect for rights can be threatened if officers do not make their law enforcement decisions professionally and with an aspiration for objectivity. If such decisions are perceived to target specific neighborhoods or particular ethnic groups, police actions might generate suspicion and hostility. People in some communities have complained that police enforce narcotics laws primarily in poor neighborhoods populated by members of minority groups. Such perceptions of the police clash with the American values of equal treatment and respect for rights.

Service

service
The police function of providing assistance to the public, usually in matters unrelated to crime.

Police perform a broad range of services, especially for lower-income citizens, that are not related to crime. This **service** function—providing first aid, rescuing animals, helping the disoriented, and so on—has become a major police function. Crime prevention has also became a major component of police services to the community. Through education and community organizing, the police can help the public take steps to prevent crime.

Research has shown how important the service function is to the community. Analysis of more than 26,000 calls to 21 police departments found that about 80 percent of requests for police assistance do not involve crimes; the largest percentage of calls, 21 percent, were requests for information (Scott, 1981). Because the police are available 24 hours a day, people turn to them in times of trouble. Many departments provide information, operate ambulance services, locate missing persons, check locks on vacationers' homes, and intervene in suicide attempts.

Some may claim that valuable resources are being inappropriately diverted from law enforcement to services. However, performing service functions can help police control crime. Through the service function, officers gain knowledge about the community, and citizens come to trust the police. Checking the security of buildings clearly helps prevent crime, but other activities—dealing with runaways, drunks, and public quarrels—may help solve problems before they lead to criminal behavior.

Implementing the Mandate

While the public may depend most heavily on the order maintenance and service functions of the police, it acts as though law enforcement—the catching of lawbreakers—is the most important function. According to public opinion polls, the crime-fighter image of the police is firmly rooted in citizens' minds and is the main reason given by recruits for joining the force.

Public support for budgets is greatest when the crime-fighting function is stressed. This emphasis can be seen in the organization of big-city departments. The officers who perform this function, such as detectives, have high status. The focus on crime leads to the creation of special units to deal with homicide, burglary, and auto theft. All other tasks are left to the patrol division. In some departments, this pattern creates morale problems because extra resources are allocated and prestige devoted to a function that is concerned with a small percentage of the problems brought to the police. In essence, police are public servants who keep the peace, but their organization reinforces their own law enforcement image and the public's focus on crime fighting.

But do the police prevent crime? David Bayley claims that they do not. He says that "the experts know it, the police know it, but the public does not know it" (Bayley, 1994:3). He bases this claim on two facts. First, no link has been found between the number of police officers and crime rates. For example, among cities with populations greater than a million in 1987, Dallas had the highest crime rate (16,282 per 100,000) and Kansas City, Missouri, the lowest (3,789 per 100,000), yet they had the same number of police per capita. Chicago, with the highest number of police per capita—4.1 per 1,000—had a crime rate only slightly above that of San Diego, where there were only 1.5 officers per 1,000 residents.

Second, the main strategies used by modern police have little or no effect on crime. Those strategies are street patrolling by uniformed officers, rapid response to emergency calls, and expert investigation of crime by detectives. Bayley says that the police believe these strategies are essential to protect public safety, yet no evidence exists that they achieve this goal (Bayley, 1994:5).

Peter Manning's observation of many years ago remains valid today: The police have an "impossible mandate":

> To much of the public the police are seen as alertly ready to respond to citizen demands, as crime-fighters, as an efficient, bureaucratic, highly organized force that keeps society from falling into chaos. The policeman himself considers the essence of his role to be the

> dangerous and heroic enterprise of crook-catching and the watchful prevention of crimes. . . . They do engage in chases, in gunfights, in careful sleuthing. But these are rare events. (Manning, 1971:157)

check point

16. What is the order maintenance function? What are officers expected to do in situations where they must maintain order?
17. How do law enforcement situations compare with order maintenance situations?

Police Policy

The police cannot enforce every law and catch every lawbreaker. Legal rules limit the ways officers can investigate and pursue offenders. For example, the constitutional ban on unreasonable searches and seizures prevents police from investigating most crimes without a search warrant.

Because the police have limited resources, they cannot have officers on every street at all times of the day and night. This means that police executives must develop policies as to how the members of their department will implement their mandate. These policies guide officers as to which offenses will receive the most attention and which tactics will be used. They develop policies, for example, on whether to have officers patrol neighborhoods in cars or on foot. Changes in policy—such as increasing the size of the night patrol or tolerating prostitution and other public order offenses—affect the amount of crime that gets official attention and the system's ability to deal with offenders. Policies with regard to high-speed pursuit, a controversial tactic in most departments, are discussed in the Close Up box.

For most of the past half-century, the police have emphasized their role as crime fighters. As a result, police in most communities focus on the crimes covered by the FBI's Uniform Crime Reports. These crimes make headlines, and politicians point to them when they call for increases in the police budget. They are also the crimes that tend to be committed by the poor. Voters pressure politicians and the police to enforce laws that help them feel safe and secure in their daily lives. Because the public views white-collar crimes such as forgery, embezzlement, or tax fraud as less threatening, they get less attention from the police.

Decisions about how police resources will be used affect the types of people who are arrested and passed through the criminal justice system. Think of the hard choices you would have to make if you were a police chief. Should more officers be sent into high-crime areas? Should more officers be assigned to the central business district during shopping hours? What should be the mix of traffic control and crime fighting? These questions have no easy answers. Police officials must answer them according to their goals and values.

American cities differ in governmental, economic, and racial and ethnic characteristics as well as in their degree of urbanization. These factors can affect the style of policing expected by the community. In a classic study, James Q. Wilson found that citizen expectations regarding police behavior are brought to bear through the political process in the choice of the top police executive. Chiefs who run their departments in ways that antagonize the community are not likely to stay in office very long. Wilson's key finding was that a city's political culture, which reflects its socioeconomic characteristics and its government organization, had a major impact on the style of policing found there. Wilson described three different styles of policing—the watchman, legalistic, and service styles (Wilson, 1968). Table 5.2 documents these styles of policing and the types of communities in which they appear.

Go to the *American System of Criminal Justice* Web site at http://www.cj.wadsworth.com/colesmith10e to explore the topic of policing styles in further detail.

High-Speed Pursuit

The suspect's pickup truck barreled across the Bridgeport, Connecticut, city line with a Trumbull police cruiser in hot pursuit. When the driver of the truck lost control, it slammed into a parked station wagon with two women inside. One, a mother of three, later died, and her sister was hospitalized for seven months. The truck continued on its way. Instead of stopping to assist the injured, the officer continued the pursuit.

Trumbull police say the pursuing officer followed departmental procedures. The suspect had broken into a house and stolen a microwave oven and other household goods. Critics say that the officer was so intent on making his collar that he never noticed others on the street.

National Highway and Traffic Safety Administration data show that about four hundred people die annually in police chases nationwide. About 1 to 3 percent of pursuits result in death. In Metro-Dade County, Florida, researchers found that 20 percent of pursuits resulted in injuries and 41 percent in accidents. Only 35 percent of pursuits were initiated to catch suspected felons, with nearly half for traffic violators.

Critics have called for strict rules banning high-speed chases, arguing that the risk to public safety is too great. Police organizations say that officers cannot be constrained too tightly or they will not be able to catch suspects. However, public pressure to restrict high-speed chases has come from accident victims and their families who, since 1980, have filed an increasing number of civil lawsuits.

Many states now require police departments to have written policies governing high-speed chases. Some departments have banned them completely. Others have guidelines requiring officers to consider such factors as driving conditions, the seriousness of the crime, and the danger the suspect poses to the community, before pursuing a suspect. Courts have considered the liability of officers for damages resulting from high-speed chases in light of departmental policies.

As in so much of police work, guidelines may exist, but it is still the officer, acting alone, who must analyze the situation and exercise discretion in a highly emotional environment.

Sources: Geoffrey P. Alpert, "Pursuit Driving: Planning Policies and Action from Agency, Officer, and Public Information," *Police Forum* 7 (January 1997): 3; *Hartford Courant*, September 12, 1997, p. 1.

Researching the Internet

To read more about police pursuit driving, go to http://www.crashprevention.org then click the link for "Find Reports & Brochures," which will lead to a link for "Police Pursuits."

Departments with a *watchman* style stress order maintenance. Patrol officers may ignore minor violations of the law, especially those involving traffic and juveniles, as long as there is order. The police exercise discretion and deal with many infractions in an informal way. Officers make arrests only for flagrant violations and when order cannot be maintained. The broad discretion exercised by officers can produce discrimination when officers do not treat members of different racial and ethnic groups in the same way. The well-known beating of Rodney King by Los Angeles police officers is an example of an abuse resulting from the watchman style.

In departments with a *legalistic* style, police work is marked by professionalism and an emphasis on law enforcement. Officers are expected to detain a high proportion of juvenile offenders, act vigorously against illicit enterprises, issue traffic tickets, and make a large number of misdemeanor arrests. They act as if there is a single standard of community conduct—that prescribed by the law—rather than different standards for juveniles, minorities, drunks, and other groups. Thus, although officers do not discriminate in making arrests and issuing citations, the strict enforcement of laws, including traffic laws, can seem overly harsh to some groups in the community.

Table 5.2 Styles of policing

James Q. Wilson found three distinct styles of policing in the communities he studied. Each style emphasizes different police functions, and each is linked with the specific characteristics of the community.

Style	Defining Characterisics	Community Type
Watchman	Emphasis on maintaining order	Declining industrial city, mixed racial/ethnic composition, blue collar
Legalistic	Emphasis on law enforcement	Reform-minded city government, mixed socioeconomic composition
Service	Emphasis on service with balance between law enforcement and order maintenance	Middle-class suburban community

Source: Drawn from James Q. Wilson, *Varieties of Police Behavior* (Cambridge, Mass.: Harvard University Press, 1968).

Suburban middle-class communities often experience a *service* style. Residents feel that they deserve individual treatment and expect the police to provide service. Burglaries and assaults are taken seriously, while minor infractions tend to be dealt with by informal means such as stern warnings. The police are expected to deal with the misdeeds of local residents in a personal, nonpublic way so as to avoid embarrassment.

In all cases, before officers investigate crimes or make arrests, each police chief decides on policies that will govern the level and type of enforcement in the community. Given that the police are the entry point to the criminal justice system, the decisions made by police officials affect all segments of the system. Just as community expectations shape decisions about enforcement goals and the allocation of police resources, they also shape the cases that will be handled by prosecutors and correctional officials.

check point

18. What are the characteristics of the watchman style of policing?
19. What is the key feature of the legalistic style of policing?
20. Where are you likely to find the service style of policing?

Police Actions

We have seen how the police are organized and which three functions of policing—law enforcement, order maintenance, and service—compose their mandate. We have also recognized that police officers must be guided by policies developed by their superiors as to how policing is to be implemented. Now let us look at the everyday actions of the police as they deal with citizens in often highly discretionary ways. We shall then discuss domestic violence to show how the police respond to serious problems.

Source: Bureau of Justice Statistics, *Sourcebook of Criminal Justice Statistics, 2000* (Washington, D.C.: U.S. Government Printing Office, 2001), Table 2.16.

Encounters between Police and Citizens

To carry out their mission, the police must have the public's confidence, because they depend on the public to help them identify crime and carry out investigations (see "What Americans Think"). Each year one in five Americans have face-to-face contact with law enforcement officers. A third of these contacts involve people seeking help or offering assistance. Another third witness or report a crime. A little less than a third say that the police initiated the contact. Men in their twenties are the most likely to have contact, while Hispanics and African Americans are 70 percent more likely than whites to do so (BJS, 1997e; *Los Angeles Times,* November 23, 1997:A18).

Although most people are willing to help the police, fear, self-interest, and other factors keep some from cooperating. Many people avoid calling the police because they think it is not worth the effort and cost. They do not want to spend time filling out forms at the station, appearing as a witness, or confronting a neighbor or relative in court. In some low-income neighborhoods, citizens are reluctant to assist the police because their past experience has shown that contact with law enforcement "only brings trouble." Without information about a crime, the police may decide not to pursue an investigation. Clearly, then, citizens have some control over the work of the police through their decisions to call or not to call them.

Officers know that developing and maintaining effective communication with people is essential to their job. As Officer Marcus Laffey of the New York Police Department says, "If you can talk a good game as a cop, you're halfway there." He says that police use of "confrontation and force, of roundhouse punches and

Corbis

Police officers often must deal with citizens in emotionally charged situations and in an environment that is apprehensive and perhaps hostile. Here, Miami police wrestle Diego Tintorero to the ground as he protested government plans to return Elian Gonzalez, a young Cuban boy, to the custody of his father in Cuba after the boy's mother drowned while fleeing to Florida from Cuba.

high speed chases" makes the movies and the news, but "what you say and how you say it come into play far more than anything you do with your stick or your gun, and can even prevent the need for them" (Laffey, 1998:38).

Citizens expect the police to act both effectively and fairly—in ways consistent with American values. Departmental policy often affects fairness in encounters between citizens and police. When should the patrol officer frisk a suspect? When should a deal be made with the addict-informer? Which disputes should be mediated on the spot and which left to more formal procedures? Surprisingly, these conflicts between fairness and policy are seldom decided by heads of departments but are left largely to the discretion of the officer on the scene. In many areas the department has little control over the actions of individual officers.

Police Discretion

Police officers have the power to deprive people of their liberty, to arrest them, take them into custody, and use force to control them. In carrying out their professional responsibilities, officers are expected to exercise discretion—to make choices in often ambiguous situations as to how and when to apply the law. Discretion can involve ignoring minor violations of the law or holding some violators to rule-book standards. It can mean arresting a disorderly person or taking that person home.

Go to the Public Policy feature on the American System of Criminal Justice CD to learn more about the issues surrounding police discretion.

In the final analysis, the officer on the scene must define the situation, decide how to handle it, and determine whether and how the law should be applied. Five factors are especially important:

1. *The nature of the crime.* The less serious a crime is to the public, the more freedom officers have to ignore it.
2. *The relationship between the alleged criminal and the victim.* The closer the personal relationship, the more variable the use of discretion. Family squabbles may not be as grave as they appear, and police are wary of making arrests because a spouse may later decide not to press charges.

3. *The relationship between the police and the criminal or victim.* A polite complainant will be taken more seriously than a hostile one. Likewise, a suspect who shows respect to an officer is less likely to be arrested than one who does not.
4. *Race/ethnicity, age, gender, class.* Although contested by many, research shows that officers are more likely to strictly enforce the law against young, minority, poor men while being more lenient to the elderly, whites, and affluent women.
5. *Departmental policy.* The policies of the police chief and city officials promote more or less discretion.

Patrol officers—who are the most numerous, the lowest-ranking, and the newest to police work—have the most discretion. For example, if they chase a young thief into an alley, they can decide, outside of the view of the public, whether to make an arrest or just recover the stolen goods and give the offender a stern warning.

Patrol officers' primary task is to maintain order and enforce ambiguous laws such as those dealing with disorderly conduct, public drunkenness, breach of the peace, and other situations in which it is unclear if a law has been broken, who committed the offense, and whether an arrest should be made. Wilson describes patrol officer's role as "unlike that of any other occupation . . . one in which subprofessionals, working alone, exercise wide discretion in matters of utmost importance (life and death, honor and dishonor) in an environment that is apprehensive and perhaps hostile" (Wilson, 1968:30).

Although some people call for detailed guidelines for police officers, such guidelines would probably be useless. No matter how detailed they were, the officer would still have to make judgments about how to apply them in each situation. At best, police administrators can develop guidelines and training that, one hopes, will give officers shared values and make their judgments more consistent.

Domestic Violence

How the police deal with domestic violence can show the links between police–citizen encounters, the exercise of discretion, and actions taken (or not taken) by officers. Domestic violence, also called "battering" and "spouse abuse," is assaultive behavior involving adults who are married or who have a prior or an ongoing intimate relationship.

Violence by an intimate (husband, ex-husband, boyfriend, or ex-boyfriend) accounts for about 21 percent of all violence experienced by female victims, compared with 3 percent for male victims. The highest rates of nonlethal violence by an intimate are among African American women, women aged 16 to 24, women in households in the lowest income categories (less than $10,000), and women residing in urban areas. A National Crime Victimization Survey estimated that during any one year, 900,000 women aged 12 or older had been victims of violence by an intimate. The survey also found that 30 percent of all female murder victims were killed by an intimate (BJS, 2000i:1, 10).

The Web site of the National Coalition Against Domestic Violence provides resources for victims of domestic violence: http://www.ncadv.org.

Despite (or perhaps because of) the high level of domestic violence in U.S. society, in the past not much was done about it. Before 1970 most citizens and criminal justice agencies viewed domestic violence as a "private" affair best settled within the family. It was thought that police involvement might make the situation worse for the victim because it raised the possibility of reprisal. Yet today, even though the largest number of calls to the police involve family disturbances, about half go unreported.

From the viewpoint of most police departments, domestic violence was a "no-win" situation in which officers responding to calls for help were often set upon by one or both disputants. If an arrest was made, the police found that the vic-

David Portnoy/Black Star

Until the 1970s most citizens and criminal justice agencies viewed domestic violence as a "private" matter best settled within the family. Today, the largest number of calls to the police involve family disturbances.

tim often refused to cooperate with a prosecution. In addition, entering a home to deal with an emotion-laden incident was thought to be more dangerous than investigating "real" crimes. Many officers believed that trying to deal with family disputes was a leading cause of officer deaths and injury. However, this belief has been challenged by researchers who have found that domestic violence cases are no more dangerous to officers than are other incidents (Garner and Clemmer, 1986; Stanford and Mowry, 1990).

Police response to domestic violence is a highly charged, uncertain, and possibly dangerous encounter with citizens in which officers must exercise discretion. In such a situation, how does an officer maintain order and enforce the law in accordance with the criminal law, department policies, and the needs of the victim? This question is addressed in the Close Up box, which presents the stories of Joanne Tremins and Tracey Thurman—two women who suffered years of abuse by their husbands without any action by the police.

check point

21. Why do patrol officers have so much discretion?
22. Why have police in the past failed to arrest in domestic violence situations?

In the past, most police departments advised officers to try to calm the parties and refer them to social service agencies rather than arrest the attacker. This policy of leniency toward male spouse abusers was studied in Chester, Pennsylvania. Researchers found that the police were less likely to arrest a man who attacked a female intimate than they would men who had committed similar violent acts against other victims (Felson and Ackerman, 2001; Fyfe, Klinger, and Flavin, 1997:455–73).

Prodded by the women's movement, police departments began to rethink this policy of leniency when research in Minneapolis found that abusive spouses who are arrested and jailed briefly are much less likely to commit acts of domestic violence again (L. W. Sherman and Berk, 1984:261). Although studies in other cities (Charlotte, Milwaukee, and Omaha) did not produce similar results (N. T. Ho, 2000), the research led some departments to order officers to make an arrest

Battered Women, Reluctant Police

As Joanne Tremins was moving some belongings out of her ramshackle house on South Main Street [Torrington, Connecticut], her 350-pound husband ran over, grabbed the family cat and strangled it in front of Tremins and her children.

For more than three years, Tremins said, she had complained to Torrington police about beatings and threats from her husband. Instead of arresting him, she said, the police acted "like marriage counselors."

The cat attack finally prompted police to arrest Jeffrey Tremins on a minor charge of cruelty to animals. But four days later, outside a local cafe, he repeatedly punched his wife in the face and smashed her against a wall, fracturing her nose and causing lacerations and contusions to her face and left arm.

That Joanne Tremins is suing this New England town of 34,000 is not without historical irony. For it was here that Tracey Thurman . . . won a $2 million judgment against the police department in a federal civil rights case that has revolutionized law enforcement attitudes toward domestic violence.

The Thurman case marked the first time that a battered woman was allowed to sue police in federal court for failing to protect her from her husband. The ruling held that such a failure amounts to sex discrimination and violates the Fourteenth Amendment.

The resulting spate of lawsuits has prompted police departments nationwide to reexamine their long-standing reluctance to make arrests in domestic assault cases, particularly when the wife refuses to press charges. State and local lawmakers, facing soaring municipal insurance costs, are also taking notice.

Here in hilly Torrington . . . Police Chief Mahlon C. Sabo said [the Thurman case] had a "devastating" effect on the town and his seventy-member force. "The police somehow, over the years, became the mediators," said Sabo. "There was a feeling that it's between husband and wife. In most cases, after the officer left, the wife usually got battered around for calling the police in the first place."

Although the law now requires them to make arrests, police officers here said, the

in every case in which evidence of an assault existed (L. W. Sherman et al., 1991:821). Police officers may have supported the arrest policy because it gave them a clear directive as to what to do (Friday, Metzger, and Walters, 1991). Officers in Minneapolis, though, told researchers they preferred to retain the discretion to do what was necessary (Steinman, 1988).

Some people have argued that if arrest stems domestic violence in some cases, arrest followed by prosecution will have an even greater impact. If so, it would seem to be a compelling reason for pursuing all cases of spouse abuse. However, a study of prosecutorial discretion in domestic violence cases in Milwaukee showed that factors such as the victim's injuries and the defendant's arrest record influenced the decision to charge, not just the fact of spouse abuse (Schmidt and Steury, 1989).

In many states, policies have been changed as a result of lawsuits by injured women who claimed that the police ignored evidence of assaults and in effect allowed the spouse to inflict serious injuries (Robinson, 2000). In addition, there is a growing sense that domestic violence can no longer be left to the discretion of individual patrol officers. Today, 23 states and the District of Columbia now require the arrest without a warrant of suspects in violent incidents, even if the officer did not witness the crime but has probable cause to believe that the suspect committed it (Hoctor, 1997). Most large departments and police academies have programs to educate officers about domestic violence.

Even though we can point to policy changes imposed to deal with domestic violence, the fact remains that the officer in the field who must handle these situations. As with most law enforcement situations, laws, guidelines, and training can help; however, as is often true in police work, in the end the discretion of the officer inevitably determines what actions will be taken.

courts toss out many domestic cases for the same reason that long hampered police.

"Unfortunately, many women just want the case dropped and fail to recognize they're in a dangerous situation," said Anthony J. Salius, director of the family division of Connecticut Superior Court. "If she really doesn't want to prosecute, it's very difficult to have a trial because we don't have a witness."

Nearly five years after the attack by her estranged husband, Tracey Thurman remains scarred and partially paralyzed from multiple stab wounds to the chest, neck and face. Charles Thurman was sentenced to fourteen years in prison.

For eight months before the stabbing, Thurman repeatedly threatened his wife and their son, two. He worked at Skee's Diner, a few blocks from police headquarters, and repeatedly boasted to policemen he was serving that he intended to kill his wife, according to the lawsuit.

In their defense, police said they arrested Thurman twice before the stabbing. The first charges were dropped, and a suspended sentence was imposed the second time. Tracey Thurman later obtained a court order barring her husband from harassing or assaulting her.

On June 10, 1983, Tracey Thurman called police and said her husband was menacing her. An officer did not arrive for twenty-five minutes and, although he found Charles Thurman holding a bloody knife, he delayed several minutes before making an arrest, giving Thurman enough time to kick his wife in the head repeatedly.

Less than a year after police were found liable in the attack on Thurman, Joanne Tremins also found that a restraining order obtained against her husband was worthless. . . . Tremins recounted how she made about sixty calls to police to complain about her husband, a cook. But she acknowledges that, on most of the occasions, when the police asked if she wanted him arrested, she said no.

"How could I say that?" she asked. "He's threatening to kill me if I have him arrested. He's threatening to kill my kids if I have him arrested. He'd stand behind the cops and pound his fist into the palm of his hand."

Hours before Tremins strangled the cat, . . . he beat and kicked his wife and her son, Stanley Andrews, fourteen. When an officer arrived, Joanne Tremins said, he told her that he could not make an arrest unless she filed a complaint at the police station.

"My son was all black and blue," Tremins said. "But [the officer] refused to come into my room and look at the blood all over the walls and the floor."

After Tremins was taken into custody for the cat incident, police did charge him with assaulting the son. He was released on bond, and his wife was issued a restraining order.

When her husband approached Tremins days later at a cafe in nearby Winsted, police refused to arrest him, despite the order. After the beating, Jeffrey Tremins was charged with assault and sentenced to two years in prison.

Source: Howard Kurtz, "Battered Women, Reluctant Police," *Washington Post,* February 28, 1988, p. A1.

The Nashville Police Department provides detailed information about domestic violence on its Web page: http://www.police.nashville.org/bureaus/investigative/domestic/default.htm.

Police and the Community

The work of a police officer in an American city can be very difficult, involving hours of boring, routine work interrupted by short spurts of dangerous crime fighting. Although police work has always been frustrating and dangerous, officers today must deal with situations ranging from helping the homeless to dealing with domestic violence to confronting shoot-outs at drug deals gone sour. Yet police actions are sometimes mishandled by officers or misinterpreted by the public, making some people critical of the police.

Special Populations

Urban police forces must deal with a complex population. City streets contain growing numbers of people suffering from mental illness, homelessness, alcoholism, drug addiction, or serious medical conditions, such as acquired immune deficiency syndrome (AIDS). In addition, they may find youthful runaways and children victimized by their parents' neglect. Several factors have contributed to increasing numbers of "problem" people on the streets. These factors include overcrowded jails, cutbacks in public assistance, and the closing of many psychiatric institutions, which must then release mental health patients. Most of these "problem" people do not commit crimes, but their presence disturbs many of their fellow citizens and thus they may contribute to fear of crime and disorder.

Patrol officers cooperate with social service agencies in helping individuals and responding to requests for order maintenance. The police must walk a fine line when requiring a person to enter a homeless shelter, obtain medical assistance, or be taken to a mental health unit (McCoy, 1986; Melekian, 1990). Police departments have developed various techniques for dealing with special populations. In Los Angeles, New York City, and Philadelphia, mobile units are equipped with restraining devices, mace, and medical equipment to handle disturbed people. Madison, Wisconsin, has educated officers about special populations and methods for dealing with them. Birmingham, Alabama, uses social workers to deal with the mentally ill, freeing police to respond to other problems (NIJ, 1988).

Clearly, dealing with special populations is a major problem for police in most cities (Finn, 2002). Each community must develop policies so that officers will know when and how they are to intervene when a person may not have broken the law but is upsetting residents. Inevitably, police officers will make mistakes in some situations or their interactions with troubled people will lead to tragic consequences that generate criticisms from the community. In 2000, for example, a Detroit police officer faced criminal charges and a civil lawsuit after shooting a man whom he believed to be threatening him with a metal rake. Tragically, he did not know that the man was deaf and mute and therefore unable to understand the officer's command to drop the rake. The officer was acquitted of manslaughter charges, but many citizens remained outraged about the shooting incident. Moreover, emotions about the incident and subsequent legal actions ran high because the police officer involved was white and the shooting victim was African American (*Detroit Free Press,* August 10, 2001). Thus the challenges police face in dealing with special populations can also intersect with the additional difficulties of policing in multicultural communities.

Policing in a Multicultural Society

Carrying out the complex tasks of policing efficiently and according to the law is a tough assignment even when the police have the support and cooperation of the public. But policing in a multicultural society like the United States presents further challenges.

In the last half-century, the racial and ethnic composition of the United States has changed. During the mid-twentieth century, many African Americans moved from rural areas of the South to northern cities. In recent years, immigrants from Puerto Rico, Cuba, Mexico, and South America have become the fastest-growing minority group in many cities. Immigrants from Eastern Europe, Russia, the Middle East, and Asia have entered the country in greater numbers than before. Since 1980 the United States has witnessed a huge increase in immigration, rivaling the stream of foreigners that arrived in the early 1900s.

Les Stone/Corbis Sygma

In multicultural America the police must be sensitive to the customs of many groups while still enforcing the law.

Policing requires trust, understanding, and cooperation between officers and the public. People must be willing to call for help and provide information about wrongdoing. But in a multicultural society, relations between the police and minorities are complicated by stereotypes, cultural variations, and language differences. Most of the newer immigrants come from countries around the world with cultural traditions and laws that differ from those in the United States. These traditions may be unfamiliar to American police officers, especially if they cannot communicate easily in English. Moreover, in the aftermath of the tragedy of September 11, law enforcement officials may have increased caution and suspicion when encountering people whom they believe to be, accurately or not, Middle Eastern or Muslim. Lack of familiarity, difficulties in communicating, and excessive suspicion can create risks that officers will violate the American value of equal treatment of all people.

Like other Americans who have limited personal experience and familiarity with people from different backgrounds, officers may attribute undesirable traits to members of minority groups. Historically, many Americans have applied stereotypes to their fellow citizens: Asian Americans are "shifty," Arab Americans are "terrorists," African Americans are "lazy," and Polish Americans are "stubborn." Stereotyping can also affect how people, including members of ethnic minorities, see the police, who are sometimes characterized as "fascists" or "pigs." Treating people according to stereotypes, rather than as individuals, creates tensions that harden negative attitudes.

Very few officers can speak a language other than English. Often, only large urban departments have officers who speak any of the many languages used by new immigrants. Those who speak little English who report crimes, are arrested, or are victimized may not be understood. Language can be a barrier for the police in responding to calls for help and dealing with organized crime. Languages and cultural diversity make it harder for the FBI or local police to infiltrate the Russian, Vietnamese, and Chinese organized crime groups now found in East and West Coast cities.

Public opinion surveys have shown that race and ethnicity are key factors shaping attitudes toward the police. As seen in "What Americans Think," questions of fair treatment by the police differ among racial groups.

Surveys have also shown that when income, education, and victimization are taken into account, African Americans are less favorably disposed toward the police than are whites (Gallup Poll, 1999). Even so, most African Americans and Hispanics are similar to most Anglo Americans in their attitudes toward the police. It is young, low-income racial-minority men who have the most negative attitudes toward the police (S. Walker, Spohn, and DeLeone, 2000). As discussed in the Close Up box, these attitudes help to explain why African Americans believed O. J. Simpson and not the police.

Inner-city neighborhoods—the areas that need and want effective policing—often significantly distrust the police; citizens may therefore fail to report crimes and refuse to cooperate with the police. Encounters between officers and members of these communities are often hostile and sometimes lead to large-scale disorders. For example, in April 2001 three nights of violent protests erupted in Cincinnati, Ohio, after a police officer shot and killed an unarmed African American teenager whom police sought for outstanding misdemeanor and traffic violations.

Same-race policing may lead to a greater willingness of residents of minority neighborhoods to report crimes and to assist investigations. Such policing may also reduce the number of unjustified arrests, misuse of force, and police harassment. The only research on this question found that same-race policing leads to a greater reduction of property crime. The researchers argue that a given number of officers will have a greater impact on crime while requiring fewer arrests, if deployed in a same-race setting (Donohue and Leavitt, 1998).

Race is not the only factor affecting attitudes toward the police. Attitudes also stem from personal experience with the police, a factor that interacts with race. In some neighborhoods, such experience may contribute to discontent with the quality of life. Thus police actions and policies clearly have a significant effect on the attitudes some citizens have about the fairness of the larger political community.

Why do some urban residents resent the police? DiIulio argues that this resentment stems from permissive law enforcement and police abuse of power (DiIulio, 1993:3). The police are charged with failure in giving protection and services to minority neighborhoods and, as we shall see in a later chapter, with abusing residents physically or verbally.

The police are seen as permissive when an officer treats an offense against a person of the same ethnic group as the offender more lightly than a similar offense in which the offender and victim are members of different groups. The

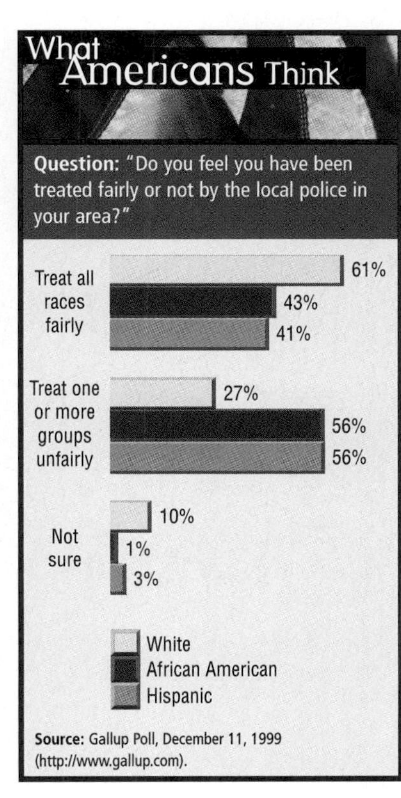

Source: Gallup Poll, December 11, 1999 (http://www.gallup.com).

Close up: Living under Suspicion

In 1995, after one of the most highly publicized criminal trials in American history, Hall of Fame football legend O. J. Simpson, an African American, was found "not guilty" of murdering his ex-wife and a man outside of her home. The trial revealed that Detective Mark Fuhrman, who claimed that he had found a bloody glove in Simpson's backyard, had previously made derogatory, racist remarks about African Americans. Fuhrman was later convicted of committing perjury when he denied ever making racist comments. In a subsequent civil lawsuit, a jury found Simpson liable for the deaths by applying a "preponderance of evidence" standard rather than the stricter "beyond a reasonable doubt" standard used in criminal cases. Public opinion polls showed that African Americans and whites were deeply divided in their views about Simpson's guilt.

If you're white and confused about why so many blacks think O. J. Simpson is innocent of murder, try a simple exercise. Take a few minutes to sit down with an African-American, preferably a male, and ask whether he has ever been hassled by the police. Chances are you'll get an education. . . .

He may have been pulled over for the offense of driving after dark through a white neighborhood, for the misdemeanor of driving with a white woman or for the felony of driving too fancy a car. He may have been questioned for making a suspicious late-night call from a public phone in a suburban mall or, as a boy, for flagrantly riding his new bike on his own street.

He may have been a student or a lawyer—even an off-duty policeman, threatened with drawn guns before he could pull out his badge. Some black parents warn their children never to run out of a store or a bank: Better to be late than shot dead.

When you grow up in vulnerability and live at the margins of society, the world looks different. That difference, starkly displayed after Mr. Simpson's acquittal in the criminal trial, has been less passionate but no less definitive since he was found liable in his civil trial. . . .

For many African-Americans, Mr. Simpson has become more symbol than individual. He is every black man who dared to marry a white women, who rose from deprivation to achievement, who got "uppity" and faced destruction by the white establishment that elevated him. He is every black man who has been pulled over by a white cop, beaten to the ground, jailed without evidence, framed for a crime he didn't commit.

Given that legacy, it is difficult for blacks not to doubt the police, and the doubts undermine law enforcement. In 1995 five Philadelphia policemen were indicted and pleaded guilty after years of fabricating evidence against poor blacks, calling into question some 1,500 prosecutions. One victim was Betty Patterson, a grandmother who spent three years in prison on a phony charge of selling crack; she later won a settlement of nearly $1 million from the city.

The indictments came as the Simpson jurors were hearing tapes of anti-black remarks by Detective Mark Fuhrman that reflected the endemic racism of the Los Angeles Police Department. As documented by the Christopher Commission, which investigated the department after the Rodney King beating in 1991, officers felt so comfortable in their bigotry that they typed racist computer messages to one another, apparently confident that they would face no punishment.

This is precisely the lesson of the black-white reactions to the Simpson case. Most policemen are not racist or corrupt, but most departments do not combat racism as vigorously as they do corruption. Many blacks have come to see the police as just another gang. Alarm bells should be going off, for the judicial system cannot function without credibility.

Of the country's institutions, police departments are probably furthest behind in addressing racism in their ranks. Some corporations are learning that a diverse work force enhances profits. The military knows that attracting volunteers and maintaining cohesion requires racial harmony. Police departments ought to understand that their bottom line is measured in legitimate convictions. They need to retrain officers and screen applicants for subtle bigotry. If morality is not argument enough, try pragmatism.

Source: David K. Shipler, "Living under Suspicion," *New York Times*, February 7, 1997, p. A33.

Researching the Internet

To read about the O.J. Simpson trial, see http://www.law.umkc.edu/faculty/projects/ftrials/ftrials.htm.

police say that such differences occur because they are working in a hostile environment. The white patrol officer may fear that breaking up a street fight among members of a minority group will provoke the wrath of onlookers, while community residents may in fact view inaction as a sign that the police do not care about their neighborhood. It is said that the police do not work effectively on

D.W.B.—Driving While Black

Dr. Elmo Randolph's commute to his office near Newark, New Jersey, usually takes only 40 minutes, but the African American dentist is often late. Since 1991 Randolph has been stopped by state troopers on the New Jersey Turnpike more than 50 times. After stopping his gold BMW by the side of the road, the officer approaches and asks him the same question: "Do you have any drugs or weapons in your car?" One time when he refused to let police search his car, they seized his license and made him wait on the side of the highway for 20 minutes. Randolph asks, "Would they pull over a white middle-class person and ask the same question?" He has sold the BMW.

Profiling—the use of race and ethnicity as clues to criminality—has become a highly charged issue in recent years because of the rising number of complaints that minority drivers were being pulled over by the police in disproportionate numbers. Often the police have justified these stops on the grounds that the drivers fit the profile of a drug runner. Studies give credence to the complaints of African Americans and Hispanics that they are so frequently stopped on highways and frisked on city streets that only their race can explain the pattern. Their leaders have called the use of the tactic blatantly racist and a violation of civil rights. In Congress and several states there have been calls for legislation to end the practice.

The police argue that race is only one characteristic used to determine if a person should be stopped for questioning. They say they are trained to develop a "sixth sense," the instinctive ability to sniff out situations or isolate individuals who seem potentially unsafe. From this viewpoint the police often act against individuals who seem "out of place"—a shabbily dressed youth in a upscale part of town or a man in a pinstriped suit prowling a gritty ghetto. Often, however, a person's furtive look or uneasy gait may give officers a vague sense that something is not right.

One of the core principles of the Fourth Amendment is that the police cannot stop and detain an individual unless there is probable cause or at least reasonable suspicion that he or she is involved in criminal activity. However, in recent years the Supreme Court has weakened this protection. *Whren v. United States* (1996) allows the police to use traffic stops—whether minor or serious, real or alleged—as a reason to stop and search a vehicle and its passengers. *Maryland v. Wilson* (1997) gave the police the power to order passengers out of a car, whether or not there is any basis to suspect they are dangerous. The American Civil Liberties Union has argued that these decisions have given the police virtually unlimited authority to stop and search any vehicle they want.

Determining when and how the police should use race to assess suspects and situations involves a complicated balancing of public safety and civil liberties. Law enforcement experts insist that effective police work depends on quick analysis and that skin color is one factor among many—like dress or demeanor—that officers must consider. But minority leaders say that racial profiling is based on the presumption that African Americans and Hispanics are linked to crime. This has led to the humiliation and physical abuse of innocent citizens.

Sources: Drawn from American Civil Liberties Union, "Driving While Black: Racial Profiling on our Nation's Highways," June 1999 (http://www.aclu.org); *New York Times*, April 9, 1999, p. A21; *Newsweek*, May 17, 1999, p. 34.

Researching the **Internet**

To read reports on allegations of racial profiling by officers in some police departments, see. http://www.aclu.org/PolicePractices/PolicePractices/main.cfm.

crimes such as drug sales, gambling, petty theft, and in-group assault, although these are the crimes that are most common in urban neighborhoods and that create the greatest insecurity and fear among residents.

Research studies reveal the existence of prejudices by many police officers toward the poor and racial minorities. These attitudes lead some officers to see African Americans or Hispanics as potential criminals; as a result these officers tend to exaggerate the extent of minority crime. If both police and citizens view each other with hostility, then their encounters will be strained and the potential for conflict great. As shown in "What Americans Think," African American men aged 18–34 have very different attitudes toward the police than do either whites or the African American population as a whole. As discussed in the Close Up box, minority group members see racial profiling as an example of police bias.

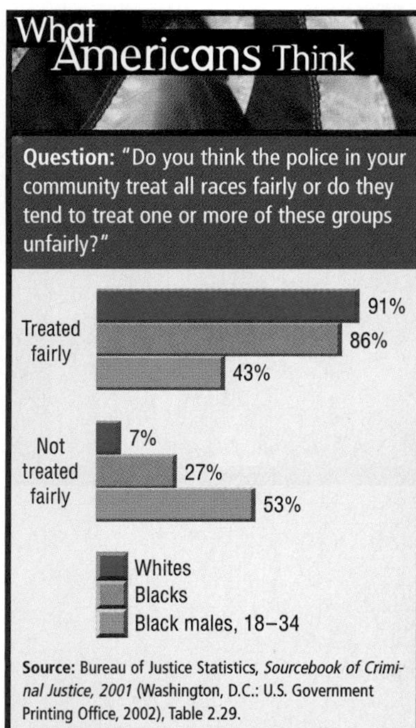

It is little wonder, therefore, that urban ghetto dwellers think of the police as an army of occupation and that the police think of themselves as combat soldiers. As noted by Jerome Skolnick and James Fyfe, the military organization of the police and the "war on crime" can lead to violence against inner-city residents, whom the police see as the enemy (Skolnick and Fyfe, 1993:160). Ultimately, stereotypes, tensions, and conflicts make it much more difficult for police officers to do their jobs effectively. All aspects of officers' responsibilities, including service, order maintenance, and crime control, can suffer when police officers and the communities that they serve lack cooperation and trust.

Community Crime Prevention

There is a growing awareness that the police cannot control crime and disorder on their own. Social control requires involvement by all members of the community. Community crime prevention can be enhanced if government agencies and neighborhood organizations cooperate. As one expert has said, "Voluntary local efforts must support official action if order is to be preserved within realistic budgetary limits and without sacrificing our civil liberties" (Skogan, 1990:125). Across the country, community programs to help the police have proliferated. We now look at several such approaches.

Citizen crime-watch groups have been formed in many communities. More than six million Americans belong to such groups, which often have direct ties to police departments. In Detroit, Neighborhood Watch covers 4,000 of the city's 12,000 blocks; in New York, the Blockwatchers are 70,000 strong and are trained at precinct houses to watch, listen, and report accurately; in Dade County, Florida, the 175,000-member Citizens Crime Watch has extended its operations into schools in an effort to reduce drug use (Garofalo and McLeod, 1989:326). Read about Agnes Brooks, a San Diego police volunteer, in "Doing Your Part."

The Crime Stoppers Program is designed to enlist public help in solving crimes. Founded in Albuquerque, New Mexico, in 1975, it has spread across the country. Television and radio stations present the "unsolved crime of the week," and cash rewards are given for information that leads to conviction of the offender. Although these programs help solve some crimes, the numbers of solved crimes are still small compared with the total number of crimes committed.

To what extent can we rely on such programs to reduce crime and maintain social order? The results are mixed. Research on 40 neighborhoods in six cities shows that while crime prevention efforts and voluntary community groups have seen some success in more affluent neighborhoods, they are less likely to be found in poor neighborhoods with high levels of disorder. In such areas, "residents typically are deeply suspicious of one another, report only a weak sense of community, perceive they have low levels of personal influence on neighborhood events, and feel that it is their neighbors, not 'outsiders,' whom they must watch with care" (McGabey, 1986:230; Skogan, 1990:130).

The National Sheriffs' Association provides information about Neighborhood Watch programs: http://www.usaonwatch.org.

However, successful community-based crime prevention programs exist in Baltimore, Boston, New York, San Francisco, and Seattle (Kelling and Coles, 1996). In each city, community-based groups worked with the police and other government agencies to restore order and control crime. Scholars say that the citizens of a community must take responsibility for maintaining civil and safe social conditions. Experience has shown that "while police might be able to *retake* a neighborhood from aggressive drug dealers, police could not *hold* a neighborhood without significant commitment and actual assistance from private citizens" (Kelling and Coles, 1996:248).

The residents of the Boyd Booth neighborhood of Baltimore have shown how citizens working together can "take back" their community from drug dealers. Before their successful efforts, many residents had "retreated into their homes, afraid to report the violence to the police, afraid that drug dealers would burn them out, or worse" (Kelling and Coles, 1996:197). Assisted by a task force of city agencies, police, the Baltimore Law Center, and community associations, the Boyd Booth residents set out to deal with the problem of abandoned housing. State money was provided to board up vacant houses, improve street lighting, and erect fences. Community members cleaned up trash, closed walkways, conducted vigils and street demonstrations, and held neighborhood picnics. The police increased their use of aggressive foot patrol and of special antidrug units. The results included a 56 percent decrease in violent crime from 1993 to 1995 and an 80 percent drop in narcotics calls to police and drug arrests (Kelling and Coles, 1996:198).

Law enforcement agencies need the support and help of the community for effective crime prevention and control. They need support when they take actions designed to maintain order. They need cooperation with investigations and information about wrongdoing. As we shall see in a later chapter, such support will not be forthcoming if the police abuse their power.

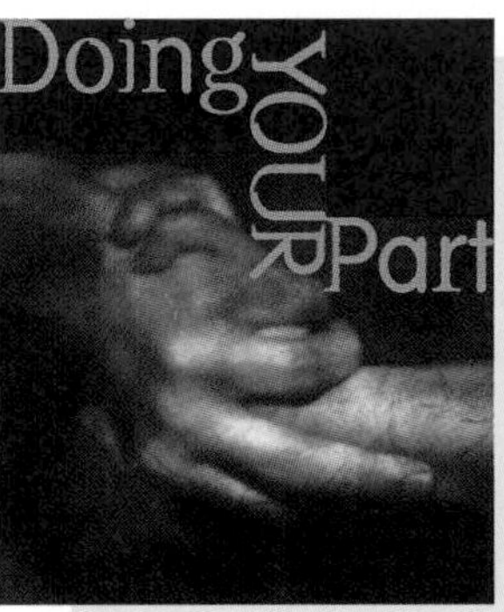

Community Policing Volunteer

San Diego has adopted a Neighborhood Policing Philosophy that emphasizes two concepts: (1) police and citizens share responsibility for identifying and solving crime problems, and (2) law enforcement is but one tool for addressing crime. As Jerry Sanders, the police chief, has said, community policing begins with a practical consideration, "Listen to the community and let them tell us what their priorities are."

One component of San Diego's approach is the 1,200 volunteers who receive police training, wear police-like uniforms and drive around in official vehicles. They help watch their neighborhood or work on police department computers so that officers can patrol.

Agnes Brooks, a 69-year-old civilian police volunteer, was assigned to figure out why a self-storage warehouse had been burglarized 150 times in six months. After studying other warehouses, she decided the problem lay with a sloppy manager, who was removed, and then she had the owner install better lighting, fencing and an electronic lock. The burglaries stopped.

As a community policing volunteer Brooks is doing her part.

Source: *New York Times,* April 4, 1999, p. WK1.

check point

23. What "special populations" pose challenges for policing?
24. What factors make policing in a multicultural society difficult?
25. What are the two basic reasons that urban residents sometimes resent the police?
26. How are citizen watch groups and similar programs helpful to the police?

Go to InfoTrac College Edition. Use the keywords *police volunteers* to learn how some departments are using senior citizens as an additional community policing asset.

Summary

- The police in the United States owe their roots to early nineteenth-century developments in policing in England.
- Like their English counterparts, the American police have limited authority, are under local control, and are organizationally fragmented.
- The three eras of American policing are the political era (1840–1920), the professional era (1920–1970), and the community policing era (1970–present).
- In the U.S. federal system of government, police agencies are found at the national, state, county, and municipal levels.
- The functions of the police are order maintenance, law enforcement, and service.
- Police executives develop policies on how they will allocate their resources according to one of three styles: the watchman, legalistic, or service styles.
- Discretion is a major factor in police actions and decisions. Patrol officers exercise the greatest amount of discretion.
- The problem of domestic violence illustrates the links between police encounters with citizens, their exercise of discretion, and the actions they take.
- Police face challenges in dealing with special populations, such as the mentally ill and homeless, who need social services yet often attract the

attention of police because they disturb or offend other citizens as they walk the streets.

- Policing in a multicultural society requires an appreciation of the attitudes, customs, and languages of minority-group members.
- For police to be effective, they must maintain their connection with the community.

Questions for Review

1. What principles borrowed from England still underlie policing in the United States?
2. What are the three eras of policing in the United States and what are the characteristics of each?
3. What are the functions of the police?
4. How do communities influence police policy and police styles?
5. How does the problem of domestic violence illustrate basic elements of police action?
6. What problems do officers face in policing a multicultural society?

Key Terms

frankpledge (p. 137)
law enforcement (p. 152)
order maintenance (p. 151)
service (p. 152)

For Further Reading

Goldstein, Herman. 1990. *Problem-oriented Policing.* New York: McGraw-Hill. Examination of the move toward problem-oriented, or community, policing. Argues for a shift to this focus.

Nadelmann, Ethan. 1993. *Cops across Borders: The Internationalization of U.S. Criminal Law Enforcement.* University Park: Pennsylvania State University Press. A major work describing the increased presence of American law enforcement agencies in foreign countries.

Skolnick, Jerome H. 1966. *Justice without Trial: Law Enforcement in a Democratic Society.* New York: Wiley. One of the first books to examine the subculture of the police and the exercise of discretion.

Tonry, Michael, and Norval Morris, eds. 1992. *Modern Policing.* Chicago: University of Chicago Press. An outstanding collection of essays by leading scholars examining the history, organization, and operational tactics of the police.

Wilson, James Q. 1968. *Varieties of Police Behavior.* Cambridge, Mass.: Harvard University Press. A classic study of the styles of policing in different types of communities. Shows the impact of politics on the operations of the force.

Going Online

For an up-to-date list of Web links, go to http://www.cj.wadsworth.com/colesmith10e

1. Using InfoTrac College Edition, enter the keywords *comprehensive care model* and access the article "The Comprehensive Care Model," *FBI Law Enforcement Bulletin,* May 1998. List the reasons why the author believes citizen participation is so important for crime prevention. Give examples of things citizen can do to prevent crime and help the police.
2. Go to http://www.FBI.gov and obtain information on entry requirements and the application process for becoming a special agent. What types of people is the FBI seeking? Do you qualify?
3. Using InfoTrac College Edition, enter the keyword *DVERT* and access the article "DVERTing Domestic Violence: The Domestic Violence Enhanced Response Team," *FBI Law Enforcement Bulletin,* June 1998. Describe the Colorado Springs DVERT approach to domestic violence. What actions are police officers expected to take when investigating a domestic violence situation? What has been the impact of the DVERT program?

Checkpoint Answers

1 Limited authority, local control, organizational fragmentation.

2 A rule requiring groups of ten families to uphold the law and maintain order.

3 Established a parish constable system. Citizens were required to pursue criminals.

4 Established the first organized police force in London.

5 To prevent crime without the use of repressive force, to manage public order nonviolently, to minimize and reduce conflict between citizens and the police, to demonstrate efficiency by the absence of crime.

6 Political era, professional era, community policing era.

7 Close ties between the police and local politicians, leading to corruption.

8 The police should be removed from politics, police should be well trained, the law should be enforced equally, technology should be used, merit should be the basis of personnel procedures, the crime-fighting role should be prominent.

9 The professional, crime-fighting role isolated the police from the community. The police should try to solve the problems underlying crime.

10 The police should be close to the community, provide services, and deal with the "little problems."

11 Enforce the laws of the federal government.

12 Because of the increase in international criminality in a shrinking world.

13 All state police agencies have traffic law enforcement responsibilities, and in two-thirds of the states they have general police powers.

14 Operate jails, move prisoners, and provide court bailiffs.

15 Local control, fragmentation.

16 Police have a broad mandate to prevent behavior that either disturbs or threatens to disturb the peace or involves face-to-face conflict among two or more people. Officers are expected to "handle" the situation.

17 The police in order maintenance situations must first determine if a law has been broken. In law enforcement situations, that fact is already known; thus, officers must only find and apprehend the offender.

18 Emphasis on order maintenance, extensive use of discretion, and differential treatment of racial and ethnic groups.

19 Professionalism and using a single standard of law enforcement throughout the community.

20 Suburban middle-class communities.

21 They deal with citizens, often in private, and are charged with maintaining order and enforcing laws. Many of these laws are ambiguous and deal with situations in which the participants' conduct is in dispute.

22 Officers are often set upon by both parties, the victim is often uncooperative, and intervention is thought to be dangerous.

23 Runaways and neglected children; people who suffer from homelessness, drug addiction, mental illness, or alcoholism.

24 Stereotyping, cultural differences, language differences.

25 Permissive law enforcement and police abuse of power.

26 They assist the police by reporting incidents and providing information.

CHAPTER 6

Police Officers and Law Enforcement Operations

William Wilson Lewis III/AP/Wide World Photos, Inc.

"Officer down!" burst over the radios of patrol cars in Bristol, Connecticut, a city of 60,000, on a Saturday evening in May 1996. As police sped to 10 Addison Street, 26-year-old Officer John Reilly lay sprawled on a driveway, bleeding from eight gunshot wounds to his arm, shoulder, abdomen, and legs.

Earlier that day Reilly had responded to a domestic disturbance call at the Addison Street address, where he found that the male suspect had already left. He returned that evening to arrest the suspect when he came home. Reilly was sitting in his patrol car across from the house when a car drove into the driveway. Assuming that he had found his man, Reilly pulled his car behind the one in the driveway. As he approached, the driver ran behind a garage. Reilly followed, but as he turned the corner the suspect fired, hitting him twice. The suspect then made a full circle around the garage, approached Reilly, and shot him six more times. Even as he lay on the ground, Reilly managed to return fire and radio for help as the suspect fled.

Four hours later the suspect, Brent McCall, was spotted limping on his wounded leg as he tried to make his way to his sister's house. When McCall saw the police, he started shooting again. He was finally subdued by the officers' bullets. But McCall, wanted for a series of armed robberies, was not the suspect that Reilly had been seeking.

The shoot-out on Addison Street is the type of incident that gets attention. In much of America, law enforcement agencies face tough situations as they deal with crime, violence, racial tensions, and drugs. Handling such situations, often without warning or with incomplete information, is a tall order for patrol officers—especially because they must try to do so within the limits of the law.

In this chapter, we focus on the actual work of the police as they pursue suspects and prevent crimes. The police must be organized so that patrol efforts can be coordinated, investigations carried out, arrests made, evidence gathered, crimes solved, and violators prosecuted.

QUESTIONS for INQUIRY

- What people become police officers, and how do they learn their jobs?
- What is the police officer's "working personality"?
- How are the police organized?
- What three factors affect police response?
- What are the main functions of police patrol, investigation, and special operations units?

Who Are the Police?

As you read the opening description of Officer Reilly's shooting and injuries, could you picture yourself in a situation that poses such dangers? Who would want to face such risks? What motivates someone to choose such a career? These questions are important because they help to determine which people will be granted the authority to carry firearms and make discretionary decisions about arrests, searches, and even ending the lives of other human beings by pulling the trigger during stressful, fast-moving, and dangerous scenarios.

Because policing is such an important occupation, society would obviously benefit from recruiting its most thoughtful, athletic, and dedicated citizens as police officers. Happily, many such individuals are attracted to this field. Yet many other people who would make fine law enforcement officers turn to other occupations because policing is such a difficult job. The modest salaries, significant job stress, and moments of danger involved in police work can deter some individuals from choosing this public service occupation.

If you or someone you know plans a career in law enforcement, ask yourself what aspects of the job make it more appealing than other kinds of work. Some people might want the adventure and excitement of investigating crimes and catching suspects. Others might be drawn to the satisfactions that come from being a public servant. Still others may be attracted to a civil service job with good benefits. Table 6.1 presents the reasons people give for choosing police work as a career.

Table 6.1 Reasons for choosing police work as a career

To what extent do the reasons for choosing police work differ from those that might be given for choosing other careers? What explains the different responses given by men and women?

Reason	Male	Female	Total
Variety	62.2%	92.1%	69.4%
Responsibility	50.4	55.3	51.6
Serve public	48.7	50.0	49.0
Adventure	49.6	39.5	47.1
Security	46.2	34.2	43.3
Pay	43.7	42.1	43.3
Benefits	36.1	31.6	35.0
Advancement	31.9	34.2	32.5
Retirement	27.7	5.3	22.3
Prestige	16.0	13.2	15.3

Source: Harold P. Slater and Martin Reiser, "A Comparative Study of Factors Influencing Police Recruitment," *Journal of Police Science and Administration* 16 (1988): 170.

Recruitment

How can departments recruit well-rounded, dedicated public servants who will represent the diversity of contemporary America? All agencies require

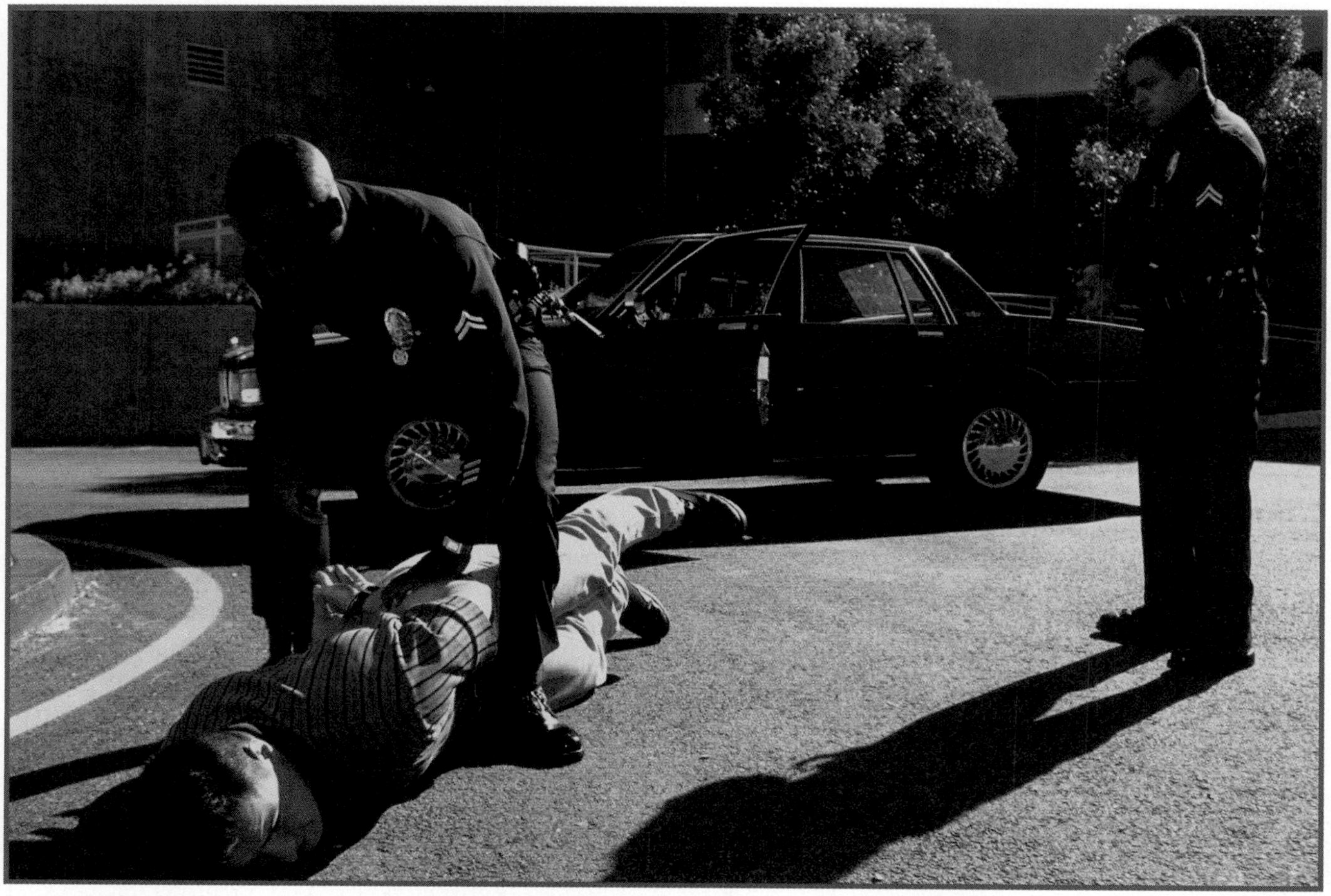

Kim Kulish/CORBIS SABA

Violent arrest training at the Los Angeles Police Academy includes hands-on demonstrations such as this one, in which a recruit arrests a handcuffed suspect while another officer provides backup.

recruits to pass physical fitness tests, and they check to see if applicants have criminal records. Agencies increasingly require recruits to undergo psychological evaluations, because each officer will ultimately make important discretionary decisions, including those that may determine life and death in stressful situations (Langworthy, Hughes, and Sanders, 1995:26).

Among the potential recruits who fulfill these requirements, what other factors determine who is hired by specific law enforcement agencies? One factor is the compensation that departments offer. The average starting salary in 2001 was more than $32,000 plus the likelihood of overtime pay (BJS, 2002e: Table 1.66). Federal agencies and others that provide good compensation and benefits tend to attract larger numbers of applicants. Because of limited budgets, rural sheriffs' departments, by contrast, may have a more difficult time recruiting a competitive applicant pool. Such departments may recruit outstanding officers who want to live in a particular rural community but they may also have officers lured away by more attractive compensation packages in other agencies.

The U.S. Department of Labor provides detailed descriptions of the job responsibilities, qualifications, and training for many different law enforcement positions: http://www.bls.gov/oco/ocos160.htm.

Another factor is the educational level of potential recruits. Most departments require only a high school diploma, yet they actually may seek to recruit people with at least some college education. Only 1 percent of local police departments require a four-year college degree, but 8 percent of departments require a two-year degree, and 14 percent require some college education (Reaves and Goldberg, 2000). The number of departments requiring college classes for officers is steadily growing. The expansion of criminal justice programs at community colleges and universities throughout the United States has produced increasing numbers of law enforcement officers who have taken college courses in criminology, law, sociology, and psychology. Competitive entry-level positions in the most sought-after agencies, including federal law enforcement agencies, state police departments, and those in the cities and suburbs (which provide the most generous pay and benefits), now often require college education. Fortunately, the expansion of college criminal justice programs has helped to provide qualified applicants.

Many law enforcement agencies encourage their personnel to continue with college courses and advanced degrees. Frequently, experienced officers finish their bachelor's degrees or earn master's degrees in order to enhance their prospects for promotion. Increasingly, universities' criminal justice departments are providing online courses that permit officers to earn degrees via the Internet.

Debate continues about whether college-educated officers perform better than those who lack advanced education (Worden, 1990). The idea that college-educated officers would be better decision makers and make more effective officers helped to spur the creation of the federal Police Corps program (Gest, 2001). Although some researchers found that a college education makes little difference for police performance, other scholars have concluded that employment of college-educated officers reduces disciplinary problems and citizens' complaints while it improves report writing and other aspects of performance (Krimmel, 1996; Lersch and Kunzman, 2001). Obviously, education alone does not determine performance; departmental training, supervision, and other factors also shape it.

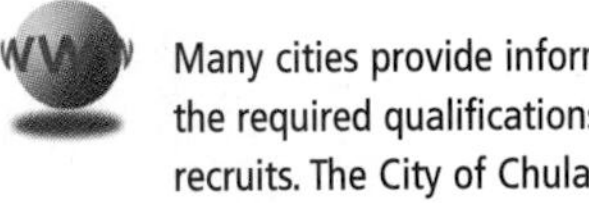

Many cities provide information on the required qualifications for police recruits. The City of Chula Vista, California, provides one such example: http://www.ci.chula-vista.ca.us/polrec.htm.

Contemporary developments pose new issues for the recruitment of law enforcement officers. First, in some agencies large cohorts of officers are approaching retirement age. Such agencies may need to undertake vigorous recruiting just as a second factor is shaping law enforcement nationally: the dramatic acceleration of hiring for federal agencies and private security positions in the aftermath of the attack on the World Trade Center and the Pentagon on September 11, 2001. Many federal agencies, including the FBI and Customs Service, faced an immediate need for new recruits. In addition, creation of the Department of Homeland Security will result in job changes within federal agencies, such as the movement of officers from various agencies into the expanded Sky Marshals program to provide security on airline flights. At the same time, private businesses throughout the country recognized a need for additional personnel to provide employee background checks, on-site security, emergency-response planning, and technical operations. As job opportunities in law enforcement and private security increase, it remains to be seen whether colleges' criminal justice programs will produce enough graduates to permit all employers to find the qualified applicants that they seek.

Figure 6.1
The changing profile of the American police officer
Today about one in ten officers is female and one in five belongs to a racial or ethnic minority.

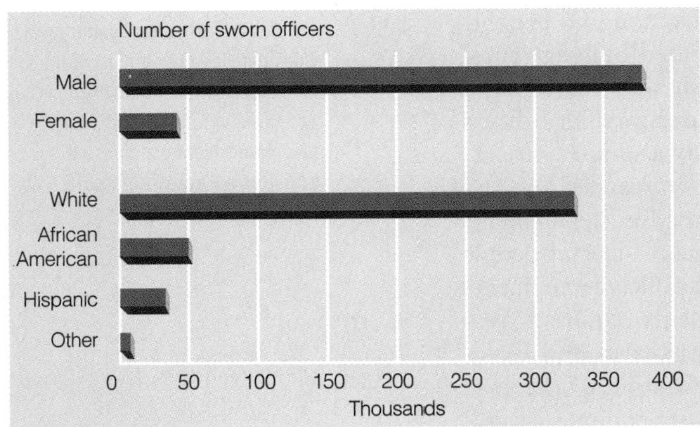

*Includes Asian, Pacific Islander, Native American, and Native Alaskan.
Source: Brian A. Reaves and Andrew L. Goldberg, *Local Police Departments, 1997* (Washington, D.C.: Bureau of Justice Statistics, U.S. Government Printing Office, 2000), 3.

The Changing Profile of the Police

For most of the nation's history, almost all police officers were white men. Today, women and minorities represent a growing percentage of police departments in many areas (see Figure 6.1). There are several reasons for this. In 1968 the National Advisory Commission on Civil Disorders found that police–minority relations greatly contributed to the ghetto riots of the 1960s. The Equal Employment Opportunity Act of 1972 bars state and local governments from discriminating in their hiring practices. Pressured by state and federal agencies as well as by lawsuits, most city police forces have mounted campaigns to recruit more minority and female officers (S. E. Martin, 1991). Since the 1970s the percentage of minority group members and women has doubled. More than 22 percent of officers nationwide belong to minority groups. The percentage is even larger—38 percent—in big-city police departments (Reaves and Hickman, 2002).

The advancement of diversity within police forces reflects the American value of equal opportunity. Although the country has a long history of racial and gender discrimination, such actions clash with the Constitution's equal protection clause. In addition to promoting equality, the expansion of employment opportunities to additional groups may provide significant benefits for law enforcement officials. If people in neighborhoods composed largely of members from a specific ethnic or racial group see the police as "outsiders" who are different and hostile, developing the community cooperation needed to prevent and investigate crimes can be difficult. When a force employs police officers from all demographic groups, the police gain legitimacy because they are seen as reflecting the interests of all people. Further, they may gain concrete benefits in communication and cooperation.

Go to the *American System of Criminal Justice* Web site at http://www.cj.wadsworth.com/colesmith10e to explore the topic of the changing profile of the police in further detail.

Unfortunately, many of the minority and female officers who served as trailblazers to desegregate many departments faced hostility and harassment from their colleagues as they attempted to prove themselves. Many of these courageous officers also faced disrespect and hostility from citizens who did not believe that they could be effective. Although employment discrimination lawsuits that arise periodically indicate that some officers believe racial and gender discrimination still exists, especially with respect to promotions, female and minority officers have become well-accepted as capable and valuable law enforcement professionals throughout the country.

Minority Police Officers

Before the 1970s many police departments did not hire nonwhites. As this practice declined, the makeup of police departments changed, especially in large cities. A study of the nation's 62 local police departments serving a population of 250,000 or more found that from 1990 to 2000 the percentage of African American officers rose to 20 percent of the force, Hispanics rose to 14 percent, and Asian/Pacific Islander/Native Americans to 3.2 percent (Reaves and Hickman, 2002). The fact that minority officers constitute 38 percent of these departments represents a dramatic change in staff composition over the past two decades.

As the population and political power shift toward minorities in some American cities, the makeup of their police forces reflects this change. Three-quarters of Detroit's population is now African American, as is about 63 percent of the city's police officers. In El Paso and San Antonio, Texas, which have large Hispanic populations, 72 percent and 42 percent respectively of those police departments are Hispanic. The extent to which the police reflect the racial composition of a city is believed to affect police–community relations and thus the quality of law enforcement. A survey of Detroit residents found that African Americans held more favorable attitudes toward the police than did whites. As researchers note, "In Detroit, the people who perform the police function are not alien to African Americans; instead they represent an indigenous force" (Frank et al., 1996:332).

The election of an African American or Hispanic mayor does not always produce an immediate change in the composition of the police force. Surprisingly, in the melting pot of New York City, the police are among the most racially imbalanced in the United States, with white officers composing 67 percent of the force but only 43 percent of the population (*New York Times,* March 3, 1999:A14).

Women on the Force

Women have been police officers since 1905, when Lola Baldwin was made an officer in Portland, Oregon. However, the number of women officers remained small for most of the twentieth century because of the belief that policing was "men's work." This attitude changed as the result of federal and state laws against employment discrimination as well as court decisions enforcing those laws. Court decisions opened up police work for women by prohibiting job assignments by gender; changing minimum height, weight, and physical fitness requirements; and insisting that departments develop job classification and promotion criteria that were nondiscriminatory (*Blake v. Los Angeles,* 1979; *Griggs v. Duke Power Company,* 1971).

The percentage of female officers rose from 1.5 percent of sworn officers in 1970 to about 10 percent today (Reaves and Goldberg, 2000). Interestingly, the larger the department, the higher the proportion of women as sworn officers. In cities of more than 250,000, women make up 16 percent of officers (Reaves and Hickman, 2002). By contrast, women make up only 2 to 5 percent of officers, on average, in cities with fewer than 50,000 inhabitants (Reaves and Goldberg, 2000). In some police departments, such as Detroit, more than 20 percent of officers are women (S. Walker and Turner, 1992). A study of 800 police departments by the International Association of Chiefs of Police (IACP) found that almost 20 percent of the departments surveyed had no women officers, and of the nation's 17,000 departments, only 123 had women serving as chiefs (IACP, 1998:5).

Although some male police officers still question whether women can handle dangerous situations and physical confrontations, most policewomen have easily met the expectations of their superiors. However, the IACP survey found that 25 percent of top law enforcement officials expressed concerns that female officers could not handle physical conflicts (IACP, 1998:23). Yet, studies done by the Police Foundation and other researchers have found that, in general, male and female officers perform in similar ways. Alissa Worden's research found few differences in the ways male and female officers viewed "their role, their clientele, or their departments" (Worden, 1993). Research has also found that most citizens have positive things to say about the work of policewomen (Bloch and Anderson, 1974; Grennan, 1987; Sichel, 1978; Worden, 1993). Some researchers believe that women have generally superior performance in avoiding excessive use of force and interviewing crime victims, especially in cases of sexual assault and domestic violence (Prussel and Lonsway, 2001). Rape victims may also specifically request to be interviewed by a female officer, so gender diversity on a police force may be valuable in investigating specific types of crimes or dealing with specific victims and witnesses (Jordan, 2002). See the Comparative Perspective for more on how social attitudes affect female officers.

Despite these findings, women still have trouble breaking into police work. Cultural expectations of women often conflict with ideas about the proper behavior of officers, as the Close Up box reveals.

Many people do not think women are tough enough to confront dangerous suspects. Also, women often find it hard to gain promotions and must contend with prejudice from their male colleagues. Especially with regard to patrol duty, questions like the following are often raised:

- Can women handle situations that involve force and violence?
- What changes must be made in training and equipment in order to accommodate women?
- Should women and men have equal opportunities to be promoted?
- Does assigning men and women as patrol partners tend to create tensions with their spouses?

As these questions reveal, women have to overcome resistance from their fellow officers and some citizens. In particular, they encounter resistance when they assert their authority. They must often endure sexist remarks and worse forms of sexual harassment. Many male officers were upset by the entry of women into what they viewed as a male world. They complained that if their patrol partner was a woman, they could not be sure of her ability to provide necessary physical help in times of danger. The challenges for female officers from minority groups may be even more difficult if they perceive others to doubt their qualifications

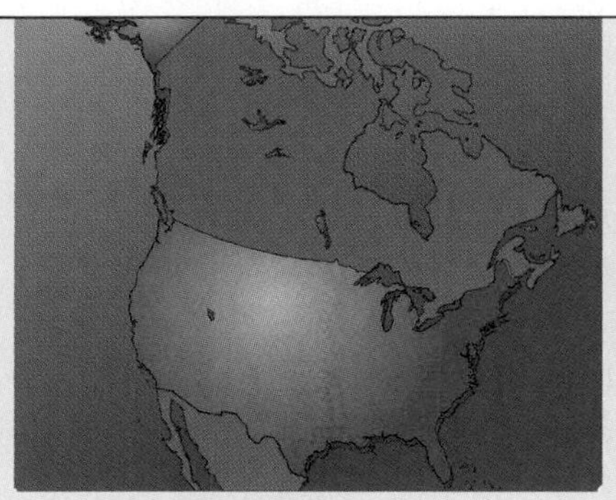

Female Police Officers and the Status of Women in Society

Opportunities for women to serve as law enforcement officers are typically affected by a society's views about the appropriate roles for women. In a country where women are expected to devote themselves to caring for their homes and children, they may not be permitted to undertake careers in law enforcement. Even if women begin to assert themselves through greater activity in business and government, government officials' concerns about women's capacity to fulfill police duties may limit their opportunities. For example, in Kuwait, a predominantly Muslim country in which men have traditionally controlled government and commerce, the government did not propose permitting women to become police officers until 2001.

Even if policy makers are receptive to the idea that women can serve as law enforcement officers, they may have concerns about whether men will accept assertions of authority by policewomen. Will men resist arrest, refuse to cooperate, and otherwise reject the authority of women serving in the police department? This is an important question because police require cooperation from the community in order to be effective.

Conversely, in societies in which women lack equal status, problems may arise from male police officers' ignoring or undervaluing the concerns of female citizens. Women who are victims of crimes, especially domestic violence, may feel that they cannot gain protection from local law enforcement authorities. One approach undertaken in a few countries to address these issues has been creation of all-women police units who focus their efforts on addressing crimes that affect women.

In 1985, after concerted lobbying by women's rights advocates, Brazil created women's police stations. Although Brazil's constitution bars discrimination against women, many women victimized by domestic violence and other crimes found that male police officers were not responsive to their complaints. By contrast, the female officers who staff the women's police stations place special emphasis on addressing domestic violence, rapes, and death threats against women.

In the 1990s the state of Tamil Nadu in India established all-women police units that were responsible for crimes against women. They handle such matters as sexual assault cases, false marriage promises, and violence against women when there are dowry disputes. Initially, officers in these units expressed satisfaction with their positions because their supervisors shared a common vision of the role of policewomen. Everyone respected the officers' needs to fulfill their own family responsibilities and, unlike officers in some other countries, they were free from sexual harassment.

These examples differ greatly from the situation in the contemporary United States, where departments are required by employment discrimination laws to integrate women into all law enforcement functions. If female officers in the United States were limited to certain tasks, that would convey a clear message about the limits of their authority and their inferior status within the department. In other societies, the process of integration may proceed more slowly, if at all, when there are no legal rules and political forces that support women's aspirations for equality. It is possible that integration and equality may never be achieved if cultural values and leaders with political power resist such developments. In the case of the female police units in Tamil Nadu, India, recent research indicates increasing dissatisfaction with heavy workloads and lack of promotion opportunities among the female officers. It remains to be seen how their aspirations for integration and equality within police departments will proceed.

Sources: "Kuwaiti Cabinet Approves Female Police," *Washington Report on Middle East Affairs* 20 (July 2001): 39; Mangai Natarajan, "Women Police in Traditional Society: Test of a Western Model of Integration," *International Journal of Comparative Sociology*, February–May 2001, pp. 211–33; Linda Robinson and Jack Epstein, "Battered by the Myth of Machismo: Violence against Women Is Endemic in Brazil," *U.S. News and World Report*, April 4, 1994, p. 40.

and ability because of their race as well as their gender (Dodge and Pogrebin, 2001).

In short, policewomen often have to prove themselves to many people. One night in 1987 Letitia Cook had the chance to do just this when she and her partner broke up a fight in a barroom. She was 21 and new to the Montville, New Jersey, department and the town's first female officer. She was "anxious to prove

Patrol Officer Cristina Murphy

Jim Dyer was drunk out of his mind when he called the Rochester Police Department on a recent Saturday night. He wanted to make a harassment complaint; a neighbor, he claimed, was trying to kill him with a chair. Officer Cristina Murphy, 27, a petite, dark-haired, soft-spoken three-year veteran of the Rochester P.D., took the call.

"What's the problem here?" she asked when she arrived at the scene. A crowd had gathered. Dyer's rage was good local fun.

"You're a woman!" Dyer complained as Murphy stepped from her squad car. "All they send me is women. I called earlier and they sent me a Puerto Rican and she didn't do nothing either."

"Mr. Dyer, what exactly is the problem?"

"Dickie Burroughs is the problem. He tried to kill me." Through a drunken haze, Dyer made certain things clear: He wanted Dickie Burroughs locked up. He wanted him sent to Attica for life. He wanted it done that night. Short of all that, Dyer hoped that the police might oblige him by roughing up his foe, just a little.

"We don't do that sort of thing," Murphy explained in the voice she uses with drunks and children. "Mr. Dyer, I can do one of two things for you. I can go find Mr. Burroughs and get his side of the story; I can talk to him. The other thing I can do is take a report from you and advise you how to take out a warrant. You'll have to go downtown for that."

Later, in her squad car, Murphy would say that she isn't usually so curt to complaining citizens. "But it's important not to take crap about being a female. Most of the stuff I get, I just let slip by. This guy, though, he really did not want service on his complaint, he wanted retribution. When he saw a woman taking his call, he figured that I wouldn't give it to him; it never struck him that no male officer would either. You know, everyone has an opinion about women being police officers—even drunks. Some people are very threatened by it. They just can't stand getting orders from a woman. White males, I think, are the most threatened. Black males seem the least—they look at me and they just see blue. Now women, they sometimes just can't stand the idea that a woman exists who can have power over them. They feel powerless and expect all women to feel that way too. As I said, everyone has an opinion."

Source: Claudia Driefus, "People Are Always Asking Me What I'm Trying to Prove," *Police Magazine,* March 1980. Reprinted by permission of the Edna McConnell Clark Foundation.

Researching the Internet

To read information about policewomen in the United States as well as other countries, see the Web site of the International Association of Women Police: http://www.iawp.org.

Read a report about the history of women in American policing: http://www.ncjrs.org/policing/fem635.htm.

her moxie to the male officers who showed up minutes later." As she said ten years later, "I got right down on the ground with everyone else. That's when they stepped back and said: 'All right, she can handle herself. She can help us' " (*New York Times,* August 7, 1997:A35).

In a few cities, such as Atlanta and Portland, Oregon, a small number of women have risen to the top ranks of police departments. Elsewhere, employment discrimination lawsuits have helped to open promotion opportunities for women. In many other departments, however, few women have been promoted to supervisory jobs. Thus it is usually left to male administrators to identify and combat any remaining barriers to the recruitment, retention, and promotion of female officers (S. Walker and Turner, 1992).

The role of women in police work will undoubtedly evolve along with changes in the nature of policing, in cultural values, and in the organization of law enforcement. As citizens become accustomed to women on patrol, female officers will find gaining their cooperation easier. Finally, there are signs that more and more citizens and policemen are beginning to take for granted that women will be found on patrol along with men (S. E. Martin, 1989).

Training

The performance of the police is not based solely on the types of people recruited; it is also shaped by their training. Most states require preservice training for all recruits. This is often a formal course at a police academy, but in some states candidates for police jobs must complete a basic training program, at their own expense, before being considered for employment. Large departments generally run their own programs, while state police academies may train their own officers as well as recruits from municipal units. Candidates for positions in rural and small-town units may have to pay their own way through training programs at community colleges in order to receive the necessary certification to become a law enforcement officer. The courses range from two-week sessions that stress the handling of weapons to academic four-month programs followed by fieldwork. Recruits hear lectures on social relations, receive foreign-language training, and learn emergency medical treatment.

To read about the training provided for law enforcement officers in Connecticut, see the Web site of the Connecticut Police Academy: http://www.post.state.ct.us.

Recruits need formal training in order to gain an understanding of legal rules, weapons use, and other aspects of the job. However, the police officer's job also demands skills in dealing with people that cannot be learned from a lecture or a book. Much of the most important training of police officers takes place during a probationary period when new officers work with and learn from experienced officers. When new officers finish their classroom training and arrive for their first day of patrol duty, they may be told by experienced officers, "Now, I want you to forget all that stuff you learned at the academy. You really learn your job on the streets."

The process of **socialization**—in which members learn the symbols, beliefs, and values of a group or subculture—includes learning the informal rather than the rule-book ways of law enforcement. New officers must learn how to look "productive," how to take shortcuts in filling out forms, how to keep themselves safe in dangerous situations, how to analyze conflicts so as to maintain order, and a host of other bits of wisdom, norms, and folklore that define the subculture of a particular department. Recruits learn that loyalty to other officers, esprit de corps, and respect for police authority are highly valued.

socialization
The process by which the rules, symbols, and values of a group or subculture are learned by its members.

In police work, the success of the group depends on the cooperation of its members. All patrol officers are under direct supervision, and their performance is measured by their contribution to the group's work. Besides supervisors, the officers' colleagues also evaluate and influence them. Officers within a department may develop strong, shared views on the best way to "handle" various situations. How officers use their personal skills and judgment can mean the difference between defusing a conflict and making it worse so that it endangers citizens and other officers. In tackling their "impossible mandate," new recruits must learn the ways of the world from the other officers, who depend on them and on whom they depend.

check point

1. What are the main requirements for becoming a police officer?
2. How has the profile of American police officers changed?
3. What type of training do police recruits need?
4. Where does socialization to police work take place?

(Answers are at the end of the chapter.)

The Police Subculture

A **subculture** is made up of the symbols, beliefs, values, and attitudes shared by members of a subgroup within the larger society. The subculture of the police helps define the "cop's world" and each officer's role in it. Like the subculture of any occupational group that sees itself as distinctive, police develop shared values that affect their view of human behavior and their role in society. As we just saw, the recruit learns the norms and values of the police subculture through a process of socialization. This begins at the training academy but *really* takes hold on the job through the interactions with experienced officers. The characteristics

subculture
The symbols, beliefs, and values shared by members of a subgroup of the larger society.

of a subculture are not static; they change as new members join the group and as the surrounding environment changes. For example, the composition of the police has changed dramatically during the past 30 years in terms of race, gender, and education. We should thus expect that these "new officers" will bring different attitudes and cultural values to the police subculture (S. Walker, 1999:332).

There are four key issues in our understanding of the police subculture: the concept of the "working personality," the role of police morality, the isolation of the police, and the stressful nature of much police work.

The Working Personality

working personality
A set of emotional and behavioral characteristics developed by a member of an occupational group in response to the work situation and environmental influences.

Social scientists have demonstrated that there is a relationship between one's occupational environment and the way one interprets events. The police subculture produces a **working personality**—that is, a set of emotional and behavioral characteristics developed by members of an occupational group in response to the work situation and environmental influences. The working personality of the police thus influences the way officers view and interpret their occupational world.

The working personality of the police is defined by two elements of police work: (1) the threat of danger and (2) the need to establish and maintain one's authority (Skolnick, 1966:44).

Danger

Because they often face dangerous situations, officers are keenly aware of clues in people's behavior or in specific situations that indicate that violence and lawbreaking may be about to happen. As they drive the streets, they notice things that seem amiss—a broken window, a person hiding something under a coat—anything that looks suspicious. As sworn officers, they are never off duty. People who know that they are officers will call on them for help at any time, day or night.

Liaison

The occupational environment and working personality are so interlocked that they greatly influence the daily experience of the police.

Throughout the socialization process, experienced officers warn recruits to be suspicious and cautious. Rookies are told about officers who were killed while trying to settle a family squabble or writing a traffic ticket. The message is clear: Even minor offenses can escalate into extreme danger. Constantly pressured to recognize signs of crime and be alert to potential violence, officers may become suspicious of everyone, everywhere. Thus, police officers are in a constant state of "high alert," always on the lookout and never letting down their guard.

Being surrounded by risks creates tension in officers' lives. They may feel constantly on edge and worried about possible attack. This concern with danger may affect their interactions with citizens and suspects. Citizens who come into contact with them may see their caution and suspicion as hostile, and such suspicion may generate hostile reactions from suspects. As a result, on-the-street interrogations and arrests may lead to confrontations.

Authority

The second aspect of the working personality is the need to exert authority. Unlike many professionals, such as doctors, psychiatrists, and lawyers, whose clients recognize and defer to their authority, police officers must *establish* authority through their actions. The officer's uniform, badge, gun, and nightstick are symbols of his or her position and power, but the officer's demeanor and behavior are what determine whether people will defer to him or her.

Victims are glad to see the police when they are performing their law enforcement function, but the order maintenance function puts pressure on officers' authority. If they try too hard to exert authority in the face of hostile reactions, officers may cross the line and use excessive force. For example, when sent to investigate a report of a fight, drunken neighbor, or domestic quarrel, they usually do not find a cooperative complainant. Instead, they must contend not only with the perpetrators but also with onlookers who might escalate the conflict. In such circumstances the officers must "handle the situation" by asserting authority without getting emotionally involved. Even when citizens challenge their conduct and their right to enforce the law, the police are expected to react in a detached or neutral manner. For officers who feel burdened with the twin pressures of danger and authority, this may not be easy. Thus, in the daily work of policing, the rules and procedures taught at the academy may have less impact on officers' actions than the need to preserve and exert authority in the face of potential danger.

At times, officers must give orders to people with higher status. Professionals, businesspeople, and others sometimes respond to the officer not as a person working for the benefit of the community but as a public servant whom they do not respect. Poor people may also challenge officers' authority when, for example, they are angry about a situation or believe officers are targeting them unfairly. Research indicates that police officers' own expressions of disrespect in encounters with citizens, such as name-calling and other kinds of derogatory statements, occur most often when those citizens had already shown disrespect to the officers (Mastrofski, Reisig, and McCluskey, 2002).

In sum, working personality and occupational environment are closely linked and constantly affect the daily work of the police. Procedural rules and the structure of policing are overshadowed by the need to exert authority in the face of potential danger in many contexts in which citizens are angry, disrespectful, or uncooperative.

Police Morality

In his field observations of Los Angeles patrol officers, Steve Herbert found a high sense of morality in the law enforcement subculture. He believes that three aspects of modern policing create dilemmas that their morality helps to overcome. These dilemmas include (1) the contradiction between the goal of preventing crime and the officers' inability to do so, (2) the fact that officers must use their discretion to "handle" situations in ways that do not strictly follow procedures, and (3) "the fact that they invariably act against at least one citizen's interest, often with recourse to coercive force that can maim or kill" (Herbert, 1996:799).

Herbert believes that justifying their actions in moral terms, such as upholding the law, protecting society, and chasing "bad guys," helps officers lessen the dilemmas of their work. Thus use of force may be condoned as necessary for ridding "evil from otherwise peaceable streets." It is the price we pay to cleanse society of the "punks," "crazies," or "terrorists." But police morality can also be applauded: Officers work long hours and are genuinely motivated to help people and improve their lives, often placing themselves at risk. Yet to the extent that police morality crudely categorizes individuals and justifies insensitive treatment of some community members, it contributes to police–citizen tensions.

Police Isolation

Police officers' suspicion of and isolation from the public may be increased by their belief that the public is hostile to them. Many officers feel that people look

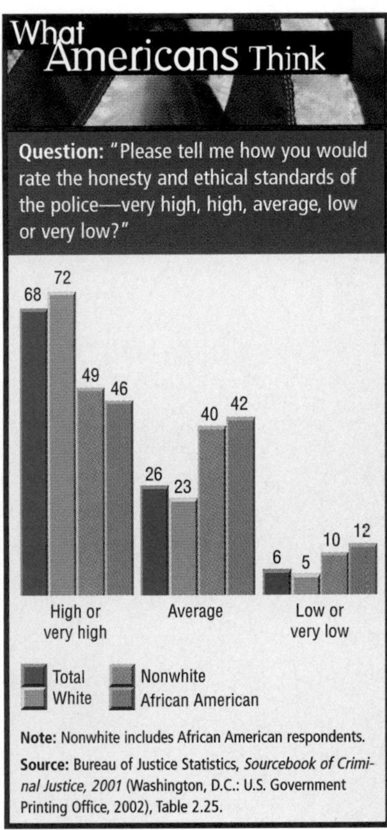

upon them with suspicion, in part because they have the authority to use force to gain compliance. Some scholars argue that this attitude increases officers' desire to use force on citizens (Regoli, Crank, and Culbertson, 1987). Public opinion polls have found that a majority of people have a high opinion of the police. However, as shown in "What Americans Think," people have different opinions regarding the police officers' ethical standards.

Police officers' isolation from the public is made worse by the fact that many officers interact with the public mainly in moments of conflict, emotion, and crisis. Victims of crimes and accidents are often too hurt or distraught to thank the police. Citizens who are told to stop some activity when the police are trying to keep order may become angry at the police. Even something as minor as telling someone to turn down the volume on a stereo can make the police the "bad guy" in the eyes of people who believe that the officers' authority limits personal freedom. Ironically, these problems may be at their worst in ghetto neighborhoods where effective policing is needed most. There, pervasive mistrust of the police may keep citizens from reporting crimes and cooperating with investigations.

Because they believe that the public is hostile to them and that the nature of their work makes the situation worse, the police tend to separate themselves from the public and to form strong in-group ties. The police culture also encourages the bonding that often occurs among people who deal with violence. This solidarity "permits fallible men to perform an arduous and difficult task, and... places the highest value upon the obligation to back up and support a fellow officer (M. K. Brown, 1981:82).

One result of the demands placed on the police is that officers often cannot separate their job from other aspects of their lives. From the time they are given badges and guns, they must always carry these symbols of the position—the tools of the trade—and be prepared to use them. Their obligation to remain vigilant even when off duty and to work at odd hours reinforces the values shared with other officers. Strengthening this bond is officers' tendency to socialize mainly with their families and other officers; indeed, they have little social contact with people other than police officers. As James Ahern, former chief of police of New Haven, Connecticut, has noted:

> When he gets off duty on the swing shift, there is little to do but go drinking and few people to do it with but other cops. He finds himself going bowling with them, going fishing, helping them paint their house or fix their cars. His family gets to know their families, and a kind of mutual protection society develops which turns out to be the only group in which the policeman is automatically entitled to respect. (Ahern, 1972:14)

Further, wherever they go, the police are recognized by people who want to talk shop; others harangue them about what is wrong with police service. This also adds to the stress and isolation felt by the police.

Job Stress

The work environment and police subculture can increase the stress felt by officers. This stress, stemming from the elements of danger and authority, can affect not only the way officers treat the citizens they encounter but also the officer's own health (G. Anderson, Litzenberger, and Plecas, 2002). Stress can also affect how officers interact with each other (Haarr and Morash, 1999).

Police officers are always on alert, sometimes face grave danger, and feel unappreciated by a public they perceive to be hostile. Thus it is not surprising that their physical and mental health suffers at times. In fact, the American Institute of Stress has stated that policing is one of the ten most stress-producing jobs (*Newsweek,* April 25, 1988:43). The effects of stress are compounded by the long hours many officers work, including double shifts that deprive them of sleep and make them work under conditions of severe fatigue (Vila and Kenney, 2002). The stress of police work may help explain why five times as many cops die by their own hands—about 300 per year—as are killed in the line of duty (*New York Times,* January 1, 1997:12; *Newsweek,* September 26, 1994:58).

In 2002 many Americans were shocked when a Nebraska state trooper killed himself after botching a background check on a man who later participated in killing five people during a bank robbery. When checking the serial number of a gun that he found on the man during a traffic stop, the trooper inadvertently typed the wrong numbers into the computer and failed to discover that the gun was stolen. Apparently, he blamed himself because he believed the homicides would have been prevented if he had arrested the man after doing a proper background check (Lorentzen, 2002). Because of their important duties and self-image as guardians of society, some police officers suffer severe stress when they cannot prevent tragic crimes from occurring.

Newspaper and magazine articles with such titles as "Time Bombs in Blue" discuss the effects of the pent-up emotions, confrontations with violence and human tragedy, and physical demands officers experience. However, only since the late 1970s have law enforcement officials been fully aware of these hazards. Researchers have noted that a higher proportion officers, compared with the general population, have marital, health, alcohol, and drug problems. It has long been held that the police have higher suicide rates than do people in other occupations. However, the evidence is mixed. A study of the Los Angeles police concluded that the suicide rate was, in fact, lower for police than for the average adult (Josephson and Reiser, 1990). But a study of the Buffalo department found that officers were three times more likely to take their own lives than were the general public (*Hartford Courant,* December 27, 1998:A1).

Psychologists have identified four kinds of stress to which officers are subject and the factors that cause each:

1. *External stress.* This is produced by real threats and dangers, such as the need to enter a dark and unfamiliar building, respond to "man with a gun" alarms, and chase lawbreakers at high speeds.
2. *Organizational stress.* This is produced by the nature of work in a paramilitary structure: constant adjustment to changing schedules, irregular work hours, and detailed rules and procedures.
3. *Personal stress.* This can be caused by an officer's racial or gender status among peers, which can create problems in getting along with other officers and adjusting to group-held values that differ from one's own. Social isolation and perceptions of bias also contribute to personal stress.
4. *Operational stress.* This reflects the total effect of dealing with thieves, derelicts, and the mentally ill; being lied to so often that all citizens become suspect; being required to face danger to protect a public that seems hostile; and always knowing that one may be held legally liable for one's actions. (Cullen et al., 1985)

Although police executives have been slow to deal with the problems of stress, psychological and medical counseling have become more available. Some departments now have stress prevention, group counseling, liability insurance, and family involvement programs. Many states have more liberal disability and retirement rules for police than for other public employees because their jobs are more stressful (Goolkasian, Geddes, and DeJong, 1989).

As we have seen, police officers face special pressures that can affect their interactions with the public and even harm their physical and mental health. How would you react to the prospect of facing danger and being on the lookout for crime at every moment, even when you were not actually working? It seems understandable that police officers become a close-knit group, yet their isolation from society may decrease their understanding of other people. It may also strengthen their belief that the public is ungrateful and hostile. As a result, officers' actions toward members of the public may be hostile, gruff, or even violent.

In sum, the effects of the police subculture on the behavior of officers are stronger in situations that produce conflict between the police and society. To endure their work, the police find they must relate to the public in ways that protect their own self-esteem. If the police view the public as hostile and police work as adding to that hostility, they will isolate themselves by developing strong values and norms to which all officers conform.

check point

5. What are the two key aspects of the police officer's working personality?
6. What are the four types of stress felt by the police?

Organization of the Police

Most police agencies are organized in a military manner with a structure of ranks and responsibilities. But police departments are also bureaucracies designed to achieve objectives efficiently. Bureaucracies are characterized by a division of labor, a chain of command with clear lines of authority, and rules to guide the activities of staff. Police organization differs somewhat from place to place depending upon the size of the jurisdiction, the characteristics of the population, and the nature of the local crime problems. However, the basic characteristics of a bureaucracy can be found in all sizeable departments.

Bureaucratic Elements

The police department in Phoenix, Arizona, reveals the elements of bureaucracy in a typical urban police force. Figure 6.2 shows the Phoenix Police Department's organizational chart, which we shall refer to in the following discussion.

Division of Labor

The Phoenix department is divided into four divisions, marked in Figure 6.2 by different colors: Headquarters, Management and Support Services, Investigation, and Field Operations (patrol). Within the Management and Support Services division and the Investigations Division, authority is further delegated to bureaus and units that have special functions (for example, property management, training, laboratory, organized crime). The Field Operations Divisions are further divided into geographic units for patrol in precincts and into specialized units to deal, for example, with traffic or special projects.

The bureaucratic organization of an urban police department such as Phoenix allows the allocation of resources and the supervision of personnel, taking into account the needs and problems of each district.

Chain and Unity of Command

The military character of police departments is illustrated by the chain of command according to ranks—officer, commander, sergeant, lieutenant, captain, major, and chief (see Figure 6.2). These make clear the powers and duties of officers at each level. Relationships between superiors and subordinates emphasize discipline, control, and accountability. Each officer has an immediate supervisor who has authority and responsibility for the actions of those below. These values help officers mobilize resources. They also ensure that civil liberties are protected; if police officers are accountable to their superiors, they are less likely to abuse their authority by needlessly interfering with the freedom and rights of citizens.

Figure 6.2 **Organization of the Phoenix, Arizona, Police Department**
This is a typical structure. Note the major divisions of headquarters, management and support services, investigations, and field operations (patrol). Specialized and geographic divisions are found within these divisions.

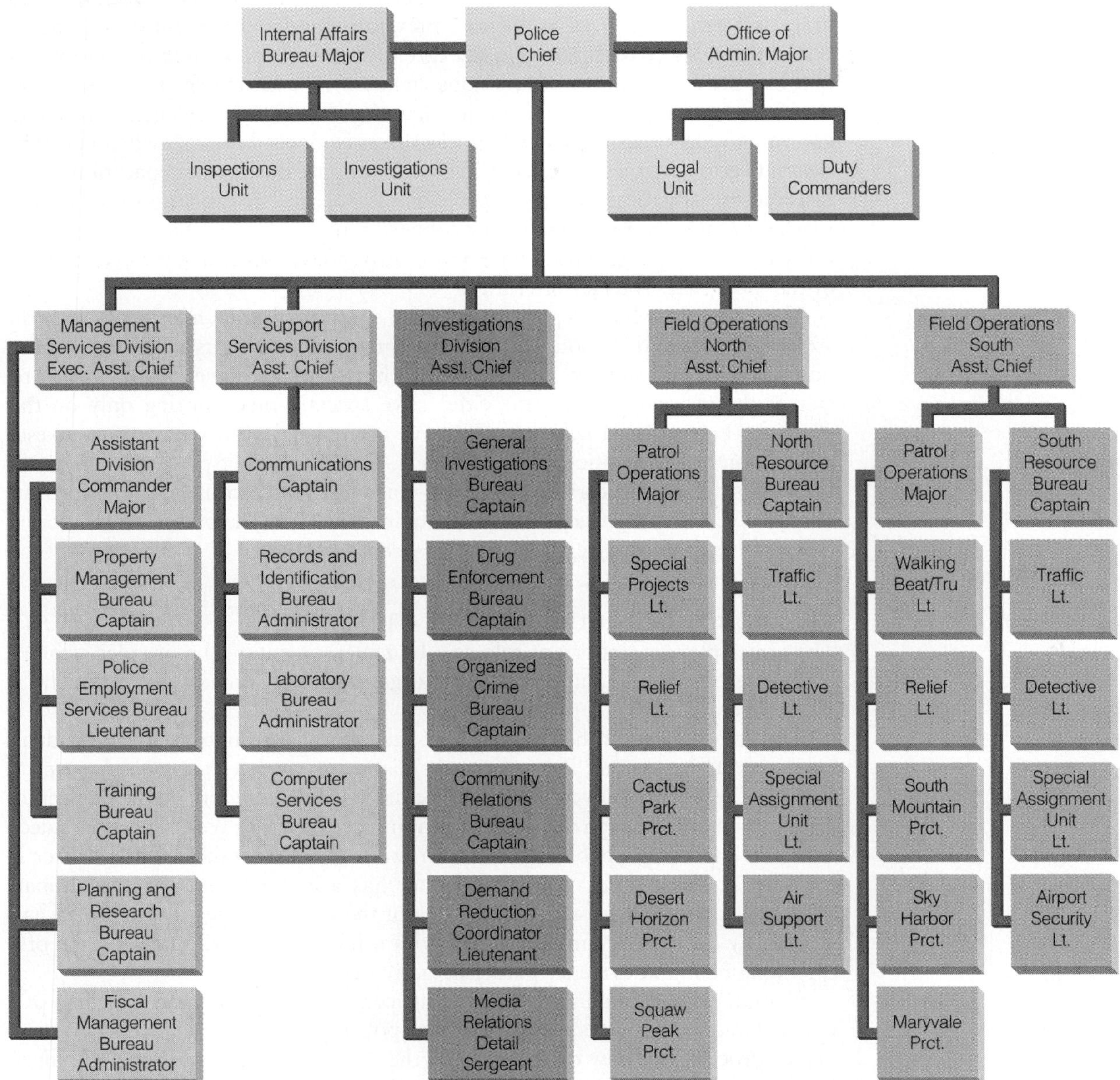

Source: City of Phoenix, Arizona, Police Department, *Annual Report,* 1990.

Rules and Procedures

Complex bureaucracies such as police departments depend on clearly stated rules and procedures to guide officers. These rules are usually found in operations manuals so that officers will know the procedures they should take when confronted by particular types of incidents. In some departments the rules are so detailed that they tell officers when they may unholster their gun, what precautions to take when stopping a vehicle, arrest procedures, and actions to take in domestic squabbles. Obviously rules cannot define all police actions, and the specificity of some rules detract from law enforcement effectiveness. Critics say that the rules of too many departments are "hidebound" and cannot possibly cover all circumstances. They argue that officers must be encouraged to use discretion without fear of sanctions for not strictly following the rules.

Operational Units

All but the smallest police departments assign officers to operational units that focus on specific functions: patrol, investigation, traffic, vice, and juvenile. These units perform the basic tasks of crime prevention and control. The patrol and investigation (detective) units form the core of the modern department. The patrol unit handles a wide range of functions, including preventing crime, catching suspects, mediating quarrels, helping the ill, and giving aid at accidents. The investigation unit identifies, apprehends, and collects evidence against lawbreakers who commit serious crimes. Because of their overlapping duties, the separation of patrol and investigation can cause problems. While the investigation unit usually focuses on murder, rape, and major robberies, the patrol unit has joint responsibility for investigating those crimes but is also solely responsible for investigation of the more numerous lesser crimes.

The extent to which departments create specialized units may depend on the size of the city and its police force. While many departments have traffic units, only those in mid-sized to large cities also have vice and juvenile units. As a result of the war on drugs, some cities have special units working only on this problem. Large departments usually have an internal affairs section to investigate charges of corruption against officers, as well as other problems associated with the staff and officers. The juvenile unit works with young people, focusing mainly on crime prevention. All special units depend on the patrol officers for information and assistance.

The Police Bureaucracy and the Criminal Justice System

The police play an important role as a bureaucracy within the broader criminal justice system. Three issues arise in the organizational context within which the police operate.

First, the police are the gateway through which information and individuals enter the justice system. Police have the discretion to determine which suspects will be arrested and moved into the system. Cases that are sent to the prosecutor for charging and then to the courts for adjudication begin with an officer's decision that there is probable cause for an arrest. The care taken by the officer in making the arrest and collecting evidence has a major impact on the ultimate success of the prosecution. The outcome of the case, whether through plea bargaining by lawyers or through a trial with a judge and jury, hinges on the officer's judgment and evidence-gathering activities.

Second, police administration is influenced by the fact that the outcome of a case is largely in the hands of others. The police bring suspects into the criminal justice process, but they cannot control the decisions of prosecutors and judges. In some cases, the police officers feel that their efforts have been wasted. For example, the prosecutor sometimes agrees to a plea bargain that does not, in the eyes of the officer, adequately punish the offender. The potential for conflict between police and other decision makers in the system is increased by the difference in social status between police officers, who often do not have college degrees, and lawyers and judges, who have graduate degrees.

Third, as part of a bureaucracy, police officers are expected to observe rules and follow the orders of superiors while at the same time making independent, discretionary judgments. They must stay within the chain of command yet also make choices in response to events on the streets. To understand the impact of these factors on police behavior, let us examine two aspects of their daily work—organizational response and productivity.

check point

7. What are three characteristics of a bureaucracy?
8. What are the five operational units of all but the smallest police departments?

Police Response and Action

In a free society, people do not want police on every street corner asking them what they are doing. Thus, the police are mainly **reactive** (responding to citizen calls for service) rather than **proactive** (initiating actions in the absence of citizen requests). Studies of police work show that 81 percent of actions result from citizen telephone calls, 5 percent are initiated by citizens who approach an officer, and only 14 percent are initiated in the field by an officer. These facts affect the way departments are organized and the way the police respond to cases.

reactive
Occurring in response, such as police activity in response to notification that a crime has been committed.

proactive
Acting in anticipation, such as an active search for potential offenders that is initiated by the police without waiting for a crime to be reported. Arrests for crimes without victims are usually proactive.

Because they are mainly reactive, the police usually arrive at the scene only after the crime has been committed and the perpetrator has fled. This means that the police are hampered by the time lapse and sometimes by inaccurate information given by witnesses. For example, a mugging may happen so quickly that victims and witnesses cannot accurately describe what happened. In about a third of cases in which police are called, no one is present when the police arrive on the scene.

Citizens have come to expect that the police will respond quickly to *every* call, whether it requires immediate attention or can be handled in a more routine manner. This expectation has produced **incident-driven policing,** in which calls for service are the primary instigators of action. Studies have shown, though, that less than 30 percent of calls to the police involve criminal law enforcement—most calls concern order maintenance and service (S. Walker, 1999:80). To a large extent, then, reports by victims and observers define the boundaries of policing.

incident-driven policing
A reactive approach to policing emphasizing a quick response to calls for service.

The police do use proactive strategies such as surveillance and undercover work to combat some crimes. When addressing crimes without victims, for example, they must rely on informers, stakeouts, wiretapping, stings, and raids. Because of the current focus on drug offenses, police resources in many cities have been assigned to proactive efforts to apprehend people who use or sell illegal drugs. Because calls from victims reporting these crimes are few, crime rates for such offenses are nearly always reported as rates of arrest rather than rates of known criminal acts. As such, the assignment of police personnel in these cases often stems from proactive efforts, as reported in the crime rate, rather than actual crimes.

Organizational Response

How the police bureaucracy is organized influences how the police respond to citizens' calls. Factors that affect the response process include the separation of police into various functional groups (patrol, vice, investigation, and so on), the quasi-military command system, and the techniques used to induce patrol officers to respond in desired ways.

Police departments are being reshaped by new communications technology, which has tended to centralize decision making. The core of the department is the communications center, where commands are given to send officers into action. Patrol officers are expected to be in constant touch with headquarters and must report each of their actions. Two-way radio, cell phone, and computers are the primary means by which administrators monitor the decisions of officers in the field. In the past, patrol officers might have administered on-the-spot justice to a mischievous juvenile, but now they must file a report, take the youth into custody, and start formal proceedings. Because officers must contact headquarters by radio or computer with reports about each incident, headquarters is better able to guide officers' discretion and ensure that they comply with departmental policies. More than 80 percent of police departments serving cities of 250,000 or more residents use computers in patrol cars. That figure drops to 50 percent for cities of 10,000 to 50,000 and only 20 percent for rural areas and towns with fewer than 10,000 (Hickman and Reaves, 2001). From these figures we can see

Read about Mobile Data Terminals, the wireless computers used in New York City patrol cars, at http://www.n2nov.net/mdt2_nyt.html.

that the availability of communications and information technology varies, depending on a department's resources.

Most residents in urban and suburban areas can now call 911 to report a crime or obtain help or information. The 911 system has brought a flood of calls to police departments—many not directly related to police responsibilities. In Baltimore a 311 system has been implemented to help reduce the number of nonemergency calls, estimated as 40 percent of the total calls. Residents have been urged to call 311 when they need assistance that does not require the immediate dispatch of an officer. A recent study found that this innovation reduced calls to 911 by almost 25 percent and resulted in extremely high public support (*New York Times,* October 10, 1997:A12). (The Close Up box examines the emotionally draining work of a 911 operator.)

differential response
A patrol strategy that assigns priorities to calls for service and chooses the appropriate response.

To improve efficiency, police departments use a **differential response** system that assigns priorities to calls for service. This system assumes that it is not always necessary to rush a patrol car to the scene when a call is received. The appropriate response depends on several factors—such as whether the incident is in progress, has just occurred, or occurred some time ago, as well as whether anyone is or could be hurt. A dispatcher receives the calls and asks for certain facts. The dispatcher may (1) send a sworn officer to the scene right away, (2) give the call a lower rank so that the response by an officer is delayed, (3) send someone other than a sworn officer, or (4) refer the caller to another agency.

Evaluations of differential response policies have found them to be successful. In Greensboro, North Carolina, only about half of the calls received warranted an immediate response by an officer, 26.9 percent received a delayed response by an officer, and no officer was dispatched in 19.5 percent of calls, most of which concerned cold burglaries. Both officers and residents were satisfied with the procedures (M. Cohen and McEwen, 1984). Research in Lansing, Michigan, found differential response both efficient and equitable. Low-priority calls received a response in an average of 16 minutes, and calls not requiring the presence of an officer were dealt with in a report given over the telephone. People across racial and income lines in Lansing were satisfied with police response (A. P. Worden, 1993).

The policy of differential response clearly saves police resources. It provides other benefits as well. For example, with trained officers answering "911," (1) more-detailed information is gathered from callers, (2) callers have a better sense of when to expect a response, and (3) patrol officers have more information about the case when they respond.

Some experts criticize centralized communications and decision making. Many advocates of community policing believe that certain technologies tend to isolate the police from citizens. Community policing strategies attempt to enhance interaction and cooperation between officers and citizens (Morash and Ford, 2002). Widespread use of motorized patrols has meant that residents get only a glimpse of officers as they cruise through their neighborhoods. Community-oriented policing attempts to overcome some of the negative aspects of centralized response.

Productivity

Go to the Public Policy feature on the American System of Criminal Justice CD to learn more about the issues surrounding measuring police productivity.

Following the lead of New York's Compstat program, police departments in Baltimore, New Orleans, Indianapolis, and other cities now emphasize precinct-level accountability for crime reduction. Through twice-weekly briefings before their peers and senior executives, precinct commanders must explain the results of their efforts to reduce crime. Essential to this management strategy is timely, accurate information. Computer systems have been developed to put up-to-date crime data into the hands of managers at all levels. This allows discussion of department-wide strategies and puts pressure on low producers (L. W. Sherman, 1998:430; Silverman, 1999). This innovation has brought major changes to police operations and raised questions as to how police work should be measured.

Holding the 911 Line

It's a new day. I walk down to the basement of the public-safety building, pass through a secured entrance and walk slowly down a long, quiet corridor. My stomach tightens a bit as I approach a final locked door. . . . I'm in the Phoenix Police Communications Center, known as "911.". . .

It's 0800 hours. I take a deep breath, say a little prayer and hope that I don't make any mistakes that might get me on the 6 o'clock news. This will be my not-so-happy home for the next 10 hours.

"911, what is your emergency?" It's my first call of the day. The woman is crying but calm. She has tried to wake her elderly husband. With the push of a button I connect her to the fire department. They ask if she wants to attempt CPR, but she says, "No, he's cold and blue . . . I'm sure he's dead." I leave the sobbing widow in the hands of the fire dispatcher. I'm feeling sad, but I just move on. I have more incoming calls to take. It's busy this morning. The orange lights in each corner of the room are shining brightly, a constant reminder that non-emergency calls have been holding more than 90 seconds. My phone console appears to be glowing, covered with blinking red lights. It's almost hypnotic, like when you sit in the dark and stare at a lit Christmas tree, or gaze into a flickering fireplace. But then I remember that each light represents a person—a person with a problem, someone in crisis.

A loud bell is ringing. It means an emergency call is trying to get through but the lines are jammed. All operators are already on a call. I quickly put my caller on hold. He's just reporting a burglary that occurred over the weekend. . . .

"911, what is your emergency?" This one's serious. A bad traffic accident, head-on collision. "Yes, sir, we'll get right out there." I get officers started and advise the fire department. Now everyone in the vicinity of the accident is calling. "Yes, ma'am, we're on the way." "We'll be out shortly, sir, thanks for calling." My supervisor comes out of his office to advise us of something. He always looks serious, but this time it's different. He looks worried and upset. He tells us that two of our detectives were involved in the collision. He doesn't know who they are or how badly they're injured. My heart stops momentarily because my husband is a detective. I quickly call the office and confirm that he is safe. I'm relieved but still stunned. . . . But there's not much time for sentiment. There are more calls to take, more decisions to make and more pressures needing attention. . . .

"911, what is your emergency?" It's just a boy on a phone getting his kicks by calling me vulgar names. He hangs up before I have a chance to educate him on correct 911 usage. We get a lot of trivial calls, pranksters, hang-ups, citizens complaining to us about a non-crime situation, something they should handle themselves. People call us because they don't know where to turn. Everyone must be treated fairly and with respect. It's a difficult balance to maintain.

My supervisor again comes out to advise us. His face shows a sadness I've never seen in him. "The officers were killed in the accident." A quietness descends over the room. I suppose the bells are still ringing and the lights flashing but I don't hear or see them. The typing stops; talking ceases. I just want to get out of here and cry, but I have to stay and do my job. I have to keep going. I can break down on my long drive home tonight; for now I have phones to answer, people to help.

Source: Tracy Lorenzano, "Holding the 911 Line," *Newsweek*, June 20, 1994, p. 10.

Researching the **Internet**

Many police departments try to educate the public about when it is appropriate to dial 911. See http://www.ci.tukwila.wa.us/police/pd911.htm.

Quantifying police work is difficult in part because of the wide range of duties and day-to-day tasks of officers. In the past, the crime rate and the clearance rate have been used as measures of "good" policing. A lower crime rate might be cited as evidence of an effective department, but critics note that this measure is affected by other factors beside policing.

The **clearance rate**—the percentage of crimes known to police that they believe they have solved through an arrest—is a basic measure of police performance. The clearance rate varies by type of offense. In reactive situations this rate can be low. For example, the police may learn about a burglary hours or even days later; the clearance rate for such crimes is only about 14 percent.

clearance rate
The percentage of crimes known to the police that they believe they have solved through an arrest; a statistic used to measure a police department's productivity.

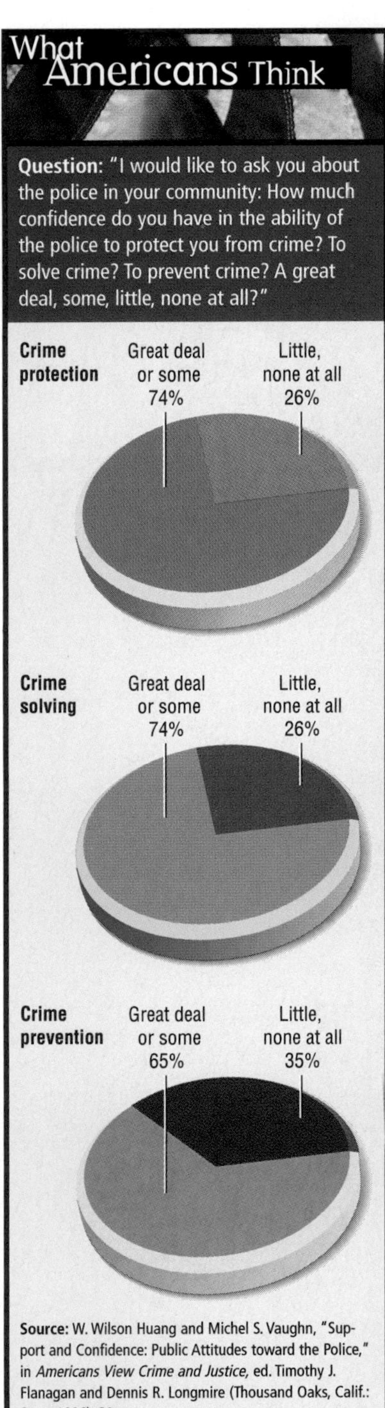

Police have much more success in handling violent crimes in which victims tend to know their assailants; the clearance rate is 48 percent (FBI, 2001:12). In proactive situations the police are not responding to the call of a crime victim; rather they seek out crimes. Hence, at least in theory, arrests for prostitution, gambling, and drug selling have a clearance rate of 100 percent, because every crime known to the police is matched with an arrest.

The arrest of a person often results in the clearance of other reported offenses because the police can link some arrested persons with similar, unsolved crimes. Interrogation and lineups are standard procedures, as is the lesser-known operation of simply assigning unsolved crimes to the suspect. When an offender enters a guilty plea, part of the bargain may be an admission that he or she committed prior crimes. Professional thieves know that they can gain favors from the police in exchange for "confessing" to unsolved crimes that they may not have committed.

These measures of police productivity are sometimes supplemented by other data, such as the numbers of traffic citations issued, illegally parked cars ticketed, and suspects stopped for questioning, as well as the value of stolen goods recovered. These additional ways of counting work done reflect the fact that an officer may work hard for many hours yet have no arrests to show for his or her efforts (Kelling, 1992:23). Yet society may benefit even more when officers spend their time in activities that are hard to measure, such as calming disputes, becoming acquainted with people in the neighborhood, and providing services to those in need. Some research indicates that officers who engage in activities that produce higher levels of measurable productivity, such as issuing citations or making arrests, also receive higher numbers of citizen complaints about alleged misconduct (Lersch, 2002). Would officers better serve the community by spending time in difficult-to-measure activities? Only further research can provide an answer.

One might think that police effectiveness would depend on a city's population, its crime level, and size of its police force. As seen in Figure 6.3, however, these variables are not always related. For example, the Dallas police force is small relative to the population, but its rates of index offenses are high. In contrast, index offenses in Washington, D.C., rank in the middle range of the cities studied, but its force is the largest. The issue grows even more complicated: Police productivity is governed in part by population density, the number of nonresidents who spend part of their day working or visiting in the area, local politics, and other factors. In sum, like other public agencies, the police have trouble gauging the quantity and quality of their work. Perhaps they need to pay greater attention to the attitudes of the consumers of police services, the public (see "What Americans Think").

check point

9. What is "incident-driven policing"?
10. What is "differential response"?
11. What is the basic measure of police productivity?

Delivery of Police Services

line functions
Police components that directly perform field operations and carry out the basic functions of patrol, investigation, traffic, vice, juvenile, and so on.

In service bureaucracies like the police, a distinction is often made between line and staff functions. **Line functions** are those that directly involve field operations such as patrol, investigation, traffic control, vice and juvenile crimes, and so on. By contrast, *staff functions* supplement or support the line functions. Staff functions are based in the chief's office and the support or services bureau, as well as in the staff inspection bureau (see Figure 6.2). An efficient department maintains an appropriate balance between line and staff duties. A department like the one in Phoenix would be about 16 percent staff and 84 percent line. Figure 6.4 shows the allocation of line personnel in the nation's six largest departments.

Figure 6.3 **Sworn officers and index offenses per 1,000 population in 15 U.S. cities**
These major cities have varying numbers of police officers and crimes for every 1,000 residents. As you can see, the amount of crime and numbers of police do not always correlate.

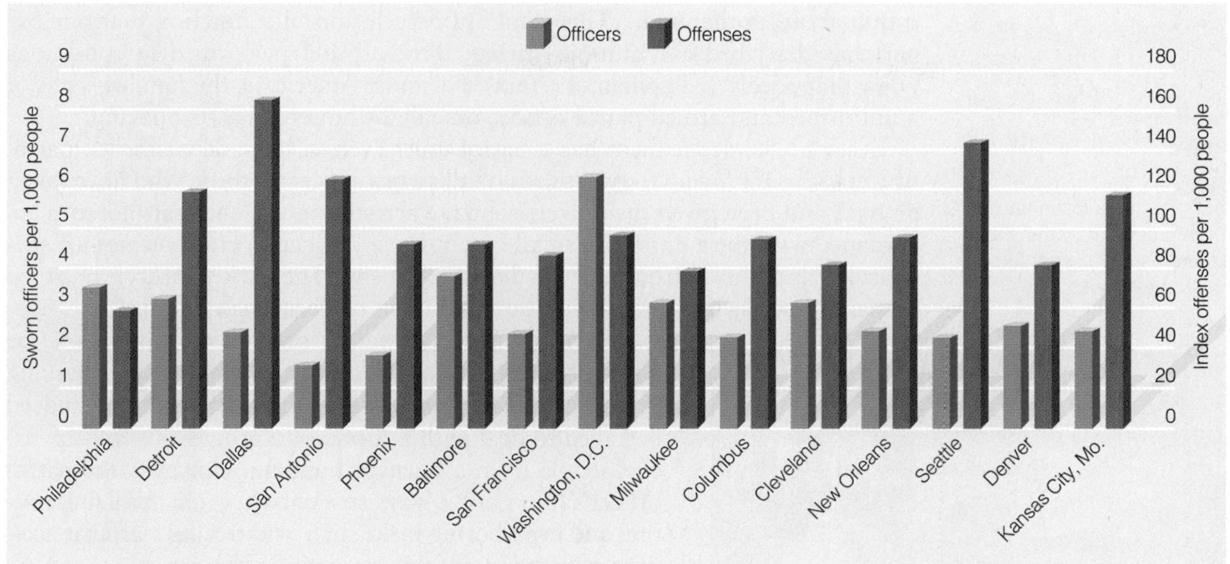

Source: *Issue Paper: Metropolitan Police Department Resource Allocation* (Washington, D.C.: Police Executive Research Forum, 1990).

Figure 6.4 **Distribution of sworn police personnel in the nation's six largest departments**
What does the distribution of officers tell us about the role of the police in urban areas? How might smaller departments differ from these large urban departments?

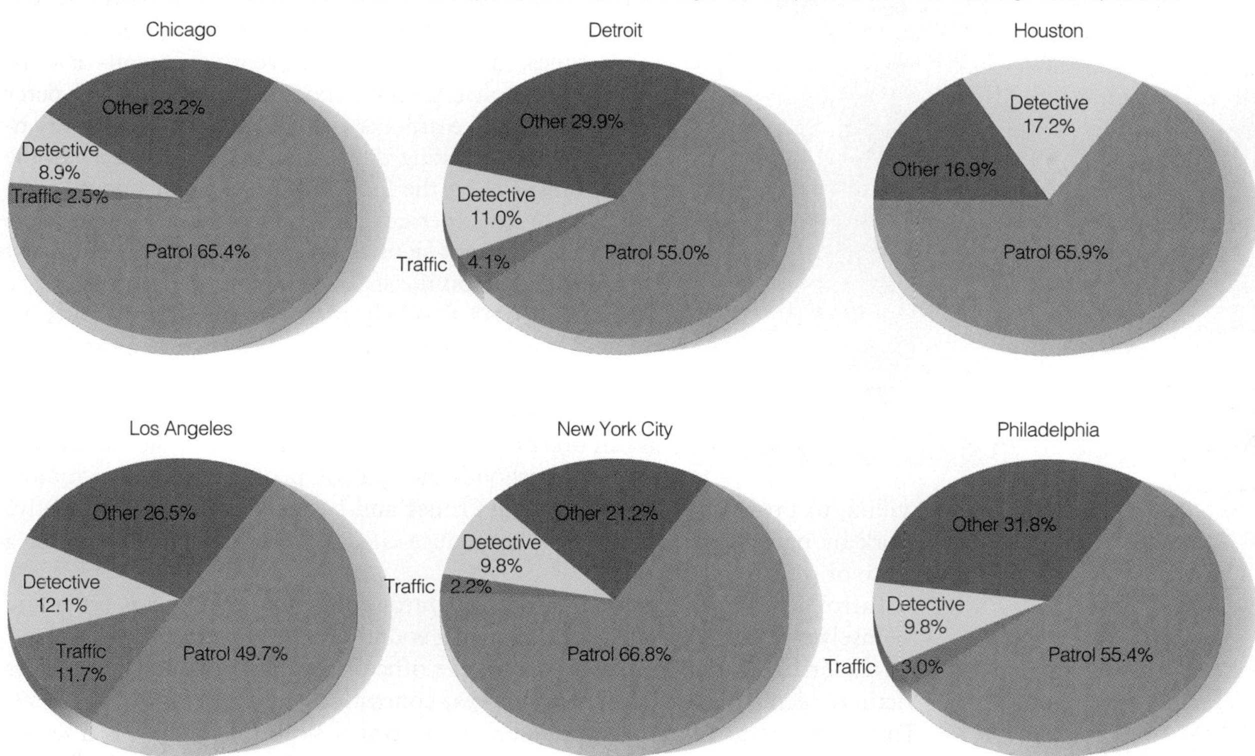

Note: *Other* refers to specialized units such as communications, antiterrorism, administration, and personnel.
Source: Adapted from Anthony Pate and Edwin Hamilton, *The Big Six: Policing America's Largest Departments* (Washington, D.C.: Police Foundation, 1990), 60.

Patrol Functions

Patrol is often called the backbone of police operations. The word *patrol* is thought to be derived from a French word, *patrouiller,* which once meant "to tramp about in the mud." This is an apt description of a function that one expert has described as "arduous, tiring, difficult, and performed in conditions other than ideal" (Chapman, 1970:ix). For most Americans the familiar sight of a uniformed and armed patrol officer, on call 24 hours a day, *is* policing.

sworn officers
Police employees who have taken an oath and been given powers by the state to make arrests and use necessary force, in accordance with their duties.

Every police department has a patrol unit. Even in large departments, patrol officers account for up to two-thirds of all **sworn officers**—those who have taken an oath and been given the powers to make arrests and use necessary force in accordance with their duties. In small communities, police operations are not specialized, and the patrol force *is* the department. The patrol officer must be prepared for any imaginable situation and must perform many duties.

Peter Turnley/CORBIS

Patrol officers often find themselves in complex situations requiring sound judgments and careful actions. How would you interpret this picture? What is the problem? What actions are the officers taking?

Television portrays patrol officers as always on the go—rushing from one incident to another and making several arrests in a single shift. A patrol officer may indeed be called to deal with a robbery in progress or to help rescue people from a burning building. However, the patrol officer's life is not always so exciting, often involving routine and even boring tasks such as directing traffic at accident scenes and road construction sites.

Most officers, on most shifts, do not make even one arrest (Bayley, 1994:20). To better understand patrol work, note in Figure 6.5 how the police of Wilmington, Delaware, allocate time to various activities.

The patrol function has three parts: answering calls for help, maintaining a police presence, and probing suspicious circumstances. Patrol officers are well suited to answering calls, because they usually are near the scene and can move quickly to provide help or catch a suspect. At other times, they engage in **preventive patrol**—that is, making the police presence known in an effort to deter crime and to make officers available to respond quickly to calls. Whether walking the streets or cruising in a car, the patrol officer is on the lookout for suspicious people and behavior. With experience, officers come to trust in their own ability to spot signs of suspicious activity that merit stopping people on the street for questioning.

Patrol officers also help maintain smooth relations between the police and the community. As the most visible members of the criminal justice system, they can profoundly affect the willingness of citizens to cooperate. When officers earn the trust and respect of the residents of the neighborhoods they patrol, people become much more willing to provide information about crimes and suspicious activities. Effective work by patrol officers can also help reduce citizens' fear of crime and foster a sense of security.

Patrol officers' duties sound fairly straightforward, yet these officers often find themselves in complex situations requiring sound judgments and careful actions. As the first to arrive at a crime scene, the officer must comfort and give aid to victims, identify and question witnesses, control crowds, and gather evidence. This calls for creativity and good communicational skills.

preventive patrol
Making the police presence known, to deter crime and to make officers available to respond quickly to calls.

Because the patrol officer has the most direct contact with the public, the image of the police and their relations with the community are based on patrol officers' actions. Moreover, successful investigations and prosecutions often depend on patrol officers' actions in questioning witnesses and gathering evidence after a crime. Think of the variety of events that come to the attention of patrol officers. How would you handle them?

Figure 6.5 **Time allocated to patrol activities by the police of Wilmington, Delaware**
The time spent on each activity was calculated from records for each police car unit. Note the range of activities and the time spent on each.

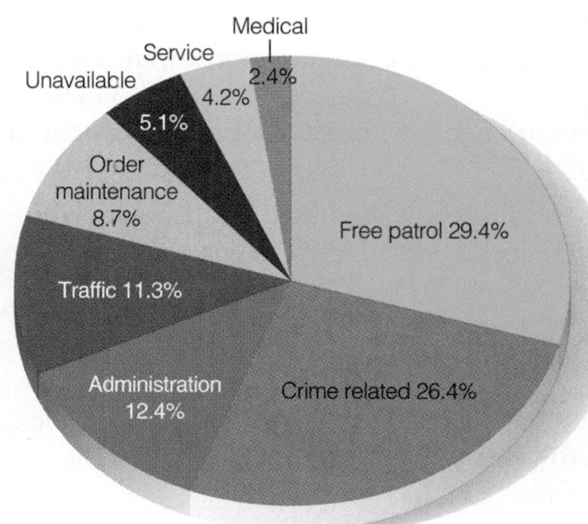

Free patrol: park and walk

Crime related: officer in trouble, suspicious person/vehicle, crime in progress, alarm, investigate crime not in progress, service warrant/subpoena, assist other police

Administration: meal break, report writing, firearms training, police vehicle maintenance, at headquarters, court related

Traffic: accident investigation, parking problems, motor vehicle driving problems, traffic control, fire emergency

Order maintenance: order maintenance in progress, animal complaint, noise complaint

Service: service related

Medical: medical emergency, at local hospital

Source: Jack R. Greene and Carl B. Klockars, "What Police Do," in *Thinking about Police,* 2nd ed., ed. Carl B. Klockars and Stephen D. Mastrofski (New York: McGraw-Hill, 1991), 279.

Because the patrol officer's job involves the most contact with the public, the best-qualified officers should be chosen to perform it. However, because of the low status of patrol assignments, many officers seek higher-status positions such as that of detective. A key challenge facing policing is to grant to patrol officers a status that reflects their importance to society and the criminal justice system.

Many cities provide descriptions of police patrol operations on their Web pages; see, for example, http://www.ci.mercer-island.wa.us/Page.asp?NaDID=517.

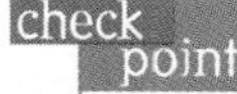

12. What is the difference between line and staff functions?
13. What are the three parts of the patrol function?

Investigation

All cities with a population of more than 250,000, and 90 percent of smaller cities, have officers called detectives assigned to investigative duties. Detectives make up 15 percent of police personnel. Compared with patrol officers, they have a higher status in the department. Their pay is higher, their hours are more flexible, and they are supervised less closely. Detectives do not wear uniforms, and their work is considered more interesting than that of patrol officers. In addition, they engage solely in law enforcement rather than in order maintenance or service work; hence, their activities conform more closely to the image of the police as crime fighters.

Detectives in small departments are generalists who investigate whatever crimes occur, but in large departments they are assigned to special units such as homicide, robbery, auto theft, forgery, and burglary. In recent years, because of public pressures, some departments have set up new special units to deal with bias crimes, child abuse, sexual assault, and computer crime (Bayley, 1994:26).

Web pages for city governments sometimes describe the organization of the detective bureau and the responsibilities of detectives; see, for example, http://www.southplainfieldnj.com/police/dets.htm.

Most investigative units are separated from the patrol chain of command. Many argue that this results in duplication of effort and lack of continuity in handling cases. It often means that vital information known by one branch is not known by the other.

Like patrol, criminal investigation is largely reactive. Detectives become involved after a crime has been reported and a patrol officer has done a preliminary investigation. The job of detectives is mainly to talk to people—victims, suspects, witnesses—in order to find out what happened. On the basis of this information, detectives develop theories about who committed the crime and then set out to gather the evidence that will lead to arrest and prosecution. David

Bayley notes that detectives do not maintain an open mind about the identity of the offender. They know that if the suspect cannot be identified by people on the scene, they are not likely to find him or her on their own. Detectives collect physical evidence to support testimony that identifies a suspect, not to *find* the suspect (Bayley, 1994:26).

Herbert Goldstein (1977:55) has outlined the process of investigation as follows:

- When a serious crime occurs and the suspect is identified and caught right away, the detective prepares the case to be presented to the prosecuting attorney.
- When the suspect is identified but not caught, the detective tries to locate him or her.
- When the offender is not identified but there is more than one suspect, the detective conducts investigations to determine which one committed the crime.
- When there is no suspect, the detective starts from scratch to find out who committed the crime.

Michael Madrid for USA TODAY. Copyright 2002, USA TODAY. Reprinted with permission.

Criminal investigation requires much dogged footwork. Here, Virginia Police Academy Cadets search for evidence at a scene where a woman was shot by the D.C. Sniper.

In performing an investigation, detectives depend not only on their own experience but also on technical experts. Much of the information they need comes from criminal files, lab technicians, and forensic scientists. Many small departments turn to the state crime laboratory or the FBI for such information. Detectives are often pictured as working alone, but in fact they are part of a team.

Although detectives focus on serious crimes, they are not the only ones who investigate crimes. Patrol, traffic, vice, and juvenile units may also be involved. In small towns and rural areas, patrol officers must conduct investigations because police departments are too small to have separate detective bureaus. In urban areas, because they are likely to be the first police to arrive at the scene of a crime, patrol officers must do much of the initial investigative work. As we have seen, the patrol unit's investigation can be crucial. Successful prosecution of many kinds of cases, including robbery, larceny, and burglary, is closely linked to the speed with which a suspect is arrested. If patrol officers cannot obtain information from victims and witnesses right away, the chance of arresting and prosecuting the suspect greatly decreases.

Apprehension

The discovery that a crime has been committed sets off a chain of events leading to the capture of a suspect and the gathering of the evidence needed to convict that person. It may also lead to several dead ends, such as a lack of clues pointing to a suspect or a lack of evidence to link the suspect to the crime.

The process of catching a suspect has three stages: detection of a crime, preliminary investigation, and follow-up investigation. Depending on the outcome of the investigation, these three steps may be followed by a fourth: clearance and arrest. As shown in Figure 6.6, these actions are designed to use criminal justice resources to arrest a suspect and assemble enough evidence to support a charge.

1. *Detection of a crime.* Although patrol officers sometimes discover crimes, information that a crime has been committed usually comes in a call to the

Figure 6.6 **The apprehension process**
Apprehension of a felony suspect results from a sequence of actions by patrol officers and detectives. Coordination of these efforts is key to solving major crimes.

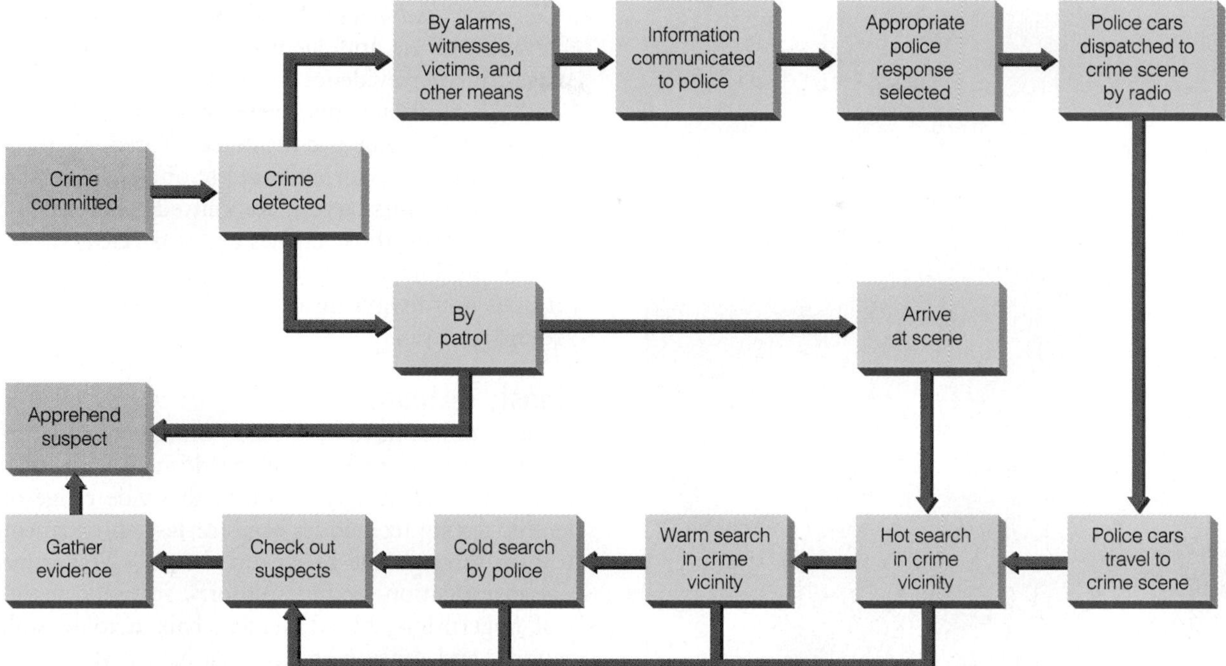

police. For example, automatic alarms linked to police headquarters could alert the police to a crime on business premises. Such direct communications help shorten response time and increase the chances of catching the suspect.

2. *Preliminary investigation.* The first law enforcement official on the scene is usually a patrol officer who has been dispatched by radio. The officer helps the victim, secures the crime scene for investigation, and documents the facts of the crime. If a suspect is present or nearby, the officer conducts a "hot" search and may apprehend the suspect. This initial work is crucial. The officer must gather the basic facts, including the name of the victim, a description of the suspect, and the names of witnesses. After the information is collected, it is sent to the investigation unit.

3. *Follow-up investigation.* After a crime has been brought to the attention of the police and a preliminary investigation has been made, the detective decides what course of action to pursue. In big-city departments, incident reports from each day are analyzed the next morning. Investigators receive assignments based on their specialties. They study the information, weigh each factor, and decide whether the crime can likely be solved.

    Some departments have guidelines for making these decisions so that resources will be used efficiently. If the detectives decide there is little chance of solving the crime quickly, the case may be dropped. Steven Brandl found that in burglary and robbery follow-up investigations, the value of the lost property and the detective's belief that the case could be resolved through an arrest were the main factors affecting how much time and effort were spent in solving the crime (Brandl, 1993:414).

    When detectives decide that a full-scale investigation is warranted, a wider search—known as a "cold" search—for evidence or weapons is carried out. Witnesses may be questioned again, informants contacted, and evidence gathered. Because of the pressure of new cases, however, an

AP/Wide World Photos, Inc.

Forensic scientist Dr. Henry Lee and members of the Connecticut State Police crime team mark a mannequin to indicate where 14-year-old Aquan Salmon was shot by Hartford Police Officer Robert Allen. Salmon was fleeing from a car, and Allen thought Salmon was reaching for a gun.

investigation may be shelved so that resources can be directed toward "warmer" cases.

4. *Clearance and arrest.* The decision to arrest is a key part of the apprehension process. In some cases, further evidence or links between suspects and others are not discovered if arrests are made too soon. A crime is considered cleared when the evidence supports the arrest of a suspect. If a suspect admits having committed other unsolved crimes, those crimes are also "cleared." When a crime is cleared in police files, however, it does not always mean that the suspect will be found guilty.

Forensic Techniques

American police have long relied on science in gathering, identifying, and analyzing evidence. The public has become increasingly aware of the wide range of scientific testing techniques used for law enforcement purposes through the television drama *CSI* (Crime Scene Investigation) and its spin-offs. Scientific analysis of fingerprints, blood, semen, hair, textiles, soil, weapons, and other materials has helped the police identify criminals (Table 6.2). It has also helped prosecutors convince jurors of the guilt of defendants. Beginning in the 1990s, these techniques have also increasingly helped defense attorneys establish that people sitting in prison were actually innocent of crimes such as rape and murder (Dwyer, Neufeld, and Scheck, 2001). All states and many large cities have forensic labs. However, this does not guarantee that the latest tests can be applied to all pieces of evidence. Not all labs have the same technical machinery and personnel. In addition, not all police departments, especially those in small towns and rural areas, have much access to crime labs and other technology (Hickman and Reaves, 2001).

The technological weapons employed to investigate many kinds of crimes include DNA "fingerprinting." This technique identifies people through their distinctive gene patterns (also called genotypic features). DNA, or deoxyribonucleic acid, is the basic component of all chromosomes; all the cells in an individual's

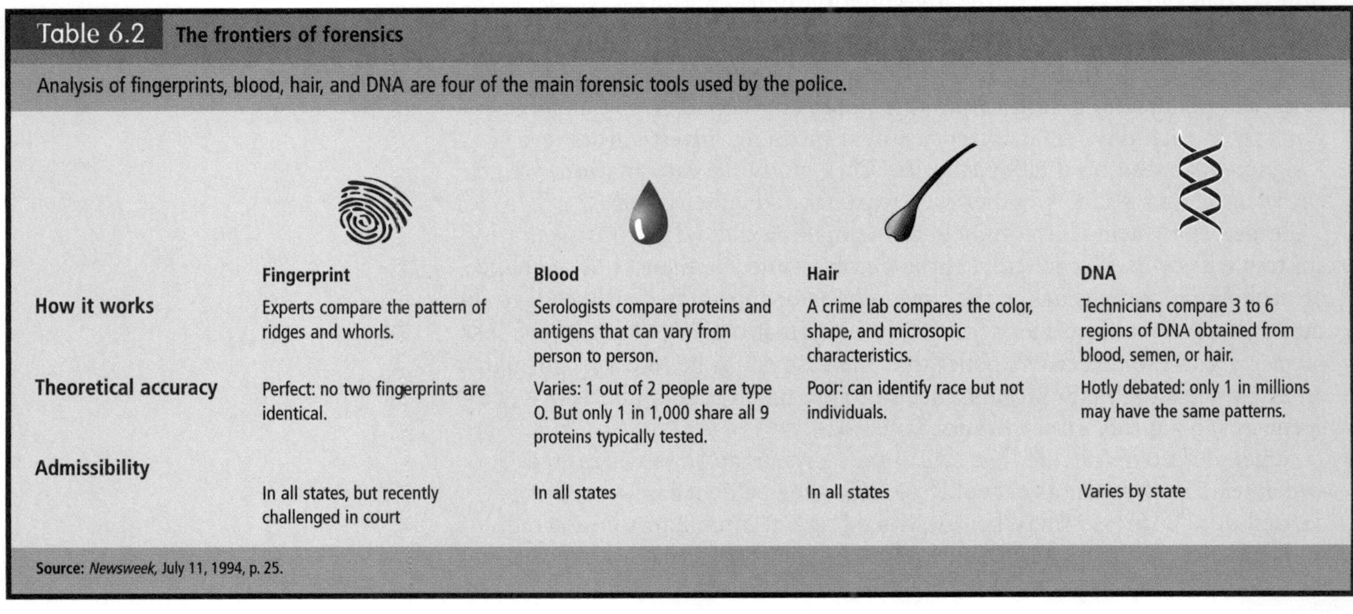

Table 6.2 The frontiers of forensics

Analysis of fingerprints, blood, hair, and DNA are four of the main forensic tools used by the police.

	Fingerprint	Blood	Hair	DNA
How it works	Experts compare the pattern of ridges and whorls.	Serologists compare proteins and antigens that can vary from person to person.	A crime lab compares the color, shape, and microsopic characteristics.	Technicians compare 3 to 6 regions of DNA obtained from blood, semen, or hair.
Theoretical accuracy	Perfect: no two fingerprints are identical.	Varies: 1 out of 2 people are type O. But only 1 in 1,000 share all 9 proteins typically tested.	Poor: can identify race but not individuals.	Hotly debated: only 1 in millions may have the same patterns.
Admissibility	In all states, but recently challenged in court	In all states	In all states	Varies by state

Source: *Newsweek,* July 11, 1994, p. 25.

new directions in criminal justice policy

National DNA Database

Many states and the federal government are building a national database of DNA records that is maintained by the FBI. Known as CODIS, which stands for Combined DNA Index System, the project began in 1990 as a pilot project serving a few state and local laboratories. CODIS has now grown to include 137 laboratories in 47 states and the District of Columbia.

In the federal corrections system, the Bureau of Prisons obtains DNA through blood samples from offenders convicted of murder, sex offenses, robbery, kidnapping, and burglary. Under federal law, offenders can be convicted of a misdemeanor for refusing to cooperate by contributing a blood sample. By taking samples from people convicted of specific crimes in the state and federal systems, officials hope that CODIS will enable them to close unsolved crimes that involve DNA evidence.

An example of the use of a DNA database to solve crimes comes from Florida. A Ft. Lauderdale detective searching old cases noticed in an unsolved 1986 murder in which a trail of blood leading away from the victim indicated the attacker had been wounded. A single droplet from a floor tile, and stored for more than a decade, matched the DNA of a convicted sex offender, Scott Edward Williams. Williams was in custody but was scheduled to be released. When confronted with the evidence, he confessed and committed suicide a week later.

Sources: Nancy Beatty Gregoire, "Federal Probation Joins the World of DNA Collection," *Federal Probation* 66 (June): 30–32; *Newsweek*, November 16, 1998, p. 69.

Researching the **Internet**

For more on CODIS access the web site of the FBI: http://www.fbi.gov/hq/lab/codis/index1.htm.

body, including those in skin, blood, organs, and semen, contain the same unique type of DNA. The characteristics of certain segments of DNA vary from person to person and thus form a genetic "fingerprint." Analysts can therefore analyze DNA from, say, samples of hair and compare them with those of suspects. See "New Directions in Criminal Justice Policy" to learn about the National DNA Database.

Use of the DNA technique has been hampered by the fact that few labs are equipped to perform DNA analysis. Moreover, many detectives and prosecutors do not make full use of these resources, and some claim that the method does not yet have a sound scientific foundation. Courts in most states now accept DNA results as evidence, however.

The Bureau of Justice Statistics regularly publishes surveys that provide information about DNA laboratories; see the latest at http://www.ojp.usdoj.gov/bjs/abstract/sdnacl01.htm.

Since 1989, DNA testing has played a role in over 20,000 convictions, particularly in sexual contact and abuse cases (Burns and Smith, 1999:1). It has also been responsible for the release from prison of an increasing number of people after testing has shown that they could not have committed the crimes for which they were imprisoned (Connors et al., 1996:2).

Research on Investigation

The results of several studies raise questions about the value of investigations and the role detectives play in apprehension. This research suggests that the police have attached too much importance to investigation as a means of solving crimes and shows that most crimes are cleared because of arrests made by the patrol force at or near the scene. Response time is key to apprehension, as is the information given by the victim or witnesses.

A classic study of 153 large police departments found that a key factor in solving crimes was identification of the perpetrator by the victim or witnesses. Of those cases that were not solved right away but were cleared later, most were cleared by routine procedures such as fingerprint searches, tips from informants, and mug-shot "show-ups." The report found that actions by the investigative staff mattered in very few cases. In sum, about 30 percent of the crimes were cleared by on-scene arrest and another 50 percent through identification by victims or witnesses when the police arrived. Thus, only about 20 percent could have been solved by detective work. Even among this group, however, the study found that most crimes "were also solved by patrol officers, members of the public who spontaneously provide further information, or routine investigative practices" (Greenwood, Chaiken, and Petersilia, 1977:227).

In some cities, the amount of serious crime has gone down during the past decade, but the number of unsolved cases has remained relatively stable. In part this may be accounted for by the lack of resources allocated to pursuing "cold cases." Detectives emphasize that although forensic tools are important, solving crimes "the old fashioned way" through much street work is still effective.

Does this research show that detectives are not important? No. Some cases are weak with little evidence, some are strong with a lot of evidence. Police need not devote a great deal of effort in these polar cases. However, in between lie cases with moderate evidence. These do require additional effort by detectives, and, as one researcher found, this "is extremely important with respect to subsequent making of follow-up arrests" (Bayley, 1998:149). This was confirmed by a study of a midwestern department's follow-up investigations of burglary and robbery (Brandl and Frank, 1994:163).

The detective's role is important in at least two ways besides solving crimes. First, the status of detective provides a goal to which patrol officers can aspire and thereby gives them an incentive to excel in their work. Second, the public expects the police to conduct investigations. Citizens may have more trust in the police or feel more willing to cooperate with them when they see investigations being conducted, even if those investigations do not always lead to arrests.

check point

14. What are the four steps of the apprehension process?
15. What is "DNA fingerprinting"?

Special Operations

Patrol and investigation are the two largest and most important units in a police department. In metropolitan areas, however, special units are set up to deal with specific types of problems. The most common such units concern traffic, vice, and juveniles. Some cities also have units to deal with organized crime and drugs. Even with special units in place, however, patrol officers and investigators continue to deal with the same problems.

Traffic

Traffic regulation is a major job of the police. On average, 7 percent of officers are assigned to traffic units (Bayley, 1994:94). The police regulate the flow of vehicles, investigate accidents, and enforce traffic laws. This work may not seem to have much to do with crime fighting or order maintenance, but in fact it does. Besides helping to maintain order, enforcement of traffic laws educates the public by promoting safe driving habits and provides a visible service to the community.

Traffic duty can also help the police catch criminals. In enforcing traffic laws, patrol officers can stop cars and question drivers. Stolen property and suspects linked to other criminal acts are often found this way. Most departments can now automatically check license numbers against lists of wanted vehicles and suspects.

Enforcement of traffic laws offers a good example of police discretion. When officers stop drivers for traffic violations, they choose among five options (Bayley, 1986):

1. Issue a citation (43 percent of stops).
2. Release the driver with a warning (20.7 percent).
3. Arrest the driver for intoxication or for another crime (14 percent).

4. Let the driver go (13.4 percent).
5. Issue a citation while also giving a stern lecture (12 percent).

Traffic work is mostly proactive, and the level of enforcement is linked to departmental policies. Guided by these policies, officers target certain kinds of violations or certain highways. Some departments expect officers to issue a certain number of citations during each shift. Although these norms may be informal, they offer a way of gauging the productivity of traffic officers. For the most part, selective enforcement is the general policy, since the police have neither the desire nor the resources to enforce all traffic laws.

Vice

Enforcement of vice laws depends on proactive police work, which often involves the use of undercover agents and informers. Most big-city police departments have a vice unit. Strict enforcement of these laws requires that officers be given wide discretion. They often must engage in degrading activities, such as posing as prostitutes or drug dealers, in order to catch lawbreakers. The special nature of vice work requires members of the unit to be well trained in the legal procedures that must be followed if arrests are to lead to convictions.

The potential for corruption in this type of police work presents some administrative problems. Undercover officers are in a position to blackmail gamblers and drug dealers and may also be offered bribes. In addition, officers must be transferred when their identities become known.

The growth of undercover work and electronic surveillance, common in vice patrols, troubles critics who favor more open policing. They fear that the use of these tactics violates civil liberties and increases government intrusion into the private lives of citizens, whether or not those citizens commit crimes.

Drug Law Enforcement

Many large cities have a bureau to enforce drug laws. These agencies may include task forces that deal with organized crime or gangs involved in drug dealing. Other groups may use sting operations to arrest drug sellers on the street or to provide drug education in the community.

Drug enforcement sometimes reflects the goal of *aggressive patrol,* or assigning resources so as to get the largest number of arrests and stop street dealing. Police executives believe that they must show dealers and the community that drug laws are enforced.

The police have used various strategies to attack drug dealing. One of these involves inspections of houses and buildings used by drug dealers. Those that do not meet city standards can be boarded up in order to rid the neighborhood of dealers. Streets where drugs are dealt openly can be flooded with officers who engage in proactive stops and questioning.

Another strategy is to disrupt the drug market. In Phoenix, Arizona, and other cities, police placed signs warning motorists entering "drug neighborhoods" that they might be stopped and questioned. In New York City's "Operation Pressure Point," a thousand police officers were moved into the Lower East Side to shut down the area's "drug supermarket." The police made thousands of arrests, abandoned buildings were torn down, and storefronts used by dealers were padlocked (Zimmer, 1987). This approach has been used in other parts of New York, in Los Angeles, and in other cities. But how effective is it? Do these efforts simply shift the drug market to another area, or do they actually reduce the availability of drugs?

The war on drugs consumes much of the resources of many urban police departments. While some officers might prefer patrolling a regular beat than being a drug cop, other officers enjoy the work. As Officer Marcus Laffey of the NYPD explained, moving to narcotics from being a beat cop was refreshing. "For one thing, you deal only with criminals. No more domestic disputes, barricaded schizophrenics, or D.O.A.s, the morass of negotiable and nonnegotiable difficulties people have with their neighbors or boyfriends or stepchildren." Laffey says that patrol cops deal with the "fluid whole of people's lives, but usually when the tide's going out." On the narcotics squad, he notes that "now all I do is catch sellers of crack and heroin, and catch their customers to show that they sold it. Patrol is politics, but narcotics is pure technique" (Laffey, 1999:29).

Although arrests for drug sale or possession have increased dramatically, some observers believe that this is not the best way to deal with the problem. Many public officials argue that drugs should be viewed as a public health problem rather than as a crime problem. Critics of current policies believe that society would benefit more if more resources were devoted to drug treatment programs than from police actions that fill prisons without doing much to reduce drug use.

check point

16. What are three kinds of special operations units that police departments often employ?

Summary

- To meet current and future challenges, the police must recruit and train individuals who will uphold the law and receive citizen support.
- Improvements have been made during the past quarter-century in recruiting more women, racial and ethnic minorities, and well-educated people as police officers.
- The police work in an environment greatly influenced by their subculture.
- The concept of the working personality helps us understand the influence of the police subculture on how individual officers see their world.
- The isolation of the police strengthens bonds among officers but can also add to job stress.
- Police operations are shaped by the department's formal organizational structures as well as social and political processes both within and outside the department.
- The police are organized along military lines so that authority and responsibility can be located at appropriate levels.
- Police services are delivered through the work of the patrol, investigation, and specialized operations units.
- The patrol function has three components: answering calls for assistance, maintaining a police presence, and probing suspicious circumstances.
- The investigation function is the responsibility of detectives in close coordination with patrol officers.
- The felony apprehension process is a sequence of actions that includes crime detection, preliminary investigation, follow-up investigation, clearance, and arrest.
- Large departments usually have specialized units dealing with traffic, drug, and vice.

Questions for Review

1. How do recruitment and training practices affect policing?
2. What is meant by the police subculture, and how does it influence an officer's work?
3. What factors in the police officer's "working personality" influence an officer's work?
4. What are some of the issues that influence police administrators in their allocation of resources?
5. What is the purpose of patrol? How is it carried out?
6. Why do detectives have so much prestige on the force?

Key Terms

clearance rate (p. 189)
differential response (p. 188)
incident-driven policing (p. 187)
line functions (p. 190)
preventive patrol (p. 192)
proactive (p. 187)
reactive (p. 187)
socialization (p. 179)
subculture (p. 179)
sworn officers (p. 192)
working personality (p. 180)

For Further Reading

Bayley, David H. 1994. *Police for the Future.* New York: Oxford University Press. Examination of policing in five countries—Australia, Canada, Great Britain, Japan, and the United States. Includes a suggested blueprint for the future.

Bratton, William. 1998. *Turnaround: How America's Top Cop Reversed the Crime Epidemic.* New York: Random House. Description by former Police Commissioner William Bratton of the efforts he took to reduce crime in New York City.

Brown, Michael K. 1981. *Working the Street.* New York: Russell Sage Foundation. A classic study of patrol work by officers of the San Diego Police Force.

Geller, William A., ed. 1985. *Police Leadership in America.* New York: Praeger. A collection of essays written by some of the most progressive police executives.

Manning, Peter K. 1977. *Police Work.* Cambridge, Mass.: MIT Press. Manning here argues that the police have an "impossible mandate." They have emphasized their crime-fighting stance, a role that they do not play successfully.

Skolnick, Jerome H., and David H. Bayley. 1986. *The New Blue Line.* New York: Free Press. A look at modern policing by two major criminal justice scholars.

Going Online

For an up-to-date list of Web links, go to http://www.cj.wadsworth.com/colesmith10e

1 Read the qualifications required of applicants who wish to become police officers at a state university: http://www.kysu.edu/UnivPolice/Qualifications.htm. Are these qualifications appropriate? Should any additional qualifications be required?

2 Why is it so important to protect the scene of a criminal event during an investigation? Find the reasons given at http://www.crime-scene-investigator.net/index.html.

3 Go to Infotrac College Edition. Use the keywords *police women* and then click on "periodicals." Read a journal article entitled "Aspects of Discriminatory Treatment of Women Police Officers Serving in Forces in England and Wales." In the British Journal of Criminology. What are the similarities and differences between the experiences of women police officers in the United States and Great Britain?

Checkpoint Answers

1 High school diploma, good physical condition, absence of a criminal record.

2 Better educated, more female and minority officers.

3 Preservice training, usually in a police academy.

4 On the job.

5 Danger, authority.

6 External stress, organizational stress, personal stress, operational stress.

7 A bureaucracy has (1) division of labor, (2) chain and unity of command, (3) rules and procedures.

8 Patrol, investigation, traffic, vice, juvenile.

9 Citizen expectation that the police will respond quickly to *every* call.

10 Policy that gives priority to calls according to whether an immediate or delayed response is warranted.

11 Clearance rate—the percentage of crimes known to the police that they believe they have solved through an arrest.

12 Personnel assigned to line functions are directly involved in field operations. Personnel assigned to staff functions supplement and support the line function.

13 (1) Answering calls for assistance, (2) maintaining a police presence, (3) probing suspicious circumstances.

14 (1) Detection of crime, (2) preliminary investigation, (3) follow-up investigation, (4) clearance and arrest.

15 A process of identifying individuals from their distinctive gene patterns.

16 Traffic, vice, narcotics.

CHAPTER 7

Police and Constitutional Law

AP Photo/Bill Janscha

Texas police officers arrived at a Dallas apartment on August 9, 2000. They were looking for Ronda Adham, a 21-year-old woman who was wanted for violating conditions of her bail in connection with pending charges concerning her alleged involvement in drug trafficking. When they entered the apartment, they found Adham's sister as well as Dallas Cowboys football star Michael Irvin. The officers also found cocaine, marijuana, and ecstasy pills. Irvin and the woman were arrested and charged with felony possession of cocaine. The arrest occurred just two months after Irvin completed a four-year probation sentence after being convicted of felony cocaine possession in 1996. In the aftermath of the arrest, Irvin, who had retired from the Cowboys one month earlier, lost his job as a television sports commentator for Fox Sports before he ever had the opportunity to cover any games ("Search without a Warrant," 2001).

A grand jury indicted Irvin in June 2001, and his trial date was set for January 14, 2002. In November 2001, however, a Texas trial judge dismissed all charges against Irvin and the woman. Although Irvin had been found in the apartment with the drugs, the judge learned that the police officers had entered the apartment without a proper warrant to conduct a search for drugs. Thus the judge ruled that the drugs in the apartment could not be used in evidence against Irvin and his companion. Without the drugs, the prosecutor had no other evidence against Irvin, so there was no basis for pursuing any criminal charges ("Search Without a Warrant," 2001).

Michael Irvin's case demonstrates the potential power of law as a limitation on police officers' efforts to investigate and combat criminal behavior. Because of the exclusionary rule (introduced in Chapter 4), when police officers violate the law by improperly obtaining evidence, they risk being denied permission to use that evidence. As a result, guilty people could be set free and society's efforts to control crime thwarted. Irvin denied that any drugs in the apartment belonged to him, so we do not know if he was a guilty person who was set free or an innocent person who was spared from an improper prosecution. Clearly, the police officers' actions in undertaking an improper warrantless search prevented the prosecutor from pursuing the question of which individual was guilty of a drug crime for keeping cocaine, marijuana, and ecstasy in the apartment.

The judge's action in Irvin's cases demonstrated that we sometimes place a higher priority on protecting individuals' rights than on pursuing criminal prosecutions. In this chapter we examine individual rights and how those legal protections define the limits of police officers' investigative and arrest powers. In particular, we look closely at two rights that were introduced in Chapter 4: the Fourth Amendment protection against unreasonable searches and seizures and the Fifth Amendment privilege against compelled self-incrimination (see Appendix A for the complete text).

QUESTIONS for INQUIRY

- What authority do police officers possess to stop and search people and their vehicles?
- When and how do police officers seek warrants in order to conduct searches and make arrests?
- Can police officers look in people's windows or their backyards to see if there is evidence of a crime there?
- In which situations can police officers conduct searches without obtaining a warrant?
- What is the purpose of the privilege against compelled self-incrimination?
- What is the exclusionary rule?
- In what situations does the exclusionary rule apply?

Legal Limitations on Police Investigations

In our democracy, the rights of individuals contained in the Bill of Rights embody important American values (see Chapter 4). They reflect the historic belief that we do not want to give government officials absolute power to pursue criminal investigations and prosecutions, because that approach to crime control would impose excessive costs on the values of individual liberty, privacy, and due process. If police could do whatever they wanted to do, then people would lack protections against arbitrary searches and arrests. On the other hand, crime control is an important policy goal. We do not want individuals' expectations about legal protections to block the ability of law enforcement officers to protect citizens from crime and punish wrongdoers. Judges must therefore interpret the Constitution in ways that seek to achieve a proper balance between crime control and the protection of individual rights.

Many police actions fall under the Fourth Amendment because they involve searches, seizures, and warrants. If officers exceed their authority by conducting an improper search of a person or a home, judges may release the arrestees or forbid certain evidence from being used. Officers might also be disciplined by their superiors or even sued by people whose rights were violated if investigatory activities violate the rules of law. Clearly, police officers need to know the legal rules that apply to their investigative activities, such as searches, arrests, and the questioning of suspects.

How can an officer know when his or her actions might violate the Fourth Amendment? The officer must depend on information and training provided at the police academy and subsequent updates from city and state attorneys who monitor court decisions. Individual police officers do not have time to follow the details of the latest court decisions. That responsibility rests with those who train and supervise law enforcement officers. Thus police officers' compliance with the law depends on their own knowledge and decisions as well as the supervision and training provided by their departments.

Go to the *American System of Criminal Justice* Web site at http://www.cj.wadsworth.com/colesmith10e to explore the topic of search and seizure in further detail.

Search and Seizure

The Fourth Amendment prohibits police officers from undertaking "unreasonable searches and seizures." The Supreme Court defines **searches** as actions by law enforcement officials that intrude on people's **reasonable expectations of privacy.** For example, someone who places a personal diary in a locked drawer within a bedroom of his or her home has demonstrated a reasonable expectation. Police officers cannot simply decide to enter the home and bedroom in order to open the locked door and read the diary. Many situations raise questions about people's reasonable expectations. For example, should people reasonably expect a police officer to reach into their pockets in order to see if they have guns? Should people reasonably expect a police officer not to walk up to their houses and peer into the windows? Although judges do not always answer these questions in clear, consistent ways, people's reasonable expectations about their privacy are important elements in judges' determinations about legal guidelines for police investigations.

search
Officials' examination of and hunt for evidence in or on a person or place in a manner that intrudes on reasonable expectations of privacy.

reasonable expectation of privacy
Standard developed for determining whether a government intrusion of a person or property constitutes a search because it interferes with individual interests that are normally protected from government examination.

In defining **seizure,** the Supreme Court focuses on the nature and extent of officers' interference with people's liberty and freedom of movement. If an officer who is leaning against the wall of a building says to a passing pedestrian, "Where are you going?" and the person replies, "To the sandwich shop down the street" as she continues to walk without interference by the officer, there is virtually no intrusion on her liberty and freedom of movement. Thus officers are free to speak to people on the street. If people voluntarily stop in order to speak with the officer, they have not been "seized," because they are free to move along whenever they choose. However, if people are not free to leave when officers' assert their authority to halt someone's movement, then a seizure has occurred, and the Fourth Amendment requires that the seizure be reasonable. One form of seizure is an arrest, which involves taking a suspect into custody. Property can also be subject to seizure, especially if it is evidence in a criminal case.

seizure
Any police use of their authority to deprive people of their liberty or property that is reasonable according to the Fourth Amendment.

When a seizure is very brief, it is called a **stop,** defined as a brief interference with a person's freedom of movement with a duration that can be measured in minutes. When police require a driver to pull over in order to receive a traffic citation, that is a stop. To be permissible under the Fourth Amendment, stops must be justified by **reasonable suspicion**—a situation in which specific aspects of the person's appearance, behavior, and circumstances lead the officer to conclude that the person should be stopped in order to investigate the occurrence of a crime. Officers cannot make stops based solely on hunches.

stop
Government officials' interference with an individual's freedom of movement for a duration that can be measured in minutes.

reasonable suspicion
A police officer's belief, based on articulable facts, that criminal activity is taking place, so that intruding on an individual's reasonable expectation of privacy is necessary.

As we shall see, courts permit police officers to make stops without reasonable suspicion, in many kinds of situations. For example, these stops can occur in locations such as border-crossing points where it is especially important to prevent illegal activities, such as smuggling and drug trafficking. Thus everyone can be stopped in these special situations even if there is no specific basis to suspect them of wrongdoing.

The Web page of the Cincinnati police explains traffic stops to help citizens understand police officers' motives and authority: http://www.iglou.com/cintipd/trafficstop.htm.

check point

1. What is a search?
2. What justification do police officers need to make a stop?
(Answers are at the end of the chapter.)

Arrest

probable cause
An amount of reliable information indicating that it is more likely than not that evidence will be found in a specific location or that a specific person is guilty of a crime.

An *arrest* is a significant deprivation of liberty, because a person is taken into police custody, transported to the police station or jail, and processed into the criminal justice system. A seizure need not be lengthy to be an arrest. Indeed, some "stops" may be longer than "arrests" if, for example, a person taken to the police station is released on bail within an hour while a person stopped along a roadside must wait a longer period for the officer to write out a slew of traffic citations. Typically, however, arrests last much longer than stops.

Because arrests involve a more significant intrusion on liberty, they necessitate a higher level of justification. Unlike stops, which require only reasonable suspicion, all arrests must be supported by probable cause. **Probable cause** requires that sufficient evidence exist to support the reasonable conclusion that a person has committed a crime. Police officers must provide a judicial officer with sufficient evidence to support a finding of probable cause in order to obtain an arrest warrant. Alternatively, police officers' on-the-street determinations of probable cause can produce discretionary warrantless arrests. A judge subsequently examines such arrests for the existence of probable cause, in a hearing that must occur shortly after the arrest, typically within 48 hours. If the judge determines that the police officer was wrong in concluding that probable cause existed to justify the arrest, then the suspect is released from custody.

Ray J. Malace

Arrest is the physical taking of a person into custody. What legal requirements must be met to make this a valid arrest? What limits are placed on the officers?

Officers may make arrests when they see people commit criminal acts or when witnesses provide them with sufficient information so that they believe probable cause exists to arrest an individual. Arrest authority is not limited to felonies and misdemeanors, however. The Supreme Court has expanded the discretionary authority of police officers to make arrests. In 2001 the justices decided that police officers can make a warrantless arrest for a fine-only traffic offense, such as a failure to wear a seatbelt, which would draw only a fine upon conviction (*Atwater v. City of Lago Vista,* 2001).

Warrants and Probable Cause

Imagine that you are a judge. Two police officers come to your chambers to ask you to authorize a search warrant. They swear that they observed frequent foot traffic of suspicious people going in and out of a house. Moreover, they swear that a reliable informant told them that he was inside the house two days earlier and saw crack cocaine being sold. Does this information rise to the level of "probable cause," justifying issuance of a search warrant? Can you grant a warrant based purely on the word of police officers, or do you need more concrete evidence?

Search Warrant Requirements

The Fourth Amendment requires that "no Warrants shall issue, but upon probable cause, supported by Oath or affirmation, and particularly describing the place to be searched, and the persons or things to be seized." These particular elements of the Amendment must be fulfilled in order to issue a warrant. If they are not fulfilled, then a defendant can later challenge the validity of the warrant. The important elements are, first, the existence of probable cause. Second, the evidence that police officers present to the judicial officer must be supported by "oath or affirmation," which typically means that police officers say "yes" when the judicial officer asks them if they swear or affirm that all the information presented is true to the best of their knowledge. Officers can also fulfill this requirement by presenting an **affidavit,** which is a written statement confirmed by oath or affirmation. Third, the warrant must describe the specific place to be searched; a "general warrant" to search many locations cannot be issued. Fourth, the warrant must describe the person or items to be seized. Thus, if the warrant authorizes a search for a person suspected of robbery, the officers should not open small dresser drawers or other places where they know a person could not be hiding.

affidavit
Written statement of fact, supported by oath or affirmation, submitted to judicial officers to fulfill the requirements of probable cause for obtaining a warrant.

The U.S. Supreme Court has attempted to guide judicial officers in identifying the existence of probable cause. Mere suspicion cannot constitute probable cause, yet the level of evidence to establish it need not fulfill the high level of proof needed to justify a criminal conviction. In essence, probable cause is a level of evidence sufficient to provide a reasonable conclusion that the proposed objects of a search will be found in a location that law enforcement officers request to search. For an arrest warrant, the essential issue is whether sufficient evidence is presented to lead to the reasonable conclusion that a specific person should be prosecuted for an arrestable criminal offense. There is no hard-and-fast definition of *probable cause* that judicial officers can apply to every situation; rather, it serves as a flexible concept that the officers can apply in different ways.

During the 1960s, the Supreme Court established a two-part test for probable cause in the cases of *Aguilar v. Texas* (1964) and *Spinelli v. United States* (1969). Under the so-called *Aguilar-Spinelli* test, the evidence presented to justify a warrant must (1) provide the basis for the law enforcement officer's knowledge about the alleged criminal activity and (2) provide substantiation for the truthfulness and reliability of the information's source. In other words, law enforcement officers could not simply say that they had heard certain information about the existence of criminal activity or seizable objects at a certain location; they were required to provide enough information to convince the judicial officer about the circumstances in which the source had gained the information. The police also had to provide information to convince the judicial officer of the truthfulness and reliability of the information source. In *Illinois v. Gates* (1983), however, the Supreme Court turned away from the two-part test in order to embrace a more flexible **totality of circumstances** test. Thus, rather than requiring each of the two components be fulfilled, judicial officers could make a more generalized determination about whether the evidence is both sufficient and reliable enough to justify a warrant.

Some organizations have formal policies and procedures for verifying warrants and communicating with officers before police search their premises; see, for example, http://www.tulane.edu/~counsel/search_warr.html.

totality of circumstances test
Flexible test established by the Supreme Court for identifying whether probable cause exists to justify a judicial officer in issuing a warrant.

check point

3. What is the difference between an arrest and a stop?
4. What do police officers need to demonstrate in order to obtain a warrant?

Plain View Doctrine

Although the warrant requirement is a central feature of the Fourth Amendment, the Supreme Court has identified situations in which warrants are not required. What if a police officer is walking down the street and sees a marijuana plant growing in the front window of a home? Has the officer conducted a search by

A. Ramey/PhotoEdit

Under the plain view doctrine, can the police legally seize the marijuana plant taken from the yard of this home without a search warrant?

looking into the window? If so, is the search legal even though it took place by chance but was not supported by reasonable suspicion or probable cause? In *Coolidge v. New Hampshire* (1971), the Court discussed the **plain view doctrine,** which permits officers to notice and use as evidence items that are visible to them when the officers are where they are permitted to be. Officers could not break into a home and then claim that the drugs found inside were in plain view on a table. However, if the drugs were visible from a public sidewalk, the plain view doctrine could apply. Because the drugs were in plain view, their owner had lost any reasonable expectation of privacy with respect to them. The officer's plain view of the drugs provides probable cause for obtaining a warrant to gain entry to the house in order to seize them.

plain view doctrine
Officers may examine and seize, without a warrant, contraband or evidence that is in open view at a location where they are legally permitted to be.

Open Fields Doctrine

Related to the plain view doctrine is the **open fields doctrine.** Under this doctrine, first announced by the Supreme Court in *Hester v. United States* (1924), property owners have no reasonable expectation of privacy in open fields on and around their property. Thus, if criminal evidence is visible, then probable cause has been established for its seizure. The Court has approved cases in which police officers, acting without a warrant, walked past "no trespassing" signs and found marijuana plants in fields on private property (*Oliver v. United States,* 1984). The Court limited this doctrine by refusing to apply it to the yard area immediately surrounding the home that is called the *curtilage.* Although protected against physical intrusion by officers, that area remains subject to the plain view doctrine if evidence of criminal activity is clearly visible from the vantage point of a location where officers can lawfully stand. For example, the plain view doctrine includes any areas visible from the air when police officers hover above property in a helicopter.

open fields doctrine
Officers are permitted to search, without a warrant, for visible evidence on private property beyond the area immediately surrounding a house.

Police and prosecutors use Web pages to share information about recent developments affecting the plain view doctrine and other issues; see http://www.clarkprosecutor.org/html/police/mar98.htm.

Plain Feel and Other Senses

If law enforcement officers may conduct a warrantless search under the plain view doctrine, what about detection of criminal evidence using other senses? If

Table 7.1 Searches by sight and feel

The Fourth Amendment's protection for reasonable expectations of privacy does not cover criminal evidence that can be seen or felt by officers in specific situations.

Case	Decision
Plain view	
Coolidge v. New Hampshire (1971)	Officers are permitted to notice and use as evidence items in plain view when the officers are where they are legally permitted to be.
Open fields	
Oliver v. U.S. (1984)	Officers are permitted to intrude on private lands that are open areas, such as fields and pastures, but they may not search the yard area immediately surrounding a house (*curtilage*) without a warrant or a specific justification for a warrantless search.
Plain feel	
Minnesota v. Dickerson (1993)	While conducting a pat-down search of a suspect's outer clothing, police may seize items in pockets or clothing as evidence if they are immediately identifiable by touch as weapons or contraband.

officers smell the distinctive odor of an illegal substance, such as marijuana, they are justified in investigating further. Bear in mind that the sense of smell may be employed by a trained police dog, too. Court decisions have established that police dogs who sniff luggage in public places are not conducting searches and therefore are not subject to the requirements of the Fourth Amendment.

Does an officer's sense of "feel" apply to searches of property? As we shall see in the discussion of stop-and-frisk searches, a police officer with reasonable suspicion may conduct a pat-down search of a person's outer clothing. If the officer feels something that is immediately recognizable as a weapon, crack pipe, or other contraband, the item may be seized (*Minnesota v. Dickerson,* 1993). However, police officers cannot aggressively feel and manipulate people's property, such as a duffel bag, in an attempt to detect criminal evidence, unless the luggage examination is part of a standard search in boarding a commercial airliner or crossing an international border into the United States (*Bond v. United States,* 2000).

Table 7.1 reviews selected cases concerning the Fourth Amendment's protection for reasonable expectations of privacy involving searches by sight and feel.

check point

5. What is the plain view doctrine?
6. May officers use senses other than sight to find evidence of crime without a warrant?

Warrantless Searches

The U.S. Supreme Court has identified specific categories of searches that do not require warrants. The Court has decided that society's law enforcement needs are so significant in these situations that police officers must have the authority to undertake searches without taking the time to seek a warrant. In the rest of this section, we examine six of these categories: (1) special needs beyond the normal purposes of law enforcement, (2) stop and frisk on the streets, (3) search incident to a lawful arrest, (4) exigent circumstances, (5)consent, and (6) automobile searches.

The Supreme Court has upheld systematic highway stops without a warrant to look for drunk drivers. Each vehicle must be stopped and the driver briefly questioned. Here, officers set up a roadblock as part of North Carolina's "Booze It and Lose It" campaign.

Special Needs beyond the Normal Purposes of Law Enforcement

Law enforcement officials have a justified need to conduct warrantless searches of every individual in certain specific contexts. The use of metal detectors to examine airline passengers, for example, is a specific context in which the need to prevent hijacking justifies a limited search of every passenger. Here the Court does not require officers to have any suspicions, reasonable or otherwise, about the illegal activities of any individual.

Permissible warrantless searches also take place at the entry points into the United States—border crossings, ports, and airports. The government's interests in guarding against the entry of people and items (e.g., weapons, drugs, toxic chemicals) that are harmful to national interests outweigh the individuals' expectations of privacy. Typically, these border stops take only a few moments as customs officers check required documents, such as passports and visas, inquire about where the person traveled, and ask what the person is bringing into the United States. The customs officers may have a trained dog sniff around people and their luggage, checking for drugs or large amounts of cash. At the Mexican and Canadian borders and at international airports, people may be chosen at random to have their cars and luggage searched. They may also be chosen for such searches because their behavior or their answers to questions arouse the suspicions of customs officers.

The U.S. Border Patrol regularly makes warrantless stops and searches based on the special needs exception to the Fourth Amendment's warrant requirement; see their home page at http://www.ins.usdoj.gov/graphics/lawenfor/bpatrol.

The handbook of the U.S. Customs Service permits an officer to base some types of searches on suspicion alone, even though mere suspicion does not meet the standard of "reasonable suspicion," which requires the support of articulable facts. The Customs Service instructs its personnel to consider six categories of factors in determining if suspicion exists to justify searching a traveler at a border crossing or airport:

1. *Behavioral analysis:* Signs of nervousness, such as flushed face, avoidance of eye contact, excessive perspiration
2. *Observational techniques:* Unexplained bulges in clothing or awkwardness in walking
3. *Inconsistencies:* Discrepancies in answers to questions posed by customs officers
4. *Intelligence:* Information provided to customs officers by informants or other law enforcement officials

5. *K-9:* Signals from law enforcement trained dogs who sniff around people and luggage
6. *Incident to a seizure or arrest:* The discovery of contraband in one suitcase, which can justify the search of the person and the rest of the person's property

Table 7.2 contains the Custom Service's policies for personal searches, including the level of suspicion required for each search and whether supervisory approval is required. Do you believe these guidelines strike a proper balance between individuals' rights and societal interests in stopping the flow of contraband?

The Supreme Court has expanded the checkpoint concept by approving systematic stops along highways within the nation's interior in order to look for drunk drivers. Specifically, they approved a sobriety checkpoint program in Michigan. State police had set up a checkpoint at which they stopped every vehicle and briefly questioned each driver. The checkpoint program was challenged as a violation of the Fourth Amendment right to be free from unreasonable seizures, but the Court found no constitutional violation (*Michigan Department of State Police v. Sitz,* 1990). Although the U.S. Supreme Court has approved vehicle checkpoints that combat drunk driving as context for permissible warrantless stops and searches, this does not mean that these checkpoints are permissible everywhere in the United States. As you read the Close Up box about legal developments in Michigan, think about how the definitions of rights and police authority can differ from state to state.

The U.S. Supreme Court has not given blanket approval for every kind of checkpoint or traffic stop that police might wish to use. The Court specifically forbids random stops of vehicles by officers on patrol (*Delaware v. Prouse,* 1979). Officers must have a basis for a vehicle stop, such as an observed violation of traffic laws. The Court has also ruled that a city cannot set up a checkpoint in order to check drivers and passengers for possible involvement in drugs. In *City of Indianapolis v. Edmond* (2000), even though police officers stopped

Table 7.2 **U.S. Customs Service policies for personal searches**

Search Type	Suspicion Level	Approval
1. Immediate pat-down (frisk): A search necessary to ensure that a person is not carrying a weapon	Suspicion that a weapon may be present	None required
2. Pat-down for merchandise: A search for merchandise, including contraband, hidden on a person's body	One articulable fact	On-duty supervisor
3. Partial body search: The removal of some clothing by a person to recover merchandise reasonably suspected to be concealed on the body	Reasonable suspicion, based on specific, articulable facts	On-duty supervisor
4. X-ray: Medical X-ray by medical personnel to determine the presence of merchandise within the body	Reasonable suspicion, based on specific, articulable facts	Port director and court order, unless person consents
5. Body-cavity search: Any visual or physical intrusion into the rectal or vaginal cavity	Reasonable suspicion, based on specific, articulable facts	Port director and court order, unless person consents
6. MBM (monitored bowel movement): Detention of a person for the purpose of determining whether contraband or merchandise is concealed in the alimentary canal.	Reasonable suspicion, based on specific, articulable facts	Port director

Source: U.S. General Accounting Office, *U.S. Customs Service: Better Targeting of Airline Passengers for Personal Searches Could Produce Better Results* (Washington, D.C.: U.S. Government Printing Office, March 2000).

State Supreme Courts and Constitutional Rights

Ironically, although the Michigan case established the legality of sobriety checkpoints for the entire nation, the Michigan Supreme Court later barred the use of such checkpoints within the state of Michigan. The Michigan Supreme Court examined the protection against unreasonable searches and seizures contained in Article I, Section 11 of the Michigan Constitution and found that such checkpoints violate its interpretation of the state constitution. Michigan's high court used a balancing test that simply struck a different balance than did the one applied by the U.S. Supreme Court majority. The Michigan court concluded that the government's interest in reducing drunk driving did not outweigh the liberty and privacy interests of individual drivers.

The *Sitz* case serves as a reminder that states can make authoritative decisions about many of their own affairs in the U.S. system of government. The U.S. Supreme Court has final authority over decisions concerning the interpretation of the U.S. Constitution, but state supreme courts control the interpretation of their own constitutions. Although state supreme courts cannot interpret their constitutions to provide fewer or weaker rights for people in their states, they can interpret their own constitutions to provide *stronger* rights than those recognized by the U.S. Supreme Court. This is what happened in the Michigan sobriety checkpoint case. It happens in other cases, too, and thus constitutional rights vary to some degree from state to state.

Since all of the states in the United States are part of one country, should rights vary from state to state? If people in Michigan are protected against surprise sobriety checkpoints as an invasion of their right against unreasonable seizures, is it fair that other Americans do not enjoy the same constitutional protection?

The California Supreme Court is often regarded as a leader in establishing its own interpretations of rights under a state constitution. You can read its opinions at http://www.courtinfo.ca.gov/opinions.

vehicles only briefly in order to ask a few questions and circle the car with a drug-sniffing dog, the Court declared that checkpoints cannot be justified by a general search for criminal evidence. Such stops must be narrowly focused on a specific objective, such as checking for drunk drivers.

check point

7. In what situations do law enforcement's special needs justify stopping an automobile without reasonable suspicion?

Stop and Frisk on the Streets

Terry v. Ohio (1968)
Supreme Court decision endorsing police officers' authority to stop and frisk suspects on the street when there is reasonable suspicion that they are armed and involved in criminal activity.

Police officers possess the authority to make stops and limited searches of individuals on the streets when specific circumstances justify such actions. As you read the Close Up box concerning the landmark case of ***Terry v. Ohio*** **(1968)**, pay particular attention to the circumstances that must exist in order for an officer to initiate a search. Also take note of how extensive such a search can be.

The Court's decision recognized that seizures short of arrest could be "reasonable" under the Fourth Amendment. In this case, the suspects were not free to leave, yet the officer would presumably have released them if he had not found the weapons. Thus the stop and search occurred as part of the investigation process before any arrest occurred. The justices were clearly concerned about striking an appropriate balance between Fourth Amendment rights and necessary police authority to investigate and prevent crimes.

stop-and-frisk search
Limited search approved by the Supreme Court in *Terry v. Ohio* that permits police officers to pat down the clothing of people on the streets if there is reasonable suspicion of dangerous criminal activity.

Although the justices supported law enforcement authority, they struck the balance by carefully specifying the circumstances in which this sort of pat-down search—more commonly known as a **stop-and-frisk search**—can occur. Look closely at the holding in the case. The Court appears to demand that several spe-

Terry v. Ohio, 392 U.S. 1 (1968)

In *Terry v. Ohio,* a police officer observed several men repeatedly walking back and forth in front of a store and peering into the window. Their behavior aroused the officer's suspicions that they could be preparing to commit a robbery. The officer approached the men, identified himself as a police officer, and patted down the exterior clothing of one man. When he found a gun in the man's coat pocket, he ordered the other two men to stand against a wall, and he discovered a weapon in the coat pocket of one of the other men. The men sought to have the guns excluded from their trial on the charge of carrying a concealed weapon. They asserted that the officer's pat-down search of their outer clothing was not justified by probable cause because the officer had no evidence to indicate that they had committed any crime. Thus, they argued that his search was unreasonable under the terms of the Fourth Amendment. Chief Justice Warren delivered the opinion of the Court, as follows.

* * *

It is quite plain that the Fourth Amendment governs "seizures" of the person which do not eventuate in a trip to the station house and prosecution for crime—"arrests" in traditional terminology. It must be recognized that whenever a police officer accosts an individual and restrains his freedom to walk away, he has "seized" that person. And it is nothing less than sheer torture of the English language to suggest that a careful exploration of the outer surfaces of a person's clothing all over his or her body in an attempt to find weapons is not a "search." Moreover, it is simply fantastic to urge that such a procedure performed in public by a policeman while the citizen stands helpless, perhaps facing a wall with his hands raised, is a "petty indignity." It is a serious intrusion upon the sanctity of the person, which may inflict great indignity and arouse strong resentment, and it is not to be undertaken lightly.

* * *

We conclude that the revolver seized from Terry was properly admitted in evidence against him. At the time he seized petitioner and searched him for weapons, Officer McFadden had reasonable grounds to believe that petitioner was armed and dangerous, and it was necessary for the protection of himself and others to take swift measures to discover the true facts and neutralize the threat of harm if it materialized. The policeman carefully restricted his search to what was appropriate to the discovery of the particular items which he sought. . . . We merely hold today that where a police officer observes unusual conduct which leads him reasonably to conclude in light of his experience that criminal activity may be afoot and that the persons with whom he is dealing may be armed and presently dangerous, where in the course of investigating this behavior he identifies himself as a policeman and makes reasonable inquiries, and where nothing in the initial stages of the encounter serves to dispel his reasonable fear for his own or others' safety, he is entitled for the protection of himself and others in the area to conduct a carefully limited search of the outer clothing of such persons in an attempt to discover weapons which might be used to assault him.

Such a search is a reasonable search under the Fourth Amendment, and any weapons seized may properly be introduced in evidence against the person from whom they were taken.

Affirmed.

Researching the Internet

Learn more about how the U.S. Supreme Court interprets the Constitution; see the Web site of the Supreme Court Historical Society: http://www.supremecourthistory.org.

cific facts exist in each situation in which a permissible stop and frisk can occur. If we break apart the Court's own words, we can see that the justices explicitly say "We merely hold today that

[1] where a police officer observes unusual conduct

[2] which leads him reasonably to conclude in light of his experience

[3] that criminal activity may be afoot and

[4] that the persons with whom he is dealing may be armed and presently dangerous,

[5] where in the course of investigating this behavior

[6] he identifies himself as a policeman and makes reasonable inquiries,

Craig Filipacchi/Gamma-Liaison

The stopping and frisking of individuals must be carried out according to the law. What does the law require in this situation?

[7] and where nothing in the initial stages of the encounter serves to dispel his reasonable fear for his own or others' safety,

[8] he is entitled for the protection of himself and others in the area to conduct a carefully limited search of the outer clothing of such persons in an attempt to discover weapons which might be used to assault him.

These specified factors imposed an obligation on police officers to make observations, draw reasonable conclusions, identify themselves, and make inquiries before conducting the stop-and-frisk search. In addition, the reasonableness of the search was justified by a reasonable conclusion that a person was armed and therefore the officer needed to act in order to protect him- or herself and the public.

Court decisions have given officers significant discretion to decide when these factors exist. For example, if officers see someone running at the sight of police in a high-crime neighborhood, their observation can provide the basis for sufficient suspicion to justify a stop and frisk (*Illinois v. Wardlow,* 2000). Thus officers need not actually see evidence of a weapon or interact with the suspect prior to making the stop.

The Supreme Court later expanded police authority by permitting officers to rely on reports from reliable witnesses as the basis for conducting the stop and frisk (*Adams v. Williams,* 1972). However, an unverified anonymous tip is not an adequate basis for a stop-and-frisk search. In ***Florida v. J. L.*** (2000), police officers received an anonymous tip that a young African American man standing at a specific bus stop and wearing a plaid shirt was carrying a gun. Police officers went to the bus stop and frisked a young man matching the description. They found a gun, and the young man was charged with unlawfully carrying a concealed weapon. The justices unanimously ruled that the gun must be excluded from evidence because the officers did not have reliable information as the basis for the search. The Court did not rule out the possibility that an anonymous tip alone might be sufficient in extraordinary circumstances in which a greater societal interest is at stake, such as a report that someone is carrying a bomb—a device with greater risk and likelihood of harm than a handgun. In the post–September 11 effort to combat terrorism, such stops may become more common.

***Florida v. J. L.* (2000)**
Police officers may not conduct a stop-and-frisk search based solely on an anonymous tip.

Search Incident to a Lawful Arrest

The authority to undertake a warrantless search incident to a lawful arrest is not limited by the crime for which the arrestee has been taken into custody. Even someone arrested for a traffic offense can be searched. Although there is no reason to suspect the person has a weapon or to believe that evidence related to the offense will be found in the person's pockets, the arrestee is subject to the same arrest scene search as someone taken into custody for murder (*United States v. Robinson,* 1973).

The justification for searches of arrestees emerged in the Supreme Court's decision in ***Chimel v. California*** **(1969).** The officers must make sure that the arrestee does not have a weapon that could endanger the officers or others in the vicinity. The officers must also look for evidence on the person of the arrestee that the arrestee might destroy or damage before or during transportation to jail. Officers can search the arrestee and the immediate area around the arrestee. Officers can also make a protective sweep through other rooms where the suspect may recently have been. However, the arrest would not justify opening drawers and conducting a thorough search of an entire house. If, after the arrest, officers have probable cause to conduct a more thorough search, they must obtain a warrant that specifies the items that they seek and the places that they will search.

Chimel v. California (1969)
Supreme Court decision that endorsed warrantless searches for weapons and evidence in the immediate vicinity of people who are lawfully arrested.

Although a lawful arrest justifies a limited search and protective sweep, the Court has been unwilling to permit thorough warrantless searches at crime scenes, even when a murder victim is discovered. Officers should obtain a warrant to open luggage, packages, and filing cabinets at the murder scene (*Flippo v. West Virginia,* 1999).

State legislatures may use statutes to define officers' authority to search incident to an arrest. You can read Idaho's statute at http://www3.state.id.us/cgi-bin/newidst?sctid=190060013.K.

check point

8. What knowledge must an officer possess in order to conduct a stop-and-frisk search on the streets?
9. Where can officers search when conducting a warrantless search incident to a lawful arrest?

Exigent Circumstances

Officers can make an arrest without a warrant when there are **exigent circumstances.** This means that officers are in the middle of an urgent situation in which they must act swiftly and do not have time to go to court to seek a warrant. With respect to arrests, for example, when officers are in hot pursuit of a fleeing suspected felon, they need not stop to seek a warrant and thereby risk permitting the suspect to get away (*Warden v. Hayden,* 1967). Similarly, exigent circumstances can justify warrantless searches. When the ex-wife of football Hall-of-Famer O. J. Simpson was stabbed to death in front of her home, police officers went to Simpson's home and climbed the wall to gain entry to his backyard. They claimed that they found a bloody glove in the backyard, and that glove was admitted into evidence against Simpson because a judge was persuaded that the officers made the warrantless entry and search based on the urgency of their need to make sure that no one at the Simpson house was injured or in danger.

exigent circumstances
When there is a threat to public safety or the risk that evidence will be destroyed, officers may search, arrest, or question suspects without obtaining a warrant or following other usual rules of criminal procedure.

In *Cupp v. Murphy* (1973), a man voluntarily complied with police officers' request that he come to the police station to answer questions concerning his wife's murder. The couple resided in separate homes at the time. At the station, officers noticed a substance on the man's fingernails that they thought might be dried blood. Over his objections, they took a sample of scrapings under his fingernails and ultimately used that tissue as evidence against him when he was convicted of murdering his wife. The Supreme Court said the search was properly undertaken under exigent circumstances. If officers had taken the time to seek a warrant, the suspect may have gone to the bathroom to wash his hands and the evidence would have been lost.

In other cases, the Supreme Court approved warrantless blood tests because of the need for fast action. For example, evidence of alcohol in the blood will dissipate and disappear if not retrieved immediately through a blood test (*Breihaupt v. Abram,* 1957).

Police officers can use the exigent circumstances justification for warrantless searches for the purpose of seeking evidence. To justify such searches, they do not need to show that there was a potential threat to public safety. As a practical matter, police officers make quick judgments about undertaking certain searches. If incriminating evidence is discovered, courts may be asked to make an after-the-fact determination of whether the urgency of the situation justified a warrantless search and whether the nature and purpose of the search were reasonable. Judges are usually quite reluctant to second-guess a police officer's on-the-spot decision that the urgency of a situation required an immediate warrantless search.

Consent

If people consent to a search, officers do not need probable cause or even any level of suspicion to justify the search. The consent effectively absolves law enforcement officers of any risk that evidence will be excluded from use at trial or that they will be found liable in a civil lawsuit alleging a violation of Fourth Amendment rights.

Consent searches provide a valuable investigatory tool for officers who wish to conduct warrantless searches. Officers in many police departments are trained to ask people if they will consent to a search. Thus some officers ask every motorist during a traffic stop, "May I search your car?" Or, if called to the scene of a domestic dispute or a citizen complaint about noise, the officers may say, "Do you mind if I look around in the downstairs area of your house?" Criminal evidence is often uncovered in such consent searches, a fact which may indicate that many citizens do not know that they have the option to say "no" when officers ask for permission to search. Moreover, some citizens may fear that they will look more suspicious to the officers if they say "no," so they agree to searches in order to act as if they have nothing to hide. In addition, in ***United States v. Drayton*** **(2002)**, the Supreme Court said very clearly that police officers do not have to inform people of their right to say "no" when asked if they wish to consent to a search.

United States v. Drayton **(2002)**
Police officers are not required to inform people of their right to decline when police ask for consent to search.

One must address two key issues in deciding if a permissible consent search has occurred. First, the consent must *voluntary.* Police officers could not have used coercion or threats in order to obtain consent. Even subtler tricks, such as dishonestly telling someone that there is a search warrant and thereby implying that the person has no choice but to consent, will result in the search being declared improper (*Bumper v. North Carolina,* 1968). Second, the consent must be given by someone who *possesses authority to give consent* and thereby waive the right. Someone cannot, for example, consent to have his or her neighbor's house searched.

check point

10. What are exigent circumstances?
11. What two elements must be present for a valid consent to permit a warrantless search?

Automobile Searches

We began a discussion of automobile searches in the section on special needs; here we look at such searches in greater detail. The U.S. Supreme Court first addressed searches of automobiles in *Carroll v. United States* (1925), a case in which federal agents searched a car looking for illegal alcohol. The *Carroll* case, in which the warrantless search was approved, provided an underlying justification for permitting such searches of automobiles. In essence, because cars are mobile, they are quite different from houses and other buildings. Automobiles can be driven away and disappear in the time that it would take officers to ask a judicial officer for a search warrant.

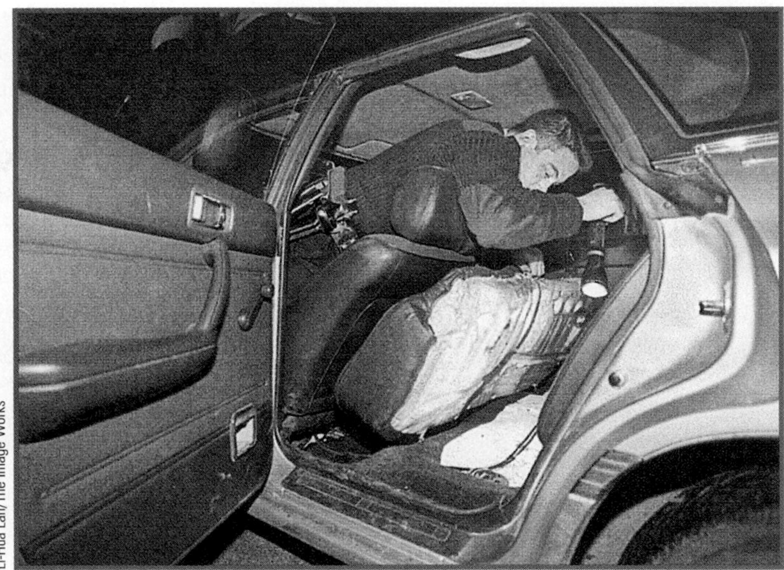
Li-Hua Lan/The Image Works

Warrantless searches of automobiles may be conducted when there is probable cause to believe that a vehicle contains evidence. Lieutenant Tim Laun checks the inside and under a car seat after he and his colleagues arrested a suspect; they found illegal drugs in the vehicle.

Police officers have significant authority to search automobiles and to issue commands to people riding in vehicles. For example, during a traffic stop, officers can order passengers as well as the driver to exit the vehicle, even if there is no basis for suspicion that the passengers engaged in any wrongdoing (*Maryland v. Wilson,* 1997).

The two key questions that arise in automobile searches are (1) When can an officer stop a car? and (2) How extensively can they search the vehicle? Many automobile searches arise as a result of traffic stops. A stop can occur when an officer observes a traffic violation, including defective safety equipment, or when there is a basis for reasonable suspicion concerning the involvement of the car, its driver, or its passengers in a crime. Police officers are free to make a visible inspection around a car's interior as they question a driver and ask for identification when preparing a citation for a traffic violation. All sworn officers can make traffic stops, even if they are in unmarked vehicles and serving in special vice or detective bureaus that do not normally handle traffic offenses (*Whren v. United States,* 1996). A traffic violation by itself, however, does not provide an officer with the authority to search an entire vehicle (*Knowles v. Iowa,* 1998). Specific factors must create reasonable suspicion or probable cause to justify officers doing anything more than looking inside the vehicle.

For example, the lawful arrest of a driver justifies a search of the entire passenger compartment of the automobile for evidence or weapons (*New York v. Belton,* 1981). Moreover, such an arrest justifies the search of a passenger's property (*Wyoming v. Houghton,* 1999). In addition, the Court has expanded officers' authority to search automobiles even when no formal arrest has yet occurred. In *Michigan v. Long* (1983), the Court approved a search of the car's interior around the driver's seat after officers found the car in a ditch and the driver standing outside the car appearing intoxicated. The Supreme Court justified the search as an expansion of the *Terry* doctrine. In effect, the officers were permitted to "frisk" the car in order to protect themselves and others by making sure no weapon was available to the not-yet-arrested driver. Such a search requires that the officers have reasonable suspicion that the person stopped may be armed and poses a potential danger to the officers.

Initially the Court treated containers and closed areas in automobiles differently from the passenger compartment. Even when officers had probable cause to search a car's trunk, they were expected to obtain a warrant for any containers found within the trunk. However, this rule changed in the Court's decision in *California v. Acevedo* (1991). Now police officers can search anywhere in the car for which they have probable cause to search. Further, unlike the situations with warrants, the officers themselves, rather than a judge, determine whether probable cause exists before conducting the warrantless search of the vehicle. If, however, a judge later disagrees with the officer's conclusion about the existence of probable cause, any evidence found in the search of the automobile will likely be excluded from use at trial.

Even if officers lack probable cause to believe that the vehicle has been stolen, an officer may enter the vehicle to see the vehicle identification number by the

Table 7.3 Warrantless searches

The Supreme Court has ruled that there are circumstances when a warrant is not required.

Case	Decision
Special needs	
Michigan Department of State Police v. Sitz (1990)	Stopping motorists systematically at roadblocks designed for specific purposes, such as detecting drunken drivers, is permissible.
City of Indianapolis v. Edmond (2000)	Police traffic checkpoints cannot be justified as a generalized search for criminal evidence; they must be narrowly focused on a specific objective.
Stop and frisk	
Terry v. Ohio (1968)	Officers may stop and frisk suspects on the street when there is reasonable suspicion that they are armed and involved in criminal activity.
Adams v. Williams (1972)	Officers may rely on reports from reliable witnesses as the basis for conducting a stop and frisk.
Illinois v. Wardlow (2000)	When a person runs at the sight of police in a high-crime area, officers are justified in using that person's flight as a basis for forming reasonable suspicion to justify a stop and frisk.
Incident to an arrest	
Chimel v. California (1969)	To preserve evidence and protect the safety of the officer and the public after a lawful arrest, the arrestee and the immediate area around the arrestee may be searched for weapons and criminal evidence.
United States v. Robinson (1973)	A warrantless search incident to an arrest is not limited by the seriousness of the crime for which the arrestee has been taken into custody.
Exigent circumstances	
Warden v. Hayden (1967)	When officers are in hot pursuit of a fleeing suspect, they need not stop to seek a warrant and thereby risk permitting the suspect to get away.
Cupp v. Murphy (1973)	Officers may seize evidence to protect it if taking time to seek a warrant creates a risk of its destruction.
Consent	
Bumper v. North Carolina (1968)	Officers may not tell falsehoods as a means of getting a suspect to consent to a search.
United States v. Drayton (2002)	An officer does not have to inform people of their right to refuse when he or she asks if they wish to consent to a search.
Automobiles	
Carroll v. United States (1925)	Because by their nature automobiles can be easily moved, warrantless searches are permissible when reasonable suspicion of illegal activity exists.
New York v. Class (1986)	An officer may enter a vehicle to see the vehicle identification number when a car has been validly stopped pursuant to a traffic violation or other permissible justification.
California v. Acevedo (1991)	Officers may search throughout a vehicle when they believe they have probable cause to do so.
Maryland v. Wilson (1997)	During traffic stops, officers may order passengers and as well as the driver to exit the vehicle, even if there is no basis for suspicion that the passengers engaged in any wrongdoing.
Knowles v. Iowa (1998)	A traffic violation by itself does not provide an officer with the authority to search an entire vehicle. There must be reasonable suspicion or probable cause before officers can extend their search beyond merely looking inside the vehicle's passenger compartment.

windshield when a car has been validly stopped pursuant to a traffic violation or other permissible justification (*New York v. Class,* 1986). In addition, the Court permits thorough searches of vehicles, without regard to probable cause, when police officers inventory the contents of impounded vehicles (*South Dakota v. Opperman,* 1976). Containers found within the course of the inventory search may also be opened and searched when the examination of such containers is consistent with a police department's inventory policies.

Table 7.3 reviews selected Supreme Court cases concerning those circumstances in which the police do not need a warrant to conduct a search or to seize evidence.

check point

12. What defines the scope of officers' authority to search containers in automobiles?

Questioning Suspects

The Fifth Amendment contains various rights, including the one most relevant to police officers' actions in questioning suspects. The relevant words of the Amendment are "No person shall... be compelled in any criminal case to be a witness against himself." The privilege against compelled self-incrimination should not be viewed as simply a legal protection that seeks to assist individuals who may be guilty of crimes. By protecting individuals in this way, the Fifth Amendment discourages police officers from using violent or otherwise coercive means to push suspects to confess.

In addition to discouraging the physical abuse of suspects, the privilege against compelled self-incrimination also diminishes the risk of erroneous convictions. When police officers use coercive pressure to seek confessions, some innocent people will succumb to the pressure by confessing to crimes that they did not commit. The worst-case scenario is illustrated by the film *In the Name of the Father,* based on a true story in England in which police officers gain a confession from a bombing suspect, whom they know to be innocent, by placing a gun in the suspect's mouth and threatening to pull the trigger.

Miranda Rules

As discussed in Chapter 4, the 1966 decision by the Supreme Court in *Miranda v. Arizona* said that as soon as the investigation of a crime begins to focus on a particular suspect and he or she is taken into custody, the so-called *Miranda* warnings must be read aloud before questioning can begin. Suspects must be told four things:

1. They have the right to remain silent.
2. If they decide to make a statement, it can and will be used against them in court.

Spencer Grant/PhotoEdit

What are the rights of suspects before and during police interrogation?

Miranda v. Arizona, 384 U.S. 436 (1966)

Ernest Miranda, a loading dock worker with a prior history of sex offenses, was arrested for rape. Two detectives took him into a private interrogation room for questioning. Eventually they emerged with his signed confession. Miranda's lawyer challenged the confession, because the questioning took place before the attorney had been appointed to provide representation. Chief Justice Warren delivered the opinion of the Court, as follows.

* * *

Our holding will be spelled out with some specificity in the pages which follow but briefly stated it is this: the prosecution may not use statements . . . stemming from custodial interrogation of the defendant unless it demonstrates the use of procedural safeguards effective to secure the privilege against self-incrimination. By custodial interrogation, we mean questioning initiated by law enforcement officers after a person has been taken into custody or otherwise deprived of his freedom of action in any significant way. As for the procedural safeguards to be employed, unless other fully effective means are devised to inform accused persons of their right to silence and to assure a continuous opportunity to exercise it, the following measures are required. Prior to any questioning, the person must be warned that he has a right to remain silent, that any statement he does make may be used as evidence against him, and that he has the right to the presence of an attorney, either retained or appointed. The defendant may waive effectuation of these rights, provided the waiver is made voluntarily, knowingly, and intelligently. If, however, he indicates in any manner and at any stage of the process that he wishes to consult with an attorney before speaking there can be no questioning. Likewise, if the individual is alone and indicates in any manner that he does not wish to be interrogated, the police may not question him. The mere fact that he may have answered some questions or volunteered some statements on his own does not deprive him of the right to refrain from answering any further inquiries until he has consulted with an attorney and thereafter consents to be questioned.

3. They have the right to have an attorney present during interrogation or to have an opportunity to consult with an attorney.
4. If they cannot afford an attorney, the state will provide one.

Prior to the *Miranda* decision, police officers in some places solved crimes by picking up poor people or African Americans and torturing them until a confession was produced. In *Brown v. Mississippi* (1936), the Supreme Court ruled that statements produced after police beat suspects were inadmissible, but it did not insist that counsel be available at the early stages of the criminal process.

Two rulings in 1964 laid the foundation for the *Miranda* decision. In *Escobedo v. Illinois,* the Court made the link between the Fifth Amendment right against self-incrimination and the Sixth Amendment right to counsel. Danny Escobedo was questioned at the police station for 14 hours without counsel even though he asked to see his attorney. He finally made incriminating statements that the police said were voluntary. The Court's ruling specified that defendants have a right to counsel when

> the investigation is no longer a general inquiry into an unsolved crime, but has begun to focus on a particular suspect, the suspect has been taken into police custody, [and] the police carry out a process of interrogations that lends itself to eliciting incriminating statements.

The Court effectively expanded the right to counsel to apply at an early point in the criminal justice process as a means to guard against law enforcement officers' actions that might violate the Fifth Amendment privilege against compelled self-incrimination. In *Massiah v. United States* (1964), the Supreme Court declared that the questioning of the defendant by a police agent outside of the presence of defense counsel violated the defendant's rights.

As you read the Close Up box containing the excerpt from *Miranda v. Arizona* (1966), think about why so many law enforcement officials harshly criticized the decision at first.

The constitutional issue we decide . . . is the admissibility of statements obtained from a defendant questioned while in custody or otherwise deprived of his freedom of action in any significant way. . . .

An understanding of the nature and setting of this in-custody interrogation is essential to our decisions today. The difficulty in depicting what transpires at such interrogations stems from the fact that in this country they have largely taken place incommunicado. From extensive factual studies undertaken in the early 1930's, including the famous Wickersham Report to Congress by a Presidential Commission, it is clear that police violence and the "third degree" flourished at that time.

In a series of cases decided by this Court long after these studies, the police resorted to physical brutality—beatings, hanging, whipping—and to sustained and protracted questioning incommunicado in order to extort confessions. . . . The use of physical brutality and violence is not, unfortunately, relegated to the past or to any part of the country. Only recently in Kings County, New York, the police brutally beat, kicked, and placed lighted cigarette butts on the back of a potential witness under interrogation for the purpose of securing a statement incriminating a third party. . . .

The examples given above are undoubtedly the exception now, but they are sufficiently widespread to be the object of concern. Unless a proper limitation upon custodial interrogation is achieved—such as these decisions will advance—there can be no assurance that practices of this nature will be eradicated in the foreseeable future. . . .

* * *

In dealing with statements obtained through interrogation, we do not purport to find all confessions inadmissible. Confessions remain a proper element in law enforcement. Any statement given freely and voluntarily without any compelling influences is, of course, admissible in evidence. . . . There is no requirement that police stop a person who enters a police station and states that he wishes to confess to a crime, or a person who calls the police to offer a confession or any other statement he desires to make. Volunteered statements of any kind are not barred by the Fifth Amendment and their admissibility is not affected by our holding today. . . .

* * *

In announcing these principles, we are not unmindful of the burdens which law enforcement officials must bear, often under trying circumstances. We also fully recognize the obligation of all citizens to aid in enforcing the criminal laws. This Court, while protecting individual rights, has always given ample latitude to law enforcement agencies in the legitimate exercise of their duties. The limits we have placed on the interrogation process should not constitute an undue interference with a proper system of law enforcement. . . .

Researching the Internet

The effort to investigate and prevent terrorist activities in the aftermath of the September 11 tragedy has triggered new debates about whether police need greater freedom to conduct interrogations without the restrictions of *Miranda*. To read about this debate, see http://jurist.law.pitt.edu/terrorism/terrorismparry.htm.

The *Miranda* warnings apply only to *custodial interrogations*. If police officers walk up to someone on the street and begin asking questions, they do not need to inform the person of his or her rights. The justices say that people know they can walk away when an officer asks them questions in a public place. When police have taken someone into custody, however, the Supreme Court sees it as an inherently coercive situation. The loss of liberty and isolation experienced by detained suspects can make them vulnerable to abusive interrogation techniques, especially when interrogations take place out of view of anyone other than police officers. When a suspect has been alone in a room with police officers, if the suspect claims to have been beaten, will anyone believe it, even if it is true? If the police say that the suspect confessed, will anyone believe the suspect who says that no confession was ever given? The *Miranda* warnings and presence of counsel during questioning are supposed to prevent such risks from occurring.

Training programs provide information for police officers about effective interrogation techniques; see, for example, http://www.tpub.com/maa/171.htm.

One circumstance in which the Court has permitted police officers to forgo *Miranda* warnings is when taking the time to provide the warnings would create a threat to "public safety." This exception is similar to the exigent circumstance justification for warrantless searches. The underlying premise is that in some urgent situations, a larger social need outweighs individuals' rights. In the case that created the **"public safety" exception,** police officers chased an armed man into a supermarket after a reported assault. When they found him with an empty shoulder holster, they asked, "Where's the gun?" after he was handcuffed but before he had been informed of his *Miranda* rights (*New York v. Quarles,* 1984). His response to the question could be used against him court because the public's safety might have been threatened if the police took the time to read him his rights before asking any questions.

"public safety" exception
When public safety is in jeopardy, police may question a suspect in custody without providing the *Miranda* warnings.

The Fifth Amendment protection against compelled self-incrimination applies only to testimonial evidence, which normally means incriminating statements made by suspects. The Fifth Amendment does *not* protect against the admission into evidence of nontestimonial evidence, such as objects or descriptions of behaviors manifested by the suspect. Thus police could use evidence of a drunken driving suspect's slurred speech and inability to answer questions, because such evidence was nontestimonial. By contrast, the police could not use as evidence a statement made by the same arrested suspect in response to a question that was posed prior to the delivery of *Miranda* warnings (*Pennsylvania v. Muniz,* 1990).

Although some legal commentators and police officials have criticized *Miranda* warnings, the Supreme Court strongly repeated its endorsement of the *Miranda* requirement in 2000 (*Dickerson v. United States*).

check point

13. What are *Miranda* rights?
14. What is the "public safety" exception?

The Consequences of *Miranda*

During oral arguments at the Supreme Court, the opponents of *Miranda* assumed that every subject would cease to talk upon being informed that there is a right to silence. However, in practice, this has not proven to be the case. Police officers have adapted their techniques in order to question suspects without any impediment from the warnings.

Miranda rights must be provided *before questions are asked* during custodial interrogations. Many departments train their officers to read the *Miranda* warnings to suspects as soon as an arrest is made. This is done in order to make sure the warnings are not omitted as the suspect is processed in the system. The warnings may be read off a standard "Miranda card" to make sure that the rights are provided consistently and correctly. However, the courts do not require that police inform suspects of their rights immediately after arrest. The warnings do not have to be provided until the police begin to ask questions. Thus, after taking a suspect into custody, some officers may use their discretion to delay providing *Miranda* warnings in order to see if the suspect will talk on his or her own. The suspect may be kept in the backseat of a car as officers drive around town, or the suspect may be left alone in a room at the police station. Some suspects will take the initiative to talk to officers because of feelings of guilt. Other suspects may start conversations with officers because they are eager to convince the officers that they have an alibi or that they want to cooperate. The suspect might thus provide contradictory statements that will help to build the case.

After suspects in custody have been informed of their *Miranda* rights, officers may attempt to defuse the potential impact of the rights by presenting them in a manner intended to encourage suspects to talk. For example, officers may inform suspects of their rights but then add, "But if you don't have anything to hide, why would you ask for an attorney or stay silent?"

Officers are also trained in interrogation techniques that are intended to encourage suspects to talk despite *Miranda* warnings. Officers may pretend to be sympathetic to the suspect (Leo, 1996b). They may say, for example, "We understand how bad stuff can happen that you never want to have happen. We know that you had a good reason to get mad and go after that guy with your knife. We probably would have done the same thing if we were in your situation. We know that you never really planned to stab him." Such statements are not honest. But police officers are allowed to use deception to induce suspects to talk. It is not uncommon for officers to say, untruthfully, "We have five witnesses that saw you do it. If you tell us everything right now, we may be able to get you a good deal. If you don't help us, we don't know what we can do for you." Do such statements constitute coercion that would be regarded as improper pressure in violation of *Miranda*? Probably not—as long as the officers do not threaten suspects in ways that make them fear for their physical safety or the safety of their loved ones.

Miranda rights have become very familiar to the American public through television shows and movies in which police officers inform arrested suspects of their rights. By the time television-watching Americans reach adulthood, they will have probably heard the *Miranda* warnings delivered hundreds of times on these shows. Many Americans can easily recite the warnings along with the television detectives. Ironically, this very familiarity with the warnings may impede the effective implementation of *Miranda,* because it interferes with suspects' ability to think about what the warnings actually mean.

Many suspects talk to the police despite being informed of their right to remain silent and their right to have an attorney present during questioning. Some suspects do not fully understand the rights. They may believe that they will look guilty by remaining silent or by asking for an attorney. Therefore they feel that they must talk to officers in order to have any hope of claiming innocence. Other suspects may be overly confident about their ability to fool the police and therefore talk to officers, despite the warnings, in an effort to act as if they have nothing to hide. More importantly, many suspects believe (often accurately) that they will gain a more favorable charge or plea bargain if they cooperate with officers as fully as possible and as early as possible. Thus a trio of suspects arrested together after a robbery who are read their *Miranda* rights and who are placed in separate interrogation rooms may, in effect, race to be the first one to tell a version of events in order to pin greater responsibility on the other arrestees and to seek police assistance in gaining a favorable deal with the prosecutor.

This incentive to cooperate can completely negate many of the fears about *Miranda*'s potentially detrimental effect on law enforcement's effectiveness. It can also create problems of its own, however. There are many cases in which the guiltiest suspect, for example, the one who pulled the trigger and killed a storeowner during a robbery, is the most eager to cooperate with the police. If the police are not sufficiently skeptical and careful, the most serious offender may get the most favorable deal by having his or her version of events accepted by authorities, and the least culpable defendant, such as the driver of the getaway car, can sometimes end up with the severest punishment if he or she loses the "race" to confess.

Table 7.4 presents selected cases concerning Supreme Court decisions on how the Fifth Amendment protects suspect's rights against self-incrimination. "New Directions in Criminal Justice Policy" examines how 9-11 has engendered a suspension of many of the rights just discussed.

check point

15. How have police officers changed their practices in light of *Miranda*?

Table 7.4 Questioning suspects

The Supreme Court has ruled that suspects' rights against self-incrimination are protected by the Fifth Amendment.

Case	Decision
***Miranda* Rules**	
Miranda v. Arizona (1966)	Before suspects in police custody may be questioned, they must be told that they have the right to remain silent, that anything they say may be used against them, and that they have the right to counsel during questioning.
Public Safety Exception	
New York v. Quarles (1984)	Officers may direct questions to arrested suspects prior to reading the *Miranda* warnings if concerns about public safety require immediate questioning.

The Suspension of Rights in a Time of Terrorism

The U.S. government's response to the terrorist attacks on New York City and Washington, D.C., in September 2001 raises questions about the nature of constitutional rights and whether the principles of the Constitution actually govern all of the arrests made by the American government.

Under the direction of President George W. Bush and Attorney General John Ashcroft, the government has jailed American citizens without charging them with any crimes, giving them access to court proceedings, or permitting them to meet with an attorney. For example, Abdullah al-Muhajir, an American formerly known as Jose Padilla, was arrested in Chicago on suspicions that he was seeking to obtain material to build a radioactive "dirty bomb." Because the government labeled him as an "enemy combatant" and jailed him in a military prison, it claims that al-Muhajir is not entitled to constitutional rights and that it need not present any evidence to a court to justify his detention. He has no access to an attorney, so any interrogations that are occurring in secret would appear to violate the principles of *Miranda.*

He is not the only American citizen being held without the provision of the constitutional rights usually available in the criminal justice process. There are at least two other citizens being held under similar circumstances. In addition, there are several hundred noncitizen detainees captured in Afghanistan and Pakistan who are being held as "enemy combatants" in the Navy base at Guantánamo, Cuba. Holding them out of the country allows the government to withhold benefits from laws that would apply if they were within the United States. These detainees face the possibility of being tried and sentenced to death by military commissions that the Bush administration has proposed to use as a legal process that is not governed by the Bill of Rights.

The American Bar Association (ABA), a national organization representing 400,000 lawyers, passed a resolution calling on the government to guarantee that defendants will receive traditional legal protections when tried before military commissions. The ABA argued that defendants should be presumed innocent, have their guilt proven beyond a reasonable doubt, and be convicted by a unanimous verdict before a death penalty could be imposed.

The government's actions, which are now being challenged in court, raise interesting questions. Does the government really have the authority to ignore the Bill of Rights by holding American citizens in detention for indefinite periods without producing evidence of guilt, providing access to legal processes, or permitting representation by an attorney? Should the principles of the Constitution not apply when the U.S. government is prosecuting noncitizens? In light of the fact that the U.S. government criticizes China and other countries for not providing human rights, is it hypocritical of the United States to detain terrorism suspects without providing those rights to them? Is there a risk that people who are innocent of terrorism might be detained indefinitely or erroneously convicted by a military commission because they did not receive the benefits of the right to counsel, rules of evidence, strict standards of proof, and the opportunity to appeal?

These questions are especially interesting because of public opinion polls indicating that Americans do not wish to sacrifice constitutional rights in the fight against terrorism (see "What Americans Think").

Sources: Anne Gearan, "ABA Urges Military Tribunal Rights," Associated Press Wire Service, February 4, 2002; "Justice Kept in the Dark," *Newsweek,* December 10, 2001, pp. 37–43; Adam Liptak, Neil A. Lewis, and Benjamin Weiser, "After Sept. 11, a Legal Battle on the Limits of Civil Liberty," *New York Times,* August 4, 2002, pp. 1, 16.

Researching the Internet

Human rights organizations have documented many instances in which the United States has criticized other countries for the very kinds of actions that it appears to be undertaking; see http://www.hrw.org/press/2001/11/tribunals1128.htm.

Go to the Public Policy feature on the American System of Criminal Justice CD to learn more about the issues surrounding Constitutional rights for terrorism suspects.

The Exclusionary Rule

As discussed in Chapter 4 and illustrated by this chapter's opening vignette about football star Michael Irvin, a primary remedy applied for rights violations by police officers is the exclusion of evidence from court. Thus police may see evidence excluded when they conduct improper stops and searches as well as improper interrogations.

In *Weeks v. United States* (1914), the U.S. Supreme Court first endorsed the exclusion of evidence from trial as a remedy for improper searches conducted by *federal* law enforcement officials. The Court clearly declared that if prosecutors were permitted to use improperly obtained evidence, then the Fourth Amendment would lose all meaning and people's rights under the Amendment would disappear. According to Justice William Day's opinion,

> If letters and private documents can thus be seized and held and used in evidence against a citizen accused of an offense, the protection of the 4th Amendment, declaring his right to be secure against such searches and seizures, is of no value, and, so far as those thus placed are concerned, might as well be stricken from the Constitution. (232 U.S. at 393)

The exclusionary rule does not necessarily require that cases against defendants be dismissed when constitutional rights have been violated. The prosecution can continue, but it may not use improperly obtained evidence. In some cases, other valid evidence of guilt may exist in the form of witness testimony or confessions. Without such alternative evidence, however, the exclusionary rule can lead to charges being dropped. The rule clearly accepts the possibility that a guilty person may go free despite the fact that evidence, although illegally obtained, exists to demonstrate his or her guilt.

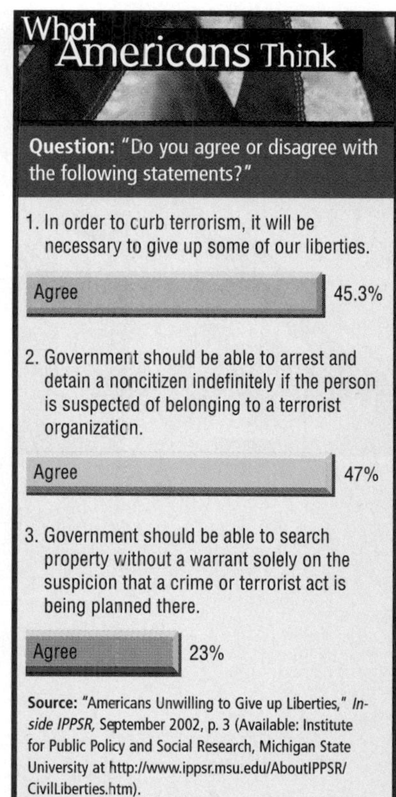

Source: "Americans Unwilling to Give up Liberties," *Inside IPPSR,* September 2002, p. 3 (Available: Institute for Public Policy and Social Research, Michigan State University at http://www.ippsr.msu.edu/AboutIPPSR/CivilLiberties.htm).

Application of the Exclusionary Rule to the States

In *Wolf v. Colorado* (1949), the Supreme Court incorporated the Fourth Amendment. However, the justices declined to apply the exclusionary rule to the states, because they believed states could develop their own remedies to handle improper searches by police. The situation changed when the appointment of Earl Warren as Chief Justice in 1953 ushered in an era in which the Supreme Court expanded the definitions of constitutional rights affecting a variety of issues, including criminal justice. During the Warren era (1953–1969), the Court incorporated most of the criminal justice–related rights in a way that required state law enforcement officials to adhere to the same rules that federal law enforcement officials had to follow. Because the Warren Court was asked to consider whether to incorporate various Fifth, Sixth, and Eighth Amendment rights, it was no surprise that they decided to apply the exclusionary rule to the actions of all law enforcement officers, including those in state and local agencies. As you read the Close Up excerpt from the landmark case of *Mapp v. Ohio,* look for reasons given by the Court for applying the exclusionary rule to state and local criminal cases as well federal cases.

Why did the Supreme Court see the exclusionary rule as necessary? Several reasons emerge in such cases as *Weeks* and *Mapp*. First, *Weeks* declared that the exclusionary rule is essential to make the Fourth Amendment meaningful. In essence, the justices believed that constitutional rights are nullified if government officials are permitted to benefit by violating those rights. Second, the *Mapp* decision indicates that the Constitution requires the exclusionary rule. Third, the majority opinion in *Mapp* concluded that alternatives to the exclusionary rule do not work. Clark's opinion noted that many states had found that nothing short of exclusion of evidence would work to correct constitutional rights violations and limit the number of violations that occur. Fourth, the *Mapp* opinion argued that the use of improperly obtained evidence by officials who are responsible for upholding the law only serves to diminish respect for the law. In Clark's words, "Thus the State, by admitting evidence unlawfully seized, serves to encourage disobedience to the Federal Constitution which it is bound to uphold." Fifth, the *Mapp* decision indicates that the absence of an exclusionary rule

Close up

Mapp v. Ohio, 367 U.S. 644 (1961)

In the events leading to *Mapp v. Ohio,* police officers came to Dolly Mapp's house looking for a bombing suspect. She would not let them enter. They forced open a door and entered. She demanded to see their search warrant. They waved a piece of paper in her face, which she grabbed and stuffed down her shirt. The officers forcibly retrieved the paper from her and it was never seen again. The officers handcuffed Mapp and rummaged through her house. In the basement they found a trunk containing books with such titles as *The Affairs of a Troubador, London Stage Affairs,* and *Memories of a Hotel Man.* Because of the books, Mapp was convicted of having obscene materials in her possession. The case was brought to the Supreme Court on a claim that the Ohio obscenity statute violated the First Amendment. However, the Court focused on the issue of whether the evidence should be excluded because the police conducted an unreasonable warrantless search. The majority opinion was given by Justice Clark, as follows.

* * *

While in 1949, prior to the *Wolf* case, almost two-thirds of the States were opposed to the use of the exclusionary rule, now, despite the *Wolf* case, more than half of those since passing upon it, by their own legislative or judicial decision, have wholly or partly adopted or adhered to the *Weeks* rule. . . . Significantly, among those now following the rule is California, which, according to its highest courts, was "compelled to reach that conclusion because other remedies have completely failed to secure compliance with the constitutional provisions". . . . In connection with this California case, we note that the second basis elaborated in *Wolf* in support of its failure to enforce the exclusionary doctrine against the States was that "other means of protection" have been afforded "the right to privacy." . . . The experience of California that such other remedies have been worthless and futile is buttressed by the experience of other States. The obvious futility of relegating the Fourth Amendment to the protection of other remedies has, moreover, been recognized by this Court since *Wolf.*

* * *

Moreover, our holding that the exclusionary rule is an essential part of both the Fourth and Fourteenth Amendments is not only the logical dictate of prior cases, but it also makes very good sense. There is no war between the Constitution and common sense. Presently, a federal prosecutor may make no use of evidence illegally seized, but a State's attorney across the street may, although he supposedly is operating under the enforceable prohibitions of the same Amendment. Thus the State, by admitting evidence unlawfully seized, serves to encourage disobedience to the Federal Constitution which it is bound to uphold. . . .

The ignoble shortcut to conviction left open to the States tends to destroy the entire system of constitutional restraints on which the liberties of the people rest. Having once recognized that the right to privacy embodied in the Fourth Amendment is enforceable against the States, and that the right to be secure against rude invasions of privacy by state officers is, therefore, constitutional in origin, we can no longer permit the right to remain an empty promise. Because it is enforceable in the same manner and to like effect as other basic rights secured by the Due Process Clause, we can no longer permit it to be revocable at the whim of any police officer who, in the name of law enforcement itself, chooses to suspend its enjoyment. Our decision, founded on reason and truth, gives to the individual no more than that which the Constitution guarantees him, to the police officer no less than that to which honest law enforcement is entitled, and, to the courts, that judicial integrity so necessary in the true administration of justice.

To read arguments favoring the exclusionary rule, see http://www.cato.org/pubs/pas/pa-319es.html.

diminishes the protection of all rights because it would permit all constitutional rights "to be revocable at the whim of any police officer who, in the name of law enforcement itself, chooses to suspend . . . [the] enjoyment [of rights]." Sixth, the exclusionary rule is justified as an effective means of deterring police and prosecutors from violating constitutional rights.

check point

16. Why was the exclusionary rule created and eventually applied to the states?

Exceptions to the Exclusionary Rule

The exclusionary rule has many critics, including justices on the Supreme Court. Earl Warren's successor, Chief Justice Warren Burger, who served from 1969 to 1986, criticized the rule as ineffective and misguided. He joined many law enforcement officials, commentators, and politicians in harshly criticizing the Court's decision in *Mapp*. Burger and his allies complained that the Court's decision would hamper police investigations and allow guilty criminals to go free. In Burger's view, there was no proof that the rule prevented officers from conducing improper searches. Moreover, he saw the rule as punishing prosecutors and society rather than the officers who violated people's rights.

Research has not clearly supported claims about the negative consequences of the exclusionary rule. Studies of the impact of the exclusionary rule have produced two consistent findings. First, only a small minority of defendants file a "motion to suppress," which is used to ask a judge to exclude evidence that has allegedly been obtained in violation of the defendant's rights. Second, only a small fraction of motions to suppress evidence are granted (Davies, 1983; Uchida and Bynum, 1991; S. Walker 2001:90–91). Despite continuing debates about the rule's impact and effectiveness, the Supreme Court began creating exceptions to the exclusionary rule after Burger became chief justice.

As discussed in Chapter 4, the Supreme Court created a **"good faith" exception** to the exclusionary rule when officers use search warrants (*United States v. Leon,* 1984). When officers have acted in good faith reliance on a warrant, the evidence will not be excluded even if the warrant was issued improperly. "Good faith" means that the officers acted with the honest belief that they were following the proper rules. In addition, the reliance and honest belief must be reasonable. If officers knew that a judge issued a warrant based on no evidence whatsoever, officers could not claim that they reasonably and honestly relied on the warrant. However, when officers presented evidence of probable cause to the judge and the judge made the error by issuing a warrant based on information that actually fell below the standard of probable cause, the officers may use evidence found in the resulting search.

"good faith" exception
When police act in honest reliance on a warrant, the evidence seized is admissible even if the warrant is later proved to be defective.

Importantly, the Supreme Court never created a general "good faith" exception to permit the admissibility of improperly obtained evidence whenever police officers make an honest mistake. In *Leon,* there was "good faith" reliance on a warrant, meaning that the fundamental error was made by the judge who issued the warrant. Evidence can still be excluded if officers undertook an improper warrantless search based on their own discretionary decision, even if they honestly (but wrongly) believed that a warrantless search was permitted.

Over the years the Supreme Court has recognized other circumstances where a "good faith" exception is applied to the exclusionary rule. For example,

1. *Reliance on a warrant found to be incorrect* (*Maryland v. Garrison,* 1987). Police relied on a warrant that incorrectly designated the wrong apartment to search. They were able to use evidence found in the apartment, even though there had been no probable cause to search that apartment in the first place.
2. *Reliance on statutes later declared unconstitutional* (*Illinois v. Krull,* 1987). Officers conducted a search of a junkyard based on a state statute that authorized warrantless searches of such regulated locations. Although the statute was later declared unconstitutional, the evidence found during the improper search could be used against the defendant.
3. *Reliance on records maintained by justice system employees* (*Arizona v. Evans,* 1995). Officers stopped a man for a traffic violation. A computer check of his license revealed that there was an outstanding warrant for his arrest. They arrested him and found marijuana in the car, which they had searched in conjunction with the arrest. Although it later turned out that there was no warrant and a court employee had failed to clear the warrant

from his record, the marijuana could be used against him even though the arrest justifying the search was invalid.

4. *Reasonable reliance on a consent to search provided by someone who lacked the authority to grant such consent* (*Illinois v. Rodriguez,* 1990). A suspect's girlfriend provided the police with a key and granted permission to search an apartment even though she did not live in the apartment and she was not supposed to have a key. Evidence was admissible against the defendant because the officers reasonably believed that the girlfriend lived in the apartment.

"inevitable discovery" exception
Improperly obtained evidence can be used when it would later have inevitably been discovered without improper actions of the police.

One important exception to the exclusionary rule is the **"inevitable discovery" exception.** This rule arose from a case involving the tragic abduction and murder of a young girl. The police sought an escapee from a psychiatric hospital who was seen carrying a large bundle. The man being sought contacted an attorney and arranged to surrender to police in a town 160 miles away from the scene of the abduction. The Supreme Court subsequently found that the police improperly questioned the suspect outside of the presence of his attorney while driving him back to the city where the abduction occurred (*Brewer v. Williams,* 1977). The Supreme Court declared that the girl's body and the suspect's statements had to be excluded from evidence because they were obtained in violation of his rights. Thus his murder conviction was overturned and he was given a new trial. At the second trial, at which he was convicted again, the prosecution used the body in evidence against him based on the claim that search parties would have found the body eventually even without his confession. There was a search team within two and one-half miles of the body at the time that it was found. In ***Nix v. Williams*** **(1984),** the Supreme Court agreed that the improperly obtained evidence can be used when it would later have been inevitably discovered anyway even without improper actions by the police.

Nix v. Williams **(1984)**
Decision in which the Supreme Court created the "inevitable discovery" exception to the exclusionary rule.

Table 7.5 summarizes selected Supreme Court decisions regarding the exclusionary rule as it applies to the Fourth and Fifth Amendments.

The Supreme Court also created exceptions to the exclusionary rule by identifying stages in the criminal justice process in which the rule will not apply. Table 7.6 lists contexts outside of the standard criminal prosecution in which evidence is *not* excluded even if officials commit rights violations in the course of gathering evidence.

State supreme courts also make decisions defining the application of the exclusionary rule within a state; see, for example, http://www.metnews.com/articles/will060402.htm.

When the Supreme Court created the exclusionary rule in *Weeks v. United States* (1914) and later expanded its coverage to state and local criminal cases in *Mapp v. Ohio* (1961), it appeared to make strong statements against the use of improperly obtained evidence. As the Court refined the application of the rule from the 1970s onward, it became clear that the exclusion of evidence would

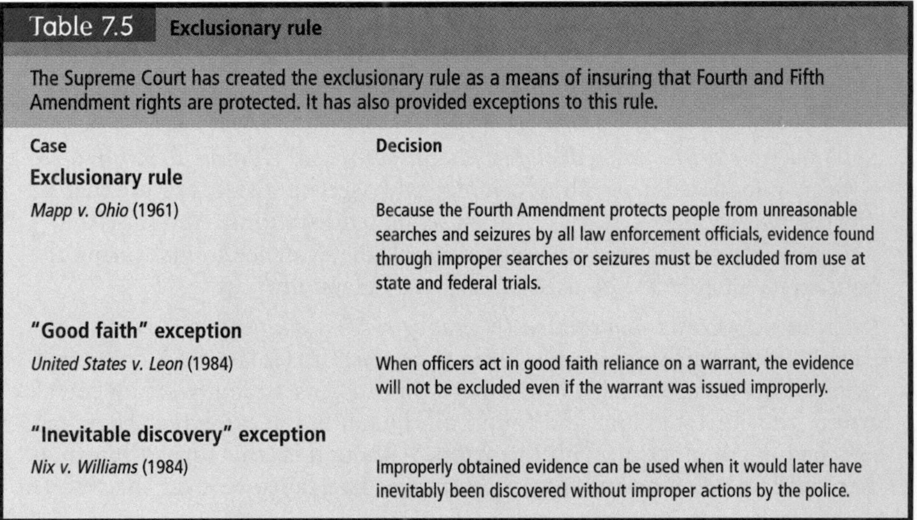

Table 7.5 Exclusionary rule

The Supreme Court has created the exclusionary rule as a means of insuring that Fourth and Fifth Amendment rights are protected. It has also provided exceptions to this rule.

Case	Decision
Exclusionary rule	
Mapp v. Ohio (1961)	Because the Fourth Amendment protects people from unreasonable searches and seizures by all law enforcement officials, evidence found through improper searches or seizures must be excluded from use at state and federal trials.
"Good faith" exception	
United States v. Leon (1984)	When officers act in good faith reliance on a warrant, the evidence will not be excluded even if the warrant was issued improperly.
"Inevitable discovery" exception	
Nix v. Williams (1984)	Improperly obtained evidence can be used when it would later have inevitably been discovered without improper actions by the police.

Table 7.6 Contexts outside of the standard criminal prosecution in which the exclusionary rule does not apply

Case	Decision
Grand jury proceedings	
United States v. Calandra (1974)	A witness summoned to appear before a grand jury cannot refuse to answer questions simply because the questions were based on evidence obtained from an improper search.
Parole revocation hearings	
Pennsylvania Board of Pardons and Parole v. Scott (1998)	Improperly obtained evidence can be used at parole revocation proceedings.
Immigration deportation hearings	
Immigration and Naturalization Service v. Lopez-Mendoza (1984)	Improperly obtained evidence can be used at deportation hearings.
Impeachment of defendant	
Harris v. New York (1971)	Improperly obtained statements can be used to impeach the credibility of defendants who take the witness stand and testify in their own trials.

arise only in specific situations. The justices have clarified their intention to apply the rule in criminal trials, but not in other kinds of proceedings, such as grand jury testimony and parole revocation hearings, that are not direct criminal prosecutions to determine guilt and punishment. In addition, the specific exceptions to the rule created by the Supreme Court show that the justices changed their approach to determining when evidence should be excluded.

When the Court issued its decisions in *Weeks* and *Mapp,* it appeared that the exclusion of evidence would be guided by a trial judge's answer to the question "Did police violate the suspect's rights?" By contrast, through the development of exceptions to the rule, the Court shifted its focus to the question "Did the police make an error that was so serious that the exclusion of evidence is required?" For example, the "good faith" exception established in *United States v. Leon* (1984) emphasizes the fact that officers did what they thought they were supposed to do. The decision did not rest on the fact that the suspect's Fourth Amendment rights were violated by a search conducted with an improper warrant. Thus the Supreme Court's creation of exceptions to the exclusionary rule has given police officers the flexibility to make specific kinds of errors without jeopardizing the admissibility of evidence that will help to establish a defendant's guilt.

check point

17. What are some of the criticisms of the exclusionary rule?
18. What are the exceptions to the exclusionary rule?

Summary

- The Supreme Court has defined rules for the circumstances and justifications for stops, searches, and arrests in light of the Fourth Amendment's prohibition on "unreasonable searches and seizures."
- Most stops must be supported by reasonable suspicion, and arrests, like search warrants, must be supported by enough information to constitute probable cause.
- The plain view doctrine permits officers to examine visually and seize any contraband or criminal evidence that is in open sight when they are in a place where they are legally permitted to be.

- Searches are considered "reasonable" and may be conducted without warrants in specific "special needs" circumstances that have purposes beyond those of normal law enforcement. For example, borders and airports often require searches without warrants.
- Limited searches may be conducted without warrants when officers have reasonable suspicions to justify a stop and frisk for weapons on the streets; when officers make a lawful arrest; under exigent circumstances; when people voluntarily consent to searches of their persons or property; and in certain situations involving automobiles.
- The Fifth Amendment privilege against compelled self-incrimination helps to protect citizens against violence and coercion by police as well as to maintain the legitimacy and integrity of the legal system.
- The Supreme Court's decision in *Miranda v. Arizona* required officers to inform suspects of specific rights before custodial questioning, although officers have adapted their practices to accommodate this rule and several exceptions have been created.
- In barring the use of illegally obtained evidence in court, the exclusionary rule is designed to deter police from violating citizens' rights during criminal investigations.
- The Supreme Court has created several exceptions to the exclusionary rule, including the "good faith" and "inevitable discovery" exceptions.

Questions for Review

1. What are the requirements for police officers with respect to stops, searches, arrests, and warrants?
2. What are the plain view doctrine and the open fields doctrine?
3. Under what circumstances are warrantless searches permissible?
4. How have police officers adapted to the requirements of *Miranda v. Arizona*?
5. What are the exceptions to the exclusionary rule?

Key Terms and Cases

affidavit (p. 207)
exigent circumstances (p. 215)
"good faith" exception (p. 227)
"inevitable discovery" exception (p. 228)
open fields doctrine (p. 208)
plain view doctrine (p. 208)
probable cause (p. 206)
"public safety" exception (p. 221)
reasonable expectation of privacy (p. 205)
reasonable suspicion (p. 205)
search (p. 205)
seizure (p. 205)
stop (p. 205)
stop-and-frisk search (p. 212)
totality of circumstances test (p. 207)
Chimel v. California (1969) (p. 215)
Florida v. J. L. (2000) (p. 214)
Nix v. Williams (1984) (p. 228)
Terry v. Ohio (1968) (p. 212)
United States v. Drayton (2002) (p. 216)

For Further Reading

Amar, Akhil Reed. 1997. *The Constitution and Criminal Procedure: First Principles.* New Haven, Conn.: Yale University Press. A detailed examination of the Fourth and Fifth Amendments, with suggestions for remedies other than the exclusionary rule.

Grano, Joseph D. 1996. *Confessions, Truth, and the Law.* Ann Arbor: University of Michigan Press. An analysis of the law related to police interrogation and confessions, including criticisms of *Miranda* rights.

Smith, Christopher E. 2003. *Criminal Procedure.* Belmont, Calif.: Wadsworth. A detailed review of constitutional rights affecting police investigations and trial processes.

Uviller, H. Richard. 1996. *Virtual Justice: The Flawed Prosecution of Crime in America.* New Haven, Conn.: Yale University Press. A critical evaluation of the exclusionary rule and other aspects of rights in criminal justice process, with an emphasis on assessing how legal rules work in the actual processes conducted by police and prosecutors.

Going Online

For an up-to-date list of Web links, go to http://www.cj.wadsworth.com/colesmith10e

1 Go to the Web site of the Alameda County, California, District Attorney's Office: http://www.co.alameda.ca.us/da/pov/POV_index.shtml. This site provides examples and discussions of various search and arrest cases in the courts. Read the brief descriptions of several of these cases, including the district attorney's opinion on the cases. Do you agree with the district attorney's perspective? Is the prosecutor biased in favor of law enforcement and insufficiently concerned about individuals' rights?

2 Go to the Web site of the American Civil Liberties Union, an advocacy organization that lobbies and files lawsuits on behalf of the protection and expansion of constitutional rights: http://www.aclu.org/PolicePractices/PolicePractices.cfm?ID=10626&c=118. Read their pamphlet about what to do if you are stopped by the police. Do you think it is proper for organizations to provide the public with information that might interfere with the ability of police officers to gather evidence about crimes?

3 Sign on at InfoTrac College Edition. Search for the term *exclusionary rule.* Read one article that supports the rule and one article that criticizes it. What is your view? Is the rule effective for its purposes? Is it too costly for society? Are there potentially effective alternative approaches?

Checkpoint Answers

1 A government intrusion into an individual's reasonable expectation of privacy.

2 Reasonable suspicion of wrongdoing based on articulable facts.

3 An arrest requires probable cause and involves taking someone into custody for prosecution, while a stop is a brief deprivation of freedom of movement based on reasonable suspicion.

4 The existence of probable cause by the totality of circumstances in the case.

5 Officers can examine and seize contraband and criminal evidence that is in open sight at a place where they are legally permitted to be.

6 Officers may use their sense of smell, especially for distinctive odors such as that of marijuana, but the Supreme Court has limited the authority to feel and manipulate luggage and other objects.

7 Warrantless stops of automobiles are permitted at international borders and sobriety checkpoints (unless barred within a specific state by its own supreme court) or when there is reasonable suspicion of a traffic violation or other wrongdoing.

8 A reasonable suspicion based on personal observation or information from a reliable informant that an individual is armed and involved in possible criminal activity.

9 Officers can search in the immediate area of the arrestee and do a protective sweep of rooms where the arrestee may have been recently located.

10 Urgent situations in which evidence may be destroyed, a suspect may escape, or the public would be endangered by taking the time to seek a warrant for a search or arrest.

11 The person must do it voluntarily and must have the proper authority to consent.

12 Officers can search any container or closed portion of an automobile for which probable cause exists to justify the search.

13 Before custodial interrogation, officers must inform suspects of the right to remain silent, the prosecution's authority to use any of the suspect's statements, the right to the presence of an attorney during questioning, and the right to have an attorney appointed if the suspect cannot afford one.

14 Officers can ask questions of suspects in custody without first providing *Miranda* warnings if public safety would be threatened by taking the time to supply the warnings.

15 Officers ask questions before suspects are in custody, use techniques to pretend to befriend or empathize with suspects being questioned, and give suspects misinformation about the existence of evidence demonstrating guilt.

16 The exclusionary rule was created to deter officers from violating people's rights, and the Supreme Court considers it an essential component of the Fourth and Fifth Amendments.

17 The rule is criticized as punishing the prosecutor and society rather than the police, imposing excessive costs on society, depriving the legal process of relevant evidence, and permitting some guilty people to go free.

18 A "good faith" exception in warrant situations, an "inevitable discovery" exception when evidence would have been discovered by the police anyway, and no application of exclusion in grand jury proceedings and other contexts that do not involve the proof of guilt in a criminal prosecution.

CHAPTER 8

Policing: Issues and Trends

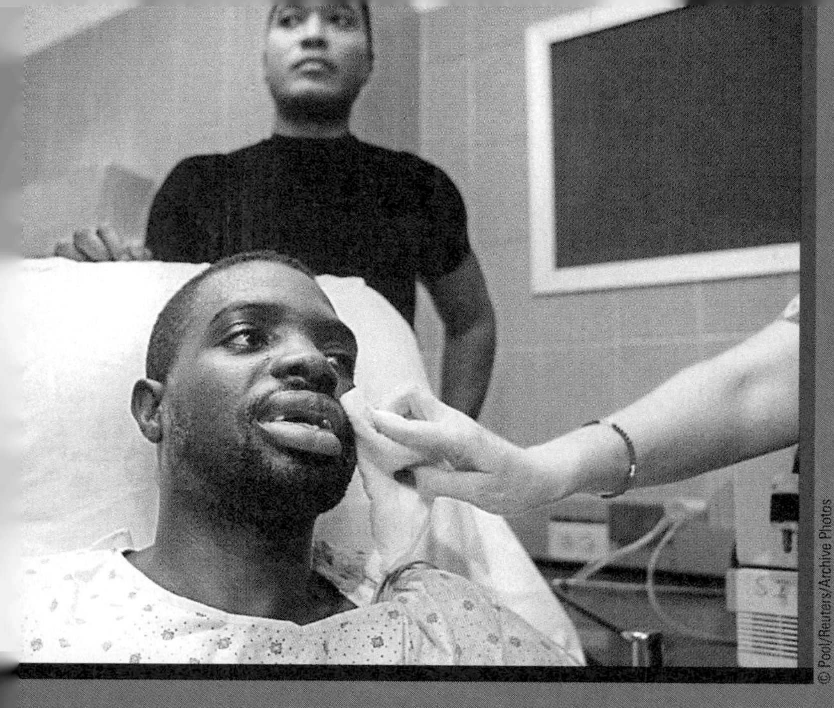
© Pool/Reuters/Archive Photos

On the night of August 9, 1997, Abner Louima, a 32-year-old Haitian immigrant, was arrested for disorderly conduct following a melee outside of the Club Rendez-Vous in Brooklyn. As he was hustled to a patrol car, Louima was struck by Officer Justin Volpe. Volpe erroneously believed that Louima was the person in the crowd who had taken a swing at him. The beatings continued in the police car as Volpe and other officers drove to the 70th Precinct station house. There, Louima was taken into the restroom where Volpe rammed a broken broomstick into his rectum and threatened to kill him if he ever told anyone about the assault. Volpe paraded around the station house brandishing the feces-covered stick. Later, Louima was taken to the hospital with broken teeth, a pierced bladder, and other serious internal injuries.

In the aftermath of the brutal assaults on Abner Louima, five officers were brought to trial on several federal civil rights and criminal charges. After trial testimony by a fellow officer that Volpe had bragged about torturing Louima with the handle, Volpe suddenly changed his plea to guilty to six of the charges, with the expectation that he would escape a life sentence. On

December 13, 1999, Justin Volpe was sentenced to 30 years in federal prison plus 5 years of probation.

The brutal attack on Abner Louima provides a particularly chilling illustration of a problem that arises with troubling regularity in various law enforcement agencies around the country. Police officers have sworn an oath to protect society against crime; thus, we are shocked when they, of all people, violate the public trust. For example, in October 2002 several officers in Detroit were charged with stealing millions of dollars' worth of cocaine from the evidence room at the police station (Schaefer, 2002). The bonds between the police and the community are often fragile, especially when racial, gender, or class bias comes into play. How can we make sure that those with authority do not misuse their power?

In this chapter we discuss several continuing issues about police and their role in society. We first look at how police deploy their personnel in attempting to control crime, maintain order, and provide service to citizens. Second, we examine how technological changes have given police new abilities to investigate criminal activity and monitor people's behavior and how these new technologies have also raised new questions about the role of police and the preservation of citizens' rights. Third, we discuss the problem of abuse of power by the police and what is being done to make police more accountable. Finally, we look at private-sector policing, which falls under the title of security management, a growing industry that is increasingly affecting police operations and requiring unprecedented cooperation between public and private agencies.

QUESTIONS for INQUIRY

- What patrol strategies do police departments employ?
- What is community policing?
- What new technologies have assisted police investigations, and how might they affect citizens' rights?
- In what ways do the police abuse their power, and how can this abuse be controlled?
- What methods can be used to make police more accountable to citizens?
- What policing and related activities does private-sector security management undertake?

Issues in Patrolling

As we saw in Chapters 5 and 6, patrol officers are the front-line personnel who bear the primary responsibility for all of the major functions of policing, including law enforcement, order maintenance, and service. The effectiveness of patrol officers will be determined, in part, by the strategies that police administrators use to distribute personnel throughout a city or county and to instruct officers about practices and priorities. For each specific problem that arises, police agencies instruct their officers to perform in ways tailored to each problem; different problems require different modes of operation. For example, when police departments throughout metropolitan Washington, D.C., desperately hunted for the sniper who picked off random victims during October 2002, they instructed officers to scrutinize light-color vans and trucks similar to those reportedly near several shootings, to remain in a high state of readiness for quick response to any reported shooting, and to be a highly visible, mobile presence in commercial areas. The police employed a "swarming strategy" by attempting to close every road and highway in the vicinity of a shooting as quickly as possible after a sniper attack was reported (Weil and Dvorak, 2002). By contrast, departments that can focus on long-term trends in crime control or service may be able to establish specific patterns of patrol that emphasize having officers walk within neighborhoods and build personal relationships with individual citizens.

In the last 30 years, much research has been done on police methods of assigning tasks to patrol officers and transporting and communicating with them. Although their conclusions have been mixed, these studies have caused experts to rethink some aspects of patrolling. However, even when researchers agree on which the patrol practices are the most effective, those practices often run counter to the desires of departmental personnel. For example, foot patrol may be key to some community policing strategies, but many officers would rather remain in squad cars rather than beat the pavement. Police administrators therefore must deal with many issues in order to develop and implement effective patrol strategies.

Assignment of Patrol Personnel

In the past it has been assumed that patrol officers should be assigned where and when they will be most effective in preventing crime, keeping order, and serving the public. For the police administrator, the question has been "Where should the officers be sent, when, and in what numbers?" There are no guidelines to answer this question, and most assignments seem to be based on the notion that patrols should be concentrated in "problem" neighborhoods or in areas where crime rates and calls for service are high. Thus, the assignment of officers is based on factors such as crime statistics, 911 calls, degree of urbanization, pressures from business and community groups, ethnic composition, and socioeconomic conditions.

Patrol officers are assigned to shifts and to geographic areas. Demands on the police differ according to the time of day, day of the week, and even season of the year. Most serious crimes occur during the evening hours, and the fewest occur in the early morning. Police executives try to allocate their patrol resources according to these variables.

The assignment of officers to specific locations is only one aspect of determining patrol strategies. Law enforcement officials must also decide how police will travel on patrol and what activities the officers will emphasize. Experimentation with different strategies in various cities has led to numerous choices for police leaders. In addition, research on these strategies sheds light on the strengths and weaknesses of various options. We shall examine several options in greater detail: (1) preventive patrol, (2) hot spots, (3) rapid response time, (4) foot versus motorized patrol, (5) one-person versus two-person patrol units, and (6) aggressive patrol.

Preventive Patrol

Preventive patrol has long been thought to help deter crime. Since the days of Sir Robert Peel, it has been argued that a patrol officer's moving through an area will keep criminals from carrying out illegal acts. In 1974 this assumption was tested in Kansas City, Missouri. The results were surprising and shook the theoretical foundations of American policing (L. W. Sherman and Weisburd, 1995).

In the Kansas City Preventive Patrol Experiment, a 15-beat area was divided into three sections, each with similar crime rates, population characteristics, income levels, and numbers of calls to the police. In one area, labeled "reactive," all preventive patrol was withdrawn, and the police entered only in response to citizens' calls for service. In another section, labeled "proactive," preventive patrol was raised to as much as four times the normal level: All other services were provided at the same levels as before. The third section was used as a control, with the usual level of services, including preventive patrol, maintained. After observing events in the three sections for a year, the researchers concluded that the changes in patrol strategies had had *no* major effects on the amount of crime reported, the amount of crime as measured by citizen surveys, or citizens' fear of crime (Kelling et al., 1974). Neither a decrease nor an increase in patrol activity had any apparent effect on crime.

Despite contradictory findings of other studies using similar research methods, the Kansas City finding "remains the most influential test of the general deterrent effects of patrol on crime" (L. W. Sherman and Weisburd, 1995:626). Because of this study, many departments have shifted their focus from law enforcement to maintaining order and serving the public. Some have argued that if the police cannot prevent crime by changing their patrol tactics, they may serve society better by focusing patrol activities on other functions while fighting crime as best they can.

Those who support the professional crime-fighting model of policing have criticized this and other studies that question the effectiveness of preventive patrol. They claim that the research attacks the heart of police work. But the research simply calls into question the inflexible aspects of preventive patrol.

Hot Spots

In the past, patrols were organized by "beats." It was assumed that crime can happen anywhere, and the entire beat must be patrolled at all times. Research shows, however, that crime is not spread evenly over all times and places. Instead, direct-contact predatory crimes, such as muggings and robberies, occur when three elements converge: motivated offenders, suitable targets, and the absence of anyone who could prevent the violation. This means that resources should be focused on "hot spots," places where crimes are likely to occur (L. E. Cohen and Felson, 1979:589).

In a study of crime in Minneapolis, researchers found that a small number of "hot spots"—3 percent of streets and intersections—produced 50 percent of calls to the police. By analyzing the places from which calls were made, administrators could identify those that produced the most crime (L. W. Sherman, Gartin, and Buerger, 1989:27).

directed patrol
A proactive form of patrolling that directs resources to known high-crime areas.

With this knowledge, officers can be assigned to **directed patrol**—a proactive strategy designed to direct resources to known high-crime areas. However, the extra police pressure may simply cause lawbreakers to move to another neighborhood. The premise of this argument is that "there are only so many criminals seeking outlets for the fixed number of crimes they are predestined to commit" (L. W. Sherman and Weisburd, 1995:629). Although some public drug markets may participate in this shifting of "the action," it does not fit all crime or even all vice—such as prostitution (L. W. Sherman, 1990; Weisburd and Green, 1995).

Police administrators know that the amount of crime varies by season and time. Rates of predatory crimes such as robbery and rape increase in the summer months, when people are outdoors. By contrast, domestic violence is more frequent in winter, when intimates spend more time indoors in close proximity to each other.

There are also "hot times," generally between 7 P.M. and 3 A.M. A one-year study done in Minneapolis found that 51.9 percent of crime calls to the police came during this period, while the fewest calls were made between 3 A.M. and 11 A.M. With this knowledge, the department increased patrol presence in hot spots and at hot times (Koper, 1995). Although this strategy resulted in less crime, many officers disliked the new tactics. Being a "presence" in a hot spot might deter criminals, but the officers grew bored. Preventing crime is not as glamorous as catching criminals (L. W. Sherman and Weisburd, 1995:646).

Rapid Response Time

Most departments are organized so that calls for help come to a central section that dispatches the nearest officers by radio to the site of the incident. Because most citizens have access to phones, most cities have 911 systems, and because most officers are in squad cars linked to headquarters by two-way radios, cell phones, and computers, police can respond quickly to calls. But are response times short enough to catch offenders?

Several studies have measured the impact of police response time on the ability of officers to intercept a crime in progress and arrest the criminal. In a classic

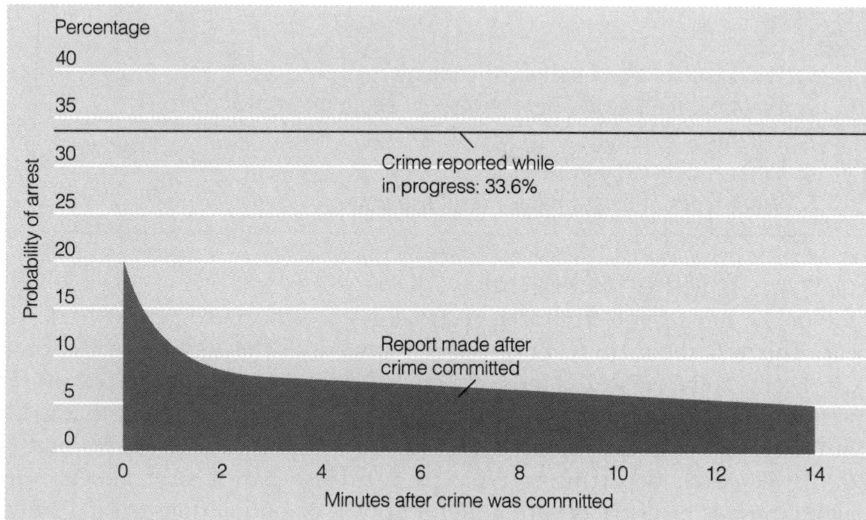

Source: William G. Spelman and Dale K. Brown, *Calling the Police: Citizen Reports of Serious Crime* (Washington, D.C.: Police Executive Research Forum, 1984), 65. Reprinted by permission.

Figure 8.1
Probability of arrest as a function of elapsed time after crime
The probability of arrest declines sharply when the police are not called within seconds. What does this imply for patrol policies?

study, William Spelman and Dale Brown (1984) found that the police succeeded in only 29 of 1,000 cases. It made little difference whether they arrived 2 minutes or 20 minutes after the call. What did matter, however, was how soon the police were called. Figure 8.1 presents these findings.

Although delayed arrival of the police is often due to slowness in calling, it seems unlikely that arrest rates would be improved merely by educating the public about their key role in stopping crime. As Spelman and Brown (1984) point out, there are three decision-making delays that slow the process of calling the police:

1. *Ambiguity delays.* Some people find the situation *ambiguous* and are not sure whether the police should be called. They might see an event but not know whether it is a robbery or two young men "horsing around."
2. *Coping delays.* Other people are so busy *coping*—taking care of the victim or directing traffic—that they cannot leave the scene to call the police.
3. *Conflict delays.* Still other people must first resolve conflicts before they call the police. For example, they may call someone else for advice about whether to call the police.

Besides these delays, communication problems can slow response. For example, a telephone may not be available, the emergency number may have to be looked up, or the dispatcher may not be able to handle the incoming call because she or he is dealing with other problems. The 911 system was designed to deal with communication delays.

Although delay is a major problem, reducing delay would only slightly increase arrest rates. In about three-quarters of crime calls, the police are reactive, in that the crimes (burglary, larceny, and the like) are discovered long after have they have occurred. A much smaller portion are "involvement" crimes (robbery, rape, assault) that victims know about right away and for which they can call the police promptly (Spelman and Brown, 1984:4).

In theory, rapid police response should prevent injury, increase arrests, and deter crime. However, as Lawrence Sherman says, "In practice, it seems to do none of these things." He notes that injuries occur during the first seconds of the event, and the chances of catching a criminal after a five-minute delay are not great. Rapid response time is valuable for only a small fraction of all calls. In sum, the costs of police resources and the danger created by high-speed response may outweigh any increase in effectiveness due to faster response times (L. W. Sherman, 1995:334).

check point

1. What factors affect patrol assignments?
2. What did the Kansas City study show about preventive patrol?
3. What is a hot spot?
4. What is directed patrol?
5. What types of delays reduce response time?

Foot versus Motorized Patrol

One of the most frequent citizen requests is for officers to be put back on the beat. This was the main form of police patrol until the 1930s, when motorized patrol came to be viewed as more effective. Of the 195 million Americans served by local police departments, 85 percent are served by a department that uses foot patrol, bicycle patrol, or both (Hickman and Reaves, 2001; Reaves and Hart, 2000). However, departments typically use these patrol strategies in selected neighborhoods or districts with a high business or population density. Most patrolling is still conducted in cars. One study found that motorized patrol accounts for 94 percent of patrol time in large cities (Reaves, 1992). Squad cars increase the amount of territory that officers can patrol. With advances in communication technologies and onboard computers, patrol officers have direct links to headquarters and to criminal information databases. Now they can be quickly sent where needed, with crucial information in their possession.

However, many citizens and some researchers claim that patrol officers in squad cars have become remote from the people they protect and less aware of their needs and problems. Motorized patrols and telephone dispatching have caused a shift from "watching to prevent crime" to "waiting to respond to crime" (L. W. Sherman, 1983:149). Because officers rarely leave the patrol car, citizens have few chances to tell them what is going on in the community: "who is angry at whom about what, whose children are running wild, what threats have been made, and who is suddenly living above his apparent means" (L. W. Sherman, 1983:149). If they do not know about problems and suspicious activities within neighborhoods, patrol officers cannot mediate disputes, investigate suspected criminal activities, and make residents feel that the police care about their well-being. Further, when officers are distant from the people they serve, citizens may be less inclined to call for help or provide information (Moore, 1992:113).

By contrast, officers on foot stay close to the daily life of the neighborhood. They detect criminal activity and apprehend lawbreakers more easily than do car patrols. Further, patrol officers who are known to citizens are less likely to be viewed as symbols of oppression by poor or minority residents. In large cities, personal contact may help reduce racial tensions and conflict.

Because of citizens' demands for a familiar figure walking through the neighborhood, the past decade has seen a revived interest in foot patrol. Studies have shown that foot patrols are costly and do not greatly reduce crime but that they make citizens less fearful of crime. In addition, citizen satisfaction with the police increases, and the officers have a greater appreciation of neighborhood values (M. Cohen, Miller, and Rossman, 1990; Kelling, 1991). In terms of the cost and benefit, foot patrols are effective in high-density urban neighborhoods and business districts.

One-Person versus Two-Person Patrol Units

The debate over one-person versus two-person patrol units has raged in police circles for years. Patrolling is costly, and two one-officer units can cover twice as much territory and respond to as many calls as can a single two-officer unit. A 1991 study of large cities found that 70 percent of patrol cars are staffed by one officer, but the cities use one-person patrol in different ways. For example, Los Angeles uses one-person cars for about half of its units during the day, but only 9 percent at night. Philadelphia, however, uses only one-officer cars (Pate and Hamilton, 1991).

Officers and their union leaders support the two-person squad car. They claim that police are safer and more effective when two officers work together in dangerous or difficult situations. However, police administrators contend that the one-person squad car is much more cost-effective and permits them to deploy more cars on each shift. With more cars to deploy, each can be assigned to a smaller area and response time can be decreased. They also contend that an officer working alone is more alert and attentive because he or she cannot be distracted by idle conversation with a colleague.

Aggressive Patrol

Aggressive patrol is a proactive strategy designed to maximize police activity in the community. It takes many forms, such as "sting" operations, firearms confiscation, raids on crack houses, programs that encourage citizens to list their valuables, and the tracking of high-risk parolees. James Wilson and Barbara Boland (1979) have shown the link between patrol tactics that increase the risk of arrest and lower crime rates. They argue that the effect of the police on crime depends less on how many officers are deployed in an area than on what they do while they are there.

aggressive patrol
A patrol strategy designed to maximize the number of police interventions and observations in the community.

The study showed that officers in an "anticrime patrol" in New York worked the streets of high-crime areas in civilian clothes. Although they accounted for only 5 percent of the officers assigned to each precinct, during one year they made more than 18 percent of the felony arrests, including more than half of the arrests for robbery and about 40 percent of the arrests for burglary and auto theft (Wilson and Boland, 1979).

The zero-tolerance policing of the 1990s in New York City is an example of aggressive patrol linked to the "broken windows" theory. This theory asserts "that if not firmly suppressed, disorderly behavior in public will frighten citizens and attract predatory criminals, thus leading to more serious crime problems (Greene, 1999:172). Thus, the police should focus on minor, public order crimes such as aggressive panhandling, graffiti, prostitution, and urinating in public. By putting more police on the streets, decentralizing authority to the precinct level, and instituting officer accountability, the zero-tolerance policy was judged to be a major factor in reducing New York City's crime rate (Silverman, 1999). However, by the end of the decade there were increasing cries of outrage from citizens, especially those living in low-income, minority neighborhoods, that the police were being too aggressive (*Newsweek,* June 21, 1997:65).

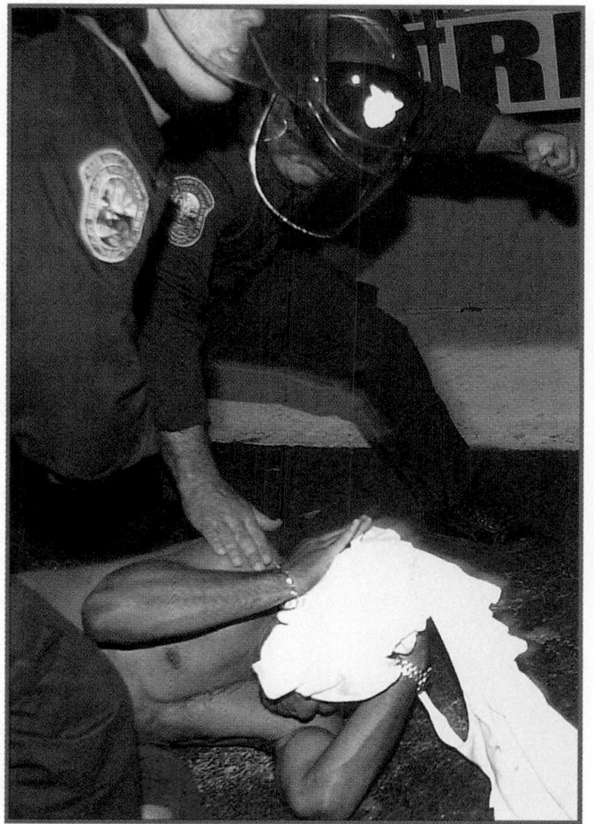

AP/L. M. Otero

Aggressive take-back-the-street tactics have made a big dent in urban crime. But in some cities a tough question is being asked: Does that style of policing come at an unacceptable price?

Handguns are the leading risk factor for criminal harm. Studies show a strong link between the number of guns in a community and rates of gun injury. James Wilson (1994) argues that the police should focus their gun-control efforts on guns being carried in high-risk places, by high-risk people, at high-risk times. The police may legally seize firearms when they are carried without a permit, when they are concealed, and when the person carrying one is on probation or parole.

In the 1990s some police departments began to seize illegally possessed firearms as a way of getting guns off the street. In Kansas City, Missouri, aggressive traffic enforcement was used as a way to seize firearms in a beat with a high homicide rate. The police seized one gun for every 28 traffic stops (L. W. Sherman and Rogan, 1995a:673). Aggressive patrol tactics were also used to seize firearms in raids on crack houses (L. W. Sherman and Rogan, 1995b:755). The result was a doubling of the gun recovery rate and a major reduction in gun violence (L. W. Sherman, 1995:340).

Release of violent felons from prison also poses a risk to community safety. The use of repeat offender squads to track high-risk parolees has proven successful in several cities. Using proactive tactics, the Washington, D.C., Repeat Offender Program targeted offenders with long records who were believed to be

Mayor Guiliani has been hired as a consultant to help devise zero-tolerance practices of aggressive policing for Mexico City. You can read more about this issue at http://www.manhattan-institute.org/html/cr_22.htm.

engaged in criminal activity. One squad, the "Hunter," focused on warrant targets, especially those sought for violent crimes; the "Trapper" squad carried out long-term investigations designed to close unsolved cases and recover stolen property. "Fisherman" squads followed up on tips, made warrant arrests, and "cruised" targeted areas to spot crimes as they occurred. The program succeeded in removing repeat offenders from the streets, but it was costly because it moved officers away from other duties (S. E. Martin and Sherman, 1986).

Antifencing efforts, often called "stings," are a widely used law enforcement technique. Typically police set up a storefront operation, then they pose as fences and buy stolen property from thieves. Large amounts of property are recovered, and thieves are arrested and successfully prosecuted. Researchers have questioned the impact of such programs, however. Robert Langworthy studied an auto theft sting conducted by police in Birmingham. He claims that, with respect to the goal of increased publicity and public support, the sting went well (Langworthy, 1989). With respect to crime prevention, however, an apparent increase in auto theft may have resulted from the sting. He notes that stings may cause police to engage in illegal behavior, a risk that may not be worth taking.

The most cost-effective of the aggressive patrol strategies seem to be those that encourage officers to carry out more field questioning and traffic stops. To implement such a strategy, the department must recruit certain kinds of officers, train them, and devise requirements and reward systems (traffic ticket quotas, required numbers of field interrogations, chances for promotion) that will encourage them to carry out the intended strategy.

Although aggressive patrol strategies reduce crime, they may also lead to citizen hostility. In New York, Pittsburgh, Charlotte, Washington, and other cities, polls show support for the strategy. However, in some neighborhoods there are rumblings that aggressive patrol has gone too far and is straining police relations with young African Americans and Hispanics. This issue pits the need to balance the rights of individuals against the community's interest in order (Kolbert, 1999:50). "Put another way, it's whose son is being hassled" (Reibstein, 1997:66). See "The Policy Debate" for more on the pros and cons of aggressive enforcement.

Community Policing

As we saw in Chapter 5, the concept of community policing has taken hold in many cities. To a great extent, community policing has been seen as the solution to problems with the crime-fighter stance that prevailed during the professional era (P. V. Murphy, 1992). In addition, many cities have turned to community policing because the federal government has provided funding for the development of community policing strategies and programs. Community policing consists of attempts by the police to involve residents in making their own neighborhoods safer. Based on the belief that citizens may be concerned about local disorder as well as crime in general, this strategy emphasizes cooperation between the police and citizens in identifying community needs and determining the best ways to meet them (Moore, 1992).

Community policing has four components (Skolnick and Bayley, 1986):

1. Community-based crime prevention
2. Changing the focus of patrol activities to nonemergency services
3. Making the police more accountable to the public
4. Decentralizing decision making to include residents

As indicated by these four components, community policing requires a major shift in the philosophy of policing. In particular, police officials must view citizens as customers to be served and partners in the pursuit of social goals rather than as a population to be watched, controlled, and served in a reactive fashion (Morash et al., 2002).

Departments that view themselves as emphasizing community policing do not necessarily have identical patrol strategies and initiatives (Thurman, Zhao, and

Should the Police Aggressively Enforce Public Order Offenses?

In "Broken Windows: The Police and Neighborhood Safety," James Wilson and George Kelling (1982) argue that disorderly behavior that is unregulated and unchecked is a signal to residents that the area is unsafe. Disorder makes residents become fearful. They then stay off the streets, avoid certain areas, and withdraw to the safety of their homes. This retreat of fearful citizens undermines the fabric of urban life, increasing a neighborhood's vulnerability to an influx of disorderly behavior, serious crime, and urban decay.

Wilson and Kelling urge the police and the community to pay attention to public order offenses: aggressive panhandling, public drunkenness, soliciting by prostitutes, urinating in public, rowdiness, and blocking of sidewalks. These "little crimes," they say, can lead to more-serious offenses. They believe the police must deal with public order offenses in an aggressive, proactive manner to prevent crime.

The connection between disorderly behavior, fear, and crime has long been recognized. Research has shown that (1) residents of a community generally agree on what constitutes disorder; (2) high levels of disorder are linked to high levels of crime, no matter how poor a community is, what its racial mix is, or how economically unstable the times are; and (3) disorder plays an important role in community decline, as fearful residents move, property values drop, and businesses close (Biderman et al., 1967; Skogan, 1990).

Until recently, researchers, policy makers, and the police have largely ignored these links, focusing instead on "serious crime," primarily the UCR index offenses of murder, rape, robbery, assault, and burglary. The professional crime-fighter role that has dominated policing in America since the 1920s has meant that the order maintenance and service functions have been considered less important.

The rise of the community policing movement has brought a shift in many cities to more targeting of public order offenses. Patrol officers assigned to "walk the beat" become acquainted with their neighborhoods, learn about local problems, and become known to residents. Officers also can use their discretion to establish informal rules defining what behavior is accepted in a particular neighborhood. They then enforce these rules by telling violators to stop, ordering panhandlers to move along, or making arrests.

How have the police responded to the findings that suggest they should shift to an order maintenance role? Many police executives are skeptical. They argue that serious crime is what the public expects them to control. They fear that law enforcement would get less political support, and therefore fewer resources, with a shift of emphasis to "little crimes." Police officers say they joined the police to fight crime, not to "do social work."

Although most departments have continued to emphasize the crime-fighting role, some—for example, New York City, Baltimore, San Francisco, and Seattle—are giving greater attention to enforcement of public order offenses, in order to improve the quality of life in their communities. To be effective, however, this focus requires the combined efforts of neighborhood groups, citizens, public officials, businesses, and the police. Community crime-fighting initiatives can reduce disorderly behavior, fear, and urban decay, thereby improving the life of citizens.

For Aggressively Enforcing Public Order Offenses

Supporters of a new focus on public order offenses argue that dealing with these "little crimes" is necessary to reduce residents' fears and prevent worse crimes. They say research has shown that preventive patrol in squad cars, rapid response, and centralized decision making isolate officers from the community. The use of community policing to deal effectively with public order offenses is a better way to control crime and make urban areas more livable. Through aggressive foot patrol, order can be restored and maintained.

Arguments for aggressively enforcing public order offenses include the following:

- Enforcing public order offenses reduces residents' fear, serious crime, and urban decay.
- When the police deal with low-level offenders, they learn about and are put in contact with those who have committed serious offenses.
- The police have a duty to improve the quality of life so residents do not have to deal with "street people" who impede pedestrian traffic and aggressively panhandle.
- Officers walking through a neighborhood become familiar with the residents and gain their cooperation and assistance when serious crime erupts.
- Police action on public order offenses encourages citizens to uphold neighborhood standards for behavior in public spaces.

Against Aggressively Enforcing Public Order Offenses

Enforcing the law and improving the quality of urban life may seem to be positive goals for any community; however, opinion is divided on this shift in policy. Some police officers say they have enough to do just dealing with the "bad guys" and they should not divert resources to lesser offenses. Many doubt that disorder and fear are actually linked to serious crime. Civil libertarians and advocates for the homeless have opposed many attempts to enforce laws against people's using public areas to panhandle, sell goods, and sleep. They say the new policies targeting public order offenses are designed to harass the poor, the homeless, and the mentally ill—the people society has pushed into the streets. They also emphasize that some officers misuse force in enforcing these policies.

The arguments against aggressive enforcement of public order offenses include the following:

- Police resources and tactics should be focused on fighting serious crime.
- The link between disorder, fear, and crime is uncertain and requires further research.
- Aggressive police tactics against people using public spaces constitute attacks on the poor. Resources could be better spent on helping the poor, the mentally ill, the homeless, and other social outcasts.
- The civil liberties of the poor are infringed on when the police aggressively enforce public order offenses.

What Should U.S. Policy Be?

How would the American people react if greater police resources were allocated to deal with public order offenses? Some researchers have argued that by aggressively dealing with disorder, the police reduce residents' fear and prevent worse crimes. They believe that ignoring these issues sends a community on a downward spiral that ends in serious crime and urban decay. However, others see this new emphasis as targeting primarily the weak—the poor and the outcasts of society. Civil liberties are trampled in the process.

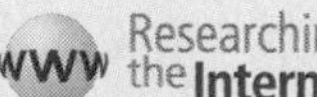

Researching the Internet

To read about the efforts on one New York City police precinct to enforce public order offenses that detract from the quality of life in the neighborhood, see http://nyc.gov/html/nypd/html/pct/pgm114.html.

Go to the *American System of Criminal Justice* Web site at http://www.cj.wadsworth.com/colesmith10e to explore this question in further detail: Should the police aggressively enforce public order offenses?

Giacomazzi, 2001). Some departments emphasize identifying and solving problems related to disorder and crime. Other departments work mainly on strengthening local neighborhoods. A department's emphasis can affect which activities become the focus of officers' working hours. In addition, organizational factors can affect the implementation of community policing. For example, community policing may be carried out by patrol officers assigned to walk neighborhood beats so that they can get to know residents better. It may entail creating police ministations in the community and police-sponsored programs for youth and the elderly. Police departments may also survey citizens to find out about their problems and needs (Reisig, 2002). The common element in community policing programs is a high level of interaction between officers and citizens and the involvement of citizens in identifying problems and assisting the development of solutions.

problem-oriented policing
An approach to policing in which officers routinely seek to identify, analyze, and respond to the circumstances underlying the incidents that prompt citizens to call the police.

A central feature of community policing for many departments is **problem-oriented policing,** a strategy that seeks to find out what is causing citizen calls for help (Goldstein, 1990). The police seek to identify, analyze, and respond to the conditions underlying the events that prompt people to call the police (DeJong, Mastrofski, and Parks, 2001). Knowing those conditions, officers can enlist community agencies and residents to help resolve them (Braga, 1999). Police using this approach do not just fight crime; they address a broad array of problems that affect the quality of life in the community.

Many departments train their officers to use the SARA strategy for problem solving (Thurman, Zhao, and Giacomazzi, 2001:206). SARA stands for a four-step process:

1. Scanning the social environment to identify problems
2. Analysis of the problem by collecting information
3. Response to the problem by developing and employing remedies
4. Assessment of the remedies to evaluate the extent to which the problem has been solved

The problem-oriented approach asks officers to look beyond the department for information. They talk to residents, businesspeople, offenders, and public officials—anyone who might offer information. They may find that incidents will cease if street lighting is improved, aggressive measures are taken against streetwalkers, or the closing hours of a local bar are enforced. Whatever the solution, it usually means getting help from other agencies (Spelman and Eck, 1987).

Syracuse, N.Y., patrol officers Ed Tagliatela and David Mathewson ride the downtown area, providing a high-visibility presence to store owners and citizens alike. What are the pros and cons of using bicycles on patrol?

The Image Works

Regardless of whether the police focus their resources on order maintenance, law enforcement, or service, they tend to respond to specific incidents. In most cases, a citizen's call or an officer's field observation triggers a police response. The police are often asked to respond to a rash of incidents in the same location. Because the police traditionally focus on *incidents,* they do not try to identify the *roots* of these incidents. By contrast, those engaged in problem-oriented policing seek to address the underlying causes.

Community policing has spread across the country and gained a great deal of support from citizens, legislators, and Congress (Bayley, 1994). This support can be seen in the emphasis on community policing in the Violent Crime

Control and Law Enforcement Act passed by Congress in 1994. Portions of the act call for increases in the numbers of officers assigned to community policing and for the development of new community policing programs.

For an explanation of the SARA strategy's role in policing, see http://www.crimereduction.gov.uk/skills04.htm.

San Diego has adopted a Neighborhood Policing Philosophy that emphasizes two concepts: (1) police and citizens share responsibility for identifying and solving crime problems and (2) law enforcement is but one tool for addressing crime (Mears, 1998). As the police chief, Jerry Sanders, said, community policing begins with a practical consideration: "listen[ing] to the community and letting them tell us what their priorities are" (Butterfield, 1999b:4). The police learned that what the people wanted them to work on were not serious crimes, but mainly abandoned cars or houses—smaller problems that attract larger ones—and in the worst areas, drug houses.

Through this approach, San Diego police have fostered connections with the community to share information, to work with citizens to address crime and disorder, and to tap other public and private agency resources to help solve problems. Examples of the neighborhood policing strategy in San Diego include the following (Greene, 1999:183):

- Support for "neighborhood watch" and citizen patrols that look for suspicious activity, identify community problems, and work on crime prevention
- Use of civil remedies and strict building-code enforcement to abate nuisance properties and close down drug houses
- Collaboration with community organizations and businesses to clear up, close down, or redesign specific locations and properties that repeatedly attract prostitution, drugs, and gang problems

Assisting the San Diego police are 1,200 volunteers who have received police training, wear policelike uniforms, and use police cars. They watch their neighborhoods so that officers can patrol (Butterfield, 1999b:4).

Although community policing has won support from police executives, the Police Foundation, the Police Executive Research Forum, and police researchers, it may be difficult to put into effect. As with any reform, change might not come easily (Schafer, 2002). Police chiefs and mid-level managers, who usually deal with problems according to established procedures, may feel that their authority is decreased when responsibility is given instead to precinct commanders and officers on the streets (Alley, Bonello, and Schafer, 2002). Another problem with implementing community policing is that it does not reduce costs; it requires either additional funds or redistribution within existing budgets. Measuring the success of this approach in reducing fear of crime, solving underlying problems, maintaining order, and serving the community is also difficult. In addition, there is the debate about how far the police should extend their role beyond crime fighting to remedying other social problems. Police officers may resist committing themselves to daily activities that emphasize goals other than the crime-fighting role that may have attracted them to careers in law enforcement (Mastrofski, Willis, and Snipes, 2002). This view is not limited to the officers themselves. In the view of former New York Mayor Rudolph Giuliani, community policing has "resulted in officers doing too much social work and making too few arrests" (*Criminal Justice Newsletter*, 1994:1).

The Future of Patrol

Preventive patrol and rapid response to calls for help have been the hallmarks of policing in the United States for the past half-century. However, research done in the past 30 years has raised many questions about which patrol strategies police should employ. The rise of community policing has shifted law enforcement toward problems that affect the quality of life of residents. Police forces need to use patrol tactics that fit the needs of the neighborhood. Neighborhoods with

Patrol in Japan

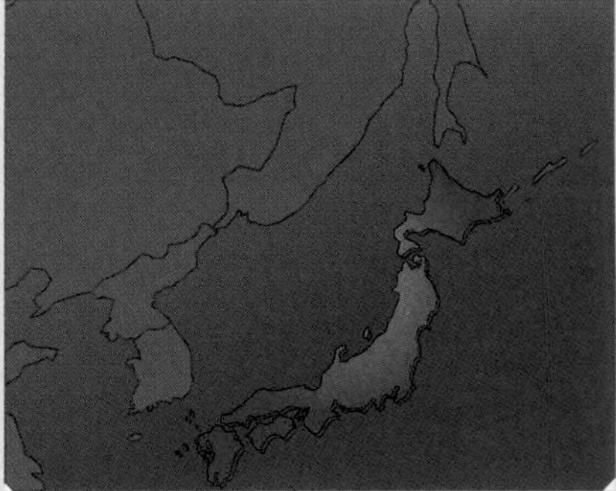

Many community policing strategies now being used in the United States have been the tradition in Japan for many years. Patrol officers walking through their assigned neighborhoods and working out of local offices are a hallmark of Japanese policing.

Japanese policemen are addressed by the public as Omawari-san—Mr. Walkabout. This is an accurate reflection of what the public sees the police doing most of the time. Foot patrolling is done out of *kobans* [mini police stations in urban neighborhoods], usually for periods of an hour. Patrols are more common at night, when officers work in pairs.... Patrolmen amble at a ruminative pace that allows thorough observation.... Patrolling by automobile, which is much less common than foot patrolling, can be frustrating too. Due to the narrow congested streets of Japanese cities... patrol cars are forced to move at a snail's pace....

Patrolling is by no means a matter of high adventure. For the most part it consists of watching and occasionally answering questions. Patrolmen rarely discover genuine emergencies; the chance of coincidence between patrolmen and sudden need are simply too great. Patrolling does not reduce reaction time or particularly enhance availability. What patrolling does is to demonstrate the existence of authority, correct minor inconveniences... such as illegally parked cars... and generate trust through the establishment of familiar personal relations with a neighborhood's inhabitants. On patrol, policemen are alert for different kinds of problems in different places. In a residential area they watch for people who appear out of place or furtive. In public parks they give attention to loitering males. Around major railroad stations they look for runaway adolescents, lured by the glamour of a big city, who could be victimized by criminal elements. They also watch for *teyhaishi*... labor contractors... who pick up and sell unskilled laborers to construction companies. In a neighborhood of bars and cabarets, patrolmen stare suspiciously at stylishly dressed women standing unescorted on street corners. They determine whether wheeled carts piled with food or cheap souvenirs are blocking pedestrian thoroughfares. Throughout every city they pay particular attention to illegally parked cars and cars that have been left with their doors unlocked....

When a Japanese policeman is out on patrol he makes a special point of talking to people about themselves, their purposes, and their behavior. These conversations may be innocent or investigatory. The law provides that

crime "hot spots" may require different strategies than do neighborhoods where residents are concerned mainly with order maintenance. Many researchers believe that traditional patrol efforts have focused too narrowly on crime control, neglecting the order maintenance and service activities for which police departments were originally formed. Critics have urged that the police become more community oriented and return to the first principle of policing: "to remain in close and frequent contact with citizens" (Williams and Pate, 1987). To see this policy in action, we look to Japan, where most patrolling is done on foot, as described in the Comparative Perspective.

How the national effort to combat terrorism will affect local police patrol operations remains uncertain. Since the attacks of September 11, 2001, state and local police have assumed greater responsibility for investigating bank robberies and other federal crimes as the FBI and other federal agencies devote significant attention to catching people connected with terrorist organizations. In addition, even local police officers in a neighborhood must be ready to spot suspicious activities that might relate to terrorist activity. They are the first responders in a bombing or other form of attack. Obviously, federal law enforcement officials

Justin Case/Corbis Outline

policemen may stop and question people only if there is reasonable ground for suspecting they have committed or are about to commit a crime or have information about a crime. Nevertheless, standard procedure on patrol is to stop and question anyone whenever the policeman thinks it may be useful. One reason for doing so is to discover wanted persons. And the tactic has proved very effective; 40 percent of criminals wanted by the police have been discovered by patrolmen on the street. Not only do officers learn to question people adroitly on the street, they become adept at getting people to agree to come to the *koban* so that more extended, less public inquiries can be made. People are under no obligation to do so, any more than they are to stop and answer questions. The key to success with these tactics is to be compelling without being coercive. This in turn depends on two factors: the manner of the police officer and a thorough knowledge of minor laws. The first reduces hostility, the second provides pretexts for opening conversations justifiably. People who park illegally, ride bicycles without a light, or fail to wear helmets when riding a motorcycle are inviting officers to stop them and ask probing questions. The importance with which the police view on-street interrogation is indicated by the fact that prefectural and national contests are held each year to give recognition to officers who are best at it. . . . Senior officers continually impress upon new recruits the importance of learning to ask questions in inoffensive ways so that innocent people are not affronted and unpleasant scenes can be avoided. . . .

The most striking aspect of the variety of situations confronted by policemen is their compelling, unforced naturalness. The police see masses of utterly ordinary people who have been enmeshed in situations that are tediously complex and meaningful only to the persons immediately involved. The outcomes are of no interest to the community at large; the newspapers will not notice if matters are sorted out or not; superior officers have no way of recording the effort patrolmen expend in trying to be helpful; and the people themselves are incapable by and large of permanently escaping their predicaments. Policemen are responsible for tending these individuals, for showing that they appreciate—even when they are tired, hurried, bored, and preoccupied—the minute ways in which each person is unique. It is perhaps, the greatest service they render.

Source: David H. Bayley, *Forces of Order: Police Behavior in Japan and the United States* (Berkeley: University of California Press, 1979), 33–34, 37, 41, 51–52. Copyright © 1976 The Regents of the University of California. Reprinted by permission.

To learn more about policing in Japan, see the English-language Web site of Japan's National Police Agency: http://www.npa.go.jp/police_e.htm.

must work closely with local police in order to be effective. Yet many local police chiefs have criticized the FBI for failing to share important information about local suspects (Bowers, 2002). The new concerns about terrorism will not alter traditional police responsibilities for crime fighting, order maintenance, and service, but they will provide an additional consideration as police administrators plan how to train and deploy their personnel.

check point

6. What are the advantages and disadvantages of foot patrol? Of motorized patrol?
7. What are the advantages and disadvantages of one-person versus two-person patrol units?
8. What is aggressive patrol?
9. What are the major elements of community policing?

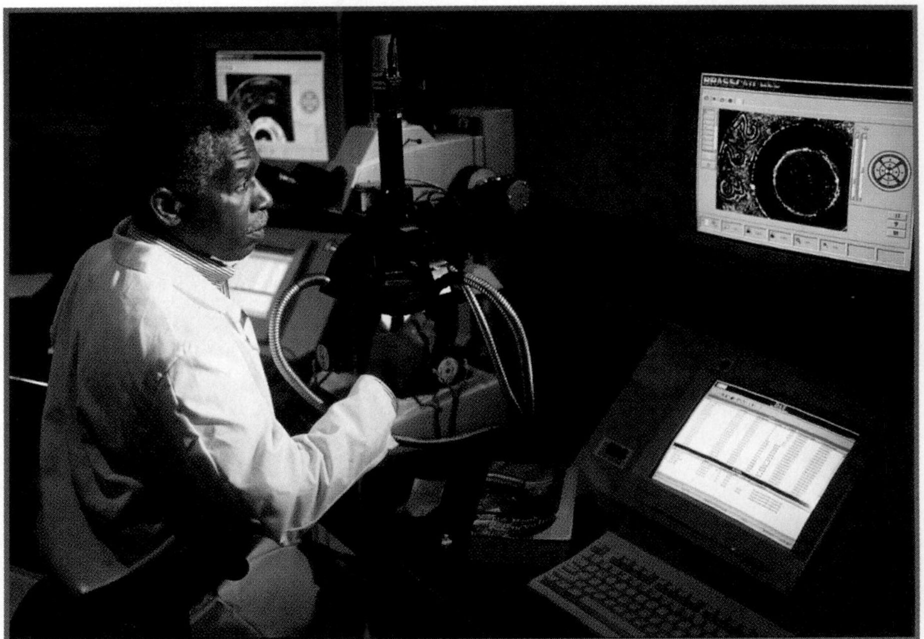

Brooks Kraft/Gamma

National databases of fingerprints and the DNA of every known felon, plus the ballistics signature of every gun ever used in a crime are now being developed. Here, the FBI's Lead Ballistics Examiner Walter Dandridge studies the grooves of a .223 slug like the one used by the D.C. snipers.

Policing and New Technology

Policing has long made use of technological developments. As discussed in Chapter 5, police departments adopted the use of automobiles and radios in order to increase the effectiveness of their patrols, including better response time to criminal events and emergencies. Technology has affected the investigation of crime as well. As early as 1911, fingerprint evidence was used to convict an offender. Police officers seek to collect fingerprints, blood, fibers, and other crime-scene materials to be analyzed through scientific methods in order to identify and convict criminal offenders. Police officers also use polygraphs, the technical name for "lie detectors," that measure people's heart rates and other physical responses as they answer questions. Although polygraph results are typically not admissible as evidence, police officers have often used these examinations on willing suspects and witnesses as a basis for excluding some suspects or for pressuring others to confess.

Several issues arise as police adopt new technologies. First, questions about the accuracy and effectiveness of technological developments persist, even though the developments were originally embraced with great confidence. For example, despite its long and confident usage in court by police and prosecutors, the accuracy of fingerprint evidence has been questioned. In 2002 a federal judge ruled that expert witnesses could compare crime-scene fingerprints with those of a defendant, but they could not testify that the prints definitely matched. The judge pointed out that, unlike DNA evidence, fingerprint evidence processes have not been scientifically verified, the error rate for such identifications has never been measured, and there are no scientific standards for determining when fingerprint samples "match" (Loviglio, 2002). Prosecutors later persuaded the judge to reverse his original decision and admit the expert testimony about a fingerprint match, but the judge's first decision raises the possibility that other judges will scrutinize fingerprint evidence more closely.

Second, some worry that new technologies will create new collisions with citizens' constitutional rights. As police gain greater opportunities for sophisticated electronic surveillance, for example, new questions arise about what constitutes a "search" that violates the reasonable expectations of privacy of citizens. The development of technology for the interception of email messages by law enforcement agencies provides an illustration of new situations that were not foreseeable in prior decades.

Investigative Tools

One of the most rapidly spreading technological tools for law enforcement officers is the computer, especially portable ones in patrol cars. Computers provide for instant electronic communication that permits the radio airwaves to be reserved for emergency calls rather than for requests to check license numbers and other routine matters. Computers also give officers quick access to databases and other information sources that help identify suspects. Depending on the software used and the organization of databases, many officers can make a quick checks of individuals' criminal histories, driving records, and outstanding warrants (A. Davis, 2001). With more-advanced computers and software, some officers can even receive mug shots and fingerprint records on their computer screens. Advances in technology provide a variety of possibilities for improving officers' ability to evaluate evidence at the scene of an event. With mobile scanners, officers can potentially run a quick check of an individual's fingerprints against the millions of fingerprint records stored in the FBI's database (Pochna, 2002). The Seal Beach, California, Police Department has worked with high-tech companies to develop streaming video capabilities that can permit officers to view live video from crime scene cameras as they approach the location of an incident. For example, if officers can tune their computers into the surveillance cameras that are standard features of banks and convenience stores, they can see the details of an unfolding robbery-in-progress as they approach the scene of an emergency call ("Law Enforcement Solution," 2002). Thus technology can improve the safety and effectiveness of police officers, especially in their crime-fighting role.

Advances in mobile computer technology raise questions about the development of law enforcement databases. The FBI has developed a significant database of fingerprints. As discussed in Chapter 6, a national database of DNA records is being constructed, although there are questions about which offenders should be required to submit samples. Local police departments may have "crime-mapping" databases that provide updated information about crime trends, especially the locations of recent criminal events. As police officers sought the sniper who terrorized Washington, D.C., in October 2002, new debates emerged about whether there should be a national database of ballistic evidence. Advocates argued that every gun sold should undergo a firing test so that its ballistic "fingerprint" could be stored in the database, just in case the weapon was later used in a crime. Opponents claimed that this was an undesirable step toward national gun registration and that such a database would be useless because the ballistic characteristics of a gun's fired bullets will change as the gun is used over time (Chaddock, 2002). The usefulness of these databases depends on the accuracy of technology to match evidence with stored information and the accessibility of database information to police departments and individual officers. In addition, as indicated by the debate about ballistic evidence, the nature and use of evidence databases will be affected by public policy debates about what information can be gathered and how it will be used.

An additional, little-noticed problem with laptop computers and new technological devices in patrol cars is the potential danger such devices pose to officers. There are increasing reports of officers being injured by flying equipment within their cars when they engage in high-speed pursuits or even get into minor collisions. Typically, automobiles were not designed to have laptop computers, video cameras, radar "guns," and other equipment mounted or otherwise available in the front seat. The deployment of the airbag in some accidents has sent equipment flying through the car with even greater velocity than would normally occur from a collision (Alonso-Zaldivar, 2002). Thus the development and deployment of technology requires further planning to integrate it safely into existing patrol car operations.

Computers have become especially important for investigating specific types of crimes, especially *cybercrimes,* which are crimes based on computer activity.

Many police departments have begun to train and use personnel to investigate people who use computers to meet children online in order to lure them into exploitative relationships. Computer investigations also involve pursuing people who commit identity theft, steal credit card numbers, and engage in fraudulent financial transactions using computers.

Police have begun using surveillance cameras in many ways. American cities increasingly use surveillance cameras at intersections to monitor and ticket people who run red lights or exceed speed limits. In Scotland, England, and Australia, law enforcement officials have adopted the use of surveillance cameras that permit police to monitor activities that occur in downtown commercial areas or other selected locations. Officials in a control room can watch everyone who passes within the cameras' fields of exposure. Advances in camera technology can enable these officials to see clearly the license plate numbers of cars and other specific information. American cities, such as New York and Washington, have made moves toward experimenting with this approach to combating crime in specific areas. Civil libertarians complain, however, that constant surveillance by government intrudes on the privacy of innocent, unsuspecting citizens and that there is insufficient evidence that this surveillance leads to reduced crime rates (Taifa, 2002). There are also allegations in some British cities that bored officers in the control booth spend their time engaged in close-up monitoring of attractive women and ignore or hide evidence of police misconduct that is caught on camera.

WWW Learn about the New York Surveillance Camera Project at http://www.mediaeater.com/cameras/.

American law enforcement officials have experimented with other surveillance and detection technologies. The National Institute of Justice is providing funding to help scientists develop devices that will assist the police. For example, scanners are being developed that will permit officers to detect whether individuals are carrying weapons, bombs, or drugs. Some of these devices detect foreign masses hidden on the human body, while others detect trace particles and vapors that are differentiated from those associated with human bodies and clothing (Business Wire, 2001b; PR Newswire, 2001). The first versions of such scanners are undergoing testing as security measures at airports, prisons, schools, and stadiums. However, officers on the streets could eventually use smaller, more mobile versions, especially if a handheld device could be pointed at an individual passerby to detect whether the person is carrying weapons or contraband.

At the Super Bowl in 2001, police officers used a surveillance system with facial-recognition technology in an attempt to identify people being sought on outstanding warrants. The police claimed that the cameras and facial-recognition software permitted them to identify 19 people wanted for crimes. Casinos in Atlantic City also use facial-recognition technology with surveillance cameras to identify people whom they know to be skilled at cheating. Conceivably, the system could also be used to identify suspected terrorists attempting to enter the country at airports (Meyer and Gorman, 2001). This technology poses problems, however. It cannot identify faces and match them with database pictures quickly enough to prevent suspects from disappearing into a crowd and thus requiring officers to search for them. In addition, questions persist about the accuracy of the facial-recognition technology. According to one researcher who has tested some systems, "One out of every 50 people looks like Carlos the Jackal, [the infamous terrorist], and the real Carlos the Jackal has only a 50 percent chance of looking like himself" (Meyer and Gorman, 2001:1).

Researchers claim that iris-recognition technology, which examines the interior of the eye and matches its unique characteristics with information in a database, is much more accurate than facial-recognition technology or technologies that attempt to match voices, fingerprints, or the palm of the hand (Business Wire, 2001a). Such iris-recognition technology was employed throughout the fictional futuristic world in the Stephen Spielberg film *Minority Report.* It is not clear, however, that such technology could be developed for use in surveillance

use in policing. Moreover, such a technology would require the development of an entirely new type of database containing records of people's eyes. As with other developing technologies, significant questions arise about the costs of developing and producing new scientific devices for wide distribution. Even if the scientific community develops new technologies that might benefit policing, the expense of implementing these devices may be far more than individual cities and counties can afford.

The U.S. Supreme Court has already given a sign that it will look critically at some new police technologies. Recall from Chapter 4 that in ***Kyllo v. United States* (2001)**, law enforcement officials pointed a thermal imaging device at a house to detect unusual heat sources that might indicate marijuana being cultivated under "grow lights." Their efforts led to a search of the home and the discovery of 100 marijuana plants. In the majority opinion Justice Scalia declared the use of the device in this manner to be an illegal search. According to Scalia, "Obtaining by sense-enhancing technology any information regarding the interior of the home that could not otherwise have been obtained without physical intrusion into a constitutionally protected area constitutes a search" and is therefore covered by the limitations of the Fourth Amendment, especially the warrant requirement (*Kyllo v. United States,* 2001:2043). Thus it is not clear how judges may evaluate the constitutionally permissible uses of new technologies.

***Kyllo v. United States* (2001)**
Law enforcement officials cannot examine a home with a thermal imaging device unless they obtain a warrant.

Scientists are working to develop technology to detect deceptions that suspects may use when questioned by police. Polygraph tests are considered insufficiently reliable, because some liars may be very calm when they lie, and thereby avoid detection, while some truthful people will be very nervous when being asked questions. Thus truthful people may look like liars on a polygraph test if their palms sweat and their heart rates increase as they answer. One approach under investigation is the use of a thermal imaging camera that can detect faint blushing in the faces of people who answer questions in an untruthful manner. Critics warn, however, that this technology may simply reproduce the problems with polygraphs by looking only at physical responses that vary by individual (R. Callahan, 2002). An alternative technology detects people's brain-wave responses to words and images. The subject wears an electronic headband while being shown words or images flashed on a screen. If the person shows a brain-wave response to words or pictures that would be familiar only to the witness or perpetrator of a crime, then law enforcement officials might be able to move forward with an investigation that ultimately solves the crimes (Bergstrom, 1999). This approach has not been fully tested, and it raises concerns that a court would regard this technique as violating the Fifth Amendment privilege against compelled self-incrimination.

Weapons Technology

As we shall see, police officers have been sued in many cases when they injured or killed people without proper justification. Some of these lawsuits have resulted in cities and counties paying millions of dollars to people who were injured when police used guns or nightsticks improperly or in an inappropriate situation. To avoid future lawsuits, departments have given greater attention to the training of officers. They have also sought alternative **nonlethal weapons** that could be used to incapacitate or control people without causing serious injuries or deaths. Traditional nonlethal weapons, such as nightsticks and pepper spray, can be used only when officers are in close contact with suspects, and they are not suitable for all situations that officers face.

nonlethal weapons
Weapons such as pepper spray and air-fired beanbags or nets that can incapacitate a suspect without inflicting serious injuries or a likelihood of death.

Police officers need to have the ability to incapacitate agitated people who are threatening to harm themselves or others. This need arises when they confront someone suspected of committing a serious crime as well as when they are attempting to control a crowd causing civil disorder. They also seek to enhance their

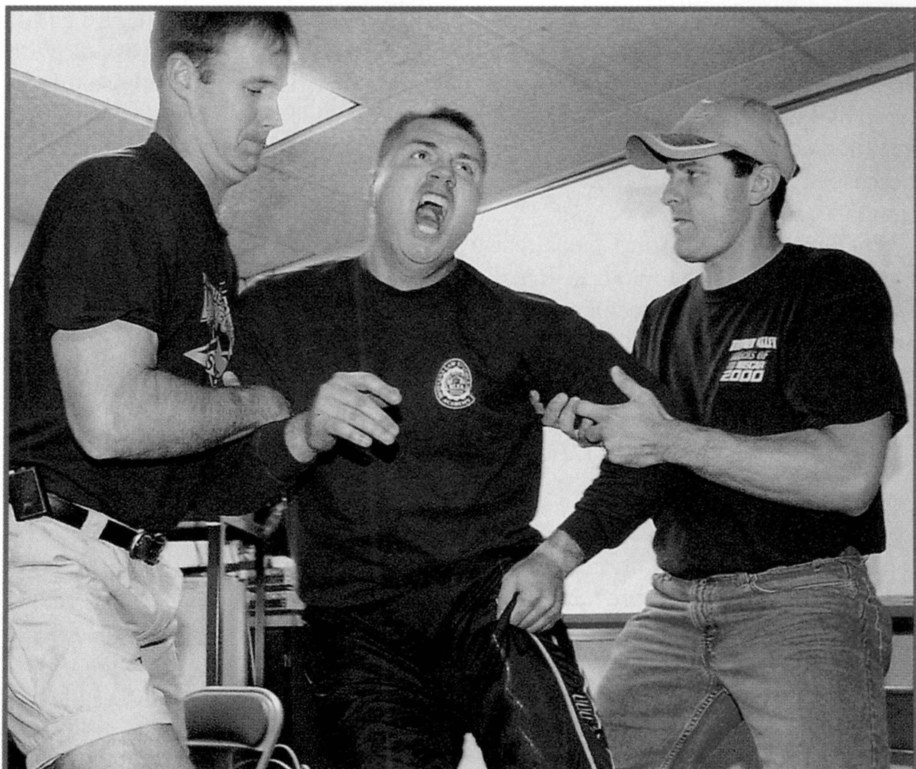

AP Photo/Daily Inter Lake, Karen Nichols

Kalispell, Montana, Police Officer Mike Whitcher reacts as he receives a jolt from a Taser gun. The Taser gun fires two filaments that send an incapacitating electric jolt into people upon contact. Whitcher had to endure the jolt for a second or two in order to become certified in the use of the weapon.

ability to stop criminal suspects from fleeing. A variety of nonlethal weapons have been developed to accomplish these goals. Police use some of them widely, while others are still undergoing testing and refinement.

Projectile weapons shoot objects at people whom the police wish to subdue. Some nonlethal projectiles, such as rubber bullets, can travel a long distance. Others are employed only when suspects are within a few yards of the officers. Rubber bullets have been used for many years. Although they are generally nonlethal, they can cause serious injuries if they hit someone in the eye or elsewhere in the head. Many departments have turned to the use of beanbags, small canvas bags containing tiny lead beads that are fired from a shotgun (Spencer, 2000). They are intended to stun people upon impact without causing lasting injury. Several police departments in the Los Angeles area, however, have abandoned the use of beanbags because of concerns about injuries and a few deaths caused by these projectiles as well as dissatisfaction with their accuracy when fired at a target (Leonard, 2002).

Other departments have begun to use airguns that shoot "pepperballs," small plastic pellets that are filled with a peppery powder that causes coughing and sneezing upon release after the suspect is stunned by the impact of the pellet. Officers can also fill the pellets with green dye in order to mark and later arrest individuals in an out-of-control crowd (Randolph, 2001). For suspects who are close at hand, many police departments use the *taser,* a weapon with prongs that send an incapacitating electric jolt into people upon contact (Ith, 2001). Other weapons under development either shoot nets that can wrap around individual suspects or spray a fountain of foam that envelops the suspect in layers of paralyzing ooze.

The development of new, nonlethal weapons has undoubtedly saved officers from firing bullets in many situations in which they previously would have felt required to shoot threatening suspects. However, as with all technologies, these weapons do not magically solve the problem of incapacitating suspects safely. Mechanical problems or misuse by the officer may make the new weapons ineffectual. In addition, officers may act too quickly in firing a nonlethal weapon in situations where patient communication and persuasion might have handled a suspect more safely. In such situations, needless minor injuries may be inflicted, or the targeted person may become more enraged and thus more threatening to the officers who later must transport the person to jail. Moreover, there are only so many weapons that an officer can carry in his or her arms. The existence of nonlethal weapons will not ensure that such weapons are actually handy when officers must make difficult, on-the-spot decisions about how to handle a threatening situation.

check point

10. What kinds of new technologies are assisting police with their investigative functions?
11. What kinds of new weaponry have police employed?

Police Abuse of Power

The misconduct of the New York City police officer described at the beginning of this chapter is not unique. The beating of Rodney King by Los Angeles police officers drew worldwide attention, as did the revenge killing by New Orleans police of Adolph Archer, who had shot an officer. The many recent police corruption scandals have made abuse of police power a major issue on the public agenda (Skolnick and Fyfe, 1993). Although such scandals have occurred throughout U.S. history, only in the past quarter-century has the public been aware of the problems of police misconduct, especially the illegal use of violence by law enforcement officers and the criminal activities associated with police corruption. Although most officers do not engage in misconduct, these problems deserve study because they raise questions about how much the public can control and trust the police.

Use of Force

Most people cooperate with the police, yet officers must at times use force to arrest, control disturbances, and deal with the drunken or mentally ill (Thompson, 2001). As noted by Jerome Skolnick and James Fyfe (1993:37),

> As long as some members of society do not comply with the law and resist the police, force will remain an inevitable part of policing. Cops, especially, understand that. Indeed, anybody who fails to understand the centrality of force in police work has no business in a police uniform.

Thus police may use *legitimate* force to do their job. It is when they use *excessive* force that they violate the law. But what is excessive force? This question has often stumped both officers and experts.

In cities where racial tensions are high, conflicts between police and residents often result when officers are accused of acting in unprofessional ways. Citizens use the term *police brutality* to describe a wide range of practices, from the use of profane or abusive language to physical force and violence. As shown in "What Americans Think," most people approve a police officer striking a citizen under certain circumstances.

Stories of police brutality are not new. However, unlike the untrained officers of the early 1900s, today's officers are supposed to be professionals who know the rules and understand the need for proper conduct. Thus, the beating of Rodney King and other incidents of brutality are particularly disturbing (Ogletree et al., 1995). Moreover, when abusive behavior by police comes to light, there is no

Source: Bureau of Justice Statistics, *Sourcebook of Criminal Justice Statistics, 1998* (Washington, D.C.: U.S. Government Printing Office, 1999), 115.

way for the public to know how often police engage in such actions, because most violence is hidden from public view (Weitzer, 2002). If a person looking on from a nearby window had not videotaped the beating of Rodney King, the officers could have claimed that they had not used excessive force, and King would have had no way to prove that they had. How can we prevent such incidents, especially when they occur without witnesses?

The concept "use of force" takes many forms in practice. We can arrange the various types of force on a continuum ranging from most severe (civilians shot and killed) to least severe (come-alongs). Table 8.1 lists many of these forms of force according to their frequency of use. How often must force be used? Most research has shown that in police contacts with suspects, force is used infrequently and the type of force used is usually at the low end of the continuum—toward the less severe. Research in Phoenix found that the single largest predictor of police use of force was use of force by the suspect to which the police then responded (Garner et al., 1995). Research in six urban jurisdictions in which 7,512 arrests were examined showed that no weapon such as a baton, flashlight, handgun, chemical agent, or canine was used by the police in 97.9 percent of the contacts (Garner and Maxwell, 1999:31). Again, it is *excessive* use of force, in violation of department policies and state laws, that constitutes abuse of police power.

By law, the police have the authority to use force if necessary to make an arrest, keep the peace, or maintain public order. But just how much force is necessary and under what conditions it may be used are complex and debatable questions. In particular, the use of deadly force in apprehending suspects has become a deeply emotional issue with a direct connection to race relations. Research has shown that the greatest use of deadly force by the police is found in communities with high levels of economic inequality and large minority populations (Holmes, 2000; Sorensen, Marquart, and Brock, 1993).

When the police kill a suspect or bystander while trying to make an arrest, their actions may produce public outrage and hostility. This was the case in November 1996 when a white officer in St. Petersburg, Florida, killed a black motorist who had refused to lower his window and appeared to be trying to drive away after a routine traffic stop. The riot that followed left more than a dozen people injured and caused $5 million in property damage. A second round of rioting was sparked after a predominantly white grand jury cleared the officer of wrongdoing (*USA Today,* November 11, 1996).

New Yorkers were outraged by the killing of Amadou Diallo, an unarmed West African immigrant, who died in a fusillade of 41 bullets fired by four members of New York City's Street Crime Unit. Unarmed and standing alone, Diallo was killed in the vestibule of his apartment building. The officers were looking for a rapist-murderer when they came upon Diallo. As they approached him, they said, they thought he was reaching for a gun. The killing resulted in massive protests and the indictment of the officers on second-degree murder charges. During their trial the officers said that they "reasonably believed" that Diallo was about to use deadly force against them (*New York Times,* February 26, 2000:A13). The Diallo killing also raised questions about New York's zero-tolerance policies and the aggressive tactics of the Street Crime Unit.

There are no accurate data on the number of people shot by the police. It is estimated that the police shoot about 3,600 people each year, with fatal results in as many as 1,000 of these incidents (Cullen et al., 1996:449).

Table 8.1 Reported uses of force by big-city police

Police have the legal right to use force to make an arrest, keep the peace, and maintain order. Of the many types of force available to police, the less severe types are used most often.

Type of Force	Rate per Thousand Sworn Officers
Handcuff/leg restraint	490.4
Bodily force (arm, foot, or leg)	272.2
Come-alongs	226.8
Unholstering weapon	129.9
Swarm	126.7
Twist locks/wrist locks	80.9
Firm grip	57.7
Chemical agents (Mace or Cap-Stun)	36.2
Batons	36.0
Flashlights	21.7
Dog attacks or bites	6.5
Electrical devices (TASER)	5.4
Civilians shot at but not hit	3.0
Other impact devices	2.4
Neck restraints/unconsciousness-rendering holds	1.4
Vehicle rammings	1.0
Civilians shot and killed	0.9
Civilians shot and wounded but not killed	0.2

Source: Drawn from Bureau of Justice Statistics, *National Data Collection on Police Use of Force* (Washington, D.C.: U.S. Government Printing Office, 1996), 43.

Although these numbers are alarming, it is important to remember that force (hit, held, choked, threatened) is used against 500,000 people each year (BJS, 1997d:12). The number of police killings should not obscure the fact that most of those killed are young African American men. However, the ratio of blacks to whites killed has declined, in part because of new police policies (L. W. Sherman and Cohn, 1986; S. Walker, Spohn, and DeLeone, 2000:95).

Until the 1980s the police had broad authority to use deadly force in pursuing suspected felons. Police in about half the states were guided by the common-law principle that allowed the use of whatever force was necessary to arrest a fleeing felon. In 1985 the Supreme Court set a new standard in ***Tennessee v. Garner* (1985)**, ruling that the police may not use deadly force in apprehending fleeing felons "unless it is necessary to prevent the escape and the officer has probable cause to believe that the suspect poses a significant threat of death or serious physical injury to the officer or others."

***Tennessee v. Garner* (1985)**
Deadly force may not be used against an unarmed and fleeing suspect unless necessary to prevent the escape and unless the officer has probable cause to believe that the suspect poses a significant threat of death or serious injury to the officers or others.

The case dealt with the killing of Edward Garner, a 15-year-old eighth grader who was shot by a member of the Memphis Police Department. Officers Elton Hymon and Leslie Wright were sent to answer a "prowler-inside" call. When they arrived at the scene, they saw a woman standing on her porch and gesturing toward the adjacent house. She told them she had heard glass breaking and someone was inside. While Wright radioed for help, Hymon went to the back of the house, heard a door slam, and saw someone run across the backyard toward a 6-foot chainlink fence. With his flashlight, Hymon could see that Garner was unarmed. He called out, "Police! Halt!" but Garner began to climb the fence. Convinced that Garner would escape if he made it over the fence, Hymon fired, hitting him in the back of the head. Garner died in the operating room, the ten dollars he had stolen still in his pocket. Hymon had acted under Tennessee law and Memphis Police Department policy.

The standard set by *Tennessee v. Garner* presents problems because it can be hard to judge how dangerous a suspect may be. Because officers must make quick decisions in stressful situations, creating rules that will guide them in every case is impossible. The Court tried to clarify its ruling in the case of *Graham v. Connor* (1989). Here the justices established the standard of "objective reasonableness," saying that the officer's use of deadly force should be judged in terms of the "reasonableness at the moment." This means that the use of the deadly force should be judged from the point of view of the officer on the scene. The Court's decision says that it must be recognized that "officers are often forced to make split-second judgments—in circumstances that are tense, uncertain, and rapidly evolving—about the amount of force that is necessary in a particular situation" (*Graham v. Connor*, 1989).

You can read the Police Use of Force and Firearms Policy for a university's police department at http://www.uca.edu/divisions/admin/board/policies/420.html.

The risk of lawsuits by victims of improper police shootings looms over police departments and creates a further incentive for administrators to set and enforce standards for the use of force. However, as long as officers carry weapons, some improper shootings will occur. Training, internal review of incidents, and disciplining or firing trigger-happy officers may help reduce the use of unnecessary force (M. Blumberg, 1989:442; Fyfe, 1993:128).

Although progress has been made in reducing police brutality and misuse of deadly force, corruption remains a major problem. We turn to this issue next.

Corruption

Police corruption has a long history in America. Early in the twentieth century, city officials organized liquor and gambling businesses for their personal gain. In many cities, ties between politicians and police officials assured that favored clients would be protected and competitors harassed. Much of the Progressive movement to reform the police aimed at combating such corrupt arrangements. Although these political ties have been reduced in most cities, corruption still exists.

Bianco's Restaurant is a popular, noisy place in a tough section of town. Open from 6:30 A.M. until midnight, it is usually crowded with regulars who like the low prices and ample portions, teenagers planning their next exploit, and people grabbing a quick bite to eat.

Officer Buchanan has just finished his late-night "lunch" before going back on duty. As he walks toward the cash register, Cheryl Bianco, the manager, takes the bill from his hand and says, "This one's on me, John. It's nice to have you with us."

Officer Buchanan protests, "Thanks, but I'd better pay for my own meal."

"Why do you say that? The other cops don't object to getting a free meal now and then."

"Well, they may feel that way, but I don't want anyone to get the idea that I'm giving you special treatment," Buchanan replies.

"Come off it. Who's going to think that? I don't expect special treatment; we just want you to know we appreciate your work."

→ What issues are involved here? If Buchanan refuses to accept Bianco's generosity, what is he saying about his role as a police officer? If he accepts the offer, what does that say? Might people who overhear the conversation draw other meanings from it? Is turning down a free $6.50 meal that important?

To read one city's code of ethics for its police officers, see http://www.massillonohio.com/police/ethics.html.

Sometimes corruption is defined so broadly that it ranges from accepting a free cup of coffee (see "A Question of Ethics") to robbing businesses or beating suspects. Obviously, *corruption* is not easily defined, and people disagree about what it includes. As a useful starting point, we can focus on the distinction between corrupt officers who are "grass eaters" and those who are "meat eaters."

Grass Eaters and Meat Eaters

"Grass eaters" are officers who accept payoffs that the routines of police work bring their way. "Meat eaters" are officers who actively use their power for personal gain. Although meat eaters are few, their actions make headlines when discovered. By contrast, because grass eaters are numerous, they make corruption seem acceptable and promote a code of secrecy that brands any officer who exposes corruption as a traitor. Grass eaters are the heart of the problem and are often harder to detect than meat eaters.

In the past, low salaries, politics, and poor hiring practices have been cited as factors contributing to corruption. However, these arguments fall short of explaining today's corruption. While some claim that a few "rotten apples" should not taint an entire police force, corruption in some departments has been so rampant that the rotten-apple theory does not fully explain the situation. Some explanations are based on the structure and organization of police work. Much police work involves enforcement of laws in situations in which there is no complainant or it is unclear whether a law has been broken. Moreover, most police work is carried out at the officer's own discretion, without direct supervision. Thus, police officers may have many opportunities to gain benefits by using their discretion to protect people who engage in illegal conduct.

Examples of meat eaters in Cleveland, Ohio, came to light in January 1998 as a result of an FBI sting operation. Forty-one officers were charged with protecting cocaine trafficking. The Cleveland case was one of a series of police-corruption investigations that have struck cities across the country in recent years. From 1994 to 1997, 508 officers in 47 cities were convicted in federal corruption cases (*New York Times,* January 1, 1998:A16).

Former New York City police commissioner William Bratton has noted a new form of corruption:

> It used to be cops took payoffs to look the other way, for what was a more benign activity like gambling, prostitution. What we're seeing now is the insidious aspect caused by the drug problem. There is more and more crossing the line to get involved in that business. (*New York Times,* January 1, 1998:A16)

In New Orleans, ten officers were convicted for their role in protecting a warehouse containing 286 pounds of cocaine. In Chicago in two unrelated cases, ten officers were charged with robbing and extorting money and narcotics from drug dealers. Thirteen Los Angeles officers were fired or suspended following exposure by former officer Rafael Perez. Perez pled guilty to stealing cocaine from an evidence locker but gained a lighter sentence by implicating his fellow officers in the shooting of an unarmed gang member and the shooting of two suspects in another incident (*New York Times,* September 26, 1999:26).

If police administrators judge success merely by the maintenance of order on the streets and a steady flow of arrests and traffic citations, they may not have any idea what their officers actually do while on patrol. Officers therefore may learn that they can engage in improper conduct without worrying about investigations by supervisors as long as there is order on the streets and they keep their activities out of the public spotlight.

When police administrators do not monitor the activities of officers, opportunities for corruption will always arise. New York's Mollen Commission found that department norms may shield corrupt cops from detection. Former police officer Kevin Hembury told the commission that at the police academy and in the locker room of the Seventy-third Precinct he had learned the "us against them" mentality and the "blue wall of silence"—that "cops never rat on other cops, that ratting on corrupt cops is worse than corruption itself." When he was exposed to the drug dealing and violence in his precinct, Hembury learned that "opportunities for money, drugs, power, and thrills were plentiful, and opportunities for friendly, productive contact with the thousands of good people who lived there were few." What startled the commission was his statement that "no commanding officer ever asked how he and his colleagues were spending their days . . . or how well they were serving the residents they were supposed to protect" (*New York Times,* November 1, 1992:A12).

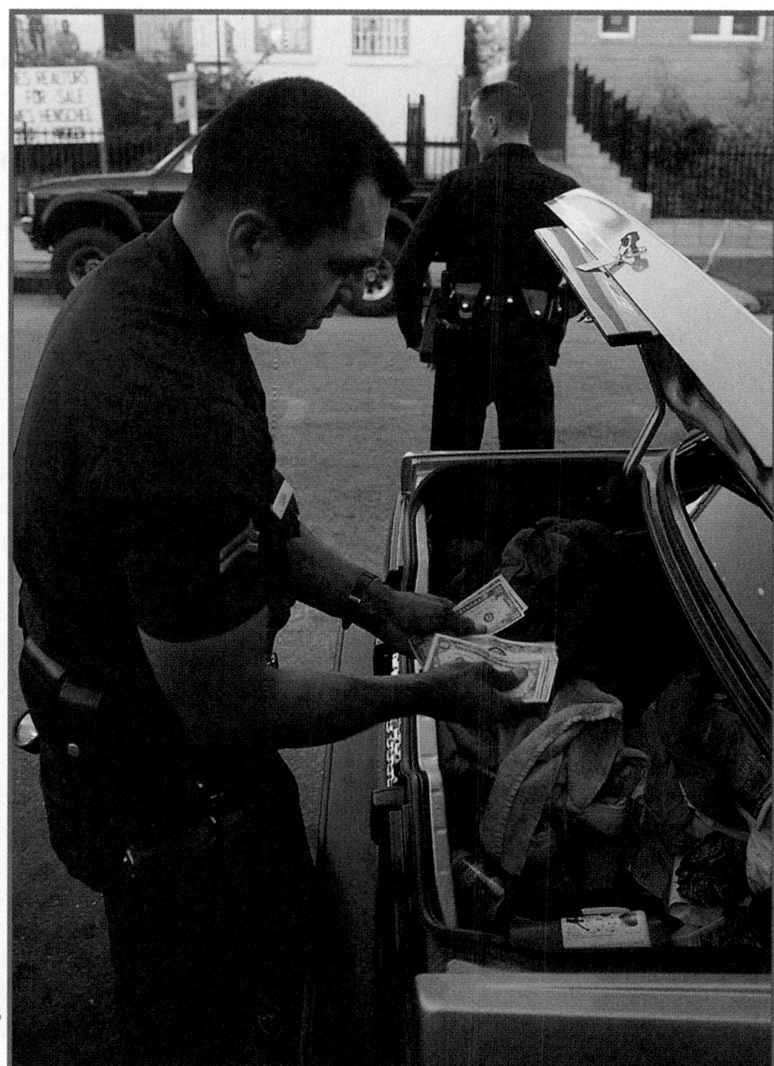
Joe Rodriguez/Black Star

Officers are often placed in situations where they can be tempted to violate the law.

Enforcement of vice laws, especially drug laws, creates major problems for police agencies. In many cities the rewards for vice offenders are so high that they can easily afford to make large payments to unethical officers to protect themselves against prosecution. That police operations against victimless crimes are proactive makes the problem worse. Unless drugs are being sold openly, upsetting the residents of a neighborhood, there are no victims to complain if officers ignore or even profit from the activities of drug dealers.

Over time, illegal activity may become accepted as normal. Ellwyn Stoddard, who studied "blue-coat crime," has said that it can become part of an "identifiable informal 'code.'" He suggests that officers are socialized to the code early in their careers. Those who "snitch" on other officers may be ostracized. When corruption comes to official attention, officers protect the code by distancing themselves from the known offender rather than stopping their own improper conduct. Activities under this blue-coat code may include the following (Stoddard, 1968:205):

- *Mooching:* Accepting free coffee, cigarettes, meals, liquor, groceries, or other items, which are thought of as compensation either for being underpaid or for future favoritism to the donor.
- *Bribery:* Receiving cash or a "gift" in exchange for past or future help in avoiding prosecution. The officer may claim to be unable to identify a criminal, may take care to be in the wrong place when a crime is to occur, or may take some other action that can be viewed as mere carelessness.

- *Chiseling:* Demanding discounts or free admission to places of entertainment, whether on duty or not.
- *Extortion:* Demanding payment for an ad in a police magazine or purchase of tickets to a police function; holding a "street court" in which minor traffic tickets can be avoided by the payment of cash "bail" to the arresting officer, with no receipt given.
- *Shopping:* Picking up small items such as candy bars, gum, and cigarettes at a store where the door has been left unlocked at the close of business hours.
- *Shakedown:* Taking expensive items for personal use during an investigation of a break-in or burglary. Shakedown is distinguished from shopping by the value of the items taken and the ease with which former ownership of items can be determined if the officer is caught.
- *Premeditated theft:* Using tools, keys, or other devices to force entry and steal property. Premeditated theft is distinguished from shakedown by the fact that it is planned, not by the value of the items taken.
- *Favoritism:* Issuing license tabs, window stickers, or courtesy cards that exempt users from arrest or citation for traffic offenses (sometimes extended to family members and friends of recipients).
- *Perjury:* Lying to provide an alibi for fellow officers engaged in unlawful activity or otherwise failing to tell the truth so as to avoid sanctions.
- *Prejudice:* Treating members of minority groups in a biased fashion, especially members of groups that lack political influence in City Hall to cause the arresting officer trouble.

Police corruption has three major effects on law enforcement: (1) suspects are left free to engage in further crime, (2) morale is damaged and supervision becomes lax, and (3) the image of the police suffers. The image of the police agency is very important in light of the need for citizen cooperation. When people see the police as not much different from the "crooks," effective crime control falls even further out of reach.

What is startling is that many people do not equate police corruption with other forms of crime. Some believe that police corruption is tolerable as long as the streets remain safe. This attitude ignores the fact that corrupt officers are serving only themselves and are not committed to serving the public.

Controlling Corruption

The public has a role to play in stopping police corruption. Scandals attract the attention of politicians and the news media, but it is up to citizens to file complaints about improper actions. Once a citizen files a complaint, however, questions remain about how best to respond. All departments have policies about proper police behavior and ways of dealing with complaints, but some departments tend to sweep corruption complaints under the rug. The most effective departments often have strong leaders who make it clear to the public and to officers that corruption will not be tolerated and that complaints will be investigated and pursued seriously.

check point

12. What kinds of practices do citizens view as police brutality?
13. When may the police use force?
14. How did the Supreme Court rule in *Tennessee v. Garner*?
15. What is the difference between grass eaters and meat eaters?
16. What are five of the ten practices cited by Stoddard as "blue-coat crime"?

Civic Accountability

Relations between citizens and the police depend greatly on citizen confidence that officers will behave in accordance with the law and with departmental guidelines. Rapport with the community is enhanced when citizens feel sure that the police will protect their persons and property and the rights guaranteed by the Constitution. Making the police responsive to citizen complaints without burdening them with a flood of such complaints is difficult. The main challenge in making the police more accountable is to use citizen input to force police to follow the law and departmental guidelines without placing too many limits on their ability to carry out their primary functions. At present, four less-than-perfect techniques are used in efforts to control the police: (1) internal affairs units, (2) civilian review boards, (3) standards and accreditation, and (4) civil liability lawsuits. We now look at each of these in some detail.

Internal Affairs Units

Controlling the police is mainly an internal matter that administrators must give top priority. The community must be confident that the department has procedures to ensure that officers will protect the rights of citizens. Many departments have no formal complaint procedures, and when such procedures do exist, they often seem designed to discourage citizen input (see Figure 8.2). Rumor has it, for example, that several years ago the Internal Affairs Bureau of the San Francisco Police Department posted a sign that said "Write your complaints here." Under the sign was a pile of 1-inch-square scraps of paper.

Depending on the size of the department, a single officer or an entire section can serve as an **internal affairs unit** that receives and investigates complaints against officers. An officer charged with misconduct can face criminal prosecution or disciplinary action leading to resignation, dismissal, or suspension. Officers assigned to the internal affairs unit have duties similar to those of the inspector general's staff in the military. They must investigate complaints against other officers. Hollywood films and television dramas depict dramatic investigations of drug dealing and murder, but investigations of sexual harassment, alcohol or drug problems, misuse of force, and violations of departmental policies are more common.

internal affairs unit
A branch of a police department that receives and investigates complaints alleging violation of rules and policies on the part of officers.

The internal affairs unit must be given enough resources to carry out its mission, as well as direct access to the chief. Internal investigators who assume that a citizen complaint is an attack on the police as a whole will shield officers against such complaints. When this happens, administrators do not get the information they need to correct a problem. The public, in turn, may come to believe that the department condones the practices they complain of and that filing a complaint is pointless. Moreover, even when the top administrator seeks to attack misconduct, he or she may find it hard to persuade police to testify against other officers.

Internal affairs investigators find the work stressful, because their status prevents them from maintaining close relationships with other officers. A wall of silence rises around them. Such problems can be especially severe in smaller departments where all the officers know each other well and regularly socialize together.

Civilian Review Boards

If a police department cannot show that it effectively combats corruption among officers, the public will likely demand that the department be investigated by a *civilian review board.* These boards allow complaints to be channeled through a committee of people who are not sworn police officers. The organization and powers of civilian review boards vary, but all oversee and review how police

Go to the Public Policy feature on the American System of Criminal Justice CD to learn more about the issues surrounding civilian review boards.

Figure 8.2
Path of citizen complaints
Compare the actions taken when a citizen is assaulted by a police officer in the course of dealing with a traffic violation and when a citizen is assaulted by a neighbor.

An officer stops a citizen for a traffic violation. An argument ensues and the officer breaks the citizen's nose as his son looks on.

Victim is charged with breach of peace and resisting arrest.

Victim calls police to report assault.

Victim is told to come to station to file complaint but is warned he could be arrested for filing a false complaint.

Victim gives complaint to internal affairs, where victim is again warned he could be charged with filing a false complaint.

Investigators question victim and son, submit written questions to officer.

Review board hears testimony from victim and son, reads internal affairs report, finds there is not enough evidence to prove the charge; nothing happens to the officer.

If review board agrees that excessive force was used, recommendation is forwarded to chief.

If chief agrees, chief either reprimands or suspends officer. Breach of peace and resisting arrest charges against victim are dropped.

A neighbor hits the victim, breaking nose, as victim's son looks on.

Victim calls police. Officers are sent to the home to take complaint and interview son.

Police arrest neighbor, who is booked on third-degree assault charge.

Neighbor goes to court, where he is arraigned and enters not guilty plea. Prosecutor, defense attorney, and judge are involved at this point.

Prosecutor offers a deal. But the neighbor rejects the deal and the victim's case goes to a pretrial hearing, where a judge determines that there is enough evidence to proceed. Prosecutor's investigators interview victim and son.

A prosecutor is assigned to case. He offers another deal.

Neighbor refuses, requesting a jury trial.

A six-member jury is selected and the victim tells how his neighbor hit him without provocation. Son testifies. Doctor testifies.

Neighbor convicted and sentenced to $1,000 fine and/or up to one year in prison.

Source: *Hartford Courant,* September 30, 1991, p. A6.

departments handle citizen complaints. The boards may also recommend remedial action. They do not have the power to investigate or discipline individual officers, however (S. Walker and Wright, 1995).

During the 1980s, as minorities gained more political power in large cities, a revival of civilian review boards took place. A survey of the 50 largest cities found that 36 had civilian review boards, as did 13 of the 50 next-largest cities (S. Walker and Wright, 1995).

The main argument made by the police against civilian review boards is that people outside law enforcement do not understand the problems of policing. The police contend that civilian oversight lowers morale and hinders performance and that officers will be less effective if they are worried about possible disciplinary actions. In reality, however, the boards have not been harsh.

Review of police actions occurs some time after the incident has taken place and usually comes down to the officer's word against that of the complainant. Given the low visibility of the incidents that lead to complaints, a great many complaints are not substantiated (Skolnick and Fyfe, 1993:229). The effectiveness of civilian review boards has not been tested; their presence may improve police–citizen relations. Even so, filing a complaint against the police can be quite frustrating, as shown in Figure 8.2.

Standards and Accreditation

One way to increase police accountability is to require that police actions meet nationally recognized standards. The movement to accredit departments that meet these standards has gained momentum during the past decade. It has the support of the Commission on Accreditation for Law Enforcement Agencies (CALEA), a private nonprofit corporation formed by four professional associations: the International Association of Chiefs of Police (IACP), the National Organization of Black Law Enforcement Executives (NOBLE), the National Sheriffs Association (NSA), and the Police Executive Research Forum (PERF).

The CALEA *Standards,* first published in 1983, have been updated from time to time. The fourth edition, published in 1999, has 439 specific standards. Each standard is a statement, with a brief explanation, that sets forth clear requirements. For example, under "Limits of Authority," Standard 1.2.2 requires that "a written directive [govern] the use of discretion by sworn officers." The explanation states, "In many agencies, the exercise of discretion is defined by a combination of written enforcement policies, training and supervision. The written directive should define the limits of individual discretion and provide guidelines for exercising discretion within those limits" (Commission for Accreditation for Law Enforcement Agencies, 1989:1). Since police departments have said almost nothing about their use of discretion, this statement represents a major shift. However, the standard still is not specific enough. For example, it does not cover stop-and-frisk actions, the handling of drunks, and the use of informants.

Police accreditation is voluntary. Departments contact CALEA, which helps them in their efforts to meet the standards. This process involves self-evaluation by departmental executives, the development of policies that meet the standards, and the training of officers. The CALEA representative acts like a military inspector general, visiting the department, examining its policies, and seeing if the standards are met in its daily operations. Departments that meet the standards receive certification. Administrators can use the standards as a management tool, training officers to know the standards and be accountable for their actions. By 1998 over 460 agencies had been accredited (S. Walker, 1999:285).

Obviously, the standards do not guarantee that police officers in an accredited department will not engage in misconduct. However, they are a major step toward providing clear guidelines to officers about proper behavior. Accreditation can also show the public that the department is committed to making sure officers carry out their duties in an ethical, professional manner.

For additional information on police accreditation, visit the Web site of the Commission on Accreditation for Law Enforcement Agencies: http://www.calea.org/index1.htm.

Civil Liability Suits

Civil lawsuits against departments for police misconduct can increase civic accountability. Only recently have citizens been allowed to sue public officials. In 1961 the U.S. Supreme Court ruled that Section 1983 of the Civil Rights Act of 1871 allows citizens to sue public officials for violations of their civil rights. This right was extended in 1978 when the Supreme Court ruled that individual officials and the agency may be sued when a person's civil rights are violated by the agency's "customs and usages." If an individual can show that harm was caused by employees whose wrongful acts were the result of these "customs, practices, and policies, including poor training and supervision," then he or she can sue (*Monell v. Department of Social Services for the City of New York,* 1978).

Lawsuits charging brutality, false arrest, and negligence are being brought in both state and federal courts. In several states people have received damage awards in the millions of dollars, and police departments have settled some suits out of court. For example, a Michigan court awarded $5.7 million to the heirs of a man who had been mistakenly shot by a Detroit officer, and Boston paid $500,000 to the parents of a teenager who had been shot to death. Over a year, city governments can end up paying quite a lot. In 1997, for example, New York paid $27.3 million to settle 521 cases of police misconduct (*New York Times,* September 17, 1997:A33).

Civil liability rulings by the courts tend to be simple and severe: Officials and municipalities are ordered to pay a sum of money, and the courts can enforce that judgment. The potential for costly judgments gives police departments an incentive to improve the training and supervision of officers (Vaughn, 2001). One study asked a sample of police executives to rank the policy issues most likely to be affected by civil liability decisions. The top-ranked issues were use of force, pursuit driving, and improper arrests (C. E. Smith and Hurst, 1996). Most departments have liability insurance, and many officers have their own insurance policies.

The courts have ruled that police work must follow generally accepted professional practices and standards. The potential for civil suits seems to have led to some changes in policy. For instance, a $2-million judgment won by Tracey Thurman against the Torrington, Connecticut, police had a profound impact (see the Close Up box "Battered Women, Reluctant Police" in Chapter 5). Plaintiffs' victories in civil suits have spurred accreditation efforts because police executives believe that liability can be avoided or reduced if they can show that their officers are meeting the highest professional standards. In fact, insurance companies that provide civil liability protection now offer discounts for accreditation.

As we shall see in the next section, private policing is a new player in the quest for security. This is yet another trend that is changing the landscape of law enforcement.

check point

17. What are the four methods used to increase the civic accountability of the police?
18. What is an internal affairs unit?
19. Why are civilian review boards relatively uncommon?
20. What is the importance of the decision in *Monell v. Department of Social Services for the City of New York*?

Security Management and Private Policing

Only a few years ago, the term *private security* called to mind the image of security guards, people with marginal qualifications for other occupations who ended up accepting minimal wages to stand guard outside factories and businesses. This imagery reflected a long history of private employment of individuals who served limited police patrol functions. Private policing existed in Europe and the United States before the formation of public police forces. Examples include Fielding's Bow Street Runners in England and the bounty hunters of the American West. In the late nineteenth century, the Pinkerton National Detective Agency provided industrial spies and strikebreakers to thwart labor union activities, and Wells, Fargo and Company was formed to provide security for banks and other businesses.

In recent years, by contrast, private-sector activities related to policing functions have become more complex and important. Today, if one speaks of people employed in "private security," it would be more accurate to envision a variety of occupations ranging from traditional security guards to computer security experts to high-ranking corporate vice presidents responsible for planning and overseeing safety and security at a company's industrial plants and office complexes around the world. The aftermath of the September 11 attack on the World Trade Center in New York has brought a heightened awareness of the importance of security management and private-sector employees in handling police functions.

Retail and industrial firms spend nearly as much for private protection as all localities spend for police protection. Many government entities hire private companies to provide security at specific office buildings or other facilities. In addition, private groups, such as residents of wealthy suburbs, have hired private police to patrol their neighborhoods. Recently, an estimated 60,000 private agencies employed more than 1.9 million people in security operations (T. Carlson, 1995:67). Each year businesses, organizations, and individuals together spend about $100 billion on private security. There are now three times as many officers hired by private-security companies as there are public police (see Figure 8.3).

Private agencies have gained success for several reasons. Private companies recognize the need to be conscientious about protecting their assets, including buildings, financial resources, and personnel. They must be prepared for fires and other emergencies as well as for criminal activity. Next, many threats have spurred an expansion in security management and private policing; these include (1) an increase in crimes in the workplace, (2) an increase in fear (real or perceived) of crime, (3) the fiscal crises of the states, which have limited public

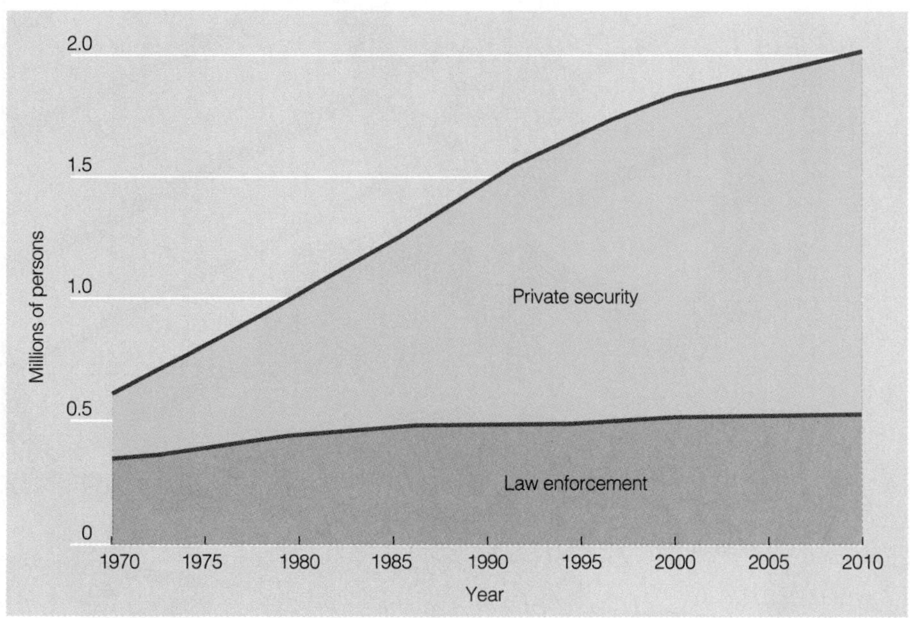

Source: Adapted from William Cunningham, John Strauchs, and Clifford Van Meter, *Private Security: Patterns and Trends* (Washington, D.C.: National Institute of Justice, U.S. Government Printing Office, 1991), 3. Trend line projection to 2010 by the authors.

Figure 8.3
Employment in private and public protection, 1970–2010 (projected)
The number of people employed by private security firms has surpassed the number employed by the public police and is growing. Such a large private force presents questions for the criminal justice system.

police protection, and (4) increased public and business awareness and use of more cost-effective private security services (Cunningham, Strauchs, and Van Meter, 1990:236).

Functions of Security Management and Private Policing

Top-level security managers have a range of responsibilities that require them to fulfill multiple roles that would be handled by separate individuals in the public sector. For their corporations, they simultaneously function as police chiefs, fire chiefs, emergency management administrators, and computer security experts. They hire, train, and supervise expert personnel to protect corporate computer systems that may contain credit card numbers, trade secrets, confidential corporate financial information, and other data sought by hackers intent on causing destruction or stealing money. Frequently they combat cybercriminals who are attacking their computer resources from overseas and are therefore beyond the reach of American law enforcement officials. They also plan security systems and fire and other disaster response plans for buildings. Such plans include provisions for evacuating large buildings and coordinating their efforts with local police and fire departments in a variety of locales. In addition, they develop security systems to prevent employee theft that may involve sophisticated schemes to use company computer systems to transfer financial assets in improper ways. Because so many American companies own manufacturing plants and office buildings overseas, security companies must often implement their services in diverse countries around the globe.

Private sector corporations own and control security for vital facilities in the United States, including nuclear power plants, oil refineries, military manufacturing facilities, and other important sites. Fires, tornadoes, or earthquakes at such sites could release toxic materials into the air and water. Thus emergency planning is essential for public safety. Moreover, because these sites are now recognized as potential targets of terrorist attacks, the role and effectiveness of security managers is even more important for society.

Security managers fulfill multiple roles usually performed by a number of individuals in the public sector. One important role is the planning of security systems for the protection of shopping malls, office buildings, power plants, and oil refineries.

Mug Shots/Corbis

At lower levels, specific occupations in private security are more directly comparable to those of police officers. Many security personnel are the equivalent of private-sector detectives. They must investigate "attacks" on company computer systems or activities that threaten company assets. Thus, for example, credit card companies have large security departments that use computers to monitor any unusual activity on individual customers' credit cards that may be a sign that the card has been stolen and is being used by a thief. Private-sector detectives must also investigate employee theft. Because this criminal activity extends beyond simple crimes such as swiping money from a store's cash register, investigations might examine whether people are making false reports on expense accounts, using company computers to run private businesses, or misspending company money.

Other activities are more directly comparable to those of police patrol officers, especially for security officers who must guard specific buildings, apartments, or stores. The activities of these private security personnel vary greatly: Some act merely as guards and call the police at the first sign of trouble, others have the power to carry out patrol and investigative duties similar to those of police officers, and still others rely on their presence, and the ability to make a "citizen's arrest," to deter lawbreakers. In most cases, citizens are authorized by law to make an arrest only when a felony has been committed in their presence. Thus private security companies risk being held liable for false arrest and violation of civil rights.

Some states have passed laws that give civil immunity to store personnel who reasonably but mistakenly detain people suspected of shoplifting. More ambiguous is the search of the person or property of a suspect by a private guard. The suspect may resist the search and file a civil suit against the guard. If such a search yields evidence of a crime, the evidence might not be admitted in court. Yet the Supreme Court has not applied the *Miranda* ruling to private police. In any case, federal law bars private individuals from engaging in wiretapping, and information so gathered cannot be entered as evidence at trial.

Security managers are often willing to accept responsibility for minor criminal incidents that occur on their employer's premises. They might perform such tasks as responding to burglar alarms, investigating misdemeanors, and carrying out preliminary investigations of other crimes. Some law enforcement administrators have indicated that they might be willing to transfer some of these tasks to private security firms. They cite several police tasks—such as providing security in public buildings and enforcing parking regulations—that private security might perform more efficiently than the police. In some parts of the country, personnel from private firms already perform some of these tasks.

Private Employment of Public Police

The officials responsible for asset protection, safety, and security at the top levels of major corporations are often retired police administrators or former military personnel. For example, New York Police Commissioner Raymond Kelly served as Senior Managing Director of Global Corporate Security for a Wall Street financial firm after he left his position as Director of the U.S. Customs Service and before he was appointed to serve as police commissioner. The reliance on people with public-sector experience for important positions in private security management reflects the fact that asset protection and security management have only recently become emphasized as topics in college and university programs. Thus relatively few professionals have yet gained specific educational credentials in this important area. As a result, the placement of retired law enforcement officials in high-level positions has often created opportunities for strategic communication and coordination between top-level security managers and public-sector police administrators. Both entities have reason to seek cooperation throughout the hierarchy of their respective organizations. Unfortunately, however, they cannot always ensure that individual police officers and lower-level security personnel will sufficiently communicate and coordinate with each other when incidents arise.

At operations levels of security management, private security and local police often make frequent contact. Private firms are usually eager to hire public police officers on a part-time basis. About 20 percent of departments forbid their officers from "moonlighting" for private employers. By contrast, some departments simultaneously facilitate and control the hiring of their officers by creating specific rules and procedures for off-duty employment. For example, the New York City police department coordinates a program called the Paid Detail Unit. Event planners, corporations, and organizations can hire uniformed, off-duty officers for $27 per hour. The police department must approve all events at which the officers will work, and the department imposes an additional 10 percent administrative fee for the hiring of its officers. Thus the department can safeguard against officers' working for organizations and events that will cause legal, public relations, or other problems for the police department. The department can also monitor and control how many hours its officers work so that private, part-time employment does not lead them to be exhausted and ineffective during their regular shifts.

For more information about New York City's program for the private employment of off-duty police officers, see http://www.nyc.gov/html/nypd/html/misc/paid_detail.html.

These officers retain their full powers and status as police personnel even when they work for a private firm while off duty. New York and other cities have specific regulations requiring an on-duty officer to be called when a situation arises in which an arrest will be made. While the use of off-duty officers expands the number and visibility of law enforcement officers, it also raises questions, two of which are discussed here.

Conflict of Interest

Police officers must avoid any appearance of conflict of interest when they accept private employment. They are barred from jobs that conflict with their public duties. For example, they may not work as process servers, bill collectors, repossessors, or preemployment investigators for private firms. They also may not work as investigators for criminal defense attorneys or as bail bondsmen. They may not work in places that profit from gambling, and many departments do not allow officers to work in bars or other places where regulated goods, such as alcohol, are sold. No department can know the full range of situations in which private employment of an officer might harm the image of the police or create a conflict with police responsibilities. Thus, departments need to keep tabs on new situations that might require them to refine their regulations for private employment of off-duty officers.

Management Prerogatives

Another issue concerns the impact of private employment on the capabilities of the local police department. Private employment cannot be allowed to tire officers and impair their ability to protect the public when they are on duty. Late-night duties as a private security officer, for example, can reduce an officer's ability to police effectively the next morning.

Departments require that officers request permission for outside work. Such permission can be denied for several reasons. Work that lowers the dignity of the police, is too risky or dangerous, is not in the "home" jurisdiction, requires more than eight hours of off-duty service, or interferes with department schedules is usually denied.

Several models have been designed to manage off-duty employment of officers. The *department contract model* permits close control of off-duty work, because firms must apply to the department to have officers assigned to them. New York City's system fits this model. Officers chosen for off-duty work are paid by the police department, which is reimbursed by the private firm, along with an overhead fee. Departments usually screen employers to make sure that the proposed use of officers will not conflict with the department's needs. When the private demand for police services exceeds the supply—and that is often the case—the department contract model provides a way of assigning staff so as to ensure that public needs are met.

The *officer contract model* allows each officer to find off-duty employment and to enter into a direct relationship with the private firm. Officers must apply to the department for permission, which is granted if the employment standards listed earlier are met. Problems can arise when an officer acts as an employment "agent" for other officers. This can lead to charges of favoritism and nepotism, with serious effects on discipline and morale.

In the *union brokerage model,* the police union or association finds off-duty employment for its members. The union sets the standards for the work and bargains with the department over the pay, status, and conditions of the off-duty employment.

Each of these models has its backers. Albert Reiss notes another complication: The more closely a department controls off-duty employment, the more liability it assumes for officers' actions when they work for private firms (Reiss, 1988).

What remains unknown is how uniformed off-duty patrol affects crime prevention and the public's perception of safety. Public fears may decrease because of the greater visibility of officers whom citizens believe to be acting in their official capacity.

The Public–Private Interface

The relationship between public and private law enforcement is a concern for police officials. Because private agents work for the people who employ them, their goals might not always serve the public interest. Questions have arisen about the power of private security agents to make arrests, conduct searches, and take part in undercover investigations. A key issue is the boundary between the work of the police and that of private agencies. Lack of coordination and communication between public and private agencies has led to botched investigations, destruction of evidence, and overzealousness.

Growing awareness of this problem has led to efforts to have private security agents work more closely with the police. Current efforts to enhance coordination

Jack Kurtz/Impact Visuals

Private security is assuming an increasingly large role in American society. Tim Hitt, security guard at the Galleria mall in Poughkeepsie, New York, says he patrols in order to provide a "certain level of calmness" in the shopping center.

involve emergency planning, building security, and the prevention of crime by individuals who are not employed by the private company in question. In other areas, private security managers still tend to act on their own without consulting the police.

One such area is criminal activity within a company. Many security managers in private firms tend to treat crimes by employees as internal matters that do not concern the police. They report UCR index crimes to the police, but employee theft, insurance fraud, industrial espionage, commercial bribery, and computer crime tend not to be reported to public authorities. In such cases the chief concern of private firms is to prevent losses and protect assets. Although some such incidents are reported, most are resolved through internal procedures ("private justice"). When such crimes are discovered, the offender may be "convicted" and punished within the firm by forced restitution, loss of the job, and the spreading of information about the incident throughout the industry. Private firms often bypass the criminal justice system so they do not have to deal with prosecution policies, administrative delays, rules that would open the firms' internal affairs to public scrutiny, and bad publicity. Thus, the question arises: To what extent does a parallel system of private justice exist with regard to some offenders and some crimes (M. Davis, Lundman, and Martinez, 1991)?

Recruitment and Training

Higher-level security managers are increasingly drawn from college graduates with degrees in criminal justice who have taken additional coursework in such subjects as business management and computer science to supplement their knowledge of policing and law. These graduates are attracted to the growing private-sector employment market for security-related occupations because the jobs often involve varied, complex tasks in a white-collar work environment. In addition, they often gain corporate benefits such as quick promotion, stock options, and other perks unavailable in public-sector policing.

By contrast, the recruitment and training of lower-level private security personnel presents a major concern to law enforcement officials and civil libertarians. These personnel carry the important responsibility of guarding factories, stores, apartments, and other buildings. Often on the scene when criminal activity occurs, they are the private security personnel most likely to interact with the public in emergency situations. Moreover, any failure to perform their duties could lead to a significant and damaging event, such as a robbery or a fire. In spite of these important responsibilities, which parallel those of police patrol officers, studies have shown that such personnel often have little education and training. Because the pay is low, the work often attracts people who cannot find other jobs or who seek temporary work. This portrait has been challenged by William Walsh (1989), who argues that differences between private and public police are not that striking. However, private security firms in San Francisco reported annual staff turnover rates as high as 300 percent because their low pay and benefits led employees continually to seek higher paying jobs, especially when better paid public-sector security work opened up, such as jobs as airport screeners (Lynem, 2002). City police departments and other public law enforcement agencies do not experience these kinds of staffing problems, because they have better pay and benefits.

The growth of private policing has brought calls for the screening and licensing of its personnel. Fewer than half of states require background checks or examine private security applicants' criminal records from states other than the one in which they currently reside. Twenty-two states have no certification or licensing requirements, and only 17 states have regulatory boards to oversee the private security industry. More than half of the states have no training requirements whatsoever for people who will assume important responsibilities in guarding buildings and other private security tasks (PR Newswire, 2002). Several national organizations, such as the National Council on Crime and Delinquency, have offered model licensing statutes that specify periods of training and orientation, uniforms that permit citizens to distinguish between public and private police, and a ban on employment of people with criminal records.

The regulations that do exist tend to focus on contractual, as opposed to proprietary, private policing. *Contractual security* services are provided for a fee by locksmiths, alarm specialists, polygraph examiners, and firms such as Brink's, Burns, and Wackenhut, which provide guards and detectives. States and cities often require contract personnel to be licensed and bonded. Similar services are sometimes provided by *proprietary security* personnel, who are employed directly by the organization they protect—for example, retail stores, industrial plants, and hospitals. Except for those who carry weapons, proprietary security personnel are not regulated by the state or city. Certainly, the importance of private security and its relation to public policing demands further exploration of these and related issues in the years to come.

check point

21. What has caused the growth of security management and private policing?
22. What are the three models for private employment of police officers?
23. What are the differences between contractual and proprietary private-policing services?

Summary

- Police administrators must make choices about possible patrol strategies, which include directed patrol, foot patrol, and aggressive patrol.
- Community policing seeks to involve citizens in identifying problems and working with police officers to prevent disorder and crime.
- The development of new technologies has assisted police investigations through the use of computers, databases, surveillance devices, and methods to detect deception.
- Police departments are seeking to identify nonlethal weapons that can incapacitate suspects and control unruly crowds without causing serious injuries and deaths.
- Police corruption and misuse of force erode community support.
- Internal affairs units, civilian review boards, standards and accreditation, and civil liability suits increase police accountability to citizens.
- The expansion of security management and private policing reflects greater recognition of the need to protect private assets and to plan for emergencies but it also produces new issues and problems concerning the recruitment, training, and activities of lower-level private security personnel.

Questions for Review

1. What has research shown about the effectiveness of patrol?
2. What controversies exist concerning new technologies employed by the police?
3. What are the major forms of police abuse of power?
4. What has the Supreme Court ruled regarding police use of deadly force?
5. What are the pros and cons of the major approaches to making the police accountable to citizens?
6. What are the problems associated with private policing?

Key Terms and Cases

aggressive patrol (p. 239)
directed patrol (p. 236)
internal affairs unit (p. 257)
nonlethal weapons (p. 249)
problem-oriented policing (p. 242)
Kyllo v. United States (2001) (p. 249)
Tennessee v. Garner (1985) (p. 253)

For Further Reading

Morash, Merry, and J. Kevin Ford, eds. 2002. *The Move to Community Policing: Making Change Happen.* Thousand Oaks, Calif.: Sage. Recent research on community policing and the challenges of implementing a new philosophy within police agencies.

Murano, Vincent. 1990. *Cop Hunter.* New York: Simon & Schuster. The story of an undercover cop who for ten years worked for the Internal Affairs Division of the New York City Police Department. Emphasizes the moral dilemmas of policing other officers.

Reiss, Albert J., Jr. 1971. *The Police and the Public.* New Haven, Conn.: Yale University Press. A classic study of the relationship of police officers to the public they serve.

Shearing, Clifford, and Philip C. Stenning, eds. 1987. *Private Policing.* Newbury Park, Calif.: Sage. An excellent volume that explores various aspects of the private security industry.

Skolnick, Jerome H., and James J. Fyfe. 1993. *Above the Law: Police and the Excessive Use of Force.* New York: Free Press. Written in light of the Rodney King beating and the riots that followed. The authors believe that only by recruiting and supporting police chiefs who will uphold a policy of strict accountability can brutality be eliminated.

Going Online

For an up-to-date list of Web links, go to http://www.cj.wadsworth.com/colesmith10e

1. Go to http://www.hrw.org/reports98/police/index.htm to read reports about police abuse cases in major American cities. After reading examples from several cities, think about the best approach to handling these problems. Is a particular approach likely to be most effective? Why?
2. Look at the Web site of the International Security Management Association: http://www.ismanet.com. Read the Press Releases. What issues are of greatest concern to top-level security managers?
3. Go to InfoTrac College Edition and use the keywords *facial recognition technology* to find and read two articles on this approach to surveillance and identification. Do you have concerns about how the technology might be used?

Checkpoint Answers

1. Crime rates, "problem neighborhoods," degree of urbanization, pressures from businesspeople and community groups, socioeconomic conditions.
2. Crime rates do not seem to be affected by changes in patrolling strategies, such as assigning more officers.
3. A hot spot is a location where there is evidence of a high number of calls for police response.
4. A proactive patrol strategy designed to direct resources to known high-crime areas.
5. Decision-making delays caused by ambiguity, coping activities, and conflicts.
6. Officers on foot patrol have greater contact with residents of a neighborhood, thus gaining their confidence and assistance. Officers on motorized patrol have a greater range of activity and can respond speedily to calls.
7. One-person patrols are more cost-efficient; two-person patrols are thought to be safer.
8. Aggressive patrol is a proactive strategy to maximize the number of police interventions and observations in the community.
9. Community policing emphasizes order maintenance and service. It attempts to involve members of the community in making their neighborhood safe. Foot patrol and decentralization of command are usually part of community-policing efforts.
10. Laptop computers in patrol cars connect to various databases, scanners, thermal-imaging devices, and facial recognition technology.
11. Nonlethal weapons, including beanbag projectiles, tasers, and pepper-ball projectiles.
12. Profanity, abusive language, physical force, violence.
13. The police may use force if necessary to make an arrest, to keep the peace, or to maintain public order.

14 Deadly force may not be used in apprehending a fleeing felon unless it is necessary to prevent the escape and unless the officer has probable cause to believe that the suspect poses a significant threat of death or serious physical injury to the officer or to others.

15 Grass eaters are officers who accept payoffs that police work brings their way. Meat eaters are officers who aggressively misuse their power for personal gain.

16 Mooching, bribery, chiseling, extortion, shopping, shakedown, premeditated theft, favoritism, perjury, prejudice.

17 Internal affairs units, civilian review boards, standards and accreditation, civil liability suits.

18 A unit within the police department designated to receive and investigate complaints alleging violation of rules and policies on the part of officers.

19 Opposition by the police.

20 Allows citizens to sue individual officers and the agency when an individual's civil rights are violated by the agency's "customs and usages."

21 Companies' recognition of the need to protect assets and plan for emergencies, problems with employee theft, computer crime, and other issues that require active prevention and investigation.

22 Department contract model, officer contract model, union brokerage model.

23 Contractual services are provided for a fee by private practitioners, such as locksmiths, alarm specialists, and organizations such as Brink's. Proprietary services are employed directly by the organizations, such as retail stores and industries, that they protect.

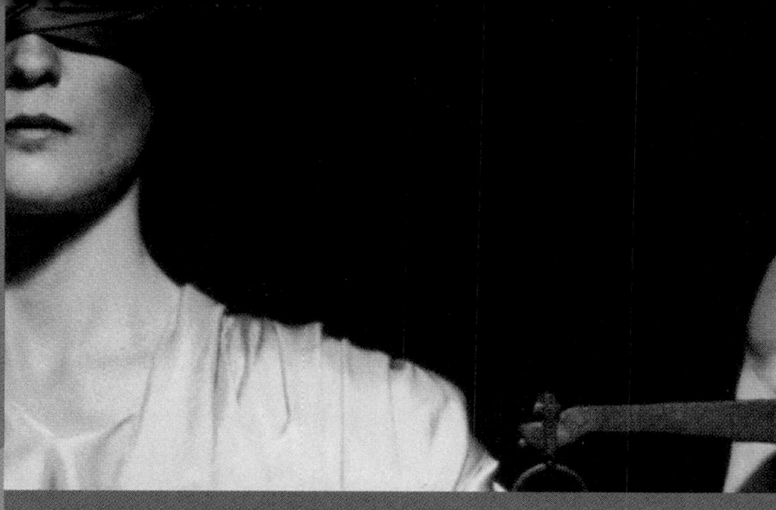

PART THREE

Courts

In a democracy, the arrest of a person is but the first part of a complex process designed to separate the guilty from the innocent. Part 3 examines the process by which guilt is determined in accordance with the law's requirements, as well as the processes and underlying philosophies of the punishment that further separates the convicted from the acquitted. Here we look at the work of prosecutors, defense attorneys, bondsmen, probation officers, and judges to understand the contribution each makes toward the ultimate decisions. In the adjudicatory stage, the goals of an administrative system blunt the force of the adversarial process prescribed by law. Although courtroom activities receive the most media attention, most decisions relating to the disposition of a case are made in less public surroundings. After the sentencing, the case recedes even further from the public eye. After studying these chapters, think about whether justice is served by processes that are more like bargaining than like the adversarial combat between two lawyers that is expected. Also consider whether the punishments our courts hand out are doing the job they are supposed to be doing in punishing offenders.

CHAPTER 9

Courts and Pretrial Processes

AP Photo/Louis Lanzano

On being arrested for a crime, suspects enter the judicial processes that will determine whether they are held in jail until their trials and, ultimately, whether they are guilty and must be punished. The processes of arrest and booking are typically the same for poor people accused of street crimes as for wealthy people accused of white-collar crimes. However, their ability to gain release from jail, while their cases are processed through the courts, often differs.

For example, John Rigas, the 78-year-old founder of Adelphia Communication Corporation, one of the nation's largest cable television systems, was arrested along with two of his sons and two company employees for improperly taking the company's money for personal use. Rigas, who had an annual salary of $1.9 million, allegedly took an additional $1 million per month from the company for a total theft of $62 million. The total amount that all of the defendants improperly took from the company allegedly exceeded $1 billion. The company eventually collapsed, and shareholders suffered massive financial losses (Farrell, 2002).

At the time of the arrest in New York City, federal law enforcement officials paraded the handcuffed defendants in front of news media cameras in order to send a message to the public that the government would take a strong stand against white-collar crime. After appearing in court to hear the formal charges, the two company employees were released on their own recognizance, meaning that they merely had to promise to appear at future court hearings. By contrast, Rigas and his two sons were each required to post $10 million in property and cash in order to gain release on bail. They would forfeit these assets if they failed to appear for scheduled hearings. Why was the bail so high? Perhaps the government and the judge feared that the family members might use their substantial wealth to attempt to flee the country (Farrell, 2002).

Why did two executive employees gain release without putting up any bail money while the Rigas family had to come up with millions of dollars? Is this disparity fair? Does it accurately reflect the seriousness of the crimes for which they were all charged, or does it only focus on perceptions of wealth? Lest you think that the wealthy suffer a disadvantage in the judicial process because they might be subjected to higher bail amounts, consider the bail set in other cases during 2002. Multimillionaire NBA basketball star Chris Webber gained immediate release when his bail was set at $10,000 after he was charged with lying in testimony to a federal grand jury investigating improper cash payments to high school and college athletes. By contrast, a German citizen, Albrecht Stromeyer, sat in a New York City jail, unable to make the $3,000 bail imposed when he was arrested and charged with stalking tennis star Serena Williams at the U.S. Open tournament. Bail was set at $2 million for a man with a lengthy criminal record who stole a city bus and drove at high speeds in Seattle, hitting cars and injuring several drivers (O'Hagan, 2002). Clearly the bail was set at an amount to ensure he would remain in jail while his case was processed. Also in Seattle, a man who allegedly had been drinking was charged with driving off the road and injuring three people on a sidewalk. Although none of his alleged victims died, he remained in jail when his bail was set at $1 million. By contrast, former NBA basketball player Jayson Williams gained release in New Jersey when bail was set at $270,000 for his charges of first-degree manslaughter and evidence tampering in the shooting death of his chauffeur, who died from a shotgun blast when Williams allegedly showed off for friends by twirling the weapon around on his hand ("Williams' Co-Defendant," 2002). When defendants are treated differently with respect to bail, the public may begin to think that the bail process clashes with the important American value on equal treatment. Moreover, when defendants cannot gain pretrial release, questions concerning liberty—another important American value—often arise.

Think about the bail amounts set for these various defendants. Which one is accused of the most serious crime? Is that the same one who might be most likely to flee? Which one might pose the greatest danger to the community while released on bail? These are not easy questions to answer. No scientific formula can permit accurate predictions about criminal suspects' behavior; judges must make the best decisions they can, case by case.

When people are arrested, they enter the court system, where the decisions of judges, prosecutors, and defense attorneys largely determine their fate. Pretrial decisions can affect the ultimate outcome of a case. If defendants are not released on bail, they might have trouble helping their lawyers prepare arguments and evidence for the defense. In some cases, additional pretrial decisions must be made about the defendant's mental competence. Defendants found to lack the necessary mental competence to stand trial might never be convicted of a crime, even in homicide cases, yet they might still spend years confined in a state institution.

Whether or not to perform a pretrial competency evaluation is one key decision that can affect the defendant's ultimate fate. Important decisions take place in several other pretrial processes as well. These processes include formal events, such as preliminary hearings to determine if enough evidence exists to pursue criminal charges, and informal interactions, such as plea bargaining discussions that might resolve the case prior to trial.

In this chapter, we examine courts, the setting in which criminal defendants' cases are processed. We look at judges and their important role in criminal cases. In particular, we look at pretrial processes that help to determine the fates of criminal defendants.

QUESTIONS for INQUIRY

- What is the structure of the American court system?
- What qualities are desired in a judge, and how are judges chosen?
- How does the bail system work, and how is bail set?

The Structure of American Courts

As we have seen, the United States has a dual court system. Separate federal and state court systems handle matters from throughout the nation. Other countries have a single national court system, but American rules and traditions permit states to create their own court systems to handle most legal matters, including most crimes.

The federal courts oversee a limited range of criminal cases. For example, they deal with people accused of violating the criminal laws of the national government. Counterfeiting, kidnapping, smuggling, and drug trafficking are examples of federal crimes. But such cases account for only a small portion of the criminal cases that pass through American courts each year. For every felony conviction in federal courts, there are more than 20 felony convictions in state courts, because most crimes are defined by state laws (BJS, 2002e). This disparity may grow wider as federal law enforcement agencies increasingly emphasize antiterrorism activities rather than traditional crime-control investigations. The gap is even greater for misdemeanors, because state courts bear primary responsibility for processing the lesser offenses, such as disorderly conduct, that arise on a daily basis.

The Mississippi Supreme Court provides an example of a state's highest court; see http://www.mssc.state.ms.us.

State supreme courts monitor the decisions of lower courts within their own states by interpreting state constitutions and statutes. The U.S. Supreme Court oversees both court systems by interpreting the U.S. Constitution, which protects the rights of defendants in federal and state criminal cases.

The complexity and coordination issues that the country's decentralized courts face are compounded by a third court system that operates in several states. Native Americans have tribal courts, whose authority is endorsed by congressional statutes and Supreme Court decisions, with **jurisdiction** over their own people on tribal land. These tribal courts permit Native American judges to apply their people's cultural values in resolving civil lawsuits and processing certain criminal offenses (Vicenti, 1995).

Both the federal and state court systems have trial and appellate courts. There are three levels of courts: **appellate courts, trial courts of general jurisdiction,** and **trial courts of limited jurisdiction.**

Cases begin in a trial court, which handles determinations of guilt and sentencing. Trial courts of limited jurisdiction handle only misdemeanors and lawsuits for small amounts of money. Felony cases and all other civil lawsuits are heard in trial courts of general jurisdiction. These are the courts in which jury

jurisdiction
The geographic territory or legal boundaries within which control may be exercised; the range of a court's authority.

appellate courts
Courts that do not try criminal cases but hear appeals of decisions of lower courts.

trial courts of general jurisdiction
Criminal courts with jurisdiction over all offenses, including felonies. In some states these courts also hear appeals.

trial courts of limited jurisdiction
Criminal courts with trial jurisdiction over misdemeanor cases and preliminary matters in felony cases. Sometimes these courts hold felony trials that may result in penalties below a specified limit.

The Supreme Court of the United States has the final word on questions concerning interpretations of the Constitution.

trials take place and judges impose prison sentences. All federal cases begin in the general jurisdiction trial courts, the U.S. District Courts.

Cases move to intermediate appellate courts if defendants claim that errors by police or the trial court contributed to their convictions. Further appeals can be filed with a state supreme court or the U.S. Supreme Court, depending on which court system the case is in and what kind of legal argument is being made. All states have courts of last resort (usually called "state supreme courts"), and all but a few have an intermediate level appellate court (usually called "courts of appeals"). In the federal system, the U.S. Supreme Court is the court of last resort, and the U.S. Circuit Courts of Appeals are the intermediate appellate courts.

Although the basic, three-tiered structure operates throughout the United States, the number of courts, their names, and their specific functions vary widely. For example, the federal system has no trial courts of limited jurisdiction. In state systems, 13,000 trial courts of limited jurisdiction handle traffic cases, small claims, misdemeanors, and other less serious matters. These courts handle 90 percent of all criminal cases. The federal system begins with the U.S. District Courts, its trial courts of general jurisdiction. In the states, these courts have a variety of names (circuit, district, superior, and others) and are reserved for felony cases or substantial lawsuits. These are the courts in which trials take place, judges rule on evidence, and juries issue verdicts. Figure 9.1 shows the basic structure of the dual court system.

Some states have reformed their court systems by simplifying the number and types of courts, while others still support a confusing assortment of lower courts. Figure 9.2 contrasts the reformed court structure of Alaska with Georgia's unreformed system. Both follow the three-tiered model, but Georgia has more courts and a more complex system for determining which court will handle which kind of case.

American trial courts are highly decentralized. Local political influences and community values affect the courts in many ways. Local officials determine their

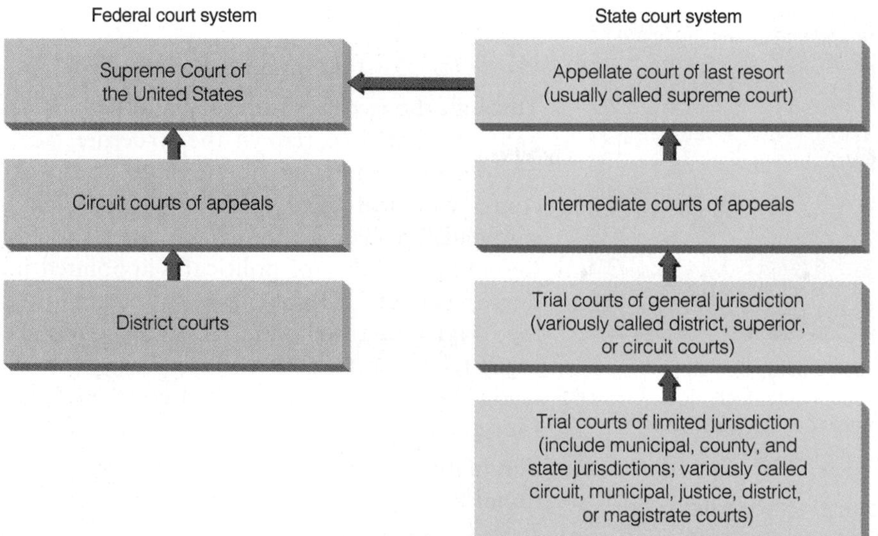

Figure 9.1
The dual court system of the United States and routes of appeal
Whether a case enters through the federal or state court system depends upon which law has been broken. The right of appeal to a higher court exists in either system.

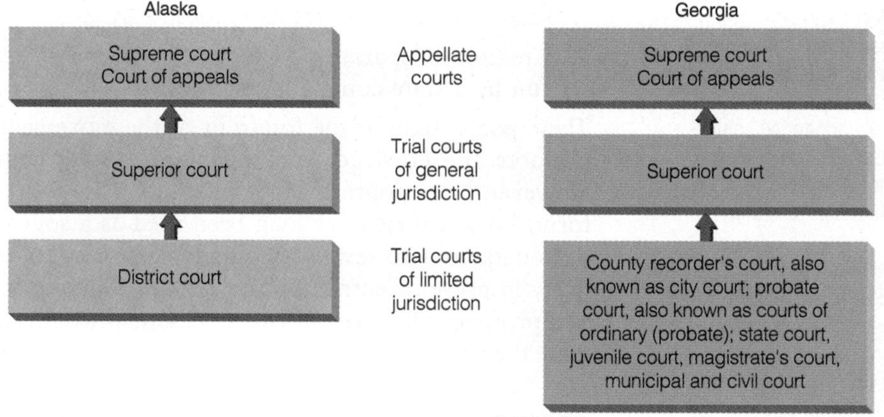

Source: National Center for State Courts, *State Court Caseload Statistics: Annual Report* (Williamsburg, Va.: National Center for State Courts, 1989), 185, 194.

Figure 9.2
Court structures of Alaska (reformed) and Georgia (unreformed)
Reformers have called on states to reduce the number of courts, standardize their names, and clarify their jurisdictions.

resources, residents make up the staff, and operations are managed so as to fit community needs. Only in a few small states is the court system organized on a statewide basis, with a central administration and state funding. In most of the country, the criminal courts operate under the state penal code but are staffed, managed, and financed by county or city government. The federal courts, by contrast, have central administration and funding, although judges in each district help to shape their own courts' practices and procedures.

Lower courts, especially at the state level, do not always display the dignity and formal procedures of general jurisdiction trial courts and appellate courts. They are not necessarily courts of record, which keep a detailed account of proceedings. Instead, they may function rather informally. In most urban areas, seemingly endless numbers of people are processed by these courts, and each defendant's "day in court" usually lasts only a few minutes.

This informality may bother the public, who expect their local courts to adhere to the standards that reflect American values of justice. Many people are critical when the courts do not meet these ideals (see "What Americans Think"). Other Americans, however, have volunteered their time in an effort to make courts more effective. As you read the Doing Your Part box (page 278) about court-appointed special advocates, think about how these volunteers may affect courts and criminal justice.

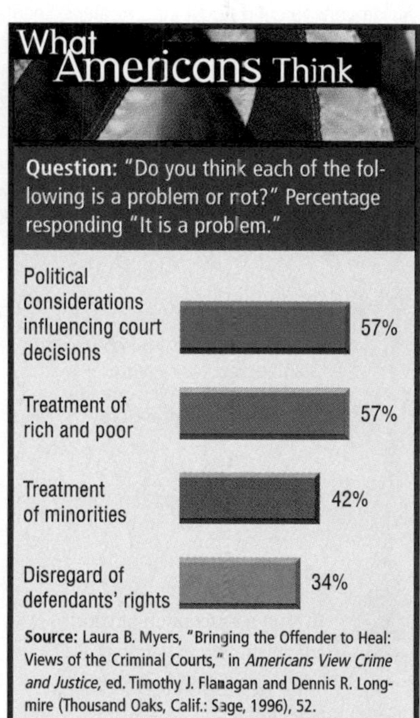

Source: Laura B. Myers, "Bringing the Offender to Heal: Views of the Criminal Courts," in *Americans View Crime and Justice*, ed. Timothy J. Flanagan and Dennis R. Longmire (Thousand Oaks, Calif.: Sage, 1996), 52.

Court-Appointed Special Advocates

Because courts are institutions operated by trained professionals with special expertise in law, imagining how the average citizen can become involved and make a contribution is challenging. Some citizens are summoned to court to serve as jurors, but few others have contact with courts unless they are brought into a case as a defendant, witness, or victim. There is, however, a little known but growing program that permits citizens to make a contribution: CASA, which stands for court-appointed special advocates.

In Boston, Massachusetts, Joanne Beauchamp received a special award in a "Light of Hope" ceremony at the local courthouse. Along with 100 other people, she volunteered her time to serve in the CASA program of the Suffolk County Juvenile Court Probation Department. As in CASA programs at courthouses throughout the country, she spent several hours every week as a court-appointed advocate for children in child abuse and neglect cases. After receiving training on the law of child abuse and neglect, on interviewing, and on advocacy, she became the advocate for specific children. The CASA volunteer advances the best interests of each child by interviewing teachers, foster parents, and others; monitoring compliance with court orders; facilitating contacts with social services agencies; and reporting to the court on the status of the child. About 52,000 CASA volunteers in more than 900 communities serve throughout the nation.

Does CASA give volunteers the opportunity to affect the criminal justice system? This is a valid question because CASA programs are typically connected not to criminal cases per se but to family courts or probate courts that have jurisdiction over child custody, parental rights, and related matters. However, CASA volunteers clearly do contribute to the criminal justice system. First, they are the "eyes and ears" of the court in supervising the child's best interests. Thus they may discover information about criminal offenses involving child abuse and neglect. Second, by attempting to protect abused and neglected children, these volunteers try to ensure a better life for them. Hopefully this will help some children to avoid influences and contexts that might lead them to commit crimes later in life.

Sources: Susan W. Miller, "Career Counselor," *Los Angeles Times,* June 9, 2002 (http://www.latimes.com); "SB Child Advocate Honored at 'Light of Hope' Ceremony," *South Boston Online,* May 2000 (http://www.southbostononline.com).

For more information on court-appointed special advocates, see the national CASA Web site at http://www.nationalcasa.org.

Effective Management of the State Courts

Through the twentieth century and beyond, many have attempted to reform the structure, administration, and financing of the state courts so the courts can deal more effectively with their huge caseloads. Problems with inadequate resources and the uneven quality of politically appointed judges hurt the courts' effectiveness, but people often see the fragmented structure of state courts as the biggest barrier to justice. Proposed solutions include the creation of a unified court system with four goals:

1. Eliminating overlapping and conflicting jurisdictional boundaries.
2. Creating a hierarchical and centralized court structure with administrative responsibility held by a chief justice and a court of last resort.
3. Having the courts funded by state government instead of local counties and cities.
4. Creating a separate civil service personnel system run by a state court administrator.

These goals stand at the forefront of the movement to promote the efficiency and fairness of state courts. However, local political interests often resist court reform. Local courts have long been used as a source of patronage jobs to reward people loyal to the political party in power. Centralization of court administration and professionalization of court personnel would eliminate the opportunities to use court jobs in this manner.

check point

1. What is the dual court system?
2. What different categories of courts exist within each court system?
3. What does it mean for courts to be decentralized?
4. What are the main goals of advocates of judicial reform?

(Answers are at the end of the chapter.)

To read a description of court administration in Vermont, visit http://www.state.vt.us/courts/admin.htm.

To Be a Judge

People tend to see judges as the most powerful actors in the criminal justice process. Their rulings and sentencing decisions influence the actions of police, defense attorneys, and prosecutors. If judges treat certain crimes lightly, for example, police and prosecutors may be less inclined to arrest and prosecute people who commit those offenses. Although judges are thought of primarily in connection with trials, they do some of their work—such as signing warrants, setting bail, arraigning defendants, accepting guilty pleas, and scheduling cases—outside the formal trial process.

More than any other person in the system, the judge is expected to embody justice, ensuring the defendant's right to due process and fair treatment. The prosecutor and the defense attorney each represent a "side" in a criminal case. By contrast, the judge's black robe and gavel are symbols of impartiality. Both within and outside the courthouse, the judge is supposed to act according to a well-defined role. Judges are expected to make careful, consistent decisions that uphold the ideal of equal justice for all citizens.

Who Becomes a Judge?

In U.S. society, the position of judge, even at the lowest level of the judicial hierarchy, carries a high status. Many lawyers take a significant cut in pay to assume a position on the bench. Public service, political power, and prestige in the community may matter more than wealth to those who aspire to the judiciary. The ability to control one's own work schedule is an additional attraction for lawyers interested in becoming judges. Unlike private practice attorneys, who often work in excess of 40 hours per week preparing cases and counseling clients, judges can usually control their own working hours and schedules. Although judges face heavy caseloads, they frequently decide for themselves when to go home at the end of the workday.

Historically, the vast majority of judges have been white men with strong political connections. Women and members of minority groups had few opportunities to enter the legal profession prior to the 1960s and thus were seldom considered for judgeships. By the late twentieth century, political factors in many cities dictated that judges be drawn from specific racial, religious, and ethnic groups. One study found that 3.6 percent of state court judges were black, most of them serving in the lower criminal courts (Graham, 1995:219). Comparing the racial and ethnic makeup of the judiciary with that of the defendants in urban courts raises many questions. Will people believe that decisions about guilt and punishment are being made in an unfair manner if middle-aged white men have nearly all the power to make judgments about people from other segments of society? Will people think that punishment is being imposed on behalf of a privileged segment of society rather than on behalf of the entire, diverse, U.S. society?

Dick Blume/The Image Works

Like all judges, the Honorable Sandra Townes, Syracuse City Court, is expected to "embody justice," ensuring that the right to due process is respected and that defendants are treated fairly.

Within these questions lurks an issue of American values. Americans often claim that equality, fairness, and equal opportunity are important values and, indeed, the Equal Protection Clause in the Fourteenth Amendment of the Constitution demonstrates a formal commitment to use law to combat discrimination. However, the political connections necessary to gain judgeships continue to disadvantage women and members of racial minority groups in many communities. Because judges symbolize the law as well as make important decisions about law, the lack of diversity in the judiciary provides a visible contrast with American values related to equal opportunity.

check point

5. What is the image of the judge in the public's eye?
6. Why might it be important for judges to represent different segments of society?

Functions of the Judge

While people usually think that the judge's job is to preside at trials, in reality the work of most judges extends to all aspects of the judicial process. Defendants see a judge whenever decisions about their future are being made: when bail is set,

Figure 9.3 **Actions of a trial court judge in processing a felony case**
Throughout the process, the judge ensures that legal standards are upheld; he or she maintains courtroom decorum, protects the rights of the accused, meets the requirement of a speedy trial, and ensures that case records are maintained properly.

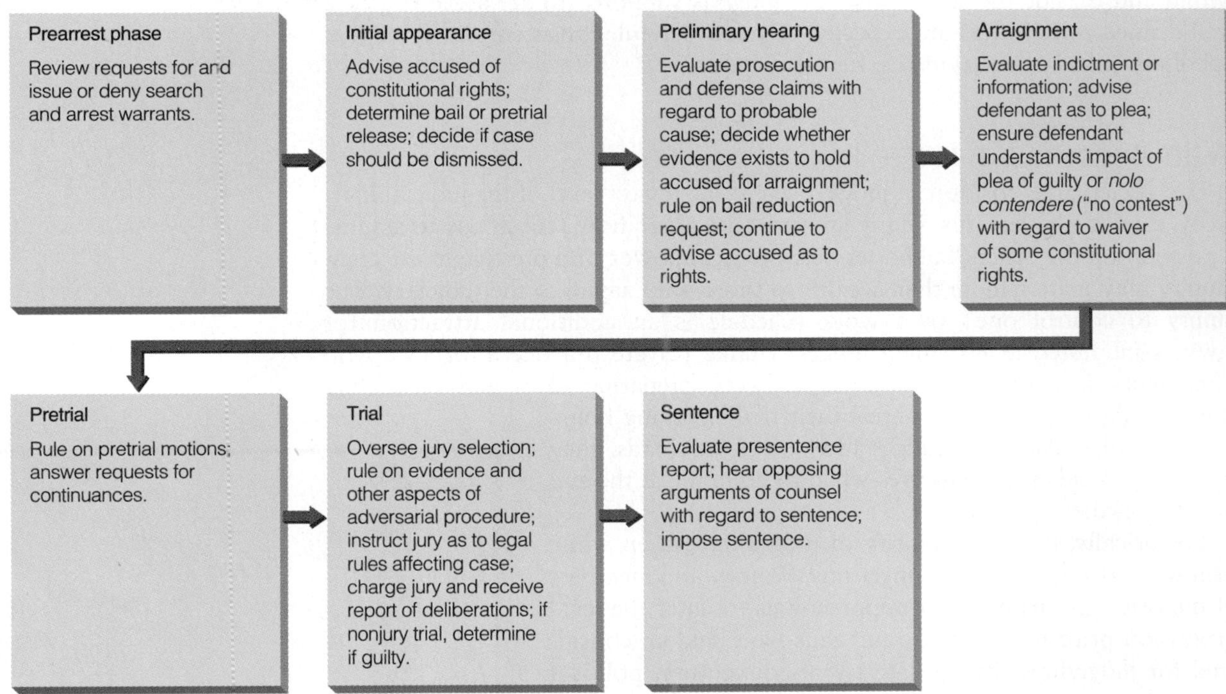

pretrial motions are made, guilty pleas are accepted, a trial is conducted, a sentence is pronounced, and appeals are filed (see Figure 9.3). However, judges also perform administrative tasks outside the courtroom. Judges have three major roles: adjudicator, negotiator, and administrator.

Adjudicator

Judges must assume a neutral stance in overseeing the contest between the prosecution and the defense. They must apply the law so that the rights of the accused are upheld in decisions about detention, plea, trial, and sentence. Judges have a certain amount of discretion in performing these tasks—for example, in setting bail—but they must do so according to law. They must avoid any conduct that could appear biased (Goldschmidt and Shaman, 1996).

Negotiator

Many decisions that determine the fates of defendants are made outside of public view, in the judge's private chambers. These decisions are reached through negotiations between prosecutors and defense attorneys about plea bargains, sentencing, and bail conditions. Judges spend much of their time in their chambers talking with prosecutors and defense attorneys. They often encourage the parties to work out a guilty plea or agree to proceed in a certain way. The judge sometimes acts as referee, keeping both sides on track in accordance with the law. Sometimes the judge takes a more active part in the negotiations, suggesting terms for an agreement or even pressuring one side to accept an agreement.

The National District Attorneys Association, an organization for prosecutors, presents a particular viewpoint on the role of judges in plea negotiations at http://www.attorneygeneral.org/plea.html. Does this viewpoint accurately recognize the judge's role as negotiator?

Administrator

A seldom-recognized function of most judges is managing the courthouse. In urban areas, professional court administrators rather than judges may actually direct the people who keep records, schedule cases, and do the many other jobs that keep a system functioning. But even then, judges are in charge of their own courtroom and staff. In rural areas, where professional court administrators are

The Image of Justice

During an arraignment in New York for a defendant charged with assaulting his wife, the judge reportedly said, "What's wrong with that? You've got to keep them in line once in a while." When authorities acted to remove the judge from office, the judge's lawyer said that the judge makes lighthearted comments from the bench but does not misuse his position.

In California, a judge reportedly indicated to a good-looking defendant that other inmates at the prison would find him attractive. The judge also allegedly called a prosecutor in a drunken-driving case a "hypocrite" who was in all probability guilty of the same offense as the defendant. The judge's attorney claimed that the comments were taken out of context when a complaint was filed with the state's Commission on Judicial Performance.

Do the statements reportedly made by these judges harm the image of the courts? If so, how? If these statements are improper, what should happen to judges who say such things? If the judges apologize, should they be forgiven and receive another opportunity to behave in a proper manner? Is there any way to make sure that judges always act according to the proper image of their judicial office?

Sources: Drawn from "Court Upholds Removal of Rockland Judge," *New York Times*, March 31, 1999 (Metro News); Richard Marosi, "Hard-Line Judge Is Being Judged Herself," *Los Angeles Times*, May 7, 1999, p. B1.

Researching the Internet

To read about ethical rules for judges, see the Code of Judicial Conduct for judges in Illinois at http://www.state.il.us/jib/conduct.htm.

not usually employed, the judge's administrative tasks may be more burdensome, including responsibility for labor relations, budgeting, and maintenance of the courthouse building.

As administrators, all judges must deal with political actors such as county commissioners, legislators, and members of the state executive bureaucracy. Chief judges in large courts sometimes also use their administrative powers to push other judges to cooperate in advancing the court's goals of processing cases efficiently (Jacob, 1973). For judges whose training as lawyers focused on courtroom advocacy skills, managing a complex organization with a sizable budget and many employees can be a major challenge (C. E. Smith and Feldman, 2001).

How to Become a Judge

The quality of justice depends to a great extent on the quality of those who make decisions about guilt and punishment. Because judges have the power to deprive a citizen of his or her liberty through a prison sentence, judges should be thoughtful, fair, and impartial. The character and experience of those appointed to federal courts and state appellate courts are examined closely (Goldman and Slotnick, 1999). Trial judges in state criminal courts undergo less scrutiny. Ironically, it is these lower courts that shape the public's image of a trial judge, because this is where citizens have the most contact with judges. When a judge is rude or hasty or allows the courtroom to become noisy and crowded, the public may lose confidence in the fairness and effectiveness of the criminal justice process (see the Close Up box).

Five methods are used to select state trial court judges: gubernatorial appointment, legislative selection, merit selection, **nonpartisan election,** and **partisan election.** Some states combine these methods; for example, in Pennsylvania a judge is initially elected by partisan election, but then at the end of the term there is a nonpartisan election (retention) for a second term. Table 9.1 shows the method used in each of the states. All the methods bring up persistent concerns about the desired qualities of judges.

nonpartisan election
An election in which candidates' party affiliations are not listed on the ballot.

partisan election
An election in which candidates openly endorsed by political parties are presented to voters for selection.

Selection by public voting occurs in more than half the states and has long been part of this nation's tradition. This method of judicial selection embodies the underlying American value of democracy, because it permits the citizens to

Table 9.1 Methods used by states to select judges

States use different methods to select judges. Note that many judges are initially appointed to fill a vacancy, giving them an advantage if they must run for election at a later date.

Partisan Election	Nonpartisan Election	Gubernatorial Appointment	Legislative Selection	Merit Selection
Alabama	Arizona (some trial courts)	Connecticut	Rhode Island (appellate)	Alaska
Arkansas	California (trial)	Delaware	South Carolina	Arizona (appellate)
Illinois	Florida (trial)	Maine	Virginia	California (appellate)
Indiana (trial)	Georgia	Massachusetts		Colorado
Mississippi	Idaho	New Hampshire		Florida (appellate)
New Mexico (retention)	Kentucky	New Jersey		Hawaii
New York (trial)	Louisiana	New York (appellate)		Indiana (appellate)
North Carolina	Michigan	Rhode Island (trial)		Iowa
Pennsylvania (initial)	Minnesota			Kansas
Tennessee (supreme and trial)	Montana			Maryland
Texas	Nevada			Missouri
West Virginia	North Dakota			Nebraska
	Ohio			New Mexico (initial)
	Oklahoma (trial)			Oklahoma (appellate)
	Oregon			South Dakota (appellate)
	Pennsylvania (retention)			Tennessee (intermediate appellate)
	South Dakota (trial)			Utah
	Washington			Vermont
	Wisconsin			Wyoming

Source: *The Book of the States, 1998–1999 Edition* (Lexington, Ky.: Council of State Governments, 1998), 135–37.

control the choice of individuals who will be given the power to make decisions in civil and criminal cases. The fulfillment of this American value also helps to ensure that judges remain connected to the community and demonstrate sensitivity to the community's priorities and concerns. The American value of democracy may, however, have detrimental consequences in the judiciary if it pressures judges to follow a community's prejudices rather than make independent decisions using their best judgment in each case.

When lawyers are first elected to serve as judges, they obviously have no prior experience in deciding cases and supervising courthouse operations. Working as a lawyer differs a great deal from working as a judge, especially in the American **adversarial system,** in which lawyers serve as advocates for one party in each case. As a result, judges must learn "on the job." This method seems to counter the notion that judges are trained to "find the law" and apply neutral judgments (M. G. Hall, 1995). In Europe, by contrast, prospective judges receive special training in law school to become professional judges in what is called an **inquisitorial system.** These trained judges must serve as assistant judges and lower court judges before they can become judges in general trial and appellate courts (Provine, 1996).

adversarial system
Basis for the American legal system in which a passive judge and jury seek to find the truth by listening to opposing attorneys who vigorously advocate on behalf of their respective sides.

inquisitorial system
Basis for legal systems in Europe in which the judge takes an active role in investigating the case and asking questions of witnesses in court.

Organizations such as the League of Women Voters often try to make information about judges available to help voters make informed choices. See the link for the Ohio league's Judicial Independence Project at http://www.lwvohio.org.

Election campaigns for lower-court judgeships traditionally tended to be low-key contests marked by little controversy. Usually only a small portion of the voters participate, judgeships are not prominent on the ballot, and ethical considerations constrain candidates from discussing controversial issues. Recent research reveals, however, that even lower-level judicial races are becoming more competitive as candidates raise money and seek connections with interest groups (Abbe and Herrnson, 2002). In addition, a 2002 decision by the U.S. Supreme Court invalidated Minnesota's ethics rule that forbade judicial candidates from announcing their views on disputed legal or political issues (*Republican Party of Minnesota v. White*). According to the Supreme Court, such rules violate candidates' First Amendment right to freedom of speech. The Court's decision will also affect similar rules in other states. Thus future judicial elections might become as controversial and combative as elections for other public offices, as candidate attack each other and openly seek to attract voters to their announced positions on issues. Observers interested in preserving the integrity of courts worry that wide-open elections will ultimately diminish the image and effectiveness of judges, who may begin to look more and more like partisan politicians.

Although the popular election of trial judges may be part of America's political heritage, until recently voters paid little attention to these elections. In many cities, judgeships are the fuel for the party machine. Because of the honors and material rewards of a place on the bench, political parties get support—in the form of donated time and money—from attorneys seeking a judgeship. Parties also want judgeships to be elected posts because they can use courthouse staff positions to reward party loyalists. When a party member wins a judgeship, courthouse jobs may become available for campaign workers because clerks, bailiffs, and secretaries are chosen by the judge.

By contrast, elections for seats on state supreme courts frequently receive statewide media attention. Because of the importance of state supreme courts as policy-making institutions, political parties and interest groups often devote substantial resources to the election campaigns of their preferred candidates. When organized interests contribute tens of thousands of dollars to judicial campaigns, questions sometimes arise about whether the successful candidates who received those contributions will favor the interests of their donors when they begin to decide court cases (Champagne and Cheek, 1996; Reid, 1996).

Some states have tried to reduce the influence of political parties in the selection of judges while still allowing voters to select judges. These states hold nonpartisan elections in which only the names of candidates, and not their party affiliations, are on the ballot. However, political parties are often strongly involved in such elections. In Ohio, for example, the Republican and Democratic political parties hold their own primary elections to choose the judicial candidates whose names will go on the nonpartisan ballot for the general election (Felice and Kilwein, 1992). In other states, party organizations raise and spend money on behalf of candidates in nonpartisan elections. When candidates' party affiliations are not listed on the ballot, voters may not know which party is supporting which candidate, especially in low-visibility elections for local trial judgeships, which do not receive the same level of media attention as elections for state supreme court seats (Lovrich and Sheldon, 1994).

Public opinion data show that Americans express concern about the influence of politics on judges, especially with respect to elected judges (see "What Americans Think"). If so many Americans are concerned about judges' involvement in political campaigns, why do so many states still rely on elections to select judges?

Merit selection, which combines appointment and election, was first used in Missouri in 1940 and has since spread to other states. When a judgeship becomes vacant, a nominating commission made up of citizens and attorneys evaluates potential appointees and sends the governor the names of three candidates, from which the replacement is chosen. After one year, a referendum is held to decide whether the judge will stay on the bench. The ballot asks, "Shall Judge X remain in office?" The judge who wins a majority vote serves out the term and can then be listed on the ballot at the next election.

Merit selection is designed to remove politics from the selection of judges and to allow the voters to unseat judges. However, studies have shown that voters in merit selection states have removed relatively few judges (W. K. Hall and Aspin, 1987). Even so, interest groups sometimes seize the opportunity to mount publicity campaigns during retention elections in order to turn out judges with whom they disagree on a single issue or to open an important court seat so that a like-minded governor can appoint a sympathetic replacement. It may be difficult for judges to counteract a barrage of inflammatory television commercials focusing on a single issue such as capital punishment (Reid, 2000). If merit-selected judges

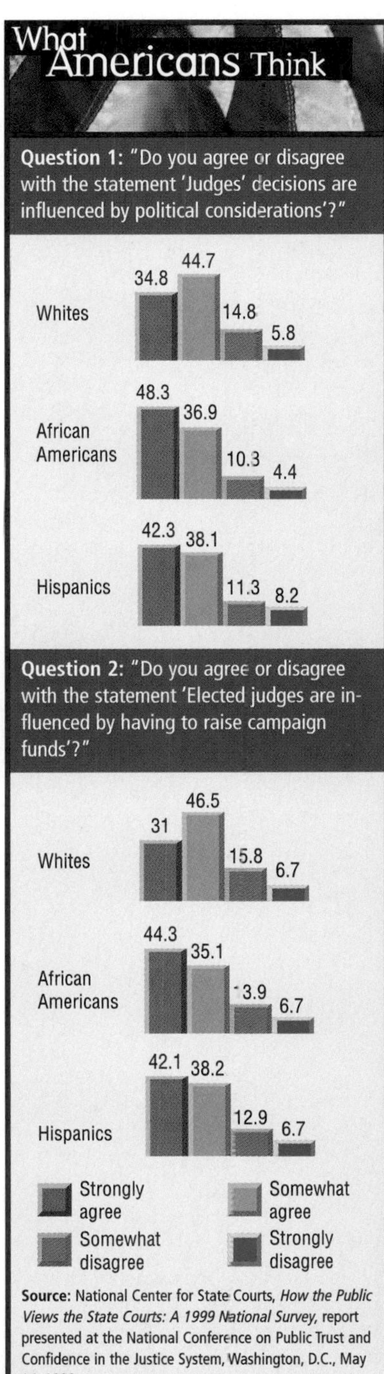

Source: National Center for State Courts, *How the Public Views the State Courts: A 1999 National Survey*, report presented at the National Conference on Public Trust and Confidence in the Justice System, Washington, D.C., May 14, 1999.

merit selection
A reform plan by which judges are nominated by a commission and appointed by the governor for a given period. When the term expires, the voters are asked to approve or disapprove the judge for a succeeding term. If the judge is disapproved, the committee nominates a successor for the governor's appointment.

feel intimidated by interest groups that might threaten their jobs at the next retention election, the independence of the judiciary will be diminished.

Despite the support of bar associations, merit selection has not gone unchallenged. Although party politics may have been removed, some argue that it has been replaced by politics within the legal profession. Many lawyers see the system as favoring "blue bloods" (high-status attorneys with ties to corporations) over the "little guy" (R. A. Watson and Downing, 1969).

check point

7. What are judges' main functions?
8. Why do political parties often prefer that judges be elected?
9. What are the steps in the merit selection process?

From Arrest to Trial or Plea

At each stage of the pretrial process, key decisions are made that move some defendants to the next stage of the process and filter others out of the system. An innocent person could be arrested based on mistaken identification or misinterpreted evidence (Huff, 2002; Kridler, 1999). However, pretrial processes are meant to force prosecutors and judges to review the available evidence and dismiss unnecessary or unjust charges. These processes are based on the American value of due process. Americans believe that people should be entitled to a series of hearings and other procedural steps in which their guilt is proven before they should be subjected to punishments such as the loss of liberty through incarceration. Although due process is an important value and is explicitly stated as a right in two different constitutional amendments, the Fifth and the Fourteenth, it can collide with Americans' interest in crime control if errors made by officials in carrying out these steps lead to the release of a guilty offender. For example, errors by judges in preliminary hearings or by police officers in lineups or other procedures can lead to the exclusion of evidence as a remedy for a rights violation. Thus due process, like other American values, can create results that undercut other priorities and objectives.

After arrest, the accused is booked at the police station. This process includes taking photographs and fingerprints, which form the basis of the case record. Usually the defendant must be taken to court for the initial appearance within 48 hours of a warrantless arrest. The purpose of this hearing is for the defendant to hear which charges are being pursued in light of the evidence gathered thus far, be advised of his or her rights, and be given the opportunity to post bail. Sometimes a separate bail hearing is scheduled shortly thereafter, especially when a case concerns serious criminal charges. At the initial appearance, the judge also must make sure that probable cause exists to believe that a crime has been committed and that the accused should be prosecuted for the crime.

If the police used an arrest warrant to take the suspect into custody, evidence has already been presented to a judge who believed that it was strong enough to support a finding of probable cause to proceed against the defendant. When an arrest is made without a warrant, the police must at the initial appearance present sufficient evidence to persuade the judge to continue the case against the defendant.

arraignment
The court appearance of an accused person in which the charges are read and the accused, advised by a lawyer, pleads guilty or not guilty.

Often, the first formal meeting between the prosecutor and the defendant's attorney is the **arraignment:** the formal court appearance in which the charges against the defendant are read and the defendant, advised by his or her lawyer, enters a plea of either guilty or not guilty. Most defendants will enter a plea of not guilty, even if they are likely to plead guilty at a later point. This is because, thus far, the prosecutor and defense attorney usually have had little chance to

Spencer Grant/PhotoEdit

"Night stalker" Richard Ramirez, flanked by his attorneys, is arraigned in a Santa Ana, California, court on rape and murder charges. When defendants are thought to pose a threat, they may have their "day in court" from within a wired cage.

discuss a potential plea bargain. The more serious the charges, the more time the prosecutor and defense attorney will likely need to assess the strength of the other side's case. Only then can plea bargaining begin.

At the time of arraignment, prosecutors begin to evaluate the evidence. The lives of the defendants hinge on this screening process, because their fate depends largely on the prosecutor's discretion (Barnes and Kingsnorth, 1996). If the prosecutor believes the case against the defendant is weak, the charges may simply be dropped. Prosecutors do not wish to waste their limited time and resources on cases that will not stand up in court. A prosecutor may also drop charges if the alleged crime is minor, if the defendant is a first offender, or if the prosecutor believes that the few days spent in jail before arraignment are enough punishment for the alleged offense. Jail overcrowding or the need to work on more serious cases can also influence the decision to drop charges. At times, prosecutors in making these decisions might discriminate against the accused because of race, wealth, or some other factor (Crew, 1991), or they might discriminate against certain victims, such as women who are sexually assaulted by an intimate partner or other acquaintance as opposed to a stranger (Spohn and Holleran, 2001). As cases move through the system, prosecutors' decisions to reduce charges for some defendants greatly affect the punishment eventually applied (J. L. Miller and Sloan, 1994). Thus, individual prosecutors play a major role in deciding which defendants will receive criminal punishment. As you read the discussion of community courts in "New Directions in Criminal Justice Policy," think about whether increasing the connections between prosecutors and the community could improve prosecutors' knowledge and decision making about criminal cases.

As Figure 9.4 shows, prosecutors use their decision-making power to filter many cases out of the system. The 100 cases illustrated are typical felony cases. The percentage of cases varies from city to city, depending on such factors as the effectiveness of police investigations and prosecutors' policies about which cases to pursue. For example, nearly half of those arrested did not ultimately face felony prosecutions. A small number of defendants were steered toward diversion programs. A larger number had their cases dismissed for various reasons—including lack of evidence, the minor nature of the charges, or first-time-offender status. Other cases were dismissed by the courts because the police and prosecutors did not present enough evidence to a grand jury or a preliminary hearing to justify moving forward.

Community Courts

Community courts represent an innovation that seeks to bring courts into closer contact with the people that they serve. Courthouses are frequently located in busy downtown commercial areas that are far removed from the daily lives of average citizens and the everyday events, including crimes, that affect their lives. A trip to a courthouse as a juror or witness can be a burdensome and expensive journey to an unfamiliar and intimidating location. As a result, reformers in several cities have sought to locate courts in residential communities and to make those courts more accessible to the public.

Community courts often focus on low-level crimes that occur within the residential communities that they serve. In seeking greater connections with local communities, the community courts often require offenders to compensate neighborhoods through community service work. Thus the punishment keeps the offender connected to the community and provides the community with a tangible benefit as compensation for harms that have occurred. Community courts seek close connections to social service agencies. Ideally, agencies have offices and service providers inside the courthouse itself. As a result, drug treatment, psychological counseling, employment assistance, and other services can be immediately accessible to low-level offenders, and the court can use its authority to pressure those offenders to use these services. Community courts also rely on citizen advisory boards to develop program ideas and provide a continuous link between the judicial professionals and neighborhood people.

In 1998 there was only one community court in the United States. It was located in New York City. Two years later, the idea spread to Portland, Oregon; Hartford, Connecticut; Austin, Texas; and other communities throughout the country.

Source: Eric Lee, *Community Courts: An Evolving Model* (Washington, D.C.: U.S. Department of Justice, Office of Justice Programs, October 2000).

To learn more about community courts in various cities, see http://www.communitycourts.org.

The proportion of cases dropped at the various stages of the pretrial process varies from city to city. In some cities, many cases are dropped before charges are filed. Prosecutors evaluate the facts and evidence and decide which cases are strong enough to carry forward. The others are quickly dismissed. In other cities, formal charges are filed almost automatically on the basis of police reports, but many cases are dismissed when the prosecutor takes the time to examine each defendant's situation closely.

During the pretrial process, defendants are exposed to the informal, assembly-line atmosphere of the lower criminal courts. Often, decisions are quickly made about bail, arraignment, pleas, and the disposition of cases. Moving cases as quickly as possible seems to be the main goal of many judges and attorneys during the pretrial process. Courts throughout the nation face pressures to limit the number of cases going to trial. These pressures may affect the decisions of both judges and prosecutors, as well as the defense attorneys who seek to maintain good relationships with them. American courts often have too little money, too few staff members, and not enough time to give detailed attention to each case, let alone a full trial.

motion
An application to a court requesting that an order be issued to bring about a specified action.

In American courts, the defense uses the pretrial period to its own advantage. Preliminary hearings provide an opportunity for defense attorneys to challenge the prosecution's evidence and make **motions** to the court requesting that an order be issued to bring about a specified action. Through pretrial motions, the defense may try to suppress evidence or learn about the prosecutor's case. The defense attorney making the motion must be able to support the claim being made about improper procedures used in the arrest, the insufficiency of the evidence, or the need for exclusion of evidence. Prosecutors also make motions, especially if they have disagreements with the defense about whether and how defense witnesses will be questioned. Judges may decide motions based on the

Figure 9.4 Typical outcomes of 100 urban felony cases
Prosecutors and judges make crucial decisions during the period before trial or plea. Once cases are bound over for disposition, guilty pleas are many, trials are few, and acquittals are rare.

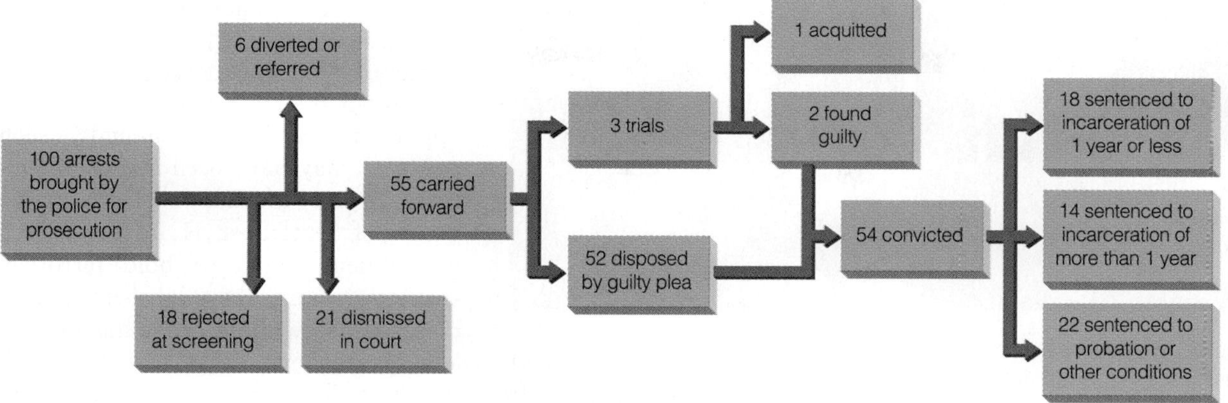

Source: Barbara Boland, Paul Mahanna, and Ronald Stones, *The Prosecution of Felony Arrests, 1988,* Bureau of Justice Statistics (Washington, D.C.: U.S. Government Printing Office, 1992), 2.

written arguments submitted by each side or they may schedule a motion hearing that will permit each attorney to present arguments about whether the motion should be granted. Decisions on motions can significantly affect the outcome of a case, especially if the motion hearing determines whether key pieces of evidence can be used in court against the defendant.

The large number of cases dismissed during pretrial proceedings need not be viewed as a sign of weakness in the system. Instead, one strength of the system is the power of prosecutors and judges to dismiss charges when a conviction would be either unfair or unlikely. A close look at Figure 9.4 shows that the offenses that a prosecutor decides to pursue have a high rate of conviction. Out of 55 typical cases carried forward, 52 will end with a guilty plea and two of the three defendants who had full trials will be convicted. These examples make it clear that the criminal justice system is effective in producing convictions when a prosecutor, with sufficient evidence, pursues a felony prosecution. In addition, recent research indicates that some of the people whose cases were dismissed will actually receive punishment. In the case of repeat offenders, for example, prosecutors may dismiss criminal charges in favor of probation violation charges that lead the offender to serve time in jail or prison despite not being convicted of a new crime (Kingsnorth, MacIntosh, and Sutherland, 2002). So the numbers of offenders punished in the process is actually higher than that indicated by Figure 9.4.

You can read both prosecution and defense motions concerning the admission of evidence in the murder trials of the Menendez brothers, wealthy young men in California who were convicted of murdering their parents, at http://www.courttv.com/casefiles/menendez/documents/.

10. What are the purposes of preliminary hearings, arraignments, and defense motions?
11. Why and how are cases filtered out of the system?

Bail: Pretrial Release

It is often stated that defendants are presumed innocent until proved guilty or until they enter a guilty plea. However, people who are arrested are taken to jail. They are deprived of their freedom and, in many cases, subjected to miserable living conditions while they await the processing of their cases. The idea that people who are presumed innocent can lose their freedom—sometimes for many months—as their cases work their way toward trial clashes with the American values of freedom and liberty. It is not clear how strongly Americans

AP/Andy Dickerman

Five men charged in connection with a double-killing carjacking appear in a Providence, Rhode Island, court for a bail hearing. What should the judge consider in granting or denying release on bail?

are committed to preserving the ideal of freedom for people who have not yet been convicted of crimes. As indicated by one public opinion study (see "What Americans Think"), members of the public may be less concerned than lawyers about the ideal of freedom when it applies to suspected criminals. Such concerns may have been further diminished in the aftermath of the tragic events of September 11, as the federal government began to hold terrorism suspects whom they labeled "enemy combatants" without providing any bail hearing, evidence of guilt, or access to defense attorneys. The outcry about such deprivations of liberty has come from specific civil rights groups and attorneys rather than from the general public.

A conflict is bound to occur between the American value of individual liberty and the reality of keeping some criminal suspects in jail because society must be protected by detaining people who are violent or may try to escape prosecution. However, every person who is charged with a criminal offense need not be detained. Thus, bail and other methods of releasing defendants are used on the condition that the accused will appear in court as required.

bail
An amount of money specified by a judge to be paid as a condition of pretrial release to ensure that the accused will appear in court as required.

Bail is a sum of money or property, specified by the judge, that the defendant must present to the court in order to gain pretrial release. The bail will be forfeited if the defendant does not appear in court as scheduled. Although people are generally entitled to a bail hearing as part of their right to due process, there is no constitutional right to release on bail, nor even a right to have the court set an amount as the condition of release. The Eighth Amendment to the U.S. Constitution forbids excessive bail, and state bail laws are usually designed to prevent discrimination in setting bail. They do not guarantee, however, that all defendants will have a realistic chance of being released before trial (Nagel, 1990).

Because the accused is presumed to be innocent, bail should not be used as punishment. The amount of bail should therefore be high enough to ensure that the defendant appears in court for trial—but no higher. But this is not the only purpose of bail. The community must be protected from further crimes that some defendants might commit while out on bail. Except in the recent cases of suspected terrorists, criminal suspects are entitled to a hearing before they are denied bail or bail is set at such a high level that they are certain to be kept in jail despite the fact that they have not yet been convicted. Congress and some of the states have passed laws that permit preventive detention of defendants when the judge concludes that they pose a threat to others or to the community while awaiting trial.

What Americans Think

Question: "Do you favor allowing the government to hold suspected criminals for more than 48 hours without being charged for a specific crime?"

Public

Oppose	No answer	Favor
68%	1%	30%

Lawyers

Oppose	No answer	Favor
87%	1%	12%

Source: Shmuel Lock, *Crime, Public Opinion, and Civil Liberties* (Westport, Ct.: Praeger, 1999), 193, 217.

The Reality of the Bail System

The reality of the bail system is far from the ideal. The question of bail may arise at the police station, at the initial court appearance in a misdemeanor case, or at the arraignment in most felony cases. For minor offenses, police officers may have a standard list of bail amounts. For serious offenses, a judge sets bail in court. In both cases, those setting bail may have discretion to set differing bail amounts for different suspects, depending on the circumstances of each case. As "A Question of Ethics" illustrates, this discretion creates the risk that officials will deprive some defendants of their freedom unfairly or for improper reasons.

In almost all courts, the amount of bail is based mainly on the judge's view of the seriousness of the crime and of the defendant's record. In part, this emphasis results from a lack of information about the accused. Because bail is typically determined 24–48 hours after an arrest, there is little time to conduct a more thorough assessment. As a result, judges in many communities have developed standard rates: so many dollars for such-and-such an offense. In some cases, a judge may set a high bail if the police or prosecutor want a certain person to be kept off the streets.

Critics of the bail system argue that it discriminates against poor people. Imagine that you have been arrested and have no money. Should you be denied a chance for freedom before trial just because you are poor? What if you have a little money, but if you use it to post bail you will not have any left to hire your own attorney? Professional criminals and the affluent have no trouble making bail; many drug dealers, for instance, can readily make bail and go on dealing while awaiting trial. In contrast, a poor person arrested for a minor violation may spend the pretrial period in jail. Should dangerous, wealthy offenders be allowed out on bail while nonviolent, poor suspects are locked up?

The problems for poor defendants are compounded by the lack of a constitutional right to representation by an attorney at bail hearings (Colbert, 1998). Defendants who cannot afford to hire an attorney may have no one to make arguments on their behalf at the bail hearing. Thus the prosecutor's arguments in favor of a high bail or a denial of bail may be the only effective arguments presented to the judge. For many poor defendants, bail is set before an attorney has been appointed to represent them in the preparation of their defense.

According to a study of felony defendants in the nation's most populous counties, 64 percent were released before disposition of their cases, 29 percent could not make bail, and 7 percent were detained without bail (Reaves, 2001). Among those who gained release, one-third had bail set at less than $5,000. Figure 9.5 shows the amounts of bail set for various types of felony offenses. Those who cannot make bail must remain in jail awaiting trial, unless they can obtain enough money to pay a bail bondsman's fee. Given the length of time between arraignment and trial in most courts and the hardships of pretrial detention, defendants in many cities depend on bondsmen. In 1998, 16,000 felony suspects in the 75 largest counties could not make bail or use the services of a bail bondsman to gain release (Reaves, 2001).

Figure 9.5

Bail amounts for felony defendants by type of offense

The amount of bail varies according to the offense.

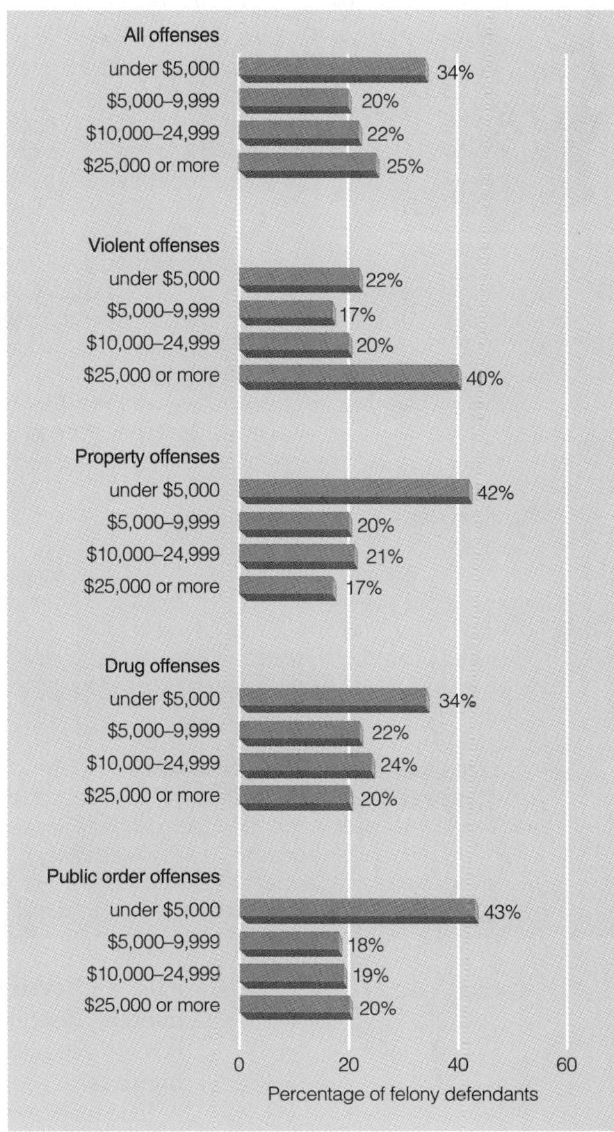

Source: Brian A. Reaves, *Felony Defendants in Large Urban Counties, 1998: State Court Processing Statistics* (Washington, D.C.: Bureau of Justice Statistics, U.S. Government Printing Office, November 2001), 18.

Bail Bondsmen

The bail bondsman is a key figure in the bail process. Bail bondsmen (or women) are private businesspeople who loan money to defendants who lack the money to make bail. They are licensed by the state and choose their own clients. In exchange for a fee, which may be 5 to 10 percent of the bail amount, the bondsman will put up the money (or property) to gain the defendant's release. Again, bondsmen are not obliged to provide bail money for every defendant who seeks to use their services. Instead, they decide which defendants are likely to return for court appearances. If the defendant skips town, the bondsman's money is forfeited.

Bondsmen may build relationships with police officers and jailers to obtain referrals. Many defendants may not know whom to call for help in making bail, and officers can steer them to a particular bondsman. This can lead to corruption if a bondsman pays a jailer or police officer to make such referrals. Moreover, these relationships can lead to improper cooperation, such as a bondsman

For the most recent statistics on pretrial release and detention, see http://www.ojp.usdoj.gov/bjs/pretrial.htm.

One national organization of bail bondsmen is the Professional Bail Agents of the United States. Visit their Web site at http://www.pbus.com.

You can read Connecticut's licensing rules and other regulations for bail bondsmen and bail enforcement agents at http://www.state.ct.us/dps/SLFU/.

Jim Rourke stood in front of Desk Sergeant Jack Sweeney at the Redwood City Police Station. Rourke was handcuffed and waiting to be booked. He had been caught by Officers Davis and Timulty outside a building in a wealthy neighborhood, soon after the police had received a 911 call from a resident reporting that someone had entered her apartment. Rourke was seen loitering in the alley with a flashlight in his back pocket. He was known to the police because of his prior arrests for entering houses at night. As Timulty held Rourke, Davis went around behind the desk and spoke to Sergeant Sweeney in a soft voice.

"I know we don't have much on this guy, but he's a bad egg and I bet he was the one who was in that apartment. The least we can do is set the bail high enough so that he'll know we are on to him."

"Davis, you know I can't do that. You've got nothing on him," said Sweeney.

"But how's it going to look in the press if we just let him go? You know the type of people who live in Littleton Manor. There will be hell to pay if it gets out that this guy just walks."

"Well, he did have the flashlight. . . . I suppose that's enough to make him a suspect. Let's make the bail $1,000. I know he can't make that."

→ What is the purpose of bail? Was the amount set appropriate in this instance? Should Rourke be held merely because of the suspicion that he might have entered the apartment? Do you think the case would have been handled in the same way if the call had come from a poorer part of town?

refusing to help a particular defendant if the police would like to see that defendant remain in jail.

The role of the bondsman poses other ethical questions as well. Is it proper for a private, profit-seeking businessperson to decide who will gain pretrial release and to profit from a person who is "presumed innocent" but is threatened with the loss of his or her freedom? If charges are dropped or a defendant is acquitted, the bondsman still keeps the fee that was paid to make bail. This can be especially costly to poor defendants. Although judges set the bail amount, the bondsmen often actually decide whether certain defendants will gain pretrial release.

Despite the problems posed by their role, bondsmen may benefit the criminal justice system. Although bondsmen act in their own interest, they contribute to the smooth processing of cases (Dill, 1975). For example, defendants who fail to appear for scheduled court appearances often do so because of forgetfulness and confusion about when and where they must appear. Courthouses in large cities are huge bureaucracies in which changes in the times and locations of hearings are not always communicated to defendants. Bondsmen can help by reminding defendants about court dates, calling defendants' relatives to make sure that the defendant will arrive on time, and warning defendants about the penalties for failing to appear.

Bounty hunters or bail enforcement agents hired by bondsmen find many of the defendants who have skipped out on bail. These independent operators have caused many problems. In highly publicized cases, bounty hunters have broken into the wrong homes, kidnapped innocent people mistaken for wanted criminals, and even shot and killed innocent bystanders (Drimmer, 1997). Bounty hunters' disregard for people's rights and public safety has led to calls for new laws to regulate the activities of bondsmen and the people they hire to hunt for fugitives.

The justice system may benefit in some ways from the activities of bondsmen. However, court and law enforcement officials could provide the same benefits as well or better if they had the resources, time, and interest to make sure that released defendants return to court. If all courts had pretrial services offices such as those in the federal courts, defendants could be monitored and reminded to return to court without the risks of discrimination and corruption associated with the use of bail bondsmen (Carr, 1993; Marsh, 1994; Peoples, 1995). See "New Directions in Criminal Justice Policy" for more on alternatives to bondsmen.

Go to the Public Policy feature on the American System of Criminal Justice CD to learn more about the issues surrounding bounty hunters.

Setting Bail

When the police set bail at the station house for minor offenses, they usually use a standard amount for a particular charge. By contrast, when a judge sets bail, the amount of bail and conditions of release stem from interactions among the judge, prosecutor, and defense attorney, who discuss the defendant's personal qualities and prior record. The prosecutor may stress the seriousness of the crime, the defendant's record, and negative personal characteristics. The defense attorney, if one has been hired or appointed at this point, may stress the defendant's good job, family responsibilities, and place in the community. Like other aspects of bail, these factors may favor affluent defendants over the poor, the un-

Bail by Credit Card and ATM

Many observers are critical of the role of bail bondsmen. Critics fear that bail bondsmen will pay bribes to police officers and jailers to steer business their way. In addition, bail bondsmen might do favors for police officers and prosecutors by denying their services to defendants that these officials would rather have stay in jail. Two counties in California experimented with techniques that bypass bail bondsmen by permitting the installation of an interactive kiosk as a means to make bail. Minutes after being booked, arrestees can slide their credit card through a device that looks like an ATM (automatic teller machine). The machine will charge the bail amount to the credit card. When the defendant returns for court appearances, the amount is recredited to the card minus a 10 percent fee. After the program's first year in the San Luis Obispo Sheriff's Department, there were 178 approved transactions with an average amount of $550.

Because the machine is operated by private businesses, the financial impact on defendants is the same as paying a bail bondsman. Only defendants with sufficient credit on a credit card can make use of the kiosk, and they are charged the same fee typically charged by bail bondsmen. However, the use of the machine may reduce critics' fears that bail bondsmen will discriminate among arrestees seeking services and develop corrupt relationships with criminal justice officials.

Courts could further reduce the impact of bondsmen by installing their own kiosks with lower fees. Such a step, by itself, would still not help those defendants who are too poor or unworthy of credit to own a credit card. Moreover, courts would need to replace a primary benefit often provided by bail bondsman, namely, reminding defendants about the time and place of their scheduled court appearances.

Are there other aspects of court operations that could be automated in order to serve the public better?

Sources: Associated Press, "Machine Bypasses Bail Bondsmen," October 5, 1998 (http://www.kiosks.org); Katherine Noyes, "Get out of Jail—But Not for Free," *CIO Magazine,* March 1, 1999 (http://www.cio.com).

Researching the **Internet**

For more information on the potential use of self-service kiosks, see http://www.kiosks.org.

employed, or people with unstable families. Yet many of these factors provide no clear information about how dangerous a defendant is or whether he or she is likely to appear in court.

Research highlights the disadvantages of the poor in the bail process. A study of Hispanic arrestees in the southwestern United States found that those who hired their own attorneys were seven times more likely to gain pretrial release than were those who were represented at public expense (M. D. Holmes et al., 1996). This result may reflect the fact that affluent defendants can more easily come up with bail money, as well as the possibility that private attorneys fight harder for their clients in the early stages of the criminal process.

The amount of bail may also reflect racial, class, or ethnic discrimination by criminal justice officials. A 1991 study by the State Bail Commission of cases in Connecticut showed that at each step in the process African American and Hispanic men with clean records were given bail amounts double those given whites. One reason for the difference might be that poor defendants often do not have jobs and a permanent residence, factors that strongly influence bail amounts. The study also recognized that the higher bail might result from the fact that African Americans and Hispanics were more likely to be charged with a felony than whites. Yet the largest disparities in bail were in felony drug cases. In these cases the average bail for African Americans and Hispanics was four times higher than for whites at the same courthouse (Houston and Ewing, 1991).

Some claim that bail setting should be guided by six principles:

1. The accused is entitled to release on his or her own recognizance.
2. Nonfinancial alternatives to bail will be used when possible.

3. The accused will receive a full and fair hearing.
4. Reasons will be stated for the decision.
5. Clear and convincing evidence will be offered to support a decision.
6. There will be a prompt and automatic review of all bail determinations.

Many people argue that these principles would hamper the ability of the justice system to deal with offenders and protect society. Others counter that personal freedom is so precious that failure to allow a person every opportunity to gain release creates an even greater injustice.

check point

12. What factors affect whether bail is set and how much money or property a defendant must provide to gain pretrial release?
13. What positive and negative effects does the bail bondsman have on the justice system?

Reforming the Bail System

Studies of pretrial detention in such cities as Philadelphia and New York raised questions about the need to hold defendants in jail. Criticisms of the bail system have focused on judges' discretion in setting bail amounts, the fact that the poor are deprived of their freedom while the affluent can afford bail, the negative aspects of bail bondsmen, and jail conditions for those detained while awaiting trial. To address such criticisms, people have attempted for many years to reform the bail system. Such efforts have led to changes in the number of defendants held in jail. One classic study of 20 cities showed that the release rate in 1962 was 48 percent (W. H. Thomas, 1976:37–38). A more recent survey found that 64 percent of felony defendants in the 75 largest counties were released before disposition of their cases. Only 7 percent of defendants were denied bail. Thus the other 29 percent of felony defendants who stayed in jail were unable to come up with the bail amount required to gain pretrial release (Reaves, 2001). The increase in defendants released on bail has occurred, in part, because of the use of certain pretrial release methods. These are listed in Table 9.2. Officers also use citations to reduce the need for booking.

Table 9.2 Pretrial release methods

Financial Bond	Alternative Release Options
Fully secured bail. The defendant posts the full amount of bail with the court.	*Release on recognizance (ROR).* The court releases the defendant on his or her promise to appear in court as required.
Privately secured bail. A bondsman signs a promissory note to the court for the bail amount and charges the defendant a fee for the service (usually 10 percent of the bail amount). If the defendant fails to appear, the bondsman must pay the court the full amount. The bondsman frequently requires the defendant to post collateral in addition to the fee.	*Conditional release.* The court releases the defendant subject to his or her following specific conditions set by the court, such as attendance at drug treatment therapy or staying away from the complaining witness.
Percentage bail. The courts allow the defendant to deposit a percentage (usually 10 percent) of the full bail with the court. The full amount of the bail is required if the defendant fails to appear. The percentage bail is returned after disposition of the case, although the court often retains 1 percent for administrative costs.	*Third-party custody.* The defendant is released into the custody of an individual or agency that promises to ensure his or her appearance in court. No monetary transactions are involved in this type of release.
Unsecured bail. The defendant pays no money to the court but is liable for the full amount of bail should she or he fail to appear.	

Source: Bureau of Justice Statistics, *Report to the Nation on Crime and Justice,* 2d ed. (Washington, D.C.: U.S. Government Printing Office, 1988), 76.

Citation

A **citation,** or summons, to appear in court—a "ticket"—is often issued to a person accused of committing a traffic offense or some other minor violation. By issuing the citation, the officer avoids taking the accused person to the station house for booking and to court for arraignment and setting of bail. Citations are now being used for more serious offenses, in part because the police want to reduce the amount of time they spend booking minor offenders and waiting in arraignment court for their cases to come up.

citation
A written order or summons, issued by a law enforcement officer, directing an alleged offender to appear in court at a specified time to answer a criminal charge.

Release on Recognizance

Pioneered in the 1960s by the Vera Institute of Justice in New York City, the **release on recognizance (ROR)** approach is based on the assumption that judges will grant releases if the defendant is reliable and has roots in the community. Soon after the arrest, court personnel talk to defendants about their job, family, prior record, and associations. They then decide whether to recommend release. In the first three years of the New York project, more than 10,000 defendants were interviewed and about 3,500 were released. Only 1.5 percent failed to appear in court at the scheduled time, a rate almost three times better than the rate for those released on bail (Goldfarb, 1965). Programs in other cities have had similar results, although Sheila Maxwell's recent research raises questions about whether women and property-crime defendants on ROR are less likely than other defendants to appear in court (Maxwell, 1999).

release on recognizance (ROR)
Pretrial release granted on the defendant's promise to appear in court, because the judge believes that the defendant's ties in the community guarantee that he or she will appear.

Ten Percent Cash Bail

Although ROR is a useful alternative to bail, not all defendants should be released on their own recognizance. Illinois, Kentucky, Nebraska, Oregon, and Pennsylvania have started bail programs in which the defendants deposit with the court 10 percent of their bail in cash. When they appear in court as required, 90 percent of this amount is returned to them. Begun in Illinois in 1964, this plan is designed to release as many defendants as possible without using bail bondsmen.

Bail Guidelines

To deal with the problem of unequal treatment, reformers have written guidelines for setting bail. The guidelines specify the standards judges should use in setting bail and also list appropriate amounts. Judges are expected to follow the guidelines but deviate from them in special situations. The guidelines take into account the seriousness of the offense and the defendant's prior record, in order to protect the community and ensure that released offenders can be trusted to return for court appearances.

Preventive Detention

Reforms have been suggested not only by those concerned with unfairness in the bail system but also by those concerned with stopping crime (Goldkamp, 1985). Critics of the bail system point to a link between release on bail and the commission of crimes, arguing that the accused may commit other crimes while awaiting trial. A study of the nation's most populous counties found that 16 percent of felony defendants released on bail were rearrested for another crime (Reaves, 2001). To address this problem, legislatures have passed laws permitting detention of defendants without bail.

For federal criminal cases, Congress enacted the Bail Reform Act of 1984, which authorizes **preventive detention.** Under the act, if prosecutors recommend that defendants be kept in jail, a federal judge holds a hearing to determine (1) if there is a serious risk that the person will flee; (2) if the person will obstruct justice or threaten, injure, or intimidate a prospective witness or juror; or (3) if the offense is one of violence or one punishable by life imprisonment or death. On finding that one or more of these factors makes setting bail without endangering the community impossible, the judge can order the defendant held in jail until the case is completed (C. E. Smith, 1990).

preventive detention
Holding a defendant for trial, based on a judge's finding that, if the defendant were released on bail, he or she would flee or would endanger another person or the community.

Close Up: Preventive Detention: Two Sides of an Issue

For Ricardo Armstrong, there is the despair of trying to reunite his family after spending four months in a Cincinnati jail for bank robbery before being acquitted of the crime.

For friends and family of Linda Goldstone, there is the anguish of knowing that she would still be alive if there had been a way to keep Hernando Williams in jail while he was facing rape and assault charges in Chicago.

Ricardo Armstrong was one of the first defendants held under the Bail Reform Act of 1984. The 28-year-old janitor, who had a prior burglary conviction, was denied bail after being charged with robbing two Ohio banks.

From the start, Mr. Armstrong had insisted that bank robbery charges against him were part of some nightmarish mix-up.

A Cincinnati jury agreed. After viewing bank photographs of the robber, the jury acquitted Mr. Armstrong in what was apparently a case of mistaken identity.

Justice, it seemed, had been served—but not before Mr. Armstrong had spent four months in jail—and his wife left their home and moved with their children a thousand miles away.

"Who's going to get me back those four months?" he now asks bitterly. "Who's going to get me back my kids?" The Bail Reform Act makes no provision for compensating defendants who are jailed and later acquitted.

Proponents of the Bail Reform Act concede that some injustices inevitably occur. But they note that other cases, involving dangerous defendants set free on bond, ring just as tragically for victims of crimes that could have been prevented.

Prosecutors point to the release of Hernando Williams as the classic example of the need for preventive detention. Even as Mr. Williams, free on $25,000 bond, drove to court to face charges [of raping and beating a woman he abducted at a shopping mall], another woman lay trapped inside his car trunk. This victim, Linda Goldstone, a 29-year-old birthing instructor, was abducted by Mr. Williams as she walked to Northwestern Hospital and was forced at gunpoint to crawl into his trunk.

Over a 4-day period, Mrs. Goldstone was removed from the trunk periodically to be raped and beaten until she was shot to death. Mr. Williams has been sentenced to death.

"Linda Goldstone might well be alive today if we'd had this law then," said Richard M. Daley, the Cook County state's attorney.

Source: Adapted from Dirk Johnston, "Preventive Detention: Two Sides of an Issue," *New York Times,* July 13, 1987, p. A13. Copyright © 1987 by The New York Times Company. Reprinted by permission.

Researching the Internet

You can read the federal government's instructions to prosecutors and court personnel about pretrial detention at http://www.usdoj.gov/usao/eousa/foia_reading_room/usam/title9/crm00026.htm.

Obviously, preventive detention provides a particularly powerful clash between important American values. The value placed on liberty for individuals seems to be denied when presumptively innocent individuals remain in jail. On the other hand, the value on all citizens' ability to enjoy the liberty of walking the streets without fear of crime may be advanced by detaining specific individuals who are found to threaten community safety.

Critics of preventive detention argue that it violates the Constitution's due process clause because the accused remains in custody until a verdict is rendered. However, the Supreme Court has ruled that it is constitutional. The preventive detention provisions of the Bail Reform Act of 1984 were upheld in ***United States v. Salerno and Cafero*** (1987). The justices said that preventive detention was a legitimate use of government power, because it was not designed to punish the accused. Instead, it deals with the problem of people who commit crimes while on bail. By upholding the federal law, the Court also upheld state laws dealing with preventive detention (M. Miller and Guggenheim, 1990).

***United States v. Salerno and Cafero* (1987)**
Preventive detention provisions of the Bail Reform Act of 1984 are upheld as a legitimate use of government power designed to prevent people from committing crimes while on bail.

Supporters of preventive detention claim that it ensures that drug dealers, who often treat bail as a business expense, cannot flee before trial. Research has shown that the nature and seriousness of the charge, a history of prior arrests, and drug use all have a strong bearing on the likelihood that a defendant will commit a crime while on bail. The Close Up box presents a case in support of this argument.

check point

14. What methods are used to facilitate pretrial release for certain defendants?
15. How did the U.S. Supreme Court rule in cases involving preventive detention? Why?

Pretrial Detention

People who are not released before trial must remain in jail. Often called "the ultimate ghetto," American jails hold over 600,000 people on any one day. Most are poor, half are in pretrial detention, and the rest are serving sentences (normally of less than a year) or are waiting to be moved to state prison or to another jurisdiction (Clear and Cole, 2003:154).

Urban jails also contain troubled people, many with mental health and drug abuse problems, who have been swept off the streets by police. Michael Welch calls this process, in which the police remove socially offensive people from certain areas, "social sanitation" (Welch, 1994:262).

Conditions in jails are often much harsher than those in prisons. People awaiting trial are often held in barracks-like cells with sentenced offenders. Thus, a "presumed innocent" pretrial detainee might spend weeks in the same confined space with troubled people or sentenced felons (Beck, Karberg, and Harrison, 2002). The problems of pretrial detention may be even worse in other countries where suspects have no opportunity for bail or face a court system that is disorganized and lacks resources. As you read the Comparative Perspective concerning pretrial detention in Russia, ask yourself whether individual U.S. jails could have similar conditions.

The period just after arrest is the most frightening and difficult time for suspects. Imagine freely walking the streets one minute and being locked in a small space with a large number of troubled and potentially dangerous cellmates the next. Suddenly you have no privacy and must share an open toilet with hostile strangers. You have been fingerprinted, photographed, and questioned—treated like the "criminal" that the police and the criminal justice system consider you to be. You are alone with people whose behavior you cannot predict. You are left to worry and wonder about what might happen. If you are female, you may be placed in a cell by yourself (Steury and Frank, 1990). Given the stressful nature of arrest and jailing, it is little wonder that most jail suicides and psychotic episodes occur during the first hours of detention.

AP/L. M. Otero

Denied bail for 279 days, nuclear scientist Wen Ho Lee was held until he pleaded guilty to one count of mishandling nuclear secrets. Fifty-eight other charges were dropped. U.S. District Judge James A. Parker said he had been misled by the prosecution into treating Lee as a dangerous spy. Judge Parker called Lee's imprisonment "draconian" and "unfair."

The shock of arrest and detention can be made even worse by other factors. Many people are arrested for offenses they committed while under the influence of alcohol or some other substance and may therefore be that much less able to cope with their new situation. Young arrestees who face the risk of being victimized by older, stronger cellmates may sink into depression. Detainees also worry about losing their jobs while in jail, because they do not know if or when they will be released.

Pretrial detention can last a long time. While most felony detainees have their cases adjudicated within three months, 25 percent must wait in jail for more than six months and 10 percent for more than a year (Reaves, 2001). Thus, the

Pretrial Detention in Russia

Prisoners almost always swear they are not guilty. In Russian pretrial detention centers, many inmates insist that they no longer care about proving their innocence. Pretrial detainees spend long periods in unhealthy conditions while investigations of their alleged offense are conducted.

"At first, all I wanted was a fair trial," Pyotr Kuznetsov, 51, said in a dank and stinking cell of Matrosskaya Tishina, one of Moscow's largest and most infamous detention centers.

He said he had been arrested and brutally beaten for stealing less than $5 and had already spent 10 months behind bars awaiting trial. His lice-ridden eighteenth-century cell, built for 30, currently warehouses more than 100 men. The inmates share beds, sleeping in three shifts.

"All I want now is to get out of here, even to a labor camp," Mr. Kuznetsov said. "I've been in prison before, and it is not as bad as this."

Perhaps the most terrifying aspect of the Russian penal system is pretrial detention. Close to 300,000 people awaiting trial are now in jail. There, a death sentence stalks people who have not yet been convicted of a crime.

Unprotected from the TB (tuberculosis) epidemic (as many as 50 percent of Russian prisoners are believed to be infected) and other infectious diseases, many detainees end up spending two, three, and even four years awaiting their day in court in cells as packed as a rush-hour subway car.

The Russian legal system is so torturous that people can find themselves detained for months or years even on minor charges. Prosecutors are legally required to complete a criminal investigation within two years, but there is no time limit for judges, who can keep a suspect waiting for trial indefinitely. The average stay in detention is 10 months.

In Soviet times, bail was dismissed as a capitalist folly. Today, bail is legal, but it remains a novelty, granted to less than 2 percent of the country's accused—usually to mobsters who have ready cash and connections to a compliant judge.

"Under our system, it is much harder to acquit than find a person guilty," Sergei Pasin, a judge in a Moscow appeals court explained. "Less than 1 percent of all cases end in an acquittal, and that is because before a judge can acquit, he must do a huge amount of work that is not done by the police: requesting information, soliciting expert testimony, etc."

psychological and economic hardships faced by pretrial detainees and their families can be major and prolonged.

Pretrial detention not only imposes stresses and hardships that can reach crisis levels, but it can also affect the outcomes of cases. People who are held in jail can give little help to their defense attorneys. They cannot help to find witnesses and perform other useful tasks on their own behalf. In addition, they may feel pressured to plead guilty in order to end their indefinite stay in jail. Even if they believe that they should not be convicted of the crime charged, they may prefer to start serving a prison or jail sentence with a definite end point. Some may even gain quicker release on probation or in a community corrections program by pleading guilty, whereas they might stay in jail for a longer period by insisting on their innocence and awaiting a trial.

check point

16. People are detained in jail for many reasons. What categories of people are found in jails?
17. What sources of stress do people in jail awaiting trial face?

J. Hill/NYT Pictures

In Russia, pretrial detention averages 10 months. Fewer than 2 percent of arrestees are given bail. In the Matrosskaya Tishina Detention Center in Moscow, 5,000 prisoners await trial in a Dickensian world of squalor, disease, and lice.

"The fact that time served before trial is subtracted from convicted prisoners' sentences can hardly be viewed as justice," Judge Pasin said. "The predetention centers are a far worse punishment than prison," he said. Prisons and labor camps in Russia are grim, but they are not nearly as overcrowded.

In a report on torture in Russia, Amnesty International said that "torture and ill-treatment occur at all stages of detention and imprisonment," but noted that it was most often reported in pretrial detention.

"Its main purpose appears to be to intimidate detainees and obtain confessions," the report said. Confessions, more than evidence, are a major part of criminal investigations in Russia.

How does the American criminal justice system differ from Russia's? How do those differences affect the conditions of pretrial detention?

Source: Alessandra Stanley, "Russians Lament the Crime of Punishment," *New York Times,* January 1, 1998, p. A1.

Summary

- The United States has a dual court system consisting of state and federal courts that are organized into separate hierarchies.
- Trial courts and appellate courts have different jurisdictions and functions.
- Despite resistance from local judges and political interests, reformers have sought to improve state court systems through centralized administration, state funding, and a separate personnel system.
- The judge is a key figure in the criminal justice process who assumes the roles of adjudicator, negotiator, and administrator.
- State judges are selected through various methods, including partisan elections, nonpartisan elections, gubernatorial appointment, legislative appointment, and merit selection.
- Merit selection methods for choosing judges have gradually spread to many states. Such methods normally use a screening committee to make recommendations of potential appointees who will, if placed on the bench by the governor, go before the voters for approval or disapproval of their performance in office.

- Pretrial processes determine the fates of nearly all defendants through case dismissals, decisions defining the charges, and plea bargains, all of which affect more than 90 percent of cases.
- Defense attorneys use motions to their advantage to gain information and delay proceedings to benefit their clients.
- The bail process provides opportunities for many defendants to gain pretrial release, but poor defendants may be disadvantaged by their inability to come up with the money or property needed to secure release. Some preventive detention statutes permit judges to hold defendants considered dangerous or likely to flee.
- Bail bondsmen are private businesspeople who charge a fee to provide money for defendants' pretrial release. Their activities create risks of corruption and discrimination in the bail process, but they may help the system by reminding defendants about court dates and by tracking down defendants who disappear.
- Although judges bear primary responsibility for setting bail, prosecutors are especially influential in recommending amounts and conditions for pretrial release.
- Initiatives to reform the bail process include release on own recognizance (ROR), police-issued citations, and bail guidelines.
- Pretrial detainees, despite the presumption of innocence, are held in difficult conditions in jails containing mixed populations of convicted offenders, detainees, and troubled people. The shock of being jailed creates risks of suicide and depression.

Questions for Review

1. Discuss the effects that partisan election of judges may have on the administration of justice. Which system of judicial selection do you think is most appropriate? Why?
2. The judge plays several roles. What are they? In your opinion, do they conflict with one another?
3. What is the method of securing pretrial release for the accused?
4. What are the criteria used to set bail?

Key Terms and Case

adversarial system (p. 282)
appellate courts (p. 275)
arraignment (p. 284)
bail (p. 288)
citation (p. 293)
inquisitorial system (p. 282)
jurisdiction (p. 275)
merit selection (p. 283)
motion (p. 286)
nonpartisan election (p. 281)
partisan election (p. 281)
preventive detention (p. 293)
release on recognizance (ROR) (p. 293)
trial courts of general jurisdiction (p. 275)
trial courts of limited jurisdiction (p. 275)
United States v. Salerno and Cafero (1987) (p. 294)

For Further Reading

Feeley, Malcolm M. 1983. *Court Reform on Trial.* New York: Basic Books. A study of court reform efforts, such as diversion, speedy trial, bail reform, and sentencing reform. The book illustrates the difficulties involved in attempting to initiate changes within courts.

Goldkamp, John. 1995. *Personal Liberty and Community Safety: Pretrial Release in Criminal Court.* New York: Plenum. An examination of issues surrounding bail and pretrial release.

Satter, Robert. 1990. *Doing Justice: A Trial Judge at Work.* New York: Simon & Schuster. A judge's view of the cases that he faces daily and the factors that influence his decisions.

Smith, Christopher E. 1997. *Courts, Politics, and the Judicial Process.* 2nd ed. Chicago: Nelson-Hall. A discussion of the structure and operations of courts, including an examination of methods for selecting judges.

Wice, Paul. 1974. *Freedom for Sale.* Lexington, Mass.: Lexington Books. A classic survey of bail and its operations.

Going Online

For an up-to-date list of Web links, go to http://www.cj.wadsworth.com/colesmith10e

1. Using the Internet, go the Web page for the judiciary of Iowa: http://www.judicial.state.ia.us. Read the section entitled "About Our Courts." What are the differences between various kinds of judges in Iowa, including judicial magistrates, associate juvenile judges, associate probate judges, district associate judges, and district court judges?
2. Using the Internet, go the Web page for the U.S. District Court for the Southern District of Texas: http://www.txs.uscourts.gov. What is the fee to file a civil lawsuit in the federal courts? Do you think the fee prevents people from making use of the courts?
3. Go to. http://bci.utah.gov/BailPI/BailHome.html. Read Utah's requirements for obtaining a license to work as a bail bondsman. Are these requirements sufficient? Should there be any additional regulations?
4. Using InfoTrac College Edition, enter the keywords *judicial selection.* Read articles about judicial elections in Texas and other states. What problems exist in using elections as the means to choose judges?

Checkpoint Answers

1. Separate federal and state court systems handling cases in the United States.
2. The federal system is made up of the Supreme Court of the United States, Circuit Courts of Appeals, and District Courts. State court systems are made up of an appellate court of last resort, intermediate courts of appeals, trial courts of general jurisdiction and trial courts of limited jurisdiction.
3. Operated and controlled by local communities, not a statewide administration. Most state and county courts are decentralized.
4. To create a unified court system with consolidated and simplified structures that has centralized management, full funding by the state, and a central personnel system.
5. That judges carefully and deliberately weigh the issues in a case before making a decision. Judges embody justice and dispense it impartially.
6. So that all segments of society will view the decisions as legitimate and fair.
7. Adjudicator, negotiator, administrator.
8. To secure the support of attorneys who aspire to become judges and to ensure that courthouse positions are allocated to party workers.
9. When a vacancy occurs, a nominating commission is appointed that sends the governor the names of approved candidates. The governor must fill the vacancy from this list. After a year's term, a referendum is held to ask the voters whether the judge should be retained.
10. Preliminary hearings inform defendants of their rights and determine if there is probable cause. Arraignments involve the formal reading of charges and the entry of a plea. Motions seek information and the vindication of defendants' rights.
11. Cases are filtered out through the discretionary decisions of prosecutors and judges when they believe that there is inadequate evidence to proceed, or when prosecutors believe that their scarce resources are best directed at other cases.
12. Bail decisions are based primarily on the judge's evaluation of the seriousness of the offense and the defendant's prior record. The decisions are influenced by the prosecutor's recommendations and the defense attorney's counterarguments about the defendant's personal qualities and ties to the community.
13. Bondsmen help the system by reminding defendants about their court dates and finding them if they fail to appear. However, bondsmen also may contribute to corruption and discrimination.
14. Bail reform alternatives include police citations, release on own recognizance (ROR), and 10 percent cash bail.
15. The U.S. Supreme Court ruled that preventive detention did not violate the Constitution's ban on excessive bail because such detentions are not punishment and are merely a way to protect the public.
16. The jail population includes (1) pretrial detainees for whom bail was not set or those who are too poor to pay the bail amount required, (2) people serving short sentences for misdemeanors, (3) people convicted of felonies awaiting transfer to prison, and (4) people with psychological or substance abuse problems who have been swept off the streets.
17. Pretrial detainees face the stress of living with difficult and potentially dangerous cellmates. They also face uncertainty about what will happen to their case, their families, their jobs, and their ability to contribute to preparing a defense.

CHAPTER 10

Prosecution and Defense

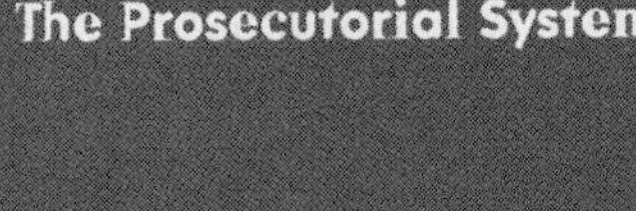

The Prosecutorial System

- Politics and Prosecution
- The Prosecutor's Influence
- The Prosecutor's Roles
- Discretion of the Prosecutor
- Key Relationships of the Prosecutor
- Decision-Making Policies

The Defense Attorney: Image and Reality

- The Role of the Defense Attorney
- Realities of the Defense Attorney's Job
- The Environment of Criminal Practice
- Counsel for Indigents
- Private versus Public Defense
- Attorney Competence

Photo Courtesy of Los Angeles County Courts/Getty Images

Security guards in the Saks Fifth Avenue store in Beverly Hills, California, observed movie actress Winona Ryder removing price tags from expensive clothing and placing the items in her bag as she shopped in December 2001. When she attempted to leave the store without paying for the items, she was stopped. Her bag allegedly contained nearly $5,000 worth of merchandise as well as unauthorized prescription painkillers. Ryder was charged with second-degree burglary, grand theft, and possession of a controlled substance—all felonies. She faced the possibility of 3 years in prison (Deutsch, 2002).

Who determined the nature and number of charges filed against Ryder? That was the job of the Los Angeles County District Attorney. Ryder's defense attorney implied that other people caught in such circumstances are charged with misdemeanors but she was facing felonies because the prosecutor wanted the publicity of winning a high-profile case (Gordon, 2002). A jury ultimately convicted Ryder of two felonies and she was sentenced to three years of probation plus community service, counseling, and restitution.

Unlike Ryder's felony trial, Rebecca Gayheart, an actress and model from the television show *Beverly Hills 90210* and youth-oriented movies such as *Scream 2* and *Urban Legend,* entered a guilty plea to the charge of misdemeanor vehicular manslaughter. While driving down a Los Angeles street in June 2001, she allegedly drove 40 miles per hour as she passed cars that were stopped to allow a 9-year-old boy to cross the street. Gayheart's vehicle struck and killed the boy. The prosecutor had originally considered filing felony charges against her but eventually decided to file a single misdemeanor count because no drugs or alcohol were involved in the accident. Unlike Ryder, who faced felony charges and several years in prison for stealing merchandise, Gayheart was only sentenced to 3 years probation, loss of her driving license, and a community-service order to make a safe-driving video. She spent no time in jail. Gayheart hired a prominent attorney to represent her, and the attorney apparently worked out a favorable plea agreement with the prosecutor as well as a financial settlement to end the civil lawsuit filed against the actress by the boy's parents ("Rebecca Gayheart," 2001; "Actress Rebecca Gayheart," 2002).

These two crimes occurred in the same county. Did the prosecutor treat the defendants in an equivalent manner? People commonly accuse the criminal justice system of favoring the rich and famous. Thus, for example, they might contrast Gayheart's probation sentence with the experience of Eve Hibbits, a less affluent woman in Jefferson County, Ohio, who spent 8 days in jail during the summer of 2002 because a deputy sheriff patrolling the county fair believed that she had not taken sufficient action to protect her children from being sunburned. She could not afford to make bail and thus she sat in jail until the prosecutor decided to drop most of the charges against her ("Mother of Sunburned Children," 2002). The case of Eve Hibbits shows that poorer people suffer disadvantages, such as the inability to make bail; it also shows the power of prosecutor's decisions. However, given the cases against Ryder and Gayheart, whether affluence determines the way prosecutors approach cases remains unclear. After all, the prosecutor in Los Angeles pursued Ryder's case more aggressively than the other two cases were pursued.

Did the criminal justice process operate fairly in its treatment of these three cases? One well-known actress faces the possibility of several years in prison for stealing merchandise from an upscale store. One rural woman who was too poor to make bail spent many days in jail facing felony charges, which were eventually dropped, because she allegedly did not do enough to prevent her children from being sunburned. Another wealthy Hollywood actress did not spend a single day behind bars after being convicted of causing the death of a young boy. The apparent inconsistencies in these cases raise an important question: What factors determined the course of events and outcomes in each case? The primary lesson demonstrated by these examples is that the prosecutor and defense attorney are the most influential figures in determining the outcomes of criminal cases. Their discretionary decisions and negotiations determine people's fates and produce apparent disparities in the way that specific cases are handled.

The American system places great power and responsibility in the hands of attorneys for each side in a criminal case. As a result, the justice system's ability to handle cases and produce fair results depends on the dedication, skill, and enthusiasm that these lawyers bring to the decisions they make in the private meetings that determine the fates of most criminal defendants.

QUESTIONS for **INQUIRY**

- What are the roles of the prosecuting attorney?
- What is the process by which criminal charges are filed, and what role does the prosecutor's discretion play in that process?
- With whom does the prosecutor interact in decision making?
- What is the day-to-day reality of criminal defense work in the United States?
- Who becomes a defense attorney?
- How is counsel provided for defendants who cannot afford a private attorney?
- What role does the defense attorney play in the system, and what is the nature of the attorney–client relationship?

The Prosecutorial System

Prosecuting attorneys make discretionary decisions about whether to pursue criminal charges, which charges to make, and what sentence to recommend. They represent the government in pursuing criminal charges against the accused. Except in a few states, no higher authority second-guesses or changes these decisions. Thus prosecutors are more independent than most other public officials. As with other aspects of American government, prosecution lies mainly in the hands of state and local governments. Because most crimes are violations of state laws, county prosecutors bring charges against suspects in court.

For cases involving violation of federal criminal laws, prosecutions are handled in federal courts by **United States attorneys.** These attorneys are responsible for a large number of drug-related and white-collar crime cases. They are appointed by the president and are part of the Department of Justice. One U.S. attorney and a staff of assistant U.S. attorneys prosecute cases in each of the 94 U.S. district courts.

United States attorney
Officials responsible for the prosecution of crimes that violate the laws of the United States; appointed by the president and assigned to a U.S. district court jurisdiction.

Each state has an elected attorney general, who usually has the power to bring prosecutions in certain cases. A **state attorney general** may, for example, handle a statewide consumer fraud case if a chain of auto repair shops is suspected of overcharging customers. In Alaska, Delaware, and Rhode Island, the state attorney general also directs all local prosecutions.

state attorney general
A state's chief legal officer, usually responsible for both civil and criminal matters.

However, the vast majority of criminal cases are handled in the 2,341 county-level offices of the **prosecuting attorney**—known in various states as the district attorney, state's attorney, commonwealth attorney, or county attorney—who pursues cases that violate state law. The number of prosecutors who work in these offices increased by more than 35 percent from 1990 to 2001 (DeFrances, 2002). Prosecutors have the power to make independent decisions about which cases to pursue and what charges to file. They also have the power to drop charges and to negotiate arrangements for guilty pleas.

prosecuting attorney
A legal representative of the state with sole responsibility for bringing criminal charges; in some states referred to as district attorney, state's attorney, or county attorney.

In rural areas the prosecutor's office may consist of merely the prosecuting attorney and a part-time assistant. By contrast, in some urban jurisdictions, such as Los Angeles, with 500 assistant prosecutors and numerous legal assistants and investigators, the office is organized according to various types of crimes. Many assistant prosecutors seek to use the trial experience gained in the prosecutor's office as a means of moving on to a better-paying position in a private law firm.

Politics and Prosecution

In all states except Connecticut and New Jersey, prosecutors are elected, usually for a 4-year term; the office thus is heavily involved in local politics. By seeking to please voters, many prosecutors have tried to use their local office as a springboard to higher office—such as state legislator, governor, or member of Congress.

Although the power of prosecutors flows directly from their legal duties, politics strongly influence the process of prosecution. Prosecutors can often mesh their own ambitions with the needs of a political party. The appointment of assistant prosecutors offers a chance to recruit bright young lawyers to the party. Prosecutors may choose certain cases for prosecution in order to gain the favor of voters, or investigate charges against political opponents and public officials to get the attention of the public. Political factors can also cause prosecutors to apply their powers unevenly within a community. As we have seen, prosecutors' discretionary power can create the impression that some groups or individuals receive harsher treatment, while others receive protection. The examples of Eve Hibbits and Rebecca Gayheart illustrate how questions can arise about whether everyone receives equal treatment from prosecutors.

The existence of discretionary decision making creates the risk that such decisions will produce discrimination. For example, some scholars claim that prosecutors' decisions reflect biases based on race, social class, and gender (Frohmann, 1997), but other researchers believe the full extent of discrimination by prosecutors has not yet been completely documented (S. Walker, Spohn, and DeLeone, 2000). Several studies do raise questions about discrimination in specific situations, such as prosecutors' decisions to seek the death penalty (Sorensen and Wallace, 1999). If prosecutors' discretionary decisions produce discriminatory results, these outcomes clearly clash with the American value of equal treatment and fairness. If the criminal justice system is going to fulfill American values concerning equality and fairness, then prosecutors must use their decision-making authority carefully to avoid inequality and injustice.

check point

1. What are the titles of the officials responsible for criminal prosecution at the federal, state, and local levels of government?

(Answers are at the end of the chapter.)

The Prosecutor's Influence

The federal government keeps statistics on prosecutions throughout the country; see http://www.ojp.usdoj.gov/bjs/pros.htm.

Prosecutors exert great influence because they are concerned with all aspects of the criminal justice process (Jacoby, 1995). By contrast, other decision makers are involved in only part of the process. Throughout the entire process—from arrest to final disposition of a case—prosecutors can make decisions that will largely determine the defendant's fate. The prosecutor chooses the cases to be prosecuted, selects the charges to be brought, recommends the bail amount, approves agreements with the defendant, and urges the judge to impose a particular sentence.

Throughout the justice process, prosecutors' links with the other actors in the system—police, defense attorneys, judges—shape the prosecutors' decisions. Prosecutors may, for example, recommend bail amounts and sentences that match the preferences of particular judges. They may make "tough" recommendations in front of "tough" judges, but tone down their arguments before judges who favor leniency or rehabilitation. Likewise, the other actors in the system may adjust their decisions and actions to match the preferences of the prosecutor. For example, police officers' investigation and arrest practices tend to reflect the prosecutor's priorities. Thus, prosecutors influence the decisions of others while also shaping their own actions in ways that reinforce their relationships with police, defense attorneys, and judges.

Prosecutors gain additional power from the fact that their decisions and actions are hidden from public view. For example, a prosecutor and a defense attorney may strike a bargain whereby the prosecutor reduces a charge in exchange for a guilty plea or drops a charge if the defendant agrees to seek psychiatric help. In such instances, decisions are reached in a way that is nearly invisible to the public.

For an example of a county prosecutor's office, see the Web page of an Indiana prosecutor at http://www.prosecutor.com.

State laws do little to limit or guide prosecutors' decisions. Most laws describe the prosecutor's duties in such vague terms as "prosecuting all crimes and civil actions to which state or county may be party." Such laws do not tell the prosecutor which cases must be prosecuted and which ones dismissed. The prosecutor has significant discretion to make such decisions without direct interference from either the law or other actors in the justice system (Caulfield, 1994). When prosecutors' decisions are challenged, judges generally reject the claim.

Because most local prosecutors are elected, public opinion influences their decisions. If they feel that the community no longer considers a particular act to be criminal, they may refuse to prosecute or try to convince the complainant not to press charges. Public influence over prosecutors can take two forms. First, because most prosecutors are elected, they must keep their decisions consistent with community values in order to increase their chances of gaining reelection. Second, because jurors are drawn from the local community, prosecutors do not want to waste their time and resources pursuing charges about which local jurors are unsympathetic or unconcerned. In some communities, for example, prostitution may be prosecuted actively, while in others it is ignored. About three-fourths of American prosecutors serve counties with populations of fewer than 100,000. There often is only one prosecutor in the community, and he or she may face strong local pressures, especially with regard to victimless crimes such as marijuana smoking, petty gambling, and prostitution. Prosecutors therefore develop policies that reflect community attitudes. As one New York prosecutor has remarked, "We are pledged to enforcement of the law, but we have to use our heads in the process."

Courtesy of Mishawaka Police Department/Getty Images

Madelyne Gorman Toogood made the national news when she was captured on videotape slapping and punching her 4-year-old daughter in a Mishawaka, Indiana, parking lot. Charged with battery to a child, Toogood said, "I am not a monster." What sort of legal, political, and social pressures might have been brought on the prosecutor in this case?

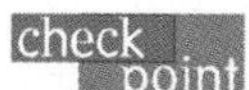

check point

2. What are the powers of the prosecuting attorney?

The Prosecutor's Roles

As "lawyers for the state," prosecutors face conflicting pressures to vigorously press charges against lawbreakers while also upholding justice and the rights of the accused. These pressures are often called "the prosecutor's dilemma." In the adversary system, prosecutors must do everything they can to win a conviction, yet as members of the legal profession they must see that justice is done even if it means that the accused is not convicted. The Canon of Ethics of the New York State Bar Association states, "The primary duty of a lawyer engaged in public prosecution is not to convict, but to see that justice is done. The suppression of facts and the secreting of witnesses capable of establishing the innocence of the accused is highly reprehensible" (A. B. Smith and Pollack, 1972:165). Even so, there is always a risk of prosecutor's bias, sometimes called a "prosecution complex." Although they are supposed to represent all the people, including the accused, prosecutors may view themselves as instruments of law enforcement. Thus, as advocates on behalf of the state, their strong desire to close each case with a conviction may keep them from recognizing unfair procedures or evidence of innocence. A comparison of prosecutors in the United States and Japan, for

Corbis/Reuters

Prosecutor Gentry Caudill makes his opening statement to the jury in the Charlotte, North Carolina, capital murder trial of former NFL wide receiver Rae Carruth. As "lawyers for the state," prosecutors must seek to win convictions; yet as members of the legal profession, they must see that justice is done.

example, found that American prosecutors often proceed with the assumption that the facts weigh against the defendant, while Japanese prosecutors are more concerned with investigating the case to discover all available facts before making any decisions (D. T. Johnson, 1998).

What happens in the United States if prosecutors make a mistake and it appears that an innocent person may have been convicted? After a trial and the completion of the appellate process, sometimes a defendant has no avenue to gain reconsideration of the conviction (Tucker, 1997). A national commission appointed by U.S. Attorney General Janet Reno recommended in 1999 that prosecutors drop their adversarial posture and cooperate in permitting DNA testing of evidence saved from old cases that had produced convictions before sophisticated scientific tests were developed (N. Lewis, 1999). Despite the fact that dozens of convicted offenders have been proved innocent in rape and murder cases through after-the-fact DNA testing, some prosecutors have resisted the reexamination of old evidence.

Prosecutors are seldom punished for mistakes they made in convicting innocent people and remain generally immune from civil lawsuits for their official actions. Moreover, even in those rare circumstances when prosecutors face criminal misconduct charges for excessive actions in seeking to convict an innocent person, juries do not always convict the prosecutors of crimes. In June 1999 an Illinois jury acquitted seven prosecutors and law enforcement officers of conspiracy and obstruction of justice charges that stemmed from their efforts to convict Rolando Cruz of a gruesome child murder. Although Cruz was eventually released from prison when someone else confessed to crime, Cruz was not a model citizen and gave inconsistent testimony about his treatment at the hands of police and prosecutors. Thus jurors were apparently reluctant to convict the prosecutors of crimes for the mistakes that they made in investigating Cruz's case (Possley and Gregory, 1999).

Although all prosecutors must uphold the law and pursue charges against lawbreakers, they can perform these tasks in different ways. Because of their personal values and professional goals, as well as the political climate of their city or county, they may define the prosecutor's role differently than do prosecutors in other places. For example, a prosecutor who believes that young offenders can be rehabilitated would likely define the role differently than one who believes that young offenders should receive the same punishments as adults. One might send juveniles to counseling programs while the other seeks to process them though the adult system of courts and corrections. A prosecutor with no assistants and few resources for conducting full-blown jury trials may be forced to stress effective plea bargaining, while a prosecutor in a wealthier county may have more options when deciding whether to take cases to trial.

Role definition is further complicated by the prosecutor's need to maintain relationships with many other actors—police officers, judges, defense attorneys, political party leaders, and so forth—who may have conflicting ideas about what the prosecutor should do. The prosecutor's decisions affect the ability of the others to perform their duties and achieve their goals. If the prosecutor decides not to prosecute, the judge and jury will not be called on to decide the case, and police officers may feel that their efforts have been wasted. If the prosecutor decides to launch a campaign against drugs or pornography, this decision will have effects in both the political and criminal justice arenas. Police may feel that they must redirect their time and energy toward the crimes emphasized by the prosecutor. However, they may also pressure the prosecutor to set new priorities by declining to devote their efforts to the kinds of crimes the prosecutor wants to concentrate on. Excessive attention to victimless crimes, such as gambling and prostitution, may produce a public backlash if citizens feel that the prosecutor should focus on more serious crimes.

We can see prosecutors as generally following one of four distinct roles:

1. *Trial counsel for the police.* Prosecutors who see their main function in this light believe they should reflect the views of law enforcement in the courtroom and take a crime-fighter stance in public.
2. *House counsel for the police.* These prosecutors believe their main function is to give legal advice so that arrests will stand up in court.
3. *Representative of the court.* Such prosecutors believe their main function is to enforce the rules of due process to ensure that the police act according to the law and uphold the rights of defendants.
4. *Elected official.* These prosecutors may be most responsive to public opinion. The political impact of their decisions is one of their main concerns.

Each of these roles involves a different view of the prosecutor's "clients" as well as his or her own responsibilities. In the first two roles, prosecutors appear to believe that the police are the clients of their legal practice. Take a moment to think about who might be the clients of prosecutors who view themselves as representatives of the court or as elected officials.

check point

3. What are the roles of the prosecutor?

Discretion of the Prosecutor

Because they have such broad discretion, prosecutors can shape their decisions to fit different interests. Their decisions might be based on a desire to impress voters through tough "throw-the-book-at-them" charges in a highly publicized case (Maschke, 1995). Their decisions might stem from their personal values, such as an emphasis on leniency and rehabilitation for young offenders. They might also shape their decisions to please local judges by, for example, accepting plea agreements that will keep the judges from being burdened by too many time-consuming trials. Such motives can shape prosecutors' decisions because there is usually no higher authority to tell prosecutors how they must do their jobs. From

Prosecution in Germany

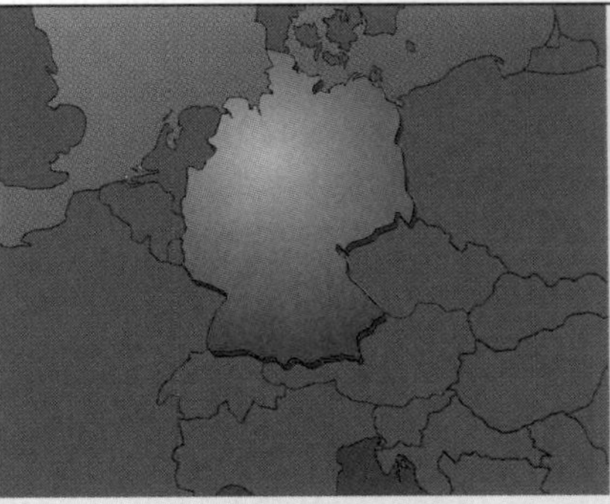

Unlike prosecutors in the United States, German prosecutors are not parties in an adversarial system; rather, they are required to act not only against, but also in favor of, the suspect at any stage of the proceedings. German prosecutors are not elected but are civil servants and thus are relatively immune from public opinion.

German prosecutors are expected to be objective above all, and thus one-third of all fraud cases studied were dismissed because of lack of sufficient evidence even though the suspect had made a confession in the course of police investigation. Another consequence of the rule of objectivity is that prosecutors need not concern themselves with winning every case. In up to 20 percent of all cases studied, the accused was acquitted by the trial judge, usually at the request of the prosecutor.

The Prosecutor's Office as an Investigating Agency

In Germany, the prosecutor controls the police investigations of each reported criminal case. Therefore, the prosecutor is often called "head of the preliminary proceedings." However, except in a few sensational cases such as murder, big commercial crimes, and, recently, terrorism, prosecutors seldom are truly in a supervisory role. Instead, a typical investigatory situation progresses as follows.

An offense will usually be reported to the police, who will then open and register a file. The police lack any discretionary power in deciding whether or not to file a case. They must follow up every suspicion and present all registered offenses—however vague the evidence may be—to the prosecutor, who alone makes the final decision. The police carry out all necessary investigations. If the police feel a case has been thoroughly investigated, they will forward it to the prosecutor, who must decide whether further investigation is necessary. The prosecutor can take over the investigation or can return the case to the police for further inquiries. The law requires the prosecutor to do

the time the police turn a case over to the prosecutor, he or she has almost complete control over decisions about charges and plea agreements.

The discretion of American prosecutors sharply contrasts with the situation of prosecutors in European countries such as Germany (see the Comparative Perspective). In Germany, the prosecutors face fewer pressures to win cases and instead bear greater responsibilities for evaluating the evidence and guilt of defendants before deciding whether to drop or pursue charges (Feeney, 1998). By contrast, American prosecutors who have doubts about whether the available evidence actually proves the defendant's guilt may just shrug their shoulders and say, "I'll just let the jury decide" rather than face public criticism for dropping charges. In Japan, prosecutors throughout the country work for a single nationwide agency and are not elected. As such, they must gain approval from superiors for many of their decisions rather than making independent decisions like those of local prosecutors in the United States (D. T. Johnson, 1998).

While the rate of dismissals varies from place to place, in most cities up to half of all arrests do not lead to formal charges. Prosecutors may decide to drop charges because of factors related to a particular case or because they have a policy of not bringing charges for certain offenses. For example, the U.S. Department of Justice gives its prosecutors guidelines for deciding whether a case should be dismissed or pursued (U.S. Department of Justice, 1980). They include the following:

1. Federal law enforcement priorities
2. The nature and seriousness of the offense

everything to solve the case—regardless of its seriousness. It does not permit him or her to "filter" out cases, as American prosecutors are authorized to do.

The Prosecutor's Office as a Charging Agency

Calling the prosecutor's office a "charging agency" is something of a misnomer because on the average three out of four cases are dropped. The label refers to the main task of the prosecutor, as it is the prosecutor's decision whether to charge or not. The charging decision involves two distinct considerations: evaluation of evidence and evaluation of guilt.

When prosecutors are *evaluating evidence,* they are more or less free in this decision. Some outside control is possible, however, since victims can file a formal complaint against the dismissal of a case. If the complaint is rejected by the attorney general (chief prosecutor of the state), the victim can file a motion for a judicial decision, which would, if successful, force the prosecutor to file a charge. Although this procedure is very seldom used, it is nonetheless feared by prosecutors. As a result, the status of victims may influence prosecutors' decisions. When the prosecutor is *evaluating guilt,* there are significant possibilities of hierarchical control over the decision. According to administrative rules issued by some of the ministries of justice of the states, deputy attorneys must present to their superiors for approval each case they want to dismiss based on minor guilt (mitigation). "In-house" instructions may also attempt to standardize the criteria by which "minor guilt" is defined.

The main task of prosecutors is to determine whether the evidence in a case is sufficient for conviction. As a result, they have large *practical* discretionary power when they describe whether "probable cause" exists in any given case. The prosecutor's "evaluation of evidence" was examined in two types of cases: petty and serious crimes. It was found that if the damage (monetary value or physical injuries) was considerable or if the suspect had previously been convicted, the prosecutor was less inclined to drop the charge even if the evidence was weak. This situation might be explained by the possibility that the more serious the crime the more likely the accused is to retain defense counsel, which may hinder police investigation.

The relationship between the suspect and the victim also markedly affects the prosecutor's evaluation of the evidence. Cases involving acquaintances or relatives of the victim rather than stranger-to-stranger cases are more likely to be dismissed if they involve the crimes of theft, robbery, or rape. However, the opposite is true if the crime is fraud or embezzlement, because of the special breach of trust connected with these types of acts.

In summary, then, it seems the prosecutor uses stricter evidentiary rules in *minor* offenses than in *serious* offenses. It may be that even though the evidence might not support a conviction in the more serious cases, the prosecutor still charges the case in order to use the charge itself as a sanction. The latter assumption is supported by the fact that prosecutors tend to regard prior criminal record as an element of proof and therefore charge recidivists more than first offenders. This tendency is in part counterbalanced by the judge, who—stressing the problem of proof more than the prosecutor—acquits more recidivists than first offenders.

Americans may wonder how the German system, with its requirement of compulsory prosecution, can be efficient. In Germany, caseloads are reduced by decriminalizing some acts, making prosecution contingent on the victim's formal request, turning felonies into misdemeanors, and extending the discretionary power of the prosecutor.

Source: Adapted from Klaus Sessar, "Prosecutorial Discretion in Germany," in *The Prosecutor,* ed. William F. McDonald (Beverly Hills, Calif.: Sage, 1979), 255–73.

3. The deterrent effect of prosecution
4. The person's culpability (blameworthiness) in connection with the offense
5. The person's history with respect to criminal activity
6. The person's willingness to cooperate in the investigation or prosecution of others
7. The probable sentence or other consequences if the person is convicted.

In addition to these formal considerations, decisions to pursue felony charges may also be affected by the staffing levels of individual prosecutor's offices (P. Walker, 1998). If offices lack sufficient resources to pursue all possible cases, prosecutors may establish priorities and then reduce or dismiss charges in cases deemed less important.

If you were a prosecutor, what would you consider the most important factors in deciding whether to pursue a case? Would you have any concerns about the possibility of prosecuting an innocent person? Is there an ethical problem if a prosecutor pursues a case against someone whom the prosecutor thinks is not really guilty of a crime? As you read "A Question of Ethics," consider what you would do if you were the prosecutor assigned to the case.

Even after deciding that a case should be prosecuted, the prosecutor has great freedom in deciding what charges to file. In criminal incidents that involve several laws, the prosecutor can bring a single charge or more than one. Suppose that Smith, who is armed, breaks into a grocery store, assaults the proprietor, and robs the cash drawer. What charges can the prosecutor file? By virtue of

Assistant County Prosecutor Adam Dow entered the office of his boss, County Prosecutor Susan Graham. "You want to see me?" he said as he closed the door.

"Yes, I do," Graham replied with a flash of anger. "I don't agree with your recommendation to dismiss charges in the Richardson case."

"But the victim was so uncertain in making the identification at the lineup, and the security video from the ATM machine is so grainy that you can't really tell if Richardson committed the robbery."

"Look. We've had six people robbed while withdrawing money at ATM machines in the past month. The community is upset. The banks are upset. The newspapers keep playing up these unsolved crimes. I want to put an end to this public hysteria. Richardson has a prior record for a robbery, and the victim picked him out of the lineup eventually." Graham stared at him coldly. "I'm not going to dismiss the charges."

Dow shifted his feet and stared at the floor. "I'm not comfortable with this case. Richardson may be innocent. The evidence just isn't very strong."

"Don't worry about the strength of the evidence. That's not your problem," said Graham. "We have enough evidence to take the case to trial. The judge said so at the preliminary hearing. So we'll just let the jury decide. Whatever happens, the community will know that we took action against this crime problem."

"But what if he's innocent? The jury could make a mistake in thinking that he's the robber in the grainy videotape. I wouldn't want that on my conscience."

→ Should Assistant Prosecutor Dow insist on the certainty of the defendant's guilt before agreeing to take a case forward? Should Prosecutor Graham consider public perceptions when she decides whether to pursue charges against Richardson? Is there an actual risk that an innocent person could be convicted in a jury trial under such circumstances if the prosecutor is reluctant to dismiss questionable charges?

To read about the proposed Federal Prosecutor Ethics Act considered by Congress, see http://www.naausa.org/initiatives/ethics.htm.

having committed the robbery, the accused can be charged with at least four crimes: breaking and entering, assault, armed robbery, and carrying a dangerous weapon. Other charges or **counts** can be added, depending on the nature of the incident. A forger, for instance, can be charged with one count for each act of forgery committed. By filing as many charges as possible, the prosecutor strengthens his or her position in plea negotiations. In effect, the prosecutor can use discretion in deciding the number of charges and thus increase the prosecution's supply of "bargaining chips."

The discretionary power to set charges does not give the prosecutor complete control over plea bargaining. Defense attorneys strengthen their position in the **discovery** process, in which the prosecutor discloses information from the case file to the defense. For example, the defense has the right to see any statements made by the accused during interrogation by the police, as well as the results of any physical or psychological tests. This information tells the defense attorney about the strengths and weaknesses of the prosecution's case. The defense attorney may use it to decide whether a case is hopeless or whether it is worthwhile to engage in tough negotiations.

The prosecutor's discretion does not end with the decision to file a certain charge. After the charge has been made, the prosecutor may reduce it in exchange for a guilty plea or enter a notation of ***nolle prosequi*** (*nol. pros.*). The latter is a freely made decision to drop the charge, either as a whole or as to one or more count. When a prosecutor decides to drop charges, no higher authorities can force him or her to reinstate them. When guilty pleas are entered, the prosecutor uses discretion in recommending a sentence.

4. How does a prosecutor use discretion to decide how to treat each defendant?

Key Relationships of the Prosecutor

Prosecutors' decisions are not based solely on formal policies and role conceptions (Fridell, 1990). They are also influenced by relationships with other actors in the justice system. Despite their independent authority, prosecutors must consider how police, judges, and others will react. They depend on these officials in order to prosecute cases successfully. In turn, the success of police, judges, and correctional officials depends on prosecutors' effectiveness in identifying and convicting lawbreakers. Thus these officials build exchange relationships in which they cooperate with each other.

Police

Prosecutors depend on the police to provide both the suspects and the evidence needed to convict lawbreakers. Most crimes occur before the police arrive at the scene; therefore, officers must reconstruct the crime on the basis of physical evidence and witnesses' reports. Police must use their training, experience, and work routines to decide whether arrest and prosecution would be worthwhile. Prosecutors cannot control the types of cases brought to them, because they can-

count
Each separate offense of which a person is accused in an indictment or an information.

discovery
A prosecutor's pretrial disclosure, to the defense, of facts and evidence to be introduced at trial.

nolle prosequi
An entry made by a prosecutor on the record of a case and announced in court to indicate that the charges specified will not be prosecuted. In effect, the charges are thereby dismissed.

not investigate crimes on their own. Thus the police control the initiation of the criminal justice process through the ways they investigate crimes and arrest suspects. Various factors, such as pressure on police to establish an impressive crime-clearance record, can influence police actions. As a result, such actions can create problems for prosecutors if, for example, the police make many arrests without gathering enough evidence to ensure conviction.

Prosecutors depend on the police, but they can still influence the actions of the police. For example, prosecutors can return cases for further investigation and refuse to approve arrest warrants. Prosecutors and police have an exchange relationship in which the success of each depends on cooperation with the other.

Police requests for prosecution may be refused for reasons unrelated to the facts of the case. First, prosecutors regulate the workload of the justice system. They must make sure that a backlog of cases does not keep the court from meeting legal time limits for processing criminal cases. To keep cases from being dismissed by the judge for taking too long, prosecutors may themselves dismiss relatively weak or minor cases and focus on those with more serious charges or clear proof of the defendant's guilt. Second, prosecutors may reject police requests for prosecution because they do not want to pursue poorly developed cases that would place them in an embarrassing position in the courtroom. Judges often scold prosecutors if weak cases are allowed to take up scarce courtroom time. Finally, prosecutors may return cases to make sure that police provide high-quality investigations and evidence.

Coordination between police and prosecutors has been a concern of criminal justice officials in recent decades. Some claim that lack of coordination causes cases to be dismissed or lost. Part of the problem is that lawyers and police have different views of crime and work for different sponsoring organizations. The police often claim that they have made a valid arrest and that there is no reason an offender should not be indicted and tried, but prosecutors look at cases to see if the evidence will result in a conviction. These different perspectives often lead to conflicts.

In response to the need for greater coordination, many jurisdictions have formed police-prosecution teams to work together on cases. This approach is often used for drug or organized-crime investigations and cases in which conviction requires detailed information and evidence. Drug cases require cooperation between the police and prosecutors because without a network of informers, drug traffickers cannot be caught with evidence that can lead to convictions. Prosecutors can help police gain cooperation from informants by approving agreements to reduce charges or even to *nol. pros.* a case. The accused person may then return to the community to gather information for the police.

To read court rules on the prosecutor's powers to dismiss criminal charges, see http://www.courtrules.org/nqxr48.htm.

Victims and Witnesses

Prosecutors depend on the cooperation of victims and witnesses. Although a case can be prosecuted whether or not a victim wishes to press charges, many prosecutors will not pursue cases in which the key testimony and other necessary evidence must be provided by a victim who is unwilling to cooperate. Prosecutors also need the cooperation of people who have witnessed crimes.

The decision to prosecute is often based on an assessment of the victim's role in his or her own victimization and the victim's credibility as a witness. If a victim has a criminal record, the prosecutor may choose not to pursue the case in the belief that a jury would not consider the victim a credible witness—despite the fact that the jury will never learn that the victim has a criminal record. In fact, the decision not to prosecute may actually reflect the prosecutor's belief that someone with a criminal record is untrustworthy or does not deserve the protection of the law. In other words, the prosecutor's own biases in sizing up victims may affect which cases he or she pursues. If a victim is poorly dressed, uneducated, or a poor communicator, the prosecutor may be inclined to dismiss charges out of fear that a jury would find the victim unpersuasive (Stanko, 1988).

Other characteristics of victims may play a similar role. For example, prosecutors might not pursue cases in which victims are prostitutes who have been raped, drug abusers who have been assaulted by drug dealers, and children who cannot stand up to the pressure of testifying in court. Research indicates that victims' characteristics, such as moral character, behavior at time of incident, and age, influence decisions to prosecute sexual assault cases more than does the actual strength of the evidence against the suspect (J. W. Spears and Spohn, 1997). Prosecutors sometimes also base their decision on whether or not the victim and defendant had a prior relationship. Studies have shown that prosecutions are most successful when aimed at defendants accused of committing crimes against strangers (Boland et al., 1983). When the victim is an acquaintance, a friend, or even a relative of the defendant, he or she may refuse to act as a witness, and prosecutors and juries may view the offense as less serious. Even if police make an arrest on the scene, a fight between spouses may strike a prosecutor as a weak case, especially if the complaining spouse has second thoughts about cooperating. A high percentage of victims of violent crimes are acquainted with their assailants. That some victims would rather endure victimization than see a friend or relative punished in the justice system creates problems for the prosecution's cases.

Based on the findings of a classic study, Figure 10.1 shows the outcomes of stranger and nonstranger robberies and burglaries in New York City. Note that 88 percent of arrests for robberies by strangers led to conviction, with 68 percent of these on a felony charge. Of those arrested, 65 percent were incarcerated, 32 percent for a year or more. In contrast, when the robbery victim knew the accused person, only 37 percent of those arrested were convicted, only 23 percent incarcerated, and none served more than a year. The same pattern can be seen in burglaries, although the punishments were less severe. Most of the burglars who were strangers were convicted, but only 8 percent on a felony charge. Prosecutors probably bargained these cases down to misdemeanors because the evidence was not strong. As with robberies of acquaintances, the burglars who knew their victims were treated more leniently than those who did not (Vera Institute, 1981).

In recent years, many people have called for measures that would force prosecutors to make victims more central to the prosecution. Because the state pursues

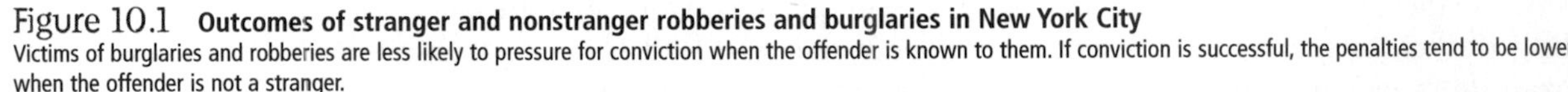

Figure 10.1 **Outcomes of stranger and nonstranger robberies and burglaries in New York City**
Victims of burglaries and robberies are less likely to pressure for conviction when the offender is known to them. If conviction is successful, the penalties tend to be lower when the offender is not a stranger.

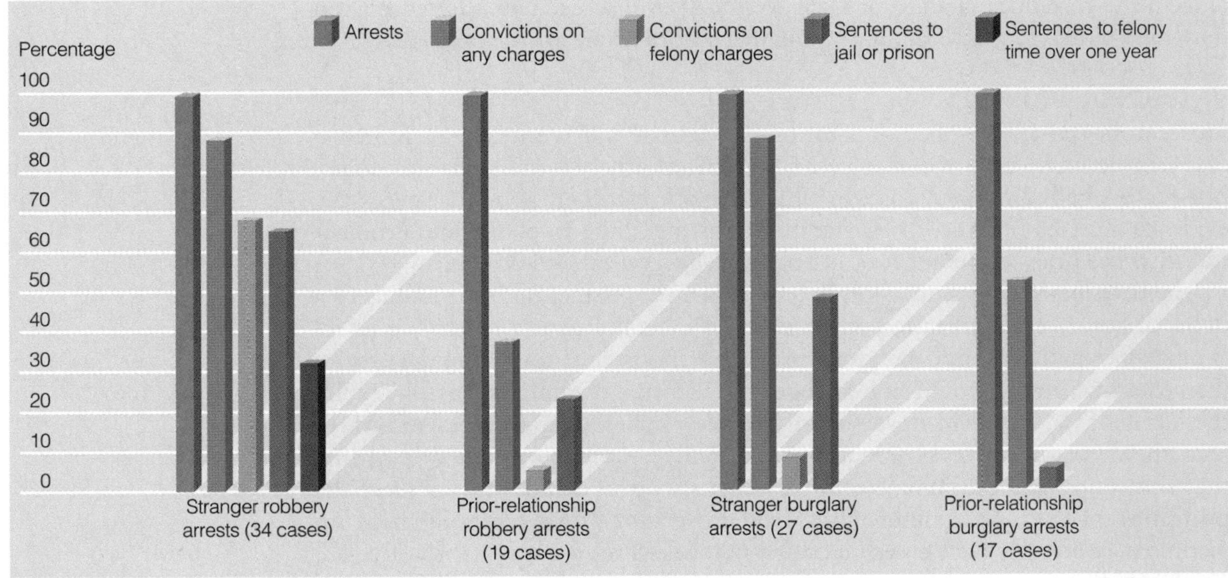

Source: Vera Institute of Justice, *Felony Arrests: Their Prosecution and Disposition in New York City's Courts* (New York: Longman, 1981), 58, 86.

charges against the accused in criminal cases, the victim is often forgotten in the process. The victims' rights movement wants victims to be given a chance to comment on plea bargains, sentences, and parole decisions. In June 1996 President Bill Clinton endorsed a proposed constitutional amendment that, if ratified, would require prosecutors to keep victims informed on the progress of criminal cases and allow them to have some input in decisions on bail, plea bargains, and sentencing.

For information on different versions of the proposed Victims' Rights Amendment, see the Web page of the Children's Protection and Advocacy Coalition: http://www.thecpac.com/cvrca.html.

Judges and Courts

The sentencing history of each judge gives prosecutors an idea of how a case might be treated in the courtroom. Prosecutors may decide to drop a case if they believe that the judge assigned to it will not impose a serious punishment. Because prosecutors' offices have limited resources, they cannot afford to waste time pursuing charges in front of a judge who shows a pattern of dismissing those particular cases.

Prosecutors depend on plea bargaining to keep cases moving through the courts. If judges' sentencing patterns are not predictable, prosecutors find it hard to persuade defendants and their attorneys to accept plea agreements. If the defendants and their lawyers are to accept a lesser charge or a promise of a lighter sentence in exchange for a guilty plea, there must be some basis to believe that the judge will support the agreement. Although some judges will informally approve plea agreements before the plea is entered, other judges believe it is improper to take part in plea bargaining. Since these judges refuse to state their agreement with the details of any bargain, the prosecutor and defense attorney must use the judges' past performance as a guide in arranging a plea that will be accepted in court.

In most jurisdictions, a person arrested on felony charges must be given a preliminary hearing within ten days. For prosecutors, this hearing is a chance to evaluate the testimony of witnesses, assess the strength of the evidence, and try to predict the outcome of the case should it go to trial. After that, prosecutors have several options: recommend that the case be held for trial, seek to reduce the charge to a misdemeanor, or conclude that they have no case and drop the charges. These decisions are greatly influenced by the prosecutor's perception of the court's caseload and the attitudes of the judges. If courts are overwhelmed with cases or if judges do not share the prosecutor's view about the seriousness of certain charges, the prosecutor may drop cases or reduce charges in order to keep the heavy flow of cases moving.

The Community

Public opinion and the media can play a crucial role in creating an environment that either supports or undermines the prosecutor. Like police chiefs and school superintendents, county prosecutors will not remain in office long if they are out of step with community values. They will likely lose the next election to an opponent who has a better sense of the community's priorities.

Public influence is especially important with respect to crimes that are not always fully enforced. Laws on the books may ban prostitution, gambling, and pornography, but a community may nonetheless tolerate them. In such a community the prosecutor will focus on other crimes rather than risk irritating citizens who believe that victimless crimes should not be strongly enforced. Other communities, however, may pressure the prosecutor to enforce morality laws and prosecute those who do not comply with local ordinances and state statutes. As elected officials, prosecutors must be sensitive to voters' attitudes.

Prosecutors' relationships and interactions with police, victims, defense attorneys, judges, and the community form the core of the exchange relations that shape decision making in criminal cases. Prosecutors' decisions are also influenced by other relationships, such as those with news media, federal and state officials, legislators, and political party officials. This long list of influences illustrates that

Community Prosecution

Community Prosecution represents an initiative to reduce crime and increase the effectiveness of the criminal justice system by bringing prosecutors into closer contact with citizens. This model program in Washington, D.C., gave individual assistant prosecutors responsibility for specific neighborhoods within the city. Some of the prosecutors were assigned exclusively to outreach functions that involved meeting with citizens and working with police to identify and remedy persistent crime problems. Other prosecutors took responsibility for prosecuting cases that arose in their assigned neighborhoods.

By having responsibility for specific neighborhoods, the prosecutors could become well-acquainted with the environment, social problems, crimes, and repeat offenders that burdened the residents of those neighborhoods. The residents could also gain personal familiarity with one or more specific prosecutors assigned to serve them. By contrast, prosecution in most cities is rather impersonal because victims and witnesses must come to the courthouse to meet with prosecutors who may either handle only specific aspects of one case or who have no reason to maintain continuing contacts with the citizens after the case is closed. Under the Community Prosecution model, individual prosecutors would become familiar to residents by working to resolve neighborhood problems and coordinate communications with police and other public service agencies.

The advocates of Community Prosecution argue that the initiative is not merely a public relations effort to gain favor with the public. Instead, it is a legitimate strategy for seeking to reduce crime, especially in neighborhoods burdened by the severest problems, and to increase cooperation between citizens and criminal justice officials.

If you were a county prosecutor, would you want to experiment with Community Prosecution? What tasks would you want your assistant prosecutors to perform in the community?

Source: Drawn from Barbara Boland, *Community Prosecution in Washington, D.C.: The U.S. Attorney's Fifth District Pilot Project* (Washington, D.C.: National Institute of Justice, U.S. Government Printing Office, April 2001).

Researching the **Internet**

To read about Community Prosecution in Montgomery County, Maryland, see http://www.communityprosecution.org.

prosecutors' decisions are not based solely on whether a law was broken. The occurrence of a crime is only the first step in a decision-making process that may vary from one case to the next. Sometimes charges are dropped or reduced. Sometimes plea bargains are negotiated quickly. Sometimes cases move through the system to a complete jury trial. In every instance, prosecutors' discretionary decisions are shaped by relationships and interactions with a variety of actors both within and outside the justice system.

As you read the accompanying box, "New Directions in Criminal Justice Policy," about the Community Prosecution program, think about how cooperation and coordination among prosecutors, police, and the public can improve by getting prosecutors closely connected with the communities that they serve.

Studies have shown that the public pays little attention to the criminal justice system. Still, the community remains a potential source of pressure that leaders may activate against the prosecutor. The prosecutor's office generally keeps the public in mind when it makes its decisions.

check point

5. What are the prosecutor's key exchange relationships?

Decision-Making Policies

Despite the many factors that potentially affect prosecutors' decisions, we can draw some general conclusions about how prosecutors approach their office. Prosecutors develop their own policies on how cases will be handled. These policies shape the decisions made by the assistant prosecutors and thus have a major impact on the administration of justice. In different counties, prosecutors may pursue different goals in forming policies on which cases to pursue, which ones to drop, and which to ones to plea bargain. For example, prosecutors who wish to maintain a high conviction rate will drop cases with weak evidence. Others, concerned about using limited resources effectively, will focus most of their time and energy on the most serious crimes.

Some prosecutors' offices make extensive use of screening and are not inclined to press charges. Guilty pleas are the main method of processing cases in some offices, while pleas of not guilty strain the courts' trial resources in others. Some offices remove cases—by diverting or referring them to other agencies—soon after they are brought to the prosecutor's attention by the police; in others, disposition occurs as late as the first day of trial. The period from the receipt of the police report to the start of the trial is thus a time of review in which the prosecutor uses discretion to decide what actions should be taken. Figure 10.2 shows how prosecutors handle felony cases in two different jurisdictions.

Implementing Prosecution Policy

Joan Jacoby analyzed the management policies that prosecutors use during the pretrial process and how they staff their offices to achieve their goals. On the basis of data from more than 3,000 prosecutors, she described three policy models: legal sufficiency, system efficiency, and trial sufficiency. The choice of a policy model is shaped by personal aspects of the prosecutor (such as role conception), external factors such as crime levels, and the relationship of prosecution to the other parts of the criminal justice system (Jacoby, 1979).

The policy model adopted by a prosecutor's office affects the screening and disposing of cases. As shown in Figure 10.3, the policy models dictate that prosecutors select certain points in the process to dispose of most of the cases

Figure 10.2 Differences in how prosecutors handle felony cases in two jurisdictions
The discretion of the prosecutor is evident in these two flowcharts. Note that different screening policies seem to be in operation: Cases are referred earlier in the process in Utah than they are in Colorado.

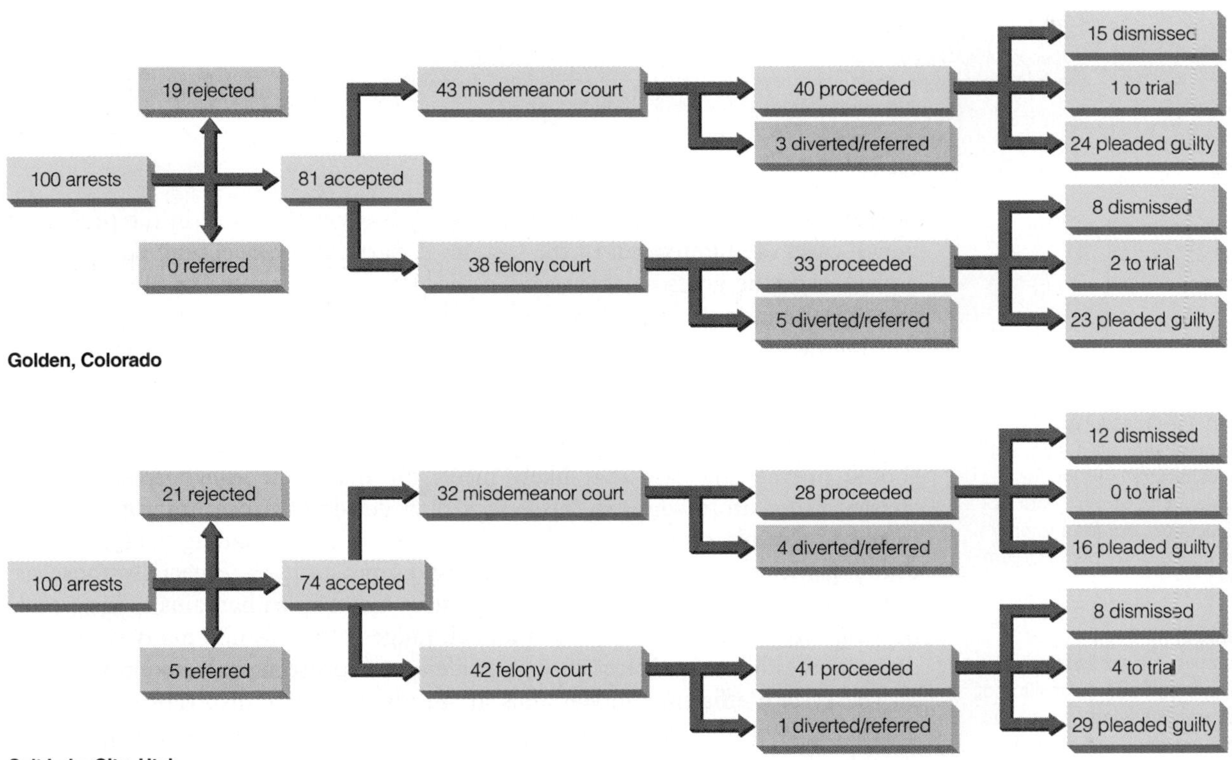

Source: Bureau of Justice Statistics, *Report to the Nation on Crime and Justice,* 2nd ed. (Washington, D.C.: U.S. Government Printing Office, 1988), 71.

Figure 10.3 **Three policy models of prosecutorial case management**
Prosecutors develop policies to guide the way their offices will manage cases. These models all assume that a portion of arrests will be dropped at some point in the system so that few cases reach trial.

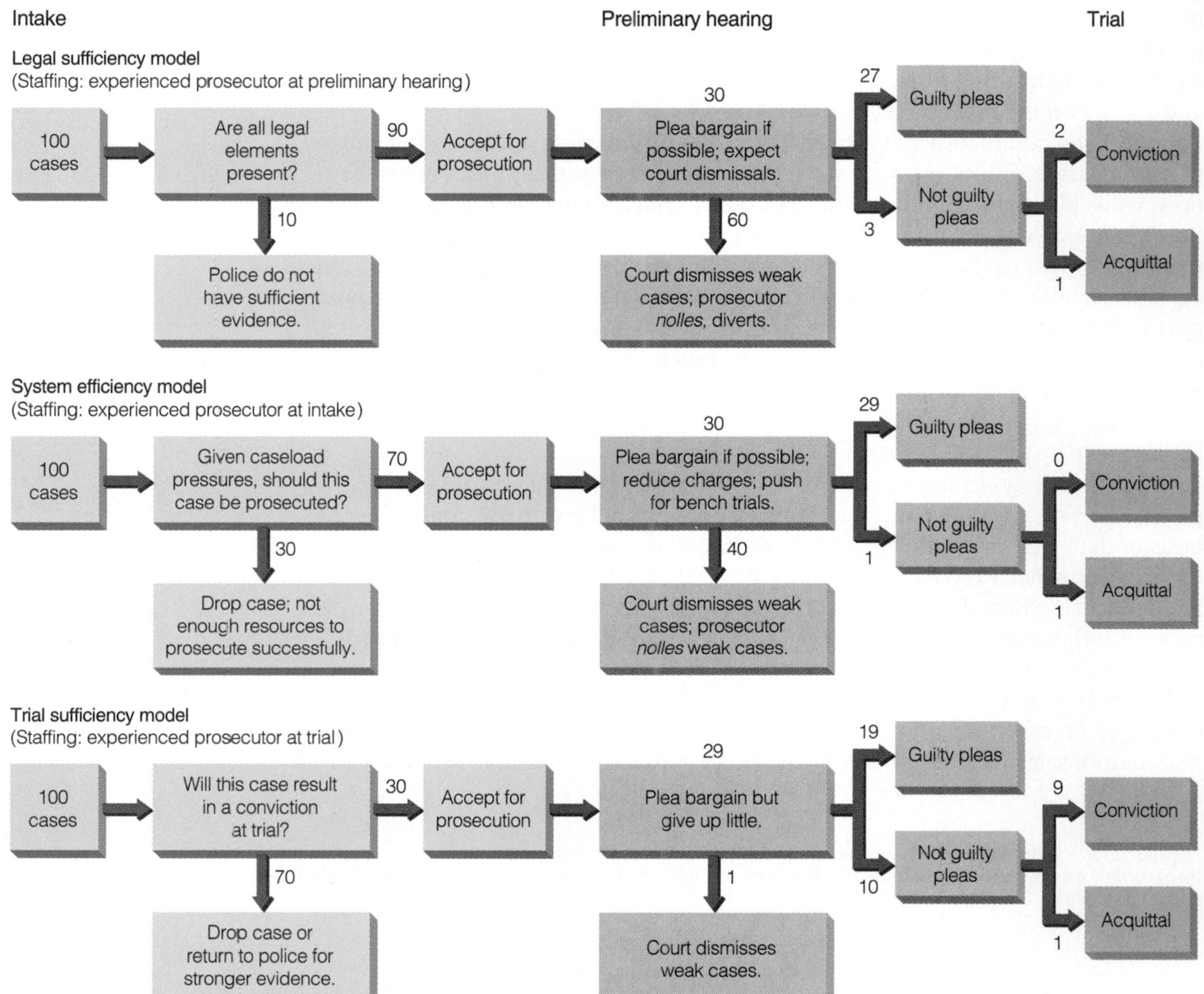

brought to them by the police. Each model identifies the point in the process at which cases are filtered out of the system. A particular model may be chosen to advance specific goals, such as saving the prosecutor's time and energy for the most clear-cut or serious cases. Each model also affects how and when prosecutors interact with defense attorneys in exchanging information or discussing options for a plea bargain.

In the **legal sufficiency** model, prosecutors merely ask whether there is enough evidence to serve as a basis for prosecution. Some prosecutors believe they should pursue any case that likely meets the minimum legal elements of the charge. Prosecutors who use this policy may decide to prosecute a great many cases. As a result, they must have strategies to avoid overloading the system and draining their own resources. Thus, assistant prosecutors, especially those assigned to misdemeanor courts, make extensive use of plea bargains to keep cases flowing through the courts. In this model, judges often dismiss many cases after determining that there is not enough evidence for prosecution to continue.

The **system efficiency** model aims at speedy and early disposition of a case. Each case is evaluated in light of the current caseload pressures. To close cases quickly, the prosecutor might charge the defendant with a felony but agree to reduce the charge to a misdemeanor in exchange for a guilty plea. According to Ja-

legal sufficiency
The presence of the minimum legal elements necessary for prosecution of a case. When a prosecutor uses legal sufficiency as the customary criterion for prosecuting cases, a great many are accepted for prosecution, but the majority of them are disposed of by plea bargaining or dismissal.

system efficiency
Policy of the prosecutor's office that encourages speedy and early disposition of cases in response to caseload pressures. Weak cases are screened out at intake, and other nontrial alternatives are used as primary means of disposition.

coby's research, this model is usually followed when the trial court is backlogged and the prosecutor has limited resources.

In the **trial sufficiency** model, a case is accepted and charges are made only when there is enough evidence to ensure conviction. For each case the prosecutor asks, "Will this case result in a conviction?" The prosecutor might not correctly predict the likelihood of conviction in every case. However, the prosecutor will make every effort to win a conviction when he or she believes there is evidence to prove that all necessary legal elements for a crime are present. This model requires good police work, a prosecution staff with trial experience, and—because there is less plea bargaining—courts that are not too crowded to handle many trials.

trial sufficiency
The presence of sufficient legal elements to ensure successful prosecution of a case. When a prosecutor uses trial sufficiency as the customary criterion for prosecuting cases, only cases that seem certain to result in conviction at trial are accepted for prosecution. Use of plea bargaining is minimal; good police work and court capacity to go to trial are required.

Clearly, these three models lead to different results. While a suspect's case may be dismissed for lack of evidence in a "trial sufficiency" court, the same case may be prosecuted and the defendant pressured to enter a guilty plea in a "legal sufficiency" court.

Case Evaluation

The **accusatory process** is the series of activities that take place from the moment a suspect is arrested and booked by the police to the moment the formal charge—in the form of an indictment or information—is filed with the court. In an *indictment,* evidence is presented to a grand jury made up of citizens who determine whether to issue a formal charge. In an *information,* the prosecutor files the charge. Although these two charging processes seem clear-cut (see Figure 10.4), in practice, variations can mix the roles of the city police, prosecutor, and

accusatory process
The series of events from the arrest of a suspect to the filing of a formal charge with the court (through an indictment or information).

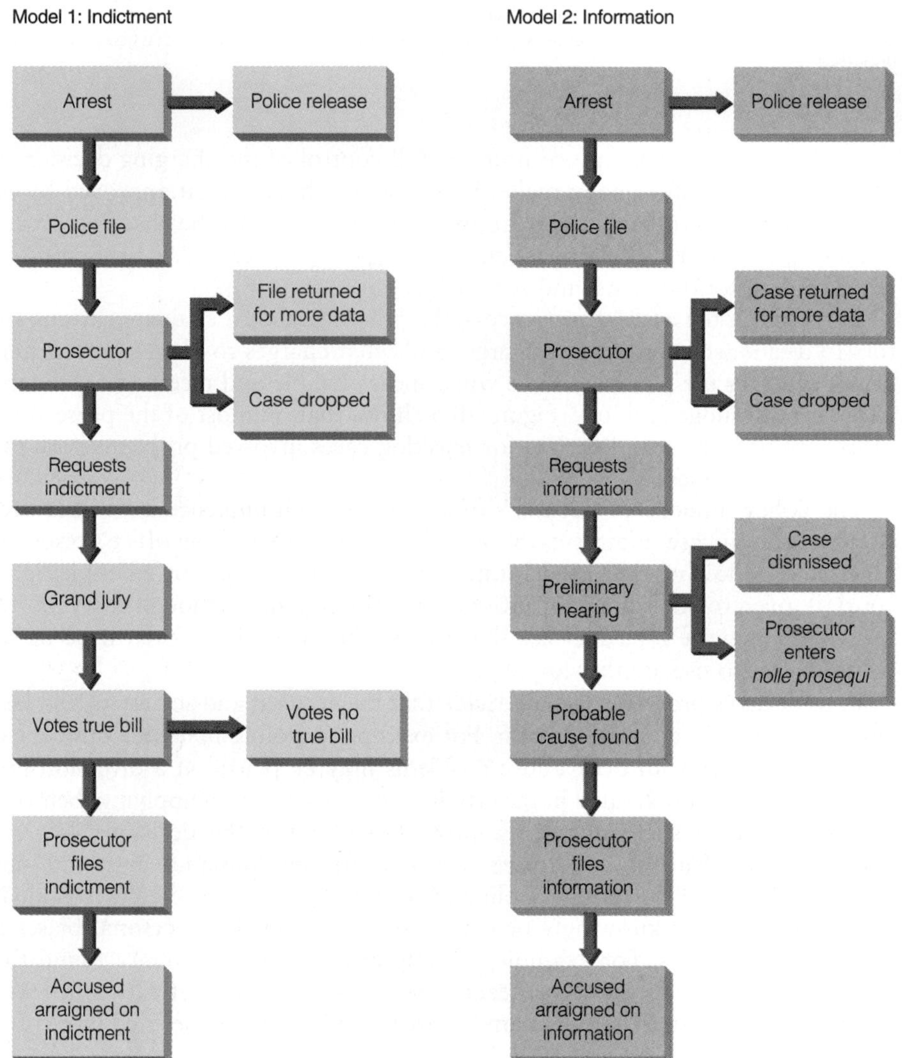

Figure 10.4
Two models of the accusatory process
Indictment and information are the two methods used in the United States to accuse a person of a crime. Note the role of the grand jury in an indictment and the preliminary hearing in an information. According to the ideal of due process, each method is designed to spare an innocent person the psychological, monetary, and other costs of prosecution.

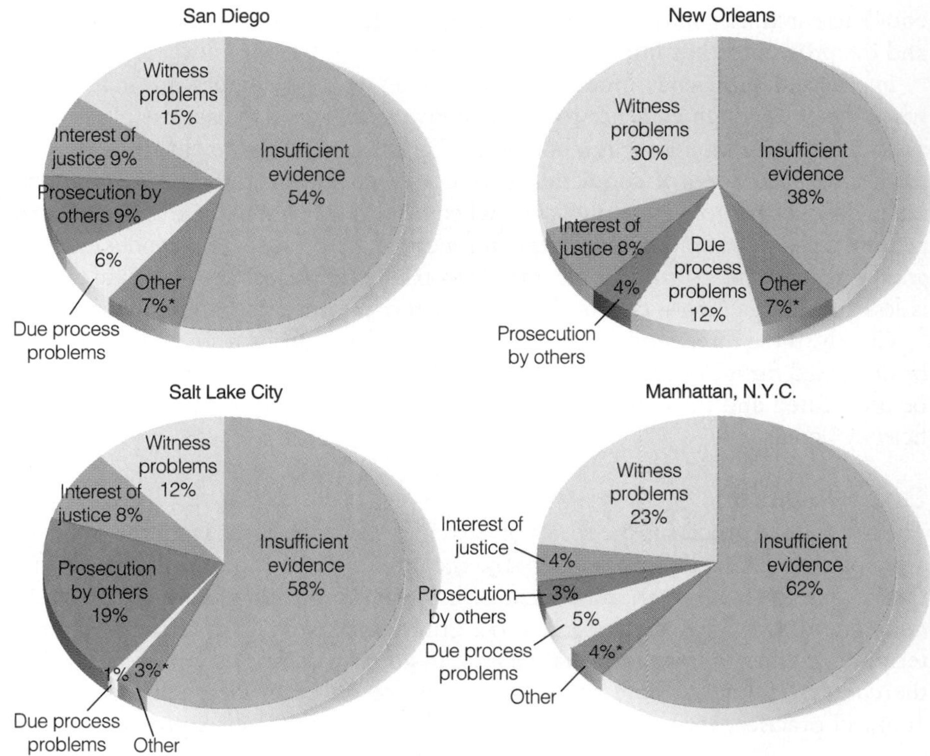

Figure 10.5
Reasons for declining to prosecute felony cases in four cities
Insufficient evidence was the main reason for declining to prosecute in the four cities studied, but note that the proportions vary.

*Includes diversion and plea to include another case.

Note: Figures may not add up to 100 percent because of rounding.

Source: Adapted from Bureau of Justice Statistics, *Report to the Nation on Crime and Justice,* 2nd ed. (Washington, D.C.: U.S. Government Printing Office, 1988), 73.

court. In some places the prosecutor has full control of the charging decision; in others, the police informally make the decision, which is then approved by the prosecutor; in still others, the prosecutor not only controls the charging process but also is involved in functions such as setting the court calendar, appointing defense counsel for indigents, and sentencing.

Throughout the accusatory process, the prosecutor must evaluate various factors to decide whether to press charges and what charges to file. He or she must decide whether the reported crime will appear credible and meet legal standards in the eyes of judge and jury. Figure 10.5 shows that, in most of the prosecution offices studied, the main reasons for rejecting cases involved problems with evidence and witnesses.

The policy model a prosecutor's office follows will influence his or her decision on a given case. However, the specifics of the case and the office's resources may make following that model impractical or impossible. For example, if the court is overcrowded and the prosecutor does not have enough lawyers, the prosecutor may be forced to use the system efficiency model even if he or she would prefer to use another approach.

In some cases prosecutors may decide that the accused and society would benefit from a certain course of action. For example, a young first-time offender or a minor offender with drug abuse problems may be placed in a diversion program rather than prosecuted in the criminal justice system. In applying their own values in making such judgments, prosecutors may make decisions that run counter to the ideals of law. Prosecutors are, after all, human beings who must respond to some of the most troubling problems in American society. In evaluating cases, they may knowingly or unknowingly permit their personal biases to affect their decisions. For example, a study in Los Angeles County found that men were more likely to be prosecuted than women and that Hispanics were prosecuted more often than African Americans, who were prosecuted more often

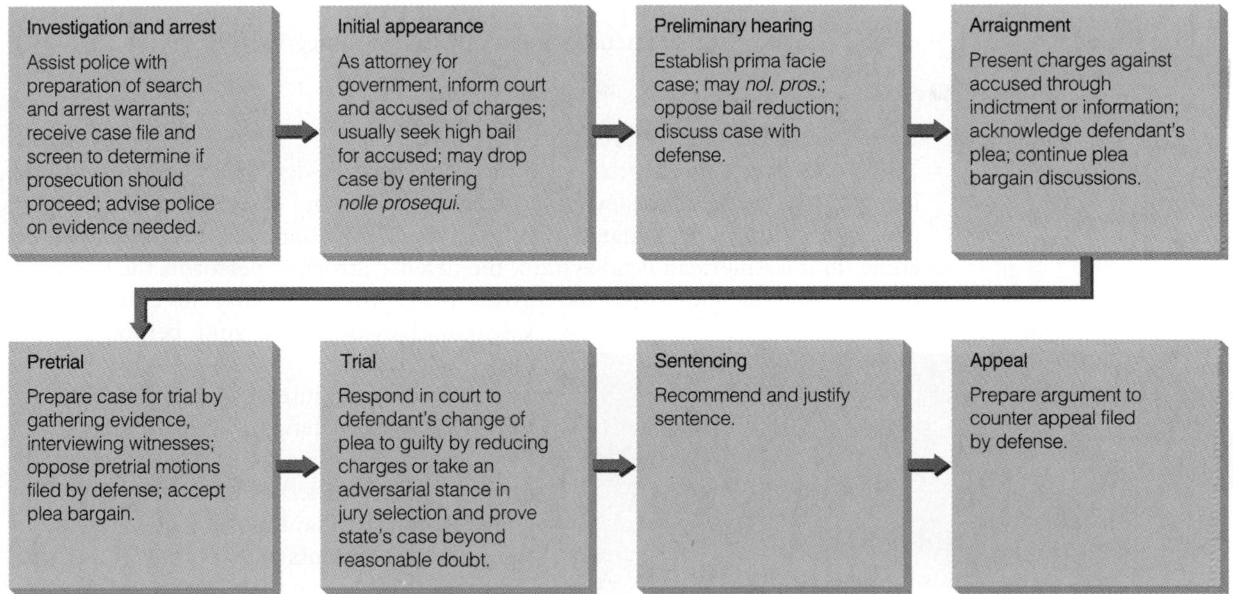

Figure 10.6 **Typical actions of a prosecuting attorney in processing a felony case**
The prosecutor has certain responsibilities at various points in the process. At each point the prosecutor is an advocate for the state's case against the accused.

than Anglos. The researchers believed that in borderline cases—those that could either be pursued or dismissed—the scale was often tipped against minorities (Spohn, Gruhl, and Welch, 1987).

Clearly, the prosecutor's established policies and decisions play a key role in determining whether charges will be filed against a defendant. Keep in mind, though, that the prosecutor's decision-making power is not limited to decisions about charges. As shown in Figure 10.6, the prosecutor makes important decisions at each stage, both before and after a defendant's guilt is determined. Because the prosecutor's involvement and influence span the justice process, from seeking search warrants during early investigations to arguing against post-conviction appeals, the prosecutor is a highly influential actor in criminal cases. No other participant in the system is involved in so many different stages of the criminal process.

6. What are the three models of prosecution policy, and how do they differ?

The Defense Attorney: Image and Reality

In an adversarial system, the **defense attorney** is the lawyer who represents accused and convicted people in their dealings with the criminal justice system. Most Americans have seen defense attorneys in action on television dramas such as *The Practice, Ally McBeal,* and *Law and Order.* In these dramas, defense attorneys vigorously battle the prosecution, and the jury often finds their clients innocent. These images are reinforced by news stories about defense attorneys such as F. Lee Bailey, Johnnie Cochran, Alan Dershowitz, and Robert Shapiro, who have gained public recognition by taking high profile, sensational cases that result in jury trials.

defense attorney
The lawyer who represents accused or convicted offenders in their dealings with criminal justice officials.

In contrast, most cases are handled by criminal lawyers who must quickly process a large volume of cases for small fees. Rather than adversarial conflict in the courtroom, they process cases through plea bargaining, discretionary dismissals, and other means. In these cases, the defense attorney may seem less like the prosecutor's adversary and more like a partner in the effort to dispose of cases as quickly and efficiently as possible through negotiation.

The Role of the Defense Attorney

To be effective, defense attorneys must have knowledge of law and procedure, investigative skills, advocacy experience, and, in many cases, relationships with prosecutors and judges that will help a defendant obtain the best possible outcome. In the American legal system, the defense attorney performs the key function of making sure that the prosecution proves its case in court or has substantial evidence of guilt before a guilty plea is entered.

AP/Nick Ut

Nationally known criminal defense specialist Robert Shapiro requests that the bailiff remove the handcuffs from actor Robert Downey, Jr., during Downey's sentencing for violating probation that had been granted during a 1996 drug conviction. Few defendants can pay the high fees commanded by attorneys such as Shapiro.

As shown in Figure 10.7, the defense attorney advises the defendant and protects his or her constitutional rights at each stage of the criminal justice process. The defense attorney advises the defendant during questioning by the police, represents him or her at each arraignment and hearing, and serves as advocate for the defendant during the appeals process if there is a conviction. Without a defense attorney, prosecutors and judges might not respect the rights of the accused. Without knowing the technical details of law and court procedures, defendants have little ability to represent themselves in court effectively.

While filling their roles in the criminal justice system, the defense attorneys also give psychological support to the defendant and his or her family. Relatives are often bewildered, frightened, and confused. The defense attorney is the only legal actor available to answer the question "What will happen next?" In short, the attorney's relationship with the client is crucial. An effective defense requires respect, openness, and trust between attorney and client. If the defendant refuses to follow the attorney's advice, the lawyer may feel obliged to withdraw from the case in order to protect his or her own professional reputation.

Realities of the Defense Attorney's Job

How well do defense attorneys represent their clients? The television image of defense attorneys is usually based on the due process model, in which attorneys are strong advocates for their clients. In reality, the enthusiasm and effectiveness of defense attorneys vary.

Attorneys who are inexperienced, uncaring, or overburdened have trouble representing their clients effectively. The attorney may quickly agree to a plea bargain and then work to persuade the defendant to accept the agreement. The attorney's self-interest in disposing of cases quickly, receiving payment, and moving on to other cases may cause the attorney to, in effect, work with the prosecutor to pressure the defendant to plead guilty.

On the other hand, although skilled defense attorneys will also consider a plea bargain in the earliest stages of a case, their use of plea bargaining will be guided by their role as an advocate for the defendant. An effective defense attor-

Figure 10.7 **Typical actions of a defense attorney processing a felony case**
Defense attorneys serve as advocates for the accused. They are obliged to challenge points made by the prosecution and to advise clients on their rights.

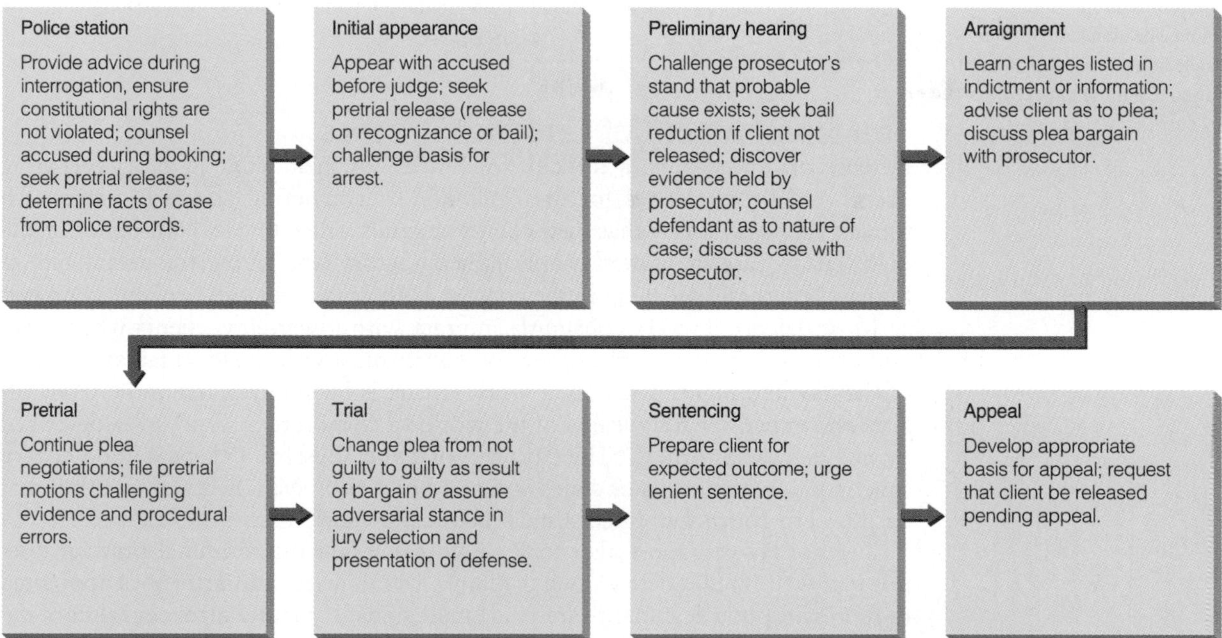

ney does not try to take every case all the way to trial. In many cases, a negotiated plea with a predictable sentence will serve the defendant better than a trial spent fending off more serious charges. Good defense attorneys seek to understand the facts of each case and to judge the nature of the evidence in order to reach the best possible outcome for their client. Even in the plea-bargaining process, this level of advocacy requires more time, effort, knowledge, and commitment than some attorneys are willing or able to provide.

The defense attorney's job is all the more difficult because neither the public nor defendants fully understand the attorney's duties and goals. The public often views defense attorneys as protectors of criminals. In fact, the attorney's basic duty is not to save criminals from punishment but to protect constitutional rights, keep the prosecution honest in preparing and presenting cases, and prevent innocent people from being convicted. Surveys indicate that lawyers place much greater emphasis on the importance of right to counsel than does the public. Look at the question presented in "What Americans Think." Do you think that the public underestimates the necessity of representation by an attorney? Alternatively, might this data indicate that the public believes criminal defendants already have too many rights?

In performing tasks that ultimately benefit both the defendant and society, the defense attorney must evaluate and challenge the prosecution's evidence. However, defense attorneys can rarely arrange for guilty defendants to go free. Keep in mind that when prosecutors decide to pursue serious charges, they have already filtered out weaker cases. The defense attorney often negotiates the most appropriate punishment in light of the resources of the court, the strength of the evidence, and the defendant's prior criminal record.

Defendants who, like the public, have watched hours of *The Practice* on television often expect their attorneys to fight vigorous battles against the prosecutor at every stage of the justice process. They do not realize that their best interest may require plea agreements negotiated in a friendly, cooperative way. Public defenders in particular are often criticized because the defendants tend to assume that if the state provided an attorney for them, the attorney must be working for the state rather than on their behalf.

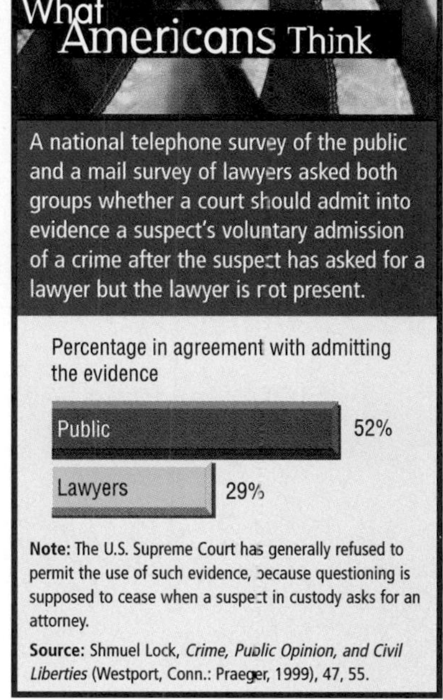

Look at the Web page for a private criminal defense attorney: http://www.davidalandarby.com. Does it provide useful information for people facing criminal charges? Would you hire this attorney? Why or why not?

check point

7. How does the image of the defense attorney differ from the attorney's actual role?

The Environment of Criminal Practice

Defense attorneys have a difficult job. Much of their work involves preparing clients and their relatives for the likelihood of conviction and punishment. Although they may know that their clients are guilty, they may become emotionally involved because they are the only judicial actors who know the defendants as human beings and see them in the context of their family and social environment.

Most defense lawyers constantly interact with lower-class clients whose lives and problems are depressing. They sometimes must visit the local jail at all hours of the day and night. Thus, their work setting is far removed from the fancy offices and expensive restaurants of the world of corporate attorneys. As described by one defense attorney, "The days are long and stressful. I spend a good deal of time in jail, which reeks of stale food and body odor. My clients often think that because I'm court-appointed, I must be incompetent" (Lave, 1998).

Defense lawyers must also struggle with the fact that criminal practice does not pay well. Public defenders have fairly low salaries, and attorneys appointed to represent poor defendants are paid small sums. If private attorneys do not demand payment from their clients at the start of the case, they may find that they must persuade the defendants' relatives to pay—because many convicted offenders have no incentive to pay for legal services while sitting in a prison cell. To perform their jobs well and gain satisfaction from their careers, defense attorneys must focus on goals other than money, such as their key role in protecting people's constitutional rights. However, usually being on the losing side can make it hard for them to feel like professionals—with high self-esteem and satisfying work.

Defense attorneys face other pressures as well. If they mount a strong defense and gain an acquittal for their client, the public may blame them for using "technicalities" to keep a criminal on the streets. If they embarrass the prosecution in court, they may harm their prospects for reaching good plea agreements for future clients. Thus, criminal practice can bring major financial, social, and psychological burdens to attorneys. As a result, many criminal attorneys are "burned out" after a few years, and few stay in the field past the age of 50.

Relationship to Court Officials

Because plea bargaining is the main method of deciding cases, defense attorneys believe they must maintain close personal ties with the police, prosecutor, judges, and other court officials. Critics point out that the defenders' independence is undermined by daily interaction with the same prosecutors and judges. When the supposed adversaries become close friends as a result of daily contact, the defense attorneys might no longer fight vigorously on behalf of their clients. Also, at every step of the justice process, from the first contact with the accused until final disposition of the case, defense attorneys depend on decisions made by other actors in the system. Even seemingly minor activities such as visiting the defendant in jail, learning about the case from the prosecutor, and setting bail can be difficult unless defense attorneys have the cooperation of others in the system. Thus defense attorneys may limit their activities in order to preserve their relationships with other courthouse actors.

For the criminal lawyer who depends on a large volume of petty cases from poor clients and assumes that they are probably guilty, the incentives to bargain are strong. If the attorney is to be assigned other cases, he or she must help make sure that cases flow smoothly through the courthouse. This requires a cooperative relationship with judges, prosecutors, and others in the justice system.

Despite their dependence on cooperation from other justice system officials to make their work go more smoothly, defense attorneys can sometimes use stubbornness as a tactic. They can, for example, threaten to take a case all the way through trial to test whether the prosecutor is really adamant about not reaching a favorable plea agreement. Some paying clients may expect their counsel to play the role of combatant in the belief that they are not getting their money's worth unless there are verbal fireworks in the courtroom. Yet even when those fireworks do occur, one cannot be sure that the adversaries are engaged in a real contest. Studies have shown that attorneys whose clients expect a vigorous defense may engage in a courtroom drama commonly known as the "slow plea of guilty," in which the outcome of the case has already been determined but the attorneys go through the motions of putting up a vigorous fight. It is often hard for defendants to understand the benefits of plea bargaining and friendly relationships between defense attorneys and prosecutors. Most cases that are pursued beyond the initial stages are not likely to result in acquittal, no matter how vigorously the attorney presents the defendant's case. In many cases the evidence of the defendant's guilt simply cannot be overcome by skilled lawyering. Thus good relationships can benefit the defendant by gaining a less-than-maximum sentence. At the same time, however, these relationships pose the risk that if the defense attorney and prosecutor are too friendly, the defendant's case will not be presented in the best possible way in plea bargaining or trial.

Relationship to Clients

Some scholars have called defense attorneys "agent-mediators" because they often work to prepare the defendant for the likely outcome of the case—usually conviction (A. Blumberg, 1967). While such efforts may help the defendant gain a good plea bargain and become mentally prepared to accept the sentence, the attorney's efforts are geared to advance the needs of the attorney and the legal system. By mediating between the defendant and the system—for example, by encouraging a guilty plea—the attorney helps save time for the prosecutor and judge in gaining a conviction and completing the case. In addition, appointed counsel and contract attorneys may have a financial interest in getting the defendant to plead guilty quickly so that they can receive payment and move on to the next case.

A more sympathetic view of defense attorneys labels them "beleaguered dealers" who cut deals for defendants in a tough environment (Uphoff, 1992). While many of their actions help push cases through the courts, defense attorneys face tremendous pressure to manage large caseloads in a difficult court environment. From this perspective, their actions in encouraging clients to plead guilty result from the difficult aspects of their jobs rather than from self-interest. Yet, as described in the Close Up box, some public defenders do maintain a personal interest in their clients.

check point

8. What special pressures do defense attorneys face?

Counsel for Indigents

Since the 1960s, the Supreme Court has interpreted the "right to counsel" in the Sixth Amendment to the Constitution as requiring that the government provide attorneys for indigent defendants who face the possibility of going to prison or jail. *Indigent defendants* are those who are too poor to afford their own lawyers. The Court has also required that attorneys be provided early in the criminal justice process to protect suspects' rights during questioning and pretrial proceedings. See Table 10.1 for a summary of key rulings on the right to counsel.

Go to the Public Policy feature on the American System of Criminal Justice CD to learn more about the issues surrounding counsel for indigents.

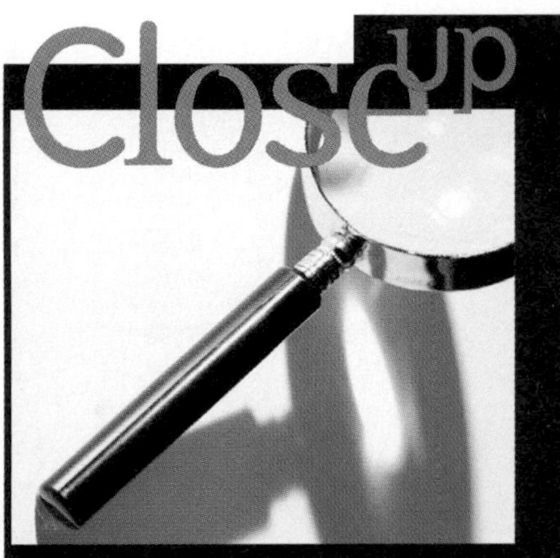

The Public Defender: Lawyer, Social Worker, Parent

Eddie, a nervous-looking heroin abuser with a three-page police record, isn't happy with his lawyer's news about his latest shoplifting arrest.

"The prosecutor feels you should be locked up for a long time," public defender William Paetzold tells Eddie in a closet-sized interview room in Superior Court. Barely big enough for a desk and two chairs, the room is known as "the pit."

Eddie, 34 and wide-eyed with a blond crew cut, twists a rolled-up newspaper in his hands. And as Paetzold goes over the evidence against him for the theft of $90.67 worth of meat from a supermarket, the paper gets tighter and tighter.

"So, you basically walked right through the doors with the shopping carriage?" Paetzold asks, scanning the police report.

"Well, there was another person involved and we really never got out of the store." Eddie replies quickly, now jingling a pocketful of change.

Eddie wants to take his case to trial. Paetzold doesn't like his chances with a jury.

"If you're going to base your whole case on that statement about not leaving the store, you're going to lose, he says. "If you lose, you're going to get 5 years."

Paetzold advises Eddie to consider pleading guilty in exchange for a lesser sentence.

Eddie rolls his eyes and grumbles. He thinks he deserves a break because he has been doing well in a methadone clinic designed to wean him from heroin.

"I'm not copping to no time." he says, shifting in his seat. "I'm not arguing the fact that I've been a drug addict my whole life, but I haven't been arrested since I've been in that program. I'm finally doing good and they want to bury me."

Paetzold says he will talk to the prosecutor and see what can be done.

"I'll be waiting upstairs," Eddie says, grabbing his newspaper and walking out past a small crowd of other clients. All are waiting to see either Paetzold or the other public defender seeing clients that morning, Phillip Armentano.

Every client wants individual attention. Many expect Paetzold or Armentano to resolve their case with little or no punishment. And they don't care that the lawyers may have 25 other clients to see that morning demanding the same.

"A lot of what we do is almost like social work, says Armentano. "We have the homeless, the mentally ill, the drug addicts, and the alcoholics. Our job just isn't to try to find people not guilty, but to find appropriate punishment, whether that be counseling, community service, or jail time."

"It's like being a parent," says Paetzold. "These clients are our responsibility and they all have problems and they want those problems solved now."

And like many parents, the lawyers often feel overwhelmed. Too many cases, not enough time or a big enough staff. Those obstacles contribute to another—the stigma that overworked public defenders are pushovers for prosecutors and judges.

"There's a perception that public defenders don't stand up for their clients," Armentano says. "We hear it all the time, 'Are you a public defender or a real lawyer?' There's a mistrust right from the beginning because they view us as part of the system that got them arrested."

With a caseload of more than a thousand clients a year, Paetzold and Armentano acknowledge that they cannot devote as much time to each client as a private lawyer can. But they insist that their clients get vigorous representation.

"Lawyers are competitors, whether you're a public defender or not," Paetzold says. "I think that under the conditions, we do a very good job for our clients."

Source: Steve Jensen, "The Public Defender: He's One Part Lawyer, One Part Social Worker and One Part Parent," *Hartford Courant,* September 4, 1994, p. H1. Reprinted with permission.

Researching the Internet

For one attempt to educate the public about the role of public defenders, see information about the Los Angeles public defender office at http://pd.co.la.ca.us.

Research on felony defendants indicates that 78 percent of those prosecuted in the 75 largest counties and 66 percent of those prosecuted in federal courts received publicly provided legal counsel (Harlow, 2000). The portion of defendants who are provided with counsel because they are indigent has increased greatly in the past three decades.

Many debate the quality of counsel given to indigent defendants (A. P. Worden, 1991). Ideally, experienced lawyers would be appointed soon after arrest to represent the defendant in each stage of the criminal justice process. However,

Table 10.1 The right to counsel: Major Supreme Court rulings

Case	Year	Ruling
Powell v. Alabama	1932	Indigents facing the death penalty who are not capable of representing themselves must be given attorneys.
Johnson v. Zerbst	1938	Indigent defendants must be provided with attorneys when facing serious charges in federal court.
Gideon v. Wainwright	1963	Indigent defendants must be provided with attorneys when facing serious charges in state court.
Douglas v. California	1963	Indigent defendants must be provided with attorneys for their first appeal.
Miranda v. Arizona	1966	Criminal suspects must be informed about their right to counsel before being questioned in custody.
United States v. Wade	1967	Defendants are entitled to counsel at "critical stages" in the process, including post-indictment lineups.
Argersinger v. Hamlin	1972	Indigent defendants must be provided with attorneys when facing misdemeanor and petty charges that may result in incarceration.
Ross v. Moffitt	1974	Indigent defendants are not entitled to attorneys for discretionary appeals after their first appeal is unsuccessful.
Strickland v. Washington	1984	To show ineffective assistance of counsel violated the right to counsel, defendants must prove that the attorney committed specific errors that affected the outcome of the case.
Murray v. Giarratano	1989	Death row inmates do not have a right to counsel for habeas corpus proceedings asserting rights violations in their cases.

inexperienced and uncaring attorneys are sometimes appointed. When this takes place during court proceedings, the attorney has no time to prepare the case. Even conscientious attorneys may be unable to provide top-quality counsel if they have heavy caseloads or are not paid enough money to spend the time required to handle the case well.

If they lack the time and desire to interview clients and prepare their cases, appointed counsels may simply persuade defendants to plead guilty right there in the courtroom during their first and only brief conversation. When the lawyers assigned to provide counsel to poor defendants cooperate with the prosecutor easily, without even asking the defendant about his or her version of events, it is little wonder that convicted offenders often believe that their interests were not represented in the courtroom. Not all publicly financed lawyers who represent poor defendants ignore their clients' interests. However, the quality of counsel received by the poor may vary from courthouse to courthouse, depending on the quality of the attorneys, conditions of defense practice, and administrative pressure to reduce the caseload.

AP/Wide World Pictures, Inc.

Public defenders are often thought to lack experience; yet research shows that they do the job well. In San Luis Obispo, California, Rex Allen Krebs appears with public defender James B. Maguire III at his arraignment. Krebs was charged with the kidnapping, sodomy, rape, and murder of college students Rachel Newhouse and Aundria Crawford.

Ways of Providing Indigents with Counsel

The three main ways of providing counsel to indigent defendants in the United States are (1) the **assigned counsel** system, in which a court appoints a private attorney to represent the accused; (2) the **contract counsel** system, in which an attorney, a nonprofit organization, or a private law firm contracts with a local government to provide legal services to indigent defendants for a specified dollar amount; and (3) **public defender** programs, which are public or private nonprofit organizations with full-time or part-time salaried staff. Figure 10.8 presents the system used in the majorities of counties in each of the 50 states. Note, however, that many counties use a combination of methods to provide representation. In particular, 23 percent of counties use both public defenders and assigned counsel (S. K. Smith and DeFrances, 1996). Counties that have sufficient resources, often send cases to assigned counsel when public defenders' caseloads become too large.

assigned counsel
An attorney in private practice assigned by a court to represent an indigent. The attorney's fee is paid by the government with jurisdiction over the case.

contract counsel
An attorney in private practice who contracts with the government to represent all indigent defendants in a county during a set period of time and for a specified dollar amount.

public defender
An attorney employed on a full-time, salaried basis by the government to represent indigents.

Assigned Counsel In the assigned counsel system, the court appoints a lawyer in private practice to represent an indigent defendant. This system is widely used in small cities and in rural areas, but even some city public defender systems assign counsel in some cases, such as in a case with multiple defendants, where a conflict of interest might result if one of them were represented by a public lawyer.

Figure 10.8 **Indigent defense system used by the majority of counties in each state**
Note that some states use a mixture of methods to provide counsel for indigents.

Source: Bureau of Justice Statistics, *Bulletin,* September 1988.

One state organization for defense attorneys is the New York State Defenders Association; see http://www.nysda.org.

But in other cities, such as Detroit, the private bar has been able to insist that its members receive a large share of the cases (see Table 10.2).

Assigned counsel systems are organized on either an ad hoc system or a coordinated basis. In ad hoc assignment systems, private attorneys tell the judge that they are willing to take the cases of indigent defendants. When an indigent requires counsel, the judge either assigns lawyers in rotation from a prepared list or chooses one of the attorneys who are known and present in the courtroom. In coordinated assignment systems, a court administrator oversees the appointment of counsel.

Use of the ad hoc system may raise questions about the loyalties of the assigned counsel. Are they trying to vigorously defend their clients or are they trying to please the judges to ensure future appointments? For example, Texas has been criticized for giving judges free rein to assign lawyers to cases without any supervising authority to ensure that the attorneys actually do a good job (Novak, 1999). Additional concerns have arisen in Texas and other states where judges run for election, because lawyers often donate money to judges' political campaigns. Judges may return the favor by supplying their contributors with criminal defense assignments. As you read the lawyers' conversation in "A Question of Ethics," consider what you would do if you were a new lawyer seeking to gain experience in criminal defense work.

Table 10.2 **Fees paid to assigned counsel in Colorado**

Colorado's statewide fee schedule states the hourly rate an attorney can charge for indigent defense. Note the maximum amounts for each case.

Standard Fees	Per Hour	
Death penalty cases	$65.00	
Type A felonies (e.g., violence)	$51.00	
Type B felonies (e.g., drugs)	$47.00	
Other (juvenile/traffic/misdemeanor)	$45.00	
Maximum Fee Payments	**With Trial**	**Without Trial**
Class 1 felonies (death penalty, life, 51+ years)	$15,000	$7,500
Class 2 felonies (41- to 50-year sentences possible)	$ 7,500	$3,750
Class 3, 4, and 5 felonies (1- to 40-year sentences possible)	$ 5,000	$2,500
Misdemeanor	$ 1,000	$ 500
Juvenile	$ 1,500	$1,000

Source: Colorado Office of Alternate Defense Counsel. 1999.

The fees paid to assigned defenders are often low compared with what a lawyer might otherwise charge (see Table 10.2). While a private practice attorney might charge clients at rates that exceed $150 per hour, hourly rates for appointed counsel in Illinois are merely $30 per hour for out-of-court tasks and $40 per hour for in-court work. These rates have remained unchanged since 1975. In many Texas counties, judges determine rates for themselves, and some pay as little as $25 per hour to attorneys who represent indigent defendants (Novak, 1999). In 1999 the average hourly overhead cost for attorneys—the amount they must make just to pay their secretaries, office rent, and telephone bills—was $58 (National Legal Aid and Defender Association, 1999). If their hourly fees do not exceed their overhead costs, then attorneys are making no money at all for spending their time on these cases.

Low fees discourage skilled attorneys from taking criminal cases. Low fees may also induce a defender to persuade clients to plead guilty to a lesser charge. Many assigned defenders find that they can make more money by collecting a preparation fee of about $50, payable when an indigent client pleads guilty, than by going to trial. Trials are very time-consuming, and appointed attorneys often feel that the fees paid by the state are not high enough to cover the amount of time required to prepare for trial, especially when the fee is a flat rate per case or trial rather than an hourly rate. It usually is more profitable to handle many quick plea bargains than to spend weeks preparing for a trial for which the fee may be only a few hundred dollars.

Many organizations of judges and lawyers lobby Congress, state legislatures, and county councils to increase the amounts paid to assigned counsel. For example, the American Bar Association, the Federal Judges Association, and the National Legal Aid and Defender Association joined forces in 1999 to urge Congress to raise the pay for assigned counsel in federal criminal cases above the rate of $45 for out-of-court work and $65 for in-court work (National Legal Aid and Defender Association, 1999). Many members of Congress, however, do not wish to spend more money for the benefit of criminal defendants.

At a county bar association luncheon to honor recent law school graduates, Sarah Schweitzer, one of the new attorneys, sought advice from Wilton Davis, an experienced criminal defense lawyer.

"Mr. Davis, how can I build my reputation so that I attract clients?"

"The most obvious way is to start seeking assignments to represent indigent defendants. Go down to the courthouse and introduce yourself to Judge Garvey. Tell her that I sent you. If she likes you, she'll start giving you some misdemeanors and, if you do okay, you might start getting some felonies, which pay a little bit better—although still not very much."

"Are cases assigned in rotation to lawyers on a list?"

Davis chuckled. "Not exactly. Judge Garvey has her own list and she decides on the order. Some people say that the attorneys who get the most assignments have two things in common. They are contributors to Judge Garvey's campaigns and their clients plead guilty quickly rather than going to trial. Working on those assigned cases will help you build a reputation, but they'll also make you appreciate the paying clients you get later. Paying clients really give you a chance to use your skills."

Schweitzer looked troubled. "Are you telling me I must donate money to Judge Garvey's campaigns and encourage my clients to plead guilty if I want to gain experience?"

Davis shook his head. "Look. I'm not telling you what to do with your clients. I'm just telling you how the system works around here."

→ What would you do if you were in Schweitzer's position as a new attorney seeking to gain experience in criminal law? If the system in this county poses ethical problems, who is at fault? The judge who runs the assignment process? The attorneys who cooperate in order to get more cases? The state and county governments that created this system for providing defense attorneys? How would you change this system to make it better?

You can read an essay on ethics by an experienced defense attorney at http://www.cardozo.net/life/winter2001/bennett/.

Contract System The contract system is used in a few counties, mainly in western states. Most states using this method do not have large populations. The government contracts with an attorney, a nonprofit association, or a private law firm to handle all indigent cases (A. P. Worden, 1994). Some jurisdictions use public defenders for most cases but contract for services in multiple-defendant cases that might present conflicts of interest, in extraordinarily complex cases, or in cases that require more time than the government's salaried lawyers can provide.

There are several kinds of contracts (L. Spears, 1991). The most common contract provides for a fixed yearly sum to be paid to the law firm that handles all cases. Some people fear that this method encourages attorneys to cut corners in order to preserve their profits, especially if there are more cases than expected for the year. Other contracts are based on a fixed price per case or per hour of work. Still other jurisdictions use a cost-plus contract, in which a new contract is negotiated when the estimated cost of counsel is surpassed. According to Robert

Counsel for the Indigent in Four Locales

Denver, Colorado

With a population of 505,000, the city and county of Denver is the largest urban area in the Rocky Mountain region. The population tends to be divided between a relatively affluent majority and an impoverished class (15 percent of the population live below the poverty line) made up primarily of the 17 percent of the population that is African American or Hispanic.

Colorado has a statewide public defender system, which is responsible for all indigent cases except for those where there is a conflict (codefendants). The federal guidelines for determining indigency are used, but the information provided by defendants is not checked for accuracy. A $10 fee, waived for those in custody, is charged to those who apply for a public defender. An estimated 85 percent of felony defendants qualify for a public defender.

Twenty-six attorneys staff the Denver public defender's office. They are assisted by ten investigators and clerical staff. New defenders tend to be recent law school graduates who stay six to seven years. Public defenders are paid less than their counterparts in the district attorney's office.

Detroit, Michigan

Wayne County has a population of 2,164,300. Half of the citizens live in the city of Detroit, making it the sixth largest city in the United States. Almost 40 percent of the population is nonwhite and about 15 percent live below the poverty level. Wayne County has a crime rate of almost 10,000 index crimes per 100,000 population.

Detroit provides attorneys to the indigent via assigned counsel and a nonprofit organization similar to a public defender agency. The assignments are distributed between two groups. Approximately 75 percent of the cases are assigned by judges to individual private attorneys; the remainder are allocated to the Legal Aid and Defenders Association, the nonprofit group. Attorneys are paid a fixed fee for their services based on the statutory punishment for the offense.

To be eligible for appointment as assigned counsel, attorneys must complete an application form listing professional experience, education,

Spangenberg and Marea Beeman (1995:49), "There are serious potential dangers with the contract model, such as expecting contract defenders to handle an unlimited caseload or awarding contracts on a low-bid basis only, with no regard to qualifications of contracting attorneys."

Public Defender The public defender is a response to the legal needs of indigent defendants. The concept started in Los Angeles County in 1914, when attorneys were first hired by government to work full-time in criminal defense. The most recent national survey of the 100 most populous counties found that public defender systems handled 82 percent of the 4.2 million indigent criminal cases in 1999, while appointed counsel handled 15 percent and contract counsel represented only 3 percent of defendants (DeFrances and Litras, 2000). The public defender system, which is growing fast, is used in 43 of the 50 most populous counties and in most large cities. There are about 20 statewide, state-funded systems; in other states the counties organize and pay for them. Only two states, North Dakota and Maine, do not have public defenders.

The Web site for the federal public defender service in Washington, D.C., provides information about attorneys who represent indigent criminal defendants: http://www.dcfpd.org.

The public defender system is often viewed as better than the assigned counsel system because public defenders are specialists in criminal law. Because they are full-time government employees, public defenders, unlike appointed counsel and contract attorneys, do not sacrifice their clients' cases to protect their own financial interests. Public defenders do face certain special problems, however.

Public defenders may have trouble gaining the trust and cooperation of their clients. Criminal defendants may assume that attorneys on the state payroll, even with the title "public defender," have no reason to protect the defendants' rights and interests. Lack of cooperation from the defendant may make it harder for the attorney to prepare the best possible arguments for use during hearings, plea bargaining, and trials.

Public defenders may also face heavy caseloads. In New York City's public defender program, for example, Legal Aid lawyers handle as many as 100 felony

and criminal trial experience. Each applicant must be favorably reviewed by a committee of five judges. Once initially certified, an attorney can be assigned only those cases in which the penalty is 20 years or less imprisonment. With additional experience, assignment can be granted for the full range of cases.

Six hundred and fifty attorneys are currently on the assigned counsel list. The pool is composed of about two hundred "hard-core" regulars who depend upon assignments for a substantial portion of their caseload and income. The remainder are "irregulars" who look to assignments to supplement their private civil and criminal practice.

The perception that the defense bar was too cozy with the judiciary and that African Americans were not receiving vigorous defense led to creation of the Legal Aid and Defenders Association (LADA) in the late 1960s. LADA is composed of 20 attorneys who by a Michigan Supreme Court order must receive 25 percent of felony case assignments.

At any one time each LADA attorney carries between 30 and 35 cases. In many ways LADA may be best understood as providing services as would a public defender organization with staff attorneys.

Oxford, Maine

With a population of only 50,200, Oxford County is located in the southwestern mountainous region of Maine. The per capita income averages $9,000, and about 13 percent of the population live below the federal poverty level. The crime rate is low by national standards, with a UCR index offense rate of 1,781 per 100,000 population. Less than one-half of 1 percent of the population are minorities.

Oxford County depends wholly on assigned counsel for indigent defense. By merely informing the court clerk, an attorney can receive assignments, which are given informally by the one visiting superior court judge who holds session for two or three weeks each month. At present only 10 of the 36 attorneys practicing in the county receive indigent cases. Most of these attorneys also do private criminal and civil work.

Assigned counsel are paid by a voucher system and are allowed to charge $40 per hour for both in- and out-of-court work. Indigent defense is funded completely by the state.

Gila County, Arizona

Gila County is a large geographic area half the size of Rhode Island. Globe, the county seat, is located about 90 miles east of Phoenix in the state's copper-mining country. The population is about 40,000, with 16 percent being Hispanic and Native American and 13 percent living below the poverty level. The violent crime rate is 2,500 per 100,000 population.

Gila County contracts with four local attorneys for the provision of defense services to the indigent. Compensation for each attorney averages $45,000 per year. The county provides additional support for investigators. All of the contract attorneys also maintain private criminal and civil practices.

Source: Roger Hanson and Joy Chapper, *Indigent Defense Systems, Report to the State Justice Institute* (Williamsburg, Va.: National Center for State Courts, 1991). Copyright © 1991 by National Center for State Courts.

For more information about criminal defense attorneys, including attorneys for indigent defendants, see the Web site of the National Association of Criminal Defense Lawyers: http://www.criminaljustice.org/public.nsf/FreeForm/PublicWelcome?OpenDocument.

cases at any time. A public defender in Atlanta may be assigned as many as 45 new cases at a *single* arraignment (Bright, 1994). Although the National Legal Aid and Defender Association recommends that defense attorneys handle no more than 400 cases per year, public defenders in Connecticut averaged 1,045 cases per year in 1994 and, despite efforts to reduce caseload pressures, still averaged 618 cases in 1999 (Casey, 1999). Such heavy caseloads do not allow time for attorneys to become familiar with each case. Public defender programs are most effective when they have enough money to keep caseloads manageable. However, these programs do not control their own budgets and usually are not seen as high priorities by state and local governments. Thus it is hard for them to gain the funds they need to give adequate attention to each defendant's case.

Some public defenders' offices try to make better use of limited resources by organizing assignments more efficiently. In some systems, every poor defendant has several public defenders, each handling a different stage or "zone" in the justice process. One attorney may handle all arraignments, another all preliminary hearings, and still another any trial work. No one attorney manages the entire case of any client. Although the zone system may increase efficiency, there is a risk that cases will be processed in a routine way, with no one taking into account special factors. With limited responsibility for a given case, the attorney is less able to advise the defendant about the case as a whole and is unlikely to develop the level of trust needed to gain the defendant's cooperation.

With or without zone systems, overburdened public defenders find it difficult to avoid making routine decisions. One case can come to be viewed as very much like the next, and the process can become routine and repetitive. Overworked attorneys cannot look closely at cases to see if there are special circumstances that would justify a stronger defense.

The Close Up box gives four views of how counsel is provided to indigents in different parts of the United States. Because state and local governments can decide how to provide defense attorneys for indigent defendants, the amount budgeted for criminal defense can vary from county to county. So, too, can the quality of counsel provided to poor defendants vary. Because state and local governments have limited funds, scholars have noted a "tendency to provide representation on the cheap," which raises concerns about the quality of representation (Spangenberg and Beeman, 1995:48).

check point

9. What are the three main methods of providing attorneys for indigent defendants?

Private versus Public Defense

Publicly funded defense attorneys now handle up to 85 percent of the cases in many places, and private defense attorneys have become more and more unusual in many courts. Retained counsel may serve only upper-income defendants charged with white-collar crimes or drug dealers and organized-crime figures who can pay the fees. This trend has made the issue of the quality of representation increasingly important.

Do defendants who can afford their own counsel get better legal services than those who cannot? Many convicted offenders say "you get what you pay for," meaning that they would have received better counsel if they had been able to pay for their own attorneys. At one time, researchers thought public defenders entered more guilty pleas than did lawyers who had been either privately retained or assigned to cases. However, studies show little variation in case outcomes by various types of defense. For example, in a study of plea bargains in nine medium-sized counties in Illinois, Michigan, and Pennsylvania, the type of attorney representing the client appeared to make no difference in the nature of plea agreements (Nardulli, 1986). Other studies have also found few differences among assigned counsel, contract counsel, public defenders, and privately retained counsel with respect to case outcomes and length of sentence (Hanson and Chapper, 1991). Table 10.3 lists data on the relationship between type of counsel and case results in four cities.

check point

10. Are public defenders more effective than private defense attorneys?

Table 10.3 Case disposition and types of defense attorneys

There are few variations in case disposition among the defense systems used in each jurisdiction. Why do the cities differ in case outcomes?

	Detroit, Michigan			Denver, Colorado		Norfolk, Virginia		Monterey, California		
Type of Disposition	Public Defender	Assigned Counsel	Private Counsel	Public Defender	Private Counsel	Assigned Counsel	Private Counsel	Public Defender	Assigned Counsel	Private Counsel
Dismissals	11.9%	14.5%	12.8%	21.0%	24.3%	6.4%	10.4%	13.5%	8.9%	3.0%
Trial acquittals	9.5	5.7	10.3	1.8	0.0	3.3	5.2	1.7	1.3	0.0
Trial convictions	22.6	14.5	24.4	5.1	9.5	5.2	2.2	7.1	11.4	18.2
Guilty pleas	54.8	64.9	52.6	72.1	66.2	85.1	81.3	76.8	78.5	78.8
Diversion	1.2	0.3	0.0	0.0	0.0	0.0	0.7	1.0	0.0	0.0
	100.0%	99.9%	100.1%	100.0%	100.0%	100.0%	99.8%	101.1%	101.1%	100.0%
Total number of cases	84	296	78	276	74	329	134	294	79	33

Source: Roger Hanson and Joy Chapper, *Indigent Defense Systems, Report to the State Justice Institute* (Williamsburg, Va.: National Center for State Courts, 1991).

AFP/Corbis

Attorney competence has increasingly become a national issue. Here, Northwestern University Professor David Protess and his students greet Anthony Porter upon his release from prison. Protess and the students developed information that led to a Wisconsin man's confession to the crime for which Porter served over 16 years on death row. Is it likely that Porter's conviction resulted from his attorney's incompetence? Might there have been other factors?

Attorney Competence

The right to counsel is of little value when the counsel is not competent and effective. The adequacy of counsel provided to both private and public clients is a matter of concern to defense groups, bar associations, and the courts (Goodpaster, 1986). There are, of course, many examples of incompetent counsel (Gershman, 1993). Even in death penalty cases, attorneys have shown up for court so drunk that they could not stand up straight (Bright, 1994). In other cases, attorneys with almost no knowledge of criminal law have made blunders that have needlessly sent their clients to death row (C. E. Smith, 1997b). Lawyers have even fallen asleep during their clients' death penalty trials, yet one Texas judge found no problem with such behavior. He wrote that everyone has a constitutional right to have a lawyer, but "the Constitution does not say that the lawyer has to be awake" (Shapiro, 1997:27). A divided appellate court later disagreed with this conclusion.

In other cases, the definition of inadequate counsel is less clear. What if a public defender's caseload is so large that he or she cannot spend more than a few minutes reviewing the files for most cases? What if, as a deliberate strategy to appear cooperative and thus stay in the judge's good graces, the defense attorney decides not to object to questionable statements and evidence presented by the prosecution? Because attorneys have discretion concerning how to prepare and present their cases, it is hard to define what constitutes a level of performance so inadequate that it violates the defendant's constitutional right to counsel.

The U.S. Supreme Court has examined the question of what requirements must be met if defendants are to receive effective counsel. In two 1984 cases, *United States v. Cronic* and *Strickland v. Washington,* the Court set standards for effective assistance of counsel. Cronic had been charged with a complex mail fraud scheme, which the government had investigated for four and a half years. Just before trial, Cronic's retained lawyer withdrew and a young attorney—who had no trial experience and whose practice was mainly in real estate law—was appointed. The trial court gave the new attorney only 25 days to prepare for the trial, in which Cronic was convicted. The Supreme Court upheld Cronic's conviction on the grounds that, although the new trial counsel had made errors, there was no evidence that the trial had not been a "meaningful" test of the prosecution's case or that the conviction had not been justified.

In *Strickland v. Washington,* the Supreme Court rejected the defendant's claim that his attorney did not adequately prepare for the sentencing hearing in a death penalty case (the attorney sought neither character statements nor a psychiatric examination to present on the defendant's behalf). As it has done in later cases, the Court indicated its reluctance to second-guess a defense attorney's actions. By focusing on whether errors by an attorney were bad enough to make the trial result unreliable and to deny a fair trial, the Court has made it hard for defendants to prove that they were denied effective counsel, even when defense attorneys perform very poorly. As a result, innocent people who were poorly represented have been convicted, even of the most serious crimes (Radelet, Bedeau, and Putnam, 1992).

When imprisoned people are proved innocent and released—sometimes after losing their freedom for many years—we are reminded that the American justice system is imperfect. The development of DNA testing has produced regular reminders of the system's imperfections as new reports surface nearly every month of innocent people released from prison after evidence was reexamined. For example, in 1996 four men, including two who had been on death row, were released from prison in Illinois after serving 18 years for murders they did not commit (D. Terry, 1996). By 2002 more than 100 innocent people had been released from death rows around the country during the preceding 25 years. Such reminders highlight the importance of having quality legal counsel for criminal defendants. However, because state and local governments have limited funds, concerns about the quality of defense attorneys' work will persist.

check point

11. How has the U.S. Supreme Court addressed the issue of attorney competence?

Summary

- American prosecutors, both state and federal, have significant discretion to determine how to handle criminal cases.
- There is no higher authority over most prosecutors that can overrule a decision to decline to prosecute (*nolle prosequi*) or to pursue multiple counts against a defendant.
- The prosecutor can play various roles, including trial counsel for the police, house counsel for the police, representative of the court, and elected official.

- Prosecutors' decisions and actions are affected by their exchange relationships with many other important actors and groups, including police, judges, victims and witnesses, and the public.
- The three primary models of prosecutors' decision-making policies are legal sufficiency, system efficiency, and trial sufficiency.
- The image of defense attorneys as courtroom advocates is often vastly different from the reality of pressured, busy negotiators constantly involved in bargaining with the prosecutor over guilty plea agreements.
- Relatively few private defense attorneys make significant incomes from criminal work, but large numbers of private attorneys accept court appointments to handle indigent defendants' cases quickly for relatively low fees.
- Defense attorneys must often wrestle with difficult working conditions and uncooperative clients as they seek to provide representation, usually in the plea negotiation process.
- Three primary methods for providing attorneys to represent indigent defendants are appointed counsel, contract counsel, and public defenders.
- Private and public attorneys provide similar quality of counsel.
- The quality of representation provided to criminal defendants is a matter of significant concern, but U.S. Supreme Court rulings have made it difficult for convicted offenders to prove that their attorneys did not provide a competent defense.

Questions for Review

1. What are the formal powers of the prosecuting attorney?
2. How do politics affect prosecutors?
3. What considerations influence the prosecutor's decision about whether to bring charges and what to charge?
4. Why is the prosecuting attorney often cited as the most powerful office in the criminal justice system?
5. What problems do defense attorneys face?
6. How is the defense attorney an agent-mediator?
7. How are defense services provided to indigents?
8. Why might it be argued that publicly financed counsel serves defendants better than does privately retained counsel?

Key Terms

accusatory process (p. 317)
assigned counsel (p. 325)
contract counsel (p. 325)
count (p. 310)
defense attorney (p. 319)
discovery (p. 310)
legal sufficiency (p. 316)
nolle prosequi (p. 310)
prosecuting attorney (p. 303)
public defender (p. 325)
state attorney general (p. 303)
system efficiency (p. 316)
trial sufficiency (p. 317)
United States attorney (p. 303)

For Further Reading

Buffa, Dudley W. 1997. *The Defense.* New York: Henry Holt; 1999. *The Prosecution: A Legal Thriller.* New York: Henry Holt. Novels focusing on court processes, judges, prosecutors, and defense attorneys; written by a former criminal attorney.

Heilbroner, David. 1990. *Rough Justice: Days and Nights of a Young D.A.* New York: Pantheon Books. The experience of an assistant district attorney learning the ropes in New York's criminal courts.

Humes, Edward. 1999. *Mean Justice: A Town's Terror, a Prosecutor's Power, a Betrayal of Innocence.* New York: Simon & Schuster. An investigative reporter's examination of prosecutions in one California county in which apparently innocent people were sent to prison for crimes they did not commit.

Lewis, Anthony. 1964. *Gideon's Trumpet.* New York: Vintage. The classic case study of *Gideon v. Wainwright.*

McIntyre, Lisa J. *The Public Defender: The Practice of Law in the Shadows of Repute.* 1987. Chicago: University of Chicago Press. A case study of the public defender's office in Cook County, Illinois.

Rowland, Judith. 1985. *The Ultimate Violation.* New York: Doubleday. A former San Diego district attorney describes her pioneering legal strategy to prosecute rapists.

Toobin, Jeffrey, *The Run of His Life: The People v. O. J. Simpson.* 1996. New York: Random House. A view of the trial from the perspectives of the prosecution and defense.

Tucker, John C. 1997. *May God Have Mercy.* New York: Norton. A former defense attorney reinvestigates and reconstructs a murder case in which the defendant, who was ultimately executed for the crime, was represented by inexperienced defense attorneys.

Turow, Scott. 1987. *Presumed Innocent.* New York: Farrar, Straus & Giroux. Fictional account of the indictment and trial of an urban prosecutor for the murder of a colleague. Excellent description of an urban court system.

Going Online

1 Go to the Web site of the National District Attorneys Association: http://www.ndaa-apri.org/, then go to the APRI home page. What purposes does the organization fulfill for prosecutors across the country? Pay particular attention to the description of the American Prosecution Research Institute. What are the Institute's goals? How might the Institute attempt to influence the development of law and policy?

2 Go to the Web site of the National Legal Aid and Defender Association: http://www.nlada.org. What purposes does the organization fulfill for defense attorneys? How does the organization attempt to influence law and policy?

3 Use InfoTrac College Edition to do the following:

a. Search for an article on *prosecutorial immunity.* Are there any circumstances in which prosecutors can be sued for misconduct? If prosecutors can rarely be sued, how can the public hold prosecutors accountable for their actions?

b. Search for an article by or about a *public defender.* Could you imagine yourself working as a criminal defense attorney? Why or why not?

Checkpoint Answers

1 United States attorney, state attorney general, prosecuting attorney (the prosecuting attorney is also called district attorney, county prosecutor, state's attorney, county attorney).

2 Decides which charges to file, what bail amounts to recommend, whether to pursue a plea bargain, and what sentence to recommend to the judge.

3 Trial counsel for the police, house counsel for the police, representative of the court, elected official.

4 The prosecutor can determine the type and number of charges, reduce the charges in exchange for a guilty plea, or enter a *nolle prosequi* (thereby dropping some or all of the charges).

5 Police, victims and witnesses, defense attorneys, judges.

6 Legal sufficiency: Is there sufficient evidence to pursue a prosecution? System efficiency: What will be the impact of this case on the system with respect to caseload pressures and speedy disposition? Trial sufficiency: Does sufficient evidence exist to ensure successful prosecution of this case through a trial?

7 The public often views defense attorneys as protectors of criminals. Defendants believe that defense attorneys will fight vigorous battles at every stage of the process. The defense attorney's actual role is to protect the defendant's rights and to make the prosecution prove its case.

8 Securing cases, collecting fees, persuading clients to accept pleas, having to lose most cases, maintaining working relationships with court officers, serving clients in unpleasant surroundings for little money, being negatively viewed by the public.

9 Assigned counsel, contract system, public defender.

10 There seems to be little difference in outcomes.

11 The Supreme Court has addressed the issue of "ineffective assistance of counsel" in two 1984 cases: *United States v. Cronic* and *Strickland v. Washington*. The court said that an attorney's actions should be judged inadequate only if a reasonably competent attorney would not have acted as did the trial counsel.

CHAPTER 11

Determination of Guilt: Plea Bargaining and Trials

W. Lopez/NYT Pictures

Kendra Webdale, a 32-year-old receptionist and aspiring screen writer, waited on a subway platform in New York City on January 3, 1999. As a subway train roared into the station, she was grabbed from behind and thrown onto the tracks in the path of the oncoming train. Webdale was killed instantly under the wheels of the train. Meanwhile, her attacker, 29-year-old Andrew Goldstein, who had never met Webdale, silently sat down as other people on the platform prevented him from leaving (Rohde, 1999). Goldstein, a mental patient who had stopped taking his schizophrenia medication, confessed to the police (L. Anderson, 1999). In his taped confession, Goldstein said, "And then the train is almost there and I said, 'Oh no, it happened.' You know,

I, I, I got into the fit again, like I've done in the past, and I pushed the woman, not meaning to push her on the tracks" (Winerip, 1999b).

Although Goldstein's confession and the witnesses on the subway platform made perfectly clear who caused Kendra Webdale's death, Goldstein had the right to a trial. He had a right to be defended by an attorney as he forced the prosecution to prove its case before 12 jurors drawn from among the citizens of New York City. At issue in Goldstein's trial was not whether he pushed Webdale, but whether he could be punished for committing a crime. Because of Goldstein's mental illness, his lawyer, Harvey Fishbein, argued that he should be found not guilty, by reason of insanity (Rohde, 1999).

In November, after the month-long presentation of evidence, the jurors, four women and eight men, spent six days locked together in a room deliberating Goldstein's fate. Occasionally they asked for testimony to be read to them again as they continued to discuss and debate. On the sixth day, they told the judge that they were hopelessly deadlocked, with ten jurors favoring conviction and two believing that Goldstein was insane. The judge declared a mistrial and thereby forced the prosecution to plan to try again in front of an entirely new jury.

The American system regards the trial as the best method for determining a defendant's guilt. Yet a trial is not a scientific process. Instead of calm, consistent evaluations of evidence, trials involve unpredictable human perceptions and reactions. When the same evidence was presented again at the second trial in March 2000, a new jury found Goldstein guilty of murder and he was given a sentence of 25 years to life in prison.

The Goldstein case occupies the top layer of Samuel Walker's criminal justice wedding cake—as one of those celebrated cases that go to trial and command great public attention (see Chapter 3). The horrific nature of the crime attracted significant public attention. The seriousness of the charge and potential punishment created little incentive for Goldstein to enter a guilty plea. And Goldstein's father, a physician, could afford to pay for defense attorneys and expert witnesses during a long, expensive trial (Italiano, 1999).

By contrast, the guilt of most defendants—even prominent defendants who can afford to pay top-notch attorneys—is determined by plea bargaining. For example, Baltimore Ravens linebacker Ray Lewis was formally charged with murder and assault for his alleged role in the stabbing deaths of two men during a fight outside a bar in January 2000. However, Lewis was not accused of actually killing the victims. He allegedly participated in the fight and helped two friends who wielded knives to escape in his limousine. In the middle of Lewis's jury trial in June 2000, he pleaded guilty to a misdemeanor charge of obstruction of justice for lying to police about what happened on the night of the killings. Lewis was sentenced to one year on probation (Roedemeier, 2000).

Although trials are relatively unusual, they are important because they provide the reference point for attorneys who must decide whether to seek a plea bargain. In calculating the risks of trial, attorneys use verdicts in other cases to predict how a judge or jury might decide their own clients' cases. Attorneys must ask themselves, "How will jurors react to the evidence that I plan to present?" In Lewis's case, the prosecutor apparently had doubts that the jury would issue a guilty verdict for murder and assault. The football player's attorney must have believed that it was better to accept conviction on a minor charge than to take the risk, however slight, that the jury might convict Lewis.

As in other cases resolved through plea bargaining, Lewis's plea negotiations involve *exchange,* the system characteristic discussed in Chapter 3. The prosecutor agreed to drop the serious felony charges and recommend a sentence of probation in exchange for Lewis's guilty plea and his promise to testify against his co-defendants.

In this chapter we discuss plea bargaining and trials as a way to examine the determination of guilt in criminal cases. We also explore the appeals process that occurs when a convicted offender challenges the validity of a criminal conviction. In all of these processes defendants' fates depend on the interactions and decisions of many individuals in important roles: judges, prosecutors, defense attorneys, and jurors.

QUESTIONS for INQUIRY

- What is the courtroom workgroup and how does it function?
- How and why does plea bargaining occur?
- What are the stages of a criminal trial?
- How are juries chosen?
- What is the basis for an appeal of a conviction?

The Courtroom: How It Functions

Similar rules and processes are used in criminal cases throughout the nation. However, courts differ in the precise ways they apply those rules and procedures. A study of criminal courts in nine communities in three states showed that similar laws and procedures can produce different results in the treatment of defendants (Eisenstein, Flemming, and Nardulli, 1988). Some courts sentence offenders to longer terms than do others. In some places, court delays and tough bail policies keep many accused people in jail awaiting trial, while in other places defendants are more likely to be released before trial or have their cases resolved quickly. Guilty pleas may make up 90 percent of dispositions in some communities but only 60 percent in others. How can differences among courts be explained—differences that are found even in the same city?

Social scientists are aware that the culture of a community greatly influences how its members behave. The definition of *culture* includes shared beliefs about proper behavior. These beliefs can span entire nations or pertain to smaller communities, including corporations, churches, or neighborhoods. In any community, large or small, the culture can exert a strong effect on people's decisions and behavior.

Researchers have identified a **local legal culture**—values and norms shared by members of a particular court community (judges, attorneys, clerks, bailiffs, and others)—about how cases should be handled, and the way court officials should behave (Church, 1985). The local legal culture influences court operations in three ways:

local legal culture
Norms shared by members of a court community as to how cases should be handled and how a participant should behave in the judicial process.

1. Norms (shared values and expectations) help participants distinguish between "our" court and other courts. Often a judge or prosecutor will proudly describe how "we" do the job differently and better than officials in a nearby county or city.
2. Norms tell members of a court community how they should treat each another. For example, mounting a strong adversarial defense may be viewed as not in keeping with the norms of one court, but it may be expected in another.
3. Norms describe how cases *should* be processed. The best example of such a norm is the **going rate,** the local view of the proper sentence for the offense, the defendant's prior record, and other factors. The local legal culture also includes attitudes on such issues as whether a judge should take part in plea negotiations, when **continuances**—lawyers' requests for delays in court proceedings—should be granted, and which defendants qualify for a public defender.

going rate
Local court officials' shared view of the appropriate sentence for the offense, the defendant's prior record, and other case characteristics.

continuance
An adjournment of a scheduled case until a later date.

Differences among local legal cultures help explain why court decisions often differ even though the formal rules of criminal procedure are basically the same. For example, while judges play a key role in sentencing, the "going rate" concept shows us that sentences are also a product of shared understandings among the prosecutor, defense attorney, and judge. In one court, shared understandings may mean a court imposes probation on a first-time thief; in other courts, different shared values may send first offenders to jail or prison for the same offense.

check point

1. How does the local legal culture affect criminal cases?
(Answers are at the end of the chapter.)

The Courtroom Workgroup

Television dramas such as *The Practice* or *Law and Order* present a particular image of the American courtroom. In these shows, prosecutors and defense attorneys lock horns in verbal combat, each side trying to persuade a judge or jury to either convict or acquit the defendant. However, this image of adversarial proceedings does not reflect the actual scene in most American courtrooms. A more realistic portrayal would stress the interactions among the actors, who are guided by the norms and expectations of the local legal culture. Many of these interactions take the form of calm cooperation among the prosecutor, defense attorney, and judge, rather than the battle of adversaries portrayed in fictional accounts (Flemming, Nardulli, and Eisenstein, 1992).

workgroup
A collection of individuals who interact in the workplace on a continuing basis, share goals, develop norms regarding how activities should be carried out, and eventually establish a network of roles that differentiates the group from others and that facilitates cooperation.

Decisions in criminal cases greatly rely on how the participants interact with each other. We can best understand how criminal justice officials and staff function when we view them as **workgroups,** or groups of people who interact with each other, share certain goals and values, and form relationships that facilitate cooperation. The better the judge, prosecutor, defense attorney, and courtroom staff can function as a workgroup, the more smoothly they can dispose of cases. The workgroup concept is especially important in analyzing urban courts, where there are many courtrooms; large numbers of lawyers, judges, and other court personnel; and a heavy caseload.

In light of the factors that define the workgroup, differences can be expected between workgroups, from courtroom to courtroom depending on the strength of these factors in each setting. For example, a rotation system that moves judges among courtrooms in a large courthouse may limit the development of workgroup norms and roles. Although the same prosecutors and defense attorneys may be present every day, the arrival of a new judge every week or month will require them to learn and adapt to new ideas about how cases should be negotiated or tried. When shared norms cannot develop, cases tend to proceed in a relatively formal manner. The actors in such a courtroom have fewer chances to follow agreed-upon routines than does a workgroup with a well-developed pattern of interactions.

AP/Wide World Pictures, Inc.

Even in the most adversarial cases, courtroom participants form a workgroup that requires constant interaction, cooperation, and negotiation.

By contrast, when there are shared expectations and consistent relationships, the business of the courtroom proceeds in a regular but informal manner, with many shared understandings among members easing much of the work (A. P. Worden, 1995). Through cooperation, each member can achieve his or her goals as well as those of the group. The prosecutor wants to gain quick convictions, the defense attorney wants fair and prompt resolution of the defendant's case, and the judge wants cooperative agreements on guilt and sentencing. All of these ac-

Figure 11.1 **Model of criminal court decision making**
This model ties together the elements of the courtroom workgroup, sponsoring organizations, and local legal culture. Note the effects on decision making. Are there other factors that should be taken into account?

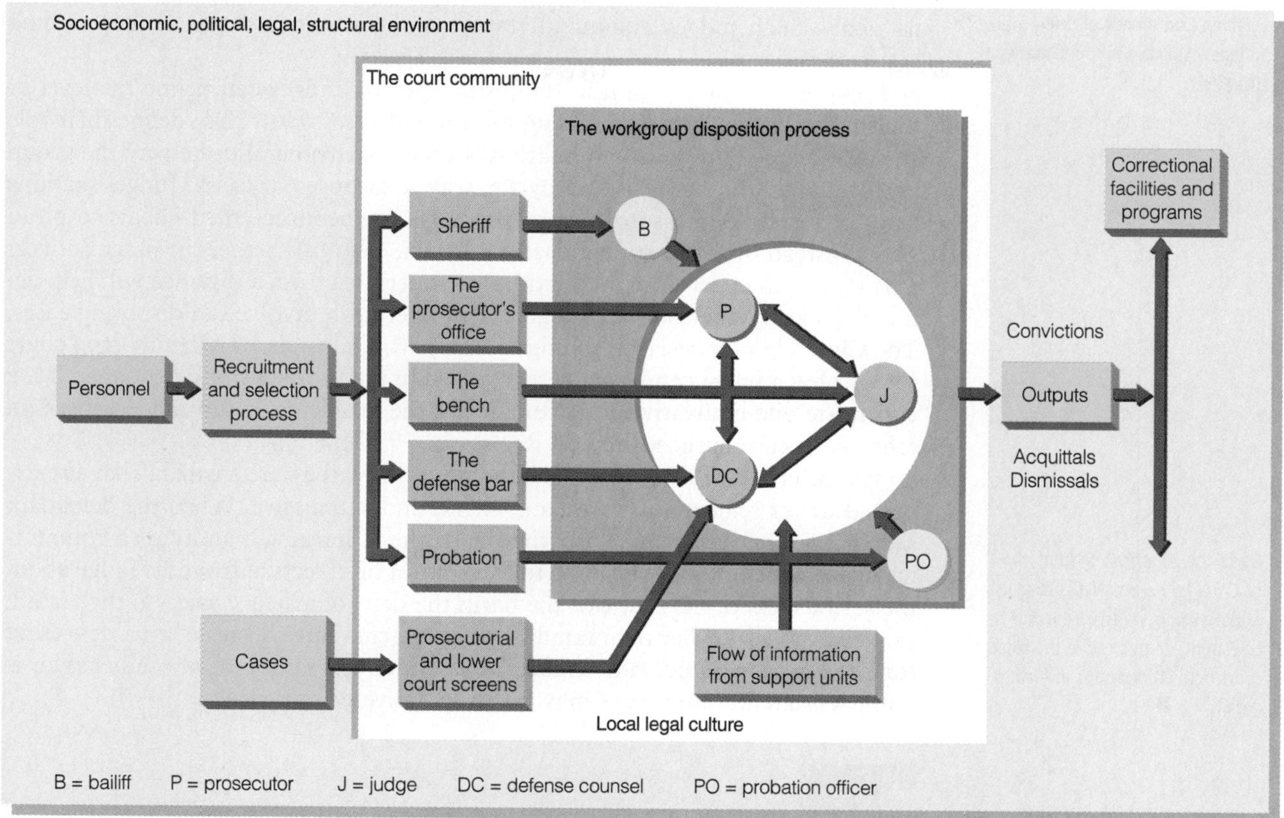

Source: Adapted from Peter Nardulli, James Eisenstein, and Roy Flemming, *Tenor of Justice: Criminal Courts and the Guilty Plea Process* (Urbana: University of Illinois Press, 1988). Copyright © 1988 by the Board of Trustees of the University of Illinois. Reprinted by permission of the University of Illinois Press.

tors want efficient processing of the steady flow of cases that burden their working lives.

Each actor in the courtroom workgroup has a specific role with unique duties and responsibilities. If a lawyer moves from the public defender's office to the prosecutor's office and later to a judgeship, each new position calls for a different role in the workgroup because each represents a different sponsoring organization (Eisenstein and Jacob, 1977:43). One organization, loosely called the court, sends judges; the prosecuting attorney's office sends assistant prosecutors; the public defender's office sends counsel for indigents. In addition, other actors who work in the courtroom contribute to the workgroup's effectiveness. In order to determine an appropriate plea agreement and sentence, for example, members of the workgroup rely on the probation officer to provide accurate information about the defendant's prior convictions and family history in the presentence report.

Figure 11.1 shows the elements of the courtroom workgroup and the influences that bear on decision making. Note that the workgroup operates in an environment in which decision making is influenced by the local legal culture, recruitment and selection processes, the nature of the cases, and the socioeconomic, political, and legal structures of the broader community.

Judges are the leaders of the courtroom team. They ensure that procedures are followed correctly. Even if prosecutors and defense attorneys appear to make the key decisions, the judge must approve them. Judges are responsible for coordinating the processing of cases. Even so, each judge can perform this role somewhat differently. Judges who run a loose administrative ship see themselves as somewhat above the battle. They give other members of the team a great deal of freedom in carrying out their duties and will usually approve group decisions—especially when the members of the group have shared beliefs about the court's

To read about ethical rules for trial judges, see the Web site of the Judicial Ethics Committee for the Pennsylvania Conference of State Trial Judges: http://www.courts.state.pa.us/ethics/.

goals and the community's values. Judges who exert tighter control over the process play a more active role. They anticipate problems; provide cues for other actors; and threaten, cajole, and move the group toward efficient achievement of its goals. Such judges command respect and participate fully in the ongoing courtroom drama.

Because of their position in the justice system, judges can define the level of their involvement in the processing of criminal cases. How they define their role strongly affects interpersonal relations in the courtroom and the way the group performs its task, as measured by the way it disposes of cases. Judges' actions can, for example, pressure defense attorneys to encourage their clients to plead guilty instead of insisting on a trial (D. Lynch, 1999). Whether the judge actively participates in courtroom interactions or supervises from a distance will help define the speed, efficiency, and degree of cooperation involved in disposing cases. The Close Up box describing Judge Stanley M. Goldstein of Miami's drug court shows how a judge can be actively involved in the problems of defendants. Drug courts are one innovative effort to address the problems of substance abusers in efficient, focused proceedings (J. R. Brown, 1999).

Go to the *American System of Criminal Justice* Web site at http://www.cj.wadsworth.com/colesmith10e to explore the topic of courtroom workgroups in further detail.

The behavior of defendants greatly affects how they are treated. They are expected to act remorseful, repentant, silent, and submissive. When the defendant admits guilt in public and states that he or she is entering a guilty plea voluntarily, acceptance of the plea can be followed by a brief lecture from the judge about the seriousness of the crime or the harm the defendant has caused to the victim, as well as to his or her own family. The judge can "give a break" to a defendant for having cooperated. A defendant who pleads not guilty or whose behavior is inappropriate in other ways may be given a severer sentence.

check point

2. How does a courtroom workgroup form and operate?

The Impact of Courtroom Workgroups

The classic research of James Eisenstein and Herbert Jacob (1977) on the felony disposition process in Baltimore, Chicago, and Detroit offers important insights into the workgroup's impact on decisions in felony cases. The researchers found that the same type of felony case was handled differently in each city, yet the outcomes of the dispositions were remarkably similar. Differences did not stem from the law, rules of procedure, or crime rate. Instead, they emerged from the structure of the courtroom workgroups, the influence of the sponsoring organizations, and sociopolitical factors.

What impact did the courtroom workgroups have on pretrial processes? Eisenstein and Jacob found that the stable courtroom workgroups in Chicago had informal procedures for screening cases. Because of the groups' close links to the trial courtrooms, they felt pressure to screen out many cases and thus spare the resources of the judges and the courts. This led to a very high dismissal rate. In Detroit, also a city with stable workgroups, the prosecutors had discretion to screen cases before they reached the courtroom; hence most of the defendants who appeared at preliminary hearings were sent to trial. Baltimore had less stable workgroups, in part because members were rotated, and sponsoring organizations did not closely supervise assistant prosecutors and defense attorneys. The unstable workgroups lacked all three workgroup criteria: close working relationships, shared values, and reasons to cooperate. As a result, there were fewer guilty pleas, and most defendants were sent on to the grand jury and thence to the trial courts.

The disposition of felony cases results from the interaction of members of the courtroom workgroup. The decisions made by each member are influenced by the policies of their sponsoring organizations. These interactions and policies

Miami's Drug Court, Judge Stanley M. Goldstein, Presiding

Standing in front of the judge in a special legal arena known as drug court, the defendant was on his own to explain why he had been arrested again for drug possession. He said he had picked up a hitchhiker who had been carrying drugs.

"I didn't do anything," the defendant said.

But in drug court, a national program for drug offenders that operates under unorthodox rules, the judge has a computer that tells him exactly what the defendant has been up to, how many urine tests have been "dirty," and how many treatment sessions have been missed. The judge also hears no prosecution or defense arguments to cloud his or her judicial instincts.

In the case involving the hitchhiker, Judge Stanley M. Goldstein's instincts told him that the defendant was playing games. "He just happened to give somebody a ride," the judge repeated, smiling, before sending the man to jail.

But the same judge looked joyous when another defendant, a woman, showed up for her last courtroom appearance. The woman, Michelle Ford, 32, had been in and out of treatment for six years and had finally quit crack.

"You get a hug and a kiss, and it's all over," he said as he beckoned Ms. Ford to the bench.

"Thank you, thank you judge," she said in his embrace, dissolving in tears.

The drama of addiction, and its intersection with crime, unfolds in courtrooms like Judge Goldstein's every workday in an experiment that has gained enthusiastic acceptance among judges and prosecutors and that criminal justice experts say offers hope amid the bleakness of rising drug use. . . .

Drug courts are small beachheads on a vast battleground. About 28,000 defendants are participating in 109 courts around the country or have graduated from them, a fraction of the more than 700,000 offenders arrested on drug possession charges each year.

In drug courts, defendants who have been charged with drug possession or related crimes in effect make a plea bargain. Judges set aside a formal trial, criminal charges, and sentences while defendants undergo treatment and court-monitored supervision. The judge can jail defendants if they violate the terms of the treatment plan. If they complete the treatment and become free of drugs, drug charges may be dismissed or sentences may be reduced.

Participants volunteer to submit to rigorous monitoring and counseling until they are classified as rehabilitated, and they receive help with searching for work and job training. . . .

Drug courts work, judges say, because they turn the judges into motivators with the power to praise, cajole and coerce defendants. . . .

But the addicts also credit their recoveries to the opportunity to talk over problems with the judge, a parental figure whom some defendants call "Daddy."

"You have moral support from an authority figure," said Kelvin Mobley, 34, a gardener who was buying cocaine on the street in June 1995 and is about to complete his treatment from Judge Goldstein. "That's a big boost."

Judge Goldstein's courtroom bustles like many others, but a visitor quickly notices differences. The prosecutor and the public defender work in agreement, tears flow easily among defendants, and the judge often says, "I love you."

But the compassion can turn into rage, as when he warned a man who was holding a yarmulke in one hand and his young son's hand in the other that if he showed cocaine in his urine in his next appointment he had better "pack a toothbrush."

"Want that kid to be a junkie?" he boomed as the man made a hasty exit. "You are the role models to your children. Don't push it off to ballplayers. You!"

Later addressing a new group of defendants, the judge made clear what they were up against if they wanted his court to dispense not punishment but a fresh start.

"There's nothing easy about this," he said. "But I know you all can do it. I also know not all of you will do it. No guts."

Source: Mireya Navarro, "Special Courts Use New Tactics in Battle against Drug Addiction," *New York Times*, October 17, 1996, p. A1. Copyright © 1996 by the New York Times Co. Reprinted by permission.

Researching the Internet

The Drug Court Program Office in the U.S. Department of Justice provides assistance and support for drug courts. See http://www.ojp.usdoj.gov/dcpo/.

may vary from courthouse to courthouse. The stability of workgroup interactions can be upset by changes such as a new docket system or changes in the policies and practices of sponsoring organizations.

3. Why are similar cases treated differently in different cities?

Plea Bargaining

As illustrated by Ray Lewis's case, for the vast majority of cases, *plea bargaining*—also known as negotiating a settlement, copping a plea, or copping out—is the most important step in the criminal justice process. Few cases go to trial; instead, a negotiated guilty plea arrived at through the interactions of prosecutors, defense lawyers, and judges determines what will happen to most defendants. Table 11.1 shows the percentages of guilty pleas in robbery and burglary cases in five jurisdictions. Note that the percentage varies little, regardless of the number of trials, judges, and prosecutors. Table 11.2 shows the types of plea bargains made in these cases. The study reported in these tables is consistent with others, which have found that up to 90 percent of felony defendants in the United States plead guilty.

To read a description of plea bargaining and why it occurs, go to http://www.nolo.com/lawcenter/index.cfm. Click the link to "Criminal Law" and then click on "Understanding Plea Bargaining."

Thirty-five years ago, plea bargaining was not acknowledged or discussed publicly; it was the criminal justice system's "little secret." Some observers felt that plea bargaining was not in accord with American values of fairness. Doubts existed about whether it was constitutional, and it clashed with the image of the courtroom as a place where prosecutors and defense attorneys engage in legal battles as the jury watches "truth" emerge from the courtroom "combat." Yet quick resolution of cases through negotiated guilty pleas have been a major means of disposing of criminal cases since at least the 1800s (Vogel, 1999). Re-

Table 11.1 Plea bargaining in five jurisdictions: Robbery and burglary

The percentage of guilty pleas is about the same in all five cities, regardless of the number of judges, the number of felony trials, and the number of indictments or informations.

	New Orleans	Seattle (King County)	Norfolk	Tucson	Delaware County, Penn.
Population	562,000	1,157,000	285,500	500,000	600,000
Estimated annual indictments or informations filed	5,063	4,500	2,800	2,309	3,000
Number of felony judges	10	8	3	7	4
Number of prosecutors	63	69	15	30	30
Percentage of robbery and burglary defendants pleading guilty	81%	86%	78%	87%	80%
Number of felony trials per year	1,069	4,567	648	270	491
Type of defense counsel and estimated percentage of defendants covered	Public 65% Assigned 10% Retained 25%	Public 64% Assigned 16% Retained 20%	Assigned 75% Retained 25%	Public 70% Assigned 3% Retained 27%	Public 65% Retained 35%
Prosecutorial restrictions on plea bargaining	Limited charge bargaining	For high-impact cases	Minimal	For career criminals	Minimal

Source: William F. McDonald, *Plea Bargaining: Critical Issues and Common Practices* (Washington, D.C.: National Institute of Justice, 1985), 7.

Table 11.2 Types of plea concessions in robbery and burglary cases in five jurisdictions

Although the percentage of cases ending in a guilty plea is similar in all of the cities (see Table 11.1), there are differences in the types of plea agreements.

Type of Concession	New Orleans	Seattle (King County)	Norfolk	Tucson	Delaware County, Penn.
Sentence recommendation only	56%	46%	32%	7%	2%
Sentence recommendation plus charge reduction and/or dismissal	4	42	37	3	31
Charge reduction and/or dismissal only	40	12	31	90	67

Source: William F. McDonald, *Plea Bargaining: Critical Issues and Common Practices* (Washington, D.C.: National Institute of Justice, 1985), 7.

AFP Photo/Shawn Thew/CORBIS

John Walker Lindh, accused of fighting for the Taliban, was charged with ten felonies, including conspiracy to kill U.S. nationals and supporting terrorist groups. He pled guilty and received a 20-year sentence. As part of the plea bargain, he agreed to provide information about the Taliban and Al Qaida.

searchers began to shed light on plea bargaining in the 1960s, and the U.S. Supreme Court endorsed the process in the 1970s. In *Santobello v. New York* (1971), for example, Chief Justice Warren Burger ruled that prosecutors were obliged to fulfill promises made during plea negotiations. According to Burger, "'Plea bargaining' is an essential component of the administration of justice. Properly administered, it is to be encouraged." Burger also listed several reasons that plea bargaining was a "highly desirable" part of the criminal justice process:

- If every case went to trial, federal and state governments would need many times more courts and judges than they now have.
- Plea bargaining leads to the prompt and largely final disposition of most criminal cases.
- Plea bargaining reduces the time that pretrial detainees must spend in jail. If they plead guilty to serious charges, they can be moved to prisons with recreational and educational programs instead of enduring the enforced idleness of jails.
- By disposing of cases more quickly than trials would, plea bargaining reduces the amount of time that released suspects spend free on bail. Therefore, the public is better protected from crimes that such suspects may commit while on pretrial release.
- Offenders who plead guilty to serious charges can move more quickly into prison counseling, training, and education programs designed to rehabilitate offenders.

In 1976, Justice Potter Stewart revealed the heart and soul of plea bargaining when he wrote in *Blackledge v. Allison* that plea bargaining "can benefit all concerned" in a criminal case. There are advantages for defendants, prosecutors, defense attorneys, and judges. Defendants can have their cases completed more quickly and know what the punishment will be, instead of facing the uncertainty of a judge's sentencing decision. Moreover, the defendant is likely to receive less than the maximum punishment that might have been imposed after a trial. Prosecutors are not being "soft on crime" when they plea bargain. Instead, they gain an easy conviction, even in cases in which enough evidence may not have been gathered to convince a jury to convict the defendant. They also save time and resources by disposing of cases without having to prepare for a trial. Private defense attorneys as well save the time needed to prepare for a trial. They earn their fee quickly and can move on to the next case. Likewise, plea bargaining helps public defenders cope with large caseloads. Judges, too, avoid time-consuming

Banning Plea Bargaining in Tennessee

In January 1997 William Gibbons, District Attorney for Shelby County, Tennessee, which includes the City of Memphis, introduced a policy of refusing to reduce charges of first- and second-degree murder and charges of robbery or rape that involved the use of a deadly weapon. These are generally considered the most violent and harmful of crimes. Under the policy, anyone indicted for these crimes must either plead guilty to the charge specified or go to trial. The operation of the policy raises interesting questions about the impact of bans on plea bargaining.

The District Attorney's Office hoped that the "no deal" policy and the resulting tough sentences for people convicted of these crimes would deter other potential offenders from committing violent crimes. Thus the ban on plea bargaining was accompanied by a public relations campaign to spread the word about the new policy. The marketing campaign, which would have cost $1 million, was produced through contributions of free advertising and private fundraising led by a former Memphis mayor, as well as $200,000 in money confiscated from drug dealers by the county sheriff. "No Deal" signs, decals, and bumper stickers were distributed to businesses and neighborhood watch groups.

The District Attorney's Office claims that the ban on plea bargaining "had a positive impact in reducing violent felonies." The Office pointed to a 12 percent reduction in criminal homicides and a 12 percent reduction in robberies from 1996 to 1997. However, violent crime nationwide dropped steadily beginning in 1992 with, for example, declines of 11.4 percent for robberies and 7.4 percent for murders in 1998. Can the District Attorney accurately conclude that the reduction in Memphis is due to the plea bargaining policy rather than reflecting a general social trend?

The District Attorney's Office says that the effectiveness of the new policy stems from cooperation between the prosecutor and local law enforcement agencies. The new policy is in large part possible due to a process by which representatives of the District Attorney's Office meet with representatives of the Memphis Police Department and the Shelby County Sheriff's Office to screen cases involving the violent crimes covered by the policy. This early review

trials and having to decide what sentence to impose on the defendant. Instead, they often adopt the sentence recommended by the prosecutor in consultation with the defense attorney, provided that it is within the range of sentences that they deem appropriate for a given crime and offender.

The attraction of plea bargaining for prosecutors and defendants was evident in the 2002 guilty plea of John Walker Lindh, the 21-year-old American captured while fighting with the Taliban in Afghanistan. He faced ten felony charges, including conspiring to kill Americans, and could have been sentenced to three life terms in prison. Instead, he received a 20 year sentence for pleading guilty to two counts, serving as a soldier for the Taliban and carrying a firearm while doing so. As part of the deal, Lindh agreed to cooperate by providing information to the government about the Taliban and the Al-Qaida network (Serrano, 2002). Lindh obviously had an incentive to avoid the risk of spending the rest of his life in prison, especially if he feared that a jury of Americans could not listen objectively to evidence about his involvement with the Taliban. It seems equally apparent that the government was eager to gain information from Lindh and was willing to settle for a lesser sentence in order to obtain that information. The government may also have had doubts about whether the evidence could support convictions on all of the charges. Does this result achieve justice? Such questions are difficult to answer when the evidence is disputed. However, these results spare the system and its decision makers from the risk of expending significant resources for uncertain outcomes.

Defenders of plea bargaining justify the practice by noting that it permits judges, prosecutors, and defense attorneys to individualize justice by agreeing to a plea and punishment that fits the offender and offense. They also claim that

process helps to insure that the D.A.'s Office has a good case with strong evidence before someone is charged and a proposed indictment is presented to the Grand Jury.

By filtering out cases for which the most serious charges are not justified and provable, does this review and screening process perhaps fulfill the function served by plea bargaining in other cities? Elsewhere, the plea negotiation process involves discussions between defense attorneys and prosecutors about the provable facts of a case so that both sides can reach agreement about the "going rate" of punishment for that particular offender and crime. In effect, then, might the Memphis screening process really just produce the same results in "no deal" cases that would have been produced anyway through plea negotiations in other cities?

In reality, the Memphis ban on plea bargaining is not absolute, even for the specified crimes to which it applies. There can be "exceptions based on legal, factual, or ethical grounds [that] must be approved by a supervisor [in the District Attorney's Office] and documented in writing." Does the possibility of exceptions create incentives for defense attorneys to seek special deals for their clients? Does it create opportunities for prosecutors to use discretion to reduce charges against particular defendants or the clients of particular attorneys?

Consider the following results from the "no deal" policy in 2001. Out of 635 indictments on eligible charges, 418 defendants entered guilty pleas to the offenses charged. Sixty-six defendants had their charges later dismissed, and 67 defendants went to trial, resulting in 62 convictions and 5 acquittals. The most interesting number is the 84 defendants who pleaded guilty to lesser charges under the "no deal" system. According to the prosecutor's office, the charge reductions were usually the result of the inability of the police to locate crucial witnesses needed for gaining a conviction at trial. In light of those numbers, does the "no deal" policy really live up to its name? Would the public be surprised to learn that a "no deal" policy permits so many plea bargains resulting in reduced charges? Alternatively, in light of how the criminal justice system operates and its dependence on witnesses and discretionary decisions, would it be unrealistic to have a policy in which there were really no charge reductions?

A critic might claim that the screening process and the opportunity to treat cases as exceptions to the "no deal" rule mean that the District Attorney's policy has probably had little impact on the outcomes of criminal cases. Arguably, many of these cases might have produced the same results in a system that relied on plea negotiations. Moreover, it is difficult to prove that any reductions in crime rates are caused by the policy when similar drops in crimes rates are simultaneously occurring throughout the country in cities that still rely on plea bargaining. Does that mean that the "no deal" policy and the accompanying advertising campaign are primarily a public relations effort to gain support and credit for the District Attorney's Office? Is it possible that the District Attorney honestly believes that the "no deal" policy has positive benefits even if it may have produced little change? What do you think?

Sources: Thomas D. Henderson, "No Deals Policy," Office of the District Attorney General, 30th Judicial District of Tennessee, 1999 (http://www.scdag.com/nodeals.htm#top); Michael J. Sniffen, "Crime Down for 7th Straight Year," Associated Press report, October 17, 1999.

To read about other efforts to abolish plea bargaining, see http://www.law.emory.edu/ELJ/volumes/spg98/guido.html.

plea bargaining is an administrative necessity because courts lack the time and resources to conduct lengthy, expensive trials in all cases. Historical studies cast doubt on the latter justification, however, because plea bargaining was a regular feature of nineteenth-century cases and even existed in courts with relatively few cases (Friedman, 1993; Heumann, 1978). Thus, instead of administrative need, the benefits of plea bargaining for the main participants appear to be the primary driving force behind the practice.

Because plea bargaining benefits all involved, it is little wonder that it existed long before it was publicly acknowledged by the legal community and that it still exists, even when prosecutors, legislators, or judges claim that they wish to abolish it. In California, for example, voters decided to ban plea bargaining for serious felony cases. Research showed, however, that when plea bargaining was barred in the felony trial courts, it did not disappear. It simply occurred earlier in the justice process, at the suspect's first appearance in the lower-level municipal court (McCoy, 1993). Efforts to abolish plea bargaining sometimes result in bargaining over the *charges* instead of over the sentence that will be recommended in exchange for a guilty plea. And if a prosecutor forbids his or her staff to plea bargain, judges may become more involved in negotiating and facilitating guilty pleas that result in predictable punishments for offenders.

As you read the Close Up box concerning the partial ban on plea bargaining in Memphis, Tennessee, consider the impact of the ban. The prosecutor claims that the ban has led to a drop in violent crime because potential criminals know that they will be severely punished under the "no deal" policy. How do we know if this is true? What other consequences might be produced by the ban on plea bargaining?

Exchange Relationships in Plea Bargaining

Plea bargaining is a set of exchange relationships in which the prosecutor, the defense attorney, the defendant, and sometimes the judge participate. All have specific goals, all try to use the situation to their own advantage, and all are likely to see the exchange as a success.

Plea bargaining does not always occur in a single meeting between prosecutor and defense attorney. One study showed that plea bargaining is a process in which prosecutors and defense attorneys interact again and again as they move farther along in the judicial process. As time passes, the prosecutor's hand may be strengthened by the discovery of more evidence or new information about the defendant's background (Emmelman, 1996). Often the prosecution rather than the defense is in the best position to obtain new evidence (Cooney, 1994). However, the defense attorney's position may gain strength if the prosecutor does not wish to spend time going farther down the path toward a trial.

check point

4. Why does plea bargaining occur?

Tactics of Prosecutor and Defense

Plea bargaining between defense counsel and prosecutor is a serious game in which friendliness and joking may mask efforts to advance each side's cause. Each side tries to impress the other with its confidence in its own case while pointing out weaknesses in the other's. An unspoken rule of openness and candor helps keep the relationship on good terms. Little effort is made to conceal information that may later be useful to the other side in the courtroom. Studies show that the outcomes of plea bargaining may depend on the relationships between prosecutors and individual attorneys, as well as the defense counsel's willingness to fight for the client (Champion, 1989).

A tactic that many prosecutors bring to plea-bargaining sessions is the multiple-offense indictment. Multiple-offense charges are especially important to prosecuting attorneys in difficult cases—in which, for instance, the victim is reluctant to provide information, the value of the stolen item is in question, and the evidence may not be reliable. The police often file charges of selling a drug when they know they can probably convict only for possession. Because the accused know that the penalty for selling is much greater, they are tempted to plead guilty to the lesser charge rather than risk a severer punishment, even though conviction on the more serious charge is uncertain.

Defense attorneys may threaten to ask for a jury trial if concessions are not made. Their hand is further strengthened if they have filed pretrial motions that require a formal response by the prosecutor. Another tactic is to seek to reschedule pretrial activities in the hope that, with delay, witnesses will become unavailable, media attention will die down, and memories of the crime will diminish by the time of the trial. Rather than resort to such legal tactics, however, some attorneys prefer to bargain on the basis of friendship.

Neither the prosecutor nor the defense attorney is a free agent. Each needs the cooperation of both defendants and judges. Attorneys often cite the difficulty of convincing defendants that they should uphold their end of the bargain. Judges might not sentence the accused according to the prosecutor's recommendation. On the other hand, although their role requires that they uphold the public interest, judges may be reluctant to interfere with a plea agreement. Thus both the prosecutor and the defense attorney often confer with the judge about the sentence to be imposed before agreeing on a plea. If a particular judge is unpredictable in supporting plea agreements, defense attorneys may be reluctant to reach agreements in that judge's court.

Pleas without Bargaining

Studies have shown that in many courts, give-and-take plea bargaining does not occur for certain types of cases, yet these cases have as many guilty pleas as they do in other courts (Eisenstein et al., 1988). The term *bargaining* may be misleading in that it implies haggling. Many scholars argue that guilty pleas emerge after an agreement to "settle the facts" is reached by the prosecutor, the defense attorney, and sometimes the judge (Utz, 1978). In this view the parties first study the facts of a case. What were the circumstances of the event? Was it really an assault or was it more of a shoving match? Did the victim antagonize the accused? Each side may hope to persuade the other that provable facts back up its view of the defendant's actions. The prosecution wants the defense to believe that strong evidence proves its version of the event. The defense attorney wants to convince the prosecution that the evidence is not solid and a jury trial would likely result in acquittal.

In some cases, the evidence is strong and the defense attorney has little hope of persuading the prosecutor otherwise. Through their discussions, the prosecutor and defense attorney seek to reach a shared view of the provable facts in the case. Once they agree on the facts, they will both know the appropriate charge, and they can agree on the sentence according to the locally defined going rate. At that point a guilty plea can be entered without any formal bargaining, because both sides agree on what the case is worth in terms of the seriousness of the charge and the usual punishment. This process may be thought of as *implicit plea bargaining* because shared understandings create the expectation that a guilty plea will lead to a less-than-maximum sentence, even without any exchange or bargaining.

The going rates for sentences for particular crimes and offenders depend on local values and sentencing patterns. Often both the prosecutor and the defense attorney are members of a particular local legal culture and thus share an understanding about how cases should be handled. On the basis of their experiences in interacting with other attorneys and judges, they become keenly aware of local practices in the treatment of cases and offenders (A. P. Worden, 1995). Thus they may both know right away what the sentence will be for a first-time burglar or second-time robber. The sentence may differ in another courthouse because the local legal culture and going rates can vary.

These shared understandings are important for several reasons. First, they help make plea bargaining more effective, because both sides understand which sentences apply to which cases. Second, they help create a cooperative climate for plea bargaining, even if there are bad feelings between the prosecutor and the defense attorney. The local legal culture dictates how attorneys are expected to treat each other and thereby reach agreements. Third, the shared understandings help maintain the relationship between the attorneys.

check point

5. What is implicit plea bargaining?

Legal Issues in Plea Bargaining

In *Boykin v. Alabama* (1969), the Court ruled that defendants must state that they made their pleas voluntarily before judges may accept those pleas. Judges have created standard forms that have questions for the defendant to affirm in open court before the plea is accepted. Trial judges also must learn whether the defendant understands the consequences of pleading guilty and ensure that the plea is not obtained through pressure or coercion.

Boykin v. Alabama (1969)
Defendants must state that they are voluntarily making a plea of guilty.

Can a trial court accept a guilty plea if the defendant claims to be innocent? In *North Carolina v. Alford* (1970), the Court allowed a defendant to enter a

North Carolina v. Alford (1970)
A plea of guilty may be accepted for the purpose of a lesser sentence by a defendant who maintains his or her innocence.

***Santobello v. New York* (1971)**
When a guilty plea rests on a promise of a prosecutor, the promise must be fulfilled.

***Ricketts v. Adamson* (1987)**
Defendants must uphold the plea agreement or suffer the consequences.

***Bordenkircher v. Hayes* (1978)**
A defendant's rights were not violated by a prosecutor who warned that not to accept a guilty plea would result in a harsher sentence.

guilty plea for the purpose of gaining a lesser sentence, even though he maintained that he was innocent. However, the Supreme Court has stated that trial judges should not accept such a plea unless a factual basis exists for believing that the defendant is in fact guilty (Whitebread and Slobogin, 2000:689).

Another issue is whether the plea agreement has been fulfilled. If the prosecutor has promised a lenient sentence, he or she must keep that promise. In ***Santobello v. New York*** **(1971)**, the Supreme Court ruled that "when a [guilty] plea rests in any significant degree on a promise or agreement of the prosecutor, so that it can be said to be part of the inducement or consideration, such promise must be fulfilled." The Court also decided, in ***Ricketts v. Adamson*** **(1987)**, that defendants must also keep their side of the bargain, such as an agreement to testify against co-defendants.

May prosecutors threaten to penalize defendants who insist upon their right to a jury trial? Yes, according to ***Bordenkircher v. Hayes*** **(1978)**. Prosecutors may, for example, threaten repeat offenders with life sentences under habitual offender statutes if they do not agree to plead guilty and accept specified terms of imprisonment. A threat of more serious charges, so long as such charges are legitimate and supported by evidence, is not considered improper pressure that makes a guilty plea involuntary and hence invalid.

Examine the scene in "A Question of Ethics." Are all of the courtroom actors behaving in an honest, ethical manner? Does this scene raise questions about how plea bargains operate?

Lisa Davidson stood silently in the courtroom of Judge Helen Iverson. Defense attorney Bill Dixon whispered in Davidson's ear as they waited for Judge Iverson to finish reading Davidson's file. "Are we ready to proceed?" asked the judge.

"Yes, your honor," came the simultaneous replies from both Dixon and the prosecutor standing nearby.

Judge Iverson stared at Davidson momentarily with a serious expression. "Ms. Davidson, you are charged with larceny. Because it is your third offense, I can send you to prison. Do you understand that?"

"Yes, your honor," replied Davidson, her voice quivering.

"Are you pleading guilty to this crime because you are guilty?" asked the judge.

"Yes, your honor."

The judge continued. "Are you pleading guilty of your own free will?"

"Yes, your honor."

"Did anyone threaten you to make you plead guilty?"

"No, your honor."

"Did anyone make any promises to you to induce you to plead guilty?"

Davidson nodded her head. "Yes. Mr. Dixon said that if I plead guilty to this charge then the prosecutor promised that my sentence would be only. . . ."

"EXCUSE ME, JUDGE IVERSON," Dixon interrupted in a loud voice. "Could I please have a moment to speak with my client?" Judge Iverson nodded. Taking Davidson by the arm, Dixon moved her three feet farther away from the judge's bench. Dixon whispered into Davidson's ear as his hands punched the air with emphatic gestures. A few moments later, they returned to their positions, standing in front of the judge. "We are ready to continue, your honor," said Dixon.

Judge Iverson looked at Davidson once again. "Did anyone promise you anything to induce you to plead guilty?"

Davidson glanced sideways at Dixon before replying "No, your honor."

"You understand that you are waiving your constitutional right to a trial and you are freely waiving that right?"

"Yes, your honor."

"Then I find you guilty as charged and I will set sentencing for one month from today at 10 A.M."

→ Should Judge Iverson have accepted the guilty plea? What role did the defense attorney play in staging the guilty plea ceremony? Were there any ethical problems? What would you have done if you were the judge?

Criticisms of Plea Bargaining

Although plea bargaining is widely used, some scholars and groups such as the American Bar Association deplore it. The criticisms are of two main types. The first stresses due process and argues that plea bargaining is unfair because defendants give up some of their constitutional rights, especially the right to trial by jury. The second criticism stresses sentencing policy and points out that plea bargaining reduces society's interest in appropriate punishments for crimes. In urban areas with high caseloads, harried prosecutors and judges are said to make concessions based on administrative needs, resulting in lighter sentences than those required by the penal code.

Plea bargaining also comes under fire because it is hidden from judicial scrutiny. Because the agreement is most often made at an early stage, the judge has little information about the crime or the defendant and thus cannot adequately evaluate the case. Nor can the judge review the terms of the bargain—that is, check on the amount of pressure put on the defendant to plead guilty. The result of "bargain justice" is that the judge, the public, and sometimes even the defendant cannot know for sure who got what from whom in exchange for what.

Other critics believe that overuse of plea bargaining breeds disrespect and even contempt for the law. They say criminals look at the judicial process as a game or a sham, much like other "deals" made in life.

Critics also contend that it is unjust to penalize people who assert their right to a trial by giving them stiffer sentences than they would have received if they had pleaded guilty. The evidence here is unclear, although it is widely believed that an extra penalty is imposed on defendants who take up the court's time by asserting their right to a trial (Spohn, 1992). Critics note that federal sentencing guidelines also encourage avoidance of trial because they include a two-point deduction from an offender's base score for a guilty plea—thus lowering the sentence—for "acceptance of responsibility" (McCoy, 1995).

Finally, another concern about plea bargaining is that innocent people will plead guilty to acts that they did not commit. Although it is hard to know how often this happens, some defendants have entered guilty pleas when they have not committed the offense. For example, the Colorado courts overturned a sentence on the ground that the defendant had been coerced by the judge's statement that he would "put him away forever if he did not accept the bargain" (*People v. Clark,* 1973). Middle-class people might find it hard to understand how anyone could possibly plead guilty when innocent. However, people with little education and low social status may lack the confidence to say "no" to an attorney who pressures them to plead guilty. Poor people may feel especially helpless in the stressful climate of the courthouse and jail. If they lack faith in the system's ability to protect their rights and find them not guilty, they may accept a lighter punishment rather than risk being convicted for a serious offense.

Go to the *American System of Criminal Justice* Web site at http://www.cj.wadsworth.com/colesmith10e to explore the topic of courtroom workgroups in further detail.

check point

6. What issues concerning plea bargaining has the Supreme Court examined?
7. What are the criticisms of plea bargaining?

Trial: The Exceptional Case

Cases not dismissed or terminated through plea bargaining move forward for trial. The seriousness of the charge is probably the most important factor influencing the decision to go to trial. Defendants charged with property crimes rarely demand a trial. However, murder, felonious assault, or rape—all charges that bring long prison terms—are more likely to require judge and jury. In a study of the nation's 75 largest counties, 26 percent of murder cases went to trial, the largest percentage for any crime. For all other crimes, trials occurred in 6 percent of cases or less (Reaves, 2001). When the penalty is harsh, many defendants seem willing to risk the possibility of conviction at trial.

Such statistics suggest a consistency in sentencing; however, the real practice varies considerably. Note in Table 11.3 the differences in the percentages of

Table 11.3 Percentage of indicted cases that went to trial, by offense

The percentages of cases that went to trial differ both by offense and by jurisdiction. It seems that the stiffer the possible penalty, the greater the likelihood of a trial.

Jurisdiction	Homicide	Sexual Assault	Robbery	Larceny	Drug Offenses
Indianapolis, Ind.	38%	18%	21%	12%	9%
Los Angeles, Calif.	29	20	12	5	7
Louisville, Ky.	57	27	18	10	11
New Orleans, La.	22	18	16	7	7
St. Louis, Mo.	36	23	15	6	6
San Diego, Calif.	37	2	12	5	3
Washington, D.C.	43	32	22	12	10

Source: Adapted from Bureau of Justice Statistics, *Report to the Nation on Crime and Justice,* 2nd ed. (Washington, D.C.: U.S. Government Printing Office, 1988), 84.

Only 9 percent of felony cases go to trial, yet they often attract great attention, as did the case of David Westerfield, convicted in San Diego of the kidnapping and murder of 7-year-old Danielle Van Dam. Such trials can be likened to morality plays, as skilled attorneys for the prosecution and defense battle in front of the jury.

defendants going to trial for several offenses in various cities. What might be the reasons for differences from one city to another and for one offense or another? Think about how prosecutors' policies or sentencing practices in different cities can increase or decrease the incentives for a defendant to plead guilty.

Most Americans are familiar with the image of the criminal trial. As portrayed in so many movies and television shows, the prosecutor and defense attorney face off in a tense courtroom conflict. Each attorney attempts to use evidence, persuasion, and emotion to convince a **jury** of citizens to favor its arguments about the defendant's guilt or innocence.

As we have seen in previous chapters, the trial process is based on the *adversary process,* an open battle between opposing lawyers that is assumed to be the best way to discover the truth. The authors of the Constitution apparently shared this assumption: The Sixth Amendment says the accused shall enjoy a speedy and public trial by an impartial jury "in all criminal prosecutions" (Langbein, 1992). In theory, each side will present the best evidence and arguments it can muster for its side, and the jury will make a decision based on thorough consideration of the available information about the case.

However, because trials are human processes, the truth might not emerge in the final verdict. Many factors may keep a trial from achieving its goal of revealing the truth. The rules of evidence can prevent one side from presenting the most useful evidence. One side may have impressive expert witnesses that the other side cannot afford to counter with its own experts. One side's attorney may be more persuasive and likeable, thus swaying the jury in spite of the evidence. The jurors or judge may bring into the courtroom their own prejudices, which cause them to favor some defendants or automatically assume the worst about others. Fundamentally, we as a society place great faith in the trial process as the best means for giving complete consideration of a defendant's potential guilt, yet the process does not always work as it should.

Trials determine the fates of very few defendants. Although the right to trial by jury is ingrained in American ideology—it is mentioned in the Declaration of Independence, three amendments to the Constitution, and countless opinions of the Supreme Court—year in and year out about 9 percent of felony cases go to trial. Of these, only 4 percent are jury trials; the rest are **bench trials** presided over by a judge without a jury. Defendants may choose a bench trial if they believe a judge will be more capable of making an objective decision, especially if the charges or evidence are likely to arouse emotional reactions in jurors.

Trials take considerable time and resources. Attorneys frequently spend weeks or months preparing—gathering evidence, responding to their opponents' motions, planning trial strategy, and setting aside from one day to several weeks to present the case in court. From the perspective of judges, prosecutors, and de-

jury
A panel of citizens selected according to law and sworn to determine matters of fact in a criminal case and to deliver a verdict of guilty or not guilty.

bench trial
Trial conducted by a judge who acts as fact finder and determines issues of law. No jury participates.

fense attorneys, plea bargaining is obviously an attractive alternative for purposes of completing cases quickly.

Going to Trial

Because the adversary process is designed to get to the truth, the rules of criminal law, procedure, and evidence govern the conduct of the trial. Trials are based on the idea that the prosecution and defense will compete before a judge and jury so that the truth will emerge. Above the battle, the judge sees to it that the rules are followed and that the jury impartially evaluates the evidence and reflects the community's interest. In a jury trial, the jury is the sole evaluator of the facts in a case. Does this adversarial, politically connected, and citizen-juried trial process provide the best mechanism for finding the truth and doing justice in our most serious criminal cases? As you read the Comparative Perspective, consider the French courts' concerns about the American process and examine whether the French trial process presents any advantages. Could the American trial process be improved by borrowing any elements from France?

The adversary process and inclusion of citizen-jurors in decision making often make trial outcomes difficult to predict. The verdict hinges not only on the nature of the evidence but also on the effectiveness of the prosecution and defense and on the attitudes of the jurors. In the aftermath of highly publicized trials, public opinion often clashes with the decisions made by judges and juries. As you examine the public opinion data on popular disagreement with trial decisions, consider whether these disagreements indicate that Americans find the trial process unsatisfactory. Do these results indicate that jurors are manipulated by attorneys in adversarial process? Alternatively, are jurors better positioned than the public to recognize the actual facts that are relevant to each case?

Eighty percent of all jury trials worldwide take place in the United States (Hans and Vidmar, 1986:109). Only in common-law countries such as Australia, Canada, Great Britain, and the United States does a group of citizens drawn from the community determine the guilt of criminal defendants. In civil-law countries, this function is usually performed by a judge or judges, often assisted by two or three nonlawyers serving as "assessors."

Juries perform six vital functions in the U.S. criminal justice system:

1. Prevent government oppression by safeguarding citizens against arbitrary law enforcement
2. Determine whether the accused is guilty on the basis of the evidence presented
3. Represent diverse community interests so that no one set of values or biases dominates decision making
4. Serve as a buffer between the accused and the accuser
5. Promote knowledge about the criminal justice system by learning about it through the jury duty process
6. Symbolize the rule of law and the community foundation that supports the criminal justice system

As a symbol of law, juries demonstrate to the public—and to defendants—that decisions about depriving individuals of their liberty will be made carefully by a group of citizens who represent the community's values. In addition, juries provide the primary element of direct democracy in the judicial branch of government. Through participation on juries, citizens use their votes to determine the outcomes of cases (C. E. Smith, 1994). This branch of government, which is dominated by judges and lawyers, offers few other opportunities for citizens to shape judicial decisions directly.

In the United States, a criminal jury traditionally comprises 12 citizens, but some states now allow as few as 6 citizens to make up a jury. This reform was recommended to modernize court procedures and reduce expenses. It costs less for the

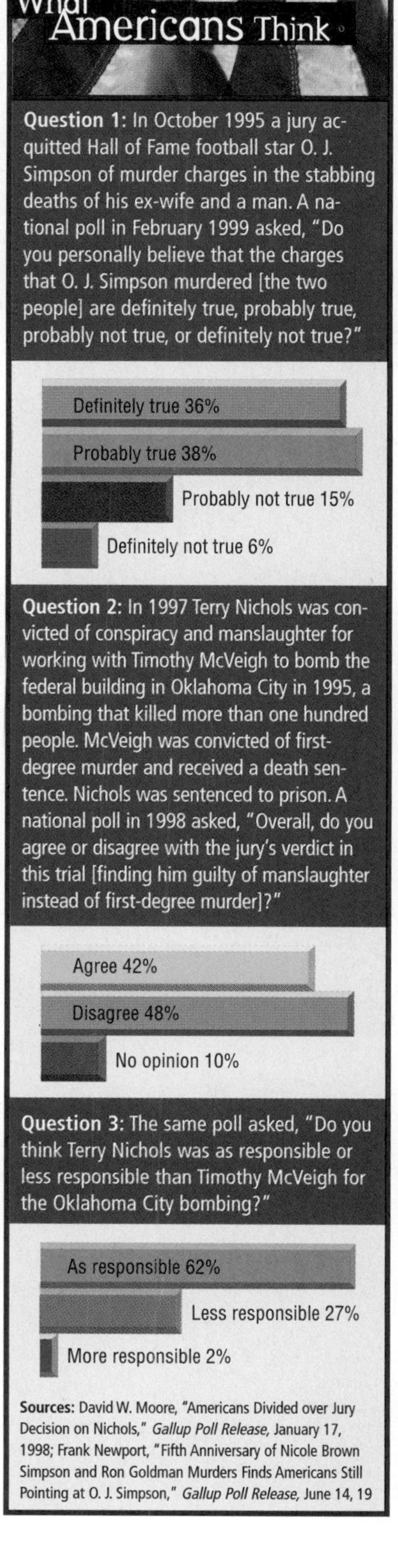

Counties often describe the trial process for people who will serve on juries. For one example, see http://www.co.alameda.ca.us/courts/jury/procedure.shtml.

Comparing Trial Processes: France and the United States

In 1977 Helen "Holly" Maddux, a 30-year-old woman from a wealthy Texas family, disappeared. She had been living in Philadelphia with her boyfriend, Ira Einhorn, a former hippie leader who had developed a network of friends among prominent people as he ran for mayor and organized artistic events and self-discovery courses. He had even spent one semester as a visiting fellow at Harvard's Kennedy School of Government. Eighteen months after Einhorn claimed that Maddux went out and never returned from a trip to the store, her decomposed remains were found in a trunk in his closet. Einhorn proclaimed his innocence and gained release on bail with the assistance of his attorney, former Philadelphia district attorney and later U.S. Senator Arlen Specter, and the support of prominent Philadelphians who thought this leading advocate of peace and love could never commit a murder.

When Einhorn's trial date approached, he disappeared. Investigators later learned that he had fled the country. Sightings of Einhorn were reported in Ireland and Sweden, but authorities could not find him. When Philadelphia's district attorney became concerned that witnesses' memories might fade over time, Einhorn was tried *in absentia* in 1993. A trial *in absentia* means that the trial was conducted even though the defendant was absent. Einhorn was convicted of murder.

Assistant District Attorney Richard DiBenedetto continued to investigate Einhorn's whereabouts, just as he had done for years. In 1997 DiBenedetto directed French police to a house where Einhorn's former Swedish girlfriend resided under an assumed name. The police found a man who said his name was "Mallon," but his fingerprints matched those of Ira Einhorn.

Einhorn hired an attorney to fight his *extradition*—the process of returning a fugitive to face charges in another jurisdiction. His attorneys argued that the United States has an unfair criminal trial process because it permits defendants to be tried *in absentia,* it uses the death penalty, and it does not obey the European Convention on Human Rights. According to an American writer who followed Einhorn's case closely, his attorneys were raising fundamental questions about the fairness of American trials and the justice process (Levy, 1997):

> *However, the underlying argument, it would appear, was to urge the French judges to send a message to the "barbarians" in the United States. . . . [They wanted France to] send a message in human rights to the new masters of the world order across the ocean.*

The French judges agreed with the attorneys' arguments. The judges refused to send Einhorn back to the United States to stand trial, and he was released from custody. Government officials in the United States protested the decision and its implication that American trial processes are unfair. In an effort to satisfy French criticisms of the trial *in absentia,* the Pennsylvania legislature passed a special law to give Einhorn a new trial if he were ever returned to the United States. After two additional years of appeals, a French court ordered Einhorn returned to the United States in 1999. He was not transported from France immediately, because he was entitled to further appeals in the French courts. Eventually, he was sent to the United States, convicted in a

Williams v. Florida (1970)
Juries of fewer than 12 members are constitutional.

court to contact, process, and pay a smaller number of jurors. The use of small juries was upheld by the Supreme Court in ***Williams v. Florida* (1970)**. In *Burch v. Louisiana* (1979), the Supreme Court ruled that 6-member juries must vote unanimously to convict a defendant, but unanimity is not required for larger juries. Some states permit juries to convict defendants by votes of 10 to 2 or 9 to 3 (see Figure 11.2 for jury size requirements in each state). Critics of the change to 6-person juries charge that the smaller group is less representative of the conflicting views in the community and too quick to bring in a verdict (Amar, 1997).

2002 murder trial, and sentenced to life without parole.

If French judges are so critical of American trial processes that they would permit a suspected murderer to live freely in their country, what does that say about their view of the United States? Moreover, in what ways might French judges view their own trial processes as superior?

Judges in France are not elected officials, and efforts are made to separate the French judiciary from electoral politics. To become a judge in France, law students must take a competitive examination to gain entry into the graduate school for future judges. Based on their performance in graduate school and their achievement on additional tests, they may gain positions at the lower levels of the judiciary, which is a branch of the national civil service. French judges have the protected tenure of civil servants and, unlike so many American state judges, never need to worry about running for reelection in order to retain their seats on the bench.

Criminal investigations and trials in France differ fundamentally from those in the United States because French judges are so deeply involved in each step of the process—from investigation of defendants through jury deliberations after a trial. Rather than a police official or prosecutor, a judge called an "examining magistrate" investigates criminal cases. Critics fear that some examining magistrates might become overly familiar with police and prosecutors and thereby lose their neutral perspective. However, the examining magistrate is positioned to be an independent investigator, unlike American police and elected prosecutors who face political pressure to gain convictions in an adversarial system.

After the investigation is completed, the trial serves as a mechanism to check the quality of the investigation. Trials for serious criminal cases take place in the Courts of Assize. A chief trial judge assumes responsibility for the case. Instead of having adversarial prosecutors and defense attorneys attempting to persuade the jury with carefully phrased and often deceptive questions, the French chief trial judge performs all questioning, and no cross examination of witnesses is permitted. The chief trial judge typically asks many questions about the defendant's background and character, because the trial does not need to focus solely on the evidence about the crime. Because judges control the pretrial investigation and the presentation of evidence in the courtroom, it may be less likely that defendants are treated differently because of their wealth. Unlike in the United States, where the quality of defense representation sometimes varies depending on whether the defendant can afford to hire his or her own attorney, French judges can ensure that sufficient and proper evidence is presented on behalf of all defendants.

Throughout the trial, the chief judge is joined by two associate judges and nine jurors from the community. Both the prosecution and defense can use peremptory challenges to eliminate a few of the jurors, but they do not engage in the extensive questioning of jurors that can occur in American trials concerning serious crimes.

At the end of the trial, the three judges and nine jurors deliberate in secret. By having judges participate in the jury's verdict, legal professionals can influence the outcome of the case. Such participation may help to keep the jurors focused on the relevant facts and law. On the other hand, it may also lead jurors to defer to the legal professionals and thereby fail to express viewpoints that reflect public sentiments about the case. Although judges do not automatically control the verdict, they influence it directly by participating in the vote. The jurors and judges vote by secret ballot. Eight of the 12 must vote in favor of conviction in order for the defendant to be found guilty. Thus a defendant can be found guilty even when four jurors disagree. The sentence is determined by a majority vote of the jurors and judges. Thus citizen-jurors have greater direct input into sentencing in France. In the United States, jurors affect the eventual sentence by determining which offenses will be the basis for the conviction. If they want to see a lighter sentence, they can convict of fewer charges or a lesser offense. However, they do not control the actual sentence because that is usually determined by a judge. By contrast, French jurors can vote directly on the sentence, and even out vote the judges in determining the sentence. Thus criminal punishment in France may be shaped directly by community representatives instead of legal professionals.

Is the French trial process superior to the processes in the United States? Would American courts benefit from giving judges greater control over criminal investigations, the presentation of evidence, and deliberations about guilt? Would they benefit from giving American jurors the direct authority to determine the sentence for each offender? The Einhorn extradition dispute between France and the United States did not rest solely on the nature of American jury trials. Instead, it seemed to reflect a broader sense that some French judges had doubts about the fairness of the American criminal justice process. The differences between the French and American systems as well as the French criticisms of the American process stem from differences in the respective countries' values and traditions.

Sources: Drawn from Henry J. Abraham, *The Judicial Process,* 6th ed. (New York: Oxford University Press, 1986); Bill Hanna, "Family of Victim Glad Fugitive's Murder Trial Finally under Way," *Fort Worth Star-Telegram,* September 24, 2002; Steven Levy, "A Guru Goes Free," *Newsweek,* December 15, 1997; Robert Moran, "Pennsylvania Governor Signs Provision for Einhorn Retrial," *Philadelphia Inquirer,* January 29, 1998; D. Marie Provine, "Court in the Political Process in France," in *Courts, Law, and Politics in Comparative Perspective* (New Haven, Conn.: Yale University Press, 1996), 177–248; Julie Stoiber, "Fugitive Ira Einhorn Loses a Round in Extradition Appeal," *Philadelphia Inquirer,* May 28, 1999.

check point

8. Approximately what percentage of felony cases reach conclusion through a trial?
9. What are three of the six functions that juries serve for the criminal justice system?
10. What has the Supreme Court decided concerning the size and unanimity requirements of juries?

The Center for Jury Studies monitors developments and reforms affecting jury trials: http://www.ncsc.dni.us/wash_dc/jury/jury.htm.

Figure 11.2 **Jury size for felony and misdemeanor trials**
All states require 12-member juries in capital cases; six states permit juries of fewer than 12 members in felony cases. Does the smaller number of people on a jury have advantages or disadvantages? Would you rather have your case decided by a 12- or a 6-person jury?

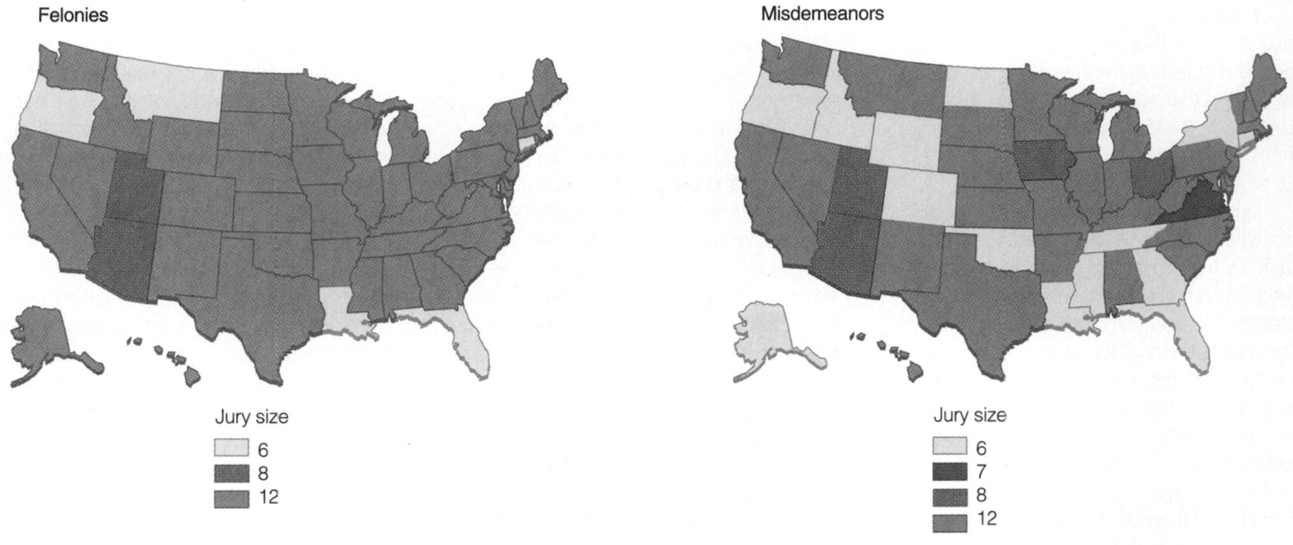

Source: Bureau of Justice Statistics, *Report to the Nation on Crime and Justice*, 2nd ed. (Washington, D.C.: U.S. Government Printing Office, 1988), 86.

The Trial Process

The trial process generally follows eight steps:

1. Selection of the jury
2. Opening statements by prosecution and defense
3. Presentation of the prosecution's evidence and witnesses
4. Presentation of the defense's evidence and witnesses
5. Presentation of rebuttal witnesses
6. Closing arguments by each side
7. Instruction of the jury by the judge
8. Decision by the jury

The details of each step may vary according to each state's rules. Although only a small number of cases go to trial, understanding each step in the process and considering the broader impact of this institution are important.

Figure 11.3 **Jury selection process for a 12-member jury**
Potential jurors are drawn at random from a source list. From this pool, a panel is selected and presented for duty. The voir dire examination may remove some, while others will be seated. The 14 jurors selected include two alternates.

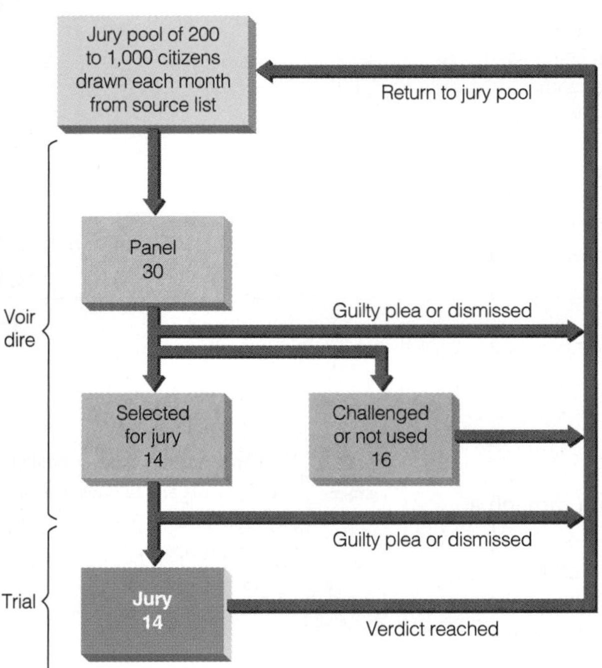

Jury Selection

The selection of the jury, outlined in Figure 11.3, is a crucial first step in the trial process. Because people always involve their experiences, values, and biases in their decision making, prosecutors and defense attorneys actively seek to identify and select potential jurors who may be automatically sympathetic to their side and to exclude potentially hostile jurors. Lawyers do not necessarily achieve these goals, because the selection of jurors involves the decisions and interactions of prosecutors, defense attorneys, and judges, each of whom has different objectives in the selection process.

Jurors are selected from among the citizens whose names have been placed in the jury pool. The composition of the jury pool tremendously impacts the ultimate composition of the trial jury. In most states, the jury pool is drawn from lists

Steve Chenn/CORBIS

During jury selection, attorneys for each side may question prospective jurors to determine whether they are biased in ways that would make them incapable of rendering a fair verdict.

of registered voters, but research has shown that nonwhites, the poor, and young people register to vote at much lower rates than do the rest of the population. As a result, members of these groups are underrepresented on juries (Fukurai, 1996). In many cases, the presence or absence of these groups may make no difference in the ultimate verdict. In some situations, however, members of these groups will likely interpret evidence differently than will their older, white, middle-class counterparts who dominate the composition of juries (Ugwuegbu, 1999). For example, the poor, nonwhites, and young people may be more likely to have had unpleasant experiences with police officers and therefore be less willing to believe that police officers always tell the truth. Today courts may supplement the lists of registered voters with other lists, such as those for driver's licenses, hunting licenses, and utility bills, in order to diversify the jury pool (Newman, 1996).

California provides a description of jury selection and service for prospective jurors; see http://www.courtinfo.ca.gov/jury/step1.htm.

Only about 15 percent of adult Americans have ever been called for jury duty. Retired people and homemakers with grown children tend to be overrepresented on juries because they are less inconvenienced by serving and are often less likely to ask to be excused because of job responsibilities or child care problems. To make jury duty less onerous, many states have moved to a system called one-day-one-trial, in which jurors serve for either one day or for the duration of one trial.

The courtroom process of **voir dire** (which means "to speak the truth") is used to question prospective jurors to screen out those who might be biased or incapable of making a fair decision. Attorneys for each side, as well as the judge, may question jurors about their background, knowledge of the case, and acquaintance with any participants in the case. Jurors will also be asked whether they or their immediate family members have been crime victims or otherwise involved in a criminal case in a manner that may prevent them from making open-minded decisions about the evidence and the defendant. If a juror's responses indicate that he or she will not be able to make fair decisions, the juror may be **challenged for cause.** The judge must rule on the challenge, but if the judge agrees with the attorney, then the juror is excused from that specific case. There is usually no limit on the number of jurors that the attorneys may challenge for cause. It is not easy, however, for attorneys to identify all of a juror's biases through brief questioning (Dillehay and Sandys, 1996).

voir dire
A questioning of prospective jurors in order to screen out people the attorneys think might be biased or otherwise incapable of delivering a fair verdict.

challenge for cause
Removal of a prospective juror by showing that he or she has some bias or some other legal disability. The number of such challenges permitted to attorneys is unlimited.

Although challenges for cause fall ultimately under the judge's control, the prosecution and defense can exert their own control over the jury's composition

peremptory challenge
Removal of a prospective juror without giving any reason. Attorneys are allowed a limited number of such challenges.

through the use of **peremptory challenges.** Using these challenges, the prosecution and defense can exclude prospective jurors without giving specific reasons. Attorneys use peremptory challenges to exclude jurors whom they think will be unsympathetic to their arguments (Hoffman, 1999). Attorneys usually use hunches about which jurors to challenge; there is little evidence that they can accurately identify which jurors will be sympathetic or unsympathetic to their side (White, 1995). Normally, the defense is allowed eight to ten peremptory challenges, and the prosecution six to eight.

Go to the Public Policy feature on the American System of Criminal Justice CD to learn more about the issues surrounding peremptory challenges.

The use of peremptory challenges has raised concerns that attorneys can use them to exclude, for example, African American jurors when an African American is on trial (Kennedy, 1997). In a series of decisions in the late 1980s and early 1990s, the Supreme Court prohibited using peremptory challenges to systematically exclude potential jurors because of their race or gender (e.g., *Batson v. Kentucky,* 1986). In practice, however, the enforcement of this prohibition on race and gender discrimination falls to the trial judge (C. E. Smith and Ochoa, 1996). If a trial judge is willing to accept flimsy excuses for race-based and gender-based exclusions, then the attorneys can ignore the ban on discrimination (Bray, 1992). As you read the Close Up box, ask yourself whether peremptory challenges have a positive or negative effect on jury selection. Do you think peremptory challenges should be abolished?

Some lawyers say that trials are won or lost in jury selection. If a lawyer succeeds in seating a favorable jury, he or she may have a receptive audience that will readily support one side's arguments and evidence.

check point

11. What is voir dire?
12. What is the difference between a peremptory challenge and a challenge for cause?

Opening Statements

After the jury has been selected, the trial begins. The clerk reads the complaint (indictment or information) detailing the charges, and the prosecutor and the defense attorney may, if they desire, make opening statements to the jury to summarize the position that each side intends to take. The statements are not evidence. The jury is not supposed to regard the attorneys' statements as proving or disproving anything about the case.

Presentation of the Prosecution's Evidence

One of the basic protections of the American criminal justice system is the assumption that the defendant is innocent until proved guilty. The prosecution must prove beyond a reasonable doubt, within the demands of the court procedures and rules of evidence, that the individual named in the indictment committed the crime. This means that the evidence excludes all reasonable doubt; it does not have to determine absolute certainty.

real evidence
Physical evidence such as a weapon, records, fingerprints, stolen property—objects actually involved in the crime.

demonstrative evidence
Evidence that is not based on witness testimony but that demonstrates information relevant to the crime, such as maps, X-rays, and photographs; includes real evidence involved in the crime.

testimony
Oral evidence provided by a legally competent witness.

By presenting evidence to the jury, the prosecution must establish a case showing that the defendant is guilty. Evidence is classified as real evidence, demonstrative evidence, testimony, direct evidence, and circumstantial evidence. **Real evidence** might include such objects as a weapon, business records, fingerprints, or stolen property. These are real objects involved in the crime. **Demonstrative evidence** is any evidence presented for jurors to see and understand without testimony. Real evidence is one form of demonstrative evidence. Other forms of demonstrative evidence are those items not involved in the crime but still used to make points to jurors. These include maps, X-rays, photographs, models, and diagrams. Most evidence in a criminal trial, however, consists of the **testimony** of witnesses. Witnesses at a trial must be legally competent. Thus the judge may be

The Peremptory Challenge Controversy

In 1987 Jimmy Elem faced trial on robbery charges in a Missouri state court. During jury selection, the prosecutor used peremptory challenges to exclude two African American men from the jury. Elem's attorney objected, claiming that the prosecutor appeared to be excluding potential jurors because of their race. Under the U.S. Supreme Court's decision in *Batson v. Kentucky* (1986), the trial judge was obligated to ask the prosecutor to provide a nonracial reason for removing the jurors when there is the appearance of race-based exclusion in a prosecutor's use of peremptory challenges. In response to the judge's question, the prosecutor replied,

> *I struck [juror] number twenty-two because of his long hair. He had long curly hair. He had the longest hair of anybody on the panel by far. He appeared to me to not be a good juror for that fact, the fact that he had long hair hanging down shoulder length, curly unkempt hair. Also he had a mustache and a goatee type beard. And juror number twenty-four also has a mustache and goatee type beard. Those are the only two people on the jury... with the facial hair.... And I don't like the way they looked, with the way the hair is cut, both of them. And the mustaches and the beards look suspicious to me.*

The trial judge accepted the prosecutor's explanation and the trial moved forward. Elem subsequently filed a habeas corpus action in the federal courts claiming that the prosecutor had used a flimsy, nonsensical excuse to cover the fact that the exclusions were really based on race. The U.S. Court of Appeals agreed with Elem and declared that peremptory challenges that appear to be based on race are only valid if actually based on reasons related to the individuals' qualifications to be a good juror. The Court of Appeals did not believe that having curly or long hair affected one's ability to be a good jurist.

Missouri carried the case forward to the U.S. Supreme Court. In a 7-to-2 decision, the Supreme Court reversed and said that prosecutors can put forward silly, superstitious, and implausible reasons as long as the trial judge accepts the exclusion as being based on something other than race or gender. Thus it is possible to violate the Constitution by using peremptory challenges in a racially discriminatory or sexist manner if the prosecutor or defense attorney can provide some alternative excuse that is accepted by the judge.

Many attorneys like the peremptory challenge because they believe that they can identify people who are biased and thereby remove them from the jury. Often these attorneys base their decisions on the jurors' facial expressions or body language. However, social science research does not support lawyers' claims that they can use such hunches to tell if a potential juror will be biased.

Although the U.S. Constitution does not say anything about peremptory challenges, Supreme Court Justice Antonin Scalia claims that peremptory challenges should be retained because they are part of such a long tradition in the jury selection process. Others argue that peremptory challenges enhance the legitimacy of the trial process by letting defendants feel as if they had some influence over the composition of the jury. By contrast, the late Supreme Court Justice Thurgood Marshall indicated that peremptory challenges should be abolished because they were frequently used to discriminate or add bias to the jury. For Marshall, if there is not enough evidence of bias to justify a challenge for cause, then the person should be allowed to serve on the jury. People should not be denied the opportunity to participate in this important aspect of judicial decision making just because one lawyer does not like the expression on their face or the color of their skin.

If you were a state legislator and someone proposed a bill to abolish peremptory challenges in jury selection, how would you vote? Do you think peremptory challenges are helpful or harmful in the trial process?

Researching the Internet

To read a proposal to abolish peremptory challenges, see http://www.apa.udel.edu/apa/archive/newsletters/v96n2/law/abolish.asp.

required to determine whether the witness whose testimony is challenged has the intelligence to tell the truth and the ability to recall what was seen. Witnesses with inadequate intelligence or mental problems can be excluded as unqualified to present testimony. **Direct evidence** refers to eyewitness accounts—for example, "I saw John Smith fire the gun." **Circumstantial evidence** requires that the jury infer a fact from what the witness observed: "I saw John Smith walk behind his house with a gun. A few minutes later I heard a gun go off, and then Mr.

direct evidence
Eyewitness accounts.

circumstantial evidence
Evidence provided by a witness from which a jury must infer a fact.

Computer Simulations in the Courtroom

In jury trials, prosecutors and defense attorneys have traditionally attempted to use their words to "paint a picture" for the jurors. Each attorney wants the jurors to envision a specific chain of events. After hearing the same presentations, individual jurors may very well leave the courtroom with quite different perceptions about what happened at the crime scene and whether the defendant played a role. In recent years, attorneys have attempted to use computer technology to present clearer images of events. The advent of realistic computer games has brought with it the development of computer-generated recreations of crime scenes. If the jury needs to understand how an injury occurred, for example, the prosecution may present a computer-generated film of a person being struck from behind or falling in a manner consistent with the victim's injuries. If a defendant has sufficient money to hire computer experts, the defendant may attempt to develop a computer presentation that recreates events in a way that absolves him or her of responsibility.

Observers have serious concerns about the use of such computer programs in trials. Such recreations are available only to those who can afford them. Thus poor defendants have little hope of using this technology to present their side of the story. In addition, the computer scenes can be developed or manipulated in ways that are not consistent with the available evidence. Jurors may believe the realistic scenes that they watch on the screen despite contrary evidence that they hear from witness testimony. In other words, the image of the recreation may stick in jurors' minds even when there is strong evidence to show that the recreation was not accurate.

Should computer-generated recreations of crimes be shown during trials? How can we reduce the risks that such recreations will distort reality or otherwise be misused?

Source: Drawn from John McCormick, "Scene of the Crime," *Newsweek*, February 28, 2000, p. 60.

Researching the **Internet**
Consultants offer computer simulation services to attorneys who conduct trials. For one example, see http://www.perspective-media-group.com.

What are the rules of evidence? Read the Federal Rules of Evidence at http://www.law.cornell.edu/rules/fre/overview.html.

Smith walked toward me holding a gun." The witness's observation that Smith had a gun and that the witness then heard a gun go off does not provide the direct evidence that Smith fired his gun; yet the jury may link the described facts and infer that Smith fired his gun. After a witness has given testimony, he or she can be cross-examined by counsel for the other side.

The attorney for each side can challenge the other side's presentation of evidence. If presented evidence violates the rules, reflects untrustworthy hearsay or opinion statements, or is not relevant to the issues in the case, an attorney will object to the presentation. In effect, the attorney is asking the judge to rule that the opponent's questionable evidence cannot be considered by the jury. See "New Directions in Criminal Justice Policy" to learn about one controversial type of evidence: computer simulations.

After the prosecution has presented all of the state's evidence against the defendant, he or she informs the court that the people's case rests. It is common for the defense then to ask the court to direct the jury to bring forth a verdict of not guilty. Such a motion is based on the defense argument that the state has not presented enough evidence to prove its case. If the motion is sustained by the judge (it rarely is), the trial ends; if it is overruled, the defense presents its evidence.

Presentation of the Defense's Evidence

The defense is not required to answer the case presented by the prosecution. As it is the state's responsibility to prove the case beyond a reasonable doubt, it is theoretically possible—and in fact sometimes happens—that the defense rests its case immediately. Usually the accused's attorney employs one strategy or a combination of three strategies: (1) contrary evidence is introduced to rebut or cast doubt on the state's case, (2) an alibi is offered, or (3) an affirmative defense is presented. The Andrew Goldstein defense team relied on the final approach in

The Gamma Liaison Network

Barry Sheck, attorney for au pair Louise Woodward, presents evidence that an earlier skull fracture, and not a shaking of 8-month-old Matthew Eappens by his client, had caused the infant's death.

presenting an insanity defense in the subway murder case. An affirmative defense is a legal excuse that permits the jury to find the defendant not responsible for the crime. As discussed in Chapter 4, defenses include self-defense, insanity, duress, and necessity.

A key issue for the defense is whether the accused will take the stand. The Fifth Amendment protection against self-incrimination means that the defendant does not have to testify. The Supreme Court has ruled that the prosecutor may not comment on, nor can the jury draw inferences from, the defendant's decision not to appear in his or her own defense. The decision is not made lightly, because if the defendant does testify, the prosecution may cross-examine him or her. *Cross-examination,* or questioning by the opposing attorney, is broader than direct examination. The prosecutor may question the defendant not only about the crime but also about his or her past, including past criminal convictions.

Although jurors are not supposed to make assumptions about the defendant's guilt, there is always a risk that some of them will do so if the defendant does not testify. For example, when Michael Skakel, a cousin of the Kennedy family, was convicted in 2002 of bludgeoning a girl with a golf club 27 years earlier as a teenager, he never took the witness stand in his own defense. The prosecution gained the conviction based on testimony from several witnesses who claimed that Skakel had told them years earlier about killing a girl with a golf club. Skakel's attorneys used an alibi defense by presenting testimony from witnesses who said that he had been at home watching television with friends at the time of the murder. The defense also sought to cast suspicion on another suspect. The jury, however, accepted the version of events presented by the prosecution's witnesses and, upon conviction, Skakel was given a sentence of 20 years to life (Goldman, 2002).

Presentation of Rebuttal Witnesses

When the defense's case is complete, the prosecution may present witnesses whose testimony is designed to discredit or counteract testimony presented on behalf of the defendant. If the prosecution brings rebuttal witnesses, the defense can question them and present new witnesses in rebuttal.

Closing Arguments by Each Side

When each side has completed its presentation of the evidence, the prosecution and defense make closing arguments to the jury. The attorneys review the evidence of the case for the jury, presenting interpretations of the evidence that favor their own side. The prosecutor may use the summation to show how individual pieces of evidence connect to form a basis for concluding that the defendant is guilty. The defense may set forth the applicable law and try to show that (1) the prosecution has not proved its case beyond a reasonable doubt and (2) the testimony raised questions but did not provide answers. Each side may remind the jury of its duty not to be swayed by emotion and to evaluate the evidence impartially. Yet, some attorneys may hope that the jurors will react emotionally to benefit their side.

Judge's Instructions to the Jury

The jury decides the facts of the case, but the judge determines the law. Before the jurors depart for the jury room to decide the defendant's fate, the judge instructs them on how the law should guide their decision. The judge may discuss basic legal principles such as proof beyond a reasonable doubt, the legal requirements necessary to show that the prosecution has proved all the elements, or the rights of the defendant. More-specific aspects of the law bearing on the decision—such as complicated court rulings on the nature of the insanity defense or the ways certain types of evidence have been gathered—may be included in the judge's instructions. In complicated trials, the judge may spend an entire day instructing the jury.

reasonable doubt
The standard used by a juror to decide if the prosecution has provided enough evidence for conviction. Jurors should vote for acquittal if they think there is a reasonable doubt.

The concept of **reasonable doubt** lies at the heart of the jury system. The prosecution is not required to prove the guilt of the defendant beyond *all* doubt. Instead, if a juror is

> satisfied to a moral certainty that this defendant . . . is guilty of any one of the crimes charged here, you may safely say that you have been convinced beyond a reasonable doubt. If your mind is wavering, or if you are uncertain . . . you have not been convinced beyond a reasonable doubt and must render a verdict of not guilty. (Phillips, 1977:214)

The experience of listening to the judge may become an ordeal for the jurors, who must hear and understand perhaps two or three hours of instruction on the law and the evidence (Bradley, 1992). It is assumed that somehow jurors will fully absorb these details upon first hearing them, so that they will thoroughly understand how they are supposed to decide the case in the jury room (G. P. Kramer and Koenig, 1990).

Decision by the Jury

After they have heard the case and have been instructed by the judge, the jurors retire to a room where they have complete privacy. They elect a foreperson to run the meeting, and deliberations begin. Until now, the jurors have been passive observers of the trial, unable to question witnesses or to discuss the case among themselves; now they can discuss the facts that have been presented. Throughout their deliberations the jurors may be *sequestered*—kept together day and night, away from the influences of newspapers and conversations with family and friends. If jurors are allowed to spend nights at home, they are ordered not to discuss the case with anyone. The jury may request that the judge reread to them portions of the instructions, ask for additional instructions, or hear portions of the transcript detailing what was said by specific witnesses.

If the jury becomes deadlocked and cannot reach a verdict, the trial ends with a hung jury and the prosecutor must decide whether to try the case all over again in front of a new jury. When a verdict is reached, the judge, prosecution, and defense reassemble in the courtroom to hear it. The prosecution or the defense may request that the jury be *polled:* Each member individually tells his or her vote in open court. This procedure presumably ensures that no juror has felt pressured to agree with the other jurors.

check point

13. What are the stages in the trial process?
14. What are the kinds of evidence presented during a trial?

Evaluating the Jury System

Early research at the University of Chicago Law School found that, consistent with theories of group behavior, participation and influence in the jury process are related to social status. Men were found to be more active participants than were women, whites more active than minority members, and the better educated more active than those less educated. Much of the discussion in the jury room was not directly concerned with the testimony but rather with trial procedures, opinions about the witnesses, and personal reminiscences (Strodtbeck, James, and Hawkins, 1957). In 30 percent of the cases, a vote taken soon after entering the jury room was the only one necessary to reach a verdict; in the rest of the cases, the majority on the first ballot eventually prevailed in 90 percent of the cases (Broeder, 1959). Because of group pressure, only rarely did a single juror produce a hung jury. Some jurors may doubt their own views or go along with the others if everyone else disagrees with them. More-recent findings have upheld the importance of group pressure on decision making (Hastie, Penrod, and Pennington, 1983).

Read about the most famous trials in American history: http://www.umkc.edu/famoustrials.

A recent examination of trials in the 75 largest counties found that 84 percent of jury trials ended in convictions, compared with only 72 percent of bench trials (Reaves and Hart, 1999). These numbers alone do not reveal whether judges and juries decide cases differently. The different conviction percentages may stem from a tendency of defendants facing more ironclad evidence to pin their hopes on the ability of the defense attorney to persuade jurors to acquit. By contrast, they may view judges as less susceptible to persuasion.

Juries tend to take a more liberal view of such issues as self-defense than do judges and are likely to minimize the seriousness of an offense if they dislike some characteristic of the victim (S. J. Adler, 1994:200–207). For example, if the victim of an assault is a prostitute, the jury may minimize the assault. Judges have more experience with the justice process. Thus, they appear more likely to label as guilty defendants whose cases were sent forward by police and prosecutors who believed that there was strong evidence of guilt.

Go to the *American System of Criminal Justice* Web site at http://www.cj.wadsworth.com/colesmith10e to explore the topic of jury trials in further detail.

15. What factors can make a jury's decision different from that of a judge?

Appeals

The imposition of a sentence does not mean that it must be served immediately. The defendant typically has the right to appeal the verdict to a higher court; indigent offenders' right to counsel continues through the first appeal (Priehs, 1999). Some states have limited the right to appeal when defendants plead guilty.

An **appeal** is based on a claim that one or more errors of law or procedure were made during the investigation, arrest, or trial process (C. E. Smith, 1999b). Such claims usually assert that the trial judge made errors in courtroom rulings or in improperly admitting evidence the police had gathered in violation of some constitutional right. A defendant might base an appeal, for example, on the claim that the judge did not instruct the jury correctly or that a guilty plea was not made voluntarily. Appeals are based on questions of procedure, not on issues of the defendant's guilt or innocence. The appellate court will not normally second-guess a jury. Instead it will check to make sure that the trial followed proper procedures. If there were significant errors in the trial, then the conviction is set aside. The defendant may be tried again if the prosecutor decides to pursue the case again. Most criminal defendants must file an appeal shortly after trial to have an appellate court review the case; however, many states provide for an automatic appeal in death penalty cases. The quality of defense representation matters a great deal because the appeal must usually meet short deadlines and carefully identify appropriate issues (Wasserman, 1990).

appeal
A request to a higher court that it review actions taken in a completed trial.

Laverne Pavlinac touches the tear-stained face of her granddaughter after being released from prison in Salem, Oregon. Pavlinac and John Sosnovske, who were convicted for the 1991 murder of Taujna Bennett, successfully appealed their conviction. The appellate judge said there was no doubt about their innocence.

A case originating in a state court is usually appealed through that state's judicial system. When a state case involves a federal constitutional question, however, it may be appealed to the U.S. Supreme Court. Even so, state courts decide almost four-fifths of all appeals.

The number of appeals in both the state and federal courts has increased during recent decades. What is the nature of these cases? A five-state study by Joy Chapper and Roger Hanson (1989) showed that (1) although a majority of appeals occur after trial convictions, about a quarter result from nontrial proceedings such as guilty pleas and probation revocations; (2) homicides and other serious crimes against people account for more than 50 percent of appeals; (3) most appeals arise from cases in which the sentence is 5 years or less; and (4) the issues raised at appeal tend to concern the introduction of evidence, the sufficiency of evidence, and jury instructions.

Most appeals do not succeed. In almost 80 percent of the cases Chapper and Hanson examined, the decision of the trial courts was affirmed. Most of the other decisions produced new trials or resentencing; only 9.4 percent of those whose convictions were overturned received acquittals on appeal. Table 11.4 shows the percentage distribution of the outcomes from the appellate process. The appellate process rarely provides a ticket to freedom for someone convicted of a crime.

habeas corpus
A writ or judicial order requesting the release of a person being detained in a jail, prison, or mental hospital. If a judge finds the person is being held improperly, the writ may be granted and the person released.

Habeas Corpus

After people use their avenues of appeal, they may pursue a writ of habeas corpus if they claim that their federal constitutional rights were violated during the lower-court processes. Known as "the great writ" from its traditional role in English law and its enshrinement in the U.S. Constitution, **habeas corpus** is a judicial order requesting that a judge examine whether an individual is being prop-

Table 11.4 Percentage distribution of alternative outcomes in five state appellate courts

Although the public thinks defendants exercising their right of appeal will be released, this study shows that 20.6 percent have their convictions reversed, but only a few are acquitted by the appellate court.

Appeal Outcome	Percentage of Appeals
Conviction affirmed	79.4
Conviction reversed	20.6
	100.0
Among convictions reversed	
Acquittal	9.4
New trial	31.9
Resentencing	35.3
Other	23.4
	100.0

Source: Joy Chapper and Roger Hanson, *Understanding Reversible Error in Criminal Appeals* (Williamsburg, Va.: National Center for State Courts, 1989).

erly detained in a jail, prison, or mental hospital. If there is no legal basis for the person to be held, then the judge may grant the writ and order the person to be released. In the context of criminal justice, convicted offenders claim that their imprisonment is improper because one of their constitutional rights was violated during the investigation or adjudication of their case. Statutes permit offenders convicted in both state and federal courts to pursue habeas corpus actions in the federal courts. After first seeking favorable decisions by state appellate courts, convicted offenders can start their constitutional claims anew in the federal trial-level district courts and subsequently pursue their habeas cases in the federal circuit courts of appeal and the U.S. Supreme Court.

Only about 1 percent of habeas petitions succeed (Flango, 1994). One reason may be that an individual has no right to be represented by counsel when pursuing a habeas corpus petition. Few offenders have sufficient knowledge of law and legal procedures to identify and present constitutional claims effectively in the federal courts (Hanson and Daley, 1995).

In the late 1980s and early 1990s, the U.S. Supreme Court issued many decisions that made it more difficult for convicted offenders to file habeas corpus petitions (Alexander, 1993; C. E. Smith, 1995a). The Court created tougher procedural rules that are more difficult for convicted offenders to follow. The rules also unintentionally created some new problems for state attorneys general and federal trial courts that must examine the procedural rules affecting cases rather than simply address the constitutional violations that the offender claims occurred (C. E. Smith, 1995c). In 1996 Congress enacted and President Bill Clinton signed the Antiterrorism and Effective Death Penalty Act, which placed additional restrictions on habeas corpus petitions. The statute was quickly approved by the U.S. Supreme Court. These reforms were based, in part, on a belief that prisoners' cases were clogging the federal courts (C. E. Smith, 1995b). Ironically, habeas corpus petitions in the federal courts have increased by 50 percent since the passage of the restrictive legislation (Scalia, 2002). By imposing strict filing deadlines for petitions, the legislation may have inadvertently focused more prisoners' attention on the existence of habeas corpus and thereby encouraged them to move forward with petitions in order to meet the deadlines.

Evaluating the Appellate Process

The public seems to believe that many offenders are being "let off" through the appellate process. Frustrated by the problems of crime, some conservatives have argued that opportunities for appeal should be limited. They claim that too many offenders delay imposition of their sentences and that others seek to evade punishment by filing appeals endlessly. This practice not only increases the workload of the courts but also jeopardizes the concept of the finality of the justice process. However, because 90 percent of accused people plead guilty, the number of cases that might be appealed is relatively small.

Consider what follows a defendant's successful appeal, which is by no means a total or final victory. An appeal that results in reversal of the conviction normally means that the case is remanded to the lower court for a new trial. At this point the state must consider whether the procedural errors in the original trial can be overcome and whether it is worth additional expenditure to bring the defendant into court again. Frequently, the prosecutor pursues the case again and gains a new, proper conviction of the defendant. The appeal process sometimes generates new plea negotiations that produce a second conviction with a lesser sentence that reflects the reduced strength of the prosecutor's case. For example, New York City police officer Charles Schwarz was one of the officers charged with participating in a brutal 1997 attack on Haitian immigrant Abner Louima (see Chapter 8). Schwarz was accused of escorting Louima to the police restroom where the attack occurred and holding Louima during the attack. After being tried and convicted, then having convictions overturned on appeal, Schwarz faced a fourth trial on federal charges of violating Louima's civil rights. In an unusual Saturday-night session at federal district court, Schwarz's attorney and the prosecution reached a last-minute plea agreement that avoided the necessity of a fourth trial. He pleaded guilty to perjury, a charge for which he had previously been convicted in a jury trial, in exchange for having the prosecutors drop the civil rights charges and recommend that Schwarz serve a sentence of less than 5 years in prison (Glaberson, 2002). After many months of proclaiming his innocence, Schwarz apparently decided not to take the risk that he might receive a 15 year sentence if convicted by a jury. The prosecution apparently decided not to take the chance that the jury might acquit Schwarz after a long, expensive, and highly publicized trial. Thus, successful appeals do not necessarily result in the defendant being set free.

The appeals process performs the important function of righting wrongs. It also helps to ensure consistency in the application of law by judges in different courts. Beyond that, its presence constantly influences the daily operations of the criminal justice system in that prosecutors and trial judges must consider how their decisions and actions might later be evaluated by a higher court.

check point

16. How does the appellate court's job differ from that of the trial court?
17. What is a habeas corpus petition?

Summary

- The outcomes in criminal cases are significantly influenced by a court's local legal culture, which defines the going rates of punishment for various offenses.
- Courtroom workgroups made up of judges, prosecutors, and defense attorneys who work together can smoothly and efficiently handle cases through cooperative plea-bargaining processes.
- Most convictions are obtained through plea bargains, a process that exists because it fulfills the self-interest of prosecutors, judges, defense attorneys, and defendants.
- Plea bargaining is facilitated by exchange relations between prosecutors and defense attorneys. In many courthouses, there is little actual bargaining, as outcomes are determined through the implicit bargaining process of settling the facts and assessing the going rate of punishment according to the standards of the local legal culture.
- The U.S. Supreme Court has endorsed plea bargaining and addressed legal issues concerning the voluntariness of pleas and the obligation of prosecutors and defendants to uphold agreements.
- Plea bargaining has been criticized for pressuring defendants to surrender their rights and for reducing the sentences imposed on offenders.
- Americans tend to presume that, through the dramatic courtroom battle of prosecutors and defense attorneys, trials provide the best way to discover the truth about a criminal case.
- Less than 10 percent of cases go to trial, and half of those are typically bench trials in front of a judge, not jury trials.
- Cases typically go to trial because they involve defendants who are wealthy enough to pay attorneys to fight to the very end, or they involve serious

disagreements between the prosecutor and defense attorney about the provable facts and the appropriate punishment.

- The U.S. Supreme Court has ruled that juries need not be made up of 12 members, and 12-member juries can, if permitted by state law, convict defendants by a supermajority vote instead of a unanimous vote.
- Juries serve vital functions for society by preventing arbitrary action by prosecutors and judges, becoming educated about the justice system, symbolizing the rule of law, and involving citizens from diverse segments of the community in judicial decision making.
- The jury selection process, especially in the formation of the jury pool and the exercise of peremptory challenges, often creates juries that do not fully represent all segments of a community.
- The trial process consists of a series of steps: jury selection, opening statements, presentation of the prosecution's evidence, presentation of the defense's evidence, presentation of rebuttal witnesses, closing arguments, judge's jury instructions, and the jury's decision.
- Rules of evidence dictate what kinds of information may be presented in court for consideration by the jury. Types of evidence include are real evidence, demonstrative evidence, testimony, direct evidence, and circumstantial evidence.
- Convicted offenders can appeal, although defendants who plead guilty—unlike those convicted through a trial—often have few grounds for an appeal.
- Appeals focus on alleged errors of law or procedure in the investigation by police and prosecutors or in the decisions by trial judges. Relatively few offenders win their appeals, and most of those simply gain an opportunity for a new trial, not release from jail or prison.
- After convicted offenders have used all of their appeals, they may file a habeas corpus petition to seek federal judicial review of claimed constitutional rights violations in their cases. Very few petitions succeed.

Questions for Review

1. What is the courtroom workgroup and what does it do?
2. Why does plea bargaining exist?
3. Given that there are so few jury trials, what types of cases would you expect to find adjudicated in this manner? Why?
4. If so few cases ever reach a jury, why are juries such an important part of the criminal justice system?
5. What is the purpose of the appeals process?

Key Terms and Cases

appeal (p. 363)
bench trial (p. 352)
challenge for cause (p. 357)
circumstantial evidence (p. 359)
continuance (p. 339)
demonstrative evidence (p. 358)
direct evidence (p. 359)
going rate (p. 339)
habeas corpus (p. 364)
jury (p. 352)
local legal culture (p. 339)
peremptory challenge (p. 358)
real evidence (p. 358)
reasonable doubt (p. 362)
testimony (p. 358)
voir dire (p. 357)
workgroup (p. 340)
Bordenkircher v. Hayes (1978) (p. 350)
Boykin v. Alabama (1969) (p. 349)
North Carolina v. Alford (1970) (p. 349)
Ricketts v. Adamson (1987) (p. 350)
Santobello v. New York (1971) (p. 350)
Williams v. Florida (1970) (p. 354)

For Further Reading

Adler, Stephen. 1994. *The Jury: Disorder in the Court.* New York: Doubleday. A newspaper reporter analyzes the jury system by interviewing jurors after publicized verdicts and reconstructing how they made their decisions.

Eisenstein, James, Roy Flemming, and Peter Nardulli. 1988. *The Contours of Justice: Communities and Their Courts.* Boston: Little, Brown. A study of nine felony courts in three states. Emphasizes the impact of the local legal culture on court operations.

Geis, Gilbert, and Leight B. Bienen. 1998. *Crimes of the Century: From Leopold and Loeb to O. J. Simpson.* Boston: Northeastern University Press. An examination of several of the most famous criminal trials in U.S. history.

McCoy, Candace. 1993. *Politics and Plea Bargaining: Victims' Rights in California.* Philadelphia: University of Pennsylvania Press. A study of the abolition of plea bargaining for serious offenses in California's Superior Courts, including the increase in plea bargaining activity elsewhere in the criminal justice system.

Pohlman, H. L. 1999. *The Whole Truth? A Case of Murder on the Appalachian Trail.* Amherst: University of Massachusetts Press. An analysis of a highly publicized murder case, including the defendant's and attorneys' considerations about whether to seek a jury trial.

Wishman, Seymour. 1986. *Anatomy of a Jury.* New York: Times Books. A dramatic account of human interactions within the jury room.

Going Online

For an up-to-date list of Web links, go to http://www.cj.wadsworth.com/colesmith10e

1 Go to http://www.ajc.state.ak.us/Reports/pleafram.htm. Read the report on banning plea bargaining in Alaska. What has been the impact of banning plea bargaining there?

2 Go to http://www.acjnet.org/youthfaq/jury.html to read about the right to a jury in criminal trials in Canada. Can you identify any differences between the jury processes there and in the United States?

3 On InfoTrac College Edition, search for *jury nullification* and read two articles on this topic. What is jury nullification? Should jurors be permitted to exercise this power?

Checkpoint Answers

1 The local legal culture consists of norms that distinguish between "our" court and other jurisdictions, that stipulate how members should treat one another, and that describe how cases should be processed.

2 The courtroom workgroup is made up of judge, prosecutor, defense counsel, and support staff assigned to a specific courtroom. Through the interaction of these members, goals and norms are shared and a set of roles becomes stabilized.

3 Several factors can vary in different cities including the structure of the courtroom workgroup and the influence of sponsoring organizations, which can affect such things as prosecution policies and public defender assignments.

4 Plea bargaining occurs because it serves the self-interest of all relevant actors: defendants gain certain, less-than-maximum sentences; prosecutors gain swift, sure convictions; defense attorneys get prompt resolution of cases; judges do not have to preside over as many time-consuming trials.

5 Implicit plea bargaining occurs when prosecutors and defense attorneys use shared expectations and interactions to settle the facts of a case and reach a resolution based on the going rate for sentences in the local legal culture.

6 The U.S. Supreme Court has examined whether the defendant pleads guilty in a knowing and voluntary way, guilty pleas from defendants who still claim to be innocent, and prosecutors' and defendants' obligations to fulfill their plea agreements.

7 The criticisms of plea bargaining include concerns about pressures on defendants to surrender their rights and concerns that society's mandated criminal punishments are improperly reduced.

8 Only 9 percent of felony cases go to trial; 4 percent are jury trials and 5 percent are bench trials.

9 The six functions of juries are to safeguard citizens against arbitrary law enforcement, determine the guilt of the accused, represent diverse community interests and values, serve as buffer between accused and accuser, become educated about the justice system, and symbolize the law.

10 The Supreme Court has said that juries can have as few as 6 jurors, except in death penalty cases, in which 12 are required, and convictions can occur

through less-than-unanimous verdicts.

11 Voir dire is the jury selection process in which lawyers and/or judges ask questions of prospective jurors and make decisions about using peremptory challenges and challenges for cause to shape the jury's composition.

12 A challenge for cause is based on an indication that a prospective juror cannot make a fair decision. Such challenges must be approved by the judge. A peremptory challenge can be made by the attorney without giving a reason, unless an allegation arises that the attorney is using such challenges systematically to exclude people because of their race or gender.

13 The stages in the trial process are jury selection, attorneys' opening statements, presentation of prosecution's evidence, presentation of defense's evidence, presentation of rebuttal witnesses, closing arguments by each side, judge's instructions to the jury, and the jury's decision.

14 The kinds of evidence are real evidence, demonstrative evidence, witness testimony, direct evidence, and circumstantial evidence.

15 Jurors may be impressed more than judges would be with defendants who take the stand or with those who have no criminal record, and jurors may discount cases in which they dislike the victims.

16 Unlike trial courts, which have juries, hear evidence, and decide if the defendant is guilty or not guilty, appellate courts focus only on claimed errors of law or procedure in trial court proceedings. Victory for a defendant in a trial court means an acquittal and instant freedom. Victory in an appellate court may mean only a chance at a new trial—which often leads to a new conviction.

17 The habeas corpus process may be started after all appeals have been filed and lost. Convicted offenders ask a federal court to review whether any constitutional rights were violated during the course of a case investigation and trial. If rights were violated, the person's continued detention in prison or jail may be improper.

CHAPTER 12

Punishment and Sentencing

Photo by CNN/Getty Images

"All rise!" Everyone stood as San Francisco County Superior Court Judge James Warren strode into court. On this day in July 2002, the courtroom was packed with attorneys, reporters, and onlookers. Judge Warren was about to sentence Marjorie Knoller for involuntary manslaughter in the fatal dog mauling of her neighbor, Diane Whipple. The case had attracted national attention because of the nature of the attack and because Judge Warren had thrown out her second-degree murder conviction for lack of evidence.

Knoller, with her husband Robert Noel (both attorneys), were engaged in a plan with their adopted son, prison inmate Paul "Cornfed" Schneider, to raise and sell the enormous Presa Canario attack dogs. Knoller's dogs attacked Whipple as she entered their apartment building. Even though Knoller tried to get the male dog, Bane, off the victim, Whipple's larynx was crushed and she lay bleeding and suffocating on the hallway floor. At trial, witnesses testified that they had been chased, bitten, or lunged at by the dogs before they attacked Whipple. It was Knoller and Noel's apparent refusal to accept responsibility or display remorse that brought national attention to the case. Robert Noel, who was not at home when the attack occurred, was convicted of involuntary manslaughter and is serving a 4 year prison sentence.

Before Judge Warren imposed sentence, Prosecutor James Hammer challenged Knoller to speak directly to the loved ones of the victim. "The one thing that might bring some peace to everyone who knew Diane would be if this woman here, this lawyer—who lied 52 times, who mocked Diane Whipple and blamed her for her own death—would stand up and as a human being say I'm sorry. I wish I hadn't done these things. I'm responsible, and I'm ready to pay the price," Hammer said. Despite the long pause Warren afforded her to speak, Knoller remained silent, looking pale and drawn in her orange prison jumpsuit.

In imposing the 4 year maximum sentence for manslaughter, Judge Warren cited Knoller's lack of remorse and her repeated lies on the witness stand. "You knowingly inserted into society two massive, dangerous and uncontrollable dogs. You knew you could not control them, you took them outside anyway, and it was clear at some point [that] someone was going to get hurt by those dogs," Warren said (*San Francisco Chronicle,* July 16, 2002 (http://www.sfgate.com); *New York Times,* July 16, 2002, p. A8).

Sentencing is a crucial point in the criminal justice system. After guilt is established, a decision must be made about what to do with the defendant. The interest of the public—even in a highly publicized case—seems to drop at this point. Usually the convicted criminal is out of sight and the case is out of the public's mind. But for the offender, sentencing is the beginning of corrections.

The criminal justice system aims to solve three basic questions: (1) What conduct is criminal? (2) What determines guilt? (3) What should be done with the guilty? Earlier chapters emphasized the first two questions. The answers given by the legal system to the first question compose the basic rules of society: Do not murder, rob, sell drugs, commit treason, and so forth. The process for determining guilt or innocence is spelled out in the law, but it is greatly influenced by the administrative and interpersonal considerations of the actors in the criminal justice system. In this chapter we begin to examine the third problem, sanction and punishment. First we consider the four goals of punishment: retribution, deterrence, incapacitation, and rehabilitation. We then explore the forms punishment takes to achieve its goals. These are incarceration, intermediate sanctions, probation, and death.

QUESTIONS for INQUIRY

- What are the goals of punishment?
- What really happens in sentencing?
- What types of sentences can judges impose?
- Does the system treat wrongdoers equally?

The Goals of Punishment

Criminal sanctions in the United States have four main goals: retribution (deserved punishment), deterrence, incapacitation, and rehabilitation. Ultimately, all criminal punishment is aimed at maintaining the social order, but the justifications for sentencing are closely tied to the American values of justice and fairness. However, the justice sought by crime victims often conflicts with fairness to offenders.

Punishments reflect the dominant values of a particular moment in history. By the end of the 1960s, for example, the number of Americans who were sentenced to imprisonment decreased because of a widespread commitment to rehabilitating offenders. By contrast, since the mid-1970s record numbers of offenders have been sentenced to prison because of an emphasis on imposing strong punishments for the purposes of retribution, deterrence, and incapacitation. (See "What Americans Think.") At the beginning of the twenty-first century, voices are calling for the addition of restorative justice as a fifth goal of the criminal sanction.

AP/Wide World Photos, Inc.

Former nurse Orville Lynn Majors, convicted of giving lethal injections to six hospital patients in Brazil, Indiana, waits with his attorney to hear his fate. The judge sentenced him to 360 years in prison. What should be the goal of his punishment?

Retribution—Deserved Punishment

Retribution is punishment inflicted on a person who has infringed on the rights of others and so deserves to be penalized. The biblical expression "An eye for an eye, a tooth for a tooth" illustrates the philosophy underlying this kind of punishment. Retribution means that those who commit a particular crime should be punished alike, in proportion to the gravity of the offense or to the extent to which others have been made to suffer. Retribution is deserved punishment; offenders must "pay their debts."

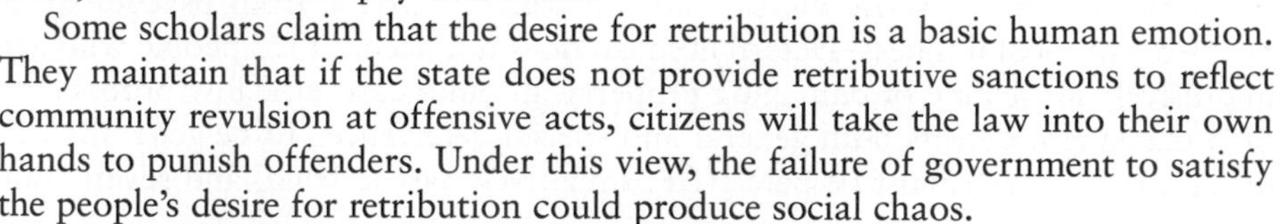

Some scholars claim that the desire for retribution is a basic human emotion. They maintain that if the state does not provide retributive sanctions to reflect community revulsion at offensive acts, citizens will take the law into their own hands to punish offenders. Under this view, the failure of government to satisfy the people's desire for retribution could produce social chaos.

This argument may not be valid for all crimes, however. If a rapist is inadequately punished, then the victim's friends, family, and other members of the community may be tempted to exact their own retribution. But what about a young adult smoking marijuana? If the government failed to impose retribution for this offense, would the community care? The same apathy may hold true for offenders who commit other nonviolent crimes that have a modest impact on society. Even in these seemingly trivial situations, however, retribution may be useful and necessary to remind the public of the general rules of law and the important values they protect.

Since the late 1970s retribution as a justification for the criminal sanction has aroused new interest, largely because of dissatisfaction with the philosophical basis and practical results of rehabilitation. Using the concept of "just deserts or deserved punishment" to define retribution, some theorists argue that one who infringes on the rights of others *deserves* to be punished. This approach rests on the philosophical view that punishment is a moral response to harm inflicted on society. In effect, these theorists believe that basic morality demands that wrongdoers be punished (von Hirsch, 1976:49). According to this view, punishment should be applied only for the wrong inflicted and not primarily to achieve other goals such as deterrence, incapacitation, or rehabilitation.

retribution
Punishment inflicted on a person who has infringed on the rights of others and so deserves to be penalized. The severity of the sanction should fit the seriousness of the crime.

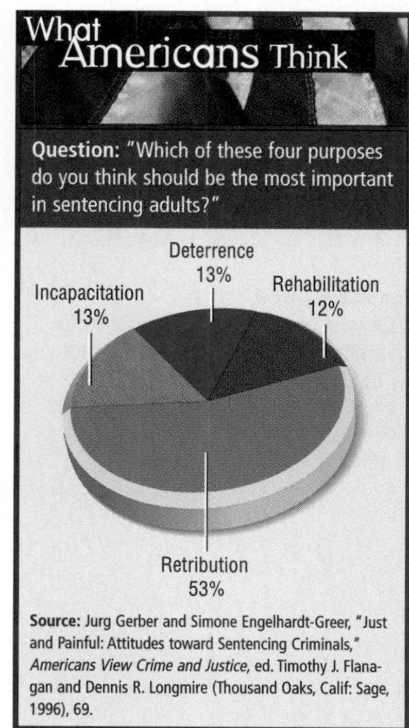

Source: Jurg Gerber and Simone Engelhardt-Greer, "Just and Painful: Attitudes toward Sentencing Criminals," *Americans View Crime and Justice*, ed. Timothy J. Flanagan and Dennis R. Longmire (Thousand Oaks, Calif: Sage, 1996), 69.

Deterrence

Many people see criminal punishment as a basis for affecting the future choices and behavior of individuals. Politicians frequently talk about being "tough on crime" in order to send a message to would-be criminals. The roots of this approach, called deterrence, lie in eighteenth-century England among the followers of social philosopher Jeremy Bentham.

Bentham was struck by what seemed to be the pointlessness of retribution. His fellow reformers adopted Bentham's theory of utilitarianism, which holds that human behavior is governed by the individual's calculation of the benefits versus the costs of one's acts. Before stealing money or property, for example, potential offenders would consider the punishment that others have received for similar acts and would thereby be deterred.

general deterrence
Punishment of criminals that is intended to be an example to the general public and to discourage the commission of offenses.

There are two types of deterrence. **General deterrence** presumes that members of the general public, on observing the punishments of others, will conclude that the costs of crime outweigh the benefits. For general deterrence to be effective, the public must be constantly reminded about the likelihood and severity of punishment for various acts. They must believe that they will be caught, prosecuted, and given a specific punishment if they commit a particular crime. Moreover, the punishment must be severe enough that they will be impressed by the consequences of committing crimes. For example, public hanging was once considered to be an effective general deterrent.

specific deterrence
Punishment inflicted on criminals to discourage them from committing future crimes.

By contrast, **specific deterrence** targets the decisions and behavior of offenders who have already been convicted. Under this approach, the amount and kind of punishment are calculated to discourage that criminal from repeating the offense. The punishment must be severe enough to cause the criminal to say, "The consequences of my crime were too painful. I will not commit another crime, because I do not want to risk being punished again."

The concept of deterrence has obvious difficulties (Stafford and Warr, 1993). Deterrence assumes that all people think before they act. Deterrence does not account for the many people who commit crimes while under the influence of drugs or alcohol, or those whose harmful behavior stems from psychological problems or mental illness. Deterrence also does not account for people who act impulsively in stealing or damaging property. In other cases, the low probability of being caught defeats both general and special deterrence. To be generally deterrent, punishment must be perceived as relatively fast, certain, and severe. But that is not always the case.

Knowledge of the effectiveness of deterrence is limited (Nagin, 1998). For example, social science cannot measure the effects of general deterrence, because only those who are *not* deterred come to the attention of researchers. A study of the deterrent effects of punishment would have to examine the impact of different forms of the criminal sanction on various potential lawbreakers. How can we truly determine how many people—or even if *any* people—stopped themselves from committing a crime because they were deterred by the prospect of prosecution and punishment? Therefore, while legislators often cite deterrence as a rationale for certain sanctions, no one really knows the extent to which sentencing policies based on deterrence achieve their objectives. Because contemporary U.S. society has shown little ability to reduce crime by imposing increasingly severe sanctions, the effectiveness of deterrence for many crimes and criminals should be questioned.

Incapacitation

incapacitation
Depriving an offender of the ability to commit crimes against society, usually by detaining the offender in prison.

Incapacitation assumes that society can keep an offender from committing further crimes by detention in prison or by execution. Many people express such sentiments, urging officials to "lock 'em up and throw away the key!" In primitive societies, banishment from the community was the usual method of incapacitation. In early America, offenders often agreed to move away or to join the army as an alternative to some other form of punishment. In contemporary America, imprisonment is the usual method of incapacitation. Offenders can be confined within secure institutions and effectively prevented from committing additional harm against society for the duration of their sentence. Capital punishment is the ultimate method of incapacitation.

Any sentence that physically restricts an offender can have the effect of incapacitating the person, even when the underlying purpose of the sentence is retribution, deterrence, or rehabilitation. Sentences based on incapacitation are future oriented. Whereas retribution requires focusing on the harmful act of the offender, incapacitation looks at the offender's potential future actions. If the offender is likely to commit future crimes, then a severe sentence may be imposed—even for a relatively minor crime.

For example, under the incapacitation theory, a woman who kills her abusive husband as an emotional reaction to his verbal insults and physical assaults could receive a light sentence. As a one-time impulse killer who felt driven to kill by unique circumstances, she is not likely to commit additional crimes. By contrast, someone who shoplifts merchandise and has been convicted of the offense on ten previous occasions may receive a severe sentence. The criminal record and type of crime indicate that he or she will commit additional crimes if released. Thus incapacitation focuses on characteristics of the offenders instead of characteristics of their offenses.

Does it offend your sense of justice that a person could receive a severer sentence for shoplifting than for manslaughter? This is one of the criticisms of incapacitation. Questions also arise about how to determine the length of sentence. Presumably, offenders will not be released until the state is reasonably sure that they will no longer commit crimes. However, can we accurately predict any person's behavior? Moreover, on what grounds can people be punished for anticipated future behavior that we cannot accurately predict?

In recent years greater attention has been paid to the concept of **selective incapacitation,** whereby offenders who repeat certain kinds of crimes are sentenced to long prison terms. Research has suggested that a relatively small number of offenders commit a large number of violent and property crimes (Clear, 1994:103). Burglars, for example, tend to commit many offenses before they are caught. Thus, these "career criminals" should be locked up for long periods (Auerhahn, 1999). Such policies could be costly, however. Not only would correctional facilities have to be expanded, but the number of expensive, time-consuming trials also might increase if severer sentences caused more repeat offenders to plead not guilty. Another difficulty with this policy is that we cannot accurately predict which offenders will commit more crimes upon release.

selective incapacitation
Making the best use of expensive and limited prison space by targeting for incarceration those individuals whose incapacity will do the most to reduce crime in society.

Rehabilitation

Rehabilitation refers to the goal of restoring a convicted offender to a constructive place in society through some form of training or therapy. Americans want to believe that offenders can be treated and resocialized in ways that allow them to lead a crime-free, productive life upon release. Over the last hundred years, rehabilitation advocates have argued for techniques that they claim identify and treat the causes of criminal behavior. If the offender's criminal behavior is assumed to result from some social, psychological, or biological imperfection, the treatment of the disorder becomes the primary goal of corrections.

rehabilitation
The goal of restoring a convicted offender to a constructive place in society through some form of vocational or educational training or therapy.

Rehabilitation focuses on the offender. Its objective does not imply any consistent relationship between the severity of the punishment and the gravity of the crime. People who commit lesser offenses can receive long prison sentences if experts believe that a long period will be required to rehabilitate them. By contrast, a murderer might win early release by showing signs that the psychological or emotional problems that led to the killing have been corrected.

According to the concept of rehabilitation, offenders are treated, not punished, and they will return to society when they are "cured." Consequently, judges should not set fixed sentences but rather ones with maximum and minimum terms so that parole boards can release inmates when they have been rehabilitated.

From the 1940s until the 1970s, the goal of rehabilitation was so widely accepted that treatment and reform of the offender were generally regarded as the only issues worth serious attention. Crime was assumed to be caused by problems affecting individuals, and modern social sciences had the tools to address those problems. During the past 30 years, however, the assumptions of the rehabilitation model have been questioned. Studies of the results of rehabilitation programs have challenged the idea criminal offenders can be cured (Martinson, 1974). Moreover, scholars no longer take for granted that crime is caused by identifiable, curable problems such as poverty, lack of job skills, low self-esteem, and hostility toward authority. Instead, some argue that we cannot identify the cause of criminal behavior for individual offenders.

Clearly, many legislatures, prosecutors, and judges have abandoned the rehabilitation goal in favor of retribution, deterrence, or incapacitation. Yet on the basis of opinion polls, researchers have found public support for rehabilitative programs (Applegate, Cullen, and Fisher, 1997).

New Approaches to Punishment

restoration
Punishment designed to repair the damage done to the victim and community by an offender's criminal act.

In keeping with the focus on community justice—police, courts, corrections—many people are calling for **restoration** (through restorative justice) to be added to the goals of the criminal sanction (Basemore and Umbreit, 1994).

The restorative justice perspective views crime as more than a violation of penal law. The criminal act practically and symbolically denies community. It breaks trust among citizens and requires community members to determine how "to contradict the moral message of the crime that the offender is above the law and the victim beneath its reach" (Clear and Karp, in press). Crime victims suffer losses involving damage to property and self. The primary aim of criminal justice should be to repair these losses. Crime also challenges the very essence of community, to the extent that community life depends on a shared sense of trust, fairness, and interdependence. Shifting the focus to restorative justice requires a three-way approach that involves the offender, the victim, and the community. This approach may include mediation in which the three actors devise ways that all agree are fair and just for the offender to repair the harm done to victim and community.

Rose Howerter/The Oregonian

Restorative justice seeks to repair the damage that an offender's criminal act has done to the victim and the community. Here, Susanna Kay Cooper sits next to David Lee Myers as she looks at a photo of his dead wife. Cooper plead guilty to vehicular homicide in the death of Elaine Myers, received a 34 month prison sentence, and agreed to enter into talks with the victim's family.

This new approach to criminal justice means that losses suffered by the crime victim are restored, the threat to local safety is removed, and the offender again becomes a fully participating member of the community. The Vermont Reparative Sentencing Boards, described in the Close Up box, exemplifies one way of implementing restoration.

To see how these goals of punishment might be enacted in real life, consider again the sentencing of Marjorie Knoller for the death of Diane Whipple. Table

Table 12.1 The goals of punishment

At sentencing, the judge usually gives reasons for the punishments imposed. Here are statements that Judge James Warren *might* have given Majorie Knoller, each promoting a different goal for the sanction.

Goal	Judge's Possible Statement
Retribution	I am imposing this sentence because you deserve to be punished for the death of Diane Whipple. Your criminal behavior is the basis of the punishment. Justice requires that I impose a sanction at a level that illustrates the importance that the community places on the sanctity of life.
Deterrence	I am imposing this sentence so that your punishment for the death of Diane Whipple will serve as an example and deter others who may contemplate similar actions. In addition, I hope that this sentence will deter you from ever again committing an illegal act.
Incapacitation	I am imposing this sentence so that you will be incapacitated and hence unable to kill a person in the free community during the length of this term.
Rehabilitation	The trial testimony and information contained in the presentence report makes me believe that there are aspects of your personality that led to the death of Diane Whipple. I am therefore imposing this sentence so that you can receive treatment that will rectify your behavior so you will not commit another crime.

Restorative Justice in Vermont

One night in Morrisville, Vermont, Newton Wells went looking for a good time and wound up in an experiment. The 22-year-old college student was charged with assault after nearly driving into two police officers who were breaking up a party. Facing a felony conviction, Wells took a different way out. He pleaded guilty to a lower charge and volunteered to be sentenced by a county "reparative" board. Instead of a judge, a businessman, a counselor, a retired chemistry teacher, and a civil servant issued his punishment.

Restorative justice programs are designed to compensate victims, rehabilitate offenders, and involve the community in a new and a direct way in the justice process. Today some Vermont offenders may be sentenced to make public apologies, make restitution, or chop wood for the elderly—to "repair" the community.

Vermont's sentencing boards, typically four to six volunteers, handle misdemeanors and low-grade felonies such as drunken driving and writing bad checks. Although such crimes normally would not merit jail time, removing the cases from the traditional criminal justice system frees up correctional department resources.

Board members meet with offenders in hour-long sessions, hear explanations and apologies, and tailor the penalties. The idea is to make the punishment relate to the crime, which often occurs in novel ways:

- In Morrisville, college student Wells was ordered to work 30 hours with troubled youths and to meet with the police he menaced so that they could vent their anger about his driving.
- In Rutland, a man who drove 105 mph down a residential street was sentenced to work with brain-injured adults, some of them survivors of high-speed crashes.
- In Hyde Park, a teenager who vandalized a home got 55 hours on a work crew. His job was repairing plaster on an aging opera house.

Panel members get involved in ways they never could if they were serving as jurors. In Rutland, Jack Aicher tells shoplifters they've committed crimes against the "community." Everyone pays higher prices, he says, to cover the store's loss.

Proponents say board sanctions are typically tougher than conventional probation. But offenders opt for the citizen panels to get their sentences concluded quickly. In Vermont, probation can last more than a year and can include special sanctions such as drug tests and rehabilitation programs. Reparative board punishments are concluded within 90 days.

The percentage of nonviolent offenders in the state's eight prisons has dropped from about 50 percent to 28 percent. The decline is ascribed, in part, to the effect of the boards. By handling low-level offenders, the community panels have freed state probation officers to deal with more serious cases. Those probation officers can then monitor criminals serving their sentences in work camps or on furlough rather than in jail, as a way of relieving overcrowding.

Source: *USA Today*, February 12, 1997 (http://www.usatoday.com).

Researching the Internet

Using InfoTrac College Edition, enter the keywords *restorative justice* and access the article by Stephani Coward-Yaskin, "Restorative Justice: What Is It? Can It Work? What Do Women Think?" *Horizons*, Spring 2002, p. 22.

12.1 show various hypothetical sentencing statements that the judge *might* have given, depending on prevailing correctional goals.

As we next consider the ways that the goals are applied though the various forms of punishment, keep in mind the underlying goal—or mix of punishment goals—that justifies each form of sanction.

For more on community/restorative justice, visit http://www.communityjustice.org.

check point

1. What are the four primary goals of the criminal sanction?
2. What are the difficulties in showing that a punishment acts as a deterrent? (Answers are at the end of the chapter.)

Forms of the Criminal Sanction

Incarceration, intermediate sanctions, probation, and death are the basic ways that the criminal sanction, or punishment, is applied. There is not a common sentencing law for the United States. The punishments are specified in the criminal code of each of the states and of the federal government. Each code differs to some extent in the severity of the punishment for specific crimes and in the amount of discretion given judges to tailor the sanction to the individual offender.

Many judges and researchers believe that sentencing structures in the United States are both too severe and too lenient. That is, many offenders who do not warrant incarceration are sent to prison, and many who should be given more restrictive punishments receive minimal probation supervision.

Advocates for more-effective sentencing practices increasingly support a range of punishment options, with graduated levels of supervision and harshness. As Figure 12.1 shows, simple probation lies at one end of this range, and traditional incarceration lies at the other. It is argued that by using this type of sentencing scheme, authorities can maintain expensive prison cells for violent offenders. At the same time, less restrictive community-based programs can be used to punish nonviolent offenders.

As we examine the various forms of criminal sanctions, bear in mind that complex problems are associated with applying these legally authorized punishments. Judges are given wide discretion in determining the appropriate sentence within the parameters of the penal code.

Although these are the sanctions used in the United States, the form and severity of punishment vary across cultures, as seen in the Comparative Perspective on the use of corporal punishment in Singapore. As you read that article, consider the reaction in the United States to the flogging of Michael Fay. Why have corporal punishments (inflicting pain on the body of the offender) disappeared in Western countries? Should flogging be reinstituted?

Figure 12.1 **Escalating punishments to fit the crime**
This list includes generalized descriptions of many sentencing options used in jurisdictions across the country.

PROBATION
Offender reports to probation officer periodically, depending on the offense, sometimes as frequently as several times a month or as infrequently as once a year.

INTENSIVE SUPERVISION PROBATION
Offender sees probation officer three to five times a week. Probation officer also makes unscheduled visits to offender's home or workplace.

RESTITUTION AND FINES
Used alone or in conjunction with probation or intensive supervision and requires regular payments to crime victims or to the courts.

COMMUNITY SERVICE
Used alone or in conjunction with probation or intensive supervision and requires completion of set number of hours of work in and for the community.

SUBSTANCE ABUSE TREATMENT
Evaluation and referral services provided by private outside agencies and used alone or in conjunction with either simple probation or intensive supervision.

Source: *Seeking Justice: Crime and Punishment in America* (New York: Edna McConnell Clark Foundation, 1997), 32–33.

Incarceration

Imprisonment is the most visible penalty imposed by U.S. courts. Although less than 30 percent of people under correctional supervision are in prisons and jails, incarceration remains the standard for punishing those who commit serious crimes. Imprisonment is thought to significantly contribute to deterring potential offenders. However, incarceration is expensive. It also creates the problem of reintegrating offenders into society upon release.

In penal codes, legislatures stipulate the type of sentences and the amount of prison time that may be imposed for each crime. Three basic sentencing structures are used: (1) indeterminate sentences (36 states), (2) determinate sentences (14 states), and (3) mandatory sentences (all states). Each type of sentence makes certain assumptions about the goals of the criminal sanction, and each provides judges with varying degrees of discretion (Bureau of Justice Assistance [BJA], 1998:4).

P. F. Bentley/Black Star

Incarceration is the greatest restriction on freedom. Since 1980 the number of Americans in prisons and jails has quadrupled.

Indeterminate Sentences

When the goal of rehabilitation dominated corrections, legislatures enacted **indeterminate sentences** (often called indefinite sentences). In keeping with the goal of

DAY REPORTING
Clients report to a central location every day where they file a daily schedule with their supervision officer showing how each hour will be spent—at work, in class, at support group meetings, etc.

HOUSE ARREST AND ELECTRONIC MONITORING
Used in conjunction with intensive supervision; restricts offender to home except when at work, school, or treatment.

HALFWAY HOUSE
Residential settings for selected inmates as a supplement to probation for those completing prison programs and for some probation or parole violators. Usually coupled with community service work and/or substance abuse treatment.

BOOT CAMP
Rigorous military-style regimen for younger offenders, designed to accelerate punishment while instilling discipline, often with an educational component.

PRISONS AND JAILS
More-serious offenders serve their terms at state or federal prisons, while county jails are usually designed to hold inmates for shorter periods.

Corporal Punishment in Singapore

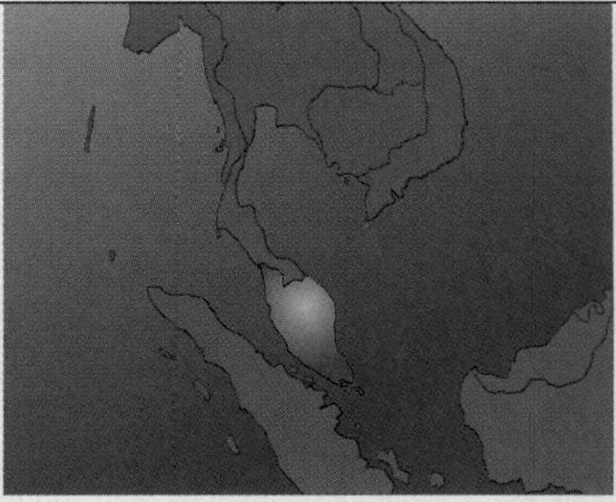

A Singapore court's decision to sentence Michael Fay, an American teenager, to receive a flogging for vandalizing cars with spray paint produced a predictable nod of approval from many Singaporeans, long accustomed to their government's firm hand. For many Americans the punishment seemed unduly harsh, yet others expressed the view that this might be the answer to the U.S. crime problem.

Michael Fay was sentenced to six strokes of the cane; 4 months in prison; and a $2,230 fine after pleading guilty to two counts of vandalism, two counts of mischief, and one count of possessing stolen property. Canings (floggings) in Singapore are carried out by a jailer trained in martial arts who uses a moistened, 4-foot rattan cane. The offender is stripped, then bound by the hands and feet to a wooden trestle. Pads covering his kidneys and groin are the only protection from the cane. Should he pass out, a doctor will revive him before the caning continues. The wounds generally take two weeks to heal; scarring is permanent.

After Singapore gained independence from Britain, the government imposed increasingly harsh penalties for a range of crimes, culminating in laws that carry a mandatory death penalty for such offenses as armed robbery and drug trafficking. Singapore has dropped some traditional safeguards, such as jury trials, on grounds that guilty criminals were manipulating the system to walk free.

According to Singaporean officials, sentences are intended not just as punishment but also as a deterrent. For example, when an 18-year-old man who was called "educationally subnormal" repeatedly kissed a woman in an elevator, he was charged with molestation. A court sentenced him to 6 months in prison. When the man's lawyer appealed, Chief Yong Pung How said that "sentences have been too light; they are not having a deterrent effect" and increased the punishment to include three whacks of the rattan cane.

For the pros and cons of corporal punishment, use InfoTrac College Edition and enter the keywords *corporal punishment* to access Abraham Andero and Allen Stewart, "Issue of Corporal Punishment: Re-examined," *Journal of Intructional Psychology,* June 2002.

Source: Adapted from Charles P. Wallace, "Singapore's Justice System: Harsh, Temptingly Effective," *Hartford Courant,* April 4, 1994, p. 1.

indeterminate sentence
A period, set by a judge, that specifies a minimum and a maximum time to be served in prison. Sometime after the minimum, the offender may be eligible for parole. Because it is based on the idea that the time necessary for treatment cannot be set, the indeterminate sentence is closely associated with rehabilitation.

treatment, indeterminate sentencing gives correctional officials and parole boards significant control over the amount of time a prisoner serves. Penal codes with indeterminate sentences stipulate a minimum and a maximum amount of time to be served in prison (for example, 1–5 years, 3–10 years, or 1 year to life). At the time of sentencing, the judge informs the offender about the range of the sentence. The offender also learns that he or she will probably be eligible for parole at some point after the minimum term has been served. The parole board determines the actual release date.

Determinate Sentences

determinate sentence
A sentence that fixes the term of imprisonment at a specific period.

presumptive sentence
A sentence for which the legislature or a commission sets a minimum and maximum range of months or years. Judges are to fix the length of the sentence within that range, allowing for special circumstances.

Dissatisfaction with the rehabilitation goal and support for the concept of deserved punishment led many legislatures in the 1970s to shift to **determinate sentences.** With a determinate sentence, a convicted offender is imprisoned for a specific period of time (for example, 2 years, 5 years, 15 years). At the end of the term, again minus credited good time, the prisoner is automatically freed. The time of release is tied neither to participation in treatment programs nor to a parole board's judgment concerning the offender's likelihood of returning to criminal activities.

Some determinate-sentencing states have adopted penal codes that stipulate a specific term for each crime category. Others allow the judge to choose a range of time to be served. Some states emphasize a determinate **presumptive sentence;**

the legislature or often a commission specifies a term based on a time range (for example, 14–20 months) into which most cases should fall. Only in special circumstances should judges deviate from the presumptive sentence. Whichever variation is used, however, the offender theoretically knows at sentencing the amount of time to be served. One result of determinate sentencing is that by reducing the judge's discretion, legislatures have tended to limit sentencing disparities and to ensure that terms correspond to those the elected body thinks are appropriate (Griset, 1993).

Mandatory Sentences

mandatory sentence
A sentence determined by statutes and requiring that a certain penalty be imposed and carried out for convicted offenders who meet certain criteria.

Politicians and the public have continued to complain that offenders are released before serving long enough terms, and legislatures have responded. All states and the federal government now have some form of **mandatory sentences** (often called mandatory minimum sentences), stipulating some minimum period of incarceration that people convicted of selected crimes must serve. The judge may not consider the circumstances of the offense or the background of the offender, and he or she may not impose nonincarcerative sentences. Mandatory prison terms are most often specified for violent crimes, drug violations, habitual offenders, or crimes in which a firearm was used. (See "What Americans Think.")

The "three strikes and you're out" laws adopted by 24 states and the federal government provide an example of mandatory sentencing (Schultz, 2000). These laws require that judges sentence offenders with three felony convictions (in some states two or four convictions) to long prison terms, sometimes to life without parole. In California and Georgia, the two states making the greatest use of them, these laws have had the unintended consequences of clogging the courts, lowering rates of plea bargaining, and causing desperate offenders to violently resist arrest (Butterfield, 1996b). One study shows that the law has had little impact on the reduction of rates for serious crime or petty theft (Stolzenberg and D'Alessio, 1997).

Although legislators may assume that mandatory sentences will be imposed and criminal behavior reduced, the decisions of judges and prosecutors may thwart this intent. California prosecutors vary greatly as to whether they charge under the three-strikes law. There is a much lower use of the law in San Francisco, for example, than in San Diego (Zimring, Hawkins, and Kamin, 2001:219) Regional voter support for the law may account for the disparity. A study of the impact of the California three-strikes law (Zimring et al., 2001:62) shows that

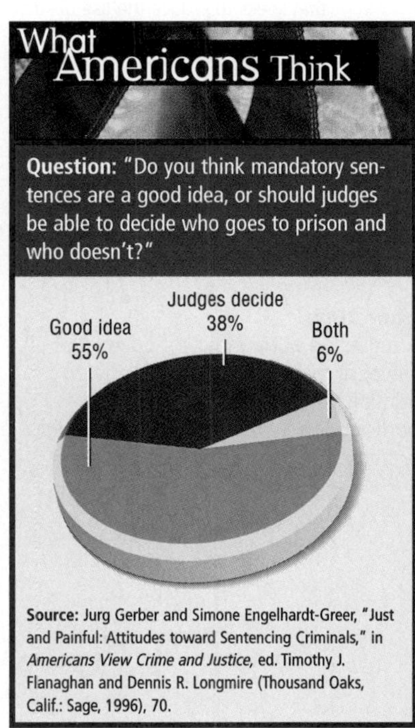

Courtesy of NYT Pictures

Gloria L. Van Winkle, with her children. Van Winkle was sentenced to life in prison under the Kansas "three strikes" law for possession of $40 worth of cocaine. The cost of the long-term incarceration of nonviolent drug offenders is raising questions about the effectiveness of mandatory sentences.

- The law does incapacitate habitual offenders for a long time, but no hard evidence proves that it has had a deterrent effect on crime commission.
- The law targets repeat felons but captures mostly nonviolent offenders.
- Wide discretion and racial disparity in applying the law raise questions of legality and fairness.
- Prison problems are exacerbated by demand for space, high costs of building and staffing, and escalation of geriatric inmate health care costs.

Use of mandatory minimum sentences was greatly expanded during the 1980s as a weapon in the "war on drugs." The result has been a great increase in drug offenders, most for nonviolent offenses, spending very long terms in America's prisons. Research has shown that these are low-level street dealers, mules, and addicts rather than the "kingpins" who import and distribute drugs to the market. Across the country, mandatory prison terms are applied more often to African American drug offenders than to their white counterparts (Crawford, 2000).

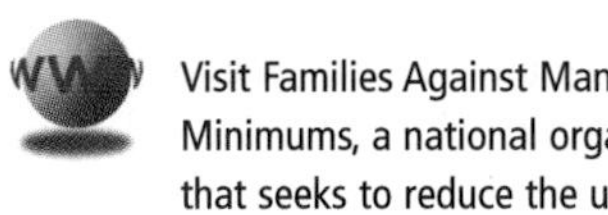
Visit Families Against Mandatory Minimums, a national organization that seeks to reduce the use of such sentences, at http://www.famm.org.

The Sentence versus Actual Time Served

Regardless of how much discretion judges have to fine-tune the sentences they give, the prison sentences that are imposed may bear little resemblance to the amount of time served. In reality, parole boards in indeterminate sentencing states have broad discretion in release decisions once the offender has served a minimum portion of the sentence. In addition, offenders can have their prison sentence reduced by earning **good time** for good behavior, at the discretion of the prison administrator.

good time
A reduction of an inmate's prison sentence, at the discretion of the prison administrator, for good behavior or participation in vocational, educational, or treatment programs.

All but four states have good time policies (BJA, 1998). Days are subtracted from prisoners' minimum or maximum term for good behavior or for participating in various types of vocational, educational, or treatment programs. Correctional officials consider these policies necessary for maintaining institutional order and reducing crowding. The possibility of receiving good-time credit is an incentive for prisoners to follow institutional rules. Prosecutors and defense attorneys also take good time into consideration during plea bargaining. In other words, they think about the actual amount of time a particular offender is likely to serve.

The amount of good time one can earn varies among the states, usually from 5 to 10 days a month. In some states, once 90 days of good time are earned, they are vested; that is, the credits cannot be taken away as a punishment for misbehavior. Prisoners who then violate the rules risk losing only days not vested.

Judges in the United States often prescribe long periods of incarceration for serious crimes, but good time and parole reduce the amount of time spent in prison. Figure 12.2 shows the estimated time actually served by offenders sent to state prisons versus the average (mean) sentence. Note that the national average for time served is 27 months, or 47 percent of the mean sentence of 57 months.

This type of national data often hides the impact of variations in sentencing and releasing laws in individual states. In many states, because of prison crowding and release policies, offenders are serving less than 20 percent of their sentences. In other states, where three-strikes and "truth-in-sentencing" laws are employed, the average time served will be longer than the national average.

"Truth-in-Sentencing"

Truth-in-sentencing refers to laws that require offenders to serve a substantial proportion (usually 85 percent for violent crimes) of their prison sentence before being released on parole. These laws have three goals: (1) providing the public with more-accurate information about the actual length of sentences, (2) reducing crime by keeping offenders in prison for longer periods, and (3) achieving a rational allocation of prison space by prioritizing the incarceration of particular classes of criminals (such as violent offenders).

For further information on truth-in-sentencing in state prisons, access http://www.ojp.usdoj.gov/bjs/abstract/tssp.htm.

Figure 12.2 **Estimated time served in state prison compared with mean length of sentence**
Most offenders serve a third or less of their mean sentences. Why is there such a difference between the sentence and actual time served?

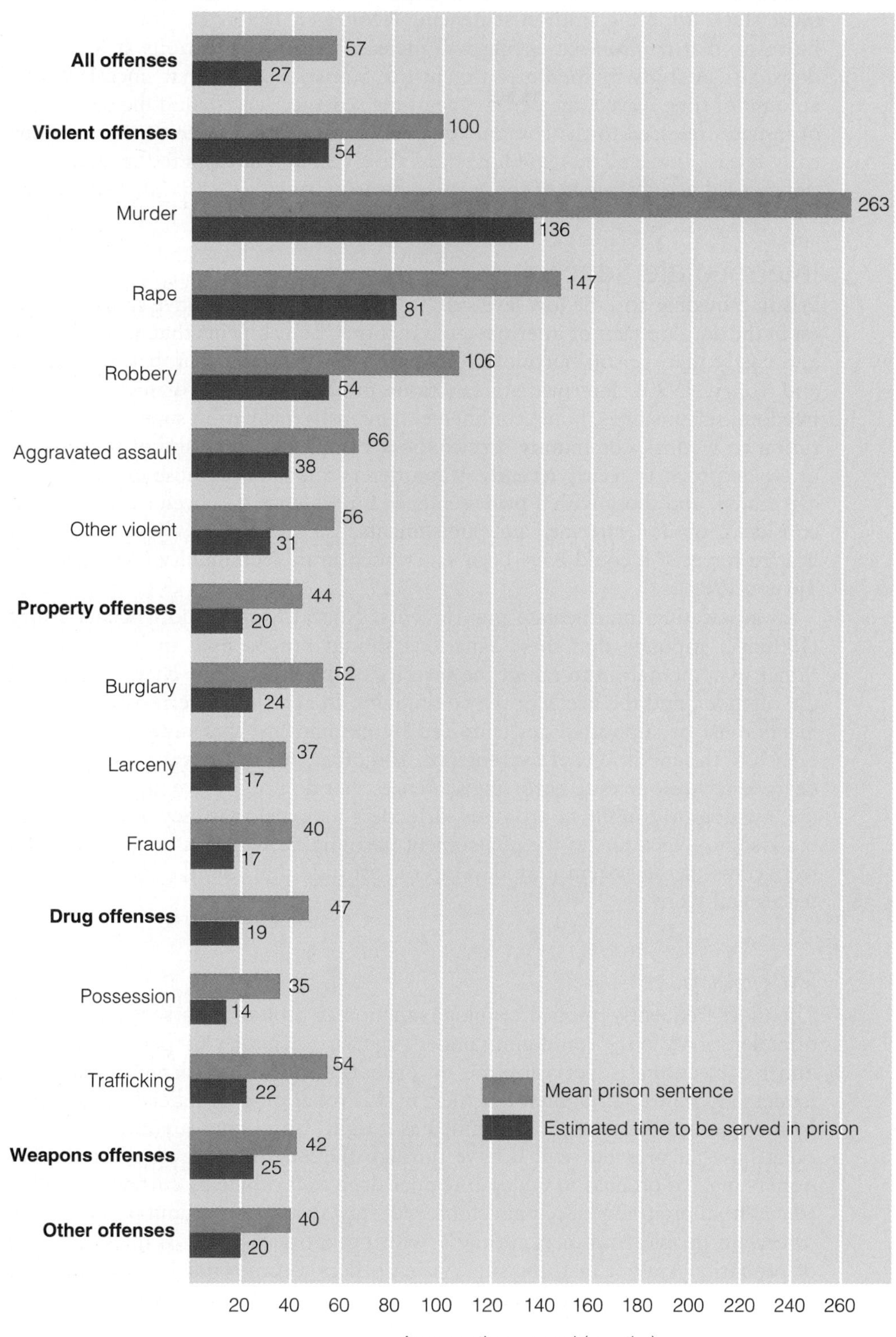

Source: Bureau of Justice Statistics, *Felony Sentences in State Courts, 1998* (Washington, D.C.: U.S. Government Printing Office, 2001).

Truth-in-sentencing has become such a politically attractive idea that the federal government has allocated almost $10 billion for prison construction to those states adopting truth-in-sentencing (Donziger, 1996:24). Critics maintain, however, that truth-in-sentencing will increase prison populations at a tremendous cost. A study by the Bureau of Justice Statistics shows that since 1990 the amount of time served, the percentage of the sentence served, and the percentage of inmates released to the community upon expiration of their sentence (versus early release) have all increased. Even relatively small increases in the amount of time served greatly augment the costs of incarceration (BJS, 1999d: 4–11).

Intermediate Sanctions

intermediate sanctions
A variety of punishments that are more restrictive than traditional probation but less severe and less costly than incarceration.

Prison crowding and the low levels of probation supervision have spurred interest in the development of **intermediate sanctions,** punishments that are less severe and costly than prison but more restrictive than traditional probation (Morris and Tonry, 1990). Intermediate sanctions provide a variety of restrictions on freedom, such as fines, home confinement, intensive probation supervision, restitution to victims, community service, boot camp, and forfeiture of possessions or stolen property. Fairly recently, if murderers and rapists, those previously incarcerated, and those with a prior sentence for violence had been excluded from consideration for intermediate punishments, 29 percent of those who were headed for prison could have been sanctioned in the community (Petersilia and Turner, 1989).

In advocating intermediate punishments, Norval Morris and Michael Tonry (1990:37) stipulate that these sanctions should not be used in isolation, but rather in combination to reflect the severity of the offense, the characteristics of the offender, and the needs of the community. In addition, intermediate punishments must be supported and enforced by mechanisms that take seriously any breach of the conditions of the sentence. Too often, criminal justice agencies have devoted few resources to enforcing sentences that do not involve incarceration. If the law does not fulfill its promises, offenders may feel that they have "beaten" the system, which makes the punishment meaningless. Citizens viewing the ineffectiveness of the system may develop the attitude that nothing but stiffer sentences will work.

Probation

probation
A sentence that the offender is allowed to serve under supervision in the community.

The most frequently applied criminal sanction is **probation,** a sentence that an offender serves in the community under supervision. Nearly 60 percent of adults under correctional supervision are on probation. Ideally, under probation, offenders attempt to straighten out their lives. Probation is a judicial act, granted by the grace of the state, not extended as a right. Conditions are imposed specifying how an offender will behave through the length of the sentence. Probationers may be ordered to undergo regular drug tests, abide by curfews, enroll in educational programs or remain employed, stay away from certain parts of town or certain people, and meet regularly with probation officers. If the conditions of probation are not met, the supervising officer recommends to the court that the probation be revoked and that the remainder of the sentence be served in prison. Probation may also be revoked for commission of a new crime.

shock probation
A sentence in which the offender is released after a short incarceration and resentenced to probation.

Although probationers serve their sentences in the community, the sanction is often tied to incarceration. In some jurisdictions, the court is authorized to modify an offender's prison sentence after a portion is served by changing it to probation. This is often referred to as **shock probation** (or *split probation*): an offender is released after a period of incarceration (the "shock") and resentenced to probation. An offender on probation may be required to spend intermittent periods, such as weekends or nights, in jail. Whatever its specific terms, a probationary sentence will emphasize guidance and supervision in the community.

Probation is generally advocated as a way of rehabilitating offenders whose crimes are not serious or whose past records are clean. It is viewed as less expensive than imprisonment, and more effective. For example, imprisonment may embitter youthful or first-time offenders and mix them with hardened criminals so that they learn more sophisticated criminal techniques.

Death

Although other Western democracies abolished the death penalty years ago, the United States continues to use it. Capital punishment was imposed and carried out regularly prior to the late 1960s. Amid debates about the constitutionality of the death penalty and with public opinion polls showing opposition to it, the U.S. Supreme Court suspended its use from 1968 to 1976. Eventually the Court decided that capital punishment does not violate the Eighth Amendment's prohibition of cruel and unusual punishments. Executions resumed in 1977 as a majority of states began, once again, to sentence murderers to death.

The numbers of people facing the death penalty has increased dramatically, as Figure 12.3 reveals. As of October 1, 2002, more than 3,700 people awaited execution in 37 of the 38 death penalty states. Two-thirds of those on death row are in the South, with the greatest number found in Alabama, Florida, North Carolina, and Texas (see Figure 12.4). Although about 250 people are sent to death row each year, since 1977 the annual number of executions has never exceeded 98 (which occurred in 1999).

Articles and information in support of the death penalty can be found at http://www.prodeathpenalty.com.

The Death Penalty and the Constitution

Death differs from other punishments in that it is final and irreversible. The Supreme Court has therefore examined the decision-making process in capital cases to ensure that it fulfills the Constitution's requirements regarding due process,

Figure 12.3 **People under sentence of death and people executed, 1953–2002**
Since 1976 about 250 new offenders have been added to death row each year, yet the number of executions has never been greater than 98. What explains this fact?

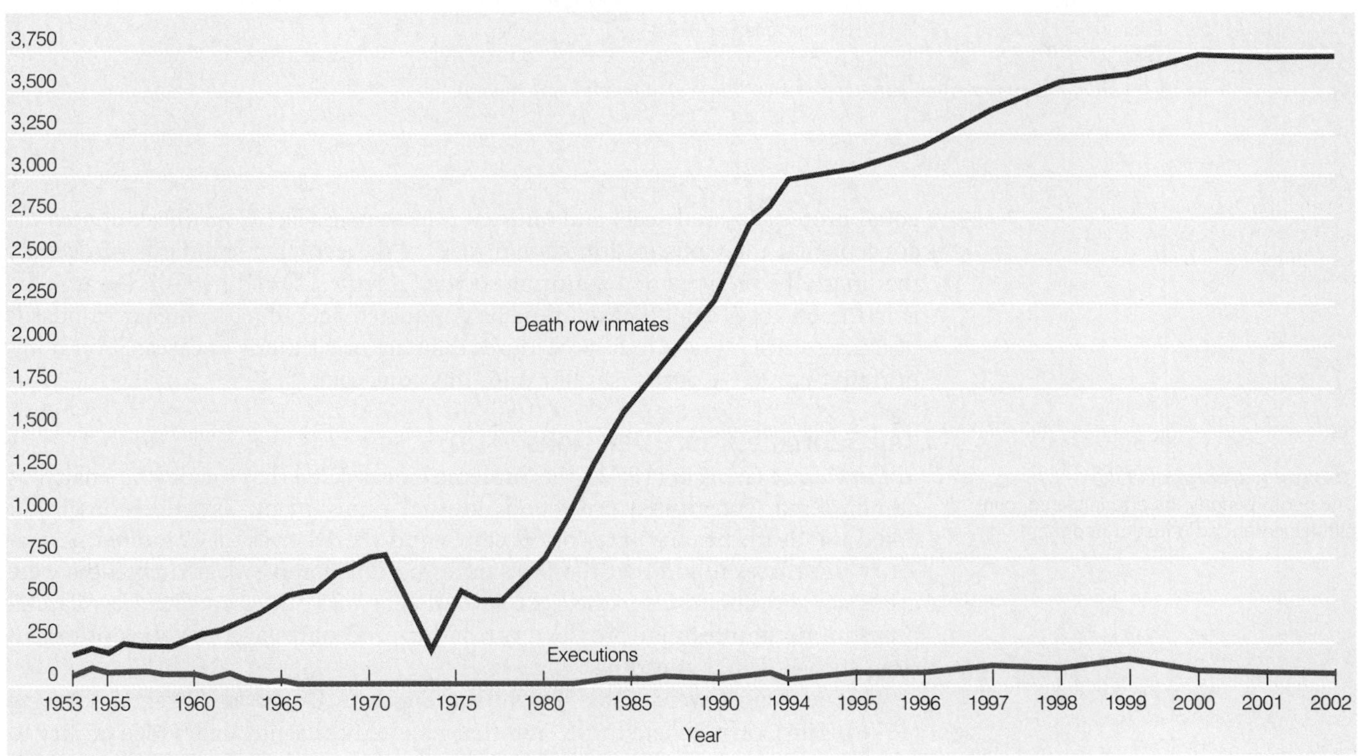

Source: NAACP Legal Defense and Education Fund, *Death Row, USA* (Fall 2002); Death Penalty Information Center at http://www.deathpenaltyinfo.org/ (January 7, 2003).

Figure 12.4 **Death row census, January 2003**

Many of the inmates on death row are concentrated in certain states. African Americans make up about 13 percent of the U.S. population, yet make up 43 percent of the death row population. How might you explain this higher percentage of death sentences in proportion to the population?

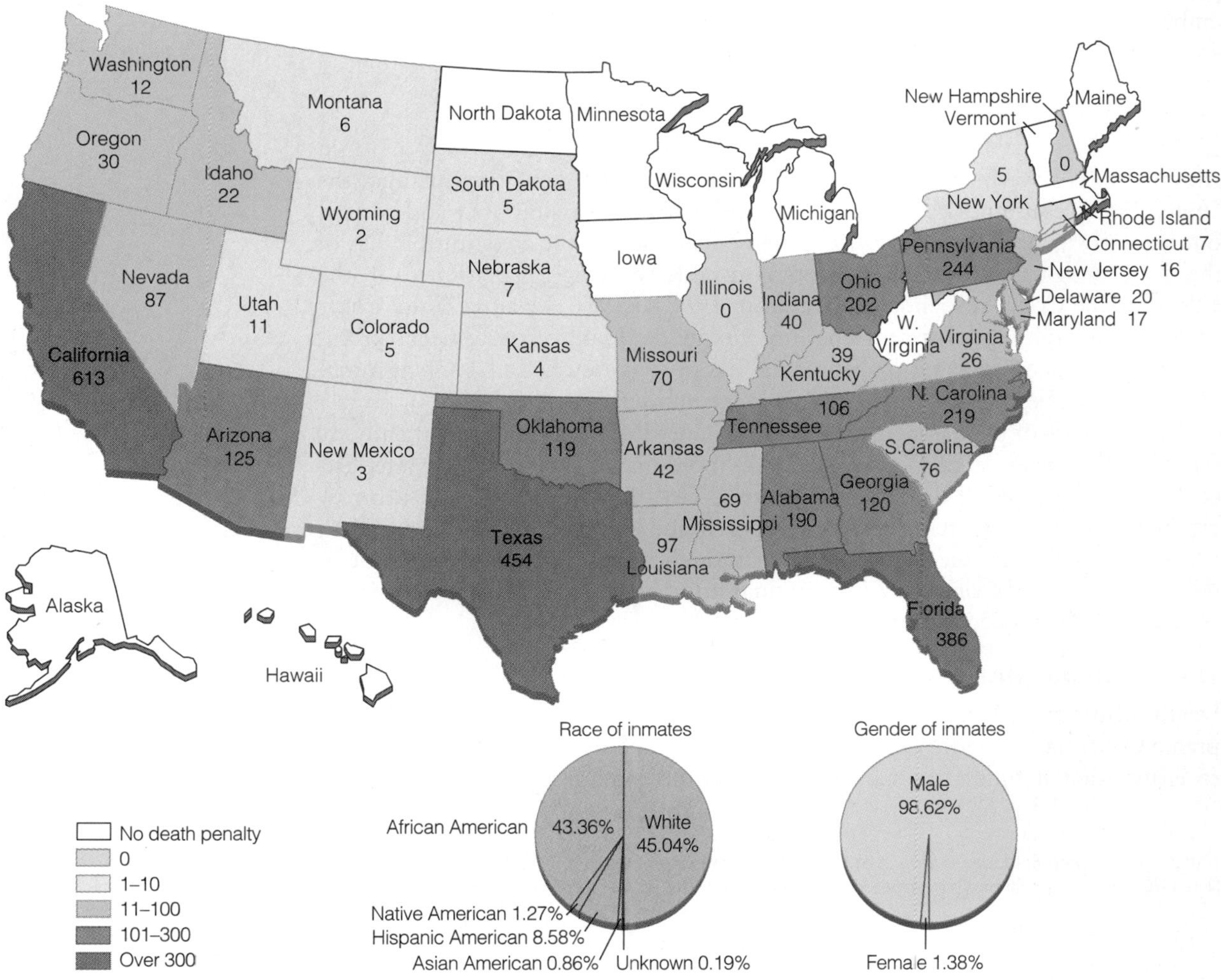

Source: NAACP Legal Defense and Education Fund, *Death Row, USA* (Fall 2002); *The New York Times,* January 12, 2003, p. A1.

equal protection, and cruel and unusual punishment. The Court has adopted the concept that the Constitution should reflect "the evolving standards of decency that mark the progress of a maturing society" (*Trop v. Dulles,* 1958). Because life is in the balance, capital cases must be conducted according to higher standards of fairness and more-careful procedures than are other kinds of cases. Several important Supreme Court cases illustrate this concern.

Key Supreme Court Decisions

Furman v. Georgia (1972)
The death penalty, as administered, constitutes cruel and unusual treatment.

In ***Furman v. Georgia*** **(1972),** the Supreme Court ruled that the death penalty, as administered, constituted cruel and unusual punishment. The decision invalidated the death penalty laws of 39 states and the District of Columbia. A majority of justices found that the procedures used to impose death sentences were arbitrary and unfair. Over the next several years, 35 states enacted new capital punishment statutes that provided for better procedures and methods of execution, such as lethal injection.

The new laws were tested before the Supreme Court in *Gregg v. Georgia* (1976). The Court upheld those laws that required the sentencing judge or jury to take into account specific aggravating and mitigating factors in deciding which convicted murderers should be sentenced to death. Further, the Court decided that, rather than having a single proceeding determine the defendant's guilt and whether the death sentence would be applied, states should use "bifurcated proceedings." In this two-part process, the defendant has a trial that determines guilt or innocence and then a separate hearing that focuses exclusively on the issues of punishment. It seeks to ensure a thorough deliberation before someone receives the ultimate punishment.

Under the *Gregg* decision, the prosecution uses the punishment-phase hearing to focus attention on the existence of aggravating factors, such as excessive cruelty or a defendant's prior record of violent crimes. The defense may focus on mitigating factors, such as the offender's youthfulness, mental condition, or lack of a criminal record. These aggravating and mitigating factors must be weighed before the judge or jury can decide to impose a death sentence. Because of the Court's emphasis on fair procedures and individualized decisions, state appellate courts review trial court procedures in virtually every capital case.

Lisa Terry/The Gamma Liaison Network

Mumia Abu-Jamal, sentenced to death in Philadelphia for the killing of a police officer, charges that the criminal justice system is racist as evidenced by his prosecution, trial, and sentence.

In ***McCleskey v. Kemp*** (1987), opponents of the death penalty felt that the U.S. Supreme Court dealt a fatal blow to their movement. In this case, the Court rejected a challenge to Georgia's death penalty law, made on the grounds of racial discrimination. Warren McCleskey, an African American, was sentenced to death for killing a white police officer. Before the U.S. Supreme Court, McCleskey's attorney cited research that showed a disparity in the imposition of the death penalty in Georgia based on the race of the victim and, to a lesser extent, the race of the defendant. Researchers had examined more than two thousand Georgia murder cases and found that defendants charged with killing whites had received the death penalty 11 times more often than had those convicted of killing African Americans. Although 60 percent of homicide victims in Georgia are African Americans, all seven people put to death in that state since 1976 had been convicted of killing white people, and six of the seven murderers were African Americans (Baldus, Woodworth, and Pulaski, 1994).

***McCleskey v. Kemp* (1987)**
Rejects a challenge of Georgia's death penalty on grounds of racial discrimination.

By a 5–4 vote, the justices rejected McCleskey's assertion that Georgia's capital sentencing practices violated the equal protection clause of the Constitution by producing racial discrimination. The slim majority of justices declared that McCleskey would have to prove that the decision makers acted with a discriminatory purpose in deciding his particular case. The Court also concluded that statistical evidence showing discrimination throughout the Georgia courts did not provide adequate proof. McCleskey was executed in 1991.

In June 2002 the Supreme Court broke new ground in a way that heartened opponents of the death penalty. In ***Atkins v. Virginia*** it ruled that execution of the mentally retarded was unconstitutional, and in ***Ring v. Arizona*** it ruled that juries, rather than judges, must make the crucial factual decisions as to whether a convicted murderer should receive the death penalty.

***Atkins v. Virginia* (2002)**
Execution of the mentally retarded is unconstitutional.

***Ring v. Arizona* (2002)**
Juries, rather than judges, must make the crucial factual decisions as to whether a convicted murderer should receive the death penalty.

Daryl Atkins, who has an IQ of 59, was sentenced to death for killing Eric Nesbitt in a 7-Eleven store parking lot. Lower courts had upheld Atkins's sentence based on *Penry v. Lynaugh* (1989), in which the Supreme Court had upheld execution of the retarded. In that decision it noted that only two states prohibited the death penalty in such cases.

Justice John Paul Stevens, writing for the *Atkins* majority, noted that since 1989 there has been a "dramatic shift in the state legislative landscape" and a national consensus had emerged rejecting execution of the retarded. He pointed out that of the 38 death penalty states, the number prohibiting such executions has gone from 2 to 18. The dissenters, Chief Justice Rehnquist and Justices Scalia and Thomas, disputed that there was a real or lasting consensus against executing the retarded. In the absence of an authentic consensus, Justice Scalia said that the majority had merely imposed their own views as constitutional law.

As the majority opinion notes, the characteristics of mentally retarded offenders, people with IQs of less than 70, "undermine the strength of the procedural protections." This point is in keeping with the argument of mental health experts who say their suggestibility and willingness to please leads retarded people to confess. At trial they have problems remembering details, locating witnesses, and testifying credibly in their own behalf.

Ring v. Arizona overturned the law of that state and four others—Colorado, Idaho, Montana, and Nebraska—where judges alone decide whether there are aggravating factors that warrant capital punishment. The decision also raised questions about the procedure in four other states—Alabama, Delaware, Florida, and Indiana—where the judge decides life imprisonment or death after hearing a jury's recommendation. The *Ring* opinion also says that any aggravating factors must be stated in the indictment, thus also requiring a change in federal death penalty laws.

The decision results from the implications of the Court's decision in *Apprendi v. New Jersey* (2000). Under New Jersey's hate crime statute, judges can impose a higher sentence when they find that a crime was committed with a biased motive. The Court said that any factor that led to a higher sentence than the statutory maximum must be charged in the indictment and found beyond a reasonable doubt by the jury. In the 7–2 majority opinion in *Ring v. Arizona,* Justice Ruth Bader Ginsburg wrote that in view of the *Apprendi* ruling, the right to a jury trial "would be senselessly diminished if it encompassed the factfinding necessary to increase a defendant's sentence by two years, but not the factfinding necessary to put him to death."

Continuing Legal Issues

The case law since *Furman* indicates that capital punishment is legal so long as it is imposed fairly. However, opponents argue that certain classes of death row inmates should not be executed, because they are insane, were underage at the time they committed the crime, did not have effective counsel, or were convicted by a death-qualified jury. A fifth issue, the length of appeals, has been a major concern of Chief Justice Rehnquist.

For current death penalty issues before the U.S. Supreme Court, go to http://www.law.cornell.edu/topics/death_penalty.html.

Execution of the Insane As we have seen, insanity is a recognized defense for commission of a crime. But should people who become mentally disabled after they are sentenced be executed? The Supreme Court responded to this question in 1986 in *Ford v. Wainwright.* In 1974 Alvin Ford was convicted of murder and sentenced to death. Only after he was incarcerated did he begin to exhibit delusional behavior.

Justice Thurgood Marshall, writing for the majority, concluded that the Eighth Amendment prohibited the state from executing the insane—the accused must comprehend both the fact that he had been sentenced to death and the reason for it. Marshall cited the common-law precedent that questioned the retributive and deterrent value of executing a mentally disabled person.

Critics have also raised questions about the morality of treating an offender's mental illness so that he or she can be executed, a policy opposed by the American Medical Association. The Supreme Court has not directly addressed this issue with regard to death row inmates.

Execution of Juveniles Twenty-three of the 38 death penalty states permit the execution of juveniles—those under age 18 when they committed murder. The laws of eight states do not specify a minimum age for offenders receiving capital punishment. In some states the minimum age is the same as the age at which a juvenile can be tried as an adult (BJS, 1997b). From colonial times to the present, about 360 juveniles, 19 since 1976, have been executed in the United States (NAACP, 2002; R. Rosenbaum, 1989). Death penalty opponents have argued that adolescents do not have the same capacity as adults to understand the consequences of their actions. The United States is one of only six nations in the world—the others being Iran, Nigeria, Pakistan, Saudi Arabia, and Yemen—who have executed juveniles since 1990.

The Supreme Court has been divided on the issue of the death penalty for juveniles. In *Thompson v. Oklahoma* (1988), the Court narrowly decided that William Wayne Thompson, who was 15 when he committed murder, should not be executed. A plurality of four justices held that executing juveniles was not in accord with the "evolving standards of decency that mark the progress of a maturing society." Within a year the Court again considered the issue in *Stanford v. Kentucky* (1989) and *Wilkins v. Missouri* (1989). This time the justices upheld the death sentences imposed on offenders who were 16 and 17 years old at the time of their crime. All the justices agreed that interpretation of the cruel and unusual punishment clause rests on the "evolving standards of decency that mark the progress of a maturing society." However, the justices disagreed as to the factors that should be used to make that determination.

The Supreme Court has sanctioned executions of juveniles under some circumstances. On May 28, 2002, Texas put to death Napoleon Beasley for a murder committed when he was 17 years old during a botched carjacking. Beazley became the tenth juvenile offender executed in Texas since 1976, the state where half of the 18 juveniles nationwide have been put to death (*New York Times,* May 27, 2002). As of October 1, 2002, there were 83 men on death rows who had been under the age of 18 at the time their offenses occurred (NAACP, 2002). In October, 2002, Justices Ginsburg, Breyer, Souter, and Stevens indicated that they were opposed to executing youths.

Effective Counsel In *Strickland v. Washington* (1984), the Supreme Court ruled that defendants in capital cases had the right to representation that meets an "objective standard of reasonableness." As noted by Justice Sandra Day O'Connor, the appellant must show "that there is a reasonable probability that, but for the counsel's unprofessional errors, the result of the proceeding would be different."

David Washington was charged with three counts of capital murder, robbery, kidnapping, and other felonies, and an experienced criminal lawyer was appointed as counsel. Against his attorney's advice, Washington confessed to two murders, waived a jury trial, pleaded guilty to all charges, and chose to be sentenced by the trial judge. Believing the situation was hopeless, his counsel did not adequately prepare for the sentencing hearing. On being sentenced to death, Washington appealed. The Supreme Court, however, rejected Washington's claim that his attorney was ineffective because he did not call witnesses, seek a presentence investigation report, or cross-examine medical experts on the defendant's behalf. In this case, the Court set standards that Washington did not meet. In other words, although his lawyer did not do as good a job as he wanted, Washington nonetheless received a fair trial.

In recent years the public has learned of cases where the defense attorney's competency has been put in doubt, even to the point of sleeping at trial. In 1999 the *Chicago Tribune* conducted an extensive investigation of capital punishment in Illinois. Reporters found that 33 defendants sentenced to death since 1977 were represented by an attorney who had been, or was later, disbarred or suspended for conduct that was " incompetent, unethical or even criminal." These attorneys included David Landau, who was disbarred one year after representing a Will County defendant sentenced to death, and Robert McDonnell, a convicted felon and the only lawyer in Illinois to be disbarred twice. McDonnell represented four men who landed on death row (Armstrong and Mills, 1999).

In March 2000 a federal judge in Texas ordered the release of Calvin Jerold Burdine after 16 years on death row. At his 1984 trial, Burdine's counsel slept through long portions of the proceedings. As the judge said, "Sleeping counsel is equivalent to no counsel at all" (*New York Times,* March 2, 2000:A19).

***Witherspoon v. Illinois* (1968)**
Potential jurors who object to the death penalty cannot be automatically excluded from service; however, during voir dire those who feel so strongly about capital punishment that they could not give an impartial verdict may be excluded.

Death-Qualified Juries Should people who are opposed to the death penalty be excluded from juries in capital cases? In ***Witherspoon v. Illinois*** **(1968)**, the Supreme Court held that potential jurors who have general objections to the death penalty or whose religious convictions oppose its use cannot be automatically excluded from jury service in capital cases. However it upheld the practice of removing, during voir dire (preliminary examination), those people whose opposition is so strong as to "prevent or substantially impair the performance of their duties." Such jurors have become known as "Witherspoon excludables." The decision was later reaffirmed in *Lockhart v. McCree* (1986).

Because society is divided on capital punishment, opponents argue that death-qualified juries do not represent a cross-section of the community. Researchers have also found that "juries are likely to be nudged toward believing the defendant is guilty and toward an imposition of the death sentence by the very process of undergoing death qualification" (Luginbuhl and Burkhead, 1994:107).

Mark Costanzo points to research that indicates that death qualification has several impacts. First, those who are selected for jury duty are more conviction prone and more receptive to aggravating factors presented during the penalty phase. A second, subtler impact is that jurors answering the questions about their willingness to vote for a death sentence often conclude that both defenders and prosecutors anticipate a conviction and a death sentence (Costanzo, 1997:24–25).

Appeals The long appeals process for death penalty cases is a source of ongoing controversy. The 85 prisoners executed in 2000 were under sentence of death an average of 11 years and 5 months (BJS, 2000c:12). During this time, sentences are reviewed by the state courts and through the writ of habeas corpus by the federal courts.

Chief Justice Rehnquist has actively sought to reduce the opportunities for capital punishment defendants to have their appeals heard by multiple courts. In 1996 President Bill Clinton signed the Anti-Terrorism and Effective Death Penalty Act that requires death row inmates to file habeas appeals within one year and requires federal judges to issue their decisions within strict time limits.

Appellate review is a time-consuming and expensive process, but it also makes an impact. From 1973 to 2000, 6,930 people entered prison under sentence of death. During those 27 years, 683 people were executed, 223 died of natural causes, and 2,654 were removed from death row as a result of appellate court decisions and reviews, commutations, or death while awaiting execution (BJS, 2000c:15).

Former death row inmates Gary Gauger, Dennis Williams, Rolando Cruz, Verneal Jimerson, and Perry Cobb are among over a hundred freed since 1976 because later evidence proved their innocence. Opponents of capital punishment argue that it is not possible to prevent such errors.

2001 Kevin Horan/Chicago

Michael Radelet and his colleagues have examined the cases of 68 death row inmates later released because of doubts about their guilt (Radelet, Lofquist, and Bedau, 1996:907). These cases are equal in number to one-fifth of the inmates executed during the period 1970–1996. Correction of the miscarriage of justice for about one-third of the defendants took four or less years, but it took nine years or longer for another third of the defendants. Had the expedited appeals process and limitations on habeas corpus been in effect, would these death sentences have been overturned?

The Death Penalty: A Continuing Controversy

On January 13, 2000, Governor George Ryan of Illinois, a longtime supporter of the death penalty, called for a moratorium on executions in his state. Ryan said that he was convinced that the death penalty in Illinois was "fraught with errors," noting that since 1976 Illinois had executed 12 people yet freed 13 from death row as innocent. He was followed by a similar call from Kansas Governor Bill Graves, Maryland Governor Paris Glen-

Should the Death Penalty Be Abolished?

The execution moratorium imposed by Illinois Governor George Ryan in January 2000 reinvigorated debate on the death penalty. His announcement was soon followed by a national poll that found support for the penalty to be the lowest in 19 years, release of a national study of appeals that found two-thirds of death sentences overturned, and research questioning the quality of counsel given to many defendants. Within months, the policy debate shifted to whether it was possible to construct a system that could ensure that innocent people were not executed.

Opponents of capital punishment continue the fight to abolish it. They argue that poor people and minorities receive a disproportionate number of death sentences. They believe also that it is barbaric to execute people who are teenagers, insane, or mentally retarded.

Even the proponents of capital punishment remain dissatisfied with how it is applied. They point to the fact that although there are more than 3,700 convicted murderers on death row, the number of executions since 1976 has never been greater than 98 in a year. The appeals process is a major factor halting this pace, given that executions are delayed for years as cases are appealed through the courts.

For the Death Penalty

Supporters argue that society should apply swift, severe punishments to killers to address the continuing problems of crime and violence. Execution should occur quite soon after conviction so that the greatest deterrent value will result. They say that justice requires that a person who murders another must be executed. To do less is to denigrate the value of human life.

The arguments for the death penalty include the following:

- The death penalty deters criminals from committing violent acts.
- The death penalty achieves justice by paying killers back for their horrible crimes.
- The death penalty prevents criminals from doing further harm while on parole.
- The death penalty is less expensive than holding murderers in prison for life.

Against the Death Penalty

Opponents believe that the death penalty lingers as a barbaric practice from a less civilized age. They point out that most other developed democracies in the world have ceased to execute criminals. Opponents challenge the death penalty's claims for effectiveness in reducing crime. They also raise concerns about whether the punishment can be applied without errors and discrimination.

The arguments against the death penalty include these:

- No hard evidence proves that the death penalty is a deterrent.
- It is wrong for a government to participate in the intentional killing of citizens.
- The death penalty is applied in a discriminatory fashion.
- Innocent people have been sentenced to death.
- Some methods of execution are inhumane, causing painful, lingering deaths.

What Should U.S. Policy Be?

With more and more people now being sentenced to death row but fewer than one hundred individuals executed each year, death penalty policy is at a significant crossroads. Will the United States increase the pace of executions, allow the number of capital offenders in prison to keep growing, or take a middle ground that satisfies neither side completely, such as life imprisonment without parole for convicted murderers?

Researching the Internet

There is much information about the death penalty on the Internet. For more on this debate, go to InfoTrac College Edition and enter the keywords *death penalty.* Access articles giving competing views of this punishment.

Go to the *American System of Criminal Justice* Web site at http://www.cj.wadsworth.com/colesmith10e to explore this question in further detail: Should the death penalty be abolished?

dening, the Louisiana Bar Association, and the Philadelphia City Council. In May 2000 the New Hampshire legislature became the first in more than two decades to vote to repeal the death penalty. In 2002 Congressional hearings were held on the bipartisan Innocent Protection Act. Passage of the act would ensure federal and state death row inmates access to DNA testing and improve the quality of legal representation provided to indigent capital defendants. In January 2003, Governor George Ryan of Illinois pardoned four death-row inmates and commuted the sentences of 167 to life imprisonment without parole.

The Death Penalty Information Center is a major organization that opposes capital punishment. Visit them at http://www.deathpenaltyinfo.org/.

Although public opinion polls show high support for the death penalty and about 250 new death sentences are imposed each year (see "What Americans Think"), the number of executions remains low. Mark Costanzo (1997:123) points to surveys that show the public is about evenly split when respondents are asked to choose between life imprisonment (without parole) and death. Does this mean that Americans are ambivalent about carrying out the punishment? What might it say about capital punishment in the next decade? Debate on this important public policy issue has gone on for more than two hundred years, yet there is still no consensus. (See "The Policy Debate" for more.)

Table 12.2 The punishment of offenders

The goals of the criminal sanction are carried out in a variety of ways, depending upon the provisions of the law, the characteristics of the offender, and the discretion of the judge. Judges may impose sentences that combine several forms to achieve punishment objectives.

Form of Sanction	Description	Purposes
Incarceration	Imprisonment.	
Indeterminate sentence	Specifies a maximum and minimum length of time to be served.	Incapacitation, deterrence, rehabilitation
Determinate sentence	Specifies a certain length of time to be served.	Retribution, deterrence, incapacitation
Mandatory sentence	Specifies a minimum amount of time that must be served for given crimes.	Incapacitation, deterrence
Good time	Subtracts days from an inmate's sentence because of good behavior or participation in prison programs.	Rewards behavior, relieves prison crowding, helps maintain prison discipline
Intermediate sanctions	Punishment for those requiring sanctions more restrictive than probation but less restrictive than prison.	Retribution, deterrence
Administered by the judiciary		
Fine	Money paid to state by offender.	Retribution, deterrence
Restitution	Money paid to victim by offender.	Retribution, deterrence
Forfeiture	Seizure by the state of property illegally obtained or acquired with resources illegally obtained.	Retribution, deterrence
Administered in the community		
Community service	Requires offender to perform work for the community.	Retribution, deterrence
Home confinement	Requires offender to stay in home during certain times.	Retribution, deterrence, incapacitation
Intensive probation supervision	Requires strict and frequent reporting to probation officer.	Retribution, deterrence, incapacitation
Administered institutionally		
Boot camp/shock incarceration	Short-term institutional sentence emphasizing physical development and discipline, followed by probation.	Retribution, deterrence, rehabilitation
Probation	Allows offender to serve a sentence in the community under supervision.	Retribution, incapacitation, rehabilitation
Death	Execution.	Incapacitation, deterrence, retribution

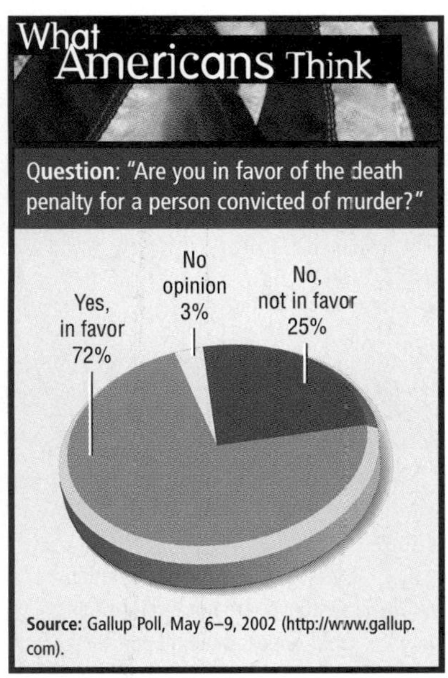

Source: Gallup Poll, May 6–9, 2002 (http://www.gallup.com).

The criminal sanction takes many forms, and offenders are punished in various ways to serve various purposes. Table 12.2 summarizes how these sanctions operate and how they reflect the underlying philosophies of punishment.

check point

3. What are the three types of sentences used in the United States?
4. What are thought to be the advantages of intermediate sanctions?
5. What requirements specified in *Gregg v. Georgia* must exist before a death sentence can be imposed?

The Sentencing Process

Regardless of how and where the decision has been made—misdemeanor court or felony court, plea bargain or adversarial context, bench or jury trial—judges have the responsibility for imposing sentences.

Sentencing is often difficult and usually involves more than applying clear-cut principles to individual cases. In one case, a judge may decide to sentence a forger to prison as an example to others, even though the offender is no threat to community safety and probably does not need rehabilitative treatment. In another case, the judge may impose a light sentence on a youthful offender who has committed a serious crime but may be a good risk for rehabilitation if moved quickly back into society. As Judge Robert Satter notes in the Close Up box, sentencing requires balancing the scales of justice between a violated society and the fallible but human defendant.

Legislatures establish the penal codes that set forth the sentences judges can impose. These laws generally give judges discretion in sentencing. Judges may combine various forms of punishment in order to tailor the sanction to the offender. The judge may specify, for example, that the prison terms for two charges are to run either concurrently (at the same time) or consecutively (one after the other), or that all or part of the period of imprisonment may be suspended. In other situations, the offender may be given a combination of a suspended prison term, probation, and a fine. Judges may also suspend a sentence as long as the offender stays out of trouble, makes restitution, or seeks medical treatment. The judge may also delay imposing any sentence but retain the power to set penalties at a later date if the offender misbehaves.

Within the discretion allowed by the code, various elements influence the decisions of judges. Social scientists believe that several factors influence the sentencing process: (1) the administrative context of the courts, (2) the attitudes and values of judges, (3) the presentence report, and (4) sentencing guidelines.

The Administrative Context of the Courts

Judges are strongly influenced by the administrative context within which they impose sentences. As a result, differences are found, for example, between the assembly-line style of justice in the misdemeanor courts and the more formal proceedings found in felony courts.

Misdemeanor Courts: Assembly-Line Justice

Misdemeanor or lower courts have limited jurisdiction because they normally can only impose jail sentences of less than one year. These courts hear about 90 percent of criminal cases. Whereas felony cases are processed in lower courts only for arraignments and preliminary hearings, misdemeanor cases are processed completely in the lower courts. Only a minority of cases adjudicated in lower courts end in jail sentences. Most cases result in fines, probation, community service, restitution, or a combination of these punishments.

Most lower courts are overloaded and allot minimal time to each case. Judicial decisions are mass produced because actors in the system share three assumptions. First, any person appearing before the court is guilty, because doubtful cases have presumably been filtered out by the police and prosecution. Second, the vast majority of defendants will plead guilty. Third, those charged

Joel Gordon Photography

Although they can tailor the sentence to the particular needs of the offender and the community, judges are influenced by the various ways justice is allocated in misdemeanor and felony courts.

A Trial Judge at Work: Judge Robert Satter

I am never more conscious of striving to balance the scales of justice than when I am sentencing the convicted. On one scale is society, violated by a crime, on the other is the defendant, fallible, but nonetheless human.

As a trial judge I am faced with the insistent task of sentencing a particular defendant who never fails to assert his own individuality. . . .

George Edwards was tried before me for sexual assault, first degree. The victim, Barbara Babson, was a personable woman in her late twenties and a junior executive in an insurance company. She described on the stand what had happened to her:

I was returning to my Hartford apartment with two armloads of groceries. As I entered the elevator, a man followed me. He seemed vaguely familiar but I couldn't quite place him. When I reached my floor and started to open my door, I noticed him behind me. He offered to hold my bags. God, I knew right then I was making a mistake. He pushed me into the apartment and slammed the door. He said, "Don't you know me? I work at Travelers with you." Then I remembered him in the cafeteria and I remembered him once staring at me. Now I could feel his eyes roving over my body, and I heard him say, "I want to screw you." He said it so calmly at first, I didn't believe him. I tried to talk him out of it. When he grabbed my neck, I began to cry and then to scream. His grip tightened, and that really scared me. He forced me into the bedroom, made me take off my clothes.

"Then," she sobbed, "he pushed my legs apart and entered me."

"What happened next?" the state's attorney asked.

"He told me he was going to wait in the next room, and if I tried to leave he would kill me. I found some cardboards, wrote HELP! on them, and put them in my window. But nobody came. Eventually I got up the courage to open the door, and he had left. I immediately called the police."

Edwards's lawyer cross-examined her vigorously, dragging her through the intimate details of her sex life. Then he tried to get her to admit that she had willingly participated in sex with the defendant. Through it all, she maintained her poise. She left the stand with her version of the crime intact.

Edwards took the stand in his own defense. A tall man with bushy hair, he was wearing baggy trousers and a rumpled shirt. In a low voice he testified that the woman had always smiled at him at work. He had learned her name and address and gone to her apartment house that day. When he offered to help her with her bundles, she invited him into her apartment. She was very nice and very willing to have sex. He denied using force.

I did not believe him. I could not conceive that Miss Babson would have called the police, pressed the charges, and relived the horrors of the experience on the stand if the crime had not been committed as she testified. The jury did not believe him either. They readily returned a verdict of guilty.

First-degree sexual assault is a class B felony punishable by a maximum of twenty years in the state prison. If I had sentenced Edwards then, I would have sent him to prison for many years. But sentencing could take place only after a presentence report had been prepared by a probation officer.

The report was dropped off in my chambers a few days before the sentencing date. Unlike the trial, which had portrayed Edwards in the

with minor offenses will be processed in volume, with dozens of cases being decided in rapid succession within a single hour. The citation will be read by the clerk, a guilty plea entered, and the sentence pronounced by the judge for one defendant after another.

Defendants whose cases are processed through the lower court's assembly line may appear to receive little or no punishment. However, people who get caught in the criminal justice system experience other punishments, whether or not they are ultimately convicted. A person who is arrested, but then released at some point in the process, still incurs various tangible and intangible costs. Time spent in jail awaiting trial, the cost of a bail bond, and days of work lost create an immediate and concrete impact. Poor people may lose their jobs or be evicted from their homes if they fail to work and pay their bills for even a few days. For most people, simply being arrested is a devastating experience. It is impossible to mea-

context of the crime, the presentence report portrayed the crime in the context of Edwards's life.

It revealed that Edwards was thirty-one years old, born of a black father and white mother. He had graduated from high school and had an associate's degree from a community college. . . . Edwards had worked successfully as a coordinator of youth programs in the inner city of Hartford. Simultaneously he had taken computer courses. At the time of the crime, he was a computer programmer at Travelers Insurance Company. Edwards was separated from his wife and child, and fellow employees had recently noticed a personality change in him; he seemed withdrawn, depressed, and sometimes confused. His only criminal offense was a disorderly conduct charge three months before the crime, which had not been prosecuted.

I gazed out the window of my chambers and reflected. What should be my sentence?

Before the rescheduled date, I had weighed the factors, made up my mind, and lived with my decision for several days. In serious criminal cases I do not like to make snap judgment from the bench. I may sometimes allow myself to be persuaded by the lawyers' arguments to reduce a preconceived sentence, but never to raise it.

I nod to the state's attorney to begin. He asks to have Miss Babson speak first. She comes forward to the counsel table. "That man," she says, pointing to Edwards, "did a horrible thing. He should be severely punished not only for what he did to me, but for what he could do to other women. I am furious at him. As far as I am concerned, Judge, I hope you lock him up and throw away the key."

She abruptly stops and sits down. The state's attorney deliberately pauses to let her words sink in before he stands up. Speaking with less emotion but equal determination, he says,

This was a vicious crime. There are not many more serious than rape. The defendant cynically tried to put the blame on the victim. But it didn't wash. She has been damaged in the most fundamental way. And the defendant doesn't show the slightest remorse. I urge the maximum punishment of twenty years in prison.

Edwards's lawyer starts off by mentioning his client's lack of a criminal record. Then he goes on, "George and his wife have begun living together again with their child, and they are trying to pick up the pieces of their lives. More important," the lawyer continues, "George started seeing a psychiatrist six weeks ago."

The lawyer concludes, "If you will give George a suspended sentence, Your Honor, and make a condition of probation that he stay in treatment, he won't be before this court again. George Edwards is a good risk."

I look at Edwards. "Do you have anything you want to say, Mr. Edwards?"

The question takes him by surprise. Gathering his thoughts, he says with emotion, "I'm sorry for what I did, Judge. I'm sorry for Barbara, and I understand how she feels. I'm sorry for my wife. I'm . . . " His voice trails off.

I gaze out the courtroom window struggling for the words to express my sentence. I am always conscious that the same sentence can be given in a way that arouses grudging acceptance or deep hostility.

Mr. Edwards, you have committed a serious crime. I am not going to punish you to set an example for others, because you should not be held responsible for the incidence of crime in our society. I am going to punish you because, as a mature person, you must pay a price for your offense. The state's attorney asks for twenty years because of the gravity of the crime. Your attorney asks for a suspended sentence because you are attempting to deal with whatever within you caused you to commit the crime. Both make valid arguments. I am partially adopting both recommendations. I herewith sentence you to state prison for six years.

Edwards wilts. His wife gasps. I continue.

However, I am suspending execution after four years. I am placing you on probation for the two-year balance of your term on the condition that you continue in psychiatric treatment until discharged by your doctor. The state is entitled to punish you for the crime that you have committed and the harm you have done. You are entitled to leniency for what I discern to be the sincere effort you are making to help yourself.

Edwards turns to his wife, who rushes up to embrace him. Miss Babson nods to me, not angrily, I think. She walks out of the courtroom and back into her life. As I rise at the bench, a sheriff is leading Edwards down the stairwell to the lockup.

Source: Robert Satter, *Doing Justice: A Trial Judge at Work* (New York: Simon & Schuster, 1990), 170–81. Copyright © 1990 by Robert Satter. Reprinted by permission of the author.

For more on the sentencing discretion of judges, go to InfoTrac College Edition and enter the keywords *judicial sentencing.* Access the article "Judicial Sentencing: The Soul of Justice or a Ghost in the Machine?" *Trial,* April 1996. How much discretion should judges have to depart from sentencing guidelines?

sure the psychic and social price of being stigmatized, separated from family, and deprived of freedom.

Felony Courts

Felony cases are processed and offenders are sentenced in courts of general jurisdiction. Because of the seriousness of the crimes, the atmosphere is more formal and generally lacks the chaotic, assembly-line environment of misdemeanor courts. Caseload burdens can affect how much time individual cases receive. Exchange relationships among courtroom actors can facilitate plea bargains and shape the content of prosecutors' sentencing recommendations. Sentencing decisions are ultimately shaped, in part, by the relationships, negotiations, and agreements among the prosecutor, defense attorney, and judge. Table 12.3 shows the types of felony sentences imposed for different conviction offenses.

Table 12.3 Types of felony sentences imposed by state courts

Although a felony conviction is often equated with a sentence to prison, almost a third of felony offenders receive probation.

Most Serious Conviction Offense	Percentage of Felons Sentenced to		
	Prison	Jail	Probation
All offenses	44%	24	32
Violent offenses	59	19	22
Murder	94	2	4
Sexual assault	67	15	18
Rape	70	14	16
Other sexual assault	64	16	20
Robbery	76	12	12
Aggravated assault	46	26	28
Other violent	41	26	33
Property offenses	43	25	35
Burglary	54	21	25
Larceny	40	34	26
Motor vehicle theft	43	33	24
Fraud	35	20	45
Drug offenses	42	22	35
Possession	36	29	35
Trafficking	45	26	29
Weapons offenses	42	26	32
Other offenses	35	28	37

Note: For persons receiving a combination of sanctions, the sentence designation came from the most severe penalty imposed—prison being the most severe, followed by jail and then probation.

Source: Bureau of Justice Statistics, *Felony Sentences in State Courts, 1998* (Washington, D.C.: U.S. Government Printing Office, 2001), 2.

Attitudes and Values of Judges

All lawyers recognize that judges differ from one another in their sentencing decisions. The conflicting goals of criminal justice, administrative pressures, and the influence of community values partly explain these differences. Sentencing decisions also depend on judges' attitudes concerning the offender's blameworthiness, protection of the community, and the practical implications of the sentence (Steffensmeier and Demuth, 2001).

Blameworthiness concerns such factors as offense severity (such as violent crime or property crime), the offender's criminal history (such as recidivist or first timer), and role in commission of the crime (such as leader or follower). For example, a judge might impose a harsh sentence on a repeat offender who organized others to commit a serious crime.

Protection of the community is influenced by similar factors, such as dangerousness, recidivism, and offense severity. However, it focuses mostly on the need to incapacitate the offender or to deter would-be offenders.

Finally, the practical implications of a sentence can affect judges' decisions. For example, judges may take into account the offender's ability to "do time," as in the case of an elderly person. They may also consider the impact on the offender's family; a mother with children may demand a different sentence than a single woman would. Finally, costs to the corrections system may play a role in sentencing, as judges consider the number of probation caseloads or prison crowding (Steffensmeier, Kramer, and Streifel, 1993).

Presentence Report

presentence report
A report, prepared by a probation officer, that presents a convicted offender's background and is used by the judge in selecting an appropriate sentence.

Even though sentencing is the judge's responsibility, the **presentence report** has become an important ingredient in the judicial mix. Usually a probation officer investigates the convicted person's background, criminal record, job status, and mental condition to suggest a sentence that is in the interests of both the offender and society. Although the presentence report serves primarily to help the judge select the sentence, it also assists in the classification of probationers, prisoners, and parolees for treatment planning and risk assessment. In the report, the probation officer makes judgments about what information to include and what conclusions to draw from that information. In some states, however, probation officers present only factual material to the judge and make no sentencing recommendation. Because the probation officers do not necessarily follow evidentiary rules, they may therefore include hearsay statements as well as firsthand information. The Close Up box gives an example of a presentence report.

Although presentence reports are represented as diagnostic evaluations, critics point out that they are not scientific and often reflect stereotypes. John Rosencrance has argued that in actual practice the presentence report primarily serves to maintain the myth of individualized justice. He found that the present offense and the prior criminal record determine the probation officer's final sentencing recommendation (Rosencrance, 1988). He learned that officers begin by reviewing the case and typing the defendant as one who should fit into a particular sentencing category. They then conduct their investigations in ways that help them gather information to buttress their early decision.

The presentence report is one means by which judges ease the strain of decision making. The report lets judges shift partial responsibility to the probation

Sample Presentence Report

STATE OF NEW MEXICO
Corrections Department
Field Service Division
Santa Fe, New Mexico 87501
Date: January 4, 2003
To: The Honorable Manuel Baca
From: Presentence Unit, Officer Brian Gaines
Re: Richard Knight

Evaluation

Appearing before Your Honor for sentencing is 20-year-old Richard Knight, who on November 10, 2002, pursuant to a Plea and Disposition Agreement, entered a plea of guilty to Aggravated Assault Upon a Peace Officer (Deadly Weapon) (Firearm Enhancement), as charged in Information Number 95-5736900. The terms of the agreement stipulate that the maximum period of incarceration be limited to one year, that restitution be made on all counts and charges whether dismissed or not, and that all remaining charges in the Indictment and DA Files 39780 be dismissed.

The defendant is an only child, born and raised in Albuquerque. He attended West Mesa High School until the eleventh grade, at which time he dropped out. Richard declared that he felt school was "too difficult" and that he decided that it would be more beneficial for him to obtain steady employment rather than to complete his education. The defendant further stated that he felt it was "too late for vocational training" because of the impending 1-year prison sentence he faces, due to the Firearm Enhancement penalty for his offense.

The longest period of time the defendant has held a job has been for 6 months with Frank's Concrete Company. He has been employed with the Madrid Construction Company since August 2002 (verified). Richard lives with his parents who provide most of his financial support. Conflicts between his mother and himself, the defendant claimed, precipitated his recent lawless actions by causing him to "not care about anything." He stressed the fact that he is now once again "getting along" with his mother. Although the defendant contends that he doesn't abuse drugs, he later contradicted himself by declaring that he "gets drunk every weekend." He noted that he was inebriated when he committed the present offense.

In regard to the present offense, the defendant recalled that other individuals at the party attempted to stab his friend and that he and his companion left and returned with a gun in order to settle the score. Richard claimed remorse for his offense and stated that his past family problems led him to spend most of his time on the streets, where he became more prone to violent conduct. The defendant admitted being a member of the 18th Street Gang.

Recommendation

It is respectfully recommended that the defendant be sentenced to 3 years incarceration and that the sentence be suspended. It is further recommended that the defendant be incarcerated for 1 year as to the mandatory Firearm Enhancement and then placed on 3 years probation under the following special conditions:

1. That restitution be made to Juan Lopez in the amount of $622.40.
2. That the defendant either maintain full-time employment or obtain his GED [general equivalency diploma].
3. That the defendant discontinue fraternizing with the 18th Street Gang members and terminate his own membership in the gang.

Researching the Internet

The United States Probation Office Web site is designed to inform the bench and bar of the purposes of the presentence investigation report. You can access it at http://www.flmp.uscourts.gov/Presentence/Explanation/explanation.htm.

department. Because a substantial number of sentencing alternatives are open to judges, they often rely on the report for guidance. "A Question of Ethics" illustrates some of the difficulties faced by a judge who must impose a sentence with little more than the presentence report to go on.

Sentencing Guidelines

Since the 1980s, **sentencing guidelines** have been established in the federal courts and in 17 states, and they are being developed in other states (BJA, 1998). Such guidelines indicate to judges the expected sanction for particular types of offenses. They are intended to limit the sentencing discretion of judges and to reduce disparity among sentences given for similar offenses. Although statutes

sentencing guidelines
A mechanism to indicate to judges the expected sanction for certain offenses, in order to reduce disparities in sentencing.

Seated in her chambers, Judge Ruth Carroll read the presentence investigation report of the two young men she would sentence when court resumed. She had not heard these cases. As often happens in this overworked courthouse, the cases had been given to her only for sentencing. Judge Harold Krisch had handled the arraignment, plea, and trial.

The codefendants had held up a convenience store in the early morning hours, terrorizing the young manager and taking $47.50 from the till.

As she read the reports, Judge Carroll noticed that they looked pretty similar. Each offender had dropped out of high school, had held a series of low-wage jobs, and had one prior conviction for which probation was imposed. Each had been convicted of Burglary 1, robbery at night with a gun.

Then she noticed the difference. David Bukowski had pleaded guilty to the charge in exchange for a promise of leniency. Richard Leach had been convicted on the same charge after a one-week trial. Judge Carroll pondered the decisions that she would soon have to make. Should Leach receive a stiffer sentence because he had taken the court's time and resources? Did she have an obligation to impose the light sentence recommended for Bukowski by the prosecutor and the defender?

There was a knock on the door. The bailiff stuck his head in. "Everything's ready, Your Honor."

"Okay, Ben, let's go."

→ How would you decide? What factors would weigh in your decision? How would you explain your decision?

provide a variety of sentencing options for particular crimes, guidelines attempt to direct the judge to more-specific actions that *should* be taken. The range of sentencing options provided for most offenses is based on the seriousness of the crime and on the criminal history of an offender.

Legislatures—and, in some states and the federal government, commissions—construct sentencing guidelines as a grid of two scores (Tonry, 1993:140). As shown in Table 12.4, one dimension relates to the seriousness of the offense, and the other to the likelihood of offender recidivism. The offender score is obtained by totaling the points allocated to such factors as the number of juvenile, adult misdemeanor, and adult felony convictions; the number of times incarcerated; the status of the accused at the time of the last offense, whether on probation or parole or escaped from confinement; and employment status or educational achievement. Judges look at the grid to see what sentence should be imposed on a particular offender who has committed a specific offense. Judges may go outside of the guidelines if aggravating or mitigating circumstances exist; however, they must provide a written explanation of their reasons for doing so (J. H. Kramer and Ulmer, 1996).

Sentencing guidelines are to be reviewed and modified periodically so that recent decisions will be included. Given that guidelines are constructed on the basis of past sentences, some critics argue that because the guidelines reflect only what has happened, they do not reform sentencing. Others question the choice of characteristics included in the offender scale and charge that some are used to mask racial criteria. However, Lisa Stolzenberg and Steward J. D'Alessio (1994) studied the Minnesota guidelines and found, compared with preguideline decisions, an 18 percent reduction in disparity for the prison/no-prison outcome and a 60 percent reduction in disparity of length of prison sentences.

The U.S. Sentencing Commission helps to define punishments for federal offenses; visit them at http://www.ussc.gov.

For more on Minnesota Sentencing Guidelines, see http://www.msgc.state.mn.us.

Go to the Public Policy feature on the American System of Criminal Justice CD to learn more about the issues surrounding sentencing guidelines.

One impact of guidelines is that sentencing discretion has shifted from the judge to the prosecutor. Prosecutors can choose the charge and plea bargain; therefore, the accused realize that to avoid the harsh sentences specified for some crimes (such as crack cocaine possession or operating a continuing criminal enterprise), they must plead guilty and cooperate. In fact, federal drug laws give prosecutors discretion to ask judges to give sentence reductions for offenders who have "provided substantial assistance in the investigation or prosecution of another person."

Although guidelines make sentences more uniform, many judges object to having their discretion limited in this manner (Weinstein, 1992). However, Peter Rossi and Richard Berk (1997) found a fair amount of agreement between the sentences prescribed in the federal guidelines and those desired by the general public.

check point

6. What are the four factors thought to influence the sentencing behavior of judges?

Table 12.4 Minnesota sentencing guidelines grid (presumptive sentence length in months)

The italicized numbers in the grid are the range within which a judge may sentence without the sentence departing from the guidelines. The criminal history score is computed by adding one point for each prior felony conviction, one-half point for each prior gross misdemeanor conviction, and one-quarter point for each prior misdemeanor conviction.

Severity of Offense (Illustrative Offenses) (Less Serious ↑ ↓ More Serious)	Criminal History Score (Less Serious ← → More Serious) 0	1	2	3	4	5	6 or more
Sale of simulated controlled substance	12	12	12	13	15	17	19 *18–20*
Theft-related crimes ($2,500 or less) Check forgery ($200–$2,500)	12	12	13	15	17	19	21 *20–22*
Theft crimes ($2,500 or less)	12	13	15	17	19 *18–20*	22 *21–23*	25 *24–26*
Non-residential burglary theft crimes (more than $2,500)	12	15	18	21	25 *24–26*	32 *30–34*	41 *37–45*
Residential burglary simple robbery	18	25	27	30 *29–31*	38 *36–40*	46 *43–49*	54 *50–58*
Criminal sexual conduct, second degree	21	26	30	34 *33–35*	44 *42–46*	54 *50–58*	65 *60–70*
Aggravated robbery	48 *44–52*	58 *54–62*	68 *64–72*	78 *74–82*	88 *84–92*	98 *94–102*	108 *104–112*
Criminal sexual conduct, first degree Assault, first degree	86 *81–91*	98 *93–103*	110 *105–115*	122 *117–127*	134 *129–139*	146 *141–151*	158 *153–163*
Murder, third degree Murder, second degree (felony murder)	150 *144–156*	165 *159–171*	180 *174–186*	195 *189–201*	210 *204–216*	225 *219–231*	240 *234–246*
Murder, second degree (with intent)	306 *299–313*	326 *319–333*	346 *339–353*	366 *359–373*	386 *379–393*	406 *399–413*	426 *419–433*

(Shaded) At the discretion of the judge, up to a year in jail and/or other nonjail sanctions can be imposed instead of prison sentences as conditions of probation for most of these offenses. If prison is imposed, the presumptive sentence is the number of months shown.

(Unshaded) Presumptive commitment to state prison for all offenses.

Note: First-degree murder is excluded from the guidelines by law and is punished by life imprisonment.

Source: *Seeking Justice: Crime and Punishment in America* (New York: Edna McConnell Clark Foundation, 1997), 24.

Who Gets the Harshest Punishment?

Harsh, unjust punishments can occur because of sentencing disparities and wrongful convictions. The prison population in most states contains a higher proportion of African American and Hispanic men than appears in the general population. Are these disparities caused by racial prejudices and discrimination, or are other factors at work? *Wrongful conviction* occurs when people who are in fact innocent are nonetheless found guilty by plea or verdict. It also includes those cases in which the conviction of a truly guilty person is overturned on appeal because of due process errors. See "New Directions in Criminal Justice Policy" for more on wrongful conviction.

Wrongful Convictions

In his Presidential Address to the American Society of Criminology, C. Ronald Huff explored the problem of wrongful convictions—people "who, notwithstanding plea or verdict, are in fact innocent." The causes of wrongful convictions include overzealous law enforcement officers and prosecutors, withholding of evidence, false or coerced confessions, perjury, inappropriate use of informants, and ineffective assistance of counsel. Although the number of wrongful convictions is unknown, it has been suggested that if only a 0.5 percent error rate is used, 7,500 people arrested for index crimes were wrongfully convicted in 2000. Huff's policy recommendations include the following:

1. States should enact laws to fairly compensate those who are wrongly convicted.
2. When biological evidence is available for testing, defendants should be able to request and receive such tests. The results should be preserved.
3. When eyewitness identification is involved, the testimony of qualified experts and witnesses should be allowed and judges should give cautionary instructions to juries informing them of the possibility of misidentification.
4. No identification procedure (such as lineups) should be conducted without the presence of counsel for the suspect/accused.
5. Police interrogations of suspects should be recorded in full.
6. Criminal justice officials who engage in unethical or illegal conduct contributing to wrongful conviction should be removed from their position and subjected to appropriate sanctions.
7. Criminal case review commissions should be established to review postappellate claims of wrongful conviction and, when appropriate, refer those cases to the appropriate courts.

Source: Drawn from C. Ronald Huff, "Wrongful Conviction and Public Policy: The American Society of Criminology 2001 Presidential Address," *Criminology* 40:1–18.

Researching the **Internet**

For a case study of Guy Paul Moren, wrongfully convicted in Canada, use InfoTrac College Edition and the keywords *wrongful conviction* to access a series of articles in *MacLean's* magazine published from July 1996 through March 1997.

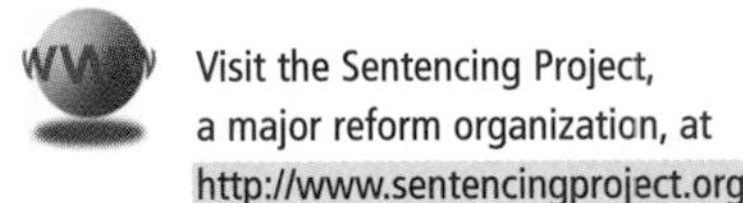
Visit the Sentencing Project, a major reform organization, at http://www.sentencingproject.org.

Racial Disparities

Research on racial disparities in sentencing are inconclusive. Studies of sentencing in Pennsylvania, for example, found that there is a "high cost of being black, young (21–29 years), and male." Sentences given these offenders resulted in a higher proportion going to prison and for longer terms (Steffensmeier, Ulmer, and Kramer, 1998:789). While supporting the Pennsylvania results, research in Chicago, Kansas City, Missouri, and Miami found variation among the jurisdictions as to sentence length (Spohn and Holleran, 2000).

Do these disparities stem from the prejudical attitudes of judges, police officers, and prosecutors? Are African Americans and Hispanics viewed as a "racial threat" when they commit crimes of violence and drug selling, which are thought to be spreading from the urban ghetto to the "previously safe places of the suburbs" (Crawford, Chircos, and Kleck, 1998:484)? Are enforcement resources distributed so that certain groups are subject to closer scrutiny than are other groups?

Scholars have pointed out that the relationship between race and sentencing is complex and that judges consider many defendant and case characteristics. According to this view, judges assess not only the legally relevant factors of blameworthiness, dangerousness, and recidivism risk, but also race, gender, and age characteristics. The interconnectedness of these variables, not judges' negative attitudes, is what culminates in the disproportionately severe sentences given young black men.

Wrongful Convictions

A serious dilemma for the criminal justice system concerns people who are falsely convicted and sentenced. Whereas much public concern is expressed over those who "beat the system" and go free, comparatively little attention is paid to those who are innocent, yet convicted.

The development of DNA technology has increased the number of people convicted by juries and later exonerated by science. Tests conducted on 18,000 cases found that more than 25 percent of the prime suspects were excluded prior to trial. Ronald Huff notes that "because the great majority of cases do not produce biological material to be tested, one can only speculate about the error rate in those cases" (Huff, 2002:2). In August 2002 Eddie Joe Loyd became the 110th person to be exonerated by DNA. Loyd was released from a Michigan prison, where he had been held for 17 years of a life sentence for murder and rape (*New York Times,* August 27, 2002:A10).

Why do wrongful convictions occur? Eyewitness error, unethical conduct by police and prosecutors, community pressure, false accusations, inadequacy of counsel, and plea bargaining pressures may all contribute to wrongful convictions (Huff, 2002). Beyond the fact that the real criminal is presumably still free in such cases, the standards of our society are damaged when an innocent person has been wrongfully convicted.

Each year several cases of the conviction of innocent people come to national attention. For example, in Illinois, Northwestern University journalism students uncovered police and prosecution bungling, thus securing the release of four men who had spent nearly 20 years on death row (*New York Times,* March 3, 1999:A1).

Whether unjust punishments result from racial discrimination or wrongful convictions, the ideals of justice are not served. Unjust punishments raise fundamental questions about the criminal justice system and its links to the society it serves.

Summary

- In the United States, the four main goals of the criminal sanction are retribution, deterrence, incapacitation, and rehabilitation.
- Restoration, a new approach to punishment, has not become mainstream yet.
- The goals of the criminal sanction are carried out through incarceration, intermediate sanctions, probation, and death.
- Penal codes vary as to whether the permitted sentences are indeterminate, determinate, or mandatory. Each type of sentence makes certain assumptions about the goals of the criminal sanction.
- Good time allows correctional administrators to reduce the sentence of prisoners who live according to the rules and participate in various vocational, educational, and treatment programs.
- Capital punishment is allowed by the U.S. Supreme Court if the judge and jury are allowed to take into account mitigating and aggravating circumstances.
- Judges have considerable discretion in fashioning sentences to take into account factors such as the seriousness of the crime, the offender's prior record, and mitigating and aggravating circumstances.
- The sentencing process is influenced by the administrative context of the courts, the attitudes and values of the judges, and the presentence report.
- Sentencing guidelines have been formulated in many states as a way of reducing disparity among the sentences given offenders in similar situations.
- Harsh, unjust punishments may result from racial discrimination or wrongful convictions.

Questions for Review

1. What are the major differences among retribution, deterrence, incapacitation, and rehabilitation?
2. What is the main purpose of restoration?
3. What are the forms of the criminal sanction?
4. What purposes do intermediate sanctions serve?
5. What has been the Supreme Court's position on the constitutionality of the death penalty?
6. Is there a link between sentences and social class? Between sentences and race?

Key Terms and Cases

determinate sentence (p. 380)
general deterrence (p. 374)
good time (p. 382)
incapacitation (p. 374)
indeterminate sentence (p. 380)
intermediate sanctions (p. 384)
mandatory sentence (p. 381)
presentence report (p. 396)
presumptive sentence (p. 380)
probation (p. 384)
rehabilitation (p. 375)
restoration (p. 376)
retribution (p. 373)
selective incapacitation (p. 375)
sentencing guidelines (p. 397)
shock probation (p. 384)
specific deterrence (p. 374)
Atkins v. Virginia (2002) (p. 387)
Furman v. Georgia (1972) (p. 386)
McCleskey v. Kemp (1987) (p. 387)
Ring v. Arizona (2002) (p. 387)
Witherspoon v. Illinois (1968) (p. 390)

For Further Reading

Abramsky, Sasha. 2002. *Hard Time Blues: How Politics Built a Prison Nation.* New York: St. Martin's Press. Examines the growth of incarceration in America, through the story of a career criminal with a long history of nonviolent crimes committed to fund his drug habit.

Costanzo, Mark. 1997. *Just Revenge.* New York: St. Martin's Press. Analyzes the costs and consequences of the death penalty. Finds that, when given an option, people give more support for life without parole than for death.

Gaylin, Willard. 1997. *The Killing of Bonnie Garland.* Rev. ed. New York: Simon & Schuster. True story of the murder of a Yale student by her boyfriend and the reaction of the criminal justice system to the crime. Raises important questions about the goals of the criminal sanction and the role of the victim in the process.

Johnson, Robert. 1998. *Death Work.* 2nd ed. Belmont, Calif.: Wadsworth. A look at those on death row—prisoners and correctional officers—and the impact of capital punishment on their lives.

Scheck, Barry, Peter Neufeld, and Jim Dwyer. 2000. *Actual Innocence.* New York: Doubleday. Describes the harrowing stories of ten men wrongly convicted and the efforts of the Innocence Project to free them.

Tonry, Michael. 1996. *Sentencing Matters.* New York: Oxford University Press. Examination of sentencing reforms over the past quarter century; critiques of the just deserts model, sentencing guidelines, and mandatory penalties.

Zimring, Franklin E., Gordon Hawkins, and Sam Kamin. 2001. *Punishment and Democracy: Three Strikes and You're Out in California.* New York: Oxford University Press. Examines the origins, politics, and impact of the three-strikes law in California.

Going Online

For an up-to-date list of Web links, go to http://www.cj.wadsworth.com/colesmith10e

1. Go to the Web site of Families Against Mandatory Minimums (FAMM): http://www.famm.org. Click on "Sentencing Issues," then "Background." Read about the history of mandatory sentences. What is the principle characteristic of this type of sentence? What has been it's impact according to FAMM?
2. The Web site of the Death Penalty Information Center—http://www.deathpenaltyinfo.org/—contains a wealth of information. Under "Information Topics," examine the data concerning the race of the victim and the race of the offender. Compare intra- versus interracial punishments.
3. Using InfoTrac College Edition, search for *capital punishment.* Find an article on the relationship between the news media and capital punishment. What impact do the news media have on public perceptions of the death penalty?

Checkpoint Answers

1 Retribution, deterrence, incapacitation, rehabilitation.

2 It is impossible to show who has been deterred from committing crimes; punishment isn't always certain; people act impulsively rather than rationally; people commit crimes while on drugs.

3 Determinate, indeterminate, and mandatory sentences.

4 Intermediate sanctions give judges a greater range of sentencing alternatives, reduce prison populations, cost less than prison, and increase community security.

5 Judge and jury must be able to consider mitigating and aggravating circumstances, proceedings must be divided into a trial phase and a punishment phase, and there must be opportunities for appeal.

6 The administrative context of the courts, the attitudes and values of judges, the presentence report, and sentencing guidelines.

PART FOUR

Corrections

Throughout history the debate has continued about the most appropriate and effective ways to punish lawbreakers. Over time the corrections system has risen to peaks of excited reform, only to drop to valleys of despairing failure. In Part 4, we examine how the American system of criminal justice now deals with offenders. The process of corrections is intended to penalize the individual found guilty, to impress upon others that violators of the law will be punished, to protect the community, and to rehabilitate and reintegrate the offender into law-abiding society.

Chapters 13 through 16 will discuss how various influences have structured the U.S. corrections system and how offenders are punished. As these chapters unfold, recall the processes that have occurred before the sentence was imposed and how they are linked to the ways offenders are punished in the correctional portion of the criminal justice system.

CHAPTER 13

Corrections

Andrew Lichtenstein/The Image Works

It is 11 A.M. in New York City. For several hours, five criminal offenders have been picking up trash in a park in the Bronx. Across town in Rikers Island, the view down a corridor of jail cells shows the prisoners' hands gesturing through the bars as they converse, play cards, share cigarettes—the hands of people doing time. About a thousand miles to the south, almost four hundred inmates sit in isolated cells on Florida's death row. In Tennessee a woman on probation reports to a "community control officer." On her ankle she wears an electronic monitoring device that signals the officer if she leaves her home at night. On a multiacre field in Texas, sunburned prisoners in stained work clothes tend crops. Almost due north in Kansas, an inmate grievance committee in a maximum-security prison reviews complaints of guard harassment. Out on the West Coast, in San Francisco, a young man on his way to work checks in with his parole officer and drops off a urine sample. All these activities are part of corrections. And all the main actors are offenders.

corrections
The variety of programs, services, facilities, and organizations responsible for the management of people who have been accused or convicted of criminal offenses.

Corrections refers to the great number of programs, services, facilities, and organizations responsible for the management of people accused or convicted of criminal offenses. In addition to prisons and jails, corrections includes probation, halfway houses, education and work release programs, parole supervision, counseling, and community service. Correctional programs operate in Salvation Army hostels, forest camps, medical clinics, and urban storefronts.

Since the early 1970s, corrections has experienced unprecedented growth. This growth means that more Americans than ever have direct experience with the corrections system. Counting all its forms—prisons, jails, probation, parole, and community corrections—a total of 6.5 million adults (more than 1 out of every 20 men and 1 out of every 100 women) are now under some form of correctional control. This represents an astounding 3 percent of the adult U.S. population. These offenders are supervised by over 700,000 administrators, psychologists, officers, counselors, social workers, and other professionals.

The expansion of corrections is particularly alarming considering that one of every six African American adult men and one of three African American men in their twenties are under some form of correctional supervision. In inner-city areas of Baltimore, Detroit, and Philadelphia, as much as half of this group is under penal supervision. Nearly 9 percent of all African American men 20–40 years old—the age of most fathers—are serving prison terms.

Corrections is authorized by all levels of government, is administered by both public and private organizations, and costs $50 billion a year (BJS, 2002a:3). This chapter will examine (1) the history of corrections, (2) the organization of corrections, (3) role of jails, and (4) the policy trends in incarceration.

QUESTIONS for INQUIRY

- How has the American system of corrections developed?
- What roles do federal, state, and local governments play in corrections?
- Why has the prison population more than doubled in the last ten years?

Development of Corrections

How did corrections get where it is today? Why are offenders now placed on probation or incarcerated instead of whipped or burned as in colonial times? Over the past two hundred years, ideas about punishment have moved like a pendulum from far in one direction to far in another (see Table 13.1). As we review the development of present-day policies, think about how future changes in society may lead to new forms of corrections.

Invention of the Penitentiary

Enlightenment
A movement, during the eighteenth century in England and France, in which concepts of liberalism, rationalism, equality, and individualism dominated social and political thinking.

The late eighteenth century stands out as a remarkable period. At that time scholars and social reformers in Europe and America were rethinking the nature of society and the place of the individual in it. During the **Enlightenment**, as this period was called, philosophers and reformers challenged tradition with new ideas about the individual, about limitations on government, and about rationalism. Such thinking was the main intellectual force behind the American Revolution and laid the foundation of American values. The Enlightenment also affected the new nation's views on law and criminal justice. Reformers began to raise questions about the nature of criminal behavior and the methods of punishment.

Table 13.1 History of corrections in America

Note the extent to which correctional policies have shifted from one era to the next and are influenced by societal factors.

	Correctional Model					
Colonial (1600s–1790s)	**Penitentiary (1790s–1860s)**	**Reformatory (1870s–1890s)**	**Progressive (1890s–1930s)**	**Medical (1930s–1960s)**	**Community (1960s–1970s)**	**Crime Control (1970s–2000s)**
Features Anglican Code Capital and corporal punishment, fines	Separate confinement Reform of individual Power of isolation and labor Penance Disciplined routine Punishment according to severity of crime	Indeterminate sentences Parole Classification by degree of individual reform Rehabilitative programs Separate treatment for juveniles	Individual case approach Administrative discretion Broader probation and parole Juvenile courts	Rehabilitation as primary focus of incarceration Psychological testing and classification Various types of treatment programs and institutions	Reintegration into community Avoidance of incarceration Vocational and educational programs	Determinate sentences Mandatory sentences Sentencing guidelines Risk management
Philosophical basis Religious law Doctrine of predestination	Enlightenment Declaration of Independence Human perfect/ability and powers of reason Religious penitence Power of reformation Focus on the act Healing power of suffering	National Prison Association Declaration of Principles Crime as moral disease Criminals as "victims of social disorder"	The Age of Reform Positivist school Punishment according to needs of offender Focus on the offender Crime as an urban, immigrant ghetto problem	Biomedical science Psychiatry and psychology Social work practice Crime as signal of personal "distress" or "failure"	Civil rights movement Critique of prisons Small is better	Crime control Rising crime rates Political shift to the right New punitive agenda

Prior to 1800, Americans copied Europeans in using physical punishment as the main criminal sanction. The methods of controlling deviance and maintaining public safety primarily included flogging, branding, and maiming. For more serious crimes, offenders were hanged on the gallows. For example, in the state of New York about 20 percent of all crimes on the books were capital offenses. Criminals were regularly sentenced to death for picking pockets, burglary, robbery, and horse stealing (Rothman, 1971:49). Jails existed throughout the country, but they served only to hold people awaiting trial or to punish people unable to pay their debts. As in England, the American colonies maintained houses of correction, where offenders were sentenced to terms of "hard labor" as a means of turning them from crime (Hirsch, 1992).

The European history of incarceration is found at http://www.homeoffice.gov.uk/prishist.htm.

French scholar Michel Foucault has written about the spread of Enlightenment ideas during the late eighteenth century (Foucault, 1977). Before the French Revolution of 1789, European governments tried to control crime by making punishments such as torture and hanging into public spectacles. Criminals were often branded to display their offense. The dismembered bodies of capital offenders were put on display. In the early nineteenth century, such practices were gradually replaced by "modern" penal systems that emphasized fitting the punishment to the individual offender. The new goal was not to inflict pain on the offender's body but to change the individual and set him or her on the right path.

Historical methods of torture and execution are described at http://www.theelectricchair.com/torture.htm.

Clearly, this constituted a major shift in policy. The change from physical (corporal) punishment to correction of the offender reflected new ideas about the causes of crime and the possibility of reforming behavior.

Many people promoted the reform of corrections, but John Howard (1726–1790), sheriff of Bedfordshire, England, was especially influential. His book, *The State of Prisons in England and Wales,* published in 1777, described his observations of the prisons he visited (Howard, 1929). Among generally horrible conditions, the lack of discipline particularly concerned him.

American Stock/Archive Photos

Until the early 1800s Americans followed the European practice of relying on punishment that was physically brutal, such as death, flogging, and branding. This whipping post and pillory in New Castle, Delaware, continued to be used well into the nineteenth century.

Public response to the book resulted in Parliament's passing the Penitentiary Act of 1779, which called for the creation of a house of hard labor where offenders would be imprisoned for up to two years. The institution would be based on four principles:

1. A secure and sanitary building
2. Inspection to ensure that offenders followed the rules
3. Abolition of the fees charged offenders for their food
4. A reformatory regime

At night prisoners were to be confined to individual cells. During the day they were to work silently in common rooms. Prison life was to be strict and ordered. Influenced by his Quaker friends, Howard believed that the new institution should be a place of industry. More important, it should be a place that offered criminals opportunities for penitence (sorrow and shame for their wrongs) and repentance (willingness to change their ways). In short, the purposes of this **penitentiary** were to punish and to reform.

Although enacted during Howard's lifetime, the penitentiary legislation was not implemented in England until 1842, 50 years after his death. Although his own country was slow to act, Howard's idea of the penitentiary traveled across the Atlantic to the United States, where it took root.

check point

1. What was the Enlightenment and how did it influence corrections?
2. What were the main goals of the penitentiary?

(Answers are at the end of the chapter.)

penitentiary
An institution intended to punish criminals by isolating them from society and from one another so they can reflect on their past misdeeds, repent, and reform.

Reform in the United States

From 1776 to around 1830, a new revolution occurred in the American idea of criminal punishment. Although based on the work of English reformers, the new correctional philosophy reflected many ideas expressed in the Declaration of Independence, including an optimistic view of human nature and of individual perfectibility. Emphasis shifted from the assumption that deviance was part of human nature to a belief that crime resulted from environmental forces. The new nation's humane and optimistic ideas focused on reforming the criminal.

In the first decades of the nineteenth century, the creation of penitentiaries in Pennsylvania and New York attracted the attention of legislators in other states and investigators from Europe. Even travelers from abroad with no special interest in corrections made it a point to include a penitentiary on their itinerary, much as they planned visits to a southern plantation, a textile mill, or a frontier town. By the mid-1800s, the U.S. penitentiary had become world famous.

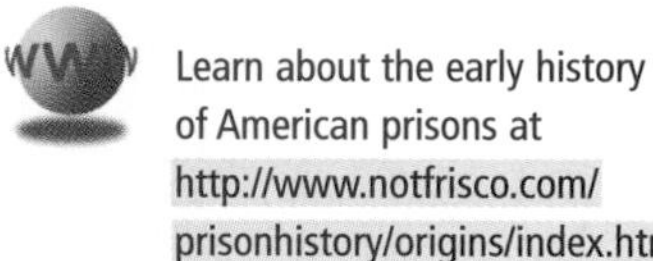
Learn about the early history of American prisons at http://www.notfrisco.com/prisonhistory/origins/index.html.

The Pennsylvania System

Several groups in the United States dedicated themselves to reforming the institutions and practices of criminal punishment. One of these groups was the Philadelphia Society for Alleviating the Miseries of Public Prisons, formed in 1787. This group, which included many Quakers, was inspired by Howard's ideas. They argued that criminals could best be reformed if they were placed in penitentiaries—isolated from one another and from society to consider their crimes, repent, and reform.

In 1790 the Pennsylvania legislature authorized the construction of two penitentiaries for the solitary confinement of "hardened and atrocious offenders."

The Library Company of Philadelphia

Eastern State Penitentiary, located outside Philadelphia, became the model for the Pennsylvania system of "separate" confinement. The building was designed to ensure that each offender was separated from all human contact so that he could reflect upon his misdeeds.

The first, created out of an existing three-story stone structure in Philadelphia, was the Walnut Street Jail. This 25-by-40-foot building had eight dark cells, each measuring 6 by 8 by 9 feet, on each floor. A yard was attached to the building. Only one inmate occupied each cell, and no communications of any kind were allowed. From a small, grated window high on the outside wall, prisoners "could perceive neither heaven nor earth."

From this limited beginning, the Pennsylvania system of **separate confinement** evolved. It was based on five principles:

1. Prisoners would not be treated vengefully but should be convinced that through hard and selective forms of suffering they could change their lives.
2. Solitary confinement would prevent further corruption inside prison.
3. In isolation, offenders would reflect on their transgressions and repent.
4. Solitary confinement would be punishment because humans are by nature social animals.
5. Solitary confinement would be economical because prisoners would not need long periods of time to repent, and so fewer keepers would be needed and the costs of clothing would be lower.

separate confinement
A penitentiary system, developed in Pennsylvania, in which each inmate was held in isolation from other inmates. All activities, including craft work, took place in the cells.

The opening of the Eastern Penitentiary near Philadelphia in 1829 culminated 42 years of reform activity by the Philadelphia Society. On October 25, 1829, the first prisoner, Charles Williams, arrived. He was an 18-year-old African American and had been sentenced to 2 years for larceny. He was assigned to a cell 12 by 8 by 10 feet with an individual exercise yard 18 feet long. In the cell was a fold-up steel bed, a simple toilet, a wooden stool, a workbench, and eating utensils. Light came from an 8-inch window in the ceiling. Solitary labor, Bible reading, and reflection were the keys to the moral rehabilitation that was supposed to occur within the penitentiary. Although the cell was larger than most in use today, it was the only world the prisoner would see throughout the entire sentence. The only other human voice heard would be that of a clergyman who would visit on Sundays. Nothing was to distract the penitent prisoner from the path toward reform.

In the years between Walnut Street and Eastern, other states had adopted aspects of the Pennsylvania system. Separate confinement was introduced by Maryland in 1809, by Massachusetts in 1811, by New Jersey in 1820, and by Maine in 1823.

Eastern Penitentiary is today a national historical landmark where visitors are welcome. Learn about current exhibits, events, and links at http://www.easternstate.org.

Within five years of its opening, Eastern endured the first of several outside investigations. The reports detailed the extent to which the goal of separate confinement was not fully observed, physical punishments were used to maintain discipline, and prisoners suffered mental breakdowns from isolation. Separate confinement had declined at Eastern by the 1860s, when crowding required doubling up in each cell, yet it was not abolished in Pennsylania until 1913 (Teeters and Shearer, 1957: ch. 4).

The New York System

congregate system
A penitentiary system, developed in Auburn, New York, in which each inmate was held in isolation during the night but worked and ate with other prisoners during the day under a rule of silence.

In 1819 New York opened a penitentiary in Auburn that evolved as a rival to Pennsylvania's concept of separate confinement. Under New York's **congregate system,** prisoners were held in isolation at night but worked with other prisoners in shops during the day. They worked under a rule of silence and were even forbidden to exchange glances while on the job or at meals (see Table 13.2).

Auburn's warden, Elam Llynds, was convinced that convicts were incorrigible and that industrial efficiency should be the overriding purpose of the prison. He instituted a reign of discipline and obedience that include the lockstep and the wearing of prison stripes.

contract labor system
A system under which inmates' labor was sold on a contractual basis to private employers who provided the machinery and raw materials with which inmates made salable products in the institution.

The men were to have the benefits of labor as well as meditation. Convict labor for profit through a **contract labor system** became an essential part of Auburn and other northeastern penitentiaries. Through this system the state negotiated contracts with manufacturers, who then delivered raw materials to the prison for conversion into finished goods. By the 1840s Auburn was producing footwear, barrels, carpets, harnesses, furniture, and clothing.

American reformers, seeing the New York approach as a great advance, copied it throughout the Northeast (see Figure 13.1). Because the inmates produced goods for sale, advocates said operating costs would be covered. At an 1826 meeting of prison reformers in Boston, the New York system was described in glowing terms:

> At Auburn, we have a more beautiful example still, of what may be done by proper discipline, in a prison well constructed.... The unremitted industry, the entire subordination, and subdued feeling among the convicts have probably no parallel among any equal number of convicts. In their solitary cells, they spend the night with no other book than the Bible, and at sunrise they proceed in military order, under the eye of the turnkey in solid columns, with the lock march to the workshops. (Goldfarb and Singer, 1973:30)

During this period, advocates of the Pennsylvania and New York plans debated on public platforms and in the nation's periodicals. Advocates of both systems agreed that the prisoner must be isolated from society and placed on a disciplined routine. They believed that criminality was a result of corruption pervading the community that the family and the church did not sufficiently counterbalance. Only when offenders were removed from the temptations and influences of society and kept in a silent, disciplined environment could they reflect on their sins and offenses and become useful citizens. The convicts were not

Table 13.2 Comparison of Pennsylvania and New York (Auburn) penitentiary systems

	Goal	Implementation	Method	Activity
Pennsylvania (separate system)	Redemption of the offender through the well-ordered routine of the prison	Isolation, penance, contemplation, labor, silence	Inmates kept in their cells for eating, sleeping, and working	Bible reading, work on crafts in cell
New York (Auburn) (congregate system)	Redemption of the offender through the well-ordered routine of the prison	Strict discipline, obedience, labor, silence	Inmates sleep in their cells but come together to eat and work	Work together in shops making goods to be sold by the state

Figure 13.1 **Early prisons in the United States**

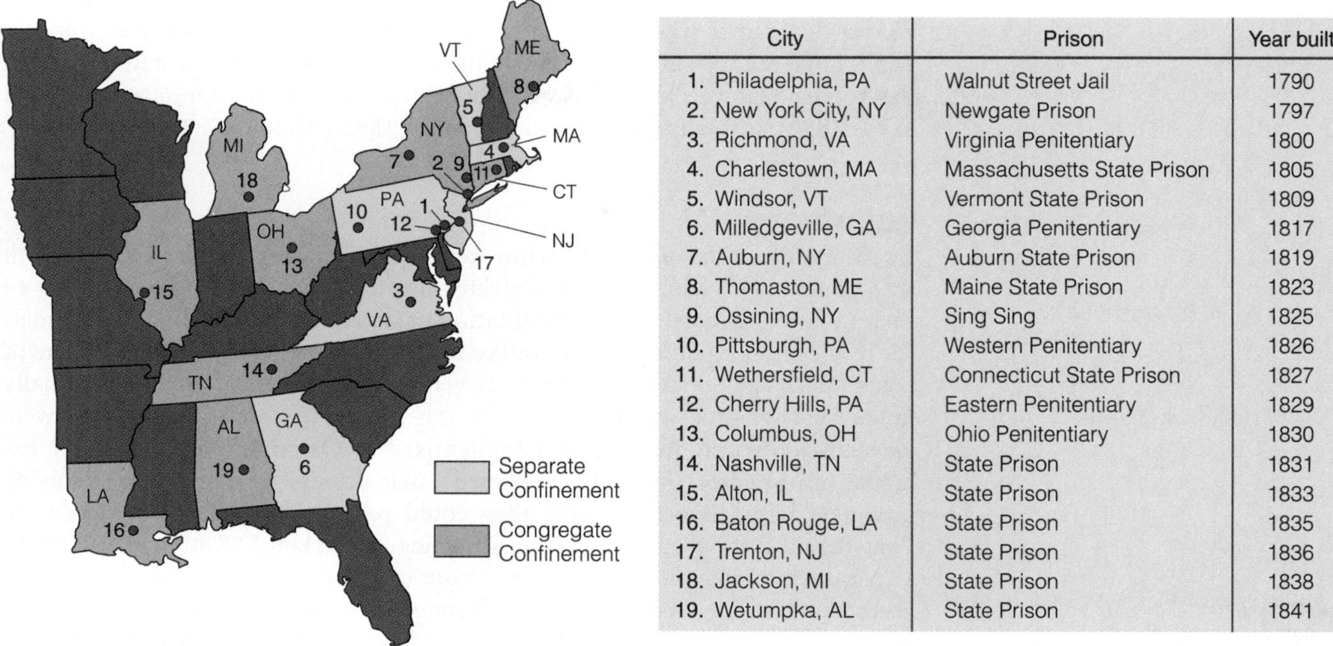

City	Prison	Year built
1. Philadelphia, PA	Walnut Street Jail	1790
2. New York City, NY	Newgate Prison	1797
3. Richmond, VA	Virginia Penitentiary	1800
4. Charlestown, MA	Massachusetts State Prison	1805
5. Windsor, VT	Vermont State Prison	1809
6. Milledgeville, GA	Georgia Penitentiary	1817
7. Auburn, NY	Auburn State Prison	1819
8. Thomaston, ME	Maine State Prison	1823
9. Ossining, NY	Sing Sing	1825
10. Pittsburgh, PA	Western Penitentiary	1826
11. Wethersfield, CT	Connecticut State Prison	1827
12. Cherry Hills, PA	Eastern Penitentiary	1829
13. Columbus, OH	Ohio Penitentiary	1830
14. Nashville, TN	State Prison	1831
15. Alton, IL	State Prison	1833
16. Baton Rouge, LA	State Prison	1835
17. Trenton, NJ	State Prison	1836
18. Jackson, MI	State Prison	1838
19. Wetumpka, AL	State Prison	1841

Source: Norman Johnston, *Forms of Constraint: A History of Prison Architecture* (Urbana: University of Illinois, 2000).

inherently depraved; rather, they were victims of a society that had not protected them from vice. While offenders were being punished, they would become penitent and motivated to place themselves on the right path.

Prisons in the South and West

Scholars tend to emphasize the nineteenth-century reforms in the populous Northeast, neglecting penal developments in the South and the West. Prisons, some following the penitentiary model, were built in four Southern states—Georgia, Kentucky, Maryland, and Virginia—before 1817. Later prisons, such as the ones in Jackson, Mississippi (1842), and Huntsville, Texas (1848), were built on the Auburn model. But further expansion ended with the Civil War. With the exception of San Quentin (1852), the sparse population of the West did not lend itself to the construction of many prisons until the latter part of the nineteenth century.

After the Civil War, southerners began the task of rebuilding their communities and primarily agricultural economy. They lacked funds to build prisons but faced an increasing population of offenders. Given these challenges, a large African American inmate labor force, and the states' need for revenue, southern states developed the **lease system.** This allowed businesses in need of workers to negotiate with the state for the labor and care of prisoners. Prisoners were leased to firms that used them in milling, logging, cotton picking, mining, and railroad construction. As Edgardo Rotman notes, these entrepreneurs, "having no ownership interest in them (the prisoners), exploited them even worse than slaves" (Rotman, 1995:176). The prisoner death rate soared.

lease system
A system under which inmates were leased to contractors who provided prisoners with food and clothing in exchange for their labor. In southern states the prisoners were used as agricultural, mining, logging, and construction laborers.

Settlement in the West did not take off until the California gold rush of 1849; only during the latter part of the nineteenth century did most western states enter the Union. Except in California, the prison ideologies of the East did not greatly influence penology in the West. Prior to statehood, prisoners were held in territorial facilities or federal military posts and prisons. Until Congress passed the Anticontract Law of 1887, restricting the employment of federal prisoners, leasing programs existed in California, Montana, Oregon, and Wyoming. In 1852 a leasee chose Point San Quentin and, using convict labor, built two prison buildings. In

1858, after reports of deaths, escapes, and brutal discipline, the state of California took over the facility. The Oregon territory had erected a log prison in the 1850s, but it was soon leased to a private company. On joining the Union in 1859, however, the state discontinued the lease system. In 1877 a state prison on the Auburn plan was built, but with labor difficulties and an economic depression in the 1890s, it was turned over to a lessee in 1895 (McKelvey, 1977:228).

Reformatory Movement

By the middle of the nineteenth century, reformers had become disillusioned with the penitentiary. Neither the Pennsylvania nor the New York systems nor any of their imitators had achieved rehabilitation or deterrence. This failure was seen as the result of poor administration rather than as a flawed idea. Within 40 years of being built, penitentiaries had become overcrowded, understaffed, and minimally financed. Discipline was lax, brutality was common, and administrators were viewed as corrupt. At Sing Sing Penitentiary in Ossining, New York, for example, investigators in 1870 discovered "that dealers were publicly supplying prisoners with almost anything they could pay for" and that convicts were "playing all sorts of games, reading, scheming, trafficking" (Rothman, 1980:18).

Meanwhile, new ideas about the nature of the prison developed in England and Ireland. In England, Alexander Maconochie urged the **mark system** of graduated terms of confinement. Release would be based on performance through voluntary labor, participation in educational and religious programs, and good behavior. A similar system was developed by Sir Walter Crofton in Ireland in 1854. After a period of solitary confinement following sentencing, prisoners were sent to public work prisons where they could earn marks. When they had enough marks, they were transferred to the intermediate stage, where they could work at outside jobs. The final test was a **ticket-of-leave,** a release under supervision that could be revoked if the offender did not live up to the conditions of his release. The modern parole system is based on these ideas (Dooley, 1981:55). Again, theory and practice bridged the continents as Maconochie's and Crofton's ideas traveled across the Atlantic and were implemented.

mark system
A system in which offenders receive a certain number of points at the time of sentencing, based on the severity of their crime. Prisoners can reduce their term and gain release by earning marks to reduce these points through labor, good behavior, and educational achievement.

ticket-of-leave
A system of conditional release from prison, first developed in Ireland by Sir Walter Crofton. An early form of parole.

Cincinnati, 1870

The National Prison Association (the predecessor of today's American Correctional Association) and its 1870 meeting in Cincinnati embodied a new spirit of reform. In its famous Declaration of Principles, the association advocated a new design for penology: that prisons should operate according to a philosophy of inmate change, with reformation rewarded by release. Sentences of indeterminate length would replace fixed sentences, and proof of reformation—rather than mere lapse of time—would be required for a prisoner's release. Classification of prisoners on the basis of character and improvement would encourage the reformation program. Penitentiary practices that had evolved during the first half of the nineteenth century—fixed sentences, the lockstep, rules of silence, and isolation—were now seen as debasing and humiliating and as destroying inmates' initiative.

Elmira Reformatory

The first **reformatory** took shape in 1876 at Elmira, New York, when Zebulon Brockway was appointed superintendent. Brockway believed that diagnosis and treatment were the keys to reform and rehabilitation. He questioned each new inmate in order to explore the social, biological, psychological, and "root cause(s)" of the offender's deviance. An individualized work and education treatment program was then prescribed. Inmates followed a rigid schedule of work during the day, followed by courses in academic, vocational, and moral subjects during the evening. Inmates who did well achieved early release.

reformatory
An institution for young offenders, emphasizing training, a mark system of classification, indeterminate sentences, and parole.

Designed for first-time felons aged 16–30, the approach at Elmira incorporated a "mark" system of classification, indeterminate sentences, and parole.

Each offender entered the institution at grade 2, and if he earned nine marks a month for six months by working hard, completing school assignments, and causing no problems, he could be moved up to grade 1—necessary for release. If he failed to cooperate and violated the rules, he would be demoted to grade 3. Only after three months satisfactory behavior could he reembark on the path toward eventual release. In sum, this system placed "the prisoner's fate, as far as possible, in his own hands" (Pisciotta, 1994:20).

By 1900 the reformatory movement had spread throughout the nation, yet by the outbreak of World War I in 1914, it was already in decline. In most institutions the architecture, the attitudes of the guards, and the emphasis on discipline differed little from those of the past. Too often, the educational and rehabilitative efforts took a back seat to the traditional emphasis on punishment. Yet the reformatory movement contributed the indeterminate sentence, rehabilitative programs, and parole. The Cincinnati Principles and the reformatory movement set goals that inspired prison activists well into the twentieth century.

check point

3. How did the Pennsylvania and the New York systems differ?
4. What was the significance of the Cincinnati Declaration of Principles?

Improving Prison Conditions for Women

Until the beginning of the nineteenth century, female offenders in Europe and North America were treated no differently than men and were not separated from them when they were incarcerated. Only with John Howard's 1777 exposé of prison conditions in England and the development of the penitentiary in Philadelphia did attention begin to focus on the plight of the female offender. Among the English reformers, Elizabeth Gurney Fry, a middle-class Quaker, was the first person to press for changes. When she and other Quakers visited London's Newgate Prison in 1813, they were shocked by the conditions in which the female prisoners and their children were living (Zedner, 1995:333).

News of Fry's efforts spread to the United States. The Women's Prison Association was formed in New York in 1844 with the goal of improving the treatment of female prisoners and separating them from men. Elizabeth Farnham, head matron of the women's wing at Sing Sing from 1844 to 1848, implemented Fry's ideas until male overseers and legislators thwarted her and she was forced to resign.

Archive Photos

In the 1860s at Wethersfield Prison for Women, the inmates were trained for ironing, laundry work, and cooking; yet time was also spent learning such "ladylike" games as croquet.

The Cincinnati Declaration of Principles did not address the problems of female offenders. It only endorsed the creation of separate treatment-oriented prisons for women. Although the House of Shelter, a reformatory for women, was created in Detroit following the Civil War, not until 1873 did the first independent female-run prison open in Indiana. Within 50 years, 13 other states had followed this lead.

Three principles guided female prison reform during this period: (1) the separation of female prisoners from men, (2) the provision of care in keeping with the needs of women, and (3) the management of women's prisons by female staff. "Operated by and for women, female reformatories were decidedly 'feminine' institutions'" (Rafter, 1983:147).

As time passed, the original ideas of the reformers faltered. In 1927 the first federal prison for women opened in Alderson, West Virginia, with Mary Belle Harris as warden. Yet, by 1935 the women's reformatory movement had "run its course, having largely achieved its objective (establishment of separate prisons run by women)" (Heffernan, 1994; Rafter, 1983:165).

check point

5. What principles guided the reform of corrections for women in the nineteenth century?

Rehabilitation Model

Go to the Public Policy feature on the American System of Criminal Justice CD to learn more about the issues surrounding rehabilitation of prisoners.

In the first two decades of the twentieth century, reformers known as the Progressives attacked the excesses of big business and urban society and advocated government actions against the problems of slums, vice, and crime. The Progressives urged that knowledge from the social and behavioral sciences should replace religious and traditional moral wisdom as the guiding ideas of criminal rehabilitation. They pursued two main strategies: (1) improving conditions in social environments that seemed to be the breeding grounds of crime and (2) rehabilitating individual offenders. By the 1920s probation, indeterminate sentences, presentence reports, parole, and treatment programs were being promoted as a more scientific approach to criminality.

Although the Progressives were instrumental in advancing the new penal ideas, not until the 1930s did reformers attempt to implement fully what became known as the **rehabilitation model** of corrections. Taking advantage of the new prestige of the social sciences, penologists helped shift the emphasis of corrections. The new approach saw the social, intellectual, or biological deficiencies of criminals as the causes of their crimes. Because the essential elements of parole, probation, and the indeterminate sentence were already in place in most states, incorporating the rehabilitation model meant adding classification systems to diagnose offenders and treatment programs to rehabilitate them.

rehabilitation model
A model of corrections that emphasizes the need to restore a convicted offender to a constructive place in society through some form of vocational or educational training or therapy.

Because penologists likened the new correctional methods to those used by physicians in hospitals, this approach was often referred to as the **medical model.** Correctional institutions were to be staffed with people who could diagnose the causes of an individual's criminal behavior, prescribe a treatment program, and determine when the offender was cured and could be safely released to the community.

medical model
A model of corrections based on the assumption that criminal behavior is caused by biological or psychological conditions that require treatment.

Maryland's Patuxent Institution is probably the best example of a prison run with a full commitment to the medical model. Learn more about it at http://www.dpscs.state.md.US/pat/history.htm.

Following World War II, rehabilitation won new followers. Group therapy, behavior modification, counseling, and several other approaches became part of the "new penology." Yet even during the 1950s, when the medical model was at its height, only a small proportion of state correctional budgets went to rehabilitation. What frustrated many reformers was that, even while states adopted the rhetoric of the rehabilitation model, the institutions were still run with custody as the overriding goal.

Because the rehabilitation model failed to achieve its goals, it became discredited in the 1970s. According to critics of rehabilitation, its reportedly high recidivism rates prove its ineffectiveness. Probably the most thorough analysis of research data from treatment programs was undertaken by Robert Martinson. Using rigorous standards, he surveyed 231 studies of rehabilitation programs, including counseling, group therapy, medical treatment, and educational and vocational training. Martinson summarized his findings by saying, "With few and isolated exceptions, the rehabilitative efforts that have been reported so far have had no appreciable effect on recidivism " (Martinson, 1974:25). The report had an immediate impact on legislators and policy makers, who took up the cry that "Nothing Works!" As a result of dissatisfaction with the rehabilitation model, new reforms emerged.

Community Model

The social and political values of particular periods have long influenced correctional goals. During the 1960s and early 1970s, U.S. society experienced the civil rights movement, the war on poverty, and resistance to the war in Vietnam. People challenged the conventional ways of government. In 1967 the President's Commission on Law Enforcement and the Administration of Justice argued that the purpose of corrections should be to reintegrate the offender into the community (President's Commission on Law Enforcement and Administration of Justice, 1967:7).

Under this model of **community corrections,** the goal of corrections was to reintegrate the offender into the community. Proponents viewed prisons as artificial institutions that hindered offenders from finding a crime-free lifestyle. They argued that corrections should focus on increasing opportunities for offenders to be successful citizens and on providing psychological treatment. Programs were supposed to help offenders find jobs and remain connected to their families and the community. Imprisonment was to be avoided, if possible, in favor of probation, so that offenders could seek education and vocational training that would help their adjustment. The small proportion of offenders who had to be incarcerated would spend a minimal amount of time in prison before release on parole. To promote reintegration, correctional workers were to serve as advocates for offenders in dealing with government agencies providing employment counseling, medical treatment, and financial assistance.

community corrections
A model of corrections based on the goal of reintegrating the offender into the community.

The community model dominated until the late 1970s. It gave way to a new punitiveness in criminal justice, in conjunction with the rebirth of the determinate sentence. Advocates of reintegration claim, as did advocates of previous reforms, that the idea was never adequately tested. Nevertheless, community corrections remains one of the significant ideas and practices in the recent history of corrections.

Crime Control Model

As the political climate changed in the 1970s and 1980s, legislators, judges, and officials responded with an emphasis on crime control through incarceration and risk containment. The critique of rehabilitation led to changes in the sentencing structures in more than half the states and the abolition of parole release in many.

Compared with the community model, this **crime control model of corrections** is more punitive and makes greater use of incarceration (especially for violent offenders and career criminals), longer sentences, mandatory sentences, and strict supervision of probationers and parolees.

crime control model of corrections
A model of corrections based on the assumption that criminal behavior can be controlled by more use of incarceration and other forms of strict supervision.

The effect of these get-tough policies is demonstrated by the record number of people incarcerated, the greater amount of time being served, the great number of parolees returned to prison, and the huge size of the probation population. In some states, the political fervor to be tough on criminals has resulted in the reinstitution of chain gangs and the removal of television sets, body-building equipment, and college courses from prisons. Some advocates point to the crime control policies as the reason for the fall of the crime rate. Others ask whether the crime control policies have really made a difference, considering the smaller number of men in the crime-prone age group and other changes in U.S. society.

The history of corrections in America reflects a series of swings from one model to another. During this early part of the twenty-first century, the time may be ripe for another look at correctional policy. The language now used in criminal justice journals differs markedly from that found in their pages 30 years ago.

The optimism that once suffused corrections has waned. The financial and human costs of the retributive crime control policies of the 1990s are now being scrutinized. Are the costs of incarceration and surveillance justified? Has crime been reduced? Is society safer today than it was, say, 25 years ago? Many researchers think not. Looking to the future, will there be a new direction for corrections? If so, what will be its focus?

check point

6. What are the underlying assumptions of the rehabilitation, community, and crime control models of corrections?

Organization of Corrections in the United States

The organization of corrections in the United States is fragmented. Each level of government has some responsibility for corrections. The federal government, the 50 states, the District of Columbia, the 3,047 counties, and most cities all have at least one correctional facility and many correctional programs. State and local governments pay about 95 percent of the cost of all correctional activities in the nation (BJS, 2002a:3).

The scope of federal criminal laws is less broad than that of state laws; as a result, only about 240,000 adults are under federal correctional supervision. In most areas, maintaining prisons and parole is the responsibility of the state, while counties have some jails for misdemeanor offenders but no authority over the short-term holding facilities operated by towns and cities. Jails are operated mainly by local governments (usually sheriff's departments), but in six states they are integrated with the state prison system. Most correctional activities fall under the executive branch of government, but most agencies of community corrections—probation and intermediate sanctions—are run by the county governments and are usually part of the judicial branch. Facilities and programs for juveniles are separate.

The fragmentation of corrections is illustrated in Table 13.3, which shows how correctional responsibilities are distributed in the Philadelphia metropolitan area. Note that all levels of government—federal, state, county, and municipal—operate correctional programs. Various departments within these levels are responsible for implementing programs.

Federal Corrections System

The correctional responsibilities of the federal government are divided between the Department of Justice, which operates prisons through the Federal Bureau of Prisons, and the Administrative Office of the United States Courts, which covers probation and parole supervision.

Federal Bureau of Prisons

The Federal Bureau of Prisons, created by Congress in 1930, now operates a system of prisons located throughout the nation and housing almost 150,000 inmates, supervised by a staff of more than thirty thousand. Facilities and inmates are classified by security level, ranging from Level 1 (the least secure, camp-type settings such as the Federal Prison Camp in Tyndall, Florida) through Level 5 (the most secure, such as the supermax penitentiary in Florence, Colorado). Between these extremes are Levels 2 through 4 federal correctional institutions—other U.S. penitentiaries, administrative institutions, medical facilities, and spe-

Table 13.3 Distribution of correctional responsibilities in Philadelphia County, Pennsylvania

Note the various correctional functions performed by different government agencies.

	Correctional Function	Level and Branch of Government	Responsible Agency
Adult corrections	Pretrial detention	Municipal/executive	Department of Human Services
	Probation supervision	County/courts	Court of Common Pleas
	Halfway houses	Municipal/executive	Department of Human Services
	Houses of corrections	Municipal/executive	Department of Human Services
	County prisons	Municipal/executive	Department of Human Services
	State prisons	State/executive	Department of Corrections
	County parole	County/executive	Court of Common Pleas
	State parole	State/executive	Board of Probation and Parole
Juvenile corrections	Detention	Municipal/executive	Department of Public Welfare
	Probation supervision	County/courts	Court of Common Pleas
	Dependent/neglect	State/executive	Department of Human Services
	Training schools	State/executive	Department of Public Welfare
	Private placements	Private	Many
	Juvenile aftercare	State/executive	Department of Public Welfare
Federal corrections	Probation/parole	Federal/courts	U.S. courts
	Incarceration	Federal/courts	Federal Bureau of Prisons

Sources: Taken from the annual reports of the responsible agencies.

cialized institutions for women and juveniles. The Bureau enters into contractual agreements with states, cities, and private agencies to provide community services such as halfway houses, prerelease programs, and electronic monitoring.

The Bureau of Prisons is responsible for the punishment of federal offenders. Visit them at http://www.bop.gov.

Because of the nature of federal criminal law, prisoners in most federal facilities differ from those in state institutions. Federal prisoners are often a more sophisticated type of criminal, from a higher socioeconomic background, who have committed crimes of extortion, mail fraud, bank robbery, and arson. However, since the beginning of the war on drugs in the 1980s, the proportion of drug offenders has increased and now makes up about 60 percent of the incarcerated population. Fewer offenders (less than 15 percent of the federal prison population) have committed crimes of violence than are found in most state institutions. About 30 percent of federal prisoners are citizens of other countries (Federal Bureau of Prisons, 2000:53).

Federal Probation and Parole Supervision

Probation and parole supervision for federal offenders are provided by the Federal Probation and Pretrial Services System, a branch of the Administrative Office of the U.S. Courts. The federal judiciary appoints probation officers, who serve the court. The first full-time federal probation officer was appointed in 1927; today 3,842 are assigned to the judicial districts across the country. They assist with presentence investigations but are primarily involved in supervising those on probation and offenders released either on parole or mandatory release. Their average caseload is 70 people (BJS, 1999e:477).

The Pretrial Services Act of 1982 required pretrial services to be established in each federal judicial district. These services are performed either by probation officers or independently in a separate office of pretrial services. The responsibilities of pretrial services officers are to “collect, verify, and report to the judicial officer information pertaining to the pretrial release of each person charged with an offense” (Administrative Office of the U.S. Courts, 1993).

State Corrections Systems

Although states vary considerably in how they organize corrections, in all states the administration of prisons falls under the executive branch of state government. This point is important because probation is often part of the judiciary, parole may be separate from corrections, and in most states jails are run by county governments. The differences can be seen in the proportion of correctional employees who work for the state. In Connecticut, Rhode Island, and Vermont, for example, 100 percent are state employees, compared with 47 percent in California. The remaining 53 percent in California work for county or municipal governments.

The Florida Department of Corrections provides an example of a state correctional agency: http://www.dc.state.fl.us.

Community Corrections

Probation, intermediate sanctions, and parole are the three major ways that offenders are punished in the community. States vary in how they carry out these punishments. In many states, probation and intermediate sanctions are administered by the judiciary, often by county and municipal governments. By contrast, parole is a function of state government. The decision to release an offender from prison is made by the state parole board in those states with discretionary release. Parole boards are a part of either the department of corrections or an independent agency. In states with a mandatory system, the department of corrections makes the release. In all states, a state agency supervises the parolees.

Central to the community corrections approach is a belief in the "least restrictive alternative," the idea that the criminal sanction should be applied only to the minimum extent necessary to meet the community's need for protection, the seriousness of the offense, and society's need for offenders to get their deserved punishment. To this end, probation and parole services are geared to assist and reintegrate the offender into the community.

State Prison Systems

A wide range of state correctional institutions and programs exists for adult felons, including prisons, reformatories, prison farms, forestry camps, and halfway houses. This variety does not exist for women because of the smaller female prisoner population.

States vary considerably in the number, size, type, and location of correctional facilities they have. Michigan's prison at Jackson, for example, can hold 3,500, whereas specialized institutions house fewer than a hundred inmates. Some states (such as New Hampshire) have centralized incarceration in a few institutions, and other states (such as California, New York, and Texas) have a wide mix of sizes and styles—secure institutions, diagnostic units, work camps, forestry centers, and prerelease centers. For example, Alabama has 13 correctional institutions (prisons), a disciplinary rehabilitation unit, an honor farm, a boot camp, a state cattle ranch, a prison for women, and a youth center for male felons under age 25, in addition to 11 community-based facilities (American Correctional Association, 1996:4)

State correctional institutions for men are usually classified by level of security: maximum, medium, and minimum. With changes in the number of prisoners and their characteristics, the distinction between maximum and medium security has disappeared in some systems. Crowding has forced administrators to house inmates requiring maximum security in medium-security facilities.

Thirty-eight states have created prisons that exceed maximum security. About 80,000 men, 7 to 9 percent of those behind bars, are currently kept in these "super max" prisons. These institutions are designed to hold the most disruptive, violent, and incorrigible offenders. California's Pelican Bay institution and Connecticut's Northern Correctional Facility are examples of prisons designed to hold the "toughest of the tough." In such institutions, inmates spend up to 23 hours a day in their cells. They are shackled whenever they are out of their cells—during recreation, showers, and telephone calls. All of these measures are designed to send a message to other inmates.

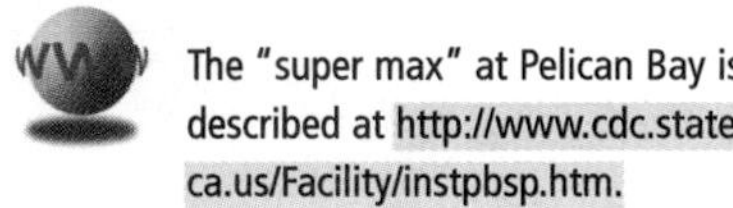

The "super max" at Pelican Bay is described at http://www.cdc.state.ca.us/Facility/instpbsp.htm.

Stephen Ferry/Liaison/Getty Images

About 80,000 inmates are now held in 360 "super max" prisons such as the Administrative Maximum Facility, Florence, Colorado, designed to house 400 of the most "predatory" convicts in the federal system. Critics charge that these facilities, designed to minimize human contact, violate human rights.

The maximum-security prison (where 35 percent of state inmates are confined) is built like a fortress, usually surrounded by stone walls with guard towers and designed to prevent escape. New facilities are surrounded by double rows of chain-link fences with rolls of razor wire in between and along the tops of the fences. Inmates live in cells that include plumbing and sanitary facilities. Some facilities' barred doors are operated electronically so that an officer can confine all prisoners to their cells with the flick of a switch. The purpose of the maximum-security facility is custody and discipline. It maintains a military-style approach to order, with prisoners following a strict routine. Some of the most famous prisons, such as Attica (New York), Folsom (California), Stateville (Illinois), and Yuma (Arizona) are maximum-security facilities.

The medium-security prison (holding 47 percent of state inmates) externally resembles the maximum-security prison, but it is organized somewhat differently and its atmosphere is less rigid. Prisoners have more privileges and contact with the outside world through visitors, mail, and access to radio and television. The medium-security prison usually places greater emphasis on work and rehabilitative programs. Although the inmates may have committed serious crimes, they are not perceived as hardened criminals.

The minimum-security prison (with 18 percent of state inmates) houses the least-violent offenders, long-term felons with clean disciplinary records, and inmates who have nearly completed their term. The minimum-security prison lacks the guard towers and stone walls associated with correctional institutions. Often, chain-link fencing surrounds the buildings. Prisoners usually live in dormitories or even in small private rooms rather than in barred cells. There is more personal freedom: Inmates may have television sets, choose their own clothes, and move about casually within the buildings. The system relies on rehabilitation programs and offers opportunities for education and work release. To the outsider, minimum-security prisons may seem to enforce little punishment, but the inmates are segregated from society and their freedoms are restricted. They are still prisons.

State Institutions for Women

Because only 6.6 percent of the incarcerated population are women, there are relatively few women's facilities. Although the ratio of arrests is approximately 6 men to 1 woman, the ratio of admissions to state correctional institutions is

18 men to 1 woman. A higher proportion of female defendants is sentenced to probation and intermediate punishments, partly as a result of male offenders' tendency to commit most of the violent crimes. However, the growth rate in number of incarcerated women has exceeded that for men since 1981. In fact, since 1990 the male population in state and federal prisons increased 77 percent, whereas that of women increased by 108 percent. During the past ten years, the number of women in state prisons for drug offenses has increased almost 450 percent (BJS, 1998c:3). The number of women now incarcerated in prisons is more than 92,000 (BJS, 2001c:3). The increased number of women in prison has significantly affected the delivery of programs, housing conditions, medical care, staffing, and security (B. Owen and Bloom, 1995:166).

Female offenders are incarcerated in 141 institutions for women and 162 coed facilities (BJS, 1997c:54). Conditions in correctional facilities for women are more pleasant than those of similar institutions for men. Usually the buildings have no gun towers and barbed wire. Because of the small population, however, most states have only one facility, which is often located in a rural setting far removed from urban centers. Thus women prisoners may be more isolated than men from their families and communities. Pressure from women's organizations and the apparent rise in the incidence of crime committed by women may bring about a greater equality in corrections for men and women.

check point

7. What agencies of the U.S. government are responsible for prisons and probation?
8. What agencies of state government are responsible for incarceration, probation, intermediate sanctions, and parole?

Private Prisons

Corrections is a multibillion-dollar government-funded enterprise that purchases supplies and services from the private sector. Many jurisdictions have long contracted with private vendors to provide specific institutional services and to operate aftercare facilities and programs. Businesses furnish food and medical services, educational and vocational training, maintenance, security, and industrial programs. All of this has been referred to as "the corrections-commercial complex" (Lilly, 1993:150).

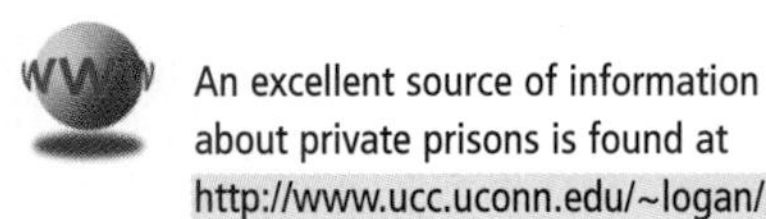
An excellent source of information about private prisons is found at http://www.ucc.uconn.edu/~logan/.

One response to prison and jail crowding and rising staff costs has come from private entrepreneurs who argue that they can build and run prisons at least as effectively, safely, and humanely as any level of government can, at a profit and at a lower cost to taxpayers. The management of entire institutions for adult felons under private contract is a relatively new approach in corrections that was launched in the 1980s (Shichor, 1995).

In 1986 Kentucky's Marion Adjustment Center became the first facility that was privately owned and operated (by the U.S. Corrections Corporation) for the incarceration of adult felons classified at least to a level of minimum security. By May 2001 there were 158 private prisons, with a total capacity of 119,813, operating in 31 states, Puerto Rico, and the District of Columbia (see Figure 13.2). The $1 billion-a-year private prison business is dominated by the Corrections Corporation of America and Wackenhut Corrections Corporation, which together hold more than three quarters of the market share of the private prison business (C. W. Thomas, 2002).

Advocates of privately operated prisons claim that they provide the same level of care as the states but more cheaply and flexibly. Charles Logan's study (1992) of private prisons points to the difficulties of measuring the costs and quality of these institutions. One issue is that many of the "true costs" (fringe benefits, con-

Figure 13.2 Private prisons for adults
The number of private correctional facilities for adults varies greatly among the 31 states, Puerto Rico, and the District of Columbia.

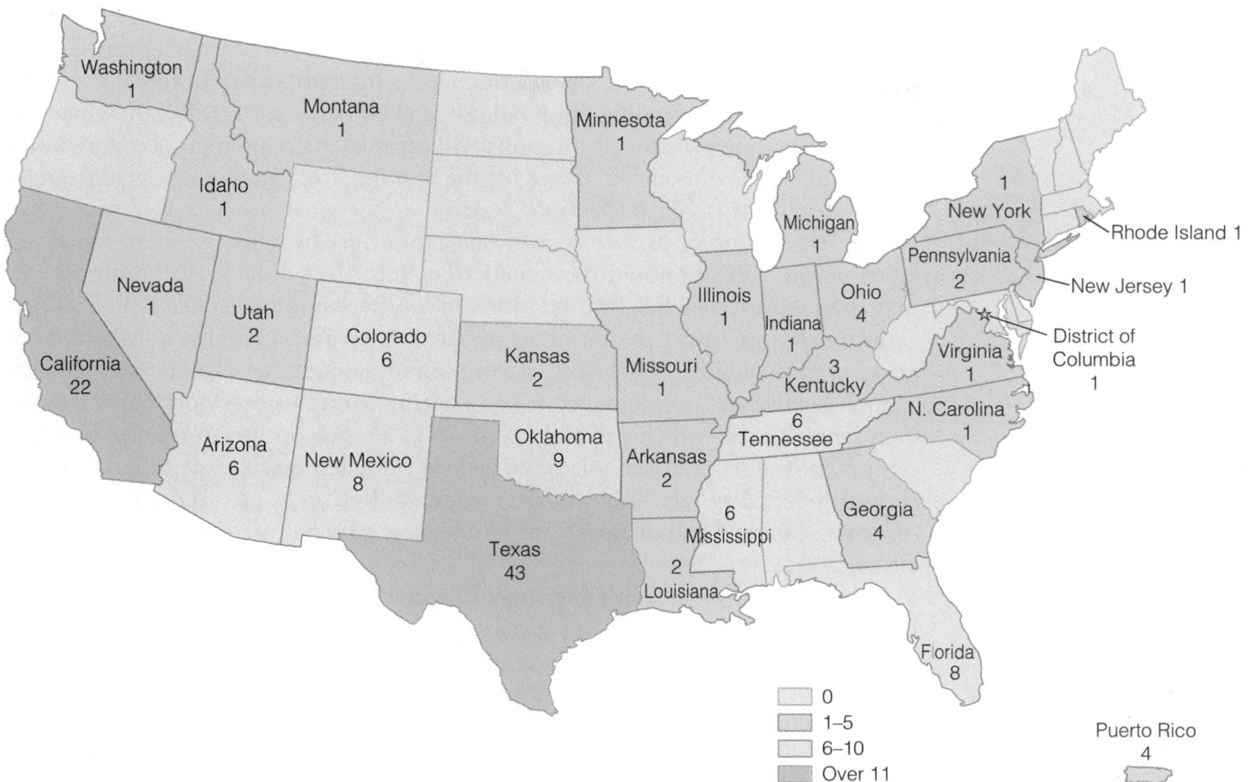

Note: The location of facilities does not necessarily indicate contracting decisions made by agencies in those jurisdictions. Some states are contracting for the housing of their prisoners in other jurisdictions. Some states are providing sites only for federal facilities. This figure represents both facilities in operation and those under construction.
Source: Center for Studies in Criminology and Law, University of Florida (http://www.crim.ufl.edu/pcp/).

tracting supervision, federal grants) are not taken into consideration. The quoted rates of existing private facilities vary widely. In Texas the state pays the private companies about $30 a day on average for each prisoner, compared with $39.50 per day in state-run facilities. However, the $39.50 figure includes expensive maximum-security prisons, which the private companies do not run. The private prison rate in Texas is equivalent to $10,950 per year, much less than the costs per inmates held in most states (*New York Times,* June 24, 1997:A19). In 1996 the U.S. General Accounting Office issued a report comparing the costs of public and private prisons. After reviewing five separate studies, it could not determine whether privatization saved money (*New York Times,* July 13, 1997:D5).

Provision of correctional services by private companies may result in lower costs, but public agencies must constantly monitor contracts to ensure compliance. The profit incentive may result in poor services, as evidenced by a 1995 detainee uprising at an Elizabeth, New Jersey, jail run by Esmore Correctional Services Corporation for the Immigration and Naturalization Service. Undercutting a bid from Wackenhut Corporation by $20 million, Esmore violated the contract by understaffing, abusing detainees, maintaining inadequate physical conditions, and presenting health hazards (*New York Times,* July 23, 1995:1). In the Northeast Ohio Correctional Center, owned by the Corrections Corporation of America, 20 inmates were stabbed, two of the fatally, during the first ten months of operations (*New York Times,* April 15,1999:1).

Political, fiscal, ethical, and administrative issues must be examined before corrections can become too heavily committed to the private ownership and operation of prisons. The political issues, including ethical questions concerning the delegation of social-control functions to people other than state employees, may be the most difficult to overcome. Some people believe that the administration of justice is a basic function of government that should not be delegated. They fear that correctional policy would be skewed because contractors would use their political influence to continue programs not in the public interest. Joseph Hallinan describes the extent to which executives and shareholders of Corrections Corporation of American and U.S. Corrections have funded political campaigns in Indiana, Kentucky, Oklahoma, and Tennessee (Hallinan, 2001:168–70). There are also fears that the private corporations will press to maintain high occupancy and will be interested only in skimming off the best inmates, leaving the most troublesome ones to the public corrections system.

The fiscal value of private corrections cannot yet be demonstrated. However, labor unions have opposed these incursions into the public sector, pointing out that the salaries, benefits, and pensions of workers in other spheres such as private security are lower than in their public counterparts. Finally, questions have arisen about quality of services, accountability of service providers to corrections officials, and problems related to contract supervision. Opponents cite the many instances in which privately contracted services in group homes, day-care centers, hospitals, and schools have been terminated because of reports of corruption, brutality, or substandard services. Research has shown that staff turnover, escapes, and drug use are problems in private prisons (S. D. Camp and Gales, 2002).

A movement for greater government regulation of private prisons is growing. In Ohio, Texas, Tennessee, and several other states, legislatures have enacted or are considering new laws to ensure that the private prison industry lives up to its contractual obligations. Several members of Congress have introduced bills to prohibit federal inmates from serving their time in private prisons (*New York Times,* April 15, 1999:1).

The idea of privately run correctional facilities has stimulated much interest among the general public and within the criminal justice community, but the future of this approach is quite uncertain. Further privatization of criminal justice services may ensue, or privatization may become only a limited venture initiated at a time of prison crowding, fiscal constraints on governments, and revival of the free-enterprise ideology. In any case, the controversy about privatization has forced corrections to rethink some strongly held beliefs. In this regard, the possibility of competition from the private sector may have a positive impact on corrections.

check point

9. What are the arguments in favor of and against privately run prisons?

Jails: Detention and Short-Term Incarceration

prison
An institution for the incarceration of people convicted of serious crimes, usually felonies.

jail
An institution authorized to hold pretrial detainees and sentenced misdemeanants for periods longer than 48 hours. Most jails are administered by county governments; in six jurisdictions, by state governments.

Most Americans do not distinguish between jails and prisons. **Prisons** are federal and state correctional institutions that hold offenders who are sentenced to terms of more than one year. **Jails** are local facilities for the detention of people awaiting trial and sentenced misdemeanants. Jails are also a holding facility for social misfits—derelicts, junkies, prostitutes, the mentally ill, and disturbers of public order.

Origins and Evolution

Jails in the United States descend from feudal practices in twelfth-century England. At that time, an officer of the crown, the *reeve,* was appointed in each *shire* (what we call a county) to collect taxes, keep the peace, and run the *gaol* (jail). Among other duties, the *shire reeve* (from which the word *sheriff* evolved) caught and held in custody, until a court hearing determined guilt or innocence, people accused of breaking the law. With the development of the workhouse in the sixteenth century, the sheriff took on added responsibilities for vagrants and the unemployed who were sent there. The sheriff made a living by collecting fees from inmates and by hiring out their labor.

English settlers brought these institutions to the American colonies. After the Revolution, the local community elected law enforcement officials—sheriffs and constables—to run the jail. As in England, the early American jails were used to detain accused people awaiting trial as well as to shelter misfits.

In the 1800s the jail began to change in response to the penitentiary movement. In addition to shouldering traditional responsibilities, jails now held offenders serving short terms. The development of probation removed some offenders, as did adult reformatories. However, even with these innovations, the overwhelming majority of accused and convicted misdemeanants were held in jail. This pattern continued to modern times.

The Contemporary Jail

Of the 3,365 jails in the United States, 2,700 have a county-level jurisdiction, and most are administered by an elected sheriff. An additional 600 or so municipal jails are in operation. Only in six states—Alaska, Connecticut, Delaware, Hawaii, Rhode Island, and Vermont—does the state administer jails for adults. There are also an estimated 13,500 police lockups (or drunk tanks) and similar holding facilities authorized to detain people for up to 48 hours. The Federal Bureau of Prisons operates 11 jails for detained prisoners only, holding a total of 11,000 inmates. There are 47 privately operated jails, under contract to state or local governments, and they house 2.4 percent of the total jail population (BJS, 2001a:2).

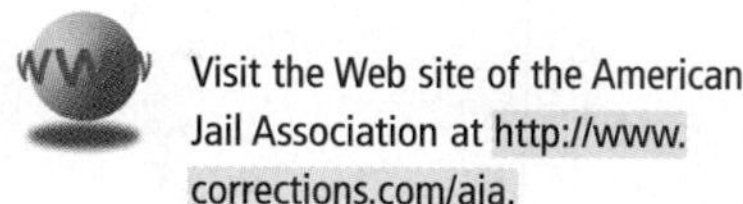

Visit the Web site of the American Jail Association at http://www.corrections.com/aja.

The primary function of jails is to hold people awaiting trial and people who have been sentenced for misdemeanors to terms of less than one year. On a national basis, about 50 percent of jail inmates are pretrial detainees. In some states, convicted felons may serve more than one year in jail instead of in prison. For 87 percent of the sentenced population, however, stays in jail are less than one month.

Jails and police lockups shoulder responsibility for housing not only criminal defendants and offenders but also those viewed as problems by society. The criminal justice system is thus linked to other government agencies. People with substance abuse and mental problems have become a part of the jail population. They are often reported to the police for their deviant acts which, although not illegal, are upsetting to the citizenry (urinating in public, appearing disoriented, shouting obscenities, and so on). Temporary confinement in a lockup or jail may be necessary if no appropriate social service facilities are available. This situation has been likened to a revolving door that shifts these "street people" from the police station to the jail. After an appearance in court, they are often released to the streets to start their cycle through the system all over again.

Jails also house sentenced felony offenders for whom state prisons have no room. They house people awaiting transportation to prison, such as those convicted of parole or probation violations. This backup of inmates has caused difficulties in some states for judges and jail administrators, who must often put misdemeanants on probation because no jail space is available.

The capacity of jails varies greatly. The 25 largest jurisdictions hold almost 30 percent of the nation's jailed inmates. The Los Angeles County Men's Central Jail alone holds more than 6,000 people, but most jails are much smaller, with 67 percent holding fewer than 50 people each (BJS, 1998a:8). However, these small facilities are dwindling in number because of new jail construction and the creation of regional, multicounty facilities.

Who Is in Jail?

With an estimated 11 million jail admissions per year, more people directly experience jails than experience prisons, mental hospitals, and halfway houses combined. Even if we consider that some people of this total are admitted more than once, probably at least six to seven million people are detained at some time during the year. Nationally, over 600,000 people, both the convicted and the unconvicted, sit in jail on any one day. However, the number of people held at any one time in jail does not tell the complete story. Many are held for less than 24 hours; others may reside in jail as sentenced inmates for up to one year; a few may await their trial for more than a year (BJS, 2000a:6).

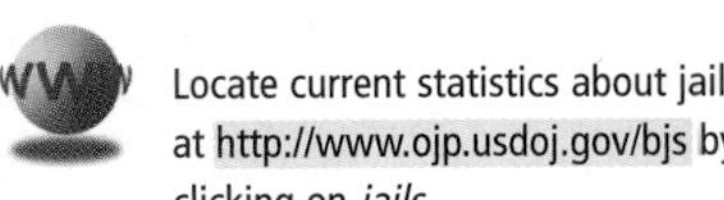

Locate current statistics about jails at http://www.ojp.usdoj.gov/bjs by clicking on *jails.*

The most recent National Jail Census shows that about 90 percent of inmates are men, most are under 30 years old, more than half are people of color, and most have very low education and incomes (BJS, 2001a:8). The demographic characteristics of the jail population differ greatly from those of the national population (see Figure 13.3).

Figure 13.3 **Characteristics of adult jail inmates in U.S. jails**
Compared with the American population as a whole, jails are disproportionately inhabited by men, minorities, the poorly educated, and those with low income.

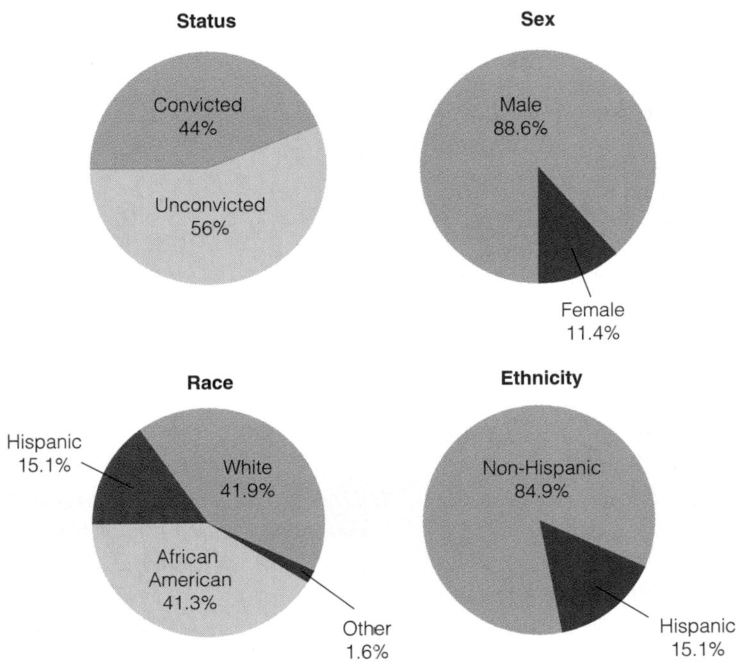

Source: Bureau of Justice Statistics, *Bulletin,* March 2001, p. 7.

Managing Jails

Jail administrators face several problems that good management practices cannot always overcome. These problems include (1) the perceived role of the jail in the local criminal justice system, (2) the inmate population, and (3) fiscal problems.

Jail: Law Enforcement or Corrections?

As facilities to detain accused people awaiting trial, jails customarily have been run by law enforcement agencies. We might reasonably expect that the agency that arrests and transports defendants to court should also administer the facility that holds them. Typically, however, neither sheriffs nor deputies have much interest in corrections. They often think of themselves as police officers and of the jail as merely an extension of their law enforcement activities. In some major cities, municipal departments of correction, rather than the police, manage the jails.

Many experts argue that jails have outgrown police administration. Jails no longer are simply holding places but now represent one of the primary correctional facilities. In fact, much correctional work is directed toward jail inmates. Probation officers conduct presentence investigations in jails, alcohol and drug abusers receive treatment in many facilities, and inmates work toward reintegration or perform community service out of some facilities. Therefore, the effective administration of jails requires skills in offender management and rehabilitation that are not generally included in law enforcement training.

Inmate Characteristics

The mixture of offenders of widely diverse ages and criminal histories is an often-cited problem in U.S. jails. Because most inmates are viewed as temporary residents, little attempt is made to classify them for either security or treatment purposes. Horror stories of the mistreatment of young offenders by older, stronger, and more violent inmates occasionally come to public attention. The physical condition of most jails aggravates this situation, because most are old, overcrowded, and lacking in basic facilities. Many sentenced felons prefer to move on to state prison, where the conditions are likely to be better.

Because of constant inmate turnover and because local control provides an incentive to keep costs down, correctional services are usually lacking in jail.

new directions in criminal justice policy

Direct Supervision Jails

To deal with jail crowding, violence, and the inefficiency of old construction, many jurisdictions have turned toward the *direct supervision jail.* This jail is both a design and a set of programs that attempts to use the physical plant to improve the staff's ability to manage and interact with the inmate population and to provide services. Three general concepts are employed: podular design, interaction space, and personal space.

The podular unit, which replaces the old cell blocks, is a living area for a group of inmates. Twelve to 25 individual cells are organized into a unit (the pod) that serves as something like a self-contained minijail. Typically the cell doors open into a common living area where the inmates of the pod are allowed to congregate.

The direct supervision jail tends to reinforce interactions of various sorts. For example, inmates have greater freedom to interact socially and recreationally. Further, in traditional jails, bars and doors separate correctional officers from inmates; the direct supervision jail places them in the same rooms with inmates.

The new structure offers several advantages over older jails. First, its flexibility makes it more economical. When jail populations are low, whole pods can be temporarily shut down, saving personnel and operational costs. Second, minimum standards for recreation time and nonlockup time can be met routinely without costly construction or renovation. Third, because staff have greater autonomy to manage their pods, supervising the staff is less demanding. Fourth, research indicates that direct supervision jails are as much as 20 percent cheaper to construct, and they provide better inmate security and supervision. Finally, some evidence suggests that this new jail concept results in less violence and fewer inmate infractions, leaving staff feeling more secure in their work.

WWW Researching the Internet

Go to InfoTrac College Edition. Enter the keywords *direct supervision jail,* then read the article in *Corrections Today,* April 1993, to learn how the design of a facility can affect inmate behavior.

Recreational facilities and treatment programs are not usually found there. Medical services are generally minimal. Such conditions add to the idleness and tensions of the inmates. Suicides and high levels of violence are hallmarks of many jails. In any one year, almost half the people who die while in jail have committed suicide.

Fiscal Problems

Because of the close links between jail administration and local politics, fiscal pressures greatly affect the management of jails. For example, pretrial release programs are a cost-efficient and proven means of reducing institutional crowding, yet the public's fear of crime often makes the programs politically infeasible. Conversely, political pressures may support expanded use of jail confinement for misdemeanants or probation violators (particularly when crime is a potent electoral issue), but the local government often lacks funds to expand or upgrade a jail's capacity to handle additional offenders. The jail controls crime but also drains revenues. The tension between these two public interests often surfaces in local debates over capital expenditures for jail construction. Because revenues often are insufficient, many jails are overcrowded and cannot house all the inmates assigned to their supervision, and some are released or placed in other facilities. See "New Directions in Criminal Justice Policy" for one approach to solving these and related problems.

As criminal justice policy has become more punitive, jails, like prisons, have become crowded. Surveys have documented increases averaging 6 percent during

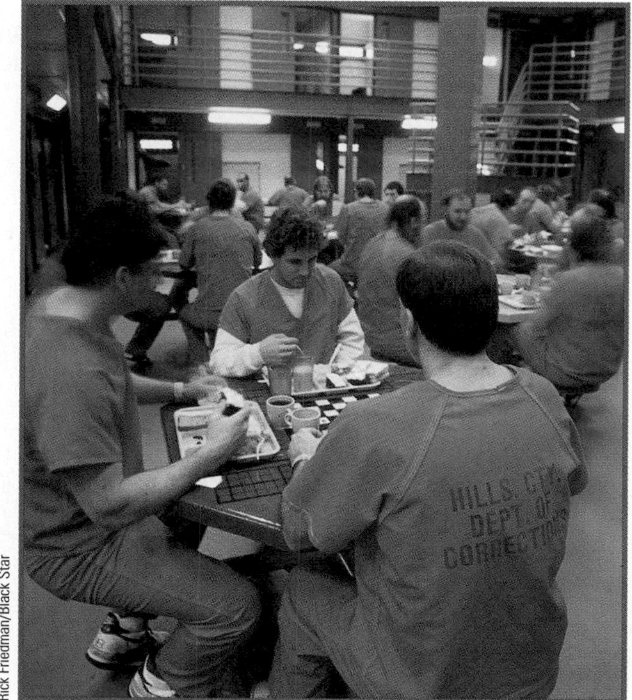

Rick Friedman/Black Star

Direct supervision jails, like this one in Manchester, New Hampshire, are designed to increase the interaction of inmates with correctional officers. What are the advantages and disadvantages of this approach?

each of the past five years. Even with new construction and with alternatives such as release on recognizance programs, diversion, intensive probation supervision, and house arrest with electronic monitoring, the jail population continues to rise. The $4.5 billion annual cost of operating jails is a great financial burden for local governments.

check point

10. What are the functions of jails?
11. What are three of the problems affecting jails?

Correctional Policy Trends

Anyone at all attentive to criminal justice issues knows that the United States has a large and expanding population under correctional supervision. Extensive media coverage has highlighted the fact that since the middle of the 1970s the United States has fought a war on crime mainly by increasing the severity of sanctions against offenders. This has led to a 500 percent increase in correctional budgets, more than 3.8 million people on probation, 2 million incarcerated in prisons and jails, and 750,000 under parole supervision. These are staggering figures, especially considering the fact that crime has been decreasing for the past decade. Figure 13.4 shows the tremendous growth in the correctional population since 1980.

Some observers believe that the drop in crime is a result of the harsher arrest and sentencing policies of the past quarter century. Critics say that the "lock 'em up" policies have had little impact on crime and that the fiscal and human costs of current policies severely damage families and communities. As discussed in "The Policy Debate," many believe that there now exists a "prison-commercial complex" that encourages increased spending on imprisonment regardless of need. Let's examine community corrections and incarceration policies so as to better understand current practices and future trends.

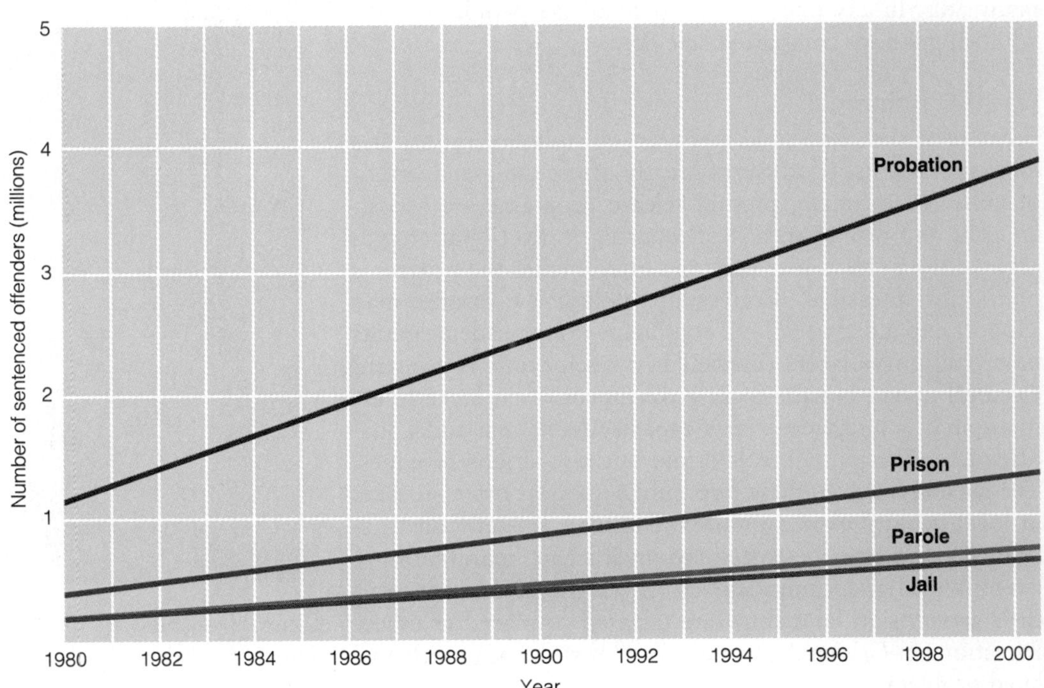

Figure 13.4
Correctional populations in the United States, 1980–2001
Although the increase in prison populations receives the most publicity, a greater proportion of correctional growth has occurred in probation and parole.

Source: Bu·eau of Justice Statistics, October 1, 2002 (http//www.ojp.usdoj.gov/bjs/).

Is There a Prison-Commercial Complex?

Forty years ago, President Dwight D. Eisenhower warned of the strong, unwarranted influence of the "military-industrial complex." He was concerned about the extent to which the armed forces of the United States and the manufacturers of military hardware shared an interest in the ever-expanding defense budget. Today critics are pointing to a similar "prison-commercial complex" made up of bureaucratic, political, and economic interests that encourage increased spending on imprisonment, regardless of need.

One of the anomalies of the past decade is that as crime rates have fallen, the prison population has continued to grow. Some have said that crime has fallen *because* of tough incarceration policies and that there is still too much violent and drug-related crime. Others believe that, with corrections costing more than $35 billion per year, many factors have encouraged expansion: the profits to be made in prison supplies and construction, the increased value of stock in corporations running private prisons, the greater number of correctional jobs, the expanded fiefdoms of prison bureaucrats, the growth of correctional officer labor unions, and the votes for politicians who pass "tough on crime" legislation.

Why are so many people in the United States locked up? Are government agencies and legislators merely responding to public demand for criminals to be isolated? Is there a prison-commercial complex that has influenced the upward spiral of the number of prisoners?

There Is a Prison-Commercial Complex

Those who believe that there is a prison-commercial complex argue that high incarceration rates during a period of falling levels of crime are influenced by the "punishment industry." They say that corporations doing business with corrections have a mutuality of interests with government agencies seeking to expand their domain and with legislators promoting tough crime policies.

People holding this view point to the 400 percent increase in correctional spending since 1979, the 600 percent increase in funds for prison construction, and the expectation that these allocations will continue to grow at an annual rate of 5 to 10 percent. They cite the spectacular growth of the private prisons industry and the billions of dollars spent to purchase goods and services. In addition to corporations, labor unions have also benefited by the rise in the number of prison employees, now set at more than 350,000. In many states, correctional officers have become a potent political force and have lobbied for expansion of the system.

The arguments supporting the existence of a prison-commercial complex that has promoted incarceration include these:

- Spending for incarceration continues to rise and in most states exceeds appropriations for most government services.
- There is a mutuality of interests among correctional agencies, businesses, and legislators that supports high incarceration.
- Correctional workers and their unions support the hiring of more employees.
- Legislators believe that voters expect them to be "tough on crime."

There Is No Prison-Commercial Complex

Those who support incarceration for offenders who have committed serious felonies say that there is no prison-commercial complex. They believe prison expansion is driven by the need to provide space for the increased number of offenders incarcerated for longer terms and not by business interests hoping to profit from the crime problem.

Defenders also say that the growth of the prison population has helped to lower crime rates because of the large numbers of offenders who have been put away. They believe that treating criminals severely is just and that incarcerated felons deserve to be punished seriously. They argue that incarceration is expensive but to allow felons to live in society where they will continue their criminal ways is many times more costly.

The arguments against the existence of a prison-commercial complex include the following:

- Increased incarceration rates are not being pushed by commercial interests but reflect current public policies.
- Justice demands that serious offenders be incarcerated.
- Incarceration policies have helped lower the crime rate.
- The public's support of incarceration policies is reflected by the actions of Congress and the state legislatures.

What Should U.S. Policy Be?

Several questions about incarceration warrant serious attention. Does incarceration have an impact—one way or the other—on the crime rate? Is incarceration rising during a period of decreased criminality because it is being promoted by economic interests? Should imprisonment be used more sparingly, only for the worst offenders?

Researching the Internet

There are now several Web sites concerning this issue, including the following: http://www.ranknfile-ue.org/policy_pi.html and http://www.theatlantic.com/issues/98dec/prisons.htm.

Go to the *American System of Criminal Justice* Web site at http://www.cj.wadsworth.com/colesmith10e to explore this question in further detail: Is there a prison-commercial complex?

Community Corrections

Escalating prison growth has captured the public's attention, yet the numbers on probation and parole have actually risen at a faster rate than the incarcerated population has risen. Many factors may explain this growth, including more arrests and successful prosecutions, the lower costs of probation compared with incarceration, prison and jail crowding, and the great numbers of felons now being released from prison.

Probation

People on probation under community supervision now make up more than 70 percent of the correctional population, yet budgets and staffing have not risen accordingly. In many urban areas, probation caseloads are growing well beyond reasonable management levels: 200- and even 300-person caseloads are no longer unusual. This has lead to a deterioration in the quality of supervision. Yet the importance of probation for public safety has never been greater. For example, up to 17 percent of felony arrests in one sample of large urban counties were of people who were on probation at the time of their alleged offense (Reaves and Hart, 1999). As a result, a renewed emphasis on public safety has arisen. Many agencies have seen a resurgence of intensive and structured supervision for selected offenders.

In many respects, then, probation finds itself at a crossroads. Although its credibility is probably as low as it has ever been, its workload is growing dramatically and, in view of the crowding in prison and jails, will probably continue to do so. Under the strain of this workload and on-again, off-again public support, probation faces a serious challenge. Can its methods of supervision and service be adapted successfully to high-risk offenders?

Parole

With the incarcerated population more than quadrupling during the past 30 years, it is not surprising that the number of parolees has also grown. Currently almost 600,000 felons are released from prison each year and allowed to live in the community under supervision. In 2000, 725,527 were under parole supervision, a threefold increase since 1980 (BJS, 2001e: Table 6.1). With the massive incarcerations of the past decades, the number on parole is likely to reach one million in the next five years.

An increasing portion of these new parolees are older, were sentenced for drug violations, have served longer prison sentences, and have higher levels of substance abuse and mental illness than those returning in 1990 (Beck, 2000). These characteristics increase reentry problems concerning the renewal of family ties, obtaining a job, and living according to parole rules. Most parolees cannot obtain the assistance necessary to reenter the community successfully.

Further, increased numbers of offenders are being returned to prison as parole violators. In 1980, 82.4 percent of those entering prison did so directly as a result of a court sentence. This percentage dropped to 64.5 percent in 1994, reflecting an increase in the number sent to prison for parole violations. Between 1990 and 1998 the number of parolees sent back to prison increased by 54 percent—half of them for a technical violation, the others for a new felony conviction (BJS, 2000b:11). A 2002 Bureau of Justice Statistics study found that 67 percent of inmates released from state prisons in 1994 committed at least one serious new crime within three years (BJS, 2002b:2). Allen Beck's analysis (1997:10) shows that much of the growth in total admissions to state prisons can be attributed to the return of parolees.

Incarceration

From 1940 until 1973, the number of people incarcerated in the United States remained fairly stable, with an incarceration rate of about 110 per 100,000 population. However, since 1973, when the overall crime rate started to level off, the incarceration rate has quadrupled. Only during 2001 did the nation's prison population rise at the lowest rate (1 percent) since 1971 and the smallest absolute increase (14,770) since 1979 (BJS, 2002c). It is difficult to judge this slowing of the increase in the prison population. Is it a one-year aberration or does it indicate the influence of lower crime rates, state budgetary problems, or correctional policy shifts?

Figure 13.5 **Incarceration in federal and state prisons per 100,000 population, 1940–2001**
Between 1940 and 1970, the incarceration rate was steady. From 1975 until the end of 2000, before declining in 2001, the incarceration rate continued to increase. The rate today is more than double what it was in 1985.

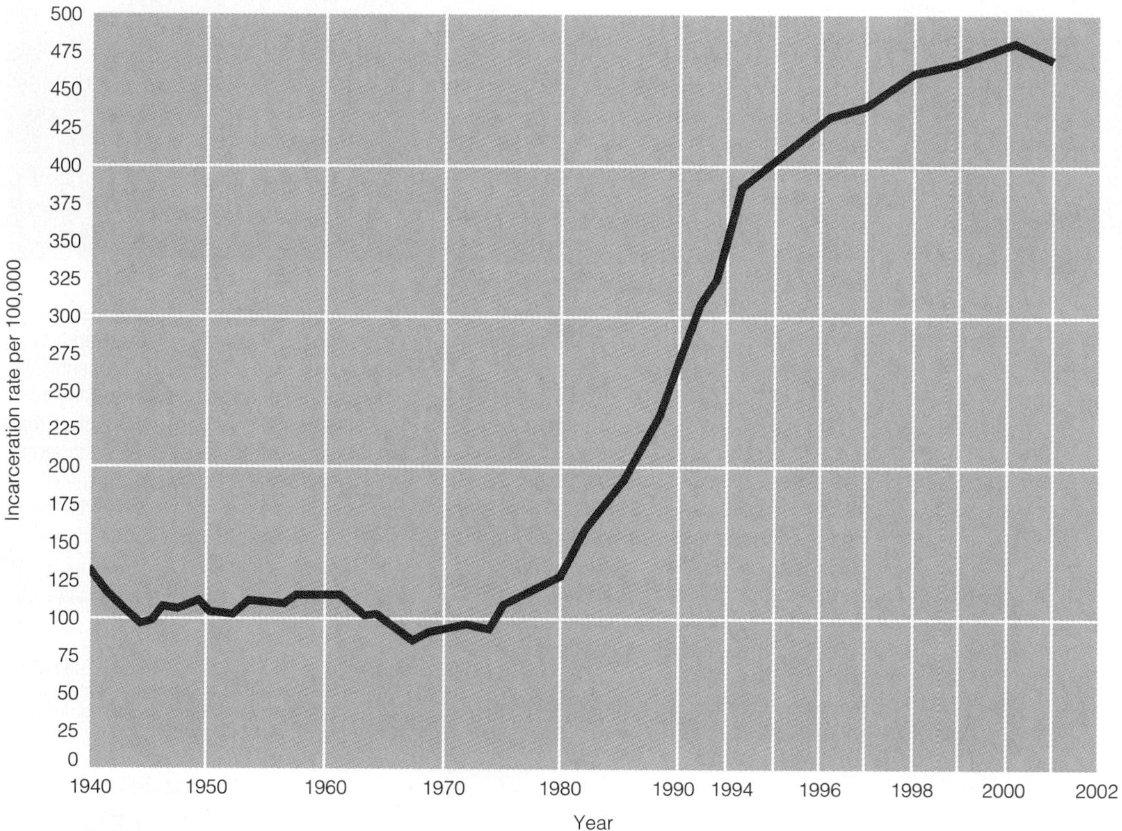

Source: Bureau of Justice Statistics, *Bulletin,* July 2002.

Every June and December, a census of the U.S. prison population is taken for the Bureau of Justice Statistics. As shown in Figure 13.5, from a low of 98 per 100,000 population in 1972, the incarceration rate has steadily risen to a high of 478 in 2000 and a slight dip in December 31, 2001 to 470 per 100,000. This corresponds to 1,406,031 men and women in state and federal prisons, or about one in every 112 men and one in every 1,724 women U.S. residents. An additional 631,240 were in local jails (BJS, 2002c). Incarceration rates are second only to Russia in North America and Europe, as shown in the Comparative Perspective.

Access the latest data from the annual prison census at http://www.ojp.usdoj.gov/bjs/prisons.htm.

Keep in mind that the size and growth of the prison population is not evenly distributed across the country. As Figure 13.6 shows, eight of the ten states with the highest incarceration rates are in the South. In 2001 the South incarcerated 526 people for each 100,000 inhabitants, a ratio much higher than the national average of 470 (BJS, 2002c:4). Because Michigan and Missouri are included in the top ten, the South is not the only area with high incarceration rates.

Why this increase? If little relationship exists between the crime rate and the incarceration rate, what factors explain the growth? Five reasons are often cited for the increase: (1) improved law enforcement and prosecution, (2) tougher sentencing, (3) prison construction, (4) the war on drugs, and (5) state politics. None of these reasons should be viewed as a single explanation or as having more impact than the others.

Increased Arrests and More Likely Incarceration

Some analysts have argued that the billions of dollars spent on the crime problem may be paying off. Not only have arrest rates increased, particularly for

Comparative Perspective

Behind Bars in North America and Europe

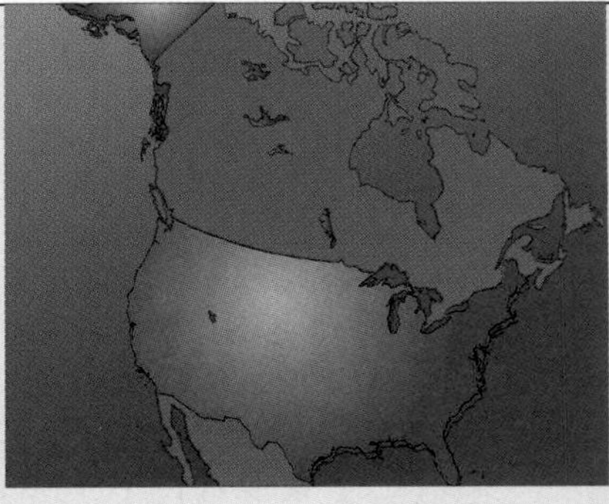

Most Western countries have put more people behind bars in recent years, but in none has the incarceration rate risen higher than in the United States. The cause of the extraordinary American figure is not higher levels of crime, for the crime rate in the United States is about the same as in western Europe (except for the rate of homicide, which is two to eight times greater, mostly because of the ready availability of guns).

The high U.S. rate—which rivals those of former Soviet nations—can be traced primarily to a shift in public attitudes toward crime that began about 30 years ago as apprehension about violence and drugs escalated. Politicians were soon exploiting the new attitudes with promises to get criminals off the streets. Congress and state legislatures, often at the prodding of presidents and governors, promoted "tough on crime" measures, including mandatory sentencing, three-strikes laws, longer sentences, and increased budgets for prison construction.

As a result, the length of sentences, already severe by western European standards, became even more punitive. Consequently, the number of those locked up rose more than fivefold between 1972 and 2000 to more than two million. Most of those sentenced in recent years are perpetrators of nonviolent crimes, such as drug possession, that would not ordinarily be punished by long prison terms in other Western countries.

Source: Roger Doyle, "By the Numbers," *Scientific American,* August 1999, p. 25.

Go to InfoTrac College Edition. Use *incarceration rate* as a key term to read more about national income levels and the size of prison populations.

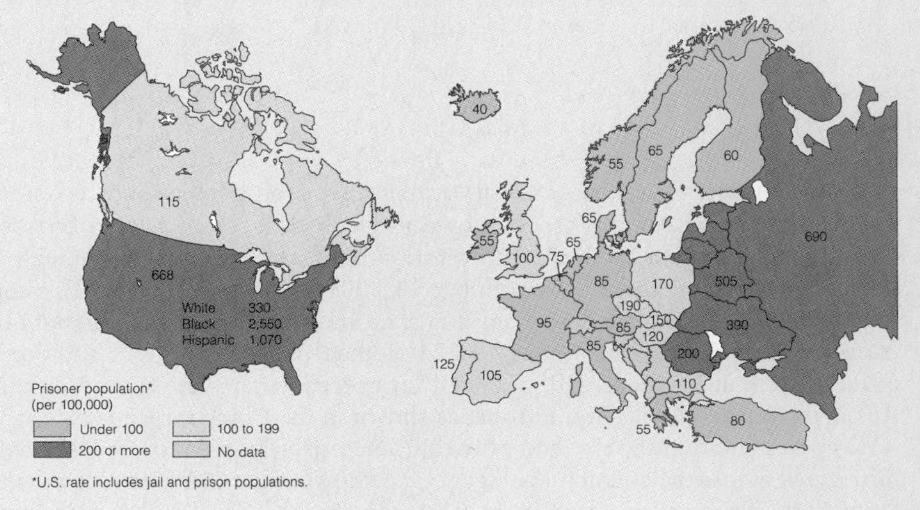

some offenses such as drug violations, aggravated assaults, and sexual assaults, but the probability of being sent to prison also has dramatically increased. Between 1980 and 1994 (the latest available data), the likelihood of incarceration upon arrest increased fivefold for drug violations, fourfold for weapons offenses, and twofold for larceny/theft, motor vehicle theft, and sexual assault other than rape. For only one crime—murder/nonnegligent manslaughter—did the likelihood of incarceration for a serious offense decrease (Beck, 1997:11).

Tougher Sentencing Practices

Some observers think that a hardening of public attitudes toward criminals is reflected in longer sentences, in a smaller proportion of those convicted getting probation, and in fewer being released at the time of the first parole hearing.

Figure 13.6 **Sentenced prisoners in state institutions per 100,000 population, December 31, 2001**
What can be said about the differences in incarceration rates among the states? There are not only regional differences but also differences between adjacent states that seem to have similar socioeconomic and crime characteristics.

Source: Bureau of Justice Statistics, *Bulletin*, August 2002.

In the past three decades, the states and the federal government have passed laws that increase sentences for most crimes. However, the tougher sentences do not seem to be the main factor keeping offenders in prison for longer periods. Between 1990 and 1998 the mean sentence of new court commitments has actually dropped. Rather, it is the 13 percent increase in the amount of time served that affects the total number of inmates (BJS, 2000b:12). The amount of time served is likely to further increase in the coming decade as the new truth-in-sentencing laws begin to make an impact and as the trend of parole boards being more restrictive continues.

Prison Construction

The increased rate of incarceration may be related to the creation of additional space in the nation's prisons. As Joseph Davey has noted, "The presence of empty state-of-the-art prison facilities can encourage a criminal court judge to incarcerate a defendant who may otherwise get probation" (1998:84).

Prison construction during the 1990s was a growth industry, building 351 adult facilities that added more than 528,000 beds during the decade (BJS, 2001c:9). The new facilities increased the capacity of state prisons by 81 percent.

For health and security reasons, crowded conditions in existing facilities cannot be tolerated. Many states attempted to build their way out of this dilemma, because the public seemed to favor harsher sentencing policies, which would require more prison space. With many states holding large budget surpluses during the booming economy of the 1990s, legislatures were willing to advance the huge sums required for prison expansion. Pressures from contractors, building material providers, and correctional officer unions spurred expansion in many states. Yet many states that tried to build their way out of their crowded facilities found that, as soon as a new prison came on line, it was quickly filled (see the Close Up box).

Connecticut: Trying to Build Its Way Out

In the early 1980s Connecticut's prison system became overcrowded, driven by the public demand that the criminal justice system "get tough" on crime. A state long wedded to the concepts of rehabilitation and community corrections, Connecticut's incarceration rate in 1981 was 95 per 100,000 population, well below the national rate of 153. As political pressures increased, however, the legislature toughened sentencing laws, eliminated supervised home release, and mandated that an increasing portion of sentences be served. Immediately the incarceration rate began to rise.

In 1987 Connecticut launched a $1-billion construction effort to double capacity by adding 13 new prisons and expanding 9 others. Connecticut's prison-building program was rivaled in scope only by California's. The expansion began at a time when the state's economy was booming and there was a budget surplus. However, by the time the new facilities came on line in the early 1990s, a recession had set in and the state had a major budget deficit. As operating costs skyrocketed, opening the new prisons became a problem. Several stood vacant, awaiting legislative appropriations to hire additional staff, yet the flow of newly sentenced offenders continued to increase.

From 1985 to 1997 the number of Connecticut inmates increased from 5,790 to 14,100; the correctional budget rose from $92.5 million to $417 million; and the incarceration rate swelled from 127 to 387 per 100,000 inhabitants (the highest in the Northeast). All of this has occurred in a state in which the amount of reported crime has not changed appreciably, although the number of arrests, especially for drug offenses, increased dramatically. In 1994 Connecticut led all states by recording a one-year prisoner growth rate of 20 percent. By 1995 the new prisons were operational—and filled. In 2002, with the highest incarceration rate in the Northeast, the Connecticut Department of Corrections had over 300 inmates incarcerated in Virginia. The department requested authorization to build an additional 1,500-bed facility.

Researching the Internet

For a different way of dealing with prison crowding, go to the North Carolina Sentencing and Policy Advisory Commission at http://www.nccourts.org. Search for the word *commission*.

The "War on Drugs"

Crusades against the use of drugs have recurred in American politics since the late 1800s. The latest manifestation began in 1982, when President Ronald Reagan declared another "war on drugs" and asked Congress to set aside more money for drug enforcement personnel and for prison space. This came at a time when the country faced the frightening advent of crack cocaine, which ravaged many communities and increased the murder rate. In 1987 Congress imposed stiff mandatory minimum sentences for federal drug law violations, and many states copied these sentencing laws. The war continued on through the Clinton administration, with each president urging Congress to appropriate billions more for an all-out law enforcement campaign against drugs.

The war on drugs succeeded on one front by packing the nation's prisons with drug law offenders, but many scholars believe that is about all it has achieved. With additional resources and pressures for enforcement, the number of people sentenced to prison for drug offenses has increased steadily. In 1980 only 19,000 or about 6 percent of state prisoners had been convicted of drug offenses; by 2000 the number had risen to 251,000. Today, 21 percent of state prisoners are incarcerated for drug offenses, and the percentage in federal prisons has reached almost 60 percent (BJS, 2001c:12). Furthermore, the average state drug sentence has increased from 13 months in 1985 to 47 months in 1998.

State Politics

It makes sense that incarceration rates vary among the regions and states, but why do states with similar characteristics differ in their use of prisons as well? Can it be that local political factors influence correctional policies?

One might think that each state would show a certain association between crime rates and incarceration rates—the more crime, the more prisoners. Even when states have similar socioeconomic and demographic characteristics—poverty, unemployment, racial composition, drug arrests—unaccountable variations among their incarceration rates exist. For example, North Dakota and South Dakota have similar social characteristics and crime rates, yet the incarceration rate in South Dakota has risen 477 percent since 1978, compared with a rise of 133 percent in its neighbor (BJS, 2000g: Table 6.27; 2001c:3). One can even find similar and contiguous states such as Connecticut and Massachusetts, Arizona and New Mexico, or Minnesota and Wisconsin, where the state with the *higher* crime rate has the *lower* incarceration rate.

Since the 1970s most politicians have felt that the public has demanded that they be "tough on crime." Governors and legislators have pushed for tougher sentences and greater use of incarceration as a way of reducing crime. Joseph Davey found that in seven states with "law-and-order" governors, there was a "rapid increase in the rate of imprisonment without regard to changes in the crime rate." In contiguous states where governors advocated less punitive policies, imprisonment rates did not increase (Davey, 1998:111).

It is difficult to point to one factor as the primary cause of the doubling of the incarceration rate during the past decade. Several plausible hypotheses exist. Given current public attitudes toward crime and punishment, fear of crime, and the expansion of prison space, incarceration rates will likely remain high (see "What Americans Think"). Perhaps only when the costs of this form of punishment have a greater impact on the pockets of taxpayers will attitudes and policies shift, with a greater emphasis being placed on alternatives to incarceration.

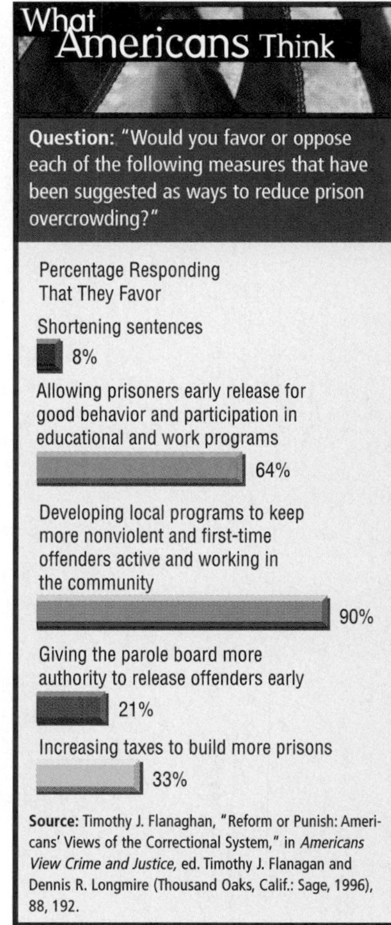

Source: Timothy J. Flanaghan, "Reform or Punish: Americans' Views of the Correctional System," in *Americans View Crime and Justice,* ed. Timothy J. Flanagan and Dennis R. Longmire (Thousand Oaks, Calif.: Sage, 1996), 88, 192.

12. What are four explanations for the great increase in the incarcerated population?
13. Why might additional construction only aggravate the problem?

Summary

- From colonial days to the present, the methods of criminal sanctions that are considered appropriate have varied.
- The development of the penitentiary brought a shift away from corporal punishment.
- The Pennsylvania and New York systems were competing approaches to implementing the ideas of the penitentiary.
- The Declaration of Principles of 1870 contained the key elements for the reformatory and rehabilitation models of corrections.
- Three principles guided female prison reform during the nineteenth century: (1) separation from male prisoners, (2) care specialized to women's needs, and (3) management by female staff.
- Although based on the social sciences, the rehabilitative model failed to reduce recidivism.
- The community model of corrections tried to increase opportunities for offenders to be successful citizens and provide psychological treatment.
- The crime control model emphasized incarceration, long and mandatory sentencing, and strict supervision.
- The administration of corrections in the United States is fragmented in that various levels of government are involved.

Go to the *American System of Criminal Justice* Web site at http://www.cj.wadsworth.com/colesmith10e to explore the topic of incarceration policy in further detail.

- The correctional responsibilities of the federal government are divided between the Federal Bureau of Prisons, of the U.S. Department of Justice, and the Administrative Office of the U.S. Courts.
- In all states the administration of prisons falls under the executive branch of state government.
- Private prisons may or may not become accepted as a way to address overcrowding.
- Jails, which are administered by local government, hold people awaiting trial and hold sentenced offenders.
- Jail administrators face several problems: (1) the perceived role of the jail in the local criminal justice system, (2) the inmate population, and (3) fiscal problems.
- Prison populations have more than doubled during the past decade; there has also been a great increase in facilities and staff to administer them.

Questions for Review

1 What were the major differences between the New York and Pennsylvania systems in the nineteenth century?

2 What are some of the pressures that administrators of local jails face?

3 What types of correctional programs does your state support? What government agencies run them?

4 Why are private prisons a corrections option that is attractive to some state legislators?

5 What explanations might be given for the increased use of incarceration during the past two decades?

Key Terms

community corrections (p. 417)
congregate system (p. 412)
contract labor system (p. 412)
corrections (p. 408)
crime control model of corrections (p. 417)
Enlightenment (p. 408)
jail (p. 424)
lease system (p. 413)
mark system (p. 414)
medical model (p. 416)
penitentiary (p. 410)
prison (p. 424)
reformatory (p. 414)
rehabilitation model (p. 416)
separate confinement (p. 411)
ticket-of-leave (p. 414)

For Further Reading

Clear, Todd R., and George F. Cole. 2003. *American Corrections.* 6th ed. Belmont, Calif.: Wadsworth. An overview of American corrections.

Davey, Joseph Dillion. 1998. *The Politics of Prison Expansion: Winning Elections by Waging War on Crime.* Westport, Conn.: Praeger. Examines increases in the crime rate and increases in the incarceration rate at the state level. Finds that political factors have influenced prison expansion since 1972.

Foucault, Michel. 1977. *Discipline and Punish.* Translated by Alan Sheridan. New York: Pantheon. Describes the transition of the focus of correctional punishment from the body of the offender to the reform of the individual.

Hallinan, Joseph T. 2001. *Going up the River: Travels in a Prison Nation.* New York: Random House. Exploration of America's biggest growth industry—its prisons.

Irwin, John, and James Austin. 2001. *It's About Time: America's Imprisonment Binge.* 3rd ed. Belmont, Calif.: Wadsworth. Argues that the "grand imprisonment experiment" that has dominated recent American crime reduction policy has failed miserably and should be abandoned.

Mauer, Marc, and Meda Chesney-Lind, eds. 2002. *Invisible Punishment: The Collateral Consequences of Mass Imprisonment.* New York: New Press. An outstanding collection of articles examining the impact of incarceration on individuals, families, and communities.

Rothman, David J. 1971. *The Discovery of the Asylum: Social Order and Disorder in the New Republic.* Boston: Little, Brown. Rothman notes that, before the nineteenth century, deviants were cared for in the community. Urbanization and industrialization brought this function to government institutions.

———. 1980. *Conscience and Convenience.* Boston: Little, Brown. Argues that conscience activated the Progressives to reform corrections, yet the new structures for rehabilitation operated for the convenience of administrators.

Going Online

For an up-to-date list of Web links, go to http://www.cj.wadsworth.com/colesmith10e

1. Write a short paper describing the organization, staffing, and facilities of the department of corrections in your state. You can access this information by using a search engine to find the Web site of your state's department of corrections.
2. Go to the Web site of the Bureau of Justice Statistics at http://www.ojp.usdoj.gov/bjs/. Click on "publications" and then access the bulletin, "Prisoners in 2001." How many prisoners were held in your state on December 31, 2001? What was the incarceration rate? Compare the numbers and rates of two adjacent states. Can you explain differences among the three states?
3. Go to InfoTrac College Edition, search for *prison reformers,* then read an article about Elizabeth Fry. What were conditions like in British prisons? What did Fry try to accomplish?

Checkpoint Answers

1. A period in the late eighteenth century when philosophers rethought the nature of society and the place of the individual in the world. New ideas about society and government arose from the Enlightenment.
2. Four principles: secure and sanitary building, systematic inspection, abolition of fees, and a reformatory regime.
3. The Pennsylvania system of separate confinement held inmates in isolation from one another. The New York congregate system kept inmates in their cells at night, but they worked together in shops during the day.
4. The Declaration of Principles advocated indeterminate sentences, rehabilitation programs, classifications based on improvements in character, and release on parole.
5. Separation of women prisoners from men, care in keeping with women's needs, women's prisons staffed by women.
6. Rehabilitation model: criminal behavior is the result of a biological, psychological, or social deficiency; clinicians should diagnose the problem and prescribe treatment; when cured, the offender may be released. Community model: the goal of corrections is to reintegrate the offender into the community, so rehabilitation should be carried out in the community rather than in prison if possible; correctional workers should serve as advocates for offenders in their dealings with government agencies. Crime control model: criminal behavior can be controlled by greater use of incarceration and other forms of strict supervision.
7. The Federal Bureau of Prisons, of the Department of Justice, and the Administrative Office of the U.S. Courts, which handles probation.
8. Prisons: department of corrections. Probation: judiciary or executive branch department. Intermediate sanctions: judiciary, probation department, department of corrections. Parole: executive agency.
9. In favor: costs are lower, yet conditions are the same or better than prisons run by the government. Opposed: incarceration should be a function of government, not an enterprise for private profit. Private interests can skew public policy.
10. Holding of offenders before trial and incarceration of offenders sentenced to short terms.
11. High population turnover, lack of services, scarce resources.
12. Increased arrests and more likely incarceration, tougher sentencing, prison construction, the war on drugs.
13. New prison beds will quickly become filled because judges will be less hesitant to sentence people to prison and because the correctional bureaucracy needs the space to be used.

CHAPTER 14

Probation, Intermediate Sanctions, and Parole

Spencer Grant/The Picture Cube

Todd Harrison raked his way across the littered lot as he and his coworkers moved about in the Bayside, Florida, recreation area. He wore the "uniform" provided by the probation department—an orange-colored hard hat and vest. He wore his own sunglasses and a T-shirt emblazoned "B.U.M." Harrison was one of ten probationers working under the watchful eye of Rich Clark, a community service supervisor employed by the nonprofit organization Upward Now, Inc. Two years before, Harrison had been sentenced to 3 years on probation and 100 hours of community service for a larceny conviction. Because Todd was 19 at the time and had no prior record, the judge had given him a community sentence instead of sending him to prison—the usual sentence for more experienced criminals convicted of the same offense. Harrison lives with his mother, works the late shift at a convenience store, reports to his probation officer monthly, and spends five hours every Saturday under the supervision of Clark to complete his community service. Things are looking up for Todd Harrison as he moves toward completion of his punishment.

Since the early nineteenth century, supervision in the community has been recognized as an appropriate punishment for some offenders. Probation was developed in the 1840s and **parole** followed in the 1870s. By the 1930s every state and the federal government used these forms of community corrections to either punish offenders without incarceration (probation) or to supervise offenders in the community after leaving prison (parole). Intermediate sanctions were developed in the 1980s when people saw the need for punishments that were less restrictive than prison but more restrictive than probation.

parole
The conditional release of an inmate from incarceration after part of the prison sentence has been served; the parolee remains under supervision for the remainder of the sentence.

In this chapter we examine the three elements of community corrections—probation, intermediate sanctions, and parole. Almost three-quarters of offenders under correctional supervision are not incarcerated, but are living in the community (see Figure 14.1).

Figure 14.1
Percentage of people in each category of correctional supervision
Although most people think of corrections as prisons and jails, in fact almost three-quarters of offenders are supervised within the community.

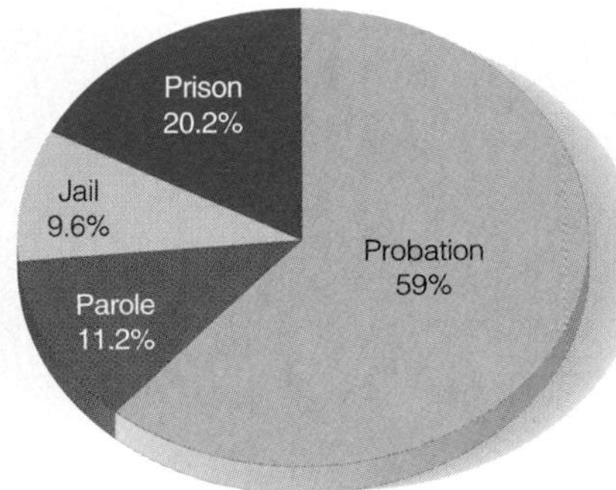

Source: Bureau of Justice Statistics, July 10, 2002 http://www.ojp.usdoj.gov/bjs/.

QUESTIONS for INQUIRY

- What philosophical assumptions underlie community corrections?
- How did probation evolve, and how are probation sentences implemented today?
- What are the types of intermediate sanctions, and how are they administered?
- What problems do parolees face in the community?
- Why has reentry become an important issue for community corrections?

Community Corrections: Assumptions

Community corrections seeks to keep offenders in the community by building ties to family, employment, and other normal sources of stability and success. This model of corrections assumes that the offender must change, but it also recognizes that factors within the community that might encourage criminal behavior (unemployment, for example) must also change.

Four factors are usually cited in support of community corrections:

1. Many offenders' criminal records and current offenses are not serious enough to warrant incarceration.
2. Community supervision is cheaper than incarceration.
3. Rates of **recidivism,** or returning to crime, for those under community supervision are no higher than for those who go to prison.
4. Ex-inmates require both support and supervision as they try to remake their lives in the community.

recidivism
A return to criminal behavior.

Community corrections is based on the goal of finding the "least restrictive alternative"—punishing the offender only as severely as needed to protect the community and to satisfy the public. Advocates call for programs to assist offenders in the community so they will have opportunities to succeed in law-abiding activities and to reduce their contact with the criminal world.

The American Probation and Parole Association is a national organization concerned with community corrections; visit them at http://www.appa-net.org.

check point

1. What are the four main assumptions underlying community corrections? (Answers are at the end of the chapter.)

Probation: Correction without Incarceration

As we have seen, probation is the conditional release of the offender into the community, under the supervision of correctional officials. Although probationers live at home and work at regular jobs, they must report regularly to their probation officers. They must also abide by certain conditions, such as submitting to drug tests, obeying curfews, and staying away from certain people or parts of town. Although probation is used mainly for lesser offenses, states are increasingly using probation for more serious felonies, as shown in Figure 14.2.

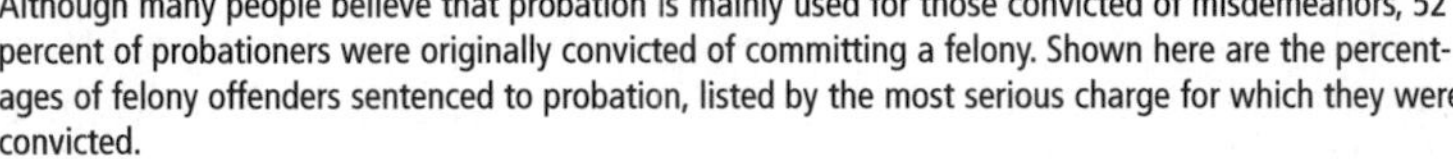

Figure 14.2 **Felony sentences to probation in state courts**
Although many people believe that probation is mainly used for those convicted of misdemeanors, 52 percent of probationers were originally convicted of committing a felony. Shown here are the percentages of felony offenders sentenced to probation, listed by the most serious charge for which they were convicted.

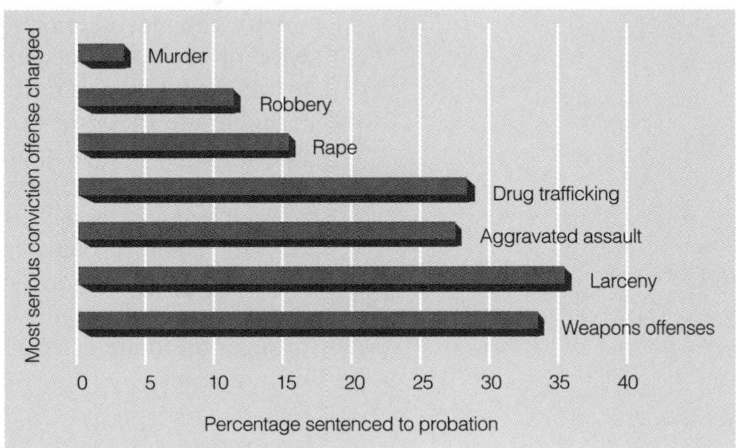

Source: Bureau of Justice Statistics, *Bulletin*, October 2001, p. 2.

Probation can be combined with other sanctions, such as fines, restitution, and community service. Fulfillment of these other sanctions may, in effect, become a condition for successful completion of probation. The sentencing court retains authority over the probationer, and if he or she violates the conditions or commits another crime, the judge can order the entire sentence to be served in prison.

The number of probationers now under supervision is at a record high and is still rising. Much has been written about overcrowded prisons, but the adult probation population has also been increasing—by about 3 percent a year, up 22 percent since 1990 (BJS, 2000f). Today, more than 3.8 million offenders are on probation, yet probation budgets in many states have been cut and caseloads increased as greater resources are diverted to prisons.

Although probation offers many benefits that cause it to be chosen over incarceration, the public often sees it as merely a "slap on the wrist" for offenders. With caseloads in some urban areas of as many as three hundred probationers, officers cannot provide the level of supervision necessary.

Origins and Evolution of Probation

The historical roots of probation lie in the procedures for reprieves and pardons of early English courts. Probation first developed in the United States when John Augustus, a Boston boot maker, persuaded a judge in the Boston Police Court in 1841 to give him custody of a convicted offender for a brief period and then helped the man to appear rehabilitated by the time of sentencing.

Massachusetts developed the first statewide probation system in 1880, and by 1920, 21 other states had followed suit. The federal courts were authorized to hire probation officers in 1925. By the beginning of World War II 44 states had probation systems.

Probation began as a humanitarian effort to allow first-time and minor offenders a second chance. Early probationers were expected not only to obey the law but also to behave in a morally acceptable fashion. Officers sought to provide moral leadership to help shape probationers' attitudes and behavior with respect to family, religion, employment, and free time.

By the 1920s the development of psychology led probation officers to shift their emphasis from moral leadership to therapeutic counseling. This shift brought three important changes. First, the officer no longer primarily acted as a community supervisor charged with enforcing a particular morality. Second, the officer became more of a clinical social worker whose goal was to help the offender solve psychological and social problems. Third, the offender was expected to become actively involved in the treatment. The pursuit of rehabilitation as the primary goal of probation gave the officer extensive discretion in defining and treating the offender's problems. Officers used their judgment to evaluate each offender and develop a treatment approach to the personal problems that presumably had led to crime.

During the 1960s a new shift occurred in probation. Rather than counseling offenders, probation officers provided them with concrete social services such as assistance with employment, housing, finances, and education. This emphasis on reintegrating offenders and remedying the social problems they faced was consistent with federal efforts to wage a "war on poverty." Instead of being a counselor or therapist, the probation officer served as an advocate, dealing with private and public institutions on the offender's behalf.

In the late 1970s the orientation of probation changed again as the goals of rehabilitation and reintegration gave way to "risk management." This approach, still dominant today, seeks to minimize the probability that an offender will commit a new offense. Risk management reflects two basic goals. First, in accord with the deserved-punishment ideal, the punishment should fit the offense, and correctional intervention should neither raise nor lower the level of punishment. Second, according to the community protection criterion, the amount and type of supervision are determined according to the risk that the probationer will return to crime.

check point

2. Who was John Augustus, and what did he do?
3. What is the main goal of probation today?

Organization of Probation

As a form of corrections, probation falls under the executive branch, and people usually see it as a concern of state government. However, in about 25 percent of the states, probation falls to county and local governments. Further, in many states it is administered locally by the judiciary. The state sets the standards and provides financial support and training courses, but about two-thirds of all people under probation supervision are handled by locally administered programs.

In many jurisdictions, although the state is formally responsible for all probation services, the locally elected county judges are in charge. This seemingly odd arrangement produces benefits as well as problems. On the positive side, having probationers under the supervision of the court permits judges to keep closer tabs on them and to order incarceration if the conditions of probation are violated. On the negative side, some judges know little about the goals and methods of corrections, and the probation responsibility adds to the administrative duties of already overworked courts.

Judicially enforced probation seems to work best when the judge and the supervising officer have a close relationship. Proponents of this system say that judges need to work with probation officers whom they can trust, whose presentence reports they can accurately evaluate, and on whom they can rely to report on the success or failure of individual cases.

For the sake of their clients and the goals of the system, probation officers need direct access to corrections and other human services agencies. However, these agencies are located within the executive branch of government. Several states have combined probation and parole services in the same agency to coordinate resources and services better. Others point out, however, that probationers differ from parolees. Parolees already have served prison terms, frequently have been involved in more serious crimes, and often have been disconnected from mainstream society. By contrast, most probationers have not developed

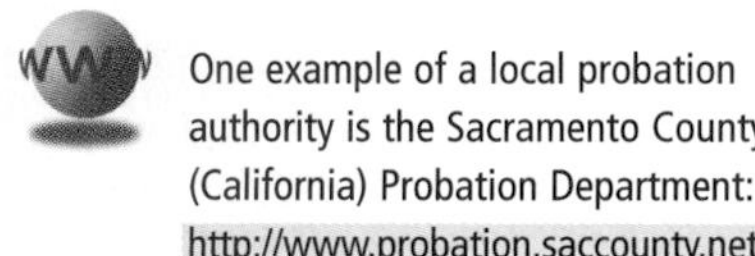

One example of a local probation authority is the Sacramento County (California) Probation Department: http://www.probation.saccounty.net/.

criminal lifestyles to the same degree and do not have the same problems of reintegration into the community.

Probation Services

Probation officers play roles similar to both the police and social workers. In addition to assisting the judiciary with presentence investigations (see Chapter 12), probation officers supervise clients to keep them out of trouble and enforce the conditions of the sentence. This law enforcement role involves discretionary decisions about whether to report violations of probation conditions. Probation officers are also expected to play a social worker role by helping clients obtain the housing, employment, and treatment services they need. The potential conflict between the roles is great. Not surprisingly, individual officers sometimes emphasize one role over the other.

For a look at one probation organization's approach to adult field services, see http://www.probation.saccounty.net/. When you reach the home page, type "adult field services" in the search function.

A continuing issue for probation officers is the size of their caseloads. How many clients can one officer effectively handle? In the 1930s the National Probation Association recommended a 50-unit caseload, and in 1967 the President's Commission on Law Enforcement and Administration of Justice reduced it to 35. However, today the national average for adult supervision is about 150, but some urban caseloads exceed 300 (Petersilia, 1998). The oversized caseload is usually cited as one of the main obstacles to successful probation. Research indicates, however, that the caseload size is less significant than the quality of the services and supervision (Petersilia and Turner, 1993).

During the past decade, probation officials have developed methods of classifying clients according to their service needs, the element of risk they pose to the community, and the chance that they will commit another offense. Risk classification fits the deserved-punishment model of the criminal sanction in that the most serious cases receive the greatest restrictions and supervision. If probationers live according to the conditions of their sentence, the level of supervision is gradually reduced.

Several factors affect how much supervision serious cases actually receive. Consider the "war on drugs." It has significantly increased probation levels in urban areas because large numbers of people convicted of drug sales or possession are placed on probation. Many of these offenders have committed violent acts and live in inner-city areas marked by drug dealing and turf battles to control drug markets. Under these conditions, direct supervision can be dangerous for the probation officer. In some urban areas, probationers are merely required to telephone or mail reports of their current residence and employment. In such cases, it is hard to see how any goal of the sanctions—deserved punishment, rehabilitation, deterrence, or incapacitation—is being realized. If none is of these objectives is being met, the offender is "getting off."

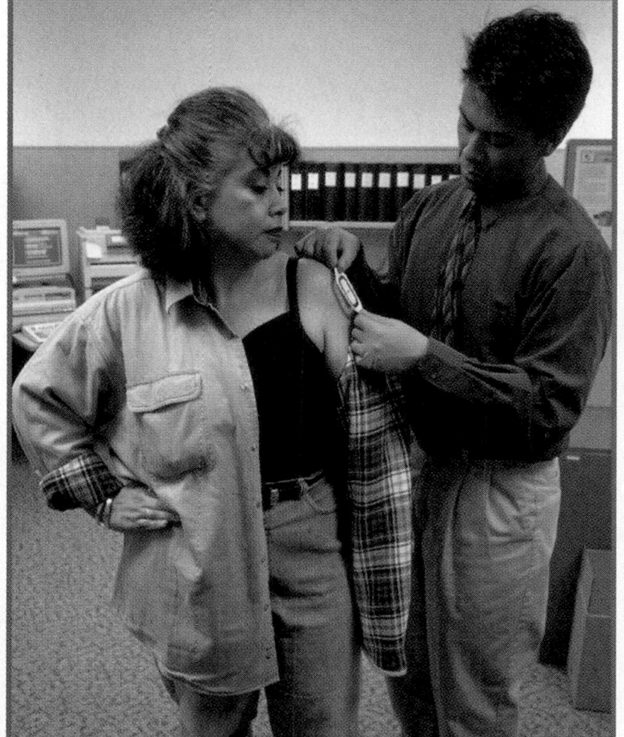

Spencer Grant/PhotoEdit

Frequent drug testing is a condition of probation for many offenders. Administering these tests has become part of the officer's supervisory role.

4. What are the major tasks of probation officers?

Revocation and Termination of Probation

Probation ends in one of two ways: (1) the person successfully completes the period of probation, or (2) the probationary status is revoked because of misbehavior. In 1998 a national survey of probationers found that 59 percent of adults

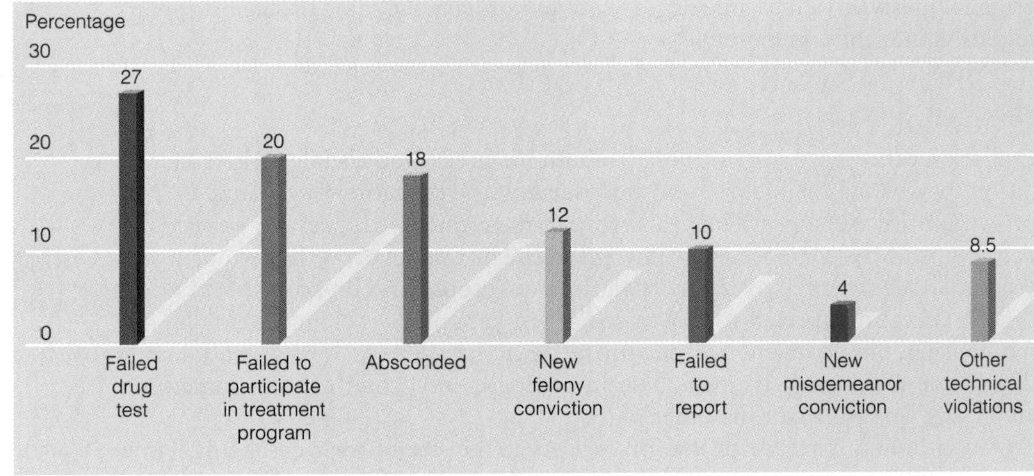

Figure 14.3
Motions for revocation of probation
Revocation can result in the imposition of incarceration or new, more stringent, probation conditions.

Source: Peter Burke, *Policy-Driven Responses to Probation and Parole Violations* (Washington, D.C.: National Institute of Corrections, 1997), 12.

released from probation successfully completed their sentences, while only 17 percent had been reincarcerated (BJS, 1999b). Revocation of probation can occur for either a **technical violation** or a new arrest.

technical violation
The probationer's failure to abide by the rules and conditions of probation (specified by the judge), resulting in revocation of probation.

Technical violations occur when a probationer fails to meet the conditions of a sentence by, for instance, violating curfew, failing a drug test, or using alcohol. Officers have discretion as to whether or not they bring this fact to the attention of the judge. Figure 14.3 presents the reasons presented to the court for revocation of probation.

Probation officers and judges have widely varying notions of what constitutes grounds for revoking probation (see "A Question of Ethics"). Once the officer calls a violation to the attention of the court, the probationer may be arrested or summoned for a revocation hearing. Because of the contemporary emphasis is on avoiding incarceration except for flagrant and continual violation of the conditions of probation, most revocations today occur because of a new arrest or conviction.

As you look over the Recommendation for Revocation Report sent to you by Officer Sawyer, you are struck by the low-level technical violations used to justify sending James Ferguson, a minor drug offender, to prison. Sawyer cites Ferguson's failure to attend all the drug treatment sessions, to complete his community service, to pay a $500 fine. You call Sawyer in to discuss the report.

"Bill, I've looked over your report on Ferguson and I'm wondering what's going on here. Why isn't he fulfilling the conditions of his probation?"

"I'm really not sure, but it seems he just doesn't want to meet the conditions. I think he's got a bad attitude, and I don't like the guys he hangs around with. He's always mouthing off about the 'system' and says I'm on his case for no reason."

"Well, let's look at your report. You say that he works for Capital Services cleaning offices downtown from midnight till 8 A.M. yet has to go to the drug programs three mornings a week and put in ten hours a week at the Salvation Army Thrift Store. Is it that he isn't trying or does he have an impossible situation?"

"I think he could do it if he tried, but also, I think he's selling cocaine again. Perhaps he needs to get a taste of prison."

"That may be true, but do you really want to revoke his probation?"

→ What's going on here? Is Sawyer recommending revocation because of Ferguson's attitude and the suspicion that he is selling drugs again? Do the technical violations warrant prison?

In 1967 the U.S. Supreme Court gave its first opinion concerning the due process rights of probationers at a revocation hearing. In ***Mempa v. Rhay* (1967)**, the justices determined that a state probationer had a right to counsel at a combined revocation-sentencing hearing, but the Court did not refer to any requirement for a hearing. This issue was addressed in ***Gagnon v. Scarpelli* (1973)**, in which the justices ruled that before probation or parole can be revoked, the offender is entitled to a preliminary and a final hearing and to specific elements of due process. The approved practice is to handle the revocation in three stages:

1. *Preliminary hearing* (sometimes waived): The facts of the arrest are reviewed to determine if there is probable cause that a violation has occurred.
2. *Hearing:* The facts of the allegation are heard and decided. The probation department presents the evidence to support the allegation, and the probationer has an opportunity to refute the evidence. The probationer has the right to see written notice of the charges, to testify, to present witnesses, to cross-examine witnesses, to be heard by a neutral

officers, and to review a written statement of findings. Unless the case raises complicated issues, the probationer has no automatic right to counsel for proceedings focused on whether violations occurred that justify revoking probation.

3. *Sentencing:* A right to counsel exists in combined revocation-sentencing proceedings for cases in which no suspended sentence of incarceration had been established at the original sentencing. After any revocation, the judge decides whether to impose a term of incarceration and, if not previously determined, the duration of the term. This stage is more than a technicality, because after a minor violation, probation is often reinstated with greater restrictions.

Mempa v. Rhay (1967)
Probationers have the right to counsel at a combined revocation-sentencing hearing.

Gagnon v. Scarpelli (1973)
Before probation can be revoked, a two-stage hearing must be held and the offender provided with specific elements of due process.

For those who successfully complete probation, the sentence ends. Ordinarily the probationer is then a free citizen again, without obligation to the court or to the probation department.

check point

5. What are the grounds for probation revocation?
6. What rights does a probationer have while revocation is being considered?

Assessing Probation

Probation is at a crossroads. Some critics see probation as nothing more than a slap on the wrist, an absence of punishment. Yet the importance of probation for public safety has never been greater: In one sample of large urban counties, 17 percent of people arrested for a felony were on probation. (Reaves and Smith, 1995). Nationally, three out of five felony probationers see their officer no more than once a month at best. Joan Petersilia (1996) found that 60 percent of all Los Angeles probationers are tracked solely by computer and have no contact with officers. While probation suffers from poor credibility in the public's eyes, its workload is growing dramatically and, in view of the crowding of prisons and jails, will probably continue to do so.

Go to the Public Policy feature on the American System of Criminal Justice CD to learn more about the issues surrounding the expanded use of probation.

Although the recidivism rate for probationers is lower than the rate for those who have been incarcerated, researchers question whether this is a direct result of supervision or an indirect result of the maturing of the offenders. Most offenders placed on probation do not become career criminals, their criminal activity is short-lived, and they become stable citizens as they obtain jobs and get married. Most of those who are arrested a second time do not repeat their mistake again.

What rallies support for probation is its relatively low cost: Keeping an offender on probation instead of behind bars costs roughly $1,000 a year, a savings of more than $20,000 a year (Abadinsky, 1997). However, these savings might not satisfy community members who hear of a sex offender on probation who repeats his crime.

In recent years as prisons have become overcrowded, increasing numbers of felony offenders have been placed on probation. Of all convicted felons, 46 percent receive probation (Petersilia, 1996:21). More than 75 percent of probationers are addicted to drugs or alcohol. These factors present new challenges for probation, because officers can no longer assume that their clients pose little threat to society and that they have the skills to lead productive lives in the community.

AP/Wide World Photos, Inc.

Scott Weiland, lead singer for the Stone Temple Pilots, pleaded guilty to a New York misdemeanor drug charge in exchange for probation and staying out of trouble for a year. Unfortunately, Weiland lasted less than six months and was jailed in California for illegal drug use. Was probation appropriate for a person such as Weiland?

To offer a viable alternative to incarceration, probation services need the resources to supervise and assist their clients appropriately. The new demands on probation have brought calls for increased electronic monitoring and for risk-management systems that provide different levels of supervision for different kinds of offenders.

Intermediate Sanctions in the Community

Dissatisfaction with the traditional means of probation supervision, coupled with the crowding and high cost of prisons, has resulted in a call for intermediate sanctions. These are sanctions that restrict the offender more than does simple probation and that constitute actual punishment for more serious offenders.

The case for intermediate sanctions can be made on several grounds, but Norval Morris and Michael Tonry said it this way: "Prison is used excessively; probation is used even more excessively; between the two is a near vacuum of purposive and enforced punishments" (1990:3). Forty-six percent of convicted felons are given prison, the severest sentence, while 47 percent receive probation, the least severe. Hence more than 90 percent of all convicted felons receive either the severest or the most lenient of possible penalties (Langan, 1994:791). Morris and Tonry urge that punishments be created that are more restrictive than probation yet match the severity of the offense and the characteristics of the offender, and that can be carried out while still protecting the community.

The Community Corrections Association of Pennsylvania provides information about the state's programs: http://www.c-cap.org/choice.html.

We can view intermediate sanctions as a continuum—a range of punishments that vary in levels of intrusiveness and control, as shown in Figure 14.4. Probation plus a fine or community service may be appropriate for minor offenses, while 6 weeks of boot camp followed by intensive probation supervision might be right for serious crimes. But some question whether offenders will be able to fulfill the conditions added to probation. Moreover, if prisons are overcrowded, is incarceration a believable threat if offenders fail to comply?

Across the country, corrections employs many types of intermediate sanctions. They can be divided into (1) those administered primarily by the judiciary (fines, restitution, and forfeiture), (2) those primarily administered in the community with a supervision component (home confinement, community service, day reporting centers, and intensive probation supervision), and (3) those that are administered inside institutions and followed by community supervision (boot camp). Furthermore, sanctions may be imposed in combination—for example, a fine and probation, or boot camp with community service and probation.

check point

7. What is the main argument for intermediate sanctions?
8. What is meant by a continuum of sanctions?

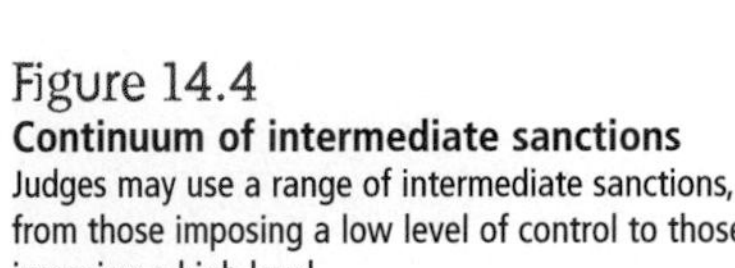

Figure 14.4
Continuum of intermediate sanctions
Judges may use a range of intermediate sanctions, from those imposing a low level of control to those imposing a high level.

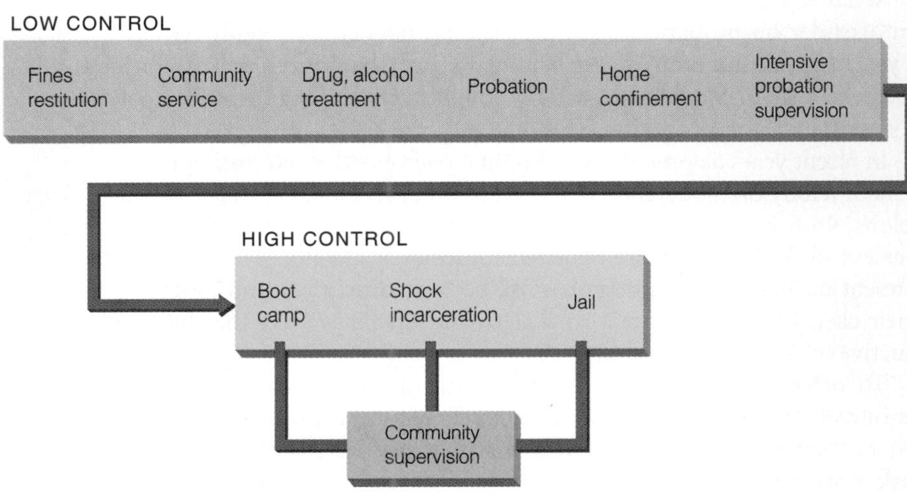

Intermediate Sanctions Administered Primarily by the Judiciary

The judiciary administers many kinds of intermediate sanctions. Here we discuss three of them—fines, restitution, and forfeiture. Because all three involve the transfer of money or property from the offender to the government or crime victim, the judiciary is considered the proper body not only to impose the sanction but also to collect what is due.

Fines

Fines are routinely imposed for offenses ranging from traffic violations to felonies. Studies have shown that the fine is used widely as a criminal sanction and that nationally well over $1 billion in fines have been collected annually (Hillsman, Sichel, and Mahoney, 1983). Yet, judges in the United States make little use of fines as the *sole* punishment for crimes more serious than motor vehicle violations. Instead, fines typically are used in conjunction with other sanctions, such as probation and incarceration; for example, 2 years of probation and a $500 fine.

fine
A sum of money to be paid to the state by a convicted person as punishment for an offense.

Many judges cite the difficulty of collecting fines as the reason that they do not make greater use of this punishment. They note that offenders tend to be poor, and many judges fear that fines will be paid from the proceeds of additional illegal acts. Other judges are concerned that relying on fines as an alternative to incarceration will let affluent offenders "buy" their way out of jail while forcing the poor to serve time.

Fines are used extensively in Europe, are enforced, and are normally the sole sanction for a wide range of crimes. In Germany, 81 percent of all sentenced offenders must pay a fine, including 73 percent of those convicted of crimes of violence. In Sweden, fines are used in 91 percent of cases; in England, 47 percent of indictable offenses (roughly equivalent to an American felony) (Tonry 1998a:698). To deal with the concern that fines exact a heavier toll on the poor than on the wealthy, Sweden and Germany have developed the day fine, which bases the penalty on offender's income. (See the Comparative Perspective.) The day fine has been tested in Arizona, Connecticut, Iowa, New York, and Washington.

Restitution

Restitution is repayment by an offender to a victim who has suffered some form of financial loss from the crime. It is *reparative* in that it seeks to repair the harm done. In the Middle Ages, restitution was a common way to settle a criminal case (Karmen, 2001:305). The offender was ordered to pay the victim or do the victim's work. The growth of the modern state saw the decline of such punishments based on "private" arrangements between offender and victim. Instead, the state prosecuted offenders, and punishments focused on the wrong the offender had done to society.

restitution
Repayment—in the form of money or service—by an offender to a victim who has suffered some loss from the offense.

Victim restitution has remained a part of the U.S. criminal justice system, though it is largely unpublicized. In many instances, restitution derives from informal agreements between the police and offenders at the station, during plea bargaining, or in the prosecutor's sentence recommendation. Only since the late 1970s has restitution been institutionalized, usually as one of the conditions of probation.

As with fines, convicted offenders differ in their ability to pay restitution, and the conditions inevitably fall more harshly on less affluent offenders who cannot easily pay. Someone who has the "good fortune" to be victimized by an affluent criminal might receive full compensation, while someone victimized by a poor offender might never receive a penny.

Restitution is more easily imposed when the "damage" inflicted can be easily measured—value of property destroyed or stolen, or medical costs, for instance. But what should be the restitution for the terror of an attempted rape?

Day Fines in Germany: Could the Concept Work in the United States?

Monetary sanctions are used extensively in Europe in part because of the existence of the day-fine system. Under this system the amount of the fine is related not only to the seriousness of the crime but also to the offender's income. Could a day-fine system work in the United States?

Modern implementation of fines related to the income of the offender began with creation of the day-fine system in Finland in 1921, followed by its development in Sweden (1931) and Denmark (1939). The Federal Republic of Germany instituted day fines in 1975. Since then, the way offenders are punished has greatly changed, so that now more than 80 percent of those convicted receive a fine-alone sentence.

Judges determine the amount of the day fine through a two-stage process. First, judges relate the crime to offense guidelines, which state the minimum and maximum number of day-fine units for each offense. For example, theft may be punished by a day fine of 10–50 units. Judges choose the number of units by considering the culpability of the offender and by examining the offender's motivation and the circumstances surrounding the crime. Second, the value of these units is determined. The German day fine is calculated as the cost of a day of freedom: the amount of income an offender would have forfeited if incarcerated for a day. One day-fine unit is equal to the offender's average net daily income (considering salary, pensions, welfare benefits, interest, and so on), without deductions for family maintenance, so long as the offender and the offender's dependents have a minimal standard of living. Finally, the law calls for publication of the number of units and their value for each day fine set by the court so that the sentencing judgment is publicly known.

For example, say a judge is faced with two defendants who have separately been convicted of theft. One defendant is a truck driver who earns an average of 100 Euros per day and the other is a business manager whose earnings average 300 Euros per day. The judge uses the guidelines and decides that the circumstances of the theft and the criminal record of each offender are the same. The judge decides that 40 day-fine units should be assessed to each. By multiplying these units by the average daily income for each, the truck driver's fine is 4,000 Euros and the manager's fine is 12,000 Euros.

Since the day-fine system was introduced in Germany, there has been an increase in the use of fines and a decrease in short-term incarceration. The size of fines has also increased, reflecting the fact that affluent offenders are now being punished at levels corresponding to their financial worth. Likewise, fines for poor offenders have remained relatively low. These results have been accomplished without an increase in the default rate.

Some Americans believe that day fines would be more equitable than the current system of low fines for all, regardless of wealth. Others believe that to levy higher fines against rich people than poor people is unjust because the wealthy person is being penalized for working hard for a high income. What do you think?

Forfeiture

With passage of two laws in 1970—the Racketeer Influenced and Corrupt Organizations Act (RICO) and the Continuing Criminal Enterprise Act (CCE)—Congress resurrected forfeiture, a criminal sanction that had lain dormant since the American Revolution. Through amendments in 1984 and 1986, Congress improved ways to implement the law. Similar laws are now found in most states, particularly to deal with trafficking in controlled substances and with organized crime.

Forfeiture is government seizure of property and other assets derived from or used in criminal activity. Assets seized by federal and state agencies through forfeiture can be quite considerable. For example, the Drug Enforcement Administration alone annually seizes assets (including cash, real estate, vehicles, vessels, and airplanes) valued at more than a half billion dollars (BJS, 1999e:378).

Forfeiture is controversial. Critics argue that confiscating property without a court hearing violates citizens' constitutional rights. Concerns have also been raised about the excessive use of this sanction, because forfeited assets often go into the budget of the law enforcement agency taking the action (Blumenson and Nilsen, 1998).

In a 1993 opinion, the Supreme Court ruled that the Eighth Amendment's ban on excessive fines requires that the seriousness of the offense be related to the property that is taken (*Austin v. United States*). The ruling places limits on the government's ability to seize property and invites the judiciary to monitor the government's forfeiture activities when convicted offenders challenge them.

Critics argue that ownership of the seized property is often unclear. For example, in Hartford, Connecticut, a woman's home was seized because her grandson, unbeknownst to her, was using it as a base for selling drugs. Under a new law passed by Congress, owners' property cannot be seized if they can demonstrate their innocence by a preponderance of evidence (*Lansing State Journal*, April 14, 2000:6A).

check point

9. Distinguish between fines, restitution, and forfeiture.
10. What are some of the problems of implementing these sanctions?

Intermediate Sanctions Administered in the Community

One basic argument for intermediate sanctions is that probation, as traditionally practiced, is inadequate for the large numbers of offenders whom probation officers must supervise today. Probation leaders have responded to this criticism by developing new intermediate sanction programs and expanding old ones. Four of these are: home confinement, community service, day reporting centers, and intensive supervision probation.

Home Confinement

With technological innovations that provide for electronic monitoring, **home confinement**, in which offenders must remain at home during specific periods, has gained attention. Offenders under home confinement (often called "house arrest") may face other restrictions such as the usual probation rules against alcohol and drugs as well as strictly monitored curfews and check-in times.

home confinement
A sentence requiring the offender to remain inside his or her home during specified periods.

Private companies provide electronic monitoring equipment and services. Visit one at http://www.compuguard.com.

Some offenders are allowed to go to a place of employment, education, or treatment during the day but must return to their homes by a specified hour. Those supervising home confinement may telephone offenders' homes at various times of the day or night to speak personally with offenders to make sure they are complying.

Home confinement offers a great deal of flexibility. It can be used as a sole sanction or in combination with other penalties. It can be imposed at almost any point in the criminal justice process: during the pretrial period, after a short term in jail or prison, or as a condition of probation or parole. In addition, home confinement relieves the government of the responsibility to provide the offender with food, clothing, and housing, as it must do in prisons. Home confinement programs have grown and proliferated.

The development of electronic monitoring equipment has made home confinement an enforceable sentencing option. The number of offenders currently being monitored is difficult to estimate, because the equipment manufacturers consider this privileged information. However, the best estimates are that about 17 different companies provide electronic monitoring of nearly 100,000 offenders (Conway, 2001:7–9).

Two basic types of electronic monitoring devices exist. Passive monitors respond only to inquiries; most commonly, the offender receives an automated telephone call from the probation office and is told to place the device on a receiver attached to the phone. Active devices send continuous signals that a receiver picks up; a computer notes any break in the signal.

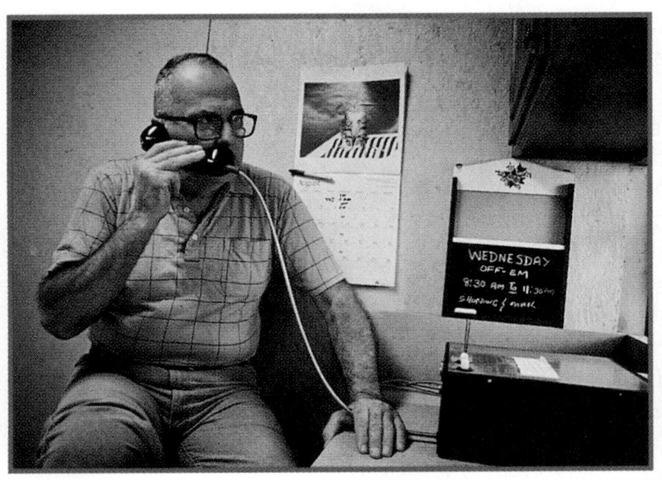

Jack Kurtz/Impact Visuals

Larry Ingles, given a one-year sentence of home confinement for driving while intoxicated (DWI), answers his electronic monitoring call. Failure to answer the telephone within three minutes can result in revocation of probation.

Despite favorable publicity, certain legal, technical, and correctional issues must be addressed before home confinement with electronic monitoring can become a standard punishment. First, some criminal justice scholars question its constitutionality. Monitoring may violate the Fourth Amendment's protection against unreasonable searches and seizures. The issue is a clash between the constitutionally protected reasonable expectation of privacy and the invasion of one's home by surveillance devices. Second, technical problems with the monitoring devices are still extensive, often giving erroneous reports that the offender is home. Third, offender failure rates may prove to be high. Being one's own warden is difficult, and visits by former criminal associates and other enticements may become problematic for many offenders (Renzema, 1992:41). Some observers believe that four months of full-time monitoring is about the limit before a violation will occur (Clear and Braga, 1995:435). Furthermore, some crimes—such as child abuse, drug sales, and assaults—can be committed while the offender is at home.

Variations in the use of electronic monitoring may alleviate some of these problems. For instance, after a time some offenders might be allowed to go to work or simply to leave home for restricted periods of the day; others might be allowed to maintain employment for their entire sentence. Whatever the details, such monitoring centers on using the offender's residence as the place of punishment.

Community Service

community service
A sentence requiring the offender to perform a certain amount of unpaid labor in the community.

A **community service** sentence requires the offender to perform a certain amount of unpaid labor in the community. Community service can take a variety of forms, including assisting in social service agencies, cleaning parks and roadsides, or helping the poor. The sentence specifies the number of hours to be worked and usually requires supervision by a probation officer. Community service can be tailored to the skills and abilities of offenders. For example, less educated offenders might pick up litter along the highway, while those with schooling might teach reading in evening literacy classes. Many judges order community service when an offender cannot pay a fine. The offender's effort to make reparation to the community offended by the crime also serves a symbolic function.

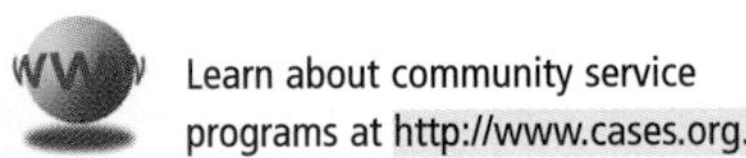

Learn about community service programs at http://www.cases.org.

Although community service has many supporters, some labor unions and workers criticize it for possibly taking jobs away from law-abiding citizens. In addition, some experts believe that if community service is the only sanction, it may be too mild a punishment, especially for upper-class and white-collar criminals.

Day Reporting Centers

day reporting center
A community correctional center where an offender reports each day to comply with elements of a sentence.

Another intermediate sanction option is the **day reporting center**—a community correctional center to which the offender must report each day to carry out elements of the sentence. Designed to ensure that probationers follow the employment and treatment stipulations attached to their sentence, day reporting centers also increase the likelihood that offenders and the general public will consider probation supervision to be credible.

Most day reporting centers incorporate multiple correctional methods. For example, in some centers offenders must be in the facility for eight hours or to report for drug urine checks before going to work. Centers that have a rehabilitation component carry out drug and alcohol treatment, literacy programs, and job searches. Others "provide contact levels equal to or greater than intensive supervision programs, in effect, creating a community equivalent to confinement" (Diggs and Peiper, 1994).

Most of these programs have not yet been formally evaluated. One study of New York City's program found that its stiff eligibility requirements resulted in few cases entering the center. In Connecticut, however, more than six thousand offenders report daily to such centers (Parent, 1990). A study of six day reporting centers in Massachusetts found that about 80 percent of offenders successfully completed the program (McDivitt and Miliano, 1992:160). In determining success with regard to recidivism, examining who is being treated is important. If such centers are used only for selected offenders with a low risk of returning to crime, knowing whether the centers themselves are effective will be difficult.

check point

11. How effective is home confinement? What are some of the problems of this type of sanction?
12. What goes on at a day reporting center?

Intensive Supervision Probation (ISP)

Intensive supervision probation (ISP) is a means of dealing with offenders who need greater restrictions than traditional community-based programs can provide. Jurisdictions in every state have programs to intensively supervise such offenders. ISP uses probation as an intermediate form of punishment by imposing conditions of strict reporting to a probation officer who has a limited caseload. ISP programs are of two general types: probation diversion and institutional diversion.

intensive supervision probation (ISP)
Probation granted under conditions of strict reporting to a probation officer with a limited caseload.

Probation diversion puts offenders under intensive surveillance who are thought to be too risky for routine supervision. Institutional diversion selects low-risk offenders sentenced to prison and provides supervision for them in the community (Clear and Braga, 1995:429). Daily contact between the probationer and the probation officer may cut rearrest rates. Such contact also gives the probationer greater access to the resources the officer can provide, such as treatment services in the community. Offenders have incentives to obey rules, knowing that they must meet with their probation officers daily and in some cases must speak with them even more frequently. Additional restrictions—electronic monitoring, alcohol and drug testing, community service, and restitution—often are imposed on offenders as well.

ISP programs have been called "old-style" probation because each officer has only 20 clients and requires frequent face-to-face contact. Nonetheless, some people question how much of a difference constant surveillance can make to probationers with numerous problems. Such offenders frequently need help to get a job, counseling to deal with emotional and family situations, and a variety of supports to avoid drug or alcohol problems that may have contributed to their criminality. Yet ISP may be a way of getting the large number of felons who are drug addicted into treatment (Gendreau, Cullen, and Bonta, 1994).

ISP has become popular among probation administrators, judges, and prosecutors because it presents a "tough" image of community supervision and addresses the problem of prison crowding. Most ISP programs require a specific number of monthly contacts with officers, performance of community service, curfews, drug and alcohol testing, and referral to appropriate job-training, education, or treatment programs.

Observers have warned that ISP is not a "cure" for the rising costs and other problems facing corrections systems. Ironically, ISP can also increase the number of probationers sent to prison. All evaluations of ISP find that, probably because of the closer contact with clients, probation officers uncover more violations of rules than they do in regular probation. Therefore, ISP programs often have higher failure rates than do regular probation, even though their clients produce fewer arrests (Tonry and Lynch, 1996:116).

Another surprising finding is that when given the option of serving prison terms or participating in ISP, many offenders have chosen prison. In New Jersey,

15 percent of offenders withdrew their applications for ISP once they learned the conditions and requirements. Similarly, when offenders in Marion County, Oregon, were asked if they would participate in ISP, one-third chose prison instead (Petersilia, 1990:24). Apparently some offenders would rather spend a short time in prison, where conditions differ little from their accustomed life, than a longer period under demanding conditions in the community. To these offenders, ISP does not represent freedom, because it is so intrusive and the risk of revocation seems high.

Despite problems and continuing questions about its effectiveness, ISP has rejuvenated probation. Some of the most effective offender supervision has been carried out by these programs (Clear and Hardyman, 1990:42). As with regular probation, the size of a probation officer's caseload, within reasonable limits, is often less important for preventing recidivism than is the quality of supervision and assistance provided to probationers. If ISP is properly implemented, it may improve the quality of supervision and services that foster success for more kinds of offenders.

check point

13. How does intensive supervision probation differ from traditional probation?

Intermediate Sanctions Administered in Institutions and the Community

boot camp
A short-term institutional sentence, usually followed by probation, that puts the offender through a physical regimen designed to develop discipline and respect for authority. Also referred to as *shock incarceration.*

Among the most publicized intermediate sanctions are the **boot camps** operated by 36 states and the Federal Bureau of Prisons. Often referred to as *shock incarceration,* these programs vary, but all are based on the belief that young offenders (usually 14- to 21-year-olds) can be "shocked" out of their criminal ways. Boot camps put offenders through a 30-to-90-day physical regimen designed to develop discipline and respect for authority. Like the Marine Corps, most programs emphasize a spit-and-polish environment and keep the offenders in a disciplined and demanding routine that seeks ultimately to build self-esteem. Most camps also include education, job-training programs, and other rehabilitation services. On successful completion of the program, offenders are released to the community. At this point probation officers take over, and the conditions of the sentence are imposed.

Joseph Rodriguez/Black Star

Military-type drilling is part of the regimen at most boot camps such as this Federal Intensive Confinement Center for Women in Bryan, Texas. Evaluations of boot camps have reduced the initial optimism about this approach.

Evaluations of boot camp programs have reduced the initial optimism about such approaches (Tonry, 1996:108–14). Critics suggest that the emphasis on physical training ignores young offenders' real problems. Some point out that, like the military, boot camp builds esprit de corps and solidarity, characteristics that can improve the leadership qualities of the young offender and therefore enhance a criminal career. In fact, follow-up studies of boot camp graduates show they do no better after release from the program than do other offenders (MacKenzie, 1995). It has also been found that, like intensive supervision probation, boot camps do not automatically reduce prison crowding (MacKenzie and Piquero, 1994).

Some correctional practitioners now recognize that boot camps have not achieved their goals. The director of the Arizona Department of Corrections asked the legislature to eliminate the program, arguing that with an 85 percent failure rate it was neither cost-effective nor successful in reducing recidivism (Petersen

After Boot Camp, a Harder Discipline

Nelson Colon misses waking up to the blast of reveille. He sometimes yearns for those 16-hour days filled with military drills and 9-mile runs. He even thinks fondly of the surly drill instructors who shouted in his face.

During his four months at New Jersey's boot camp, Mr. Colon adapted to the rigors of military life with little difficulty. He says it was a lot easier than what he faces now. He is back in his old neighborhood, trying to stay away from old friends and old ways.

So far, Colon, at age 18, has managed to stay out of trouble since he graduated with the camp's first class of 20 cadets in June. Yet each day, he said, he fears he will be pulled back onto the corner, only two blocks away, where he was first arrested for selling drugs at age 15.

A 10 P.M. curfew helps keep Colon off the streets. His parole officer checks in with him almost daily, sometimes stopping by at 11 to make sure he is inside. He is enrolling in night classes to help him earn his high school equivalency certificate, and he plans on attending Narcotics Anonymous meetings.

His biggest problems are the same ones that tens of thousands of Camden residents confront daily. Camden's unemployment rate exceeds 20 percent. There are few jobs in this troubled city, particularly for young men who have dropped out of high school. Colon has found work as a stock clerk in a sneaker store, but it is miles away at a shopping center on a busy highway, and he has no transportation there.

Selling drugs paid a lot more than stacking shoe boxes, and it did not require commuting. Mr. Colon says he pushes those thoughts of easy money out of his head and tries to remember what the boot camp's drill instructors told him over and over again.

"They used to tell us, 'It's up to you.' You have to have self-accountability. You have to be reliable for your own actions, not because some person wanted you to do it. They taught us not to follow, to lead. That was one of the most important things."

Mr. Colon said his immediate goal was to find a job that he could get to more easily, and then save enough to get as far away from Camden as possible. "I want to get out of here," he said.

"The people's mentality here is real petty. Life isn't nothing to them. The other night, they killed one of the guys I grew up with. They shot him a couple of times. My old friends came around and knocked on my door at one o'clock in the morning to tell me." He said it was his eighth childhood friend to die.

Source: Adapted from *New York Times,* September 3, 1995, p. B1.

Researching the Internet

For more on boot camps, use InfoTrac College Edition to access the article by Claire Souryal and Doris Layton MacKenzie, "Shock Therapy: Can boot camps provide effective drug treatment?" *Corrections Today,* February 1994.

and Palumbo, 1997:85). California, Colorado, and North Dakota have closed their camps. Georgia, one of the first states to implement boot camps, is phasing out its program, while Florida is scaling back its program as well.

Defenders of boot camps argue that the camps are accomplishing their goals; the failure lies in the lack of educational and employment opportunities in the participants' inner-city communities (see the Close Up box). A national study found that few boot camp graduates received any aftercare assistance on returning to their communities (Bourque, Han, and Hill, 1996). Because boot camps have been popular with the public, which imagines that strict discipline and harsh conditions will instill positive attitudes in young offenders, such camps are likely to continue operating whether or not they are more effective than probation or prison. Some criminal justice experts believe the entire boot camp experiment has been a cynical political maneuver. As Franklin Zimring has said, "Boot camps are rapidly becoming yesterday's enthusiasm" (*Newsweek,* February 21, 1994:26).

check point

14. What are some typical activities at a boot camp?

Implementing Intermediate Sanctions

Although the use of intermediate sanctions has spread rapidly, three major questions have emerged about their implementation: (1) Which agencies should implement the sanctions? (2) Which offenders should be admitted to these programs? (3) Will the "community corrections net" widen as a result of these policies so that more people will come under correctional supervision?

As in any public service organization, administrative politics is an ongoing factor in corrections. In many states, agencies compete for the additional funding needed to run the programs. The traditional agencies of community corrections, such as probation offices, could receive the funding, or the new programs could be contracted out to nonprofit organizations. Probation organizations argue that they know the field, have the experienced staff, and—given the additional resources—could do an excellent job. They correctly point out that a great many offenders sentenced to intermediate sanctions are also on probation. Critics of giving this role to probation services argue that the established agencies are not receptive to innovation. They say that probation agencies place a high priority on the traditional supervision function and would not actively help clients solve their problems.

The different types of offenders who are given intermediate sanctions prompt a second issue in the implementation debate. One school of thought focuses on the seriousness of the offense and the other on the problems of the offender. If offenders are categorized by the seriousness of their offense, they may be given such close supervision that they will not be able to abide by the sentence. Sanctions for serious offenders may accumulate to include, for example, probation, drug testing, addiction treatment, and home confinement (Blomberg and Lucken, 1993). As the number of sentencing conditions increases, even the most willing probationers find fulfilling every one of them difficult.

Some agencies want to accept into their intermediate sanctions program only those offenders who *will* succeed. These agencies are concerned about their success ratio, especially because of threats to future funding if the program does not reduce recidivism. Critics point out that this strategy leads to "creaming," taking the most promising offenders and leaving those with worse problems to traditional sanctions.

net widening
Process in which new sentencing options increase instead of reduce control over offenders' lives.

The third issue concerns **net widening,** a process in which the new sanction increases instead of reduces the control over offenders' lives. This can occur when a judge imposes a more intrusive sentence than usual. For example, rather than merely giving an offender probation, the judge might also require that the offender perform community service. Critics of intermediate sanctions argue that they have created the following:

- Wider nets. Reforms increase the proportion of individuals in society whose behavior is regulated or controlled by the state.
- Stronger nets. By intensifying the state's intervention powers, reforms augment the state's capacity to control individuals.
- Different nets. Reforms transfer jurisdictional authority from one agency or control system to another.

The creation of intermediate sanctions have been advocated as a less costly alternative to incarceration and a more effective alternative to probation. But how have they been working? Michael Tonry and Mary Lynch have discouraging news: "Few such programs have diverted large numbers of offenders from prison, saved public monies or prison beds, or reduced recidivism rates" (1996:99). With incarceration rates still at record highs and probation caseloads increasing, intermediate sanctions will probably play a major role in corrections through the first decade of this century. However, correctional reform has always had its limitations, and intermediate sanctions may not achieve the goals of their advocates (Cullen, Wright, and Applegate, 1996:69).

Go to the *American System of Criminal Justice* Web site at http://www.cj.wadsworth.com/colesmith10e to explore the topic of intermediate sanctions in further detail.

15. What are three problems in the implementation of intermediate sanctions?

Parole Supervision in the Community

In this chapter, we begin a discussion of parole supervision that will continue in Chapter 16, where we discuss the mechanisms of release. This chapter focuses on parole from the standpoint of the community and the corrections system.

Parolees are released from prison on condition that they abide by laws and follow rules, known as **conditions of release,** designed to aid their readjustment to society and control their movement. As in probation, the parolee may be required to abstain from alcohol, keep away from undesirable associates, maintain good work habits, and not leave the state without permission. If they violate these conditions, they could be returned to prison to serve out the rest of their sentence. All states except Maine have some requirement for post-prison supervision, and nearly 80 percent of released prisoners are subject to some form of conditional community supervision release (Petersilia, 1999:489).

conditions of release
Conduct restrictions that parolees must follow as a legally binding requirement of being released.

The restrictions are justified on the ground that people who have been incarcerated must readjust to the community so that they will not fall back into preconviction habits and associations. The strict enforcement of these rules may create problems for parolees who cannot fulfill all of the demands placed on them. For example, it may be impossible for a parolee to be tested for drugs, attend an Alcoholics Anonymous meeting, and work full-time while also meeting family obligations.

Parolees have the added handicap of former convict status. In most states, laws prevent former prisoners from working in certain types of establishments—where alcohol is sold, for example—thus ruling out many jobs. In many trades, workers must belong to a union, and unions often have restrictions on the admission of new members. Finally, many parolees, as well as other ex-convicts, face a significant dilemma. If they are truthful about their backgrounds, many employers will not hire them. If they are not truthful, they can be fired for lying if the employer ever learns about their conviction. Some problems that parolees encounter when they reenter the community are illustrated in the Close Up box. As you read about Jerome Washington's experience, ask yourself what problems you might encounter after a long term in "max."

Other reentry problems plague parolees. For many, the transition from the highly structured life in prison to open society is too difficult to manage. Many just do not have the social, psychological, and material resources to cope with the temptations and complications of modern life. For these parolees, freedom may be short-lived as they fall back into forbidden activities such as drinking, using drugs, and stealing.

Community Programs Following Release

There are various programs to assist parolees. Some help prepare offenders for release while they are still in prison; others provide employment and housing assistance after release. Together, the programs are intended to help the offender progress steadily toward reintegration into the community.

Among the many programs developed to help offenders return to the community, three are especially important: work and educational release, furloughs, and residential programs. Although similar in many ways, each offers a specific approach to helping formerly incarcerated individuals reenter the community.

Returning to America

Returning to America after living in France, China, Swaziland, or the high Himalayas is one thing, but returning to America after serving sixteen years and three months in maximum security, mostly in Attica, is something altogether different.

In 1972 when I went to prison, Richard M. Nixon was president and politicians were still thought to be ethical; . . . the Supreme Court was reasonably balanced; the Vietnam War was winding down, but the weekly body count was still news. The HIV virus was unknown and free sex had more fans than the Super Bowl. Although everybody was not living the American Dream, and some people felt that life was hopeless, most were optimistic about their future and many had a strong commitment to social activism. People cared, and even the most disadvantaged could still dream without fear of having nightmares.

Soon after I got out I was with my brother Freddy. We were standing at Columbus Circle, a major hub, a New York City crossroads. Freddy was my guide. He asked where I'd like to go; what I'd like to do; what I'd like to see. Did I want to meet new people, or just hang out, drift from place to place? Suddenly, life was a smorgasbord, a cornucopia of enticements and alluring temptations. I didn't know where to start, what to do first. Prison was my immediate reference point and, there, decisions related to physical movement were made by the guards, not by me. "We can't stand here all day," my brother said, over and over.

"Go slow," I told myself as I recalled a number of prisoners who shortly after release returned to prison with new convictions, and new sentences. They tried to make everything happen at once, all at the same time. Like children, they wanted instant gratification. Played all their cards at the same time, swung before the ball got to the plate, struck out and found themselves back in a cell where their only landscape was the sun setting against the prison wall.

I decided to do life the same way I did prison. Nothing fancy. One step at a time, one day at a time, and most of all, don't forget to breathe.

Freddy was supportive and sensitive. He understood that I needed to relearn the rhythm of the streets, tune in on the city, explore my new freedom and tune out on prison. I had no preference which direction we'd walk, or which street we'd take. Freddy didn't seem to have any preference either. He just started off, leaving me to stay where I was or to catch up. I learned a quick but important lesson. It was this kind of small, ordinary decision—often taken for granted and overlooked—that I missed most in prison. Now, by just walking off and letting me decide what to do, Freddy was tuning me in again to this level of free choice.

The morning after my release found me in Harlem. I was staying with Bert, a long-time family friend. I awoke at dawn. There was no excitement. No stage fright or butterflies to signal the first day of the rest of my life. Looking up from sleep I could have dreamed my release from prison the day before. The sky was as gray as a prison sky—the same sky I had seen for the past sixteen years and three months.

Not long after I went to prison, I woke in the middle of the night and sat up on the side of the bed. The cell was so quiet I could hear cockroaches foraging in my garbage.

"When I get out of prison," I said to myself, "sex can wait." Thinking of what I would most like to do, I said, "I'm going to eat strawberries! Big! Fresh! Red strawberries!" And that became my mantra for the rest of the time I was in prison.

On the day I was released, Kathrin, a friend, a sister, my confidante, came to pick me up. She was there with her camera, taking photos of me as I walked through the last gate to freedom. She drove me to the house where she lived with her husband and son, and fed me steamed shrimp, French champagne, and *strawberries*!

Note: Jerome Washington, a writer, is now discharged from parole supervision and is living in California.

Source: Jerome Washington, *Iron House: Stories from the Yard* (New York: Vintage, 1994), 155–63.

To learn about reentry services offered to parolees, go to http://www.cdc.state.ca.us/program/prevent.htm.

Work and Educational Release

work and educational release The daytime release of inmates from correctional institutions so they can work or attend school.

Programs of **work and educational release,** in which inmates are released from correctional institutions during the day to work or attend school, were first established in Vermont in 1906. However, the Huber Act, passed by the Wisconsin legislature in 1913, is usually cited as the model on which such programs are based. By 1972 most states and the federal government had instituted these programs.

Lara Jo Regan/SABA Press

Finding and holding a job is one of the major problems faced by those released from prison. San Francisco's Delancey Street Foundation for many years has been a leader in training ex-offenders in such skills as floristry, baking, and carpentry.

Although most work and educational release programs are justifiable in terms of rehabilitation, many correctional administrators and legislators also like them because they cost relatively little. In some states a portion of the inmate's earnings from work outside may be deducted for room and board. One problem with these programs is that they allegedly take jobs from free citizens, a complaint often given by organized labor. Furthermore, the releasee's contact with the community increases the chances that contraband will be brought into the institution. To deal with such bootlegging and to assist in the reintegration process, some states and counties have built special work and educational release units in urban areas, where offenders live away from the prison.

Furloughs

Isolation from loved ones is one of the pains of imprisonment. Although correctional programs in many countries include conjugal visits, only a few U.S. corrections systems have used them. Many penologists view the **furlough**—the temporary release of an inmate from a correctional institution for a visit home—as a meaningful approach to inmate reintegration.

furlough
The temporary release of an inmate from a correctional institution for a brief period, usually one to three days, for a visit home. Such programs help maintain family ties and prepare inmates for release on parole.

Furloughs are thought to offer an excellent means of testing an inmate's ability to cope with the larger society. Through home visits, the inmate can renew family ties and relieve the tensions of confinement. Most administrators also feel that furloughs are good for prisoners' morale. The general public, however, does not always support the concept. Public outrage is inevitable if an offender on furlough commits another crime or fails to return. Correctional authorities are often nervous about using furloughs, because they fear being blamed for such incidents.

Residential Programs

The **community correctional center** houses soon-to-be-released inmates and connects them to community services, resources, and support. This institution takes several forms, such as halfway houses, prerelease centers, and correctional service centers, and it serves a variety of offender clients. Most programs require offenders to reside at the facility while they work in the community or visit with their families. Other facilities are designed primarily to provide services and programs for parolees. Often these correctional centers are established in former private homes or small hotels, creating a homey, less institutional environment.

community correctional center
An institution, usually in an urban area, that houses inmates soon to be released. Such centers are designed to help inmates establish community ties and thus promote their reintegration with society.

Individual rooms, group dining rooms, and other homelike features are maintained whenever possible.

halfway house
A correctional facility housing convicted felons who spend a portion of their day at work in the community but reside in the halfway house during nonworking hours.

The term **halfway house** has been applied to a variety of community correctional facilities and programs in which felons work in the community but reside in the halfway house during nonworking hours. Halfway houses range from secure institutions in the community, with programs designed to assist inmates who are preparing for release on parole, to group homes where parolees, probationers, or others diverted from the system live with minimal supervision and direction. Some halfway houses deliver special treatment services, such as programs designed to deal with alcohol, drug, or mental problems.

The Delancey Street Foundation provides residential and employment assistance to ex-prisoners in San Francisco and at five other sites; see http://www.delanceystfndtn.citysearch.com/.

Residential programs have problems. Few neighborhoods want to host halfway houses or treatment centers for convicts. Community resistance has significantly impeded the development of community-based correctional facilities and even has forced some successful facilities to close. Many communities, often wealthier ones, have blocked placement of halfway houses or treatment centers within their boundaries. One result of the NIMBY ("not in my backyard") attitude is that many centers are established in deteriorating neighborhoods inhabited by poor people, who lack the political power and resources to block unpopular programs.

The future of residential programs is unclear. Originally advocated for both rehabilitative and financial reasons, they do not seem to be saving as much money for the corrections system as officials had hoped. Medical care, education, vocational rehabilitation, and therapy are expensive. Effective programs require the services of teachers, counselors, and other professional personnel. Moreover, to be truly effective, these officials must work with small numbers of offenders. The savings realized from the use of fewer custodial personnel may be offset by the costs of counseling and other professional services.

Learn how the Fortune Society helps ex-offenders; go to http://www.fortunesociety.org and click on "About Us" to learn about the mission, history, and services of the organization.

If recidivism rates of offenders who have been involved in community treatment were proven to be lower, the expenditures might more readily be justified. However, the available data are discouraging. The excitement and optimism that greeted the community correctional movement may have been unwarranted.

check point

16. What are three programs designed to ease the reentry of offenders into the community?

Parole Officer: Cop or Social Worker?

After release, a parolee's principal contact with the criminal justice system is through the parole officer, who has the dual responsibility of providing surveillance and assistance. Thus, parole officers are asked to play two different, some might say incompatible, roles: cop and social worker. Whereas parole was originally designed to help offenders make the transition from prison to the community, supervision has shifted ever more toward surveillance, drug testing, monitoring curfews, and collecting restitution. Safety and security have become major issues in parole services.

The Parole Officer as Cop

In their role as police officer, parole officers have the power to restrict many aspects of the parolee's life, to enforce the conditions of release, and to initiate revocation proceedings if parole conditions are violated. Like other officials in the criminal justice system, the parole officer has extensive discretion in low-visibility situations. In many states, parole officers have the authority to search the parolee's house without warning, to arrest him or her without the possibility of bail for suspected violations, and to suspend parole pending a hearing before the board. This authoritarian component of the parole officer's role can give the ex-offender a sense of insecurity and hamper the development of mutual trust.

The parole officer is responsible for seeing that the parolee follows the conditions imposed by the parole board. Typically the conditions require the parolee to follow the parole officer's instructions; permit the officer to visit the home and place of employment; maintain employment; not leave the state without permission; not marry without permission; not own a firearm; not possess, use, or traffic in narcotics; not consume alcohol to excess; and comply with all laws and be a good citizen.

Parole officers are granted law enforcement powers so as to protect the community from offenders who are coming out of prison. However, because these powers diminish the possibility for the officer to develop a close relationship with the client, they can weaken the officer's other role of assisting the parolee's readjustment to the community (Clear and Latessa, 1993:441).

Chang W. Lee/NYT Pictures

Parole Officer Corey Burke drops by unannounced to visit a paroled sex offender in the man's apartment. Burke sees his job as neither to exact retribution nor to offer compassion, but to keep parolees from committing another crime.

The Parole Officer as Social Worker

Parole officers must act as social workers by helping the parolee find a job and restore family ties. Officers channel parolees to social agencies, such as psychiatric, drug, and alcohol clinics, where they can obtain help. As caseworkers, officers work to develop a relationship that allows parolees to confide their frustrations and concerns.

Because parolees are not likely to do this if they are constantly aware of the parole officer's ability to send them back to prison, some researchers have suggested that parole officers' conflicting responsibilities of cop and social worker should be separated. Parole officers could maintain the supervisory aspects of the position, and other personnel—perhaps a separate parole counselor—could perform the casework functions. Another option would be for parole officers to be charged solely with social work duties, while local police check for violations. In Japan and a few other countries, citizen volunteers are involved in helping newly released offenders adjust to the community and become law-abiding citizens (see the Comparative Perspective).

The Parole Bureaucracy

Although parole officers have smaller caseloads than do probation officers, parolees require more extensive services. One reason is that parolees, by the very fact of their incarceration, have generally committed much more serious crimes. Another reason is that parolees must make a difficult transition from the highly structured prison environment to a society in which they have previously failed to live as law-abiding citizens. It is exceptionally difficult for a parole officer to monitor, control, and assist clients who may have little knowledge of or experience with living successfully within society's rules.

The parole officer works within a bureaucratic environment. Like most other human services organizations, parole agencies are short on resources and expertise. Because the difficulties faced by many parolees are so complex, the officer's job is almost impossible. As a result, parole officers frequently must classify parolees and give priority to those most in need. For example, most parole officers spend extra time with the newly released. As the officer gains greater confidence in the parolee, the level of supervision can be adjusted to "active" or "reduced" surveillance. Depending on how the parolee has functioned in the community, he or she may eventually be allowed to check in with the officer

Parole Supervision in Japan

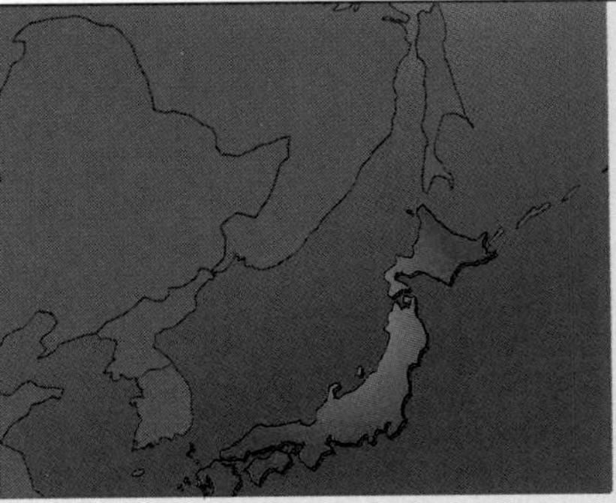

Parole supervision and aftercare services in Japan are characterized by the extensive participation of community volunteers. Would Americans be willing to volunteer to play such a role?

When Japan reorganized its correctional services after World War II, it was argued that probation and parole supervision should be organized to combine a professional staff and volunteer community corrections workers. A shortage of funds precluded an expanded professional service, but Japan already had a history of volunteer services that had contributed to the rehabilitation of offenders. Japan also had a tradition of voluntary social welfare systems firmly rooted in the community. The Offender's Rehabilitation Law called on all people to "render help, in accordance with their position and ability, in order to achieve the goals (of rehabilitation of offenders, etc.)." With passage of the Volunteer Probation Officer Law in 1950, people were nominated to serve in this capacity. They were charged with helping offenders to rehabilitate themselves in society and with fostering a constructive public attitude that would help to promote crime prevention.

Today, almost fifty thousand volunteers work on an individual basis with the one to ten cases assigned to them and are supervised by eight hundred professional officers. Appointed for two-year terms, volunteers are assigned according to their place of residence to one of 764 "rehabilitation areas." The volun-

periodically instead of submitting to regular home visits, searches, and other intrusive monitoring.

check point

17. What are some of the rules most parolees must follow while they are supervised in the community?
18. What are the major tasks of parole officers?

Adjustments to Life outside Prison

General Adjustments

With little preparation, the ex-offender moves from the highly structured, authoritarian life of the institution into a world that is filled with temptations and complicated problems. Suddenly, ex-convicts who are unaccustomed to undertaking even simple tasks such as going to the store for groceries are expected to assume pressing, complex responsibilities. Finding a job and a place to live are not the only problems the newly released person faces. The parolee must also make significant social and psychological role adjustments. A male ex-convict, for example, is suddenly required to become not only a parolee but also an employee, a neighbor, a father, a husband, and a son. The expectations, norms, and social relations in the free world are very different from those learned in prison. The relatively predictable inmate code is replaced by society's often unclear rules of behavior—rules that the offender had failed to cope with during his or her previous life in free society.

The Texas Department of Criminal Justice operates Project RIO (Re-Integration of Offenders), which helps ex-prisoners find employment; see http://www.tdcj.state.tx.us/ex-offender-employ.htm.

Public Opinion

The public's assumptions about ex-offenders are shaped by news reports of brutal crimes committed by parolees. The murder of 12-year-old Polly Klaas by a

teers in each area form an association of officers that is nationally linked to provide for volunteer solidarity, to coordinate training, and to gain resources.

Volunteer officers tend to be older (more than half are over 50) and come from a variety of backgrounds. The largest group (23 percent) comes from such primary industries as agriculture, fishing, and forestry. The second largest category (18 percent) comprises individuals officially classified as unemployed but composed mainly of homemakers and the retired. Religious professionals comprise the next largest category. Only 5 percent of the officers are lawyers, doctors, and other professionals, somewhat in contrast to the community activities of this group in Western countries. Although from diverse backgrounds, most volunteers are middle class.

The volunteer regularly meets a client at home and also visits the client's family. The volunteer continues to observe the offender during these meetings and tries to advise, assist, and support him or her. Assistance is also given to the offender's family, with due respect to the dignity and freedom of the parolee. Sometimes the volunteer has to visit the client's place of employment. The greatest concern of the volunteer is how to maintain client contact while at the same time keeping knowledge of the offender's criminal background from neighbors and employers. The volunteers usually meet their clients twice a month, but in special cases they do so almost every day. Volunteers feel they should be readily available to their clients and their families, even during weekends or late at night in case of emergency, particularly in remote areas with few professional services.

The volunteer probation and parole service in Japan is believed to have unique merits lacked by the professional officer. The nonofficial nature of the relationship between volunteer and offender is thought to be positive. It is believed that through this relationship the offender can regain self-respect and identify with the law-abiding culture. Another merit is the "local" nature of the volunteers. As members of the community where their clients live, volunteers know the particular setting and local customs. Yet some of the professional officers believe that they could do a better job at the grassroots level than can the volunteers.

The nature of probation and parole in Japan draws heavily on that country's unique sense of community. By sharing a common culture and social experience, the Japanese are closely bound to one another in a consensual society. For offenders, rehabilitation requires earning one's way back into community membership.

The Japanese approach to probation and parole is quite different from that in the United States. Perhaps it can succeed only in a country without great cultural diversity and where community pressures are a major aspect of social control. Do you agree?

Sources: Drawn from Elmer H. Johnson, *Japanese Corrections* (Carbondale: Southern Illinois University Press, 1996); Kenichi Nakayama, "Japan," in *Major Criminal Justice Systems*, 2nd ed., ed. George F. Cole, Stanislaw Frankowski, and Marc G. Gertz (Newbury Park, Calif.: Sage, 1987), 168; L. Craig Parker, Jr., *Parole and the Community Based Treatment of Offenders in Japan and The United States* (New Haven, Ct.: University of New Haven Press, 1986); Yasuyoshi Shiono, "Use of Volunteers in the Non-institutional Treatment of Offenders in Japan," *International Review of Crime Policy* 27 (1969): 25–31.

parolee and the rape and murder of 7-year-old Megan Kanka by a paroled sex offender spurred legislators in more than 35 states to enact "sexual offender notification" laws. These laws require that the public be notified of the whereabouts of "potentially dangerous" sex offenders. In some states, paroled sex offenders must register with the police, while in others, the immediate neighbors must be informed. Many states now have publicly accessible sex offender Web sites listing the names and addresses of those registered.

The impact of these laws have had several unintended consequences. Incidents have occurred in which parolees have been "hounded" from communities, where the media have televised the parolee's homecoming, where homes have been burned, and where neighbors have assaulted parolees they erroneously thought were sex offenders. In some states the legislation was written so broadly that statutory rape, consensual sodomy, and third-degree assault that might constitute inappropriate touching or sexual contact are included in the notification mandate. Real estate agents have also found it difficult to sell property in neighborhoods where registered sex offenders live (*Hartford Courant*, April 7, 1999).

The fact of repeat violence fuels a public perception that parolees represent a continuing threat to the community. Although the new laws are directed primarily at people who have committed sex offenses against children, some fear that the community will target all parolees. This preoccupation with potential parolee criminality makes it even more difficult for ex-offenders to successfully reenter society.

In November 2002 the U.S. Supreme Court heard oral arguments in two cases involving the sex offender laws of Connecticut and Alaska. The constitutionality of the Connecticut law was challenged because it makes no distinctions among the registrants as to the seriousness of their offense or to the identity of those who are no longer a danger to the community. Alaska's law includes the names of those whose crime predated enactment of the 1994 statute. Opponents claim that this is an additional punishment and a violation of the Constitution's ex post facto clause. Decisions on these cases are expected by June 2003.

Revocation of Parole

Always hanging over the ex-inmate's head is the potential revocation of parole for committing a new crime or violating the conditions of release. The public tends to view the high number of revocations as a failure of parole. Corrections officials point to the great number of parolees who are required to be drug-free, be employed, and pay restitution—conditions that are difficult for many to fulfill.

Morrissey v. Brewer (1972)
Due process rights require a prompt, informal inquiry before an impartial hearing officer before parole may be revoked. The parolee may present relevant information and confront witnesses.

As decided in ***Morrissey v. Brewer*** **(1972)**, if the parole officer alleges that a technical violation has occurred, the U.S. Supreme Court requires a two-step revocation proceeding. In the first stage the parole authority determines whether there is probable cause to believe the conditions have been violated. The parolee has the right to be notified of the charges, to be informed of the evidence, to be heard, to present witnesses, and to confront the witnesses. In the second stage the parole authority decides if the violation is severe enough to warrant return to prison.

The number of parole violators returned to prison has increased dramatically during the past 20 years. In 1999, 35 percent of new admissions to state prisons were parole violators, up from 17 percent in 1980. Parole violators accounted for more than half of prison admissions in California (67 percent), Utah (55 percent), and Louisiana (53 percent) but less than 10 percent in Alabama and Florida. As shown in Table 14.1, 70 percent of parole violators were returned to prison because of an arrest or conviction for a new offense. The percentage of parolees returned for technical violations also varies. For example 17 percent of California's prison population (29,000 beds) consists of inmates who were returned for a technical violation. In the State of Washington only 1 percent was returned for technical violations (Austin, 2001:319). As seen in "What Americans Think," much of the public believes that those who recidivate should not be released on parole.

Table 14.1 Reasons for revocation among parole violators in state prison

An increasing number of parolees are being returned to prison because of new arrests or technical violations. What factors might be causing this increase?

Reason for Revocation	
Arrest/conviction for new offense	69.9%
Drug-related violations	16.1
Positive test for drug use	7.9
Possession of drugs	6.6
Failure to report for drug testing	2.3
Failure to report for drug treatment	1.7
Absconders	22.3%
Failure to report/absconded	18.6
Left jurisdiction without permission	5.6
Other reasons	17.8%
Possession of gun(s)	3.5
Failure to report for counseling	2.4
Failure to meet financial obligations	2.3
Failure to maintain employment	1.2
Maintained contact with known offenders	1.2

Source: Bureau of Justice Statistics, *Special Report*, October 2001, p. 14.

check point

19. What are "offender notification laws?"
20. What two conditions can result in the revocation of parole?
21. What due process requirements must be followed in the parole revocation process?

What Americans Think

Question: "Tell me whether you think the following proposal is a good idea or a bad idea."

Refuse parole to any prisoner who has been paroled before for a serious crime.

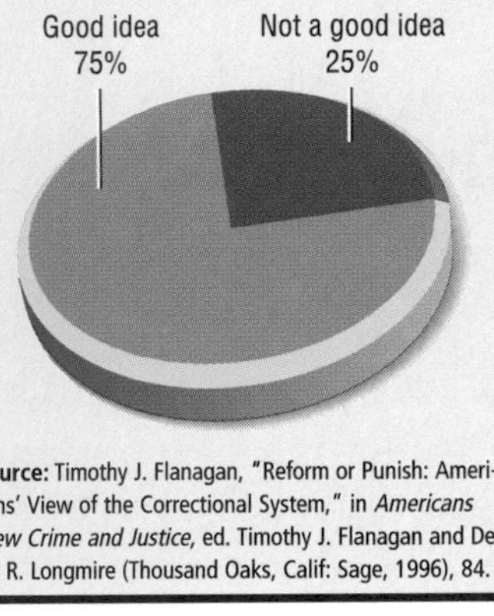

Good idea 75%
Not a good idea 25%

Source: Timothy J. Flanagan, "Reform or Punish: Americans' View of the Correctional System," in *Americans View Crime and Justice*, ed. Timothy J. Flanagan and Dennis R. Longmire (Thousand Oaks, Calif: Sage, 1996), 84.

The Reentry Problem

The rising number of parolees returned to prison is a problem that has only recently come to the attention of policy makers. One underrecognized impact of the incarceration policies of the 1980s was that "more prisoners in prison means that, eventually, more prisoners will be let out" (Butterfield, 2000). There is now a sudden flood of offenders leaving prison—about 600,000 per year—and probably about a third will return to prison, often within a year of their release. The recidivism rate demonstrates a failure of the criminal justice system to deal with the reentry problems of ex-felons. What is at the crux of this problem?

Jeremy Travis and Joan Petersilia point to several factors that seem to have contributed to the reentry problem. They argue that beginning in the 1970s the power of parole boards to decide whether a prisoner was "ready" to be released was abolished in mandatory release states and severely restricted in discretionary release states. This means that more inmates are automatically leaving prison, ready or not, when they meet the requirements of their sentence. It also means that there has been little or no prerelease planning so that the new parolee has a job, housing, and a supportive family when he or she hits the streets. There is

new directions in criminal justice policy

Reentry Courts

Courts play only a marginal role in the reentry to the community of former prisoners. Traditionally, a judge's responsibility ends when the defendant is sentenced; prison administrators and parole officers are the ones to prepare prisoners for release and supervise their transition as members of the community. Officials, however, are considering policy alternatives that can deal with the reentry crisis, in which so many ex-prisoners are returned to prison because of new offenses or technical violations.

One suggestion for dealing with this problem is the creation of "reentry courts," patterned after drug courts. Judges would maintain active oversight of parolees they had originally sentenced. Parolees would appear before the court on a regular basis so that the judge, together with the parole officer, could assess the ex-inmates' progress in following the parole conditions and adjusting to life in society. Other core elements of the reentry court include (1) the involvement of the judge and correctional officials in assessing the needs of a prisoner prior to release and in building linkages to family, social services, housing, and work opportunities that would support reintegration; (2) the provision of supportive services such as substance abuse treatment, job training, and family assistance; and (3) a system of sanctions and rewards to encourage positive behavior.

The failure of so many ex-prisoners to succeed on parole has only recently been recognized as a serious problem requiring policy changes. Proponents of reentry courts point to the success of drug courts and say that with continuing judicial oversight and supportive services a greater percentage of ex-felons succeed on parole. Skeptics are concerned that this is only the latest "enthusiasm" to strike corrections and that the supportive services will not be funded so as to make reentry viable.

Researching the Internet

To learn more about reentry courts, go to the Web site of the U.S. Department of Justice, Office of Justice Programs, at http://www.ojp.usdoj.gov/reentry/.

also an increasing percentage of prison releasees who "max out" and hence are not on parole because they served their full sentences in prison.

A second factor believed to contribute to the recidivism rate is the curtailment of prison education, job training, and other rehabilitation programs designed to prepare inmates for reentry into the community.

Finally, Travis and Petersilia note that the profile of returning prisoners has changed in ways that pose new challenges to successful reentry. In particular the conviction offense and time served is different than it was 20 years ago. Now, more than a third of prisoners released to parole are incarcerated for a drug offense—up from 12 percent in 1985. While the average time served has also increased by almost a half year since 1990, some drug and violence offenders are exiting prison after very long terms, perhaps 20 or more years. The longer time in prison means a longer period the prisoner has been absent from family and friends. See "New Directions in Criminal Justice Policy" for a look at one way proposed to alleviate the problem of reentry.

check point

22. What are some of the major problems faced by parolees?
23. Why are recidivism rates high?

The Future of Parole

Parole has been under attack since the 1970s as a symbol of leniency whereby criminals are "let out" early (Petersilia, 1999). Public outrage is heightened when the media report the gruesome details of violent crimes committed by parolees. Calls by legislators for the abolition of parole have been politically popular. Some people argue that without parole criminals would serve longer terms and there would be greater honesty in sentencing. Where discretionary release has been retained, many boards have limited the number of prisoners granted parole.

Correctional experts argue that parole plays an important role in the criminal justice system, given that early release from prison must be earned. Discretionary release enables parole boards to individualize punishment, place offenders in treatment programs, and provide incentives for early release. Neither mandatory nor expiration release provides the tools to prepare felons to reenter the community, because the parole date is based solely on the sentence minus good time (see Chapter 16 for more on parole and the forms of reentry).

As prison populations rise, demands that felons be allowed to serve part of their time in the community will undoubtedly mount. These demands will not come from the public, which typically believes that all offenders should serve their full sentences. Instead, they will come from legislators and correctional officials who recognize that the money and facilities to incarcerate all offenders for the complete terms of their sentences are lacking. Although many offenders are not successfully integrated into the community, most will end up back in free society whether or not they serve their full sentences. Parole and community programs represent an effort to address the inevitability of their return. Even if such programs do not prevent all offenders from leaving the life of crime, they do help some to turn their lives around.

The Future of Community Corrections

In 1980 there were 1.4 million Americans under community supervision; by 1999 this figure had grown to 3.9 million, an increase of more than 250 percent (BJS, 2001e: Table 6.1). Despite this tremendous growth, community corrections still lacks public support. Community corrections suffers from the image of being "soft on crime." As a result, some localities provide adequate resources for prisons and jails but not for community corrections.

Community corrections also faces the challenge that offenders today require closer supervision. (Petersilia and Turner, 1990). The crimes, criminal records, and drug problems of these offenders are often worse than those of lawbreakers of earlier eras. In New York, for example, 77 percent of probationers are convicted felons, and about a third of these have been found guilty of violent crimes. Yet, those people are supervised by probation officers whose caseloads number in the hundreds (Petersilia, 1993:61). Such officers, and their counterparts in parole, cannot provide effective supervision and services to all their clients.

Community corrections is burdened by even greater caseload pressures than in the past. With responsibility for about three-fourths of all offenders under correctional supervision, community corrections needs an infusion of additional resources.

To succeed, public support for community corrections is essential, but it will come only if citizens believe that offenders are being given appropriate punishments. Citizens must realize that policies designed to punish offenders in the community yield not mere "slaps on the wrists" but meaningful sanctions, even while these policies allow offenders to retain and reforge their ties to their families and society. Joan Petersilia has argued that too many crime control policies are focused solely on the short term. She believes that long-term investments in community corrections will pay off for both the offender and the community (Petersilia, 1996). But before new policies can be put in place, public opinion must shift toward support of community corrections.

Summary

- Community supervision through probation, intermediate sanctions, and parole are a growing part of the criminal justice system.
- Probation is imposed on more than half of offenders. People with this sentence live in the community according to conditions set by the judge and under the supervision of a probation officer.
- Intermediate sanctions are designed as punishments that are more restrictive than probation and less restrictive than prison.
- The range of intermediate sanctions allows judges to design sentences that incorporate one or more of these punishments.
- Some intermediate sanctions are implemented by courts (fines, restitution, forfeiture), others in the community (home confinement, community service, day reporting centers, intensive supervision probation), and others in institutions and the community (boot camps).
- Parolees are released from prison on the condition that they do not violate the law and they live according to rules designed to help them adjust to society.
- Parole officers are assigned to assist ex-inmates make the transition to society and to ensure that they follow the conditions of their release.
- The problem of reentry has become a major policy issue.

Questions for Review

1 What is the aim of community corrections?

2 What is the nature of probation, and how is it organized?

3 What is the purpose of intermediate sanctions?

4 What are the primary forms of intermediate sanctions?

5 What problems confront parolees upon their release?

Key Terms and Cases

boot camp (p. 452)
community correctional center (p. 457)
community service (p. 450)
conditions of release (p. 455)
day reporting center (p. 450)
fine (p. 447)
furlough (p. 457)
halfway house (p. 458)
home confinement (p. 449)
intensive supervision probation (ISP) (p. 451)
net widening (p. 454)
parole (p. 440)
recidivism (p. 440)
restitution (p. 447)
technical violation (p. 444)
work and educational release (p. 456)
Gagnon v. Scarpelli (1973) (p. 445)
Mempa v. Rhay (1967) (p. 445)
Morrissey v. Brewer (1972) (p. 462)

For Further Reading

Anderson, David. 1998. *Sensible Justice: Alternatives to Prison.* New York: New Press. A comprehensive review of the arguments for alternatives to incarceration. Develops a politically feasible case for expanded use of alternatives.

Byrne, James M., Arthur J. Lurigio, and Joan Petersilia. 1992. *Smart Sentencing: The Emergence of Intermediate Sanctions.* Newbury Park, Calif.: Sage. A collection of papers exploring various issues in the design and implementation of intermediate sanctions programs.

Clear, Todd R., and Harry Dammer. 2000. *The Offender in the Community.* Belmont, Calif.: Wadsworth. A comprehensive description of community corrections issues and programs.

Morris, Norval, and Michael Tonry. 1990. *Between Prison and Probation: Intermediate Punishments in a Rational Sentencing System.* New York: Oxford University Press. Urges development of a range of intermediate punishments that can be used to sanction offenders more severely than probation but less severely than incarceration.

Simon, Jonathan. 1993. *Poor Discipline: Parole and Social Control of the Underclass.* Chicago: University of Chicago Press. Explores the use of parole to control poor and disadvantaged members of society.

Tonry, Michael, and Kate Hamilton, eds. 1995. *Intermediate Sanctions in Overcrowded Times.* Boston: Northeastern University Press. Summaries of research on intermediate sanctions in the United States and England.

Going Online

For an up-to-date list of Web links, go to **http://www.cj.wadsworth.com/colesmith10e**

1. Go to the Web site of the New York State Probation Officers association: http://www.nyspoa.com. Click on "Research Info" and then access the probation salaries for the last few years. Are you surprised by the salaries for probation officers? Do these officers receive adequate pay for the kind of work they do?
2. Go to the Carolina Correctional Services Web site at http://www.ccs-incorporated.com/. Write a short paper describing one of the services they provide.
3. Using InfoTrac College Edition, search for *community corrections.* Read about a community corrections program in New York. Does this program offer advantages over incarceration?

Checkpoint Answers

1. Many offenders' crimes and records do not warrant incarceration; community supervision is cheaper; recidivism rates for those supervised in the community are no higher than for those who serve prison time; incarceration is more destructive to the offender and society.
2. A Boston boot maker who became the first probation officer by taking responsibility for a convicted offender before sentencing; called the "father of probation."
3. Risk control.
4. To assist judges by preparing presentence reports and to provide assistance and supervision to offenders in the community.
5. An arrest for a new offense or a technical violation of the conditions of probation that were set by the judge.
6. Right to a preliminary and final hearing, right to cross-examine witnesses, right to notice of the alleged violations, and right to a written report of the proceedings. Right to counsel is determined on a case-by-case basis.
7. Judges need a range of sentencing options that are less restrictive than prison and more restrictive than simple probation.
8. A range of punishments reflecting different degrees of intrusiveness and control over the offender.
9. A fine is a sum of money paid to the government by the offender. Restitution is a sum of money paid to the victim by the offender. Forfeiture is the taking by the government of assets derived from or used in criminal activity.
10. Most offenders are poor and cannot pay, offenders may commit additional crimes to pay monetary sanctions, and the courts do not allocate resources for collection and enforcement.
11. Home confinement may violate the Fourth Amendment's protections against unreasonable searches, monitoring devices have technical problems, and failure rates are high because offenders cannot tolerate home confinement for very long.
12. Drug and alcohol treatment, job searches, educational programs, and sometimes just offenders reporting in.
13. In ISP the offender is required to make stricter and more frequent reporting to an officer with a much smaller caseload.
14. Boot camps maintain a spit-and-polish environment and strict discipline, involve offenders in physical activity, and provide educational, vocational, and rehabilitative services.
15. Deciding which agencies should implement the sanctions, deciding which offenders should be admitted to these programs, and the possible widening of the "community corrections net."

16 Work and educational release programs, furlough programs, and residential programs.

17 Make required reports to parole officer, do not leave the state without permission, use no alcohol or drugs, maintain employment, and attend required treatment programs.

18 Surveillance and assistance.

19 Laws requiring certain types of parolees (usually sex offenders) to notify the police or residents that they are living in the community.

20 Arrest for a new crime or a technical violation of one or more of the conditions of parole.

21 In a two-step hearing process, the parolee has the right to be notified of the charges, to know the evidence against him or her, to be heard, to present witnesses, and to confront witnesses.

22 Finding housing and employment, having enough money, and reestablishing relationships with family and friends.

23 Many parolees are career criminals, and reentry and close parole supervision require difficult adjustments.

CHAPTER 15

Prisons: Their Goals and Management

Ralf-Finn Hestoft/SABA Press

On Easter a fight broke out in the recreation yard at the Southern Ohio Correction Facility in Lucasville, a "supermax" prison reserved for the most violent and incorrigible offenders. Within minutes the fight grew into a full-scale riot. Eight correctional officers were taken hostage by the 450 prisoners, who barricaded themselves inside Cellblock L. The prisoners held their ground—and their hostages—for more than a week. During the uprising, prisoners murdered others whom they regarded as "snitches," and six inmate bodies were dumped into the recreation yard.

When the prisoners threatened to kill one of the hostages, a spokesperson for the state said it was a "standard threat they've been issuing." Shortly thereafter, correctional officer Robert Vallandingham was murdered. Another hostage told the media that the officer was killed because the prisoners were angry that their threats were not being taken seriously. Eventually, the prisoners negotiated their surrender, the remaining hostages were released, and the state began prosecuting some prisoners on criminal charges stemming from the riot and murders.

These periodic eruptions of prisoners bring public attention to life behind bars. Maximum-security prisons such as Lucasville are not the only correctional institutions that simmer with trouble. Many others—even most—experience the racial conflict, gangs, allegations of brutality, and inmate violence that can bring tensions inside to the boiling point. Violence is relatively infrequent only because most institutions manage to keep the lid on the cauldron.

Incarceration—what does it mean to the inmates, the officers, and the public? What goes on inside U.S. prisons? In this chapter the goals of the more than 1,600 American prisons are examined, as well as how prisons are managed, the crucial role of the correctional officer, the problem of prison violence, and the constitutional rights of prisoners.

QUESTIONS for INQUIRY

- How is a prison organized?
- How do contemporary institutions differ from the old-style "big-house" prisons?
- What assumptions does each model of incarceration make?
- How is a prison governed?
- What is the role of correctional officers?
- What is the nature of prison violence?
- What constitutional rights do prisoners have?

The Modern Prison: Legacy of the Past

American correctional institutions have always been more varied than movies or novels portray them to be. Fictional depictions of prison life are typically set in a fortress, the "big house"—the maximum-security prisons where the inmates are tough and the guards are just as tough or tougher. Although big houses predominated in much of the country during the first half of the twentieth century, many prisons were built on another model. In the South, for instance, prisoners worked outside at farm labor, and the massive walled structures were not so common.

The typical big house of the 1940s and 1950s was a walled prison with large, tiered cell blocks, a yard, shops, and industrial workshops. The prisoners, in an average population of about 2,500 per institution, came from both urban and rural areas, were usually poor, and outside the South, were predominantly white. The prison society was essentially isolated; access to visitors, mail, and other communication was restricted. Prisoners' days were strictly structured, with rules enforced by the guards. A basic division stood between inmates and staff; rank was observed and discipline maintained. In the big house, few treatment programs existed; custody was the primary goal.

During the 1960s and early 1970s, when the rehabilitation model prevailed, many states built new prisons and converted others into "correctional institutions." Treatment programs administered by counselors and teachers became a major part of prison life, although the institutions continued to give priority to the custody goals of security, discipline, and order.

During the past 30 years, as the population of the United States has changed, so has the prison population. The number of African American and Hispanic inmates has greatly increased. More inmates come from urban areas, and more have been convicted of drug-related and violent offenses. Former street gangs, often organized along racial lines, today regroup inside prisons, and in many institutions they have raised the level of violence.

Now the focus of corrections has shifted to crime control, which emphasizes the importance of incarceration. Not only has the number of people in prison greatly increased, but many states have removed educational and recreational amenities from institutions. Some states have even reinstated the chain gang as a way of "getting tough" on inmates.

Over the last two decades the number of people held in prisons has more than quadrupled, and tensions have built within the overcrowded institutions. Although today's correctional administrators seek to provide humane incarceration, they must struggle with limited resources and shortages of cell space. Thus, the modern prison faces many of the difficult problems that confront other parts of the criminal justice system: racial conflicts, legal issues, limited resources, and growing populations. Despite these challenges, can prisons still achieve their objectives? The answer to this question depends, in part, on how we define the goals of incarceration.

1. How does today's prison differ from the "big house" of the past?
(Answers are at the end of the chapter.)

Goals of Incarceration

Citing the nature of inmates and the need to protect staff and the community, most people consider security the dominant purpose of a prison. High walls, barbed-wire fences, searches, checkpoints, and regular counts of inmates serve the security function: Few inmates escape. More importantly, the features set the tone for the daily operations. Prisons are expected to be impersonal, quasi-military places where strict discipline, minimal amenities, and restrictions on freedom serve to punish criminals.

Three models of incarceration have predominated since the early 1940s: the custodial, rehabilitation, and reintegration models. Each is associated with one style of institutional organization.

1. The **custodial model** assumes that prisoners have been incarcerated for the purpose of incapacitation, deterrence, or retribution. It emphasizes security, discipline, and order as they subordinate the prisoner to the authority of the warden. Discipline is strict, and most aspects of behavior are regulated. This model prevailed in corrections before World War II, and it dominates most maximum-security institutions today.
2. The rehabilitation model, developed during the 1950s, emphasizes treatment programs designed to reform the offender. According to this model, security and housekeeping activities are viewed primarily as preconditions for rehabilitative efforts. As all aspects of the organization should be directed toward rehabilitation, professional treatment specialists have a higher status than do other employees. Since the rethinking of the rehabilitation goal in the 1970s, treatment programs still exist in most institutions, but few prisons conform to this model today.
3. The **reintegration model** is linked to the structures and goals of community corrections. Recognizing that prisoners will be returning to society, this model emphasizes maintaining the offenders' ties to family and community as a method of reform. Prisons following this model gradually give inmates greater freedom and responsibility during their confinement, moving them to halfway houses or work release programs before giving them community supervision.

custodial model
A model of incarceration that emphasizes security, discipline, and order.

reintegration model
A model of a correctional institution that emphasizes maintaining the offender's ties to family and community as a method of reform, recognizing that the offender will be returning to society.

Steve Lehman/SABA Press

Some legislators have argued that weightlifting, basketball, and other prison physical activities are frills that should be restricted. Wardens, however, believe that these activities are important means of keeping prisoners busy and reducing tensions.

Although one can find correctional institutions that conform to each of these models, most prisons are mainly custodial. Nevertheless, treatment programs do exist, and because almost all inmates return to society at some point, even the most custodial institutions must prepare them for their reintegration. See "What Americans Think" for a look at how the public views the goals of incarceration.

Much is asked of prisons. As Charles Logan notes, "We ask them to correct the incorrigible, rehabilitate the wretched, deter the determined, restrain the dangerous, and punish the wicked" (Logan, 1993:19). Because prisons are expected to pursue many different and often incompatible goals, they are almost doomed to fail as institutions. Logan believes the mission of prisons is confinement. He argues that the basic purpose of imprisonment is to punish offenders fairly and justly through lengths of confinement proportionate to the seriousness of their crimes. He summarizes the mission of prison as follows: "to keep prisoners—to keep them in, keep them safe, keep them in line, keep them healthy, and keep them busy—and to do it with fairness, without undue suffering, and as efficiently as possible" (Logan, 1993). If the purpose of prisons is punishment through confinement under fair and just conditions, what are the implications of this purpose for correctional managers?

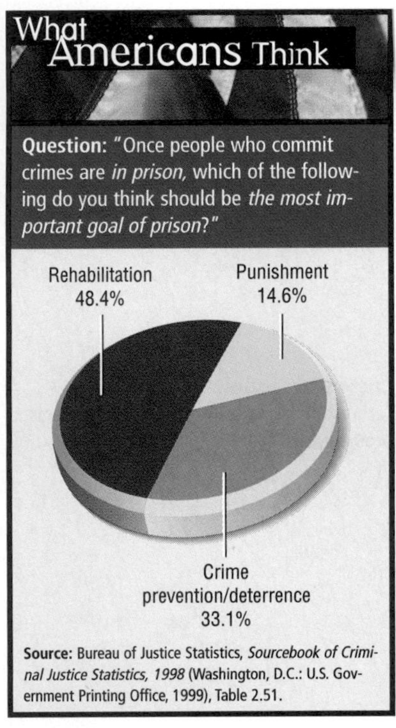

Question: "Once people who commit crimes are *in prison,* which of the following do you think should be *the most important goal of prison?*"

Source: Bureau of Justice Statistics, *Sourcebook of Criminal Justice Statistics, 1998* (Washington, D.C.: U.S. Government Printing Office, 1999), Table 2.51.

check point

2. What three models of prison have predominated since the 1940s?

Prison Organization

The prison's physical features and function set it apart from almost every other institution and organization in modern society. It is a place where a group of employees manage a group of captives. Prisoners must live according to the rules of their keepers, and their movements are sharply restricted. Unlike managers of other government agencies, prison managers

- Cannot select their clients
- Have little or no control over the release of their clients
- Must deal with clients who are there against their will
- Must rely on clients to do most of the work in the daily operation of the institution—work they are forced to do and for which they are not paid
- Must depend on the maintenance of satisfactory relationships between clients and staff

Given these unique characteristics, how should a prison be run? What rules should guide administrators? As the description just given indicates, wardens and other key personnel are asked to perform a difficult job, one that requires skilled and dedicated managers.

Most prisons are expected to fulfill goals related to keeping (custody), using (working), and serving (treating) inmates. Because individual staff members are not equipped to perform all functions, separate lines of command organize the groups of employees that carry out these different tasks. One group is charged with maintaining custody over the prisoners, another group supervises them in their work activities, and a third group attempts to treat them.

The custodial employees are the most numerous. They are normally organized along military lines, from warden to captain to officer, with accompanying pay

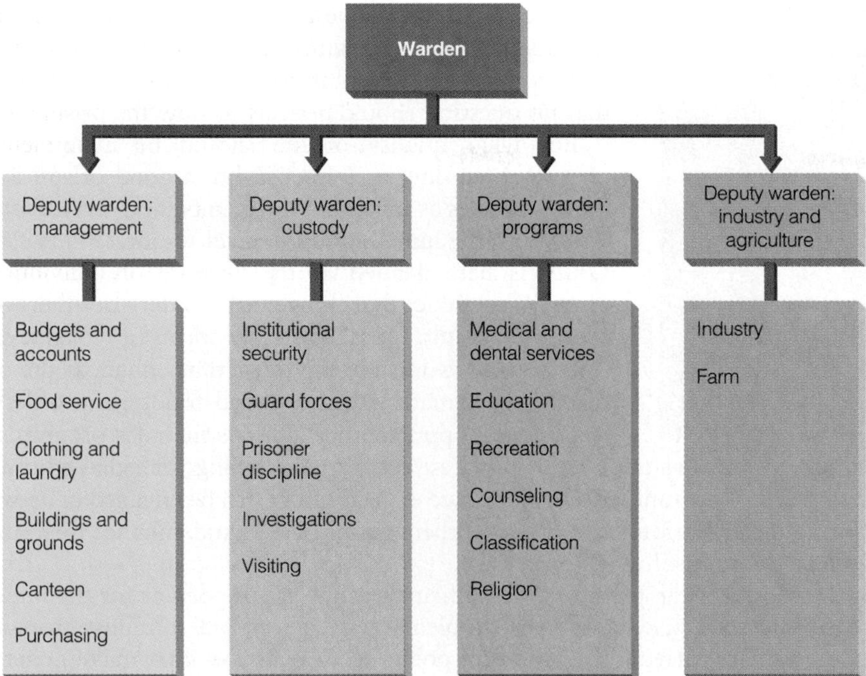

Figure 15.1
Formal organization of a prison for adult felons
Prison staff are divided into various sections consistent with the goals of the organization. Custodial employees are the most numerous.

differentials down the chain of command. The professional personnel associated with the using and serving functions, such as industry supervisors, clinicians, and teachers, are not part of the custodial structure and have little in common with its staff. All employees are responsible to the warden, but the treatment personnel and the civilian supervisors of the workshops have their own salary scales and titles. Figure 15.1 presents the formal organization of staff responsibilities in a typical prison.

The multiple goals and separate lines of command often cause ambiguity and conflict in the administration of prisons. For example, the goals imposed on prisons are often contradictory and unclear. Conflict between different groups of staff (custodial versus treatment, for instance), as well as between staff and inmates, presents significant challenges for administrators.

How, then, do prisons function? How do prisoners and staff try to meet their own goals? Although the U.S. prison may not conform to the ideal goals of corrections and the formal organization may bear little resemblance to the ongoing reality of the informal relations, order *is* kept and a routine *is* followed.

check point

3. How do prisons differ from other organizations in society?
4. What are the multiple goals pursued in today's prisons?
5. What problems do these goals present to administrators?

Governing a Society of Captives

Much of the public believes that prisons are operated in an authoritarian manner. In such a society, correctional officers give orders and inmates follow orders. Strictly enforced rules specify what the captives may and may not do. Staff members have the right to grant rewards and to inflict punishment. In theory, any inmate who does not follow the rules could be placed in solitary confinement.

Jeffry D. Scott/Impact Visuals

"Management by walking around" is a style that successful wardens have adopted. This means that they must be "hands on" and proactive, paying close attention to details rather than waiting for problems to arise.

Because the officers have a monopoly on the legal means of enforcing rules and can be backed up by the state police and the National Guard if necessary, many people believe that no question should arise as to how the prison is run.

But what quality of life should be maintained in prison? According to John DiIulio, a good prison is one that "provides as much order, amenity, and service as possible given the human and financial resources" (1987:12). *Order* is here defined as the absence of individual or group misconduct that threatens the safety of others—for example, assault, rapes, and other forms of violence or insult. *Amenities* include anything that enhances the comfort of the inmates, such as good food, clean cells, and recreational opportunities. *Service* includes programs designed to improve the lives of inmates: vocational training, remedial education, and work opportunities. Here, too, we expect inmates to be engaged in activities during incarceration that will make them better people and enhance their ability to lead crime-free lives upon release.

If we accept the premise that well-run prisons are important for the inmates, staff, and society, what are the problems that correctional administrators must address? The correctional literature points to four factors that make governing prisons different from administering other public institutions: (1) the defects of total power, (2) the limitation on the rewards and punishments officials can use, (3) the co-optation of correctional officers by inmates, and (4) the strength of inmate leadership. After we review each of these research findings, we shall ask what kind of administrative systems and leadership styles ensure that prisons are safe and humane and serve inmates' needs.

The Defects of Total Power

Imagine a prison society that comprises hostile and uncooperative inmates ruled by force. Prisoners can be legally isolated from one another, physically abused until they cooperate, and put under continuous surveillance. Although all of these things are possible, such practices would probably not be countenanced for long because the public expects correctional institutions to be run humanely.

In reality, the power of officers is limited, because many prisoners have little to lose by misbehaving, and unarmed officers have only limited ability to force compliance with rules. Perhaps more important is the fact that forcing people to follow commands is an inefficient way to make them carry out complex tasks; efficiency is further diminished by the ratio of inmates to officers (typically 40 to 1) and by the potential danger (Hepburn, 1985).

Rewards and Punishments

Correctional officers often rely on rewards and punishments to gain cooperation. To maintain security and order among a large population in a confined space, they impose extensive rules of conduct. Instead of using force to ensure obedience, however, they reward compliance and punish rule violators by granting and denying privileges.

Several policies can be followed to promote control. One is to offer cooperative prisoners rewards such as choice job assignments, residence in the honor unit, and favorable parole reports. Inmates who do not break rules are given good time. Informers may also be rewarded, and administrators may ignore conflict among inmates on the assumption that it keeps prisoners from uniting against authorities.

The system of rewards and punishments has some deficiencies. One is that the punishments for rule breaking do not represent a great departure from the pris-

oners' usual circumstances. Because inmates are already deprived of many freedoms and valued goods—heterosexual relations, money, choice of clothing, and so on—not being allowed to attend, say, a recreational period does not carry much weight. Further, authorized privileges are given to the inmate at the start of the sentence and are taken away only if rules are broken, but few rewards are authorized for progress or exceptional behavior. However, as an inmate approaches release, opportunities for furloughs, work release, or transfer to a halfway house can serve as incentives to obey rules.

Gaining Cooperation: Exchange Relationships

One way that correctional officers obtain inmate cooperation is by tolerating minor rule infractions in exchange for compliance with major aspects of the custodial regime. The correctional officer plays the key role in these exchange relationships. Officers and prisoners are in close association both day and night—in the cell block, workshop, dining hall, recreation area, and so on. Although the formal rules require a social distance between officers and inmates, the physical closeness makes them aware that each relies on the other. The officers need the cooperation of the prisoners so that they will look good to their superiors, and the inmates count on the officers to relax the rules or occasionally look the other way. For example, officers in a Midwestern prison told researcher Stan Stojkovic that flexibility in rule enforcement was especially important as it related to the ability of prisoners to cope with their environment. As one officer said, "Phone calls are really important to guys in this place.... You cut off their calls and they get pissed. So what I do is give them a little extra and they are good to me." Yet the officers also told Stojkovic that they would be crazy to intervene to stop illicit sex or drug use (Stojkovic, 1990:214).

Correctional officers must be careful not to pay too high a price for the cooperation of their charges. Under pressure to work effectively with prisoners, officers may be blackmailed into doing illegitimate favors in return for cooperation. Officers who establish *sub-rosa,* or secret, relationships can be manipulated by prisoners into smuggling contraband or committing other illegal acts. See "A Question of Ethics" for a dilemma that correctional officers frequently face.

Inmate Leadership

In the traditional prison of the big-house era, administrators enlisted the inmate leaders to help maintain order. Inmate leaders had been "tested" over time so that they were neither pushed around by other inmates nor distrusted as stool pigeons. Because the staff could rely on them, they served as the essential communications link between staff and inmates. Their ability to acquire inside information and gain access to higher officials brought inmate leaders the respect of other prisoners and special privileges from officials. In turn, they distributed these benefits to other prisoners, thus bolstering their own influence within the prison society.

Descriptions of the contemporary maximum-security prison, however, raise questions about administrators' ability to run institutions in this way. In most of today's institutions, prisoners are divided by race, ethnicity, age, and gang affiliation, so that no single leadership structure exists.

After three years of daily contact, correctional officer Bill MacLeod and Jack Douglas, who was serving a 3–5 year sentence, knew each other very well. They were both devoted to the Red Sox and the Celtics. Throughout the year they would chat about the fortunes of their teams and the outlook ahead. MacLeod got to know and like Douglas. They were about the same age and had come from similar backgrounds. Why they were now on opposite sides of the cell bars was something that MacLeod could not figure out.

One day Douglas called to MacLeod and said that he needed money because he had lost a bet gambling on the Red Sox. Douglas said that his wife would send him the money but that it couldn't come through the prison mail to him in cash. And a check or money order would show on his commissary account.

"The guy wants cash. If he doesn't get it, I'm dead." Douglas took a breath and then rushed on with his request. "Could you bring it in for me? She'll mail the money to you at home. You could just drop the envelope on my bed."

"You know the rules. No gambling and no money," said MacLeod.

"But I'm scared shitless. It will be no big deal for you and it will make all the difference for me. Come on, we've gotten along well all these years. I think of you as being different from those other officers."

→ What should MacLeod do? Is this kind of request likely to be a one-time occurrence with Douglas? What if MacLeod's sergeant finds out? What if other inmates learn about it?

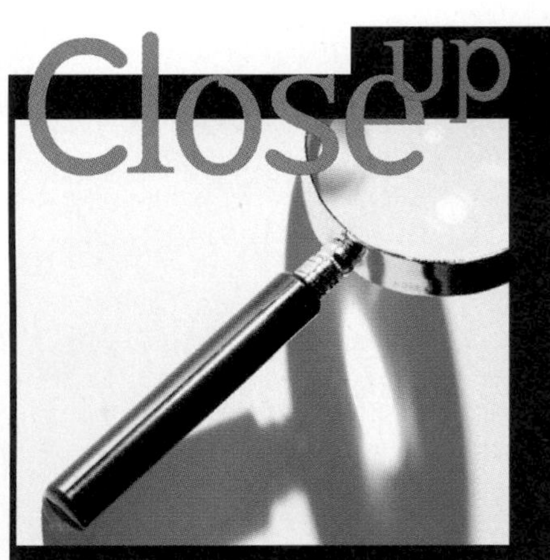

A Model Prison

In the woods outside of Bradford, Pennsylvania, stands the Federal Correctional Institution, McKean. Opened in 1989 as a medium-security facility, it houses more than one thousand male inmates. Until he retired in July 1995, Dennis Luther was McKean's warden, an administrator who, during this 16 years in prison work, gained a reputation for unorthodox policies.

At a time when politicians were railing against "country club" prisons and the need to "make 'em bust rocks," Warden Luther ran an institution that earned a 99.3 accreditation rating from the American Correctional Association, the highest in the Bureau of Prisons. Although badly overcrowded and with an increasing number of violent offenders, McKean cost taxpayers $15,370 a year for each inmate, well below the federal average of $21,350. Amazingly in six years there were no escapes, no murders, no suicides, and only three serious assaults against staff and six recorded against inmates.

How did Warden Luther do it? According to Luther, each prison has its own culture, which is often violent and abusive, based on gangs. The staff in such institutions feel they cannot change it. At McKean, Warden Luther set out to build a different type of culture, one based on unconditional respect for the inmates as people. As he says, "If you want people to behave responsibly and treat you with respect, then you treat other people that way." This credo has been translated into 28 beliefs, the product of Luther's years of experience. These "Beliefs about the Treatment of Inmates" are posted all over the institution to remind both staff and inmates alike of their responsibilities. They include the following:

1. Inmates are sent to prison *as* punishment and not *for* punishment.
2. Correctional workers have a *responsibility* to ensure that inmates are returned to the community no more angry or hostile than when they were committed.
3. Inmates are *entitled* to a safe and humane environment while in prison.
4. You must believe in man's *capacity* to change his behavior.
10. *Be responsive* to inmate requests for action or information. Respond in a timely manner and respond the first time an inmate makes a request.
12. It is important for staff to *model* the kind of behavior they expect to see duplicated by inmates.
14. There is an *inherent value* in self-improvement programs such as education, whether or not these programs are related to recidivism.
18. Staff *cannot,* because of their own insecurities, lack of self-esteem, or concerns

The Challenge of Governing Prisons

The factors of total power, rewards and punishments, exchange relationships, and inmate leadership exist in every prison and must be managed. How they are managed greatly influences the quality of prison life. John DiIulio's research (1987) challenges the common assumption of many correctional administrators that "the cons run the joint." Instead, successful wardens have made their prisons function well by applying management principles within the context of their own style of leadership. Prisons can be governed, violence can be minimized, and services can be provided to the inmates if correctional executives and wardens exhibit leadership. Governing prisons is an extraordinary challenge, but it can be and has been effectively accomplished. The Close Up box describes the unique management practices of Warden Dennis Luther.

check point

6. What four factors make the governing of prisons different from administering other public institutions?
7. How would you characterize Warden Luther's management style?

about their masculinity, condescend or degrade inmates.

26. Inmate discipline must be consistent and fair.

Merely posting the "Beliefs" in prominent places will not create a superior prison culture. The credo must be put into practice. Here are some examples:

1. *Front-Line Staff.* To get front-line staffers to treat inmates with respect, top managers must treat staffers with respect. As Luther has said, "Line-level people have good ideas, not only about how to do their job, but about how to do *your* job better." With this in mind he created the Line Staff Advisory Board, a rotating group of front-line workers who meet with him to talk through complaints, suggestions, and rumors.
2. *"Management By Walking Around."* Through contact with staff and inmates in the dining hall, on the yard, and in the cell blocks, a warden becomes a visible presence who can hear suggestions and complaints. Often he or she can nip problems before they fester and explode. This presence sets an example of the extent to which the warden is concerned about the problems of inmates and staff.
3. *Inmate Involvement.* Regular "town hall" meetings with inmates provide opportunities for two-way communications. Proposed changes in regulations or procedures are first brought to the inmates for comment. For example, items to be offered in the commissary would be discussed.
4. *Inmate Benefit Fund.* The Inmate Benefit Fund (IBF) was created to generate money inmates could use to purchase items for which taxpayer dollars were not available. Using their own funds, inmates could order items from Bradford stores and restaurants that would ease their stay in McKean. Orders were placed with the IBF and delivered to the institution for a modest handling charge. With 2,000 inmates, substantial sums were generated by these surcharges. The inmates could use these funds to purchase additional educational and recreational programs for the population. Besides helping inmates gain access to these programs, the IBF spending contributed to the local economy.
5. *Education.* McKean has a higher percentage of inmates enrolled in classes than does almost any other federal prison. Luther believes that prison time should be spent preparing offenders for their return to the community. Courses are taught by staff members of the prison's education department, professors from neighboring colleges, and inmates. The inmates teach Adult Continuing Education courses and act as mentors and tutors.

Luther expects inmates to be responsible, and he holds them to a higher standard than found in most prisons. After a few minor incidents, the warden ordered "closed movement" during evening hours. This restricted inmate activity and was meant to be permanent. A group of inmates asked if he would restore "open movement" if the prison was incident-free for 90 days. Luther agreed and the prison has remained "open."

Inmates who meet the standards receive rewards. Weekly inspections are held in each cell block, and inmates who score high are given additional privileges. Those whose disciplinary record is clean and excel in the programs can earn their way to the "honor unit." Those who show consistently good behavior are allowed to attend supervised picnics on Family Day.

Dennis Luther is convinced that his methods will work in any prison, even those plagued by violence, overcrowding, and gangs. Many staff members feel the same way. They believe that McKean is a shining example of the difference good management can make.

Source: Drawn from Tom Peters, *Liberation Management* (New York: Knopf, 1992), 247–55; Robert Worth, "A Model Prison," *Atlantic Monthly,* November 1995, pp. 38–44.

For a different management approach, use InfoTrac College Edition to access the article "Missouri's Parallel Universe: A Blueprint for Effective Prison Management," *Corrections Today,* April 2001.

Correctional Officers: The Linchpin of Management

A prison is simultaneously supposed to keep, use, and serve its inmates. The achievement of these goals depends heavily on the performance of its correctional officers. Their job is not easy. Not only do they work long and difficult hours with a hostile client population, but their superiors also expect them to do so with few resources or punishments at their disposal. Most of what they are expected to do must be accomplished by gaining and keeping the cooperation of the prisoners.

The Officer's Role

Over the past 25 years, the correctional officer's role has changed greatly. No longer responsible merely for "guarding," the correctional officer is now considered a crucial professional who has the closest contact with the prisoners and performs a variety of tasks. Officers are expected to counsel, supervise, protect, and process the inmates under their care. But the officer also works as a member of a complex bureaucratic organization and is expected to deal with clients impersonally and to follow formal procedures. Fulfilling these contradictory role

Rich Pedroncelli/AP/Wide World Photos

Much of the work of correctional officers involves searching and counting. Such officers have a saying: "We're all doing time together, except guards are doing it in eight-hour shifts."

expectations is difficult in itself, and the difficulty is exacerbated by the physical closeness of the officer and inmate over long periods. Yet John Hepburn and Paul Knepper found that officers who played a human services role rather than a purely custodial role had greater job satisfaction (1993:315).

Recruitment of Officers

Employment as a correctional officer is not a glamorous and popular occupation. The work is thought to be boring, the pay is low, and career advancement barely exists. Studies have shown that one of the primary incentives for becoming involved in correctional work is the security that civil service status provides. In addition, because most correctional facilities are located in rural areas, prison work often is better than other available employment. Because correctional officers are recruited locally, most of them are rural and white, in contrast to the majority of prisoners who come from urban areas and are often either African American or Hispanic (see Figure 15.2). Yet some correctional officers see their work as a way of helping people, often the people most in need in U.S. society.

Today, because they need more well-qualified correctional officers, most states recruit quality personnel. Salaries have been raised so that the yearly average entry-level pay runs from $16,000 in some southern and rural states to over $30,000 in states such as Massachusetts and New Jersey (C. G. Camp and Camp, 2001:150). In addition to their salaries, most officers can earn overtime pay, supplementing base pay by up to 30 percent. However, low salaries in a competitive economy, the massive increase in the prison population, and a tougher, more violent class of prisoners have all probably contributed to a severe shortage of correctional officers (Belluck, 2001).

Information about a career as a correctional officer can be found at the *Occupational Outlook Handbook* Web site: http://www.bls.gov/oco/ocos156.htm.

Special efforts have been made to recruit women and minorities. Today approximately 34 percent of correctional officers are members of minority groups and 22 percent are women (C. G. Camp and Camp, 2001:134). Female officers are no longer restricted to working with female offenders. For example, women represent 25 percent of Alabama's correctional officers, and 97 percent of these women work in male institutions (BJS, 1999c:81).

How do these increases in the number of minority and female officers shape the work environment among correctional officers? Dana Britton found in her study that black male and female officers are less satisfied with their jobs than are their white male counterparts. She also found that black and Hispanic male officers felt they were more effective working with the inmates than did their white counterparts (Britton, 1997). Contrary to the assumption of some male officers that women cannot handle the job, Denise Jenne and Robert Kersting (1996) found that female officers tended to respond to violent situations as aggressively as their male coworkers. In some states, male prisoners raised the issue of privacy when female officers were assigned to cell-block duty; courts have upheld inmate objections with regard to women supervising shower and toilet facilities (Pogrebin and Poole, 1997).

Figure 15.2 **Racial/ethnic composition of correctional officers and inmates, adult systems, nationwide**

Although the racial/ethnic composition of correctional officers does not equal the racial/ethnic composition of the inmate population, great strides have been made during the past quarter century.

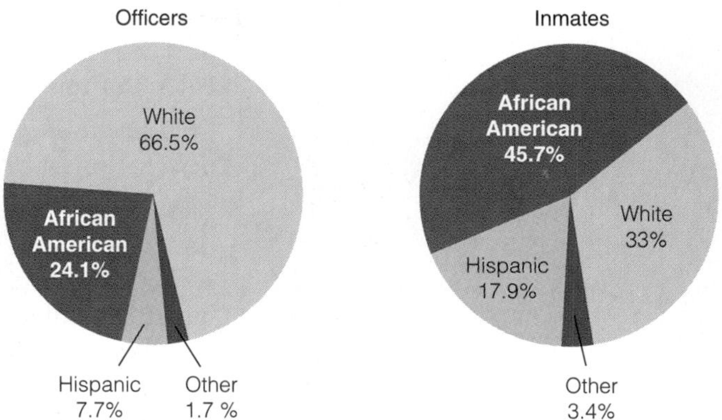

Sources: Bureau of Justice Statistics, *Bulletin* (Washington, D.C.: U.S. Government Printing Office, August, 2000), 9; Camille Camp and George Camp, *Corrections Yearbook, 2000* (Middletown, Conn.: Criminal Justice Institute, 2001), 134.

Most states now have training programs for correctional officers. Ted Conover compares his experience as a "newjack" (recruit) at the Corrections Academy of the State of New York to that of the military's basic training (Conover, 2000:12–56). During the typical six-week programs, recruits receive at least a rudimentary knowledge of job requirements and correctional rules. The classroom work, however, often bears little resemblance to problems confronted in the cell block or on the yard. Therefore, on completing the course, the new officer is placed under the supervision of an experienced officer. On the job, the new officer experiences real-life situations and learns the necessary techniques and procedures. Through encounters with inmates and officers, the recruit becomes socialized to life behind the walls and gradually becomes part of that subculture (Crouch and Marquart, 1994:301).

For most correctional workers, being a custodial officer is a dead-end job. Although officers who perform well may be promoted to higher ranks such as correctional counselor, few ever move into administrative positions. However, in some states and in the Federal Bureau of Prisons, people with college degrees can move up the career ladder to management positions.

Use of Force

The use of force by correctional officers, as by the police, is a controversial issue. Although corporal punishment and the excessive use of force are not permitted, correctional officers use force in many situations. They often confront inmates who challenge their authority or are attacking other inmates. Though unarmed and outnumbered, officers must maintain order and uphold institutional rules. Under these conditions they feel justified in using force.

When and how much force may be used? All correctional agencies now have formal policies and procedures with regard to the legitimate use of force. In general these policies allow only levels of force necessary to achieve legitimate goals. Officers violating these policies may face an inmate lawsuit and dismissal. There are five situations in which the use of force is legally acceptable:

1. *Self-defense:* If officers are threatened with physical attack, they may use a level of force that is reasonable to protect themselves from harm.

2. *Defense of third persons:* As in self-defense, an officer may use force to protect an inmate or another officer. Again, only reasonably necessary force may be used.
3. *Upholding prison rules:* If prisoners refuse to obey prison rules, officers may need to use force to maintain safety and security. For example, if an inmate refuses to return to his or her cell it may be necessary to use handcuffs and forcefully transfer the prisoner.
4. *Prevention of a crime:* Force may be used to stop a crime, such as theft or destruction of property, from being committed.
5. *Prevention of escapes:* Officers may use force to prevent escapes, because they threaten the well-being of society and order within correctional institutions. Although escape from a prison is a felony, officials may not shoot the fleeing inmate at will as in the past. Today, agencies differ as to their policies toward escapees. Some limit the use of deadly force to prisoners thought to be dangerous, while others require warning shots. However, officers in Nebraska and Texas may face disciplinary action if they fail to use deadly force. Although the U.S. Supreme Court has limited the ability of police officers to shoot fleeing felons, the rule has not been applied to correctional officers.

Correctional officers face challenges to self-control and professional decision making. Inmates often "push" officers in subtle ways such as moving slowly, or they use verbal abuse to provoke officers. Correctional officers are expected to run a "tight ship" and maintain order, often in situations where they are outnumbered and dealing with troubled people. In confrontational situations they must defuse hostility yet uphold the uphold the rules—a difficult task at best.

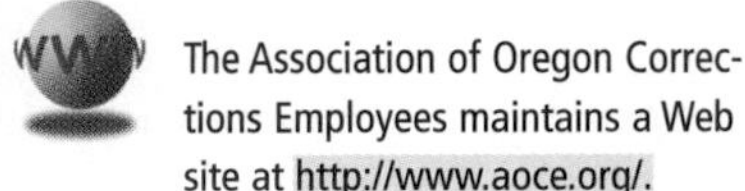
The Association of Oregon Corrections Employees maintains a Web site at http://www.aoce.org/.

8. Why are correctional officers called the "linchpin of management?"
9. Name three of the five legally acceptable reasons for the use of force.

Violence in Prison

Prisons provide a perfect recipe for violence. They confine in cramped quarters a thousand men, some with histories of violent behavior. While incarcerated, these men are not allowed contact with women and live under highly restrictive conditions. Sometimes these conditions spark collective violence, as in the riots at Attica, New York (1971), Santa Fe, New Mexico (1980), Atlanta, Georgia (1987), and Lucasville, Ohio (1993).

Although prison riots are widely reported in the news, few people know the level of everyday interpersonal violence in U.S. prisons. For example, each year about 150 prisoners commit suicide, about 90 perish in deaths "caused by another," and 400 die of unknown causes that were apparently not natural, self-inflicted, accidental, or homicide (BJS, 2000d:91). Annually about 27,000 assaults by other inmates and about 15,000 assaults against staff take place. Great numbers of prisoners live in a state of constant uneasiness, always on the lookout for people who might demand sex, steal their few possessions, or otherwise hurt them. Some researchers suggest that the level of violence varies by offender age, institutional security designation, and administrative effectiveness (Maitland and Sluder, 1998:55).

Assaultive Behavior and Inmate Characteristics

For the person entering prison for the first time, the anxiety level and fear of violence is especially high. Gary, an inmate at Leavenworth, told Pete Earley, "Every convict has three choices, but only three. He can fight (kill someone), he

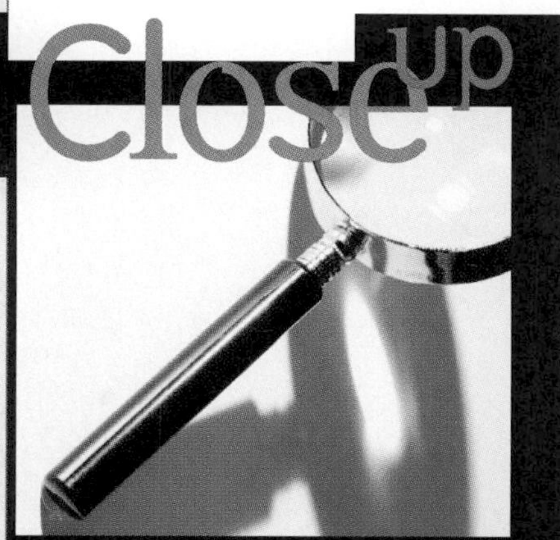

On Prison Rape

The problem of sexual assault in prison receives little attention from policy makers and the public. There are no reliable national data on prison rape; only a few small-scale studies indicate the scope of the problem. If these findings reflect the national picture, then at least 140,000 prisoners have been raped. Prison rape is a crime hidden by a curtain of silence.

Victims of prison rape tend to be young, physically small, first-timers who are gay, have "feminine" characteristics, and were convicted of sexual offense against a minor. Not only are such attacks traumatic, but the victim also becomes a target for further exploitation.

Although the characteristics of prison rapists are somewhat less clear, Human Rights Watch found certain patterns. The perpetrators tend to be young, if not always as young as their victims—generally well under 35 years old. Frequently larger or stronger than their victims, they are generally more assertive, physically aggressive, and more at home in the prison environment. They are "street smart"—often gang members—and have typically been convicted of more-violent crimes than their victims have.

Incidents occasionally come to public attention when the victim goes to the press or to court. For example, Edward Dillard, a 120-pound inmate serving time for assault at California's Corcoran State Prison, was repeatedly raped by Wayne Robertson, a 230-pound sexual predator serving life without parole for a murder conviction.

Dillard had previously clashed with Robertson and placed his name on a list of known enemies with whom he should not share a cell. Yet Dillard was moved into Robertson's cell, where he was raped numerous times over a weekend. On Monday Robertson was taken to a hearing, and when he returned Dillard ran out and refused to reenter the cell.

Dillard's case is one of the few to come to both criminal and civil trials. In court papers he charged that prison guards set up the rape. Robertson backed up the complaint saying that Robert Decker, a correctional officer, agreed to place Dillard with him so that he "could show Mr. Dillard 'how to do his time.'" Although Decker and three other officers were charged with aiding and abetting sodomy, they were acquitted at trial. Dillard is now out of prison and is pursuing a civil suit against the four.

In the age of AIDS, rape can be a death penalty. Kenneth Spruce, an Arkansas prisoner serving time on a fraudulent check conviction, was raped by 20 inmates in one year and contracted AIDS as a result. He sued prison officials, charging cruel and unusual treatment. Warden Willis Sargent testified that prisoners bore the responsibility for fighting off sexual advances, by letting others know they are "not going to put up with that." A Federal District Court found that even if the warden knew of the risks to Spruce, his actions did not amount to "deliberate indifference," the legal standard holding him accountable.

Some correctional departments are taking steps to train correctional officers to prevent inmate rape, to bring criminal charges against the perpetrators, and to provide medical and psychological care for the victim. But these initiatives are the exception. Prison rape remains a crime for which the victims receive little sympathy or remedy.

Sources: Drawn from Stephen Donaldson, "The Rape Crisis behind Bars," *New York Times,* December 29, 1993; Human Rights Watch, *No Escape: Male Rape in U.S. Prisons* (http://www.hrw.org/reports/2001/prison/report1.html); Tamar Lewin, "Little Sympathy or Remedy for Inmates Who Are Raped," *New York Times,* April 15, 2001, p. A1; *Prison Journal* 80 (December 2000) [special issue on prison sexuality].

Researching the **Internet**

Learn more about prison rape at the Web site of Stop Prison Rape, a national nonprofit organization: http://www.spr.org.

can hit the fence (escape), or he can fuck (submit)" (1992:55). Correctional officers find it difficult to distinguish between consensual sexual acts and rapes. Most have not caught inmates in the act, and only a few officers said they ignored violations when they discovered them (Eigenberg, 2000). See the Close Up box for more on prison rape.

Violent behavior in prisons is related to the characteristics of the inmates. Christopher Innes and Vicki Verdeyen suggest that violent offenders can be divided into those who (1) have learned to be violent, (2) cannot regulate their violence, because of mental disabilities, and (3) are violent and have severe personality disorders (1997:1). Three characteristics underlie these behavioral factors: age, attitudes, and race.

Age

Young men aged 16–24, both inside and outside prison, are more prone to violence than are their elders (L. M. S. Simon, 1993:263). Not surprisingly, 96 percent of adult prisoners are men, with an average age at the time of admission of 27.

Besides greater physical strength, young men also lack the commitments to career and family that can restrict antisocial behavior. In addition, many have difficulty defining their position in society. Thus they interpret many things as challenges to their status.

"Machismo," the concept of male honor and the sacredness of one's reputation as a man, requires physical retaliation against those who insult one's honor. Observers have argued that many homosexual rapes are not sexual but political—attempts to impress on the victim the aggressor's male power and to define the target as passive or "feminine" (Rideau and Wikberg, 1992:79). Some inmates adopt a preventive strategy of trying to impress others with their bravado, which may result in counterchallenges and violence. The potential for violence among such prisoners is clear.

Attitudes

One sociological theory of crime suggests that a subculture of violence exists among certain socioeconomic, racial, and ethnic groups. In this subculture, found in the lower class and in its value system, violence is "tolerable, expected, or required" (Wolfgang and Ferracuti, 1967:263). Arguments are settled and decisions are made by the fist rather than by verbal persuasion. Many inmates bring these attitudes into prison with them.

Race

Race has become a major divisive factor in today's prisons. Racist attitudes, common in the larger society, have become part of the "convict code," or implicit rules of life. Forced association—having to live with people one would not likely associate with on the outside—exaggerates and amplifies racial conflict. Violence against members of another race may be how some inmates deal with the frustrations of their lives. The presence of gangs organized along racial lines contributes to violence in prison.

Prisoner–Prisoner Violence

Although prison folklore may attribute violence to brutal guards, most prison violence occurs between inmates. Matthew Silberman (1995:9) found a rate at "Central" of 32.64 attacks per 1,000 inmates, and Ben Crouch and James Marquart (1989:201) found a similar rate in eight Texas prisons. These levels of violence are not necessarily related to the size of the population in a particular facility. Uncounted inmates are injured by assaults. As Hans Toch has observed, the climate of violence in prisons has no free-world counterpart: "Inmates are terrorized by other inmates, and spend years in fear of harm. Some inmates request segregation, others lock themselves in, and some are hermits by choice" (1976:47–48).

Prison Gangs

Racial or ethnic gangs (also referred to as "security threat groups") are now linked to acts of violence in most prison systems. Gangs make it difficult for wardens to maintain control. By continuing their street wars inside prison, gangs make some prisons more dangerous than any American neighborhoods. Gangs are organized primarily to control an institution's drug, gambling, loan-sharking, prostitution, extortion, and debt-collection rackets. In addition, gangs protect their members from other gangs and instill a sense of macho camaraderie (Hunt et al., 1993:398).

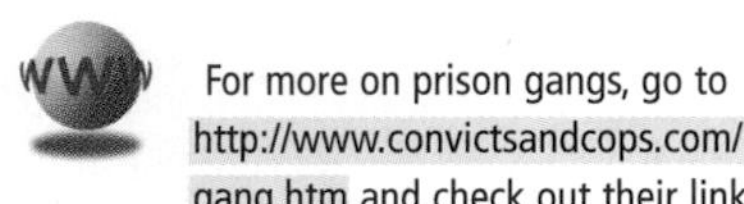

For more on prison gangs, go to http://www.convictsandcops.com/gang.htm and check out their links.

Contributing to prison violence is the usual "blood-in, blood-out" basis for gang membership: A would-be member must stab a gang's enemy to be admitted and, once in, cannot drop out without endangering his own life. Given the racial and ethnic foundation of the gangs, violence between them can easily spill into the general prison population. Some institutions have programs that offer members "a way out" of the gang. Often referred to as "deganging," these programs educate members and eventually encourage them to renounce their gang membership. Critics say that for many this supposed change is only a "way of getting out of lock-down status; proponents counter with 'So what? Their behavior within the prison setting has been modified'" (P. M. Carlson, 2001:13).

Prison gangs exist in the institutions of most states and the federal system. In Illinois as much as 60 percent of the population belongs to gangs (Hallinan, 2001:95). The Florida Department of Corrections has identified 240 street gangs operating in their prisons (Davitz, 1998). A study by the American Correctional Association found more than 46,000 gang members in the federal system and in the prisons of at least 35 states (1994:21).

Although the gangs are small, they are tightly organized and have even arranged the killing of opposition gang leaders housed in other institutions. Administrators say that prison gangs, like organized crime groups, tend to pursue their "business" interests, yet they are also a major source of inmate–inmate violence as they discipline members, enforce orders, and retaliate against other gangs (Buentello, 1992:58).

The racial and ethnic basis of gang membership has been documented in several states. In California, for example, a Chicano gang called the Mexican Mafia—whose membership had known each other in Los Angeles—took over the rackets in San Quentin in the late 1960s. In reaction, other gangs were formed, including a rival Mexican gang, La Nuestra Familia; CRIPS (Common Revolution in Progress); the Texas Syndicate; the Black Guerrilla Family; and the Aryan Brotherhood (see Table 15.1). Recent immigration patterns are reflected in new Chinese, Southeast Asian, and Central American gangs entering U.S. prisons (Huff and Meyer, 1997:11).

Many facilities segregate rival gangs by housing them in separate units of the prison or moving members to other facilities (Knox, 2000). Administrators have also set up intelligence units to gather information on gangs, particularly about illegal acts both in and outside of prison. In some prisons, however, these policies created a power vacuum within the convict society that newer groups with new codes of behavior soon filled (Hunt et al., 1993).

Table 15.1 Characteristics of major prison gangs

These gangs were founded in the California prison system during the late 1960s and 1970s. They have now spread across the nation and are viewed as major security threat groups in most corrections systems.

Name	Makeup	Origin	Characteristics	Enemies
Aryan Brotherhood	White	San Quentin, 1967	Apolitical. Most in custody for crimes such as robbery.	CRIPS, Bloods, BGF
Black Guerrilla Family (BGF)	African American	San Quentin, 1966	Most politically oriented. Antigovernment.	Aryan Brotherhood, EME
Mexican Mafia (EME)	Mexican American/Hispanic	Duel Vocational Center, Los Angeles, late 1950s	Ethnic solidarity, control of drug trafficking.	BGF, NF
La Nuestra Familia (NF)	Mexican American/Hispanic	Soledad, 1965	Protect young, rural Mexican Americans.	EME
Texas Syndicate	Mexican American/Hispanic	Folsom, early 1970s	Protect Texan inmates in California.	Aryan Brotherhood, EME, NF

Source: Florida Department of Corrections, "Major Prison Gangs" (http://www.dc.state.fl.us/pub/gangs/prison.html).

Protective Custody

For many victims of prison violence, protective custody offers the only way to escape further abuse. About 5,000 state prisoners are in protective custody (C. G. Camp and Camp, 2001:26). Life is not pleasant for these inmates. Often they are let out of their cells only briefly to exercise and shower (McGee, Warner, and Harlow, 1998). Inmates who ask to "lock up" have little chance of returning to the general prison population without being viewed as a weakling—a snitch or a punk—to be preyed on. Even when they are transferred to another institution, their reputations follow them through the grapevine.

Prisoner–Officer Violence

The mass media have focused on riots in which guards are taken hostage, injured, and killed. However, violence against officers typically occurs in specific situations and against certain individuals. Yearly, inmates assault more than 14,000 staff members (*USA Today,* August 8, 1997:1). Correctional officers do not carry weapons within the institution, because a prisoner might seize them. However, prisoners do manage to obtain lethal weapons and can use the element of surprise to injure an officer. In the course of a workaday an officer may encounter situations that require the use of physical force against an inmate—for instance, breaking up a fight or moving a prisoner to segregation. Because such situations are especially dangerous, officers may enlist others to help them minimize the risk of violence. The officer's greatest fear is unexpected attacks, such as a missile thrown from an upper tier or an officer's "accidental" fall down a flight of stairs. The need to constantly watch against personal attacks adds stress and keeps many officers at a distance from the inmates.

Officer–Prisoner Violence

A fact of life in many institutions is unauthorized physical violence by officers against inmates. Stories abound of guards giving individual prisoners "the treatment" when supervisors are not looking. Many guards view physical force as an everyday, legitimate procedure. In some institutions, authorized "goon squads" composed of physically powerful officers use their muscle to maintain order.

Perhaps the worst cases of officer–prisoner violence in recent years have occurred at the California State Prison at Corcoran. Between 1989 and 1995, 43 inmates were wounded and 7 killed by officers firing assault weapons—the most killings in any prison. Guards even instigated fights between rival gang members. During those "gladiator days," tower guards often shot the gladiators after they had been ordered to stop fighting. Each shooting was justified by state-appointed reviewers (Arax and Gladstone, 1998:1).

How do we tell when prison officers are using force legitimately and when they are using physical violence to punish individual prisoners? Correctional officers are expected to follow departmental rules in their dealings with prisoners, yet supervisors generally cannot observe staff–prisoner confrontations directly. Further, prisoner complaints about officer brutality are often not believed until the officer involved gains a reputation for harshness. Even in this case, wardens may feel they must support their officers in order to retain their officer's support.

Decreasing Prison Violence

As listed by Lee Bowker, five factors contribute to prison violence: (1) inadequate supervision by staff members, (2) architectural design that promotes rather than inhibits victimization, (3) the easy availability of deadly weapons, (4) the housing of violence-prone prisoners near relatively defenseless people, and (5) a general high level of tension produced by close quarters (1982:64). The physical

Joe Jines/Southern Illinoisan/AP/Wide World Photos

Preemptive strikes to rid prisons of drugs and weapons is one way to reduce violence. Here a tactical team at Big Muddy Correctional Center, Illinois, searches every inmate and cell.

size and condition of the prison and the relations between inmates and staff also affect violence.

The Effect of Architecture and Size

The fortresslike prison certainly does not create an atmosphere for normal interpersonal relationships, and the size of the larger institutions can create management problems. The massive scale of the megaprison, which may hold up to 3,000 inmates, provides opportunities for aggressive inmates to hide weapons, dispense private "justice," and engage more or less freely in other illicit activities. The size of the population in a large prison may also result in some inmates' "falling through the cracks"—being misclassified and forced to live among more-violent offenders.

The Role of Management

The degree to which inmate leaders are allowed to take matters into their own hands can affect the level of violence among inmates. When administrators run a tight ship, security measures prevent sexual attacks in dark corners, the making of "shivs" and "shanks" (knives) in the metal shop, and open conflict among inmate groups. A prison must afford each inmate defensible space, and administrators should ensure that every inmate is secure from physical attack.

Prison management can decrease the level of assaultive behavior by limiting opportunities for attacks. Wardens and correctional officers must therefore recognize the types of people with whom they are dealing, the role of prison gangs, and the structure of institutions. John DiIulio argues that no group of inmates is "unmanageable [and] no combination of political, social, budgetary, architectural, or other factors makes good management impossible" (DiIulio, 1991:12).

He points to such varied institutions as the California Men's Colony, New York City's Tombs and Rikers Island, the Federal Bureau of Prisons, and the Texas Department of Corrections under the leadership of George Beto. At these institutions, good management practices have resulted in prisons and jails where inmates can "do time" without fearing for their personal safety. Wardens who exert leadership can manage their prisons effectively, so that problems do not fester and erupt into violent confrontations.

In sum, prisons must be made safe places. Because the state puts offenders there, it has a responsibility to prevent violence and maintain order. To exclude violence from prisons, officials may have to limit movement within institutions, contacts with the outside, and the right of inmates to choose their associates. Yet these measures may run counter to the goal of producing men and women who will be accountable when they return to society.

Prisoners' Rights

hands-off policy
Judges should not interfere with the administration of correctional institutions.

***Ruffin v. Commonwealth* (1871)**
By committing a crime, the prisoner has become a slave of the state and has forfeited all personal rights.

Prior to the 1960s, most courts maintained a **hands-off policy** with respect to prisons. Judges in some states applied their state's constitution to correct abuses in jails and prisons. However most judges followed the belief of the Virginia judge in ***Ruffin v. Commonwealth*** **(1871)** that prisoners did not have rights. In addition, judges argued that the separation of powers among the three branches of government prevented them from interfering in the operations of any executive agency, such as a prison. Judges supposed that because they were not penologists, their intervention in the internal administration of prisons would disrupt discipline.

Since the 1960s, however, prisoners have gained access to the courts to contest decisions made by officers and aspects of their incarceration that they believe violate basic rights. Judicial decisions have defined and recognized the constitutional rights of incarcerated offenders and the need for correctional policies and procedures that respect those rights.

***Cooper v. Pate* (1964)**
State prisoners are entitled to the protection of the Civil Rights Act of 1871 and may challenge in federal courts the conditions of their confinement.

The U.S. Supreme Court decision in ***Cooper v. Pate*** **(1964)** signaled the end of the hands-off policy. The court said that through the Civil Rights Act of 1871 (referred to here as Section 1983), state prisoners were *persons* whose rights are protected by the Constitution. The act imposes *civil liability* on any person who deprives another of constitutional rights. It allows suits against state officials to be heard in the federal courts. Because of *Cooper v. Pate,* the federal courts now recognize that prisoners may sue state officials over such things as brutality by guards, inadequate nutrition and medical care, theft of personal property, and the denial of basic rights.

The first successful prisoners' rights cases involved the most excessive of prison abuses: brutality and inhumane physical conditions. Gradually, however, prison litigation has focused more directly on the daily activities of the institution, especially on the administrative rules that regulate inmates' conduct. The result has been a series of court decisions concerning the First, Fourth, Eighth, and Fourteenth Amendments to the Constitution. (See Appendix A for the full text of these amendments.)

For news of the current actions of the Supreme Court see the Web site of On the Docket: http://www.medill.nwu.edu/docket/index.html.

check point

10. What is meant by the hands-off policy?
11. Why is the case of *Cooper v. Pate* important to the expansion of prisoners' rights?

Table 15.2 Prisoners' rights under the First Amendment: Selected interpretations

The Supreme Court and other courts have made several decisions affecting prisoners' rights to freedom of speech and expression and freedom of religion.

Case	Decision
Fulwood v. Clemmer (1962)	The Muslim faith must be recognized as a religion, and officials may not restrict members from holding services.
Gittlemacker v. Prasse (1970)	The state must give inmates the opportunity to practice their religion but is not required to provide a member of the clergy.
Cruz v. Beto (1972)	Prisoners who adhere to other than conventional beliefs may not be denied the opportunity to practice their religion.
Theriault v. Carlson (1973)	The First Amendment does not protect so-called religions that are obvious shams, that tend to mock established institutions, and whose members lack religious sincerity.
Procunier v. Martinez (1974)	Censorship of mail is permitted only to the extent necessary to maintain prison security.
Kahane v. Carlson (1975)	An orthodox Jewish inmate has the right to a diet consistent with his religious beliefs unless the government can show cause why it cannot be provided.
O'Lone v. Estate of Shabazz (1987)	The rights of Muslim prisoners are not violated when work assignments make it impossible for them to attend religious services if no alternative exists.
Turner v. Safley (1987)	Inmates in different institutions do not have a right to receive mail from one another, and this mail can be banned if "reasonably related to legitimate penological interests."
Thornburgh v. Abbott (1989)	Rules permitting wardens to reject incoming publications deemed detrimental to security, good order, and discipline are constitutional.

First Amendment

The First Amendment guarantees freedom of speech, press, assembly, petition, and religion. Many of the restrictions of prison life—access to reading materials, censorship of mail, and rules affecting some religious practices—have been successfully challenged by prisoners in the courts.

Since 1970, courts have extended the rights of freedom of speech and expression to prisoners. They have required correctional administrators to show why restrictions on these rights must be imposed (see Table 15.2). For example, in 1974 the Supreme Court ruled that censorship of mail was permissible only when officials could demonstrate a compelling government interest in maintaining security (*Procunier v. Martinez*). The result has been a marked increased in communications between inmates and the outside world. However, in *Turner v. Safley* (1987), the Court upheld a Missouri ban on correspondence between inmates in different institutions, as a means of combating gang violence and the communication of escape plans.

The First Amendment prevents Congress from making laws respecting the establishment of religion or prohibiting its free exercise. Cases concerning the free exercise of religion have caused the judiciary some problems, especially when the religious practice may interfere with prison routine and the maintenance of order.

The growth of the Black Muslim religion in prisons set the stage for suits demanding that this group be granted the same privileges as other faiths (special diets, access to clergy and religious publications, opportunities for group worship). In the early 1960s many prison administrators believed that the Black Muslims were primarily a radical political group posing as a religion. They did not grant them the benefits accorded to those who practiced conventional religions.

In ***Fulwood v. Clemmer* (1962)**, however, a federal court ruled that officials must recognize the Black Muslims as a religion and allow them to hold worship services as do inmates of other faiths. In ***Cruz v. Beto* (1972)**, the Supreme Court

***Fulwood v. Clemmer* (1962)**
Black Muslims have the same right to worship and practice their religion that inmates of other faiths have.

***Cruz v. Beto* (1972)**
Inmates whose faiths are not the conventional ones practiced in the United States should have reasonable opportunities to practice their faiths.

CORBIS

The First Amendment to the Constitution provides for the free exercise of religion. The Black Muslims have been a major factor in forcing correctional administrators to recognize that right.

declared that a Buddhist prisoner must be given reasonable opportunities to practice his faith, like those given to prisoners belonging to religions more commonly practiced in the United States.

However, in *O'Lone v. Estate of Shabazz* (1987), the court ruled that a Muslim's rights were not violated by prison officials who would not alter his work schedule so that he could attend Friday afternoon Jumu'ah services. Shabazz's assignment took him outside of the prison, and officials claimed that returning him for services would create a security risk. The justices ruled that the policy was related to a legitimate penological interest.

Muslim, Orthodox Jewish, Native American, and other prisoners have gained some of the rights considered necessary for the practice of their religions. Court decisions have upheld prisoners' rights to be served meals consistent with religious dietary laws, to correspond with religious leaders and possess religious literature, to wear a beard if religious belief requires it, and to assemble for religious services. In sum, members of these religious minorities have broken new legal ground in First Amendment issues.

Fourth Amendment

The Fourth Amendment was designed to safeguard various types of privacy, protecting people from government intrusions. However, on entering a correctional institution, prisoners surrender most of their rights to privacy. The amendment prohibits only "unreasonable" searches and seizures. Thus regulations viewed as reasonable to maintain security and order in an institution may be justified.

Table 15.3 outlines some of the U.S. Supreme Court's Fourth Amendment opinions. They reveal the fine balance between the right to privacy and institutional need.

Table 15.3 Prisoners' rights under the Fourth Amendment: Selected interpretations

The Supreme Court and other courts identify very limited protection against searches and seizures.

Case	Decision
Lanza v. New York (1962)	Conversations recorded in a jail visitor's room are not protected by the Fourth Amendment.
U.S. v. Hitchcock (1972)	A warrantless search of a cell is not unreasonable, and documentary evidence found there is not subject to suppression in court. It is not reasonable to expect a prison cell to be accorded the same level of privacy as a home or automobile.
Bell v. Wolfish (1979)	Strip searches, including searches of body cavities after contact visits, may be carried out when the need for such searches outweighs the personal rights invaded.
Hudson v. Palmer (1984)	Officials may search cells without a warrant and seize materials found there.

Two principal types of searches occur in prisons: searches of cells and searches of persons. In ***Hudson v. Palmer* (1984)**, the Supreme Court upheld the right of officials to search cells and confiscate any materials found. Searches of the person may be conducted at different levels of intrusiveness: metal detectors, pat-down searches of clothed inmates, visual "strip" (nude) searches, and body cavity searches. Correctional administrators must craft regulations to demonstrate clearly that the level of intrusiveness is related to a legitimate institutional need and not conducted with the intent to humiliate or degrade (*Smith v. Fairman,* 1982).

***Hudson v. Palmer* (1984)**
Prison officials have a right to search cells and confiscate from inmates any materials found.

Courts have ruled that staff members of one sex may not supervise inmates of the opposite sex during bathing, use of the toilet, or strip searches (*Lee v. Downs,* 1981). Here the inconvenience of ensuring that the officer is of the same sex as the inmate does not justify the intrusion. Yet the authority of female guards to "pat down" male prisoners, excluding the genital area, has been upheld (*Smith v. Fairman,* 1982).

Eighth Amendment

The Constitution's prohibition of cruel and unusual punishments has been tied to prisoners' need for decent treatment and minimum health standards. The courts have applied three principal tests under the Eighth Amendment to determine whether conditions are unconstitutional:(1) whether the punishment shocks the conscience of a civilized society, (2) whether the punishment is unnecessarily cruel, and (3) whether the punishment goes beyond legitimate penal aims.

Federal courts have ruled that, although some aspects of prison life may be acceptable, the combination of various factors—the *totality of conditions*—may be such that life in the institution constitutes cruel and unusual punishment. When courts have found brutality, unsanitary facilities, overcrowding, and inadequate food, judges have used the Eighth Amendment to order sweeping changes and, in some cases, even to take over administration of entire prisons or corrections systems. In these cases judges have ordered wardens to follow specific internal procedures and to spend money on certain improvements (see Table 15.4).

Several dramatic cases demonstrate this point. In Georgia, for example, prison conditions were shown to be so bad that judges demanded change (Chilton, 1991). In ***Ruiz v. Estelle* (1980)**, the court ordered the Texas prison system to address a series of unconstitutional conditions (Crouch and Marquart,

***Ruiz v. Estelle* (1980)**
Conditions of confinement in the Texas prison system were unconstitutional.

Table 15.4 Prisoners' rights under the Eighth Amendment: Selected interpretations

In several key cases, the Supreme Court has ruled on whether correctional actions constitute cruel and unusual punishments.

Case	Decision
Estelle v. Gamble (1976)	Deliberate indifference to serious medical needs of prisoners constitutes the unnecessary and wanton infliction of pain, and thus violates the Eighth Amendment.
Ruiz v. Estelle (1980)	Conditions of confinement in the Texas prison system are unconstitutional.
Rhodes v. Chapman (1981)	Double-celling and crowding do not necessarily constitute cruel and unusual punishment. It must be shown that the conditions involve "wanton and unnecessary infliction of pain" and are "grossly disproportionate" to the severity of the crime warranting imprisonment.
Whitley v. Albers (1986)	A prisoner shot in the leg during a riot does not suffer cruel and unusual punishment if the action was taken in good faith to maintain discipline rather than for the mere purpose of causing harm.
Wilson v. Seiter (1991)	Prisoners must not only prove that prison conditions are objectively cruel and unusual but also show that they exist because of the deliberate indifference of officials.

1989; Martin and Ekland-Olson, 1987). Judicial supervision of the system continued for a decade, finally ending in 1990.

Many conditions that violate the rights of prisoners may be corrected by administrative action, training programs, or a minimal expenditure of funds, but remedying an overcrowded population requires expanding facilities or reducing the intake rate. Prison officials have no control over the capacities of their institutions or over the number of offenders sent to them by the courts. New facilities are expensive, and they require appropriations by legislatures and, often, approval of bond measures by voters.

check point

12. Which amendments to the Bill of Rights have been most influential in expanding prisoners' rights?

Fourteenth Amendment

One word and two clauses of the Fourteenth Amendment are relevant to the question of prisoners' rights. The relevant word is *state,* which is found in several clauses of the Fourteen Amendment. It was not until the mid-twentieth century that the Supreme Court ruled that through the Fourteenth Amendment, the Bill of Rights restricts state governments.

The first important clause concerns procedural due process, which requires that government officials treat all people fairly and justly and that official decisions be made according to procedures prescribed by law. The second important clause is the equal protection clause. Assertions that prisoners have been denied equal protection of the law are based on claims of racial, gender, or religious discrimination.

Due Process in Prison Discipline

In the 1970s the Supreme Court began to insist that procedural due process be part of the most sensitive of institutional decisions: the decisions by which inmates are sent to solitary confinement and the method by which good-time credit is taken away because of misconduct.

***Wolff v. McDonnell* (1974)**
Basic elements of procedural due process must be present when decisions are made about the disciplining of an inmate.

In *Wolff v. McDonnell* (1974), the Supreme Court extended certain due process rights. The Supreme Court specified that when a prisoner faces serious disciplinary action that could result in the withdrawal of good time or segregation, the state must follow certain minimal procedures that conform to the guarantee of due process. Specifically, prisoners have a right to receive notice of the complaint, to have a fair hearing, to confront witnesses, to get help in preparing for the hearing, and to be given a written statement of the decision. However, the Court also recognized special conditions of incarceration; it also stated that prisoners do not have a right to cross-examine witnesses and that the evidence presented by the offender shall not be unduly hazardous to institutional safety or correctional goal.

As a result of these Supreme Court decisions, some of which are outlined in Table 15.5, prison officials have established rules that provide elements of due process in disciplinary and other proceedings. In many institutions, a disciplinary committee receives the charges, conducts hearings, and decides guilt and punishment. Such committees usually include only administrative personnel but sometimes include inmates or citizens from the outside. Even with these protections, prisoners are still powerless and may risk further punishment if they challenge the warden's decisions too vigorously.

Equal Protection

In 1968 the Supreme Court firmly established that racial discrimination may not be official policy within prison walls (*Lee v. Washington*). Segregation can be justified only as a temporary expedient during periods when violence between

Table 15.5 Prisoners' rights under the Fourteenth Amendment: Selected interpretations

The Supreme Court has ruled in several key cases concerning procedural due process.

Case	Decision
Wolff v. McDonnell (1974)	The basic elements of procedural due process must be present when decisions are made concerning the disciplining of an inmate.
Baxter v. Palmigiano (1976)	Although due process must be accorded, an inmate has no right to counsel in a disciplinary hearing.
Vitek v. Jones (1980)	The involuntary transfer of a prisoner to a mental hospital requires a hearing and other minimal elements of due process such as notice and the availability of counsel.
Sandin v. Conner (1995)	Prison regulations do not violate liberty in a way that requires due process protection, unless they place atypical and significant hardships on a prisoner.

races is demonstrably imminent. Equal protection claims have also been upheld in relation to religious freedoms and access to reading materials of interest to racial minorities. For instance, the cases brought by members of the Black Muslim religion concerned both the First Amendment right to religious freedom and the Fourteenth Amendment right to equal protection.

The most recent cases concerning equal protection deal with issues concerning female offenders. Although the Supreme Court has yet to rule, state and lower federal courts have considered several cases. In *Pargo v. Elliott* (1995), female inmates in Iowa argued that their equal protection rights were violated because programs and services were not as good as those provided to male inmates. The court ruled that because of differences and needs, identical treatment is not required for men and women. It concluded that there was no evidence of "invidious discrimination."

checkpoint

13. Which two clauses of the Fourteenth Amendment have been interpreted by the Supreme Court to apply to prisoners' rights?

Redress of Grievances

Decisions of the U.S. Supreme Court make headlines, but the public never hears about many prisoners' rights suits. In 2000, state prisoners filed 25,500 suits in the federal courts under the Civil Rights Act of 1871 (42 U.S.C. 1983) contesting conditions of their confinement. In these Section 1983 civil rights suits, prisoners sought improvements in prison conditions, medical care, return of property, or compensation for abuse by officers.

Go to the Public Policy feature on the American System of Criminal Justice CD to learn more about the issues surrounding prisoner litigation.

Few of these suits succeed. Researchers found that 74 percent of Section 1983 cases disposed of in one year were dismissed because there was no evidence of a constitutional rights violation (Hanson and Daley, 1995:19). Most prisoner petitions are written without the assistance of counsel and are often filed in error because of misinterpretations of the law. Ultimately only 2 percent of the cases went to trial and only half were decided in favor of the prisoner.

Although successful Section 1983 cases are few, individual inmates have won redress, or remedy, of their grievances. Some have received monetary compensation for neglect; others have been given the medical attention they desired; still other cases have brought judicial orders that have ended certain correctional practices.

Courts may respond to prisoners' requests in specific cases, but judges cannot possibly oversee the daily activities within institutional walls. As a result of the increase in conditions-of-confinement cases, correctional authorities have acted to ensure that fair procedures are followed and that unconstitutional practices are stopped. Publication of institutional rules, obligations, and procedures is one of the first and most important steps required to meet these goals. Grievance procedures have been developed so that prisoner complaints can be addressed before they result in a lawsuit.

check point

14. What has been the function of 42 U.S.C. 1983 in relation to prisoners' rights?
15. What procedures are required in disciplinary proceedings for prisoners?

A Change in Judicial Direction?

Wilson v. Seiter (1991)
The standard of review of official conduct is whether state policies or actions by correctional officers constitute "deliberate indifference" to constitutional rights.

During the past 25 years, the Supreme Court has been less supportive of expanding prisoners' rights, and a few decisions reflect a retreat. The concept of deliberate indifference surfaced in *Daniels v. Williams* (1986). Here the Court ruled that prisoners could sue for damages only if officials had inflicted injury intentionally or deliberately. This reasoning was extended in ***Wilson v. Seiter* (1991)**, where the Court ruled that a prisoner's conditions of confinement are not unconstitutional unless it can be shown that prison administrators had acted with "deliberate indifference" to basic human needs (Call, 1995; C. E. Smith, 1993). Even with regard to First Amendment rights (inmate to inmate correspondence and attendance at Black Muslim religious services) the Court upheld prison policies(*Turner v. Safley,* 1987; *O'Lone v. Estate of Shabazz,* 1987).

In 1996 Congress passed the Prison Reform Litigation Act, making it more difficult for prisoners to file civil rights lawsuits and for judges to make decisions affecting prison operations. To stem the number of Section 1983 cases, the act made it difficult for prisoners to seek a waiver of court fees. Since the act became law, the number of Section 1983 lawsuits filed in federal courts have dropped by about 48 percent, even though the number of state prisoners has continued to rise (Cheesman, Hanson, and Ostrom, 1998).

Robert McElroy/Woodfin Camp & Associates

Until *Ruiz v. Estelle,* the staff in many Texas prisons relied on a select group of inmates known as "building tenders" (BTs) to handle the rank and file. These BTs had extensive power over their fellow inmates.

Impact of the Prisoners' Rights Movement

The prisoners' rights movement can be credited with general changes in American corrections since the late 1970s (Feeley and Hanson, 1990). The most obvious are improvements in institutional living conditions and administrative practices. Law libraries and legal assistance are now generally available, communication with the outside is easier, religious practices are protected, inmate complaint procedures have been developed, and due process requirements are emphasized. Prisoners in solitary confinement undoubtedly suffer less neglect than they did before. Although overcrowding is still a major problem, many conditions are much improved and the most brutalizing elements of prison life have diminished (Jacobs, 1995:63).

Individual cases may have made only a dent in correctional bureaucracies, but over time real changes have occurred. The prisoners' rights movement has clearly influenced correctional officials. The threat of lawsuits and public exposure has placed many in the correctional bureaucracy on guard. On the one hand, this wariness may have merely further bureaucratized corrections, requiring staff to prepare extensive and time-consuming documentation of their actions to protect themselves from lawsuits. On the other hand, judicial intervention has forced corrections to rethink existing procedures and organizational structures. As part of the wider changes in the "new corrections," new administrators, increased funding, reformulated policies, and improved management procedures have been, at least in part, influenced by the prisoners' rights movement.

Extending constitutional rights to prisoners has by no means been a speedy process, and the courts have addressed only limited areas of the law. No one has yet measured the impact of these decisions on the actual behavior of correctional officials, but evidence suggests that court decisions have had a broad effect. Wardens and their subordinates may now be refraining from traditional disciplinary actions that might result in judicial intervention. In sum, after two hundred years of judicial neglect of the conditions under which prisoners are held, courts have looked more closely at the situation of the incarcerated.

The position of the American Civil Liberties Union on the Prison Litigation Reform Act is found by clicking on "Prisons" at http://www.aclu.org.

For a perspective on the treatment of prisoners around the world, read information published by Human Rights Watch at http://www.hrw.org/prisons/.

Go to the *American System of Criminal Justice* Web site at http://www.cj.wadsworth.com/colesmith10e to explore the topic of prisoners' rights in further detail.

Summary

- Three models of incarceration have predominated since the 1940s. (1) The custodial model emphasizes the maintenance of security. (2) The rehabilitation model views security and housekeeping activities as mainly a framework for treatment efforts. (3) The reintegration model recognizes that prisoners must be prepared for their return to society.
- The public's belief that the warden and officers have total power over the inmates is outdated.
- Good management through effective leadership can maintain the quality of prison life as measured by levels of order, amenities, and services.
- Most prisons are expected to fulfill goals related to keeping (custody), using (working), and serving (treating) inmates.
- Four factors make managing prisons different from administering other public institutions: defects of total power, limited use of rewards and punishments, exchange relationships, and strength of inmate leadership.
- Correctional officers, because they are constantly in close contact with the prisoners, are the real linchpins in the prison system. The effectiveness of the institution lies heavily on their shoulders.
- Violence in prison depends on such things as administrative effectiveness, the architecture and size of prisons, and inmate characteristics such as age, attitudes, and race.
- Violence occurs between prisoners, often through gangs, and between prisoners and guards.
- The prisoners' rights movement, through lawsuits in the federal courts, has brought many changes to the administration and conditions of American prisons. Prisoners' rights moved from a hands-off policy before the 1960s to a great increase in rights through the present day, when the pendulum has begun to swing back from the expansion of rights.

Questions for Review

1. How do modern prisons differ from those in the past?
2. What are the characteristics of prisons that make them different from other institutions?
3. What must a prison administrator do to ensure successful management?

4 What are the forms and causes of prison violence?

5 What Supreme Court decisions are most significant to corrections today? What effect has each had on correctional institutions?

Key Terms and Cases

custodial model (p. 471)
hands-off policy (p. 486)
reintegration model (p. 471)
Cooper v. Pate (1964) (p. 486)
Cruz v. Beto (1972) (p. 487)
Fulwood v. Clemmer (1962) (p. 487)
Hudson v. Palmer (1984) (p. 489)
Ruffin v. Commonwealth (1871) (p. 486)
Ruiz v. Estelle (1980) (p. 489)
Wilson v. Seiter (1991) (p. 492)
Wolff v. McDonnell (1974) (p. 490)

For Further Reading

Conover, Ted. 2000. *Newjack: Guarding Sing Sing*. New York: Random House. Denied permission to write about the lives of correctional officers, Conover became one himself and served a year at Sing Sing. The book provides an officer's view of a maximum-security institution.

DiIulio, John J., Jr. 1987. *Governing Prisons*. New York: Free Press. A critique of the sociological perspective on inmate society. DiIulio argues that governance by correctional officers is the key to the maintenance of good prisons and jails.

Jacobs, James B. 1977. *Stateville*. Chicago: University of Chicago Press. A classic study of the management of a large state prison over half a century.

Johnson, Robert. 2002. *Hard Time: Understanding and Reforming the Prison*. 3rd ed. Belmont, Calif.: Wadsworth. A significant contribution to understanding prison society.

Kauffman, Kelsey. 1988. *Prison Officers and Their World*. Cambridge, Mass.: Harvard University Press. Looks at the work of correctional officers, their roles, and their place within the prison environment.

Martin, Steve J., and Sheldon Ekland-Olson. 1987. *Texas Prisons: The Walls Came Tumbling Down*. Austin: Texas Monthly Press. Impact of the federal courts on the Texas prison system.

Useem, Bert, and Peter Kimball. 1989. *States of Siege: U.S. Prison Riots, 1971–1986*. New York: Oxford University Press. Surveys prison riots with case studies of the upheavals at Attica, Joliet, Santa Fe, Jackson, and Moundsville and considers the nature and causes of prison riots.

Going Online

For an up-to-date list of Web links, go to http://www.cj.wadsworth.com/colesmith10e

1 Go to the Web site of the Massachusetts Department of Corrections roster of prison gangs: http://www.state.ma.us/doc/gang/othgang.htm. Read about the gangs represented in Massachusetts prisons. How should officials address the problem of multiple, diverse gangs within prisons?

2 Using InfoTrac College Edition, enter the keywords *prison administration*. Access the article by John W. Roberts, "A Century's Legacy: Five Critical Developments in the Evolution of American Prisons, 1900–2000," *Corrections Today*, August 2000. What are the five critical developments and why are they important?

3 Go to InfoTrac College Edition and search for *prisoners' rights*. Click on "religion." Find and read an article that will help you understand the impact of the U.S. Supreme Court's decision in *O'Lone v. Estate of Shabazz*. Did the Court make a good decision?

Checkpoint Answers

1 The characteristics of the inmate population have changed, more inmates are from urban areas and have been convicted for drug-related or violent offenses, the inmate population is fragmented along racial and ethnic lines, prisoners are less isolated from the outside world, and correctional officers have used collective bargaining to improve their working conditions.

2 The custodial, rehabilitation, and reintegration models.

3 It is a place where a group of workers manages a group of captives.

4 Keeping (custody), using (working), serving (treatment).

5 The goals often mean the administration of prisons is marked by ambiguity and conflict.

6 The defects of total power, a limited system of rewards and punishments, exchange relations between correctional officers and inmates, and the strength of inmate leadership.

7 Management by "walking around."

8 They are in daily contact with the inmates.

9 Self-defense, defense of third person, upholding prison rules, prevention of crime, prevention of escapes.

10 Judges' belief that prisoners do not have protected rights and that the courts should not become involved in the administration of prisons.

11 *Cooper v. Pate* allowed state prisoners to challenge the conditions of their confinement in the federal courts.

12 First Amendment concerning speech and religion; Eighth Amendment concerning prison conditions.

13 The due process and equal protection clauses.

14 42 U.S.C. 1983 is the provision of the United States Code that allows state prisoners to challenge conditions of their confinement in the federal courts.

15 The prisoner should receive notice of the complaint, a fair hearing, assistance in preparing for the hearing, and written notice of the decision. The prisoner should also be able to confront witnesses.

CHAPTER 16

Prison Society and Release

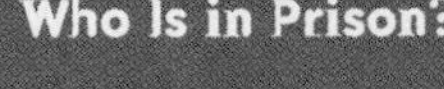

AP Photo/Robert F. Bukaty

We're crowded into the department of corrections' bus, 40 convicts en route to the state prison. I'm handcuffed to two other men, the chains gleaming dully at wrists and ankles. The man on my right lifts his hand to smoke, the red eye of his cigarette burning through the darkness of the van. When he exhales, the man at my left coughs, the sound in his lungs suggesting that he's old, maybe sick. I want to ask what he's in for. But I don't speak, restrained by my fear, a feeling that rises cold up the back of my spine. For a long time no one else speaks either, each man locked

Close up: One Man's Walk through Atlanta's Jungle

Michael G. Santos

I was not expecting to receive the southern hospitality for which Atlanta is famous when the bus turned into the penitentiary's large, circular drive, but neither did I expect to see a dozen uniformed prison guards—all carrying machine guns—surround the bus when it stopped. A month in transit already had passed by the time we made it to the U.S. Penitentiary (USP) in Atlanta, the institution that would hold me (along with over two thousand other felons) until we were transferred to other prisons, we were released, or we were dead.

I left the jail in Tacoma, Washington, on the first of August, but I didn't see the huge gray walls that surround USP Atlanta until the first of September. That month was spent in a bus operated by the U.S. Marshal Service as it moved across the country, picking up federal prisoners in local jails and dropping them off at various Bureau of Prison facilities.

As I crossed the country, I listened to tales from numerous prisoners who sat beside me on the bus. There wasn't much to discuss except what was to come. Each of us was chained at the hands and feet. There were neither magazines to read nor music playing. Mostly people spoke about a riot that had taken place behind USP Atlanta's walls a few months earlier. A lot of the men had been to prison before, and Atlanta would be nothing new. Those prisoners only talked about reuniting with old friends, explaining prison routine, or sat like stone-cold statues waiting for what was to come. I'd never been confined before, so it was hard to tune out the stories that others were telling. While I was listening, though, I remember telling myself that I *would* survive this sentence. No matter what it took, I *would* survive.

I was in my early twenties, younger than perhaps every other prisoner on the bus. Pimples spotted my face as I began my term, but I was certain my black hair would be white by the time I finished. I had been sentenced to 45 years by a U.S. district court judge in Tacoma on charges related to cocaine trafficking. I was expected to serve close to 30 years before release. It was hard then—just as it is hard now—to believe the sentence was real. The best thing I could do, I reasoned, was to stay to myself. I'd heard the same rumors that every suburban kid hears about prison. I was anxious about what was to come, but I was determined to make it out alive and with my mind intact. Now it was all to begin!

After the bus stopped, the guards began calling us off by last name and prison number. It is not easy to walk with a 12-inch chain connected to each ankle, and wrists bound to a chain that runs around the waist, but when my name was called, I managed to wobble through the bus's aisle, hop down the steps, and then begin the long march up the stairs leading to the fortress. As I was moving to the prison's doors, I remember glancing over my

in his own thoughts. It's someone up front, a kid, his voice brittle with fear, who speaks first. "What's it like down there—in the joint? Is it as bad as they say?"

"Worse," someone answers. "Cell blocks are dirty. Overcrowded. Lousy chow. Harassment. Stabbings."

"How do you live there?"

"You don't exactly live. You go through the motions. Eat, sleep, mind your own business. Do drugs when you can get them. Forget the world you came from."

This description of the "way in" was written by an inmate who was incarcerated in the Arizona penal system for seven years. It conveys much of the anxiety not only of the new "fish" but also of the old con. What is it like to be incarcerated? What does it mean to the inmates, the guards, and the administrators? Are the officers in charge or do the prisoners "rule the joint?" This chapter explores the lives of the incarcerated, both in prison and as they face release into the community.

As we examine the social and personal dimensions of prison life, imagine visiting a foreign land and trying to learn about its culture and daily activities. The prison may be located in the United Sates, but the traditions, language, and relationships are unlike anything you are used to.

QUESTIONS for INQUIRY

- What are the characteristics of the incarcerated population?
- What is it like to be in prison, and how do prisoners adapt to "life in the joint?"

shoulder, knowing it would be the last time I'd see the world from the outside of prison walls for a long time.

Once inside the institution, the guards began unlocking my chains. About 50 other prisoners arrived with me that day, so the guards had plenty of chains to unlock, but their work didn't stop there. They also had to squeeze us through the dehumanizing admissions machine. The machine begins with photographs, fingerprints, and interrogations. Then comes the worst part, the strip search, where each prisoner stands before a prison official, naked, and responds to the scream: "Lift up your arms in the air! Let me see the back of your hands! Run your fingers through your hair! Open your mouth! Stick your tongue out! Lift your balls! Turn around! Bend over! Spread your ass! Wider! Lift the bottom of your feet! Move on!" The strip search, I later learned, is a ritual Atlanta's officers inflict on prisoners every time they have contact with anyone from outside the walls, and sometimes randomly as prisoners walk down the corridor.

There was a lot of hatred behind those walls. Walking through the prison must be something like walking through a jungle, I imagined, not knowing whether others perceive you as predator or prey, knowing that you must remain always alert, watching every step, knowing that the wrong step may be the one that sucks you into the quicksand. The tension is ever present; I felt it wrapped all over, under and around me. I remember it bothering me that I didn't have enough hatred, because not hating in the jungle is a weakness. As the serpents slither, they spot that lack of hatred and salivate over a potential target.

Every prisoner despises confinement, but each must decide how he or she is going to do the time. Most of the men run in packs. They want the other prisoners either to run with them or run away from them. I wasn't interested in doing either. Instead of scheming on how I could become king of the jungle, I thought about ways that I could advance my release date. Earning academic credentials, keeping a clean record, and initiating projects that would benefit the communities both inside and outside of prison walls seemed the most promising goals for me to achieve. Yet working toward such goals was more dangerous than running with the pack; it didn't take me long to learn that prisoners running in herds will put forth more energy to cause others to lose than they will to win themselves. Prison is a twisted world, a menagerie.

I found that a highly structured schedule would not only move me closer to my goals but also would limit potential conflicts inside the prison. There is a pecking order in every prison, and prisoners vying for attention don't want to see others who are cutting their own path. I saw that bullies generally look for weaker targets, so I began an exercise routine that would keep me physically strong. If I were strong, I figured, others would be more reluctant to try me. Through discipline, I found, I could develop physical strength. Yet I've never figured out how to develop the look of a killer, or the hatred off which that look feeds.

I don't know whether the strategies I have developed for doing time are right for everyone. But they are working for me. Still, I know that I may spend many more years in prison. The only fear I have—and as I'm working on my eighth year, it's still here—is that someone will try me and drag me into an altercation that may jeopardize my spotless disciplinary record. I've been successful in avoiding the ever-present quicksand on my walk through the jungle so far, but I know that on any given day, something may throw me off balance, or I may take a wrong step. And one wrong step in this jungle can drown me in quicksand, sucking me into the abysmal world of prison forever. That wrong step also could mean the loss of life, mine or someone else's.

In prison, more than anywhere else I know, understanding that some things are beyond an individual's sphere of control is vital. No matter how much preparation is made, the steel and concrete jungle is a dangerous place in which to live.

Source: Written for this book by Michael G. Santos, currently finishing the 15th year of a 45 year sentence for drug trafficking.

Michael Santos is now incarcerated at the Federal Correctional Institution—Ft. Dix, New Jersey. While in prison, he has completed his bachelor's and master's degrees. You can contact Michael at http:// www.prisonerlife.com/.

- How do social relationships among female prisoners differ from those among male prisoners?
- What programs are available to prisoners?
- What is the process of release from prison to the community?

Who Is in Prison?

In many ways the American maximum-security prison is a foreign land. Observers of the criminal justice system need to gain an awareness of the social dimensions of prison life: its traditions, the roles played there, and the patterns of interpersonal relations. The age, education, and criminal history of the inmate population help determine how correctional institutions function. What are the characteristics of inmates in our nation's prisons? Do most offenders have long records of serious offenses, or are many of them first-time offenders who have committed minor crimes? Do some inmates have special needs that dictate their place in prison? These questions are crucial to an understanding the work of wardens and correctional officers. In the Close Up, Michael Santos, a long-term prisoner, describes his entry to the U.S. Federal Penitentiary—Atlanta.

Not much data on the characteristics of prisoners exist. However, in a national survey of state prisons, the Bureau of Justice Statistics found that most prisoners are men in their late twenties to early thirties, have less than a high

Figure 16.1
Sociodemographic and offense characteristics of state prison inmates
These data reflect the types of people found in state prisons. What do they indicate about the belief that many offenders do not "need" to be incarcerated?

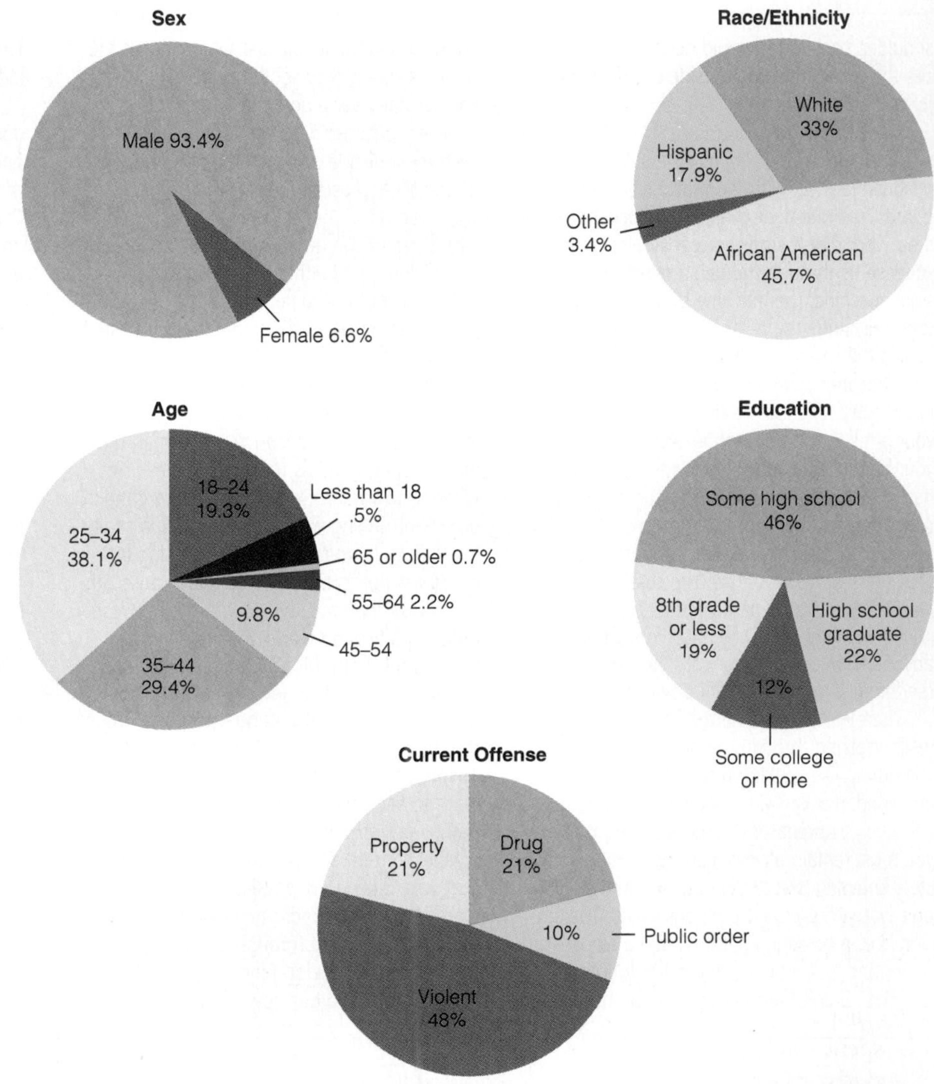

Sources: Bureau of Justice Statistics [BJS], *Survey of State Prison Inmates* (Washington, D.C.: U.S. Government Printing Office, 1993), 3; BJS, *Bulletin*, August 2000; BJS, *Correctional Populations in the United States*, November 2000, p. iv.

school education, and are disproportionately members of minority groups (see Figure 16.1).

The most recent studies indicate that inmates who are recidivists and who are convicted of violent crimes make up a significant portion of the prison population. More than 60 percent of inmates have been either incarcerated or on probation at least twice; 45 percent of them, three or more times; and nearly 20 percent, six or more times. Two-thirds of the inmates were serving a sentence for a violent crime or had previously been convicted of a violent crime. These are major shifts from the prison populations of earlier decades, when only about 40 percent of all inmates had committed such offenses. Beyond these shifts in the prison population, four additional factors affect correctional operations: the increased number of elderly prisoners, the many prisoners with HIV/AIDS, the thousands of prisoners who are mentally ill, and the increase in long-term prisoners.

Elderly Prisoners

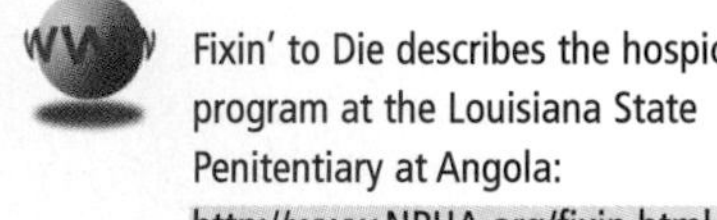

Fixin' to Die describes the hospice program at the Louisiana State Penitentiary at Angola: http://www.NPHA.org/fixin.html.

Correctional officials have only recently become aware of the increasing number of elderly inmates. In 1999 U.S. prisons held more than 43,000 offenders over 55 years old, an increase of over 50 percent compared with the elderly population in 1996 (BJS, 2000b).

directions in criminal justice policy new

Release of the Elderly

Severe sentencing laws, including mandatory minimums, have resulted in a major increase in the number of prisoners over age 55. Research has shown that age is the most reliable predictor of recidivism. As people get older, most become less dangerous—they undergo a criminal "menopause." Although people over 60 commit only 1 percent of serious crime, incarceration of the elderly costs more than three times that of holding younger inmates, because of health issues.

The Project for Older Prisoners (POPS) was organized at Tulane Law School in 1989 to cull low-risk geriatrics from overcrowded prisons so that they can live in the community. Chapters of POPS are now found at law schools in Louisiana, Maryland, Michigan, North Carolina, Virginia, and the District of Columbia. POPS is meticulous in selecting candidates for release. Prisoners must acknowledge their guilt, have an exemplary record while incarcerated, and meet age and medical criteria. POPS then considers supporting the prisoner for a pardon, commutation, parole release, or some other alternative to incarceration such as a halfway house. Given the size of the elderly prison population across the nation, the more than two hundred geriatric inmates who have secured release through POPS is small; however, their recidivism rate is zero.

Many states and the federal government are considering legislation that will deal with the problem of elderly prisoners in overcrowded times. Programs such as POPS is one answer. What are others?

Researching the Internet

Using InfoTrac College Edition, type in the key words *Project for Older Prisoners.* Read the article by George Anderson, "Growing Old Behind Bars." Is the release of elderly prisoners a policy direction that all states and the federal government should undertake?

To some extent, the prison population is growing older because it reflects the aging of the overall citizenry, but more so because sentencing practices have changed. Consecutive lengthy sentences for heinous crimes, long mandatory minimum sentences, and life sentences without parole mean that more people who enter prison will spend most or all the rest of their lives behind bars.

Elderly prisoners have security and medical needs that differ from those of the average inmate. In many states, special sections of the institution have been designated for this older population so they will not have to mix with the younger, tougher inmates. Elderly prisoners are more likely to develop chronic illnesses such as heart disease, stroke, and cancer. The costs for maintaining an elderly inmate averages about $69,000 per year, triple the average cost (*Hartford Courant,* February 18, 1997). Ironically, while in prison the offender will benefit from much better medical care and live a longer life than if he or she were discharged (Morris and Rothman, 1995:253). See "New Directions in Criminal Justice Policy" for more on the release of the elderly.

Angel Franco/The New York Times

An increasing portion of the prison population is elderly. In some states their numbers have grown to such a degree that nursing home wings have been added to prisons. How should these Angola, Louisiana, offenders be treated?

Prisoners with HIV/AIDS

In the coming years, AIDS is expected to be the leading cause of death among men aged 35 and younger. With 57 percent of the adult inmate population under age 35, correctional officials must cope with the problem of HIV as well as AIDS and related health issues. In 1999 there were more than 25,000 HIV-positive inmates (2.1 percent of the prison population) and over 6,000 offenders (0.5 percent) with AIDS. The rate of confirmed AIDS cases in state and federal prisons is five times higher than in the total U.S. population. More than 250 inmates have been dying each year of AIDS, the second largest single cause of inmate

Follow the latest regarding HIV in prison at the Correctional HIV Consortium: http://www.silcom.com/~chc/.

death (BJS, 2001b:1). Because many inmates who are HIV infected are undiagnosed, these numbers underestimate the scope of the problem.

The high incidence of HIV/AIDS among prisoners can be traced to increased incarceration of drug offenders. Many of these inmates engaged in intravenous drug use, shared needles, and/or traded sex for drugs or money. Male homosexual activity is also a major way that HIV is transmitted. Some argue that government has a compelling interest to educate prisoners about the risk of unprotected sex or drug use in prison and even beyond the walls (Merianos, Marquart, and Damphousse, 1997).

To deal with offenders who have AIDS symptoms or who test positive for the virus, prison officials can develop policies on methods to prevent transmission of the disease, housing of those infected, and medical care for inmates with the full range of symptoms. Administrators are confronting a host of legal, political, medical, budgetary, and attitudinal factors as they decide what actions the institution should take.

Mentally Ill Prisoners

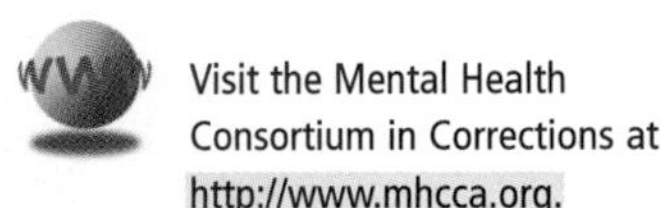

Visit the Mental Health Consortium in Corrections at http://www.mhcca.org.

Mass closings of public hospitals for the mentally ill began in the 1960s. At the time new antipsychotic drugs made treating patients in the community seem a more humane and less expensive alternative to long-term hospitalization, but it soon became apparent that community treatment works only if the drugs are taken and that clinics and halfway houses do not exist to assist the mentally ill.

Homelessness has become the most public sign of the lack of programs for the mentally ill. But with the expansion of prisons and the greater emphasis on public order offenses, arrest and incarceration have become the price many people pay for their illness. Mentally ill inmates tend to follow a revolving door from homelessness to incarceration and then back to the streets, with little treatment.

Currently far more mentally ill are in the nation's jails and prisons (almost 300,000) than in state hospitals (62,000) (BJS, 1999e). The incarceration rate of the mentally ill is four times that of the general population. The prison has become the largest psychiatric facility in some states. For example, New York City's Riker's Island houses three thousand mentally ill inmates (Winerip, 1999a:42). Over the past ten years, the mentally ill portion of Connecticut's prison population has gone from 24 to 40 percent (G. Watson, 1999). In Los Angeles, 50 percent of those entering the county jail are identified as mentally ill (Butterfield, 1998b).

Although some inmates benefit from the regular medication they receive in jail or prison, others suffer as the stress of confinement deepens their depressions, intensifies delusions, or leads to mental breakdown. Many commit suicide.

Correctional workers are usually unprepared to deal with the mentally ill. Cell-block officers, for instance, often do not know how to respond to disturbed inmates. Although most corrections systems have mental health units that segregate the ill, many inmates with psychiatric disorders live among other prisoners in the general population, where they are teased and otherwise exploited.

Few states have well-developed mental health treatment programs in prisons. An exception is Ohio, where mental health units have been created in each facility and one prison has been set aside to house only the mentally ill. In any case, most prisons rely on the generous dispensing of medication to keep the mentally ill stable and functioning.

Long-Term Prisoners

More prisoners in the United States serve longer sentences than do prisoners in other Western nations. While the average first-time offender serves about 22 months, an estimated 11 to 15 percent of all prisoners—well over 100,000—will serve more than seven years in prison. About 9 percent are serving life sentences, and another 24 percent are serving sentences of over 25 years. These long-term prisoners are often the same people who will become elderly offenders, with all of the attendant problems (Flanagan, 1995:10).

Studies show substantial differences in the way the long-termer responds to incarceration. Some, but not others, experience severe stress, depression, and other health problems (Bonta and Gendreau, 1995). Such emotional stress tends to take place earlier rather than later in the sentence.

Long-term prisoners are generally not seen as control problems. They are charged with disciplinary infractions about half as often as are short-term inmates. However, they do represent a management problem for administrators, who must find ways of making long terms livable. According to Timothy Flanagan (1995:256), a leading authority on long-term inmates, administrators follow three main principles: (1) maximize opportunities for the inmate to exercise choice in living circumstances, (2) create opportunities for meaningful living, and (3) help the inmate maintain contact with the outside world. Most long-term inmates will eventually be released after spending their prime years incarcerated. Will offenders be able to support themselves when they return to the community at age 50, 60, or 70?

The contemporary inmate population presents several challenges to correctional workers. Resources may not be available to provide rehabilitative programs for most inmates. Even if the resources exist, the goal of maintaining a safe and healthy environment may tax the staff's abilities. These difficulties are multiplied still further by AIDS and the increasing numbers of elderly and long-term prisoners. The contemporary corrections system must also deal with a different type of inmate, one who is more prone to violence, and with a prison society where racial tensions are great. How well it meets this correctional challenge will greatly affect American society.

1. What are the major characteristics of today's prisoners?
(Answers are at the end of the chapter.)

The Convict World

The 1934 publication of Joseph Fishman's *Sex in Prison* marked the beginning of the scientific study of inmate subcultures in maximum-security institutions (Fishman, 1934). Since that time, social scientists have studied the prison as a functioning community with its own values, roles, language, and customs (Sykes, 1958). In other words, the inmates of a maximum-security prison do not serve their time in isolation. Rather, prisoners form a society with traditions, norms, and a leadership structure. Some choose to associate with only a few close friends; others form cliques along racial or "professional" lines (Carroll, 1974). Still others serve as the politicians of the convict society; they attempt to represent convict interests and distribute valued goods in return for support. Just as there is a social culture in the free world, there is a prisoner subculture on the "inside." Membership in a group provides mutual protection from theft and physical assault, the basis of wheeling and dealing activities, and a source of cultural identity (Irwin, 1980).

As in any society, the convict world has certain norms and values. Often described as the **inmate code,** these norms and values develop within the prison social system and help to define the inmate's image of the model prisoner. As Robert Johnson notes, "The public culture of the prison has norms that dictate behavior 'on the yard' and in other public areas of the prison such as mess halls, gyms, and the larger program and work sites" (2002:100). An overriding fact is

inmate code
The values and norms of the prison social system that define the inmates' idea of the model prisoner.

Andrew Lichtenstein/Sygma

Contemporary prison society is divided along racial, ethnic, and gang subgroups. There is no longer an inmate code to which all prisoners subscribe. As a correctional officer, how would you deal with these members of the white supremacist Aryan Brotherhood gang incarcerated in Ferguson Prison, Texas?

The Prison Zone contains photographs, as well as inmate poetry, writing, and art: http://www.prisonzone.com.

that prison is an ultramasculine world. Prison culture breathes masculine toughness and insensitivity, impugning softness, caring, and femininity. The culture emphasizes the use of hostility and manipulation in one's relations with fellow inmates and staff. It makes caring and friendly behavior, especially with respect to the staff, look servile and silly (Sabo, Kupers, and London, 2001:7).

Chuck Terry, a former inmate with 12 years of personal experience on the "inside" says that male prisoners must project an image of "fearlessness in the way they walk, talk and socially interact" (1997:26). Because showing emotion is seen as a weakness, inmates must suppress expressions of their true feelings.

The code also emphasizes the solidarity of all inmates against the staff. For example, inmates should never inform on one another, pry into one another's affairs, "run off at the mouth," or put another inmate on the spot. They must be tough and not trust the officers or the principles for which the guards stand. Further, guards are "hacks" or "screws"; the officials are wrong and the prisoners are right.

Some sociologists believe that the code emerges within the institution as a way to lessen the pain of imprisonment (Sykes, 1958); others believe that it is part of the criminal subculture that prisoners bring with them (Irwin and Cressey, 1962). The inmate who follows the code can be expected to enjoy a certain amount of admiration from other inmates as a "right guy" or a "real man." Those who break the code are labeled "rat" or "punk" and will probably spend their prison life at the bottom of the convict social structure, alienated from the rest of the population and targeted for abuse (Sykes, 1958:84).

A single, overriding inmate code probably does not exist in today's prisons. Instead, convict society has divided itself along racial lines (Carroll, 1974; Irwin, 1980). The level of adherence to the inmate code also differs among institutions, with greater modifications to local situations found in maximum-security prisons. Still, the core commandments described by Sykes almost 50 years ago remain. For a somewhat different perspective, see the Close Up box "Survival Tips for Beginners."

Recent interviews with ex-convicts in California painted a picture of prison society in a greater degree of turmoil than in the past. This turmoil was created by the presence of gangs, changes in the type of person now incarcerated, and

Survival Tips for Beginners

TJ Granack

Okay, so you just lost your case. Maybe you took a plea bargain. Whatever. The point is you've been sentenced. You've turned yourself over to the authorities and you're in the county jail waiting to catch the next chain to the R Units (receiving) where you'll be stripped and shaved and photographed and processed and sent to one of the various prisons in your state.

So what's a felon to do? Here are some survival tips that may make your stay less hellish:

1. *Commit an Honorable Crime.* Commit a crime that's considered, among convicts, to be worthy of respect. I was lucky. I went down for first-degree attempted murder, so my crime fell in the "honorable" category. Oh, goodie. So I just had to endure the everyday sort of danger and abuse that comes with prison life.
2. *Don't Gamble.* Not cards, not chess, not the Super Bowl. And if you do, don't bet too much. If you lose too much, and pay up (don't even think of doing otherwise), then you'll be known as rich guy who'll be very popular with the vultures.
4. *Never Loan Anyone Anything.* Because if you do, you'll be expected to collect one way or another. If you don't collect, you will be known as a mark, as someone without enough heart to take back his own. . . .
6. *Make No Eye Contact.* Don't look anyone in the eye. Ever. Locking eyes with another man, be he a convict or a guard, is considered a challenge, a threat, and should therefore be avoided.
7. *Pick Your Friends Carefully.* When you choose a friend, you've got to be prepared to deal with anything that person may have done. Their reputation is yours, and the consequences can be enormous.
8. *Fight and Fight Dirty.* You have to fight, and not according to Marquis of Queensbury rules, either. If you do it right, you'll only have to do it once or twice. If you don't, expect regular whoopings and loss of possessions. . . .
10. *Mind Your Own Business.* Never get in the middle of anyone else's discussion/argument/confrontation/fight. Never offer unsolicited knowledge or advice.
11. *Keep a Good Porn Collection.* If you *don't* have one, the boys will think you're funny. . . .
14. *Don't Talk to Staff, Especially Guards.* Any prolonged discussions or associations with staff makes you susceptible to rumor and suspicion of being a snitch.
15. *Never Snitch.* Or even *appear* to snitch. And above all, avoid the real thing. And if you do, you'd better not get caught.

Source: Drawn from TJ Granack, "Welcome to the Steel Hotel: Survival Tips for Beginners," in *The Funhouse Mirror,* ed. Robert Gordon Ellis (Pullman: Washington State University Press, 2000), 6–10.

Researching the **Internet**

See the survival tips for beginners that are presented at http://www.prisonerlife.com/advice.cfm.

changes in prison policy. As the researchers found, "All these elements coalesced to create an increasingly unpredictable world in which prior loyalties, allegiances, and friendships were disrupted" (Hunt et al., 1993:399).

In a changing society that has no single code of behavior accepted by the entire population, the tasks of administrators become much more difficult. They must be aware of the different groups, recognize the norms and rules that members hold, and deal with the leaders of many cliques rather than with a few inmates who have risen to top positions in the inmate society.

check point

2. What are the key elements of the inmate code?
3. Why is it unlikely that a single, overriding inmate code exists in today's prisons?

Adaptive Roles

On entering prison, a newcomer ("fish") is confronted by the question, "How am I going to do my time?" Some decide to withdraw and isolate. Others decide to become full participants in the convict social system. The choice, influenced by

Steve Lehman/SABA Press

Every prisoner must answer the question, "How am I going to do my time?" Some, like these San Quentin inmates, will glean as much as they can from prison programs, while others will adopt the role of "jailing" by making the prison their "home."

prisoners' values and experiences, helps determine strategies for survival and success.

Most male inmates use one of four basic role orientations to adapt to prison: "doing time," "gleaning," "jailing," and functioning as a "disorganized criminal" (Irwin, 1970:67).

Doing Time

Men "doing time" view their prison term as a brief, inevitable break in their criminal careers, a cost of doing business. They try to serve their terms with the least amount of suffering and the greatest amount of comfort. They avoid trouble by living by the inmate code, finding activities to fill their days, forming friendships with a few other convicts, and generally doing what they think is necessary to survive and to get out as soon as possible.

Gleaning

Inmates who are "gleaning" try to take advantage of prison programs to better themselves and improve their prospects for success after release. They use the resources at hand: libraries, correspondence courses, vocational training, schools. Some make a radical conversion away from a life of crime.

Jailing

"Jailing" is the choice of those who cut themselves off from the outside and try to construct a life within the prison. These are often "state-raised" youths who have spent much of their lives in institutional settings and who identify little with the values of free society. These are the inmates who seek power and influence in the prison society, often becoming key figures in the politics and economy of prison life.

Disorganized Criminal

A fourth role orientation—the "disorganized criminal"—describes inmates who cannot develop any of the other three orientations. They may be of low intelligence or afflicted with psychological or physical disabilities, and they find functioning in prison society difficult. They are "human putty" to be manipulated by others. These are also the inmates who cannot adjust to prison life and who develop emotional disorders, attempt suicide, and violate prison rules (Adams, 1992).

As these roles suggest, prisoners are not members of an undifferentiated mass. Individual convicts choose to play specific roles in prison society. The roles they choose reflect the physical and social environment they have experienced and also influence their relationships and interactions in prison. How do most prisoners serve their time? Although the media generally portray prisons as violent, chaotic places, research shows that most inmates want to get through their sentence without trouble. As journalist Pete Earley found in his study of Leavenworth, roughly 80 percent of inmates try to avoid trouble and do their time as easily as possible (1992:44).

check point

4. What are the four role orientations found in adult male prisons?

The Prison Economy

In prison, as outside, individuals want goods and services. Although the state feeds, clothes, and houses all prisoners, amenities are sparse. Prisoners are deprived of everything but bare necessities. Their diet and routine are monotonous and their recreational opportunities scarce. They experience a loss of identity (due to uniformity of treatment) and a lack of responsibility. In short, the prison is relatively unique in having been deliberately designed as "an island of poverty in the midst of a society of relative abundance" (V. Williams and Fish, 1974:40).

In recent years the number of items that a prisoner can purchase or receive through legitimate channels has increased. In some state institutions, for example, inmates may own television sets, civilian clothing, and hot plates. However, these few luxuries are not enjoyed by all prisoners, nor do they satisfy lingering desires for a variety of other goods. Some state legislatures have prohibited amenities, claiming that prisoners should live in a Spartan environment.

Recognizing that prisoners do have some needs that are not met, prisons have a commissary or "store" from which inmates may, on a scheduled basis, purchase a limited number of items—toilet articles, tobacco, snacks, and other food products—in exchange for credits drawn on their "bank accounts." The size of a bank account depends on the amount of money deposited on the inmate's entrance, gifts sent by relatives, and amounts earned in the low-paying prison industries.

However, the peanut butter, soap, and cigarettes of the typical prison store in no way satisfy the consumer needs and desires of most prisoners. Consequently, an informal, underground economy is a major element in prison society. Many items taken for granted on the outside are inordinately valued on the inside. For example, talcum powder and deodorant become more important because of the limited bathing facilities. Goods and services that a prisoner would not have consumed at all outside prison can have exaggerated importance inside prison. For example, unable to get alcohol, offenders may seek a similar effect by sniffing glue. Or to distinguish themselves from others, offenders may pay laundry workers to iron a shirt in a particular way, a modest version of conspicuous consumption.

Many studies point to the pervasiveness of this economy. When David Kalinich (1980) studied the State Prison of Southern Michigan in Jackson, he learned that a market economy provides the goods (contraband) and services not available or not allowed by prison authorities. Mark Fleisher (1989:151) found an inmate running a "store" in almost every cell block in the U.S. Penitentiary at Lompoc, California. Food stolen (from the kitchen) for late-night snacks, homemade wine, and drugs (marijuana) were available in these "stores."

As a principal feature of prison culture, this informal economy reinforces the norms and roles of the social system and influences the nature of interpersonal relationships. The extent of the underground economy and its ability to produce desired goods and services—food, drugs, alcohol, sex, preferred living conditions—vary according to the scope of official surveillance, the demands of the consumers, and the opportunities for entrepreneurship. Inmates' success as "hustlers" determines the luxuries and power they can enjoy.

Because real money is prohibited and a barter system is somewhat restrictive, the standard currency of the prison economy is cigarettes. They are not contraband, are easily transferable, have a stable and well-known standard of value, and come in "denominations" of singles, packs, and cartons. Furthermore they are in demand by smokers. Even those who do not smoke keep cigarettes for prison currency. Postage stamps and soap may also serve as currency.

Certain positions in the prison society enhance opportunities for entrepreneurs. For example, inmates assigned to work in the kitchen, warehouse, and administrative office steal food, clothing, building materials, and even information to sell or trade to other prisoners. The goods may then become part of other market transactions. Thus, the exchange of a dozen eggs for two packs of cigarettes may result in the reselling of the eggs in the form of egg sandwiches made on a hot plate for five cigarettes each. Meanwhile, the kitchen worker who stole the eggs may use the income to get a laundry worker to starch his shirts, to get drugs from a hospital orderly, or to pay a "punk" for sexual favors.

Economic transactions can lead to violence when goods are stolen, debts are not paid, or agreements are violated. Disruptions of the economy can occur when officials conduct periodic "lockdowns" and inspections. Confiscation of contraband can result in temporary shortages and price readjustments, but gradually business returns. The prison economy, like that of the outside world, allocates goods and services, rewards and sanctions, and it is closely linked to the society it serves.

check point

5. Why does an underground economy exist in prison?
6. Why are prison administrators wary of the prison economy?

Women in Prison

Most studies of prisons have been based on institutions for men. How do prisons for women differ, and what are the special problems of female inmates?

Women constitute only 6.6 percent (about 92,000) of the entire U.S. prison population. However, the growth rate in the number of incarcerated women has exceeded that of men since 1981. In fact, since 1990 the population of men in state and federal prisons increased 77 percent, whereas that of women increased by 108 percent. This growth is particularly acute in the federal system, which, because of the war on drugs has had to absorb an additional six thousand female inmates during the past 20 years (BJS, 2001c). During the 1990s the number of women incarcerated in state prisons for drug offenses increased almost 450 percent (*The New York Times Magazine,* June 2, 1996:35). The increased number of women in prison has significantly affected the delivery of programs, housing conditions, medical care, staffing, and security.

Hollywood's depiction of female prisoners may be understood by reading the reviews of the many films about them. See http://www.prisonflicks.com/.

Life in the nation's 141 women's prisons both resembles and differs from that in institutions for men. Women's prisons are smaller, with looser security and less structured relationships; the underground economy is not as well developed; and female prisoners seem less committed to the inmate code. Women also serve shorter sentences than do men, so their prison society is more fluid as new members join and others leave.

Most women's prisons have the outward appearance of a college campus, often seen as a group of "cottages" around a central administration/dining/program building. Generally these facilities lack the high walls, guard towers, and cyclone fences found at most prisons for men. In recent years, however, the trend has been to upgrade security for women's prisons by adding barbed wire, higher fences, and other devices to prevent escapes.

The characteristics of correctional facilities for women are offset by geographic remoteness and inmate heterogeneity. Few states operate more than one institution for women, so inmates are generally far from children, families, friends, and attorneys. In many institutions the small numbers of inmates limit the extent to which the needs of individual offenders can be recognized and treated. Housing classifications are often so broad that dangerous or mentally ill inmates are mixed with women who have committed minor offenses and have no psychological problems. Similarly, available rehabilitative programs are often not used to their full extent, because correctional departments fail to recognize women's problems and needs.

Richard Lord/PhotoEdit

In contrast to male convicts, many female prisoners, such as these in Little Rock, Arkansas, develop strong bonds of support and friendship.

In most respects, we can see incarcerated women, like male prisoners, as disadvantaged losers in this complex and competitive society (Pollock, 1998:7). However the two groups differ with regard to types of offenses and length of sentences. Twenty-eight percent of female prisoners are sentenced for violent offenses (compared with 49 percent of male prisoners) and 34 percent for drug-related offenses (versus 20 percent of men). Overall, women receive shorter maximum sentences than do men. Half of the women have a maximum sentence of 5 years or less, whereas half of the men have a sentence of 10 years or less (BJS, 2000b). Figure 16.2 summarizes some characteristics of female prisoners.

check point

7. What accounts for the neglect of facilities and programs in women's prisons?

The Subculture of Women's Prisons

Studies of the subculture of women's prisons have been less extensive than those of male convict society. Further, just as there have been few ethnographic studies of men's prisons during the past two decades, there have been very few of women's prisons.

Much early investigation of women's prisons focused on types of social relationships among female offenders. As in all types of penal institutions, same-sex relationships were found, but unlike in male prisons, such relationships among women appeared more voluntary than coerced. Perhaps more importantly, scholars reported that female inmates tended to form pseudofamilies in which they adopted various roles—father, mother, daughter, sister—and interacted as a unit, rather than identifying with the larger prisoner subculture (Girshick, 1999; Propper, 1982). Esther Hefferman views these "play" families as a "direct, conscious substitution for the family relationships broken by imprisonment, or . . . the development of roles that perhaps were not fulfilled in the actual home environment" (1972:41–42). She also notes the economic aspect of the play families and the extent to which they are formed to provide for their members. Such cooperative relationships help relieve the tensions of prison life, assist the socialization of new inmates, and permit individuals to act according to clearly defined roles and rules. (For a survival method that one woman chose, see the Close Up box).

Figure 16.2
Characteristics of female inmates in state prisons
Like their male counterparts, female prisoners typically are young, have little education, are members of minority groups, and are incarcerated for a serious offense.

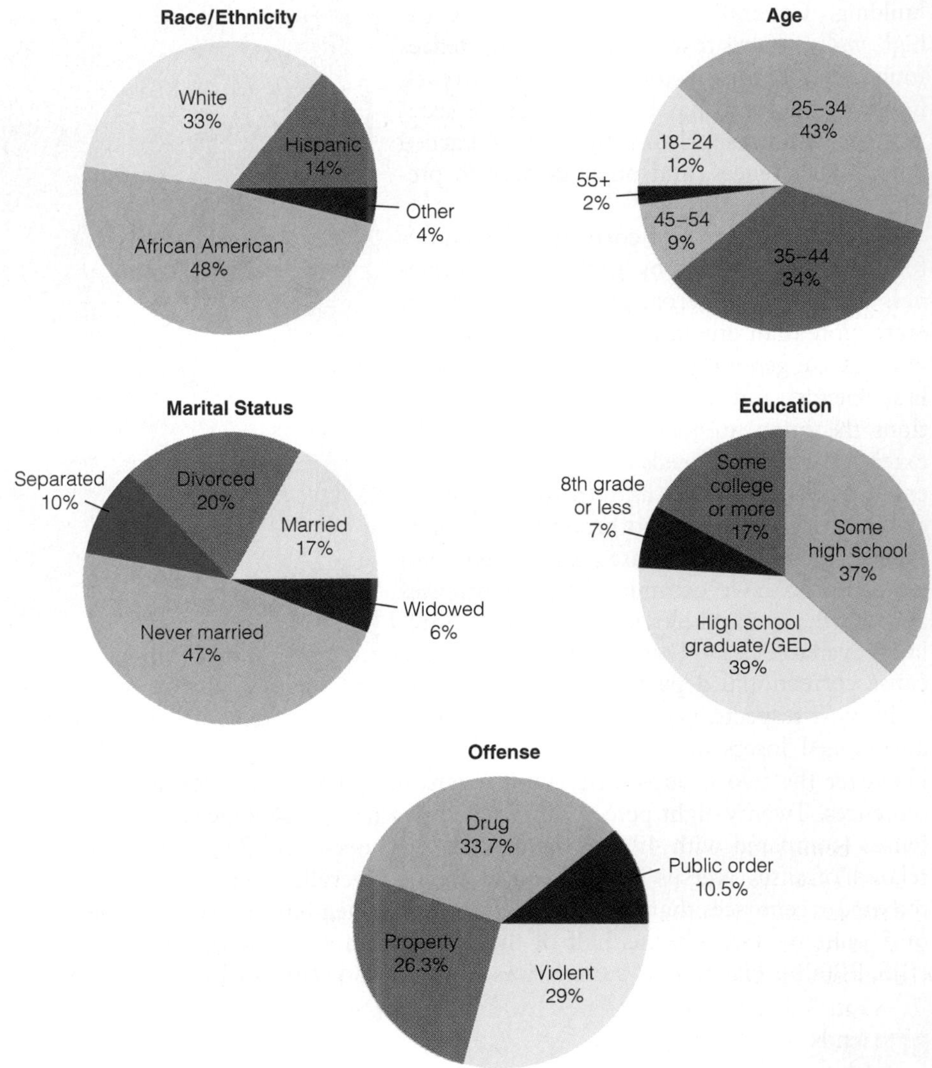

Sources: Bureau of Justice Statistics [BJS], *Special Report*, December 1999; BJS, *Bulletin*, August 2001.

In considering the available research on women in prison, we need to consider the most recent shifts in prison life. Just as the subculture of male prisons has changed since the pioneering research of the 1950s, the climate of female prisons has undoubtedly changed. Kimberly Greer (2000) found support for the idea that prisons for women are less violent, involved less gang activity, and do not have the racial tensions existing in men's prisons; however, the respondents indicated that their interpersonal relationships may be less stable and less familial than in the past. They reported higher levels of mistrust among women and greater economic manipulation.

In one of the few recent studies of prison culture, Barbara Owen (1998) found that the inmates at the Central California Women's Facility, holding over 4,500 women, developed various styles of doing time. Based on the in-prison experience, these styles correspond to the day-to-day business of developing a program of activities and settling into a routine. Owen found that one's style of doing time is influenced by the commitment to a deviant identity and the stage of one's criminal and prison career. These facts influence the extent to which an inmate is committed to the "convict code" and participating in "the mix."

She observed that the vast majority wanted to avoid "the mix"—"behavior that can bring trouble and conflict with staff and other prisoners." A primary feature of "the mix" is anything for which one can lose "good time" or can re-

Surviving in Prison

I was scared when I went to Bedford Hills. But I knew a few things by then. Like if you act quiet and hostile, people will consider you dangerous and won't bother you. So when I got out of isolation and women came up and talked to me, I said, "I left my feelings outside the gate, and I'll pick 'em up on my way out." I meant I wasn't going to take no junk from anyone. I made a promise if anybody hit me, I was gonna send 'em to the hospital.

When you go in, if you have certain characteristics, you're classified in a certain way. First of all, if you are aggressive, if you're not a dependent kind of woman, you're placed in a position where people think you have homosexual tendencies. If you're in that society long, you play the game if it makes it easier to survive. And it makes it easier if people think you're a stud broad. I played the game to make it easier so they would leave me alone. I didn't have money to use makeup and I couldn't see going through any changes. You're in there and the women are looking for new faces. Since I was quiet and not too feminine-looking, I was placed in a certain box in other people's minds. I let them think that's what box I was in—'cause it was a good way to survive. My good friends knew better. But I had three good friends and they were considered "my women"—so they in turn were safe, too. You have to find ways to survive. You cultivate ways to survive. It's an alien world and it has nothing to do with functioning in society better. What I learned there was to survive there.

Source: Kathryn Watterson Burkhart, *Women in Prison* (New York: Doubleday, 1976), 89–90.

Researching the Internet
The California Coalition for Women Prisoners is a reform group with a Web site at http://www.prisonactivist.org/ccwp/.

sult in being sent to administrative segregation. Being in "the mix" was related to "'homo-secting,' involvement in drugs, fights, and 'being messy,' that is being involved in conflict and trouble." Owen found most women want to do their time and go home, but some "are more at home in prison and do not seem to care if they 'lost time'." The culture of being "in the mix" is not imported from the outside but is internal to the prison, as some inmates prefer the pursuit of drugs, girlfriends, and fighting (Owen, 1998:179).

Male versus Female Subcultures

Comparisons of male and female prisons are complicated by the nature of the research: Most studies have been conducted in single-sex institutions, and most follow theories and concepts first developed in male prisons. However, the following facts may explain the differences in subculture:

- Nearly half of male inmates but only a third of female inmates are serving time for violent offenses.
- There is less violence in prisons for women than in prisons for men.
- Women show greater responsiveness to prison programs.
- Men's prison populations are divided by security level, but most women serve time in facilities where the entire population is mixed.
- Men tend to segregate themselves by race; this is less true with women.
- Men rarely become intimate with their keepers, but many women share their lives with officers.

A major difference between the two types of prisons relates to interpersonal relationships. Male prisoners act for themselves and are evaluated by others according to how they adhere to subcultural norms. As James Fox (1982) noted in his comparative study of one women's prison and four men's prisons, men believe they must demonstrate physical strength and consciously avoid any mannerisms that might imply homosexuality. To gain recognition and status within the convict community, the male prisoner must strictly adhere to these values. Men form cliques, but not the family networks found in prisons for women. Male norms stress autonomy, self-sufficiency, and the ability to cope with one's own problems, and men are expected to "do their own time." Fox found little sharing in the men's prisons.

Women place less emphasis on achieving status or recognition within the prisoner community. Fox writes that women are also less likely "to impose severe restrictions on the sexual (or emotional) conduct of other members" (1982:100). As noted previously, in prisons for women, close ties seem to exist among small groups akin to extended families. These family groups provide emotional support and share resources.

The differences between male and female prisoner subcultures have been ascribed to the nurturing, maternal qualities of women. Some critics charge that such an analysis stereotypes female behavior and imputes a biological basis to personality where none exists. Of importance as well is the issue of inmate–inmate violence in male and female institutions. The few data that exist indicate that women are less likely to engage in violent acts against other inmates than are men (Kruttschnitt and Krmopotich, 1990:371). In any case, it will be interesting to see whether such gender-specific differences continue to be found among prisoners as the feminist perspective gains influence among researchers and as society comes to view women and men as equals.

check point

8. How do the social relationships among female prisoners differ from those of their male counterparts?

Issues in the Incarceration of Women

As noted, the number of incarcerated women has greatly increased over the past ten years. Under pressures for equal opportunity, states seem to believe that they should run women's prisons as they do prisons for men, with the same policies and procedures. Joycelyn Pollock (1998) believes that when prisons emphasize parity, then use a male standard, women lose. She says that with the increased number of woman in prison and more equality in programming, there are also more security measures and formalistic approaches to supervision.

Although correctional departments have been playing "catch up" to meet the challenges of the influx of women offenders, sexual misconduct by officers, demands for education and training, medical services, and methods for dealing with the problems of mothers and their children persist. We next examine each of these issues and the policy implications they pose for the future.

Sexual Misconduct

As the number of female prisoners has increased, cases of sexual misconduct by male correctional officers have escalated. The case of murderer Susan Smith's relationship with Houston Cagle, an officer with 13 years of service, received much attention by the media when he was arrested, but there are countless other women who have remained silent. As a result of an investigation of sexual misconduct by officers in the women's prisons of five states—California, Georgia, Illinois, Michigan and New York—Human Rights Watch reported that male officers had raped, sexually assaulted, and abused female inmates. Guards had also "used their near total authority to provide or deny goods and privileges to female prisoners to compel them to have sex or, in other cases, to reward them for having done so" (*New York Times,* December 27, 1996:A18).

Monetary civil judgements awarded to women for mistreatment while in prison have grown. Officials in California, Georgia, and the District of Colum-

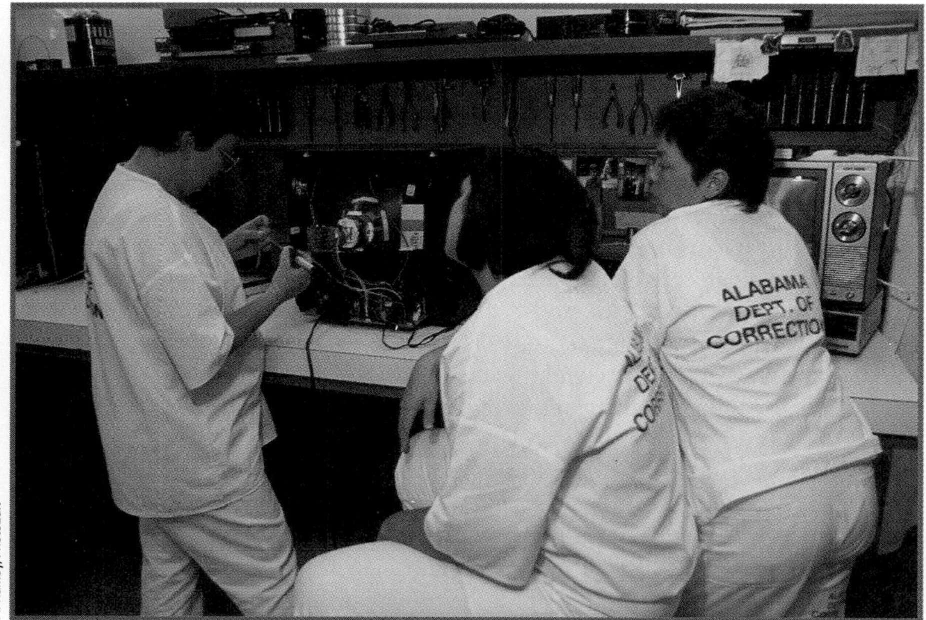

A. Ramey/PhotoEdit

Though these Alabama prisoners are taking an electronics course, critics charge that many training programs in women's prisons are for jobs that are stereotypically "feminine."

bia have reached out-of-court settlements in class-action suits brought on behalf of women who said they were sexually harassed or assaulted by guards while incarcerated. A District of Columbia plaintiff was awarded $5 million in punitive damages and $350,000 in compensatory damages.

To deal with the problem of sexual abuse in prison, all but eight states have enacted statutes prohibiting sexual misconduct with correctional clients. While some of these laws are directed at correctional officers, several states are revising their statutes to include anyone who supervises offenders (*Criminal Justice Research Reports,* 2001). Beyond the new laws, corrections faces a great need for the implementation of effective sexual harassment policies, the training of officers, and tougher screening of recruits.

Some administrators say that part of the problem is the large number of men guarding women. The Human Rights Watch report noted that the majority of correctional officers in women's prisons are men and in some states, such as Illinois, males outnumber female guards three to one in women's prisons.

Educational and Vocational Training Programs

A major criticisms of women's prisons is that they lack the variety of vocational and educational programs available in male institutions. Critics also charge that existing programs tend to conform to sexual stereotypes of "female" occupations—cosmetology, food service, housekeeping, sewing. Such training does not correspond to the wider employment opportunities available to women in today's world. Both men's and women's faculties usually offer educational programs so inmates can become literate and earn general equivalency diplomas (GEDs). Such programs are important, considering that upon release most women must support themselves and many are financially responsible for children.

Research conducted in the 1970s by Ruth Glick and Virginia Neto (1977) confirmed that fewer programs were offered in women's than in men's institutions and that the existing programs lacked variety. Merry Morash and her colleagues noted changes during the 1980s, but they too found that gender stereotypes shaped vocational programs (Morash, Haarr, and Rucker, 1994). The American Correctional Association (1990) reported that the few work assignments available for incarcerated women do teach marketable job skills.

To get a good job, workers must have the education necessary to meet the needs of a complex workplace. However, the educational level of most female offenders limits their access to these occupations. In some institutions less than half of the inmates have completed high school. Some corrections systems assign these women to classes so they can earn a GED, and other inmates can do college work through correspondence study or courses offered in the institution.

Medical Services

Women's prisons lack proper medical services. Yet women usually have more serious health problems because of their socioeconomic status and limited access to preventive medical care. Compared to men, they have a higher incidence of asthma, drug abuse, diabetes, and heart disorders, and many women also have gynecological problems (Bershard, 1985; Yang, 1990). A higher percentage of women than men report receiving medical services in prison, yet women's institutions are less likely than men's to have a full-time medical staff or hospital facilities.

HIV, tuberculosis, drug addiction, and mental illness affect female prisoners more than they do male ones. A national survey revealed that a higher percentage of female than male state prison inmates (4.0 percent versus 2.3 percent) tested positive for HIV. In addition, more than 11 percent of HIV-positive women had spent a night in a mental hospital before incarceration, and 54 percent had used drugs during the month before entering prison (BJS, 1999e).

Surveys show that about 25 percent of incarcerated women were pregnant on admission or had given birth during the previous year. Pregnancies raise numerous issues for correctional policy, including special diets, abortion rights, access to delivery rooms and medical personnel, and length of time that newborns can remain with incarcerated mothers. Most pregnant inmates have characteristics (older than 35, history of drug abuse, prior multiple abortions, and sexually transmitted diseases) that indicate the potential for a high-risk pregnancy requiring special medical care. Many prison systems are attempting to address this problem by allowing nursing infants to stay with their mothers, creating in-prison nurseries, instituting counseling programs, and improving standards of medical care (Wooldredge and Masters, 1993).

Saying that corrections must "defuse the time bomb," Leslie Acoca (1998) argues that failure to provide female inmates with basic preventive and medical treatments such as immunizations, breast cancer screenings, and management of chronic diseases "is resulting in the development of more serious health problems that are exponentially more expensive to treat." She says that poor medical care for the incarcerated merely shifts costs to overburdened community health care systems after release.

Mothers and Their Children

Of greatest concern to incarcerated women is the fate of their children. Over 65 percent of women inmates are mothers with, on average, two dependent children. Thus on any given day, 167,000 American children—two-thirds of whom are under ten years old—have mothers who are in jail or prison. Roughly half of these children do not see their mothers the entire time they are in prison (BJS, 2000j:1).

Because about 65 percent of incarcerated mothers were single caretakers of minor children before they entered prison, they do not have partners to take care of the children. Nearly 78 percent of these children are cared for by relatives, while 10 percent are in state-funded foster care (Acoca, 1997).

In most states, babies born in prison must be placed with a family member or social agency within three weeks. However, critics have expressed great concern about such early termination of the developmentally crucial mother–infant bonding, so some innovative programs now let them stay together longer. For example, at the Women's Correctional Institution at Bedford Hills, New York, women and their newborns move to a special nursery wing and can stay there for up to one year. Their primary responsibility is to care for their children and to learn parenting skills.

Chicago Legal Advocacy for Incarcerated Mothers assists families of female prisoners. Visit their site at http://www.c-l-a-i-m.org/.

AP/Kathy Willens

Through the Children of Incarcerated Mothers Initiative, Rikers Island, New York, Damara Quiles has weekly visits with her daughter and son. Most incarcerated mothers have difficulty maintaining contact with their children.

Imprisoned mothers have difficulty maintaining contact with their children. Because most states have only one or two prisons for women, mothers may be incarcerated 150 miles or more away. Transportation is thus difficult, visits are short and infrequent, and phone calls uncertain and irregular. When the children do visit the prison, the surroundings are strange and intimidating. In some institutions, children must conform to the rules governing adult visitations: strict time limits and no physical contact.

Other correctional facilities, however, seek ways to help mothers maintain links to their children. For example, the Dwight Correctional Center in Illinois schedules weekend retreats, similar to camping trips, for women and their children. In some states, children can meet with their mothers at almost any time, for extended periods, and in playrooms or nurseries where contact is possible. Some states transport children to visit their mothers; some institutions even let children stay overnight with their mothers. A few prisons have family visitation programs that let the inmate, her legal husband, and her children be together, often in a mobile home or apartment, for up to 72 hours.

The future of women's correctional institutions is hard to predict. More women are being sent to prison now, and more have committed the violent crimes and drug offenses that used to be more typical of male offenders. Will these changes affect the adaptive roles and social relationships that differentiate women's prisons from men's? Will women's prisons need to become more security conscious and to enforce rules through more formal relationships between inmates and staff? These important issues need further study.

check point

9. What are some of the problems encountered by female prisoners in maintaining contact with their children?
10. How are children cared for while their mothers are incarcerated?

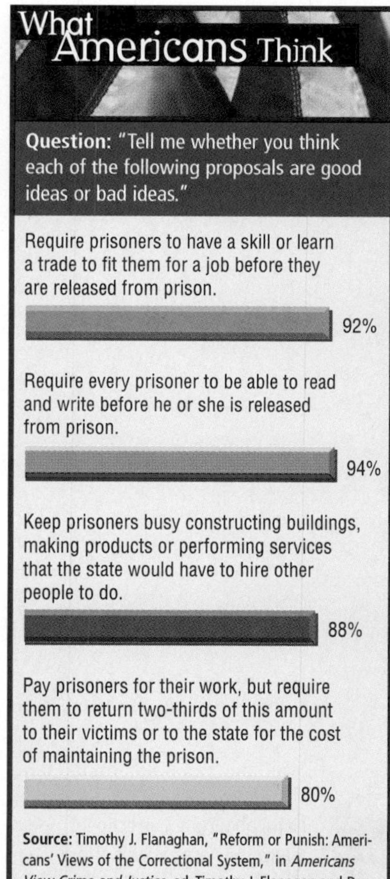

Question: "Tell me whether you think each of the following proposals are good ideas or bad ideas."

Require prisoners to have a skill or learn a trade to fit them for a job before they are released from prison. 92%

Require every prisoner to be able to read and write before he or she is released from prison. 94%

Keep prisoners busy constructing buildings, making products or performing services that the state would have to hire other people to do. 88%

Pay prisoners for their work, but require them to return two-thirds of this amount to their victims or to the state for the cost of maintaining the prison. 80%

Source: Timothy J. Flanaghan, "Reform or Punish: Americans' Views of the Correctional System," in *Americans View Crime and Justice*, ed. Timothy J. Flanagan and Dennis R. Longmire (Thousand Oaks, Calif.: Sage, 1996), 84.

Prison Programs

Modern correctional institutions differ from those of the past in the number and variety of programs provided for inmates. Early penitentiaries included prison industries; educational, vocational, and treatment programs were added when rehabilitation goals became prevalent. During the last 30 years, as the public called for harsher punishment of criminals, legislators have gutted prison educational and treatment programs as "frills" that only "coddled" inmates. In addition, the great increase in the number of prisoners has limited access to those programs that are still available. Yet, respondents to one survey support some prison programs (see "What Americans Think").

Steve Lehman/SABA Press

As the saying goes, "Idle hands are the Devil's playground." Experienced administrators know that the more programs are offered, the less likely inmates' boredom will translate into "mischief making."

Administrators argue that programs help them deal with the problem of time on the prisoners' hands. They know that the more programs prisons offer, the less likely that inmate idleness will turn into hostility—the less cell time, the fewer tensions. Evidence suggests that inmate education and jobs may positively affect the running of prisons, as well as reduce recidivism (Butterfield, 1995a).

Classification of Prisoners

Determining the appropriate program for an individual prisoner usually involves a process called **classification.** A committee—often comprising the heads of the security, treatment, education, and industry departments—evaluates the inmate's security level, treatment needs, work assignment, and eventually readiness for release.

classification
The process of assigning an inmate to a category specifying his or her needs for security, treatment, education, work assignment, and readiness for release.

Classification decisions are often based on the institution's needs rather than those of the inmates. For example, inmates from the city may be assigned to farm work because that is where they are needed. Further, certain popular programs may remain limited, even though the demand for them is great. Thus inmates may find that the few places in, for example, a computer course are filled and that there is a long waiting list. Prisoners are often angered and frustrated by the classification process and the limited availability of programs. Release on parole can depend on a good record of participation in these programs, yet entrance for some inmates is blocked.

check point

11. Why are prison programs important from the standpoint of prison administrators?
12. How are inmates assigned to programs?

Educational Programs

Surveys have shown that programs offering academic courses are the most popular in corrections systems. Offenders constitute one of the most undereducated groups in the U.S. population. In many systems, all inmates who have not completed eighth grade are assigned full-time to prison school. Many programs provide remedial help in reading, English, and math. They also permit prisoners to earn their GED. Some institutions offer courses in cooperation with a college or

Learn about the Correctional Education Association's efforts regarding prisoner education at http://www.ceanational.org.

university, although funding for such programs has come under attack. The Comprehensive Crime Control Act of 1994 bans federal funding to prisoners for postsecondary education (Kunen, 1995). Some state legislatures have passed similar laws, under pressure from people who argue that tax dollars should not be spent on the tuition of prisoners.

Studies have shown that prisoners assigned to education programs tend to avoid committing crimes after release (Andrews and Bonta, 1994). However, it is unclear whether education helps to rehabilitate these offenders or whether the types of prisoners ("gleaners") assigned to education programs tend to be those motivated to avoid further crimes. See "Doing Your Part" for more on prisoner education.

Vocational Education

Vocational education programs attempt to teach offenders a marketable job skill. Unfortunately, too many programs train inmates for trades that already have an adequate labor supply or in which new methods have made the skills taught obsolete.

Offenders often lack the attitudes necessary to obtain and keep a job—punctuality, accountability, deference to supervisors, cordiality to coworkers. Therefore most prisoners need to learn not only a skill but also how to act in the work world.

Yet another problem is perhaps the toughest of all. In one state or another, the law bars ex-felons from practicing certain occupations including nurse, beautician, barber, real estate salesperson, chauffeur, worker where alcoholic beverages are sold, cashier, and insurance salesperson. Unfortunately, some prison vocational programs actually train inmates for jobs they can never hold.

Prison Industries

Prison industries, which trace their roots to the early workshops of New York's Auburn Penitentiary, are intended to teach work habits and skills that will assist prisoners' reentry into the outside workforce. In practice, institutions rely on prison labor to provide basic food, maintenance, clerical, and other services. In addition, many prisons contain manufacturing facilities that produce goods, such as office furniture and clothing, to be used in correctional and other state institutions.

The prison industries system has had a checkered career (Conley, 1980). During the nineteenth century, factories were established in many prisons, and inmates manufactured items that were sold on the open market. With the rise of the labor movement, however, state legislatures and Congress passed laws restricting the sale of prison-made goods so that they would not compete with those made by free workers. In 1979 Congress lifted restrictions on the interstate sale of prison-made products and urged correctional administrators to explore with the private sector possible improvements for prison industry programs. Industrial programs would relieve idleness, allow inmates to

Mentor to Prisoners

Dr. R. Bruce McPherson

About ten years before Dr. R. Bruce McPherson retired as Professor of Education at the University of Illinois at Chicago, a colleague asked him to send a copy of one of his published articles to her brother, incarcerated at the Federal Correctional Institution, Butner, North Carolina. That initial contact led to a visit to the prison and a friendship. The brother was studying at the college level, and McPherson became interested as to how these courses were made available to prisoners. He contacted the administrator for all Bureau of Prison educational programs, who alerted supervisors at half a dozen prisons with strong college programs of McPherson's interest in visiting, observing, and assisting inmates with their education.

Since 1987, Professor McPherson has been a teacher, mentor, and friend to 18 prisoners. He believes that his most effective contributions have been to four men with long sentences who are still incarcerated but are especially prepared for release. He argues that the criminal justice system has no effective, commonsensical means of assessing the readiness of prisoners for release and acting on that knowledge.

Ten of the eighteen have been released and McPherson remains in close touch with eight, all of whom are doing well. One runs a clothing store and plans to purchase it soon, one is a corporate manager, another works for a major airline, another is studying at a fine university, another has published two books and aspires to a literary career, another married and is now a salesman, and another works as a union painter and part-time evangelist.

Bruce McPherson has been a provider of books, a mentor and tutor as college courses were selected and completed and degrees attained, an advocate, an advice giver, an editor, an information provider, and—perhaps most important—a friend. He is distressed that in 1994 Congress banned federal funding (Pell Grants) to prisoners for postsecondary education. This decision has all but eliminated college courses in state and federal prisons, yet research shows that participation in educational programs is one of the best predictors of inmate success in the community upon release.

Professor McPherson says that he has considered all of these men and women as his students.

I learned never to overestimate or underestimate my impact on them. Inmates need strong contacts with mainstream citizens who will befriend them, help them in practical ways, serve as role models and give them faith in themselves and hope for a decent, productive life after prison. A part of my contribution remains with those who now live among us. My heart remains with those who are still incarcerated.

McPherson believes that education, coupled with attention to religious/spiritual needs, typically proves to be the strongest force in rehabilitation and atonement. He says, "If I could design a prison, I would have the chapel and the classroom at its core."

Learn more about opportunities for Missouri's program for volunteers in corrections at http://www.corrections.state.mo.us/division/prob/news22.htm.

earn wages that they could save until release, and reduce the costs of incarceration. The Federal Bureau of Prisons and some states have developed industries, but generally their products are not sold on the free market and the percentage of prisoners employed varies greatly. For example, in North Carolina and Utah more than 20 percent of prisoners work in prison industries, while in most states 5 percent or less do (C. G. Camp and Camp, 1999:96). In 1999 the governing board of the Federal Prison Industries approved plans to expand the exclusive government contract work and to enter new commercial markets (Weis, 2001:253).

Visit the Web site of Prison Blues, which features a line of denim jeans, shirts, and jackets made by the inmates at Eastern Oregon Correctional Institution: http://www.prisonblues.com.

Although the idea of employing inmates sounds attractive, the inefficiencies of prison work may offset its economic value. Turnover is great because many inmates are transferred among several institutions or released over a two-year period. Many prisoners have little education and lack steady work habits, making it difficult for them to perform many of the tasks of modern production. An additional cost to efficiency is the need to stop production periodically to count heads and to check that tools and materials have not been stolen (Flanagan and Maguire, 1993).

Rehabilitative Programs

Rehabilitative programs seek to treat the personal defects thought to have brought about the inmate's criminality. Most people agree that rehabilitating offenders is a desirable goal, but they disagree a great deal on the amount of emphasis that these programs should receive.

Reports in the 1970s cast doubt on the ability of treatment programs to stem recidivism. They also questioned the ethics of requiring inmates to participate in rehabilitative programs in exchange for the promise of parole (Martinson, 1974). Supporters of treatment programs argue that certain programs, if properly run, work for certain offenders (Andrews et al., 1990; Palmer, 1992).

Most corrections systems still offer a range of psychological, behavioral, and social services programs. How much they are used seems to vary according to the goals of the institution and the attitudes of the administrators. Nationally, little money is spent on treatment services, and these programs reach only 5 percent of the inmate population. Although rehabilitative programs remain a part of correctional institutions, then, their emphasis has diminished. Incarceration's current goal of humane custody implies no effort to change inmates.

Medical Services

Most prisons offer medical services through a full-time staff of nurses, augmented by part-time physicians under contract to the corrections system. Nurses take care of routine health care and dispense medicines from a secure in-prison pharmacy; regularly scheduled visits to the prison by doctors can enable prisoners to obtain checkups and diagnoses. For cases needing a specialist, surgery, or emergency medical assistance, prisoners must be transported to local hospitals under close supervision by correctional staff. The aim is for the prison system to be able to provide a range of medical assistance to meet the various needs of the population as a whole.

For information on medical services for prisoners in Louisiana, see http://www.ci.baton-rouge.La.US/DEPT/EMS/prison.htm.

While inmates' needs for health care echo those of the general population, prisoners pose two special needs, one due to poverty and the other to aging. Because prisoners as a group are very poor, they often bring to the prison years of neglect of their general health. Other consequences of being poor, such as an inadequate diet and poor hygiene, also affect the general health of the prison population.

Go to the *American System of Criminal Justice* Web site at http://www.cj.wadsworth.com/colesmith10e to explore the topic of rehabilitative programs in further detail.

As we have seen, by far the most extraordinary health problem in contemporary corrections is the burgeoning number of elderly prisoners. Elderly inmates have more complicated and more numerous health problems overall, and they eventually reach an age where they cannot productively participate in prison assignments. Prisons are difficult places in which to grow old and die. Some prison

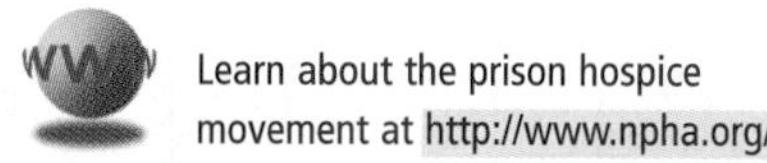

systems have formed hospice facilities where younger inmates can care for the elderly as they spend their last days on earth behind bars.

Learn about the prison hospice movement at http://www.npha.org/.

check point

13. Why have legislatures and the general public been so critical of educational and rehabilitative programs in prisons?
14. What problems are encountered in vocational training programs?
15. Why have legislatures restricted prison industries?

Release to the Community

Go to the Public Policy feature on the American System of Criminal Justice CD to learn more about the issues surrounding parole.

In Chapter 14 we looked at parole from the perspective of the criminal justice system and the community. Here, we take another look at release from prison, this time focusing on the issues as they affect the inmates themselves.

Except for the small number who die in prison, all inmates will eventually be released to live in the community. Currently about 80 percent of felons will be released on parole and will remain under correctional supervision for a specific period of time. Recall that parole is the *conditional* release of an offender from incarceration but not from the legal custody of the state. Thus offenders who comply with parole conditions and do not further conflict with the law receive an absolute discharge from supervision at the end of their sentences. If a parolee breaks a rule, parole can be revoked and the person returned to a correctional facility. Parole rests on three concepts:

The Oklahoma Pardon and Parole Board provides information to the public about its responsibilities at http://www.ppb.state.ok.us.

1. *Grace:* The prisoner could be kept incarcerated but the government extends the privilege of release.
2. *Contract:* The government enters into an agreement with the prisoner whereby the prisoner promises to abide by certain conditions in exchange for being released.
3. *Custody:* Even though the offender is released from prison, he or she is still a responsibility of the government. Parole is an extension of correctional programs into the community.

Only felons are released on parole; adult misdemeanants are usually released immediately after they have finished serving their sentences. Almost 600,000 felons are released from prison each year and allowed to live under supervision in the community. Today about 725,000 people are under parole supervision, a three-fold increase since 1980 (Travis and Petersilia, 2001). In Chapter 14 we read about parole supervision in Japan; in the Comparative Perspective, we revisit this topic from a different perspective.

Release Mechanisms

From 1920 to 1973 there was a nationwide sentencing and release policy. During this period all states and the federal government used indeterminate sentencing, authorized discretionary release by parole boards, and supervised prisoners after release, and they did this all in the interest of the rehabilitation of offenders.

With the 1970s critique of rehabilitation, the move to determinate sentencing, and the public's view that the system was "soft" on criminals, 14 states eventually abolished their parole boards (Petersilia, 1999:480). Further, some of the states that kept release by parole boards have been reluctant to grant it. In Texas, for

Bob Daemmrich/Stock Boston

Until the 1970s discretionary release by a parole board was the primary way that offenders left prison. Mandatory release now accounts for 40 percent of felons released to the community. What are the advantages and disadvantages of each mechanism?

Parole Release in Japan

Japan is probably the safest country in the developed world. To understand why Japan's crime rate is so low, we might talk to a short, squat man with rumpled clothes, a gentle smile, and big, leathery hands who once crushed his neighbor's head with a hammer.

This 62-year-old man, who killed his neighbor after robbing him of money, is on parole after 15 years in prison. No one in his family ever visited him. His wife and son have told him never to return to their village. His three daughters have even refused to see him. "I have four grandchildren—I think," he said. He has never even seen their pictures.

More than any other developed country, Japan has resolved to "just say no" to crime. Japanese society ostracizes offenders and demands that they not just be caught but that they also confess and show remorse. But, as in the United States, few Japanese offenders die in prison; almost all are released on parole to live under supervision in the community.

Aftercare programs have been available for Japanese offenders since the 1880s. But not until the 1950s were all elements of community treatment for ex-offenders—probation, parole, and aftercare—brought together on a national basis.

Today, decisions to release offenders from prison and place them under supervision in the community are made by eight regional parole boards (RPBs). Sitting in panels of three, the members review applications for parole from prisons and training schools. They also have the authority to revoke an individual's parole on the recommendation of a local office.

The service units of the RPBs coordinate parole. One-third of the sentence must be served. The warden, not the inmate, files the application; he thus clearly uses parole to manage prisoners. The prison directly helps select parolees by sending information to the RPB for parole.

A parole officer visits the home specified in the inmate's job/living plan. The officer checks the situation over and recommends changes, if necessary. The report goes to the prison and the RPB. Sometimes the inmate has to revise and submit another plan.

Then the regional parole board looks at the inmate's character, behavior, and other circumstances. A board member interviews the inmate. Parole conditions are set partly by law and partly by administrative actions. For example, Parker (1986:53–54) writes that parolees must

> *(1) maintain a fixed residence and pursue a lawful occupation; (2) refrain from associating with persons having criminal or delinquent tendencies; (3) maintain good behavior; (4) obtain advance permission from a parole supervisor before changing a place of residence or traveling for an extended period; and (5) comply with any special conditions imposed by the parole board at the time of release.*

Japanese probation, parole, and aftercare focus on community. As we saw in Chapter 14, unpaid volunteers do the supervision; private organizations administer aftercare, paid only partly by governmental subsidies.

The Japanese public largely believes that people can correct themselves. Repentant offenders tend to get out; others end up in prison. "Rehabilitation" is a way to earn the right to be reincluded in society.

Sources: Adapted from Elmer H. Johnson, *Japanese Corrections: Managing Convicted Offenders in an Orderly Society* (Carbondale: Southern Illinois University Press, 1996), 266–67, 294; Nicholas D. Kristof, "Japanese Say No to Crime: Tough Methods at a Price," *New York Times,* May 14, 1995, p. 1; L. Craig Parker, Jr., *Parole and the Community Based Treatment of Offenders in Japan and The United States* (New Haven, Conn.: University of New Haven Press, 1986), 53–54.

example, 57 percent of all cases considered for parole release in 1988 were approved; by 1998 that figure had dropped to just 20 percent (Fabelo, 1999).

There are now four basic mechanisms for people to be released from prison: (1) discretionary release, (2) mandatory release,(3) other conditional release, and (4) expiration release. Figure 16.3 shows the percentage of felons released by the various mechanisms.

discretionary release
The release of an inmate from prison to conditional supervision at the discretion of the parole board within the boundaries set by the sentence and the penal law.

Discretionary Release

States retaining indeterminate sentences allow **discretionary release** by the parole board within the boundaries set by the sentence and the penal law. This is a conditional release to parole supervision. This approach (illustrated in the Close Up box) lets the parole board assess the prisoner's readiness for release within the minimum and maximum terms of the sentence. In reviewing the prisoner's file and asking questions, the parole board focuses on the nature of the offense, the inmate's behavior, and his or her participation in rehabilitative programs. This process places great faith in the ability of parole board members to predict the future behavior of offenders. See "A Question of Ethics" for more.

Figure 16.3 **Methods of release from state prison**
Felons are released from prison to the community, usually under parole supervision, through various means depending upon the law.

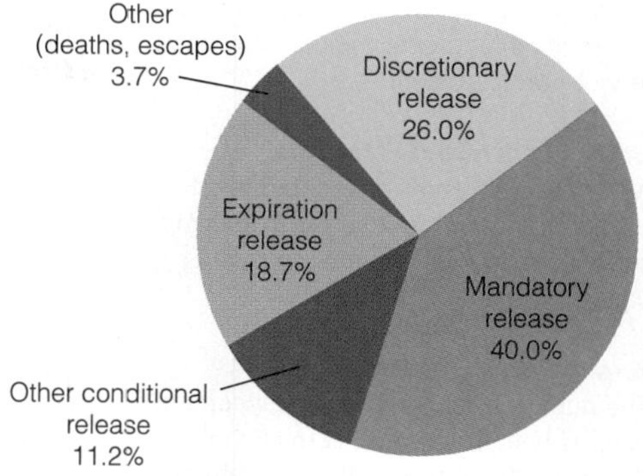

Source: Jeremy Travis and Joan Petersilia, "Reentry Reconsidered," *Crime and Delinquency* 47 (July 2001): 295.

Mandatory Release

Mandatory release occurs after an inmate has served time equal to the total sentence minus good time, if any, or to a certain percentage of the total sentence as specified by law. Mandatory release is found in federal jurisdictions and states with determinate sentences and good time provisions (see Chapter 12). Without a parole board to make discretionary decisions, mandatory release is a matter of bookkeeping to check the correct amount of good time and other credits and make sure the sentence has been accurately interpreted. The prisoner is conditionally released to parole supervision for the rest of the sentence.

Other Conditional Release

Because of the growth of prison populations, many states have devised ways to get around the rigidity of mandatory release by placing inmates in the community through furloughs, home supervision, halfway houses, emergency release, and other programs (BJS, 2000d; Griset, 1995:307). These types of **other conditional release** also avoid the appearance of the politically sensitive label "discretionary parole."

Expiration Release

An increasing percentage of prisoners receive an **expiration release.** These inmates are released from any further correctional supervision and cannot be returned to prison for their current offense. Such offenders have served the maximum court sentence, minus good time—they have "maxed out."

check point

16. How do discretionary release, mandatory release, other conditional release, and expiration release differ?

Impact of Release Mechanisms

Parole release mechanisms do more than simply determine the date at which a particular prisoner will be sent back into the community. Parole release also has an enormous impact on other parts of the system, including sentencing, plea bargaining, and the size of prison populations.

One important effect of discretionary release is that an administrative body—the parole board—can shorten a sentence imposed by a judge. Even in states that have mandatory release, various potential reductions built into the sentence mean that the full sentence is rarely

The five members of the parole board questioned Jim Allen, an offender with a long history of sex offenses involving teenage boys. Now approaching 45 and having met the eligibility requirement for a hearing, Allen respectfully answered the board members.

Toward the end of the hearing, Richard Edwards, a dentist who had recently been appointed to the board, spoke up: "Your institutional record is good, you have a parole plan, a job has been promised, and your sister says she will help you. All of that looks good, but I just can't vote for your parole. You haven't attended the behavior modification program for sex offenders. I think you're going to repeat your crime. I have a 13-year-old son, and I don't want him or other boys to run the risk of meeting your kind."

Allen looked shocked. The other members had seemed ready to grant his release.

"But I'm ready for parole. I won't do that stuff again. I didn't go to that program because electroshock to my private area is not going to help me. I've been here 5 years of the 7-year max and have stayed out of trouble. The judge didn't say I was to be further punished in prison by therapy."

After Jim Allen left the room, the board discussed his case. "You know, Rich, he has a point. He has been a model prisoner and has served a good portion of his sentence," said Brian Lynch, a long-term board member. "Besides we don't know if Dr. Hankin's program works."

"I know, but can we really let someone like that out on the streets?"

→ Are the results of the behavior-modification program for sex offenders relevant to the parole board's decision? Is the purpose of the sentence to punish Allen for what he *did* or for what he *might* do in the future? Would you vote for his release on parole? Would your vote be the same if his case had received media attention?

mandatory release
The required release of an inmate from incarceration to community supervision upon the expiration of a certain period, as specified by a determinate-sentencing law or parole guidelines.

other conditional release
A term used in some states to avoid the rigidity of mandatory release by placing convicts in various community settings under supervision.

expiration release
The release of an inmate from incarceration, without any further correctional supervision; the inmate cannot be returned to prison for any remaining portion of the sentence for the current offense.

served. Good time, for example, can reduce punishment even if there is no parole eligibility.

To understand the impact of release mechanisms on criminal punishment, we must compare the amount of time actually served in prison with the sentence specified by the judge. In some jurisdictions, up to 60 percent of felons sentenced to prison are released to the community after their first appearance before a parole board. Eligibility for discretionary release is ordinarily determined by the minimum term of the sentence minus good time and jail time.

Although states vary considerably, on a national basis felony inmates serve an average of just over two years before release. Offenders who receive long sentences actually serve a smaller proportion of such sentences than do offenders given shorter sentences. For example, a robbery offender may be given a term of 12 to 60 months and serve 69 percent of the term before being released after 23 months. By contrast, an offender sentenced to a term of 181 to 240 months will actually serve 38 percent of the term, 83 months. Figure 16.4 shows the average time served for selected offenses.

Supporters of discretion for the paroling authority argue that parole benefits the overall system. Discretionary release mitigates the harshness of the penal code. If the legislature must establish exceptionally strict punishments as a means of conveying a "tough on crime" image to frustrated and angry voters, parole can effectively permit sentence adjustments that make the punishment fit the crime. Everyone convicted of larceny may not have done equivalent harm, yet some legislatively mandated sentencing schemes may impose equally strict sentences. Early release on parole can be granted to an offender who is less deserving of strict punishment, such as someone who voluntarily makes restitution, cooperates with the police, or shows genuine regret.

Figure 16.4
Estimated time to be served (in months) by state prisoners for selected offenses
The data indicate that the average felony offender going to prison for the first time spends about two years in prison. How would you expect the public to react to that fact?

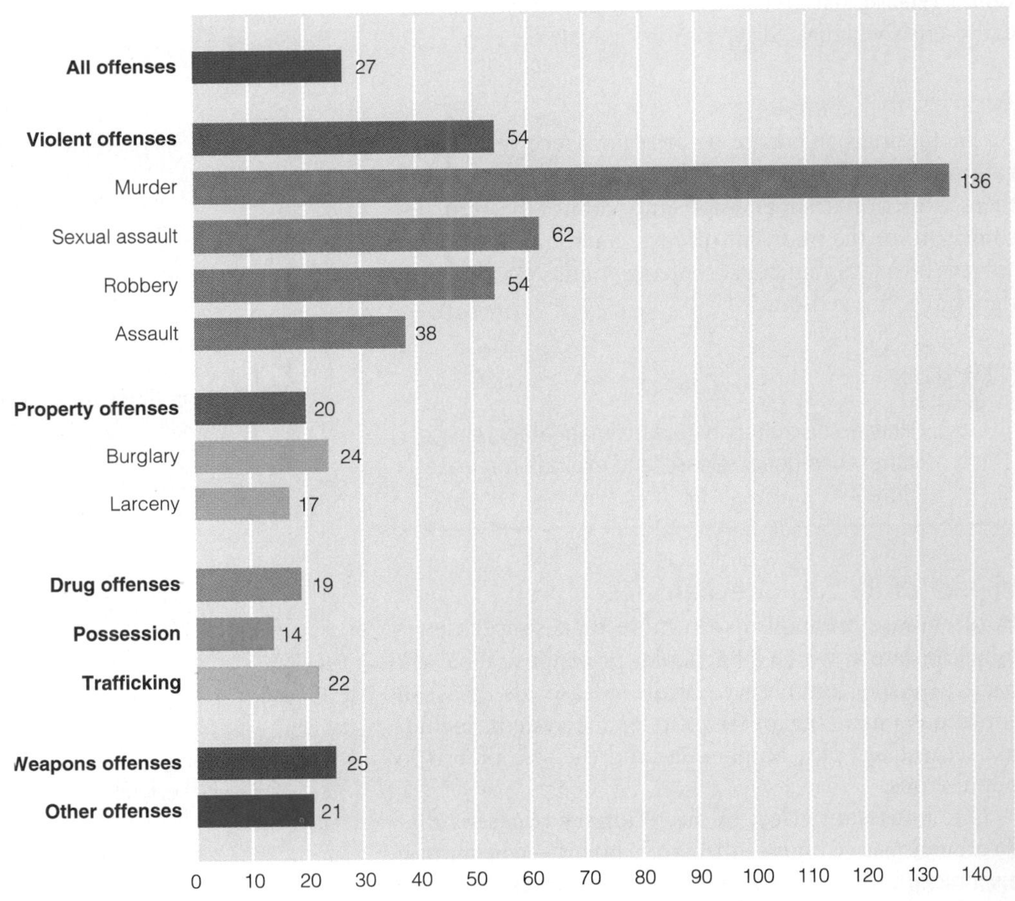

Source: Bureau of Justice Statistics, *Bulletin*, October 2001, p. 5.

A Roomful of Strangers

After three years, three months, and four days in Stanhope Correctional Facility, Ben Brooks was ready to go before the Board of Parole. He woke with butterflies in his stomach, realizing that at nine o'clock he was to walk into the hearing room to confront a roomful of strangers. As he lay on his bunk he rehearsed the answers to the questions he thought the board members might ask: "How do you feel about the person you assaulted? What have you done with your time while incarcerated? Do you think you have learned anything here that will convince the board that you will follow a crime-free life in the community? What are your plans for employment and housing?" According to prison scuttlebutt, these were the types of questions asked, and you had to be prepared to answer that you were sorry for your past mistakes, had taken advantage of the prison programs, had a job waiting for you, and planned to live with your family. You had to "ring bells" with the board.

At breakfast, friends dropped by Ben's table to reassure him that he had it made. As one said, "Ben, you've done everything they've said to do. What else can they expect?" That was the problem, *What did they expect?*

At eight-thirty, Officer Kearney came by the cell. "Time to go, Ben." They walked out of the housing unit and down the long prison corridors to a group of chairs outside the hearing room. Other prisoners were already seated there. "Sit here, Ben. They'll call when they're ready. Good luck."

At ten minutes past nine the door opened and an officer called, "First case, Brooks." Ben got up, walked into the room. "Please take a seat, Mr. Brooks," said the African American seated in the center at the table. Ben knew he was Reverend Perry, a man known as being tough but fair. To his left was a white man, Mr. MacDonald, and to his right a Hispanic woman, Ms. Lopez. The white man led the questioning.

"Mr. Brooks. You were convicted of armed robbery and sentenced to a term of 6–10 years. Please tell the board what you have learned during your incarceration."

Ben paused and then answered hesitantly, "Well, I learned that to commit such a stupid act was a mistake. I was under a lot of pressure when I pulled the robbery and now am sorry for what I did."

"You severely injured the woman you held up. What might you tell her if she were sitting in this room today?"

"I would just have to say, I'm sorry. It will never happen again."

"But this is not the first time you have been convicted. What makes you think it will never happen again?"

"Well this is the first time I was sent to prison. You see things a lot differently from here."

Ms. Lopez spoke up. "You have a good prison record—member of the Toastmaster's Club, gotten your high school equivalency diploma, kept your nose clean. Tell the board about your future plans should you be released."

"My brother says I can live with him until I get on my feet, and there is a letter in my file telling you that I have a job waiting at a meat-processing plant. I will be living in my hometown but I don't intend to see my old buddies again. You can be sure that I am now on the straight and narrow."

"But you committed a heinous crime. That woman suffered a lot. Why should the board believe that you won't do it again?"

"All I can say is that I'm different now."

"Thank you Mr. Brooks," said Reverend Perry. "You will hear from us by this evening." Ben got up and walked out of the room. It had only taken eight minutes, yet it seemed like hours. Eight minutes during which his future was being decided. Would it be back to the cell or out on the street? It would be about ten hours before he would receive word from the board as to his fate.

For more on this subject, see http://www.crjustice.org/rolparol htm.

A major criticism of discretionary release is that it shifts responsibility for many primary criminal justice decisions from a judge, who holds legal procedures uppermost, to an administrative board, where discretion rules. Judges know a great deal about constitutional rights and basic legal protections, but parole board members may not have such knowledge. In most states with discretionary release, parole hearings are secret, with only board members, the inmate, and correctional officers present. Often no published criteria guide decisions, and prisoners are given no reason for denial or granting of parole. However, an increasing number of states permit oral or written testimony by victims, as well as members of the offender's family. (See the Close Up box for a look at how discretionary release can put pressure on inmates.)

See the Web site that helps Nebraska crime victims learn about the parole system: http://www.corrections.state.ne.us/victim_assistance/faqs.html.

Should society place such power in the hands of parole boards? Because there is so little oversight over their decision making and so few constraints on their decisions, some parole board members will make arbitrary or discriminatory decisions that are inconsistent with the values underlying our constitutional system and civil rights. Generally, the U.S. legal system seeks to avoid determining people's fate through such methods.

check point

17. How does parole release influence the rest of the criminal justice system?

Problems Facing Parolees

The day they come out of prison, parolees face a staggering array of problems. In most states, they are given only clothes, a token amount of money, a list of rules governing their conditional release, and the name and address of the parole officer to whom they must report within 24 hours. Although a promised job is often a condition for release, an actual job may be another matter. Most former convicts are unskilled or semiskilled, and the conditions of release may prevent them from moving to areas where they could find work. If the parolee is African American, male, and under 30, he joins the largest group of unemployed in the country. (Parole supervision is fully discussed in Chapter 14.)

Civil Disabilities of Ex-Felons

Once a person has been released from prison, paid a fine, or completed parole or probation, the debt to society—in theory—has been paid and the punishment has ended. For many offenders, however, a criminal conviction is a lifetime burden. In most states, certain civil rights are forfeited forever, some fields of employment are closed, and some insurance or pension benefits may be denied. It does not matter if an ex-convict successfully obtains steady employment, raises a family, and contributes time to community organizations.

civil disabilities
Legal restrictions that prevent released felons from voting, serving on juries, and holding public office.

The **civil disabilities** of ex-felons include loss of the right to vote and hold public office. In all but four states prisoners convicted of felonies are disenfran-

With a set of cheap clothes, a check for $50, and a state voucher good for one bus ticket out of town, about one hundred inmates are released every weekday from Huntsville Prison in Texas. What problems will released offenders face in today's world?

Phillippe Diederich

chised. In more than 30 states they may reapply only when they are off parole. In 12, mostly southern, states they are barred for life from voting. The Sentencing Project (1998) estimates that 3.9 million Americans, including 1.4 million African American men (13 percent of all black men), cannot vote because of their felony convictions. Thus in Alabama and Florida, 31 percent of African American men are permanently ineligible to vote, and in Iowa, Mississippi, New Mexico, Virginia, Washington, and Wyoming, fully a quarter of black men are not eligible to vote (Abramsky, 1999). Florida's 204,600 African American men probably would have swayed the 2000 election to Al Gore if they were not disenfranchised. In many states, felons are denied other civil rights, such as serving on juries, maintaining parental rights, and having access to public employment (Love and Kuzma, 1996).

Critics of civil disability laws point out that, upon fulfilling the penalty imposed for a crime, the former offender should be assisted to full reintegration into society. They argue that it is counterproductive for the government to promote rehabilitation with the goal of reintegration while at the same time preventing offenders from fully achieving that goal. Supporters of these laws respond that they are justified by the possibility of recidivism and the community's need for protection.

Between these two extremes is the belief that not all people convicted of felonies should be treated equally. In other words, to be protected, society needs to place restrictions only on certain individuals.

Pardon

References to **pardon** are found in ancient Hebrew law, and the church and the monarchies had the power of clemency in medieval Europe. Pardon later became known as the "royal prerogative of mercy" in England.

pardon
An action of the executive branch of state or federal government excluding an offense and absolving the offender from the consequences of the crime.

In the United States, the president or the state governor may grant clemency in individual cases. In each state the executive receives recommendations from the state's board of pardons (often combined with the board of parole) concerning individuals who are thought to be deserving of the act. Pardons serve three main purposes: (1) to remedy a miscarriage of justice, (2) to remove the stigma of a conviction, and (3) to mitigate a penalty. Although full pardons for miscarriages of justice are rare, from time to time society is alerted to the story of some individual who has been released from prison after the discovery that he or she was incarcerated by mistake. The more typical activity of pardons boards is to erase the criminal records of first-time offenders—often young people—so they may enter those professions whose licensing procedures keep out former felons, may obtain certain types of employment, and in general will not have to bear the stigma of a single mistake.

check point

18. What is a civil disability? Give three examples.
19. What purposes does pardoning serve?

Summary

- Prison administrators must deal with the special needs of some groups, including elderly prisoners, prisoners with HIV/AIDS, mentally ill prisoners, and long-term prisoners.
- Inmates do not serve their time in isolation but are members of a subculture with its own traditions, norms, and leadership structure. Such norms are often described the inmate code.

- Today's prisons, unlike those of the past, do not have a uniform inmate code but several, in part because of the influence of gangs.
- Inmates deal with the pain of incarceration by assuming an adaptive role and lifestyle.
- To meet their needs for goods and services not provided by the state, prisoners run an underground economy.
- Women make up only a small portion of the inmate population. This is cited as the reason for the limited programs and services available to female prisoners.
- Social relationships among female inmates differ from those of their male counterparts. Women tend to form pseudofamilies in prison. Many women experience the added stress of being responsible for their children on the outside.
- Educational, vocational, industrial, and treatment programs are available in prisons. Administrators believe these programs are important for maintaining order.
- Release to the community takes four main forms: discretionary release, mandatory release, other conditional release, and expiration release. Pardons are granted in few cases.

Questions for Review

1. What is meant by an adaptive role? Which roles are found in male prison society? In female prison society?
2. What is the currency used in the underground prison economy?
3. How does the convict society in institutions for women differ from that in institutions for men?
4. What are the main forms of prison programs, and what purposes do they serve?
5. How do the four types of release from prison affect inmates both before and after release?

Key Terms

civil disabilities (p. 524)
classification (p. 516)
discretionary release (p. 520)
expiration release (p. 522)
inmate code (p. 503)
mandatory release (p. 522)
other conditional release (p. 522)
pardon (p. 525)

For Further Reading

Earley, Pete. 1992. *The Hot House: Life inside Leavenworth Prison.* New York: Bantam Books. An eyewitness account of daily life in the United States Penitentiary in Leavenworth, Kansas, written by the first journalist given unlimited access to a maximum-security institution of the Federal Bureau of Prisons.

Lerner, Jimmy R. 2002. *You Got Nothing Coming: Notes from a Prison Fish.* New York: Broadway Books. True story of a middle-class, middle-aged, Jewish man from Brooklyn, serving a 12-year term for voluntary manslaughter, in a Nevada correctional facility. As a fish, Lerner quickly learns the ropes from Kansas, his "cellie." For Lerner, prison is a world of petty corruption, racial strife, and crank-addicted neo-Nazis.

Rideau, Wilbert, and Ron Wilkburg. 1992. *Life Sentences: Rage and Survival behind Bars.* New York: Times Books. Describes life inside the Louisiana State Penitentiary. Written by two former editors of *The Angolite,* the prison newspaper.

Rierden, Andi. 1997. *The Farm: Life inside a Women's Prison.* Amherst: University of Massachusetts Press. A case study of changes in the inmate population and administration from the late 1980s to the early 1990s at Connecticut's Niantic Correctional Institution.

Sheehan, Susan. 1978. *A Prison and a Prisoner.* Boston: Houghton Mifflin. A fascinating description of life in Green Haven Prison and the way one prisoner "makes it" through "swagging," "hustling," and "doing time." It contains an excellent discussion of the inmate economy.

Stanley, David T. 1976. *Prisoners among Us.* Washington, D.C.: Brookings Institution. Still the only major published account of parole-release decision making with an emphasis on parole board discretion.

Going Online

For an up-to-date list of Web links, go to http://www.cj.wadsworth.com/colesmith10e

1. Go to the Web page of the Correctional Industries Association: http://www.corrections.com/industries/. Find and read the Association's Legislative Position Statement. Does the Association invite or discourage state regulation of prison industries? Why?
2. Go to InfoTrac College Edition and search for *prisoners*. Click on "woman prisoners." Find an article about the daily life of four women in prison in Maryland. How has prison affected the lives of these women and their outlook on the future?
3. Using the keyword *parole,* use a search engine to find the Web site of an attorney offering services to inmates at release hearings. What services are offered? Do you think an attorney would be helpful?

Checkpoint Answers

1. Today's prisoners are largely men in their late twenties to early thirties with less than a high school education. They are disproportionately members of minority groups.
2. The values and norms of prison society that emphasize inmate solidarity.
3. The prison society is fragmented by racial and ethnic divisions.
4. Doing time, gleaning, jailing, and functioning as a disorganized criminal.
5. To provide goods and services not available through regular channels.
6. The prison economy is responsible for the exploitation of prisoners by other prisoners and has the potential for violence.
7. The small number of female inmates compared with the number of male inmates.
8. Men are more individualistic and their norms stress autonomy, self-sufficiency, and the ability to cope with one's own problems. Women are more sharing with one another.
9. The distance of prisons from homes, intermittent telephone privileges, and unnatural visiting environment.
10. Children are either with relatives or in foster care.
11. Programs keep prisoners busy and reduce security problems.
12. Classification by a committee according to the needs of the inmate or of the institution.
13. They are thought to "coddle" prisoners and give them resources not available to free residents.
14. Too many programs train inmates for trades for which there is already an adequate labor supply or in which the skills are outdated. They are inefficient because of the low education level and poor work habits of the prisoners. Production has to be stopped for periodic head counts and checks on tools and materials.
15. Pressures from labor unions whose members make competing products at higher wages.
16. Discretionary release is the release of an inmate from incarceration to conditional supervision at the discretion of the parole board within the boundaries set by the sentence and the penal law. Mandatory release is the required release of an inmate from incarceration to community supervision upon the expiration of a certain period as specified by a determinate sentencing law. Other conditional release is the release of an inmate who has received a mandatory sentence from incarceration to a furlough, halfway house, or home supervision by correctional authorities attempting to deal with a crowding problem. Expiration release is the release of an inmate from incarceration without any further correctional supervision; the inmate cannot be returned to prison for any remaining portion of the sentence for the current offense.
17. It affects sentencing, plea bargaining, and the size of prison populations.
18. Ex-felons forfeit certain civil rights such as the right to vote, to serve on juries, and to hold public office. Ex-felons are restricted from certain types of employment as well.
19. To remedy a miscarriage of justice, to remove the stigma of a conviction, to mitigate a penalty.

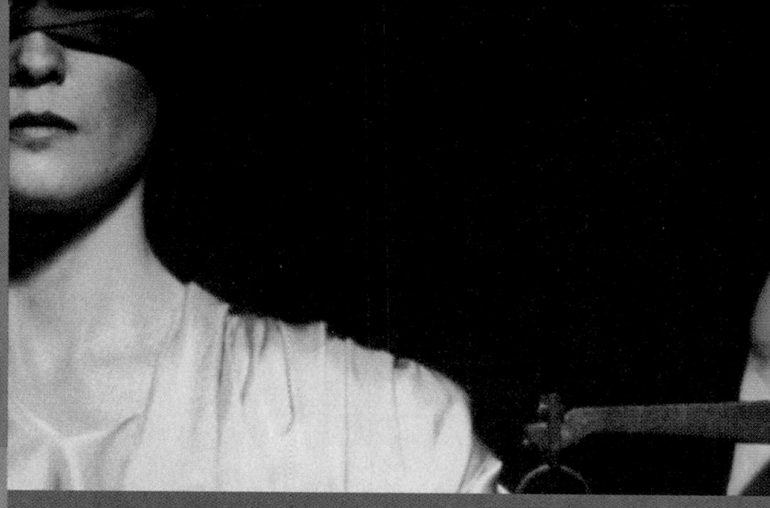

PART FIVE

The Juvenile Justice System

Crimes committed by juveniles are a serious national problem. The Uniform Crime Reports show that just over one-third of the people arrested for an index crime are under 18 years of age. Children who are charged with crimes, who have been neglected by their parents, or whose behavior is otherwise judged to require official action enter the juvenile justice system, an independent process that is interrelated with the adult system.

Many of the procedures used in handling juvenile problems are similar to those used with adults, but the overriding philosophy of juvenile justice is somewhat different, and the state may intrude into the lives of children to a much greater extent. In recent years political and legal moves have been made to reduce the differences in the procedures of the two systems.

CHAPTER 17

Juvenile Justice

David Peters Photography

On the night of October 12, 2001, 14-year-old Devin Lyman and three friends—Andrew Anderson, aged 16, and two other juveniles, aged 11 and 13, sneaked out of their homes and wandered around downtown Canaan, Connecticut, a community of two thousand located in the Litchfield Hills. Around 1:30 A.M., the boys set fire to leaves under a wooden platform near Keilty's Depot, a popular restaurant in the 130-year-old Canaan Railroad Station. As the fire spread to the building, the boys fled. The two younger boys wanted to call 911 from a nearby pay phone, but Anderson and Lyman talked them out of it. The blaze consumed the historic landmark, caused more than $2 million in damage, wrecked several businesses, and cost dozens of jobs.

In the police investigation, suspicion focused on the four juveniles. Under questioning, Devin made up a false alibi but later confessed. Because Devin and Andrew Armstrong where older than 14 at the time of the incident, the juvenile court judge waived jurisdiction and they were indicted in the adult court. The 11- and 13-year-old boys were dealt with in juvenile court and their names have not been released.

In May 2002 Devin Lyman pleaded guilty to third-degree arson and first-degree criminal mischief. In a June court appearance before Judge Alexandra DiPentima, Devin said that he didn't mean to burn down the building: "I can't describe the sorrow I feel toward these people (the victims). I hope they somehow can forgive." Devin's mother pointed out that her son had never been in trouble before and that he was only six months too old for protection by the juvenile justice system. Defense attorney Michael Sconyers argued that Lyman was only one of four boys and wasn't the instigator. "Devin is only 15, he's an unformed human being. Devin is not a criminal."

Judge DiPentima disagreed with Sconyers. "Punishment must fit the criminal as well as the crime. And while attorney Sconyers has indicated Devin is not a criminal, he indeed is." She then sentenced Devin to a 10 year prison term to be suspended after eight months, followed by 5 years probation, 800 hours of community service, and payment of symbolic restitution of $8,000. Addressing the offender she said, "What you did and didn't do changed people's lives in a permanent and devastating way. Your parents and teachers support you. Don't let them down again, and more importantly, don't let yourself down" (*Hartford Courant,* June 27, 2002:A1).

At the same time that society confronts the frightening fact that young offenders can commit terrible acts, no consensus has been reached on how to solve this problem. Should juveniles continue to be treated differently from adults when they commit crimes, assuming that juveniles can be taught to change their ways? Or should all criminals be treated alike? Should we be tough on everyone who commits violent crimes?

Although juvenile justice is separate from the adult criminal justice system, the key values of freedom, fairness, and justice undergird both systems. The formal processes of each differ not in values but mainly in emphasis. Although different, the systems are interrelated. The activities and concerns of policing, courts, or corrections cannot be separated from the problems of youth. With juveniles committing a significant portion of criminal offenses, officials in the adult system must pay serious attention to the juvenile system as well.

QUESTIONS for INQUIRY

- What is the extent of youth crime in the United States?
- How did the juvenile justice system develop, and what assumptions was it based on?
- What determines the jurisdiction of the juvenile justice system?
- How does the juvenile justice system operate?
- What are some of the problems facing the American system of juvenile justice?

Youth Crime in the United States

In Denver a child visiting the zoo was hit by a bullet intended by one teenager for another. A 17-year-old Salt Lake City boy was kicked and then shot to death by a group of his fellow high school students. A British tourist was killed while at a rest stop; a 13-year-old boy was one of the suspects. Such dramatic criminal

acts make headlines. Are these only isolated incidents, or is the United States facing a major increase in youth crime?

The juvenile crime incidents just described are rare. In a nation with 70 million people under 18, there are about 2.4 million arrests of juveniles each year, 99,000 (4 percent) of which are for violent crime. After rising from 1988 to 1994, the juvenile violent crime rate has now returned to 1985 levels (OJJDP, 2002). Yet when Americans are asked to identify the two or three most serious problems facing children, they cite drugs and crime (BJS, 2000g:102).

As shown in Figure 17.1, youth crimes range from UCR Index Crimes (for example murder, rape, robbery, assault) to "youthful crimes" such as curfew violations, loitering, and being a runaway. About 1 in 20 people in the under-18 cohort is taken into police custody each year and nearly a million are processed by juvenile courts. Most juvenile crimes are committed by young males; only 28 percent of arrestees under 18 years of age are females (OJJDP, 2002. Online). Some researchers have estimated that one boy in three will be arrested by the police at some point before his 18th birthday.

The "epidemic" of violent youth crime of the early 1990s coincided with an increase in drug arrests, particularly in nonwhite urban areas. As Alfred Blumstein

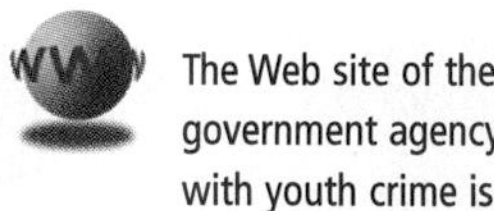

The Web site of the leading government agency dealing with youth crime is found at http://ojjdp.ncjrs.org.

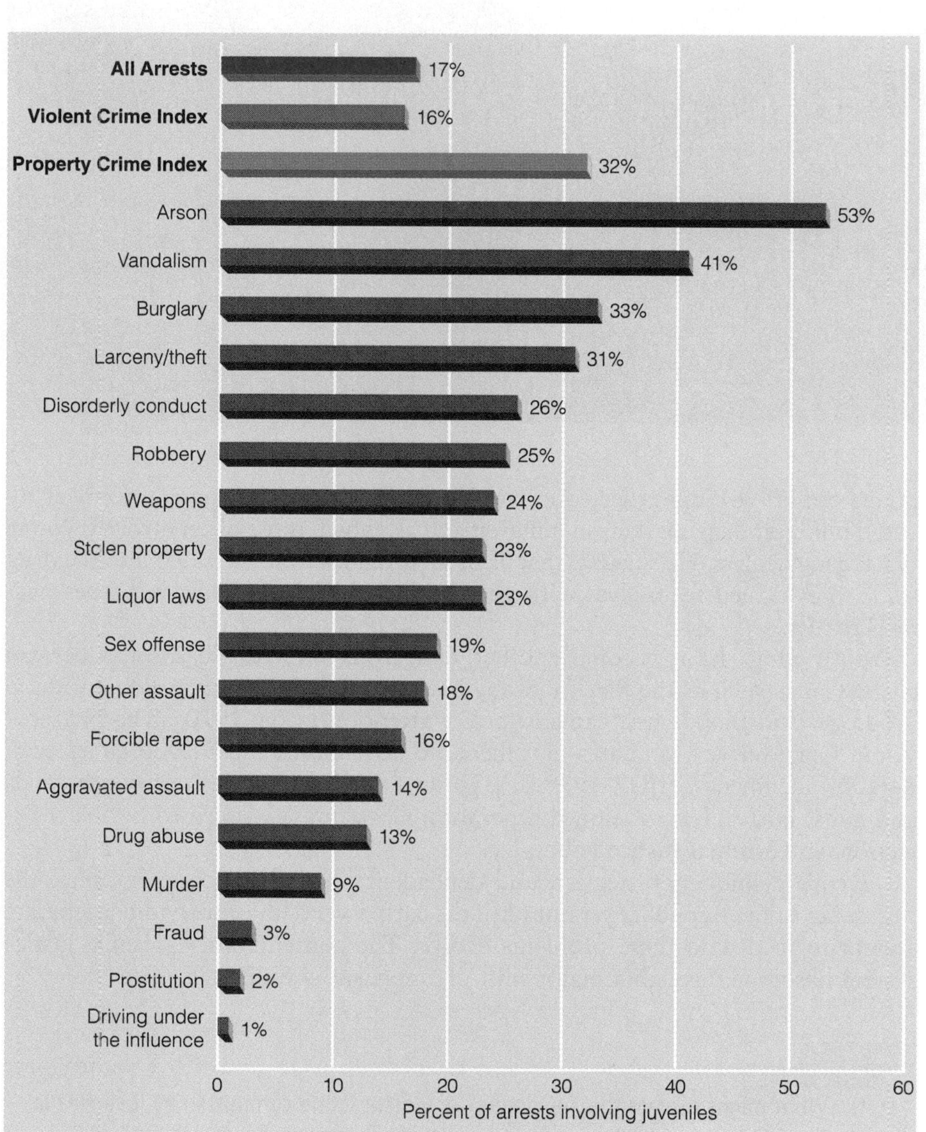

Source: Office of Juvenile Justice and Delinquency Prevention, July 25, 2002 (http://ojjdp.ncjrs.org).

Figure 17.1

Percentage of arrests of people under 18 years old

Juveniles are arrested for a wide range of offenses. For some offenses—such as arson, vandalism, motor vehicle theft, and burglary—juveniles account for a larger proportion of arrests than the percentage of juveniles in the general population would suggest.

AP Photo/Ed Andrieski

A mother and daughter are reunited following the shooting at Columbine High School, Littleton, Colorado. The 2 teenaged killers, 12 students, and a teacher died; 23 students were wounded.

points out (1996), this reflected in part the extent to which drug enforcement focused on street drug markets in inner-city areas, which more often involved young black drug dealers. He suggests that as more juveniles were recruited into the drug trade, they armed themselves with guns and used those firearms in battles over market turf.

Youth gangs have become another dangerous presence in most American cities. Gangs such as the Black P Stone Nation, CRIPS (Common Revolution in Progress), and Bloods first came to police attention in the 1970s. The National Youth Gang Survey estimates that there are now more than 31,000 gangs with 846,000 members (OJJDP, 1999:77). To deal with the problem of youth gangs and guns, Boston has developed Operation Ceasefire, as described in "New Directions in Criminal Justice Policy."

The National Center for Juvenile Justice presents research about youthful offenders at http://www.ncjj.org.

Juvenile delinquency, neglect, and dependency have been concerns since the beginning of the Republic, yet not until the early twentieth century did a separate system to deal with these problems evolve. The contemporary juvenile justice system has gone through a major shift of emphasis as well.

check point

1. What might explain the "epidemic" of violent crime committed by juveniles in the 1990s?

(Answers are at the end of the chapter.)

Operation Ceasefire

There can be no higher priority than reducing gang street violence. Boston's Operation Ceasefire is a coordinated attempt to end gang gun violence. Ceasefire is based on the knowledge that a few offenders account for a substantial portion of all crime and that these offenders are often concentrated in particular city neighborhoods.

Operation Ceasefire uses two strategies. First, interagency collaboration identifies individuals and gangs at risk for committing violence. A task force of federal, state, and municipal criminal justice and social service agencies regularly meet to share information, identify gang members to be targeted, discuss tactics to increase investigation effectiveness, and develop a repertoire of interventions and strategies.

A second strategy is aimed at increasing deterrence through swift and certain sanctions. When a violent act is committed, the various agencies can at their discretion not only arrest suspects but also shut down drug markets, strictly enforce probation restrictions, make disorder arrests, deal more strictly with cases in adjudication, deploy federal enforcement power, and so on.

Operation Ceasefire develops in gang members a new set of expectations regarding violent behavior. When gang members seek rehabilitative services, the program assists them. But when they persist in violent activity, the coordinated agencies hit them with undesirable sanctions until the violence stops.

The Boston program has been going strong since late 1992 and has had unexpected success. Firearm homicides by juveniles dropped from ten to an astounding zero for two years running. National attention has been focused on Boston's success story.

Source: Adapted from Todd R. Clear and David R. Karp, *Community Justice: Preventing Crime and Achieving Justice, Report to the National Institute of Justice* (Tallahassee: Florida State University, 1999).

Researching the Internet

For more on Boston's youth violence policy, go to InfoTrac College Edition. Enter the keywords *operation ceasefire* and access the article "Swift and Certain Punishment" in *U.S. News and World Report,* December 29, 1997. What problems do you see with Boston's strategy?

The Development of Juvenile Justice

The system and philosophy of juvenile justice that began in the United States during the social reform period of the late nineteenth century was based on the idea that the state should act as would a parent in the interest of the child. This view remained unchallenged until the 1960s, when the Supreme Court ushered in the juvenile rights period. With the rise in juvenile crime in the 1980s, the juvenile justice system shifted again to one focusing on the problem of controlling youth crime. Today, people are again reexamining the philosophy and processes of the juvenile justice system.

The idea that children should be treated differently from adults originated in the common law and in the chancery courts of England. The common law had long prescribed that children under seven years of age were incapable of felonious intent and were therefore not criminally responsible. Children aged 7 to 14 could be held accountable only if it could be shown that they understood the consequences of their actions.

The English chancery courts, established during the Middle Ages, heard only civil cases, mainly concerning property. However, under the doctrine of ***parens patriae,*** which held the king to be the father of the realm, the chancery courts exercised protective jurisdiction over all children, particularly those involved in questions of dependency, neglect, and property. At this time the criminal courts, not a separate juvenile court, dealt with juvenile offenders. In legitimizing the actions of the state on behalf of the child, however, the concept of *parens patriae* laid the groundwork for the development of juvenile justice.

parens patriae
The state as parent; the state as guardian and protector of all citizens (such as juveniles) who cannot protect themselves.

Table 17.1 Juvenile justice developments in the United States

Period	Major Developments	Causes and Influences	Juvenile Justice System
Puritan 1646–1824	Massachusetts Stubborn Child Law (1646).	A Puritan view of child as evil B Economically marginal agrarian society	Law provides A Symbolic standard of maturity B Support for family as economic unit
Refuge 1824–1899	Institutionalization of deviants; House of Refuge in New York established (1825) for delinquent and dependent children.	A Enlightenment B Immigration and industrialization	Child seen as helpless, in need of state intervention.
Juvenile court 1899–1960	Establishment of separate legal system for juveniles; Illinois Juvenile Court Act (1899).	A Reformism and rehabilitative ideology B Increased immigration, urbanization, large-scale industrialization	Juvenile court institutionalized legal irresponsibility of child.
Juvenile rights 1960–1980	Increased "legalization" of juvenile law; Gault decision (1967); Juvenile Justice and Delinquency Prevention Act (1974) calls for deinstitutionalization of status offenders.	A Criticism of juvenile justice system on humane grounds B Civil rights movement by disadvantaged groups	Movement to define and protect rights as well as to provide services to children.
Crime control 1980–present	Concern for victims, punishment for serious offenders, transfer to adult court of serious offenders, protection of children from physical and sexual abuse.	A More-conservative public attitudes and policies B Focus on serious crimes by repeat offenders	System more formal, restrictive, punitive; increased percentage of police referrals to court; incarcerated youths stay longer periods.

Sources: Adapted from Barry Krisberg, Ira M. Schwartz, Paul Litsky, and James Austin, "The Watershed of Juvenile Justice Reform," *Crime and Delinquency* 32 (January 1986): 5–38; U.S. Department of Justice, *A Preliminary National Assessment of the Status Offender and the Juvenile Justice System* (Washington, D.C.: U.S. Government Printing Office, 1980), 29.

check point

2. Until what age were children exempt from criminal responsibility under common law?
3. What was the jurisdiction of the English chancery court?
4. What is meant by the doctrine of *parens patriae?*

Table 17.1 outlines the shifts in how the United States has dealt with the problems of youth. These shifts fall into five periods of American juvenile justice history. Each was characterized by changes in juvenile justice that reflected the social, intellectual, and political currents of the time. During the past two hundred years, population shifts from rural to urban areas, immigration, developments in the social sciences, political reform movements, and the continuing problem of youth crime have all influenced how Americans have treated juveniles.

The Puritan Period (1646–1824)

The English procedures were maintained in the American colonies and continued into the nineteenth century. The earliest attempt by a colony to deal with problem children was passage of the Massachusetts Stubborn Child Law in 1646. With this law, the Puritans of the Massachusetts Bay Colony imposed the view that the child was evil and they emphasized the need of the family to discipline and raise youths. Those who would not obey their parents were dealt with by the law.

The Refuge Period (1824–1899)

As the population of American cities began to grow during the early 1800s, the problem of youth crime and neglect became a concern for reformers. Just as the Quakers of Philadelphia had been instrumental during the same period in reforming correctional practices, other groups supported changes toward the education and protection of youths. These reformers focused their efforts primarily on the urban immigrant poor, seeking to have parents declared "unfit" if their children roamed the streets and were apparently "out of control." Not all such children were engaged in criminal acts, but the reformers believed that children whose parents did not discipline and train them to abide by the rules of society would end up in prison. The state's power was to be used to prevent delinquency. The solution was to create institutions where these children could learn good work and study habits, live in a disciplined and healthy environment, and develop "character."

The first of these institutions was the House of Refuge of New York, which opened in 1825. This half-prison, half-school housed destitute and orphaned children as well as those convicted of crime (Friedman, 1993:164). Similar facilities followed in Boston, Philadelphia, and Baltimore. Children were placed in these homes by court order usually because of neglect or vagrancy. They often stayed until they were old enough to be legally regarded as adults. The houses were run according to a strict program of work, study, and discipline.

Topham/The Image Works

During the nineteenth century, reformers were alarmed by the living conditions of inner-city youth. Reformers in Chicago ushered in the juvenile justice system.

Some states created "reform schools" to provide the discipline and education needed by wayward youth in a "homelike" atmosphere, usually in rural areas. The first, the Lyman School for Boys, opened in Westboro, Massachusetts, in 1848. A similar Massachusetts reform school for girls was opened in 1855 for "the instruction . . . and reformation, of exposed, helpless, evil disposed and vicious girls" (Friedman, 1993:164). Institutional programs began in New York in 1849, Ohio in 1850, and Maine, Rhode Island, and Michigan in 1906.

Despite these reforms, children could still be arrested, detained, tried, and imprisoned. Even in states that had institutions for juveniles, the criminal justice process for children was the same as that for adults.

The Juvenile Court Period (1899–1960)

With most states providing services to neglected youth by the end of the nineteenth century, the problem of juvenile criminality became the focus of attention. Progressive reformers pushed for the state to provide individualized care and treatment to deviants of all kinds—adult criminals, the mentally ill, juvenile delinquents. They urged adoption of probation, treatment, indeterminate sentences, and parole for adult offenders and succeeded in establishing similar programs for juveniles.

Referred to as the "child savers," these upper-middle-class reformers sought to use the power of the state to "save" children from a life of crime (Platt, 1977). They shared a concern about the role of environmental factors on behavior and a belief that benevolent state action could solve social problems. They also believed the claim of the new social sciences that they could treat the problems underlying deviance.

Reformers wanted a separate juvenile court system that could address the problems of individual youths by using flexible procedures that, as one reformer said, "banish entirely all thought of crime and punishment" (Rothman, 1980:213). They put their idea into action with the creation of the juvenile court.

Passage of the Juvenile Court Act by Illinois in 1899 established the first comprehensive system of juvenile justice. The act placed under one jurisdiction cases of dependency, neglect, and delinquency ("incorrigibles and children threatened by immoral associations as well as criminal lawbreakers") for children under 16. The act had four major elements:

- A separate court for delinquent, dependent, and neglected children.
- Special legal procedures that were less adversarial than those in the adult system.
- Separation of children from adults in all portions of the justice system.
- Programs of probation to assist the courts in deciding what is in the best interest of the state and the child.

Activists such as Jane Addams and Julia Lathrop, both of the settlement house movement; Henry Thurston, a social work educator; and the National Congress of Mothers successfully promoted the juvenile court concept, so that by 1904 ten states had implemented procedures similar to those of Illinois. By 1917, all but three states provided for a juvenile court.

The philosophy of the juvenile court derived from the idea that the state should deal with a child who broke the law much as a wise parent would deal with a wayward child. The doctrine of *parens patriae* again helped legitimize the system. Procedures would be informal and private, records would be confidential, children would be detained apart from adults, and probation and social workers would be appointed. Even the vocabulary and physical setting of the juvenile system were changed to emphasize diagnosis and treatment instead of findings of guilt. The term *criminal behavior* was replaced by *delinquent behavior* when it referred to the acts of children. The terminology reflected the underlying belief that these children could be "cured" and returned to society as law-abiding citizens.

Because procedures were not to be adversarial, lawyers were unnecessary. Psychologists and social workers, who could determine the juvenile's underlying behavioral problem, were the main professionals attached to the system. But these reforms were instituted in a system in which children lacked the due process rights held by adults.

The Juvenile Rights Period (1960–1980)

Until the early 1960s few questioned the sweeping powers of juvenile justice officials. When the U.S. Supreme Court expanded the rights of adult defendants, however, lawyers and scholars began to criticize the extensive discretion given to juvenile justice officials. In a series of decisions (see Figure 17.2), the U.S. Supreme Court expanded the rights of juveniles.

In the first of these cases, *Kent v. United States* (1966), the Supreme Court ruled that juveniles had the right to counsel at a hearing at which a juvenile judge may waive jurisdiction and pass the case to the adult court.

***In re Gault* (1967)**
Juveniles have the right to counsel, to confront and examine accusers, and to have adequate notice of charges when confinement is a possible punishment.

In re Gault **(1967)** extended due process rights to juveniles. Fifteen-year-old Gerald Gault had been sentenced to 6 years in a state training school for making a prank phone call. Had he been an adult, the maximum punishment for making such a call would have been a fine of $5 to $50 or imprisonment for 2 months at most. Gault was convicted and sentenced in an informal proceeding without being represented by counsel. The justices held that a child in a delinquency hearing must be given certain procedural rights, including notice of the charges, right to counsel, right to confront and cross-examine witnesses, and protection against self-incrimination. Writing for the majority, Justice Abe Fortas emphasized that due process rights and procedures have a place in juvenile justice: "Under our Constitution the condition of being a boy does not justify a kangaroo court."

***In re Winship* (1970)**
The standard of proof beyond a reasonable doubt applies to juvenile delinquency proceedings.

The precedent-setting *Gault* decision was followed by a series of cases further defining the rights of juveniles. In the case of ***In re Winship*** **(1970)**, the Court held that proof must be established "beyond a reasonable doubt" and not on "a preponderance of the evidence" before a juvenile may be classified as a delinquent for committing an act that would be a crime if it were committed by an adult. The Court was not willing to give juveniles every due process right, how-

Figure 17.2 **Major decisions by the U.S. Supreme Court regarding the rights of juveniles**
Since the mid-1960s the Supreme Court has gradually expanded the rights of juveniles but has continued to recognize that the logic of the separate system for juvenile offenders justifies differences from some adult rights.

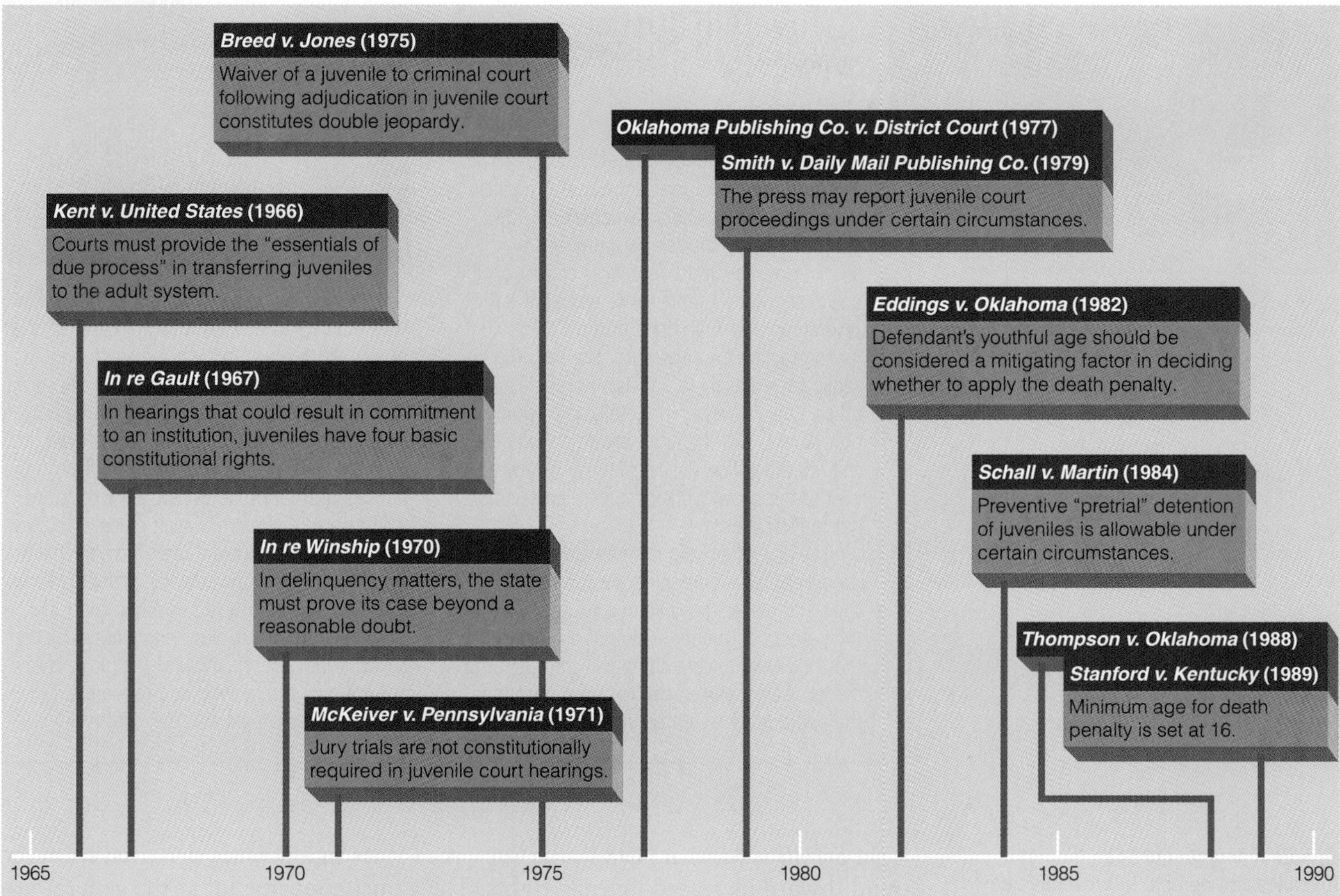

Note: For discussion of death penalty cases, see Chapter 12.
Source: Office of Juvenile Justice and Delinquency Prevention, *1999 National Report* (Washington, D.C.: U.S. Government Printing Office, 1999), 90–91.

ever: It held in ***McKeiver v. Pennsylvania*** (1971) that "trial by jury in the juvenile court's adjudicative stage is not a constitutional requirement." But in ***Breed v. Jones*** (1975), the Court extended the protection against double jeopardy to juveniles by requiring that, before a case is adjudicated in juvenile court, a hearing must be held to determine if it should be transferred to the adult court.

Another area of change concerned **status offenses**—acts that are not illegal if committed by an adult; these include skipping school, running away from home, or living a "wayward, idle or dissolute life" (Feld, 1993:203). In 1974 Congress passed the Juvenile Justice and Delinquency Prevention Act, which included provisions for taking status offenders out of correctional institutions. Since then, people have worked on diverting such children out of the system, reducing the possibility of incarceration, and rewriting status offense laws.

As juvenile crime rates continued to rise during the 1970s, the public began calling for tougher approaches in dealing with delinquents. In the 1980s, at the same time that stricter sanctions were imposed on adult offenders, juvenile justice policies shifted to crime control.

***McKeiver v. Pennsylvania* (1971)**
Juveniles do not have a constitutional right to a trial by jury.

***Breed v. Jones* (1975)**
Juveniles cannot be found delinquent in juvenile court and then transferred to adult court without a hearing on the transfer; to do so violates the protection against double jeopardy.

status offense
Any act committed by a juvenile that is considered unacceptable for a child, such as truancy or running away from home, but that would not be a crime if it were committed by an adult.

The Crime Control Period (1980–Present)

Since 1980 the public has demanded a "crackdown on crime." Legislators have responded in part by changing the juvenile system. Greater attention is now being focused on repeat offenders, with policy makers calling for harsher punishment for juveniles who commit crimes.

The Hidden Juvenile Justice System in Norway

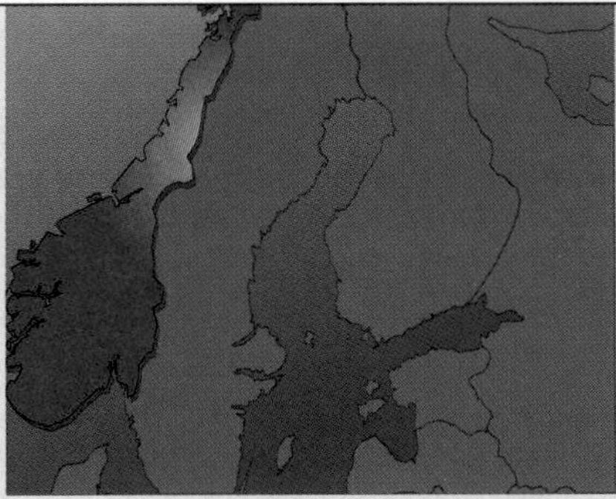

There is no punishment for crimes in Norway for a child who is under fifteen. Thus, there are no special courts to try criminal cases against juvenile offenders. Older teenagers may be tried in ordinary courts and sentenced to prison. However, most sentences consist of only a suspended sentence or probation or several months in an open prison.

In practice, the prosecutor transfers the juvenile case directly to a division of the "social office," the *barnevern*—literally, child protection. After a trial the judge may also refer the child to this office. Police evidence is turned over to the social workers, not for prosecution, but for "treatment."

The usual first step in treatment is that the *barnevern* takes emergency custody of the child and places the child in a youth home. If the parents or guardians do not give consent, the child welfare committee will consider arguments against placement. Here the question is the appropriate treatment for the child.

The *barnevern* is most often associated in the public mind with handling of cases of child abuse and neglect. In such a case, the board will turn over custody of the child to the social workers for placement in a foster home or youth home. Once the custody is removed from the parents, the burden of proof is on the parents to retain custody. Social workers are well aware of numerous such cases of recovering alcoholics who, even after recovery, have been unable to retain custody of their children.

In contrast to the U.S. juvenile court, the Norwegian model is wholly dominated by the social worker. The function of the judge is to preside over the hearing and to maintain proper legal protocol, but the child welfare of-

***Schall v. Martin* (1984)**
Juveniles can be held in preventive detention if there is concern that they may commit additional crimes while awaiting court action.

In *Schall v. Martin* (1984), the Supreme Court significantly departed from the trend toward increased juvenile rights. The Court confirmed that the general notion of *parens patriae* was a primary basis for the juvenile court, equal in importance to the Court's desire to protect the community from crime. Thus, juveniles may be held in preventive detention before trial if they are deemed a "risk" to the community.

The *Schall* decision reflects the ambivalence permeating the juvenile justice system. On one side are the liberal reformers, who call for increased procedural and substantive legal protections for juveniles accused of crime. On the other side are conservatives devoted to crime control policies and alarmed by the rise in juvenile crime.

The present crime control policy has brought many more juveniles to be tried in adult courts. As noted by Alex Kotlowitz, "the crackdown on children has gone well beyond those accused of violent crimes" (1994:40). Data from the National Juvenile Court Data Archive show that delinquency cases adjudicated in the adult criminal courts have increased 47 percent since 1987 (OJJDP, 1999:170).

In spite of the increasingly tough policies directed at juvenile offenders, changes that occurred during the juvenile rights period continue to affect the system profoundly. Lawyers are now routinely present at court hearings and other stages of the process, adding a note of formality that was not present 20 years ago. Status offenders seldom end up in secure, punitive environments such as training schools. The juvenile justice system looks more like the adult justice system than it did, but it remains less formal. Its stated intention is also less harsh: to keep juveniles in the community whenever possible.

Public support for a get-tough stance toward older juveniles seems to be growing. The juvenile court, where the use of discretion and the desire to rehabilitate were uppermost, has become a system of rules and procedures similar to adult courts. With deserved punishment more prominent as a correctional goal, juve-

fice presents the evidence and directs the case. The five laypeople who constitute the [social welfare committee] are advised by the child welfare office well before the hearing of the "facts" of the case. Before the hearing, the youth will have been placed in a youth home or mental institution "on an emergency basis"; the parents' rights to custody will have already been terminated.

The hearing is thus a mere formality after the fact. There is overwhelming unanimity among members of the board and between the board and social worker administrators. The arguments of the clients and of their lawyers seem to "fall on deaf ears."

Proof of guilt brought before the committee will generally consist of a copy of the police report of the offenses admitted by the accused and a school report written by the principal after he or she has been informed of the lawbreaking. Reports by the *barnevern*-appointed psychologist and social worker are also included. The *barnevern,* in its statement, has summarized the reports from the point of view of its arguments (usually for placement). Otherwise, the reports are ignored.

The hearing itself is a far cry from standard courtroom procedure. The youth and his or her parents may address the board briefly. The attorney sums up the case for a return to the home. Expert witnesses may be called and questioned by the board concerning, for instance, their treatment recommendations.

Following the departure of the parties, the *barnevern* office presents what amounts to "the case for the prosecution." There is no opportunity to rebut the testimony and no opportunity for cross-examination.

Placement in an institution is typically for an indefinite period. No notice of the disposition of the matter is given to the press. This absence of public accountability may serve more to protect the social office than the child.

Children receive far harsher treatments than do adults for similar offenses. For instance, for a young adult first offender the typical penalty for thievery is a suspended sentence. A child, however, may languish in an institution for years for the same offense.

A *barnevern*'s first work ought to be to create the best possible childhood. However, the *barnevern* also has a control function in relation to both the parents and the child, and the controller often feels a stronger duty to the community than to the parents and child. The institutionalization of children with behavioral problems clearly reflects this social control function. Approximately half of the children under care of the child welfare committee were placed outside the home and the other half placed under protective watch.

The system of justice for children accused of crimes is therefore often very harsh. This is in sharp contrast to the criminal justice system for adults, which is strikingly lenient. Where punishment is called *treatment,* however, the right of the state can almost become absolute. The fact that the state is represented by social work administrators creates a sharp ethical conflict for those whose first duty is to the client.

What we see in Norway is a process of juvenile justice that has not changed substantially since the 1950s. Due to flaws within the system, including the lack of external controls, the best intentions of social workers "have gone awry." Where care and protection were intended, power and secrecy have prevailed. Juvenile justice in Norway today is the justice of America yesterday.

Source: Condensed from Katherine Van Wormer, "The Hidden Juvenile Justice System in Norway: A Journey Back in Time," *Federal Probation,* March 1990, pp. 57–61.

niles who are repeat offenders are receiving severer sentences. Examine how Norway deals with youth crime by reading the Comparative Perspective.

check point

5. What was the function of a House of Refuge?
6. What were the major elements of the Illinois Juvenile Court Act of 1899?
7. What was the main point of the decision in *In re Gault?*

The Juvenile Justice System

Juvenile justice operates through a variety of procedures in different states; even different counties within the same states vary. Because the offenses committed by juveniles are mostly violations of state laws, there is little federal involvement in the juvenile justice system. Despite internal differences, the juvenile justice system is characterized by two key factors: (1) the age of clients and (2) the categories of cases under juvenile instead of adult court jurisdiction.

Age of Clients

Age normally determines whether a person is processed through the juvenile or adult justice system. The upper age limit for a juvenile varies from 16 to 18. In 38 states and the District of Columbia, it is the 18th birthday; in 8 states, the 17th; and in the remainder, the 16th. In 49 states, judges have the discretion to transfer juveniles to adult courts through a waiver hearing. Figure 17.3 shows the age at which juveniles can be transferred to adult court.

Figure 17.3 **The youngest age at which juveniles may be transferred to adult criminal court by waiver of juvenile jurisdiction**
The waiver provisions of states vary greatly, and no clear regional or other factor explains the differences.

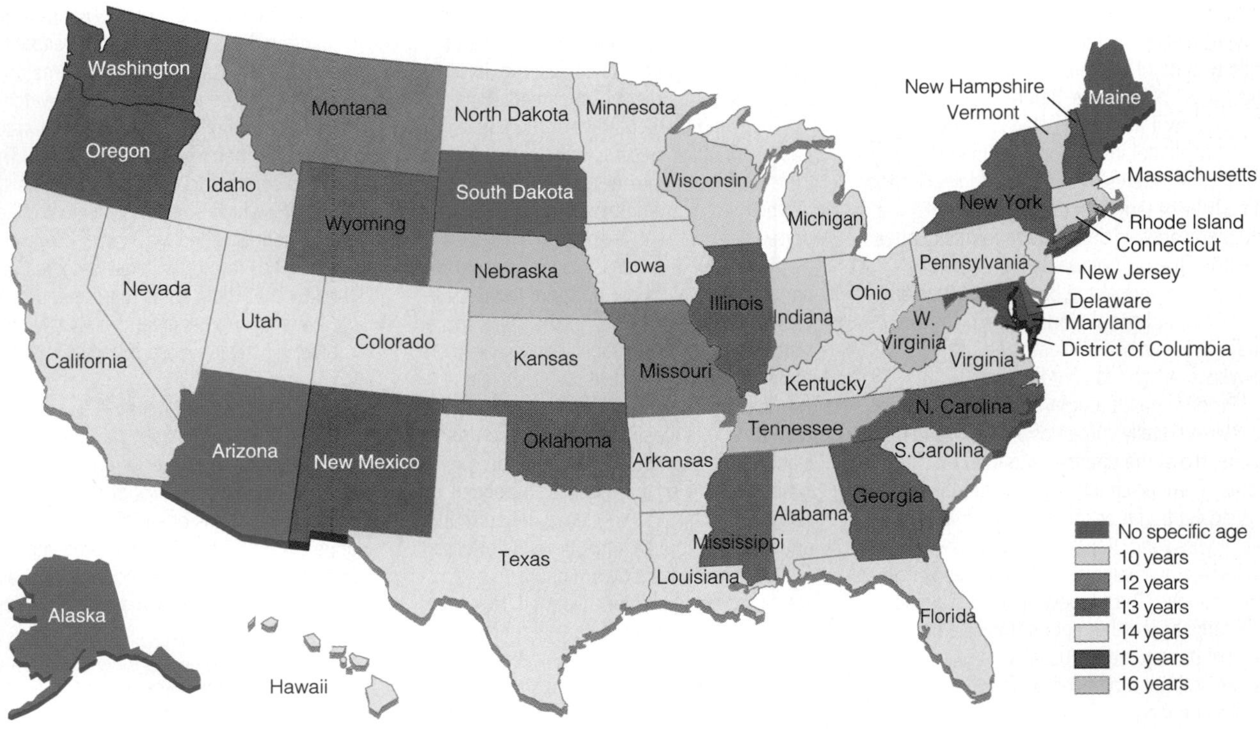

Source: Offiice o Juvenile Justice and Delinquency Prevention, *Trying Juveniles as Adults in Criminal Court* (Washington, D.C.: U.S. Government Printing Offiice, 1998), 4–15.

Categories of Cases under Juvenile Court Jurisdiction

Four types of cases fall under the jurisdiction of the juvenile justice system: delinquency, status offenses, neglect, and dependency. Mixing together young criminals and children who suffer from their parents' inadequacies dates from the earliest years of juvenile justice.

delinquent
A child who has committed an act that if committed by an adult would be criminal.

Delinquent children have committed acts that if committed by an adult would be criminal—for example, auto theft, robbery, or assault. Juvenile courts handle about 1.8 million delinquency cases each year, 77 percent involving male delinquents, and 30 percent involving African Americans. Among the criminal charges brought before the juvenile court, 22 percent are for crimes against the person, 50 percent for property offenses, 10 percent for drug law violations, and 19 percent for public order offenses (OJJDP, 1999:144). Table 17.2 shows the distribution of delinquency cases that are referred to juvenile court.

PINS
Acronym for "person in need of supervision," a term that designates juveniles who are either status offenders or thought to be on the verge of trouble.

Recall that status offenses are acts that are illegal only if they are committed by juveniles. Status offenders have not violated a penal code; instead they are charged with being ungovernable or incorrigible: as runaways, truants, or **PINS** (persons in need of supervision). Status offenders make up about 10 percent of the juvenile court caseload. Although female offenders account for only 15 percent of delinquency cases, they are involved in 42 percent of the status offense cases.

Some states do not distinguish between delinquent offenders and status offenders; they label both as juvenile delinquents. Those judged to be ungovernable and those judged to be robbers may be sent to the same correctional institution. Beginning in the early 1960s, many state legislatures attempted to distinguish between status offenders and to exempt them from a criminal record. In states that have decriminalized status offenses, juveniles who participate in these activities may now be classified as dependent children and placed in the care of child-protective agencies.

Juvenile justice also deals with problems of neglect and dependency—situations in which children are viewed as being hurt through no fault of their own because their parents have failed to provide a proper environment for them. People see the state's proper role as acting as a parent to a child whose own parents are unable or unwilling to provide proper care. Illinois, for example, defines a **neglected child** as one who is not receiving proper care because of some action or inaction of his or her parents. This may include not being sent to school, not receiving medical care, being abandoned, living in an injurious environment, or not receiving some other care necessary for the child's well-being. A **dependent child** either has no parent or guardian or is not receiving proper care because of the physical or mental disability of the parent. The law governing neglected and dependent children is broad and includes situations in which the child is viewed as a victim of adult behavior.

neglected child
A child who is not receiving proper care, because of some action or inaction of his or her parents.

dependent child
A child who has no parent or guardian or whose parents cannot give proper care.

Nationally about 75 percent of the cases referred to the juvenile courts are delinquency cases, 20 percent of which are status offenses. Twenty percent are dependency and neglect cases, and about 5 percent involve special proceedings, such as adoption. The system, then, deals with both criminal and noncriminal cases. Often juveniles who have done nothing wrong are categorized, either officially or in the public mind, as delinquents. In some states little effort is made in prejudicial detention facilities or in social service agencies to separate the classes of juveniles.

Table 17.2 Distribution of delinquency cases referred to juvenile court

About 75 percent of the juvenile court caseload involves criminal charges against youths.

	Percentage of Total Cases Referred	
22%	**Crimes against persons**	
	Homicide	less than 1%
	Forcible rape	less than 1
	Robbery	2
	Aggravated assault	5
	Simple assault	12
	Other personal offenses	1
	Other violent sex offenses	1
50%	**Property crimes**	
	Burglary	8%
	Larceny/theft	24
	Motor vehicle theft	3
	Arson	1
	Vandalism	7
	Trespassing	4
	Stolen property offenses	2
	Other property offenses	2
10%	**Drug violations**	**10%**
19%	**Public order offenses**	
	Obstruction of justice	7%
	Disorderly conduct	5
	Weapons offenses	2
	Liquor law violations	1
	Nonviolent sex offenses	1
	Other public order offenses	3

Source: Offiice of Juvenile Justice and Delinquency Prevention, *Juvenile Offenders and Victims: 1999 National Report* (Washington, D.C.: U.S. Government Printing Offiice, 1999), 144

8. What are the jurisdictional criteria for the juvenile court?

The Juvenile Justice Process

Underlying the juvenile justice system is the philosophy that the police, judges, and correctional officials should be primarily concerned with the interests of the child. Prevention of delinquency is the system's justification for intervening in the lives of juveniles who are involved in either status or criminal offenses.

In theory at least, juvenile proceedings are to be conducted in a nonadversarial environment, and the juvenile court is a place where the judge, social workers, clinicians, and probation officers work together to diagnose the child's problem and select a treatment program to attack that problem.

Juvenile justice is a bureaucracy based on an ideology of social work and is staffed primarily by people who think of themselves as members of the helping professions. Even the recent emphasis on crime control and punishment has not removed the treatment philosophy from most juvenile justice arenas. However, political pressures and limits on resources may stymie the implementation of this philosophy by focusing on the punishment of offenders rather than the prevention of delinquency.

Like the adult system, juvenile justice functions within a context of exchange relationships between officials of various government and private agencies that influence decisions. The juvenile court must deal not only with children and their parents, but also with patrol officers, probation officers, welfare officials, social workers, psychologists, and the heads of treatment institutions—all of whom have their own goals, perceptions of delinquency, and concepts of treatment.

The National Council of Juvenile and Family Court Judges is a national organization concerned with juvenile justice: http://www.ncjfcj.unr.edu.

Figure 17.4 outlines the sequence of steps that are taken from the point of police investigation through to correctional disposition. As you examine this figure, compare the procedures with those of the criminal justice system for adults. Note the various options available to decision makers and the extensive discretion that they may exercise.

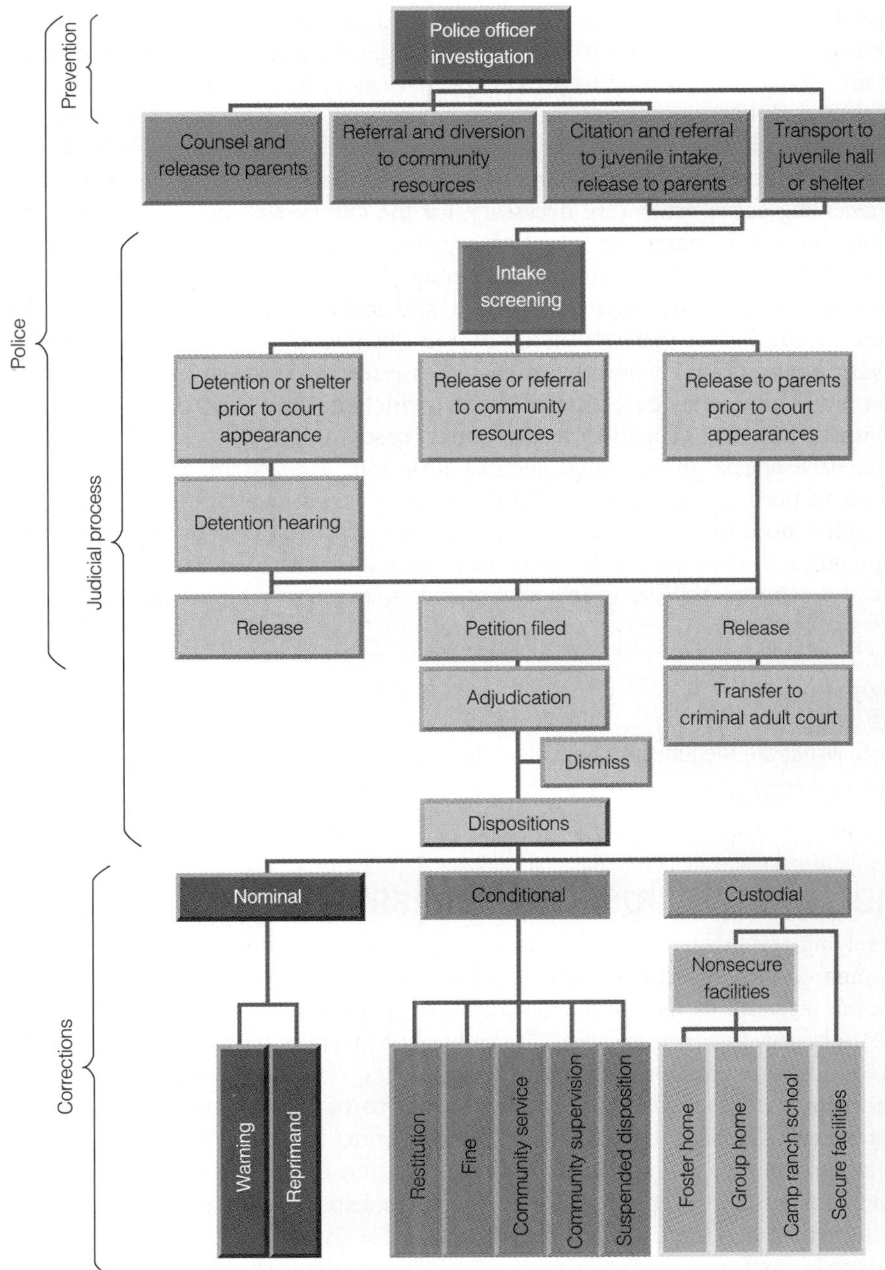

Figure 17.4
The juvenile justice system
Decision makers have more options for the disposition of juvenile offenders, compared with options in the criminal justice system for adults.

Source: National Advisory Commission on Criminal Justice Standards and Goals, *Report of the Task Force on Juvenile Justice and Delinquency Prevention* (Washington, D.C.: Law Enforcement Assistance Administration, 1976).

Police Interface

Many police departments, especially in cities, have special juvenile units. The juvenile officer is often selected and trained to relate to youths, knows much about relevant legal issues, and is sensitive to the special needs of young offenders. This officer also serves as an important link between the police and other community institutions, such as schools and other organizations serving young people.

Most complaints against juveniles are brought by the police, although an injured party, school officials, and even the parents can initiate them as well. The police must make three major decisions with regard to the processing of juveniles:

1. Whether to take the child into custody
2. Whether to request that the child be detained following apprehension
3. Whether to refer the child to court

The police exercise enormous discretion in these decisions. They do extensive screening and make informal adjustments in the street and at the stationhouse. In communities and neighborhoods where the police have developed close relationships with the residents or where policy dictates, the police may deal with violations by giving warnings to the juveniles and notifying their parents. Figure 17.5 shows the disposition of juveniles taken into police custody.

Initial decisions about what to do with a suspected offender are influenced by such factors as the predominant attitude of the community; the officer's attitude toward the juvenile, the juvenile's family, the offense, and the court; and the officer's conception of his or her own role. The disposition of juvenile cases at the arrest stage also relies on the seriousness of the offense, the child's prior record, and his or her demeanor. To summarize, several key factors influence how the police dispose of a case of juvenile delinquency:

Figure 17.5 **Disposition of juveniles taken into police custody**
The police have discretion in the disposition of juvenile arrest cases. What factors can influence how a case is disposed?

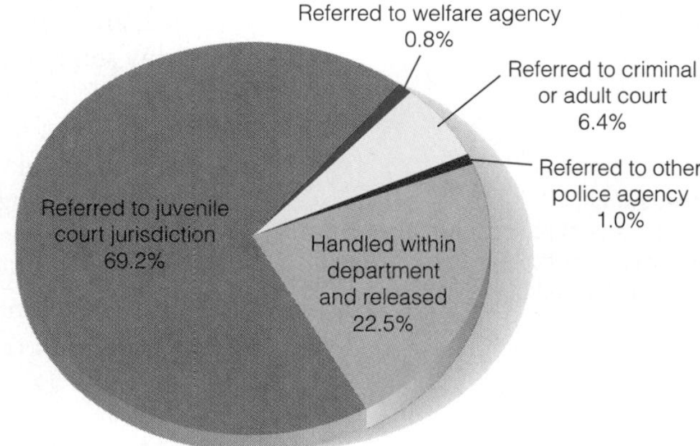

Source: Bureau of Justice Statistics, *Sourcebook of Criminal Justice Statistics, 2000* (Washington, D.C.: U.S. Government Printing Offiice, 2001), Table 4.25

1. The seriousness of the offense.
2. The willingness of the parents to cooperate and to discipline the child.
3. The child's behavioral history as reflected in school and police records.
4. The extent to which the child and the parents insist on a formal court hearing.
5. The local political and social norms concerning dispositions in such cases.
6. The officer's beliefs and attitudes

In dealing with juveniles, police often confront issues concerning the *Miranda* warnings and the *Mapp* unreasonable search and seizure rulings. Although the language of these decisions is not explicit, most jurisdictions now provide the *Miranda* protections. But questions remain as to the ability of juveniles to waive these rights. In 1979 the Supreme Court ruled in ***Fare v. Michael C.*** that a child may waive his or her rights to an attorney and to protections against self-incrimination. But the Court said that juvenile court judges must evaluate the totality of circumstances under which the minor made these decisions to ensure that they were voluntary.

***Fare v. Michael C.* (1979)**
By examining the totality of circumstances, trial court judges must evaluate the voluntariness of juveniles' waiving their rights to an attorney and to protections against self-incrimination.

On the issue of unreasonable searches and seizures prohibited by the Fourth Amendment, the Court has not been as forthcoming. State courts interpreted *Gault* to extend these provisions, but in 1985 the Supreme Court ruled in ***New Jersey v. T.L.O.*** that school officials can search students and their lockers. The justices recognized that children do have Fourth Amendment rights, yet a search could be viewed as reasonable if (1) it is based on a suspicion of lawbreaking and (2) it is required to maintain order, safety, and discipline in the school.

***New Jersey v. T.L.O.* (1985)**
School officials may search a student if they have a reasonable suspicion that the search will produce evidence that a school or a criminal law has been violated.

Although young people commit many serious crimes, the juvenile function of police work is concerned largely with order maintenance. In most incidents of this sort, the law is ambiguous, and blame cannot easily be assigned. Many offenses committed by juveniles that involve physical or monetary damage are minor infractions: breaking windows, hanging around the business district, disturbing the peace, public sexual behavior, and shoplifting. Here the function of the investigating officer is not so much to solve crimes as to handle the often legally uncertain complaints involving juveniles. The officer seeks both to satisfy the complainant and to keep the youth from future trouble. Given this emphasis on settling cases within the community—instead of strictly enforcing the law—the police power to arrest is a weapon that can be used to deter juveniles from criminal activity and to encourage them to conform to the law.

Intake Screening at the Court

The juvenile court processing of delinquency cases begins with a referral in the form of a *petition*, not an arrest warrant as in the adult system. When a petition is filed, an *intake hearing* is held, which is presided over by a hearing officer. During this stage, the officer determines whether the alleged facts are sufficient for the juvenile court to take jurisdiction or whether some other action would be in the child's best interest.

diversion
The process of screening children out of the juvenile justice system without a decision by the court.

Nationally, 45 percent of all referrals are disposed of at this stage, without formal processing by a judge. **Diversion** is the process of screening children out of the system without a decision by the court. In 47 percent of these cases, the charges are dismissed, with about one-third diverted to an informal probation, 6 percent placed in a mental health facility or other treatment facility, and 21 percent dealt with through some agreed-on alternative sanction.

Pretrial Procedures

When a decision is made to refer the case to the court (55 percent of cases), the court holds an initial hearing. Here, the juveniles are informed of their rights and told that if a plea is given it must be voluntary.

detention hearing
A hearing by the juvenile court to determine if a juvenile is to be detained or released prior to adjudication.

waive
Procedure by which the juvenile court waives its jurisdiction and transfers a juvenile case to the adult criminal court.

If the juvenile is to be detained pending trial, most states require a **detention hearing,** which determines if the youth is to be released to a parent or guardian or to be held in a detention facility until adjudication. Some children are detained to keep them from committing other crimes while awaiting trial. Others are held to protect them from the possibility of harm from gang members or parents. Still others are held because if released they will likely not appear in court as required. Nationally, about 18 percent of all delinquency cases involve detention between referral to the juvenile court and disposition of the case (OJJDP, 1999:152).

The conditions in many detention facilities are poor; abuse is often reported. In some rural areas juveniles continue to be detained in adult jails even though the federal government has pressed states to hold youths in separate facilities. Although much attention is focused on the adjudication processes of the juvenile court and the sanctions imposed by judges, many more children are punished through confinement in detention centers and jails before any court action has taken place than are punished by the courts.

Transfer to Adult Court

One of the first decisions to be made is whether a case should be transferred to the criminal (adult) justice system. In 49 states, juvenile court judges may **waive** their jurisdiction. This means that after considering the seriousness of the charge, the age of the juvenile, and the prospects of rehabilitation, the judge can transfer the case to adult court (OJJDP, 1998). In 13 states, prosecutors have the authority to file a case directly with the adult court. In 26 states, certain violent crimes such as murder, rape, and armed robbery are excluded by law from the jurisdiction of the juvenile courts (NIJ, 1997). See "What Americans Think" for a look at public attitudes about transferring juveniles to the adult court.

AP Photo/Jim Cole

Following a guilty plea, Robert Tulloch, 18, listens with his attorneys in Grafton County, Vermont, Superior Court as he is sentenced to life in prison without parole for the January 2001 murders of two Dartmouth College professors. Tulloch's accomplice, James Parker, was 16 at the time of the murders. His case was initiated in juvenile court but was transferred to adult court for sentencing. In a plea bargain Parker agreed to testify against Tulloch and was sentenced to 25 years to life as an accomplice to second-degree murder.

Since a "tougher" approach to juvenile crime took hold in the 1970s, the number of cases transferred has increased dramatically. However, waived cases still represent less than 2 percent (about 11,000) of delinquency cases. The likelihood of waiver varies by offense, of-

Should Juvenile Offenders Be Tried as Adults?

Arrests of juveniles for violent crimes more than doubled between 1988 and 1994. Since their peak in 1994, juvenile violent crime arrests have declined, yet cases still come up that are so serious that the public demands severe punishment. Youths are also the primary victims of violent crime. The availability of guns, the prevalence of urban youth gangs, and the problem of drugs are cited as the causes of violent youth crimes.

In the face of crimes such as the schoolyard shootings of the late 1990s, the public has loudly called for "getting tough with these young hoods." Politicians and criminal justice planners have urged that steps be taken to ensure that juveniles accused of serious crimes be dealt with in the adult courts.

For Trying Juveniles as Adults

Those who want to make trying juveniles as adults easier point not only to the continuing high levels of violence but also to the heinous nature of some crimes committed by youths. They see the juvenile courts as "coddling" these young predators. Often, only when a youth is transferred to the adult system is his or her long record of felonies revealed—felonies for which little punishment was ordered by the juvenile court. The current level of violence by juveniles requires that offenders be dealt with swiftly and quickly so as to deter the upcoming generation from following in the footsteps of their older siblings.

The arguments for trying serious juvenile offenders in the adult criminal justice system include these:

- Violence by juveniles is a serious problem and must be dealt with in a swift and certain manner.
- Juvenile courts have not been effective in stemming the tide of violence by young people.
- Procedures for waiving juvenile jurisdiction are cumbersome in many states.
- Justice demands that heinous crimes, regardless of the age of the accused, be dealt with to the full extent the law provides.

Against Trying Juveniles as Adults

Although they recognize that serious youth crime is a problem, many experts believe that trying juveniles as adults only makes things worse. They point out that treating adolescents as adults ignores the fact that they are at a different stage of social and emotional development. They argue that children should not be held to the same standards as adults. In an increasingly violent world, children need help to navigate the temptations and threats of adolescence.

The arguments against trying serious juvenile offenders in the adult criminal justice system include these:

- The juvenile justice system is better able to deal with the social and emotional problems of young offenders.
- The basic foundations of criminal law recognize that children carry diminished responsibility for their acts.
- Punishing juveniles in adult institutions robs them of their childhood and threatens their future.
- The problem of violent crime by juveniles must be dealt with by changing the environment within which they live.

What Should U.S. Policy Be?

Under pressure to "do something" about violent juvenile crime, legislators have proposed that the age of adulthood be lowered and that the cases of serious offenders be tried in the adult criminal justice system. Is this the best way to protect community safety—to punish youthful offenders in the adult criminal justice system? Is the juvenile corrections system equipped to treat and guide juvenile offenders in a way that will return them to their communities as productive people? How should the juvenile justice system deal with the coming generation of crime-prone youths?

Researching the Internet

You can find the article "Delinquents or Criminals: Policy Options for Young Offenders" at http://www.urban.org/crime/delinq.html.

fender age, and offender race. One result of the increased use of waiver is the more than doubling in ten years of juveniles sent to adult state prison. In 1997 (the last data), 7,400 prisoners were under age 18, 69 percent of them for violent offenses (BJS, 2000h:1).

Many states now place on the youth the burden of proving that he or she is amenable to treatment in the juvenile instead of the adult court. Transferring juveniles to be tried in the adult criminal courts remains controversial, as outlined in "The Policy Debate."

Go to the *American System of Criminal Justice* Web site at http://www.cj.wadsworth.com/colesmith10e to explore this question in further detail: Should juvenile offenders be tried as adults?

Go to the Public Policy feature on the American System of Criminal Justice CD to learn more about the issues surrounding juveniles and the death penalty.

Juvenile Justice Magazine can be accessed online at http://www.juvenilejustice.com/online.html.

Adjudication

Juvenile courts deal with almost a million delinquency cases a year (OJJDP, 1999:157). Adjudication is the trial stage of the juvenile justice process. If the child has not admitted to the charges and the case has not been transferred to the adult court, an adjudication hearing is held to determine the facts in the case and, if appropriate, label the juvenile "delinquent."

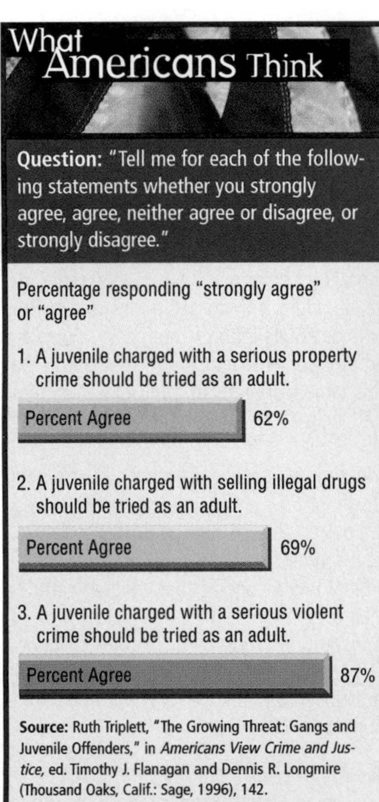

Source: Ruth Triplett, "The Growing Threat: Gangs and Juvenile Offenders," in *Americans View Crime and Justice,* ed. Timothy J. Flanagan and Dennis R. Longmire (Thousand Oaks, Calif.: Sage, 1996), 142.

The Supreme Court's decision in *Gault* (1967) and other due process rulings mandated changes in criminal proceedings that have changed the philosophy and actions of the juvenile court. Contemporary juvenile proceedings are more formal than those of the past, although still more informal than adult courts. Copies of petitions with specific charges must be given to the parents and child; counsel may be present, and free counsel can be appointed if the juvenile cannot pay; witnesses can be cross-examined; and a transcript of the proceedings must be kept.

As with other Supreme Court decisions, local practice may differ sharply from the procedures spelled out in the high court's rulings. Juveniles and their parents often waive their rights in response to suggestions from the judge or probation officer. The lower social status of the offender's parents, the intimidating atmosphere of the court, and judicial hints that the outcome will be more favorable if a lawyer is not present are reasons the procedures outlined in *Gault* may not be followed. The litany of "getting treatment," "doing what's right for the child," and "working out a just solution" may sound enticing, especially to people who are unfamiliar with the intricacies of formal legal procedures. In practice, then, juveniles still lack many of the protections given to adult offenders. Some of the differences between the juvenile and adult criminal justice systems are listed in Table 17.3.

The increased concern about crime has given prosecuting attorneys a more prominent part in the system. In keeping with the traditional child-saver philosophy, prosecuting attorneys rarely appeared in juvenile court prior to the *Gault* decision. Now that a defense attorney is present, the state often retains legal counsel as well. In many jurisdictions, prosecutors are assigned to deal specifically with juvenile cases. Their functions are to advise the intake officer, administer diversion

Table 17.3 The adult and juvenile criminal justice systems

Compare the basic elements of the adult and juvenile systems. To what extent does a juvenile have the same rights as an adult? Are the different decision-making processes necessary because a juvenile is involved?

		Adult System	Juvenile System
Philosophical assumptions		Decisions made as result of adversarial system in context of due process rights	Decisions made as result of inquiry into needs of juvenile within context of some due process elements
Jurisdiction		Violations of criminal law	Violations of criminal law, status offenses, neglect, dependency
Primary sanctioning goals		Retribution, deterrence, rehabilitation	Retribution, rehabilitation
Official discretion		Widespread	Widespread
Entrance		Official action of arrest, summons, or citation	Official action, plus referral by school, parents, other sources
Role of prosecuting and defense attorneys		Required and formalized	Sometimes required; less structured; poor role definition
Adjudication		Procedural rules of evidence in public jury trial required	Less formal structure to rules of evidence and conduct of trial; no right to public jury in most states
Treatment programs		Run primarily by public agencies	Broad use of private and public agencies
Application of Bill of Rights amendments			
Fourth:	Unreasonable searches and seizures	Applicable	Applicable
Fifth:	Double jeopardy	Applicable	Applicable (re waiver to adult court)
	Self-incrimination	Applicable (*Miranda* warnings)	Applicable
Sixth:	Right to counsel	Applicable	Applicable
	Public trial	Applicable	Applicable in less than half of states
	Trial by jury	Applicable	Applicable in less than half of states
Fourteenth:	Right to treatment	Not applicable	Applicable

programs, negotiate pleas, and act as an advocate during judicial proceedings (BJS, 1997a).

Juvenile proceedings and court records have traditionally been closed to the public to protect the child's privacy and potential for rehabilitation. However, judges in the adult courts may not have access to juvenile records. This means that people who have already served time on juvenile probation or in institutions are erroneously perceived to be first offenders when they are processed for crimes as adults. Some people argue that adult courts should have access to juvenile records and that young criminals should be treated more severely than adults to deter them from future illegal activity.

Monty Davis/The Wichita Eagle

In Wichita, Kansas, Judge Richard Shull sentences a juvenile drug offender. With discretion and a range of sanctions, juvenile court judges can tailor the sentence to the particular needs of the offender and the community.

Disposition

If the court makes a finding of delinquency, the judge will schedule a dispositional hearing to decide what action should be taken. Typically, before passing sentence the judge receives a predispositional report prepared by a probation officer. Similar to a presentence report, it serves to assist the judge in deciding on a disposition that is in the best interests of the child and is consistent with the treatment plan developed by the probation officer.

Few juveniles are found by the court to be not delinquent at trial, because the intake and pretrial processes normally filter out cases in which a law violation cannot be proved. Besides dismissal, four other choices are available: (1) probation, (2) alternative dispositions, (3) custodial care, and (4) community treatment.

Juvenile court advocates have traditionally believed that rehabilitation is the only goal of the sanction imposed on young people. For most of the twentieth century, judges sentenced juveniles to indeterminate sentences so that correctional administrators could decide when release was appropriate. As in the adult criminal justice system, indeterminate sentences and unbridled discretion in juvenile justice have been under attack during the last three decades. Several states have tightened the sentencing discretion of judges, especially with regard to serious offenses. The State of Washington, for example, has adopted a determinate sentencing law for juveniles. In other states, a youth can be transferred more readily to the adult court for adjudication and sentencing. Jurisdictions such as the District of Columbia, Colorado, Florida, and Virginia have passed laws requiring mandatory sentences for certain offenses committed by juveniles.

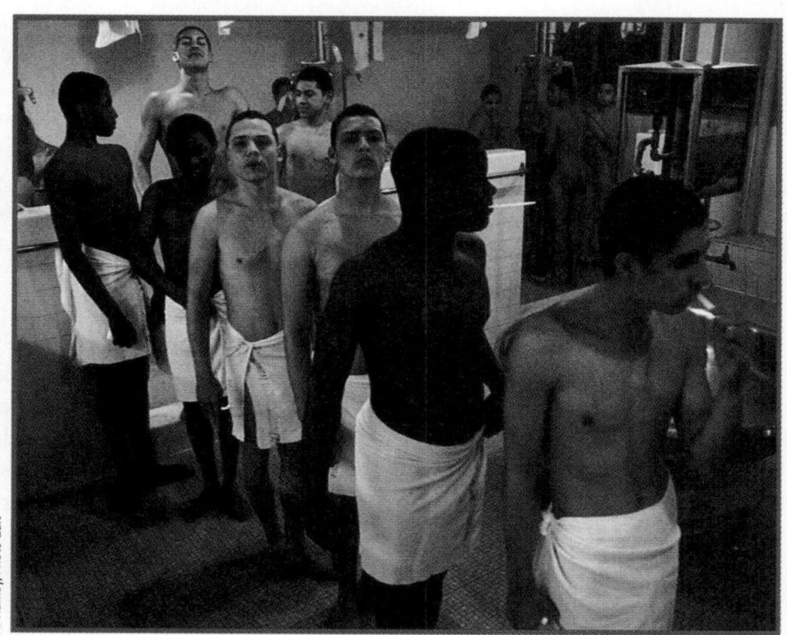
A. Ramey/Photo Edit

At Camp Karl Holton, California, youthful offenders line up for showers. Nationally almost 100,000 youths are held in institutional care, usually for six months. What lies ahead for these delinquents?

Corrections

Many aspects of juvenile corrections resemble those of adult corrections. Both systems, for example, mix rehabilitative and retributive sanctions. However, juvenile corrections differs in many respects from the adult system. Some of the differences flow from the *parens patriae* concept and the youthful, seemingly innocent people with whom the system deals. At times, the differences are expressed in formal operational policies, such as contracting for residential treatment. At other times, the differences are apparent only in the style and culture of an operation, as they are in juvenile probation.

One predominant aim of juvenile corrections is to avoid unnecessary incarceration. When children are removed from their homes, they

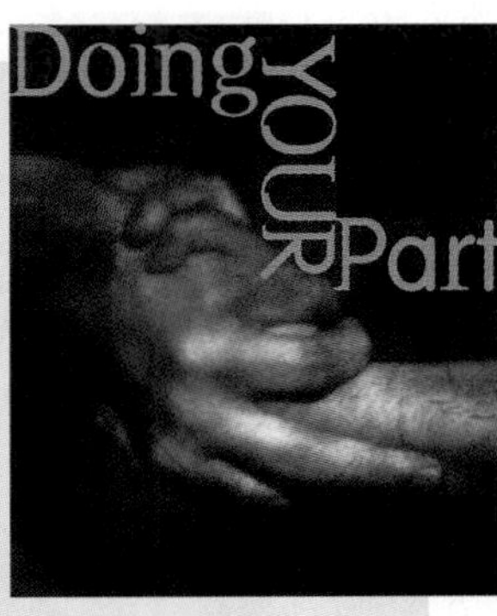

Teen Court

Tim Nadon, a social studies teacher at Plymouth High School in Michigan, volunteers his time to arrange for his students to serve as jurors in criminal cases. Very few of his students are actually old enough to be called for jury duty at the local courthouse. Instead, they serve as jurors in a "Teen Court" program that enables them to determine appropriate punishments for their peers who have committed misdemeanors and petty offenses. More than 600 Teen Court programs exist throughout the United States. The defendants are teenagers who have committed a variety of lesser offenses, including theft, minor assault, vandalism, alcohol possession, truancy, and traffic violations. The defendants must be first offenders who agree to plead guilty. If so, juvenile probation officers can refer them to the local Teen Court where their punishments will be determined by a jury of teenage volunteers who have been trained in the Teen Court's processes and goals. In many Teen Courts, teenagers who have gained experience as jurors later serve as "attorneys" in these cases, either arguing for specific punishments as "prosecutors" or as "defense attorneys" who support the defendant's explanation for why the offenses occurred. The jury carefully questions the defendant and then reaches a unanimous decision about punishment. Punishments often emphasize restorative justice by requiring community service and restitution. Defendants may also be required to write letters of apology to victims and essays that will force them to think about and learn from their experiences. An adult volunteer, often a local attorney, serves as the "judge" who ensures that the proceedings remain serious and that fair procedures are followed. The courts are relatively informal in the sense that they do not follow formal trial rules, but they are serious affairs in which the defendant and other participants are expected to be well-dressed and respectful of the process.

Sources: Drawn from Sheri Hall, "Teen Court Changes Venue," *Detroit Free Press*, August 21,2002 (http://www.freep.com); Sharon J. Zehner, "Teen Court," *FBI Law Enforcement Bulletin*, March 1997 (http://www.fbi.gov/publications).

Learn more about the Teen Court concept at http://www.geocities.com/uncteencourt/.

are inevitably damaged emotionally, even when the home life is harsh and abusive, for they are forced to abandon the only environment they know. Further, placing children in institutions has labeling effects; the children begin to perceive themselves as "bad" because they have received punitive treatment, and children who see themselves as bad are likely to behave that way. Finally, treatment is believed to be more effective when the child is living in a normal, supportive home environment. For these reasons, noninstitutional forms of corrections are seen as highly desirable in juvenile justice and have proliferated in recent years.

Probation

In 54 percent of cases, the juvenile delinquent is placed on probation and released to the custody of a parent or guardian. Often the judge orders that the delinquent undergo some form of education or counseling. The delinquent can also be required to pay a fine or make restitution while on probation.

Juvenile probation operates in much the same way that adult probation does, and it is sometimes carried out by the same agency. In two respects, however, juvenile probation can differ markedly from adult probation. First, juvenile probation officers have smaller caseloads. Second, the juvenile probation officer is often infused with the sense that the offender is worthwhile and can change and that the job is valuable and enjoyable. Such attitudes make for greater creativity than adult probation officers usually express. For example, a young offender can be paired with a "big brother" or "big sister" from the community.

Alternative Dispositions

Although probation and commitment to an institution are the system's two main dispositional options, intermediate sanctions served in the community now account for 15 percent of adjudicated juvenile cases. Judges have wide discretion to warn, to fine, to arrange for restitution, to refer a juvenile for treatment at either a public or a private community agency, or to withhold judgment.

Judges sometimes suspend judgment—that is, continue a case without a finding—when they wish to put a youth under supervision but are reluctant to apply the label "delinquent." The judge holds off on giving a definitive judgment but can give one should a youth misbehave while under the informal supervision of a probation officer or parents.

Custodial Care

Of those juveniles declared delinquent, 29 percent are placed in public or private facilities. The national incarceration rate per 100,000 juveniles aged 10–18 is 368. Like the adult incarceration rate, these rates vary widely among the states, with the highest rate in Louisiana (583) and the lowest in Vermont (71). Nationally, 74 percent of incarcerated juveniles are held in public facilities, with the remainder in private facilities (Stickmund, 2000).

Policy makers are concerned about the overrepresentation of incarcerated African American juveniles. One study (Figure 17.6) found that the disproportionate confinement of minority juveniles often stems from disparity at the early stages of case processing. Thus, if more African Americans are detained than oth-

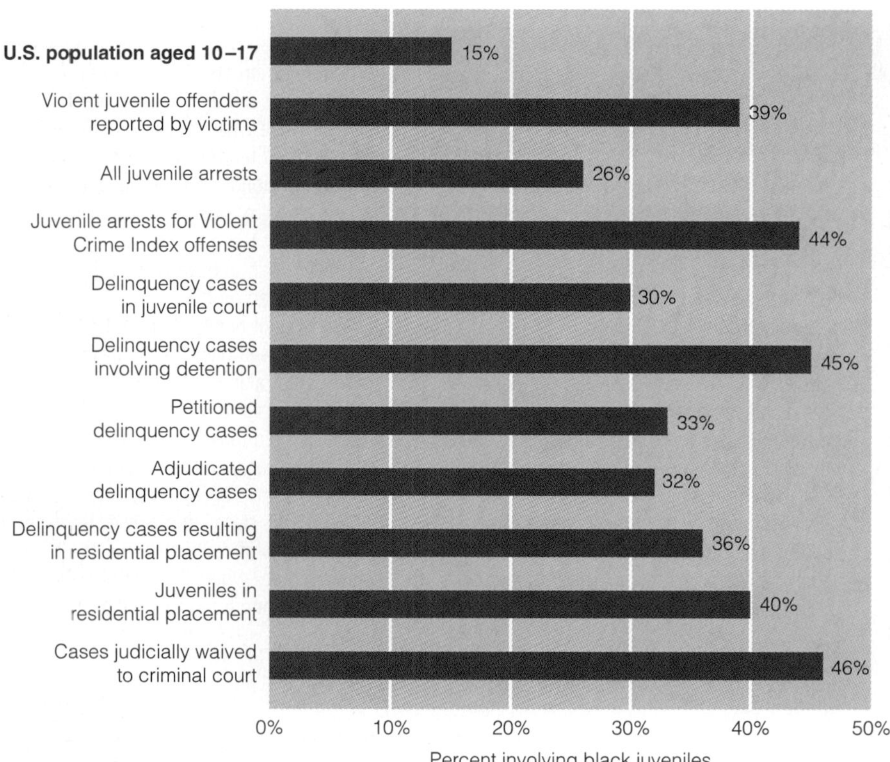

Figure 17.6
Representation of African American juveniles in the juvenile justice system compared with their proportion in the population

Source: Office of Juvenile Justice and Delinquency Prevention, "Minorities in the Juvenile Justice System," *1999 National Report Series,* December 1999, p. 2.

ers, more of them will likely be adjudicated in juvenile court, and more placed in residential facilities.

Institutions for juvenile offenders are classified as either nonsecure or secure. Nonsecure placements (foster homes, group homes, camps, ranches, or schools) include a significant number of nonoffenders—youths referred for abuse, neglect, or emotional disturbance. Secure facilities, such as reform schools and training schools, deal with juveniles who have committed serious violations of the law and have serious personal problems. Most secure juvenile facilities are small, designed to hold 40 or fewer residents. However, many states have at least one facility holding two hundred or more hard-core delinquents who are allowed limited freedom. Because the residents are younger and somewhat more volatile than adults, behavioral control is often an everyday issue, and fights and aggression are common. Poor management practices, such as those described in "A Question of Ethics," can lead to difficult situations.

Boot camps for juvenile offenders had a spurt of growth in the early 1990s. By 1997 more than 27,000 teenagers were passing through 54 camps in 34 states annually. However, as with boot camps for adults, the results have not been promising. A national study showed that recidivism among boot camp attendees ranged from 64 percent to 75 percent, slightly higher than for youths sentenced to adult prisons (*New York Times,* January 2, 2000:WK3). States are rethinking their policies.

Residents of the Lovelock Home had been committed by the juvenile court because they were either delinquent or neglected. All 25 boys, aged 12 to 16, were streetwise, tough, and interested only in getting out. The institution had a staff of social services professionals who tried to deal with the educational and psychological needs of the residents. Because state funding was short, these services looked better in the annual report than to an observer visiting Lovelock. Most of the time the residents watched television, played basketball in the backyard, or just hung out in one another's rooms.

Joe Klegg, the night supervisor, was tired from the eight-hour shift that he had just completed on his "second job" as a daytime convenience-store manager. The boys were watching television when he arrived at seven. Everything seemed calm. It should have been, because Joe had placed a tough 15-year-old, Randy Marshall, in charge. Joe had told Randy to keep the younger boys in line. Randy used his muscle and physical presence to intimidate the other residents. He knew that if the home was quiet and there was no trouble, he would be rewarded with special privileges such as a "pass" to go see his girlfriend. Joe wanted no hassles and a quiet house so that he could doze off when the boys went to sleep.

→ Does the situation at Lovelock Home raise ethical questions, or does it merely raise questions of poor management practices? What are the potential consequences for the residents? For Joe Klegg? What is the state's responsibility?

Fernando, 16, Finds a Sanctuary in Crime

Fernando Morales was glad to discuss his life as a 16-year-old drug dealer. He had recently escaped from Long Lane School, a [Connecticut] correctional institution that became his home after he was caught with $1,100 worth of heroin known as P.

"The Five-O caught me right here with the bundles of P," he said, referring to a police officer, as he stood in front of a boarded-up house on Bridgeport's East Side. "They sentenced me to eighteen months, but I jetted after four. Three of us got out a bathroom window. We ran through the woods and stole a car. Then we got back here and the Five-O's came to my apartment, and I had to jump out the side window on the second floor."

What Future?

Since his escape, Fernando has been on the run for weeks. He still went to the weekly meetings of his gang, but he was afraid to go back to his apartment, afraid even to go to a friend's place to pick up the three guns he had stashed away. "I would love to get my baby Uzi, but it's too hot now."

"Could you bring a photographer here?" he asked. "I want my picture in the newspaper. I'd love to have me holding a bundle right there on the front page so the cops can see it. They're going to bug out."

The other dealers on the corner looked on with a certain admiration. They realized that a publicity campaign might not be the smartest long-term career move for a fugitive drug dealer—"Man, you be the one bugging out," another dealer told him—but they also recognized the logic in Fernando's attitude. He was living his life according to a common assumption on these streets: There is no future.

When you ask the Hispanic teenagers selling drugs here what they expect to be doing in five years, you tend to get a lot of bored shrugs. Occasionally they'll talk about being back in school or being a retired drug dealer in a Porsche. But the most common answer is the one that Fernando gave without hesitation or emotion: "Dead or in jail."

The story of how Fernando got that way is a particularly sad one, but the basic elements are fairly typical in the lives of drug dealers and gang members in any urban ghetto. He has grown up amid tenements, housing projects, torched buildings, and abandoned factories. His role models have been adults who use "the city" and "the state" primarily as terms for the different types of welfare checks. His neighborhood is a place where 13-year-olds know by heart the visiting hours at local prisons.

The Family: A Mother Leaves, a Father Drinks

Fernando Morales was born in Bridgeport, Connecticut, and a few months after his birth his mother moved out. Since then he has occasionally run into her on the street. Neither he nor his relatives can say exactly why she left—or why she didn't take Fernando and her other son with her—but the general assumption is that she was tired of being hit by their father.

The father, Bernabe Morales, who was 24 years old and had emigrated from Puerto Rico as a teenager, moved the two boys in with his mother at the P. T. Barnum public housing project. Fernando lived there until the age of 8, when his grandmother died. . . .

After that Fernando and his brother Bernard lived sometimes with their father and his current girlfriend, sometimes with relatives in Bridgeport or Puerto Rico. They eventually

Figure 17.7 **Juveniles in public facilities: Types of offenses and nondelinquent reasons for placement**

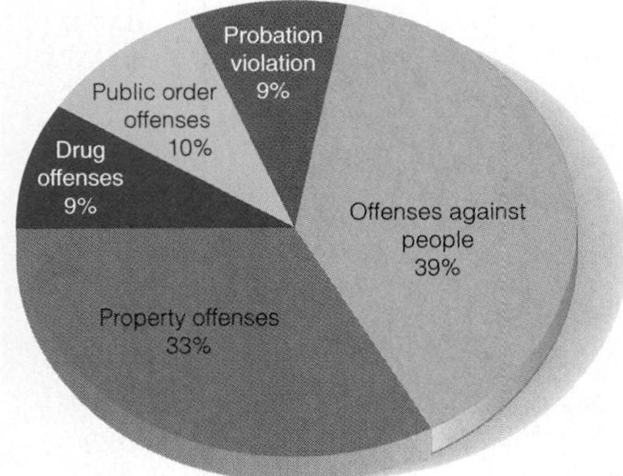

Source: Offiice of Juvenile Justice and Delinquency Prevention, *Juvenile Offenders and Victims: 1999 National Report* (Washington, D.C.: U.S. Government Printing Offiice 1999), 188.

A national survey of public custodial institutions showed that 39 percent of juveniles were incarcerated for violent offenses, 60 percent used drugs regularly, and 50 percent said that a family member had been in prison at some time in the past. Also, 88 percent of the residents were male, only 30 percent had grown up in a household with both parents, and the percentages of African Americans (40 percent) and Hispanics (18 percent) were greater than the percentage of those groups in the general population (OJJDP, 1999:195). The Close Up box tells the story of Fernando, whose background matches this profile. Figure 17.7 shows the types of offenses and nondelinquent reasons for the placement of juveniles in public correctional facilities.

Institutional Programs

Because of the emphasis on rehabilitation that has dominated juvenile justice for much of the past 50 years, a wide variety of treatment programs has been used. Counseling, education, vocational train-

settled with their father's cousin, Monserrate Bruno, who already had ten children living in her two-bedroom apartment. . . .

His father, by all accounts, was a charming, generous man when sober but something else altogether when drinking or doing drugs. He was arrested more than two dozen times, usually for fighting or drugs, and spent five years in jail while Fernando was growing up. He lived on welfare, odd jobs, and money from selling drugs, a trade that was taken up by both his sons.

The "Industry": Moving Up in the Drug Trade

Fernando's school days ended two years ago, when he dropped out of ninth grade. "School was corny," he explained. "I was smart, I learned quick, but I got bored. I was just learning things when I could be out making money."

Fernando might have found other opportunities—he had relatives working in fast-food restaurants and repair shops, and one cousin tried to interest him in a job distributing bread that might pay $700 a week—but nothing with such quick rewards as the drug business flourishing on the East Side.

He had friends and relatives in the business, and he started as one of the runners on the street corner making sales or directing buyers to another runner holding the marijuana, cocaine, crack, or heroin. The runners on each block buy their drugs—paying, for instance, $200 for fifty bags of crack that sell for $250—from the block's lieutenant, who supervises them and takes the money to the absentee dealer called the owner of the block.

By this winter Fernando had moved up slightly on the corporate ladder. "I'm not the block lieutenant yet, but I have some runners selling for me," he explained as he sat in a bar near the block. Another teenager came in with money for him, which he proudly added to a thick wad in his pocket. "You see? I make money while they work for me."

Fernando still worked the block himself, too, standing on the corner watching for cars slowing down, shouting "You want P?" or responding to veteran customers for crack who asked, "Got any slab, man?" Fernando said he usually made between $100 and $300 a day, and that the money usually went as quickly as it came.

He had recently bought a car for $500 and wrecked it making a fast turn into a telephone pole. He spent money on gold chains with crucifixes, rings, Nike sneakers, Timberland boots, an assortment of Russell hooded sweatshirts called hoodies, gang dues, trips to New York City and his 23-year-old girlfriend.

His dream was to get out of Bridgeport. "I'd be living fat somewhere. I'd go to somewhere hot, Florida or Puerto Rico or somewhere, buy me a house, get six blazing girls with dope bodies." In the meantime, he tried not to think about what his product was doing to his customers.

"Sometimes it bothers me. But see, I'm a hustler. I got to look out for myself. I got to be making money. Forget them. If you put that in your head, you're going to be caught out. You going to be a sucker. You going to be like them." He said he had used marijuana, cocaine, and angel dust himself, but made a point of never using crack or heroin, the drugs that plagued the last years of his father's life. . . .

The Gangs: "Like a Family" of Drug Dealers

"I cried a little, that's it," was all that Fernando would say about his father's death. But he did allow that it had something to do with his subsequent decision to join a Hispanic gang named Neta. He went with friends to a meeting, answered questions during an initiation ceremony, and began wearing its colors, a necklace of red, white, and blue beads.

"It's like a family, and you need that if you've lost your own family," he said. "At the meetings we talk about having heart, trust, and all that. We don't disrespect nobody. If we need money, we get it. If I need anything they're right there to help me."

Neta is allied with Bridgeport's most notorious gang, the Latin Kings, and both claim to be peaceful Hispanic cultural organizations opposed to drug use. But they are financed at least indirectly by the drug trade, because many members like Fernando work independently in drug operations, and the drug dealers' disputes can turn into gang wars. . . .

"I like guns, I like stealing cars, I like selling drugs, and I like money," he said. "I got to go to the block. That's where I get my spirit at. When I die, my spirit's going to be at the block, still making money. Booming.". . .

"I'll be selling till I get my act together. I'm just a little kid. Nothing runs through my head. All I think about is doing crazy things. But when I be big, I know I need education. If I get caught and do a couple of years, I'll come out and go back to school. But I don't have that in my head yet. I'll have my little fun while I'm out."

Source: John Tierney, *New York Times*, April 13, 1993, pp. Al, B6.

Researching the **Internet**

Using InfoTrac College Edition, enter the keywords *youth gangs.* Access the article "Understanding and Responding to Youth Gangs: A Juvenile Corrections Approach," published in *Corrections Today,* August 1999.

ing, and an assortment of psychotherapy methods have been incorporated into the juvenile correctional programs of most states. Unfortunately, research has raised many questions about the effectiveness of rehabilitation programs in the juvenile corrections setting. For example, incarceration in a juvenile training institution primarily seems to prepare many offenders for entry into adult corrections. John Irwin's concept of the state-raised youth is a useful way of looking at children who come in contact with institutional life at an early age, lack family relationships and structure, become accustomed to living in a correctional facility, and cannot function in other environments (Irwin, 1970).

Aftercare

The juvenile equivalent of parole is known as **aftercare.** Upon release the offender is placed under the supervision of a juvenile parole officer who assists with educational, counseling, and treatment services. As with the adult system, juveniles may be returned to custodial care should they violate the conditions of their parole.

aftercare
Juvenile justice equivalent of parole, in which a delinquent is released from a custodial sentence and supervised in the community.

Community Treatment

In the past decade, treatment in community-based facilities has become much more common. Today there are many private, nonprofit agencies that contract with states to provide services for troubled youths. Community-based options include foster homes in which juvenile offenders live with families, usually for a short period, and group homes, often privately run facilities for groups of 12–20 juvenile offenders. Each group home has several staff personnel who work as counselors or houseparents during 8- or 24-hour shifts. Group home placements can allow juveniles to attend local schools, provide individual and group counseling, and offer a more structured life than most of the residents received in their own homes. However, critics suggest that group homes often are mismanaged and may do little more than "warehouse" youths.

check point

9. What three discretionary decisions do the police make with regard to processing juveniles?
10. What five factors influence the police in deciding the disposition of a case?
11. What is the purpose of diversion?
12. What are five sentencing dispositions available to the judge?

Problems and Perspectives

Much of the criticism of juvenile justice has emphasized the disparity between the treatment ideal and the institutionalized practices of an ongoing bureaucratic system. Commentators have focused on how the language of social reformers has disguised the day-to-day operations that lack the elements of due process and in which custodial incarceration is all too frequent. Other criticisms claim that the juvenile justice system does not control juvenile crime.

The juvenile court, in both theory and practice, is a remarkably complex institution that must perform a wide variety of functions. The juvenile justice system must play such a range of roles that goals and values will inevitably collide. In many states the same judges, probation officers, and social workers are asked to deal with both neglected children and young criminals. Although departments of social services usually deal primarily with cases of neglect, the distinction between the criminal and the neglected child is often not maintained.

In addition to recognizing that the juvenile system has organizational problems, society must acknowledge that little is known about the causes of delinquency and its prevention or treatment. Over the years, people have advanced various social and behavioral theories to explain delinquency. One generation looked to slum conditions as the cause of juvenile crime, and another pointed to the affluence of the suburbs. Psychologists sometimes point to masculine insecurity in a matriarchal family structure, and some sociologists note the peer group pressures of the gang. This array of theories has led to an array of proposed—and often contradictory—treatments. In such confusion, those interested in the problems of youth may despair. What is clear is that we need additional research on the causes of delinquency and the treatment of juvenile offenders.

What trends may foretell the future of juvenile justice? The conservative crime control policies that have hit the adult criminal justice system—with their emphasis on deterrence, retribution, and getting tough—have apparently also influenced juvenile justice. One can point to growing levels of overcrowding in juvenile institutions, increased litigation challenging the abuse of children in training schools and detention centers, and higher rates of minority youth incarceration. All of these problems have emerged during a period of declining youth populations and fewer arrests of juveniles. With the demographic trend now reversing and the concern about drugs increasing, one can see a surge of adolescents going through their criminally high-risk years in a system and community that simply cannot cope with them.

Summary

- Crimes committed by juveniles have increased since 1980 even though crimes of violence in general have decreased.
- The history of juvenile justice comprises five periods: Puritan, Refuge, juvenile court, juvenile rights, and crime control.
- Creation of the juvenile court in 1899 established a separate juvenile justice system for dealing with delinquency, neglected children, and dependent children.
- The *In re Gault* decision by the U.S. Supreme Court in 1967 brought due process to the juvenile justice system.
- Decisions by police officers and juvenile intake officers dispose of a large portion of cases that are never referred to the court.
- In juvenile court most cases are settled through a plea agreement.
- After conviction or plea, a disposition hearing is held. The judge reviews the offense and the juvenile's social history before passing sentence.
- Possible dispositions of a juvenile case include suspended judgment, probation, community treatment, or institutional care.
- Juvenile court jurisdiction is increasingly being waived so that youths can be tried in the adult criminal justice system.
- Options for juvenile corrections include probation, alternative dispositions, custodial care, institutional programs, aftercare, and community treatment.

Questions for Review

1. What are the major historical periods of juvenile justice in the United States?
2. What is the jurisdiction of the juvenile court system?
3. What are the major processes in the juvenile justice system?
4. What are the sentencing and institutional alternatives for juveniles who are judged delinquent?
5. What due process rights do juveniles have?

Key Terms and Cases

aftercare (p. 553)
delinquent (p. 542)
dependent child (p. 543)
detention hearing (p. 546)
diversion (p. 546)
neglected child (p. 543)
parens patriae (p. 535)
PINS (p. 542)
status offense (p. 539)
waive (p. 546)
Breed v. Jones (1975) (p. 539)
Fare v. Michael C. (1979) (p. 545)
In re Gault (1967) (p. 538)
In re Winship (1970) (p. 538)
McKeiver v. Pennsylvania (1971) (p. 539)
New Jersey v. T.L.O. (1985) (p. 545)
Schall v. Martin (1984) (p. 540)

For Further Reading

Ayers, William. 1997. *A Kind and Just Parent: The Children of Juvenile Court.* Boston: Beacon Press. Examination of the lives of offenders in the Chicago juvenile court system through the eyes of one of their teachers.

Decker, Scott H., and Barick Van Winkle. 1996. *Life in the Gang: Families, Friends, and Violence.* New York: Cambridge University Press. Follows the life of a juvenile gang in St. Louis for a year, documenting their trouble with the law. Examines juvenile justice efforts to deal with family and community problems.

Feld, Barry C. 1999. *Bad Kids: Race and the Transformation of the Juvenile Court.* New York: Oxford University Press. Examination of the recent shift in policies regarding youth crime and the juvenile justice system in the context of race issues in U.S. society.

Klein, Malcolm W. 1996. *The American Street Gang: Its Nature, Prevalence, and Control.* New York: Oxford University Press. A study of street gangs in the American city. Argues the need for investment in jobs, schools, and social services to serve the needs of the poor and to discourage the growth of gangs.

Kotlowitz, Alex. 1992. *There Are No Children Here: The Story of Two Boys Growing up in the Other America.* New York: Anchor. True story of two boys growing up in a Chicago housing project surrounded by street gangs, gunfire, violence, and drugs.

Matza, David. 1974. *Delinquency and Drift.* New York: Viking. A classic examination of the role of the juvenile court. Describes the influence of "kadi" justice (in which the judge exercises great discretion) on the system.

Going Online

For an up-to-date list of Web links, go to http://www.cj.wadsworth.com/colesmith10e

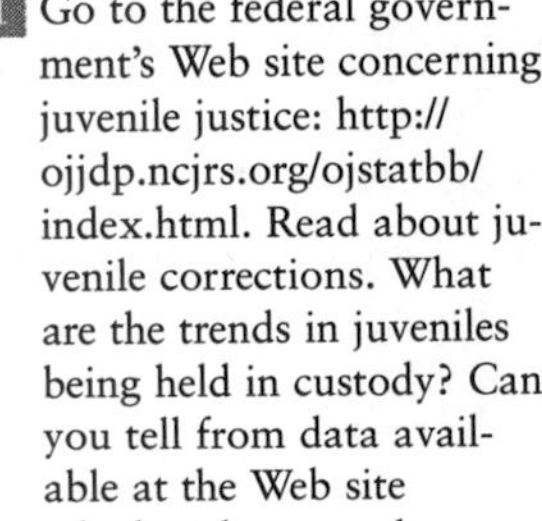

1. Go to the federal government's Web site concerning juvenile justice: http://ojjdp.ncjrs.org/ojstatbb/index.html. Read about juvenile corrections. What are the trends in juveniles being held in custody? Can you tell from data available at the Web site whether these trends are caused by changes in the crime rates or by changes in custody policies?
2. Read about Florida's County Juvenile Councils and District Juvenile Justice Boards at http://www.djj.state.fl.us/RnD/asp/1997/asp7.htm. Do these organizations appear to be good mechanism for dealing with juvenile justice problems? How well would they work in your community?
3. Using InfoTrac College Edition, search for *juvenile delinquency.* Click on "juvenile detention facilities" and read several articles that will help you answer the question "Should juveniles ever be held in adult jails or prisons?"

Checkpoint Answers

1. Juveniles, armed with guns, recruited into the inner-city drug trade.
2. Age seven.
3. Chancery courts had protective jurisdiction over children, especially those involved in cases concerning dependency, neglect, and property.
4. The state acting as parent and guardian.
5. To provide an environment where neglected children could learn good work and study habits, live in a disciplined and healthy environment, and develop character.
6. A separate court for delinquent, dependent, and neglected children; special legal procedures that were less adversarial than in the adult system; separation of children from adults throughout the system; programs of probation to assist judges in deciding what is in the best interest of the state and the child.
7. Procedural rights for juveniles, including notice of charges, right to counsel, right to confront and cross-examine witnesses, and protection against self-incrimination.
8. The age of the juvenile, usually under 16 or 18, and the type of case: delinquency, status offense, neglect, or dependency.
9. (1) Whether to take the child into custody, (2) whether to request that the child be detained, (3) whether to refer the child to court.
10. The seriousness of the offense, the willingness of the parents to cooperate, the child's behavioral history, the extent to which the child and the parents insist on a formal court hearing, and local political and social norms.
11. To avoid formal proceedings when the child's best interests can be served by treatment in the community.
12. Suspended judgment, probation, community treatment, institutional care, judicial waiver to an adult court.

Constitution of the United States

Criminal Justice Amendments

The first ten amendments to the Constitution, known as the Bill of Rights, became effective on December 15, 1791.

IV. The right of the people to be secure in their persons, houses, papers, and effects, against unreasonable searches and seizures, shall not be violated, and no warrants shall issue but upon probable cause, supported by oath or affirmation, and particularly describing the place to be searched, and the persons or things to be seized.

V. No person shall be held to answer for a capital or otherwise infamous crime, unless on a presentment or indictment of a grand jury, except in cases arising in the land or naval forces or in the militia when in actual service in time of war or public danger; nor shall any person be subject for the same offense to be twice put in jeopardy of life or limb; nor shall be compelled in any criminal case to be a witness against himself, nor be deprived of life, liberty, or property, without due process of law; nor shall private property be taken for public use without just compensation.

VI. In all criminal prosecutions the accused shall enjoy the right to a speedy and public trial, by an impartial jury of the State and district wherein the crime shall have been committed, which district shall have been previously ascertained by law, and to be informed of the nature and cause of the accusation; to be confronted with the witnesses against him; to have compulsory process for obtaining witnesses in his favor, and to have the assistance of counsel for his defense.

VIII. Excessive bail shall not be required, nor excessive fines imposed, nor cruel and unusual punishments inflicted.

The Fourteenth Amendment became effective on July 28, 1868.

XIV. SECTION 1. All persons born or naturalized in the United States, and subject to the jurisdiction thereof, are citizens of the United States and of the State wherein they reside. No State shall make or enforce any law which shall abridge the privileges or immunities of citizens of the United States; nor shall any State deprive any person of life, liberty, or property, without due process of law; nor deny to any person within its jurisdiction the equal protection of the laws.

Understanding and Using Criminal Justice Data

When it comes to numbers, criminal justice is somewhat like baseball. Both require a wealth of quantitative data to answer a variety of questions. Casual baseball fans want to know who has the highest batting average in the league or how many runs a certain pitcher gives up per game. More-serious fans might want information that can help them judge whether statistics on various events (home runs, stolen bases, sacrifice bunts) support one or more of the manager's strategies. Similarly, people interested in criminal justice need quantitative data to describe events as well as to make inferences about trends or about the impact of different policies. They want to know, for example, how much crime there is; whether crime is on the increase and which types of crimes are increasing or decreasing; whether strong gun control laws are linked to a decrease in violent crime; or what effects correctional policies have on the likelihood that criminals will break the law in the future.

Researchers constantly gather, analyze, and disseminate quantitative information that fosters an understanding of the dimensions of crime and the workings of the criminal justice system. As a student in this course and as an informed citizen, you need to be able to read about these data intelligently and to make valid inferences about them.

In this text, as in most criminal justice books and articles, quantitative data often are reported in graphs and tables that organize the information and highlight certain aspects of it. The way the information is presented reflects the writer's choices about what is important in the raw data that underlie the graphic display. So that you can better interpret and use quantitative information, this appendix provides some pointers on reading graphic presentations and on interpreting raw data.

Reading Graphs and Tables

Writers use graphs and tables to organize information so that key factors stand out. Although you may be tempted to try to take in the meaning of such displays in a quick glance, you will need to *analyze* what is being presented so that you do not misinterpret the material.

To begin, read the title and descriptive caption carefully to find out what the data do and do not represent. For example, consider the title of Figure B.1: "Violent crime trends measured by UCR and NCVS." The title tells you that the data presented pertain to *violent* crime (not all crime) and that the *sources* of the information are reports to police (Uniform Crime Reports) and victimization surveys (National Crime Victimization Survey). Knowing where the data come from is important, because different means of data collection have their own strengths and weaknesses. So what this figure presents is not a directly observed picture of crime trends, but a picture that has been filtered through two distinct

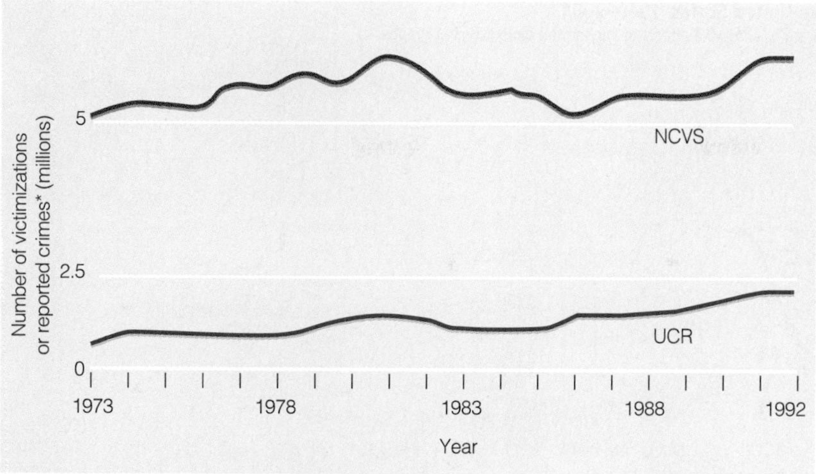

*Includes NCVS violent crimes of rape, robbery, aggravated assault, and simple assault and UCR violent crimes of murder and nonnegligent manslaughter, forcible rape, robbery, and aggravated assault.
Source: Bureau of Justice Statistics, *Highlights from Twenty Years of Surveying Crime Victims,* August 1993, p. 4.

Figure B.1
Violent crime trends measured by UCR and NCVS
Note that these data are for the *number* of violent victimizations reported, not for the victimization *rate* from 1973 to 1992.

methods of measuring crime. (These measures of crime are described in Chapter 1.) In general, always note the sources of the data before drawing conclusions from a graphic display.

After reading the title and caption, study the figure itself. Note that the graph compares the number of crimes from 1973 to 1992 as reported by the two types of surveys. As indicated in the caption, the data are presented in terms of the *number* of victimizations, not the relative *frequency* of crime (a crime *rate*). For this reason you need to be cautious in making inferences about what the data show about crime trends. In baseball, a graph showing an increase in the number of home runs hit over a certain period would not prove that home runs were becoming more common if, during the same period, new teams were added to the league. More teams and more games being played would naturally lead to an increase in the total number of home runs. Similarly, given the increases in the U.S. population over the 20-year period of the data, part of the increase in the *number* of crimes can be attributed to the greater number of Americans.

Also note that the data show what has happened over the past two decades. Even though the lines in the graph depict trends during that period, they do *not* in themselves forecast the future. There are statistical procedures that could be used to predict future trends based on certain assumptions, but such projections are not a part of this figure.

A final caution about graphic display in general: the form in which data are presented can affect or even distort your perception of the content. For example, a graph showing incarceration rates in the United States from 1940 to 2001 could be drawn with a shorter or longer time line (see Figure B.2). Figure B.2a shows the graph in normal proportions. If the time line is made shorter in relation to the incarceration rate scale, as in Figure B.2b, the changes in incarceration rates will appear to be more drastic than if the line is longer, as in Figure B.2c. By the same token, the height chosen for the vertical axis affects the appearance of the data and can influence the way the data are interpreted. How does your impression of the same data change when you compare Figure B.2d with B.2e?

Although much more could be said about interpreting graphical displays, these brief comments alert you to the need to carefully review data presented in graphic form. In criminal justice, as in baseball, you need to actively question and think about the information you encounter, in order to become a serious student of the game.

Figure B.2 Incarceration rates in the United States, 1940–2001

The panels of this graph are intentionally distorted to show the effects of varying the dimensions of graphs.

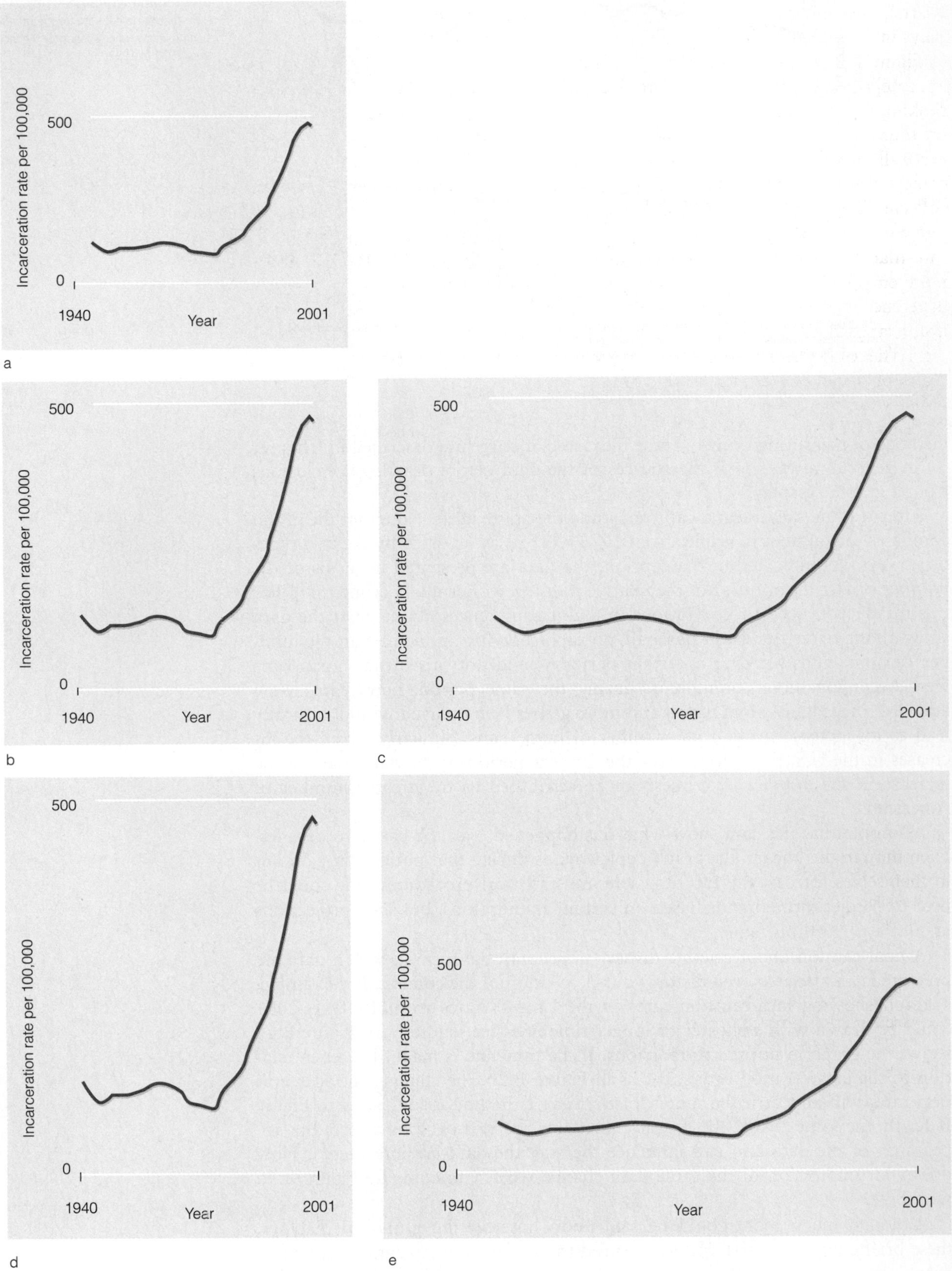

a

b

c

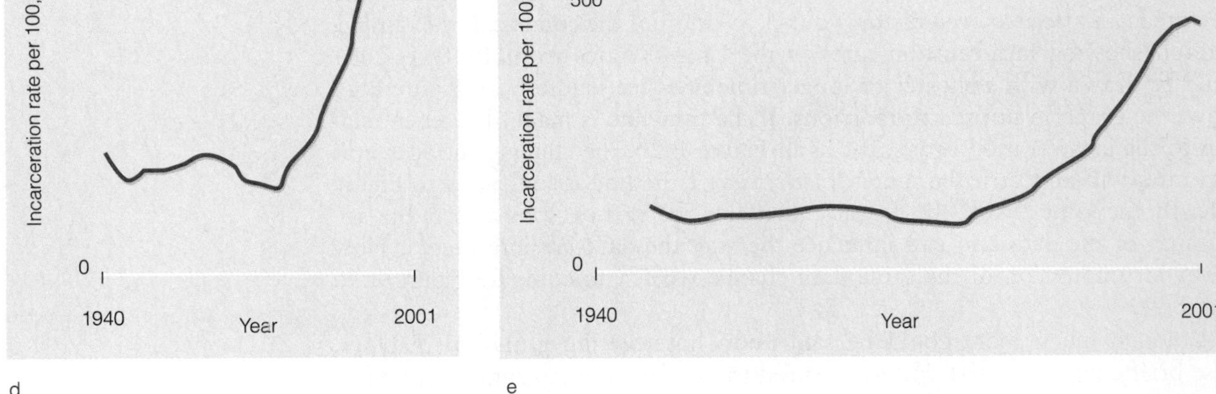

d

e

Sources: Bureau of Justice Statistics *Bulletin,* June 1997; August 1998; August 2001; August 2002.

Three Types of Graphs

You will find three types of graphs in this book: bar graphs, pie graphs (or pie charts), and line graphs. All three are represented in Figure B.3. Each graph displays information concerning public opinion about crime.

Figure B.3a is a bar graph. Bar graphs compare quantities organized in different categories. In this case, each bar represents the percentage of poll respondents ranking the indicated problem as "the most important problem facing this country today." The lengths of the bars (or their heights, when a bar graph is oriented vertically) allow for a visual comparison of the quantities associated with each category of response. In this case, you can readily see that when the data were collected in September 1993, health care outranked crime as the public's number one concern by nearly 2 to 1. The creator of a graph of this type needs to take care that the sizes of the bars are visually proportionate to the quantities they represent. A bar graph that is drawn unscrupulously or carelessly can make the difference in quantities appear larger or smaller than it really is. Intentionally or not, graphs that appear in the mass media often exaggerate some effect in this way. The lesson here is to go beyond looking at the shape of the graph. Use the scales provided on the axes to directly compare the numbers being depicted and verify your visual impression.

Figure B.3b is a pie graph. Pie graphs show the relative sizes of the parts of a single whole. Usually these sizes are reported as percentages. In this case, respondents were asked if there is more, less, or about the same amount of violence as there was five years ago. The whole consists of all the responses taken together, and the portions of the "pie" represent the percentage of respondents who chose each option. The pie graph indicates that a substantial majority (86 percent) of respondents in the survey believe that violence has increased. The same data could have been reported in a bar graph, but it would not have been as clear that a single whole was divided into parts.

Whenever data are presented as percentages of a whole—whether in a pie graph, table, or other display—the percentages should add up to 100 percent. Often, however, the sum may be slightly over or under 100 because of what is known as *rounding error.* Rounding error can occur when percentages are rounded to the nearest whole number. For instance, suppose the percentage of

Figure B.3 **Crime: In the nation, in our neighborhood**

Crime remains one of the most important problems facing Americans. More than eight in ten people surveyed believed society is more violent than it was five years ago. A plurality say there is more crime in their neighborhood than there was a year ago.

A. Question: What do you think is the most important problem facing this country today?

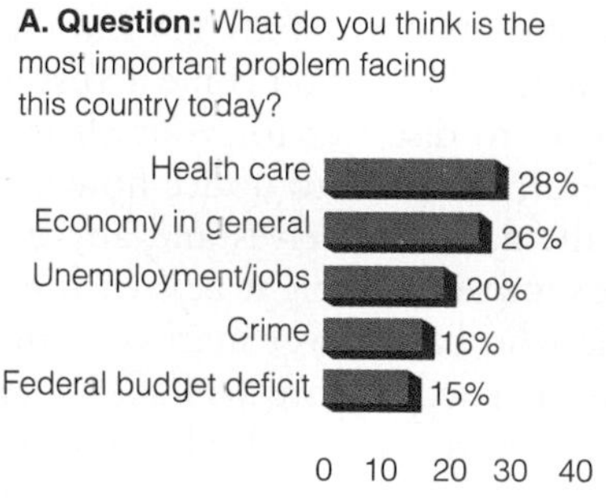

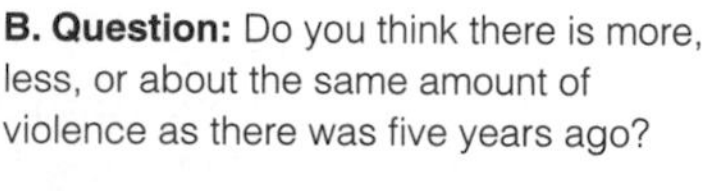

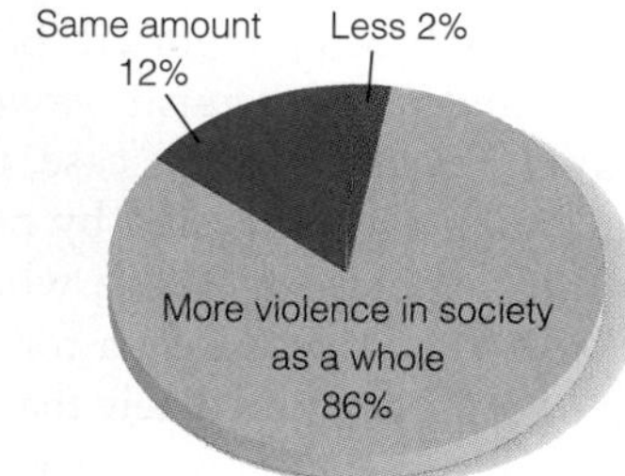

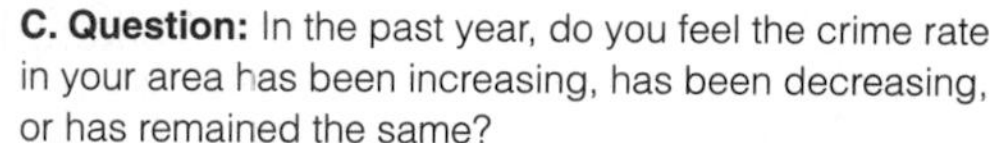

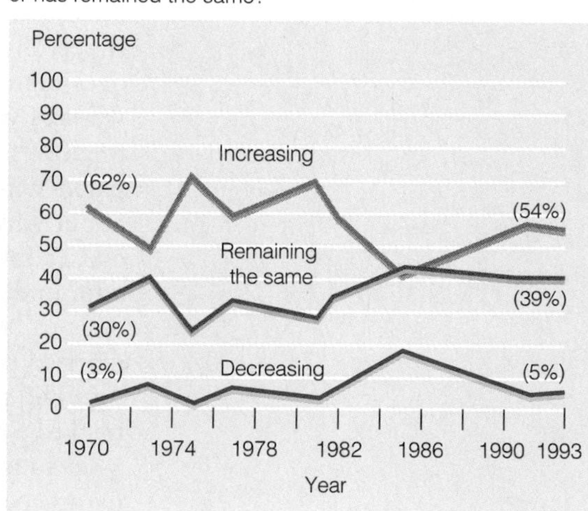

Source: "Public Opinion and Demographic Report," *The Public Perspective* 5 (November–December 1993): 78.

"more violence" responses was calculated as 86.7 percent. The figure might be reported as 87 percent. Unless rounding of the other percentages compensated for the error, the total of the reported percentages would add up to 101 percent. Where rounding error occurs, the figure or table will usually have a note indicating this fact.

Figure B.3c is a line graph. Line graphs show the relationship between two variables. The variables in question are indicated by the labels on the vertical axis and the longitudinal (horizontal) axis of the graph. In this case, the variable on the vertical axis is the percentage of people who say that crime has been increasing, decreasing, or staying about the same in the past year. The variable on the longitudinal axis is time, reported as years when the survey question was asked. In 1970, for instance, 62 percent of respondents said that crime had been increasing in the past year. Drawing a line through the points that show the percentage associated with each response for each year allows for a graphic presentation of how opinions have changed over time. The same data could have been presented in a table, but this would have made it harder to see the direction of change in opinion. Line graphs are especially well suited to showing data about trends.

Analyzing Tables

All these points about graphic presentations in general apply also to tables. When you see a table, read the title and descriptive information carefully, note the source of the data, and be aware of how the presentation itself affects your perception of the content.

Tables relate two or more variables by organizing information in vertical columns and horizontal rows. In Table B.1, the columns give data about victimization rates for two categories of crime: violent crime and personal theft. The rows of the table show categories of victims organized by sex, age, race, Hispanic origin, household income, and so forth. Reading *down* a column allows you to compare information about personal theft, for example, for different types of victims. By inspecting each column in turn, you can see that the rates for both types of crime victimization are higher for Hispanics than for non-Hispanics, for people aged 16–19 than for those in all other age groups, for urban than for rural groups, and so on. Reading *across* a row, for example, "Divorced/separated," allows you to compare the different categories of crime victimization for the same type of victim.

Like other types of data displays, tables often require close study beyond the particular information being highlighted by the writer. When you come across a table, read down the columns and across the rows to discover for yourself the shape of the information being reported. Be careful, however, to notice how the data are organized and to distinguish between the data themselves and any *inferences* you draw from them. In this case, for example, you might be struck by the lower victimization rates reported by people who have never married compared with the rates reported by those who are married. Before you speculate about why this is so, note that the data for marital status are not broken out by age. People under age 25 are more likely than those older to be victimized (see the data under "age"). Because these younger people are far more likely than older ones to be unmarried, the difference in victimization rates for married and unmarried people may be largely accounted for by age rather than by marital status. The table does not provide enough information to tell to what extent this might be the case.

In summary, data are presented in tables and graphs so they can be more easily grasped. But before you decide that you have truly understood the information, read the item and accompanying commentary attentively and be aware of

Table B.1 Who are the victims of violent crimes and personal theft?

NCVS data help clarify the characteristics of crime victims.

		Rate per 1,000 persons age 12 or older	
	Victims	Violence*	Personal Theft**
Sex	Male	33	1.0
	Female	23	1.4
Age	12–15	60	1.8
	16–19	64	3.0
	20–24	49	1.1
	25–34	35	1.5
	35–49	22	1.0
	50–64	14	.5
	65 or older	4	1.2
Race	White	27	1.1
	African American	35	1.0
	Other	21	1.8
Hispanic origin	Hispanic	28	2.4
	Non-Hispanic	28	1.1
Household income	Less than $7,500	60	2.3
	$7,000–$14,999	38	2.1
	$15,000–$24,999	32	1.2
	$25,000–$34,999	30	1.4
	$35,000–$49,999	29	.6
	$50,000–$74,999	24	1.0
	$75,000 or more	22	1.2
Marital Status	Never married	51	2.3
	Married	13	.5
	Divorced/separated	42	1.3
	Widowed	22	1.3
Region	Northeast	51	2.3
	Midwest	30	1.2
	South	25	.6
	West	34	1.3
Residence	Urban	35	2.3
	Rural	27	.4

*Rounded
**Personal theft includes only purse snatching and pocket picking.
Source: Bureau of Justice Statistics, *National Crime Victimization Survey*, June 2001, pp. 6, 7.

the ways the writer has chosen to organize and display the data. By working with graphic presentations and posing questions to yourself as you read them, you also make the important information easier to remember.

Understanding Raw Data

Data that you see in graphs and tables have already been sifted and organized. As a student of criminal justice, you also encounter raw (or "whole") data. For example, the *Sourcebook of Criminal Justice Statistics, 2000* reports that there were 14,790 arrests for murder in the United States in 1999. Data often are expressed in terms of the *rate* at which an event occurs for a certain number of people in the population. The murder rate in 1999 was 5.7 murders per 100,000 people in the United States. The formula for determining the rate is

$$\frac{\text{Number of murders}}{\text{Total U.S. population}} \times 100{,}000 = \text{Rate per } 100{,}000$$

For some purposes, the total figures (the raw data) are needed; for other purposes, percentages are more informative; and for still other purposes, expressing data as a rate is most useful. To illustrate this point, consider the following example of data about incarceration in two different states.

On December 31, 2000, 47,718 offenders were held in the prisons of Michigan and 35,047 in the prisons of Louisiana. How does incarceration in these states compare? Just knowing the number of prisoners does not allow you to draw many conclusions about incarceration in these states. If, however, the numbers are expressed as a *rate,* the difference in the sizes of the two state populations would be taken into consideration and a much clearer picture would result. Although Louisiana has fewer prisoners than Michigan, the incarceration rate in Louisiana (801 prisoners per 100,000 population) is considerably higher than in Michigan (480 per 100,000). On a national basis, the number of incarcerated people in 2000 represented a rate of 478 prisoners for every 100,000 U.S. residents, so the rate in Louisiana is significantly higher than in the United States as a whole. In fact, Louisiana has the highest incarceration rate in the country.

Sources of Criminal Justice Data

To a large extent, criminal justice researchers depend on data collected and analyzed by agencies of the government. Many of these sources are cited throughout this book. In particular, the Bureau of Justice Statistics of the U.S. Department of Justice produces the *Sourcebook of Criminal Justice Statistics,* an annual compilation of data on most aspects of crime and justice (found on the Internet at http://www.albany.edu/sourcebook); the *Bulletin,* regularly published issues focusing on a single topic related to police, courts, and corrections; and the *Special Report,* a publication that presents findings from specific research projects (see http://www.ojp.usdoj.gov/bjs/). The National Institute of Justice, also an arm of the U.S. Department of Justice, publishes *Research in Brief,* summary versions of major research studies (http://www.ojp.usdoj.gov/nij/). *Crime in the United States,* published each August by the Department of Justice, contains data collected through the FBI's Uniform Crime Reports system (http://www.fbi.gov).

The libraries of most colleges and universities hold these publications in the government documents or reference section. Ask your librarian to help you find them. If you would like to get on the mailing list to receive the free publications of the Bureau of Justice Statistics, fill out the form on the last page of the *Bulletin.* You can also access most of these publications through the Internet. Go to the Web site for the agencies, as noted earlier.

references

Abadinsky, H. 1997. *Probation and Parole.* 6th ed. Upper Saddle, N.J.: Prentice-Hall.

———. 2003. *Organized Crime.* 7th ed. Belmont, Calif.: Wadsworth.

Abbe, O. G., and P. S. Herrnson. 2002. "How Judicial Election Campaigns Have Changed." *Judicature* 85:286–95.

Abrams, J. 2000. "Congress Passes Asset Forfeiture Bill." *Topeka Capital Journal,* April 12 (http://cjonline.com/stories/).

Abramsky, S. 1999. "When They Get Out." *Atlantic Monthly,* June, pp. 30–36.

———. 2002. *Hard Time Blues: How Politics Built a Prison Nation.* New York: St. Martin's Press.

Acker, J. R., and C. S. Lanier. 1994. "In Fairness and Mercy: Statutory Mitigating Factors in Capital Punishment Cases." *Criminal Law Bulletin* 30: 299–345.

———. 1995. "Matters of Life or Death: The Sentencing Provisions in Capital Punishment Statutes." *Criminal Law Bulletin* 31:3–18.

Acoca, L. 1997. "Hearts on the Ground: Violent Victimization and Other Themes in the Lives of Women Prisoners." *Corrections Management Quarterly* 1 (Spring): 44–55.

———. 1998. "Defusing the Time Bomb: Understanding and Meeting the Growing Health Care Needs of Incarcerated Women in America." *Crime and Delinquency* 44 (January): 49–69.

"Actress Rebecca Gayheart." 2002. Associated Press Wire Service, January 23 (available on Lexis-Nexis).

Adams, K. 1992. "Adjusting to Prison Life." In *Crime and Justice: A Review of Research,* vol. 16, ed. M. Tonry. Chicago: University of Chicago Press, 275–359.

Adler, F. 1975. *Sisters in Crime: The Rise of the New Female Criminal.* New York: McGraw-Hill.

Adler, S. J. 1994. *The Jury: Disorder in the Court.* New York: Doubleday.

Administrative Office of the U.S. Courts. 1993. *Guide to Judiciary Policies and Procedures: Probation Manual,* vol. 10. [mimeograph]

Ahern, J. F. 1972. *Police in Trouble.* New York: Hawthorne Books.

Alarid, L. F., J. M. Marquart, V. S. Burton, Jr., and S. J. Cuvelier. 1996. "Women's Roles in Serious Offenses: A Study of Adult Felons." *Justice Quarterly* 13 (September): 431–54.

Albanese, J. 1991. "Organized Crime: The Mafia Myth." In *Criminology: A Contemporary Handbook,* ed. J. Sheley. Belmont, Calif.: Wadsworth, 201–18.

Alexander, R., Jr. 1993. "The Demise of State Prisoners' Access to Federal Habeas Corpus." *Criminal Justice Policy Review* 6:55–70.

Alley, M. E., E. M. Bonello, and J. A. Schafer. 2002. "Dual Responsibilities: A Model for Immersing Midlevel Managers in Community Policing." In *The Move to Community Policing: Making Change Happen,* ed. M. Morash and J. Ford. Thousand Oaks, Calif.: Sage, 112–25.

Almeida, C. 2002. "Abducted Girls Rescued from Remote Desert Area; Suspect Shot and Killed." Associated Press Wire Service, August 2.

Alonso-Zaldivar, R. 2002. "Police Officers Face New Hazard: Assault by Air Bag." *Los Angeles Times,* August 7, p. 24.

Amar, A. R. 1997. *The Constitution and Criminal Procedure: First Principles.* New Haven, Conn.: Yale University Press.

American Correctional Association. 1990. *The Female Offender: What Does the Future Hold?* Alexandria, Va.: Kirby Lithographic Company.

———. 1994. *Gangs in Correctional Facilities: A National Assessment.* Laurel Md.: American Correctional Association.

———. 1996. *Juvenile and Adult Correctional Facilities Directory.* College Park, Md.: American Correctional Association.

Anderson, D. 1998. *Sensible Justice: Alternatives to Prison.* New York: New Press.

Anderson, G., R. Litzenberger, and D. Plecas. 2002. "Physical Evidence of Police Officer Stress." *Policing* 25:399–420.

Anderson, L. 1999. "Attacks Spur Call to Force Medications." *Chicago Tribune,* June 1, p. 1.

Andrews, D. A., and J. Bonta. 1994. *The Psychology of Criminal Behavior.* Cincinnati, Ohio: Anderson.

Andrews, D. A., I. Zinger, R. D. Hoge, J. Bonta, P. Gendreau, and F. T. Cullen. 1990. "Does Correctional Treatment Work? A Clinically Relevant and Psychologically Informed Meta-Analysis." *Criminology* 28:369–404.

Applegate, B. K., F. T. Cullen, and B. S. Fisher. 1997. "Public Support for Correctional Treatment: The Continuing Appeal of the Rehabilitative Ideal." *Prison Journal* 77:237–58.

Arax, M., and M. Gladstone. 1998. "State Thwarted Brutality Probe in Corcoran Prison, Investigators Say." *Los Angeles Times,* July 5, p. 1.

Armstrong, K., and S. Mills. 1999. "Death Row Justice Derailed." *Chicago Tribune,* November 14, 15, p. 1.

Auerhahn, K. 1999. "Selective Incapacitation and the Problem of Prediction." *Criminology* 37:703–34.

Ayers, William. 1997. *A Kind and Just Parent: The Children of Juvenile Court.* Boston: Beacon Press.

Baldus, D. C., G. Woodworth, and C. A. Pulaski. 1994. *Equal Justice and the Death Penalty: A Legal and Empirical Analysis.* Boston: Northeastern University Press.

Bandy, D. 1991. "$1.2 Million to Be Paid in Stray-Bullet Death." *Akron Beacon Journal,* December 3, p. B6.

Barnes, C. W., and R. Kingsnorth. 1996. "Race, Drug, and Criminal Sentencing: Hidden Effects of the Criminal Law." *Journal of Criminal Justice* 24:39–55.

Basemore, G., and M. S. Umbreit. 1994. Foreword to *Balanced and Restorative Justice: Program Summary.* Washington, D.C.: Office of Juvenile Justice and Delinquency Prevention, U.S. Government Printing Office.

Bast, C. M. 1995. "Publication of the Name of a Sexual Assault Victim: The Collision of Privacy and Freedom of the Press." *Criminal Law Bulletin* 31: 379–99.

Bayley, D. H. 1986. "The Tactical Choice of Police Patrol Officers." *Journal of Criminal Justice* 14:329–48.

———. 1994. *Police for the Future.* New York: Oxford University Press.

———. 1998. *What Works in Policing?* New York: Oxford University Press.

Beck, A. 1997. "Growth, Change, and Stability in the U.S. Prison Population, 1980–1995."*Corrections Management Quarterly* 8 (January): 1–14.

———. 2000. "State and Federal Prisoners Returning to the Community: Findings from the Bureau of Justice Statistics." Paper presented at the First Reentry Courts Initiative Cluster Meeting, Washington, D.C., April 13.

Becker, Howard S. 1963. *Outsiders: Studies in the Sociology of Deviance.* New York: Free Press.

Bell, D. 1967. *The End of Ideology.* 2nd. rev. ed. New York: Collier.

Belluck, P. 2001. "Desperate for Prison Guards, Some States Even Rob Cradles." *New York Times,* April 21, p. A1.

Benson, M., and D. Wood. 2002. "U.S. Terror Suspect's Case Cause of Concern." *Seattle Times,* June 14 (http://www.seattletimes.com).

Bergstrom, K. 1999. "Source of Evidence: The Suspect's Brain." *Lansing State Journal,* August 30, p. 4.

Bershard, L. 1985. "Discriminatory Treatment of the Female Offender in the Criminal Justice System." *Boston College Law Review* 26:389–438.

Biderman, A. D., L. A. Johnson, J. McIntyre, and A. W. Weit. 1967. *Report on a Pilot Study in the District of Columbia on Victimization and Attitudes toward Law Enforcement.* Washington, D.C.: U.S. Government Printing Office.

BJS (Bureau of Justice Statistics). 1988. *Report to the Nation on Crime and Justice.* 2nd ed. Washington, D.C.: U.S. Government Printing Office.

———. 1997a. *Bulletin,* January.

———. 1997b. *Bulletin,* December.

———. 1997c. *Correctional Populations in the United States, 1995.* Washington, D.C.: U.S. Government Printing Office.

———. 1997d. *Police Use of Force.* Washington, D.C.: U.S. Government Printing Office.

———. 1997e. *Press Release,* November 22.

———. 1998a. *Bulletin,* January.

———. 1998b. *Bulletin,* June.

———. 1998c. *Bulletin,* August.

———. 1998d. *Crime and Justice in the United States and in England and Wales, 1981–1996.*Washington, D.C.: U.S. Government Printing Office.

———. 1999a. *American Indians and Crime.* Washington, D.C.: U.S. Government Printing Office.

———. 1999b. *Bulletin,* August.

———. 1999c. *Sourcebook of Criminal Justice Statistics, 1998.* Washington, D.C.: U.S. Government Printing Office.

———. 1999d. *Special Report,* January.

———. 1999e. *Special Report,* July.

———. 2000a. *Bulletin,* April.

———. 2000b. *Bulletin,* August.

———. 2000c. *Bulletin,* December.

———. 2000d. *Correctional Populations in the United States, 1997.* Washington, D.C.: U.S. Government Printing Office.

———. 2000e. *Law Enforcement Management and Administration Statistics (LEMAS) Survey, 1999.* Washington, D.C. U.S. Government Printing Office.

———. 2000f. *Press Release,* July 23.

———. 2000g. *Sourcebook of Criminal Justice Statistics, 1999.* Washington, D.C.: U.S. Government Printing Office.

———. 2000h. *Special Report,* February.

———. 2000i. *Special Report,* May.

———. 2000j. *Special Report,* August.

———. 2001a. *Bulletin,* March.

———. 2001b. *Bulletin,* July.

———. 2001c. *Bulletin,* August.

———. 2001d. "Criminal Victimization" (http://www.ojp.usdoj.gov/bjs/).

———. 2001e. *Sourcebook of Criminal Justice Statistics, 2000.* Washington, D.C. U.S. Government Printing Office.

———. 2002a. *Bulletin,* February.

———. 2002b. *Bulletin,* June.

———. 2002c. *Bulletin,* July.

———. 2002d. "Justice Expenditure and Employment in the United States, 1999." Bureau of Justice Statistics *Bulletin,* February.

———. 2002e. *Sourcebook of Criminal Justice Statistics, 2001.* Washington, D.C.: U.S. Government Printing Office.

———. 2002f. *Special Report,* May.

Blankenship, M., J. Luginbuhl, F. Cullen, and W. Redick. 1997. "Juror's Comprehension of Sentencing Instructions: A Test of the Death Penalty Process in Tennessee." *Justice Quarterly* 14: 325–51.

Bloch, P., and D. Anderson. 1974. *Policewomen on Patrol: First Report.* Washington, D.C.: Police Foundation.

Blomberg, T. G., and K. Lucken. 1993. "Intermediate Punishments and the Piling up of Sanctions." In *Criminal Justice: Law and Politics,* 6th ed., ed. G. F. Cole. Belmont, Calif.: Wadsworth, 470–82.

Blumberg, A. 1967. "The Practice of Law as a Confidence Game." *Law and Society Review* 1: 11–39.

Blumberg, M. 1989. "Controlling Police Use of Deadly Force: Assessing Two Decades of Progress." In *Critical Issues in Policing,* ed. G. Dunham and G. Alpert. Prospect Heights, Ill.: Waveland Press.

Blumenson, E., and E. Nilsen. 1998. "The Drug War's Hidden Economic Agenda." *The Nation.* March 9, p. 11.

Blumstein, A. 1996. "Youth Violence, Guns, and Illicit Drug Markets." In *NIJ Research Preview.* Washington, D.C.: National Institute of Justice, U.S. Government Printing Office.

Boland, B., E. Brady, H. Tyson, and J. Bassler. 1983. *The Prosecution of Felony Arrests.* Washington, D.C.: Bureau of Justice Statistics, U.S. Government Printing Office.

Bonta, J., and P. Gendreau. 1995. "Reexamining the Cruel and Unusual Punishment of Prison Life." In *Long-Term Imprisonment,* ed. T. J. Flanagan. Thousand Oaks, Calif.: Sage, 75–94.

Bourque, B. B., M. Han, and S. M. Hill. 1996. "A National Survey of Aftercare Provisions for Boot Camp Graduates." In *Research in Brief.* Washington, D.C.: National Institute of Justice, U.S. Government Printing Office.

Bowers, F. 2002. "The Intelligence Divide: Can It Be Bridged?" *Christian Science Monitor,* October 8, p. 2.

Bowker, L. H. 1982. "Victimizers and Victims in American Correctional Institutions." In *Pains of Imprisonment,* ed. R. Johnson and H. Toch. Beverly Hills, Calif.: Sage.

Bradley, C. 1992. "Reforming the Criminal Trial." *Indiana Law Journal* 68:659–64.

Braga, A. A. 1999. "Problem-oriented Policing in Violent Crime Places: A Randomized Controlled Experiment." *Criminology* 37:541–80.

Brandl, S. 1993. "The Impact of Case Characteristics of Detectives' Decision Making." *Justice Quarterly* 10 (September): 395–415.

Brandl, S., and Frank, J. 1994. "The Relationship between Evidence, Detective Effort, and the Disposition of Burglary and Robbery Investigations." *American Journal of Police,* 13: 149–68.

Brandon, K. 1999. "Legal Abortions Tied to Decline in Crime." *Hartford Courant,* August 8, p. A5.

Bratton, William. 1998. *Turnaround: How America's Top Cop Reversed the Crime Epidemic.* New York: Random House.

Bray, K. 1992. "Reaching the Final Chapter in the Story of Peremptory Challenges." *U.C.L.A. Law Review* 40: 517–55.

Brennan, P. A., S. A. Mednick, and J. Volavka. 1995. "Biomedical Factors in Crime." In *Crime,* ed. J. Q. Wilson and J. Petersilia. San Francisco: ICS Press.

Bright, S. B. 1994. "Counsel for the Poor: The Death Sentence Not for the Worst Crime but for the Worst Lawyer." *Yale Law Journal* 103:1850.

Britt, C. 2000. "Social Context and Racial Disparities in Punishment Decisions." *Justice Quarterly* 17:707–32.

Britton, D. M. 1997. "Political Attacks on the Judiciary." *Judicature* 80:165–73.

Broeder, D. W. 1959. "The University of Chicago Jury Project." *Nebraska Law Review* 38:774–803.

Brown, J. R. 1999. "Drug Diversion Courts: Are They Needed and Will They Succeed in Breaking the Cycle of Drug-Related Crime?" In *Criminal Courts for the 21st Century,* ed. L. Stolzenberg and S. D'Alessio. Saddle River, N.J.: Prentice-Hall.

Brown, M. K. 1981. *Working the Street.* New York: Russell Sage Foundation.

Buentello, S. 1992. "Combating Gangs in Texas." *Corrections Today* 54 (July): 58–60.

Buffa, D. W. 1997. *The Defense.* New York: Holt.

———. 1999. *The Prosecution: A Legal Thriller.* New York: Holt.

Bureau of Justice Assistance (BJA). 1998. *1996 National Survey of State Sentencing Structures.* Washington, D.C.: U.S. Government Printing Office.

Burns, R., and J. Smith. 1999. "DNA: Fingerprint of the Future?" *ACJS Today.* November–December, p. 1.

Bushway, S. D., and A. M. Piehl. 2001. "Judging Judicial Discretion: Legal Factors and Racial Discrimination in Sentencing." *Law and Society Review* 35:733–64.

Business Wire. 2001a. "Study Shows Iris Recognition Technology Is Superior Among Biometrics; Britain's National Physical Laboratory Publishes Performance Evaluation of Seven Biometric Systems." May 17 (available on Lexis-Nexis).

Business Wire. 2001b. "WorldNet Technologies, Creators of a State of the Art Weapons Detection System, Signs Consulting Deal with NuQuest." November 27 (available on Lexis-Nexis).

Butterfield, F. 1995a. "Idle Hands within the Devil's Own Playground." *New York Times,* July 16, p. E3.

———. 1995b. "More Blacks in Their 20's Have Trouble with the Law." *New York Times,* October 5, p. A18.

———. 1996a. *All God's Children: The Bosket Family and the American Tradition of Violence.* New York: Avon.

———. 1996b. "Three Strikes Rarely Invoked in Courtrooms." *New York Times,* September 10, p. A1.

———. 1998a. "Decline in Violent Crimes Is Linked to Crack Market." *New York Times,* December 18, p. A16.

———. 1998b. "Prisons Replace Hospitals for the Nation's Mentally Ill." *New York Times,* March 5, p. A26.

———. 1999a. "Crime Fell 7 Percent in '98 Continuing a 7-Year Trend." *New York Times,* May 17, p. A12.

———. 1999b. "Rethinking the Strong Arm of the Law." *New York Times,* April 4, p. WK1.

———. 2000. "Often, Parole Is One Stop on the Way Back to Prison." *New York Times,* November 29:A1.

Byrne, J. M., A. J. Lurigio, and J. Petersilia. 1992. *Smart Sentencing: The Emergence of Intermediate Sanctions.* Newbury Park, Calif.: Sage.

Calhoun, F. 1990. *The Lawmen.* Washington, D.C.: Smithsonian Institution.

Call, J. E. 1995. "Prison Overcrowding Cases in the Aftermath of *Wilson v. Seiter.*" *Prison Journal* 75 (September): 390–405.

Callahan, L. A., M. A. McGreevy, C. Cirincione, and H. J. Steadman. 1992. "Measuring the Effects of the Guilty But Mentally Ill (GBMI) Verdict." *Law and Human Behavior* 16:447–62.

Callahan, R. 2002. "Scientists: Liars Are Betrayed by Their Faces." Associated Press Wire Service, January 2.

Camp, C. G., and G. M. Camp. 1999. *Corrections Yearbook, 1999.* Middletown, Conn.: Criminal Justice Institute.

———. 2001. *Corrections Yearbook, 2000.* Middletown, Conn.: Criminal Justice Institute.

Camp, D. D. 1993. "Out of the Quagmire: After *Jacobson v. United States:* Toward a More Balanced Entrapment Standard." *Journal of Criminal Law and Criminology* 83:1055–97.

Camp, S. D., and G. G. Gales. 2002. "Growth and Quality of U.S. Private Prisons: Evidence from a National Survey." *Criminology and Public Policy* 1:427–50.

Carlson, P. M. 2001. "Prison Interventions: Evolving Strategies to Control Security Threat Groups." *Corrections Management Quarterly* 5 (Winter): 10–22.

Carlson, T. 1995. "Safety, Inc." *Policy Review,* Summer, pp. 67–73.

Carr, J. G. 1993. "Bail Bondsmen and the Federal Courts." *Federal Probation* 57 (March): 9–14.

Carroll, L. 1974. *Hacks, Blacks, and Cons: Race Relations in a Maximum Security Prison.* Lexington, Mass.: Lexington Books.

Carter, C. J. 2002. "Army Officer, Four Others Indicted." Associated Press Wire Service, July 3.

Casey, M. 1999. "Defense Lawyers for Poor Clients May Get Pay Raise." *New York Times,* April 11, p. 5.

Cassell, P., and R. Fowles. 1998. "Handcuffing the Cops? A Thirty-Year Perspective on *Miranda*'s Harmful Effects on Law Enforcement." *Stanford Law Review* 50:1055–145.

Caulfield, S. L. 1994. "Life or Death Decision: Prosecutorial Power vs. Equality of Justice." *Journal of Contemporary Criminal Justice* 5:233–47.

Chaddock, G. R. 2002. "Sniper Revives Prospects for Gun-Tracking Moves." *Christian Science Monitor,* October 17, p. 1.

Champagne, A., and K. Cheek. 1996. "PACs and Judicial Politics in Texas." *Judicature* 80:26–29.

Champion, D. J. 1989. "Private Counsels and Public Defenders: A Look at Weak Cases, Prior Records, and Leniency in Plea Bargaining." *Journal of Criminal Justice* 17:253–63.

Chapman, S. G. 1970. *Police Patrol Readings.* 2nd ed. Springfield, Ill.: Thomas.

Chapper, J. A., and R. A. Hanson. 1989. *Understanding Reversible Error in Criminal Appeals.* Williamsburg, Va.: National Center for State Courts.

Cheesman, F., R. A. Hanson, and B. J. Ostrom. 1998. "To Augur Well: Future Prison Population and Prisoner Litigation." Paper presented at the Federal Judicial Center, Washington, D.C., May 20.

Chermak, S. M. 1995. *Victims in the News: Crime and the American News Media.* Boulder, Colo.: Westview Press.

Chilton, B. S. 1991. *Prisons under the Gavel: The Federal Court Takeover of Georgia Prisons.* Columbus: Ohio State University Press.

Chiricos, T. G., and W. D. Bales. 1991. "Unemployment and Punishment: An Empirical Assessment." *Criminology* 29:701–24.

Chiricos, T. G., and C. Crawford. 1995. "Race and Imprisonment: A Contextual Assessment of the Evidence." In *Ethnicity, Race, and Crime: Perspectives across Time and Place,* ed. D. F. Hawkins. Albany: State University of New York Press.

Chiricos, T. G., S. Escholz, and M. Gertz. 1997. "Crime, News, and Fear of Crime." *Social Problems* 44:342–57.

Chiricos, T., K. Padgett, and M. Gertz. 2000. "Fear, TV News, and the Reality of Crime." *Criminology* 38:755–85.

Christopher, R. L. 1994. "Mistake of Fact in the Objective Theory of Justification." *Journal of Criminal Law and Criminology* 85:295–332.

Church, T. W. 1985. "Examining Local Legal Culture." *American Bar Foundation Research Journal* 1985 (Summer): 449.

Clear, T. R. 1994. *Harm in American Penology.* Albany: State University of New York Press.

Clear, T. R., and A. A. Braga. 1995. "Community Corrections." In *Crime,* ed. J. Q. Wilson and J. Petersilia. San Francisco: ICS Press, 421–44.

Clear, T. R., and G. F. Cole. 2003. *American Corrections.* 6th ed. Belmont, Calif.: Wadsworth.

Clear, T. R., and H. Dammer. 2000. *The Offender in the Community.* Belmont, Calif.: Wadsworth.

Clear, T. R., and P. L. Hardyman. 1990. "The New Intensive Supervision Movement." *Crime and Delinquency* 36:42.

Clear, T. R., and D. R. Karp. In press. *Community Justice: Preventing Crime and Achieving Justice.* Washington, D.C.: National Institute of Justice, U.S. Government Printing Office.

Clear, T. R., and E. J. Latessa. 1993. "Surveillance vs. Control: Probation Officers' Roles in Intensive Supervision." *Justice Quarterly* 10:441.

Cohen, L. E., and M. Felson. 1979. "Social Change and Crime Rates: A Routine Activity Approach." *American Sociological Review* 44:588–608.

Cohen, M., and J. T. McEwen. 1984. "Handling Calls for Service: Alternatives to Traditional Policing." In *NIJ Reports.* Washington, D.C.: U.S. Government Printing Office, 4–8.

Cohen, M., T. R. Miller, and S. B. Rossman. 1990. "The Costs and Consequences of Violent Behavior in the United States." Paper prepared for the Panel on the Understanding and Control of Violent Behavior, National Research Council, National Academy of Sciences, Washington, D.C.

Colbert, D. 1998. "Thirty-five Years after *Gideon:* The Illusory Right to Counsel at Bail Proceedings." *University of Illinois Law Review* 1998:1–58.

Cole, D. 1999. *No Equal Justice: Race and Class in American Criminal Justice.* New York: New Press.

Commission on Accreditation for Law Enforcement Agencies. 1989. *Standards for Law Enforcement Accreditation.* Fairfax, Va.: Author.

Conley, J. A. 1980. "Prisons, Production, and Profit: Reconsidering the Importance of Prison Industries." *Journal of Social History* 14:257.

Connors, E., T. Lundregan, N. Miller, and T. McEwen. 1996.

Convicted by Juries, Exonerated by Science: Case Studies in the Use of DNA Evidence to Establish Innocence after Trial. Washington, D.C.: National Institute of Justice, U.S. Government Printing Office.

Conover, T. 2000. *Newjack: Guarding Sing Sing.* New York: Random House.

Constanzo, M. 1997. *Just Revenge.* New York: St. Martin's Press.

Conway, P. 2001. "The 2001 Electronic Monitoring Survey." *Journal of Electronic Monitoring* 14 (Winter–Spring): 7–9.

Cooney, M. 1994. "Evidence as Partisanship." *Law and Society Review* 28:833–58.

Crawford, C. 2000. "Gender, Race, and Habitual Offender Sentencing in Florida." *Criminology* 38 (February): 263–80.

Crawford, C., T. Chiricos, and G. Kleck. 1998. "Race, Racial Threat, and Sentencing of Habitual Offenders." *Criminology* 36 (August): 481–512.

Crew, B. K. 1991. "Race Differences in Felony Charging Sentencing: Toward an Integration of Decision-Making and Negotiation Models." *Journal of Crime and Justice* 14:99–122.

"Crime Rate Rising Again." 2002. *BBC News.* June 16 (http://www.bbc.com).

Criminal Justice Newsletter. 1994. January 8, p. 1.

Criminal Justice Research Reports. 2001. July–August, p. 87.

Crocker, L. 1993. "Can the Exclusionary Rule Be Saved?" *Journal of Criminal Law and Criminology* 84:310–51.

Crouch, B. M., and J. M. Marquart. 1989. *An Appeal to Justice.* Austin: University of Texas Press.

———. 1994. "On Becoming a Prison Guard." In *The Administration and Management of Criminal Justice Organizations,* 2nd ed., ed. S. Stojokovic, J. Klofas, and D. Kalinich. Prospect Heights, Ill.: Waveland Press.

Cullen, F. T., L. Cao, J. Frank, R. H. Langworthy, S. L. Browning, R. Kopache, and T. J. Stevenson. 1996. "'Stop or I'll Shoot': Racial Differences in Support for Police Use of Deadly Force on Fleeing Felons." *American Behavioral Scientist* 39 (February): 449.

Cullen, F. T., T. Leming, B. Link, and J. Wozniak. 1985. "The Impact of Social Supports in Police Stress." *Criminology* 23:503–22.

Cullen, F. T., J. P. Wright, and B. K. Applegate. 1996. "Control in the Community: The Limits of Reform?" In *Choosing Correctional Options that Work: Defining the Demand and Evaluating the Supply,* ed. A. T. Harland. Thousand Oaks, Calif.: Sage, 69–116.

Cunningham, W. C., J. J. Strauchs, and C. W. Van Meter. 1990. *Private Security Trends, 1970 to the Year 2000.* Boston: Butterworth-Heinemann.

Daly, K. 1998. "Gender, Crime, and Criminology." In *The Handbook of Crime and Punishment,* ed. M. Tonry. New York: Oxford University Press, 85–108.

Daly, K., and M. Chesney-Lind. 1988. "Feminism and Criminology." *Justice Quarterly* 5:497.

Davitz, T. 1998. "The Gangs Behind Bars." *Insight on the News,* September 28.

Davey, J. D. 1998. *The Politics of Prison Expansion: Winning Elections by Waging War on Crime.* Westport, Conn.: Praeger.

Davies, T. Y. 1983. "A Hard Look at What We Know (and Still Need to Learn) About the 'Costs' of the Exclusionary Rule: The NIJ Study and Other Studies of 'Lost' Arrests." *American Bar Foundation Research Journal* 1983:611–90.

Davis, A. 2001. "Laptop Computers in Police Cars Keep Officers Informed, on Streets." *Arkansas Democrat-Gazette,* February 24, p. B3.

Davis, M., R. Lundman, and R. Martinez, Jr. 1991. "Private Corporate Justice: Store Police, Shoplifters, and Civil Recovery." *Social Problems* 38: 395–408.

Dawson, M., and R. Dinovitzer. 2001. "Victim Cooperation and the Prosecution of Domestic Violence in a Specialized Court." *Justice Quarterly* 18:593–622.

Decker, S. H., and B. Van Winkle. 1996. *Life in the Gang: Families, Friends, and Violence.* New York: Cambridge University Press.

Decker, S., R. Wright, A. Redfern, and D. Smith. 1993. "A Woman's Place Is in the Home: Females and Residential Burglary." *Justice Quarterly* 10 (March): 142.

DeFrances, C. J. 2002. "Prosecutors in State Courts, 2001." Bureau of Justice Statistics *Bulletin,* May.

DeFrances, C. J., and J. Litras. 2000. "Indigent Defense Services in Large Counties, 1999." Bureau of Justice Statistics *Bulletin,* November.

DeJong, C., S. Mastrofski, and R. Parks. 2001. "Patrol Officers and Problem Solving: An Application of Expectancy Theory." *Justice Quarterly* 18:31–61.

Deutsch, L. 2002. "Trial Date Set in Winona Ryder Shoplifting Case after Plea Deal Efforts Fail." Associated Press Wire Service, September 18.

Diggs, D. W., and S. L. Peiper. 1994. "Using Day Reporting Centers as an Alternative to Jail." *Federal Probation* 58 (March): 9–13.

DiIulio, J. J., Jr. 1987. *Governing Prisons.* New York: Free Press.

———. 1991. *No Escape: The Future of American Corrections.* New York: Basic Books.

———. 1993. "Rethinking the Criminal Justice System: Toward a New Paradigm." In *Performance Measures for the Criminal Justice System.* Washington, D.C.: Bureau of Justice Statistics, U.S. Government Printing Office.

———. 1994. "The Question of Black Crime." *The Public Interest* (Fall): 3–32.

Dill, F. 1975. "Discretion, Exchange, and Social Control: Bail Bondsmen in Criminal Courts." *Law and Society Review* 9:644–74.

Dillehay, R. C., and M. R. Sandys. 1996. "Life under *Wainwright v. Witt:* Juror Dispositions and Death Qualification." *Law and Human Behavior* 20:147–65.

Dodge, J., and M. Pogrebin. 2001. "African-American Policewomen: An Exploration of Professional Relationships." *Policing* 24:550–52.

Donohue, J. J., and S. D. Levitt. 1998. "The Impact of Race on Policing, Arrest Patterns, and Crime." American Bar Foundation Working Paper #9705 (Revision).

Donziger, S. R., ed. 1996. *The Real War on Crime: The Report of the National Criminal Justice Commission.* New York: Harper Collins.

Dooley, E. E. 1981. "Sir Walter Crofton and the Irish or Intermediate System of Prison Discipline." *New England Journal of Prison Law* 575 (Winter).

Dreitzler, B., and M. Lafferty. 2001. "Missing Car Leads to Body in Trailer." *Columbus Dispatch,* December 12, p. 1A.

Drimmer, J. 1997. "America's Least Wanted: We Need New Rules to Stop Abuses." *Washington Post,* September 21, p. C6.

Dugan, L. 1999. "The Effect of Criminal Victimization on a Household's Moving Decision." *Criminology* 37:903–30.

Dugdale, R. 1910. *The Jukes: Crime, Pauperism, Disease, and Heredity.* 4th ed. New York: Putnam.

Dumaine, B. 1998. "Beating Bolder Corporate Crooks." *Fortune,* April 25, p. 193.

Dwyer, J., P. Neufeld, and B. Scheck. 2001. *Actual Innocence: When Justice Goes Wrong and How to Make It Right.* New York: New American Library.

Earley, P. 1992. *The Hot House: Life inside Leavenworth Prison.* New York: Bantam Books.

Egan, T. 1999. "A Drug Ran Its Course, Then Hid with Its Users." *New York Times,* September 19, p. A1.

Eigenberg, H. 2000. "Correctional Officers, and their Perceptions of Homosexuality, Rape, and Prosecution in Male Prisons." *Prison Journal* 80 (December): 415–33.

Eisenstein, J., R. B. Flemming, and P. F. Nardulli. 1988. *The Contours of Justice: Communities and Their Courts.* Boston: Little, Brown.

Eisenstein, J., and H. Jacob. 1977. *Felony Justice: An Organizational Analysis of Criminal Courts.* Boston: Little, Brown.

Eitle, D. J. 2000. "Regulatory Justice: A Re-Examination of the Influence of Class Position on the Punishment of White-Collar Crime." *Justice Quarterly* 17:809–35.

Emmelman, D. S. 1996. "Trial by Plea Bargain: Case Settlement as a Product of Recursive Decisionmaking." *Law and Society Review* 30:335–60.

Engel, R. S., J. M. Calnon, and T. J. Bernard. 2002. "Theory and Racial Profiling: Shortcomings and Future Directions in Research." *Justice Quarterly* 19:249–73.

Erikson, Kai T. 1966. *Wayward Puritans.* New York: Wiley.

Estrich, S. 1998. *Getting away with Murder: How Politics Is Destroying the Criminal Justice System.* Cambridge, Mass.: Harvard University Press.

Fabelo, T. 1999. *Biennial Report to the 76th Texas Legislature.* Austin, Texas: Criminal Justice Policy Council.

Farrell, M. 2002. "No Surrender: Rigases Arrested; Adelphia Five Face Charges They 'Looted on Massive Scale'." *Multichannel News* (Reed Business Information), July 29 (available on Lexis-Nexis).

FBI (Federal Bureau of Investigation). 2001. *Crime in the United States—2000.* Washington, D.C.: U.S. Government Printing Office.

———. 2002. *National Press Release: Crime Trends, 2001 Preliminary Figures.* June 24 (http://www.fbi.gov).

Federal Bureau of Prisons. 2000. *State of the Bureau: Accomplishments and Goals.* Washington, D.C.: U.S. Government Printing Office.

Feeley, M. M. 1983. *Court Reform on Trial.* New York: Basic Books.

Feeley, M. M., and R. A. Hanson. 1990. "The Impact of Judicial Intervention on Prisons and Jails: A Framework of Analysis and a Review of the Literature." In *Courts, Corrections, and the Constitution,* ed. J. J. DiIulio, Jr. New York: Oxford University Press.

Feeney, F. 1998. *German and American Prosecution: An Approach to Statistical Comparison.* Washington, D.C.: Bureau of Justice Statistics, U.S. Government Printing Office.

Feld, B. C. 1993. "Criminalizing the American Juvenile Court." In *Crime and Justice: A Review of Research,* vol. 17, ed. M. Tonry. Chicago: University of Chicago Press, 197–280.

———. 1999. *Bad Kids: Race and the Transformation of the Juvenile Court.* New York: Oxford University Press.

Felice, J. D., and J. C. Kilwein. 1992. "Strike One, Strike Two . . . : The History and Prospect for Judicial Reform in Ohio." *Judicature* 75:193–200.

Felson, R. B., and J. Ackerman. 2001. "Arrest for Domestic and Other Assaults." *Criminology* 39:655–75.

Finn, M. A. 2002. "Police Handling of the Mentally Ill in Domestic Violence Situations." *Criminal Justice and Behavior* 29:278–307.

Fishbein, D. H. 1990. "Biological Perspectives in Criminology." *Criminology* 28:27.

Fishman, J. 1934. *Sex in Prison.* New York: National Liberty Press.

Flanagan, T. J., ed. 1995. *Long-Term Imprisonment.* Thousand Oaks, Calif.: Sage.

Flanagan, T. J., and K. Maguire. 1993. "A Full Employment Policy for Prisons in the United States: Some Arguments, Estimates, and Implications." *Journal of Criminal Justice* 21: 117–30.

Flango, V. E. 1994. *Habeas Corpus in State and Federal Courts.* Williamsburg, Va.: National Center for State Courts.

Fleisher, M. 1989. *Warehousing Violence.* Newbury Park, Calif.: Sage.

Flemming, R. B., P. F. Nardulli, and J. Eisenstein. 1992. *The Craft of Justice: Politics and Work in Criminal Court Communities.* Philadelphia: University of Pennsylvania Press.

Fletcher, George P. 1988. *A Crime of Self-Defense: Bernhard Goetz and the Law on Trial.* New York: Free Press.

Foucault, M. 1977. *Discipline and Punish.* Translated by A. Sheridan. New York: Pantheon.

Fox, J. G. 1982. *Organizational and Racial Conflict in Maximum Security Prisons.* Lexington, Mass.: Lexington Books.

Foy, Paul. 1999. "Utah Liquor Laws Gaining Notoriety." *Lansing State Journal,* June 26, p. 5A.

Frank, J., S. G. Brandl, F. T. Cullen, and A. Stichman. 1996. "Reassessing the Impact of Race on Citizens' Attitudes toward the Police: A Research Note." *Justice Quarterly* 13 (June): 320–34.

Friday, P. C., S. Metzger, and D. Walters. 1991. "Policing Domestic Violence: Perceptions, Experience, and Reality." *Criminal Justice Review* 16:198–213.

Fridell, L. 1990. "Decision Making of the District Attorney: Diverting or Prosecuting Intrafamilial Child Sexual Abuse Offenders." *Criminal Justice Policy Review* 4:249–67.

Friedman, L. M. 1993. *Crime and Punishment in American History.* New York: Basic Books.

Friedrichs, D. O. 1996. *Trusted Criminals: White-Collar Crime in Society.* Belmont, Calif.: Wadsworth.

Frohmann, L. 1997. "Convictability and Discordant Locales: Reproducing Race, Class, and Gender Ideologies in Prosecutorial Decisionmaking." *Law and Society Review* 31:531–56.

Fukurai, H. 1996. "Race, Social Class, and Jury Participation: New Dimensions for Evaluating Discrimination in Jury Service and Jury Selection." *Journal of Criminal Justice* 24:71–88.

Fyfe, J. 1993. "Police Use of Deadly Force: Research and Reform." In *Criminal Justice: Law and Politics,* 6th ed, ed. G. F. Cole. Belmont, Calif.: Wadsworth.

Fyfe, J., D. A. Klinger, and J. M. Flavin, 1997. "Differential Policy Treatment of Male-on-Female Spousal Violence." *Criminology* 35 (August): 454–73.

Gallup Poll. 1999. "Racial Attitudes toward the Police." December 11 (http://www.gallup.com).

Gardner, M. A. 1993. "Section 1983 Actions under *Miranda:* A Critical View of the Right to Avoid Interrogation." *American Criminal Law Review* 30: 1277–328.

Garner, J., and E. Clemmer. 1986. *Danger to Police in Domestic Disturbances—A New Look.* Washington, D.C.: Bureau of Justice Statistics, U.S. Government Printing Office.

Garner, J. H., and C. D. Maxwell. 1999. "Measuring the Amount of Force by and against the Police in Six Jurisdictions." In *Use of Force by the Police.* Washington, D.C.: National Institute of Justice, U.S. Government Printing Office.

Garner J., T. Schade, J. Hepburn, and J. Buchanan. 1995. "Measuring the Continuum of Forced Used by and against the Police." *Criminal Justice Review* 20 (Autumn): 146–68.

Garofalo, J., and M. McLeod. 1989. "The Structure and Operation of Neighborhood Watch Programs in the United States." *Crime and Delinquency* 35:326–44.

Gaylin, W. 1997. *The Killing of Bonnie Garland.* Rev. ed. New York: Simon & Schuster.

Geis, G., and L. B. Bienen. 1998. *Crimes of the Century: From Leopold and Loeb to O. J. Simpson.* Boston: Northeastern University Press.

Geller, W. A., ed. 1985. *Police Leadership in America.* New York: Praeger.

Geller, W. A., and Morris, N. 1992. "Relations between Federal and Local Police." In *Modern Policing,* ed. M. Tonry and N. Morris. Chicago: University of Chicago Press, 231–348.

Gendreau, P., F. T. Cullen, and J. Bonta. 1994. "Intensive Rehabilitation Supervision: The Next Generation in Community Corrections?" *Federal Probation* 58:72–78.

Gershman, B. L. 1993. "Themes of Injustice: Wrongful Convictions, Racial Prejudice, and Lawyer Incompetence." *Criminal Law Bulletin* 29:502–15.

Gest, T. 2001. *Crime and Politics: Big Government's Erratic Campaign for Law and Order.* New York: Oxford University Press.

Gill, M. S. 1997. "Cybercops Take a Byte out of Computer Crime." *Smithsonian,* May, pp. 114–24.

Girshick, L. B. 1999. *No Safe Haven: Stories of Women in Prison.* Boston: Northeastern University Press.

Glaberson, W. 2002. "On Eve of Trial, Ex-Officer Agrees to Perjury Term in Louima Case." *New York Times,* September 22, p. 1.

Glick, R. M., and V. V. Neto. 1977. *National Study of Women's Correctional Programs.* Washington, D.C.: U.S. Government Printing Office.

Goddard, H. H. 1902. *The Kallikak Family.* New York: Macmillan.

Goldfarb, R. L. 1965. *Ransom: A Critique of the American Bail System.* New York: Harper & Row.

Goldfarb, R. L., and L. R. Singer. 1973. *After Conviction.* New York: Simon & Schuster.

Goldkamp, J. S. 1985. "Danger and Detention: A Second Generation of Bail Reform." *Journal of Criminal Law and Criminology* 76:1–75.

———. 1995. *Personal Liberty and Community Safety: Pretrial Release in Criminal Court.* New York: Plenum.

———. 2002. "Skakel Is Found Guilty of 1975 Moxley Murder." *Los Angeles Times,* June 8.

Goldman, S., and Slotnick, E. 1999. "Clinton's Second Term Judiciary: Picking Judges under Fire." *Judicature* 82:264–85.

Goldschmidt, J., and J. M. Shaman. 1996. "Judicial Disqualifications: What Do Judges Think?" *Judicature* 80:68–72.

Goldstein, H. 1977. *Policing a Free Society.* Cambridge, Mass.: Ballinger.

———. 1979. "Improving Policing: A Problem-oriented Approach." *Crime and Delinquency* 25:236–57.

———. 1990. *Problem-oriented Policing.* New York: McGraw-Hill.

Goodman, J. 1994. *Stories of Scottsboro.* New York: Random House.

Goodpaster, G. 1986. "The Adversary System, Advocacy, and Effective Assistance of Counsel in Criminal Cases." *New York University Review of Law and Social Change* 14:90.

Goolkasian, G. A., R. W. Geddes, and W. DeJong. 1989. "Coping with Police Stress." In *Critical Issues in Policing,* ed. R. G. Dunham and G. P. Alpert. Prospect Heights, Ill.: Waveland Press, 489–507.

Gordon, D. 2002. "Reality Bites." *Newsweek,* June 17, p. 62.

Gottfredson, M., and T. Hirschi. 1990. *A General Theory of Crime.* Stanford, Calif.: Stanford University Press.

Graham, B. L. 1995. "Judicial Recruitment and Racial Diversity on State Courts." In *Courts and Justice,* ed. G. L. Mays and P. R. Gregware. Prospect Heights, Ill.: Waveland Press.

Grano, J. D. 1996. *Confessions, Truth, and the Law.* Ann Arbor: University of Michigan Press.

Green, G. S. 1992. *Occupational Crime.* 2nd ed. Chicago: Nelson-Hall.

Greene, J. A. 1999. "Zero Tolerance: A Case Study of Police Policies and Practices in New York City." *Crime and Delinquency* 45 (April): 171–87.

Greenwood, P., J. M. Chaiken, and J. Petersilia. 1977. *Criminal Investigation Process.* Lexington, Mass.: Lexington Books.

Greer, K. R. 2000. "The Changing Nature of Interpersonal Relationships in a Women's Prison." *Prison Journal* 80 (December): 442–68.

Grennan, S. A. 1987. "Findings on the Role of Officer Gender in Violent Encounters with Citizens." *Journal of Police Science and Administration* 15:78–85.

Griffin, A., and F. Rhee. 1999. "Twins, 11, Held in Gory Shooting of Parents, Sister." *Charlotte Observer,* April 3.

Griset, P. L. 1993. "Determinate Sentencing and the High Cost of Overblown Rhetoric: The New York Experience." *Crime and Delinquency* 39 (April): 552.

———. 1995. "The Politics and Economics of Increased Correctional Discretion over Time Served: A New York Case Study." *Justice Quarterly* 12 (June): 307.

Haarr, R. N., and M. Morash. 1999. "Gender, Race and Strategies of Coping with Occupational Stress in Policing." *Justice Quarterly* 16:303–36.

Hagan, F. E. 1997. *Political Crime: Ideology and Criminality.* Needham Heights, Mass.: Allyn and Bacon.

Hagan, J., and R. D. Peterson. 1995. "Criminal Inequality in America: Patterns and Consequences." In *Crime and Inequality,* ed. J. Hagan and R. D. Peterson. Stanford, Calif.: Stanford University Press, 14–36.

Haghighi, B., and J. Sorensen. 1996. "America's Fear of Crime." In *Americans View Crime and Justice,* ed. T. Flanaghan and D. R. Longmire. Thousand Oaks, Calif.: Sage, 16–30.

Hall, J. 1947. *General Principles of Criminal Law.* 2nd ed. Indianapolis: Bobbs-Merrill.

Hall, M. G. 1995. "Justices as Representatives: Elections and Judicial Politics in the United States." *American Politics Quarterly* 23:485–503.

Hall, W. K., and L. T. Aspin. 1987. "What Twenty Years of Judicial Retention Elections Have Told Us." *Judicature* 70:340.

Hallinan, J. T. 2001. *Going up the River: Travels in a Prison Nation.* New York: Random House.

Hans, V., and N. Vidmar. 1986. *Judging the Jury.* New York: Plenum Press.

Hanson, R. A., and J. Chapper. 1991. *Indigent Defense Systems.* Williamsburg, Va.: National Center for State Courts.

Hanson, R. A., and H. W. K. Daley. 1995. *Challenging the Conditions of Prisons and Jails: A Report on Section 1983 Litigation.* Washington, D.C.: Bureau of Justice Statistics, U.S. Government Printing Office.

Harlow, C. 2000. "Defense Counsel in Criminal Cases." Bureau of Justice Statistics *Bulletin,* November.

Hastie, R., S. Penrod, and N. Pennington. 1983. *Inside the Jury.* Cambridge, Mass.: Harvard University Press.

Hathaway, W. 2002. "A Clue to Antisocial Behavior: Study Finds Gene Marker for Which Abused Children May Become Troubled Adults." *Hartford Courant,* August 2, p. A17.

Heffernan, E. 1972. *Making It in Prison.* New York: Wiley.

Heidensohn, F. M. 1985. *Women and Crime.* New York: New York University Press.

Heilbroner, David. 1990. *Rough Justice: Days and Nights of a Young D.A.* New York: Pantheon Books.

Henning, P. J. 1993. "Precedents in a Vacuum: The Supreme Court Continues to Tinker with Double Jeopardy." *American Criminal Law Review* 31:1–72.

Hensley, T. R., and C. E. Smith. 1995. "Membership Change and Voting Change: An Analysis of the Rehnquist Court's 1986–1991 Terms." *Political Research Quarterly* 48:837–56.

Hepburn, J. R. 1985. "The Exercise of Power in Coercive Organizations: A Study of Prison Guards." *Criminology* 23: 145–64.

Hepburn, J. R., and P. E. Knepper. 1993. "Correctional Officers as Human Services Workers: The Effect of Job Satisfaction." *Justice Quarterly* 10 (June): 315.

Herbert, S. 1996. "Morality in Law Enforcement: Chasing 'Bad Guys' with the Los Angeles Police Department." *Law and Society Review* 30:799–818.

Herrnstein, R. J. 1995. "Criminogenic Traits." In *Crime,* ed. J. Q. Wilson and J. Petersilia. San Francisco: ICS Press.

Heumann, M. 1978. *Plea Bargaining.* Chicago: University of Chicago Press.

Hickey, T. J. 1993. "Expanding the Use of Prior Act Evidence in Rape and Sexual Assault." *Criminal Law Bulletin* 29: 195–218.

———. 1995. "A Double Jeopardy Analysis of the Medgar Evers Murder Case." *Journal of Criminal Justice* 23:41–51.

Hickman, M. J., and B. A. Reaves. 2001. *Local Police Departments, 1999.* Washington, D.C.: Bureau of Justice Statistics, U.S. Government Printing Office.

Hillsman, S. T., J. L. Sichel, and B. Mahoney. 1983. *Fines in Sentencing.* New York: Vera Institute of Justice.

Hirsch, A. J. 1992. *The Rise of the Penitentiary.* New Haven, Conn.: Yale University Press.

Hirschi, T. 1969. *Causes of Delinquency.* Berkeley: University of California Press.

Ho, N. T. 2000. "Domestic Violence in a Southern City: The Effects of a Mandatory Arrest Policy on Male-Versus-Female Aggravated Assault Incidents." *American Journal of Criminal Justice* 25:107–18.

Ho, T. 1998. "Retardation, Criminality, and Competency to Stand Trial among Mentally Retarded Criminal Defendants: Violent versus Non-violent Defendants." *Journal of Crime and Justice* 21:57–70.

Hoctor, M. 1997. "Domestic Violence as a Crime against the State." *California Law Review* 85 (May): 643.

Hoffman, M. 1999. "Abolish Peremptory Challenges." *Judicature* 82:202–4.

Holmes, M. D. 2000. "Minority Threat and Police Brutality: Determinants of Civil Rights Criminal Complaints in U.S. Municipalities." *Criminology* 38:343–67.

Holmes, M. D., H. M. Hosch, H. C. Daudistel, D. A. Perez, and J. B. Graves. 1996. "Ethnicity, Legal Resources, and Felony Dispositions in Two Southwestern Jurisdictions." *Justice Quarterly* 13:11–29.

Holmes, O. W., Jr. 1881. *The Common Law.* Boston: Little, Brown.

Horney, J., and C. Spohn. 1991. "Rape Law Reform and Instrumental Change in Six Urban Jurisdictions." *Law and Society Review* 25:117–53.

Houston, B., and J. Ewing. 1991. "Justice Jailed." *Hartford Courant,* June 16, p. A1.

Howard, J. 1929. *The State of Prisons in England and Wales.* London: J. M. Dent.

Huff, C. R. 2002. "Wrongful Conviction and Public Policy: The American Society of Criminology 2001 Presidential Address." *Criminology* 40:1–18.

Huff, C. R., and M. Meyer. 1997. "Managing Prison Gangs and Other Security Threat Groups." *Corrections Management Quarterly* 1 (Fall): 11.

Humes, E. 1999. *Mean Justice: A Town's Terror, a Prosecutor's Power, a Betrayal of Innocence.* New York: Simon & Schuster.

Hunt, G., S. Riegel, T. Morales, and D. Waldorf. 1993. "Changes in Prison Culture: Prison Gangs and the Case of the Pepsi Generation." *Social Problems* 40:398–409.

Ianni, F. A. J. 1973. *Ethnic Succession in Organized Crime.* Washington, D.C.: U.S. Government Printing Office.

Innes, C. A., and V. D. Verdeyen. 1997. "Conceptualizing the Management of Violent Inmates." *Corrections Management Quarterly* 1 (Fall): 1–9.

International Association of Chiefs of Police. 1998. *The Future of Women in Policing: Mandates for Action.* Alexandria, Va.: Author.

Irwin, J. 1970. *The Felon.* Englewood Cliffs, N.J.: Prentice-Hall.

———. 1980. *Prisons in Turmoil.* Boston: Little, Brown.

Irwin, J., and J. Austin. 2001. *It's About Time: America's Imprisonment Binge.* 3rd ed. Belmont, Calif.: Wadsworth.

Irwin, J., and D. Cressey. 1962. "Thieves, Convicts, and the Inmate Culture." *Social Problems* 10:142–55.

Italiano, 1999. "Kendra's Kin Despair at Hung Jury." *New York Post,* November 3.

Ith, I. 2001. "Taser Fails to Halt Man with Knife; Seattle Officer Kills 23-Year-Old." *Seattle Times,* November 28, p. A1.

Jacob, H. 1973. *Urban Justice.* Boston: Little, Brown.

Jacobs, J. B. 1977. *Stateville.* Chicago: University of Chicago Press.

———. 1995. "Judicial Impact on Prison Reform." In *Punishment and Social Control,* ed. T. G. Blomberg and S. Cohen. New York: Aldine DeGruyter, 63–76.

Jacobs, J. B., and C. Panarella. 1998. "Organized Crime." In *The Handbook of Crime and Punishment,* ed. M. Tonry. New York: Oxford University Press, 159–77.

Jacobs, J. B., C. Panarella, and J. Worthington. 1994. *Busting the Mob:* United States v. Cosa Nostra. New York: New York University Press.

Jacoby, J. 1979. "The Charging Policies of Prosecutors." In *The Prosecutor,* ed. W. F. McDonald. Beverly Hills, Calif.: Sage.

———. 1995. "Pushing the Envelope: Leadership in Prosecution." *Justice System Journal* 17:291–307.

Jenne, D. L., and R.C. Kersting. 1996. "Aggression and Women Correctional Officers in Male Prisons." *Prison Journal* 76:442–60.

Johnson, D. T. 1998. "The Organization of Prosecution and the Possibility of Order." *Law and Society Review* 32:247–308.

Johnson, R. 1998. *Death Work.* 2nd ed. Belmont, Calif.: Wadsworth.

Johnson, R. 2002. *Hard Time: Understanding and Reforming the Prison.* 3rd ed. Belmont, Calif.: Wadsworth.

Jordan, J. 2002. "Will Any Woman Do? Police, Gender and Rape Victims." *Policing* 25:319–44.

Josephson, R. L., and M. Reiser. 1990. "Officer Suicide in the Los Angeles Police Department." *Journal of Police Science and Administration* 17:227–29.

Kadlec, D. 2002. "WorldCon." *Time Magazine,* July 8, pp. 20–26.

Kalinich, D. B. 1980. *Power, Stability, and Contraband.* Prospect Heights, Ill.: Waveland Press.

Kampeas, R. 2001. "Terror Attacks Bring Profound Changes in FBI Focus, Challenges for New Director." Associated Press News Service, October 27.

Kappeler, V. E., M. Blumberg, and G. W. Potter. 1996. *The Mythology of Crime and Criminal Justice.* 2nd ed. Prospect Heights, Ill.: Waveland Press.

Karmen, A. 2001. *Crime Victims.* 4th ed. Belmont, Calif.: Wadsworth.

Katz, J. 1988. *Seductions of Crime: Moral and Sensual Attractions of Doing Evil.* New York: Basic Books.

Katz, L. 1987. *Bad Acts and Guilty Minds.* Chicago: University of Chicago Press.

Kauffman, K. 1988. *Prison Officers and Their World.* Cambridge, Mass.: Harvard University Press.

Kelling, G. L. 1985. "Order Maintenance, the Quality of Urban Life, and Police: A Line of Argument." In *Police Leadership in America,* ed. W. A. Geller. New York: Praeger.

———. 1991. *Foot Patrol.* Washington, D.C.: National Institute of Justice, U.S. Government Printing Office.

———. 1992. "Measuring What Matters: A New Way of Thinking about Crime and Public Order." *City Journal* 2 (Spring): 21–31.

Kelling, G. L., and C. M. Coles. 1996. *Fixing Broken Windows: Restoring and Reducing Crime in Our Communities.* New York: Free Press.

Kelling, G. L., and M. Moore. 1988. "The Evolving Strategy of Policing." In *Perspectives on Policing,* no. 13. Washington, D.C.: National Institute of Justice, U.S. Government Printing Office.

Kelling, G. L., T. Pate, D. Dieckman, and C. E. Brown. 1974. *The Kansas City Preventive Patrol Experiments: A Summary Report.* Washington, D.C.: Police Foundation.

Kennedy, R. 1997. *Race, Crime, and the Law.* New York: Pantheon.

Kenney, D. J., and J. O. Finckenauer. 1995. *Organized Crime in America.* Belmont, Calif.: Wadsworth.

Kerry, J. S. 1997. *The New War.* New York: Simon & Schuster.

King, N. J. 1994. "The Effects of Race-Conscious Jury Selection on Public Confidence in the Fairness of Jury Proceedings: An Empirical Puzzle." *American Criminal Law Review* 31: 1177–202.

Kingsnorth, R., R. MacIntosh, and S. Sutherland. 2002. "Criminal Charge or Probation Violation? Prosecutorial Discretion and Implications for Research in Criminal Court Processing." *Criminology* 40:553–77.

Klein, Malcolm W. 1996. *The American Street Gang: Its Nature, Prevalence, and Control.* New York: Oxford University Press.

Kleinknecht, W. 1996. *The New Ethnic Mobs: The Changing Face of Organized Crime in America.* New York: Free Press.

Klockars, C. B. 1985. "Order Maintenance, the Quality of Urban Life, and Police: A Different Line of Argument," *Police Leadership in America,* ed. W. A. Geller. New York: Praeger.

Klofas, J., and J. Yandrasits. 1989. "'Guilty but Mentally Ill' and the Jury Trial: A Case Study." *Criminal Law Bulletin* 24:424.

Knox, G. W. 2000. "A National Assessment of Gangs and Security Threat Groups (STGs) in Adult Correctional Institutions: Results of the 1999 Adult Corrections Survey." *Journal of Gang Research* 7:1–45.

Kolbert, E. 1999. "The Perils of Safety." *New Yorker,* March 22, p. 50.

Koper, C. 1995. "Just Enough Police Presence: Reducing Crime and Disorderly Behavior by Optimizing Patrol Time in Crime Hot Spots." *Justice Quarterly* 12 (December): 649–72.

Kotlowitz, A. 1992. *There Are No Children Here: The Story of Two Boys Growing up in the Other America.* New York: Anchor.

———. 1994. "Their Crimes Don't Make Them Adults." *The New York Times Magazine,* February 13, p. 40.

Kramer, G. P., and D. M. Koenig. 1990. "Do Jurors Understand Criminal Justice Instructions? Analyzing the Results of the Michigan Juror Comprehension Project." *University of Michigan Journal of Law Reform* 23:401–37.

Kramer, J. H., and J. T. Ulmer. 1996. "Sentencing Disparity and Departures from Guidelines." *Justice Quarterly* 13 (March): 81.

Krauss, C. 1994. "No Crystal Ball Needed on Crime." *New York Times,* November 13, sec. 4, p. 4.

Kridler, C. 1999. "Sergeant Friday, Where Are You?" *Newsweek,* May 17, p. 14.

Krimmel, J. T. 1996. "The Performance of College-Educated Police: A Study of Self-Rated Performance Measures." *American Journal of Policing* 15: 85–96.

Kruttschnitt, C., and S. Krmopotich. 1990. "Aggressive Behavior among Female Inmates: An Exploratory Study." *Justice Quarterly* 7 (June): 371.

Kunen, J. S. 1995. "Teaching Prisoners a Lesson." *New Yorker,* July 10, p. 34.

Kurtz, H. 1997. "The Crime Spree on Network News." *Washington Post,* August 12, p. 1.

Labaton, S. 2002. "Downturn and Shift in Population Feed Boom in White-Collar Crime." *New York Times,* June 2, pp. 1, 22.

Laffey, M. 1998. "Cop Diary" *New Yorker,* August 10, pp. 36–39.

———. 1999. "Cop Diary." *New Yorker,* February 1, pp. 29–32.

Langan, P. A. 1994. "Between Prison and Probation: Intermediate Sanctions." *Science* 264 (May): 791–93.

Langbein, J. H. 1992. "On the Myth of Written Constitutions: The Disappearance of the Criminal Jury Trial." *Harvard Journal of Law and Public Policy* 15:119–27.

Langworthy, R. H. 1989. "Do Stings Control Crime? An Evaluation of a Police Fencing Operation." *Justice Quarterly* 6 (March): 27.

Langworthy, R. H., T. Hughes, and B. Sanders. 1995. *Law Enforcement Recruitment Selection and Training: A Survey of Major Police Departments.* Highland Heights, Ill.: Academy of Criminal Justice Sciences.

Lauritsen, J., and N. White. 2001. "Putting Violence in Its Place: The Influence of Race, Ethnicity, Gender, and Place on the Risk for Violence." *Criminology and Public Policy* 1:37–59.

Lave, T. R. 1998. "Equal before the Law." *Newsweek,* July 13, p. 14.

"Law Enforcement Solution." 2002. October 10 (http://www.cisco.com).

Lear, E. T. 1995. "Contemplating the Successive Prosecution Phenomenon in the Federal System." *Journal of Criminal Law and Criminology* 85:625–75.

Lee, M. S., and J. T. Ulmer. 2000. "Fear of Crime among Korean Americans in Chicago Communities." *Criminology* 38: 1173–206.

Leo, R. A. 1996a. "The Impact of *Miranda* Revisited." *Journal of Criminal Law and Criminology* 86:621–92.

Leo, R. A. 1996b. "*Miranda*'s Revenge: Police Interrogation as a Confidence Game." *Law and Society Review* 30:259–88.

Leonard, J. 2002. "Dropping 'Nonlethal' Beanbags as Too Dangerous." *Los Angeles Times,* June 3, p. 1.

Lerner, J. R. 2002. *You Got Nothing Coming: Notes from a Prison Fish.* New York: Broadway Books.

Lersch, K. M. 2002. "Are Citizen Complaints Just Another Measure of Officer Productivity? An Analysis of Citizen Complaints and Officer Activity Measures." *Police Practices and Research* 3:135–47.

Lersch, K. M., and L. Kunzman. 2001. "Misconduct Allegations and Higher Education in a Southern Sheriff's Department." *American Journal of Criminal Justice* 25:161–72.

Levine, J. P. 1992. *Juries and Politics.* Belmont, Calif.: Wadsworth.

Levy, S. 1997. "A Guru Goes Free." *Newsweek,* December 15, p. 44.

Lewis, A. 1964. *Gideon's Trumpet.* New York: Vintage.

Lewis, N. 1999. "Prosecutors Urged to Allow Appeals on DNA." *New York Times,* September 28, p. 14.

Lilly, J. R. 1993. "The Corrections-Commercial Complex." *Crime and Delinquency* 39 (April): 150.

Liptak, A. 2002. "Citing Cost, Judge Rejects Death Penalty." August 18 (http://www.nytimes.com).

Liptak, A., N. Lewis, and B. Weiser. 2002. "After Sept. 11, a Legal Battle on the Limits of Civil Liberty." *New York Times,* August 4, pp. 1, 16.

Liska, A. E., and S. F. Messner. 1999. *Perspectives on Crime and Deviance.* 3rd ed. Upper Saddle River, N.J.: Prentice-Hall.

Logan, C. 1992. "Well Kept: Comparing Quality of Confinement in Private and Public Prisons." *Journal of Criminal Law and Criminology* 83 (Fall): 577.

———. 1993. "Criminal Justice Performance Measures in Prisons." In *Performance Measures for the Criminal Justice System.* Washington, D.C.: Bureau of Justice Statistics, U.S. Government Printing Office, 19–60.

Logan, C., and J. J. DiIulio, Jr. 1993. "Ten Deadly Myths about Crime and Punishment in the United States." In *Criminal Justice: Law and Politics,* ed. G. F. Cole. Belmont, Calif.: Wadsworth, 486–502.

Lombroso, C. 1968 [1912]. *Crime: Its Causes and Remedies.* Montclair, N.J.: Patterson Smith.

Loof, S. 1999. "Both Sides Argue over Boy's Confession." *Lansing State Journal,* January 7.

Lorentzen, A. 2002. "Trooper Who Had Stopped Bank Suspect Kills Self." *Seattle Times,* September 28 (http://www.seattletimes.com).

Love, M., and S. Kuzma. 1996. *Civil Disabilities of Convicted Felons.* Washington, D.C.: Office of the Pardon Attorney, U.S. Government Printing Office.

Loviglio, J. 2002. "Judge Reverses Himself, Will Allow Fingerprint-Analysis Testimony." Associated Press Wire Service, March 13 (available on Lexis-Nexis).

Lovrich, N. P., and C. H. Sheldon. 1994. "Is Voting for State Judges a Flight of Fancy or a Reflection of Policy and Value Preferences?" *Justice System Journal* 16:57–71.

Luginbuhl, J., and M. Burkhead. 1994. "Sources of Bias and Arbitrariness in the Capital Trial."*Journal of Social Issues* 7:103–112.

Lynch, D. 1999. "Perceived Judicial Hostility to Criminal Trials: Effects on Public Defenders in General and on Their Relationships with Clients and Prosecutors in Particular." *Criminal Justice and Behavior* 26:217–34.

Lynch, J. 1995. "Crime in International Perspective." In *Crime,* ed. J. Q. Wilson and J. Petersilia. San Francisco: ICS Press, 11–38.

Lynem, J. N. 2002. "Guards Call for Higher Wages, More Training: Industry Faces Annual Staff Turnover Rate of up to 300%." *San Francisco Chronicle,* August 22, p. B3.

MacCoun, R. J., A. Saiger, J. P. Kahan, and P. Reuter. 1993. "Drug Policies and Problems: The Promises and Pitfalls of Cross-National Comparisons." In *Psychoactive Drugs and Human Harm Reduction: From Faith to Science,* ed. N. Heather, E. Nadelman, and P. O'Hare. London: Whurr.

MacKenzie, D. L. 1995. "Boot Camp Prisons and Recidivism in Eight States." *Criminology* 33:327–58.

MacKenzie, D. L., and A. Piquero. 1994. "The Impact of Shock Incarceration Programs on Prison Crowding." *Crime and Delinquency* 40 (April): 222–49.

Maitland, A. S., and R. D. Sluder. 1998. "Victimization and Youthful Prison Inmates: An Empirical Analysis." *Prison Journal* 78:55.

Mann, C. R. 1993. *Unequal Justice: A Question of Color.* Bloomington: Indiana University Press.

Manning, P. K. 1971. "The Police: Mandate, Strategies, and Appearances." In *Crime and Justice in American Society,* ed. J. D. Douglas. Indianapolis, Ind.: Bobbs-Merrill, 149–193.

———. 1977. *Police Work.* Cambridge, Mass.: MIT Press.

Marsh, J. R. 1994. "Performing Pretrial Services: A Challenge in the Federal Criminal Justice System." *Federal Probation* 58 (December): 3–10.

Martin, S. E. 1989. "Women in Policing: The Eighties and Beyond." In *Police and Society,* ed. D. Kenney. New York: Praeger.

———. 1991. "The Effectiveness of Affirmative Action." *Justice Quarterly* 8:489–504.

Martin, S. E., and L. W. Sherman. 1986. "Selective Apprehension: A Police Strategy for Repeat Offenders." *Criminology* 24 (February): 155–73.

Martin, S. J., and S. Eckland-Olson. 1987. *Texas Prisons: The Walls Came Tumbling Down.* Austin: Texas Monthly Press.

Martinson, R. 1974. "What Works? Questions and Answers about Prison Reform." *The Public Interest,* Spring, p. 25.

Maschke, K. J. 1995. "Prosecutors as Crime Creators: The Case of Prenatal Drug Use." *Criminal Justice Review* 20: 21–33.

Mastrofski, S. D., M. D. Reisig, and J. D. McCluskey. 2002. "Police Disrespect Toward the Public: An Encounter-Based Analysis." *Criminology* 40: 519–52.

Mastrofski, S. D., J. J. Willis, and J. B. Snipes. 2002. "Styles of Patrol in a Community Policing Context." In *The Move to Community Policing: Making Change Happen,* ed. M. Morash and J. Ford. Thousand Oaks, Calif.: Sage, 81–111.

Matza, David. 1974. *Delinquency and Drift.* New York: Viking.

Maudsley, H. 1974. *Responsibility in Mental Disease.* London, England: Macmillan.

Mauer, Marc, and Meda Chesney-Lind, eds. 2002. *Invisible Punishment: The Collateral Consequences of Mass Imprisonment.* New York: New Press. An outstanding collection of articles examining the impact of incarceration on individuals, families, and communities.

Maxwell, S. R. 1999. "Examining the Congruence between Predictors of ROR and Failures to Appear." *Journal of Criminal Justice* 27:127–41.

Mayhew, P., and J. J. M. van Dijk. 1997. *Criminal Victimisation in Eleven Industrial Countries.* The Hague, Netherlands: Dutch Ministry of Justice.

McCoy, C. 1986. "Policing the Homeless." *Criminal Law Bulletin* 22 (May–June): 263.

———. 1993. *Politics and Plea Bargaining: Victims' Rights in California.* Philadelphia: University of Pennsylvania Press.

———. 1995. "Is the Trial Penalty Inevitable?" Paper presented at the annual meeting of the Law and Society Association, Phoenix, Arizona, June.

McDivitt, J., and R. Miliano. 1992. "Day Reporting Centers: An Innovative Concept in Intermediate Sanctions." In *Smart Sentencing: The Emergence of Intermediate Sanctions,* ed. J. M. Byrne, A. J. Lurigio, and J. Petersilia. Newbury Park, Calif.: Sage, 152–65.

McGabey, R. 1986. "Economic Conditions: Neighborhood Organizations and Urban Crime." In *Crime and Justice,* vol. 8, ed. A. J. Reiss and M. Tonry. Chicago: University of Chicago Press.

McGee, R. A., G. Warner, and N. Harlow. 1998. "The Special Management Inmate." In *Incarcerating Criminals,* ed. T. A. Flanagan, J. W. Marquart, and K. G. Adams. New York: Oxford University Press, 99–106.

McIntyre, Lisa J. 1987. *The Public Defender: The Practice of Law in the Shadows of Repute.* Chicago: University of Chicago Press.

McKelvey, B. 1977. *American Prisons.* Montclair, N.J.: Patterson Smith.

Mears, T. 1998. "Place and Crime." *Chicago-Kent Law Review* 73:669.

Meier, R. F., and T. D. Miethe. 1993. "Understanding Theories of Criminal Victimization." In *Crime and Justice: A Review of Research,* ed. M. Tonry. Chicago: University of Chicago Press.

Melekian, B. 1990. "Police and the Homeless." *FBI Law Enforcement Bulletin* 59:1–7.

Menard, S. 2000. "The 'Normality' of Repeat Victimization from Adolescence through Early Adulthood." *Criminology* 17:541–74.

Mentzer, A. 1996. "Policing in Indian Country: Understanding State Jurisdiction and Authority." *Law and Order* (June): 24–29.

Merianos, D. E., J. W. Marquart, and K. Damphousse. 1997. "From the Outside In: Using Public Health Data to Make Inferences about Older Inmates." *Crime and Delinquency* 43 (July): 298–314.

Messner, S. F., and R. Rosenfeld. 1994. *Crime and the American Dream.* Belmont, Calif.: Wadsworth.

Meyer, C., and T. Gorman. 2001. "Criminal Faces in the Crowd Still Elude Hidden ID Camera Security." *Los Angeles Times,* February 2, p. 1.

Miethe, T. D. 1995. "Fear and Withdrawal from Urban Life." *Annals of the American Academy of Political and Social Science* 539 (May): 14–27.

Miller, J. L., and J. J. Sloan. 1994. "A Study of Criminal Justice Discretion." *Journal of Criminal Justice* 22:107–23.

Miller, M., and M. Guggenheim. 1990. "Pretrial Detention and Punishment." *Minnesota Law Review* 75:335–426.

"Mistrial in Landmark DUI Case." 2002. *CBS News.* August 9 (http://www.cbsnews.com).

Monkkonen, E. H. 1981. *Police in Urban America, 1869–1920.* Cambridge, England: Cambridge University Press.

———. 1992. "History of the Urban Police." In *Modern Policing,* ed. M. Tonry and N. Morris. Chicago: University of Chicago Press.

Moore, M. 1992. "Problem-Solving and Community Policing." In *Modern Policing,* ed. M. Tonry and N. Morris. Chicago: University of Chicago Press, 99–158.

Moore, M., and G. L. Kelling. 1983. "To Serve and to Protect: Learning from Police History." *The Public Interest,* Winter, p. 55.

Morash, M., and J. K. Ford, eds. 2002. *The Move to Community Policing: Making Change Happen.* Thousand Oaks, Calif: Sage.

Morash, M., J. K. Ford, J. P. White, and J. G. Boles. 2002. "Directing the Future of Community-Policing Initiatives." In *The Move to Community Policing: Making Change Happen,* ed. M. Morash and J. Ford. Thousand Oaks, Calif.: Sage, 277–88.

Morash, M., R. N. Haarr, and L. Rucker. 1994. "A Comparison of Programming for Women and Men in the U.S. Prisons in the 1980s." *Crime and Delinquency* 40 (April): 197.

Morris, N. 1982. *Madness and the Criminal Law.* Chicago: University of Chicago Press.

Morris, N., and D. J. Rothman, eds. 1995. *The Oxford History of the Prison.* New York: Oxford University Press.

Morris, N., and M. Tonry. 1990. *Between Prison and Probation: Intermediate Punishments in a Rational Sentencing System.* New York: Oxford University Press.

"Mother of Sunburned Children." 2002. Associated Press Wire Service, August 21 (available on Lexis-Nexis).

Murano, V. 1990. *Cop Hunter.* New York: Simon & Schuster.

Murphy, D. 2002. "Grief and Dread at Girls' Burial Site in Oregon." *New York Times,* August 27 (http://www.nytimes.com).

Murphy, P. V. 1992. "Organizing for Community Policing." In *Issues in Policing: New Perspectives,* ed. J. W. Bizzack. Lexington, Ky.: Autumn Press, 113–28.

NAACP Legal Defense and Educational Fund. 2002. *Death Row USA.* New York: Author, Winter.

Nadelmann, E. A. 1993. *Cops across Borders: The Internationalization of U.S. Criminal Law Enforcement.* University Park: Pennsylvania State University Press.

Nagel, R. F. 1990. "The Myth of the General Right to Bail." *The Public Interest* (Winter): 84–97.

Nagin, D. S. 1998. "Criminal Deterrence Research at the Outset of the Twenty-First Century." In *Crime and Justice,* vol. 23, ed. M. Tonry. Chicago: University of Chicago Press, 1–42.

Nardulli, P. F. 1983. "The Societal Costs of the Exclusionary Rule: An Empirical Assessment." *American Bar Foundation Journal* 1983:585–690.

———. 1986. "Insider Justice: Defense Attorneys and the Handling of Felony Cases." *Journal of Criminal Law and Criminology* 79:416.

National Legal Aid and Defenders Association. 1999. "Full-Court Press on Federal CJA Rate Increase." *Press release,* April 21.

Naughton, K. 2002. "More 'Ridiculousness'." *Newsweek,* July 8, p. 46.

NBC News. 2002. "Sheriff Larry Waldie Discusses the Rescue of the Two Girls Kidnapped in California." *Today Show* transcript, August 2 (available on Lexis-Nexis).

New York Office of Justice Systems Analysis. 1991. *The Incarceration of Minority*

Defendants: An Identification of Disparity in New York State, 1985–1986. Albany: New York: State Division of Criminal Justice Services.

Newman, T. C. 1996. "Fair Cross-Section and Good Intention: Representation in Federal Juries." *Justice System Journal* 18:211–32.

NIJ (National Institute of Justice). 1988. *Research in Action.* Washington, D.C.: U.S. Government Printing Office.

———. 1996. *Victim Costs and Consequences: A New Look.* Washington, D.C.: U.S. Government Printing Office.

———. 1997. *Research in Brief,* January.

Novak, V. 1999. "The Cost of Poor Advice." *Time,* July 5, p. 38.

O'Hagan, M. 2002. "$2 Million Bail Set in Bus Hijack." *Seattle Times,* August 31 (http://www.seattletimes.com).

Ogletree, C. J., Jr., M. Prosser, A. Smith, and W. Talley, Jr. 1995. *Beyond the Rodney King Story: An Investigation of Police Misconduct in Minority Communities.* Boston: Northeastern University Press.

OJJDP (Office of Juvenile Justice and Delinquency Prevention). 1998. *Trying Juveniles as Adults in Criminal Court: An Analysis of State Transfer Provisions.* Washington, D.C.: U.S. Government Printing Office.

———. 1999. *Juvenile Offenders and Victims: 1999 National Report.* Washington, D.C.: U.S. Government Printing Office.

———. 2002. http://www.ojjdp.ncjrs.org/ojstatbb/html.

Olivares, K., V. Burton, and F. Cullen. 1996. "The Collateral Consequences of a Felony Conviction: A National Study of State Legal Codes 10 Years Later." *Federal Probation* 60:10–18.

Oliver, W. M. 2002."9-11, Federal Crime Control Policy, and Unintended Consequences." *ACJS Today* 22 (September–October): 1–6.

Owen, B. 1998. *"In the Mix": Struggle and Survival in a Woman's Prison.* Albany: State University of New York Press.

Owen, B., and B. Bloom. 1995. "Profiling Women Prisoners: Findings from National Surveys and a California Sample." *Prison Journal* 75 (June): 165–85.

Packer, H. L. 1968. *The Limits of the Criminal Sanction.* Stanford, Calif.: Stanford University Press.

Palmer, T. 1992. *The Re-Emergence of Correctional Intervention.* Newbury Park, Calif.: Sage.

Parent, D. G. 1990. *Day Reporting Centers for Criminal Offenders: A Descriptive Analysis of Existing Programs.* Washington, D.C.: National Institute of Justice, U.S. Government Printing Office.

Parenti, C. 1999. *Lockdown America: Police and Prisons in the Age of Crisis.* New York: Verso.

Parker, L. C., Jr. 1986. *Parole and the Community Based Treatment of Offenders in Japan and The United States.* New Haven, Conn.: University of New Haven Press.

Pate, A. M., and E. H. Hamilton. 1991. *The Big Six: Policing America's Large Cities.* Washington, D.C.: Police Foundation.

Peoples, J. M. 1995. "Helping Pretrial Services Clients Find Jobs." *Federal Probation* 59 (March): 14–18.

Perito, R. M. 1999. "Managing U.S. Participation in International Police Operations." In *Civilian Police and Multinational Peacekeeping—A Workshop Series.* Washington, D.C. National Institute of Justice, U.S. Government Printing Office, 9–11.

Perkins, D. B., and J. D. Jamieson. 1995. "Judicial Probable Cause Determinations after *County of Riverside v. McLaughlin.*" *Criminal Law Bulletin* 31: 534–46.

Petersen, R. D., and D. J. Palumbo. 1997. "The Social Construction of Intermediate Punishments." *Prison Journal* 77 (March): 77–91.

Petersilia, J. 1990. "When Probation Becomes More Dreaded Than Prison." *Federal Probation,* March, p. 24.

———. 1993. "Measuring the Performance of Community Corrections." In *Performance Measures for the Criminal Justice System.* Washington, D.C.: Bureau of Justice Statistics, U.S. Government Printing Office.

———. 1996. "A Crime Control Rationale for Reinvesting in Community Corrections." *Perspectives* 20 (Spring): 21–29.

———. 1998. "Probation and Parole." In *The Handbook of Crime and Punishment,* ed. M. Tonry. New York: Oxford University Press, 563–88.

———. 1999. "Parole and Prisoner Reentry in the United States." In *Prisons,* ed. M. Tonry and J. Petersilia. Chicago: University of Chicago Press.

Petersilia, J., and S. Turner. 1987. "Guideline-based Justice Prediction and Racial Minorities." In *Crime and Justice,* vol. 15, ed. N. Morris and M. Tonry. Chicago: University of Chicago Press.

———. 1990. *Intensive Supervision for High-Risk Probationers: Findings from Three California Experiments.* Santa Monica, Calif.: Rand Corporation.

———. 1993. "Intensive Probation and Parole." In *Crime and Justice,* vol. 17, ed. M. Tonry. Chicago: University of Chicago Press.

Phillips, S. 1977. *No Heroes, No Villains.* New York: Random House.

Pisciotta, A. W. 1994. *Benevolent Repression: Social Control and the American Reformatory-Prison Movement.* New York: New York University Press.

Platt, A. 1977. *The Child Savers.* 2nd ed. Chicago: University of Chicago Press.

Pochna, P. 2002. "Computers on Patrol; Cops Linking up with National Data Network." *Bergen County (N.J.) Record,* March 16, p. A1.

Pogrebin, M. R., and E. D. Poole. 1997. "The Sexualized Work Environment: A Look at Women Jail Officers." *Prison Journal* 77 (March): 41–57.

Pohlman, H. L. 1999. *The Whole Truth? A Case of Murder on the Appalachian Trail.* Amherst: University of Massachusetts Press.

Pollock, J. M. 1998. *Counseling Women in Prison.* Thousand Oaks, Calif.: Sage.

Possley, M., and T. Gregory. 1999. "DuPage 5 Win Acquittal." *Chicago Tribune,* June 5, p. 1.

PR Newswire. 2001. "Ion Track Instruments Unveils New Technology to Aid in Fight Against Terrorism and Drug Trafficking." March 22 (available on Lexis-Nexis).

PR Newswire. 2002. "As Homeland Security Bill Approaches House Vote, It Still Neglects Problems with Massive Private Security Industry." July 24 (available on Lexis-Nexis).

President's Commission on Law Enforcement and Administration of Justice. 1967. *The Challenge of Crime in a Free Society.* Washington, D.C.: U.S. Government Printing Office.

Priehs, R. 1999. "Appointed Counsel for Indigent Criminal Appellants: Does Compensation Influence Effort?" *Justice System Journal* 21:57–79.

Priest, D., and D. Farah. 2002. "Al-Qaida Reportedly Teaming with Hezbollah." *Seattle Times,* June 30 (http://www.seattletimes.com).

Propper, A. 1982. "Make Believe Families and Homosexuality among Imprisoned Girls." *Criminology* 20:127–39.

Provine, D. M. 1996. "Courts in the Political Process in France." In *Courts, Law, and Politics in Comparative Perspective,* ed. H. Jacob, E. Blankenburg, H. Kritzer, D. M. Provine, and J. Sanders. New Haven, Conn.: Yale University Press, 177–248.

Prussel, D., and K. Lonsway. 2001. "Recruiting Women Police Officers." *Law and Order* 49 (July): 91–96.

Pyle, R. 2002. "Swaggering Mafia Boss John Gotti Dies in Prison Hospital." *Seattle Times,* June 11 (http://www.seattletimes.com).

Radelet, M. L., H. A. Bedeau, and C. E. Putnam. 1992. *In Spite of Innocence.* Boston: Northeastern University Press.

Radelet, M. L., W. S. Lofquist, and H. A. Bedau. 1996. "Prisoners Released from Death Rows Since 1970 Because of Doubts about Their Guilt." *Thomas M. Cooley Law Review* 13:907.

Rafter, N. H. 1983. "Prisons for Women, 1790–1980." In *Crime and Justice,* 5th ed., ed. M. Tonry and N. Morris. Chicago: University of Chicago Press.

Randolph, E D. 2001. "Inland Police Like New Weaponry." *Riverside (Calif.) Press-Enterprise,* November 24, p. B4.

Reaves, B. A. 1992. *State and Local Police Departments, 1990.* Washington, D.C.: Bureau of Justice Statistics, U.S. Government Printing Office.

———. 2001. *Felony Defendants in Large Urban Counties, 1998: State Court Processing Statistics.* Washington, D.C.: Bureau of Justice Statistics, U.S. Government Printing Office.

Reaves, B. A., and A. L. Goldberg. 2000. *Local Police Departments, 1997.* Washington, D.C.: Bureau of Justice Statistics, U.S. Government Printing Office.

Reaves, B. A., and T. C. Hart. 1999. *Felony Defendants in Large Urban Counties, 1996: State Court Case Processing Statistics.* Washington, D.C.: Bureau of Justice Statistics, U.S. Government Printing Office.

———. 2000. *Law Enforcement Management and Administrative Statistics, 1999.* Washington, D.C.: Bureau of Justice Statistics, U.S. Government Printing Office.

Reaves, B. A., and M. J. Hickman. 2002. "Police Departments in Large Cities, 1999–2000." Bureau of Justice Statistics *Special Report* (May).

Reaves, B. A., and P. Z. Smith. 1995 *Felony Defendants in Large Urban Counties, 1992.* Washington, D.C.: U.S. Government Printing Office.

"Rebecca Gayheart." 2001. City News Service, August 8 (available on Lexis-Nexis).

Regoli, R. M., J. P. Crank, and R. G. Culbertson. 1987. "Rejoinder—Police Cynicism: Theory Development and Reconstruction." *Justice Quarterly* 4:281–86.

Regoli, R. M., and J. D. Hewitt. 1994. *Criminal Justice.* Englewood Cliffs, N.J.: Prentice-Hall.

Reibstein, L. 1997. "NYPD Black and Blue." *Newsweek,* June 2, p. 66.

Reichers, L. M., and R. R. Roberg. 1990. "Community Policing: A Critical Review of Underlying Assumptions." *Journal of Police Science and Administration* 17:105–14.

Reid, T. V. 1996. "PAC Participation in North Carolina Supreme Court Elections." *Judicature* 80:21–25.

———. 2000. "The Politicization of Judicial Retention Elections: The Defeat of Justices Lamphier and White." In *Research on Judicial Selection 1999.* Chicago: American Judicature Society, 45–72.

Reiman, J. 1996. . . . *And the Poor Get Prison: Economic Bias in American Criminal Justice.* Boston: Allyn and Bacon.

Reisig, M. D. 2002. "Citizen Input and Police Service: Moving beyond the "Feel Good" Community Survey." In *The Move to Community Policing: Making Change Happen,* ed. M. Morash and J. Ford. Thousand Oaks, Calif.: Sage, 43–60.

Reiss, A. J., Jr. 1971. *The Police and the Public.* New Haven, Conn.: Yale University Press.

———. 1988. *Private Employment of Public Police.* Washington, D.C.: National Institute of Justice, U.S. Government Printing Office.

———. 1992. "Police Organization in the Twentieth Century." In *Crime and Justice: A Review of Research,* vol. 15, ed. M. Tonry and N. Morris. Chicago: University of Chicago Press, 51–97.

Renzema, M. 1992. "Home Confinement Programs: Development, Implementation, and Impact." In *Smart Sentencing: The Emergence of Intermediate Sanctions,* ed. J. M. Byrne, A. J. Lurigio, and J. Petersilia. Newbury Park, Calif.: Sage, 41–53.

Rhodes, R. 1999. *Why They Kill: The Discoveries of a Maverick Criminologist.* New York: Knopf.

Richardson, J. E. 1993. "It's Not Easy Being Green: The Scope of the Fifth Amendment Right to Counsel." *American Criminal Law Review* 31:145–67.

Richtel, M. 2002. "Credit Card Theft Online as Global Market." *New York Times,* May 13 (http://www.nytimes.com).

Rideau, W., and R. Wikberg. 1992. *Life Sentences: Rage and Survival behind Bars.* New York: Times Books.

Rierden, A. 1997. *The Farm: Life inside a Women's Prison.* Amherst: University of Massachusetts Press.

Robinson, A. L. 2000. "The Effect of a Domestic Violence Policy Change on Police Officers' Schemata." *Criminal Justice and Behavior* 27:600–24.

Robinson, P. H. 1993. "Foreword: The Criminal-Civil Distinction and Dangerous Blameless Offenders." *Journal of Criminal and Criminology* 83:693–717.

Roedemeier, C. 2000. "Linebacker Pleads Guilty to Lesser Charge, Avoids Jail Time." Associated Press Wire Service, June 5.

Rohde, D. 1999. "Rage against Women Said to Prompt Shove." *New York Times,* October 8, p. B3.

Rosen, L. 1995. "The Creation of the Uniform Crime Report: The Role of Social Science." *Social Science History* 19 (Summer): 215–38.

Rosenbaum, J. L. 1989. "Family Dysfunction and Female Delinquency." *Crime and Delinquency* 35:31.

Rosenbaum, R. 1989. "Too Young to Die?" *New York Times Magazine,* March 12, p. 60.

Rosencrance, J. 1988. "Maintaining the Myth of Individualized Justice: Probation Presentence Reports." *Justice Quarterly* 5:235.

Rossi, P. H., and R. A. Berk. 1997. *Just Punishments: Federal Guidelines and Public Views Compared.* New York: Aldine DeGruyter.

Rothman, D. J. 1971. *The Discovery of the Asylum: Social Order and Disorder in the New Republic.* Boston: Little, Brown.

———. 1980. *Conscience and Convenience.* Boston: Little, Brown.

Rotman, E. 1995. "The Failure of Reform." In *Oxford History of the Prison,* ed. N. Morris and D. J. Rothman. New York: Oxford University Press.

Rousey, D. C. 1984. "Cops and Guns: Police Use of Deadly Force in Nineteenth-Century New Orleans." *American Journal of Legal History* 28:41–66.

Rowland, J. 1985. *The Ultimate Violation.* New York: Doubleday.

Sabo, D., T. A. Kupers, and W. London. 2001. "Gender and the Politics of Punishment." In *Prison Masculinities,* ed. D. Sabo, T. A. Kupers, and W. London. Philadelphia: Temple University Press.

Sampson, R. J., and J. L. Lauritsen. 1997. "Racial and Ethnic Disparities in Crime and Criminal Justice in the United States." In *Crime and Justice,* vol. 21, ed. M. Tonry. Chicago: University of Chicago Press, 311–74.

Samuelson, R. J. 1999. "Do We Care about Truth?" *Newsweek,* September 6, p. 76.

Satter, R. 1990. *Doing Justice: A Trial Judge at Work.* New York: Simon & Schuster.

Scalia, J. 2002. "Prisoners Petitions Filed in U.S. District Courts, 2000, with Trends 1980–2000." Bureau of Justice Statistics *Special Report,* January.

Schaefer, J. 2002. "8 From Detroit Police Indicted in Drug Theft." *Detroit Free Press,* October 5, p. 1.

Schafer, J. A. 2002. "The Challenge of Effective Organizational Change: Lessons Learned in Community-Policing Implementation." In *The Move to Community Policing: Making Change Happen,* ed. M. Morash and J. Ford. Thousand Oaks, Calif.: Sage, 243–63.

Scheck, B., P. Neufeld, and J. Dwyer. 2000. *Actual Innocence.* New York: Doubleday.

Scheingold, S. A. 1995. *Politics, Public Policy, and Street Crime.* Philadelphia: Temple University Press.

Schmidt, J., and E. H. Steury. 1989. "Prosecutorial Discretion in Filing Charges in Domestic Violence Cases." *Criminology* 27:487.

Schultz, D. 2000. "No Joy in Mudville Tonight: The Impact of Three Strikes' Laws on State and Federal Corrections Policy, Resources, and Crime Control." *Cornell Journal of Law and Public Policy* 9:557–83.

Scott, E. J. 1981. *Calls for Service: Citizen Demand and Initial Police Response.* Washington, D.C.: U.S. Government Printing Office.

"Search without a Warrant Leads to Dismissal." 2001. November 5 (http://www.espn.com).

Security Industry Association. 2000. "Economic Crime Cost Reaches $200 Billion in 2000." *Research Update,* January, p. 1.

Sentencing Project. 1998. *Losing the Vote.* Washington, D.C.: Author.

Serrano, R. 2002. "Lindh Pleads Guilty, Agrees to Aid Inquiry." *Los Angeles Times,* July 16, p. 1.

Shapiro, B. 1997. "Sleeping Lawyer Syndrome." *The Nation,* April 7, pp. 27–29.

Shearing, C., and P. C. Stenning, eds. 1987. *Private Policing.* Newbury Park, Calif.: Sage.

Sheehan, S. 1978. *A Prison and a Prisoner.* Boston: Houghton Mifflin.

Sheehan, T. 2002. "Judge Won't Let Budget Hinder Case." *Columbus Dispatch,* August 14, p. 1B.

Sherman, A. 1994. *Wasting America's Future.* Boston: Beacon Press.

Sherman, L. W. 1983. "Patrol Strategies for Police." In *Crime and Public Policy,* ed. J. Q. Wilson. San Francisco: ICS Press, 149–54.

———. 1990. "Police Crackdowns: Initial and Residual Deterrence." In *Crime and Justice,* ed. M. Tonry and N. Morris. Chicago: University of Chicago Press, 1–48.

———. 1995. "The Police." In *Crime,* ed. J. Q. Wilson and J. Petersilia. San Francisco: ICS Press, 327–48.

———. 1998. "Police." In *Handbook of Crime and Punishment,* ed. M. Tonry. New York: Oxford University Press, 429–56.

Sherman, L. W., and R. A. Berk. 1984. "The Specific Effects of Arrest for Domestic Assault." *American Sociological Review* 49:261–72.

Sherman, L. W., and E. G. Cohn. 1986. "Citizens Killed by Big City Police: 1970–84." Unpublished manuscript, Crime Control Institute, Washington, D.C., October.

Sherman, L. W., P. R. Gartin, and M. E. Buerger. 1989. "Hot Spots of Predatory Crime: Routine Activities and the Criminology of Place." *Criminology* 27:27–55.

Sherman, L. W., and D. P. Rogan. 1995a. "Effects of Gun Seizures on Gun Violence: 'Hot Spots' Patrol in Kansas City." *Justice Quarterly* 12 (December): 673–93.

———. 1995b. "Deterrent Effects of Police Raids on Crack Houses: A Randomized Controlled Experiment." *Justice Quarterly* 12 (December): 755–81.

Sherman, L. W., J. D. Schmidt, D. P. Rogan, P. R. Gartin, E. G. Cohn, D. J. Collins, and A. R. Bacich. 1991. "From Initial Deterrence to Long-Term Escalation: Short Custody Arrest for Poverty Ghetto Domestic Violence." *Criminology* 29:821–50.

Sherman, L. W., and D. A. Weisburd. 1995. "General Deterrent Effects of Police Patrol in Crime 'Hot Spots': A Randomized Controlled Trial." *Justice Quarterly* 12 (December): 625–48.

Shichor, D. 1995. *Punishment for Profit: Private Prisons/Public Concerns.* Thousand Oaks, Calif.: Sage.

Shover, N. 1998. "White-Collar Crime." In *The Handbook of Crime and Punishment,* ed. M. Tonry. New York: Oxford University Press, 133–58.

Silberman, M. 1995. *A World of Violence.* Belmont, Calif.: Wadsworth.

Silverman, E. 1999. *NYPD Battles Crime.* Boston: Northeastern University Press.

Simon, J. 1993. *Poor Discipline: Parole and Social Control of the Underclass.* Chicago: University of Chicago Press.

Simon, L. M. S. 1993. "Prison Behavior and the Victim–Offender Relationships among Violent Offenders." *Justice Quarterly* 10 (September): 263.

Simon, R. 1975. *Women and Crime.* Lexington, Mass.: D.C. Heath.

Simpson, A. W. B. 1984. *Cannibalism and the Common Law.* Chicago: University of Chicago Press.

Skogan, W. G. 1990. *Disorder and Decline: Crime and the Spiral of Decay in America.* New York: Free Press.

———. 1995. "Crime and Racial Fears of White Americans." *Annals of the American Academy of Political and Social Science* 539 (May): 59–71.

Skogan, W. G., and M. G. Maxfield. 1981. *Coping with Crime.* Newbury Park, Calif.: Sage.

Skolnick, J. H. 1966. *Justice without Trial: Law Enforcement in a Democratic Society.* New York: Wiley.

Skolnick, J. H., and D. H. Bayley. 1986. *The New Blue Line.* New York: Free Press.

Skolnick, J. H., and J. J. Fyfe. 1993. *Above the Law: Police and Excessive Use of Force.* New York: Free Press.

Smith, A. B., and H. Pollack. 1972. *Crimes and Justice in a Mass Society.* New York: Xerox.

Smith, C. E. 1990. *United States Magistrates in the Federal Courts: Subordinate Judges.* New York: Praeger.

———. 1993. "Justice Antonin Scalia and Criminal Justice Cases." *Kentucky Law Journal* 81:207.

———. 1994. "Imagery, Politics, and Jury Reform." *Akron Law Review* 28:77–95.

———. 1995a. "The Constitution and Criminal Punishment: The Emerging Visions of Justices Scalia and Thomas." *Drake Law Review* 43:593–613.

———. 1995b. "Federal Habeas Corpus Reform: The State's Perspective." *Justice System Journal* 18:1–11.

———. 1995c. "Judicial Policy Making and Habeas Corpus Reform." *Criminal Justice Policy Review* 7:91–114.

———. 1997a. *Courts, Politics, and the Judicial Process.* 2nd ed. Chicago: Nelson-Hall.

———. 1997b. *The Rehnquist Court and Criminal Punishment.* New York: Garland.

———. 1999a. "Criminal Justice and the 1997–98 U.S. Supreme Court Term." *Southern Illinois University Law Review* 23:443–67.

———. 1999b. *Law and Contemporary Corrections.* Belmont, Calif.: Wadsworth.

———. 2003. *Criminal Procedure.* Belmont, Calif.: Wadsworth.

Smith, C. E., C. DeJong, and J. D. Burrow. 2002. *The Supreme Court, Crime, and the Ideal of Equal Justice.* New York: Peter Lange.

Smith, C. E., and S. B. Dow. 2002. "Criminal Justice and the 2000–2001 U.S. Supreme Court Term." *University of Detroit-Mercy Law Review* 79:189–227.

Smith, C. E., and H. Feldman. 2001. "Burdens of the Bench: State Supreme Courts' Non-Judicial Tasks." *Judicature* 84:304–9.

Smith, C. E., and J. Hurst. 1996. "Law and Police Agencies' Policies: Perceptions of the Relative Impact of Constitutional Law Decisions and Civil Liabilities Decisions." Paper given at the annual meeting of the American Society of Criminology, Chicago.

———. 1997. "The Forms of Judicial Policy Making: Civil Liability and Criminal Justice Policy." *Justice System Journal* 19:341–54.

Smith, C. E., and R. Ochoa. 1996. "The Peremptory Challenge in the Eyes of the Trial Judge." *Judicature* 79:185–89.

Smith, S. K., and C. J. DeFrances. 1996. "Indigent Defense." Bureau of Justice Statistics *Bulletin,* February.

Sorensen, J. R., J. M. Marquart, and D. E. Brock. 1993. "Factors Related to Killings of Felons by Police Officers: A Test of the Community Violence and Conflict Hypotheses." *Justice Quarterly* 10:417–40.

Sorenson, J. R., and D. H. Wallace. 1999. "Prosecutorial Discretion in Seeking Death: An Analysis of Racial Disparity in the Pretrial Stages of Case Processing in a Midwestern County." *Justice Quarterly* 16:561–78.

Souryal, S. S., D. W. Potts, and A. I. Alobied. 1994. "The Penalty of Hand Amputation for Theft in Islamic Justice." *Journal of Criminal Justice* 22:249–65.

Spangenberg, R. L., and M. L. Beeman. 1995. "Indigent Defense Systems in the United States." *Law and Contemporary Problems* 58:31–49.

Sparrow, M. K., M. H. Moore, and D. M. Kennedy. 1990. *Beyond 911: A New Era for Policing.* New York: Basic Books.

Spears, J. W., and C. C. Spohn. 1997. "The Effect of Evidence Factors and Victim Characteristics on Prosecutors' Charging Decisions in Sexual Assault Cases." *Justice Quarterly* 14:501–24.

Spears, L. 1991. "Contract Counsel: A Different Way to Defend the Poor—How It's Working in North Dakota." *American Bar Association Journal on Criminal Justice* 6:24–31.

Spelman, W. G., and D. K. Brown. 1984. *Calling the Police: Citizen Reporting of Serious Crime.* Washington, D.C.: Police Executive Research Forum.

Spelman, W. G., and J. Eck. 1987. "Problem-Oriented Policing." In *Research in Brief.* Washington, D.C.: National Institute of Justice, U.S. Government Printing Office.

Spencer, C. 2000. "Nonlethal Weapons Aid Lawmen: Police Turn to Beanbag Guns, Pepper Spray to Save Lives of Defiant

Suspects." *Arkansas Democrat-Gazette,* November 6, p. B1.
Spitzer, S. 1975. "Toward a Marxian Theory of Deviance." *Social Problems* 22:639.
Spohn, C. 1992. "An Analysis of the 'Jury Trial Penalty' and Its Effect on Black and White Offenders." *The Justice Professional* 7:93–97.
Spohn, C., J. Gruhl, and S. Welch. 1987. "The Impact of the Ethnicity and Gender of Defendants on the Decision to Reject or Dismiss Felony Charges." *Criminology* 25:175–91.
Spohn, C., and D. Holleran. 2000. "The Imprisonment Penalty Paid by Young, Unemployed Black and Hispanic Male Offenders." *Criminology* 38:281–306.
———. 2001. "Prosecuting Sexual Assault: A Comparison of Charging Decisions in Sexual Assault Cases Involving Strangers, Acquaintances, and Intimate Partners." *Justice Quarterly* 18:651–85.
Stafford, M. C., and M. Warr. 1993. "A Reconceptualization of General and Specific Deterrence." *Journal of Research in Crime and Delinquency* 30 (May): 123.
Stahl, M. B. 1992. "Asset Forfeiture, Burden of Proof, and the War on Drugs." *Journal of Criminal Law and Criminology* 83:274–337.
Stanford, M. R., and B. L. Mowry. 1990. "Domestic Disturbance Danger Rate." *Journal of Police Science and Administration* 17:244–49.
Stanko, E. 1988. "The Impact of Victim Assessment on Prosecutors' Screening Decisions: The Case of the New York District Attorney's Office." In *Criminal Justice: Law and Politics,* 5th ed., ed. G. F. Cole. Pacific Grove, Calif.: Brooks/Cole.
Stanley, David T. 1976. *Prisoners among Us.* Washington, D.C.: Brookings Institution.
Steffensmeier, D., and S. Demuth. 2001. "Ethnicity and Judges' Sentencing Decisions: Hispanic-Black-White Comparisons." *Criminology* 39:145–78.
Steffensmeier, D., J. Kramer, and C. Streifel. 1993. "Gender and Imprisonment Decisions." *Criminology* 31:411–46.
Steffensmeier, D., J. Ulmer, and J. Kramer. 1998. "The Interaction of Race, Gender, and Age in Criminal Sentencing: The Punishment Cost of Being Young, Black, and Male." *Criminology* 36:763–97.
Steinberg, J. 1999. "The Coming Crime Wave Is Washed Up." *New York Times,* January 3, p. 4WK.
Steinman, M. 1988. "Anticipating Rank and File Police Reactions to Arrest Policies Regarding Spouse Abuse." *Criminal Justice Research Bulletin* 4:1–5.
Steury, E. 1993. "Criminal Defendants with Psychiatric Impairment: Prevalence, Probabilities, and Rates." *Journal of Criminal Law and Criminology* 84:352–76.
Steury, E., and N. Frank. 1990. "Gender Bias and Pretrial Release: More Pieces of the Puzzle." *Journal of Criminal Justice* 18:417–32.
Stickmund, M. 2000. "State Custody Rates, 1997." In *Juvenile Justice Bulletin,* December (Washington, D.C.: U.S. Government Printing Office).
Stoddard, E. R. 1968. "The Informal 'Code' of Police Deviancy: A Group Approach to Blue-Coat Crime." *Journal of Criminal Law, Criminology, and Police Science* 59:204–11.
Stojkovic, S. 1990. "Accounts of Prison Work: Corrections Officers' Portrayals of Their Work Worlds." *Perspectives on Social Problems* 2:211–30.
Stolzenberg, L., and S. J. D'Alessio. 1994. "Sentencing and Unwarranted Disparity: An Empirical Assessment of the Long-Term Impact of Sentencing Guidelines in Minnesota." *Criminology* 32:301–10.
———. 1997. "Three Strikes and You're Out: The Impact of California's New Mandatory Sentencing Law on Serious Crime Rates." *Crime and Delinquency* 43:457.
Strodtbeck, F., R. James, and G. Hawkins. 1957. "Social Status in Jury Deliberations." *American Sociological Review* 22:713–19.
Sutherland, E. H. 1947. *Criminology.* 4th ed. Philadelphia: Lippincott.
———. 1949. *White-Collar Crime.* New York: Holt, Rinehart, and Winston.
———. 1950. "The Sexual Psychopath Laws." *Journal of Criminal Law and Criminology* 40 (January–February): 543.
Sykes, G. M. 1958. *The Society of Captives.* Princeton, N.J.: Princeton University Press.

Taifa, N. 2002. Testimony on Behalf of American Civil Liberties Union of the National Capital Area Concerning Proposed Use of Surveillance Cameras, before the Joint Public Oversight Hearing Committee on the Judiciary, Council of the District of Columbia, June 13 (http://www.dcwatch.com).
Tanveer, K. 2002. "Pakistani Council Doles out Brutal Punishment: Gang Rape." *Lansing (Mich.) State Journal,* July 4, p. 2A.
Teeters, N. K., and J. D. Shearer. 1957. *The Prison at Philadelphia's Cherry Hill.* New York: Columbia University Press,.
Terry, C. 1997. "The Function of Humor for Prison Inmates." *Journal of Contemporary Criminal Justice* 13:26.
Terry, D. 1996. "After 18 Years in Prison, 3 Are Cleared of Murders." *New York Times,* July 3, p. A8.
Thomas, C. W. 2002. "A 'Real Time' Statistical Profile of Private Prisons for Adults" (http://web.crim.ufl.edu/pcp/census).
Thomas, W. H., Jr. 1976. *Bail Reform in America.* Berkeley: University of California Press.
Thompson, R. A. 2001. "Police Use of Force against Drug Suspects: Understanding the Legal Need for Policy Development." *American Journal of Criminal Justice* 25:173–97.
Thurman, Q., J. Zhao, and A. Giacomazzi. 2001. *Community Policing in a Community Era.* Los Angeles: Roxbury.
Toch, H. 1976. *Peacekeeping: Police, Prisons, and Violence.* Lexington, Mass.: Lexington Books.
Tonry, M. 1993. "Sentencing Commissions and Their Guidelines." In *Crime and Justice,* vol. 17, ed. M. Tonry. Chicago: University of Chicago Press.
———. 1995. *Malign Neglect: Race, Crime, and Punishment in America.* New York: Oxford University Press.
———. 1996. *Sentencing Matters.* New York: Oxford University Press.
———. 1998a. "Intermediate Sanctions." In *Handbook of Crime and Punishment,* ed. M. Tonry. New York: Oxford University Press, 683–711.
———. 1998b. Introduction to *Handbook of Crime and Punishment,* ed. M. Tonry. New York: Oxford University Press, 22–23.
Tonry, M., and K. Hamilton, eds. 1995. *Intermediate Sanctions in Overcrowded Times.* Boston: Northeastern University Press.
Tonry, M., and M. Lynch. 1996. "Intermediate Sanctions." In *Crime and Justice,* vol. 20, ed. M. Tonry. Chicago: University of Chicago Press, 99–144.
Tonry, M., and N. Morris, eds. 1992. *Modern Policing.* Chicago: University of Chicago Press.
Toobin, J. 1996. *The Run of His Life: The People v. O. J. Simpson.* New York: Random House.
Torriero, E. A., and R. Manor. 2002. "Andersen Convicted; Most Work Will Cease." *Seattle Times,* June 16 (http://www.seattletimes.com).
Travis, J., and J. Petersilia. 2001. "Reentry Reconsidered: A New Look at an Old Question." *Crime and Delinquency,* July, pp. 291–313.
Tucker, J. 1997. *May God Have Mercy.* New York: Norton.
Turley, J. 2002. "Detaining Liberty." *Lansing State Journal,* August 18, p. 11A.
Turow, S. 1987. *Presumed Innocent.* New York: Farrar, Straus, and Giroux.

Uchida, C., and T. Bynum. 1991. "Search Warrants, Motions to Suppress and 'Lost Cases': The Effects of the Exclusionary Rule in Seven Jurisdictions." *Journal of Criminal Law and Criminology* 81:1034–66.
Ugwuegbu, D. 1999. "Racial and Evidential Factors in Juror Attributions of Legal Responsibility." In *The Social Organization of Law,* 2nd ed., ed. M. P. Baumgartner. San Diego: Academic Press.
U.S. Department of Justice. 1980. *Principles of Prosecution.* Washington, D.C.: U.S. Government Printing Office.
U.S. President's Commission on Law Enforcement and Administration of Justice. 1967. *The Challenge of Crime in a Free Society.* Washington, D.C.: U.S. Government Printing Office.

Uphoff, R. J. 1992. "The Criminal Defense Lawyer: Zealous Advocate, Double Agent, or Beleaguered Dealer?" *Criminal Law Bulletin* 28:419–56.

Useem, B., and P. Kimball. 1989. *States of Siege: U.S. Prison Riots, 1971–1986.* New York: Oxford University Press.

Utz, P. 1978. *Settling the Facts.* Lexington, Mass.: Lexington Books.

Uviller, H. Richard. 1996. *Virtual Justice: The Flawed Prosecution of Crime in America.* New Haven, Conn.: Yale University Press.

Vaughn, M. S. 2001. "Assessing the Legal Liabilities in Law Enforcement: Chiefs' Views." *Crime and Delinquency* 47: 3–27.

Vaughn, M. S., and R. del Carmen. 1997. "The Fourth Amendment as a Tool of Actuarial Justice: The 'Special Needs' Exception to the Warrant and Probable Cause Requirements." *Crime and Delinquency* 43:78–103.

Vera Institute of Justice. 1981. *Felony Arrests: Their Prosecution and Disposition in New York City's Courts.* New York: Longman.

Vicenti, C. N. 1995. "The Reemergence of Tribal Society and Traditional Justice Systems." *Judicature* 79:134–41.

Vila, B., and D. J. Kenney. 2002. "Tired Cops: The Prevalence and Potential Consequences of Police Fatigue." *National Institute of Justice Journal* 248: 16–21.

Vogel, M. 1999. "The Social Origins of Plea Bargaining: Conflict and the Law in the Process of State Formation, 1830–1860." *Law and Society Review* 33:161–246.

von Hirsch, A. 1976. *Doing Justice.* New York: Hill and Wang.

Walker, P. 1998. "Felony and Misdemeanor Defendants Filed in the U.S. District Courts during Fiscal Years 1990–95: An Analysis of the Filings of Each Offense Level." *Journal of Criminal Justice* 26:503–11.

Walker, S. 1984. "'Broken Windows' and Fractured History: The Use and Misuse of History in Recent Police Patrol Analysis." *Justice Quarterly* 1 (March): 88.

———. 1993. *Taming the System: The Control of Discretion in Criminal Justice 1950–1990.* New York: Oxford University Press.

———. 1999. *The Police in America.* 3rd ed. New York: McGraw-Hill.

———. 2001. *Sense and Nonsense about Crime and Drugs: A Policy Guide.* 5th ed. Belmont, Calif.: Wadsworth.

Walker, S., C. Spohn, and M. DeLeone. 2000. *The Color of Justice.* 2nd ed. Belmont, Calif.: Wadsworth.

Walker, S., and K. B. Turner. 1992. "A Decade of Modest Progress: Employment of Black and Hispanic Police Officers, 1983–1992." Omaha: Department of Criminal Justice, University of Nebraska at Omaha.

Walker, S., and B. Wright. 1995. "Citizen Review of the Police, 1994: A National Survey." In *Fresh Perspectives.* Washington, D.C.: Police Executive Research Forum.

Walsh, W. 1989. "Private/Public Police Stereotypes: A Different Perspective." *Security Journal* 1:21–27.

Warr, M. 1993. "Fear of Victimization." *The Public Perspective,* November–December, pp. 25–28.

Wasserman, D. T. 1990. *A Sword for the Convicted: Representing Indigent Defendants on Appeal.* New York: Greenwood Press.

Watson, G. 1999. "Prisons Struggling to Deal with Mental Illness." *Hartford Courant,* May 23, p. A1.

Watson, R. A., and R. G. Downing. 1969. *The Politics of the Bench and Bar: Judicial Selection under the Missouri Nonpartisan Court Plan.* New York: Wiley.

Weil, M., and P. Dvorak. 2002. "Authorities Link Virginia Shooting to Sniper Case." *Washington Post,* October 15, p. 1.

Weinstein, J. B. 1992. "A Trial Judge's Second Impression of the Federal Sentencing Guidelines." *Southern California Law Review* 66:357.

Weis, R. P. 2001. "'Repatriating' Low-Wage Work: The Political Economy of Prison Labor Reprivatization in the Postindustrial United States." *Criminology* 39:253–91.

Weisburd, D. A., and L. Green. 1995. "Measuring Immediate Spatial Displacement: Methodological Issues and Problems." In *Crime and Place: Crime Prevention Studies,* vol. 4, ed. D. A. Weisburd and J. E. Eck. Monsey, N.Y.: Criminal Justice Press.

Weitzer, R. 2002. "Incidents of Police Misconduct and Public Opinion." *Journal of Criminal Justice* 30:397–408.

Welch, M. 1994. "Jail Overcrowding: Social Sanitation and the Warehousing of the Urban Underclass." In *Critical Issues in Crime and Justice,* ed. A. Roberts. Thousand Oaks, Calif.: Sage, 249–74.

White, M. S. 1995. "The Nonverbal Behaviors in Jury Selection." *Criminal Law Bulletin* 31:414–45.

Whitebread, C. H., and C. Slobogin. 2000. *Criminal Procedure: An Analysis of Cases and Concepts.* 4th ed. Westbury, N.Y.: Foundation Press.

Wice, Paul. 1974. *Freedom for Sale.* Lexington, Mass.: Lexington Books.

Wilbanks, W. 1987. *The Myth of a Racist Criminal Justice System.* Pacific Grove, Calif.: Brooks/Cole.

"Williams' Co-Defendant Pleads Guilty to Tampering." 2002. *Seattle Times,* August 22 (http://www.seattletimes.com).

Williams, H., and P. V. Murphy. 1990. "The Evolving Strategy of Police: A Minority View." In *Perspectives on Policing,* no. 13. Washington, D.C.: National Institute of Justice, U.S. Government Printing Office.

Williams, H., and A. M. Pate. 1987. "Returning to First Principles: Reducing the Fear of Crime in Newark." *Crime and Delinquency* 33 (January): 53–59.

Williams, V., and M. Fish. 1974. *Convicts, Codes, and Contraband.* Cambridge, Mass.: Ballinger.

Willott, S., C. Griffin, and M. Torrance. 2001. "Snakes and Ladders: Upper-Middle Class Male Offenders Talk about Economic Crime." *Criminology* 39:441–66.

Wilson, J. Q. 1968. *Varieties of Police Behavior.* Cambridge, Mass.: Harvard University Press.

———. 1994. "Just Take away Their Guns." *The New York Times Magazine,* March 20, p. 47.

Wilson, J. Q., and B. Boland. 1979. *The Effect of the Police on Crime.* Washington, D.C.: U.S. Government Printing Office.

Wilson, J. Q., and R. Herrnstein. 1985. *Crime and Human Nature.* New York: Simon & Schuster.

Wilson, J. Q., and G. L. Kelling. 1982. "Broken Windows: The Police and Neighborhood Safety." *Atlantic Monthly,* March, pp. 29–38.

Wilson, J. Q., and J. Petersilia, eds. 1995. *Crime.* San Francisco: Institute for Contemporary Studies Press.

Windlesham, David. 1998. *Politics, Punishment, and Populism.* New York: Oxford University Press.

Winerip, M. 1999a. "Bedlam in the Streets." *The New York Times Sunday Magazine,* May 23, p. 42.

———. 1999b. "The Juror's Dilemma." *The New York Times Magazine,* November 21.

Winick, B. J. 1995. "Reforming Incompetency to Stand Trial and Plead Guilty." *Journal of Criminal Law and Criminology* 85:571–624.

Winkeljohn, M. 2002. "A Random Act of Hate: Duckett's Attack Linked to Racism." *Atlanta Journal and Constitution,* August 4, p. E1.

Wishman, S. 1986. *Anatomy of a Jury.* New York: Times Books.

Wolfgang, M. E., and F. Ferracuti. 1967. *The Subculture of Violence.* London: Tavistock.

Wooldredge, J. D., and K. Masters. 1993. "Confronting Problems Faced by Pregnant Inmates in State Prisons." *Crime and Delinquency* 39 (April): 195.

Worden, A. P. 1991. "Privatizing Due Process: Issues in the Comparison of Assigned Counsel, Public Defenders, and Contracted Indigent Defense Counsel." *Justice System Journal* 15:390–418.

———. 1993. "The Attitudes of Women and Men in Policing: Testing Conventional and Contemporary Wisdom." *Criminology* 31 (May): 203–24.

———. 1994. "Counsel for the Poor: An Evaluation of Contracting for Indigent Criminal Defense." *Justice Quarterly* 10:613–37.

———. 1995. "The Judge's Role in Plea Bargaining: An Analysis of Judges' Agreement with Prosecutors' Sentencing Recommendations." *Justice Quarterly* 12:257–78.

Worden, R. 1990. "A Badge and a Baccalaureate: Policies, Hypotheses, and Further Evidence." *Justice Quarterly* 7:565–92.

Worth, R. F. 2001. "73 Tied to Genovese Family Are Indicted, Officials Say." *New York Times,* December 6, p. A27.

Wright, J. P., and F. Cullen. 2000. "Juvenile Involvement in Occupational Deliquency." *Criminology* 38:863–96.

Yang, S. S. 1990. "The Unique Treatment Needs of Female Substance Abusers: The Obligation of the Criminal Justice System to Provide Parity Services." *Medicine and Law* 9:1018–27.

Zagaris, B. 1998. "U.S. International Cooperation against Transnational Organized Crime." *Wayne Law Review* 44 (Fall): 1401–64.

Zedner, L. 1995. "Wayward Sisters." In *The Oxford History of Prisons,* ed. N. Morris and D. J. Rothman. New York: Oxford University Press, 329–61.

Zimmer, L. 1987 "Operation Pressure Point: The Disruption of Street-Level Trade on New York's Lower East Side." Occasional paper from the Center for Research in Crime and Justice, New York University School of Law.

Zimring, F. 1994. *Newsweek,* February 21.

Zimring, F. E., G. Hawkins, and S. Kamin. 2001. *Punishment and Democracy: Three Strikes and You're Out in California.* New York: Oxford University Press.

Court Cases

Adams v. Williams, 407 U.S. 143 (1972).

Aguilar v. Texas, 378 U.S. 108 (1964).

Apprendi v. New Jersey, 500 U.S. 466 (2000).

Argersinger v. Hamlin, 407 U.S. 25 (1972).

Arizona v. Evans, 514 U.S. 1 (1995).

Atkins v. Virginia, 122 S.Ct. 2242 (2002).

Atwater v. City of Lago Vista, 532 U.S. 318 (2001).

Austin v. United States, 61 LW 4811 (1993).

Barron v. Baltimore, 32 U.S. 243 (1833).

Batson v. Kentucky, 476 U.S. 79 (1986).

Baxter v. Palmigiano, 425 U.S. 308 (1976).

Bell v. Wolfish, 441 U.S. 520 (1979).

Bennis v. Michigan, 116 S.Ct. 994 (1996).

Blackledge v. Allison, 431 U.S. 71 (1976).

Blake v. Los Angeles, 595 F.2d 1367 (1979).

Bond v. United States, 529 U.S. 334 (2000).

Bordenkircher v. Hayes, 343 U.S. 357 (1978).

Boykin v. Alabama, 395 U.S. 238 (1969).

Breed v. Jones, 421 U.S. 519 (1975).

Breihaupt v. Abram, 352 U.S. 432 (1957).

Brewer v. Williams, 430 U.S. 387 (1977).

Brown v. Board of Education, 347 U.S. 483 (1954).

Brown v. Mississippi, 297 U.S. 281 (1936).

Bumper v. North Carolina, 391 U.S. 543 (1968).

Burch v. Louisiana, 441 U.S. 130 (1979).

California v. Acevedo, 500 U.S. 565 (1991).

Carroll v. United States, 267 U.S. 132 (1925).

Chimel v. California, 395 U.S. 752 (1969).

City of Indianapolis v. Edmond, 531 U.S. 32 (2000).

Coolidge v. New Hampshire, 403 U.S. 443 (1971).

Cooper v. Oklahoma, 116 S.Ct. 1373 (1996).

Cooper v. Pate, 378 U.S. 546 (1964).

Cruz v. Beto, 450 U.S. 319 (1972).

Cupp v. Murphy, 412 U.S. 291 (1973).

Daniels v. Williams, 474 U.S. 327 (1986).

Delaware v. Prouse, 440 U.S. 648 (1979).

Dickerson v. United States, 530 U.S. 428 (2000).

Douglas v. California, 372 U.S. 353 (1963).

Durham v. United States, 214 F.2d 862 (D.C. Cir. 1954).

Escobedo v. Illinois, 378 U.S. 478 (1964).

Estelle v. Gamble, 429 U.S. 97 (1976).

Fare v. Michael C., 442 U.S. 707 (1979).

Flippo v. West Virginia, 528 U.S. 11 (1999).

Florida v. J.L., 529 U.S. 266 (2000).

Ford v. Wainwright, 477 U.S. 399 (1986).

Fulwood v. Clemmer, 206 F.Supp. 370 (D.C. Cir. 1962).

Furman v. Georgia, 408 U.S. 238 (1972).

Gagnon v. Scarpelli, 411 U.S. 778 (1973).

Gideon v. Wainwright, 372 U.S. 335 (1963).

Gittlemacker v. Prasse, 428 F.2d 1 (1970).

Graham v. Connor, 490 U.S. 396 (1989).

Gregg v. Georgia, 428 U.S. 153 (1976).

Griggs v. Duke Power Company, 401 U.S. 424 (1971).

Harris v. New York, 401 U.S. 222 (1971).

Hester v. United States, 265 U.S. 57 (1924).

Hudson v. Palmer, 52 L.W. 5052 (1984).

Illinois v. Gates, 462 U.S. 213 (1983).

Illinois v. Krull, 480 U.S. 340 (1987).

Illinois v. Rodriguez, 497 U.S. 177 (1990).

Illinois v. Wardlow, 528 U.S. 119 (2000).

Immigration and Naturalization Service v. Lopez-Medoza, 468 U.S. 1032 (1984).

In re Gault, 387 U.S. 9 (1967).

In re Winship, 397 U.S. 358 (1970).

Johnson v. Zerbst, 304 U.S. 458 (1938).

Kahane v. Carlson, 527 F.2d 592 (2d Cir. 1975).

Kansas v. Hendricks, 117 S.Ct. 2072 (1997).

Kent v. United States, 383 U.S. 541 (1966).

Knowles v. Iowa, 525 U.S. 113 (1998).

Kyllo v. United States, 533 U.S. 27 (2001).

Lanza v. New York, 370 U.S.139 (1962).

Lee v. Downs, 641 F.2d 318 (4th Cir. 1981).

Lee v. Washington, 390 U.S. 333 (1968).

Lewis v. United States, 116 S.Ct. 2163 (1996).

Lockhart v. McCree, 476 U.S. 162 (1986).

M'Naughten's Case, 8 Eng. Rep. 718 (1843).

Mapp v. Ohio, 367 U.S. 643 (1961).

Maryland v. Garrison, 480 U.S. 79 (1987).

Maryland v. Wilson, 519 U.S. 408 (1997).

Massiah v. United States, 377 U.S. 201 (1964).

McCleskey v. Kemp, 478 U.S. 1019 (1987).

McKeiver v. Pennsylvania, 403 U.S. 528 (1971).

Mempa v. Rhay, 389 U.S. 128 (1967).

Michigan Department of State Police v. Sitz, 496 U.S. 440 (1990).

Michigan v. Long, 463 U.S. 1032 (1983).

Minnesota v. Dickerson, 508 U.S. 366 (1993).

Miranda v. Arizona, 384 U.S. 436 (1966).

Monell v. Department of Social Services of the City of New York, 436 U.S. 658 (1978).

Montana v. Egelhoff, 116 S.Ct. 2013 (1996).

Morrissey v. Brewer, 408 U.S. 471 (1972).

Murray v. Giarratano, 492 U.S. 1 (1989).

New Jersey v. T.L.O., 105 S. Ct. 733 (1985).

New York v. Belton, 453 U.S. 454 (1981).

New York v. Class, 475 U.S. 321 (1986).

New York v. Quarles, 467 U.S. 649 (1984).

Nix v. Williams, 467 U.S. 431 (1984).

North Carolina v. Alford, 400 U.S. 25 (1970).

O'Lone v. Estate of Shabazz, 482 U.S. 342 (1987).

Oliver v. United States, 466 U.S. 170 (1984).

Pargo v. Elliott, 69 F.3d 280 (8th Cir. 1995).

Pennsylvania Board of Pardons and Parole v. Scott, 524 U.S. 357 (1998).

Pennsylvania v. Muniz, 496 U.S. 582 (1990).

Penry v. Lynaugh, 492 U.S. 302 (1989).

Powell v. Alabama, 287 U.S. 45 (1932).

Procunier v. Martinez, 416 U.S. 396 (1974).

Queen v. Dudley and Stephens, 14 Q.B.D. 273 (1884).

R.A.V. v. City of St. Paul, 112 S.Ct. 2538 (1992).

Republican Party of Minnesota v. White, 122 S.Ct. 2528 (2002).

Rhodes v. Chapman, 452 U.S. 337 (1981).

Ricketts v. Adamson, 481 U.S. 1 (1987).

Ring v. Arizona, 122 S.Ct. 2428 (2002).

Robinson v. California, 370 U.S. 660 (1962).

Ross v. Moffitt, 417 U.S. 660 (1974).

Ruffin v. Commonwealth, 62 Va. 790 (1871).

Ruiz v. Estelle, 503 F.Supp. 1265 (S.D.Tex. 1980).

Sandin v. Conner, 115 S.Ct. 2293 (1995).

Santobello v. New York, 404 U.S. 260 (1971).

Schall v. Martin, 467 U.S. 253 (1984).

Scott v. Illinois, 440 U.S. 367 (1979).

Skinner v. Oklahoma, 316 U.S. 535 (1942).

Smith v. Fairman, 678 F.2d 52 (7th Cir. 1982).

South Dakota v. Opperman, 428 U.S. 364 (1976).

Spinelli v. United States, 393 U.S. 410 (1969).

Stanford v. Kentucky, 492 U.S. 361 (1989).

Strickland v. Washington, 466 U.S. 686 (1984).

Tennessee v. Garner, 471 U.S. 1 (1985).

Terry v. Ohio, 392 U.S. 1 (1968).

Theriault v. Carlson, 339 F.Supp 375 (N.D. Ga. 1973).

Thompson v. Oklahoma, 108 S.Ct. 1687 (1988).

Thornburgh v. Abbott, 490 U.S. 401 (1989).

Trop v. Dulles, 356 U.S. 86 (1958).

Turner v. Safley, 482 U.S. 78 (1987).

United States v. Bajakajian, 118 S.Ct. 2028 (1998).

United States v. Brawner, 471 F.2d 969 (D.C. Cir. 1972).

United States v. Calandra, 414 U.S. 338 (1974).

United States v. Cronic, 444 U.S. 654 (1984).

United States v. Drayton, 122 S.Ct. 2105 (2002).

United States v. Hitchcock, 992 F.2d 1107 (CA9 1972).

United States v. Leon, 468 U.S. 897 (1984).

United States v. Robinson, 414 U.S. 218 (1973).

United States v. Salerno and Cafero, 481 U.S. 739 (1987).

United States v. Ursery, 116 S.Ct. 2135 (1996).

United States v. Wade, 388 U.S. 218 (1967).

Vitek v. Jones, 445 U.S. 480 (1980).

Warden v. Hayden, 387 U.S. 294 (1967).

Weeks v. United States, 232 U.S. 383 (1914).

Whitley v. Albers, 475 U.S. 312 (1986).

Whren v. United States, 517 U.S. 806 (1996).

Wilkins v. Missouri, 492 U.S. 361 (1989).

Williams v. Florida, 399 U.S. 78 (1970).

Wilson v. Seiter, 111 S.Ct. 232 (1991).

Wisconsin v. Mitchell, 113 S.Ct. 2194 (1993).

Witherspoon v. Illinois, 391 U.S. 510 (1968).

Wolf v. Colorado, 338 U.S. 25 (1949).

Wolff v. McDonnell, 418 U.S. 539 (1974).

Wyoming v. Houghton, 526 U.S. 295 (1999).

glossary

accusatory process The series of events from the arrest of a suspect to the filing of a formal charge with the court (through an indictment or information).

adjudication The process of determining whether the defendant is guilty or not guilty.

administrative regulations Rules made by government agencies to implement specific public policies in areas such as public health, environmental protection, and workplace safety.

adversarial system Basis for the American legal system in which a passive judge and jury seek to find the truth by listening to opposing attorneys who vigorously advocate on behalf of their respective sides.

affidavit Written statement of fact, supported by oath or affirmation, submitted to judicial officers to fulfill the requirements of probable cause for obtaining a warrant.

aftercare Juvenile justice equivalent of parole, in which a delinquent is released from a custodial sentence and supervised in the community.

aggressive patrol A patrol strategy designed to maximize the number of police interventions and observations in the community.

anomie A breakdown in and disappearance of the rules of social behavior.

appeal A request to a higher court that it review actions taken in a completed trial.

appellate courts Courts that do not try criminal cases but hear appeals of decisions of lower courts.

arraignment The court appearance of an accused person in which the charges are read and the accused, advised by a lawyer, pleads guilty or not guilty.

arrest The physical taking of a person into custody on the grounds that probable cause exists to believe that he or she has committed a criminal offense. Police may use only reasonable physical force in making an arrest. The purpose of the arrest is to hold the accused for a court proceeding.

assigned counsel An attorney in private practice assigned by a court to represent an indigent. The attorney's fee is paid by the government with jurisdiction over the case.

Atkins v. Virginia **(2002)** Execution of the mentally retarded is unconstitutional.

bail An amount of money specified by a judge to be paid as a condition of pretrial release to ensure that the accused will appear in court as required.

Barron v. Baltimore **(1833)** The protections of the Bill of Rights apply only to actions of the federal government.

bench trial Trial conducted by a judge who acts as fact finder and determines issues of law. No jury participates.

biological explanations Explanations of crime that emphasize physiological and neurological factors that may predispose a person to commit crimes.

boot camp A short-term institutional sentence, usually followed by probation, that puts the offender through a physical regimen designed to develop discipline and respect for authority. Also referred to as *shock incarceration.*

Bordenkircher v. Hayes **(1978)** A defendant's rights were not violated by a prosecutor who warned that not to accept a guilty plea would result in a harsher sentence.

Boykin v. Alabama **(1969)** Defendants must state that they are voluntarily making a plea of guilty.

Breed v. Jones **(1975)** Juveniles cannot be found delinquent in juvenile court and then transferred to adult court without a hearing on the transfer; to do so violates the protection against double jeopardy.

case law Court decisions that have the status of law and serve as precedents for later decisions.

challenge for cause Removal of a prospective juror by showing that he or she has some bias or some other legal disability. The number of such challenges permitted to attorneys is unlimited.

Chimel v. California **(1969)** Supreme Court decision that endorsed warrantless searches for weapons and evidence in the immediate vicinity of people who are lawfully arrested.

circumstantial evidence Evidence provided by a witness from which a jury must infer a fact.

citation A written order or summons, issued by a law enforcement officer, directing an alleged offender to appear in court at a specified time to answer a criminal charge.

civil disabilities Legal restrictions that prevent released felons from voting, serving on juries, and holding public office.

civil forfeiture The confiscation of property by the state as punishment for a crime. In recent years the police have used civil forfeiture to seize property that they believe was purchased with drug profits.

civil law Law regulating the relationships between or among individuals, usually involving property, contract, or business disputes.

classical criminology A school of criminology that views behavior as stemming from free will, demands responsibility and accountability of all perpetrators, and stresses the need for punishments severe enough to deter others.

classification The process of assigning an inmate to a category specifying his or her needs for security, treatment, education, work assignment, and readiness for release.

clearance rate The percentage of crimes known to the police that they believe they have solved through an arrest; a statistic used to measure a police department's productivity.

common law The Anglo-American system of uncodified law, in which judges follow precedents set by earlier decisions when they decide new but similar cases. The substantive and procedural criminal law was originally developed in this manner but was later codified—set down in codes—by state legislatures.

community correctional center An institution, usually in an urban area, that houses inmates soon to be released. Such centers are designed to help inmates establish community ties and thus promote their reintegration with society.

community corrections A model of corrections based on the goal of reintegrating the offender into the community.
community service A sentence requiring the offender to perform a certain amount of unpaid labor in the community.
conditions of release Conduct restrictions that parolees must follow as a legally binding requirement of being released.
congregate system A penitentiary system, developed in Auburn, New York, in which each inmate was held in isolation during the night but worked and ate with other prisoners during the day under a rule of silence.
constitutions The basic laws of a country defining the structure of government and the relationship of citizens to that government.
continuance An adjournment of a scheduled case until a later date.
contract counsel An attorney in private practice who contracts with the government to represent all indigent defendants in a county during a set period of time and for a specified dollar amount.
contract labor system A system under which inmates' labor was sold on a contractual basis to private employers who provided the machinery and raw materials with which inmates made salable products in the institution.
control theories Theories holding that criminal behavior occurs when the bonds that tie an individual to society are broken or weakened.
***Cooper v. Pate* (1964)** State prisoners are entitled to the protection of the Civil Rights Act of 1871 and may challenge in federal courts the conditions of their confinement.
corrections The variety of programs, services, facilities, and organizations responsible for the management of people who have been accused or convicted of criminal offenses.
count Each separate offense of which a person is accused in an indictment or an information.
crime A specific act of commission or omission in violation of the law, for which a punishment is prescribed.
crime control model A model of the criminal justice system that assumes freedom is so important that every effort must be made to repress crime; it emphasizes efficiency, speed, finality, and the capacity to apprehend, try, convict, and dispose of a high proportion of offenders.
crime control model of corrections A model of corrections based on the assumption that criminal behavior can be controlled by more use of incarceration and other forms of strict supervision.
crimes without victims Offenses involving a willing and private exchange of illegal goods or services that are in strong demand. Participants do not feel they are being harmed, but these crimes are prosecuted on the ground that society as a whole is being injured.
criminogenic Factors thought to bring about criminal behavior in an individual.
***Cruz v. Beto* (1972)** Inmates whose faiths are not the conventional ones practiced in the United States should have reasonable opportunities to practice their faiths.
custodial model A model of incarceration that emphasizes security, discipline, and order.
cybercrimes Offenses that involve the use of one or more computers.

dark figure of crime A metaphor that emphasizes the dangerous dimension of crime that is never reported to the police.
day reporting center A community correctional center where an offender reports each day to comply with elements of a sentence.
defense attorney The lawyer who represents accused or convicted offenders in their dealings with criminal justice officials.
delinquent A child who has committed an act that if committed by an adult would be criminal.
demonstrative evidence Evidence that is not based on witness testimony but that demonstrates information relevant to the crime, such as maps, X-rays, and photographs; includes real evidence involved in the crime.
dependent child A child who has no parent or guardian or whose parents cannot give proper care.
detention hearing A hearing by the juvenile court to determine if a juvenile is to be detained or released prior to adjudication.
determinate sentence A sentence that fixes the term of imprisonment at a specific period.
differential response A patrol strategy that assigns priorities to calls for service and chooses the appropriate response.
direct evidence Eyewitness accounts.
directed patrol A proactive form of patrolling that directs resources to known high-crime areas.
discovery A prosecutor's pretrial disclosure, to the defense, of facts and evidence to be introduced at trial.
discretion The authority to make decisions without reference to specific rules or facts, using instead one's own judgment; allows for individualization and informality in the administration of justice.
discretionary release The release of an inmate from prison to conditional supervision at the discretion of the parole board within the boundaries set by the sentence and the penal law.
discrimination Differential treatment of individuals or groups based on race, ethnicity, gender, sexual orientation, or economic status, instead of on their behavior or qualifications.
disparity The unequal treatment of one group by the criminal justice system, compared with the treatment accorded other groups.
diversion The process of screening children out of the juvenile justice system without a decision by the court.
double jeopardy The subjecting of a person to prosecution more than once in the same jurisdiction for the same offense; prohibited by the Fifth Amendment.
dual court system A system consisting of a separate judicial structure for each state in addition to a national structure. Each case is tried in a court of the same jurisdiction as that of the law or laws broken.
due process model A model of the criminal justice system that assumes freedom is so important that every effort must be made to ensure that criminal justice decisions are based on reliable information; it emphasizes the adversarial process, the rights of defendants, and formal decision-making procedures.

Enlightenment A movement, during the eighteenth century in England and France, in which concepts of liberalism, rationalism, equality, and individualism dominated social and political thinking.
entrapment The defense that the individual was induced by the police to commit the criminal act.
***Escobedo v. Illinois* (1964)** An attorney must be provided to suspects when they are taken into police custody.

exchange A mutual transfer of resources; a balance of benefits and deficits that flow from behavior based on decisions about the values and costs of alternatives.

exclusionary rule The principle that illegally obtained evidence must be excluded from a trial.

exigent circumstances When there is a threat to public safety or the risk that evidence will be destroyed, officers may search, arrest, or question suspects without obtaining a warrant or following other usual rules of criminal procedure.

expiration release The release of an inmate from incarceration, without any further correctional supervision; the inmate cannot be returned to prison for any remaining portion of the sentence for the current offense.

Fare v. Michael C. **(1979)** By examining the totality of circumstances, trial court judges must evaluate the voluntariness of juveniles' waiving their rights to an attorney and to protections against self-incrimination.

federalism A system of government in which power is divided between a central (national) government and regional (state) governments.

felonies Serious crimes usually carrying a penalty of death or incarceration for more than one year.

filtering process A process by which criminal justice officials screen out some cases while advancing others to the next level of decision making.

fine A sum of money to be paid to the state by a convicted person as punishment for an offense.

Florida v. J. L. **(2000)** Police officers may not conduct a stop-and-frisk search based solely on an anonymous tip.

frankpledge A system in old English law in which members of a *tithing,* a group of ten families, pledged to be responsible for keeping order and bringing violators of the law to court.

Fulwood v. Clemmer **(1962)** Black Muslims have the same right to worship and practice their religion that inmates of other faiths have.

fundamental fairness A legal doctrine supporting the idea that so long as a state's conduct maintains basic standards of fairness, the Constitution has not been violated.

furlough The temporary release of an inmate from a correctional institution for a brief period, usually one to three days, for a visit home. Such programs help maintain family ties and prepare inmates for release on parole.

Furman v. Georgia **(1972)** The death penalty, as administered, constitutes cruel and unusual treatment.

Gagnon v. Scarpelli **(1973)** Before probation can be revoked, a two-stage hearing must be held and the offender provided with specific elements of due process.

general deterrence Punishment of criminals that is intended to be an example to the general public and to discourage the commission of offenses.

Gideon v. Wainwright **(1963)** Defendants have a right to counsel in felony cases. States must provide defense counsel in felony cases for those who cannot pay for it themselves.

going rate Local court officials' shared view of the appropriate sentence for the offense, the defendant's prior record, and other case characteristics.

"good faith" exception When police act in honest reliance on a warrant, the evidence seized is admissible even if the warrant is later proved to be defective.

good time A reduction of an inmate's prison sentence, at the discretion of the prison administrator, for good behavior or participation in vocational, educational, or treatment programs.

Gregg v. Georgia **(1976)** Capital punishment statutes are permissible if they provide careful procedures to guide decision making by judges and juries.

habeas corpus A writ or judicial order requesting the release of a person being detained in a jail, prison, or mental hospital. If a judge finds the person is being held improperly, the writ may be granted and the person released.

halfway house A correctional facility housing convicted felons who spend a portion of their day at work in the community but reside in the halfway house during nonworking hours.

hands-off policy Judges should not interfere with the administration of correctional institutions.

home confinement A sentence requiring the offender to remain inside his or her home during specified periods.

Hudson v. Palmer **(1984)** Prison officials have a right to search cells and confiscate from inmates any materials found.

In re Gault **(1967)** Juveniles have the right to counsel, to confront and examine accusers, and to have adequate notice of charges when confinement is a possible punishment.

In re Winship **(1970)** The standard of proof beyond a reasonable doubt applies to juvenile delinquency proceedings.

incapacitation Depriving an offender of the ability to commit crimes against society, usually by detaining the offender in prison.

inchoate offense Conduct that is criminal even though the harm that the law seeks to prevent has been merely planned or attempted but not done.

incident-driven policing A reactive approach to policing emphasizing a quick response to calls for service.

incorporation The extension of the due process clause of the Fourteenth Amendment to make binding on state governments the rights guaranteed in the first ten amendments to the U.S. Constitution (the Bill of Rights).

indeterminate sentence A period, set by a judge, that specifies a minimum and a maximum time to be served in prison. Sometime after the minimum, the offender may be eligible for parole. Because it is based on the idea that the time necessary for treatment cannot be set, the indeterminate sentence is closely associated with rehabilitation.

indictment A document returned by a grand jury as a "true bill" charging an individual with a specific crime on the basis of a determination of probable cause as presented by a prosecuting attorney.

"inevitable discovery" exception Improperly obtained evidence can be used when it would later have inevitably been discovered without improper actions of the police.

information A document charging an individual with a specific crime. It is prepared by a prosecuting attorney and presented to a court at a preliminary hearing.

inmate code The values and norms of the prison social system that define the inmates' idea of the model prisoner.

inquisitorial system Basis for legal systems in Europe in which the judge takes an active role in investigating the case and asking questions of witnesses in court.

intensive supervision probation (ISP) Probation granted under conditions of strict reporting to a probation officer with a limited caseload.

intermediate sanction A sentence that is served in the community and that is more restrictive than probation and less restrictive than incarceration.

internal affairs unit A branch of a police department that receives and investigates complaints alleging violation of rules and policies on the part of officers.

jail An institution authorized to hold pretrial detainees and sentenced misdemeanants for periods longer than 48 hours. Most jails are administered by county governments; in six jurisdictions, by state governments.

jurisdiction The geographic territory or legal boundaries within which control may be exercised; the range of a court's authority.

jury A panel of citizens selected according to law and sworn to determine matters of fact in a criminal case and to deliver a verdict of guilty or not guilty.

Kyllo v. United States **(2001)** Law enforcement officials cannot examine a home with a thermal imaging device unless they obtain a warrant.

labeling theories Theories emphasizing that the causes of criminal behavior are not found in the individual but in the social process that labels certain acts as deviant or criminal.

law enforcement The police function of controlling crime by intervening in situations in which the law has clearly been violated and the police need to identify and apprehend the guilty person.

learning theories Theories that see criminal behavior as learned, just as legal behavior is learned.

lease system A system under which inmates were leased to contractors who provided prisoners with food and clothing in exchange for their labor. In southern states the prisoners were used as agricultural, mining, logging, and construction laborers.

legal responsibility The accountability of an individual for a crime because of the perpetrator's characteristics and the circumstances of the illegal act.

legal sufficiency The presence of the minimum legal elements necessary for prosecution of a case. When a prosecutor uses legal sufficiency as the customary criterion for prosecuting cases, a great many are accepted for prosecution, but the majority of them are disposed of by plea bargaining or dismissal.

line functions Police components that directly perform field operations and carry out the basic functions of patrol, investigation, traffic, vice, juvenile, and so on.

local legal culture Norms shared by members of a court community as to how cases should be handled and how a participant should behave in the judicial process.

mala in se Offenses that are wrong by their very nature.

mala prohibita Offenses prohibited by law but not wrong in themselves.

mandatory release The required release of an inmate from incarceration to community supervision upon the expiration of a certain period, as specified by a determinate-sentencing law or parole guidelines.

mandatory sentence A sentence determined by statutes and requiring that a certain penalty be imposed and carried out for convicted offenders who meet certain criteria.

Mapp v. Ohio **(1961)** The Fourth Amendment protects citizens from unreasonable searches and seizures by state officials.

mark system A system in which offenders receive a certain number of points at the time of sentencing, based on the severity of their crime. Prisoners can reduce their term and gain release by earning marks to reduce these points through labor, good behavior, and educational achievement.

McCleskey v. Kemp **(1987)** Rejects a challenge of Georgia's death penalty on grounds of racial discrimination.

McKeiver v. Pennsylvania **(1971)** Juveniles do not have a constitutional right to a trial by jury.

medical model A model of corrections based on the assumption that criminal behavior is caused by biological or psychological conditions that require treatment.

Mempa v. Rhay **(1967)** Probationers have the right to counsel at a combined revocation-sentencing hearing.

mens rea "Guilty mind" or blameworthy state of mind, necessary for legal responsibility for a criminal offense; criminal intent, as distinguished from innocent intent.

merit selection A reform plan by which judges are nominated by a commission and appointed by the governor for a given period. When the term expires, the voters are asked to approve or disapprove the judge for a succeeding term. If the judge is disapproved, the committee nominates a successor for the governor's appointment.

Miranda v. Arizona **(1966)** Confessions made by suspects in custody who were not notified of their due process rights cannot be admitted as evidence.

misdemeanors Offenses less serious than felonies and usually punishable by incarceration of no more than a year, probation, or intermediate sanction.

money laundering Moving the proceeds of criminal activities through a maze of businesses, banks, and brokerage accounts so as to disguise their origin.

Morrissey v. Brewer **(1972)** Due process rights require a prompt, informal inquiry before an impartial hearing officer before parole may be revoked. The parolee may present relevant information and confront witnesses.

motion An application to a court requesting that an order be issued to bring about a specified action.

National Crime Victimization Surveys (NCVS) Interviews of samples of the U.S. population conducted by the Bureau of Justice Statistics to determine the number and types of criminal victimizations and thus the extent of unreported as well as reported crime.

National Incident-Based Reporting System (NIBRS) A reporting system in which the police describe each offense in a crime incident, together with data describing the offender, victim, and property.

neglected child A child who is not receiving proper care, because of some action or inaction of his or her parents.

net widening Process in which new sentencing options increase instead of reduce control over offenders' lives.

New Jersey v. T.L.O. **(1985)** School officials may search a student if they have a reasonable suspicion that the search will produce evidence that a school or a criminal law has been violated.

Nix v. Williams **(1984)** Decision in which the Supreme Court created the "inevitable discovery" exception to the exclusionary rule.

nolle prosequi An entry made by a prosecutor on the record of a case and announced in court to indicate that the charges specified will not be prosecuted. In effect, the charges are thereby dismissed.

nonlethal weapons Weapons such as pepper spray and air-fired beanbags or nets that can incapacitate a suspect without inflicting serious injuries or a likelihood of death.

nonpartisan election An election in which candidates' party affiliations are not listed on the ballot.

North Carolina v. Alford **(1970)** A plea of guilty may be accepted for the purpose of a lesser sentence by a defendant who maintains his or her innocence.

occupational crime Criminal offenses committed through opportunities created in a legal business or occupation.

open fields doctrine Officers are permitted to search, without a warrant, for visible evidence on private property beyond the area immediately surrounding a house.

order maintenance The police function of preventing behavior that disturbs or threatens to disturb the public peace or that involves face-to-face conflict among two or more people. In such situations the police exercise discretion in deciding whether a law has been broken.

organized crime A framework for the perpetration of criminal acts—usually in fields such as gambling, drugs, and prostitution—providing illegal services that are in great demand.

other conditional release A term used in some states to avoid the rigidity of mandatory release by placing convicts in various community settings under supervision.

pardon An action of the executive branch of state or federal government excluding an offense and absolving the offender from the consequences of the crime.

parens patriae The state as parent; the state as guardian and protector of all citizens (such as juveniles) who cannot protect themselves.

parole The conditional release of an inmate from incarceration after part of the prison sentence has been served; the parolee remains under supervision for the remainder of the sentence.

partisan election An election in which candidates openly endorsed by political parties are presented to the voters for selection.

penitentiary An institution intended to punish criminals by isolating them from society and from one another so they can reflect on their past misdeeds, repent, and reform.

peremptory challenge Removal of a prospective juror without giving any reason. Attorneys are allowed a limited number of such challenges.

PINS Acronym for "person in need of supervision," a term that designates juveniles who are either status offenders or thought to be on the verge of trouble.

plain view doctrine Officers may examine and seize, without a warrant, contraband or evidence that is in open view at a location where they are legally permitted to be.

plea bargain A defendant's plea of guilty to a criminal charge with the reasonable expectation of receiving some consideration from the state for doing so, usually a reduction of the charge. The defendant's ultimate goal is a penalty lighter than the one formally warranted by the charged offense.

political crime An act, usually done for ideological purposes, that constitutes a threat against the state (such as treason, sedition, or espionage) or a criminal act by the state.

positivist criminology A school of criminology that views behavior as stemming from social, biological, and psychological factors. It argues that punishment should be tailored to the individual needs of the offender.

Powell v. Alabama **(1932)** An attorney must be provided to a defendant facing the death penalty.

presentence report A report, prepared by a probation officer, that presents a convicted offender's background and is used by the judge in selecting an appropriate sentence.

presumptive sentence A sentence for which the legislature or a commission sets a minimum and maximum range of months or years. Judges are to fix the length of the sentence within that range, allowing for special circumstances.

preventive detention Holding a defendant for trial, based on a judge's finding that, if the defendant were released on bail, he or she would flee or would endanger another person or the community.

preventive patrol Making the police presence known, to deter crime and to make officers available to respond quickly to calls.

prison An institution for the incarceration of people convicted of serious crimes, usually felonies.

proactive Acting in anticipation, such as an active search for potential offenders that is initiated by the police without waiting for a crime to be reported. Arrests for crimes without victims are usually proactive.

probable cause An amount of reliable information indicating that it is more likely than not that evidence will be found in a specific location or that a specific person is guilty of a crime.

probation A sentence that the offender is allowed to serve under supervision in the community.

problem-oriented policing An approach to policing in which officers routinely seek to identify, analyze, and respond to the circumstances underlying the incidents that prompt citizens to call the police.

procedural criminal law Law defining the procedures that criminal justice officials must follow in enforcement, adjudication, and correction.

procedural due process The constitutional requirement that all people be treated fairly and justly by government officials. An accused person can be arrested, prosecuted, tried, and punished only in accordance with procedures prescribed by law.

prosecuting attorney A legal representative of the state with sole responsibility for bringing criminal charges; in some states referred to as district attorney, state's attorney, or county attorney.

psychological explanations Explanations of crime that emphasize mental processes and behavior.

public defender An attorney employed on a full-time, salaried basis by the government to represent indigents.

public policy Policies developed by government as to the ways public resources will be used to deal with issues affecting society.

"public safety" exception When public safety is in jeopardy, police may question a suspect in custody without providing the *Miranda* warnings.

reactive Occurring in response, such as police activity in response to notification that a crime has been committed.

real evidence Physical evidence such as a weapon, records, fingerprints, stolen property—objects actually involved in the crime.

reasonable doubt The standard used by a juror to decide if the prosecution has provided enough evidence for conviction. Jurors should vote for acquittal if they think there is a reasonable doubt.

reasonable expectation of privacy Standard developed for determining whether a government intrusion of a person or property constitutes a search because it interferes with individual interests that are normally protected from government examination.

reasonable suspicion A police officer's belief, based on articulable facts, that criminal activity is taking place, so that intruding on an individual's reasonable expectation of privacy is necessary.

recidivism A return to criminal behavior.

reformatory An institution for young offenders, emphasizing training, a mark system of classification, indeterminate sentences, and parole.

rehabilitation The goal of restoring a convicted offender to a constructive place in society through some form of vocational or educational training or therapy.

rehabilitation model A model of corrections that emphasizes the need to restore a convicted offender to a constructive place in society through some form of vocational or educational training or therapy.

reintegration model A model of a correctional institution that emphasizes maintaining the offender's ties to family and community as a method of reform, recognizing that the offender will be returning to society.

release on recognizance (ROR) Pretrial release granted on the defendant's promise to appear in court, because the judge believes that the defendant's ties in the community guarantee that he or she will appear.

restitution Repayment—in the form of money or service—by an offender to a victim who has suffered some loss from the offense.

restoration Punishment designed to repair the damage done to the victim and community by an offender's criminal act.

retribution Punishment inflicted on a person who has infringed on the rights of others and so deserves to be penalized. The severity of the sanction should fit the seriousness of the crime.

Ricketts v. Adamson **(1987)** Defendants must uphold the plea agreement or suffer the consequences.

Ring v. Arizona **(2002)** Juries, rather than judges, must make the crucial factual decisions as to whether a convicted murderer should receive the death penalty.

Ruffin v. Commonwealth **(1871)** By committing a crime, the prisoner has become a slave of the state and has forfeited all personal rights.

Ruiz v. Estelle **(1980)** Conditions of confinement in the Texas prison system were unconstitutional.

Santobello v. New York **(1971)** When a guilty plea rests on a promise of a prosecutor, the promise must be fulfilled.

Schall v. Martin **(1984)** Juveniles can be held in preventive detention if there is concern that they may commit additional crimes while awaiting court action.

search Officials' examination of and hunt for evidence in or on a person or place in a manner that intrudes on reasonable expectations of privacy.

seizure Any police use of their authority to deprive people of their liberty or property that is reasonable according to the Fourth Amendment.

selective incapacitation Making the best use of expensive and limited prison space by targeting for incarceration those individuals whose incapacity will do the most to reduce crime in society.

self-incrimination The act of exposing oneself to prosecution by being forced to respond to questions whose answers may reveal that one has committed a crime. The Fifth Amendment protects defendants against self-incrimination. In any criminal proceeding, the prosecution must prove the charges by means of evidence other than the testimony of the accused.

sentencing guidelines A mechanism to indicate to judges the expected sanction for certain offenses, in order to reduce disparities in sentencing.

separate confinement A penitentiary system, developed in Pennsylvania, in which each inmate was held in isolation from other inmates. All activities, including craft work, took place in the cells.

service The police function of providing assistance to the public, usually in matters unrelated to crime.

shock probation A sentence in which the offender is released after a short incarceration and resentenced to probation.

social conflict theories Theories that assume criminal law and the criminal justice system are primarily a means of controlling the poor and the have-nots.

social process theories Theories that see criminality as normal behavior. Everyone has the potential to become a criminal, depending on (1) the influences that impel one toward or away from crime and (2) how one is regarded by others.

social structure theories Theories that blame crime on the existence of a powerless lower class that lives with poverty and deprivation and often turns to crime in response.

socialization The process by which the rules, symbols, and values of a group or subculture are learned by its members.

sociological explanations Explanations of crime that emphasize the social conditions that bear on the individual as causes of criminal behavior.

specific deterrence Punishment inflicted on criminals to discourage them from committing future crimes.

state attorney general A state's chief legal officer, usually responsible for both civil and criminal matters.

status offense Any act committed by a juvenile that is considered unacceptable for a child, such as truancy or running away from home, but that would not be a crime if it were committed by an adult.

statutes Laws passed by legislatures. Statutory definitions of criminal offenses are found in penal codes.

stop Government officials' interference with an individual's freedom of movement for a duration that can be measured in minutes.

stop-and-frisk search Limited search approved by the Supreme Court in *Terry v. Ohio* that permits police officers to pat down the clothing of people on the streets if there is reasonable suspicion of dangerous criminal activity.

strict liability An obligation or duty that when broken is an offense that can be judged criminal without a showing of *mens rea,* or criminal intent; usually applied to regulatory offenses involving health and safety.

subculture The symbols, beliefs, and values shared by members of a subgroup of the larger society.

substantive criminal law Law that defines the acts that are subject to punishment and specifies the punishments for such offenses.

sworn officers Police employees who have taken an oath and been given powers by the state to make arrests and use necessary force, in accordance with their duties.

system A complex whole consisting of interdependent parts whose operations are directed toward goals and are influenced by the environment within which they function.

system efficiency Policy of the prosecutor's office that encourages speedy and early disposition of cases in response to caseload pressures. Weak cases are screened out at intake, and other nontrial alternatives are used as primary means of disposition.

technical violation The probationer's failure to abide by the rules and conditions of probation (specified by the judge), resulting in revocation of probation.

***Tennessee v. Garner* (1985)** Deadly force may not be used against an unarmed and fleeing suspect unless necessary to prevent the escape and unless the officer has probable cause to believe that the suspect poses a significant threat of death or serious injury to the officers or others.

***Terry v. Ohio* (1968)** Supreme Court decision endorsing police officers' authority to stop and frisk suspects on the street when there is reasonable suspicion that they are armed and involved in criminal activity.

testimony Oral evidence provided by a legally competent witness.

theory of differential association Theory that people become criminals because they encounter more influences that view criminal behavior as normal and acceptable than influences that are hostile to criminal behavior.

ticket-of-leave A system of conditional release from prison, first developed in Ireland by Sir Walter Crofton. An early form of parole.

totality of circumstances test Flexible test established by the Supreme Court for identifying whether probable cause exists to justify a judicial officer in issuing a warrant.

trial courts of general jurisdiction Criminal courts with jurisdiction over all offenses, including felonies. In some states these courts also hear appeals.

trial courts of limited jurisdiction Criminal courts with trial jurisdiction over misdemeanor cases and preliminary matters in felony cases. Sometimes these courts hold felony trials that may result in penalties below a specified limit.

trial sufficiency The presence of sufficient legal elements to ensure successful prosecution of a case. When a prosecutor uses trial sufficiency as the customary criterion for prosecuting cases, only cases that seem certain to result in conviction at trial are accepted for prosecution. Use of plea bargaining is minimal; good police work and court capacity to go to trial are required.

Uniform Crime Reports (UCR) An annually published statistical summary of crimes reported to the police, based on voluntary reports to the FBI by local, state, and federal law enforcement agencies.

United States attorney Officials responsible for the prosecution of crimes that violate the laws of the United States; appointed by the president and assigned to a U.S. district court jurisdiction.

***United States v. Drayton* (2002)** Police officers are not required to inform people of their right to decline when police ask for consent to search.

***United States v. Salerno and Cafero* (1987)** Preventive detention provisions of the Bail Reform Act of 1984 are upheld as a legitimate use of government power designed to prevent people from committing crimes while on bail.

victimology A field of criminology that examines the role the victim plays in precipitating a criminal incident.

visible crime An offense against persons or property committed primarily by members of the lower class. Often referred to as "street crime" or "ordinary crime," this type of offense is the one most upsetting to the public.

voir dire A questioning of prospective jurors in order to screen out people the attorneys think might be biased or otherwise incapable of delivering a fair verdict.

waive Procedure by which the juvenile court waives its jurisdiction and transfers a juvenile case to the adult criminal court.

warrant A court order authorizing police officials to take certain actions: for example, to arrest suspects or to search premises.

***Williams v. Florida* (1970)** Juries of fewer than 12 members are constitutional.

***Wilson v. Seiter* (1991)** The standard of review of official conduct is whether state policies or actions by correctional officers constitute "deliberate indifference" to constitutional rights.

***Witherspoon v. Illinois* (1968)** Potential jurors who object to the death penalty cannot be automatically excluded from service; however, during voir dire those who feel so strongly about capital punishment that they could not give an impartial verdict may be excluded.

***Wolff v. McDonnell* (1974)** Basic elements of procedural due process must be present when decisions are made about the disciplining of an inmate.

work and educational release The daytime release of inmates from correctional institutions so they can work or attend school.

workgroup A collection of individuals who interact in the workplace on a continuing basis, share goals, develop norms regarding how activities should be carried out, and eventually establish a network of roles that differentiates the group from others and that facilitates cooperation.

working personality A set of emotional and behavioral characteristics developed by a member of an occupational group in response to the work situation and environmental influences.

name index

subject index

photo credits

Part-opening photo: Benny De Gove, The Image Bank/Getty Images

Chapter-opening photos (left-hand pages):

Chapters 1–4: G. K. & Vikki Hart, The Image Bank/Getty Images
Chapters 5–8: Hans Neleman, The Image Bank/Getty Images
Chapters 9–12: Jeffrey M. Spielman, The Image Bank/Getty Images
Chapters 13–16: Marks Productions, The Image Bank/Getty Images
Chapter 17: Garry Wade, Stone/Getty Images

Chapter 1: p. 3 © AFP Photo/Seth McAllister/CORBIS; p. 4 © Parker Hank/CORBIS Symga; p. 9 © Joseph Sohm;ChromoSohm Inc./Corbis; p. 11 © AP/Wide World Photos/J. Scott Applewhite; p. 15 © AP/Wide World Photos/Louis Lanzano; p. 20 © Getty Images; p. 21 © Hollyman/The Gamma Liaison Network; p. 22 © David Butow/SABA Press

Chapter 2: p. 35 © Casey Christie/Bakersfield Californian/Corbis Sygma; p. 39 © Alon Reininger/Woodfin Camp & Associates; p. 46 © Ted Soqui/Sygma; p. 52 © A. Fredrickson/Sipa Press; p. 54 © Larry Downing/Woodfin Camp & Associates; p. 59 © Bill Lovejoy/Santa Cruz Sentinel

Chapter 3: p. 63 © Columbus Dispatch; p. 63 © Bill Graham Photography/Athens, Ohio; p. 65 © Yong Kim/Philadelphia Daily News/The Image Works; p. 68 © AP/Wide World Photos/Bill Feig; p. 74 © Steven Rubin/The Image Works; p. 84 © AFP Photo/Doug Canter/CORBIS; p. 87 © AP/Wide World Photos

Chapter 4: p. 95 © Mark E. Gibson/CORBIS; p. 99 © Archive Photos; p. 102 © AP/Wide World Photos; p. 106 © AFP/CORBIS; p. 109 © A. Ramey/PhotoEdit; p. 116 © AP/Wide World Photos/Image from video pool; p. 119 © Corbis/Bettmann; p. 122 © Getty Images

Chapter 5: p. 135 © René Clement/AURORA; p. 139 © Culver Pictures; p. 141 © Jeff Shere/Black Star; p. 143 © Cynthia Johnson/The Gamma Liaison Network; p. 146 © AP/Wide World Photos/Don Heupel; p. 157 © Reuters New Media/CORBIS; p. 159 © David Portnoy/Black Star; p. 162 © Les Stone/Corbis Sygma

Chapter 6: p. 171 © AP/Wide World Photos/William Wilson Lewis III; p. 173 © Kim Kulish/Corbis SABA; p. 180 © Miami Herald/Liaison Agency; p. 187 © AP/Wide World Photos; p. 192 © Peter Turnley/CORBIS; p. 194 Michael Madrid for USA TODAY; Copyright 2002, USA TODAY. Reprinted with permission; p. 196 © AP/Wide World Photos

Chapter 7: p. 203 © AP/Wide World Photos/Bill Janscha; p. 206 © Ray J. Malace; p. 208 © A. Ramey/PhotoEdit; p. 210 © AP/Wide World Photos/Karen Tam; p. 214 © Craig Filapacci/Gamma-Liason; p. 217 © Li-Hua Lan/The Image Works; p. 219 © Spencer Grant/PhotoEdit

Chapter 8: p. 233 © Pool /Reuters/Archive Photos; p. 242 © Albert Fanning/The Image Works; p. 245 © Justin Case/Corbis Outline; p. 246 © Brooks Kraft/Gamma; p. 250 © AP/Wide World Photos/Daily Inter Lake, Karen Nichols; p. 255 © Joe Rodriguez/Black Star; p. 262 © Mug Shots/CORBIS; p. 265 © Jack Kurtz

Chapter 9: p. 273 © AP/Wide World Photos/Louis Lanzano; p. 276 © Collection, The Supreme Court of the United States, courtesy of the Supreme Court Historical Society; p. 279 © Dick Blume/The Image Works; p. 285 © Spencer Grant/PhotoEdit; p. 288 © AP/Wide World Photos; p. 297 © J. Hill/NYT Pictures; p. 295 © AP/Wide World Photos

Chapter 10: p. 301 Photo Courtesy of Los Angeles County Courts/Getty Images; p. 305 Courtesy of Mishawaka Police Department/Getty Images; p. 320 © AP/Wide World Photos; p. 325 © AP/Wide World Photos; p. 331 © AFP/Corbis

Chapter 11: p. 337 © W. Lopez/NYT Pictures; p. 340 © AP/Wide World Photos; p. 345 © AFP Photo/Shawn Thew/CORBIS; p. 352 © AP/Wide World Photos/Dan Trevan; p. 357 © Steve Chenn/Corbis; p. 361 © The Gamma Liaison Network; p. 364 © AP/Wide World Photos

Chapter 12: p. 371 © Photo by CNN/Getty Images; p. 373 © AP/Wide World Photos; p. 376 © Rose Howerter/The Oregonian; p. 379 © P. F. Bentley/Black Star; p. 381 Courtesy of NYT Pictures; p. 387 © Lisa Terry/The Gamma Liaison Network; p. 390 © Kevin Horan/Chicago; p. 393 © Joel Gordon Photography

Chapter 13: p. 407 © Andrew Lichtenstein/The Image Works; p. 410 © American Stock/Archive Photos; p. 411 © The Library Company of Philadelphia; p. 415 © Archive Photos; p. 421 © Stephen Ferry/Liaison/Getty Images; p. 427 © Rick Friedman/Black Star

Chapter 14: p. 439 © Spencer Grant/The Picture Cube; p. 443 © Spencer Grant/PhotoEdit; p. 445 © AP/Wide World Photos; p. 450 © Jack Kurtz; p. 452 © Joseph Rodriquez/Black Star; p. 457 © Lara Jo Regan/SABA Press; p. 459 © Chang W. Lee/NYT Pictures

Chapter 15: p. 469 © Ralf-Finn Hestoft/SABA Press; p. 472 © Steve Lehman/SABA Press; p. 474 © Jeffry D. Scott; p. 478 © AP/Wide World Photos/Rich Pedroncelli; p. 485 © AP/Wide World Photos/Joe Jines/Southern Illinoisan; p. 488 © CORBIS; p. 492 © Robert McElroy/Woodfin Camp & Associates

Chapter 16: p. 497 © AP/Wide World Photos/Robert F. Bukaty; p. 501 © Angel Franco/The New York Times; p. 504 © Andrew Lichtenstein/Sygma; p. 506 © Steve Lehman/SABA Press; p. 509 © Richard Lord/PhotoEdit; p. 513 © A. Ramey/PhotoEdit; p. 515 © AP/Wide World Photos; p. 516 © Steve Lehman/SABA Press; p. 519 © Bob Daemmrich/Stock, Boston; p. 524 © Phillippe Diederich

Chapter 17: p. 531 © David Peters Photography; p. 534 © AP/Wide World Photos/Ed Andrieski; p. 537 © Topham/The Image Works; p. 546 © AP/Wide World Photos/Jim Cole; p. 549, top, © Monty Davis/The Wichita Eagle; p. 549, bottom, © A. Ramey/PhotoEdit